A Review of the Events of 1967

The 1968 World Book Year Book

The Annual Supplement to The World Book Encyclopedia

Field Enterprises Educational Corporation

Chicago London Rome Stockholm Sydney Toronto

Staff

Editorial Director: William H. Nault

Executive Editor: A. Richard Harmet

Executive Art Director: Gordon J. Kwiatkowski

Managing Editor: Wayne Wille

Associate Editors: Louis Mariano, Paul C. Tullier

Senior Editors: Allan Davidson, Robert A. Irwin, Foster P. Stockwell, Wade Tilleux

Assistant Editors: Mary Jane Bailey, Helen Howell Dixon, Jessie Kalinowski, Lillian Zahrt

Editorial Assistant: Roberta Perusich

Associate Art Director: Clifford L. Birklund

Senior Artist: James P. Weren

Artists: Peter E. Martin, Robert Schemmel, Donald M. Taka

Photography Director: Donald E. Stebbing

Photographs Editors: Fred C. Eckhardt, Jr., Carol A. Kuharich

Cartographic Coordinator: Leon Bishop

Art Production Editor: Barbara J. McDonald

Director of Research: Kenneth H. Petchenik

Director of Educational Services: John Sternig

Director of Editorial Services: Carl A. Tamminen

Executive Editor, The World Book Encyclopedia: Robert O. Zeleny

Executive Director, Manufacturing: Philip B. Hall

Manufacturing Department: John M. Babrick, Steve Hycner, Patrick Kelly, Henry Koval, Joseph C. LaCount

Board of Editors

Merchandise Mart Plaza, Chicago, Illinois 60654.

Printed in the United States of America
Library of Congress Catalog Card Number: 62-4818

Preface

If one were to select the most spectacular photograph of 1967, it might well be the photograph of the earth shown below. It is one of the first color photographs of the full earth and, not surprisingly, the earth looks pretty much the way our geography books said it would. Four continents are visible beneath the cloud cover, the most prominent being South America in the approximate middle of the picture. This wonderful overview of the world was taken from an altitude of 22,300 miles by the Applications Technology Satellite III, launched from Cape Kennedy, Fla., on November 5.

Another kind of overview of the world is provided by this 1968 edition of *The World Book Year Book*. The details of 1967 are recorded in the Year on File, more than 400 alphabetically arranged articles written by authorities from around the world. In their Focus Reports, *The Year Book's* distinguished Board of Editors analyzes these events from the perspective of a year. The Special Reports extend this matter of perspective, drawing from the past or looking to the future in examining subjects of current importance. Thus *The Year Book* attempts to relate the events of the year to the fast-changing world in which we live–or put more simply, to bring the world into sharper focus. A.R.H.

Contents

13 **Section One: The Year in Focus**
The members of *The Year Book* Board of Editors focus their attention on the significant developments of 1967.

14 **Paul-Henri Spaak: Focus on The World**
Distinguished world statesman and Belgian Minister of State; first president of the United Nations General Assembly.

20 **James B. Reston: Focus on The Nation**
Associate Editor of *The New York Times;* a Pulitzer prize medalist for national reporting.

26 **Sylvia Porter: Focus on The Economy**
Financial writer; columnist for the Publishers-Hall newspaper syndicate; Editor, *Reporting on Government.*

32 **Harrison Brown: Focus on Science**
Professor of Geochemistry, California Institute of Technology; Foreign Secretary, National Academy of Sciences.

38 **Lawrence A. Cremin: Focus on Education**
Frederick Barnard Professor of Education, Teachers College, Columbia University.

44 **John H. Glenn, Jr.: Focus on Space**
Former United States Astronaut; the first American to orbit the earth; NASA adviser.

50 **Alistair Cooke: Focus on The Arts**
Journalist; broadcaster; Chief U.S. Correspondent for *The Guardian,* Manchester, England.

56 **Red Smith: Focus on Sports**
Sports columnist for the Publishers-Hall newspaper syndicate.

61 **Section Two: Special Reports**
Seven special articles and *The Year Book* Trans-Vision® give special treatment to subjects of current importance.

62 **The Economics of Politics** by Fletcher Knebel
A noted Washington correspondent describes how the need for money can affect government, candidates for office, and officeholders.

78 **The Mekong River Project** by Gilbert F. White and James A. Harder
A report on an experiment in international cooperation that should serve as an example for action in other parts of the world.

96 **Where the Jobs Will Be** by A. H. Raskin
In America's fast-changing work picture, versatility and brains, not narrow skills and brawn, will be needed by more and more workers.

110 **Mao's Last Revolution** by Mark Gayn
China's aging titan is creating turmoil by his efforts to re-instill a revolutionary spirit in his countrymen.

126 **The Killing of a Great Lake** by Barry Commoner
Man's unwitting destruction of Lake Erie shows how our ignorance of our environment can rob us of the resources we need for survival.

144 **The Pop Music Scene** by Leonard G. Feather
An eminent music critic details the changes bright young songwriters are making in our notions about what is acceptable in popular music.

160 **In Search of the Mayan Past** by William R. Coe
The story of the ancient Mayan site of Tikal is told by the archaeologist who directed its 12-year-long study.

177 **Tikal**—*The Year Book* Trans-Vision®
This exclusive unit uses transparent overlays to show the centuries-long growth of the temple-studded religious center at Tikal.

191 **Section Three: The Year on File**
Year Book contributors report on the major developments of 1967 in more than 400 alphabetically arranged articles.

543 **Section Four: World Book Supplement**
Ten wide-ranging and significant articles reprinted from the 1968 edition of *The World Book Encyclopedia.*

591 **Section Five: Dictionary Supplement**
Six new articles and features that will be included in the introductory pages of the 1968 edition of *The World Book Dictionary.*

597 **Section Six: The Index**
A 21-page cumulative index covering the contents of the 1964, 1965, 1966, 1967, and 1968 editions of *The Year Book.*

A chronology of the most important events of 1967 will be found on pages 8 to 12. A preview of 1968 will be found on pages 621 and 622.

Contributors

Alexiou, Arthur G., M.S., E.E.; Program Director, Institutional Support Office of Sea Grant Programs, National Science Foundation. [OCEAN]

Anderson, Jon, B.A., B.C.L.; Correspondent, *Chicago Sun-Times*. [CANADA (Close-Up)]

Anderson, Joseph P., Ph.B., LL.D.; Executive Director, National Association of Social Workers. [MEDICARE; Social Organizations]

Andrews, James H., M.A.; Assistant Professor, Political Science, Ohio State University. [STATE GOVERNMENT]

Baker, John C.; Public Information Officer, Bureau of the Census. [CENSUS]

Bautz, Laura P., Ph.D.; Assistant Professor of Astronomy, Dearborn Observatory, Northwestern University. [ASTRONOMY]

Berkwitt, George J., B.S.J.; Senior Editor, *Modern Industry*. [MANUFACTURING]

Bhote, Keki R., B.E., M.S.; Author; Lecturer. [INDIA; PAKISTAN]

Bradley, Van Allen, B.J.; Literary Editor, *Chicago Daily News*. [LITERATURE]

Brdlik, Mel F., B.A.; Senior Editor, *Dun's Review* Magazine. [MINES AND MINING; STEEL INDUSTRY]

Brooks, Gwendolyn; Winner, Pulitzer Prize for Poetry, 1950; Lecturer, Northwestern Illinois University and Columbia College; Poet Laureate of Illinois. [DEATHS OF NOTABLE PERSONS (Sandburg Close-Up)]

Brown, Kenneth; European Journalist. [Western Europe Articles]

Bryan, Leslie A., Ph.D., LL.B.; Director, Institute of Aviation, University of Illinois. [AVIATION]

Burnet, Alastair, B.A.; Editor, *The Economist*. [GREAT BRITAIN]

Cain, Charles C., III, B.A.; Automotive Editor, Associated Press. [AUTOMOBILE]

Carruth, Hayden, M.A.; Poet. [LITERATURE (Poetry)]

Coe, William R., Ph.D.; Associate Professor of Anthropology, University of Pennsylvania. [Special Report]

Commoner, Barry, Ph.D.; Chairman, Department of Botany, Washington University; Director, Washington University's Center for the Biology of Natural Systems. [Special Report]

Conley, Clare, B.A.; Managing Editor, *Field & Stream*. [HUNTING AND FISHING]

Cook, Robert C.; President, Population Reference Bureau, Inc. [POPULATION, WORLD]

Cromie, William J., B.S.; Associate Editor, World Book Encyclopedia Science Service, Inc. [ASTRONAUTS]

Csida, June Bundy; Former Radio-TV Editor, *Billboard* Magazine. [RADIO; TELEVISION]

Dale, Edwin L., Jr., B.A.; Reporter, *The New York Times*, Washington Bureau. [INTERNATIONAL TRADE AND FINANCE]

Darby, Edwin W., B.S.J.; Financial Editor, *Chicago Sun-Times*. [Business Articles]

Dewald, William G., Ph.D.; Associate Professor of Economics, Ohio State University. [Finance Articles]

Dumouchel, J. Robert; Director of Public Affairs, National Association of Housing and Redevelopment Officials, Washington, D.C. [CITY AND REGIONAL PLANNING; HOUSING]

Dunaway, James O., B.S.; Eastern Editor, *Track and Field News;* Author, *The Sports Illustrated Book of Track and Field*. [Sports Articles]

Farr, David M. L., Ph.D.; Dean of Arts, Carleton University, Ottawa. [CANADA]

Feather, Leonard G.; Author, *New Encyclopedia of Jazz*. [Special Report; Music Articles]

Feinberg, Harold, Ph.D.; Associate Professor, University of Illinois, Department of Pharmacology. [BIOCHEMISTRY; BIOLOGY]

Fenner, Frank E., B.S.; Fellow of the Photographic Society of America. [PHOTOGRAPHY]

Fleischer, Everly B., Ph.D.; Associate Professor of Chemistry, University of Chicago. [CHEMISTRY]

Freeman, Leslie G., Jr., Ph.D.; Assistant Professor, Department of Anthropology, University of Chicago. [ANTHROPOLOGY; ARCHAEOLOGY]

French, Charles E., Ph.D.; Department Head, Agricultural Economics, Purdue University. [AGRICULTURE]

Freudenheim, Milt, B.A.; National/Foreign Editor, Director of Foreign Service, *Chicago Daily News*. [DISARMAMENT; UNITED NATIONS]

Froslid, E. Kenneth, B.A.; Public Affairs Analyst, International Business Machines. [CITY (Close-Up); DEATHS OF NOTABLE PERSONS (Luce Close-Up)]

Gayn, Mark, B.A., B.S.; Chief, Asia Bureau, *The Toronto Star*. [Special Report; CHINA]

Goy, Robert W., Ph.D.; Chairman and Senior Scientist, Department of Reproductive Physiology and Behavior, Oregon Regional Primate Research Center. [PSYCHOLOGY]

Griffin, Alice, Ph.D.; Associate Professor of English, Hunter College. [THEATER]

Hanson, Donald D., M.A.; Chairman, Department of Architecture, Chicago Circle Campus, University of Illinois. [ARCHITECTURE]

Harris, Allen, LL.B.; Member, faculty of law, University of Missouri at Kansas City; Director of Community Legal Education and Legal Research. [SUPREME COURT]

Harder, James A., Ph.D.; Associate Professor of Hydraulic Engineering, University of California, Berkeley. [Special Report]

Hasson, Rachelle Joy, B.A.; Fashion Writer. [FASHION]

Havighurst, Robert J., Ph.D.; Professor of Education, University of Chicago; Author, *Older People*. [OLD AGE]

Hechinger, Fred M., B.A.; Education Editor, *The New York Times*. [EDUCATION]

Holmes, Jay E., B.S.; Special Assistant to Director, Manned Space Flight Field Center Development, NASA. [SPACE EXPLORATION]

Jessup, Mary E., B.A.; News Editor, *Civil Engineering*. [Engineering Articles]

Joseph, Lou, B.A.; Assistant Director, Bureau of Public Information, American Dental Association. [DENTISTRY]

Kavaler, Arthur R., M.S.; Managing Editor, *Oil, Paint and Drug Reporter*. [CHEMICAL INDUSTRY; DRUGS]

Klein, Fannie J., LL.B., LL.M.; Professor of Law, New York University School of Law. [COURTS AND LAWS]

Knebel, Fletcher, B.A.; Former Washington, D.C., Correspondent; Author, *Vanished*, and Coauthor, *Seven Days in May* and *Convention*. [Special Report]

Knight, Arthur, B.A.; Adjunct Professor, University of Southern California Cinema Department; Contributing Editor, *The Saturday Review*. [MOTION PICTURES]

Koenig, Louis W., Ph.D., L.H.D.; Professor of Government, New York University. [CIVIL RIGHTS]

Lach, Alma; Diplome de Cordon Bleu; Author. [FOOD]

Lake, John E., B.A.; Sports Editor, *Newsweek* Magazine. [Sports Articles; SPORTS (Close-Up)]

Leakey, L. S. B., Ph.D., D.Sc., LL.D.; Fellow of the British Academy; Honorary Director of the Coryndon Centre of Pre-History and Palaeontology, Nairobi, Kenya; Author, *Olduvai Gorge*. [ANTHROPOLOGY (Close-Up)]

Lewis, Ralph H., M.A.; Chief, Museum Branch, National Park Service. [MUSEUMS]

Lief, Donald W., M.A.; Deputy Director, Urban Information Center, Urban America, Inc. [City Articles]

Lohman, Joseph D., M.A.; Dean and Professor, School of Criminology, University of California. [CRIME]

MacFarland, Douglas C., Ph.D.; Chief, Division of Services to the Blind, Department of Health, Education, and Welfare. [BLINDNESS]

Maki, John M., Ph.D.; Vice-Dean, College of Arts and Sciences, University of Massachusetts. [JAPAN]

Malia, Thomas M., Ph.B.; Executive Editor, *Telecommunications Reports*. [COMMUNICATIONS]

Manchester, P. W.; Managing Editor, *Dance News;* New York Dance Critic, *Christian Science Monitor*. [DANCING]

Marsh, Robert C., M.A., Ed.D.; Music Critic, *Chicago Sun-Times*. [MUSIC]

Marty, Martin E., B.D., S.T.M., Ph.D; Associate Editor, *The Christian Century*. [PROTESTANT; RELIGION]

Maxon, John, Ph.D.; Associate Director, The Art Institute of Chicago. [PAINTING AND SCULPTURE]

McCaul, Eugene B.; Director, Statistical Department, American Transit Association. [TRANSIT]

McGaffin, William, B.A., B.S.; Washington Correspondent, *Chicago Daily News*. [U.S. Government Articles]

Merritt, Malcolm, B.A.; Editor, Research Institute Bulletin, American Newspaper Publishers Association. [PUBLISHING]

Morse, Walter F., B.A.; Assistant City Editor, *Chicago Sun-Times*. [Biographies]

Morton, Elizabeth H., B.A.; Executive Director, Canadian Library Association. [CANADIAN LIBRARY ASSOCIATION; CANADIAN LITERATURE]

Mullen, Frances A., Ph.D.; Consultant on Education of the Handicapped, U.S. Office of Education. [CHILD GUIDANCE; CHILD WELFARE]

Nelson, Larry L., M.S.; Instructor, Agricultural Economics Department, Purdue University. [AGRICULTURE]

Newman, Andrew L., M.A.; Deputy Director of Information, U.S. Department of the Interior. [Conservation Articles]

Norman, Lloyd H., B.S.; Military Affairs Correspondent, *Newsweek* Magazine. [ARMED FORCES OF THE WORLD; ESPIONAGE; NATIONAL DEFENSE]

O'Connor, James J., E.E.; Executive Editor, *Power* Magazine. [ELECTRIC POWER AND EQUIPMENT]

O'Leary, Theodore M., B.A.; Regional Correspondent, *Sports Illustrated* Magazine. [BRIDGE, CONTRACT; CHESS; GAMES, MODELS, AND TOYS; HOBBIES; PETS]

Patterson, William D., B.A.; Associate Publisher, *Saturday Review*. [FAIRS AND EXHIBITIONS; TRAVEL]

Pearre, James A., B.S.; News Supervisor, Illinois Institute of Technology Research Institute. [Science Articles]

Perkins, R. Marlin; Director, St. Louis Zoological Gardens. [ZOOS AND AQUARIUMS]

Pyle, Howard; President, National Safety Council. [SAFETY]

Raskin, A. H., B.A.; Assistant Editor, Editorial Page, *The New York Times*. [Special Report]

Rue, Eloise, M.A.; Associate Professor of Library Science, University of Wisconsin, Milwaukee. [LITERATURE FOR CHILDREN]

Schaefle, Kenneth E., B.S., M.B.A.; Director, Management Programs Transportation Center at Northwestern University. [TRANSPORTATION]

Schmemann, The Reverend Alexander, S.T.D., LL.D., D.D.; Dean, St. Vladimir's Orthodox Theological Seminary. [EASTERN ORTHODOX]

Schubert, Helen C., B.S.; Home Furnishing Editorial Consultant; Former Administrative Director, National Design Center. [INTERIOR DESIGN]

Shaw, Robert J., B.S.B.A.; Head, Information Service, Library Technology Program, American Library Association. [LIBRARY]

Shearer, Warren W., Ph.D.; Professor of Economics and Dean of the college, Wabash College. [ECONOMY, THE]

Silverman, David Wolf, Rabbi, M.A., M.H.L.; Director, Department of Special Education, Jewish Theological Seminary, N.Y. [JEWS AND JUDAISM]

Skilling, H. Gordon, Ph.D.; Professor of Political Science; Director, Center for Russian and East European Studies, University of Toronto. [COMMUNISM; RUSSIA; East European Countries]

Spencer, William, Ph.D.; Director, Institute of Non-Western Studies, The American University, Washington, D.C. [Middle East and North African Countries]

Stalker, John N., Ph.D.; Director, Office of International Programs, University of Hawaii. [ASIA; Asia Articles]

Steffek, Edwin F., B.S.; Editor, *Horticulture* Magazine, and other publications of the Massachusetts Horticultural Society. [GARDEN AND LAWN]

Stern, James L., Ph.D.; Professor of Economics, University of Wisconsin. [LABOR]

Thomas, Benjamin E., M.A., M.S., Ph.D.; Professor of Geography, University of California. [AFRICA; Africa Articles]

Thompson, Carol L., M.A.; Editor, *Current History* Magazine. [U.S. Government Articles]

Treuting, Theodore F., M.D., F.A.C.P.; Professor of Medicine, Psychiatry, and Neurology, Tulane University School of Medicine. [Health Articles]

Webster, Mary C., B.A.; Editor, *Noticias* and *Breve* Magazines. [Latin America Articles]

White, Gilbert, Ph.D.; Head, Department of Geography, University of Chicago. [Special Report]

White, Ruth M., B.S. in Ed., B.S. in L.S., M.A.; Headquarters Librarian, American Library Association. [AMERICAN LIBRARY ASSOCIATION]

White, Thomas O., Ph.D.; Research Associate, Department of Physics, Northwestern University. [PHYSICS]

Zahony, Kathryn, B.A.; Copy Editor and Fashion Writer *Harper's Bazaar*. [FASHION (Close-Up)]

Chronology 1967

January

Sun	Mon	Tue	Wed	Thu	Fri	Sat
1	2	3	4	5	6	7
8	9	10	11	12	13	14
15	16	17	18	19	20	21
22	23	24	25	26	27	28
29	30	31				

2 **New Year's truce in Vietnam ends.** United States reports Viet Cong and North Vietnamese violated three-day cease-fire 178 times.

6 **Latin America's longest suspension bridge opens** in Venezuela, first across Orinoco River. Four-lane 5,507-foot span links Ciudad Bolívar and Soledad.

10 **90th Congress of U.S. opens** its first session. President Johnson delivers State of the Union message. Asks for 6 per cent surcharge on all income taxes. House of Representatives declines to seat New York Democrat Adam Clayton Powell, Jr., pending investigation of his behavior.

11 **Lani Bird II satellite launched** at Cape Kennedy, also named Intelsat II for International Telecommunications Satellite Consortium.

13 **Coup d'état in Togo.** Army Chief of Staff Lieutenant Colonel Etienne Eyadema deposes President Nicolas Grunitzky.

16 **First all-Negro government in Bahamas.** Lynden O. Pindling also islands' first Negro prime minister.
First U.S. Secretary of Transportation, Alan Stephenson Boyd, takes office.
Chicago's McCormick Place burns, multimillion dollar lakefront exposition center.

18 **Eight military communications satellites launched** by a Titan-3C rocket at Cape Kennedy.

26 **ESSA IV launched** at Vandenberg Air Force Base, California.

27 **United Nations arms in space ban treaty signed** by 62 countries at ceremonies in Washington, London, and Moscow.
First U.S. space disaster. Flash fire inside Apollo spacecraft kills Air Force Lieutenant Colonels Virgil I. Grissom and Edward H. White II and Navy Lieutenant Commander Roger B. Chaffee during test at Cape Kennedy.

February

Sun	Mon	Tue	Wed	Thu	Fri	Sat
			1	2	3	4
5	6	7	8	9	10	11
12	13	14	15	16	17	18
19	20	21	22	23	24	25
26	27	28				

4 **Lunar Orbiter III launched to moon** at Cape Kennedy.

6 **Tanzania nationalizes commercial banks.** Management delegated to finance minister.

6-13 **Russian premier in Great Britain.** Aleksei N. Kosygin and Prime Minister Harold Wilson discuss Vietnam and agree on direct Teletype communications line between Kremlin and 10 Downing Street, London.

8-12 **Four-day truce in Vietnam.** Eighteen U.S. soldiers killed by enemy during cease-fire.

9-10 **King of Morocco in Washington, D.C.** Hassan II confers with President Johnson and Secretary of State Dean Rusk.

13-14 **Emperor of Ethiopia in Washington, D.C.** Haile Selassie I confers with President Johnson.

14 **Treaty banning nuclear weapons in Latin America signed** by 14 countries in Mexico City.

15 **Diadem II launched** in Algerian Sahara, France's fourth space satellite.

15-26 **OAS foreign ministers confer** in Buenos Aires, Argentina. Approve admission of Trinidad and Tobago as 22nd member of Organization of American States.

21 **United Nations Disarmament Committee reconvenes** in Geneva, Switzerland. Recessed on Aug. 25, 1966.

23 **U.S. Constitution Amendment 25 proclaimed** by President Johnson on succession to presidency and vice-presidency in event of disability.

28 **South Arabia violence.** Five persons killed in Aden at funeral for six victims of terrorist bomb the day before.

March

Sun	Mon	Tue	Wed	Thu	Fri	Sat
			1	2	3	4
5	6	7	8	9	10	11
12	13	14	15	16	17	18
19	20	21	22	23	24	25
26	27	28	29	30	31	

1 **Uruguay inaugurates president.** Oscar Diego Gestido, country's first permanent chief executive in 15 years, replaces nine-man national council.
Adam Clayton Powell barred from U.S. House of Representatives following its inquiry into the New York Democrat's behavior.

7 **James R. Hoffa enters federal penitentiary** at Lewisburg, Pa. International Brotherhood of Teamsters' president to serve eight-year sentence for jury tampering.

8 **OSO III launched** at Cape Kennedy, Orbiting Solar Observatory satellite.

10 **New U.S. Attorney General.** William Ramsey Clark takes office as Department of Justice head.

15 **Brazil inaugurates president.** Arthur da Costa e Silva elected to five-year term in 1966.

20-21 **Guam conference.** President Johnson and South Vietnam Premier Nguyen Cao Ky discuss Vietnam war and nonmilitary matters.

22 **Canary Bird launched into orbit** at Cape Kennedy, Communications Satellite Corporation's (Comsat) fourth satellite.

24-27 **Coup d'état in Sierra Leone.** Military National Reformation Council established, with Lieutenant Colonel Andrew Juxon-Smith as chairman.

27 **U.S. Vice-President in Europe.** Hubert H. Humphrey arrives in Geneva, Switzerland, on a diplomatic mission to seven West European countries.

29 **First French nuclear submarine launched** at Cherbourg, 7,900-ton *Redoubtable.*
Federal Reserve Board chairman to remain. William McChesney Martin, Jr., is to continue in post until Jan. 31, 1970.

30 **U.S. Department of Transportation established.** President Johnson signs executive order for its official existence to begin on April 1.

30-31 **NATO completes withdrawal from France.** North Atlantic Treaty Organization opens its Supreme Headquarters Allied Powers Europe (SHAPE) in Casteau, Belgium.

31 **U.S.-Soviet consular treaty signed** by President Johnson. Ratified by Senate on March 16.

April

Sun	Mon	Tue	Wed	Thu	Fri	Sat
						1
2	3	4	5	6	7	8
9	10	11	12	13	14	15
16	17	18	19	20	21	22
23/30	24	25	26	27	28	29

1 **South Vietnam's new constitution signed** by Chief of State Nguyen Van Thieu.

4 **New premier in Netherlands.** Petrus J. S. de Jong ends 47-day government crisis.

5 **International Court of Justice elects president,** José Luis Bustamante y Rivero of Peru.
ATS II launched at Cape Kennedy, Applications Technology Satellite.

10 **Radio-television strike ends** after 13 days. American Federation of Television and Radio Artists settle differences with American, Mutual, and National Broadcasting systems.

11 **New prime minister in Jamaica.** Hugh H. Shearer succeeds the late Sir Donald B. Sangster.
New York re-elects Democrat Adam Clayton Powell to seat denied him in U.S. House of Representatives in March.

12-14 **Organization of American States presidents conference** in Punta del Este, Uruguay, attended by President Johnson. Declaration of the Presidents of America includes a Latin American common market and other programs.

14 **New government in Hungary** with Pal Losonczi as president and Jenö Fock as premier.
Togo abolishes national reconciliation committee. Lieutenant Colonel Etienne Eyadema heads country as president.

17 **Canada inaugurates governor-general.** Daniel Roland Michener succeeds the late Georges Philias Vanier.
Surveyor III launched at Cape Kennedy.

19 **Konrad Adenauer dies at 91.** West Germany's first chancellor also a leader in the European unification movement.
Surveyor III soft-lands on moon, second U.S. spacecraft to achieve this feat.

20 **U.S. planes bomb Haiphong for first time.** Hit power plants in North Vietnam city.
ESSA V launched at Vandenberg Air Force Base, California.

21 **Coup d'état in Greece.** Civilian Premier Constantine Kollias installed by the army.
Joseph Stalin's daughter defects to U.S. Svetlana Alliluyeva arrives in New York City.

23 **New premier in Jordan.** Saad Jumma appointed by King Hussein following recent elections.
***Soyuz I* launched** by Russia. Cosmonaut Colonel Vladimir M. Komarov aboard.

23-26 **President Johnson in West Germany.** Attends state funeral of Konrad Adenauer. Also talks with West German Chancellor Kurt Georg Kiesinger, British Prime Minister Harold Wilson, Italian Premier Aldo Moro, and briefly with President Charles de Gaulle of France.

24 **Cosmonaut Komarov first man known to die in space flight.** Parachute trouble fatal as *Soyuz I* crashes to earth.

25 **Swaziland achieves internal self-government,** with Prince Makhosini Dlamini as prime minister of British protectorate.

27 **Male heir to Netherlands throne born** to Crown Princess Beatrix, first since birth of Crown Prince Alexander in 1851.

27-28 **Canadian Universal and International Exhibition opens in Montreal.** Official inauguration by Prime Minister Lester B. Pearson followed by general public admission.

28 **Five-in-one launching** at Cape Kennedy. Single Titan-3C rocket launches five satellites.

May

Sun	Mon	Tue	Wed	Thu	Fri	Sat
	1	2	3	4	5	6
7	8	9	10	11	12	13
14	15	16	17	18	19	20
21	22	23	24	25	26	27
28	29	30	31			

1 **Nicaragua inaugurates President.** Anastasio Somoza Debayle elected to five-year term on Feb. 5, 1967.

4 **Lunar Orbiter IV launched** at Cape Kennedy on photographic mission to moon.

5 **Ariel III launched** at Vandenberg Air Force Base, California, first satellite entirely designed and built in Great Britain.

11 **Great Britain applies for European Economic Community membership** a second time.

14 **India inaugurates its first Moslem president.** Zakir Husain, formerly vice-president, elected to five-year term May 9, 1967.
Liverpool consecrates Cathedral of Christ the King, its first since English city made a Roman Catholic archdiocese in 1850.

15 **Children under arrest entitled to Bill of Rights protections,** the same as adults, Supreme Court of United States rules.

17 **New York Stock Exchange celebrates 175th birthday.** Founded May 17, 1792.

19 **United Nations ends peace-keeping patrols in Gaza and Sinai** on request of United Arab Republic.
United Nations votes on South West Africa. General Assembly resolution provides for UN commissioner and council to rule territory now under South Africa control.

20 **Male heir to Greek throne born** to King Constantine II and Danish-born Queen Anne-Marie.

22-23 **United Arab Republic closes Gulf of Aqaba to Israel.** Blocks ships to and from country.

24 **IMP-F launched** at Vandenberg Air Force Base, California. Interplanetary Monitoring Platform is also Explorer XXXIV.

25 **President Johnson in Canada.** Confers with Prime Minister Lester B. Pearson and visits Expo 67.
Fifth *Molniya I* launched by Russia, a communications satellite.

29 **ESRO II launched** at Vandenberg Air Force Base, California, European Space Research Organization satellite.

30 **Nigeria's Eastern Region secedes** as independent Republic of Biafra.

June

Sun	Mon	Tue	Wed	Thu	Fri	Sat
				1	2	3
4	5	6	7	8	9	10
11	12	13	14	15	16	17
18	19	20	21	22	23	24
25	26	27	28	29	30	

2-5 **Riots in Boston's Negro Roxbury district** follow Mothers for Adequate Welfare sit-in.
5-10 **Israel victor in war with Arabs.** Opens Gulf of Aqaba. Takes Sinai and Gaza from United Arab Republic, Old Jerusalem from Jordan, and border areas from Syria.
5-14 **United Nations debates Arab-Israeli war.** Security Council fails to approve Russian resolution to condemn Israel as the aggressor.
6 **Astronaut killed in Houston,** Tex. Air Force Major Edward G. Givens' automobile crashes in ditch.
10 **New president in Somalia.** Abdirascid Ali Scermarche elected by National Assembly.
11-15 **Race riots in Tampa and Cincinnati.** National Guards called out in the Florida and Ohio cities.
12 **Supreme Court of U.S. ends 1966-1968 term.** Associate Justice Tom C. Clark retires. Served since Aug. 24, 1949.
Venus IV launched on four-month journey to planet Venus by Russia.
14 **Mariner V launched on journey to Venus** at Cape Kennedy.
New U.S. Secretary of Commerce, Alexander B. Trowbridge, takes office.
17 **Communist China explodes hydrogen bomb,** its first.
19-20 **Negro killed in Atlanta riots.** Stokely Carmichael meets with group in Georgia city.
20 **South Arabian troops mutiny in Aden,** killing 11 Britons and two Arab policemen.
21 **President Johnson a grandfather.** Daughter Luci gives birth to a boy in Austin, Tex.
23 **U.S. Senate censures Thomas J. Dodd.** Connecticut Democrat used "funds obtained from public through political testimonials and a political campaign" for personal benefit.
23, 25 **Glassboro Summit.** President Johnson and Russian Premier Aleksei N. Kosygin confer in New Jersey college town.
26 **Twenty-seven new Roman Catholic cardinals.** Pope Paul VI elevates prelates at secret consistory.
27-28 **Violence in Buffalo,** N.Y. East Side Negroes engage in widespread vandalism.
30 **International tariff reduction pact signed** by 46 nations at GATT (General Agreement on Tariffs and Trade) organization headquarters in Geneva, Switzerland. Results of Kennedy Round negotiations dating back to May, 1964.

July

Sun	Mon	Tue	Wed	Thu	Fri	Sat
						1
2	3	4	5	6	7	8
9	10	11	12	13	14	15
16	17	18	19	20	21	22
23/30	24/31	25	26	27	28	29

1 **Queen Elizabeth II addresses Canadian parliament** on Dominion Day, 100th anniversary of the Canadian Confederation.
El Salvador inaugurates president. Fidel Sánchez Hernández elected to five-year term on March 5.
Moise Tshombe's plane hijacked over Mediterranean and forced to land in Algeria. Former Congo premier imprisoned in Algiers.
South Korea inaugurates president. Chung Hee Park elected to second term in May.
3-5 **Queen Elizabeth II visits Expo 67,** and ends visit to Canada which began on June 30.
5-7 **Fighting in Congo.** White mercenaries and Katangese followers rebel in Kisangani and Bukavu.
6 **Civil war in Nigeria.** Secessionist Republic of Biafra attacked by federal troops.
12-17 **Twenty-six persons killed in Newark.** Most of the New Jersey city dead were Negroes.
14-16 **Surveyor IV launched to moon** at Cape Kennedy, but destroyed on impact.
17 **United Nations patrols Suez Canal area.** Peace-keeping force takes up positions to supervise Israel-United Arab Republic cease-fire.
19 **Explorer XXXV launched** at Cape Kennedy.
23-30 **Detroit wrecked by rioters.** More than 40 persons killed in the Michigan city.
24 **National Baseball Hall of Fame inducts new members:** the late Branch Rickey, 105th, and Lloyd Waner, 106th member.
25-26 **Pope Paul VI on peace pilgrimage in Turkey.** The first Roman Catholic pontiff to enter an Eastern Orthodox cathedral since 1054, exchanges vows of ecumenical unity with Patriarch Athenagoras I in Istanbul.
26 **French president ends Canadian visit.** Charles de Gaulle cancels meeting with Prime Minister Lester B. Pearson after "Vive Quebec Libre" speech in Montreal on July 24.
27-28 **Commission on racial disorders established** by President Johnson. Illinois Governor Otto Kerner, Jr., heads investigative panel.
28 **Great Britain nationalizes steel industry.** New British Steel Corporation takes over 13 major companies.
OGO-IV launched at Vandenberg Air Force Base, Orbiting Geophysical Laboratory.
29 **Aircraft carrier *Forrestal* swept by fire** in Gulf of Tonkin. At least 134 men killed.
30-31 **Rioters loot and set fires in Milwaukee.** Wisconsin sends in National Guard units.

August

Sun	Mon	Tue	Wed	Thu	Fri	Sat
		1	2	3	4	5
6	7	8	9	10	11	12
13	14	15	16	17	18	19
20	21	22	23	24	25	26
27	28	29	30	31		

1 **Lunar Orbiter V launched** at Cape Kennedy.
6-8 **Association of South East Asian Nations established** by Indonesia, Malaysia, the Philippines, Singapore, and Thailand during two days of talks in Bangkok, Thailand.
9 **White mercenaries in Congo recapture Bukavu** and escort 300 refugees across Ruzizi River into Rwanda.
Nigeria's Mid-western Region taken by Biafra forces in secessionists' first major offensive against federal troops.
District of Columbia reorganization plan approved by U.S. House of Representatives, and unopposed by Senate, gives Washington, D.C., a single chief executive and a nine-member city council nominated by the President and subject to Senate approval.
10 **Council for South West Africa created** by United Nations. José Piñera, Chile's permanent UN representative, installed as president.
19-23 **New Haven curbs racial violence** with a curfew. Connecticut city arrests some 350 persons.
25 **American Nazi leader killed** in Arlington, Va. George Lincoln Rockwell is shot to death by John Patler, aide he dismissed in March.
Argentina curbs communists. Twenty-eight-article law is signed by President Juan Carlos Onganía.
28 **Prime minister takes control of Britain's Economic Department.** Harold Wilson retains

Michael Steward, however, as first Secretary of State for Home Affairs.

30 **Algeria seizes five U.S. oil companies,** under state control since Arab-Israeli war in June.

31 **Indonesia and Malaysia establish diplomatic relations,** broken during Sukarno dictatorship.

September

Sun	Mon	Tue	Wed	Thu	Fri	Sat
					1	2
3	4	5	6	7	8	9
10	11	12	13	14	15	16
17	18	19	20	21	22	23
24	25	26	27	28	29	30

3 **South Vietnam elections.** Lieutenant General Nguyen Van Thieu elected president, and Nguyen Cao Ky, vice-president. Senators also elected.

6-12 **French president in Poland.** Charles de Gaulle visits an East European Communist country for the first time.

7 **Iran provides for a regency.** Empress Farah to serve as regent if the Shah should die or be unable to carry out his duties before Crown Prince Riza Pahlevi, now six, comes of age.

7-9 **Biosatellite II launched** at Cape Kennedy, and returned to earth near Hawaii.

9 **John G. Diefenbaker defeated** in Canada. His Progressive Conservative party elects Robert L. Stanfield, Nova Scotia premier, as leader.

10 **Gibraltar elects to remain with Britain.** Only 44 votes favor return to Spanish rule.

Surveyor V soft-lands on moon in Sea of Tranquillity.

11-14 **Organization of African Unity conference** in Kinshasa, Congo, considers white mercenaries in eastern Congo and civil war in Nigeria.

18 **United Nations General Assembly ends emergency session.** Votes to place Middle East issue on agenda of regular session.

19 **United Nations General Assembly opens.** Elects Romanian Foreign Minister Corneliu Mănescu president of 22nd regular session.

20 **Nigeria frees Mid-western Region.** Federal troops capture capital city of Benin from secessionist Biafra forces.

21 **First Thai combat troops in South Vietnam.** Royal Thai army regiment arrives in Saigon.

24 **Organization of American States acts on Cuban subversion.** Resolution includes condemnation of "forcefully" continuing intervention in Bolivia, Venezuela, and other Western Hemisphere nations.

27 **Pacific II launched** at Cape Kennedy by Comsat, Communications Satellite Corporation, as a radio relay station over the central Pacific.

28 **National Capital's first commissioner a Negro.** Walter E. Washington takes office as chief executive of Washington, D.C.

October

Sun	Mon	Tue	Wed	Thu	Fri	Sat
1	2	3	4	5	6	7
8	9	10	11	12	13	14
15	16	17	18	19	20	21
22	23	24	25	26	27	28
29	30	31				

2 **Supreme Court of U.S. opens 1967-1968 term.** First Negro associate justice, Thurgood Marshall, replaces Tom C. Clark.

4 **Barbados admitted to OAS.** Approval by the Organization of American States Council increases OAS membership to 23 nations.

4-12 **World Series won by St. Louis Cardinals** for eighth time. Defeat Boston Red Sox four games to three.

5 **U.S. astronaut killed in plane crash.** Marine Major Clifton C. Williams, Jr., crashes in a T-38 jet northeast of Tallahassee, Fla.

6 **New director of Office of Emergency Planning.** Price Daniel is confirmed by U.S. Senate.

7 **Jordan installs new premier.** Bahjat Talhouni succeeds Saad Jumma.

9 **Cuba's Ernesto "Che" Guevara killed,** an official Bolivian army dispatch reports.

12 **New U.S. Solicitor General.** Erwin N. Griswold, Harvard Law School dean, is confirmed by the Senate.

16 **NATO in new headquarters** near Brussels. Belgian Prime Minister Paul Vanden Boeynants makes official presentation to Manlio Brosio, Secretary-General of the North Atlantic Treaty Organization.

18 **Venus IV lands on planet Venus.** Russian satellite is first to succeed in this feat.

OSO IV launched at Cape Kennedy, Orbiting Solar Observatory.

19 **Mariner V passes planet Venus** by some 2,480 miles.

21 **Israeli destroyer sunk off Sinai Coast.** *Elath* miles outside United Arab Republic waters.

21-22 **End-the-Vietnam-war marchers in Washington,** D.C., storm the Pentagon.

24 **Israel shells port of Suez.** Destroys United Arab Republic fuel tanks and refineries.

26 **Coronation in Iran.** Shah Mohammed Riza Pahlevi crowns self on 48th birthday and his wife. Farah is nation's first crowned empress.

27-28 **Cosmos 186 and 187 launched** by Russia.

28 **President Johnson in Mexico.** Formally transfers to President Gustavo Díaz Ordaz the El Chamizal area at Texas-Mexico border as provided for in 1963 treaty.

30 **Cosmos 188 launched.** Joins and docks with Cosmos 186 in first Russian docking feat and world's first docking of two unmanned spacecraft.

31 **South Vietnam inaugurates president.** Lieutenant General Nguyen Van Thieu then appoints a civilian, Nguyen Van Loc, premier.

November

Sun	Mon	Tue	Wed	Thu	Fri	Sat
			1	2	3	4
5	6	7	8	9	10	11
12	13	14	15	16	17	18
19	20	21	22	23	24	25
26	27	28	29	30		

1 **New prime minister in Afghanistan.** Nour Ahmad Etemadi succeeds Mohammed Hashim Maiwandwal.

1-8 **U.S. Vice-President ends Asian tour.** Hubert H. Humphrey discusses Vietnam and other problems with Malaysian Prime Minister Tunku Abdul Rahman and his cabinet. In Indonesia, he counters talk and rumors unfavorable to the United States and its Asian policies.

4 **Congolese troops take Bukavu.** Capital of Kivu Province held by white mercenaries and Katangese rebels since August 9.

5 **ATS III launched** at Cape Kennedy, Applications Technology Satellite.

7 **Surveyor VI launched to moon** at Cape Kennedy.
United Nations adopts rights for women declaration by unanimous vote in General Assembly. Declaration "calls on governments, organizations, and individuals to work toward obtaining equal rights for women in employment, politics, education, and cultural life."

9 **Surveyor VI soft-lands on moon** in Sinus Medii, or Central Bay, area.
Saturn V test flight a success. Launched at Cape Kennedy, the 6,200,000-pound moon rocket sends Apollo IV spacecraft into orbit. Apollo IV comes down in Pacific some eight hours later.

10 **ESSA VI launched into polar orbit** at Vandenberg Air Force Base, California.

15 **Fighting erupts on Cyprus,** in villages of Ayios Theodoros and Kophinou, where 24 Turkish and two Greek Cypriots are killed.

18 **Great Britain devalues pound sterling** by 14.3 per cent. Drops from $2.79 to $2.40 in U.S. dollars.

22 **U.S. forces take Hill 875.** Some 290 Americans killed in South Vietnam Dakto battle since November 3, and an estimated 1,600 North Vietnamese.
United Nations votes on Middle East crisis. Security Council adopts British resolution calling for "eventual withdrawal of Israeli forces from Arab areas taken in June, and end of Arabs' state of belligerency with Israel."

28 **Communist China barred from United Nations** for 17th time by vote in General Assembly.
President of Gabon dies. Leon M'Ba, country's first president, was elected in 1961.

29 **New chancellor of the exchequer** in Great Britain. Roy Jenkins succeeds James Callaghan, who takes Jenkins' post as Secretary of State for the Home Department.
Robert S. McNamara new president of International Bank for Reconstruction and Development. He accepts the World Bank post, but continues as Secretary of Defense until early 1968.

30 **People's Republic of South Yemen founded,** with Republican Council President Abdul Rahman al-Iryani and Premier Hassan al-Amri. The former Federation of South Arabia was proclaimed an independent country by Great Britain on November 28.

December

Sun	Mon	Tue	Wed	Thu	Fri	Sat
					1	2
3	4	5	6	7	8	9
10	11	12	13	14	15	16
17	18	19	20	21	22	23
24/31	25	26	27	28	29	30

1 **East African Community inaugurated** by Kenya, Tanzania, and Uganda.

2 **Twentieth Century Limited ends** 65 years of service. Leaves New York's Grand Central Station on last run to Chicago. New York Central Railroad replaces it with No. 61, devoid of observation cars and other luxuries.

3 **Cyprus accord accepted** by Greece, Turkey, and Cyprus. Terms include withdrawal of Greek and Turkish troops from Cyprus not authorized by 1960 independence accord.
World's first successful human heart transplant performed by Christian N. Barnard in Cape Town, South Africa. Louis Washkansky given heart of Denise Ann Darvail, a traffic accident victim.

5 **War and draft protestors demonstrate** in New York City. Some 260 persons arrested, including the noted Dr. Benjamin Spock and the poet Allen Ginsberg.

6 **President of Uruguay dies.** Oscar D. Gestido served only nine months. Vice-President Jorge Pacheco Areco succeeds to presidency.

8 **Astronaut killed in California.** Air Force Major Robert H. Lawrence, Jr., first Negro astronaut, crashed on training flight at Edwards Air Force Base.
First Greek troops leave Cyprus. Some 400 soldiers board ship in Famagusta harbor, and sail for Athens.

9 **White House wedding.** Lynda Bird Johnson and Marine Captain Charles S. Robb are married in the East Room. First daughter of a President to be married in the executive mansion since the Wilson-McAdoo wedding in 1914.

10 **Thermonuclear blast in San Juan Basin,** New Mexico, some 4,000 feet underground. First in government-industry Plowshare program.

13 **Two-in-one launching** at Cape Kennedy. A communications satellite and Pioneer VIII put into different orbits by single rocket, ending U.S. launching program for 1967.

13-14 **Greek king fails to depose military junta.** Constantine II and family fly to Rome when broadcast appeal to people fails. Premier Constantine Kollias, also in exile, is replaced by Colonel George Papadopoulas.

14 **Canadian prime minister to retire.** Lester B. Pearson announces plan to leave post in spring or early summer of 1968.
United Nations admits South Yemen as organization's 123rd member.

15 **Denmark government falls.** Parliament rejects wage freeze bill. Prime Minister Jens Otto Krag calls for election on Jan. 23, 1968.
90th U.S. Congress adjourns first session in Washington, D.C., after 340 days and final action on such major legislation as Social Security and aid to elementary and secondary education.

17 **Australian prime minister feared drowned.** Harold E. Holt disappears off Portsea, near Melbourne.

17-18 **Coup d'état in Dahomey.** President Christophe Soglo under house arrest. Major Maurice Kouandete heads provisional government.

19 **United Nations approves space rescue treaty.** Spacemen down in high seas or alien territory should be assisted and safely and speedily returned to homeland.
John McEwen, prime minister of Australia. Harold E. Holt officially presumed drowned.

20 **United Nations General Assembly adjourns** 22nd regular session in New York City.

21 **President Johnson in Australia.** Confers with South Vietnam President Nguyen Van Thieu.
Heart transplant patient dies. Double pneumonia causes death of Louis Washkansky in Cape Town, South Africa.

22 **Harold E. Holt memorial services** in Melbourne, Australia, attended by world leaders.

23 **President Johnson visits U.S. servicemen** in Thailand and South Vietnam. Stops in Pakistan, flies to Rome, talks with Italian President Giuseppe Saragat and Prime Minister Aldo Moro, and confers with Pope Paul VI at the Vatican.

24 **Communist China nuclear test detected** by U.S. Atomic Energy Commission.
President Johnson completes global journey. Returns to Washington, D.C., for Christmas.

25 **Christmas truce in Vietnam ends** at 6 P.M. Enemy killed at least seven allied combatants during 24-hour cease-fire.

30 **Vice-President Hubert H. Humphrey in Africa.** Ivory Coast first on his 13-day tour.

31 **Truce in Vietnam.** Allies begin 36-hour cease-fire at 6 P.M. shortly after nine Americans are killed in a Viet Cong ambush.

Section One

The Year In Focus

The Year Book Board of Editors analyzes the significant developments of 1967 and considers their impact upon contemporary affairs. The Related Articles list following each report directs the reader to *The Year Book's* additional coverage of related subjects.

14 **Paul-Henri Spaak: Focus on The World**

20 **James B. Reston: Focus on The Nation**

26 **Sylvia Porter: Focus on The Economy**

32 **Harrison Brown: Focus on Science**

38 **Lawrence A. Cremin: Focus on Education**

44 **John H. Glenn, Jr.: Focus on Space**

50 **Alistair Cooke: Focus on The Arts**

56 **Red Smith: Focus on Sports**

Paul-Henri Spaak: Focus on The World

The spirit of violence intensified throughout the world in 1967; nevertheless, it does not appear that a world-wide conflict will arise

It would be difficult for even the most optimistic of observers to draw much encouragement from the international events of 1967, a year during which the spirit of violence intensified and major problems seemed farther than ever from solution.

In Vietnam, the war remained in a blind alley. A military victory by the United States and its allies appeared out of reach without a considerable step-up in the fighting, a course of action that would confront the United States with both political and military obstacles. Increased warfare, primarily heavier and unrestricted bombing or a land invasion of North Vietnam, could cause widespread casualties among its civilian population, result in disaffection for the United States by many countries, and possibly even lead to intervention in the fighting by Communist China.

A U.S. military victory in Vietnam seemed hopeless, as did a peace by negotiations

At the same time, a negotiated peace seemed equally unattainable, as the Hanoi government of North Vietnam continued to insist that any negotiations must be preceded by a cessation of bombing and complete American withdrawal from South Vietnam. This was a condition no President of the United States could dare to accept because of its unforeseeable military and political consequences.

Nevertheless, a growing number of persons felt that the United States should, at least temporarily, suspend its bombing as a test of North Vietnam's intentions. A gesture of this type, it was thought, would give Hanoi the alternatives of modifying its intransigent position without loss of face or persisting in its present attitude.

In either case, the situation would be clarified. The first alternative, a change in Hanoi's position, could lead to negotiations and, hopefully, peace. The second alternative, no change by Hanoi, would, in turn, present the United States itself with two difficult alternatives: It could feel free to continue the war, but without any restraints–and with the possibility of Communist China's intervention and all that might follow, or it could renounce its policy of attempting to protect certain nations from unwillingly falling under Communist domination.

This policy has proved completely successful in Europe, chiefly because of the Marshall Plan and the Atlantic Alliance. But there is no certainty that this same policy can be pursued equally effectively in Asia or Africa, where conditions are obviously extremely different. The great, basic question for the United States to answer, then, is: Should this policy be pursued outside Europe?

The answer to this question would have ramifications far wider than is at first apparent. For a quarter of a century, one of the constants of United States foreign policy has been to remain steadfastly loyal to commitments, whatever be the cost of this loyalty in men and money. Thus, if the United States were to answer "no" to the question and disavow its commitments in South Vietnam or elsewhere in Southeast Asia, it would be obliged to re-examine its commitments throughout the world. And it is difficult to conceive of a logical and workable third position between total commitment and withdrawal into isolationism. It is no exaggeration to say that the world's future would be greatly influenced by how the U.S. answered that basic policy question.

Tragically, too many persons throughout the world seem unable to grasp the nature of the broader issues that hang in the balance in Vietnam. Affected emotionally by the immensity of the effort there and by all the horrors that war inevitably entails, this part of public opinion desires peace without being able to determine the necessary conditions for it or being prepared to face the long-term consequences of a United States defeat or withdrawal from South Vietnam. The government of the United States is thus confronted with a problem growing ever more difficult to solve, even as the need and pressures for a tenable solution grow greater and greater. The United States' inability to extricate itself from the situation in Vietnam is jeopardizing its relations with many countries and is weakening its moral position in a great portion of the world.

The government of the U.S. is faced with a problem growing ever more difficult to solve

Elsewhere in Asia, the information that came out of Communist China during 1967, while plentiful, was vague, contradictory, and confusing. Consequently, one must be prudent when speaking of developments in mainland China and their significance.

China's internal strife, it appears, stemmed from the fact that Mao Tse-tung suffered a significant loss in power and influence during 1964 and 1965. The Cultural Revolution, which began in late 1966 and continued through 1967, represented Mao's attempt to recover his leadership position and consolidate his philosophy of a permanent revolution. China's internal turmoil was thus a struggle for power as well as a quarrel over doctrine.

The struggle for power was an understandable one. Indeed, it can be viewed as a logical step in the classic history of a dictatorship. The time is not far off when a successor to Mao must be selected, and the transfer of power in an authoritarian regime is seldom as tranquil as that in a democracy.

Vietnam reinforcements

The doctrinal quarrel between those Chinese who would like to relax, enjoy the fruits of victory, and normalize the situation, and those like Mao who–always unsatisfied–demand new efforts and perpetual changes, is also classical. In a situation where uncertainty appears to be the only certainty, everything may change, and, in consequence, it is impossible to predict which viewpoint will eventually triumph. It would therefore be extremely hazardous for nations to base their long-term policies toward Communist China on the situation that obtains at any given moment.

At present, little more can be said than that the internal conflicts of Communism–primarily in China, but also in other Communist countries–seem to be steadily worsening. And the growing hostility of Communist China toward Russia adds a conflict between Communist nations to that existing within them.

The Soviet Union has been visibly embarrassed by this continuing conflict with the Peking government of Communist China, as a result of which it feels itself physically threatened along a frontier of several thousands of miles and finds its long-time role as leader of the Communist world contested. To maintain its pre-eminent position, Russia cannot allow Peking to accuse it of revolutionary weakness. Therefore, the Soviet Union has been obliged to adopt certain attitudes–for example, its strongly anti-United States stand on the Vietnam problem –that do not fit in with its desire to pursue a policy of peaceful coexistence with the West.

Much depends upon how the Sino-Soviet split resolves itself. A reconciliation between Communist China and the Soviet Union cannot definitely be ruled out; it seems improbable, but it is not impossible. If, on the contrary and more likely, there is further aggravation of the differences between the two Communist powers, the Soviet Union will be forced into more and more of a rapprochement with the West–and particularly with the United States. The world's two mightiest military powers may thus reach the point where they have a common enemy. This perfectly plausible hypothesis, if it should be realized, would naturally have important consequences for the world.

Further quarrels between Russia and Communist China may force Russia closer to the West

In the Middle East, the conflict that had long been smoldering burst into flame in June, 1967. The war itself was fortunately a very short one, but the victorious military operations of Israel and the sporadic clashes that followed, served only to intensify the problems in this highly troubled area.

Israel's rapid military success surprised the world. And the diplomacy of the Arab countries–both before and after the fighting–seemed little more effective than their military efforts. They held numerous meetings and conferences but seemingly were unable to agree upon a common policy with respect to future relations with Israel. They were staggered and infuriated by the fact that Israel had occupied parts of three Arab states–Egypt, Jordan, and Syria–and did not seem prepared to hand them back. Yet the longer the Arabs delayed in arriving at a workable plan for the future, the more their situation was aggravated, and the more the Israeli occupation of Arab territory became an accomplished fact.

Egyptian President Nasser

The six-day war, not unexpectedly, found the great powers of the world aligned on opposite sides but, happily, not to such a grave extent as might have occurred. The role of the powers during and after the war took the form mainly of propaganda, both inside and outside the chambers of the United Nations.

Russia was taken aback by the speed of the Israeli victory–and disappointed and embarrassed by the weakness of the Arab states, whose cause it had supported. Russia, however, which had supplied many of the armaments used by the Arab states, obviously did not want to risk a widespread war by intervening militarily. The Communist power instead relied on diplomatic initiatives on behalf of the Arabs, a course of action that was not crowned with notable success. One must not lose sight, however, of the fact that Russia did obtain in 1967, through the Middle Eastern conflict, what czarist policy had vainly attempted for centuries: It was now installed in the Mediterranean. A Soviet fleet cruised there, with a base at Alexandria, Egypt. This development was less significant than it would have been during the 19th century, but it nevertheless demonstrated Russia's desire to feel out more zones in which it could exert its influence and counter that of the West. During the six-day war of June, 1967, though, despite that desire, Russia was not prepared to overstep certain limits.

In North America and Europe, public opinion and government statements were generally favorable to Israel. This instinctive reaction was a sound one. Opinions may differ on the wisdom of the decision by the United Nations in 1947 to create the state of Israel. But this decision is now international law and must be accepted.

Arab refusal to accept Israel's existence is the root of Middle East difficulties

It is of no value to look back at the history of the Middle East, as some wish, in an effort to determine the rights of the parties concerned. This would lead only to interminable discussions with nothing fruitful emerging from them. One must, instead, start from indisputable fact. The creation and existence of Israel is one such fact; indeed, it is the only fact that can serve as a basis for the start of productive discussions. Any solution to the Middle East problem must have as a prerequisite the Arab acceptance of international law and the existence of Israel. It is this fundamental truth, however, that the Arab countries will not accept, and their refusal to do so is at the root of the Middle East's difficulties. Not until this acceptance is forthcoming will it be possible to hold discussions aimed at a peace that takes into account the long-term interests of both the Arabs and the Israelis. It will then be the duty of the richer nations of the world to assist in the alleviation of the economic problems that underlie the political nature of the continual strife in the Middle East.

The only major Western nation to side with the Arabs in 1967 was France. This was just one example of the policies of President Charles de Gaulle, whose attitude continued to perturb and perplex Europe in 1967. While it became increasingly difficult to understand precisely what he wants, it appeared that two complementary passions animated him: intense nationalism, and hostility toward England and the United States.

French President Charles de Gaulle

He demonstrated his feelings toward the United States by weakening, as much as he could, the Atlantic alliance and in siding against the United States on most of the important issues that arose. His animosity to England was shown by his continued arbitrary opposition to that country's entry into the European Economic Community (EEC). His attitude toward both countries was apparent in France's antagonistic role in the events that led to the devaluation of the British pound and in its refusal to help defend the soundness of the U.S. dollar. France's actions during the troubled weeks following devaluation threatened the health of the world monetary system.

General De Gaulle apparently believes that if United States and British influence can be reduced in the world–especially in Europe–this will automatically increase the influence of France. He is increasingly the champion of nationalism, even as this is becoming more and more an outdated doctrine. Today, the great problems of the world can be solved only by more, not less, cooperation among nations. Yet General De Gaulle asserts that the nation is the immutable base on which all policy is founded. This is a false concept. Nations, as they exist today, have not always existed, and it is probable that they will not always exist in their present form. At a time when scientific and technological progress is transforming everything, it is inconceivable to believe that political formations will remain unchanged.

Whatever may be the case concerning these doctrinal questions, General De Gaulle is becoming ever more difficult to deal with. He has withdrawn French forces from the North Atlantic Treaty Organization and let it be known that he intends to abandon the alliance entirely in 1969. At the same time that he is thus detaching himself from his Western allies, he is courting Russia and the Communist countries of East Europe.

It is a dangerous paradox that world peace depends on the existence of atomic weapons

The dangers of his actions are clear. The alliance has given peace to Europe for the past 20 years. Sheltered by this peace, Europe has reached a high level of economic and social development without precedent in its history. By working to destroy the alliance, General De Gaulle is tearing down a system of proven success. The fact that he has been unable to propose another valid system to replace it only emphasizes the gravity of his misdeeds. If he should succeed in his efforts to dismantle the alliance, the result would be a state of disorder dangerous for all and for peace. The other European members of the alliance have resisted these efforts but, unfortunately, not always with all the energy that might be desired. And yet, they must have this energy if they want to pass safely through this crisis that threatens the security of the alliance.

This brief glance at world politics in 1967 is not, as I have said, a very encouraging one. Nevertheless, despite all, it does not seem that a world conflict will arise. The two great powers–the United States and Russia–appear anxious to avoid one. That peace depends on the existence of atomic weapons and the ability of the powers to retaliate effectively despite any attacks that might be made upon them–this is indeed a paradox. But it has also produced a situation in which the slightest error, the least miscalculation, could lead to unthinkable events. To forestall such miscalculations and assure lasting security for all nations, men must in the future display more imagination and good will in their international affairs.

Related Articles

For a complete report on international relations in 1967, see Section One, Sylvia Porter: Focus on The Economy; Section Two, Mao's Last Revolution; and articles on the various nations in Section Three. In the same section, see also the following:

Africa
Asia
Banks and Banking
Communism
Democracy
Europe
International Trade and Finance
Latin America
Middle East
North Atlantic Treaty Organization
United Nations

James B. Reston: Focus on The Nation

The national mood of violent protest and disillusionment increased despite progress in the war abroad and in the slums at home

For the United States, 1967 was a year of internal crisis. The nation was more divided over the war in Vietnam than at any other time since the Spanish-American War. The contention between the races flared up into something approaching rebellion in Detroit, Mich., Newark, N.J., and other American cities. Civil disobedience not only was widely practiced by young antiwar demonstrators in the universities, but also was condoned and even encouraged by influential religious leaders. By the end of the year, President Lyndon B. Johnson could not go freely into any of the great cities of the nation without being picketed by his antiwar critics.

The nation was more divided over the war in Vietnam than ever before in this century

"This is a day," Secretary of Health, Education, and Welfare John W. Gardner said in October, "of dissent and divisiveness. Everyone speaks with unbridled anger in behalf of his point of view or his party or his people. More and more, hostility and venom are the hallmarks of any conversation on the affairs of the nation.

"There used to be only a few chronically angry people in our national life. Today all seem caught up in mutual recriminations–Negro and white, rich and poor, conservative and liberal, dove and hawk, Democrat and Republican, labor and management, North and South, young and old."

What produced this mood of self-questioning and self-doubt? Was it as bad as it sounded? And why did these symptoms of something like a nervous breakdown suddenly seem so much more serious in 1967? These were the questions of the year.

The crisis was basically psychological, and while there was a general sense of uneasiness and even anxiety over the war and the race riots, the majority of the people–even the majority of the university students–went along about as in other years, doing their jobs and staying apart from the agitation. In this sense, the turmoil was primarily the work of a minority of the people in the political parties, the radical and activist Negro organizations, the press, and the churches–in short, that very minority of articulate people who usually bring about political change in most nations.

Paradoxically, the internal crisis could not be explained by any decline in the fortunes of the war in Vietnam or any drop in our standard of living. In fact, there was visible progress in 1967 both on the battlefield abroad and in the slums at home.

The American expeditionary force in South Vietnam took over large areas previously occupied by the enemy. The infiltration of enemy troops from North into South Vietnam and the recruitment of Viet Cong guerrilla fighters in the South dropped substantially, and the U.S. and South Vietnamese armies held the military initiative through most of 1967. In fact, President Johnson brought back his civilian and military leaders from Vietnam in November, and they talked not only about the progress being made, but also about the prospects of a difficult but inevitable victory.

The record on the home front in 1967 was even more encouraging. By the end of the year, the economy had completed 82 consecutive months of boom conditions. The rich were certainly getting richer, but even the very poor, including the Negroes in the city slums, got more jobs in 1967, and more training for better jobs, and ended up with a higher standard of living than they had in 1966.

Despite the fact that the war was costing more than $2,000,000,000 a month, the government was spending more and more on urgent domestic problems. In 1960, for example, federal government aid to the poor was $9,900,000,000; in 1967, it was $25,600,000,000. In 1960, federal appropriations for education, health, and training were $6,600,000,000; in 1967, they were more than $22,000,000,000.

The accumulated grievances over foreign policy surfaced in 1967

Nevertheless, the mood of violent protest and disillusionment increased. Many factors contributed to it, and the war was clearly one of them. Though progress was undoubtedly made on the battlefield during the year, its cost was high. More Americans were killed in Vietnam in 1967–more than 9,000–than in the previous five years. The nature of the war also contributed to the anxiety. It was difficult to prove that a war 7,000 miles away was essential to the security of the United States. Many Americans felt there was something morally wrong in a large country using the modern weapons of war against a small, primitive country. During 1967, the United States dropped more bombs on Vietnam than it did on Europe or on Korea in any year of those two wars, and yet there seemed to be little hope that this would bring the fighting to an end in the foreseeable future.

Nor did the opponents of the war seem to offer any solution acceptable to the government or to a majority of the people. The most popular attitudes were that the United States should increase the violence and win the war, or get out. But after all the argument and debate, nobody had a satisfactory formula for doing either.

Accordingly, the accumulated grievances of the past over foreign policy came to the surface. In 1945, the United States came out of World War II with a set of attitudes, assumptions, and expectations it has been testing ever since. Its dominant attitude was one of optimism. The old empires were collapsing, but the New World would redress the balance of the Old World. It was widely assumed that while other countries might fail to maintain order and lose wars, the United States could do anything it made up its mind to do.

On this assumption, the United States had taken the lead in organizing the United Nations. It had helped restore and defend Europe with the Marshall Plan and the North Atlantic Treaty Organization (NATO), and it had committed itself to oppose Communist aggression in the Middle East and Southeast Asia. It also had spent hundreds of billions of dollars on aid to nations throughout the world.

Great progress was made in many places, but there was always the assumption that somehow these exertions would one day come to an end, that other nations would play a larger role in the common defense, and that aid to underdeveloped countries would end after they established stable governments.

The Cold War was the first disappointment, then the Korean War and the disaster at Cuba's Bay of Pigs. Our allies did not take on more responsibility but less as the years went by. The population of the poor countries consumed all the foreign aid we could provide, and the events of 1967 added more disappointments that brought the whole trend of our postwar foreign policy under heavy attack.

France, for example, evicted NATO from that country in 1967. Israel went to war against the Arab states in defiance of Washington's advice. The colonels in Greece staged a coup d'état against the legitimate government in April, 1967. And while Washington kept its commitments in Vietnam under the Southeast Asia Collective Defense Treaty, most of the other nations that had signed it did not.

The Negro protest movement became more menacing, even as living conditions improved

Thus, the war alone did not explain the unrest among the American people. It was merely the symbol of a far deeper dissatisfaction with a wider set of circumstances. Government statements that "progress" was being made on the battlefield, therefore, did not satisfy the opposition, for what was being seriously questioned for the first time in a quarter of a century was the larger concept of America fighting wars and pouring out its wealth to nations throughout the world.

On the home front, the violent Negro uprisings also added to the feeling that something was fundamentally wrong with the social structure of the country. Again, the young militant Negro leaders were not saying that progress had not been made; instead, they were demanding a radical transformation of Negro housing, education, and employment. The Negro revolution of 1967 followed the pattern of most revolutions: It began to feed on itself. The revolutions of depressed peoples do not usually subside at the first sign of improved economic conditions, but tend to become more violent and more demanding. Thus, Negro family income, Negro employment, and Negro education all improved in 1967, but at the same time, the Negro protest movement became more menacing.

The U.S. Departments of Labor and Commerce made these points about the condition of the Negro in the United States in 1967:

- Family income, while rising steadily, was only 58 per cent as high as white family income.
- Unemployment was twice as high as white unemployment, and teen-age Negro unemployment remained very high, at 26 per cent.
- In 8 of the 12 largest cities in the country, segregation of residential housing had actually increased during the previous seven years.
- About half a million poor families–10 per cent of the total–had lived all their lives in rural areas with very limited opportunities for improvement in education, employment, housing, or income. Another half million families had incomes below the poverty line and lived in comparatively wretched conditions in the large cities.

A grim President Johnson

With all this inflammable material around, the violent outbreaks of looting and burning in Detroit and Newark in 1967 produced a mood of inquiry and foreboding and forced thoughtful people, in and outside government, to re-examine the scope of the problem.

Gunnar Myrdal, the Swedish social philosopher, who made the classic study of the American Negro in the 1920s, returned to America in 1967 and called for a readjustment of our political priorities and a dramatic upward estimate of the cost of dealing with the poor. A reliable plan to eradicate the slums and rehabilitate the slum dwellers, he said, would take a generation and cost "trillions of dollars."

"I draw the further conclusion," he said, "that in this light, the common idea that America is an immensely rich and affluent country is very much an exaggeration. . . The even more serious fact is that Congress is not only far more willing to provide vast sums for defense than for the slums, but that Congress apparently reflects how the American voters feel about this question of national priorities."

Powerful groups were challenging basic assumptions of our domestic and foreign policies

In short, the war in Vietnam and the racial struggles in the American cities made 1967 a particularly significant year, because powerful intellectual and racial minorities were challenging not only the violence at home and abroad, but also the basic assumptions of both American domestic policy and foreign policy. And in the process, they were questioning many of the traditional American attitudes toward the presidency, the political parties, the press, the church, the university, and even the family.

They were challenging, primarily, the assumption that the United States could deal effectively with all these foreign and domestic problems at the same time. To put it another way, two fundamental charges were being made against the American people and their government: first, that we did not know what kind of society we wanted to be; and, second, that we were not clear about what our relations should be with other nations. In sum, we were confused about our priorities, not knowing what came first at home or abroad, or which areas of the world were vital to us and which were unimportant.

Draft resisters

The debate itself produced something new and something very old in American life. The new thing was a strong element of doubt. For almost the first time since World War II, some officials in Washington were saying quite plainly that many of the problems of the world were beyond our control or influence, and that if we tried to deal with them all we would end up by not dealing with our problems at home.

The old theme that resurfaced in 1967 was isolationism. Nobody was saying that, since the country could not do everything abroad, it should withdraw and do nothing. But the supporters of the war in Vietnam were saying that the opponents of the war wanted to get out and isolate America. And the opponents of the war were saying that a continuance of the struggle at the present level of violence would create such a reaction against our foreign policy that the government would be obliged to adopt a more isolationist stand.

The psychological reactions of the American people to all of this were extremely varied. In the first place, most people were not touched personally by either the war or the race riots, and they seemed inclined to leave both questions to the government. On the fringes, however, many young persons were deeply engaged in the debate. There was a rise of extremist politics, with young militants leading New Left, New Right, and Black Power political organizations. There was also a rising degree of escapism among young persons seeking a way out of the complexities of modern life through the use of drugs. And everywhere there were thoughtful persons troubled by the gathering of the American people into larger and larger urban areas, larger and larger universities and corporations, and larger and more expensive political parties.

Accordingly, one of the complicating and depressing factors in the self-examination of America in 1967 was the widespread feeling that the individual's views had little effect on all these momentous questions and mammoth organizations. This sense of impotence was well described by Governor Nelson Rockefeller of New York in the January, 1968, issue of the magazine *Foreign Affairs.*

At issue was nothing less than whether life can be given meaning

"What is at issue," he wrote, "is nothing less than whether life can be given meaning. . . The deepest problem before America is moral or psychological. Since much of the current uneasiness reflects a search less for solutions than for meaning, remedies depend for their effectiveness on the philosophy or values which inspire them. The student unrest is impressive, not because some of it is fomented by agitators, but because it includes some of the most idealistic elements of our youth. In fact, much that disquiets us today gives cause for hope, for it reflects not cynicism but disappointed idealism."

Whatever else can be said about America in 1967, then, nobody can say it was not dealing with great questions. In general, it had prosperity, but it was not satisfied with the material rewards of an 82-month economic boom. It had glorified technical proficiency and specialization, but it seemed to be longing for some general philosophy. It thought it could win any war against any country in the world, but it found itself bogged down in an endless conflict against a primitive enemy and could not quite remember how it had got into the war in the first place.

America was struggling in 1967 with the great questions of life: peace and order, the relationship of the individual to the state, technology and philosophy, the education of the individual to the extent of his capacities, the problem of leadership, and the priorities of life and politics. It did not find the answer in 1967, but at least it argued about some good questions.

Related Articles

For a complete report on the year 1967 in national affairs, see also Section One, Sylvia Porter: Focus on The Economy; Section Two, The Economics of Politics; and the following articles in Section Three:

City
Civil Rights
Congress of the United States
Democratic Party
Economy, The
Housing
Johnson, Lyndon B.
Labor
Manufacturing
National Defense
Poverty
President of the U.S.
Republican Party
State Government
Supreme Court
Taxation
U.S. Government

Sylvia Porter: Focus on The Economy

The U.S. economic boom took on nightmarish aspects in 1967; but internationally, tariff cuts and a new "money" were hopeful signs

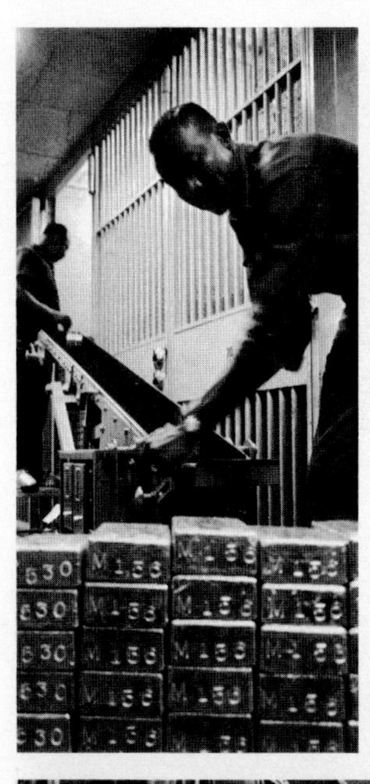

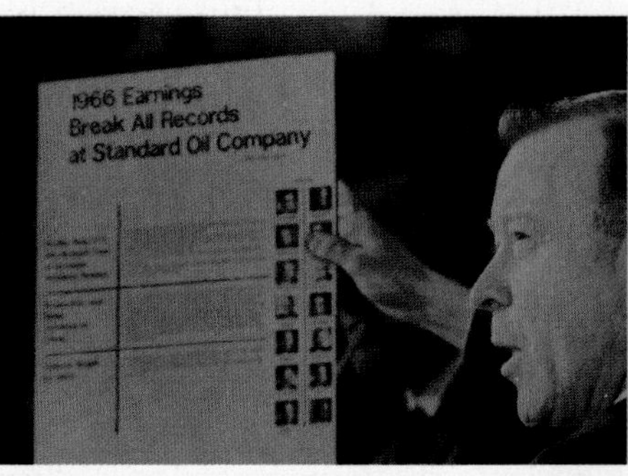

America's prolonged prosperity took on aspects of an economic nightmare in 1967. True, the great boom itself continued, for the fact that the United States is now a "service economy" has made us an increasingly stable society. Far more workers are employed in rendering services than in producing goods, and the services continued to expand without interruption in 1967. Thus, although industrial production fell early in the year, and the pace of the nation's economic growth slowed perceptibly, the overall rate of unemployment remained low; joblessness among skilled adults stayed at a minimum; and personal incomes climbed to all-time peaks.

The longest economic upswing in 110 years was marred by several blemishes

The slowdown turned out to be merely a short-lived "adjustment" brought about primarily by the restraints of tight and expensive money. By November, the economic expansion that got underway in February, 1961, had lasted 81 months–beating the 80-month expansion that spanned World War II and becoming the longest upswing in 110 years. And, in the final months of 1967, the pace of economic advance was again quickening.

But the distortions that first emerged in 1966 as a direct result of the escalation of the war in Vietnam, deepened and broadened in 1967. Among the nightmarish aspects that blemished the overall pattern of prosperity were these:

- There was a rapidly accelerating rise in the cost of living, indicated by an increase in the government's Consumer Price Index of some 3 per cent. Coming on top of a 3.3 per cent rise in 1966, this meant a loss of more than 6¢ in the purchasing power of the dollar in only 24 months. The price increases involved goods and services across the board. For millions of workers, businessmen, and housewives, this alone was enough to erase much of the glitter from the prosperity.
- Interest rates climbed, while there was fierce competition for the amount of credit available. Tens of billions of dollars in cash were sought by the federal government to cover its war-swollen budget deficit; by business corporations to expand their plants and equipment; by states, cities, and other public bodies to finance their activities; and by individuals to pay for such goods and services as houses, automobiles, appliances, and college educations. Against this background, a climbing price for borrowed money was only to be expected. Then, starting in late November, interest rates in the United States were deliberately jacked up higher by the Federal Reserve System to protect the dollar in the wake of Britain's devaluation of the pound. The highest interest rates since Civil War days emerged to help cool the economy, curb the price-wage spiral, and make sure that funds would not pour out of the country in search of richer interest rates offered abroad. As a result of all this, the nation's bond and money markets were in a chaotic upheaval throughout the latter months of 1967.
- A stickily high jobless rate among unskilled and minority workers existed side by side with shortages of many types of skilled workers. The unemployment rate among all adult breadwinners was at an effective low of less than 2 per cent throughout most of the year. Among nonwhites, however, the rate hung around 7 to 8 per cent, and

among unskilled 16-to-19-year-olds, it centered on 12 to 13 per cent. Thus, shortages of skilled workers threatened economic growth, while surpluses of unskilled workers were social-economic-political dynamite.

▪ The federal budget was flooded with red ink, despite tax money pouring in from record-high paychecks and from huge corporation profits. The budget deficits chalked up in 1967 and projected for 1968 were the result of the skyrocketing expenses of the Vietnam war–not of expansion of spending for desirable domestic programs–a fact that intensified the difficulties of cutting spending to bring outgo more in line with income. But instead of cooperating to restore the budget to a semblance of balance, the administration and congressional leaders remained deadlocked to the very end of the year in a destructive squabble about the desirability of raising income taxes and/or cutting federal spending. As a result, the deficit in the federal budget swelled to the largest total since World War II.

Devaluation of the pound led to fears the dollar might fall next

▪ More red ink in our international financial accounts (balance of payments) signaled an unceasing drain on our already seriously depleted gold reserves. Despite the United States' firm resolve in 1965 to bring its balance of payments into approximate equilibrium, we continued in 1967 to spend far more abroad than we earned abroad, and our balance of payments deficit soared back to a critical $2,500,000,000 to $3,000,000,000. The position of the dollar was delicate enough through most of 1967; then, on November 18, came Britain's decision to devalue the pound by 14.3 per cent–in terms of the dollar, from $2.80 to $2.40. Behind this action was the fact that for years, Britain also had been running a deficit in its balance of payments, and there had been an almost constant drain on its holdings of gold and of such "hard" currencies as the United States dollar. When balance of payments pressures finally toppled the pound, fears mounted that the dollar, the pivot of the international monetary system, might be next.

▪ Social Security taxes, state taxes, and local taxes all climbed, and uncertainty about the timing of higher federal income taxes continued to the last day of 1967. Because the heavier tax bite came from so many directions at once, it seemed harsher than ever and added to the general feeling of "squeeze" in an era of pervasive prosperity.

Kennedy Round negotiators exult

A grim listing? Yes. Each force by itself would have been a grave enough challenge. Together, they badly marred the boom. But, one might ask, could not the policies of the "New Economics" that had worked so well to fuel the present boom also have worked to restrain it when it developed inflationary excesses? The answer again is yes. But the reality is that the New Economics failed miserably in 1967–and the blunt reason why the theories failed is that the White House and Congress failed to provide the tools to make them work.

The essence of the New Economics is this: Our national economic goal is a strong, sustained growth that will create high employment, production, paychecks, and profits–all with reasonably stable prices.

When our economy is operating below capacity, it is imperative to put into effect a combination of fiscal and monetary (tax-spending-credit) policies that will speed up the rate of growth. Among the appropriate stimulants would be income tax cuts to spur consumer and business spending, tax incentives to encourage business investment in plants and equipment, increased government spending, and easy and relatively inexpensive credit to stimulate borrowing of money.

When our economy reaches the desired rate of growth, the policies should be carefully moderated to sustain the trend.

When our economy overheats–because of too many stimulants or some overwhelming development such as the war in Vietnam–it is imperative to switch to an entirely different set of tax-spending-credit policies to restrain the rate of growth. Among the appropriate restraints would be income tax increases to curtail consumer and business spending, suspension of tax incentives to encourage postponement of business investment, stretching out of government expenditures, and tighter and more expensive credit to limit borrowing of money.

Congress and the White House argued about who should move first to fight inflation

From early 1961 to late 1965, the New Economics performed magnificently. Our economy was put into and held in a powerful, beautifully balanced expansion by tax incentives, income tax cuts, easy credit, and rising government spending.

But with the acceleration of United States involvement in the Vietnam war in late 1965 and early 1966, the need arose for reversing the policies to provide restraint. The White House, though, did not respond. President Lyndon B. Johnson did not ask for tax hikes early in the inflationary upswing. He did not take the lead in cutting back federal spending. The beautiful balance in our economy evaporated; price stability was shattered; the basis for inflation was laid.

In 1967, with further escalation of the war in Vietnam, the danger of a 1967 inflation built on that of 1966 became very real. But this time it was Congress that did not respond. President Johnson asked for an income tax surcharge, but congressional leaders insisted that he must first slash federal spending before they would consider a tax hike. Mr. Johnson, in turn, insisted that Congress move first. Even the shock of devaluation of the pound failed to break the stalemate.

The Durations of Business Upturns Since World War II

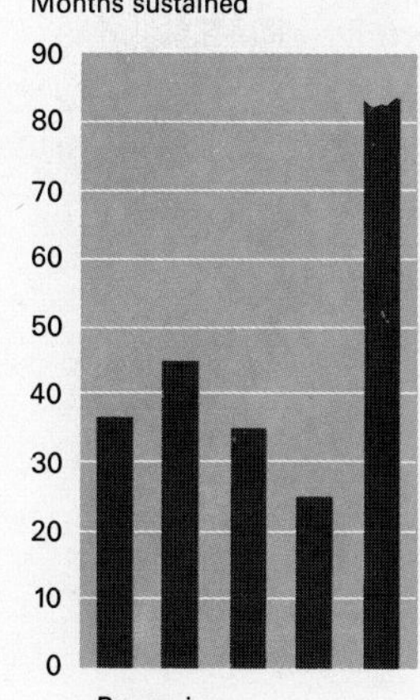

Of course, there were bright aspects, too, in 1967. In May, in Geneva, Switzerland, after three years of relentlessly hard bargaining, delegates of 53 nations finally reached agreements that will lower tariff walls on some 60,000 items an average of 33 to 35 per cent between 1968 and 1972. This was the most far-reaching step ever taken to lower tariffs and liberalize international trade. The United States entered the bargaining by authority of the Trade Expansion Act passed in 1962 during President John F. Kennedy's administration–hence the name for the negotiations was the "Kennedy Round."

The Kennedy Round tariff cuts will mean many different things to many different groups in the United States. Consumers will find more imported goods on store shelves, with possibly some small price cuts on items ranging from the German Volkswagen to Italian pottery. American manufacturers competing with imports will be faced with tougher competition. Manufacturers using imported materials will benefit from some easing of production costs. Farmers and businessmen exporting goods will have a chance to increase sales abroad, because of lower foreign barriers against American products.

But over and beyond all this was the Kennedy Round's wider implication that the world was not to be engulfed in a new wave of protectionism. Even though protectionist sentiment was clearly on the rise in the United States and other nations in 1967, the greatest round of world-wide tariff-cutting in history did succeed.

The Kennedy Round indicated the world would not see a wave of protectionism

Then, in August, in London, England, the "Group of Ten" agreed to create a new type of world money for governments to use in addition to gold and dollars to finance the vast trade expansion spurred by the Kennedy Round. The Group of Ten are the leading trading nations of the free world: Belgium, Britain, Canada, France, Italy, Japan, The Netherlands, Sweden, the United States, and West Germany. The plan was approved by the 106 nations belonging to the International Monetary Fund (IMF) at its annual meeting, in September, in Rio de Janeiro, Brazil. The timetable calls for the plan to be ratified by the lawmaking bodies of each IMF member nation in 1968 and 1969, with establishment in 1969 and 1970 of machinery to issue the new world money.

Under the plan, the IMF would create Special Drawing Rights (SDRs) and issue them to each member nation in amounts determined by the percentage of the nation's contribution to existing IMF funds. Thus, as an example, the United States would be allotted $245,000,000 of every $1,000,000,000 of SDRs created. The SDRs would exist only on the books of the IMF and the member nations, and they would be used only by government central banks to settle debts. A country drawing on its SDRs would never have to repay most of them–meaning that most of the credit truly would be money created out of the air. Thus, the new world money would expand the volume of world currency reserves as the volume of trade expanded.

Effects of The Present Boom

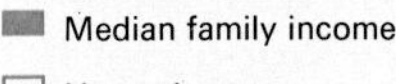

Median family income

Unemployment

Consumer prices

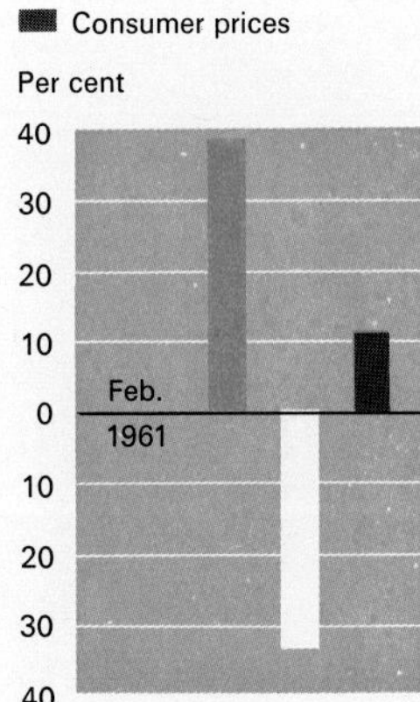

The use of SDRs to underwrite the growth of world trade should reduce the burden on the United States dollar, lessen the pressure on our dwindling gold reserves, and erase the danger of world-wide depression caused by a shortage of money to finance essential trade. They imply a move–small and tentative, but still a move–toward the eventual creation of a single world currency.

In a world turning back toward economic nationalism, the tariff cuts and the invention of a new means for financing the resulting expansion of trade stand out as magnificent accomplishments.

Less than eight weeks after the Rio meeting, though, even these accomplishments were dimmed by the British devaluation of the pound and the warning implicit in this disaster that the United States must strengthen the defenses of the dollar.

Britain was forced to devalue its currency and impose a new series of severe economic restraints on the British people by the need to reduce the deficit in its balance of payments. Although there is no direct parallel between the balance of payments position of Britain and the United States, the sobering fact is that the United States has run a balance of payments deficit in all but one of the past 17 years. In reflection of this outpouring of dollars, qualified foreign creditors of the U.S. held more than $28,000,000,000 in dollar claims in late 1967 for which they could demand gold at $35 an ounce. At the same time, our total gold reserve was only a little more than $12,000,000,000.

The United States must have the will to preserve the present period of prosperity

The reason this situation does not spell "bankruptcy" for the dollar is that most of America's creditors have faith in our paper money and refrain from exercising their right to demand gold in exchange. They would rather hold dollars, on which they can earn interest, than gold, on which they would earn nothing and which would cost them money to store. The key word is "faith." If our creditors ever lost that and staged a run on the dollar, the United States could be drained of every ounce of its gold–and still not have enough. Long before that point was reached, however, the dollar would have forfeited its eminent position as the world's key currency; the scheduled reform of the world monetary system would be shelved, and the system itself would be dead; and a violent contraction in international trade would be in progress. The West would face massive bankruptcies, spiraling joblessness, socioeconomic chaos, and a retreat to the financial barbarism that preceded World War II.

It was against a background of need to protect the dollar and to curb the price-wage upswing that thoughtful observers in the United States called with increasing urgency during 1967 for income tax increases, government spending cuts, even higher interest rates, stiffer restrictions on American investments abroad, new and direct incentives to exports, much stronger emphasis on travel at home and restraint of tourism overseas, and sharp reductions in spending for our soldiers and their dependents in noncombat areas. It was in an effort to awaken the nation to these needs that the chairman of the Federal Reserve Board, William McChesney Martin, Jr., warned at year's end: "The entire world is looking to the United States to see if it has the capability, the will, and the determination to preserve and maintain this period of prosperity."

If we in the United States fail because we do not have the capability, failure will be at least excusable. But if we fail because we do not have the will and the determination to do what we are capable of doing, it will be inexcusable.

Related Articles

For a complete report on the 1967 year in economics, see Section Two, Where the Jobs Will Be, and the following articles in Section Three:

Agriculture
Banks and Banking
Economy, The
International Trade and Finance
Labor
Manufacturing
Money
Poverty
Retailing
Steel Industry
Stocks and Bonds
Taxation
Transportation

Harrison Brown: Focus on Science

Next to the search for peace, the greatest challenge to the world is the race between food supply and a mushrooming population

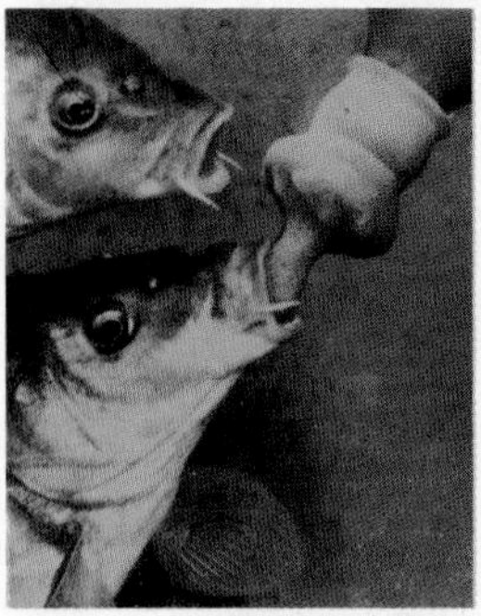

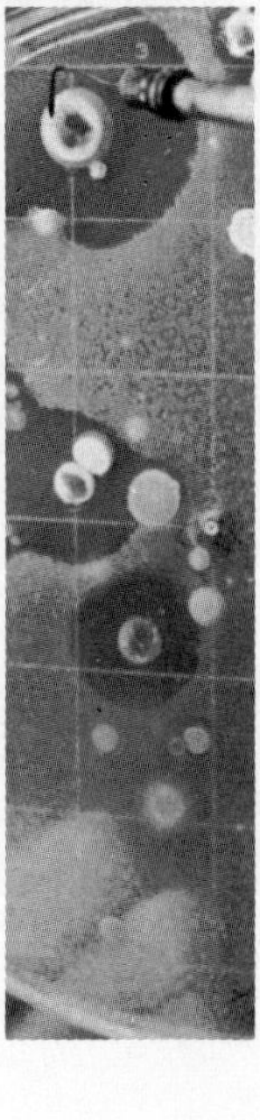

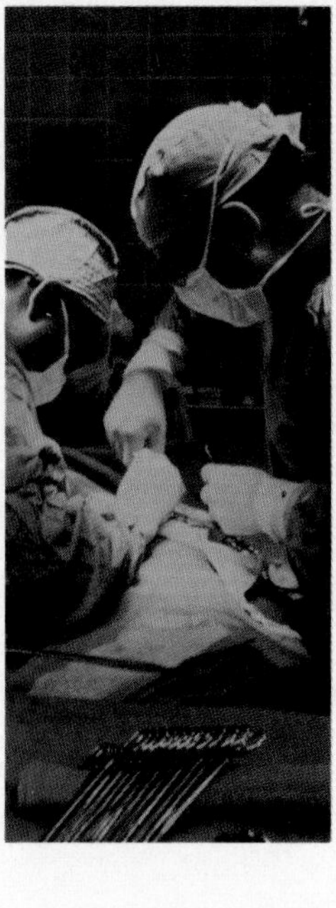

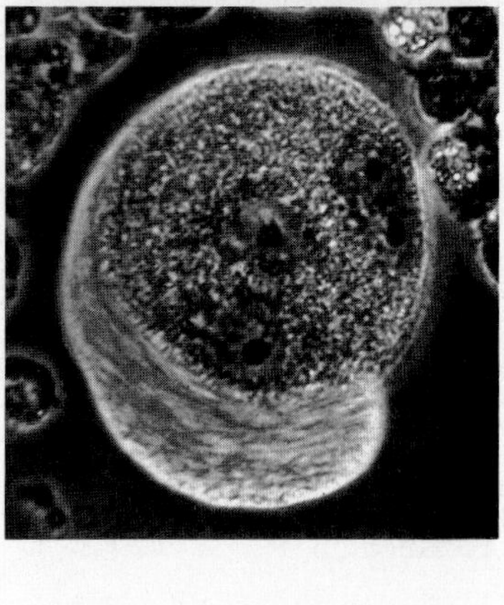

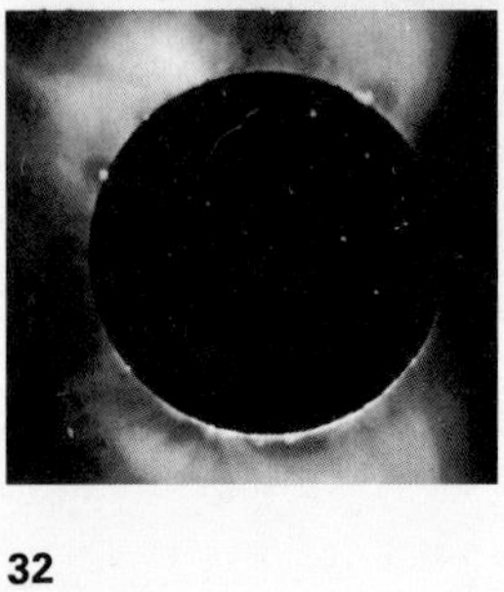

In the fast-moving world of 1967, man's science and technology–and his ambitions–seemed limitless. Heart transplants vied with facts about the moon's surface for prime space in newspapers and on television. More new elements were made. A virus was put together in a laboratory from assemblages of large molecules, and man drew closer to an understanding of life processes and the origin of life-like things. The race to the moon and planets continued.

The problems are solvable, but they probably will get worse before they get much better

But another "race" received scant attention in 1967, save for a little-noticed landmark report. It is not an exciting race, but a tragic one; it is not a new development, but is centuries old; it is right here on earth, and it may be the most important race of all, deserving of full attention from our science, our technology–and our ambition. President Lyndon B. Johnson referred to it early in the year, in his State of the Union address on January 10, when he said:

"Next to the pursuit of peace, the really greatest challenge to the human family is the race between food supply and population increase. That race tonight is being lost."

President Johnson was pointing out that population is mushrooming tremendously in Africa, Asia, and Latin America and that most persons in those areas are poorly fed and have even less to eat today than they had a decade ago. During the last 10 years 500,000,000 persons were added to the world's population and about 400,000,000 of them are destined to be hungry, malnourished, or starving for the rest of their short lives.

Aware that hunger could spur world-wide civil strife and revolution on an unprecedented scale, President Johnson had in 1966 directed his Science Advisory Committee to "search out new ways to apply all of the resources of technology to increasing food production." The committee reacted by appointing a special panel of experts in many fields to study the situation intensively. Little more than a year later, in May, 1967, the first two volumes of the *Report of the Panel on the World Food Supply* were issued by the White House. A third volume was released in September.

The report is the most comprehensive examination of the twin problems of food and population ever made. Its conclusions constitute a modern horror story. Although the problems of food and population are basically solvable, and the approaches to their solution are fairly well understood, it is evident that, at best, the situation will get considerably worse before it gets better.

Throughout its deliberations, the panel continually asked, "Why is the race between food and population being lost?" It concluded that "the problem, at first glance, seems deceptively straightforward" but in reality "is so large and so extremely complex that it is almost impossible for the casual or even the moderately trained observer to comprehend its true dimensions."

From a purely technical point of view, most of the hungry regions of the world can greatly increase their food production. For example, the average yield of rice per acre in Japan is some 3.5 times that obtained in India. One might conclude, then, that if the Indians adopted Japanese farming practices, their rice production would increase severalfold. But before we get too excited, let us examine the steps that would have to be taken.

The Japanese apply huge quantities of fertilizer to their rice paddies. The Indians, by contrast, use almost no fertilizer. This tempts us to conclude that if the Indians also added large quantities of fertilizer to their rice paddies, their crop yields would approach those of the Japanese. In fact, however, if the Indians did apply such heavy concentrations of fertilizer to their paddies, the rice plants would die. Rice grown in India has been selected to thrive under local conditions and to draw nutrients directly from the natural environment. The plants are unable to cope with an abundance of nitrogen, phosphorus, and potassium supplied artificially through fertilizers.

Boosting crop yields is far more complex than is at first apparent

This, in turn tempts us to conclude that if the varieties of rice grown in Japan were transplanted in India and heavily fertilized, the Indians would achieve rice yields like those in Japan. This conclusion would also be wrong. In reality, special varieties of rice would have to be bred that are adapted to the Indian environment, resistant to local diseases and pests, and able to utilize high concentrations of fertilizer. In general, these varieties must be bred in the local environment, and this requires the availability of laboratories, experimental stations, and trained researchers.

Let us assume, though, that Indian research workers do develop satisfactory strains of rice plants. The next task is to produce adequate quantities of fertilizer. This means supplies of materials from which to make the fertilizer must be located. Factories must be built. Large quantities of steel must be manufactured to construct the factories. All of this, in turn, requires substantial quantities of electricity and large resources of energy in the form of coal, petroleum, water power, or possibly even uranium.

Given satisfactory species of rice plants and adequate quantities of fertilizers, the next problem is fighting off a variety of pests and diseases. Most of these can be controlled by chemicals and other means, but again, factories must be built to manufacture them.

Given seeds, fertilizers, and pesticides, the next task is to get them all to the farmer. In physical terms, this means highways and trucks, railroads and trains, gasoline, coal, and oil. In monetary terms, it means creating the economic institutions–such as credit–that will make it possible for farmers to use these developments. In social terms, it means teaching the farmers how to use the new developments effectively and persuading them that their crop yields will increase substantially if they change their farming practices. Convincing the farmers to use new techniques is not easy. When we ask a farmer to change his agricultural practices, we are asking him to gamble that the new techniques will bring him larger crops. The trained agricultural scientist knows they will, but the farmer, understandably, needs considerable convincing, because the stakes for him and his family are high. For all he knows, changes might bring crop failure.

Waiting to be fed

Because of such problems, agricultural extension workers are extremely important. The personal contacts of farmers with such workers–a large proportion of whom are college-trained–have contributed substantially to the large increases in crop yields in Japan, the United States, and Western Europe. But to be effective, the number of extension workers in most of the poorer countries must be greatly increased. In Japan, for example, well over 7,000 agriculturalists are college-trained each year, and there is more than one well-trained adviser for every 600 farms. But in Indonesia, where per capita food production has been decreasing, there is only one adviser for every 100,000 farms. And the entire continent of South America trains only about 1,100 agriculturalists annually.

Poor countries must industrialize to bring about great increases in food production

Increasing the amount of farmland, another way to increase food production, appears to be fully as difficult as increasing the crop yields from land already under cultivation. In theory, more than three times the area now harvested could be cultivated. But the technological difficulties of doing so are considerable. More than half the potential farmland lies in the tropics, primarily in Africa and South America; and at present, we do not have the technical knowledge needed to farm effectively in those environments. Further, heavily populated Asia, where the problems of hunger are vast, has almost no new land that can be placed under cultivation. If food supplies in Asia are to be increased, more food must grow on the land already being farmed. It does not appear that we can look forward to rapid amelioration of the world food problem by a sudden expansion of farmland.

World Population Increase from 1965 to 1985

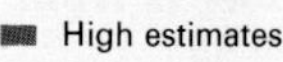
High estimates

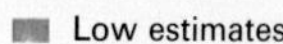
Low estimates

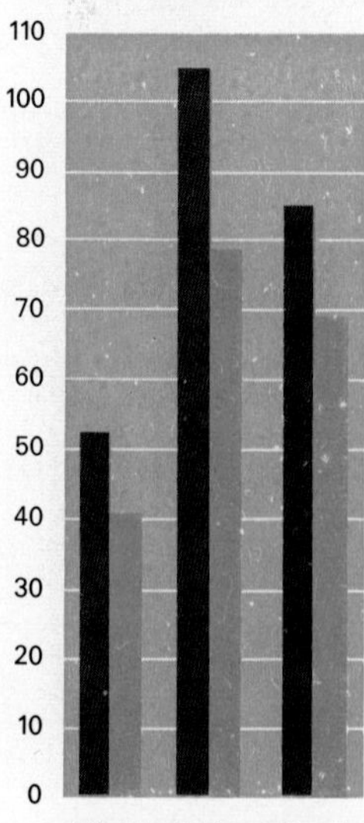

When we examine all that must be done to increase agricultural productivity, it becomes clear that simply changing agricultural practices is not enough. Increasing Indian rice productivity to the Japanese level, for example, really necessitates the creation of a full-fledged industrial society with factories, transportation and communication systems, schools, universities, and research facilities. All this must be coupled with the necessary social and economic institutions that will make possible and encourage the transition from traditional agricultural practices to modern methods. The problem far transcends simply teaching old-fashioned farmers new tricks.

In the last few years it has become apparent that economic development of the poorer countries is enormously difficult, requiring far greater efforts than those applied so far. Food production in the poorer countries actually has been increasing about as rapidly as in the richer countries. But in most of the poorer regions, population growth is so rapid that it equals or exceeds the agricultural gains, and there is no real sign of a letup. The panel estimated that the world's population will climb from today's 3,438,000,000 to about 5,000,000,000 in 1985 and to more than 6,000,000,000 in the year 2000.

It is obvious that if birth rates could be greatly diminished, the world food situation would be eased considerably, and it has been proposed that intensive campaigns of birth control be waged in the poorer countries. Some countries have in fact established population-control policies and started nationwide family planning programs. Birth rates in most of the developing countries undoubtedly will decrease during the next few decades, but the World Food Panel warns that family planning programs can have little effect on the crisis immediately ahead. In India, for example, the most critical food situation will occur in about 1980, long before any decrease in the birth rate can have any substantial effect. Nevertheless, in the long run, it is absolutely essential that population control be widely practiced. The panel concluded that "although the efforts to promote family planning cannot replace the effort to increase food production, they are of coordinate importance; unless both programs are successful, the world faces catastrophe."

The rich nations must help out with far more money and technical aid

Recent experience indicates that the current high rates of population growth, coupled with relatively meager basic resources, make it almost impossible for the poorer countries to save enough capital to invest in such a way that development will proceed smoothly and swiftly. So the poorer countries must have help from the richer ones. Some persons suggest that such help must amount to several hundred billion dollars during the next 25 years. This would require annual contributions from the richer nations of some 1 per cent of their gross national products–an amount far greater than current contributions. The annual United States contribution, for example, would be more than $7,000,000,000.

But while capital is an essential ingredient of economic development, it is not sufficient by itself. If, by some miracle, capital assistance from the richer countries to the poorer nations were suddenly doubled, it is doubtful that the additional funds could be put to really effective use. There simply are not enough persons in the poorer countries who have the education and experience to make the correct decisions about what to do–and to solve the problems associated with those decisions. This deficiency can be alleviated by expanded use of trained persons from the developed countries, but in the long run, the poorer countries must have adequate numbers of their own highly trained people.

World Caloric Requirements from 1965 to 1985

High estimates

Low estimates

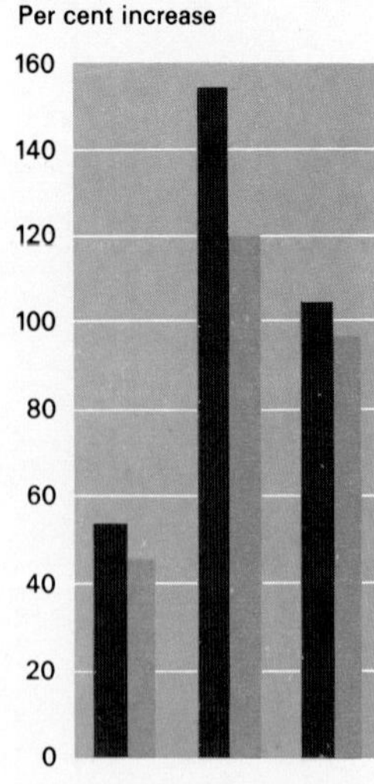

Under the circumstances, it appears that the poorer countries' greatest need is for technical assistance aimed at rapid improvement of the scope and quality of educational systems and the building up of strong research, development, and problem-solving competence. Arrangements must be made for large numbers of professional persons from the richer countries to spend a substantial portion of their professional careers teaching and doing research in developing countries and helping to build schools, universities, research laboratories, government departments, and industries.

The *Report of the Panel on the World Food Supply* has, unfortunately, received little attention. Congress, in particular, has shown a remarkable lack of interest in the study. Since the appearance of the report, foreign aid funds have been cut to the lowest figure in 20 years. Public protests have been inaudible in spite of the fact that important officials have termed congressional insensitivities to this problem "irresponsible." Further, in the face of the critical nature of the world food situation, the United States announced a cutback in wheat production only hours after release of the panel's report. Clearly, important branches of government were out of touch with each other. The behavior of other rich countries has been little better. Indeed, there is every indication that their foreign assistance also is dropping–at least relative to their ability to contribute.

"Freedom" may not be a meaningful term to someone who is hungry

When I visited India for the first time a number of years ago, I had thought I was emotionally prepared to take the shock of seeing hunger and deprivation on a massive scale. It turned out that my preparation, like that of most first-time visitors from the richer countries, was inadequate.

I shall never forget one afternoon shortly before Christmas when I was strolling with my wife and an Indian friend through the beautiful ruins of Mahabalipuram, an ancient temple near Madras. We felt thirsty, and because no safe water was easily available, we bought coconuts and drank the juice. Having drained my coconut dry, I casually tossed it into a grove of trees, knowing that, unlike a tin can, it would quickly disintegrate and become part of the soil.

Almost as soon as my drained coconut had hit the ground, I heard the sounds of children shouting angrily. I turned and saw a group of youngsters, averaging no more than eight years in age, fighting over the coconut, much like dogs will fight over a bone. Earlier, I had noticed the children following us and had concluded that they were simply curious about strangers. Instead, as it turned out, they had followed us with the hope that we might throw away some "garbage." Stated simply, they were terribly hungry.

I have often wondered since then what those children–now in their early 20s, if they are still alive–are doing and thinking today. What are their politics? What do they think of us? Are such concepts as "freedom" and "democracy" in any sense meaningful to them? Or are such terms simply hollow expressions uttered by persons who have never known, and do not understand the problem of, hunger?

Related Articles

For a complete report on the 1967 year in science and technology, see Section One, John H. Glenn, Jr.: Focus on Space; Section Two, The Mekong River Project and The Killing of a Great Lake; and the following articles in Section Three:

Awards and Prizes (Science and Industry)
Biochemistry
Biology
Botany
Chemistry
Communications
Energy
Engineering
Geology
Health and Disease
Medicine
Nobel Prizes
Ocean
Physics
Science and Research
Weather
Zoology

Lawrence A. Cremin: Focus on Education

The militancy in American education in 1967 might make the real debate over the means and ends of education more difficult to carry on and resolve

Labor Day came early in September, 1967, on the fourth of the month, and the following morning, in communities across the United States, the school year began. As always, some youngsters were enthusiastic, some a bit reluctant. Many, no doubt, had the mixed feelings that often mark the end of the long summer vacation. Most arrived to find their teachers in assigned classrooms, eager to begin. More than a million of them, however, found their teachers on strike and their schools shut down, for 1967 was the year the American teacher went militant, and the effects reverberated throughout the nation's education system.

There are huge gaps in quality between the slum schools and the suburban schools

The impact of the new militancy was greatest in Detroit, Mich., and New York City, where a combined total of 56,000 teachers stayed out for two weeks. But there were more limited walkouts in 35 other Michigan communities, as well as in Illinois and Kentucky. In Florida, a threatened state-wide resignation by 32,000 teachers was only narrowly averted when Governor Claude R. Kirk, Jr., agreed at the last minute to call the legislature into special session to seek additional taxes for education. "We have a new type of more aggressive, more alert teacher all over this nation who wants to help determine the policies that affect him," declared Braulio Alonso, president of the National Education Association (NEA). "This is the beginning of a real revolution in the teaching profession."

However far the revolution ultimately would go, there was no denying that it had been some time in the making. There were, of course, the usual matters of salaries and benefits during a period when inflation was slowly shrinking the value of the dollar. But even more fundamental were three problems at the very heart of teacher unrest: (1) the conditions of teaching; (2) the sharp competition for members between the NEA and the American Federation of Teachers (AFT); and (3) the desire of teachers to play a more significant role in the making of educational policy.

Viewed nationally, teaching conditions have improved since the end of World War II. There has been a vast school-building program. A vigorous reform movement launched in the mid-1950s has injected new life into virtually every phase of the school curriculum. And since the passage of the National Defense Education Act of 1958 and the Elementary and Secondary School Improvement Act of 1965, there has been a massive infusion of federal dollars. But all these improvements have gone forward unevenly, creating huge gaps in quality between the slum schools in the centers of our great cities and the suburban schools on their perimeters. These gaps have been widened further by the continuing migration of impoverished rural families–mostly Negro–from the South to the northern cities.

As the gaps have widened, the American people seem to have taken more seriously than ever the right of every child, as President Lyndon B. Johnson once stated it, "to all of the education, of the highest quality, which his or her ambition demands and his or her mind can absorb." Taking that right seriously has placed herculean burdens on teachers. The American commitment to universal education is about a hundred years old, but the sad fact is we are just beginning to learn how to realize it. One might say that educators have solved the easier problems, such as how to educate children favored with stable homes, good health, and loving parents with adequate incomes. But they are only beginning to contend seriously with the intractable problems of educating children who have been denied these advantages. Formerly, most such children simply dropped out in droves, found unskilled jobs, and led lives of drudgery, though, of course, there were always the few who managed to finish school through sheer determination and perseverance. Today, the unskilled jobs are disappearing. Society is demanding that young people be given a chance to learn the skills they will need. And, most importantly, parents are insisting that children be accorded their full educational rights—now.

The problem is one of getting ideas, material, and people to do the educational job

It is one thing, however, for society to demand but quite another for society to deliver; and it is here that teachers have been caught, in the gap between rising educational expectations and sharpening educational difficulties. The problem is not merely one of money, though money has always been central; it is, rather, one of getting the ideas and the material and the people to do the job. In the absence of sound knowledge, tested pedagogical procedures, and professional training appropriate to the task, classroom work in many American schools—especially city schools—has become a fatiguing, frightening, and frustrating experience. It is this sense of frustration, compounded by the feeling of being underpaid and undervalued, that seems to have led teachers to the picket lines.

Striking teachers

Other factors have aggravated the situation. For more than a half-century, there have been two leading organizations of teachers in the United States—the NEA, founded in 1857, and the AFT, founded in 1916. Of the two, the NEA, which sees itself as a "professional association" embracing principals, supervisors, and superintendents of schools as well as classroom teachers, has always been the larger and more powerful, the dominant voice of the teacher. The AFT, a union that restricts membership to classroom teachers, has been smaller but more militant.

In about 1960, however, a decision was made within the American Federation of Labor-Congress of Industrial Organizations (AFL-CIO) to assist the AFT in a drive to extend its influence. Membership increased from about 50,000 at that time to some 140,000 in 1967. But more importantly, the union assumed an increasingly militant posture in matters of salaries, rights, and working conditions, and in 1961 it won a critically important teacher representation election in New York City. Since that time, the AFT has become more and more the voice of urban teachers as they wrestle with the problem of Baltimore, Boston, Chicago, Detroit, and Washington, though it should be pointed out that vigorous NEA locals remain the negotiating agents in Buffalo, Denver, Milwaukee, Newark, and Rochester.

The AFT's drive for influence inevitably challenged the more conservative NEA, which responded with a much more militant posture of its own and with a campaign that increased its membership to more than 1,000,000 in 1967. As its counterpart of the AFT's "collective bargaining," the NEA developed "professional negotiations." As its counterpart of the "strike," the NEA worked out a system of "professional sanctions," and indeed, at its 1967 convention, the NEA actually endorsed the "strike" itself as a last resort. Yet, however much the two organizations are coming to use similar tactics–and there even have been occasional suggestions of a merger–there is no doubt that they are competing vigorously for the loyalty of American teachers. The NEA still dominates what one commentator has called "the struggle for blackboard power," having worked out 1,336 contracts to the AFT's 41 by mid-September, 1967. But the competition continues and has obviously contributed to the growing militancy of local teacher groups.

What organized teachers want is greater influence over the conditions of teaching

Finally, there is the matter of the teacher's role in policymaking. Traditionally, American educational policy has been set by laymen working through local school boards, state legislatures, and the Congress of the United States. In the classic textbook formulation, the school board makes policy, and the superintendent and his staff carry it out. Actually, the process is infinitely more complicated than that. On the one hand, the superintendent is frequently the source of policies the school board eventually adopts; and on the other hand, the board itself works within tightly defined legal limits and is subject to a host of pressures from parents, from church and civic groups, and from business, labor, and patriotic organizations.

What organized teachers ultimately want is greater influence over the conditions of teaching so that they can carry on their work more effectively. Hence, they are seeking to achieve a variety of goals in realms that have traditionally been the domain of school administrators or boards of education–for example, disciplinary procedures for unruly children or limitations on class size. The efforts to obtain such goals through direct bargaining between teacher organizations and boards of education injected some of the thorniest elements into the negotiations of 1967.

Militancy often gets results. But it also evokes counter-militancy, and one of the unexpected outcomes of the big-city strikes of 1967 was growing parent militancy directed against the teachers. The case of New York City is instructive. There, a movement had been developing for at least a year, sparked by aggressive civil rights groups in Harlem and the Bedford-Stuyvesant section of Brooklyn, to transfer control of the schools from the citywide Board of Education to neighborhood councils of parents. While groups in different neighborhoods had come up with somewhat different programs, they were unanimous in their insistence that the Board of Education had lost the confidence of the Negro community, that Negro children were receiving a substandard education in the city's public schools, and that the only way to rectify this intolerable situation was to transfer control of the schools to elected representatives of the Negro community. By August,

1967, the Board of Education, aided by grants from the Ford Foundation, had actually moved to experiment with such neighborhood councils in three slum localities. These councils were just beginning to function–some fairly well, some rather poorly–when the United Federation of Teachers (UFT), the AFT local in New York, went on strike in September.

The conflict between predominantly Negro slum parents and predominantly white teachers sharpened

A collision was inevitable. From the outset, the strike was opposed by both the United Parents Associations, a confederation of more than 450 of the city's local Parent-Teacher Associations, and the African-American Teachers Association (AATA), an organization claiming to represent half the city's 4,800 Negro teachers. "The UFT," said the AATA's president, Albert Vann, "is concerned with teachers' rights and salaries, but not so much with community problems." And it was precisely at the point of the strike's impact on "community problems" in the Negro ghettos that the collision came. At the same time that Negro parents were proposing year-round schools, the teachers were asking for shorter hours. At the same time that Negro parents were insisting that the most experienced teachers be assigned to the most difficult schools–namely, the slum schools–the teachers were standing fast on their right to transfer from school to school on the basis of seniority. At the same time that Negro parents were demanding an extension of educational opportunity to even the least fortunate of the community's children, the teachers were seeking new procedures for the removal of disruptive youngsters from their classrooms. And though the UFT steadfastly insisted that it was demonstrating its devotion to the improvement of ghetto education through its unqualified support of the city's "More Effective Schools" program, under which additional teachers and guidance counselors were assigned to designated slum schools, the More Effective Schools were themselves being charged with ineffectiveness.

Vacant school desks

These differences served only to sharpen conflicts that had long been developing between predominantly Negro slum parents and predominantly white slum teachers. They thereby injected into the controversy racial considerations that persisted well beyond the settlement of the 14-day strike. In November, a commission appointed by Mayor John V. Lindsay and headed by McGeorge Bundy, president of the Ford Foundation, put forth a plan to reorganize the city's school system into 30 to 60 separate community school districts, each with its own neighborhood board and the power to set curriculums, employ teachers and administrators, choose textbooks, and propose and administer budgets for designated neighborhood schools. Predictably, hostility between militant parents and militant teachers mounted.

"I think it is the most innovative and radical proposal we've had in education in this city in 15 years," said Eugene Callender, executive director of the New York City Urban League. "I enthusiastically endorse it." On the other hand, Albert Shanker, president of the UFT, said the proposal, if adopted, would promote "years of chaos and the eventual destruction of the city's school system. Negro teachers would be hired in Negro areas, and white teachers in white areas." Reliable leadership would be lacking in many districts because "extremists would have veto power." Not surprisingly, the Board of Education sided with Shanker.

It was abundantly clear by the year's end that the collisions in 1967 had vastly deepened the crisis in urban education and that the public school systems of the great cities stood at a crossroads. If they failed to respond to the demands of ghetto parents, the grim prospect was more widespread and more bitter unrest. If they did respond, but with unwise or unrealistic remedies, it could mean the disruption and ultimate collapse of inner city school systems. It was a painful dilemma, one that did not lend itself to prompt or easy resolution.

The public school systems of the great cities stood at a crossroads

It had become fashionable during the 1950s to talk of a "great debate" over education, in which the ends and means of the public schools were being fundamentally reappraised and redefined. Had the debate of the 1950s deteriorated into the bitter confrontations of the 1960s? Many feared it had, to the detriment of the schools.

The new militancy portended many things for American education. It was really a struggle for political influence over the schools at a time when the quality of education had become a central issue of public policy. The great collisions of 1967 actually represented, as they had throughout American history, clashes between rival views of the kind of society Americans wanted to live in and the best means of bringing that society into being. Some of the black power and white power enthusiasts really envisioned an America in which apartheid would eventually prevail. Other men and women continued to dream of an America in which citizens of every race, color, and creed could live together peacefully and creatively.

The militancy of 1967 would doubtless result in some useful short-term ends, and it might well direct attention to needs and problems that had too long been ignored. But the new militancy might also make the real debate over the means and ends of education more difficult to carry on and to resolve. And if the lines between groups were to harden, and if riots or political stalemates became the only possible outcomes, the shouting would have come at a high price indeed, and the schoolchildren would ultimately have been the losers.

Related Articles

For a complete report on the 1967 year in education, see Section Two, WHERE THE JOBS WILL BE, and the following articles in Section Three:

American Library Association
Canadian Library Association
Canadian Literature
Child Guidance
Child Welfare
City
Congress of the United States
Education
Foundations
Handicapped, The
Library
Literature
Literature for Children
Parents and Teachers, National Congress of
Poverty
State Government
Television

John H. Glenn, Jr.: Focus on Space

The Space Age was 10 years old in 1967, but despite its many accomplishments, budget limitations placed future projects in jeopardy

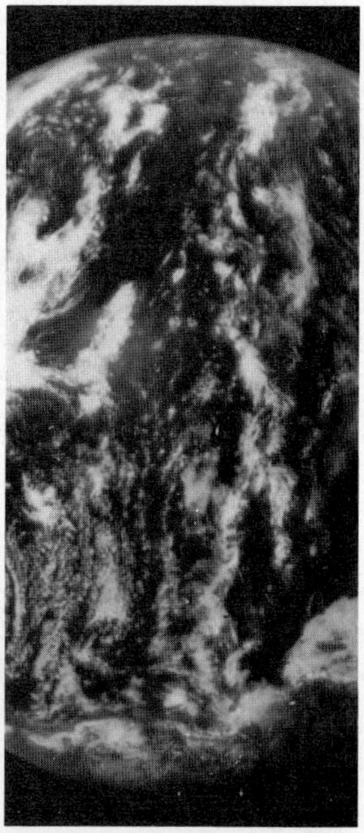

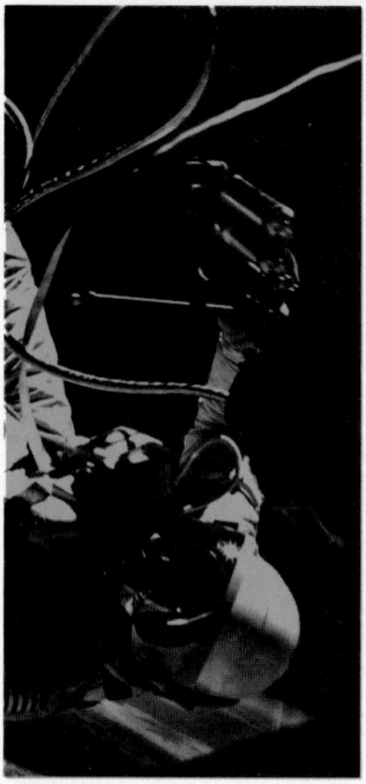

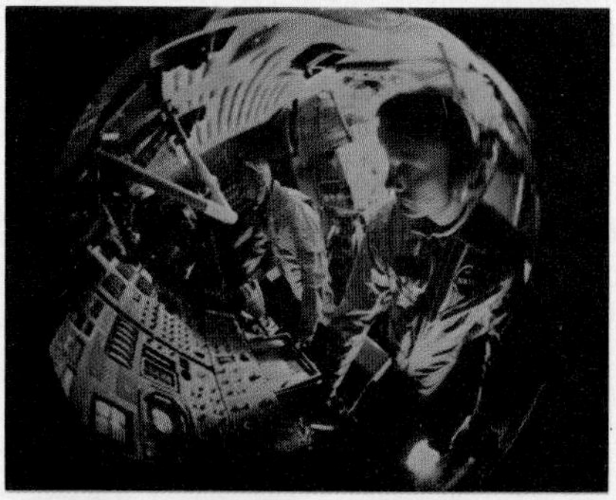

"U.S. Faces Technological Pearl Harbor," screamed one headline on Oct. 4, 1957. Russia's orbiting of the 183-pound Sputnik I had surprised the nation and the world. The United States supremacy in scientific matters had long been unchallenged; now, suddenly, our complacency was shattered by the Soviet accomplishment. In the period of soul-searching that followed, we questioned not only our science and technology, but also our educational system, industrial know-how, military capability, foreign policy–indeed, the whole fabric of our society. Magazines and newspapers were filled with articles criticizing various aspects of American life. Typical was one entitled "The Crisis in Education" that commented: "It is hard to deny that American schools have degenerated into a system for coddling and entertaining the mediocre."

Our complacency was shattered by the launch of Russia's sputnik

At the end of the first decade of the Space Age, in October, 1967, I leafed through the local newspaper one evening, casually glancing at the headlines. Back on page 16, tucked in between an advertisement for tennis shoes and another for a garden guide, was a one-inch, single-column item that stated in its entirety: "Moscow–AP. The Soviet Union launched another in its long series of unmanned satellites for space research Wednesday. The 181st satellite in the Cosmos series was reported to be functioning normally." From banner headlines in 1957 to page 16 in 1967 eloquently expresses, I think, the rate of progress and acceptance of the Space Age in the past 10 years.

The United States space effort was not mounted solely in response to Russian achievements. On July 29, 1955, President Dwight D. Eisenhower had announced that the United States would attempt to launch a series of satellites during the International Geophysical Year, which was to begin in 1957. Project Vanguard, organized under the sponsorship of the Naval Research Laboratory, the National Academy of Sciences, and the National Science Foundation, was the name of that effort. But the Russians beat us to the punch with Sputnik I and followed it up a month later with a 1,120-pound sputnik carrying a dog.

The hue and cry following this double scientific humiliation resulted in a series of Senate hearings and President Eisenhower's appearance on television in November, 1957, to appoint James R. Killian of the Massachusetts Institute of Technology to the newly created post of Special Assistant to the President for Science and Technology. Then, in July, 1958, Congress established the National Aeronautics and Space Administration (NASA) to coordinate the nation's space activities.

After the navy's Vanguard exploded on the launch pad on Dec. 6, 1957, the decision was made to give the army's Jupiter-C rocket, developed by Wernher von Braun's group at Huntsville, Ala., a chance. Finally, on Jan. 31, 1958, the four-stage booster roared off the launch pad at Cape Canaveral and placed the 30.8-pound Explorer I in orbit. America had entered the Space Age.

President John F. Kennedy gave the first clear definition of our goals in space in August, 1961, when he presented Congress with a program aimed at putting a man on the moon before 1970. Also proposed as distinct U.S. space goals were the development of communications satellites, a system of weather satellites, and the creation of nuclear propulsion systems for eventual use in deep space exploration. Despite President Kennedy's estimate that the undertaking would cost billions of dollars, Congress wholeheartedly approved the program.

Many of the goals proposed by President Kennedy have already been achieved

As we mark the 10th anniversary of the Space Age, many of these goals have already been achieved. Global communications via satellite is a reality, as evidenced by a June, 1967, telecast that was transmitted to an estimated 500,000,000 viewers in 30 nations by three U.S. communications satellites. The ESSA II weather satellite, launched on Feb. 28, 1966, circles the globe taking pictures of cloud formations and beaming them to more than 150 ground stations in 45 countries. Nuclear propulsion systems will probably be ready when needed. The Phoebus-IB developmental reactor ran for 45 minutes in February, 1967, establishing a new record for a full-power run.

The manned lunar landing objective is also well underway with Project Apollo, the successor to the Mercury and Gemini projects. Development of its transportation system received a big boost in November, 1967, with the highly successful first launching of the Saturn V vehicle. Many of you no doubt watched it on television as 7,500,000 pounds of thrust boosted a payload of 280,000 pounds–by far the largest yet–into earth orbit.

Meanwhile, Ranger, Surveyor, and Lunar Orbiter spacecraft have photographed, soft-landed on, and analyzed the moon's surface. Besides collecting as much advance information about lunar landing conditions as possible, these craft have made significant contributions to man's knowledge of the moon.

Saturn V lift-off

The Soviet Union, of course, has not been idle during this first decade. And the Russians have taken great pride in their accomplishments, even setting up a Cosmonaut monument in Moscow in 1964 with an engraved list of claimed "firsts" for the Soviet space program.

The United States has never stressed our major "firsts," but we could probably compile an equally impressive list. The "race" aspect of space remains far overemphasized to my way of thinking. It is true that some 60 nations around the world have come into existence or received their national identity since World War II and that they may well look to nations in the forefront of progress for guidance and political alignment. There are also military implications in space. But to me, the "race" argument for continuing our space program is far less significant than the fact that this is the beginning of the greatest adventure into the unknown–the greatest exploration–of all time. The U.S. program has been, and should be, a broad-based scientific approach to gathering information about the greater environment outside the earth's atmosphere.

There have been many setbacks in this first decade, and it was considerable time after the start of orbital launches before even a 50 per cent probability of success on any individual launch could be confidently forecast. Still, the safety record of the manned space program had been perfect until January, 1967, when the first fatalities occurred.

Gus Grissom, Ed White, and Roger Chaffee were killed on January 27 at Cape Kennedy when a fire swept through their Apollo capsule during a routine test of the spacecraft. And later in the year, on April 24, Russian Cosmonaut Vladimir M. Komarov lost his life while returning from space in the new Soyuz spacecraft.

What can one say when one's friends' lives are taken? To speak of their obvious determination, dedication, and purpose cannot fill the void. Together we shared moments of elation, of accomplishment, and of triumph. Now we who survive taste the sobering balance of tragedy. Man's feet remain on earth while he reaches for the stars, and his fallibility lurks in the background even during his moments of greatest accomplishment. In a tragic instant, the dark shadow of ultimate sacrifice became starkly vivid. But man tries–and succeeds; or man fails–but rises to try again. Such is his nature. To those who give their lives to this quest, our debt can never be repaid.

What can one say when one's friends' lives are taken?

It is difficult to summarize the benefits of the first decade in space. One must look at not only what we have learned about space and man's ability to venture away from his home planet, but also at the impact of the space program on the whole of American life.

Some scientists have criticized the emphasis on the manned space program; I think too many results have been expected too soon. We have been, and still are, working out the problems of man and his transportation system in space. Earlier explorers solved their ship's problems and trained their crews before setting sail, and we are at that same point today "on this new ocean," as President Kennedy termed it.

Results from unmanned space efforts have obviously been more rapid. We have discovered much about the earth: that it is slightly pear-shaped, for instance; that it is surrounded by the Van Allen radiation belts; that our previous concepts about the atmosphere and its upper reaches were erroneous; that a solar wind streams around the earth in a huge teardrop pattern. Our probes to the moon, Mars, and Venus have similarly increased our knowledge of our solar system neighbors. These few examples are indicative of the main purpose of exploration–the encountering of the unknown and the unexpected.

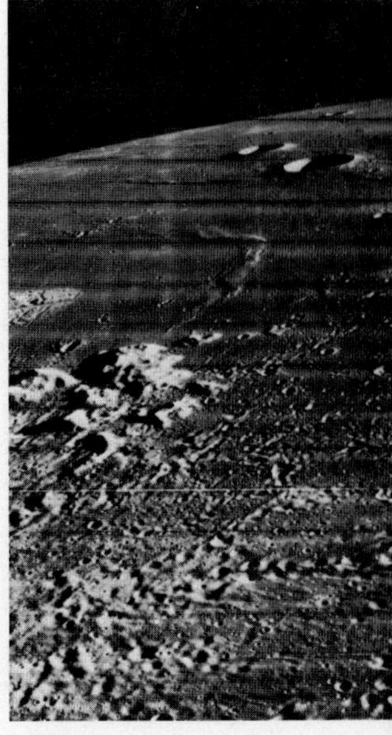

Moonscape from Lunar Orbiter III

One of the least emphasized results of the space program to date, but one that is already having considerable impact, has been the development of the systems analysis approach to problems. It brings together specialists from many fields to identify a problem, consider the various alternatives to that problem, and determine the appropriate solutions. In terms of the space program, this interdisciplinary approach has marshaled the efforts of government, industry, and our university system toward a common objective. It has been a successful approach, and perhaps it can be used to organize assaults on such problems as air and water pollution and urban difficulties.

Because of security reasons, little is known about the role of satellite reconnaissance in national defense. President Lyndon B. Johnson has been reported as saying that the surveillance satellites alone more than justify the vast sums we have spent on the space program. The wake of underwater submarines can be discerned from space, and heat measurement and other observation techniques can be used to determine the launching of not only other spacecraft, but also of boosters launched for any purpose. Within the next few years, the Manned Orbiting Laboratory will be able to station crews in space for extended detailed observation and experiments. There is little doubt that the Russians have similar programs under investigation and development.

The effect of such expenditures and employment on the nation's economy is obvious

As I have mentioned, the launch of the Russian sputnik triggered a questioning of our whole educational system. If questioning was already overdue, then this was the catalyst that touched off the reaction and that resulted in, among other things, the National Defense Education Act of 1958, increased federal school aid, and improved science curriculums. It is estimated that the United States spent approximately $13,600,000,000 on elementary and secondary education in 1957. By 1966, the estimate had risen to $28,300,000,000. Some of this growth would have occurred as a natural course of events, for our Gross National Product (GNP) was rising during this period. But the percentage of GNP being spent on all educational costs also rose–from 4.8 per cent in 1957 to 6.7 per cent in 1965.

The space program has also had salutary effects on the economy. U.S. space expenditures since 1957 are estimated at $37,600,000,000, with $2,000,000,000 of this spent on construction of facilities. Peak employment in the space industries reached approximately 450,000 men and women in 20,000 companies across the nation. The direct effect of such expenditures and employment on the country is obvious.

So-called "fallout products" from the space program number in the thousands–from improved house paints that will last as long as your house to cardiac monitoring devices that enable the doctor to check your heart via leads attached to your home telephone. But even though these space spin-offs may prove of tremendous value, the real purpose of our space effort remains research and exploration.

The doubts, fears, and uncertainties attendant at the birth of the Space Age 10 years ago have given way as the United States has met the Soviet challenge and pioneered the exploration of space. There is no limit to our horizons. There is growing concern, however, that other national problems may very seriously limit our future activities in space. Indicative of this is the fact that in 1967, Congress slashed NASA's proposed budget for 1968 from $5,100,000,000 to $4,600,000,000. Funding for current projects probably will not be drastically affected by this $500,000,000 cut, but the organizing of government, industry, and university teams to plan and execute future programs will undoubtedly suffer. Project Apollo, for instance, will not be hindered by the budgetary limitations. But beyond 1969, NASA has no approved planetary flights and few scientific flights of any kind. Cut off or at least delayed are the Mariner flights to Mars, scheduled to be launched in 1971. Also in jeopardy are the Voyager missions to Mars planned for 1973 and 1975 and the Nerva II nuclear engine planned to be used on the Saturn V booster in 1975.

There is one decision that probably can wait another year, and that involves a manned Mars landing. This requires a national commitment similar to that made for Project Apollo. But the decision will have to be made no later than 1969 if we expect to accomplish such a feat in the 1975 to 1980 time period.

Why the budget cuts in 1967? While there is still a deep interest in getting on with space research and exploration, we have, of course, many other national problems of importance. The war in Vietnam is the concern of every American. With more than 15,000 Americans killed and 50,000 wounded, no effort must be spared in bringing it to a successful conclusion. Monetarily, that effort is running at $30,000,000,000 per year. The smoldering urban problems that flamed in the summer of 1967 must be administered to, and their solutions can be found only by digging deep into the inequities of our society. The despoliation of our environment through the indiscriminate dumping of wastes into our air and water must be curtailed.

These are major problems, and while money alone will not solve them, it is a most necessary ingredient for whatever solutions are contemplated. I am realistic enough to realize that monetary restrictions will not permit us to do all the things we would wish. But if current cuts are maintained, I sincerely hope that the public will not lose its long-term interest and appreciation for the importance of space research and exploration, and that we will return to its emphasis just as soon as we have better control of these more pressing matters.

An important aspect of American life is at stake

An important aspect of American life is at stake. More than any other country, we Americans have forged ahead because of an almost innate desire to "get things done and do them better." Perhaps it was built into our national character by the way this country was expanded –from the East Coast, over the Appalachians, across the Mississippi and the Rockies, and on to the West Coast. There was always something unknown over the next hill. Were there better homesites? We had to find out. Was there gold? Was this good farmland? There was always something we did not know, but wanted to learn. We had to find the answers and to somehow make a better life, to "do it better" than anyone had ever done before.

There is still no limit to our ability and ingenuity today, whether it be probing the secrets of the cell or building a better automobile. We do have great problems that require great solutions. But we must not lose the curiosity, drive, and desire to know the new and the unknown that have characterized America and made it pre-eminent.

Related Articles

For a complete report on the 1967 year in space, see the following articles in Section Three:

Astronauts
Astronomy
Communications
Disarmament
Electronics
Space Exploration
Weather

Alistair Cooke: Focus on The Arts

The explosion in the arts of "total honesty, total freedom" raises the crucial question of where freedom ends and anarchy begins

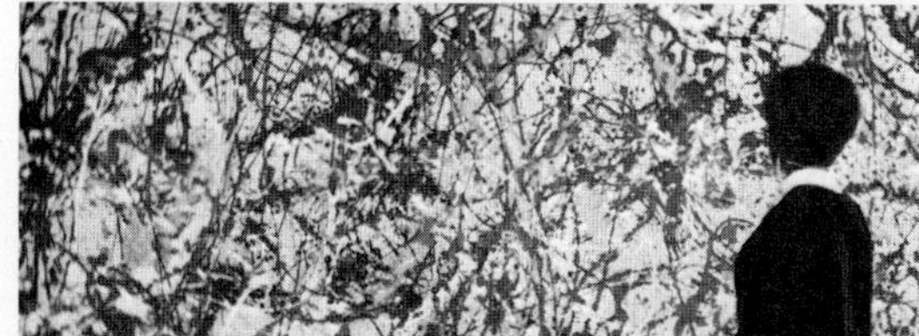

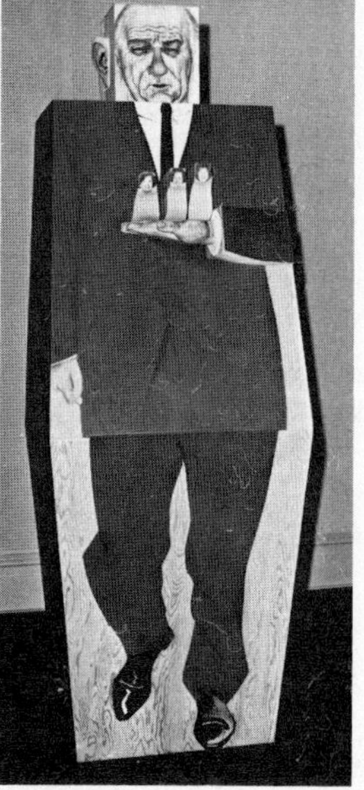

You can say for certain that the Byzantine Empire ended when Constantinople fell to the Ottoman Turks in 1453. You can safely date the American Revolutionary War from April 19, 1775–the day the minutemen clashed with British soldiers at Lexington, Mass. You can be sure that the British devalued the pound in November, 1967, and you can go on to use that month as a dividing line between one condition of the British economy and another.

A "Revolt of the Young Against the Establishment" took place in 1967

But, as I have hinted before now, it is dangerous and usually naive to try to pin any revolution in the arts to the calendar. The arts are an incomparable barometer of the tastes, manners, and morals of a country or a culture. But the reading of any barometer–whether of morals or of atmospheric pressure–requires a good deal of caution. As with climate, fundamental changes in weather systems happen slowly; a shift of the wind or a drop in the atmospheric pressure is no proof that a hurricane is on the way, or even a shower. No scientists are so cautious and hedging in their predictions as the men of the weather bureau, for the blunt reason that they can be proved wrong within 24 hours. Yet film critics, drama critics, book critics, and pontiffs on painting do not hesitate to proclaim revolutions, "breakthroughs," or the dawn and nightfall of eras on the evidence of a single movie, play, novel, or painting.

In December, 1967, *Time* was only one of many magazines that saw in the motion picture *Bonnie and Clyde* a turning point, "the shock of freedom," a "watershed picture," a landmark in the history of the motion picture comparable to *The Birth of a Nation* and *Citizen Kane*. This may be true in the sense that the movie industry will no doubt act as if it *were* true and mount a whole assembly line of *Bonnie and Clyde* retreads. But I myself doubt that it is more of a radical departure than the 60-year-old Keystone Kops, the 35-year-old *Scarface* or the 10-year-old *Cat on a Hot Tin Roof*, each of whose exhilarating elements–the comic evasion of justice, the romanticizing of the gangster, the "daring" exploitation of impotence–*Bonnie and Clyde* very slickly compounds in its rattling tribute to the 1930s.

But I have to admit, for the first time since these annual reports began, that it is possible to say–without feeling either fraudulent or superficial–that in one year a revolution has happened in the arts. It is far more general and dramatic than the isolated success of *Bonnie and Clyde* or any other single movie, play, book, painting, or happening. It is nothing less than a general "Revolt of the Young Against the Establishment."

Obviously, the movement was brewing before Jan. 1, 1967. For two or three years I have, in fact, reported on several preliminary sorties and bombardments: the sudden savagery of political satire in night clubs, off-Broadway revues, and "underground" periodicals; the increasing distrust by the Supreme Court of the United States of the old statutes that defined obscenity; the rise of publishing houses that are making a killing in the marketing of four-letter words and specific sexuality; the increasingly shaky status in England of the Lord Chamberlain, the official censor of plays and films. But 1967 was the year in which the recognition burst on an apprehensive world that, in the words of a national magazine, "the old taboos are dead or dying, a new, more permissive society is taking shape (whose) outlines are etched most prominently in the blunt, often obscene language seemingly endemic in American novels and plays, in the candid lyrics of pop songs and the *avant-garde* ballet, in erotic art and television talk shows, in freer fashions and franker advertising." Cole Porter put it more succinctly:

Little happens at any one time that has not happened before

In olden days a glimpse of stocking
Was looked on as something shocking;
Now, Heaven knows,
*Anything goes.**

How has this come about? How revolutionary is the "New Freedom of the New Left"–the hippies, the voluble and self-conscious new movie directors, the rebellious young in the schools and colleges? How original is the esthetic theory behind what one young poet has called "the breakthrough toward total honesty, total freedom"? How total can honesty be, without the risk of doing what Henrik Ibsen's Peer Gynt did, which was to hurt and crush everybody around him by telling all the truth all the time? How unlimited can the commitment to freedom be, without committing society itself to anarchy? These are the questions that I believe students of the arts ought to be asking themselves today.

I also believe it to be the function of this annual report not only to report contemporary trends, but also to relate them to the experience of the Western tradition. By "tradition" I do not mean a set of rules or doctrines laid down at any given time. I mean, rather, the whole accumulation of ideas, values, and creative genius and talent that has produced the rich body of Western art–an ungainly body but a body nonetheless. It has entertained the most varied and conflicting impulses, and only a little of what happens at any one time has not happened sometime earlier. It would be far more remarkable than the prophets of "total honesty, total freedom" seem to be aware if what we are now witnessing in the arts was something quite new in the history of civilization. Of course, it is the instinct and privilege of youth to believe that it *is* new and to make the appropriately convincing noises.

Bonnie and Clyde

As I understand it, the first tenet of the "Rebel's Creed" is: Whoever is over 30 or is middle class is a member of the Establishment, and the Establishment is rotten and must be destroyed. Forty years ago, when H. L. Mencken opened the eyes of the college generation to the frivolity of what he called "the booboisie," a group Sinclair Lewis immortalized in the person of Babbitt, the indictment of the elders by the young went this way: "They are bourgeois, they know they are bourgeois, therefore they stink."

The target of the rebels is always very much the same, whether it is called the Establishment, the "system," or the bourgeoisie. It is the

*"Anything Goes." Copyright © 1934 by Harms, Inc. Used by permission.

middle class, the average sensual men, the drones of society who are moderate in most things, know what they like, pay their taxes, and believe in patriotism, marriage, a comfortable home, sport, and a Saturday night party.

We learn from Aristotle (if we care to) that those societies are most durable that have the largest middle class and in which more people than fewer have reasonable access to *becoming* middle class. Granted, Aristotle did not have much experience with a variety of civilizations; nevertheless, the Greek city-state had gone through its ups and downs, and since it was the most successful democracy in human experience until the 19th century, there is the chance that its wisdom might apply to us.

The middle class has always been a target for attack because of its great stability

In modern political experience, there seems to be little doubt that the larger the middle class, the more likely has been the survival of a democratic form of government–unless, as happened in Germany after World War I, there was a depression so far-reaching that it impoverished even the middle class and left it with only the mockery of its tastes, habits, and convictions.

A proof of Aristotle's contention is the fact that the middle class has always been under attack by the bright boys, precisely because it is stable and can therefore so easily be made to seem lumpish and unimaginative. In the late 18th and early 19th centuries, the attack came from above, from the wits of the gentry, who ridiculed the manners and vulgar pretensions of the rising merchants and their new white-collar employees. The middle class was next under attack from the radical intelligentsia–a gamut that took in Charles Dickens as well as Karl Marx–for being hypocritical, sanctimonious, and politically indifferent.

Today, it is attacked for materialism, for an obsession with comfort and money values, for smugness and hypocrisy, and for preaching one kind of life and leading another. This time, the attack comes from the more comfortable, perhaps more indulged, children of the middle class itself, the drop-outs from "the system" who, like reformed Communists, are always the most implacable enemies of their sires. And today, through the arts, the indictment is reduced to a series of short, snappy theorems. To wit: The Establishment wants entertainment only, and is therefore Commercial, and is therefore Corrupt. Conversely, the Rebel (that is, the hippie, the off-Broadway playwright, the underground moviemaker, the New Left poet) is Serious and makes no money, and therefore he is Profound.

There is nothing new in this. The whole "Bohemian" movement of the mid-19th century was a variation of it that reacted against the prosperous, respectable, and inartistic bourgeoisie by being consciously artistic, unrespectable, and indigent. The first duty of the Bohemians was to shock the bourgeoisie. They devised their own flamboyant conventions of dress, which often interchanged the usual attributes of the sexes. They flaunted their easygoing morals. They reacted against the success of high-priced, successful artists by cherishing the belief that the true artist is unrecognized and poverty-stricken and dies young in a garret. The most admired of them, like Mimi in *La Bohème*, suffered from tuberculosis.

This odd form of Romanticism, which had as many adherents as today's hippies and mods, was succeeded by a movement that is notable for the esthetic doctrine of "Art for Art's Sake," the idea that art exists by itself and for itself and has no kind of connection with morality or ethics.

The elements of fantasy and realism combine in the current New Romanticism

I think it is no accident that the mods, the New Romantics, or whatever you care to call them, have made a cult of reviving William Morris, the Pre-Raphaelites, *art nouveau*, Aubrey Beardsley, and the whole "pure art" philosophy of the *Yellow Book*, a British literary magazine of the 1890s. It is a pretty frail philosophy and depends for its survival on the very young and the very gauche. Sooner or later it is brought home to even the most determined amoralist that art is not only inseparable from life–though of course its method is to refine, or interpret, or imaginatively distort the stuff of life–but is a *view* of life; it cannot for long shed the human values that human beings attach to everything they do. A piece of "pure beauty" is thus a nonsensical idea. The new twist is to pretend that beauty and ugliness are merely two facets of truth and that "the truth"–whether it is the representation of a wallpaper design or the movie of a bank holdup–has no moral significance: It "simply is." (The reduction to total audience boredom of this grim whimsy was an Andy Warhol motion picture called *Sleep*. The film was exactly that. It showed a man sleeping. It was several hours long. Nothing but sleep. The sleep simply "was"–ghastly.)

What appears to me to be new–and not necessarily valuable–in the New Romanticism, however, is that it combines the elements of fantasy and realism that have hitherto always been in conflict. In other words, the New Romantics do not seek to escape the squalor of actual life through the medium of something called "pure beauty." Only the hippies can be got to admit that they find organized society too gross to wrestle with and have consequently chosen to drop out and drop off into dreamland. The more aggressive and gifted new rebels–in the movies, in novels, and in painting–are really romantics about the most raw and brutal side of life. They believe that if there are such things as truth and beauty, they can be found in the "total honesty, total freedom" of obscenity (pick a paperback), nudity (name your movie), saying the worst that is on your mind (the plays of Harold Pinter), and therefore often erupting into violence and brutality (the staple of popular television drama).

Signs of indignation

I can end only with the personal conclusion that I believe this philosophy is rooted in a fundamental misunderstanding of the work of Sigmund Freud. It exploits in art, as Hitler did in life, a popular fallacy about the Unconscious as being something that must first be tapped and then allowed to explode. Because Freud's most profound discovery was that in the Unconscious opposites are the same, this new confusion of romanticism and realism could have a frightening and socially damaging sort of life. Freud's intention was never to encourage anyone to act out his Unconscious, except in the miniature and carefully controlled situation of an analysis. On the contrary, the whole aim of his therapy was to reveal to disturbed people the destructiveness that lies beneath the civilized surface of all of us; the point was to enable the patient to know enough of his motives that were formerly unknown to him so as to be able to allow for them and to control them, not to live them out. What the new rebels are doing is jeering at the mass of us for not knowing that beneath the solid middle-class house there is a cellar stacked with dynamite. But with no training as mining engineers or fire-watchers, they go down there with lighted matches and hail the subsequent explosions as art.

To guarantee liberty, we must not demand too much of it

The pessimists say that it all goes to show that we are on the way to a 20th century Babylon. The optimists say that out of this explosion of "total honesty, total freedom" may come such a tyrannical reaction, an impulse to censor and police and restrain, that the Rebels–or, let us hope, the sons and daughters of the Rebels–will pull back in time and save their free society by recognizing that the first guarantee of liberty is the willingness not to demand too much of it. The flywheel of liberty is responsibility.

Related Articles

For a complete report on the 1967 year in the arts, see Section Two, The Pop Music Scene; and the following articles in Section Three:

Albee, Edward
Architecture
Dancing
Davis, David Brion
Fashion
Goetzmann, William H.
Interior Design
Kaplan, Justin
Kirchner, Leon
Library
Literature
Malamud, Bernard
Merrick, David
Motion Pictures
Museums
Music
Nobel Prizes
Painting and Sculpture
Photography
Pulitzer Prizes
Radio
Sexton, Anne
Television
Theater
Wyeth, Andrew

Red Smith: Focus on Sports

The old firm of Musial & Schoendienst charmed the fans during a year when they were confronted with new names like the Whips, Amigos, and Penguins

Quickly, identify the following: Anaheim Amigos, Washington Whips, Minnesota Muskies, Seattle SuperSonics, Dallas Chaparrals, San Diego Rockets, St. Louis Blues, Pittsburgh Penguins, Houston Apollos, Minnesota North Stars, New Orleans Buccaneers, Fort Wayne Komets, Chicago Bulls, Houston Mavericks.

Those are the names of a few of the basketball, hockey, and soccer teams that have been springing up as rich men come clamoring into professional sports seeking status, tax deductions, and television loot.

Rich men clamored into pro sports seeking status, tax deductions, and television loot

Even major league baseball, which traditionally has moved at a glacial pace, got back into the act in 1967. The American League, having given Charles O. Finley permission to move the Athletics to Oakland, promised to replace the A's with a new team in Kansas City and assign another franchise to Seattle, both to start play in 1969. The 10-club National League grudgingly voted to add two more teams by 1971, in cities not yet chosen.

For a newcomer in the Great Expansion, costs can be hair-raising. Even before the buyers in Kansas City and Seattle were selected, the American League set their initiation fees at $5,350,000, most of it to be paid out for $1.98 ballplayers at $175,000 a man. In 1961, it had cost the New York Mets only $2,200,000 to join the National League.

Yet if the investment is frightening, the returns can be astronomical. Last fall, Bernie Parrish, a former defensive back with the Cleveland Browns, started a campaign to organize players of the National Football League (NFL) into a union affiliated with the International Brotherhood of Teamsters. He cited these figures: gross NFL income–for 1956, $12,370,074; for 1967, "approximately" $81,000,000. Profit–for 1956, $1,159,747; for 1967, "about" $50,000,000.

The almost frantic eagerness of bidders for professional franchises and their readiness to pay the prices demanded underscore three phenomena peculiar to our time:

First, when a man has made a fortune manufacturing, say, a deodorant, he becomes obsessed by an urge to be pointed out instead as the sportsman who owns the local team.

Second, with manufacturers of beer, hair oil, and razor blades constantly reaching out for new markets, he is confident that he can recover his investment from television sponsors.

Third, financial risk does not deter him, because the tax laws enable him to write off losses.

But if money and status beguile the owners, it still is the competition on the field that captivates the public. Never was this demonstrated more emphatically than in 1967.

An uneasy peace between warring football leagues brought about the first super-spectacular of the year. Having at last agreed upon a merger that would end their ruinous competition for talent, the NFL and the American Football League (AFL) arranged for a showdown meeting of their champions–the Green Bay Packers of the NFL and the Kansas City Chiefs of the AFL.

Somebody gave this promotion the slightly unappetizing name of Super Bowl, and it set off a war of words as the network televising

NFL games and the one handling AFL action each dedicated itself to showing sponsors it could attract the larger viewing audience. For weeks before the event, not even the residents of *Peyton Place* were safe from interruption by an unctuous voice reminding viewers that only on this channel could they hear super-commentators describing the super-action of two super-teams in the Super Bowl on Super Sunday.

Football's Super Bowl was regarded as the worst flop since Goliath took a dive for David

Armageddon could not have lived up to that billing. It was not the dullest game ever played; it was close for a half, and after that the Packers romped. But because the entertainment stopped so far short of the glories promised, it was regarded as the sorriest flop since Goliath took a dive for David.

The next topic to preoccupy the sports public in 1967 was Cassius Clay's dustup with the Selective Service System. When the heavyweight boxing champion, who prefers to be known as Muhammad Ali, was called for induction, he refused to take the oath.

The World Boxing Association (WBA) and the New York State Athletic Commission declared his title vacant. Clay was convicted of violating the Selective Service Act, a verdict he is appealing. Meanwhile, a television network underwrote an elimination tournament to establish a new champion. The WBA gave its benediction to the tournament, but the public did not, because such leading championship contenders as Joe Frazier and Buster Mathis were not participating.

By the time Clay slid out of the headlines, baseball was in. For a change, the American League race monopolized the excitement, but the National League produced a Damon-and-Pythias story that charmed the fans as much as the rise of the Boston Red Sox delighted them.

Super Bowl action

This was the third season of Albert Fred Schoendienst's administration as manager of the St. Louis Cardinals. In his first season, the Cards had finished seventh; in his second, sixth.

Red Schoendienst was a skinny, freckled farm kid out of Germantown, Ill., with terra-cotta hair. When he was 19, he rode a train to St. Louis to attend a tryout. (Ever since 1920, when the Cardinals answered a boyish scrawl from a kid in Nokomis, Ill., and for their 2¢ stamp got a wonderful first baseman named Jim Bottomley, it has been the club policy never to turn a boy away without a tryout.)

Lacking the price of a room, Schoendienst spent his first night in the big town on a bench in the grassy plaza in front of Union Station. The next day he walked the three miles or so to Sportsman's Park, carrying his spiked shoes and infielder's glove. He got a job, but it was not until he had served three years on farm teams that he was brought up to the parent club. That was in 1945, and Stan Musial, off in the navy, read about the new boy but had not yet met him.

Musial, perhaps the greatest player the Cardinals ever had and certainly the most popular, had been a country boy like Schoendienst. Stan came out of Donora, Pa., as a bush league pitcher, injured his shoulder, and became an outfielder. In 1943, he had won the National League batting championship with an average of .357 and been named most valuable player in the league before entering the service.

Rejoining the Cardinals in 1946, Musial met Schoendienst. With Red playing second base, third base, and shortstop–he had been the regular left fielder while Musial was away–and with Stan back in the outfield hitting .365, the Cards won the pennant and the World Series.

The next spring, the pair decided to room together. It was a success from the start. Both enjoyed the theater and good food. They liked to sleep late and would breakfast together and split taxi fare to the park after the other players had caught a subway or bus. Neither of them snored, talked in his sleep, or paced the floor brooding about a slump.

Stan Musial met Red Schoendienst in 1946–and the Cardinals won the World Series

Through nine seasons they were inseparable. Theirs became the most famous room in baseball, containing more talent–it was agreed–than any other cell except the one in Sing Sing occupied by Willie the Actor Sutton, the world's greatest bank robber.

Musial, married before he joined the Cardinals, was a year-round resident of St. Louis. Schoendienst married Mary Eileen O'Reilly of St. Louis, and they also made their home there. Even in the winter, the roommates were together so often that if one chanced to be encountered alone, nobody asked, "How are you?" The question always was, "Where's Red?" or "Where's Stan?"

In 1956, Schoendienst was traded to the New York Giants. The partnership was dissolved. A year later, Red was helping to win a world championship for Milwaukee. After the 1958 World Series, in which he played all seven games and batted .300, he entered a hospital with tuberculosis and had part of a lung removed.

He licked that, as he had licked a vision defect in boyhood by becoming a switch-hitter. He was back with the Braves in 1960, rejoined the Cardinals in 1961 as a pinch-hitter, became a coach, then was named manager late in 1964.

At the end of the 1963 season, Musial retired. The Cardinals gave him the title of vice-president, but he was not really active with the club during Schoendienst's first two seasons as manager. Then, in the winter of 1966, Stan became general manager.

The partners were reunited, but on terms that raised many doubts. Sooner or later, almost all managers get fired. Suppose the day came when Musial would have to fire Schoendienst. How could Stan, America's Nice Guy, face up to that? "It won't happen," said people who knew both men. "If such a situation came up, Red would anticipate it and quit before Stan had to do anything." The situation did not come up. The team that had finished sixth in 1966 breezed to the pennant in 1967. Musial & Schoendienst had done it again.

The Cardinals' Red Schoendienst

Meanwhile, in the American League, Detroit, Minnesota, Chicago, and–of all people–the Boston Red Sox were locked in a death struggle. Every sentimentalist in America was rooting for the Red Sox, who had not won a pennant in 21 years.

In 1966, Boston had lost more games than any other team in the American League. Fenway Park was called the "Country Club." The Red Sox dropped in when they were in town, picked up their mail and paychecks, went through the motions, and departed.

Manager Dick Williams turned the Red Sox into a baseball team

After the 1966 season, the Red Sox hired a new manager named Dick Williams, a crew-cut gentleman of 37 whose keen brown eyes had not enabled him to break down fences when he was swinging a stick for the Brooklyn Dodgers. The keen brown eyes, however, seemed to see what was inside the young men playing for Boston.

"You know what I think?" said Boston's Police Commissioner, Edmund L. McNamara. "I think these Red Sox are the young generation that we worry about so much, but with discipline. Somebody has taught them to accept discipline, and it's got to be Williams. Some of those kids would like to wear their hair down to here, but Williams won't let 'em."

Whatever he did, the Red Sox became a team. They won the pennant on the last day of the season. They had been the longest of long shots when the season opened, and they were not supposed to be a match for the seasoned professionals from St. Louis. But they carried the Cardinals into the seventh game of a wonderfully exciting World Series, and seven games is as far as a World Series can go.

A 24-year-old pitcher named Jim Lonborg won the second and fifth games for Boston. If he had not been called on to pitch the final game of the season, Lonborg would have been ready to start the first game of the World Series. He could then have come back for the fourth and would have had three days' rest before the seventh.

To say that he might then have won the seventh game and the world championship, however, is to suggest that he could have outpitched the Cardinals' incomparable Bob Gibson, who beat Boston three times. Working the seventh game with only two days' rest, Lonborg had nothing, Gibson had it easy, and the Cardinals won.

Musial, Schoendienst, & Company had it made. It looked as though the firm could go on forever, but in December a startling announcement was made: Musial was resigning. He had many business interests in St. Louis, including a big, busy, and prosperous restaurant. His partner in the restaurant had died, and Stan did not feel he could tend to his businesses and still give the time his baseball job demanded.

So he backed off. For a second time, the firm of Musial & Schoendienst was dissolved. Before that happened, though, they had made a deal. They had consented to sing a duet at the annual show of the New York Baseball Writers Association. Their song? "Friendship."

Related Articles

For a complete report on the 1967 year in sports, see the following articles in Section Three:

Automobile
Baseball
Basketball
Boats and Boating
Bowling
Boxing
Football
Golf
Horse Racing
Ice Hockey
Ice Skating
Skiing
Soccer
Sports
Swimming
Tennis
Track and Field
Wrestling

Section Two

Special Reports

Seven articles and the exclusive *Year Book* Trans-Vision® give special treatment to subjects of current importance and lasting interest.

62 **The Economics of Politics** by Fletcher Knebel

78 **The Mekong River Project** by Gilbert F. White and James A. Harder

96 **Where the Jobs Will Be** by A. H. Raskin

110 **Mao's Last Revolution** by Mark Gayn

126 **The Killing of a Great Lake** by Barry Commoner

144 **The Pop Music Scene** by Leonard G. Feather

160 **In Search of the Mayan Past** by William R. Coe

177 **Tikal:** *The Year Book* Trans-Vision®

A Year Book Special Report

By Fletcher Knebel

The Economics Of Politics

A noted Washington correspondent examines "the kinship of the buck and the ballot"–where money for political expenses comes from, where it goes, and how it can corrupt

The year 1968 will see candidates for public office–from President of the United States down to city councilman and township trustee–spend an estimated $250,000,000, the largest sum in American history, to get elected.

The year 1967 saw the dirty wash of American politics–the undershirts and shorts liberally adorned with dollar signs–hung on the line for public inspection.

These two related events have caused thousands of thoughtful citizens to re-examine a problem almost as old as the republic itself: the economics of the nation's politics or, more bluntly put, the kinship of the buck and the ballot.

To place the sum of $250,000,000 in perspective, we should note, however, that the problem lies not so much in the amount spent, but rather in the way much of this money is raised and in the way contri-

Plan to Foot the Mounting Cost of

butions from special interests to a candidate or officeholder can lead to corruption and political payoffs.

As for the dirty wash of 1967, it fortified existing knowledge about political corruption, dollar deceit, and the diversion of public and campaign funds for personal use. Robert G. "Bobby" Baker, former secretary to the U.S. Senate Democratic majority, was convicted of income tax evasion, theft, and conspiracy to defraud the government in a case involving misuse of political influence for private gain. The House of Representatives excluded from membership Congressman Adam Clayton Powell of New York, who, among other things, used public funds for private travel and high living. The U.S. Senate, by a vote of 92 to 5, censured Senator Thomas J. Dodd of Connecticut for converting campaign and testimonial funds to his personal use.

In all three cases, it was not so much what the men did as the extent to which they did it. Bobby Baker became the symbol of the adroit, shady political manipulator, yet the use of political influence for private gain is a practice as old as human history. Practitioners of the art can be found in every political system from democracy to dictatorship, from monarchy to Marxism. If every American politician who joy rides at the taxpayers' expense, as Powell did, were to be ousted from office, vacancy signs would appear in many offices in state capitals. If every officeholder who diverted campaign funds to personal use were to be publicly censured, as Dodd was, the list would resemble the telephone directory of a medium-size city. In effect, then, Baker, Powell, and Dodd were guilty of two of the grossest of political crimes: (1) they pushed common political practices to excess, and (2) they got caught.

If this assessment seems unduly cynical, it nevertheless conforms to the reality of politics in the United States, as almost any candid politician will concede—at least in private. A few anecdotes serve to illustrate the point:

- Gordon St. Angelo, Democratic state chairman of Indiana, opened his speech to a 1965 Jefferson-Jackson Day fund-raising dinner by saying: "Honored guests, vendors and would-be vendors, jobholders and would-be jobholders, successful lobbyists and unsuccessful lobbyists, Democratic party faithful, and contributors all. . . ." This was a frank summation of the political facts of life in Indiana, one of the states in which it is taken for granted that political contributions will be extracted largely from those who benefit financially from the administration in power, be it in the form of jobs, highway contracts, or special-interest proposals to the legislature.
- One of the nation's most esteemed legislators, a man renowned for his probity and financial rectitude, met one day with his campaign manager and a prospective campaign contributor. The contributor, representing a commercial interest, offered the legislator $5,000 for his campaign. The legislator promptly rejected this offer of "silent money" that would not appear on contribution reports. The contributor, abashed, left the office. The campaign manager hurried after him,

The author:
Fletcher Knebel formerly wrote about the political scene as a Washington, D.C., correspondent and columnist. He is now a free-lance writer. His most recent book, *Vanished,* a political novel, was published in January, 1968. Books of which he is coauthor include *Convention* and *Seven Days in May.*

Illustrations
by Phil Renaud

"Current regulatory laws on campaign finances are a farce."

caught him in the hall, and said: "We'll take the money. We need it. The candidate doesn't have to know." The money changed hands, the campaign fund was $5,000 fatter, and the legislator, unknowingly, had contracted a political debt on which the donor might someday expect payment in legislation.

■ Senator Everett McKinley Dirksen of Illinois, the Republican leader of the U.S. Senate and a mellifluent sage of things political, took the witness stand for a fellow Illinois Republican accused of tax evasion and said: "I have never yet found a substitute for money in the political field." Dirksen added that political monetary demands upon him averaged $100 a day. In short, Dirksen was saying that the practices and amenities of politics cost a U.S. Senator $36,500 a year–or $6,500 more than his salary.

■ When the late John F. Kennedy mounted his drive for the presidency, he faced countless charges that his wealthy father, former Ambassador Joseph P. Kennedy, intended to "buy" the election for his son. A key critic was Mrs. Eleanor Roosevelt, widow of President Franklin D. Roosevelt. She declared on television that the elder Kennedy was guilty of lavish spending to advance his son's presidential ambitions. In 1958, speaking to the Gridiron Club in Washington, D.C., Senator Kennedy touched off a roar of laughter by reading to the audience a purported telegram from his father: "Dear Jack: Don't buy a single vote more than is necessary. I'm damned if I'm going to pay for a landslide."

All of these stories emphasize, in one form or another, what every successful politician knows–money is the bone and the marrow of politics. Yet money in politics is one of the least understood, most neglected subjects on the American scene. The vast bulk of voters long has seemed little concerned about exactly where political money comes from, where it goes, what it is used for, and what is done in repayment.

Why? A basic reason, perhaps, can be found in the whole context of our society. In this era of high taxes, the process of squeezing dollars away from the grasp of the tax collector has become a hobby as refined and as socially acceptable as the ancient art of smuggling. We live in an expense-account economy, artificially distorted by tax pressures, where people play fast and loose with the dollar. Executives go hunting at company lodges on company money that then becomes deductible from taxes as a "business expense." Employees pad expense accounts. University professors fly to the ends of the earth on extravagant and questionable missions for foundations, the Department of Defense, or government contractors. Subtle, and not so subtle, conflicts of interest touch the bulk of society. Cheating, from petty thefts in supermarkets to inflated deductions on income tax returns, is endemic. In short, politics is not–indeed, has never been–the only field where the suspect dollar flits among the shadows.

Further, there is an American tradition protecting the privacy of the bank account. If a man's home is his castle, his pocketbook is deemed to be his inviolate secret. You can ask a man for his most intimate views of life, religion, the Middle East, or hippies, but ask to see his income tax return and you are guilty of unmitigated effrontery. Few Californians waxed indignant when Edmund G. "Pat" Brown, then governor, refused to disclose his complete financial resources for the *Los Angeles Times*. "It's nobody's business but my own," wrote Brown in answer to written questions. The customs of the nation decree sanctuary for a man's dollar, whether or not he holds public office, and Pat Brown's reply must surely represent a prevailing emotion.

Experts in the field of political finance recognize the pervasiveness of these public attitudes and emotions, and they also point to a few more tangible truths:

Current regulatory laws on campaign finances are a farce. All have loopholes. Most are outrageously unrealistic. Few are enforced. If every federal, state, and local campaign finance law were enforced to the letter, thousands of our public officials might be jailed or fined. For example, the Federal Corrupt Practices Act of 1925 restricts senatorial candidates to campaign expenditures of $25,000 and House candidates to $5,000. Compare this to the realities: In large states, such as California and New York, a campaign for the U.S. Senate costs about $1,000,000. Even in the small states, a man proposing to run for

"Rising campaign costs, soaring with each new election, are attributable in large part to the television set, a device the American politician invests with magic properties."

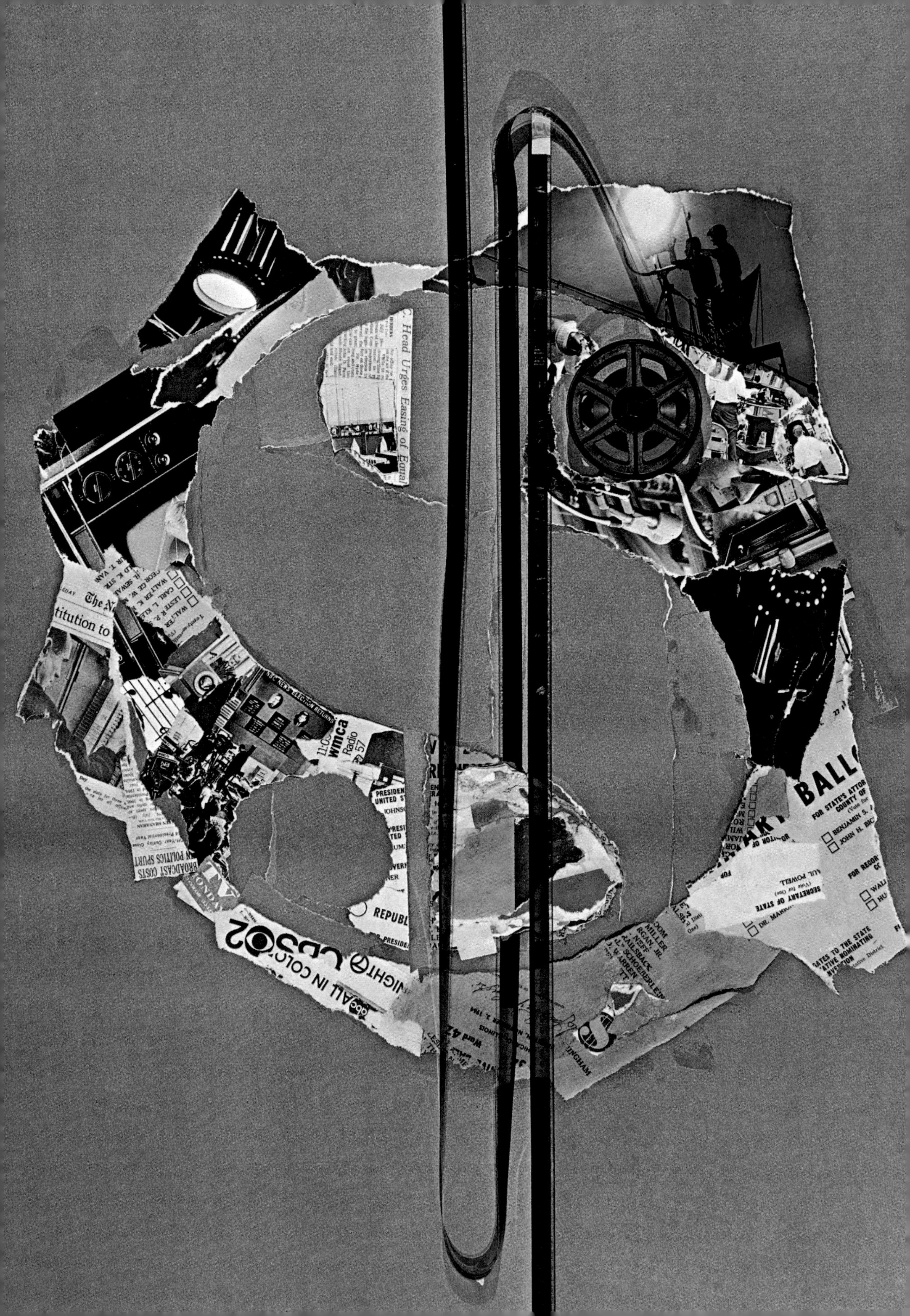
Head Urges Easing of Equal
stitution to
BROADCAST COSTS
IN POLITICS SPURT
wmca
Radio
57
BALLO
FOR STATE'S ATTOR
REPUBL
SECRETARY OF STATE

the Senate with less than $100,000 in campaign funds is deemed foolhardy. The law is evaded by a proliferation of committees. Thus, while candidate Smith may spend only $25,000 in his own name, a hundred Smith-for-Senate committees under a variety of names can spend the dollars as fast as they come in.

It is unlawful for national banks, corporations, or labor unions to contribute to candidates for federal office, whether in elections, primaries, or conventions. Many state laws duplicate the prohibition for state elections. Yet corporations and unions pour untold millions into political campaigns. The unions do it through auxiliary committees financed by so-called "voluntary" contributions by union members. Corporations do it by more discreet methods: reimbursing executives who contribute as individuals to the right candidates, or supplying office space, manpower, and services, instead of money, to candidates.

Rising campaign costs, soaring with each new election, are attributable in large part to the television set, a device the American politician invests with magic properties. The average candidate believes, with justification, that failure to place his features on the television screen means almost certain defeat. Costs of paid political broadcasts jumped 60 per cent in four years, according to a Federal Communications Commission study. Candidates for office in the nonpresidential year of 1962 spent $20,000,000 for television and radio. In 1966, another nonpresidential year, they spent $32,000,000. Presidential years mean still greater spending for television and radio, $34,600,000 in 1964 and an estimated $45,000,000 in 1968.

Total spending reaches heights that would have seemed incredible two decades ago. The elections of 1966, a midterm year, cost $120,000,000. A single office, that of governor of California, fetched $6,000,000 in primary and general election spending before Ronald Reagan was proclaimed the winner. In New York, more than $5,000,000 was spent to elect the Republican state ticket headed by Governor Nelson Rockefeller. In 1967, Democrats and Republicans poured about $300,000 into one district in San Francisco in an effort to elect a state senator who would give control of the California senate to whichever party won the seat. Never before had so much money been spent on one seat in a state legislature. In all these elections, the bulk of the money was raised from well-heeled persons and organizations and not from the citizenry at large. Experts see the accelerating cost of campaigning as imposing rigid and often unbreakable shackles on the highly qualified candidate of modest means who shuns the financial help of special interests.

There are scores of accepted political practices that raise ethical questions. Indeed, so questionable are these practices that the more scrupulous politicians strive to avoid them.

Foremost among these is the mixed career of the lawyer-legislator. Lawyers lead all other professions in representation in the Congress of the United States and in the state legislatures. It is accepted practice

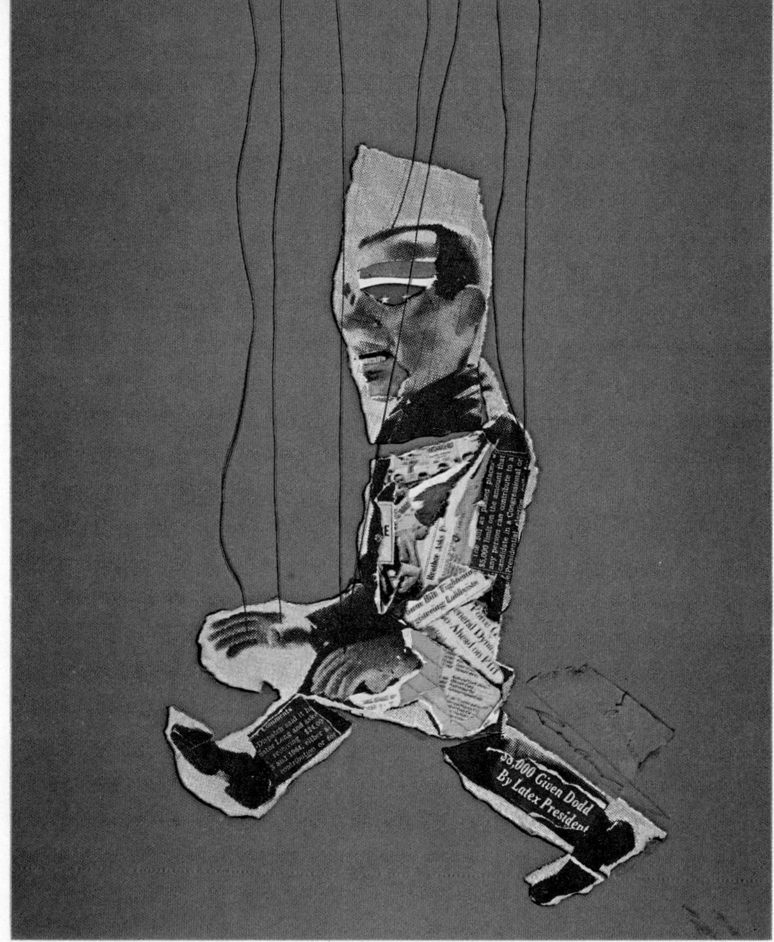

"... the problem lies ... in the way ... contributions from special interests can lead to corruption and political payoffs."

for a legislator to pursue his legal career and represent clients with a special interest in pending legislation–railroads, unions, manufacturing concerns, highway contractors, defense empires, vending machines, insurance companies. Such arrangements fairly shout "conflict of interest." The legislator who accepts a $20,000 bribe for pressing a special interest bill faces a prison term if caught, but the legislator who receives a $20,000 legal fee from a company whose interests he champions in the legislature faces no penalty. He is doing what comes naturally in American politics.

In 1967, the Dodd case illuminated a number of questionable practices. The Senate Ethics Committee, on whose findings the Senate's censure vote was based, cited Dodd for converting campaign and testimonial funds to "his personal benefit" and for seeking double reimbursement for travel. The Senate censured Dodd on the first count but exonerated him of intentional double-billing.

But the hearings of the Dodd investigation revealed other actions for which the Senate did not censure the Connecticut Democrat. Testimony showed that:

- Dodd's office employees combed the files and withdrew the names of about a thousand Connecticut "businessmen and individuals" for whom the Senator's office had done favors. These people were then rated as to whether they were "likely prospects for solicitation" for funds. This is common fund-raising practice in the well-organized political office.

- A fund-raiser was hired on a percentage basis–a cut of the total take –to solicit patrons for a testimonial dinner. While this is not a routine procedure in politics, it is by no means unusual.
- Most of Dodd's office staff, whose salaries are paid by the taxpayer, had the chores of arranging testimonial dinners and preparing solicitation lists. One staff member on government salary paid Dodd's personal bills and kept his personal accounts. This is another common practice in many levels of state government and among Congressmen.
- Dodd used staff members of at least two Senate subcommittees–Internal Security and Juvenile Delinquency–in the business of arranging dinners and soliciting political funds. It is routine for members of Congress to "raid" committee staffs, which are supposedly laboring for the nation, and enlist the personnel as campaign aides. In effect, then, the opposition candidate is paying taxes to help beat himself.

Treasurers of Dodd fund-raising committees had poverty-stricken memories when it came to remembering what vouchers, invoices, and

"It is accepted practice for a legislator to pursue his legal career and represent clients with a special interest in pending legislation . . ."

checks they signed. This, too, is routine. A campaign treasurer is the more highly prized the less reliable his memory and the less sensitive he is to ethical standards of solicitation.

Dodd's income tax return for 1961, printed in full in the committee hearings, showed that on March 6, 1961, he received a $50,000 legal fee from the International Brotherhood of Teamsters for services rendered from August, 1957, through February, 1961. During three of those years, 1959, 1960, and 1961, Dodd was a member of the U.S. Senate. An enormous amount of Teamster money has been paid out to congressmen and state legislators as legal fees or contributions.

The Teamster money, however, did not become a prominent issue in the Dodd case. Rather, Senate debate centered on the ethical use of political contributions. In his effort to escape censure, Dodd contended that he did not convert such contributions to personal use. Instead, he argued, the contributions were intended as personal gifts to be used as he saw fit. The Senate did not accept this defense.

The treatment of contributions as gifts for personal use is a time-worn, if not honored, practice among American politicians. Hardly had the dust settled on the Dodd vote when it was revealed that Representative Thaddeus J. Dulski of Buffalo, N.Y., Democratic chairman of the House Post Office and Civil Service Committee, had accepted for personal use about $11,000 raised at a political testimonial dinner. Contributors included agents of large mailers and postal unions whose interests come within the purview of Dulski's committee.

Said *The New York Times* in an editorial: "If these gentlemen had come to his office and offered him the cash straight across the desk, even Mr. Dulski would, presumably, have recognized it by its ugly, five-letter name: bribe. But since it was masquerading as a public dinner, the Congressman is able to say: 'Mrs. Dulski and I felt it was entirely in keeping with the accepted practices of American political life.' As the Dodd case, the Powell case . . . and now the Dulski case amply demonstrate, no one is quite sure what these 'accepted practices' are. . . ."

The personal gift became politically enshrined in a well-publicized case in 1965 when a federal jury in Chicago acquitted former Governor William G. Stratton of Illinois of income tax evasion charges.

Government prosecutors contended that during his last four years as governor (1957 to 1960) Stratton failed to report about $93,000 of income, chiefly in the form of political contributions that he had diverted to personal use.

The defense argued that the money–much of it in cash–came to Stratton as straight gifts and thus was not subject to tax. The donors placed no strings on the money, said the defense. Stratton could use it as he pleased. Much of the money was deductible in any event, it was contended, since it was used to advance Stratton's political career. The government contended the money went for such things as a $63,000 lodge along the Sangamon River and a $4,750 houseboat.

The story on the facing page tells how one Congressman, J. Edward Roush (D., Ind.), is affected by the high cost of politics. The photo shows him with his family. Left to right are Robin, Joel, Melody, Representative Roush, Dave, and Mrs. Roush.

Stratton's acquittal elicited cheers from some politicians. Two Illinois Congressmen declared the jury verdict meant that politicians could use campaign contributions for anything they wished. A commentator agreed. He said the jury had placed politicians in a privileged class–beneficiaries of tax-free money that could be used to enhance personal standards of living.

The Stratton jury's verdict left two major questions unanswered: What is a political contribution? What is "personal use" in politics? The Internal Revenue Service (IRS) and the Congress have failed to answer the questions definitively. A ruling of the IRS holds that campaign funds are not taxable unless and until the candidate converts them to personal use. But the tax authorities admit that "personal use" is a murky phrase. "If a candidate buys a new suit for campaigning," asked one tax official, "is that a personal or political expense?"

That the bulk of the money raised to finance political campaigns comes from special interests–individuals, corporations, or unions standing to profit financially by the election of one candidate over another–has long been recognized, but seldom carefully documented. A *Los Angeles Times* survey, however, showed that the overwhelming majority of the members of the California legislature, both Democrats and Republicans, received campaign funds from registered lobbyists.

In sum, American political financing is something less than a system ordained in heaven. Almost everyone but the troglodytes of politics concedes that changes are long overdue. In general, reformers advocate three main lines of attack:

- Broadening the base of political contributions to free officeholders from the pressures of the special-interest dollar. To accomplish this, many persons urge some form of public financing of campaigns, either through subsidy or tax deductions for political contributions.
- Adoption of codes of ethics by Congress, state legislatures, and city councils so that members and the public may know precisely which

One Man's Balance Sheet

A typical member of the United States House of Representatives receives about $35,000 a year, $30,000 of it in salary and the remainder in office allowances.

This would appear to place him in an attractive financial bracket. Yet, if he has no outside income, he frequently finds himself struggling to make ends meet. The necessity to maintain dual residences, one in his home city and one in Washington, D.C., and the myriad political and charitable demands on a public man drain his pocketbook.

Such a Congressman is J. Edward Roush, a Democrat of Huntington, Ind., representing the 5th District of Indiana. Roush, 47, is a lawyer, a World War II infantry veteran, and the father of four children. He has not practiced law since entering Congress in January, 1959. When Roush finishes paying his fixed costs, he has about $11,400 left for all family expenses–and $1,900 of this goes toward the cost of a son in college. This year, Mrs. Roush began teaching school to help swell the family income.

"I believe it's obvious that one does not get rich serving in the Congress," says Roush. "My family and I live on my income, but there are times when it is a struggle."

Although Roush's campaign expenses are defrayed by contributions to a "Roush-for-Congress Club," the trade of politics puts a dent in his own wallet between elections. Examples: A recent questionnaire mailing to constituents cost him $1,600 for printing alone; a ticket to a fund-raising dinner cost another $250.

"I severely limit my business entertaining," he says. "I turn down scores of offers to speak, partly because it means additional travel costs.

"I help share the burden of my church and hometown charities, but I am besieged with requests for contributions. I mention these various items not in the spirit of complaint but rather for the sake of providing information. After all, I have the most satisfying and personally rewarding job in the world."

Here is his personal balance sheet as provided by him:

Income			
Salary	$30,000		
Stationery allowance	3,000		
Home office allowance	1,200		
Travel allowance	741		
			$34,941
Expenditures			
Fixed:			
Taxes	$5,064		
Contribution to retirement fund	2,250		
Insurance premiums	1,203		
		8,517	
Office expenses:			
Stationery and office supplies	4,010		
Newspapers and periodicals	273		
Taxis, parking, and hotels	245		
Entertainment	858		
Commercial travel	1,043		
Car expenses (business only)	1,550		
Miscellaneous	312		
		8,291	
Expenses required by office:			
Political	3,400		
Maintaining apartment in Washington and expenses	3,350		
		6,750	
			$23,558
Balance left for family and personal expenses			**$11,383**

forms of fiscal behavior are illegal, which are cause for expulsion from the legislative body, and which are merely to be frowned upon.

- Public disclosure of all campaign contributions and expenditures, as well as the officeholder's financial status, in such manner that the data are readily available and intelligible to the press, politicians, and public.

A fourth line of attack aims not at policing officeholders or controlling contributions but at alleviating the problem of high television costs. In July, 1967, Rosel H. Hyde, chairman of the Federal Communications Commission, suggested federal legislation that would allow broadcasters to give free time to major political candidates without having to grant equal time to minor candidates. This would encourage stations to give more free exposure to candidates, thus relieving them of at least some of the high costs of broadcasting. A bill introduced in 1967 by Senator Hugh Scott (R., Pa.) would do much the same thing, except that minor candidates would receive some, but not equal, free time, the amount depending on how their party had fared in the previous election.

Of the three main lines of attack, the first has stirred the most recent action and controversy. All hands agree that the climate would be much more wholesome if the lists of campaign contributors could be swelled tenfold, so that every voter became a contributor and candidates no longer had to depend on huge special-interest funds. Much progress has been made already. At the turn of the century, presidential campaigns were financed by a handful of wealthy men in each party. By contrast, some 12,000,000 people gave money for the 1964 campaigns. If 25,000,000 people gave $10 each, the entire cost of all 1968 campaigns for all offices could be defrayed–with no candidate under obligation to wealthy donors.

But "common man" financing of campaigns is much easier imagined than accomplished. As a sample, two bipartisan fund-raising experiments failed in 1964. One, a mailing by R. L. Polk & Company, endorsed by former President Dwight D. Eisenhower and Adlai E. Stevenson, was termed a "dismal failure" by professional observers. Another, a door-to-door solicitation in Saginaw, Mich., raised only $410.86, and sponsors reported the response of the average citizen was "overwhelmingly negative."

Seeking to attain the objective by federal subsidy, Congress passed a law in 1966 permitting a taxpayer to allocate $1 of his income tax to the financing of presidential campaigns. The fund would have yielded $30,000,000 each to the Republican and Democratic parties in 1968. But in 1967, the Senate revolted against the plan, partly because of possible difficulty in administering it and partly because of a belief that permitting a taxpayer to specify a particular use for his tax dollar might be unconstitutional. The Senate voted to render the subsidy plan inoperative.

Those who challenge subsidies contend they fail to remedy current evils and merely provide more ammunition for a bad system. Robert

J. McNeil of Wayne State University pointed out a danger sign after a study of Indiana political financing. McNeil propounded another "Parkinsonian" law: "Campaign expenses tend to increase in direct proportion to the money available to meet them." This is so, said McNeil, because politicians are not sure what works in a campaign, "and if they get more money they do more of everything."

Tax deductions or tax credits for political contributions encounter less opposition, although they are a form of subsidy, since they would reduce the government's tax revenue. Herbert E. Alexander, director of the Citizens' Research Foundation of Princeton, N.J., which devotes itself exclusively to studies of money's role in politics, favors a $10 federal tax credit for $20 political contributions. The objective, says Alexander, is not to sterilize or artificially purify politics, but realistically "to relieve as many politicians as possible of as many pressures as possible." For those who favor subsidies, this approach seems to be the most reasonable, but no miracles are to be expected via the subsidy route.

The second line of attack–the adoption and, equally important, the enforcement of effective codes of ethics from city hall to Congress–cries out for implementation.

The 85th Congress passed a "code of ethics" that took effect on July 11, 1958, but it is so platitudinous and general that it offers Congressmen few solid guidelines. The 10 points covered in this code include such statements as "Give a full day's labor for a full day's

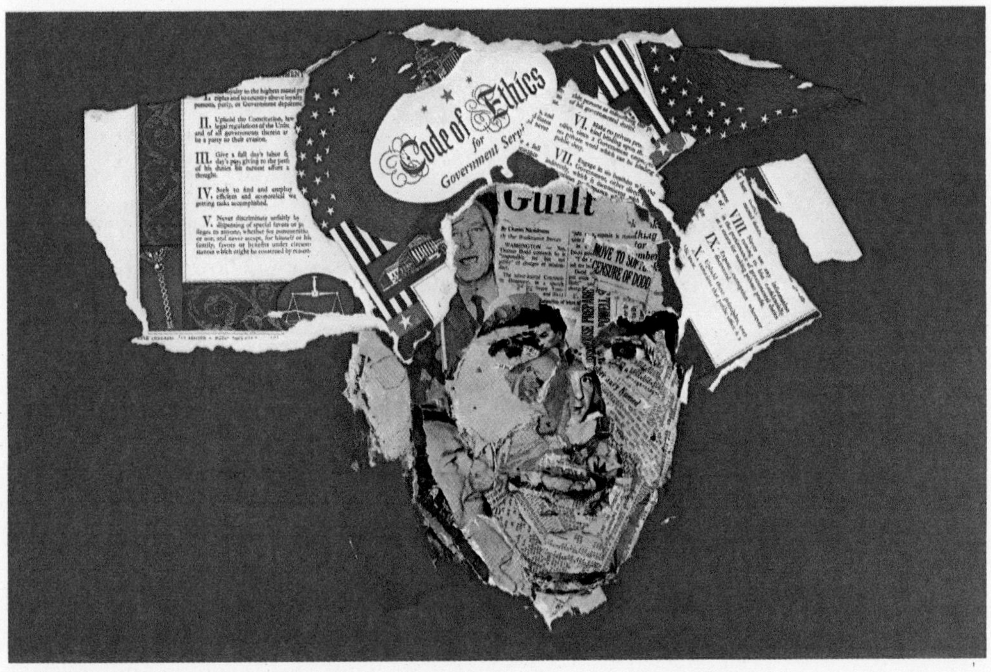

"... the politician owes it to himself and to the voters to codify the rights and wrongs of his financial conduct..."

pay . . ."; "Never discriminate unfairly by the dispensing of special favors or privileges to anyone, whether for remuneration or not; and never accept for himself or his family, favors or benefits under circumstances which might be construed by reasonable persons as influencing the performance of his governmental duties"; and "Expose corruption wherever discovered."

The resulting scene is a wilderness of rights, wrongs, and maybes. Is it unethical for a legislator to vote on a measure benefiting a company in which he holds stock? Is it wrong for a member of a public roads committee in a state legislature to accept campaign contributions from highway contractors? Should a lawyer-legislator receive legal fees from a client with legislative interests? What type of gift may a legislator reasonably accept from a lobbyist–none at all, a $10 dinner, a $50 wrist watch, a $500 color television set? As in all human behavior, there are no absolutes. But the politician owes it to himself and to the voters to codify the rights and wrongs of his financial conduct and to narrow the gray area as much as possible.

There is reason to hope that the U.S. Senate may adopt such a code of ethics. The Senate Ethics Committee, headed by Senator John Stennis (D., Miss.), is working on a code in the wake of the highly emotional Dodd debate in which Dodd himself pleaded with the committee to propound a list of "do's and don'ts." The Association of the Bar of the City of New York is undertaking a two-year study, with a $160,000 Ford Foundation grant, of "ethical standards and conflict of interest" in Congress. While the subject is a thorny one, some type of congressional action, probably in the Senate, may be forthcoming. And if the U.S. Senate acts, the stage will be set for a drive to adopt similar codes in state legislatures and city councils.

Some advances have already been made. President Lyndon B. Johnson issued an executive order in 1965 that imposes a fairly strict code of ethics on federal employees, other than members of Congress, and requires financial disclosure by most officials appointed by the President. Eight states have adopted ethical codes covering legislators, state employees, and officials. All of this action has taken place since New York adopted the first comprehensive code in 1954. A few municipalities and county governments also have adopted standards for official conduct. But in the vast majority of state and local governments, a code of ethics still is a rare item.

The third advocated reform, that of public disclosure, is perhaps the most promising of all. The voter has every right to know exactly where a candidate gets his money and what he does with it. The voter also has a right to know an officeholder's sources of outside income, so that the voter can weigh the official's actions against financial interests. Such disclosure of a Congressman's assets and income has long been advocated by former Senator Paul H. Douglas of Illinois, who made public his own financial status during his 18 years in the Senate. "Being a Congressman or Senator is a great honor, and in return for that you owe an extra obligation," Douglas said. This argument has been rejected by other Congressmen, including Senator Dirksen, who has said that forcing Congressmen to disclose their financial status would make them second-class citizens.

Despite the prevalence of the latter attitude, a House subcommittee on elections made a good start in 1967 with a bill that would set up a Federal Elections Commission with power to demand accurate and detailed reporting of campaign receipts and expenditures. It would also require candidates for federal office and members of Congress to reveal gifts and honorariums. Finally, the measure would repeal absurdly unrealistic limits on campaign spending and ban the proliferation of committees that make a mockery of campaign accounting. The ultimate hope is a federal law that could serve as a model upon which all 50 states could base their own legislation.

As Congress neared adjournment in 1967, however, there was little assurance that the House would pass the bill. The Senate, though, in September, 1967, did pass a bill, 87 to 0, that: (1) calls for full disclosure of contributions and expenditures, (2) removes all ceilings on political spending by a candidate, and (3) places a $5,000 limit on the amount any person can contribute to a candidate in a congressional or presidential election. At the same time, the Senators rejected, 46 to 42, an amendment that would have required all Congressmen and candidates for Congress to disclose the sources of their personal income.

Today, 43 of the 50 states have some sort of campaign finance laws, but they vary widely in effectiveness–or, more accurately, in ineffectiveness. Some have no teeth at all. Others permit information to be filed in such a haphazard manner that only an accountant could sort the material into an intelligible form. Almost all the laws are flouted. Enforcement is virtually nil.

Public disclosure, it must be admitted, is no cure-all. The voters of Harlem re-elected Adam Clayton Powell to the House after his financial transgressions had been spread across the newspapers of the nation. Legislators and mayors have been re-elected while in prison for fraud and income tax evasion. Public disclosure will not turn American politics into a forum of angels, but it will at least illuminate the hundreds of transactions that now take place in the shadows.

Advocates of a reasonable, simple, and enforceable financial public disclosure law make but one claim for it: The voter has a right to know where the political dollar comes from and where it goes. What the voter does with that information is his business, to be decided finally in the privacy of the voting booth. What is sought is not a financial millenium, but a long-needed ray of light. From all available evidence, that light will be forthcoming, if not in 1968, certainly within the next few years.

See also Section One, James Reston: Focus on The Nation; Section Three, Congress of the United States; Democratic Party; Elections; President of the United States; Republican Party.

A Year Book Special Report

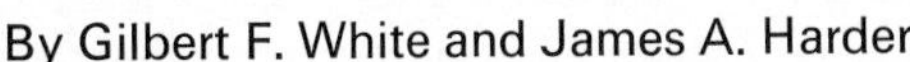

By Gilbert F. White and James A. Harder

The Mekong River Project

A total of 27 nations are cooperating to harness the waters of the Mekong. After 10 years, the project has begun to change the lives and lift the hopes of millions of persons in Southeast Asia

The village headman–lean, wiry, and bronzed by his years in the fields–looked out over the partly completed irrigation canal to the dry fields beyond. "This time of year," he said stoically, "it should all be green out there." It was late August, 1967, well into the rainy season, and northeastern Thailand was experiencing one of its worst droughts in 50 years. In some areas of the Khorat plateau there had been no rain for more than two months.

In his village of Nong Ben (Pond of the Frogs) it had rained enough in early June to wet the land in the lowest parts, where the rice seed-beds could be started. Thus, the cycle of the seasons centered on the cultivation of transplanted rice had begun, a cycle that has molded village life of Southeast Asia for generations. The seedlings normally get a month's head start while the main fields are prepared for transplanting; only with the coming of early rains can the water buffalo pull a plow through the soil, baked hard by the heat of March and April.

In this section of the vast Mekong River basin, as in most parts of Southeast and East Asia, rice is the basis of livelihood. It provides food for the upland farmers, who shift from one jagged clearing in the forest to another every two to five years, and it is the staple of the continuously cropped lowlands. Making more water available in the lowlands around Nong Ben could change the rice economy in three important ways: The drought losses to rain-dependent crops could be reduced; a second crop could be gained during the dry season; and the resulting prosperity could be reinvested in new fertilizers, new seeds, and other improvements that, in turn, would spur a new rise in productivity. As a result, the destructive pressure of shifting cultivation in the nearby uplands would be lessened.

Nong Ben's irrigation canal-to-be represented an ambitious effort to manage the previously unharnessed waters of the Mekong and its tributaries. It, as well as the nearby Nam Pong dam and its power lines, was part of a larger, unprecedented international program called the Lower Mekong Basin Project. The project was started under United Nations (UN) auspices in 1957, when representatives of Cambodia, Laos, South Vietnam, and Thailand agreed to join in a series of coordinated studies of the Lower Mekong basin. They set out to plan the development of the whole basin scientifically and dispassionately—before any disputes over the allocation of its waters could arise.

The project started slowly. Over the next decade, 23 other, non-basin nations contributed heavily with funds, professional services, and materials. Unprecedented, too, was the wide scope of the initial studies. They went beyond determining the hydrological, soil, and other basic physical and engineering data; they took into account the effects of the project on the whole ecology of the basin and on the lives of its 27,000,000 inhabitants.

By 1967, the venture had reached a crucial stage. Not only was the political turmoil surrounding the war in Vietnam jeopardizing its future, but the effectiveness of its first projects in changing the conditions of peasant life was being tested on the Khorat plateau.

If the plateau had had its usual rains, the soil surface in the fields around Nong Ben would have been puddled into a slick mud that would have slowed the downward penetration of rain water. Under normal monsoon-season conditions, the rainfall would have exceeded the amount of water consumed by plant growth and lost to evaporation. If all had gone well, the seedlings would have been transplanted in early July, in well-spaced rows for the best yield. And by August, as the headman knew, "it should all be green out there."

Con Chalong shifted his keen gaze from the parched fields to his visitors. "If we could have a crop every year," he continued, "we would be prosperous." But in August, 1967, the early seedbeds were already too old; new ones had been planted, but still there was no heavy rain. Water buffalo grazed on weeds that had sprung up in the paddy fields; men slouched under trees, having done all they could to repair the dikes for the retention of the rain that had not fallen.

In other parts of Khon Kaen province, water for cooking and drinking had to be carried for long distances in carts or in pails balanced on carrying sticks slung across the shoulders of women and children. Open wells, used mainly during the dry season when rain water could not be collected, were already going dry. One, about 30 feet deep, had but three inches of water. Boys and girls were taking turns lowering

The authors:
Gilbert F. White heads the Department of Geography at the University of Chicago and is an international authority in the field of water management. In 1961 and 1962, he conducted a pioneering Ford Foundation study of the lower Mekong.

James A. Harder, associate professor of hydraulic engineering at the University of California, Berkeley, inspected the Mekong project during the summer of 1967.

The Lower Mekong Basin

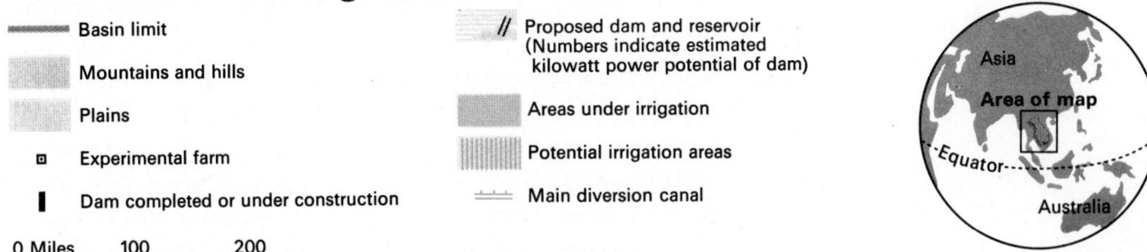

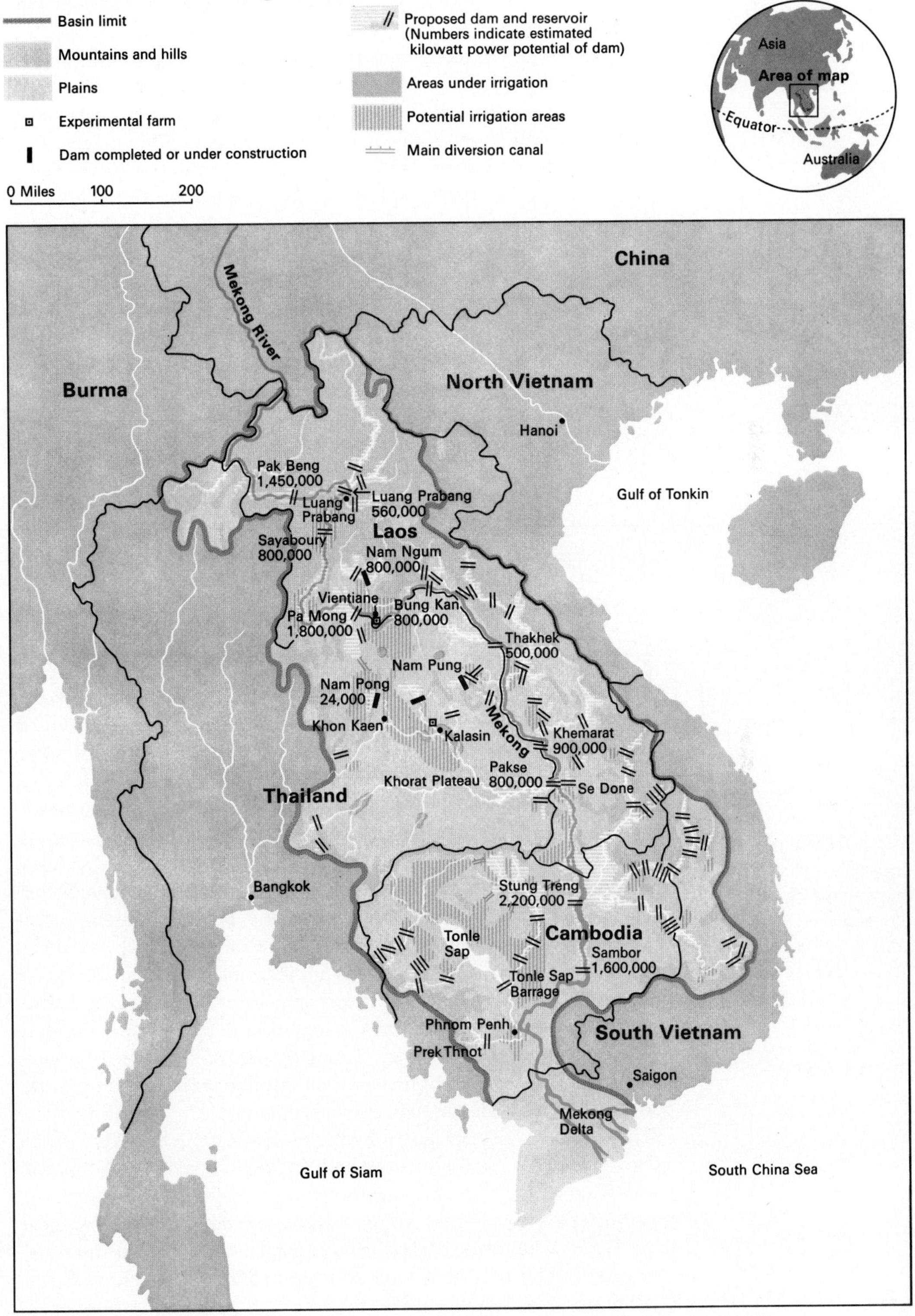

pails into it and waiting for more water to seep in from the sides. Then the pail was raised and emptied, and the slow process was repeated time after time to fill one carrying can.

How were the farmers managing to live through the drought? Con Chalong was asked. Some, he said, had savings from the sale of rice the year before, when there was a bumper crop. Others, with larger fields, had stores of rice left over. Some had nothing; they were working, or seeking work, in distant towns so that their families could eat until the next harvest. Still others had planted a cash crop–kenaf, a fiber-producing plant that can be used as a substitute for hemp or jute. This provided money to buy rice. Nearly everyone tried his hand at fishing–the principal source of protein in the villagers' diet.

Fortunately Thailand, though poor, is not food-poor; no one need starve, even during a drought. Financial disaster may strike, but there is no mass starvation, despite the fact that the quality of a villager's diet is seldom adequate. So the people cope with the caprice of the seasons. With them it is a way of life. As one old villager, Con Lek, said, philosophically, "We are born, we live, and we grow old. Then we experience pain, and we die–that is the way it is." He was not expressing Buddhist resignation, as popular Western thought would interpret it. No one who saw that old man would believe that he suffered pain and anticipated death with any more acceptance than would his Western and richer brothers. He, like the village farmer, just had fewer ways of coping with nature.

The four Mekong nations are on the rack of political tensions and have levels of living ranging from a per capita gross national product of only $66 (in Laos) to $132 (in Cambodia), placing them among the poorer lands of the world. Yet they all share one great natural asset–the untamed Mekong River and the untapped riches of its vast basin. All four also have the Mekong project, a start on a pioneering attempt at international cooperation in dealing with the problem of putting natural resources to work. Even in the densely populated plains and delta regions of the Mekong, large stretches of land await more intensive development. Traditionally, many of the basin's people have been exporters of rice, for, so far, their numbers have not put as heavy pressure on the land as have the people in nearby parts of India, China, and North Vietnam. Yet, population in places such as Nong Ben is growing at a rapid rate. It may double in 20 years. Measures are needed to help the people plan their families and curb the growth. Fortunately, the basin has many resources to tap.

The Mekong, one of the world's longest rivers, flows for about 2,600 miles from its headwaters high in the Himalayas of Tibet to South Vietnam's Delta and into the South China Sea. It drains more than 307,000 square miles–an area about 40,000 square miles larger than Texas. The lower Mekong basin, which begins 1,900 miles upstream at the borders of Burma and the People's Republic of China (Communist China), comprises an area of 236,000 square miles. It

With ample water for planting covering the rice paddy, Cambodian farmers stand atop their plows to help force the blades down into the submerged soil.

The *Bun Bang Fai,* or rocket festival, is held each May in northeast Thailand to appease the rain gods just before the onset of the monsoon season.

In the Mekong basin, housing must be adapted to the river's whims. This thatched hut in Laos is on stilts to protect the people from rising floodwaters.

The Mekong project must cope with the fact that at any given time, the lower basin may have too little water–as the parched fields and muddy pond on the Khorat plateau attest–or too much–as on these rice paddies near Cambodia's Tonle Sap.

takes in most of Laos and Cambodia, as well as northeastern Thailand and the delta area and a long, narrow band of South Vietnam.

The Mekong is a powerful river. In flood stage, its flow has exceeded by one-third the largest ever recorded on the lower Mississippi. Its minimum flow at a point 190 miles upstream is about 60,000 cubic feet per second, more than twice the minimum flow at the mouth of the Columbia, one of the largest rivers in North America.

But unlike the Columbia or the Mississippi or almost any other of the world's great rivers, the Mekong has remained undeveloped. It is unbridged, undammed, and–for its upper 2,300 miles–unnavigable, without portages. It is a "sleeping giant," in the words of C. Hart Schaaf, and "a source of tremendous potentialities for power production, irrigation, navigation, and flood control, but a source virtually unutilized." Schaaf is executive agent of the Committee for Coordination of Investigations of the Lower Mekong (the Mekong Committee).

The committee has been a prime mover in the efforts to unlock the resources of the Mekong. From its headquarters in Bangkok, Thailand, the committee coordinates the multination research and engineering task force. At the outset, the UN provided technical support, and it since has helped with staff and funds. Much heavier support has come, however, from the 23 nonbasin nations. The four Mekong Committee nations provide the remainder of the funds, about 40 per cent. They give direction to the work under a regional agency of the UN, the Economic Commission for Asia and the Far East (ECAFE) in Bangkok. Their decisions must be unanimous.

Their studies are aimed at finding out how much water flows in the main river and its tributaries, what soils can be irrigated, where floods can be controlled to the advantage of the farmers and city dwellers, and how much electric power can be generated and what markets they can expect for it. Management of the water is seen as one important means of improving the lot of the peasant and of increasing the income of the worker in the growing cities.

So thorough and painstaking have been the studies and the planning that only one of the committee's major river development projects has reached near-completion. It is the multipurpose Nam Pong project on a remote tributary of the Mekong in northeastern Thailand. It was the water from its rock-fill dam, completed in 1966, that was needed so urgently by the village of Nong Ben in the summer of 1967. The dam, named Ubol Ratana, was producing power; its ultimate installed capacity will be 24,000 kilowatts (kw). Its network of irrigation canals, however, would not be completed until sometime in 1968. When the gates do open, the life-giving water will irrigate some 113,000 acres of land. Other benefits from the $28,000,000 project include flood control, the development of fisheries behind the dam, and provision for recreational facilities.

Not only is the Nam Pong a multipurpose project, it is a multinational one as well–as is the whole Mekong program. France and Japan made the preliminary studies. The UN Special Fund spent $6,000,000 on a feasibility report, on the basis of which West Germany offered a low-interest loan of $16,000,000 to get the project started. Other loans or contributions were made by Pakistan, the Republic of China (Nationalist China), and Thailand. The Mekong Committee served as the coordinator. Thailand was reponsible for all the con-

Lower Mekong Annual Rainfall

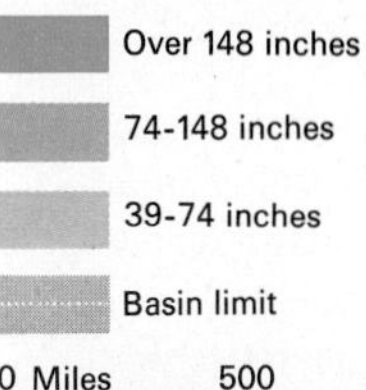

Map shows how various areas of the lower Mekong share the copious average yearly rainfall. The chart graphically demonstrates the extreme unevenness of rainfall, as measured at Udon Thani on the Khorat plateau.

Monthly Rainfall in Udon Thani

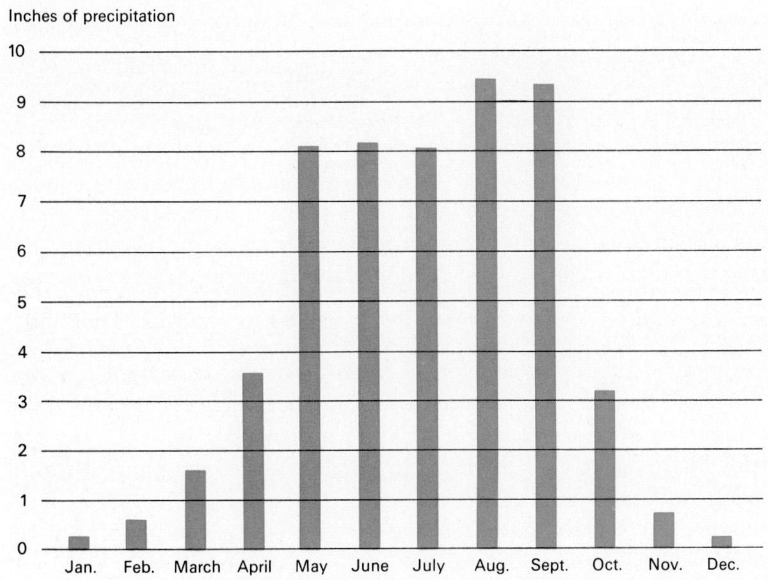

Lower Mekong Rice Growing Areas

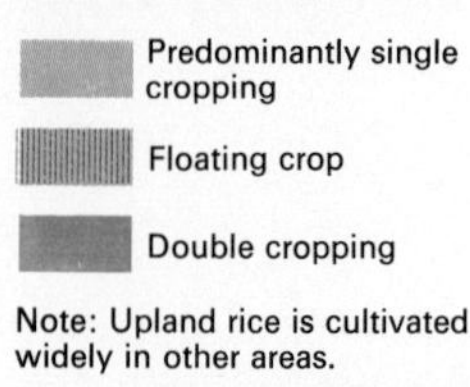

Note: Upland rice is cultivated widely in other areas.

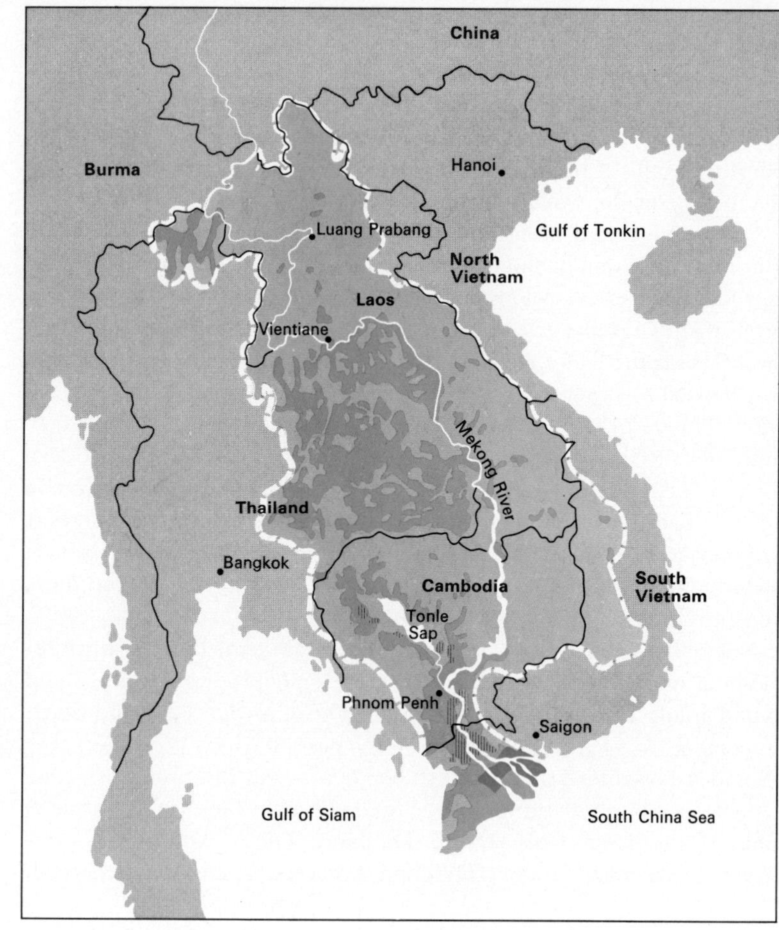

Double cropping of rice, which is now confined to the lower delta region of South Vietnam, could be extended to the irrigable single-cropping areas as the Mekong projects are completed.

struction. Machinery was used for excavation and other heavy phases of the construction. Local labor–some of it by young, unmarried women at 50 cents a day–was employed for the finishing work.

The Nam Pong and other tributary projects were deliberately given priority over mainstream developments. The Mekong Committee will use the experience gained in the construction and operation of these small-scale projects in carrying out its plans on the Mekong itself. Some of the planned mainstream projects are gigantic. All told, the proposed mainstream lower Mekong water development projects will have a total installed hydroelectric power capacity of about 2,000,000 kw and will supply enough water to irrigate almost 2,500,000 acres.

About 35 miles downstream from the Ubol Ratana dam lies the village of Nong Ben–146 houses and 1,700 persons. It represents only a miniscule part of the whole Mekong project. But how this remote little village meets and solves its problems–engineering, agricultural, social, and political–can be of inestimable value in planning and carrying out the larger and more costly elements of the overall Lower Mekong Basin Project. Nong Ben is typical of more than a hundred

Lower Mekong Population Density

Persons per square mile

More than 260

130-260

26-130

0-26

0 Miles 100 200 300

The region's population density roughly coincides with the rice areas—the heavier the rice cultivation, the more persons per square mile.

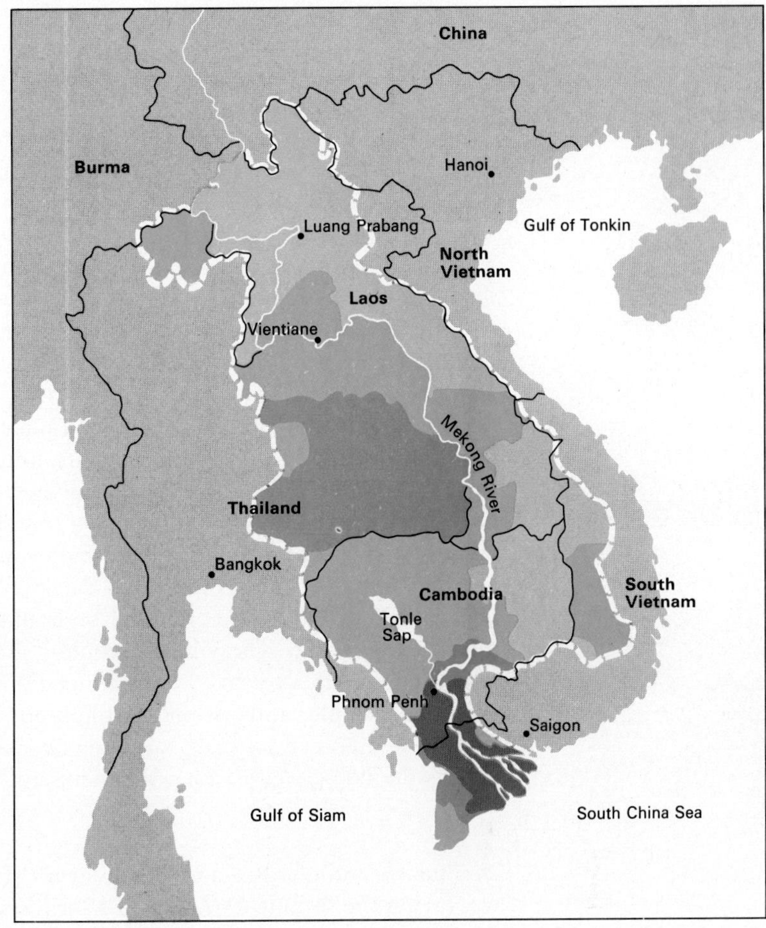

villages in the Nong Wai Irrigation District of the Nam Pong part of the project. The Mekong Committee has recognized that the mere provision of irrigation water would be pointless unless the local farmers knew how to make use of it. It has taken advantage of the delays in the planning and financing of irrigation at Nam Pong to foster an experimental and demonstration farm at nearby Kalasin. There a small dam makes it possible to irrigate about 750 acres of demonstration plots owned by local farmers as well as a 25-acre experimental farm used to test new strains of rice and their response to fertilizer. The farm is run by the UN's Food and Agriculture Organization (FAO).

It is at such test farms that the FAO comes to grips with the potentially gravest problem in increasing agricultural production: How to close the gap between what is known by the experts and what is practiced by the farmers. It is an oversimplification to assert that subsistence farmers resist change because they are lazy, stupid, or stubborn. Over the centuries, they have developed a relatively successful system of agriculture sensitively adjusted to the realities of soil, climate, and trade. Their strains of rice have been well selected to give a reasonable yield on land too low in nutrients for our modern strains. Their agricultural practices are well geared to the seasons, though not to the occasional droughts. Their conservatism is based on realization that they have little margin for error.

The people of Nong Ben take an interest in the Mekong Committee's activities on the Khorat plateau–but they are biding their time. Their way of life, which depends on the vicissitudes of the weather, is not one that engenders excitement about new hopes; there have been too many disappointments within everyone's memory for that. So, as the villagers see the new canals being dug, they remain realistic. In two years there will be water; they accept this good fortune, but not with jubilation. Time enough for that when the water actually starts to irrigate their fields.

This is not to say that they do not have plans. The village leaders say they will be able to plant corn, peanuts, and other field crops–when they have water. The village headman knew what was possible. He had already helped his fellow villagers raise $200 from their meager savings to build a road to the main highway, two miles to the west, and had obtained a $500 grant from the government to surface it with hard laterite, a reddish soil rich in iron or aluminum and common to much of the basin. The villagers could see the advantage of better access to markets, and they were acting on their vision. These were an adaptable people, and within the limitations of their circumstances –all too well known to them, but often overlooked by outside experts –they were doing well in adapting themselves to the changing world.

In the meantime, at Kalasin, the farm's staff of four professionals was laying the technical groundwork for a revolution in the villagers' age-old methods of agriculture. The agronomists and soil experts there know that the large investments in dams and canals for the Nam Pong and other projects can be justified only on the basis of an intensive and changed use of the irrigable land. Further, if a visible result is to be obtained before the increasing population overtakes the gains in productivity, those gains must be substantial and immediate.

The Kalasin Experimental Farm has demonstrated that rice yields can be increased fourfold. It achieved this by the combined use of new seeds, fertilizer, irrigation, and pesticides. This increase was for just one crop a year. With irrigation, the same land can produce a second crop during the dry season. What is required, however, is a basically new system of agricultural management. Increased productivity requires fertilizer, certainly. But fertilizer alone, applied to the traditional strains of rice, increases the yield by only a nominal amount. Most of the new strength goes into stems and blades, not into the rice itself. So the need for developing new seeds is urgent. In addition, there must be irrigation systems, drainage, and tools. Most of the farmer's needs–the seeds, the fertilizer, the tools–must be paid for in advance of the harvest. Thus, cash must be available ahead of time, either from the farmer's own savings or in the form of credit. Then too, not all of the increased productivity is a clear gain; some of the harvest must be sold on the market. This introduces still another factor: There must be roads to give the farmer access to markets.

This welter of new factors overwhelms most of the local farmers. Despite the impressive performance by the FAO experts, the farmers remain convinced that they would have difficulty matching it. They doubt their own ability to marshal all the necessary resources and apply all the new, sophisticated, western-style farming methods.

The inherent complexity of modern agriculture becomes dramatically apparent when its techniques are suddenly applied to a subsistence-level, peasant economy. Yet agriculture is only one part of the larger economic, political, and educational system necessary to a developed society. In the past, most cultures have had time to innovate and gradually adjust the various other components of their systems to improved technology–and time to correct any errors. Today, in the short time that remains before population growth gets out of hand, all of these parts of the system must be modified nearly simultaneously. Developing nations cannot afford to complete some portions of a plan only to find that 10 years have been lost because another essential factor has been neglected. Nor, on the other hand, should the sheer magnitude of the task serve as an excuse for making no start at all. In the lower Mekong basin, a start has been made on the more manageable parts of the whole development plan.

Before a bulldozer could be started, a dam built, or a power line strung, painstaking, long-term planning and scientific studies had to be carried out. *At left,* an international team is briefed on the day's work —surveying, *above,* along the Nam Ngum in Laos.

Manipulating the waters of a great basin to advance the welfare of its people is an exceedingly complex job. When a river system is tampered with, the interactions of all living things with one another and with their environment (the *biological ecosystems*) are bound to be affected. The human patterns of production and communication will be changed as well. It is difficult to predict the nature and extent of all these changes. The predictions can be no better than the knowledge of the basic processes involved. These are some of the problems already encountered by engineers:

- How would the regulation of the river's flow into and out of Tonle Sap (Great Lake) in Cambodia affect the fish that live in the waters of the lake and the Mekong? It would influence their movement, of course, but what else? Unless the life cycle of the fish and their ecological requirements are understood, the full effects of the changes in the water flow cannot be judged.
- Some of the tropical lateritic soils are especially subject to deterioration under irrigation. Therefore, it is essential either to avoid trying to till them–as often is done–and concentrate on alluvial soils, or to manage them with delicate care. Soil tests, laboratory analyses, and experiments in the field should provide data to base these decisions on.
- How can the amount of available stream water be estimated reliably when the records cover only a few years or are entirely lacking, as in most of the basin? Pains must be taken to avoid overestimating the amounts of stream discharge and underestimating evaporation losses based on a few years' records that may not be representative.

Workers from Nong Ben and from other nearby villages do concrete finishing work on the Nong Wai canal. In 1968, it should be irrigating the unplanted rice paddies in the background, where water buffalo forage for dry weeds and grass.

These and a score of other biological and physical relationships must be examined in a rigorous way if the engineers are to avoid unexpected and unwanted results.

Even greater hazard attaches to predicting the social consequences of investment in massive water-control structures. As already distressfully shown in Nong Ben and other villages served by Nam Pong canals, the water stored behind an efficient dam is of little use until the distribution facilities are constructed. And when the water does flow through the canals during the dry season as the surrounding lands lie parched, the farmers may not be able to use it to good advantage unless he has the right seeds and fertilizers, as well as available credit and the means of getting his produce to market. Changing from a one-crop, rain-fed rice culture to double-cropping irrigation that may introduce other cash crops is a drastic step for a peasant to take. When he does take it, his progress is likely to be slow and awkward.

Likewise, there is no automatic assurance that the low-cost electricity from the project's generators will find an economic market or will be sold on terms that will build productivity and allow the worker to share in his country's growth. Suitable arrangements must be made for new manufacturing and for power distribution.

Pilot farms, such as those operated by FAO in cooperation with national agencies near Kalasin and Vientiane, may help bring about an understanding of the physical problems and the social complications that go with them. New projects often are built without attention to the full range of their possible effects. At places such as the Helmand

The Ubol Ratana dam at Nam Pong, Thailand, was the first major result of the Mekong project. Although the dam was completed in 1966, its irrigation canals are not scheduled to open before sometime in 1968.

valley in Afghanistan, heavy investments have gone unused because the soil was unsuitable, the peasants would not adopt new practices, or the government failed to take the required auxiliary action.

One of the more troublesome problems is finding the proper balance between river management works and other types of national investment. The expenditures for a new dam, canal, or power plant may promise a future stream of benefits in excess of costs. But that is no assurance that such an investment would be right for the welfare of the economy. In a developing country, the savings of individual workers are small, the government's assets are likely to be modest, and the balance of cash from international trade is slim. The local savings must be husbanded for work that will yield large and early returns. To divert them to low-return purposes, such as a drainage project that would increase crop production only slightly over a long period of time, is to squander opportunity for social advance. Roads or education or some other form of investment may take precedence.

From the outset, some observers of the lower Mekong experiment have said it could not work. They have pointed to experience in other areas to bear out their skepticism. Although international rivers drain a large proportion of the continents, most large development usually has been that of a single nation on its own section of such a river–the French, for instance, on the lower Rhône or the Iraqi on the lower Tigris and Euphrates. Whatever international river development there has been usually came after squabbles over water rights and after one or both countries had taken independent steps in its own territory. Thus, the United States collaborated with Canada on the Columbia and St. Lawrence and with Mexico on the lower Rio Grande only after having gone through long negotiations.

The lower Mekong countries began with a virtually untouched river and in an atmosphere of political tension. Internal strife in Vietnam curtailed the power of the Saigon government and prevented a program of national construction. Laos was unsettled by domestic divisions, which were quieted only in part by the Geneva accords of 1962. Long-standing differences between Cambodia and Thailand veered into a breakdown of diplomatic relations; and as the Vietnamese conflict grew, Cambodia and South Vietnam also broke relations. Yet the Mekong Committee continued to function, and representatives of the four countries met around the committee's tables after other communication had halted. Mekong cooperation, continuing in spite of

This bountiful rice field in the productive delta area of South Vietnam symbolizes hope for the future, when harnessing of the Mekong will enable many thousands of additional acres to be double-cropped.

With flags of their nations and of the UN behind them, the Mekong Committee meets to set policy and coordinate the many aspects of the multinational project.

political antagonism, kept open some interchange among the nations in furthering what they regard as a common interest.

The temptation to use the Mekong activity for diplomatic purposes has been a constant hazard. Communist China–not being a member of the UN and, consequently, of the ECAFE–has not been involved in the project, but neither has it interposed formal objections to what has been done. Communist nations have given economic aid to Cambodia but have not joined in assistance to the Mekong Committee. The United States has contributed heavily. Late in 1966, however, Congress barred U.S. support for the tributary project on the Plek Thnot in Cambodia on the ground that the United States should not assist countries trading with North Vietnam. This seriously impaired the committee's operations until the fall of 1967, when Cambodia ended its boycott of committee affairs and resumed full participation.

While war prevented access of survey parties to much of South Vietnam's delta after 1963, it did not hinder work in most other sectors of the basin. Parts of Laos were blocked off, and the Khorat plateau was hazardous because of guerrilla activity. Yet, the Nam Ngum power-irrigation-flood control project was started in 1966 in a section of Laos where government control had been in doubt.

By late 1967, the Mekong Committee could point to 10 years of existence and some tangible results. An elaborate set of studies of hydrology and of preliminary plans for new construction on both the main stem of the Mekong and its major tributaries had been completed at a cost of approximately $50,000,000. In these, the 23 countries had taken part, often in collaboration with other groups. France was the first nation to help. The United States contributed the largest amount. Pakistani engineers used U.S. hydrology and Canadian air photos. Israeli technicians drew on French soil surveys and Japanese reconnaissance engineering. Certain of the studies, such as the hydrological and biological observations, were only the beginning. Others, such as the power market analysis, went as far as practicable and would require later revision.

Construction had been completed on the Nam Pong project's dam and the smaller Nam Pung power and irrigation project, also in Thailand. Building was going forward on the Nam Ngum project near Vientiane and on two smaller power projects at Nam Dong and Lower Se Done in Laos. Total construction and study commitments were in excess of $125,000,000, a modest amount considering a possible expenditure of several hundred million dollars over the next decade if the more promising works are undertaken. It is not uncommon for 10 to 20 years to pass between the first planning of a water project and its operation. In the lower Mekong, there has been a fierce sense of urgency to get on with the job in the face of obstacles that less bold supporters might have regarded as insurmountable.

Whether it survives or not, the lower Mekong experiment is an example of international cooperation that must be followed widely if the people of developing countries are to have a chance to bridge the economic gulf that separates them from their prospering Western brethren. The needs at Nong Ben are the same as those in countless other areas of Asia, Africa, and Latin America. But ingrained customs and practices that have served these people for centuries must be changed before they can put the new technology to effective use.

Infinite patience and tact must temper a thoroughgoing education and development effort by the technical experts. And this must be done in a manner that will strengthen, not disrupt, the integrity of community life. When the peasants of Nong Ben and similar villages finally get the promised water, new strains of rice seed, fertilizers, more efficient tools, roads, power, and credit facilities–it all still may be to no avail. The farmers must not only know how to use their new technological tools, but they must be thoroughly convinced they should do so. Unless they are, they would do as well by continuing with their old, time-tested methods. A Nong Ben farmer, for instance, must be convinced that he will reap a larger total harvest by sowing a slightly lower-yielding strain of rice twice a year than by planting his old, higher-yielding variety only once a year. If he does not sow two crops, he will be no better off than in any year of normal rainfall, and his costs will be higher.

By late 1967, there was hope that the farmers of Nong Ben were realizing this and that they would be fully prepared to enter into the new agricultural economy. If they do succeed in taking that step, the hopes for realizing all the exciting opportunities in the entire lower Mekong basin will rise as well. Such success, in turn, would point the way toward similar productive collaboration among other developing nations and one way of closing the widening gap between the have and have-not nations of the world.

See also Section One, Harrison Brown: Focus on Science.

A Year Book Special Report

By A. H. Raskin

Where the Jobs Will Be

The fast-changing world of work is demanding brains not brawn, versatility not narrow skills. Will today's youth be ready for 1975?

More Americans had jobs in 1967 than in any other year in America's history. Not even under the forced draft of total war were so many people employed in making the goods and performing the services that go into the complex economy of the most productive country the world has ever known.

Yet the fact that public and private employment passed the 76,000,000 mark failed to erase apprehension over two troublesome aspects of the job situation. One was the persistent exclusion from any share in the general prosperity of some 3,000,000 men and women, a disturbingly large proportion of them youthful Negroes, Puerto Ricans, and Mexican-Americans. The frustrations engendered by their idleness were part of the social dynamite that erupted in rioting and looting in the slums of Detroit, Mich.; Newark, N.J.; and other cities.

The second focus of concern stemmed from uncertainty about the effect of a fast-changing technology on jobs. Would personnel requirements be altered in such a way that people who had invested a lifetime in acquiring occupational skills might one day find their talents surplus and themselves on the industrial scrapheap? An equally pressing question: Where will the jobs be in 1975, and what kind of training and education will students now in school need to fill them?

The mappers of tomorrow's economy have acquired a sounder perspective on the pace and nature of changing industrial technology than many of them exhibited only a few years ago. Then, the conviction was strong that automation was wiping out traditional sources of employment at supersonic speed. Some scholars even envisaged a technological Armageddon in which displaced man would fight a despairing battle to destroy the machines that had reduced him to impotence by their fantastic productivity.

The experience of the last five years has provided a much more balanced view. The new technology creates opportunities as well as problems. Social inventiveness will have to keep pace with scientific inventiveness if constructive answers are to be found for all the problems of human adjustment. But it is already clear that Americans will have plenty to do for the rest of the 20th century if full use is made of the arm-stretching and mind-stretching potentialities opened up by research and development.

The U.S. Bureau of Labor Statistics (BLS), which makes a specialty of substituting fact for fancy in its evaluation of job currents, estimates that 89,000,000 persons will be gainfully employed in 1975 –an increase of 13,000,000 in eight years. This means a gain of about 1,600,000 a year in the overall number of jobs, despite the fact that increased efficiency from technological improvements will make it possible to turn out more products with fewer workers.

The explanation for this seeming paradox lies in two trends: (1) the expanding appetite of a population growing in both numbers and wealth, and (2) a sharp shift in job dominance away from the production of goods to the supplying of an ever-wider variety of services–personal, commercial, and governmental.

One clear benefit of mechanization and automation has been the removal of much of the drudgery from human toil. Machines now take the sweat out of labor, and computers perform tedious mental chores. They have eliminated many of the menial, dirty, or dull–and usually low-paying–jobs that no one liked to do. They have added new dimensions to man's capabilities.

But these new dimensions also entail challenges that can be met only by a better prepared work force. More education and more skill

The author:
A. H. Raskin, for many years a labor writer for *The New York Times* and now assistant editor of its editorial page, has written widely on employment problems.

Changing Pattern of Jobs: 1964-1975

Per cent decrease in jobs Per cent increase in jobs

−50 −40 −30 −20 −10 0 10 20 30 40 50 60 70

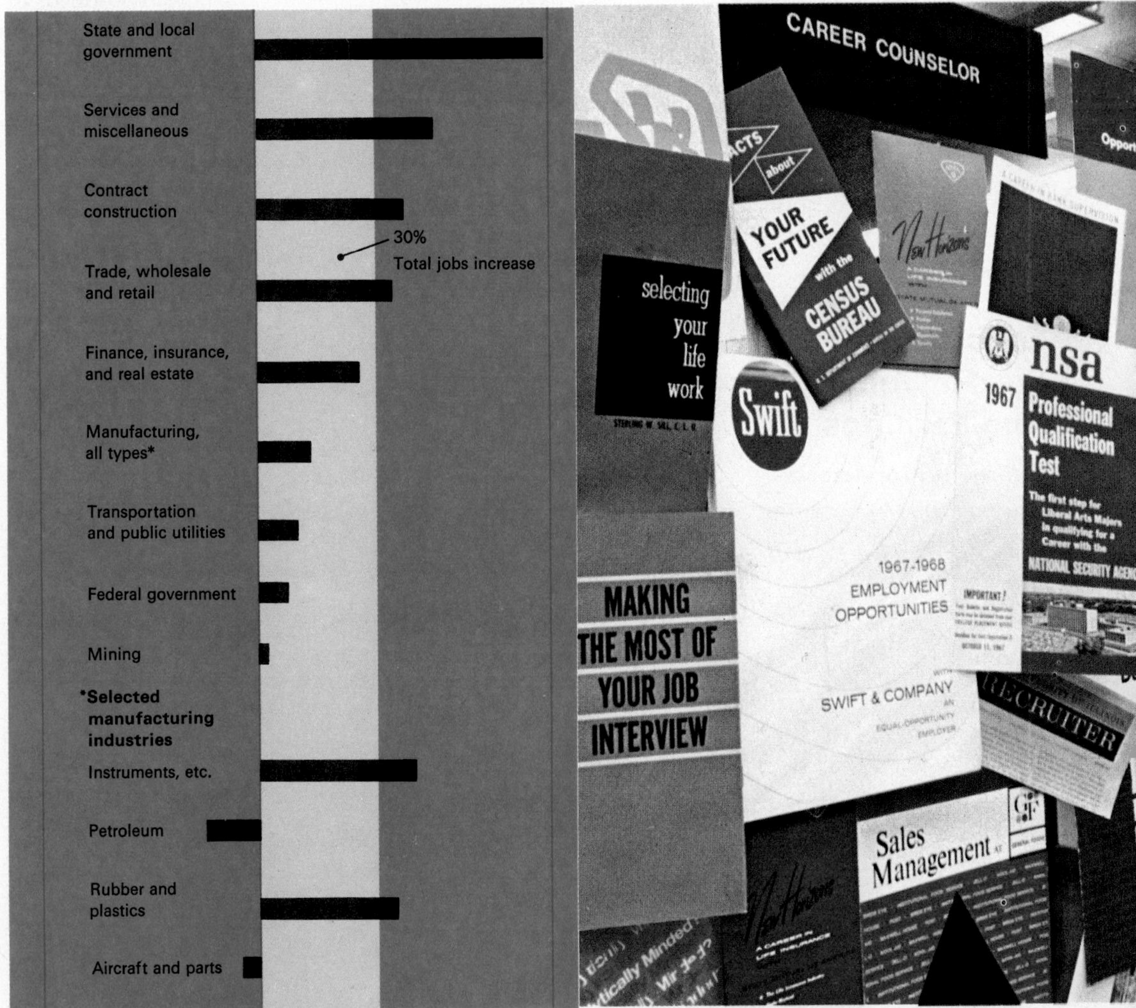

will be the chief requisites for a job in 1975. The most substantial increases in employment opportunities will be in professional and technical fields. They will be the jobs that offer the greatest satisfactions in interest and income–and also the jobs that will demand the most advanced schooling.

The biggest single age group competing for the jobs will be the 25-to-34-year-olds, whose numbers will increase twice as fast in the next decade as the rest of the labor force. An unusually rapid displacement of older workers by those in the first flush of maturity will be caused by two post-World War II developments: the "baby boom" and earlier retirements resulting from the growth of industrial pensions over and above Social Security benefits.

The 25-to-34 age group of 1975 will consist in large measure of those now in high school, college, or graduate school. They will bring to their jobs more education than did any other generation of Americans. Three-fourths will have high school diplomas, as against two-thirds in 1967. The proportion with baccalaureate degrees will go up from one-fifth to more than one-fourth, and there will be many more with master's degrees and doctorates. Yet even that upgrading in career preparation will leave many unprepared. U.S. Department of Labor officials stress that education will have to be a lifetime process for even the most learned if they are to stay abreast of the continuing knowledge explosion.

For those without education, the outlook will approach hopelessness. The extent to which the school drop-out will be the left-out in tomorrow's labor market is underscored by a projection made by the BLS in its assessment of 1975 job opportunities. It shows that young workers who do not finish elementary school will have an unemploy-

Education Pays in Jobs And Earnings

Managers, Proprietors

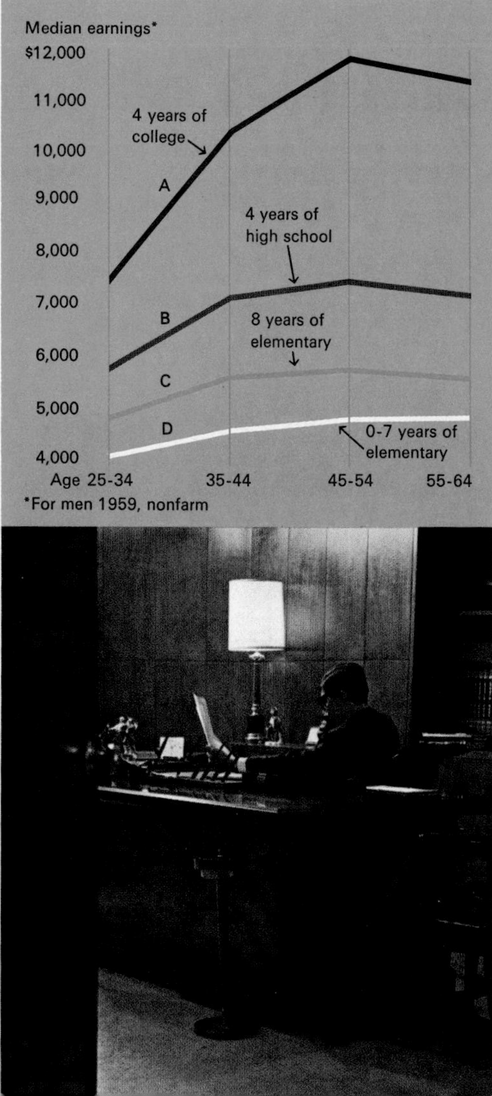

Laborers

ment rate seven times as high as that for college graduates. Likewise, when comparisons are made on the basis of occupational skills, laborers will be seven times as likely to be out of work as professionals. In crassest terms–in the total amount of money a person can expect to earn in his lifetime–education pays dividends, quite apart from the help it provides in enjoying the fullness and happiness of life.

A broad educational background has a further virtue in this era of cyclonic change. Even now, a 20-year-old entering on his first job might expect to change employers or lines of work six or seven times before retiring. For both men and women, education is an aid to adaptability and to the ability to be effectively retrained.

But if education is to add to man's flexibility, it must not itself suffer from an excessively narrow focus. In a perceptive article in the *Saturday Review*, Robert M. Hutchins, once chancellor of the University of Chicago and now president of the Fund for the Republic at the Center for the Study of Democratic Institutions, Santa Barbara,

Machinists

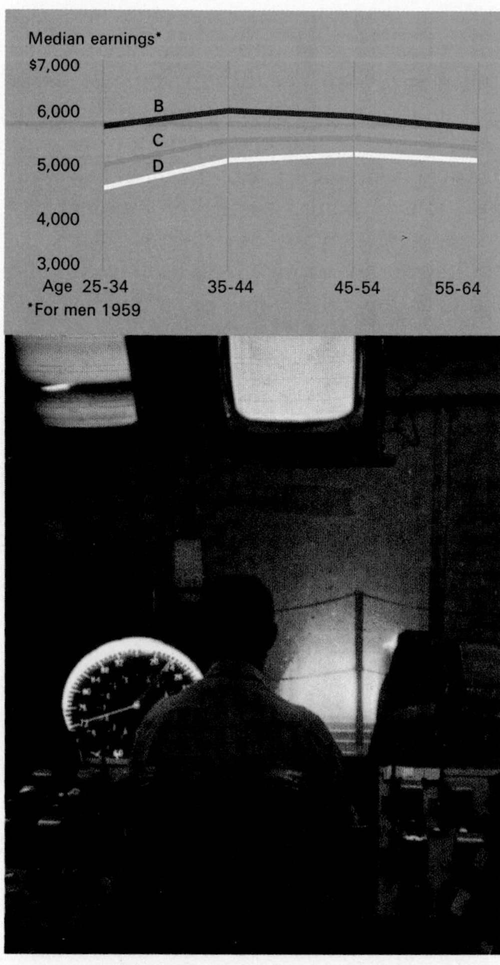

Office Workers

Calif., observed that under current industrial conditions "the more specifically education is directed to jobs, the more ineffective it is bound to be."

"What education can and should do is help people become human," Hutchins continued. "The object of education is not manpower but manhood. . . . The man who is truly educated, rather than narrowly trained, is ready for anything. He has developed his human powers and is able to use them and his understanding of the world to meet any new problem he has to face. He is prepared by his education to go on with his learning."

In line with this philosophy, there is growing support for the idea that rigid job training should be subordinate to a broad education, one that will provide a sound foundation in English, mathematics, the arts, and the physical and social sciences. The aim is the versatile man. "How can we tell what skills to teach?" Hutchins asks, or "How do we know what skill will be marketable when he (the student) tries to sell it?"

Educators have been trying to cope with this problem. One trend has been toward the comprehensive high school, with both college-preparatory and vocational courses taught under one roof. Two-year community and junior colleges–which teach academic, business, and technical courses–have multiplied. Many of their graduates decide they need more schooling and go on to regular colleges and universities. Skill centers are being planned in many large cities to provide training and retraining for youngsters who leave high school and want to qualify for skilled occupations in industry or subprofessional and technical jobs in health, science, and many other service fields. In addition, there are technical institutes under federal sponsorship and a vast range of in-school and on-the-job training programs financed by labor and industry. Corporations and unions alike have embraced the concept that their prosperity will be enhanced by a better educated work force–with social awareness and skill in human relations as prized as managerial or mechanical adeptness.

The disadvantages of inability to adjust have been painfully illustrated by the experience of two groups dispossessed by the march of technological progress–farm families and coal miners. Farming, which once provided employment for more than half of all American workers, now accounts for less than 5 per cent of the job total, and it is still declining. The tragedy of this great shakeout of rural families has been that most of the refugees have headed for the cities. They have flocked into the fetid slums–uneducated, unskilled, and unable to escape from their new prison, the heartbreak of slum existence. They have traded rural poverty for urban degradation.

The story in coal is just as grim, except that the numbers are smaller. The story began a half century ago in the anthracite mines, which gave work to more than 100,000 men. Since then, oil and natural gas have taken over almost all of the hard-coal market, and

Growth Jobs Require Training

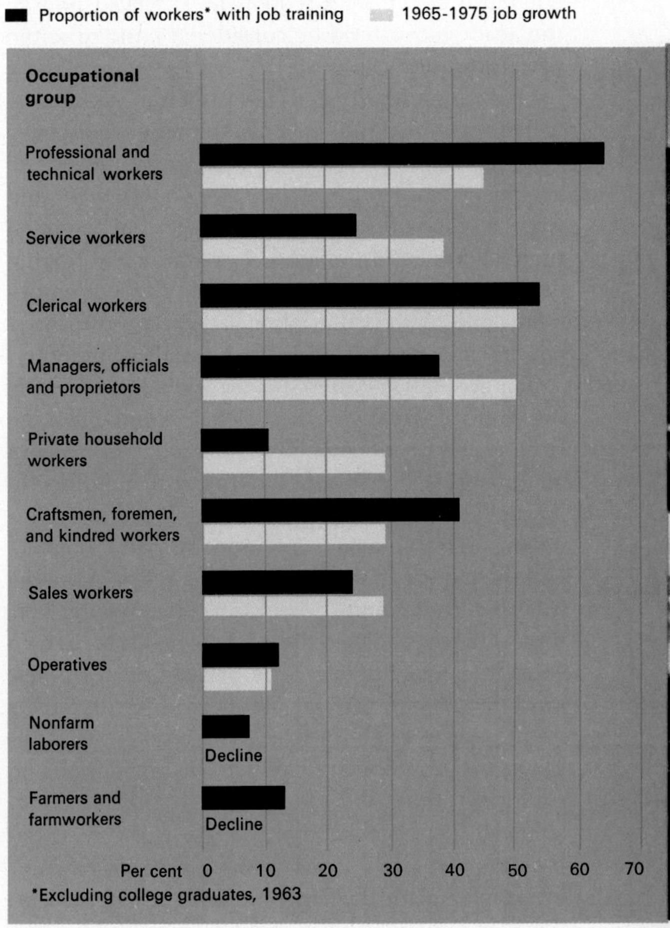

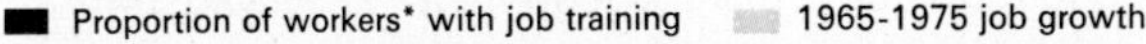

*Excluding college graduates, 1963

those 100,000 jobs have dwindled to about 10,000. Attrition in the bituminous, or soft coal, field was much more precipitous. But it was a drop attributable more to displacement of men by machines than to inroads by rival fuels. Mechanized mining now makes it possible for 100,000 miners to dig as much soft coal as 500,000 did only 20 years ago. Most of those who were squeezed out, many after 20 or 30 years in the mines, have found it difficult to adjust to above-the-ground jobs. They vegetate with their families in Appalachia, waiting for the mine whistle that will never blow.

This is what happened to the fathers. For their sons and daughters, the best hope lies in an education that will help them play a meaningful part in the new society away from the silo and the slag heap. Unhappily, however, the children's deprived neighborhoods often offer only the poorest quality of schools. For all young people, in fact, the accident of where they happen to live more often than not determines the quality of their education. James B. Conant, president emeritus of Harvard University and perhaps the foremost critic of U.S. second-

Less School, Less Work

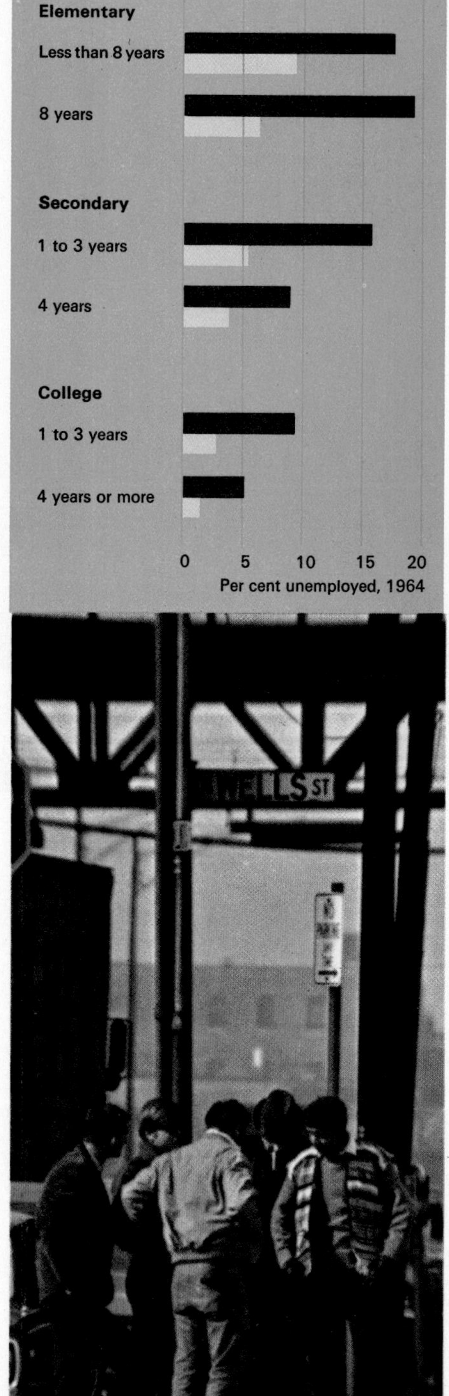

ary schools, reported in February, 1967, that only one-tenth of the high schools he surveyed met all the academic criteria he considered basic to sound preparation for life.

Had Conant directed his attention to the so-called vocational high schools, the ratio would have been far lower. The aim of these institutions is to provide "marketable skills" to young men and women who will never go to college. But too often such schools become a kind of educational dumping ground with inadequate teachers, obsolete equipment, and courses that bear little relation to present-day job opportunities in the outside community.

The federal Vocational Educational Act of 1963 has overcome many of these deficiencies by making sizable new grants available for modernizing both courses and equipment. But the real question remains: Is any type of specifically job-oriented education desirable before high school graduation?

At whatever level of career he aims, two factors are obviously going to be crucial in a young person's ultimate choice. One is a knowledge of his own capacities and interests; the other is the soundest possible estimate of the job horizon, with all its murkiness, to establish where the most fruitful employment prospects are likely to lie. Ideas are being translated from the laboratory to the industrial scene with an astounding rapidity. World-wide demand for all kinds of goods and services is expanding in pace with the "revolution of rising expectations" in underdeveloped areas–from our own racial ghettos to the slums and jungles of Asia and South America. Both of these developments have created an astonishing range of new career choices for young people.

Fields that once seemed promising roads to stability and success no longer offer the same security. Many new fields of greater promise are opening up. Tens of thousands of men and women are working in fields that were virtually unknown a decade ago –space technology, systems analysis, microelectronics, a list that grows longer each year.

The first necessity is to recognize how completely the United States has turned the corner from an economy rooted in manual labor to one built on white-collar activities and services. Now, only 45 per cent of all jobs are directly concerned with production–not just with the manufacture of everything from safety pins to locomotives, but also with the building of homes, office buildings, and factories, the construction of dams and other giant projects, the raising of food on the farm, and the mining of coal, copper, lead, and other minerals.

As vast as the number of workers producing goods is, it has become overshadowed by the 55 per cent of the labor force producing services. These gray-collar and white-collar workers are engaged in repairing and maintaining the goods that come out of the factories, in selling, in transportation, in banking and insurance, in providing utilities, in teaching, and in other services such as health care and recreation. Government at all levels, with more than 11,000,000 workers, has become the biggest service of all.

Two decades ago, in 1948, the ratio of production to service jobs was just the reverse–55 to 45. By 1975, only one out of three jobs is expected to be in production. And along with this production-to-service shift goes a more pronounced trend to higher skill-level jobs in all fields. Professional, technical, and clerical jobs–in both production and service–are expected to be held by almost half of all the 1975 work force of 89,000,000. Blue-collar, gray-collar, and farm employment combined will just barely exceed the white-collar total, a balance that economists would have pronounced ludicrously improbable half a century ago.

Fastest growing of all has been–and will continue to be–professional and technical employment. In 1947, these jobs represented 6.6 per cent of the national aggregate. Now the ratio is nearly double that, and it will keep climbing to about 15 per cent by 1975. This means that today's roughly 10,000,000 teachers, engineers, physicians, lawyers, clergymen, microbiologists, cyrogenicists, and innovators or researchers in a thousand specialties will have to be joined by at least 4,000,000 more highly skilled workers in less than a decade.

Office procedures and production methods alike will be revolutionized through the application of techniques developed as part of man's thrust into space and into the heart of the atom. One technique with impact on business management has been systems analysis, which treats every element from the acquisition of raw materials to the distribution of finished products as a factor in an integrated operation intended to achieve maximum output with minimum effort, cost, and waste. The result will be

Less Skill, Less Work

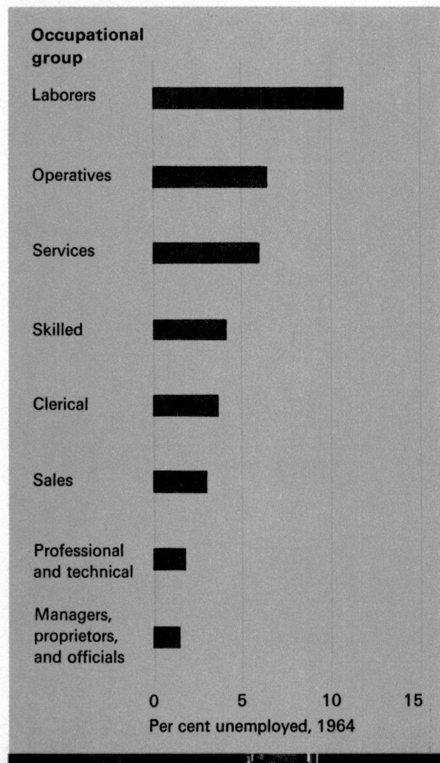

More College Degrees Ahead

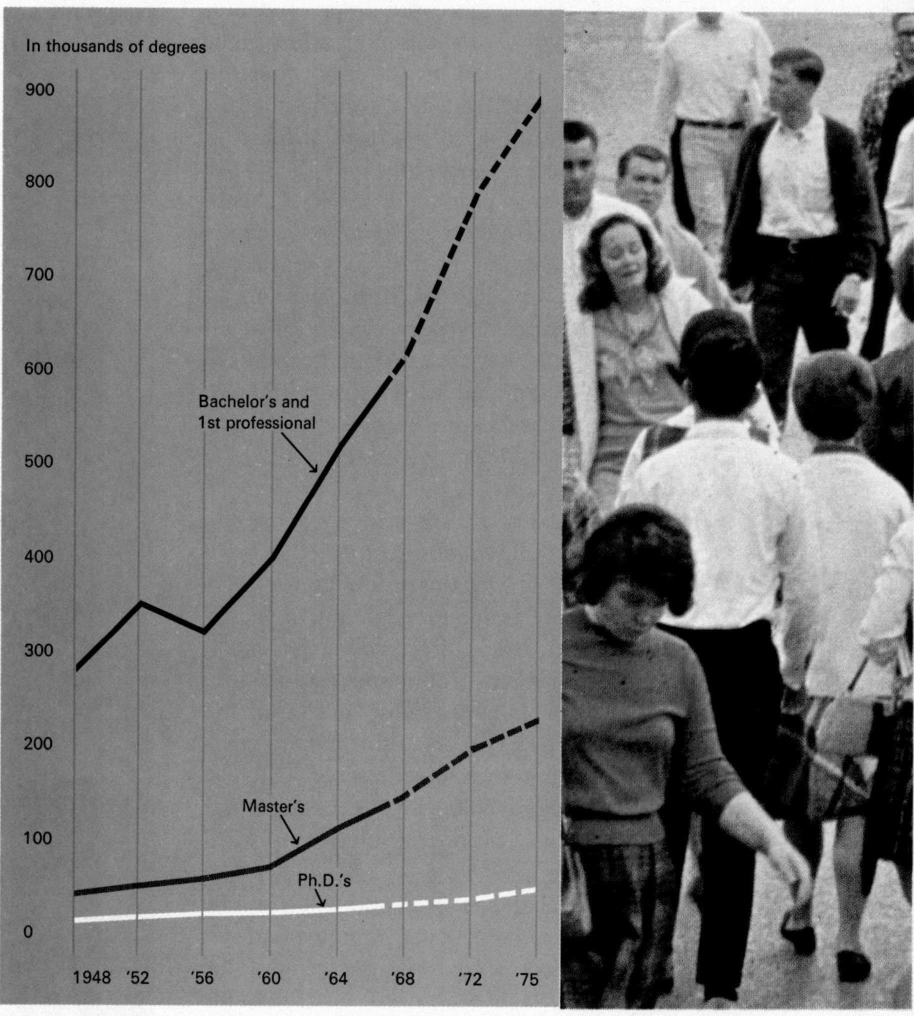

a rising need for clerical personnel to operate computers and office machines, keep records, take dictation, and type. One-sixth of all employment will be in these fields.

The executive suite will also be affected by the new technology. Mergers and diversification will mean bigger–and fewer–corporations. Fewer people will own their own businesses. Management will become increasingly a profession requiring graduate training, and it will continue to make up about one-tenth of the work force.

In blue-collar occupations, skills will remain in strong demand, particularly in construction. Prefabrication and other technological advances, however, could radically affect these jobs–a disturbing reality for youngsters setting out on three-to-five-year apprenticeship training. If today's standard skills should become obsolete by 1975, the impact will be even sharper on semiskilled and laboring jobs. Adaptability will be a must for all who enter blue-collar work, however subordinate their function might be.

Gray-collar service job openings will grow at a faster rate than will opportunities in goods production. People with more money to spend and more leisure time in which to spend it already are reaching out for a fantastically expanded range of services, from manicurists for poodles to "genuine hippies" as tour guides through San Francisco's Haight-Ashbury district.

The biggest of "growth industries," however, will be in the public sector. Demands for schools, improved health and hospital facilities, and a host of other public services will cause the 8,500,000 workers now on state and municipal payrolls to rise to 12,250,000 by 1975. Uncle Sam, though, is expected to keep the federal civilian job total fairly stable at a range between 2,500,000 and 3,000,000.

Another area of growth lies in the ever-opening scope of job opportunities for women. The proportion of women in nonfarm jobs increased from 31 per cent in 1950 to 37 per cent in 1967. Attitudes toward the working woman have also undergone profound changes.

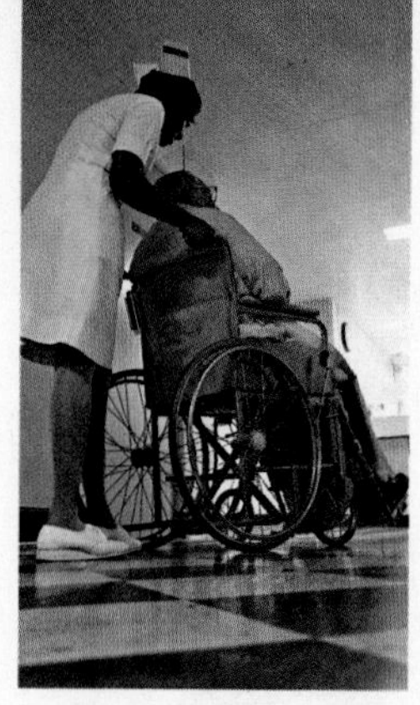

The equal employment opportunity provision of the Civil Rights Act of 1964 gave recognition to the fact that there was no longer any basis for discriminating against women- in their hiring, pay, or working conditions. With few exceptions, sex no longer is a valid employment determinant. The increasingly higher level of economic activity needed to maintain prosperity could not be achieved without women. President Lyndon B. Johnson has called "the under-utilization of American women . . . the most tragic and the most senseless waste of this century. It is a waste we can no longer afford."

The most challenging of immediate job problems is how to draw into meaningful employment the bulk of the 3,000,000 left on the side-lines. The proportion of Negroes on the unemployment rolls is twice the white rate. And it is highest of all among Negro teen-agers–out of school, out of work, out of hope. About 25 per cent of this group is idle, as against a national unemployment rate of 3.5 to 4 per cent.

In a real sense, the problem transcends unemployment. Of the 30,000,000 people in families with incomes below $3,000 a year, half are in households whose breadwinners have fulltime jobs. In New York City alone, 20,000 heads of families earn so little at their jobs that they must receive supplemental relief from the city to keep their families at some level of decency.

Health Service Job Demand In Steep Climb

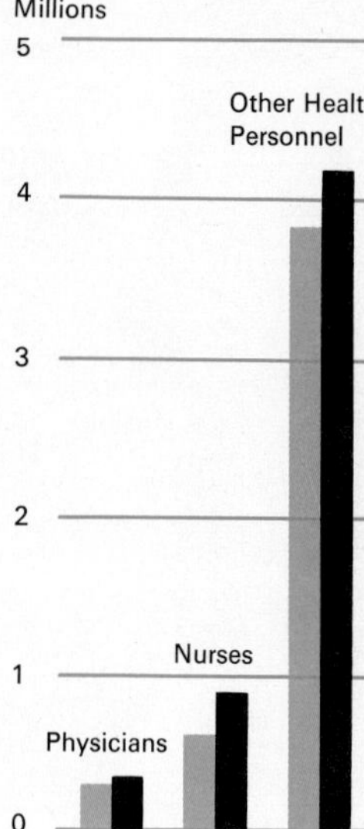

This realization of how inadequate anti-poverty efforts have been so far has stimulated stocktaking on how to lift families permanently out of their generation-after-generation need for help. One concept would make the federal government the "employer of last resort"–the guarantor of useful employment for all able and willing to work but unable to find jobs through regular channels. A companion concept would establish a negative income tax–or minimum income allowance –under which the government would pay a tax to the poor in the same way that those with higher incomes pay a tax to the government. Some critics, fearful that such assured payments would foster dependency rather than cure it, favor monthly allowances for every child–a system almost universal in Europe. The high cost of the war in Vietnam shut out serious consideration of any of these ideas in the first session of the 90th Congress. There was no dearth of effort, however–in government, education, private foundations, and collective bargaining–to carry forward the long-range social engineering essential to prepare all young people to live in a world in which everything will change, except the need for new ideas, new skills, and new idealism.

At his inauguration in April, 1967, as president of one of New York City's new community colleges, James A. Colston advised his students that three-fourths of them would live to work at jobs that do not now exist. The need for the individual to adapt to new jobs is complicated further by the accelerating pace of corporate, as well as technological, change. The upheavals that have occurred in less than a decade in one old-line enterprise with roots in the late 19th century illustrate both of these aspects of job adjustment.

In 1955, Textron, Inc., took over the American Woolen Company, the largest U.S. producer of woolens and worsteds. Textron itself had started as the Franklin Rayon Corporation in 1928. But Royal Little, Textron's chief, saw the company's future in diversification, not in textiles. Little led Textron into turning out both entirely new, sophisticated products of the Space Age and well-established products with strong markets.

American Woolen's sales had dwindled from $253,000,000 in 1951 to $73,000,000 in 1953. In 1963, Textron got out of textiles altogether. And by 1967, its 126 plants were turning out a staggering range of products–from highly complex aerospace components to ballpoint pens, chain saws, optical goods, helicopters, paint, machine tools; the list goes on and on. Total annual sales exceeded $1,000,000,000. Similar changes have occurred in almost every other major industry. Spindle watchers and shoe-last makers have had to learn to make diodes, servocontrols, automated scanners, or other items unheard of when they started to work.

At all levels of the work force, including the top reaches of management, the individuals who have fared best in these changes have been those with the liveliest imagination and the greatest resiliency. Schools and colleges are equally in need of imagination and resiliency in molding their curricula to a society that throws a mass-education burden on them but must also have free and individual–not machine-made–minds.

Secretary of Labor W. Willard Wirtz has said that machines can now do, on the average, what a high school graduate can do. Obviously, no young person is going to make any dent in the job market if that is all he has to offer. Even college and university training will be of dubious value if its sole result is to convert the graduate into a more efficient instrument of production, however rare his single-purpose skill.

The demand for versatility is certain to rise because of both the fantastic shift in vocational capacities attendant on automation and the trend in collective bargaining toward lifetime income security for industrial employees. A guaranteed annual wage coupled with pensions tends to make employers more selective in hiring. They want workers who will be able to adjust to radically altered corporate requirements, not those who will be frozen onto the payroll as unusables if the need for their original skill evaporates.

The same criterion holds with even greater force in the growing roster of professional, technical, and managerial posts in all sectors of the economy. Education will be a more important ingredient in occupational success than specific experience, and education will be adequate only if it extends beyond any narrow field of specialization to the fullest development of the total person.

See also Section One, Sylvia Porter: Focus on The Economy; Lawrence A. Cremin: Focus on Education; Section Three, Economy, The; Education; Labor; Poverty; Science and Research.

R & D Funds Spur Growth In Science Jobs

Billions of dollars
25
Nonprofit organizations
20
Total R & D funds
15
Industry
10
5
Federal government
0
1953 '55 '57 '59 '61 '63 '65

A Year Book Special Report

By Mark Gayn

Mao's Last Revolution

The aging titan is trying to move China ahead by looking back, and the result is turmoil

The party headquarters stood hidden in the narrow, pale-yellow gulley a few miles from the bombed town of Yenan. Mao Tse-tung and his closest companions lived in caves on a mountain ledge, and a rickety wooden footbridge linked them with the top story of the headquarters building. Behind the building was a small patch of land where Mao raised tobacco and vegetables.

I first met him here one night early in 1947 at a weekly dance for the party elite. A few days later I saw him again in his own cave, ill furnished and so cold my writing hand was numbed. For 10 hours, with only a break for a meal, Mao spoke of war, hunger, and "the coming American revolution."

An ocean of red sweeps through the Square of Heavenly Peace in Peking as a multitude of youths, holding booklets of Mao's thoughts, pass in review before him.

Mao in the 1920s.

Above all, he spoke of the rebellious Chinese villager. He saw China's history as a succession of peasant revolutions, and he took me on an exciting verbal tour of them, from the revolt of the Red Eyebrows, who fought during the Han dynasty at about the time of Christ, to the revolt in 1899 of the Society of Righteous and Harmonious Fists, whom the West called Boxers.

He explained why each of these uprisings failed–this one because of errors in policy and that one because of soft and undecided leadership. Mao saw his own as the last and the greatest of all the peasant revolutions. "Ours," he said firmly, "will not fail."

He and his companions spoke almost patronizingly of the Russian revolution. "Ours has lasted longer, has cost more lives, and will affect a greater number of people," he said. With pride, they spoke of the breed of men, heroic, selfless, and dedicated, who brought the revolution its victories and its glory.

Yenan was evacuated soon after I left, and Mao, his wife, and a few bodyguards struck north on sturdy Mongolian ponies. Two critical years of civil war still lay ahead, but in 1947 Mao was already certain the revolution he began in 1927 would triumph.

In 1965, when Mao was 72 years old, he launched his new, and undoubtedly his last, revolution. In many ways he was now a different man. His health was only fair. He appeared to have had a stroke the year before, and his face and body betrayed it. He shuffled his feet when he walked. Now and then his face lost its animation.

But more cruel than these infirmities of the flesh must have been the frustrations of the spirit. Mao was a titan who had devoted his life to changing the destiny of China and its millions. He had seen his dreams come true, yet now, in the final years of a long life, he sensed that what had happened to the revolutions of China's past was happening to his own. Yesterday's selfless rebels had become bureaucrats. The heroes who had made the revolution were being elbowed out by the new technocrats. Voices now cried it was less important to be Red than Expert. The Communist party he created was willing to adore him but not to follow his leadership. A chasm was widening between the cities, smug and arrogant and swollen enormously, and the villages, still mired in an 18th century way of life.

The revolution of the pure was being destroyed by the corrupt, and Mao was prevented from doing anything about it. Back in 1959, when his Great Leap Forward faltered badly, he handed over the active rule of China to other leaders of the party. Later, when he called on the party to cleanse itself, they listened politely. After all, he was the peerless revolutionary. But the governors were too busy trying to stave off famine and prevent economic collapse to worry about those who might be faithless.

Mao grew impatient and angry. A new revolution was needed, and the people had to be shaken fiercely out of their bourgeois ways. The name of Mao's new upheaval was "Cultural Revolution." It was a

The author:

Mark Gayn, who was born in China and now lives in Hong Kong, is head of the Asia bureau of the *Toronto Star.* He was one of the few Western reporters to interview Mao Tse-tung during the 1940s and has since made several trips into China to report on current conditions.

strange happening in which senseless destruction often stood side by side with idealism, millions of children became instruments of political power, slogans often replaced ideas, and people fought for goals that were never clearly defined. Lenin had offered the Russians "bread, peace, and land." Mao told his people only to "prevent the restoration of capitalism."

Not the least remarkable thing about Mao's new revolution was that even as he told his people he was leading them into a happier, purer tomorrow, he kept looking back over his shoulder at the past. Behind this new violence lay a nostalgia for the old uncomplicated era in which all men were dedicated heroes.

Not surprisingly, the main thrust of the new revolution was directed at the cities. Mao increasingly has insisted that all true virtue reposes in the countryside, that the cities are wicked, and that intellectuals can be used but never trusted. This is easy to understand if we remember that he spent the 22 most important years of his life, 1927 to 1949, in the wilderness, in caves, and mud-hut hamlets. In those years of glory and isolation, Mao came to view China, the world and revolution, morality, and the arts from a village crossroads. Now the aging giant seemed to want to punish and cleanse the cities, which he neither trusted nor understood. Whether it was a revolution or simply an upheaval, the Cultural Revolution clearly bore the imprint of this remarkable old man, with his passions and prejudices, his view of history, his old hatreds, his flaws, his virtues–and his peasant origins–all lovingly preserved.

Mao was born in the Hunan village of Shaoshan, in the heartland of rural China, on Dec. 26, 1893. Although his father was well-to-do, every member of the family had to work hard. Mao was sent to labor in the fields before he was seven years old. A year later, he entered school but still worked in the early mornings and after sunset.

At 10 years of age, Mao rebelled against his harsh schoolmaster and ran away. He was not sure where the city lay, and when the family

Communist casualties were carried through the streets of Shanghai in 1927, after Chiang Kai-shek, whose Nationalists had worked sporadically with the Communists, turned on them and had some 6,000 killed in a single night. Mao was in Hunan at the time, organizing peasants.

Mao in the 1930s.

found him three days later, he discovered he had never been more than two and a half miles from home. He later liked to recall the conflicts of his youth. Mao candidly admitted hating his father. And even when he jokingly described the two "parties" in his family–the "Ruling Power," which was his father, and the "Opposition," which was the rest of the family–his humor remained bitter.

Childhood yielded other impressions, none more memorable than the rice riots in the famine year of 1906. Some of the starving people who stormed the government offices were beheaded, and Mao was troubled by it. His family, unlike many others, did not suffer when famines came, but teen-aged Mao had a close look at extreme want, for on his winter vacations he served as a debt collector for his father, who dabbled in moneylending.

At his father's insistence, Mao quit school at age 13 and went to work in the fields. He also looked after the pigs, kept books, and collected debts. Because he was doing an adult's job, Mao was given a bit of meat, fish, and eggs twice a month–delicacies denied to his mother and brothers. At the age of 14, following a Chinese custom, he was married to a woman six years his senior. The marriage was not consummated.

At 16, Mao moved to a middle school at the provincial capital of Changsha. By now he was a tall and sturdy youth with a natural curiosity and an independent spirit nurtured by his feuds with his father, his teachers, and even his classmates.

The pathetic last emperor of the Ch'ing dynasty was still on the Chinese throne when Mao arrived in Changsha, and the country was aflame. One day a revolutionary came to Mao's school to deliver a fiery speech. Mao, then 18, was so impressed he decided to join the revolutionary army. Six months later, the revolution was over and he was back in Changsha. His time in the army was not wasted, however. He spent much of his monthly pay of seven yuan, at that time equal to about three and a half U.S. dollars, to buy revolutionary newspapers, in which he saw, for the first time, mention of socialism.

Instead of peace and order, the fall of the Ch'ing dynasty ushered in the era of warlords. In this milieu, Mao entered adulthood. For six months, he spent many hours in a library, reading everything from the writings of ancient Sun dynasty philosophers to the economics of Adam Smith. He was, he recalled later, like "an ox loose in a vegetable garden." It was only his father's threat to cut off a tiny allowance that forced Mao to enter Changsha's First Normal School, which trained teachers. Mao remained there for five years.

The First Normal was perhaps China's most famous nursery of young rebels, and Mao stood out among his schoolmates there. His intellectual hunger was insatiable, his physical strength formidable, and his habits unusual. He was known to cut off the white margins of newspapers and use them for note-taking. Eventually, he had a trunkful of these slips filled with his delicate brushwork.

Mao soon caught the eye of Yang Ch'ang-chi, his teacher of logic, psychology, and ethics, who had studied in Japan and England. Yang broadened the mind of this peasant youth, giving Mao not only a taste of the liberal ideas abroad but also a fascination with China's classical philosophers. He also infected Mao with his faith in the simple and rigorous life.

Mao was studious, but he was also an extrovert and somewhat of a bully. His village accent, his manner, and even his frayed black tunic made him an outsider in the Changsha school. But he was big and strong, and he did not hesitate to display his muscle. Revolutionary storms were sweeping across Hunan, and he felt their vigor. He organized Hunan's first student union. In 1917, he and a few friends formed "The New People's Study Society." The group began with 13 members, who met to discuss how they could best serve their country. By the following year, the membership had risen to about 80. Most of them were shot or strangled as Communists a decade later.

The five years in Changsha were stimulating, but Mao still had not found himself. His mind, he later confessed, was at this point "a curious mixture of ideas of liberalism, democratic reformism, and utopian socialism." It was only after he went to Peking, at a friend's urging, that he discovered a faith he could fervently embrace. It was a compound of Marx, poorly translated and not always understood, and of Mao's own romantic notions. Mao worked in the Peking University library and, figuratively, sat at the feet of two brilliant writers, librarian Li Ta-chao and dean of the faculty of letters Ch'en Tu-hsiu, the Leftist idols of China's youth. Peking to Mao that fall and winter of 1918-1919 was Li and Ch'en, innumerable

The "Long March" ended in 1935 at Yenan, where the Communists set up their capital. Here, Mao, *below,* and his followers worked and lived for 10 years in caves carved out of the cliffs.

Mao in the 1940s.

books, debates on Russia and Marxism, very lean living, and love. His old professor, Yang, had come from Changsha to teach in Peking, and he had brought his daughter Yang Kai-hui.

Soon after Mao returned to Changsha in 1919, his mother died. She was Mao's last bond with the village of Shaoshan, and he did not wish to go back there. Instead, he immersed himself in the campaign against Japan, then trying to take over the pieces of Chinese territory once held by Germany. He published a magazine, and then another one. The local warlord suppressed both. A little later, Mao ran a bookstore in which he sold works on Communism. He also formed a circle for the study of the Soviet Union. This group sponsored student trips to Russia. Among those who took advantage of one of these trips was another Changsha student, Liu Shao-chi, who, by the irony of fate, became Mao's principal target of attack in 1967.

In 1920, Mao's beloved, Yang Kai-hui, joined him in Changsha. They were married in the winter of 1921, and she bore Mao a son and a daughter. In 1930, she would be arrested and ordered to renounce Mao. Refusing, she was subsequently killed.

Also in 1920, agents of the *Comintern* (Communist International) began to arrive in China. They made contacts with the Chinese Leftists, talked of Bolshevism, and gave practical hints on revolution-making. As a result of their trips, a call was issued for a "national conference" of Marxists. A dozen conspirators attended this initial meeting in Shanghai on July 1, 1921. The police were soon on their trail, and the men fled to a lake resort a hundred miles away. There, in a pleasure boat, on a rainy day, the Chinese Communist party was born.

Professor Ch'en Tu-hsiu, who was absent from the picnic, was chosen to lead the party. Mao, then 28 years old, acted as secretary of the conference and was given the task of setting up Communist cells in Hunan. In this summer of 1921, the Communist party numbered 57 persons, and most of them were anarchists.

But if Moscow had played the role of a midwife, it was not prepared to entrust its hopes in China to this infant. Instead, it wooed Sun Yat-sen, then the best known of all Chinese revolutionaries. In 1923, the Russians instructed the tiny Communist party to cooperate with

Jubilant troops of the Japanese army stood on the shell-shattered wall around Nanking and shouted "Banzai" as the Chinese capital fell.

Jack Wilkes, *Life* © Time Inc.

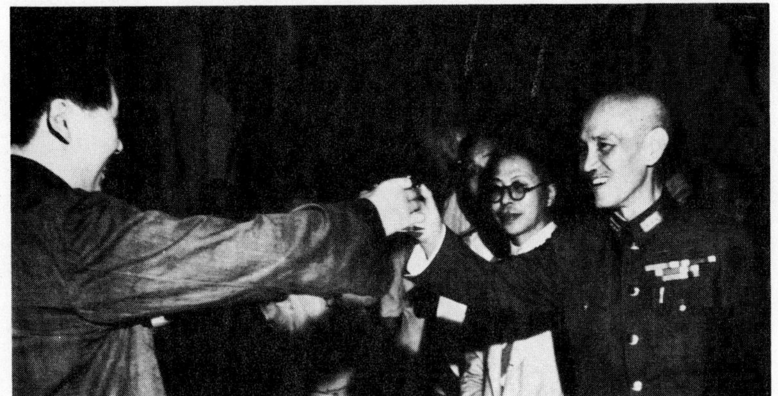

After defeating the Japanese invaders, Mao and Chiang toasted each other during negotiations to end a growing conflict between their two armies.

Sun's Nationalist party, the Kuomintang. The alliance with Russia brought Sun weapons, rubles, and a host of advisers. Soon there was a military academy at Whampoa, under a thin and intense officer named Chiang Kai-shek.

Mao played only a minor part in all this. He worked briefly with the Nationalists, but the Kuomintang patricians looked down on this rumpled peasant. He was also at odds with his Communist leaders. At the party's congress in 1925, he was even dropped from the Central Committee.

Sun died in 1925. Though his revolution had succeeded, he had not yet reunified the country. A year later, Chiang Kai-shek, who replaced Sun, began his historic Northern Expedition against the warlords. Finally, in April, 1927, assured of support from Shanghai's moneyed men and secret societies, Chiang turned on his Communist allies, killing some 6,000 persons on the Night of the Long Knives.

Mao was not directly involved in this drama. Since August, 1926, he had been organizing peasant unions in Hunan. In the early part of 1927, he spent 32 days traveling across five rural counties. He was

Troops of Mao's Communist People's Liberation Army captured all of northeast China in 1948 after a series of bloody battles with Chiang's forces.

At the height of the Cultural Revolution, Chairman Mao Tse-tung and his comrades in arms, Marshal Lin Piao, center, and Premier Chou En-lai, stand on a Peking rostrum and review Red Guards.

electrified by what he saw–peasants in control, violence, and landlords and officials denounced at "struggle" meetings. In the famous report Mao wrote, he said: "A revolution is not the same as inviting people to dinner, or writing an essay, or painting a picture, or doing fancy needlework; it cannot be anything so refined, so calm, so gentle, or so mild, kind, courteous, restrained, and magnanimous. A revolution is an uprising, an act of violence whereby one class overthrows another." During the next 40 years, with a few lapses, he continued to preach violence as the only true way to revolutionary triumph.

Increasingly, Mao thought Stalin wrong in his insistence that only the city worker could make a revolution. But when orders came, Mao obeyed. Thus, in 1927, he led the ill-conceived and hopeless Autumn Harvest Uprising. When it was drowned in blood, he walked up the Chingkang Mountains in Hunan province at the head of a tattered force of about 1,000 men. Mao was not consciously moving the revolution to the countryside; he was simply a wounded animal fleeing to the best refuge, with the hunters in pursuit. But eventually, out of necessity, came the realization that a revolution could grow mighty in the villages. His first base was five primitive hamlets, with a total population of only about 2,000. There he began to develop his strategy and tactics of guerrilla warfare, the patterns of political organization, and the techniques of propaganda. There, too, he learned the crucial need for the good will of the peasantry.

Driven out of his mountain lair in 1928, Mao moved east to Kiangsi province. He remained there for six years, suffering from malaria (Moscow reported him dead in 1930), wrangling with his rivals, and trying to survive Chiang Kai-shek's punitive campaigns. In 1931, he was elected chairman of the first Chinese "Soviet." But the real power still rested with the successive groups of young Communists trained in Moscow and sent back to Kiangsi to translate Stalin's misconcep-

Dwarfed by a giant portrait of himself, Mao, second from left, is flanked by North Vietnam's Ho Chi Minh and Russia's Nikita S. Khrushchev as Communist leaders from Asia and Europe review a parade in Peking in 1959.

tions about China into abortive uprisings. There was also a new element in the drama: In Manchuria, in 1931, the Japanese army made its first move to fragment and conquer China.

By 1934, the Communists broke out of Chiang's iron ring. This was the beginning of their "Long March," an epic, year-long, 7,000-mile retreat that ended in Shensi province. Some 300,000 men and women began it. A year later, when they reached the barren hills of the northwest, only about 30,000 remained. Fighting a battle a day, the columns crossed turbulent rivers, climbed over the Great Snow Mountains, and stumbled across the swampy grasslands of western China.

At a congress held during the march in January, 1935, Mao won control of the party for the first time. He also came to recognize the importance of the wave of anti-Japanese sentiment sweeping the country as the Japanese gobbled up Chinese territory. He demanded an end to the civil war with Chiang Kai-shek's forces and insisted that the two deadly enemies join in fighting the still deadlier foreign foe.

Mao was to remain in the loess mountains of Shensi for a dozen years–10 of them in Yenan. This was a crucial period. Even as they fought the Japanese, the Communists set up "Liberated Areas," which after the war became their bases against Chiang Kai-shek. By 1947, Mao governed some 100,000,000 people in these immense enclaves.

In 1939, Mao divorced his third wife, Ho Tzu-chen, and married a young Shanghai actress who

Carrying flags and posters of Mao, Red Guards, the spearhead of the Cultural Revolution, parade in Peking. Girl, *right,* holds book of Mao's quotations.

This billboard with Mao's thoughts in Chinese and English was erected in Shumchun. It was big enough to be seen across the river in Hong Kong.

had come to Yenan. In the mid-1960s, under the name of Chiang Ching, she would become one of the most powerful and, some said, vengeful leaders of the Cultural Revolution. But when I met her in Yenan in 1947, I found her attractive, poised, and housewifely.

Mao's control of the party at the time was complete. From the ledge outside his cave, he could summon his companions to a conference with just a shout. There were several of them living in the caves nearby–including Liu Shao-chi, who ran the party machine and was already regarded as Mao's heir apparent, and Chou En-lai, Mao's top diplomat. Though the top leaders argued freely, it was Mao who always made the final decision. There were reverses and horrendous errors of judgment, especially on land reform. But Mao, then 54 and a man at the height of his resources, never lost his confidence. He told me his timetable for victory over Chiang, and though I doubted him at the time, he erred by only a few months. A few weeks after our talks, Chiang Kai-shek's Nationalists took Yenan. But just two years later, Peking surrendered to Mao without a shot. His armies, led by Lin Piao, were already sweeping south in pursuit of Chiang Kai-shek, who finally fled to Formosa. Mao now controlled China.

If a graph of Mao's life could be drawn, the apogee would lie somewhere in the mid-1950s. He was both the king and the philosopher of this immense nation, hundreds of millions cried his glory, and his achievements were beyond measure. The wounds of the civil, Japanese, and Korean wars were healed with miraculous speed. The country was united and well governed. After the years of stagnation, there was now a sense of purpose, enthusiasm, and great pride. Russian equipment and advisers poured into the country to produce an industrial boom. Mao was now about 60, in power, and able to do what all the other revolutionaries in China's long history never could do.

Big-character posters (Ta Tze-pao) such as this one in Canton are used to carry Mao's messages to the people. Posters are pasted one over the other and in some places are 20 or 30 thick.

But the tragedy was that he had outlived his time. He spoke of a permanent revolution, while his people yearned for a respite, and he preached a philosophy that no longer suited the new society. In the mid-1950s, Mao began to dream of a huge new effort that would convert his primitive country into a major industrial and military power.

In 1958, with great fanfare, Mao launched his "Great Leap Forward" and began a program of establishing village communes. Both soon ran into trouble. Friction with Moscow, always evident, grew steadily worse until one week in July, 1960, all the Russian advisers went home and their aid was halted. Beginning with 1959, China went through a succession of lean years, through droughts, floods, and pestilence. With acute food shortages and no funds, Peking began to retrench. At times, it looked like a fight for survival.

Also in 1959, possibly under pressure, Mao gave up active direction of the party and the state. After this, he watched with anguish as his companions whittled away at his pristine revolution with "revisionist" compromise. The great man's bitterness grew, until, in 1965, his moment of revenge arrived. Oddly, the opportunity was provided by the American build-up in Vietnam. Out of the nationwide debate on Washington's intentions and on how China could best prepare for an expected invasion, emerged Mao's incredible Cultural Revolution.

Many ingredients went into the cauldron–dreams, resentments, a dash of desperation. The errant intellectuals who had been taking potshots at him had to be punished. The young had to be saved from the corruptions of city and campus. The leaders who had become faithless had to be eliminated.

Mao poured all his genius at political warfare into this struggle. His methods were direct, violent, and usually crude, but they caught his enemies unprepared. He created the Red Guards, millions of youngsters who soon filled the streets with tumult and violence. As in the past, he allied himself with the army, or at least that part of it controlled by Lin Piao. He put the little red books of his quotations into the hands of a hundred million people, partly to produce a sort of religious fervor, but also to create a political climate in which no one could dare to stand up and oppose him.

The leaders opposed to Mao were disunited, and Mao picked them off one by one. Chief of State Liu Shao-chi spent 50 days trying to stop Mao. He tried to recruit enough members of the party's Central Committee to read Mao out of the faith. But the committeemen were intimidated by Mao's fury and Lin Piao's troops.

When the Central Committee met on Aug. 1, 1966, the only members present were those who would back the old giant. Mao beefed up the committee with loyal party members and filled the hall with a claque of youngsters. On August 5, Mao presented the audience with his own *Ta Tze-pao* (big-character poster), denouncing "those party persons in authority who have taken the capitalist path." When Liu Shao-chi rose to defend himself, the claque shouted him down. He had no friends bold enough to speak in his defense, except for Marshal Chen Yi, vice-premier and foreign minister. For his effort, Chen Yi soon found himself under attack by bands of Red Guards.

The session produced a number of significant decisions. Marshal Lin Piao replaced Liu Shao-chi as heir apparent. The seven-man group that had long ruled China was purged, and now included two of Mao's lieutenants, his former political secretary, Chen Po-ta, and the intelligence specialist Kang Sheng. Most important, it proclaimed the principle, "Do not be afraid of disorder," and ordered the nation's officialdom to stay out of the way of the rampaging youngsters.

In the next few weeks, the Red Guards swept across the nation like wildfire. They stormed party offices and manhandled party bosses opposed to Mao. They covered the walls of China with millions of big-character posters that denounced officials. They paraded the "enemies" through the street, their heads forced down in penitence, derisive signs on their chests, dunce caps on their heads.

Not until late fall of 1966 did opposition begin to emerge in the provinces. It was disunited, it had no national leader, and it certainly had no program. Some of the opposing generals and party bosses may have felt that, if allowed to have his way, Mao would tear the nation apart. But for most it was just a matter of survival.

Thus, in one province after another, local Red Guards, obedient to the provincial boss, battled Maoist Red Guards. The "workers' militia" in some areas beat up Red Guards trying to enter factories to "make revolution." And in some provinces, peasants and former servicemen went to war against the Maoist youngsters. The confusion was compounded when all of them, friend or foe, called themselves Maoists.

Some provinces, mostly along China's borders, defied orders from the Maoist center. At other places, local bosses began to woo the workers by giving them unaccustomed wage increases, better housing, and extra welfare benefits. Moreover, they encouraged the workers by the thousands to go to Peking to "present grievances." This added to the strain on the railroad system, already heavily taxed by the movement of millions of Red Guards. The opposition was obviously trying to stop Mao by compounding the chaos he began.

An effort to deify Mao was part of the Cultural Revolution, as typified by these busts awaiting shipment in a warehouse.

The maneuver was devilishly clever. A provincial governor could take chances on national anarchy, but Mao, who still tried to govern the state, could not. In January, 1967, Mao was driven to desperate steps. He helped loyal Red Guards and army units throw out the party machine in Shanghai. The party leaders were displaced by a "revolutionary rebel committee." At about the same time, Mao asked the army to come in and help him crush the opposition. With the help of the military, he seized power in four carefully selected provinces, one each in the east, west, north, and south. But the opposition was equal to the challenge. It began to stage its own "power seizures" and set up its own "revolutionary committees," which promptly turned on the Maoists. Bloody battles were fought.

The extremists in Mao's "inner circle," who included Chen Po-ta, Kang Sheng, and Mao's wife, finally gave in to the entreaties of Premier Chou En-lai. On Sept. 1, 1967, the civilians, including the Red Guards, were ordered to turn in their weapons to the army, which was charged with keeping the peace. The Red Guards were also ordered to return to their cities and schools, where all formal education had been suspended since late May, 1966. Workers in the factories were ordered to stay on their jobs, and the peasants were forbidden to go into the cities to "make revolution."

The new turn produced a host of unanswerable questions. Was the old giant in retreat? Was this yet another aspect of his famous tactical program–one step back to make two steps forward? Or did he feel that he had achieved his main goal of destroying his enemies in the party leadership and could now, at a slower pace, create Maoist "revolutionary rebel committees" in the hinterland? Whatever the answers, Mao still dominated the nation's landscape.

But even if Mao was still gaining ground in his last battle for China, it was certain to be an impermanent victory. Now, for the first time in his long career, he was in conflict with history. In effect, he was calling on his people to march forward to their glorious past, and this ran against all the instincts and urges of the new society.

A titan, he had united, inspired, and built up this immense nation. But if in 1957 China seemed to stand on the threshold of greatness, in 1967 Mao and his aides had to plead with the people to stop fighting each other. The strong government it had in the 1950s had been badly weakened, and the party lay shattered. The faith many had in the integrity and competence of their governors had been undermined. National decision-making had been postponed, for the policymakers were too busy settling quarrels all over China.

Mao's Cultural Revolution had one more crucial by-product. Until 1965, the state he created had been run by the Old Guard, men from the caves of Yenan. They jealously had allowed no young men near the sources of power. But after the upheaval began, these oldsters were eliminated one by one. Liu Shao-chi, a stern ascetic, was presented to the nation as an old rake. The party's general secretary, Teng Hsiao-ping, was pictured as a bridge addict who flew his cronies by private plane from Peking to wherever he was for a game of bridge. The sordid list went on and on. But the trouble was that once this top echelon was destroyed, there were few tested men left to govern the nation and rebuild what Mao had brought down.

In 1967, younger men were elbowing their way up–Mao's quotations on their lips, ambition in their hearts, and violence in their methods. These hopefuls made alliances with the Red Guard and army factions, and engaged in demagoguery and intrigue. Other aspirants for power would yet come from the provinces or from the army, disjointed but still the most powerful political force in the land.

Thus, a future of lengthy turmoil has been handed to his people by one of the giants of our time–the man who, in unifying China, achieved what few kings could, but who then tore down his own creation because he thought it imperfect. A dreamer, an incurable romantic with long memories, a political fanatic who wanted to purify a revolution gone corrupt–which one was he? Whatever the answer, only in Greek dramas–or in the history of China's own peasant revolts–can one find a figure more tragic.

See also Section One, PAUL-HENRI SPAAK: FOCUS ON THE WORLD and Section Three, ASIA; CHINA; COMMUNISM.

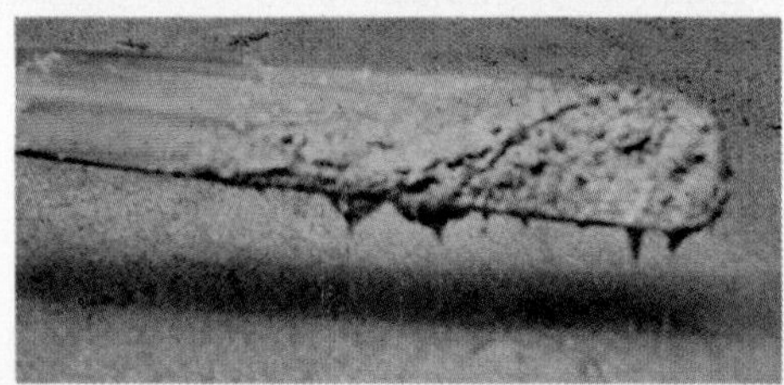

UNSAFE
FOR
SWIMMING
MICH. DEPT. OF HEALTH

A Year Book Special Report

By Barry Commoner

The Killing of A Great Lake

The unwitting destruction of Lake Erie is a tragic example of how man's lack of knowledge of his natural environment can rob him of the precious resources on which human survival depends

The Great Lakes, the huge inland seas that lie on the boundary between the United States and Canada, have long provided man with wealth and beauty. But now, because of man's folly, one of them–Lake Erie–is becoming a wasteland. Listless waves lap along its shore, sucking in and out among the slimy green rocks, deserted beaches, and oily pilings of seldom-used piers.

In recent years, Lake Erie has deteriorated so badly that the game fish that once abounded there are almost entirely gone, and beaches are open only occasionally. Swimming is often curtailed because of high bacterial counts in the water and the revolting stench of rotting algae and dead fish on the beaches. Boat owners are hesitant to take their craft into areas where oily material will cling to the hull.

In some parts of the lake, the waters are a murky green from algae that thrive on the wastes dumped into the water. During the summer months, the western basin of Lake Erie contains a mass of algae that sometimes covers 800 square miles and has a thickness of two feet.

The variety of floating and rotting wastes is a constant reminder that man can indeed kill a lake. Much of the pollution comes from the large industrial cities near and along its southern and western shores. Detroit dumps in wastes from its automotive, chemical, paper, and steel plants, as well as from its petroleum refineries. Toledo adds wastes from glass industries and more automotive, petroleum, and steel plants. Cleveland also pours in acids, oils, cyanides, and phenols from automotive, chemical, and steel industries, while Erie throws in pulp and paper wastes. Buffalo contributes pollution from flour mills and from chemical, portland cement, and steel plants. Added to all this is the common refuse of every urban center–treated and untreated human sewage–and fertilizers, insecticides, and weedkillers in the run-off water from the surrounding farmlands.

The lake is threatened with death. It is slowly choking from its heavily polluted tributaries and shoreline. Water experts warn there is little relief in sight. Some even say the lake is dying so fast it will soon be an aquatic desert–America's Dead Sea.

Lake Erie was born about 12,000 years ago after a great advancing ice sheet gouged out the beds of the Great Lakes and then melted and filled the newly made depressions with clear water. The biological life of the lake began as soon as minerals from the surrounding rocks and soil washed into the water. Microscopic plants–algae–grew and reproduced by using hydrogen from water, nitrogen and phosphorus from dissolved nitrate and phosphate salts, and carbon from the air.

Algae can sustain a complex web of life. Microscopic animals eat the algae, digesting the algal organic substance and reconverting it into their own. Fish, in turn, feed on the microscopic animals. When the fish and other living things die, their organic substances are attacked by the bacteria of decay. This process returns the carbon, nitrogen, and phosphorus to inorganic forms–carbon dioxide, nitrate, and phosphate–that can support the growth of fresh algae and thus complete the cycle.

The first recorded observations of Lake Erie in the 17th and 18th centuries showed that it supported a large and varied population of fish. The waters of the lake were clear, for the nutrient salts leaching into it were enough to produce only a limited crop of algae. The animals that fed on the algae also kept it in check.

Fish gave the first warning that the life of Lake Erie was changing. Until 1900, each of a number of valuable fish species–sturgeon, whitefish, cisco, northern pike, walleye, and blue pike–yielded annual crops of 1,000,000 pounds or more. After the turn of the century, there were successive reports of abrupt reductions in these fish crops. Typical is the history of the cisco catch. From 1885 to 1925 it averaged about 25,000,000 pounds annually–about half the total Lake Erie fish crop. In 1926, the cisco catch suddenly dropped to about 6,000,000 pounds. With some fluctuations, the catch has since declined even more, reaching a scant 1,000 pounds in 1965. Today, the total Lake Erie catch is

The author:
Barry Commoner is director of the Center for the Biology of Natural Systems at Washington University, St. Louis, Mo., which studies the effects of contamination on the environment. He also is professor of plant physiology and chairman of the university's Department of Botany.

about the same as it was in 1900, but the more valuable fish have been replaced by "rough" fish–sheepshead, catfish, smelt, and carp. As a result, the money value of the catch has declined sharply.

In 1928, the Buffalo Society of Natural Sciences made a detailed study of the lake to find reasons for the decline in the cisco catch. One suspected cause was pollution from sewage and industrial wastes from the cities on the lakeshore. But the report concluded, "... It is possible to safely say that the lake as a whole is remarkably free from pollution. In harbors and along the shore in places the water is often badly polluted, but these are purely local problems and affect in no way the lake as a whole."

Another suspected cause of the fish kills was that the lake water contained insufficient oxygen to support the more active species. The 1928 survey did find that the water was sometimes less than saturated with oxygen but concluded that the deficit was an expected conse-

The Great Lakes

Direction of flow

Water depth (feet): 0-100 100-400 over 400

Population: one dot equals 30,000 persons

0 Miles 100 200 300

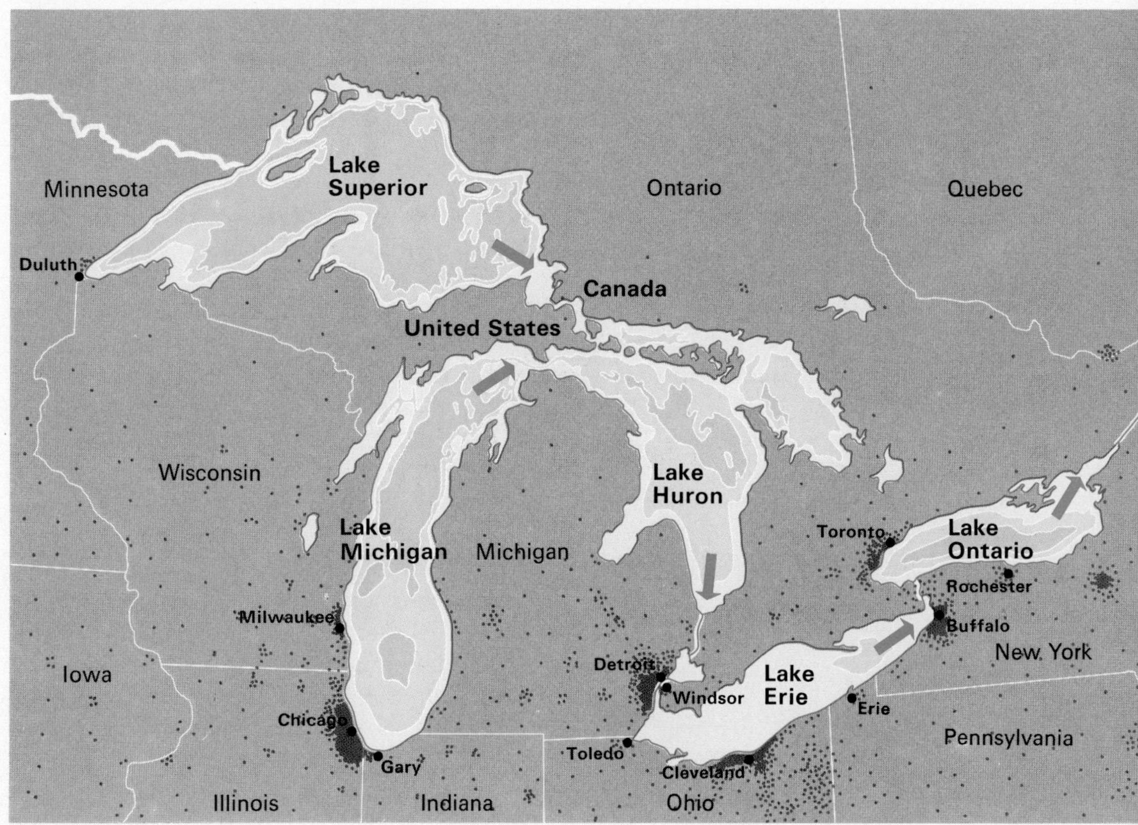

The Change in Lake Erie's Fish Production

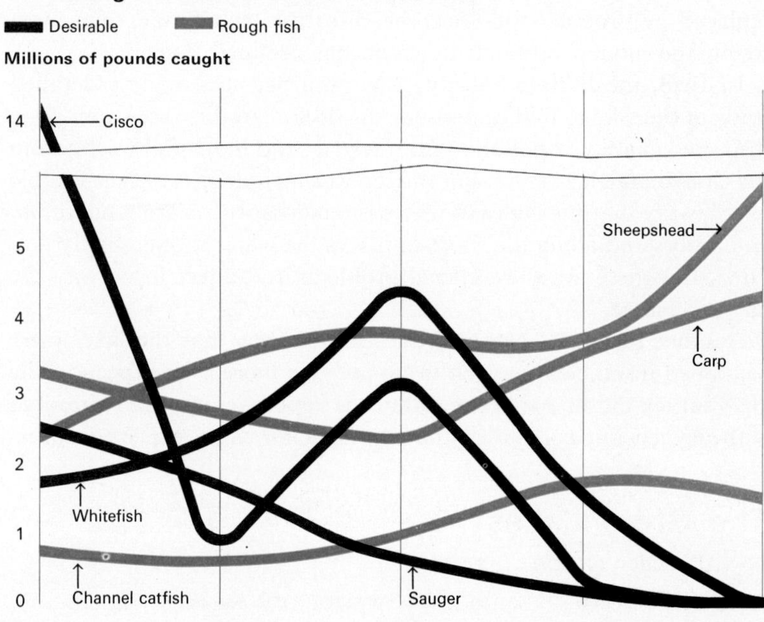

Dead fish on the shore of Lake Erie is a dramatic reminder that man can indeed kill a lake.

quence of biological activity in the lake and was not sufficient to account for the loss of fish. We now are reasonably certain, at least in this respect, that the 1928 report was wrong.

The oxygen level of lake water is a sensitive index of pollution. Raw, untreated sewage contributes a large amount of organic matter to the water. The organic wastes are broken down by bacteria of decay, a process that consumes oxygen. The more organic matter in the lake, the greater the amount of oxygen needed to convert it to inorganic salts. This biological oxygen demand (BOD) is a useful measure of the organic pollution in the water. Oxygen enters the water from the air and is also produced by the photosynthetic activity of algae. But only a limited amount of oxygen can be dissolved in a given volume of water. If the water contains enough organic matter to generate a large BOD, oxygen will be used up so fast that the oxygen content of the water will fall below the saturation level.

Certain features of water movement in a lake also affect the oxygen content. Oxygen enters the water from its surface, where contact is made with the air and where light, which is necessary for photosynthetic oxygen production, is most intense. Oxygen reaches the deeper parts of a lake only when there is good top-to-bottom circulation of the water. Such circulation is easily attained where a lake is shallow, as in Lake Erie's western basin, and where wave action churns the entire water mass to circulate it. In deeper lake water, such as Lake Erie's central basin, this vertical circulation takes place only intermittently.

In the winter, especially with ice covering the lake, there is little circulation, and oxygen becomes depleted in the lower levels of the water. In the spring, the surface water warms up and begins to sink. This movement sets up a vertical circulation that is greatly assisted by the strong spring winds. Oxygen then becomes evenly distributed through the depth of the lake.

When summer comes, the warmest water is near the surface of the lake, and the cooler water below is separated from it by a narrow zone in which the water temperature shows a sharp drop. This separating zone is called the *thermocline* and is an effective barrier between the upper and lower waters of the lake. Oxygen is readily stirred into the water above the thermocline but fails to penetrate into the underlying water. Sewage wastes, which consume oxygen as they decay, further increase the BOD of the lake water and produce low oxygen levels near the lake bottom in the summer months. Rapid consumption of oxygen in the deep lake water, or on the lake bottom, may reduce the oxygen content of the water below the thermocline to the vanishing point.

Fish that seek the bottom water because of its cool temperatures may find insufficient oxygen there. In Lake Erie, many fish spend their first months of growth on the lake bottom, where they die if the oxygen content of the water becomes too low. This helps to explain the near-disappearance of the lake's desirable fish, which require more oxygen than the "rough" varieties.

May fly nymphs, *top,* and adult May flies, *above,* were once a plentiful food for fish. In the changing lake, they have been replaced by bloodworms, *below.*

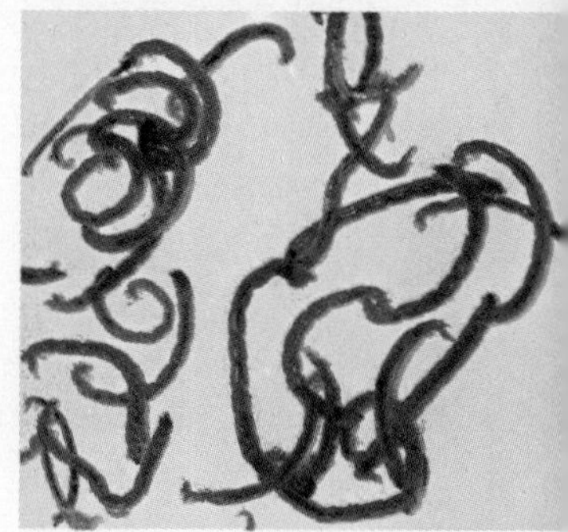

In late August, 1953, a hot month with little wind, the western basin of Lake Erie, where the waters are usually well mixed with oxygen throughout the year, experienced one of its occasional periods of thermal stratification. The warm upper water was separated from the bottom layer by a thermocline. N. Wilson Britt of Ohio State University's Institute of Hydrobiology cruised among the islands of the western basin recording water temperatures, measuring oxygen content, and studying samples of the lake bottom. His records show that the water at the bottom of the lake was badly depleted of oxygen.

As an ecologist, Britt was concerned not only with the physical environment in the lake but also with its affect on the lake's living creatures. He had a particular interest in the May fly, which was long a familiar summer feature of the Lake Erie area. Each summer lacy-winged adult May flies emerged from the lake in hordes as the May fly nymphs at the lake bottom matured. Once on the wing, they congregated around nearby lights during the summer nights. May flies, adult and nymphs, are a favorite food of the lake fish. In fact, the "gray drake," a famous dry fly among fishermen, is made in imitation of the adult May fly. But May fly nymphs can live only in bottom areas that are well supplied with oxygen.

A number of careful bottom surveys of the western basin of Lake Erie, beginning in 1929, with the last one in the spring of 1953, had shown that May fly nymphs were the most common lake bottom animals. Counts of 300 to 500 nymphs per square meter were typical. On Sept. 5, 1953, Britt dredged up some sediment from the lake

Outfall from a sewage-treatment plant on Detroit River, *left,* merging with industrial wastes from River Rouge, will finally reach Lake Erie.

At Cleveland, a major Lake Erie harbor, the Cuyahoga River spews its polluted waters into the lake.

bottom and washed it on a fine-mesh screen. He identified and counted the animals remaining on the screen. There were 93 May fly nymphs in the sample, indicating a normal count of 465 nymphs per square meter–but they were all dead and partly decomposed. Since decomposition would be rapid in the warm summer temperatures of the lake, Britt concluded that the nymphs "had been dead only a few hours, or at most only a few days." They had died, he decided, because of the brief thermal stratification and the resulting low oxygen content of the water between September 1 and 4.

From September 14 to 26, a total of 61 bottom samples were taken in the area. Where, in previous years, biologists had found hundreds of May fly nymphs per square meter of lake bottom, there was now an average of only 44. Britt had recorded a vital turning point in the biology of the western basin of Lake Erie. Although the May fly nymphs made a brief recovery in 1954, they essentially disappeared thereafter. Clouds of May flies are no longer seen in the summer nights, and the fish that once fed on them are deprived of a vital source of nutrition. The May fly nymph population on the lake bottom has been replaced by bloodworms and fingernail clams–animals that do not have such high oxygen requirements.

Although the 1928 study of the lake had recorded no bottom areas depleted of oxygen, investigations between 1955 and 1964 showed that serious oxygen deficiencies now clearly existed. In 1964, one-fourth of the total lake bottom fell to two parts of oxygen or less per million parts of water during the summer thermal stratification. Only in the eastern basin were fish able to find cool waters well-saturated with oxygen throughout the year. This area is so deep that the water contains sufficient oxygen near the bottom even during the summer stratification.

Some of the oxygen loss in Lake Erie results from the sad fact that our efforts to reduce pollution by means of modern sewage-treatment plants have backfired on us; in alleviating one part of the pollution problem, we have created another. In effect, a treatment plant domesticates the microbial activities that degrade wastes in natural streams and lakes. Sewage treatment involves a primary step in

The run-off of fertilizer, insecticides, and sprays from farmland bordering rivers and streams, *above*, contributes to pollution of Lake Erie, as does this paper mill, *right*, on the banks of Chagrin River.

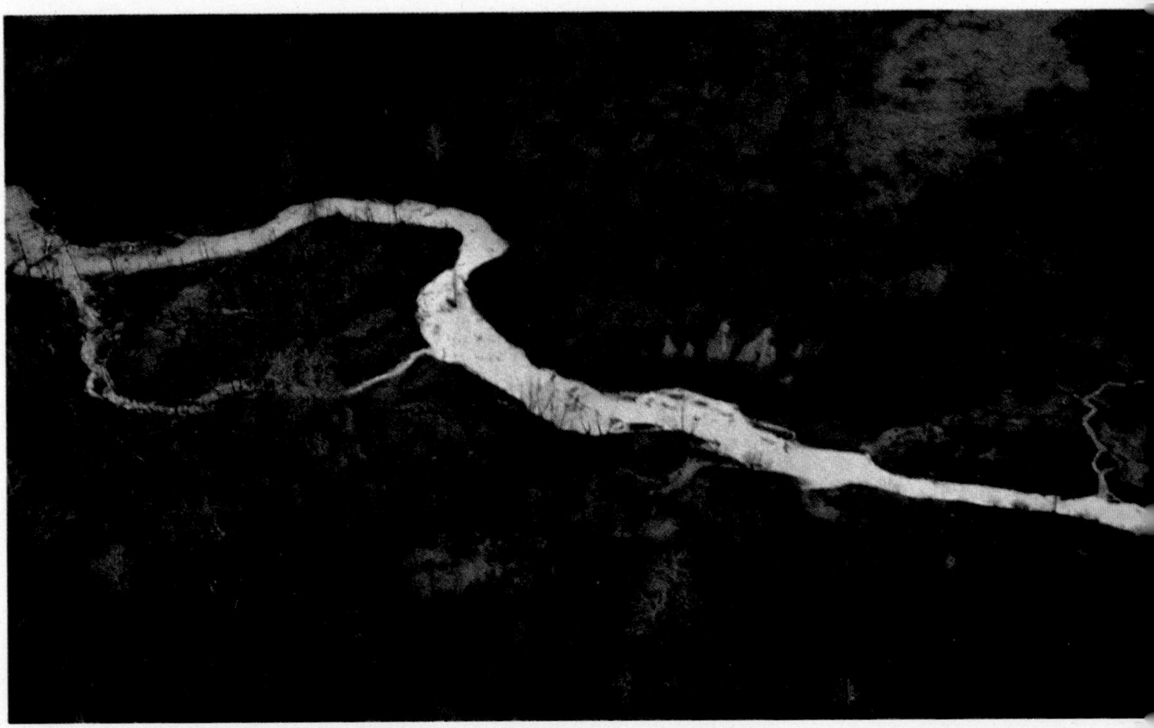

Five chemical industries pour wastes into Fields Brook, *above,* near Ashtabula, Ohio, turning it white or sometimes green or red. Detergents foam from a sewage-treatment plant into the Cuyahoga River, *left,* near Akron, Ohio.

which indigestible solids are removed, and secondary treatment in a tank or pond rich in microbial decay organisms. During secondary treatment, the organic materials, usually artificially supplied with oxygen, are converted by microbial oxidation to inorganic substances. If the system works well, the resulting water is a clear, dilute solution of the inorganic products, of which nitrate and phosphate are most important to the Lake Erie story. The inorganic products of sewage treatment, now free of BOD, presumably can be released to rivers and lakes without causing any immediate drain on the oxygen in them.

About 10,000,000 people live in communities that discharge their sewage into Lake Erie or its tributaries. Of this total population, about 45 per cent are served by sewage systems that use both primary and secondary treatment; 50 per cent have systems in which the sewage receives only primary treatment; and 5 per cent have sewage systems that provide no treatment. The total mass of organic waste that reaches Lake Erie each year requires, for its conversion to inorganic salts, the consumption of about 180,000,000 pounds of oxygen. Most of this oxygen demand comes from sewage waste.

The recent oxygen losses in the lake can be only partly explained by the action involved in oxidizing organic wastes dumped into the lake. Detailed measurements of the 1964 summer oxygen deficit permit us to calculate the minimum amount of oxygen that would have had to be withdrawn from the water to bring about this deficit.

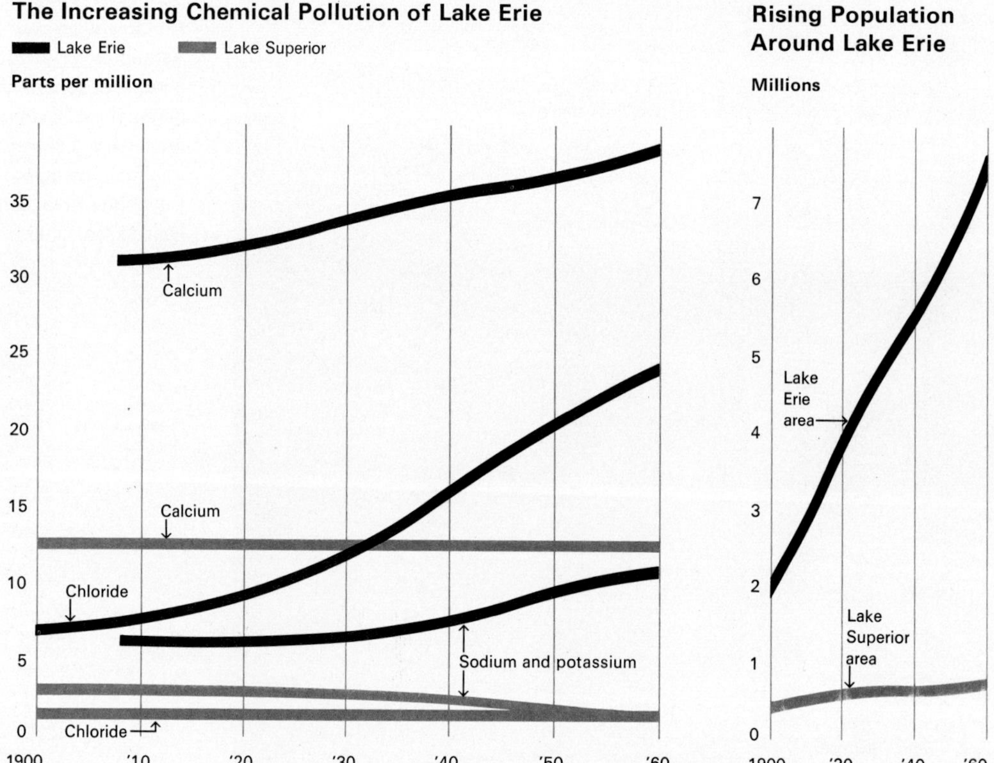

The oxygen deficit in the bottom water of the central basin alone, in 1964, was 270,000,000 pounds of oxygen. This deficit developed over a period of several weeks in only a part of the total mass of lake water and must have been partly mitigated by oxygen entering the lake water. If the organic wastes reaching the lake in a year can account for a calculated consumption of only 180,000,000 pounds of oxygen, there must be a much larger source of oxygen demand somewhere in the lake.

In seeking it, we need to recall that an effective primary and secondary sewage-treatment plant will convert nearly all (about 90 per cent) of the organic matter originally present in the raw sewage into inorganic products, especially nitrate and phosphate. These leave the treatment plant in its outflow water and eventually reach the lake. But most of these inorganic products do not, as once believed, flow out of the lake and into the sea. Instead, they are reconverted into organic matter, much of which remains in the lake, where it contributes to the huge demand for oxygen that has been so disastrous.

Eutrophication

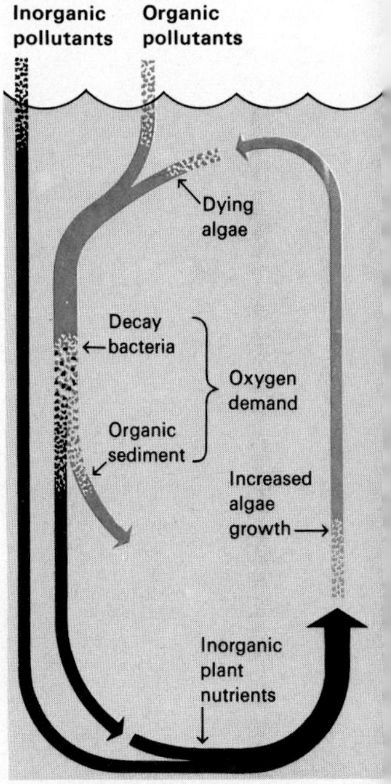

Inorganic pollutants
Organic pollutants
Dying algae
Decay bacteria
Oxygen demand
Organic sediment
Increased algae growth
Inorganic plant nutrients

The eutrophication, or overfertilization, of lakes is caused by pollutants and the cycle of algae growth and decay.

Algae are crucial in this process. Nitrate and phosphate are necessary for the growth of all green plants and, for this reason, are major constituents of fertilizer. Dumped into the lake, they fertilize the growth of algae that readily convert these inorganic materials into their own organic cell-substance. This process, called *eutrophication* (overfertilization), is clearly responsible for much of Lake Erie's oxygen deficit. One of the symptoms of the sickness has been the appearance each summer of huge algal "blooms." In vast areas of the lake, algal growths, under the impact of excessive nutrients, give it the appearance and consistency of pea soup. In recent years, great mounds of algae have even washed up on beaches to foul the shoreline. Algal blooms grow quickly; they die off equally fast and sink into the lake, fouling it with algal organic matter.

The amount of phosphate reaching the lake from treated wastes and other sources has been estimated at 174,000 pounds a day, and the amount that leaves the lake via the Niagara River has been measured as 24,000 pounds daily. The difference, 150,000 pounds of phosphate a day, or almost 55,000,000 pounds a year, stays in the lake in the overgrowths of algae stimulated by the excess nutrients.

The annual BOD resulting from organic matter produced by the lake's algae–at least in part from nutrients provided by treated organic wastes–causes an oxygen demand 27 times greater than the annual BOD of the organic matter that reaches the lake directly from waste systems. Thus, the resynthesis of organic matter by the algae undoes the work of the sewage and industrial waste-treatment systems and renders ineffective their efficient conversion of waste organic matter to inorganic salts.

The farmland surrounding the lake is another source of nutrients that stimulate algal overgrowth. Though the proportion varies with local soil conditions, probably about 10 to 25 per cent of a chemical

Unsightly algae that have washed ashore cover a beach on Kelly's Island in Lake Erie, *left and above.*

Algae grow profusely in the West Branch of the Black River, one of Lake Erie's tributaries, *below.* White pleasure craft moored off one of the Bass Islands, *right,* stands out sharply against the water turned pea-green by the algae.

fertilizer fails to enter the crop and drains out of the soil into rivers and lakes. This is especially true of nitrogen, but eroding soil also carries with it some of the added phosphates. Concentrated chemical fertilizers, with great amounts of nitrogen and phosphates, are plentiful and inexpensive. Their use has raised U.S. crop production to record heights since 1940.

Unfortunately, an inventory of such plant nutrients reaching Lake Erie from surrounding farms is not yet available. A 1947 study of Wisconsin lakes, however, showed that nitrogen run-off into the water from a square mile of farmland was equivalent to the annual sewage output of 750 people. The Lake Erie basin contains about 30,000 square miles of farmland. On the basis of the Wisconsin data, we would expect the nitrogen run-off into Lake Erie to be equivalent to the sewage nitrogen produced by a population of about 22,500,000 people. This is more than twice the actual population of the surrounding communities. Even allowing for a heavier use of fertilizer in the Wisconsin dairyland, it seems quite probable that nitrogen run-off from the farmland around Lake Erie might contribute about one-third, or even one-half, of the nitrogen that pollutes the lake. The remainder comes from municipal and industrial wastes.

The nitrogen and phosphorus salts added to the lake finally accumulate in dead algae, which, as they die, sink to the bottom–where their substance remains. Thus, instead of Lake Erie forming a waterway for sending wastes to the sea, it has become a trap that is gradually storing much of the waste material dumped into it over the years –a kind of huge underwater cesspool.

This situation is clearly reflected in the state of the lake bottom. Soundings show that most of the lake bottom is now covered with mud 30 to 125 feet thick, in which are found huge concentrations of phosphorus and nitrogen compounds. Thus, the bottom of the lake has accumulated a vast reservoir of potential plant nutrients.

Sediment from industrial wastes and decaying algae leave sludge banks such as this at Cattaraugus Creek, about 30 miles south of Buffalo, N.Y. Footprints indicate its depth.

The chemistry of the mud on the lake bottom adds another aspect to the Lake Erie story. A careful study of lake mud in England was made in 1941 by Clifford H. Mortimer. Though no such detailed study of Lake Erie mud has yet been completed, one of the lakes Mortimer examined was in a eutrophic condition of the same general state as Lake Erie–that is, it received a large amount of plant nutrients in run-off from the surrounding land, developed a heavy crop of algae, and became oxygen-depleted in the summer months, when thermal stratification separated the bottom water from the top layer. Mortimer found that the bottom mud of this lake, Esthwaite Water, underwent profound changes when the bottom became oxygen-depleted.

Most important was the behavior of iron. Two main forms of iron compounds are known to chemists. In one type, the iron atom carries a double positive electric charge. This type of iron is designated as ferrous iron, or iron II. In the other type, the iron atom has a triple positive charge and is known as ferric iron, or iron III. The salts formed by iron II are soluble in water, while iron III forms insoluble salts and tends to develop firm, insoluble combinations with a wide variety of substances. Iron II can exist only in the absence of oxygen. In fact, when iron II is exposed to oxygen, it is converted to iron III, and when oxygen is removed from the vicinity of iron III, it may, under certain conditions, be converted to iron II. Such conditions occur when hydrogen-rich organic compounds, such as those found in wastes or dead algae, are present.

Mortimer discovered that when oxygen is present in the water at the lake bottom, the mud is covered by a skin of material in which all the iron is of the iron III form. Its insolubility prevents the material in the underlying mud from dissolving into the lake water. When the bottom water loses all its oxygen, however, the iron III in the mud's surface skin is converted to iron II. Then the materials in the underlying mud are freed and may readily dissolve. Among the materials thus liberated into the water of the lake are the salts of nitrogen and phosphate–in other words, plant nutrients.

Corresponding research on Lake Erie mud, although much less detailed, substantiates the importance of the Esthwaite Water phenomenon Mortimer described in 1941. Since the area was first settled, Lake Erie has been increasingly burdened with organic wastes and with inorganic nutrients that the lake's algae convert to organic materials. These organic materials would long ago have asphyxiated most of the lake's living things had it not been for the peculiar power of iron III to form insoluble complexes with the materials of the bottom mud. The protective skin of iron III has held the enormous accumulation of potential oxygen-demanding material in the muddy bottom of the lake. But this protective skin can remain intact only so long as there is sufficient oxygen present in the water over the mud.

Lake Bottom Breakup

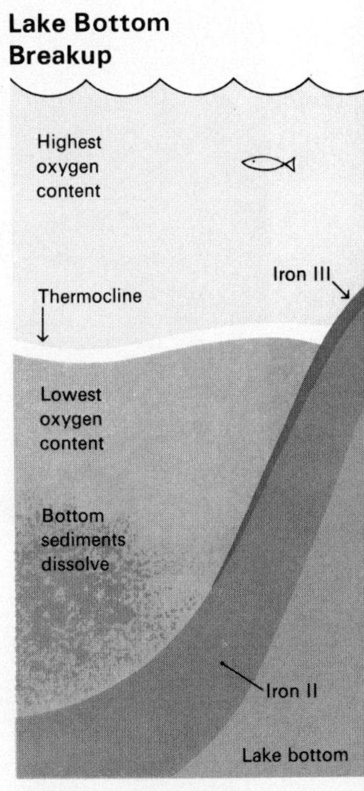

Wastes that settle on the bottom of Lake Erie are held in the mud by a layer of iron III salts. But when the water is depleted of oxygen, the protective layer breaks up, and the wastes enter the water again.

For many years this was so, and the layer of iron III held the accumulating mud materials out of the lake water. But a serious oxygen depletion now occurs in the summer months. As a result, the protective layer of iron III has begun to break down–exposing the lake to the heavy impact of the accumulated algal nutrients long stored in the mud. If the process continues, we may face a sudden biological cataclysm that will exhaust, for a time, most of the oxygen in the greater part of the lake water. Such a catastrophe would make the lake's present difficulties seem slight by comparison.

Thus, the summer depletion of oxygen at the bottom of Lake Erie's central and western basins not only kills May fly nymphs and fish embryos, but it may also release into the lake, from the vast accumulation in the bottom mud, nutrients that will add enormously to the already serious overfertilization of the lake.

The historical record of the algal population of Lake Erie has shown a continuing increase. This record can be found in the tabulations of the Cleveland Waterworks, which since 1919 has made a daily count of the number of algal cells found in one cubic centimeter of Lake Erie

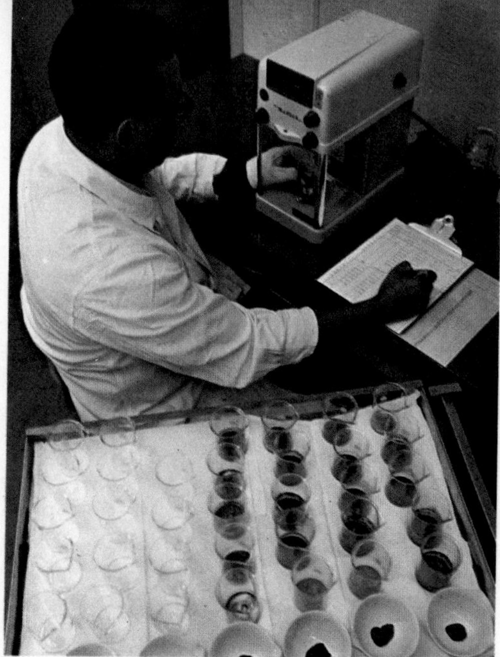

Federal Water Pollution Control Administration engineers take daily samples of bottom from Lake Erie. These are analyzed at a laboratory in Cleveland, Ohio.

water at the point of the city's water supply intake. These counts show that, since 1927, the cell population has shown a marked increase. Since 1960, the rate of increase has accelerated.

The algal counts also show that in recent years increasing numbers of blue-green algae have appeared in the lake. This adds to the lake's troubles, for unlike other algae, the blue-green types can absorb nitrogen from the air, converting it into their own organic substance, thereby adding to the oxygen-demanding burden of organic waste.

In the last few years, efforts have been made to control the pollution of Lake Erie. The Federal Water Pollution Control Act provides funds for construction of new waste-treatment systems and improvement of old plants. City and state agencies have joined with federal departments in a series of conferences on the problem. In August, 1967, the Department of the Interior created a task force to make recommendations for a program of controlling eutrophication.

At best, all these efforts aimed at cutting back the amount of pollutants that are added to the overburdened waters can be only a small start toward the solution of the Lake Erie problem. At worst, they may fail to come to grips with the problem at all.

Obviously, we need to know in greater detail what pollutants enter the lake and where they come from. The general pattern of nitrate and phosphate pollution is already clear. One-third or more of the nitrogen enters the lake from fertilizer run-off, and the rest from municipal and industrial wastes. In the case of phosphate, about 70 to 90 per cent comes from municipal sewage, particularly from synthetic detergents. Phosphate compounds are incorporated into these soap substitutes to improve their cleansing action. Unfortunately, there are no detailed records of the increase of phosphate for Lake Erie itself, but the national figures are revealing–and startling. In 1900, U.S. sewage systems as a whole discharged fewer than 10,000,000 pounds of phosphorus annually. This figure increased gradually, reaching about

40,000,000 pounds in 1940. But from then on–following the appearance of synthetic detergents on the market–the phosphorus output of municipal sewage rose so sharply that it was more than 250,000,000 pounds a year by 1964.

Phosphate levels could be drastically reduced by forbidding the further use of phosphate-containing detergents or by removing phosphate in the course of sewage treatment. Both phosphate and nitrate could be reduced by adding a third stage to the sewage-treatment plant. This would remove soluble salts from the outflow water, using the same kinds of desalting techniques that were developed to produce fresh water from seawater. These "advanced waste-treatment" systems would probably cost about five times more to operate than good current primary-secondary treatment plants. And, of course, they would require huge initial expenditures for their construction.

There is no technical control measure in sight, however, for that part of the nitrogenous wastes that originates in the run-off and evaporation of fertilizer from farmlands. The only way to reduce this form of pollution is to regulate the amounts of fertilizer used by farms in the lake drainage basin. But intensive use of cheap chemical fertilizer is the farmer's most profitable way to invest his available capital, and a huge chemical industry has been created by this demand. Thus, the economic and political difficulties involved in controlling fertilizer run-off will be enormous.

Unfortunately, any effort to halt new pollution and "flush out" the lake, however enormous a task, would still leave Lake Erie in a badly polluted condition. The sediments accumulated in the lake bottom from a century of pollution would remain to be dealt with.

The story of Lake Erie is not a happy one. We have used this great national–and international–resource to build an important part of the nation's wealth. But our stewardship has been grossly irresponsible. For nearly 100 years we have used the lake as a depository for agricultural, urban, and industrial wastes. We were not aware, until recently, that these wastes were gradually accumulating in the lake bottom. Changes such as those that have occurred in Lake Erie are also appearing in Lake Michigan and Lake Ontario. The mounting burden of wastes is putting stresses on rivers and lakes everywhere. A 1966 report of the Government's National Research Council warned that in 20 years the anticipated biological oxygen demand of the nation's municipal wastes will become equal to the oxygen available in the entire summertime flow of the nation's river systems.

The deterioration of Lake Erie warns of a great impending crisis in our environment, one that threatens to destroy the suitability of the earth for human habitation. It is a crisis born of our unwitting destruction of the natural system that supports us. The lake damage suggests that the conviction that science and technology can "conquer" nature is indeed a dangerous illusion. If we are to survive, we must remake our urban, industrial, and agricultural technologies so that they will conform to the unconquerable demands of the natural environment on which human welfare and survival depend.

A Year Book Special Report

By Leonard G. Feather

The Pop Music Scene

Today's bright young songwriters are fast making a forgotten street of Tin Pan Alley and yesterday's moon-June-spoon ballads

Have you heard the latest smash hit by the Doors? Are you keeping up with the newest creations of the Turtles, the Tokens, the Seeds, the Happening, the Who, the Buckinghams, the Jefferson Airplane, Moby Grape, the Canned Heat, the Love Generation, Country Joe and the Fish, the Grateful Dead, Booker T. and the M.G.'s, the Monkees?

If these names mean nothing to you, color yourself red for embarrassment and shape yourself square–for these and others like them are the improbable names of only a few of the offspring of a bright new generation of pop musicians.

Today, the music of young America is no longer controlled by middle-aged Tin Pan Alley publishers who had determined what song would be plugged next week. There are new administrators;

almost all are under 30 years of age, some under 20. So many new performers were flooding the market in 1967 that disk jockeys could not keep pace. They were inundated with about 150 new single records every week, and up to 100 new album releases.

For all practical purposes, the mythical Tin Pan Alley, long a symbol of music as big business, is a forgotten street. Broad new highways are being built that carry an immense load of teens-to-20s traffic.

What about today's music–which many adults find so puzzling and often annoying? Where did it come from? What distinguishes its sounds and lyrics from the music that preceded it? What is the significance of the music and lyrics? Does it have any real quality? Why should anyone but a mop-topped teeny bopper take it seriously?

The answers to these questions are often more complex than is readily apparent to the older generation, and I will deal with all of them in the course of this article. But one point should be made at the outset: the new music is the most important vehicle that a large segment of today's young people uses to express its thoughts and feelings. While it is true that much of the new music may be melodically, rhythmically, and harmonically valueless, it is also true that some of it is fresh, stimulating, and wholly original, and that all of it reflects the young culture of today, a culture that is quite different from almost everything that preceded it.

Said no less an authority than Leonard Bernstein, the distinguished musical director of the New York Philharmonic, on a CBS-TV special in April, 1967: "What I like of the new pop music is maybe 5 per cent of the whole output . . . it's mostly trash. But that 5 per cent is so exciting, and . . . so significant, that it claims the attention of every thinking person."

One difficulty in approaching the new pop style is that many adults tend to herd all of the new music under a single umbrella labeled rock 'n' roll. But rock 'n' roll is only one aspect of the scene, and rock music itself comprises a variety of shapes and styles.

The dangers of oversimplification can easily be demonstrated. All one has to do is listen to the music of a dozen top-selling artists in any given week or just review some of the terms that have been coined to describe the many forms and variations that are involved: rhythm and blues, psychedelic sounds, the Motown sound, folk rock, raga rock, Latin rock, gospel rock, and perhaps a dozen more.

Many of these terms are indefinable, for every day the boundary lines between them become thinner. And this puzzles adults who grew up in a day when popular music was made up of clearly separate categories labeled jazz, ballads, swing, and folk music.

The mingling of these categories is an important aspect of the present scene. For example, Ray Charles, the famed "rhythm and blues" man, has actually incorporated elements of almost all the categories into his singing and piano playing. Thus, any attempt to neatly pigeonhole today's pop music would be doomed to failure.

The author:
Leonard G. Feather is a composer and music critic whose books include the *New Encyclopedia of Jazz.* He also is a regular contributor of music articles to *The World Book Year Book.*

The independent attitude of the young writers, performers, and producers has been a key factor in the widening of the generation gap. No longer do the new vocalists sing a melody or mouth a lyric built around sugar-coated sentiments embodied in rhymes involving "moon-June-spoon-croon." No longer do they wait for a Tin Pan Alley or Hollywood songwriter, no matter how gifted, to dictate what they shall hear or perform.

Instead, they pick up their own guitars and devise their own melodies to lyrics that reflect their own ideas. Sometimes they form their own publishing and recording companies. The products of their work are usually far more honest reflections of their lives and values than any "songsmith"–and that word is itself significant, for it suggests one who works by formula–was interested in producing.

The young man or woman of today is often unprecedentedly sensitive in evaluating human relationships, more aware socially and politically than his parents were at the same age. Listen to some of the best lyrics in their songs, and this will become evident. It should come as no surprise, then, that the teen-age musician finds the old-line popular song to be a series of trite harmonic formulas or predictable melodies based on a long-familiar system of chord patterns and tried and true story lines. He has turned to different concepts in melody, harmony, rhythm, tone, and lyrics.

Elvis Presley, *above,* gyrated rhythm and blues to the fore in 1956. Chubby Checker popularized the "twist."

The songs of the previous generation too often gave the impression that life was a lounge full of cocktails for two; that the singer was bound for some far-off state of the Union, often a southern one, where, upon his arrival, he would find nostalgic happiness ("I'm Alabamy Bound," "Georgia on My Mind"); or, setting the very tone for this whole world of unreality, that "wishing will make it so."

But in the cultural environment of 1967, most boys and girls over 14 refused to accept this musical pabulum. They were all too well aware that the stars that fall on Alabama, as the old song had it, might be seen at any moment through a haze of atomic fallout.

Many of today's teen pop songs attest to this awareness and reflect the desperation that haunts the world they have inherited, and often their anger at it. This is detectable in the volume and aggressiveness of the music, as well as in the socially significant lyrics. For example, in a haunting song with a lyric that is a crude but powerful form of surrealistic poetry, young Bob Dylan warns that "A Hard Rain's Gonna Fall." Again, this should not come as a surprise. Many of the young people in Dylan's world-wide audience were born under the mushroom clouds of Hiroshima and Nagasaki.

These characteristics–social significance and angry or subtle protest–though predominant, are not inescapable. While the frenetic group that calls itself the Jefferson Airplane turns its guitars up to ear-cracking volume, a sextet known as the Association may offer a soft, gentle performance without a trace of hostility, and Brian Wilson's Beach Boys may contribute another example of the California-born "surfing

Beatles "yeh-yeh-yeh'd" on television in 1964, *right.* Chuck Berry, *below,* who helped get rock rolling, was big influence on Beatles.

sound" that enabled them to sell 10,000,000 records in three years. In 1965, a hit record by Barry McGuire warned of "The Eve of Destruction"; in the same year, the extent of the message on a release by a British group, Herman's Hermits, could be found in its title: "Mrs. Brown, You've Got a Lovely Daughter."

Rock 'n' roll in its raw form is a direct descendant of rhythm and blues, a hard-driving, earthy music usually played with four emphatic beats to the bar. Rhythm and blues was, and is, a branch of folk-jazz. Some authorities contend that Louis Jordan, the saxophonist and singer who sold millions of records during the 1940s, made the first real rhythm and blues impact. Others believe that the form goes farther back, to obscure Negro artists who sang and played in southern delta country, and whose laments were later given far wider exposure by their successors, men such as Lightnin' Hopkins and Chuck Berry.

Following a classic pattern of Negro origination and white imitation, a pattern that shaped the history of U.S. jazz, Elvis Presley of Tupelo, Miss., stormed the North and brought rhythm and blues to the white American public in 1956. His gyrating hips, long sideburns, and countrified voice combined to create an image that induced near-hysteria among mobs of teen-agers of the late 1950s. Some of his songs were only a slightly more sophisticated form of pure rhythm and blues (he acknowledges two Negro singers, Big Joe Turner and Bill Crudup, as his main influences), but it was with Presley and his successors that rock 'n' roll won national prominence.

In 1960, rock 'n' roll achieved a more clearly defined visual dimension when Chubby Checker, a Negro singer from Philadelphia, popularized a churning, hip-wiggling dance known as the "twist." Very soon, twisters, dancing to rock records, became to the early 1960s what the jitterbugs, with a dance known as the "Lindy," had been to the swing era of the 1930s, when the big bands were in vogue.

Beatles, in background, *above,* record "Sergeant Pepper." Paul McCartney and John Lennon, *left,* in studio where the group worked on album for three months.

Ravi Shankar, *above,* taught Beatle George Harrison, second from left, *below,* how to play the Indian sitar.

Then, as rock became an international phenomenon, four young men in Liverpool, England, well indoctrinated in the shapes and sounds of the American Negro music, suddenly shifted the focus of interest eastward across the Atlantic. Like Presley, the Beatles relied not only on their music, but also on visual shock value. In February, 1964, some 68,000,000 viewers watching the Ed Sullivan Show, one of the largest audiences in the history of television, saw their long, shaggy hair and their convention-defying clothes and heard the "yeh-yeh-yeh" enthusiasm of their songs. That evening may have been the pivotal one in the pop revolution. For about two years, English groups such as the Rolling Stones, the Animals, the Dave Clark Five, and Herman's Hermits dominated the international scene.

As Leonard Bernstein and others have observed, pure volume seems to have been used for its own sake, especially in the early days of the

new music. Amateurish lyrics, sung out of tune, were, perhaps fortunately, drowned out by the deafening noise of amplified guitars, basses, percussion, just plain shouting, and electronic sound effects. In many instances, this is still the case.

It is less important, however, to examine such defects than to turn the microscope on that small percentage of excellent material admired by Bernstein and other sociomusicologists.

The growth of rock and allied forms can best be measured by tracing the Beatles' evolution. In 1963, they were singing cheerful nonsense such as "A Hard Day's Night," to a melody based on the ancient 12-bar blues formula. Nothing was heard but the sounds of their voices and instruments, without overdubbing or special effects of any kind. Today, their songs, almost all of them written by John Lennon and Paul McCartney, provide a spectrum of the wild and wonderful steps forward in the evolution of words, music, and recording techniques.

Lyrically, the Beatles may cover any topic, serious or comic, that is likely to appeal to the adolescent and the young adult. For example, they are concerned with romantic love, as in "Michelle," a ballad that has already become a standard. But under the influence of Bob Dylan and their own restless curiosity about life, the Beatles also have written songs of a more serious nature. Lack of meaningful communication between people and the resulting loneliness is the main theme of the Beatles' "Sergeant Pepper's Lonely Hearts Club Band," which was the most unusual pop recording of 1967. The album was discussed endlessly by pop music writers and culture commentators, most of whom considered it a musical breakthrough.

Essentially, all the songs, while diverse in technique, are variations on the theme of the alienation of the individual in the modern world. The album could have had the celebrated phrase of Henry David Thoreau, "The masses of men lead lives of quiet desperation," for its

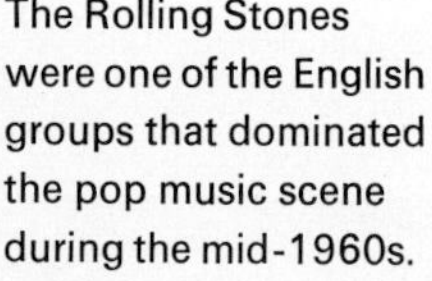

The Rolling Stones were one of the English groups that dominated the pop music scene during the mid-1960s.

motto. The album contains many kinds of music. There is the delightful and touching spoof of the oompah-oompah music of the 1920s and of the boredom of the lives of the lower class man in England who worries if his wife will still love him "when I'm 64":

When I get older, losing my hair,
Many years from now,
Will you still be sending me a valentine,
*Birthday greetings bottle of wine . . .**

Perhaps the most touching track is "She's Leaving Home." The song describes the consternation produced in a family when the young daughter rises early one morning, "silently closing her bedroom door," and goes down the stairs, "leaving the note that she hoped would say more." The parents discover her flight, and the mother ruefully complains, "Daddy, our baby's gone . . . what did we do that was wrong . . . we gave her most of our lives."

The apparent drug messages in some popular songs have been the subject of endless discussion. Sometimes the reference may be found in the title, through the use of the letters of the hallucinogenic drug LSD, as in "Love Special Delivery" or the Lennon-McCartney "Lucy in the Sky with Diamonds," which is a part of the "Sergeant Pepper" album. Marijuana seems to be indicated in "Along Comes Mary" (Mary Jane, a slang term and a direct translation from the Spanish for marijuana) and "Acapulco Gold" (the "in" name for a grade of the drug). Dozens of teen-directed tunes deal with fanciful flights from worldly reality in such a manner that adults have difficulty in determining the presence or absence of alleged narcotic subversion. They include: "Eight Miles High," "Up, Up, and Away," "The Trip," and "Running Around the World." One of Bob Dylan's biggest hits, "Mr. Tambourine Man," popularized by the Byrds, also contains lines that some persons believe refer to narcotics.

The Monkees were created to perform in a television series. Their popularity has mushroomed thanks to frenzied talents of, *left to right,* Davy, Micky, Mike, and Peter.

Bob Dylan and Janis Ian are modern troubadors who write and sing their poetry of protest.

Most of the composers have denied that such references are covert word pictures of LSD trips. McCartney sweetened the brew of controversy for a time, however, with a verbal sugar cube that paid elaborate tribute to the dangerous drug as a panacea for world ills. "After I took it, it opened my eyes . . . if the politicians would take LSD, there wouldn't be any more war, poverty, or famine." The stress on politicians is important, because it implies that the young who resort to drugs do so to escape the emptiness or bitterness of a life that might be changed by political action. But it should be noted that McCartney later stated that he does not recommend LSD. "It can open a few doors, but it's not the answer," he said.

Bob Dylan, the slender, young songwriter with the gravel voice, guitar, and long, long hair, has been called the Robert Burns of the pop revolution. Possibly he would rather be compared with Dylan Thomas, from whom he took his professional name. Originally a folk artist who accompanied himself on guitar and harmonica, he later added the heavy rhythms and electronic sounds that placed him squarely in the folk rock category. He has been called the most genuine representative of the rebellious members of his generation. His concern for the new, youth-dominated world order is expressed in general terms in his song, "The Times They Are A-Changin'."

One of his earlier hits, the 1962 "Blowin' in the Wind," is a rallying cry for freedom and against war. But Dylan's lesser works are often trivial ("Mama, You Been on My Mind") or incoherent ("Subterranean Homesick Blues," a rambling series of sometimes arbitrarily rhymed couplets). His songs are generally of little or no melodic interest.

Paul Simon of Simon and Garfunkel has written some of the most cogent and poetic songs of the new generation. Like the vast majority of young singers and writers, he has joined battle with the Establishment. Simon and his partner are opposed to the U.S. involvement in

Simon and Garfunkel sing the poetic and literate songs written by Paul Simon, at right in this photo of the pair.

the war in Vietnam, and have aligned themselves, in song, with many causes meaningful to the young, politically involved American. In the pop revolt, almost all social and political thinking lists to portside; Republican folk or rock singers can be counted on the fingers of the right hand.

A Simon and Garfunkel version of "Silent Night" begins as an orthodox treatment of the Christmas carol. As the record progresses, a distant voice is heard, that of a radio announcer. Gradually, as the announcer offers his 7 o'clock news summary–reports of violent anti-Negro housing demonstrations, the death of comedian Lenny Bruce from an overdose of narcotics, the stabbing and strangling by Richard Speck of eight young nurses in Chicago, the eviction of demonstrators at a House Un-American Activities Committee probe into anti-Vietnam war activity, the call by Richard Nixon for a stepped-up effort in Vietnam–the detached voice of the announcer grows louder and louder, and the sounds of the carol grow fainter and fainter. No single performance could come closer than this spine-chilling record to a summation of how tomorrow's leaders feel about situations for most of which they hold yesterday's children responsible.

The lyrics of Paul Simon are subtle and often contain delicate poetry. One of his most perceptive songs is "The Sound of Silence," which treats of the lack of communication in a characteristically subtle and searching manner:

In the naked light I saw
Ten thousand people, maybe more,
People talking without speaking
People hearing without listening
People writing songs that voices never shared,
No one dared
*Disturb the sound of silence.**

This song also contains the memorable line: "The words of the prophets are written on subway walls, and tenement halls."

Happily, this pair can also celebrate life, as they do in their popular "Feelin' Groovy":

Got no deeds to do, no promises to keep,
I'm dappled and drowsy and ready for sleep,
Let the morning drop all its petals on me,
*Life I love you–feelin' groo-vy.**

Protest songs have stemmed from the unlikeliest of sources. In 1967, "Society's Child," a poignant and beautiful song, both melodically and lyrically, was written and performed by a 15-year-old white girl named Janis Ian. The melody, in the key of A minor, starts somewhat somberly, almost monotonously. It builds slowly. The notes climb upward. Then there is a sudden key shift up to B minor, and a dramatic climax leaves the melody suspended on an unresolved note, with an even more unexpected final chord in the key of A major. Such procedures are inexcusably wrong by the now-discarded standards of the traditional popular ballad.

Even more unconventional are the lyrics, which are clearly a plea for interracial romance. A few years ago, no company would have dared to publish, no network would have allowed an artist to broadcast, such a controversial message.

Just as the words of the better new pop songs represent a rebellion against blandness and babbitry, their musical aspects indicate a desire to find new, sometimes radically different, avenues of expression.

The academic precision and harmonic charm of a melody by a Richard Rodgers, Cole Porter, or Duke Ellington are almost never found in the new songs. Instead, many young composers have gone back into musical history to find material that is fresh because its sound is startling. Some groups have used the Oriental-sounding modes of

John Sebastian, *below,* is one of the Lovin' Spoonful, a versatile quartet that ranges from hard rock to jug-band music; the Who, *center,* is an English group that added smoke bombs to its singing at the 1967 Monterey Pop Festival; and Motown's Supremes, *far right,* sing both new and old pop songs.

the ancient Greeks. The Beatles found inspiration in Elizabethan madrigals. Others have used basic, unadorned triads. For example, "Take a Giant Step," sung by the Monkees, is based almost entirely on the chords of C, G, and F. Such a primitive set of values can be easily played on the guitar, which, during the 1960s, has surpassed the piano as the most-played instrument in pop.

Soon after the first success of the Beatles many young musicians became convinced that all they needed for fun and profit was a guitar, an amplifier, and a knowledge of half a dozen simple chords. But this attitude became outmoded when the Beatles, again leading the pack, brought still more new sounds into pop music. They supplemented their guitar with related, if exotic, instruments, such as the sitar, which Beatle George Harrison studied for two months in India with Ravi Shankar, a master of the instrument, and the oud, a sort of Middle Eastern lute. Another form of rebellion in which the Beatles played a major role was the destruction of the myth that all songs must be symmetrically packaged in four- and eight-bar segments. The Lennon-McCartney hit, "Michelle," for example, uses a main strain that is seven measures long and a release that runs to nine measures.

By 1967, the Beatles had discovered how to make use of a string quartet, an electric organ, a strange computerized instrument known as a mellotron, tape played backward and forward at different speeds, *fuzz tones* (electronic distortions), reverberation, shifts from 4/4 to 5/4 and other meters, paper-and-comb humming effects, and even a 41-piece orchestra, some of whose pride-swallowing members were regulars in London's Royal Philharmonic.

Most of these extramusical effects were used in "Sergeant Pepper," and this points to another aspect of the new pop scene: recording technology has come to play an important role. The devices used by the Beatles in "Pepper" were sifted, blended, and added to each other in

Eardrum-defying volume is a trademark of such groups as Paul Revere and the Raiders, *left,* and the Jefferson Airplane, *above,* here performing outdoors without their usual "psychedelic" strobe lights.

Flashing lights, wild sounds, dancing, and far-out clothes all make the scene at San Francisco's Fillmore Auditorium—a mecca of pop.

the recording studio in much the same way that a baker mixes the ingredients of a cake. In short, the man in the control booth, with his tapes, dials, and switches, can choose sounds he thinks will enhance a particular performance from a library of sounds. Hence, a single three-minute track is sometimes the product of weeks of night-after-night concentration in the recording studio.

Closely allied to these electronic developments is the phenomenon of so-called psychedelic music. The term is a loose one. If it has any firm meaning, it can be defined as music that aims to produce a mind-extending–perhaps distorting is more accurate–effect. Much of this music is performed at eardrum-defying volume with the visual aid of flashing strobe lights by groups with names that are no less defiantly unorthodox: the Jefferson Airplane, the Grateful Dead, and Dr. West's Medicine Show and Junk Band.

That we have reached a point in our culture capable of producing such tradition-shattering sounds may be partly the consequence of the disillusionment of the performers with our society. The more these young musicians find distasteful in their parents' way of life, the more determined they become to find ways to reject its entire frame of reference. Many have moved so far in this direction that the result resembles a man who, disgusted with the inconsistencies of the English lan-

Musicologists differ on what specific roots nourished today's forms of music. The family tree on the facing page is a composite of the opinions of a number of musicians, critics, and other devotees of pop.

A Genealogy of Pop

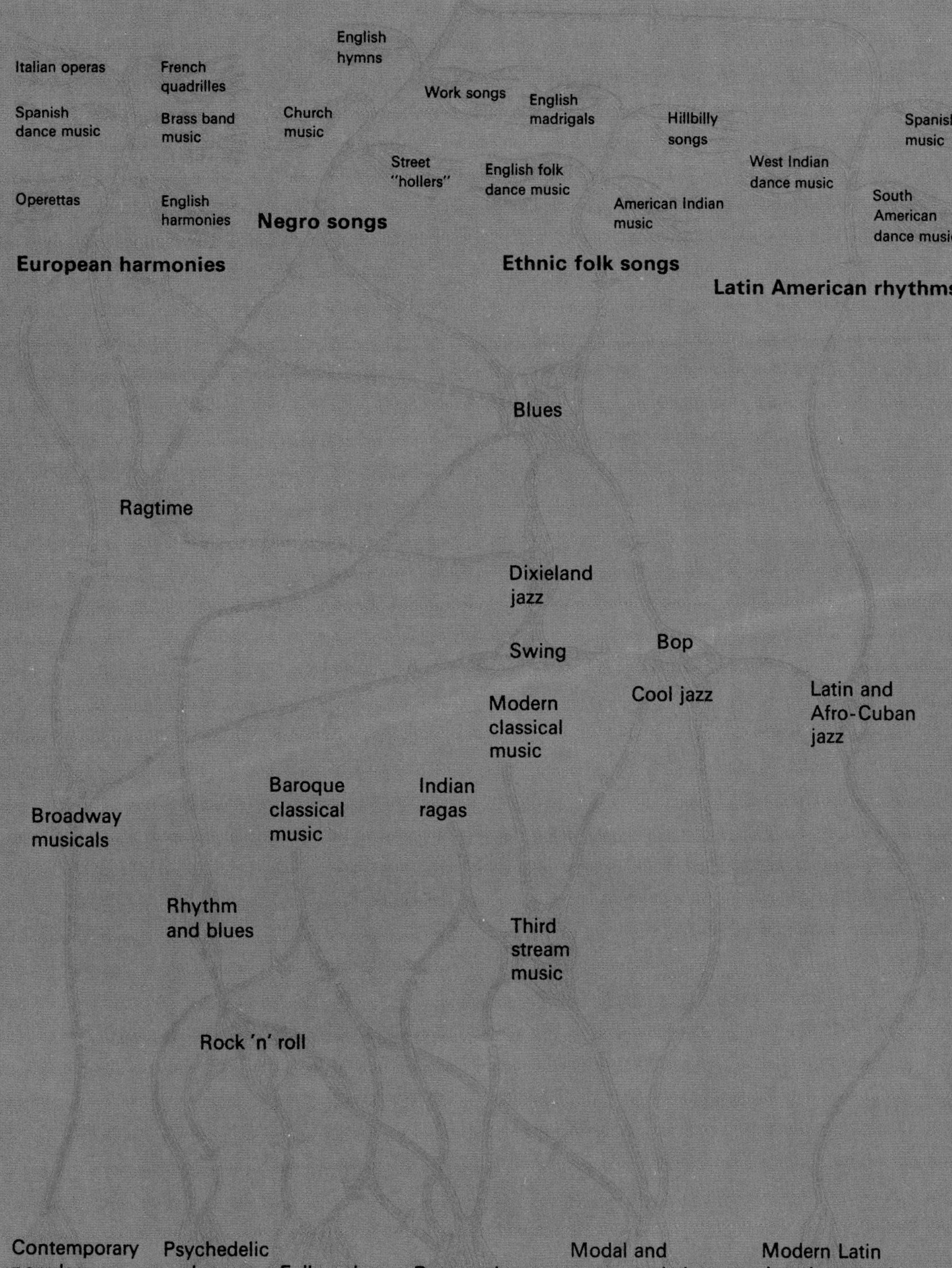

guage, resorts to a tirade of double talk. Thus, the shock-rock groups often use reverse psychology to appeal to other angry adolescents. For example, the Mothers of Invention, an all-male unit, not only present what may seem to some adults a singularly unpleasant appearance, but they also have advertised their albums with such slogans as: "Hateful, Repugnant, and a Waste of Money."

The Negro segment of the new pop scene has been underplayed in the national press, on television, and even in public performances. Critics at the 1967 Monterey Pop Festival complained about the inadequate representation of Negro groups. Of those present, Jimi Hendrix, a singer who had gained greater popularity in England than at home, made the most startling impression with a literally flaming finale. He kissed his guitar, set it down on the stage, poured gasoline on it, set it afire, then stamped out the burning pieces and threw them at his delighted audience.

Many of the leading Negro pop units are products of the so-called Motown sound named for a record company founded in 1959 in the Motor City (Detroit, Mich.) by Negro Berry Gordy with the aid of a $700 loan. It is now estimated to be worth $15,000,000. The Supremes, one of the very few female vocal groups to achieve a million-selling blend, is a Motown product, as is Smokey Robinson and the Miracles. Robinson writes not only for his own group, but also for many other Motown artists. "The Tracks of My Tears," a love lament with no social significance whatever, is representative of the lyrical content of most Motown music. The poetry of a Bob Dylan or a Paul Simon and, surprisingly, the protest of a Janis Ian is far more a part of the white than the black pop scene. Nina Simone is among the few top Negro pop artists strongly identified with protest songs.

Blind singer and composer Ray Charles was an early and potent force in "soul music."

An important aspect of the Negro pop scene is so-called "soul music." An early and potent force in soul was Ray Charles, in the days when his repertoire consisted largely of blues and related material. The most soulful singers are older men who have "paid their dues" and who sing with a passionate voice of experience. Charles, still a master of soul when he is not purveying maudlin ballads against a bank of strings, was born in 1932. Joe Williams, the former Count Basie band singer whose blues are as soulful as his ballads are tender, is 14 years Charles' senior.

These men and, to a lesser degree, such blues specialists as Aretha Franklin, B. B. King, Jimmy Reed, John Lee Hooker, and Otis Spann are tied to jazz. Their music has an elusive rhythmic quality found only in crude, watered-down form in many rhythm and blues works. It has barely influenced rock 'n' roll performances. But the authenticity of their songs and the passion with which they perform them have reached the young rock fans, black and white alike. Hence, during the late 1960s, young rock aficionados helped to bring many of the older blues artists out of obscurity and created a growing audience for them and made them a part of the current pop scene.

Just as some rock groups have improved themselves musically by listening to Indian raga music, jazz, and other forms, so have their fans assumed a broader listening attitude by giving an enthusiastic reception to certain jazz groups. Gary Burton, the avant-garde jazz vibraphonist, has performed with equal success for jazz and rock audiences. It is no coincidence that his brilliant young guitarist, Larry Coryell, is a former member of rock groups and has combined the forms in his present style. The intense, probing quartet of Charles Lloyd has performed with consistent success at San Francisco's Fillmore Auditorium, the Gibraltar of rock. And Gabor Szabo, the Hungarian guitarist, has similarly attracted young audiences with his own mixture of Indian music and jazz dubbed "raga rock." But, generally speaking, jazz with a straight 4/4 beat has little appeal for the typical teeny rocker. He prefers a touch of rhythm and blues, often including a Latin beat. More popular than any of the instrumental jazz groups is the Tijuana Brass, led by trumpeter Herb Alpert. The clean, happy sound of Alpert's non-protest music reaches all age groups.

When the dust of the pop revolution has settled, what will remain? It has been said that pure jazz had become too abstract, that the earlier popular jazz idiom had reached a dead end, and that, therefore, rock and folk rock were needed to give the audience a sense of involvement.

Surely, quality pop compositions, the kind still referred to by the older generation as "good music," will survive. "Yesterdays," by Jerome Kern and Otto Harbach (1933), and "Yesterday," by John Lennon and Paul McCartney (1965), will both be with us tomorrow. So will innumerable top-drawer songs from Broadway shows and motion picture or television specials. And these are based on formulas established decades ago by the George Gershwins, Irving Berlins, and Cole Porters. The proof of their durability can be found in the best-selling album charts. Pop composers in the grand tradition are dependent more on albums, and less on single records, than are most of the young pop writers. The growing trend represented by such LPs as "The Supremes Sing Rodgers & Hart," a big favorite in 1967, has played a significant role in narrowing what was once believed to be an unspannable generation gap.

With few exceptions, pop hits of the younger set are short-lived. The charts of single-record best sellers, 90 per cent of which represent sales to the teen market, show an astonishing turnover. Of the top 100 records in a recent week in *Billboard*, the music trade weekly, only two had been on the chart more than 12 weeks.

Nevertheless, the best of the new pop musicians have produced first-rate songs that would seem to be as durable as any. Perhaps more important, they have added a verbal honesty and curiosity about the world and a musical inventiveness that has altered our notions of what is acceptable in popular music. Because of a few young men and women in their teens and 20s, our ears will never be quite the same again.

A Year Book Special Report

By William R. Coe

In Search Of the Mayan Past

The story of Tikal, the largest of the ancient Mayan sites, is revealed by the archaeologist who directed its study

The journey from the city of Guatemala to the ancient Mayan center of Tikal in the jungles of northeastern Guatemala covers only 200 miles by plane, but it is a trip that carries the visitor to another world and another time.

The twin-engine plane leaves the airport at 8 o'clock in the morning and climbs to 10,000 feet to clear the mountains that ring the broad valley in which the city of Guatemala lies. The mountains become more rugged as the plane flies north over coffee plantations and scattered cornfields. Suddenly, the mountains drop away as the plane reaches the jungles of El Petén, one of the great rain forests of the

Limestone-crested temples of Tikal, built by the Maya a thousand years ago, rise impressively above the jungles of northeastern Guatemala.

world, its dense foliage often obscured by the morning mists. Where the clouds part, we see muddy, serpentine rivers and, here and there, solitary farms hacked laboriously from the forest. Soon, the jungles are broken further by great tracts of almost treeless grasslands, or savannas.

After flying north for an hour, the aircraft lands at Santa Elena on the shores of Lake Petén Itzá. In the middle of the lake lies the island of Flores, the capital of El Petén and the scene, in 1697, of the final military conquest of the Maya by the Spaniards. The airport is a transfer point serving the small Petén communities of farmers, loggers, and chicleros who harvest the valuable sap of the sapodilla trees for shipment to the chewing gum factories of the world. The plane remains on the ground only long enough to unload and load cargos. Families on visits to relatives in the bush climb aboard, joining the archaeologists and tourists bound for Tikal. It always seems to be a test of how much a plane can hold: drums of gasoline, beds, pots and pans, even chickens, some crated, some held squawking in the arms of women with children clinging to their skirts.

The plane is in flight again. It is now almost 10 o'clock. The sun has cleared the mists from the jungle, and soon the limestone-crested summits of the temples of Tikal appear. For more than a thousand years these gigantic temples have humbled the forest and now mark the site of the vanished Mayan civilization. Within minutes, the aircraft lands on the airstrip maintained by the Guatemalan government for the archaeologists and thousands of tourists who come to Tikal.

The author:
William R. Coe directed the Tikal Project of the University of Pennsylvania's University Museum and now is in charge of the massive publications program that will tell the full story of Tikal. He is an associate professor of anthropology at the university.

Settled at least six centuries before the birth of Christ, Tikal rose while the Greek and Roman worlds flourished and fell. Its builders raised Tikal and other Mayan centers in Guatemala, Honduras, and Yucatán to their peaks while Europe was plunged in the Dark Ages. Then, for reasons that still elude us, the Mayan civilization faded–long before Columbus came ashore in the New World. There still are a few million descendants of the ancient Maya in the mountains and in jungle settlements, but they live meagerly. They are no longer the lords of what the archaeologist and anthropologist call southeastern Mesoamerica, and, though it seems strange, they go about their everyday business with little or no knowledge of their glorious past.

A Land-Rover takes the visitor to a comfortable thatched-roof inn that can accommodate 36 guests. Belongings are stored away, and, after a 15-minute ride on a dirt road over causeways built a thousand years ago, we arrive at the Great Plaza, the ceremonial heart of Tikal. Here, masses of people once gathered to watch their priest-rulers, the most elite clothed in many pounds of jade, rich fabrics, jaguar skins, and the emerald plumes of the sacred quetzal bird, as they climbed the temple steps to the sounds of drums, flageolets, and wood trumpets and the moan of conch shells. It is awesome to think that for centuries no human voice sounded here as Tikal fell into ruin.

The sight is unforgettable. The white limestone temples and palaces –magnificent by any standard and all built without the aid of metal

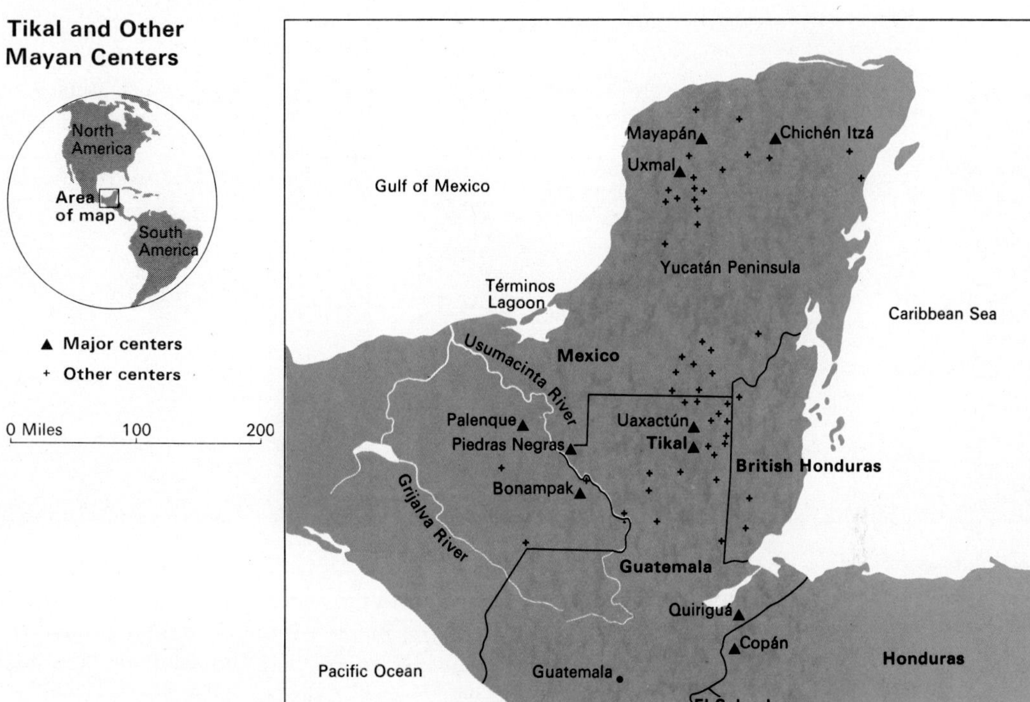

Map shows that part of Mesoamerica ruled by the ancient Maya. Mesoamerica comprises the Yucatán Peninsula and parts of Mexico, Guatemala, British Honduras, Honduras, and El Salvador.

or the wheel–stand out brilliantly against the green background of lianas and palm, cedar, and mahogany trees. Fragrant orchids and scarlet air plants bloom high in the branches, and monkeys, brilliantly colored parrots, hummingbirds, and toucans chatter and dart in the trees. Volumes have been written about the birds of Tikal. More than 200 species may be identified by the visitor today.

Facing north, one sees the splendid Temple of the Giant Jaguar. Known to archaeologists as Temple I, it is 150 feet tall. To the left is the slightly smaller Temple of the Masks (Temple II). Both were built about A.D. 700 in typical Mayan temple style: a pyramid topped by a roof comb, with a frighteningly steep staircase running up one side. Farther north, behind two rows of sculptured *stelae* (stone shafts) and altars, is the temple-studded North Acropolis. To the south, facing the Acropolis, are the great palaces of the nobles. The complex covers about four and one-half acres, but the great city–if it was a city–was at least six square miles in area. In addition, remains of buildings have been found in all directions from the city.

Because of its inaccessibility, Tikal came to the attention of the world only a century ago through the published report of two Guatemalan officials who traveled to the overgrown ruins. The men, Ambrosio Tut and Modesto Mendez, were seeking to learn the truth of tales of a lost city in the jungle. In the following years, maps were made, photographs of monuments taken, and plans of buildings drawn. By 1900, it was clear that Tikal (a delightfully musical name pronounced Tee-kahl, which is traditional and need not have been its original one) was archi-

Six flights a week land at Tikal's airfield. The landing strip was hacked from jungle in 1950. All supplies for the Tikal Project were flown in, including trucks and a sawmill. The nine-terraced Temple of the Giant Jaguar, *above right,* rises some 150 feet and is the most beautifully proportioned building in Tikal. Photo shows it after restoration work.

tecturally the most extensive and impressive of all the Mayan centers. A landing strip hacked from the jungle by the Guatemalan government in 1950 was essential for intensive archaeological work. Another essential was the steel ax, which was needed to clear, and keep clear, the miles of ruins lying beneath the 150-foot canopy of trees and vines. One is always aware how close the forest is at Tikal and of how quickly, without the steel machete and ax, it would envelop Tikal again.

Large-scale excavation and study of the sprawling site began in 1956 under the auspices of the University Museum of the University of Pennsylvania, which had long taken an active part in Mayan research.

The work at Tikal has involved incalculable hours of mapping and digging, to say nothing of the time devoted to the careful cataloging and recording of hundreds of thousands of artifacts and the study of pottery, the fragments of which, called sherds, total almost a million. The detailed contour map of central Tikal now shows nearly 3,000 surface constructions–plazas, causeways, temples, shrines, palaces, ball courts, and small- to medium-size residences. More than 200 stone monuments, the stelae and altars, were found on the surface of central Tikal. Approximately 750 excavations were carried out, some requiring no more than an hour, others spanning as much as six years. These revealed acres of Mayan constructions and in some cases a thousand years of development. Some 450 structures were revealed to one degree or another by our excavations.

The excavations within central Tikal came to a close in 1966 with the conviction that only a small part of the whole had been seen, much less understood. In the last years of our work at the site, an enormous effort was made to balance our knowledge of central Tikal by exploring, mapping, and testing its outlying portions.

The point of the entire exploration has been to translate architecture, figurines, burials, sherds by the carload, and stone, bone, and shell artifacts into a people with defined status and functions within the social structure of the huge community that once was Tikal. To do so might reveal much about the causes of the rise of a great culture, in this case a culture that not only produced a barely rivaled art and architecture, but also developed mathematicians and astronomers–all in what strikes us as an unpromising, economically rarefied environment. Analysis of the countless facts recovered over the years of work might yield the causes of the end of this civilization that had endured successfully for more than a thousand years.

But perhaps most intriguing of all, we hope to learn what caused the apparently sudden downfall of all Classic Mayan civilizations. For the abandonment to the jungle of the seemingly endless centers of temples and palaces went hand in hand with a startling depopulation of northern Guatemala and adjacent regions. Where once settlements appeared to have been almost continuous, one can now ride for hours, even days, with little or no sign of human life beyond the sight of protruding mounds or of an occasional temple toppled by a thousand years of clawing trees.

To date, we have been only partly successful in interpreting the almost overwhelming amount of field data that we have collected, including 50,000 photographs, piles of field notebooks, and bales of architectural drawings. During the coming years, we hope, the mil-

Map shows 2-square-mile area of central Tikal, with the five main temples indicated by Roman numerals. Areas in white are reservoirs. Buildings have been discovered for miles in all directions.

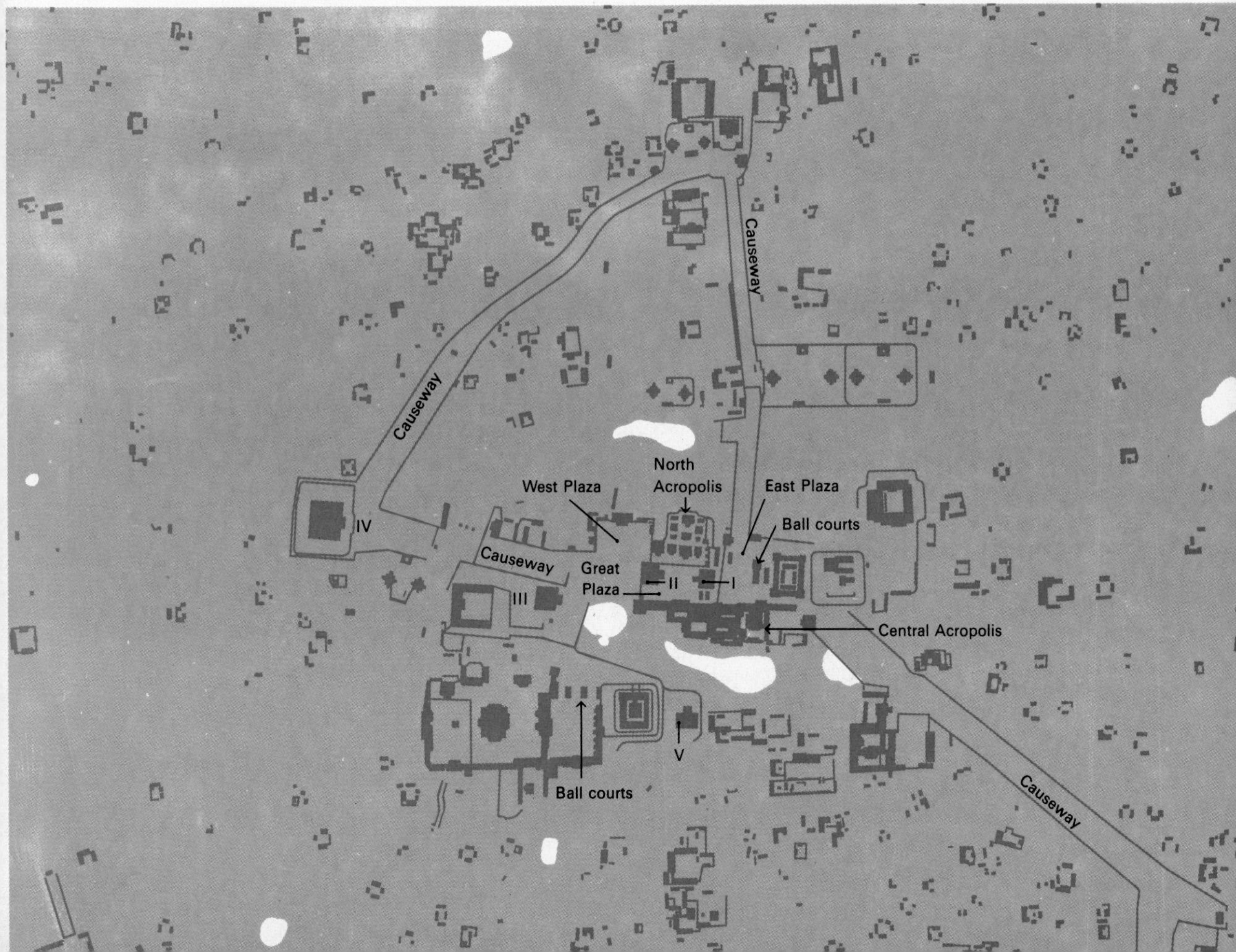

One of the first tasks as the Tikal Project began work in 1956 was clearing the jungle to establish a temporary camp. It was built at the edge of an ancient Mayan rain reservoir. Constant work with ax and machete was necessary to keep the jungle from reclaiming the site.

lions of facts at hand will yield insights worthy of the investigations. This might come to seem almost simple compared to the task of interpretation that lies ahead, for Tikal resembles the proverbial iceberg—impressive enough above, but gigantic in what remains invisible.

In the meantime, we present here our interim report on the rise and fall of an extraordinary city built in our own hemisphere. What follows are paragraphs recovered from the still largely illegible pages of the Mayan story.

In dealing with Mayan and other Mesoamerican cultures, archaeologists speak of three basic time periods: Preclassic (or Formative), Classic, and Postclassic. These terms obviously beg a definition of Classic. Perhaps maturation, or culmination of earlier trends, comes close to defining the Classic period. It was a time that, at Tikal, lasted roughly from A.D. 250 to 900, during which the distinctively lowland (jungle as opposed to mountain) Mayan ceramic, sculptural, and architectural styles emerged and were slowly fulfilled. It was a period when the thousand-odd known hieroglyphic texts of the Maya were incised upon stone and other materials. During these centuries, which in the Old World ran from roughly the fall of Rome through the Dark Ages, one of the great eras in the history of art came into being amid the myriad architectural centers then dotting southeastern Mesoamerica.

The Preclassic era, at Tikal from about 600 B.C. to A.D. 250, was a time of beginnings, of early yet impressive expressions of unmistakably Mayan civilization. It was a time of experimentation with the resources of a difficult environment. It was probably also a time of adaptation to the brilliant trends of the Maya's Mesoamerican neighbors. During the long centuries of the Preclassic period, the priest-rulers emerged with their richly staged ceremonies built on an economic base supplied by a peasantry that worked cornfields cut from the forest.

The term "Postclassic," in contrast, covers an era of collapse of sacred rulers, of once-powerful retinues dead or in exile forever. Grandeur, for whatever reason, had run its course in these lowland forests. Throughout Mesoamerica, following at least A.D. 900, the warrior replaced the effete, though often barbaric, priest. It was a time of social turbulence. At Tikal, it was also a period when survivors of the collapse of the priestly, institutionalized power lingered on in a failing attempt to emulate the past.

The Project renovated this ancient rain-water reservoir, since the Tikal area has no lakes, springs, or constantly flowing rivers.

The earliest traces of occupation of Tikal date from about 600 B.C., and consist of little more than trash, a single burial, and a human skull that appears to have been severed from its body. We know nothing else of these people. We have named their ceramics "Eb." From their refuse, we know that they traded with the Guatemalan highlands for obsidian, a black, volcanic, glasslike rock. We know that they also imported quartzite, probably from neighboring British Honduras, and used it to make *manos* and *metates* (stones to grind corn meal). We can only guess what material they used for trade, but it may have been flint, for flint abounds at Tikal. Most of the basic Mayan tools were made of it, and everything suggests that in later times Tikal was an important manufacturing center of flint tools.

The flint deposits probably were a primary attraction that caused the Eb people to settle at Tikal. Another incentive may have been the slight elevation, which provided relative dryness as well as drainage into reservoirs during the torrential rains that occur in the area. Further, Tikal is situated on the edge of a huge *bajo* (seasonal swamp). Hence, its soil may once have been comparatively rich and productive. It is no easy task to explain the origins and presence of the earliest known farmers of Tikal. But there is nothing known to contradict the assumption that they were Maya whose ancestors, like those of the Indians of North America, came to this continent from Asia over the land bridge that joined Asia to Alaska 10,000 years ago. Dark skinned, almond eyed, and stocky, the ancient lowland Maya, as well as their present-day descendants, are strikingly oriental in appearance.

Over the centuries, the pottery of the early settlers changed. Ceramics and figurines of the *Tzec* period (approximately 500 B.C. to 300 B.C.) have been found at Tikal. But we have been unable to locate architecture and burials surely belonging to these times. The propensity of the Tikal Maya to demolish and scoop up old construction as fill for new buildings and platforms is at least partly responsible for our lack of knowledge in so many areas.

The known beginnings of architecture at Tikal, in which carefully shaped stone masonry and plaster surfaces were used, coincides with the appearance (300 B.C. to 200 B.C.) of a new and more sophisticated ceramics, called *Chuen*. The architectural growth of the North Acropolis spurted during this time. There was a successive construction of small and large masonry platforms upon which probably stood buildings of wood and thatch used for religious purposes. Elsewhere at Tikal, we found some evidence of the houses of this period. These, too, were probably built of wood and thatch.

Photo shows the Temple of the Giant Jaguar as it appeared in 1957, partly cleared of the thick vegetation that had grown on it since it had last been cleared about 1900. Much of the destruction of Tikal's many temples and palaces was caused by the spread of tree roots.

Some of the most elaborately decorated temples known from the Mayan world were built in the first century before Christ. During this period, the so-called *Cauac* pottery appears, along with the first known use of corbel vaulting in some temples and tombs. Corbel vaulting later became a hallmark of the Classic period. The term is used to describe a "false" arch made by laying a stone slab across the top of two walls built to slant toward each other.

By the time of Christ, the ceremonial nucleus of Tikal had spread over several square miles. It was particularly concentrated in the area of the Great Plaza and stretched well to the southwest, where we found one spectacular pyramidal temple from these times, nearly 100 feet high, with four steep staircases.

Despite the work that had been done over the years among Classic Mayan temples, much remains to be learned of their function, evolution, and composition. Too tall to have been totally enveloped by the jungle, these man-made mountains of Tikal have long intrigued travelers and scholars. The tallest, Temple IV, is 212 feet high, approximately the height of a 20-story building. The temples of Tikal are basically pyramids with flat tops that hold one or more platforms. On the uppermost platforms are buildings with one to three rooms. The buildings are usually crowned with tapered roof combs and decorated with facades heavily embellished with painted masks and figures of modeled plaster. Stairs ascend the front of the pyramids. On gaining the top, one reaches the rooms by way of one or more small supplementary stairways.

There are some 50 temples within the center of Tikal and hundreds more lie concealed beneath more recent construction. There is little doubt of their ritual role. The great buildings command plazas suitable for religious assemblies and processions. The floors of their rooms are often found charred from the burning of copal, a resin incense still sacred to the Maya. The temples held strange and fascinating offerings that were placed in the floors just before construction. Jade, flint, obsidian, and shell were the common substances of these ritual caches, the flint and obsidian chipped into exotic shapes.

In Late Classic times, marine material came to be favored as offerings, even though the Caribbean is easily a week away on foot. It is startling today to see a plaster patch in the floor of an eighth century temple, open it, and discover a cluster of coiled sea fans and seaweed, sponge, coral, barnacles, and even fish amid a welter of red pigment and large flakes of obsidian on which images of Maya deities were incised.

The temples are the sites of the richest burials. Over and over again we ran across tombs placed in conjunction with their building. In some cases, a tomb was put into a temple immediately before it was abandoned and a new temple built over it. The Tikal Maya also occasionally opened the floors of their temples while they were in use and constructed chambers for their important dead.

The term "tomb" is appropriate for the majority of these burials, for the grave is in a chamber that is often vaulted, and the floor area is far in excess of that needed to lay out the principal corpse. Such chambers were elaborately stocked with pottery and other objects. Some of these were lifetime belongings, even heirlooms; others apparently were

This trench dug in the North Acropolis revealed centuries of superimposed architecture underlying the final version of the temple-studded Acropolis. In the background is a temple built about 100 B.C. and, above it, one from about A.D. 500.

made for the occasion. The tombs also contain the remains of individuals laid out with jewelry–necklaces, bracelets, and anklets of jade, even of pearls–which attests to their high position in life. Interestingly, the main occupants of Tikal's classic tombs tended to be larger than those buried in more prosaic circumstances. Presumably this was a matter of genetics and diet.

A major architectural feature of Tikal is the so-called palace, a relatively low-lying building with several rooms, usually arranged with other buildings to form courts. Some archaeologists believe these structures were the residences of the ruling families and their retinues. Others believe they functioned as secular administrative units, or as residential retreats for priests engaged in ceremonies, or perhaps as storehouses for the paraphernalia of ceremony and rule.

Speaking for myself, I find it difficult to believe that the arrogant, elite families of Tikal would have settled for less residentially than these magnificent buildings. I believe this to be the case even though these buildings, so elaborate without and so dark and severe within, would have required a manner of living well removed from anything in our own lives.

The largest known grouping of these structures is the Central Acropolis. This comprises an area of somewhat more than four acres that stretches east to west for 750 feet along the south side of the Great Plaza and the adjacent East Plaza. Four seasons of excavation of thousands of tons of debris and construction fill uncovered nearly 45 buildings here, the construction of which spanned 500 years. Some were two, others three, stories tall. Our knowledge of what lies beneath them and the six courts formed by them is sparse, but it is enough to suggest that a nearly equal number of buildings lies below them.

Truly a maze, the Central Acropolis must have baffled the unwary ancient visitor as much as the archaeologist trying to unscramble its parts. Centuries of construction produced situations where, to reach a nearby building, one was forced to descend some stairs and climb others, pass through alleys and over roofs, and even through what may have been narrow checkpoints. Development of the Central Acropolis thus seems to have involved an increasing degree of privacy and traffic control.

The rule appears to have been to leave nothing alone. The structures underwent repeated changes and additions. Second stories were added, as were benchlike platforms and transverse walls, the latter used to subdivide rooms. Some benches are centrally located in principal rooms and appear suitable as thrones. Those of us who are bent on seeing these buildings as true residences, however, face the difficult

Excavation revealed this large mask of stone and plaster that depicts a grotesque human head with snake attributes. The mask, probably portraying a Maya deity, decorates the base of a temple built about A.D. 450.

A tomb, *above,* can provide insights into the life and customs of the buried person. Hours of careful cleaning with brushes and penknives are followed by many more hours spent recording every feature of the tomb on paper and film. The two-part pottery idol, *above right,* dates from about A.D. 800 and probably was used in incense-burning rites. The figure holds a plaque and is seated on the grotesque head of a deity.

tasks of explaining how they were provisioned and of justifying their adaptability to the usual facets of living. For example, we found no contemporary trash in or near them.

But archaeology is more than the investigation of grandiose temples and palaces. What about the other people of Tikal? How many were they and how far did their settlements extend from the ceremonial nucleus? Were they all farmers? Was Tikal a city, or, at the least, did it have some kind of urban status? In an attempt to answer these crucial questions we undertook the decidedly unglamorous work of opening up more than 100 of the thousands of low-level mounds scattered over the area.

This work led to invaluable insights. We now know that there was a fairly dense and permanent population at Tikal during Late Classic times. Great differences in houses, burials, and other features found in these mounds suggest extensive functional and social diversity throughout a population that must have numbered at least 10,000 within the central six square miles of Tikal. Small residences formed distinct clusters, usually quadrangular in layout and well separated from neighboring groups, perhaps by back-yard gardens. Many such groups fit a pattern in which the west-facing structure contains a large number of burials and signs of ceremonies once performed there. These facts combine to suggest its use as a shrine. The most reasonable conclusion is that these patterned groups of structures were once residential compounds, each perhaps populated by an extended family incorporating married sons with their own families. The economic basis for such living is still not known, though signs of manufacturing specialties have been found in the excavations.

The cornfields on which the economy of Tikal was based required large tracts of land chopped and burned from the forests. They must

Pottery figurines such as these from the Late Classic era, *above left,* abound in Tikal. They probably were religious objects. Figurine at far right in photo is about 3 inches tall. The 4-inch-tall Early Classic dancing figure, *above,* is one of the finest of Tikal jades and was found in a North Acropolis cache. Jade was the ancient Maya's most precious material.

have been located far beyond the center of Tikal. How far out, it is almost impossible to calculate. Exploration of the outlying portions of Tikal has shown that there are about as many structures two to three miles out from the Great Plaza as there are in the city's center. But, as the terrain drops, so does the frequency of visible ruins, until, as one enters the vast bajos, there are no ruins at all.

It has been argued that Tikal and jungle sites like it were not populated in an urban sense simply because corn agriculture, as practiced by the Maya in the thin soils of the region, could never have produced enough to feed a largely nonfarming city population. The arguments, back and forth, are ponderous and usually suffer from the difficulties in gauging ancient crop yields. Optimists, however, see present-day yields as indicative of a potential for supporting large numbers of people per square mile in ancient Tikal.

In general, Tikal Project members are convinced that the site's population qualifies as urban. Tikal was obviously far more than a center of ceremony, and its population was fairly dense and diversified. In some manner, this population fed itself successfully for centuries. If corn alone could not have done the job, as some specialists believe, we have to search for other means of support. One member of our group is studying the possibility that the Tikal Maya grew various yamlike tubers, which are highly nutritive and capable of greater yields per acre than corn, under local conditions. In this view, corn might have been the favored food for the elite, and the fundamental staple of the average Maya would have been tubers, which are of quite minor importance today.

Finally, we must not forget that a surplus of wealth, with which provisions could have been purchased from other Maya centers, was almost certainly a factor in the economic health of Tikal. It was a manufacturing center of the flint tools basic to Mayan life. It is almost inconceivable that Tikal's superb artisans created solely for local consumption. And we can almost assume that the antiquity and sacredness of Tikal resulted in outside contributions, if not outright tribute, to its welfare from the Maya of the surrounding areas.

How was this great city built in the jungle? It has often been suggested that farmers living on the outskirts of Tikal were annually pressured into laboring on the staggering religious and residential edifices of their rulers. I personally doubt this. Did they have the time to do so, in the annual round of planting, harvesting, weeding, and cutting? And if they did, where would they have lived during these periods of forced labor? Who fed them and with what? Moreover, construction of the highly complex buildings would have been not only dangerous, but also technically demanding work for Sunday builders. Furthermore, building activity appears in the Tikal record as almost constant. Hence, it seems more likely that a highly specialized, permanent work force, skilled in quarrying and building, and perhaps working in some form of bondage, raised Tikal under the eyes of master architects.

The basic communal bond of the center, pervading life at all levels, is thought to have been religion. Another institution that might have helped bind all of Tikal together was a market economy, such as that described by the Spaniards for Tenochtitlán, the much later Aztec capital that now lies beneath the streets of Mexico City. While we have yet to identify a market area at Tikal, we have located and partly excavated an enormous quadrangular group of buildings with long galleries that would have been unsuited for habitation. Two lengthy causeways meet here, just north of the Central Acropolis. No debris such as one might expect in a market was found in these galleries, but then, nothing has been recovered to suggest another reason for this unique group–a usual paradox in this type of work.

In discussing Tikal's communal bonds, we cannot lose sight of the way in which the dank bajos physically surround much of it. In addition, in 1966 we discovered a wall, really a combined ditch and an embankment, that runs east and west for almost six miles about two and one-half miles north of the Great Plaza. What purpose did the wall serve? Was it built to control commerce between Tikal and Uaxactun, the closest major center? Or was it built–at a fantastic cost in labor–as a response to hostility? Whatever its true purpose, it could only have further consolidated the population of Tikal.

The bonds that had kept Tikal together so long came apart rapidly. From around A.D. 900, convincing evidence of a continuing, creative rulership disappears from our records. Buildings fall into disrepair, their roofs and vaults crashing into the rooms below as the weeds and trees take over. Monuments and new buildings cease to be commissioned. The near-magicians who had so long manipulated their time-bound gods simply disappear. All of this seems to occur suddenly, but it is difficult to follow because the record of the last years of Tikal as a classic power comes from unsealed, and hence unprotected, deposits just beneath the soil.

We are sure of one thing. Tikal was by no means suddenly depopulated. The Maya who remained there in the 10th century were extremely active in the once hallowed precincts. They plundered the Great Plaza and the North Acropolis. Temple floors were opened, and caches and tombs as old as 500 years were robbed. The lure seems to have been jade. Cached offerings about the bases of stelae were pillaged, and in some instances other objects were installed to replace the stolen ones. Such behavior points to a need to pacify past powers.

The Central Acropolis is littered with evidence of these lingering people. One would like to think of them as having taken advantage of the abandoned palaces of their past rulers–as intruders into the massive settings of pride and power. At any rate, if these buildings had

A program of repair and restoration went along with excavations at Tikal. Photo shows two of the buildings that occupy one of the six courts that form the Central Acropolis. At left is a two-story, multiroom palace.

never before been lived in on a day-to-day basis, they certainly were then. Hearths were made in the rooms, even on fallen vault debris. As trash accumulated, it was thrown into corners.

We see fleeting glimpses of still later Postclassic Tikal in rare discoveries: a partial skeleton found high up in collapsed construction, branches of wild orange trees, the remains of a house, a church bell. Or we find evidence of people who ransacked a Late Classic burial within the rooms of Temple I and who burned copal in other temples. These and various other signs are evidence that handfuls of people lived at Tikal as late as the 18th and 19th centuries.

What caused the dissolution of Classic period Tikal? The problem is inseparable from that of the breakdown of the whole of Classic civilization throughout the vast, forested lowlands.

In the case of Tikal, we can safely rule out invasion. And we can rule out ideas of drastic weather change, for the birds and animals vividly depicted by the ancient Maya are still all about us. We can also rule out earthquakes, because serious earthquakes are not known in northern Guatemala. Nor is there evidence that disease wiped out the population.

A knife-edge economic balance, if in fact conditions were this precarious, might be cited as a reasonable cause of collapse, especially in light of an expanding population. And various bits of evidence do indicate a sharply increasing population during Late Classic times. A logical outcome of this would have been wars to expand Tikal's agricultural support. But Tikal may not have had the economic power to sustain both expansion and a workable local society.

Some scholars have envisioned disruptive power games developing among the rulers and bringing chaos to the tightly knit community. Another explanation sees those in control of the highly authoritarian religious life of Tikal becoming, over the many centuries, truly lost amid their incense, jades and pearls, and emerald-green feathers. The rulers may have grown more and more separated from the peasantry by a ritual that had become disastrously expensive, elaborate, aloof, and meaningless. Add to these possibilities a run of bad agricultural years. Add also the knowledge that great civilizations in Mexico, centered on Monte Alban and Teotihuacán, had already fallen. Great social changes in the midst of heavy militarism had become the rule of the world beyond the vast forests of the lowland Maya. As a result, the highlands of Guatemala, Tikal's source of many raw materials, may have been cut off from the lowlands.

The collapse of this civilization surely must have had multiple causes. Many events conspired at a point in history to bring down an extraordinary group of rulers who had early devised the content and course of what became their utterly magnificent world. Their record of success is impressive–more than a thousand years of continuous development that seems to have seen no need to greatly change in the hothouse atmosphere of their jungles.

A.D.100 - A.D.750

Up rose the North Acropolis, level by level. The 14th construction stage, in about A.D. 200, buried everything again and led to the creation of a totally new Acropolis. The final result, the 19th stage, was one of the greatest architectural achievements in pre-Columbian America. By A.D. 750, at least 10,000 Maya were residing in the central section of Tikal, with thousands more in the surrounding food-producing area. Then, after about A.D. 900, this great, rich Tikal rapidly collapsed. Perhaps there were internal power struggles. Perhaps the peasantry rose up against the ruling families. Whatever the reasons, Tikal fell into ruins bit by bit, though a dwindling population lived on there for a century or so. Finally, the jungle totally reclaimed the site, and it remained for archaeologists a thousand years later to uncover and study the long-buried remains of this once-great civilization.

Lift flap below for artist's conception of North Acropolis as viewed from the north.

Tikal's Pottery "Calendar"

The pottery found at an ancient site is a valuable tool for archaeologists. By studying the pottery, they can draw inferences as to a people's values and desires during the period in which it was made. They also can establish a relative chronology, or calendar, of pottery styles that can help them to determine time sequences at other areas of the site where pottery and other artifacts are later found.

Eb, about 600 B.C.

Cauac, about A.D. 1

Manik, about A.D. 400

Imix, about A.D. 700

Eznab, about A.D. 950

At Tikal, Nothing Was Forever

After more than a thousand years of effective blending of man, gods, and jungle soils, the collapse of Tikal ended the extravagant process of building, destroying, and rebuilding that was such an integral part of the city's life.

Why this interminable need to create and destroy? Final answers must await the correlation of immense amounts of information obtained during years of research at Tikal. Archaeologists, however, have reached some conclusions. They point out that some destruction and rebuilding is natural when a population center exists, as Tikal did, for 12 centuries or more. Also, there undoubtedly was change for the sake of change. There also may have been a religious motivation to replace temples with ever loftier ones, in a striving to reach nearer and nearer to the gods.

The fate of this heavy stele, or inscribed stone shaft, typifies the energy devoted to destruction. It was broken from its base, carried up a stairway, and reset in a temple room (see final overlay).

But what sets Tikal apart is its ritualized approach to destruction. Everything at Tikal seemingly had a calculated span of life. Temples, monuments, fine jades, and superb pottery–the Maya at Tikal eventually demolished almost everything they considered to be of worth. Thus, we can picture skilled artisans working for months to create a beautiful facade on a temple, knowing they might live to see their work destroyed.

Archaeologists see behind this methodical demolition the possibility that the more important temples and monuments were associated with the priests or other elite Maya who used or commissioned them. Generally, when a priest died, his temple and monument were not allowed to survive him. They too were "killed," the dead priest was entombed in front of or beneath his mutilated temple, and a new temple was erected. Even the tombs were not inviolable. Occasionally, when dismantling buildings, the Maya came across these rich interments from earlier times. Having done so, they apparently sought to destroy the potency of the dead priests by smashing and burning the tombs' contents and carefully reburying everything elsewhere. Some of the theories may prove to be correct, some not, as archaeologists continue their search for answers to the many questions about the politics, social structure, and economics of Tikal.

Prepared by the staff of THE WORLD BOOK YEAR BOOK.

Consultant: Dr. William R. Coe,
University Museum, University of Pennsylvania.
Cover Photograph: Joya Hairs.
Reconstruction Drawing: H. Stanley Loten.
Reconstruction Rendering: George Suyeoka.
Pottery and Stele Photographs: Dr. William R. Coe.

Printed in U.S.A. by the Trans-Vision® Division, Milprint Incorporated.

Section Three

The Year On File, 1967

Contributors to *The World Book Year Book* report on the major developments of 1967 in their respective fields. The names of these contributors appear at the end of the articles they have written. A complete roster of contributors, giving their professional affiliation and listing the articles they have prepared, appears on pages 6 and 7.

Articles in this section are arranged alphabetically by subject matter. In most cases, titles refer directly to articles in *The World Book Encyclopedia*. Numerous cross references (in bold type) are a part of this alphabetical listing. Their function is to guide the reader to a subject or to information that may be a part of some other article, or that may appear under an alternative title. *See* and *See also* cross references appear within and at the end of articles and similarly direct the reader to related information contained elsewhere in *The Year Book*.

ADEN. See South Arabia, Federation of.

ADVERTISING, along with the general economy, lost some of its steam in 1967. Although the industry suffered, it still was a good year for advertising rather than the great year it might have been. Total spending on advertising increased in pace with inflation, or by less than 4 per cent versus 7 per cent in 1966, to about $17,000,000,000. In terms of profits, it was an even more disappointing year for the advertising agencies, whose rising costs cut into earnings.

As usual, television scored the best gain, 11 per cent, with about $2,500,000,000 of the total pie. Network radio slipped about 6 per cent. Newspapers were not quite able to hold their own. Their total volume, national and local advertising, fell about 1 per cent to approximately $4,800,000,000. Magazines gained roughly 4 per cent to $1,600,000,000.

The cost factor also meant the advertiser had to spend more to cover the same bases. For instance, toward the end of the year *Look* magazine announced that while it was increasing its circulation guarantee from 7,600,000 to 7,750,000 it also was substantially raising its advertising rates. Under the old schedule, the rate for a one-time full-color page in *Look* was $52,920. The new cost was $55,500.

Race to "Cuteness." Judging by the speeches and the writings of advertising executives, the big controversy within the industry in 1967 revolved around the "cult of creativity." The charge was that in the race to be ever more imaginatively different, the agencies were getting so dangerously close to the "cute" that they were losing sight of the basic function of advertising – to sell merchandise.

A facet of the controversy was the number of new agencies, following in the footsteps of Doyle, Dane Bernbach (the Volkswagen), and Jack Tinker & Partners (Braniff's pastel-hued jetliners), which were popping up under the "creative" banner. Notable was Wells, Rich, Greene, Inc., founded early in 1966. Its chic, blonde president, Mary Wells, and her two partners, Richard Rich and Stewart Greene, had developed the Braniff campaign at Tinker's.

Late in 1967, they had launched a series of ads for American Motors' Javelin that poked fun at its Detroit rivals. The ads stressed the car's low cost and observed: "Either we're charging too little or everyone else is charging too much." One ad on TV showed a composite rival sporty car being worked over by a sledge-hammer gang of critics. They were bashing in all the rival car's poor features.

Fighting back against this kind of competition, at least 12 of the largest agencies had formed special creative units or "think tanks," divorced from the demanding routine of agency-client relations but charged with solving special problems and called upon to create out-of-the-ordinary campaigns.

The Big Get Bigger. Despite the new-agency competition and despite the fact that some 750 agencies of varying size were operating in New York City alone, the largest U.S. agencies were growing much faster than the industry as a whole. The top 25 had increased their billings by a whopping 566 per cent from 1946 to 1966.

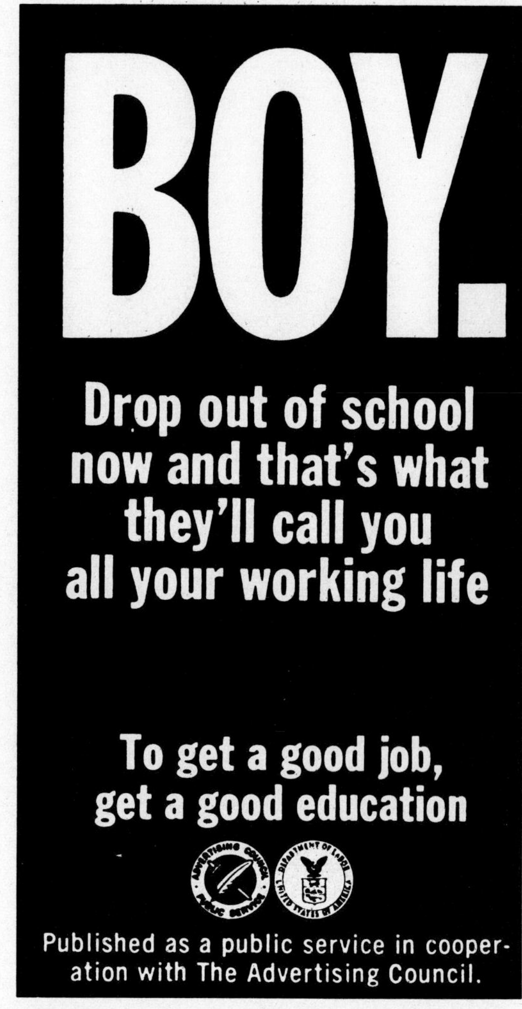

This eye stopper in the U.S. Department of Labor's Continue Your Education campaign won the Institute of Outdoor Advertising's 1967 public service award.

One reason the big were growing bigger was simply that the advertisers they serve – the major corporations – were also growing and increasing their advertising outlays faster than business in general. The top 125 national advertisers boosted their spending in 1966 by 12 per cent, against a total advertising gain of only 7 per cent. The top five advertisers increased their budgets the most. In order, they were Procter & Gamble, General Motors, General Foods, Ford Motor, and Bristol-Myers, according to the rankings published annually by *Advertising Age.*

The direct approach—as portrayed in this frank comparison between the Mustang and her client's Javelin—was typical of Mary Wells' creative advertising.

Conflict of Interest. Their clients' growth posed an unusual problem for some agencies. The startling increase in the number of corporate mergers and acquisitions during the year created conflict-of-interest problems. For instance, Agency Z may have been long handling the advertising for both Company A's breakfast food and Company B's frozen foods. Suddenly, Company A (breakfast food) buys Company C, which produces frozen food. Immediately, Agency Z has a problem: Two of its clients (A and B) now become direct competitors in the frozen food market. The agency therefore has to drop one of the accounts. Because of this situation, a number of agencies lose not only important accounts but also clients.

The continuing boom in advertising in Canada, Mexico, and overseas also contributed to the accelerated growth of large agencies. Naturally enough, only such agencies had the economic strength to establish foreign branches. Canada's increase in gross advertising revenues rose an estimated 6.6 per cent in 1967 to a total of about $904,000,000 in Canadian dollars. Another significant international development: France was getting ready to follow England in allowing commercial television advertising along with the long-established system of state-supported telecasts. [Edwin W. Darby]

See also Drugs; Publishing; Radio; Retailing; Television.

AFGHANISTAN. Prime Minister Mohammed Hashim Maiwandwal visited the United States in March for the first time since 1963, when he ended his term as Afghanistan's ambassador. One result of the visit, which included a meeting with U.S. President Lyndon B. Johnson, was the formation of a U.S. agricultural survey mission to evaluate Afghan agriculture. Its recommendations were incorporated into a third five-year plan, which went into effect in March. In October, Maiwandwal resigned because of ill health. He was succeeded by Deputy Prime Minister Nour Ahmad Etemadi.

The major part of the Soviet-financed Nangarhar Canal project was completed in 1967. It will put 40,000 acres of unused land under cultivation. A British firm, Woodrow Taylor Construction, Ltd., was awarded an $11,000,000 contract to build a 200-room hotel in Kabul. France made its first loan to Afghanistan—$18,000,000 for mining development.

This economically impoverished nation played an unaccustomed role in world affairs in July when the president of the United Nations General Assembly, Abdul Rahman Pazhwak of Afghanistan, led the debate on the Middle East crisis. [William Spencer]

Facts in Brief. Population: 16,300,000. Government: King Mohammed Zahir Shah; Prime Minister Nour Ahmad Etemadi. Monetary Unit: afghani (77.25= U.S. $1). Foreign Trade: exports, $72,800,000; imports, $74,400,000. Principal Exports: fruits and nuts, cotton.

AFRICA

Two of Africa's most populous nations, Nigeria and Congo (Kinshasa), suffered internal revolts and armed clashes throughout 1967. Nigeria was torn by civil war. In parts of the Congo, white mercenaries and supporters of the exiled former premier, Moise Tshombe, seized control, and threatened to unseat the weak central government.

The United Arab Republic (U.A.R.) received staggering military and economic blows in the war with Israel in June. President Gamal Abdel Nasser temporarily resigned, but his great popularity kept him in control of the U.A.R., and he remained the key spokesman for the Arab bloc. See MIDDLE EAST.

Military leaders seized control of the government in Sierra Leone and Togo. Coups or assassinations were blocked in Ghana, Senegal, and Uganda.

Rhodesia maintained its independence as an illegal government despite an international boycott. The United Nations (UN) was also unable to wrest South West Africa from the control of the racist government of the Republic of South Africa. The British territory of Swaziland and Spanish Equatorial Guinea moved closer toward independence.

Northern Africa

The Arab countries north of the Sahara were briefly united against Israel during the six-day Arab-Israeli war in June. But of these, only the U.A.R. was actively involved. After the war, however, the Arab countries could not agree on a common policy. See ALGERIA; LIBYA; MOROCCO; SUDAN; TUNISIA; UNITED ARAB REPUBLIC (U.A.R.).

Western Africa

A breakup of the federal government system and armed revolts kept Nigeria in turmoil. Ghana put down an attempted coup, but civilian governments in Togo and Sierra Leone fell to army leaders.

The entente states of Dahomey, Ivory Coast, Niger, Togo, and Upper Volta met at Abidjan, Ivory Coast, on January 13 and 14, where they made common plans for economic development, cooperation with France, and their joint operation of Air Afrique airline. On February 24, Mali, Mauritania, and Senegal agreed to develop the upper basin of the Niger River with assistance from the UN International Development Association. See GHANA; NIGERIA; SIERRA LEONE; TOGO.

Dahomey announced in March that it would receive loans from Italy, the United States, and the UN to help develop its water supplies, agriculture, and a textile industry.

Gambia continued friendly relations with Great Britain and the West. Britain assisted Gambia by providing several small ships and over $8,000,000 in aid as part of a four-year development program.

Guinea, fighting a declining standard of living, took steps to improve relations with the United States. Foreign Minister Louis Beauvogui visited the United States in March, and President Sékou Touré conferred with U.S. Undersecretary of State Nicholas deB. Katzenbach in Guinea in May to express his country's desire for American friendship and assistance. The two countries' relations had been damaged in 1966 by disputes, the expulsion of U.S. Peace Corps workers, and the suspension of U.S. aid. In September, both Guinea and Ivory Coast released hostages, thus easing tensions between the two countries.

Ivory Coast. In January, 315 University of Abidjan students were arrested for rioting against the

government's close association with moderate and pro-Western African nations. Of those arrested, 26 foreign students were expelled. Three local students were called up for military service.

Liberia. President William V. S. Tubman officially opened a $27,000,000 hydroelectric plant financed by a loan from the U.S. Export-Import Bank. U.S. Assistant Secretary of State Joseph Palmer attended the January ceremony.

Mali returned to more friendly relations with France, its former colonial ruler. Mali-French agreements in April provided for additional French financial aid and the re-entry of Mali into the franc bloc. Under a new agreement, up to 100 Malis per year will be given free treatment in Soviet hospitals.

Tribal tensions bloodied Africa in 1967. In Nigeria, a war between federal troops, shown here in chains, and secessionists endangered national unity.

Mauritania signed agreements with the Anglo-American Corporation and a group of French companies that will administer its copper mines. Assistance was also accepted from Communist China, especially for the improvement of rice cultivation in southern Mauritania.

Niger and the adjoining Republic of Chad agreed on April 13 to avoid border difficulties by adopting new regulations on immigration, customs, arms control, and the extradition of prisoners.

Portuguese Guinea. Portugal reported intensified guerrilla attacks by African insurgents assisted by Cubans. It sent army patrols throughout the colony to quell agitation for independence.

Senegal. Demba Diop, a prominent political leader, was assassinated on February 3. The assassin was executed, and four conspirators were given sentences ranging from four years to life imprisonment. An attempt also was made to kill President Léopold Sédar Senghor at Dakar on March 22. The would-be assassin was executed in June. This plot was blamed on followers of former Premier Mamadou Dia, now serving a life sentence.

Upper Volta. President Sangoulé Lamizana, military ruler of Upper Volta, declared early in 1967 that the army would have to stay in power for another four years to prevent disorder. France, the United States, and West Germany sent food and financial aid to ease shortages caused by drought and lean harvests.

Central Africa

Congo (Kinshasa) continued to make news headlines because of clashes between government forces and white mercenaries, demands on Algeria for the return of condemned former Premier Moise Tshombe, and new Belgian-Congolese mining disputes.

In line with UN recommendations, Spain moved to give full independence to Equatorial Guinea in 1968. The country, consisting of Río Muni on the mainland and the two islands of Fernando Póo, has had autonomy since 1964. See CONGO (KINSHASA).

Cameroon. More than 100 persons were killed and scores wounded in January as the result of a local fight in which Bamiléké workers killed four Bakossi tribesmen. The incident led the Bakossi to retaliate against Bamiléké families. Police and army units ended the massacre.

Central African Republic. Southern refugees from the north-south conflict in neighboring Sudan reached an estimated total of 37,000 in the Central African Republic, straining relations between the two countries.

Chad. Fighting between government forces and rebels in southern Chad in February resulted in the deaths of 56 persons. President François Tombalbaye visited the region to investigate security conditions and to help lessen tensions. He also visited France and West Germany to obtain economic aid.

Congo (Brazzaville) received a total of $45,000,000 in loans from the International Bank for Reconstruction and Development (World Bank), European Investment Bank, and Banque Nationale de Paris to develop its potash mining industry. The UN International Monetary Fund provided $3,000,000 more for mineral prospecting. Aid was also accepted from Russia and Communist China.

Gabon. Vice-President Albert Bongo shuffled the cabinet, ran the government, and obtained economic aid for road building from West Germany while ailing President Léon M'Ba received treatment in Paris. Both leaders were re-elected in March. M'Ba died in November.

Rwanda sought to end the border conflict and build closer trade relations with Burundi. It also attempted to increase exports through the acceptance of aid from West Germany and the International Monetary Fund.

Eastern Africa

Sudan was involved in an internal struggle between the north and the south, a border clash with Ethiopia in July, and the Arab-Israeli war in June.

Somali nationalists objected to the continued control of French Somaliland by France. In northeastern Kenya, intermittent fighting continued between Somalis and government forces. Ethiopia attempted to subdue dissidents in Eritrea, and claimed French Somaliland, but the territory voted in March to remain under French control.

President Julius Nyerere of Tanzania favored increased socialism and the replacement of European bankers and school principals by Africans. Uganda blocked a February plot against the government. See ETHIOPIA; KENYA; SOMALIA; SUDAN; TANZANIA; UGANDA.

Southern Africa

The Rhodesian situation, assistance for Zambia, and continued control of South West Africa by the Republic of South Africa were of international concern in 1967. The nations of Botswana, Lesotho, and Malawi cooperated with South Africa through economic necessity. See RHODESIA; SOUTH AFRICA, REPUBLIC OF; ZAMBIA.

Angola. Rival exile liberation movements continued their struggle for power. The Movimento Popular de Libertação de Angola, in Brazzaville, and the Gouvernement Révolutionnaire de l'Angola en Exil in Kinshasa, each held members of the rival group as hostages. Both issued reports of armed raids into Angola and reported heavy casualties to Portuguese forces. But the Portuguese army reported only light losses. Indications of substantial offshore petroleum resources in 1967 increased the potential value of Angola to Portugal.

Botswana. President Seretse Khama adopted a policy of friendship toward both black African nations and white-dominated Rhodesia and the Republic of South Africa for his year-old country.

Lesotho. In January, Prime Minister Leabua Jonathan arrested opposition leaders and forced King Motlotlehi Moshoeshoe II, the titular and ceremonial ruler, to agree not to exceed his constitutional powers. This ended a power struggle that threatened to disrupt the new nation.

Jonathan met in January with Prime Minister Balthazar Johannes Vorster of the Union of South Africa after being received with full honors. They agreed on policies of friendship, economic cooperation, and relaxed border controls.

Facts in Brief on the African Countries

Country	Population	Government	Monetary Unit	Foreign Trade (million U.S. $) Exports	Imports
Algeria*	12,113,000	President Houari Boumedienne	dinar (4.9 = $1)	704	626
Angola	5,304,000	Governor-General Rebocho Vaz	escudo (28.75 = $1)	221	209
Botswana	601,000	President Seretse Khama	rand (1 = $1.41)	no information	
Burundi	2,989,000	President Michel Micombero	franc (87.5 = $1)	14.7	16.4
Cameroon	5,384,000	President Ahmadou Ahidjo	CFA franc (246.85 = $1)	139	129
Central African Republic	1,391,000	President/Premier Jean-Bedel Bokassa	CFA franc (246.85 = $1)	30.9	35.2
Chad	3,416,000	President François Tombalbaye	CFA franc (246.85 = $1)	23.9	32.5
Congo (Brazzaville)	869,000	President Alphonse Massamba-Debat; Premier Ambroise Noumazalay	CFA franc (246.85 = $1)	43.5	69.7
Congo (Kinshasa)*	16,508,000	President Joseph Mobutu	zaire (1 = $2.00)	329	320
Dahomey	2,486,000	Head of Government Maurice Kouandété	CFA franc (246.85 = $1)	14	34
Ethiopia*	23,600,000	Emperor Haile Selassie I; Prime Minister T. T. Akilou Abte-Wold	dollar (2.50 = $1)	111	162
Gabon	470,000	President/Prime Minister Léon M'Ba Died in November	CFA franc (246.85 = $1)	100.7	66.8
Gambia	350,000	Prime Minister David K. Jawara	pound (1 = $2.40)	14	16
Ghana*	8,274,000	Council Chairman Joseph A. Ankrah	new cedi (1.02 = $1)	244	352
Guinea	3,696,000	President Sékou Touré	franc (246.85 = $1)	42.9	48.9
Ivory Coast	4,030,000	President Félix Houphouet-Boigny	CFA franc (246.85 = $1)	311	268
Kenya*	9,911,000	President Jomo Kenyatta	shilling (7.14 = $1)	174	314
Lesotho	777,000	King Motlotlehi Moshoeshoe II; Prime Minister Leabua Jonathan	rand (1 = $1.41)	no information	
Liberia	1,106,000	President William V. S. Tubman	dollar (1 = $1)	135	104
Libya*	1,732,000	King Idris; Premier Abd Al-Qadir Badri	pound (1 = $2.79)	995	405
Malagasy Republic	6,672,000	President Philibert Tsiranana	CFA franc (246.85 = $1)	98	140
Malawi	4,284,000	President Hastings Kamuzu Banda	pound (1 = $2.40)	49	85
Mali	4,836,000	President Modibo Keita	franc (493.7 = $1)	13.2	36.2
Mauritania	971,000	President Moktar Ould Daddah	CFA franc (246.85 = $1)	46	16
Morocco*	14,270,000	King Hassan II; Prime Minister Mohammed Benhima	dirham (5.06 = $1)	428	477
Mozambique	7,178,000	Governor-General José da Costa Almeida	escudo (28.75 = $1)	108	173
Niger	3,541,000	President Hamani Diori	CFA franc (246.85 = $1)	25.5	37.9
Nigeria*	60,450,000	Federal Military Government Head Yakubu Gowon	pound (1 = $2.79)	793	718
Rhodesia*	4,612,000	Prime Minister Ian D. Smith	pound (1 = $2.79)	274	266
Rwanda	3,203,000	President/Prime Minister Grégoire Kayibanda	franc (100 = $1)	14.1	17.9
Senegal	3,634,000	President Léopold Sédar Senghor	CFA franc (246.85 = $1)	128	156
Sierra Leone*	2,412,000	Council Chairman Andrew T. Juxon-Smith	leone (1 = $1.20)	83	100
Somalia*	2,617,000	President Abdirascid Ali Scermarche; Prime Minister Mohammed Ibrahim Egal	shilling (7.14 = $1)	33.8	50.5
South Africa*	18,948,000	Acting State President Jozua F. T. Naude; Prime Minister Balthazar Johannes Vorster	rand (1 = $1.39)	1,706	2,530
Sudan*	14,458,000	Supreme Council of State President Ismail al-Azhari; Premier Mohammed Ahmed Mahgoub	pound (1 = $2.87)	203	217
Swaziland	309,000	King Sobhuza II; Prime Minister Prince Makhosini Dlamini	rand (1 = $1.41)	42	37
Tanzania*	11,078,000	President Julius K. Nyerere	shilling (7.14 = $1)	235	180
Togo*	1,728,000	President Etienne Eyadema	CFA franc (246.85 = $1)	36.2	47.6
Tunisia*	4,920,000	President Habib Bourguiba	dinar (1 = $1.93)	140	250
Uganda*	7,916,000	President A. Milton Obote	shilling (7.14 = $1)	188	120
United Arab Republic*	31,855,000	President/Premier Gamal Abdel Nasser	pound (1 = $2.30)	605	1,070
Upper Volta	5,063,000	President/Prime Minister Sangoulé Lamizana	CFA franc (246.85 = $1)	11	40
Zambia*	3,983,000	President Kenneth David Kaunda	pound (1 = $2.79)	691	388

*Indicates countries that have separate articles.

Malagasy Republic. President Philibert Tsiranana continued his moderate pro-Western stand and reorganized government departments to cut red tape and increase efficiency.

Malawi. President Hastings Kamuzu Banda gave partial support to UN sanctions against Rhodesia by stopping imports of Rhodesian chrome ore, copper, iron, and tobacco. But he insisted that Malawi had to continue importing Rhodesian meat and sugar. Malawi also signed new trade agreements with the Republic of South Africa and Portuguese-controlled Mozambique. This led to criticism by African nationalists who favored the UN boycott.

Mozambique. Portugal continued to repulse terrorist attacks by African nationalists operating from bases in Tanzania and guerrilla camps in northern Mozambique. It reported 81 terrorist casualties and the capture of 176 rebels in February. Rebel leaders countered by claiming that their losses were light.

South West Africa. A UN committee worked on plans for UN administration of South West Africa but found no way to force the Republic of South Africa to withdraw from the territory it acquired as a mandate from the League of Nations in 1920.

Swaziland. The monarchy party, the Imbokodvo National Movement, made a clean sweep of the elections of April 19 and 20. King Sobhuza II and Prince Makhosini Dlamini were thus in leading positions to govern Swaziland when it is granted independence by Great Britain. [Benjamin E. Thomas]

AGRICULTURE. U.S. farmers were restless in 1967. Their high hopes for a continuation of 1966's gains dimmed. They had expected a healthy increase in exports, and had not expected the decline in farm prices and incomes. Greater production, at home and abroad, raised fears of returning surpluses. Farm-related industries suffered along with the farmers. Farm equipment sales, for example, were up only 3 per cent, against manufacturers' expectations of 10 per cent and an actual 1966 increase of 20 per cent.

Fear of the future pervaded many small family operations as narrow profit margins accelerated the trend toward larger farms. Scattered droughts, poor harvest seasons, hurricane and frost damage, labor problems, and other natural and man-made hazards of farming took on added weight in such an unfavorable year. The flight from the farm continued. As of Jan. 1, 1967, there were 2,880,000 farms, or 74,000 fewer than a year before; and there were 5,200,000 farmworkers – down about 400,000.

Public policy for agriculture was uncertain. Farm leaders were preparing to do battle to prevent the expiration of farm income-support legislation. The farmers' political strength was being challenged in legislative halls, especially where re-apportionment had radically altered previous urban-rural relationships. Relief from burdensome taxes on property at the state and local level was often disappointing.

A study by the President's Commission on Rural Poverty reported the stark realities of rural poverty. The thought that agriculture might have outgrown its need for government subsidy was shattered in March, 1967, when a U.S. Department of Agriculture (USDA) report predicted that without subsidies realized farm incomes would drop more than 30 per cent.

There were still long-run hopes for agricultural gains, however. They stemmed from: (1) growing foreign purchasing power; (2) improvements in agricultural technology; (3) the success of farmer bargaining coalitions; and (4) the promise of rural gains on "rural-urban imbalance" problems. But long-run hopes did little to dispel short-run farmer disillusion and alarm.

U.S. Farmers in 1967 learned that their minority status was more than a matter of numbers. They could observe a strong rise in nonfarm personal income, increased industrial production, and some improvement in business profits. Yet, their own situation was much less favorable. The farmer's share of the consumer's food dollar dropped to only 38 cents, from 40 cents the year before. Realized net farm income for the first nine months of the year declined 10 per cent to $14,800,000,000 on an annual rate basis. The 3 per cent rise in volume of farm

World Food Production Climbs

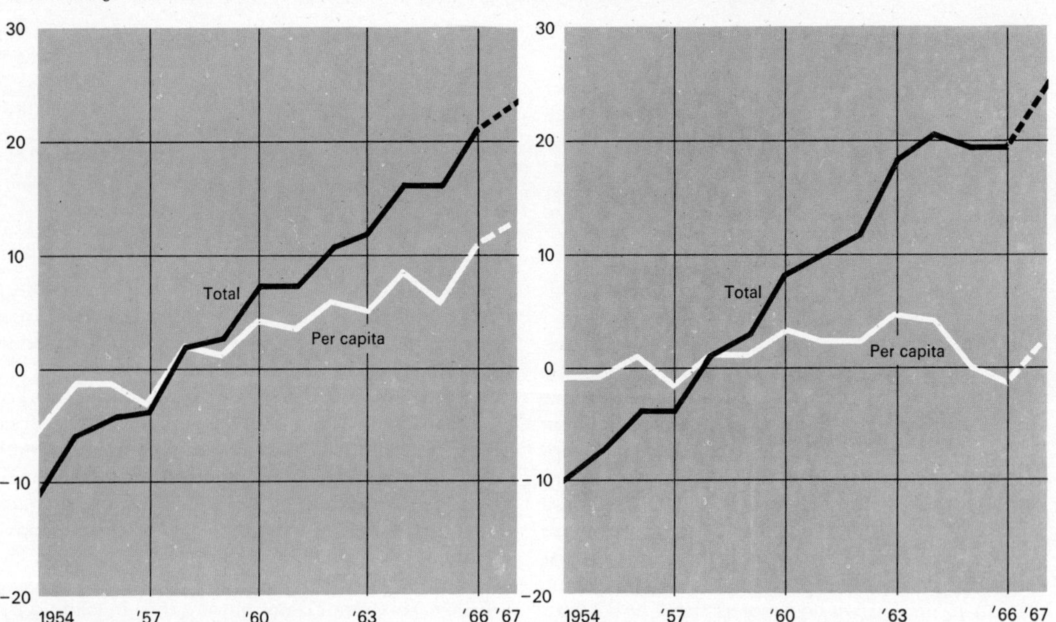

*North America, Europe, U.S.S.R., Japan, Republic of South Africa, Australia, New Zealand

*Latin America, Asia (except Japan and Communist Asia), Africa (except Republic of South Africa)

marketings was more than offset by lower prices and higher costs. Prices were down 7 per cent to 75 per cent of parity before adjustment for government payments, and down to 80 per cent with government payments included.

Total assets of U.S. agriculture on Jan. 1, 1967, were approximately $269,500,000,000; total debt was $45,700,000,000. The farmers' equities, at $223,800,000,000, increased about 4.5 per cent during 1966. The cost of farm production items and land values were up. Average investment per farm was $73,164, twice that reported for 1958. Farm debt continued to climb – up 10 per cent from the previous year. Generally, however, farmers were in sound financial condition. Farm foreclosures, at fewer than one per 1,000, were the lowest on record.

Hired workers on farms in 1967 averaged only 1,331,000, down 31 per cent from 1957. Farmers seemed finally reconciled to the fact that they would have to pay wages competitive with those in industry. Obtaining needed hired labor of sufficient competence, even with a 10 per cent higher wage rate, remained a key problem. See LABOR.

Crop Production was the highest in history, up 6 per cent from 1966 and nearly 20 per cent above the 1957 level. The all-crops production index was 4 1/2 per cent above 1966, and overall yield per acre for 28 leading crops was up 1 per cent. Corn output reached a record 4,717,000,000 bushels, and yields were up a phenomenal 5 bushels per acre. Soybean production pushed toward a billion-bushel crop, only a dream 10 years ago.

Of the major crops, only cotton continued to slump. Its estimated 8,100,000-bale total was 16 per cent below 1966 and only 65 per cent of the 1957-1959 average crop. The general increases in crop production were partly a reflection of an acreage increase of 19,700,000, or 7 per cent, from 1966. Acreage planted to food grains was up 22 per cent. Feed grain and oilseed acreage rose 4 per cent.

Food Expenditures Rise, But Income Rises Faster

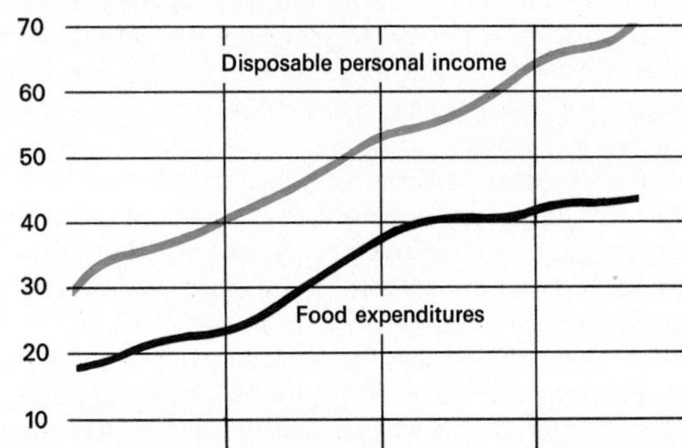

Food Takes Smaller Share of Income

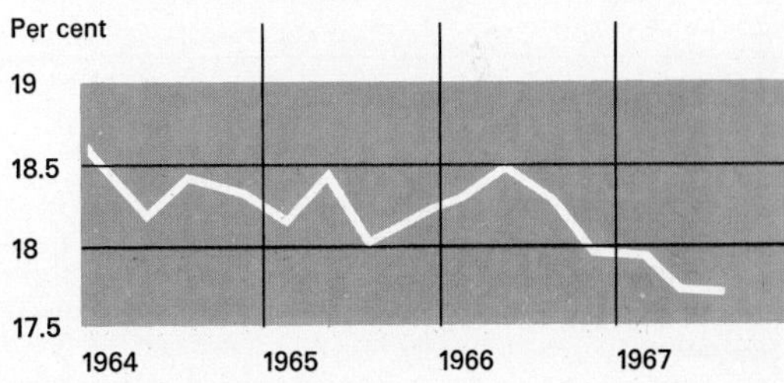

Source: U.S. Department of Agriculture

Prices Paid to Farmers Take Downturn

Per cent change since 1947-1949

40, 30, 20, 10, 0, −10, −20

Retail food prices

Prices paid to farmers

1947-'49 '55 '60 '65 '67

Source: U.S. Department of Agriculture *9-month period

Output of Major U.S. Crops

(millions of bushels)

Crop	1967*	1966	1961-1965†
Corn	4,717	4,103	3,758
Sorghums	789	720	548
Oats	806	798	953
Wheat	1,554	1,311	1,214
Soybeans	994	931	719
Rice (a)	906	851	680
Potatoes (b)	302	307	272
Sugar (c)		5,425	
Cotton (d)	81	96	149
Tobacco (e)	2,011	1,890	2,160

*Preliminary; † average
(a) 100,000 cwt; (b) 1,000,000 cwt; (c) 1,000 tons;
(d) 100,000 bales; (e) 1,000,000 pounds.

AGRICULTURE

Livestock and Poultry farmers generally kept the markets well supplied. Total red meat production gained more than 3 per cent from 1966, with the output of beef up 2 per cent, veal off 13 per cent, and pork up 6 per cent. Total poultry production rose 12 per cent. Egg production reached a record high, 5 per cent over last year, as more hens laid more eggs faster.

For the 21st consecutive year, the production of broiler chickens increased, up 3 per cent from 2,570,000,000 birds in 1966. Although the number of turkeys produced rose 8 per cent, turkey meat production gained 12 per cent in the year.

By the end of 1967, the numbers of livestock on U.S. farms were generally reduced. Cattle inventory declined for the third consecutive year to less than 108,000,000. Sheep and lambs dropped to less than 23,000,000, lowest since records were started in 1867. Milk cow herds had been culled another 4 per cent from the 15,183,000 total of Jan. 1, 1967. But because of larger output per cow, 1967 milk production approaching 120,000,000,000 pounds was expected, only slightly below 1966's total.

U.S. Production of Animal Products
(millions of pounds)

	1967*	1966	1957-1959†
Beef	20,200	19,725	13,704
Veal	790	910	1,240
Lamb and mutton	620	650	711
Pork	12,020	11,337	10,957
Eggs (a)	5,799	5,538	5,475
Chicken		7,303	4,880
Turkey		1,678	1,065
Total milk (b)	1,198	1,202	1,233
Cheese	1,895	1,856	1,396
Ice Cream		3,610	3,212
Butter	1,250	1,128	1,477

*Preliminary; † average
(a) 1,000,000 dozens; (b) 100,000,000 pounds.

The U.S. farmer's increased output of food and fiber brought him lower prices in 1967. The USDA's index of prices received by farmers was down 6 per cent, with the crop index declining 5 per cent and livestock and products index falling more than 6 per cent below 1966 levels.

Consumers continued to spend a declining percentage of disposable income for food. At 17.7 per cent, it was at an all-time low. Per capita consumption of beef continued its climb to over 105 pounds, pork was up 8 per cent to 62.8 pounds, and total red meat increased from 170.5 to 175.9 pounds.

Administration Concern. Secretary of Agriculture Orville L. Freeman, during a Midwest tour of regional farm policy conferences in Hutchinson, Kans.; Ames, Iowa; and Decatur, Ind., reassured farmers that he was, "deeply concerned" over the farmer's plight, and, he added, "I can assure you the President is concerned."

Dairy farmers "strike" by dumping milk into the Wabash River near Terre Haute, Ind., in an effort to get an additional 2 cents a quart for their milk.

In February, 1967, 400 representatives of 50 farm organizations gathered in Washington, D.C., for a one-day National Farm Policy Conference called by Freeman. President Lyndon B. Johnson met with them at a White House luncheon and assured them that "parity of income between the farmer and the rest of the economy is our constant goal."

To help the farmer achieve that income goal, the President, in a news conference on August 18, supported the principle of collective bargaining for farmers. He said, "I would hope that the administration . . . could find some legislation that would give to the farmer the means of bargaining reasonably . . . as we permit our workers to do."

Farm Groups. National Farmers Organization (NFO) members gave their officers the authority to call for the withholding of all farm products from market. Meeting in Des Moines, Iowa, in mid-August, 35,000 members of NFO also voted possible selective two-day or four-day strikes to hold milk or livestock off the market. They also voted to establish an NFO grain bank to hold back wheat, corn, and soybeans.

The American Farm Bureau Federation pushed hard for some type of marketing rights legislation. Its major provisions would:

- Uphold producers' rights to join in an association of producers.
- Prohibit dealers or handlers from refusing to deal

with such organized producers, from discriminating against them, or from coercing them in any way.
- Forbid false reports about the finances, management, or activities of an association.

"Rural-Urban Imbalance" was the second most discussed issue in agricultural policy. Secretary Freeman noted that ". . . we have on the one hand a depopulation of the countryside—because of lack of employment opportunity. . . . On the other hand, we are faced with an overpopulation of ill-planned, unplanned, and misplanned cities. . . . The real solution, I am convinced, is to bring about a readjustment of the capital assets of our country so as to result in a sensible and viable rural-urban balance."

The *Report of the President's National Advisory Commission on Food and Fiber* was released on July 14, 1967. The 29-man commission split, with 16 favoring tightening of agricultural policy controls and 13 for loosening them. The report held that the heart of the farm problem was that new technology increased production faster than effective demand could use the output. Thus, it concluded, some resources must be held out of production. Among its remedies, the report recommended programs that:
- Rely more heavily on direct payments to protect the farmer's income.
- Make use of two-price systems to better compete in world markets.
- Encourage better job opportunities for rural persons displaced from agriculture.
- Guarantee farmworkers the same benefits deemed desirable for other workers.
- Discard the historical concept of parity prices as obsolete.
- Establish a national security food reserve.

The Feed Grain Program for 1967 remained basically the same as that of 1966. Changes included a higher loan rate, higher total price support, and elimination of voluntary diversion for payment except on small farms that could earn diversion payments higher than in 1966.

As the efficiency of U.S. agriculture was climbing—by almost 7 per cent in 1966—advances in technology promised to make agriculture even more productive. The USDA in August, 1967, reported that one farmworker in 1966 produced enough to supply himself and 38.56 other persons, a 158 per cent increase since 1950, when he supplied only 14.47 other persons.

Among 1967 farm-technology developments were:
- A continuous pipe-laying machine for field drainage that utilizes a laser beam to control the depth of trenching. This economical technique may also be used to maintain a constant level in earth moving, land leveling, ditching, and road grading.
- The first steps toward using remote-sensing devices on orbiting satellites to collect agricultural data. The technique, developed in conjunction with the space program, involves the use of infrared photography and radar to survey soil conditions and moisture, diseased crops, insect pests, and amount of yields swiftly and accurately. Other possible uses are identification of species of crops and information about animal species, such as age, breed, and sex.
- The use of controlled atmospheres for the storage of perishable commodities. Nine weeks of storage in atmospheres of 1 per cent oxygen and 5 per cent carbon dioxide produced peaches and nectarines with better color, flavor, and softness, more like freshly harvested fruit than similar fruit from ordinary air storage.
- A new Bermuda grass hybrid that puts 30 per cent more weight on cattle than do the common varieties.

World Agriculture. Generally favorable weather helped production of most crops. Wheat production was estimated at a near record 10,218,000,000 bushels, slightly below the 1966 production figure, which was revised to show a record output of 10,276,000,000 bushels. Total land planted to wheat increased 2 per cent to a record 532,000,000 acres.

World Crop Production

(000,000 omitted)

Crop	1960-1964	1966	1967*	%U.S.
Barley (bu.)	3,860	4,593	4,821	7.7
Corn (bu.)		8,867		
Oats (bu.)	3,356	3,108	3,021	26.7
Wheat (bu.)	8,473	10,276	10,218	15.2
Rice (metric tons)†	160.1	163.0		
Sugar (tons)		71.9		
Coffee (bags‡)	65.4	61.9	69.8	0
Cotton (bales)	48.3	47.4	47.4	17.1
Soybeans (bu.)	1,018	1,279	1,354	73.4

*Estimated; † excluding Communist Asia; ‡ 132.276 pounds.

Livestock numbers continued to increase. At the beginning of 1967, cattle totaled 1,140,000,000 head, up 1 per cent from 1966 and 17 per cent over the 1956-1960 average. Hogs rose for the third straight year to 498,000,000 head, 2 per cent above 1966 and 16 per cent above 1956-1960. Sheep were up 1.3 per cent from 1966 and 9.4 per cent above 1956-1960 to 1,027,400,000 head. World wool production was estimated at 6,028,000,000 pounds, up 2 per cent from 1966.

Even though total food output was high, there were few gains on a per capita basis, especially in the developing nations, where populations were rising faster than production. Grain imports by developing countries rose from 20,700,000 metric tons per year in 1959-1961 to 29,000,000 metric tons in 1964-1965 and are projected at more than 50,000,000 metric tons by 1980. (A metric ton equals 2,204.62 pounds.) To avoid their rapidly expanding dependence on imports, the developing nations need to double food production by 1985. That would mean an annual increase of approximately 4 per cent, compared with the current 2.5 per cent growth rate. The President's Science Advisory Committee estimated that to reach that 1985 goal, investments of $21,200,000,000 would have to be made for fertilizer, machinery, pesticides, and seed, as well as additional large investments for education, training of personnel, marketing, research, storage, and transportation.

World attention focused sharply on these problems and some developments were encouraging. With the new U.S. policy of making food aid available only to countries committed to a concerted effort to improve their own agriculture, development of new techniques and improvement of seed and livestock strains received high priority in many developing nations.

Varieties of Mexican dwarf wheat were widely grown in Afghanistan, India, Pakistan, and Turkey. Indian scientists reported the discovery of a high-lysine wheat, with a protein content comparable to that of milk. High-lysine (high-protein) corn seed was expected to be distributed to Brazilian farmers by 1968. World fertilizer use increased rapidly. In India, fertilizer use was about double that of 1963-1964 and four times that of 1959-1960.

U.S. Agricultural Trade, as well as production, remained dominant. Exports rose slightly to a record high of $6,778,000,000 in the year ended June 30, 1967, with production from one out of every four harvested cropland acres being exported. Export gains over 1966 were largely in cotton (43 per cent), tobacco (41 per cent), and oilseeds (2 per cent). Animal product exports were down 8 per cent, and total grain exports down 6 per cent despite a 33 per cent increase in rice exports.

U.S. agricultural imports in fiscal 1967 were $4,500,000,000, about the same as the year before. Coffee imports fell 16 per cent, while those of beef and veal, dairy products, fruits, and sugar rose.

President Johnson signed a proclamation on June 30, 1967, reducing dairy imports, including butter and cheese, to 1,110,000,000 pounds of milk equivalent annually beginning July 1, 1967. Dairy imports had risen from 900,000,000 pounds of milk equivalent in 1965 to 2,800,000,000 pounds in 1966, and were 4,300,000,000 pounds in the first half of 1967. The spurt in imports had aroused U.S. dairy farmers, who had been caught in a cost-price squeeze in their battle for the lagging domestic market.

The Kennedy Round of trade negotiations was concluded in 1967 (see INTERNATIONAL TRADE AND FINANCE). The United States received concessions of $866,000,000 and, in return, it gave concessions of $860,000,000, including $260,000,000 in tropical products. [CHARLES E. FRENCH AND LARRY L. NELSON]

See also FISHERY; FOOD; FOREST PRODUCTS.

AIR FORCE, U.S. See NATIONAL DEFENSE.
AIR POLLUTION. See CONSERVATION.
AIR RACE. See AVIATION.
AIRPLANE. See ARMED FORCES OF THE WORLD.

ALBANIA completed its 21st year as a people's republic with its basic course unchanged. Although it maintained trade with other Communist countries, Albania's foreign relations generally remained cool. Its sole ally remained Communist China, whose policies it continued to defend.

After some hesitation, the Tiranë regime endorsed the Chinese Cultural Revolution and introduced a modified version of it at home in 1967. Communist party leader Enver Hoxha, in a major speech made on February 6, called for "the further revolutionizing" of the party and the government. Albania's Communist youth groups were enlisted in the campaign as volunteers but, unlike the Red Guards of China, they remained under the firm control of the party Politburo. Meetings of criticism were held in many parts of the country.

According to reports, farm collectivization was completed in April and agricultural development was given major emphasis in the new five-year plan announced by the government. Urban citizens, as well as the nation's youth, were mobilized for work on the collective farms. [H. GORDON SKILLING]

Facts in Brief. Population: 2,013,000. Government: Communist Party First Secretary Enver Hoxha; Premier Mehmet Shehu. Monetary Unit: lek (12.5=U.S. $1). Foreign Trade: exports, $66,000,000; imports, $98,000,000. Principal Exports: metal ores, crude petroleum, cotton textiles.

ALBEE, EDWARD FRANKLIN (1928-), was awarded the 1967 Pulitzer prize for the best original American play. The play, *A Delicate Balance*, presented a drama of tension in family relationships in an eastern suburban community. Albee probably is most widely known for his powerful *Who's Afraid of Virginia Woolf?*, awarded the New York Drama Critics Circle Award as the best play of the 1962-1963 season.

Earlier works, all one-act plays, were *The Zoo Story* (1958), *The Death of Bessie Smith* (1959), *The Sandbox* (1959), and *The American Dream* (1960). Recent works, *The Ballad of the Sad Cafe* (1963), *Tiny Alice* (1964), and *Malcolm* (1965), were full-length plays. Albee described the impact of his plays as stemming from his efforts to try to dig "so deep under the skin that it becomes practically intolerable."

Albee was born in Washington, D.C., on March 12, 1928, and was adopted by Mr. and Mrs. Reed A. Albee. His father was an executive of the Keith-Albee vaudeville chain. Albee was graduated from the Choate School in Wallingford, Conn., and attended Trinity College in Hartford, Conn., for one and a half years when "it was suggested that he not come back."

A bachelor, Albee lives in New York City in an old carriage house he bought from actor Maurice Evans. [WALTER F. MORSE]

ALBERTA. See CANADA.

ALGERIA mobilized its armed forces and went on a wartime footing for the June conflict with Israel. The fighting stopped, however, before Algerian troops reached the battlefront. Algerian aircraft were sent to aid the United Arab Republic (U.A.R.), but French-speaking Israeli officers tricked 42 MIG jets into landing on Israeli airfields, where they were captured. See MIDDLE EAST.

Algeria's belligerence, before and after the Arab-Israeli war, extended to the United States and Great Britain. Denunciations of "imperialist America" by the press became so violent that U.S. Ambassador John D. Jernegan demanded a public apology. In June, Algeria broke relations with both countries, put a number of U.S. firms under state control, and subscribed to an Arab oil embargo on exports to the Western countries.

Major U.S. oil companies, affiliates of Esso and Mobil, were nationalized and placed under SONATRACH, the state oil company, in August.

Algeria and Tunisia demarcated their border satisfactorily, but the Algerian-Moroccan boundary dispute continued to simmer. Russia supplied equipment with an estimated value of $180,000,000 to the Algerian armed forces.

Internal Issues. The government was plagued by internal dissension. The assassination of exiled National Liberation Front (FLN) leader Mohammed Khider in Madrid, Spain, in January underlined political rivalries. Khider, a former FLN treasurer, had been accused of secreting $11,000,000 in party funds in Swiss banks.

Algeria received an unwanted guest when a plane carrying Congolese rebel leader Moise Tshombe was hijacked and forced to land in Algiers. The Algerian supreme court refused to extradite Tshombe but Algerian authorities indicated in November that they would keep him under house arrest as a hostage because of his threat to the "anti-imperialist" struggle in Africa.

Algeria held local elections in February, the first since Algeria gained independence in 1962. The voters elected 10,158 members to 475 communal assemblies. To decentralize decision-making, the new assemblies chose two officers each to form an advisory council to the ruling National Revolutionary Council.

With 75 per cent unemployment, population growing faster than the economy, and restrictions on emigration of Algerian workers to France, the government was forced to take drastic measures. The first family planning center was established in Algiers, imports were curtailed, and export-import firms were nationalized. [WILLIAM SPENCER]

Facts in Brief. Population: 12,113,000. Government: President Houari Boumedienne. Monetary Unit: dinar (4.9=U.S. $1). Foreign Trade: exports, $704,000,000; imports, $626,000,000. Principal Exports: crude petroleum, wine, citrus fruit.

ALLILUYEVA, SVETLANA (1926-), the only daughter of Joseph Stalin, startled the world by asking, and obtaining, asylum in the United States. Her request was made March 6, 1967, at the U.S. embassy at New Delhi, India. She reached New York April 21, after speculation in the world's press as to her motives and intentions.

The red-haired, modest-mannered woman was born in the Kremlin to Stalin's second wife, Nadezhda Sergeyevna Alliluyeva. She attended public schools in Moscow and studied poetry and literature at Moscow State University. She said in an interview carried by National Educational Television on October 2, that her decision to defect from Russia was not the result of a long, thought-out plan, but was made in India. She went to India Dec. 20, 1966, to bury the ashes of her third husband, Brijesh Singh, who had died in Moscow.

When she left Russia she brought with her the manuscript of a book of her reminiscences, *Twenty Letters to a Friend*, which she had secretly written in 1963. Many publishers expressed interest in it without ever seeing the text. Published in October, 1967, the book became an immediate best seller.

Miss Alliluyeva has a son Joseph, 21, by her first husband, Grigory Morozov, and a daughter Ekaterina, 15, by her second husband, Yuri Zhdanov. Both live in Moscow. [WALTER F. MORSE]

AMERICAN LEGION. See VETERANS.

AMERICAN LIBRARY ASSOCIATION (ALA) members voted to keep their headquarters in Chicago, Ill., home of the ALA since 1909. Of the more than 36,000 members, an increase of 4,000 in 1967, 9,781 voted by mail to remain and 6,997 voted to move to Washington, D.C. In keeping with the vote, the executive board moved ahead on plans to expand its facilities in Chicago. Soon after the vote, arrangements were announced to purchase the office building of the American Federation of Teachers whose membership, coincidentally, had voted to move its headquarters to Washington, D.C.

The ALA and its members contributed approximately $11,000 to provide assistance to the libraries in Florence, Italy, following the disastrous flood of November, 1966. A library expert was also sent to the National Library in Florence to consult with its director, Dr. Emanuele Casamassima, in the task of modernizing the library.

ALA Conference. The 86th annual conference, held in San Francisco, Calif., from June 25 to July 1, was the second largest ever held. Attendance was 8,116. The recommendations for future action of the ALA president's special program, "Crisis in Library Manpower: Myth and Reality," included emphasis on recruitment, education, and examination of present position classifications. A recurring suggestion was for a national study of work goals and the levels of education and skills needed to fulfill them.

In other actions, the conference:

- Revised the Library Bill of Rights to clarify and strengthen its language and to reaffirm ALA's position on unrestricted access to libraries.
- Accredited four library schools, making a total of 42 in the United States and Canada.
- Voted an honorary life membership in the ALA to Verner W. Clapp, retiring president of the Council on Library Resources, Inc.

Also at the conference, the ALA council adopted a revised federal legislative policy. The policy described the ALA's concern with present and future federal legislation and its relationship to the objectives of the association.

Foster E. Mohrhardt, director of the National Agricultural Library, in Washington, D.C., was installed as president for 1967-1968. Roger H. McDonough, director of the Division of State Library, Archives, and History, New Jersey State Department of Education, was elected vice-president. The 87th annual conference will be held in Kansas City, Mo., June 23 to 29, 1968.

Awards in 1967 included.

Beta Phi Mu Award for distinguished service to education for librarianship and the **Isadore Gilbert Mudge Citation** for distinguished contributions to reference librarianship to Louis Shores, retired dean of the library school at Florida State University, Tallahassee, Fla.

Melvil Dewey Medal for creative professional achievement, to Walter H. Kaiser, librarian, Wayne County Library, Wayne, Mich.

E. P. Dutton-John Macrae Award of $1,000 for advanced study in the field of library work for children, to Clayton E. Rhodes, school liaison librarian, Enoch Pratt Free Library, Baltimore, Md.

Grolier Award of $1,000, to Lura E. Crawford, librarian and director of library services, Oak Park and River Forest High School, Oak Park, Ill., for achievement in guiding and stimulating the reading of children and young people.

The J. Morris Jones-World Book Encyclopedia-ALA Goals Award for 1967, a sum of $25,000, to the Association of College and Research Libraries, a division of ALA, for establishing a junior college library information center, and to the American Library Trustee Association, another ALA division, for an extensive program to strengthen, revitalize, and organize state associations.

Lippincott Award of $1,000 for distinguished service in the library profession, to Edmon Low, librarian, Oklahoma State University, Stillwater, Okla.

Melcher Scholarship of $2,000 for graduate study in children's library services, to Mrs. Florence L. Wilson of Prince George, B.C.

Halsey W. Wilson Library Recruitment Award of $1,000, to the Pioneer Library System of Rochester, N.Y., for its summer internship program to interest college students in library careers. [RUTH M. WHITE]

See also CANADIAN LIBRARY ASSOCIATION; CANADIAN LITERATURE; EDUCATION; LITERATURE FOR CHILDREN (Awards).

ANGOLA. See AFRICA.

ANGUILLA. See WEST INDIES.

ANIMAL. See AGRICULTURE; LIVESTOCK SHOW; PET; ZOOLOGY; ZOOS AND AQUARIUMS.

ANTHROPOLOGY. Louis S. B. Leakey announced the discovery of several new skeletal fragments and identification of a new hominid species, *Kenyapithecus africanus*. The bones came from two fossil sites in Kenya, Rusinga and Songhor. One of the fossils was a jaw fragment different in form than that in apes, and, according to Leakey, shows that the family of man was already well differentiated more than 19,000,000 years ago.

Also in Kenya, John Martyn, a geology student from the University of London, found a new source of fossils on the west side of Lake Baringo. He was mapping geological formations in Kenya's Northern Rift Valley at the time. These new beds yielded bones of animals of Early Villafranchian age (1,500,000 years ago). One of the bone fragments that Martyn found has been identified by Phillip V. Tobias, of the University of Witwatersrand in South Africa, as a hominid skull fragment similar to fragments of *Australopithecus* or *Homo habilis* skulls.

Other Fossil Men. International teams from Kenya, France, and the United States explored the Omo River basin in Ethiopia for early human occupation sites. All three groups were successful in their search. The team from Kenya, led by Richard Leakey, recovered a human jawbone of the Middle or Upper Pleistocene Epoch. The French team recovered skull fragments of a form which has been described by Camille Arambourg as a new hominid genus, *Paraustralopithecus ethiopicus*. The French team indicated that the skull fragments were associated with fragments of fossil animals that probably lived before those found by L. S. B. Leakey in association with *Homo habilis* in Bed I of Olduvai Gorge. Thus these remains may be more than 1,750,000 years old, the accepted age for *Homo habilis*. The American team, led by F. Clark Howell of the University of Chicago, found two sites with hominid teeth, of an age probably comparable with that of Olduvai Bed I. It is likely that more fragments will be recovered from these important sites.

Andor Thoma, a Hungarian anthropologist, published a complete description of the human remains from the site of Vértesszöllös in Hungary. This site has yielded the earliest European human skeletal fragments known to date. Also found there were numerous stone tools in a series of early human occupations. The skeletal material, discovered in 1965, consists of several teeth of a child and a skull fragment apparently from a young adult male. The detailed study of this skull fragment has led Thoma to identify it as either *Homo erectus* or *Homo sapiens*, placing it in the new subspecies *paleohungaricus* (old Hungarian).

Jan Jelinek of the Moravian Museum at Brno, Czechoslovakia, described a human upper jaw fragment found with stone tools in Kulna cave, about 45 miles north of Brno, as that of a Neanderthal Man with many advanced features. The find is thought to

Pushing Back the Age Of Man

A new chapter in the story of human evolution was added in 1967 when it was determined that the roots of man's family tree date back more than 20,000,000 years. Previously, it had been assumed that the zoological family to which man belongs, the Hominidae, came into existence in more recent times, perhaps only about 5,000,000 years ago. The finding also destroyed the popular textbook theory that man evolved from an apelike tree-dwelling primate.

We can now be relatively sure that the oldest known ancestor of man, *Kenyapithecus africanus*, evolved into mankind at the same time the true apes were evolving into gorillas and chimpanzees. The remains that we have so far uncovered indicate that both the manlike and the apelike creatures lived in comparatively open country.

The various *Kenyapithecus* fossils had been found by my co-workers and me over the last 18 years, but only recently have we been able to ascertain carefully their position on man's family tree. The fragmentary remains of at least eight individuals of a stage we have called *Kenyapithecus africanus* were found at two sites in Kenya, Songhor and Rusinga Island. They must be clearly placed within the family of man because of a number of characteristics that distinguish them from apes, either living or fossil.

The characteristics that show these differences are all related to the teeth and to the jaw structure. First, the upper central incisors are like other primitive human shovel-shaped incisors, as are the structures of the cheek teeth. Next, the lower jaw is fundamentally hominid in its detail and so is the shortening of the face, as shown by the jawbone. The position of the lower premolars in relation to the canine teeth is more human than apelike and the compressed short roots of the canines are distinctly human. Finally, the chin of *Kenyapithecus africanus* is more rounded, whereas in apes the chin slopes backward.

After we had distinguished the special features of *Kenyapithecus africanus* we were able to establish the fact that the fossil *Kenyapithecus wickeri* from Fort Ternan, Kenya, also was a member of the Hominidae. This fossil was found some years ago by my African assistant, Heslon Mukiri. It represents a later staff in the evolution of *Kenyapithecus* in the direction of man and dates to approximately 14,000,000 years. We also now realize that *Ramapithecus brevirostis*, found in 1935 by G. Edward Lewis in the Silawik Hills of India, must also be regarded as a member of the human family.

Prior to these discoveries, the view was widely held that the genus *Proconsul*, also from Songhor and Rusinga Island in Kenya, was a reasonable claimant for the title of "common ancestor of apes and man." Following the discovery of fragments of *Proconsul* in 1927 and 1931, I found the first nearly complete *Proconsul* skull in 1948. Such creatures lived at least 25,000,000 years ago. Now that Hominidae have been found that were living at the same time as *Proconsul*, we must dispense with the idea that this creature was a common ancestor to man and the apes. They should be regarded rather, as a side branch leading neither to modern ape nor to man.

It is here interesting to note that in the period from 1910 to 1920 leading scientists such as Sir Arthur Keith and Professor Boule argued that the separation of hominids from *pongids* (apes) must have occurred at least during the Early Miocene Epoch. They reached the conclusion on purely theoretical evidence, because they noted that nearly every family of mammals had become established by that time. They did not, then, realize how remote the Early Miocene was.

One other important study affected the world of anthropology in 1967—a study of the brain case of *Homo habilis*. Professor Phillip V. Tobias of the University of Witwatersrand in Johannesburg, South Africa, found that *Homo habilis* had a brain capacity that was consistently larger than that of even the largest known Australopithecines, thus firmly establishing the hominid status of this species. As a result, few scientists any longer contend that *Homo habilis* was merely an aberrant member of the Australopithecines, and many agree that *Homo habilis* could have evolved directly into modern man. [Louis S. B. Leakey] date from just before the appearance of fully modern *Homo sapiens* in Europe, about 30,000 B.C.

Fossil Ape. On November 16, Professor Elwyn L. Simons of Yale University's Peabody Museum announced the discovery of the partial skull of an ape that had lived some 28,000,000 years ago. It was found by Grant E. Meyer of the Peabody Museum in the fossil-rich Fayum desert region of Egypt, about 60 miles southwest of Cairo. The fossil skull was embedded in rock 300 feet below a deposit of lava that had previously been dated by the potassium-argon method.

Professor Simons called the unique specimen important "as the skull of a species which stands near the base of the genealogical tree leading to later great apes and man." He said that the skull belonged to a small animal "about the size of an organ-grinder's monkey." Its skull and jaw were the approximate size of the lesser apes or gibbons.

Simons named the new find *Aegyptopithecus zeuxis*, which means the linking Egyptian ape. Jawbones of this creature had been found in the past, one as early as 1906, but not until this discovery had any other part of its skull been uncovered. Simons said that this specimen is better preserved than other apelike fossils older than 300,000 years.

"As the most primitive Old World higher primate skull," Simons said, "this specimen tends to confirm the correctness of the association binding the higher primates of the New World with those of the Old World in the suborder Anthropoidea.

Espionage. A crisis arose in 1967 that had repercussions on the work of cultural anthropologists throughout the world. This was the discovery that intelligence agencies of various governments, including the U.S. Central Intelligence Agency, have used "anthropological research" as a cover for their espionage activities.

Intelligence agents, masquerading as anthropologists have gathered information and engaged in political manipulation in several newly developing nations and traditionally independent nations that are not aligned with any of the "great powers."

In an attempt to remedy this situation, the American Anthropological Association took steps to clarify the relationship between anthropology and government. While recognizing that there are governmental projects and bureaus that require anthropological advice and assistance, such as the Bureau of Indian Affairs, the association requested that the U.S. government respect the integrity of universities and research agencies engaged in work abroad, and not involve such agencies in intelligence operations. Anthropologists were advised to refuse any employment that does not permit them to conduct their research and publish their results without governmental interference. [LESLIE G. FREEMAN, JR.]

ANTI-POVERTY. See POVERTY.

ARABIA. See SAUDI ARABIA.

ARCHAEOLOGY. Two potentially useful means of dating archaeological materials received attention in 1967. These were dating by obsidian hydration and by archaeomagnetism. It was also suggested that obsidian dating be combined with radiocarbon (C-14) dating, so that obsidian hydration time scales could fill the gaps between more widely spaced C-14 dates at a given site. Since many obsidian hydration dates can be calculated for the price of a single C-14 dating, this system seems to have merit.

Obsidian, or volcanic glass, absorbs water from the atmosphere or from the ground in which it is buried. This process of absorption, proceeding from the outside of the stone to the interior, forms a progressively advancing weathered layer that is clearly distinct from the unweathered part of the stone. In the past, it had been suggested that this absorption process proceeds continuously at a uniform rate. If the rate of hydration had been constant, one could determine the length of time that had elapsed since weathering began by measuring the thickness of the hydration layer.

The process of water absorption, however, is now known to vary with the temperature of the surrounding air or earth, and with the kind of obsidian involved. Since these factors are variable, obsidian dating can at best be used only for establishing limited regional time scales.

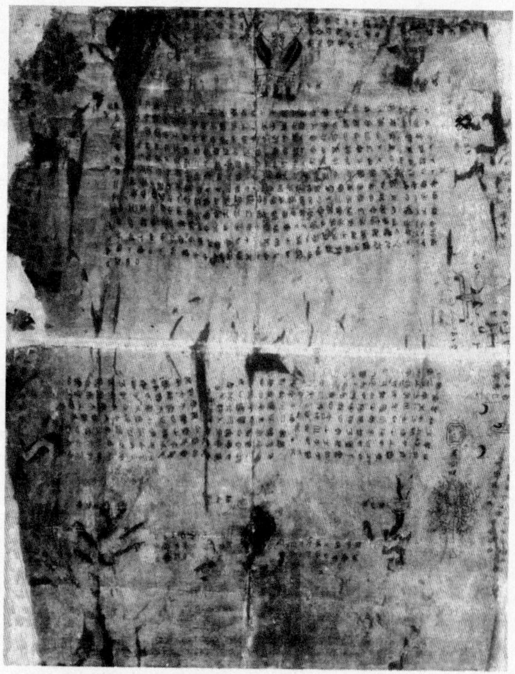

A 2,500-year-old Chinese silk manuscript, oldest ever found, was shown by a New York art collector. It is expected to help decipher archaic Chinese.

Archaeomagnetism as a dating method was also used effectively for the first time. The method is based on the fact that while the earth behaves like a magnet, the poles of its magnetic fields constantly shift. When clay is heated to about 1100°F., as it is in baking pots in a kiln or in burning a fire in a clay-lined hearth, the electrons in the clay particles begin to move in a direction that reflects the orientation of the earth's magnetic field. The clay thus becomes magnetized, and its poles align with the magnetic field of the earth. This polarization is maintained after the clay cools.

Robert DuBois of the University of Arizona used this method to determine that Hohokam Indians at Snaketown, Ariz., were practicing irrigation before 300 B.C. This would make them the earliest full-fledged users of irrigation in the United States.

Bronze Patterns. For many years it had been assumed that Southeast Asia was outside of most major developments in prehistory. This was because little was known about the area. Similar geometric designs had been found on bronze axes from Southeast Asia and on Bronze and Iron Age items from Europe and the Middle East. But the similarity was assumed to be an indication that the patterns, as well as the technique of bronzeworking, were imported to Southeast Asia from Central or Eastern Europe from about 800 to 300 B.C. Now, radiocarbon dates on some Southeast Asiatic finds make this hypothesis questionable, according to Wilhelm Solheim of the University of Hawaii. The site of Non Nok Tha in Thailand, a neolithic level with some of the patterns in question, has been dated at about 3400 B.C., and Bronze Age levels at the same site date about 2300 B.C. These early dates suggest that it is even possible that the stylistic elements were imported to Europe from Southeast Asia.

Israeli Hunting Settlement. While large, permanent settlements of hunting and gathering peoples existed in favored areas of the Americas well into historic times, only recently have scholars been willing to believe that such settlements could have also existed in Europe and Asia before the advent of agriculture. One important site that seems to represent this kind of adaptation is the multilevel Natufian site at Mallaha in Israel. The site, near the west shore of Lake Houleh, has been studied for many years by Jean Perrot of the French Archaeological Mission there. Perrot suggests that the site probably housed from 200 to 300 individuals on a relatively permanent basis. There is no indication that the Natufians at Mallaha had any knowledge of domesticated animals or plants. Of course, to support a permanent village of some 200 hunting and gathering people, there must have been abundant natural resources. [LESLIE G. FREEMAN, JR.]

Site of Minoan City

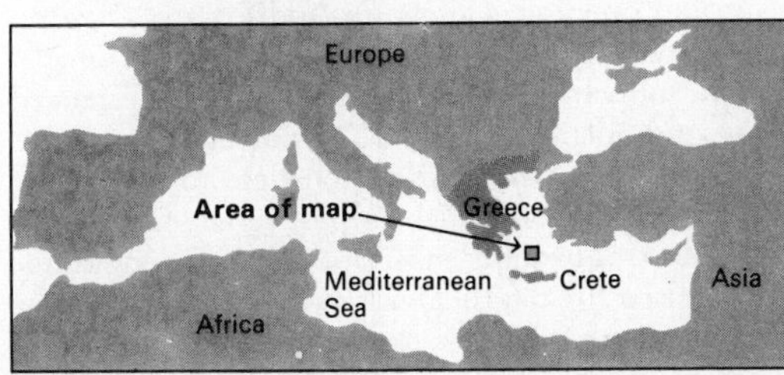

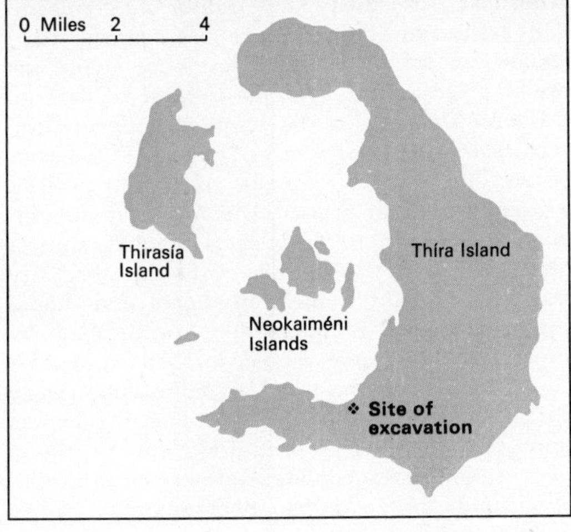

Wine jars, *above,* were found during the excavation of an archaeological site on Thíra Island near Crete. The site is thought by some to be a part of the lost continent of Atlantis, destroyed by volcanic ash.

© Ezra Stoller

The Rocky Mountains near Boulder, Colo., provide the background for the severe cluster of concrete towers of the new National Center for Atmospheric Research.

ARCHITECTURE. Although there were few hallmark projects during 1967, there was a significant recognition of the architect's role and responsibilities in a rapidly changing society. Discussions in articles, books, and at international conferences dealt less with styles and more with the processes and strategies of solving problems. Though the exploration of these problems would require time, the American Institute of Architects (AIA) took one immediate action during the year – an investment in research, both professionally and educationally, to help solve some of the problems of the relationship of architecture to today's society.

One of the year's best examples of the new approach to architectural problems was the National Center for Atmospheric Research (NCAR) near Boulder, Colo. The architects, I. M. Pei & Partners, designed a cluster of combined monolithic concrete forms that contrast with a mountain background. What might have been a series of individual buildings was expressed collectively, resulting in a concept of integration rather than segregation.

In the NCAR, the architects attempted to deal with a research establishment in a rational but not a mechanical way. A range of environments, internal and external, consisting of an office complex, a laboratory complex, and a conference building, all arranged in clusters, was provided to create an atmosphere conducive to research.

The Auditorium Theatre. Some 78 years after its grand opening, Chicago's Auditorium Theatre, designed by the famous 19th-century architects, Louis Sullivan and Dankmar Adler, experienced its second opening in 1967. The citizens of Chicago recognized the visual and acoustical merits of the theater, which had fallen into disrepair from years of neglect. Through subscription, sufficient funds were raised for the theater's reconstruction. Under the direction of Chicago architect Harry Weese, the theater was restored to its original elegance and acoustical perfection. The Auditorium's cultural and architectural importance has scarcely been equaled to this day, and it was once again, the proud possession of a proud city. See CHICAGO.

Urban Design. As the result of a devastating earthquake in 1963, the city of Skopje, Yugoslavia, became the focus of a major rebuilding project. Through the joint efforts of the Yugoslav government and a special fund of the United Nations, a plan for restoring the center of the damaged city was selected in 1967 in international invitational competition. An architectural team headed by Japan's Kenzo Tange, winner in 1966 of the AIA Gold Medal of Honor, won the commission to work out a detailed plan for the city. The project was significant because the local government grasped the occasion of tragedy and transformed it into an opportunity for creating a city of tomorrow, rather than allowing haphazard and piecemeal reconstruction. The reconstruction was to be supported by multigovernment cooperation on an international scale. Many highly qualified professional talents were being brought together to coordinate this significant undertaking. If successful, the Skopje reconstruction project will serve as a prototype for 21st century city development. It could also be considered a coming of age for the architect in his attempt to serve the demands of burgeoning societies. This role requires that creative talents accept the constraints and opportunities offered by a new era of architectural possibilities.

Expo 67. In the past, large international exhibitions established themselves as integral parts of architectural history by serving both as a retardant and as a promoter in the evolution of architectural ideas. Few, however, will be remembered as being more influential than Expo 67, the Canadian Universal and International Exposition of 1967, in inspiring the popular image of what is possible through comprehensive design. Expo 67 succeeded in going beyond the normal practice of being just a proving ground for architectural experimentation. Expo 67 demonstrated developing ideas about environment, and how to use and construct space to the best advantage. The exhibition confirmed the importance of links as well as objects in a man-made environment. In Expo 67, these links were developed so that the elements of an environment were coordinated in ways that were often complementary to each other.

"Habitat 67," Expo's experimental housing project, designed by 29-year-old Moshe Safdie of Israel, proved to be one of the most popular and influential exhibitions. Aside from its stimulating appearance, it succeeded in demonstrating the meaningfulness of architecture that includes social as well as physical factors. The West German pavilion, designed by the architects Frei Otto and Rolf Gutbrod, was regarded as a successful demonstration of an appropriate application of theoretical structural experiments. The suspended structure was covered with a translucent membrane that created an effect of light and space that held much promise for future large-scale space enclosures that would require a minimum of visual restriction.

Architect-inventor R. Buckminster Fuller, in collaboration with the Cambridge Seven Associates, architects and designers, was responsible for the U.S. pavilion. Fuller's geodesic dome and its construction technique served as a hallmark of large space enclosure with a minimum of material and weight. This type of construction is adaptable to covering entire cities, permitting the family of man to live, work, and play in a microclimate of his own selection. [DONALD D. HANSON]

See also CANADA; CITY; CITY AND REGIONAL PLANNING; FAIRS AND EXHIBITIONS.

ARGENTINA made dramatic progress during 1967 in its efforts to recover from its economic doldrums. Restrictions on capital and services transfers were eliminated. Imports were liberalized. Scaled wage increases, to be in effect until December, 1968, were established. The government also reached a cost-price agreement with industry, and granted tax deductions to spur production.

Foreign exchange reserves, including stand-by credits, totaled more than $900,000,000 for the first six months of 1967, a rise of about $456,000,000 over the same period in 1966. During the first half of 1967, the overall national product increased by 3.7 per cent, including a 13 per cent hike in agriculture due to increased production of cereals and beef. The balance of payments for the period was favorable by $336,500,000. In September, Argentina became a full member of the General Agreement on Tariffs and Trade (GATT). See INTERNATIONAL TRADE AND FINANCE.

On March 13, the republic devalued the peso by approximately 40 per cent. It simultaneously made the currency freely convertible and promised "no further devaluations." The government also placed export duties on such profitable products as beef, wheat, unprocessed animal hides, and wool.

In May, the government announced arrangements had been completed for a $400,000,000 aid package from the International Monetary Fund, the U.S. Treasury, and various foreign banks. The sum would be used to raise the nation's currency reserves, stabilize the peso, and improve the balance of payments.

Labor Curbs. Argentina's labor unions, once the most powerful in Latin America, became disorganized and demoralized in 1967 in the face of a tough attitude on the part of the military government. When the unions staged a general 24-hour strike on March 1, the government cracked down. Six unions lost their legal status and their funds were frozen.

Meanwhile, to put the deficit-ridden, state-owned enterprises on a sounder financial basis, the government ordered the dismissal of unnecessary personnel and the elimination of nonessential jobs.

Other Government Actions. In April, the government published a sweeping law under which students and graduates were no longer allowed a vote in the schools' governing bodies. On August 25, President Juan Carlos Onganía signed a law barring Communists from public office and providing severe penalties for Communist activities. Meanwhile, the congress remained dissolved and all political parties were banned. There were no indications at year's end, however, that the general elections would be held soon. [MARY C. WEBSTER]

Facts in Brief. Population: 23,266,000. Government: President Juan Carlos Onganía. Monetary Unit: peso (350=U.S. $1). Foreign Trade: exports, $1,593,200,000; imports, $1,124,300,000. Principal Exports: wheat, meat.

ARMED FORCES OF THE WORLD. The balance of nuclear might teetered precariously in 1967. In June, Communist China, far ahead of U.S. estimates, exploded a three-megaton hydrogen bomb less than three years after its first atomic bomb test on Oct. 16, 1964. By the end of 1968, it was expected that China could have a number of medium-range missiles with nuclear warheads. By the early 1970s, China could have missiles that could reach the United States.

In November, U.S. Secretary of Defense Robert S. McNamara announced that the Soviet Union was "almost certainly" developing a space-launched bomb. Called Fractional Orbital Bombardment System (FOBS), it could aim a nuclear warhead from a partial orbit. The warhead itself, McNamara stated, would be about the same size and megaton range as the U.S. submarine-launched Polaris missile, about one megaton.

"Thin" Antimissile System. In light of these developments, the United States decided to deploy an antiballistic-missile (ABM) defense system for the first time. This system, called the Sentinel, was to be a "thin" ABM system. It would utilize a radically different type of nuclear missile warhead. The warhead would use bursts of X rays for destructive power. The system would be developed not to ward off a Soviet attack, McNamara explained, but primarily to provide protection against Communist China's intercontinental ballistic missile (ICBM) threat, expected to be in operation by 1973. The thin system was expected to cost about $5,000,000,000, as opposed to the $40,000,000,000 required for a full network ABM system, which was rejected by McNamara as unrealistic.

The nuclear arms race thus entered a new phase. The missile counting of past years would no longer be meaningful. The United States could maintain its 3 to 1 superiority over the Soviet missile force by adapting cluster warheads to its 1,000 Minuteman ICBMs and 656 Polaris submarine missiles. The United States was well along in the development of the Minuteman III multiple warheads, and 31 of the 41 Polaris submarines were scheduled to be equipped with the new Poseidon systems of multiple warheads and decoy devices. In addition, the United States had 54 Titan II ICBMs, which will be retired by 1970, 540 long-range jet bombers, and 78 medium-range jet bombers.

The Soviets, in addition to their orbiting nuclear bomb system, were installing new ICBMs in deep underground launchers at the rate of about 150 to 200 a year. These were advanced SS-11 solid-fuel rockets similar to the Minuteman. By the end of 1967, the Soviet Union had approximately 500 ICBMs, 200 submarine missiles, and 150 long-range bombers that could carry 300 nuclear bombs.

However, McNamara emphasized that this "nuclear superiority" did not give the United States any power advantage because the Soviet Union could destroy the United States in a nuclear war, just as the United States could annihilate the Soviet Union. In this kind of nuclear stalemate, relative superiority in numbers or megatons has limited significance.

In Europe, this mutual respect for the other's nuclear power sustained the relative détente that has existed since the Berlin crisis of 1961. The Soviet Union made no move, however, to respond favorably to U.S. and British announcements of troop cuts in West Germany in 1968. The United States will withdraw 30,000 ground troops and 5,000 airmen from a total of about 260,000 in West Germany. The British will cut their army of the Rhine by 5,000.

Comparative Military Manpower

As of Aug. 31, 1967

	United States	Russia	Communist China
Army	1,472,307	2,200,000	2,450,000
Navy	1,048,509*	450,000	130,000
Air Force	895,123	500,000†	90,000
Total	3,415,939	3,150,000	2,670,000

*Includes 300,817 marines.
†Includes 200,000 strategic rocket force.

These reductions were motivated primarily by economic pressures. West Germany, faced by a $350,000,000 cut in its $4,500,000,000 defense budget for 1968, planned to drop 15,000 to 19,000 men from its 460,000-man armed force.

Britain continued to shrink overseas deployments. In the Mediterranean, two-thirds of the British garrison in Malta will be withdrawn by 1972, leaving only 1,400 men. British military forces in the Far East would be cut 5,000 to 10,000 men from a total of 50,000 by April, 1968. Another cut of 20,000 men is planned in 1971. About 14,000 British troops were withdrawn from Aden.

France, however, was pushing ahead in nuclear arms. It expected to test its first H-bomb of 500 kilotons in 1968 and to operate the first of at least three missile submarines in 1970. Its air force included 62 Mirage IV bombers, each with one 60-kiloton atomic bomb. And by 1969, France hoped to have 25 intermediate-range missiles in underground launchers in Provence.

On the Communist side of Europe, the Warsaw Pact nations made few changes in the power balance. The Soviet Union continued to base 20 divisions in East Germany, 2 in Poland, and 4 in Hungary. At least a dozen Soviet divisions were in the Far East covering the Communist Chinese border. The Communist Chinese army reportedly did not expand or change its deployments significantly in 1967. [Lloyd Norman]

See also National Defense; and articles on the various countries.

ART. See Architecture; Dancing; Literature; Music; Painting and Sculpture.

ASIA. The fate of Asia revolved more and more around Communist China and its 723,000,000 people in 1967. This was primarily because the massive conflict within China between the followers of Mao Tse-tung and the more orthodox forces of Chinese Communism had begun to spill over China's borders and affect all parts of Asia. What seemed to be at issue was the Maoist doctrine demanding "Wars of National Liberation" in Asia. It was a doctrine central to the internal political conflict, but, in reality, it often masked a naked power fight within China. As the more orthodox forces asserted their ascendancy over the Maoists inside China, the latter took their cause overseas.

A Prime Example of the open and bitter hostility was best seen in Vietnam, where North Vietnam's Viet Cong guerrillas continued their fight against South Vietnam and its chief supporter, the United States. About half a million Americans were involved in the war, and they were gradually being joined by the troops of other nations who sensed the nature of the Maoist threat in Vietnam. Australia, New Zealand, the Philippines, the Republic of (South) Korea, and Thailand all joined in the war. Expressions of support for the South Vietnamese cause began to come from Japan and Malaysia. Despite these hopeful signs, the conflict between Maoism and orthodoxy remained a virulent force.

Symbol of a divided nation, and a tense continent, is this 600-yard swath, *left,* being carved out of the jungle in Vietnam as a demilitarized zone by U.S. soldiers. An armed North Vietnamese woman, *above,* keeps a sharp lookout for approaching U.S. bombers.

New housing development rising above Singapore slums reflects the progress being made in some parts of Asia to raise living standards through better housing.

In an immediate sense, the Portuguese province of Macao was forced to bend to Red Guard pressures through a series of humiliating concessions to the Chinese. Hong Kong's government was beset with subversion and terrorist acts as the Maoists sought to break British control of the Crown colony. Even in areas formerly friendly to Communist China – such as North Korea and Cambodia – Maoists sought to discredit those governments through activities centered in their embassies. So excessive were their actions in Cambodia that Norodom Sihanouk deported many of them and threatened to break relations with Peking. Both Indonesia and Burma, beset with their own internal problems, reacted sharply to Maoist subversion efforts by expelling Chinese officials as well as alien Chinese residents. Indonesia, for all intents and purposes, broke relations with Communist China. Even Japan moved closer to support of the American position in Vietnam.

Overseas Effects. The conflict spread to far-off Africa where Kenya broke relations with China, partly because of a quarrel over Tanzania. Even Great Britain felt the shock of Red Guard violence (see GREAT BRITAIN). China's internal convulsion, as it spread beyond its borders, worked against the Maoist cause, however; late in the year, the United Nations predictably turned down China's bid for membership by a vote of 58 to 45 (see UNITED NATIONS [UN]).

Successful Democracy. Despite the uneasiness created in Asia by China's internal anarchy, the continent scored some significant political gains. Representative government proved its staying power in 1967 in a series of elections that were held with only minor irregularities. Both Japan and South Korea held orderly national elections, and so did the Philippines.

Perhaps the most significant election was that held in beleaguered South Vietnam. There, despite threats and terrorism from the Viet Cong and boycotts from the Buddhists, almost 80 per cent of the eligible voters trooped to the polls (see VIETNAM). Ceylon and Malaysia managed to maintain their elected governments despite social disturbances aimed at disrupting them. Cambodia, Laos, and Thailand were able to survive subversion and corruption, and at the same time register significant social gains. Asia's two military strongmen, Acting President Suharto in Indonesia and Revolutionary Council Chairman Ne Win in Burma, not only consolidated control over their none-too-stable countries, but also were able to ease some of their more oppressive restrictions. Pakistan continued under the rule of President Mohammed Ayub Khan. India managed to hold a national election during the year, but the results from some standpoints were not encouraging (see INDIA).

Economic Developments. Asia experienced a series of pluses and minuses in economic developments. Japan, as the foremost industrial power in the Orient, scored substantial gains in its exports. So substantial were the gains that Japanese capital was behind many Southeast Asian development plans (see JAPAN).

Further efforts to straighten out the tangled fiscal affairs of Southeast Asia continued in 1967. Most important were the stringent but effective measures being taken in Indonesia, where the government set about re-funding its foreign debts while at the same time adopting policies designed to restore development and stabilize the currency. Malaysia, the Philippines, and South Korea registered significant breakthroughs in their economic development.

The picture, however, was not quite so bright in other areas of Asia. Burma and Thailand slipped in their general production levels. Ceylon struggled with labor disputes. India and Pakistan continued to require massive infusions of capital just to break even in their struggle with the population growth.

In contrast to the previous year, 1967 was, in general, a good one for agriculture with crop projections being met and even exceeded. One good year, however, did not necessarily mean that the continent of Asia was winning the race between population increase and food production. See FOOD; POPULATION, WORLD. [JOHN N. STALKER]

See also Section One, HARRISON BROWN: FOCUS ON SCIENCE.

ASTRONAUTS. "Mayday, Mayday, NASA 922 ejecting near Tallahassee!" Astronaut Clifton C. Williams' tone was crisp and businesslike as he radioed that he was going to bail out of his T-38 training plane because of an oxygen system failure on October 6. It was speculated he then blacked out and slumped forward on the controls because his jet, traveling at 460 mph, crashed at a steep angle in a heavily wooded area near Tallahassee, Fla. Williams, a 35-year-old marine major, had been on a routine flight from Cape Kennedy, Fla., to Houston, Tex.

He was the sixth astronaut to die in 1967 and the ninth since the U.S. space program began. Astronaut Edward G. Givens, 37, was killed on June 6, when he failed to make a sharp turn in his car and crashed into a ditch near the Manned Spacecraft Center in Houston.

Air Force Major Robert H. Lawrence, Jr., 31, the first Negro astronaut, was killed in December when his F-104 jet slammed into the runway at Edwards Air Force Base, California, during a routine proficiency flight.

A tragic fire at a Cape Kennedy launch pad on Jan. 27, 1967, the first fatal accident in the manned space program, took the lives of Air Force Lieutenant Colonel Virgil I. "Gus" Grissom, 40; Air Force Lieutenant Colonel Edward H. White II, 36; and

Ralph Morse, *Life* © Time Inc.

Astronauts Roger B. Chaffee, Edward H. White, and Virgil I. Grissom review flight plans prior to the capsule fire that took their lives on Jan. 27, 1967.

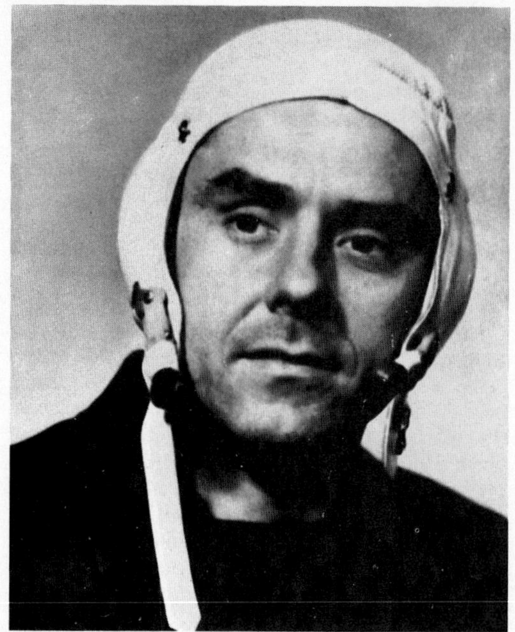

Soviet cosmonaut Vladimir M. Komarov, 40, was the first man known to have been killed in an actual space flight. He died on April 24, 1967.

Navy Lieutenant Commander Roger B. Chaffee, 31. See SPACE EXPLORATION.

M. Scott Carpenter, one of the original seven astronauts, resigned from the space program in August and went back to active navy duty as an aquanaut in the Sealab project of the navy's Man in-the-Sea program.

At the end of 1967, there were 55 astronauts assigned to the National Aeronautics and Space Administration (NASA) – 39 pilot-astronauts and 16 scientist-astronauts. Of these, 15 have made space flights. Because of the fire in the Apollo spacecraft there were no manned U.S. space flights in 1967.

The Next Flight, and the first of the three-man Apollo missions, was scheduled for the summer of 1968. NASA has designated this mission Apollo 7 and named to the prime crew Navy Captain Walter M. Schirra, 44, as commander; Air Force Major Donn F. Eisele, 37; and civilian astronaut Walter Cunningham, 35. Prime crew assignments for the second and third Apollo flights remained the same.

At a meeting in May, 1967, Schirra outlined the changes that were being made to prevent disastrous fires in the spacecraft he and other astronauts will fly. A new type hatch had been installed to allow the crew to get out of the spacecraft in 20 to 30 seconds. Flammable nylon netting that once covered some of the instrument panels had been replaced with metal covers, and all electronics, paper, wires, and pipes that might be damaged or cause fire were now encased in metal.

Survival Training. While some of the older, experienced astronauts worked with contractors on these changes, 20 pilots and scientists selected in 1965 and 1966 underwent survival training, and, in May, 1967, field geology training in New Mexico.

In June, these astronauts went to Panama to learn how to survive in case they were forced to land a spacecraft in the jungle. Only a month later the same hardy group was in Iceland studying and interpreting geological features.

New Appointments. NASA announced the selection of 11 new scientist-astronauts in August, 1967. For the first time, naturalized citizens were considered for selection and two were chosen – Philip K. Chapman, a native of Australia, and John A. Llewellyn of Wales.

Ten of these scientist-astronauts reported to the Manned Spacecraft Center in October. They are: Joseph P. Allen, 30, physicist; Philip K. Chapman, 32, physicist; Anthony W. England, 25, geophysicist; Karl G. Henize, 40, astronomer; Dr. Donald L. Holmquest, 28, physician; William B. Lenoir, 28, electrical engineer; John A. Llewellyn, 34, chemist; Dr. Franklin S. Musgrave, 31, physician; Brian T. O'Leary, 27, astronomer; Robert A. Parker, 30, astronomer; and Dr. William E. Thornton, 38, physician. [WILLIAM J. CROMIE]

ASTRONOMY. Intensive research, in 1967, centered on objects whose existence was unknown to astronomers only five years before. Such objects included quasars and X-ray sources. The study of them, together with the subject matter of cosmology and cosmic ray research, was combined into a new branch of astronomy called *relativistic astrophysics*, in which the distinction between physics and astronomy had virtually disappeared. The new field of study deals with the physical characteristics of celestial bodies in relation to the general theory of relativity

Quasars. Quasi-stellar objects, or quasars, continued to puzzle observational and theoretical astronomers, and each newly discovered fact about them brought more confusion to the theorists. Several hundred of these blue, starlike objects have been identified. Some emit radio waves and some do not. Light from all the quasars is shifted strongly toward the longer wave lengths of the spectrum, suggesting that they are moving at great speed. There is some disagreement as to their distances or their intrinsic brightnesses, although it is generally accepted that they are outside our Galaxy, the Milky Way.

In August, two English radio astronomers, George H. McDonald and Sidney Kenderdine of Cambridge University, announced the discovery of an object that had many of the radio properties associated with quasars, but which could not be seen. At the same time, quasars with exceedingly large red shifts were found to have dark lines in their spectra, and these showed a different degree of shift from the bright lines in the same spectra. As yet, there is no adequate explanation for these effects.

Oblateness of the Sun. An experiment performed by Robert H. Dicke and H. Mark Goldenberg, both of Princeton University, indicated that the sun is not a perfect sphere. They contend that the distance from the center of the sun to its surface is 22 miles shorter when measured at the pole than when measured at the equator.

Although the reported variance is small, it may cause major revisions in theories of astronomy and physics. For instance, the oblateness should cause a minute shift, 3.4 seconds of arc per century, in the position of Mercury's closest approach to the sun. This reduces the unexplained motion of Mercury from 43 seconds of arc per century to about 40 seconds per century. The general theory of relativity would then be in doubt, for it predicted the former value but not the latter. See PHYSICS.

Breakup of Galaxies. Jose Sersic of the observatory at Córdoba, Argentina, proposed in 1967 that certain giant galaxies may explode, throwing out huge fragments of matter. Each of these fragments might include enough material to condense into several smaller galaxies, each containing billions of stars. According to Sersic, the giant galaxies would become unstable as they shrank in size, causing the explosion. The fragments would turn into independent systems as they moved away from the parent galaxy. At some stage in this process, the new galaxies would emit radio waves and exhibit peculiar properties when seen through optical telescopes.

The chemical composition of lunar soil was analyzed by this alpha scattering instrument, which was put on the moon's surface, on September 10, by Surveyor V.

The theory was offered as an explanation of an effect noticed in 1966 by Halton C. Arp of the Mount Wilson and Palomar Observatories in California. He found radio sources occurring in pairs near galaxies whose chaotic appearance indicated recent explosions. Such explosions may have ejected the material that formed the radio sources. Arp now suspects that entire clusters of galaxies may be built by successive explosions in a large central galaxy. These explosions would probably be the most violent events in the lifetime of a galaxy.

Birth of Star Cluster. D. E. Kleinman and Frank J. Low of Rice University discovered a large cloud in the region of the Great Nebula in Orion when they were studying radiation with a wave length of about one-thousandth of an inch. This is believed to be the first observation of an interstellar cloud, or nebula, in the process of contraction. It had not been observed before because it is too cool on its surface, −336°F., to radiate detectable amounts of light at visible wave lengths.

Kleinman and Low estimate that the nebula is at least 1,600 light-years away. The cloud contains enough mass to form a cluster of hundreds of stars. Some stars may have already formed at the center of the nebula, but they cannot be seen because their light is absorbed by gas and dust in the cool outer parts of the cloud.

Saturn's Satellite. A new satellite of Saturn was discovered by Audouin Dollfus of the Meudon Observatory near Paris, France, around the beginning of 1967. He named it Janus, after the two-faced Roman god. It is the 10th satellite of this planet to be discovered.

Dollfus had predicted the existence of the satellite from his investigations of dark spaces in Saturn's rings, which are caused by the gravitational perturbations of the satellites on the icy fragments which form the rings. Dollfus surmised that the planet must have a 10th moon when he could not account for all the dark spaces in the rings with the nine known satellites.

On Dec. 18, 1966, the earth passed through the plane of the rings. For a few days before and after that date the rings were nearly invisible, thus allowing faint objects near Saturn to be seen more easily. Janus was found on photographs taken by observatories in France and at the U.S. Naval Observatory in Flagstaff, Ariz.

The orbit of Janus is nearly circular and has a radius of 98,000 miles. Janus has a diameter of about

190 miles and revolves about Saturn in 18 hours. It is the largest satellite of Saturn to be discovered in this century.

Spacecraft launchings produced information on two other members of the solar system–the moon and Venus. Surveyor III, launched in April, was able to scratch the lunar surface with a tiny shovel and show that it had a consistency somewhat like turned soil. Surveyor V, which landed 850 miles east of Surveyor III on September 10, had a device to test the chemical composition of the surface. In October, Mariner V passed within 2,480 miles of Venus and measured the density and pressure of its atmosphere. Both Mariner V and a Soviet craft that hit the planet on October 18 showed the surface to be too hot to support life. See SPACE TRAVEL.

New Telescopes. Three large telescopes were planned for the Southern Hemisphere, two to be built in Chile and one in Australia. The cost of building one of the Chilean instruments, a 150-inch reflecting telescope, will be shared by the Ford Foundation and the National Science Foundation. It will be located at the Cerro Tololo Inter-American Observatory in the Andes near La Serena, Chile. The other, a 140-inch telescope, will be constructed by the European Southern Observatory, an installation to be shared by astronomers from Belgium, France, the Netherlands, Sweden, and West Germany. This instrument will also be placed in the Chilean Andes. The Australian and British governments are planning a 150-inch telescope to be built in New South Wales, Australia. All three are scheduled to be in operation by the early 1970s, and will double the distance to which astronomers can see in the southern skies.

The Russian Academy of Sciences announced that it is building a 236-inch telescope in the Caucasus Mountains. When completed, this will be the largest optical telescope in the world, greatly surpassing the 200-inch Hale reflector at the Mt. Palomar Observatory.

Condon Committee. Sightings of unidentified flying objects (UFOs) have been reported to the U.S. Air Force for more than 20 years. Several well-publicized sightings in recent years have aroused intense public interest in the subject. For this reason, the Air Force Office of Scientific Research appointed a committee, in 1966, to thoroughly investigate some of the more important cases. The committee is headed by Edward U. Condon, a physicist from the University of Colorado, and consists of physical and social scientists. Their report is due in 1968.

While it is not really an astronomical phenomenon, UFO sightings are sometimes associated with astronomy because many of the unidentified objects can be explained as stars, planets, or meteors seen under unusual circumstances. [LAURA BAUTZ]

ASTURIAS, MIGUEL ANGEL. See NOBEL PRIZES.
ATOMIC ENERGY. See ENERGY.

AUSTRALIA

The nation was deeply shocked in December by news that Prime Minister Harold E. Holt had vanished while swimming off a beach near Melbourne. When search by land, sea, and air failed to locate either the prime minister or his body, he was officially declared dead and his deputy, John McEwen, was named interim prime minister. Requiem services held in Melbourne were attended by 10 heads of state, including U.S. President Lyndon B. Johnson. See DEATHS OF NOTABLE PERSONS.

McEwen, the leader of the Country party, was chosen by Lord Casey, the governor general, to succeed Holt temporarily because he had not only served for many years as deputy prime minister but because he had acted as prime minister when the cabinet chiefs had been out of the country. His party, and the bigger Liberal party, together made up the coalition government. It was the Liberal party, however, with rare exceptions, that had always provided the prime ministers for the coalition governments and on Jan. 9, 1968, it elected John Gorton, the minister of science, to the post. McEwen resigned immediately so that Gorton could take over.

Prime Minister Harold E. Holt, a sports enthusiast, shown preparing for a swim in 1966, perished on an undersea adventure off Melbourne in 1967.

Towering steel-and-glass skyscrapers, rising above winding streets and old houses of another era, give a new metropolitan air to Sydney, Australia's largest city.

The prime minister's death came as a sobering event to a nation enjoying unprecedented prosperity. Dramatic progress in the development of mineral resources continued in Australia in 1967. Spectacular new finds in oil and natural gas were made in underwater fields in Bass Strait, which separates Victoria from Tasmania, as well as in fields in the Gippsland Basin. Other offshore drilling sites with vast proven commercial quantities were being developed off western Victoria.

Oil and gas discoveries on land continued, notably in the Roma district of Queensland and on Pasco Island. Barron Island, however, off the north west coast of the state of western Australia, remained the country's largest oil-producing area.

Untapped Ore Deposits. During the year, plans were made to develop one of the world's richest but hitherto unexploited iron ore deposits in Western Australia. In April, an international consortium of five companies announced it had reached an agreement with the Australian government to develop the first mine in the area. One formation alone was estimated to contain more than 1,000,000 tons of high grade ore.

The consortium, capitalized at about $200,000,000, also announced plans to build, among other facilities, the largest privately owned railroad in Australia. It would reach from Port Hedland on the northwest coast, to Mount Whaleback, about 250 miles inland.

Plans for the development of Australian mineral resources other than oil continued to expand during the year. On the Gove Peninsula, about 450 miles east of Darwin, a syndicate was studying the possibilities of mining extensive bauxite deposits in the area. Development costs for mining the vast deposits of coal were also under study.

Facilities for the mining of manganese ore deposits on Groote Eylandt, south of Gove Peninsula, were being expanded. Test borings at Rum Jungle, located about 60 miles south of Darwin, indicated rich deposits of silver, lead, and zinc. In Shark Bay, due south of Carnavon, and at Port Hedland, extensive facilities for the production of salt through solar evaporation was being developed.

Immigration Encouraged. To meet the demands for labor created by developments in mining and in industry, Australia continued to encourage large-scale immigration. In June, the Australian government announced that it had reached an agreement with Great Britain under which the British government would continue to pay $308,000 annually toward transportation of emigrants to Australia.

Legislative Actions. A nationwide referendum on two proposals to change the federal constitution was held in May. One of the proposals called for an end to existing discrimination against Australia's aborigines by (1) repealing Section 127, which stated that the aborigines were not to be included in the census; and (2) amending Section 51 by empowering the federal government to make laws in respect to the aborigines. The proposal was approved by approximately 90 per cent of the electorate. In October, Prime Minister Harold E. Holt announced the opening of an Office of Aboriginal Affairs in Canberra to help the aborigines become an integral part of Australian community life.

The second proposal submitted to the voters called for a change in the numerical makeup of the federal house of representatives. It was defeated.

At the state level, a referendum was held in the northern area of New South Wales on April 29. Its purpose was to decide whether that region should separate from the rest of the state and form a new state in the Australian federation. The issue–one that had preoccupied the area for nearly 50 years–was rejected by a vote of 184,823 to 155,544.

Political Changes. On February 22, the ruling Liberal-Country coalition lost its one-seat majority in the 60-member senate when Senator Douglas Hannaford resigned from the Liberal party. Hannaford, whose resignation was in protest against Australia's military involvement in the war in Vietnam, became an Independent.

Another resignation of political interest during the year was that of Arthur Calwell, who gave up

Engineering News-Record © McGraw-Hill, Inc.

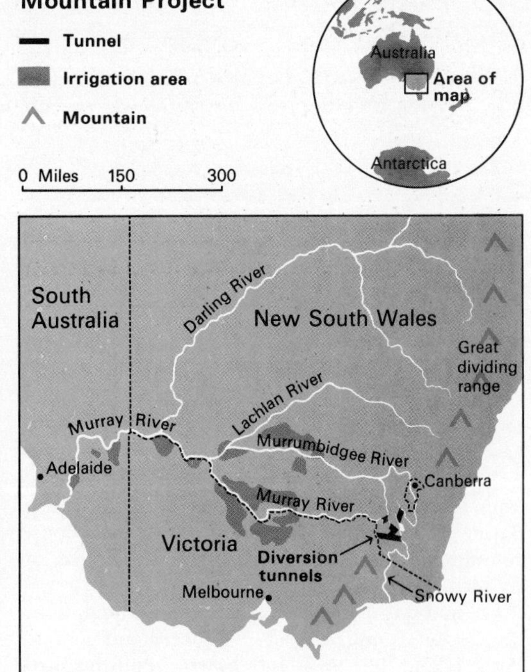

Australia's giant Snowy Mountain project, *right*, will greatly increase irrigation and power facilities when completed in 1975. Waterpipes and transmission lines, *above*, already snake through most of the huge area.

his post as Labour party leader. Calwell, who was succeeded by (Edward) Gough Whitlam, had promised to resign after Labour's defeat in the November, 1966, elections. Calwell had taken an active role in organizing antiwar demonstrations during a visit to Australia by South Vietnamese Premier Nguyen Cao Ky. See VIETNAM.

Communications Center. On September 16, one of the world's largest radio communications centers was officially opened at North West Cape in Western Australia. Built at a cost of about $80,000,000 by the U.S. Navy, the facility was to be used to maintain contact with submerged U.S. nuclear-powered submarines as well as for general naval communications.

Immediately following the commissioning of the station, Australia's newest town–Exmouth–was officially opened. Exmouth, with a population of approximately 3,000, had been built to house the Americans and Australians working on the project.

Disaster Strikes. On February 7, one of the worst bush fires in Australia's history devastated a large area in southern Tasmania. [KENNETH BROWN]

Facts in Brief. Population: 12,000,000. Government: Governor-General Lord Richard Gardiner Casey; Interim Prime Minister John McEwen. Monetary Unit: dollar (1=U.S. $1.11). Foreign Trade: exports, $3,166,000,000; imports, $3,636,000,000. Principal Exports: wool, iron ore, minerals, meat.

AUSTRIA saw its hopes of entering the European Economic Community (EEC, or Common Market) dashed in 1967, when Italy opposed negotiations for Austrian membership because of the Austro-Italian dispute involving the border region of Trentino-Adige. Rome blamed the Austrian government for spasmodic bombing near the border.

Economy Crisis. Although a member of the European Free Trade Association (EFTA), Austria was dependent mainly on EEC countries for its trade, and it was being increasingly handicapped by EEC tariff barriers against nonmember countries. The seriousness of the nation's trading position was emphasized in July when the Austrian Institute for Economic Research reported that the national economy was "in the doldrums," with industrial production static and mineral output down. The report was issued against the gloomy background of a rising cost of living and a growing trade deficit that rose to $643,000,000 during the year. To reduce these pressures, the government ordered a sizable cutback in imports, particularly agricultural products. [KENNETH BROWN]

Facts in Brief. Population: 7,339,000. Government: President Franz Jonas; Chancellor Josef Klaus. Monetary Unit: schilling (25.85=U.S. $1). Foreign Trade: exports, $1,684,000,000; imports, $2,327,000,000. Principal Exports: iron and steel, machinery, wood.

AUTOMATION. See LABOR.

AUTOMOBILE. The auto industry ran into rough going in 1967 and had to settle for its third best year in sales and sixth best in production. Labor problems were regarded as the prime roadblock.

Just as Ford Motor Company, the world's second largest automaker was getting into full production of its 1968 models, it was hit by a 49-day strike. After the contract was accepted, on Oct. 25, 1967, a rash of local plant walkouts continued, and others broke out at Chrysler Corporation and General Motors Corporation (GM) plants. Ford estimated the tie-ups cost it a production loss of 575,000 cars and trucks. It put its earnings loss in the third quarter at about $73,900,000.

The United Automobile Workers union agreement with Ford, and later with Chrysler and GM, provided boosts of over 90 cents an hour in wages and benefits over three years. American Motors Corporation (AMC), the smallest and the weakest of the "Big Four," asked for special consideration, which the union took under advisement. See LABOR.

Sales of new cars, including an astounding new high of 785,000 imports, totaled about 8,500,000 in the calendar year, well behind 1966's 9,008,488 and the all-time high of 9,313,912 in 1965. Import sales totaled 658,123 units in 1966 and 569,415 a year earlier. Through Dec. 23, 1967, the four U.S. auto firms built 7,260,702 cars, compared with 8,493,156 in the same 1966 period. Henry Ford II, chairman of Ford's board, in December, 1966, had predicted 1967 new car sales of close to 8,500,000 if there was a strike. He did not, however, forecast that his company would be its target.

The sales pace trailed that of 1966 through virtually the entire year. Aside from the unsettled labor problems, other causes of the sales lag included the auto safety issue, tight money, and the war in Vietnam. Draft calls and enlistments–actual and potential–took hundreds of thousands of young men out of the auto market. Other potential buyers may have deferred purchases until the appearance of the 1968 models, which offered more safety features than the 1967 cars.

Production Figures for the calendar year totaled 7,406,449 units, far behind the 8,611,776 built in 1966–and the record 9,329,104 assemblies in 1965. The industry wound up with about 1,580,000 truck assemblies for calendar 1967, its third best year. The figure was topped only by 1966 (1,764,377), and 1965 (1,885,109).

Despite the smaller number of cars sold, the car buyers' total bill was about the same–some $36,000,000,000–because of higher price tags and more optional equipment purchases in 1967.

Price tags of the 1968 models were marked higher at introduction time than on the comparable 1967 models. Another price boost by early 1968 seemed likely. Manufacturing costs were rising because of additional safety items and higher wages, as well as costs of materials – especially steel and copper. A government decision late in 1967 to stick with its original plan of requiring shoulder harnesses on 1968 cars manufactured after Jan. 1, 1968, made it virtually certain that much of the cost of this $25 item would be passed along to the car buyer.

Automotive News, in its yearly study of price increases, figured that the sticker prices of 1968 models were up an average of $116.25 a car, or 3.63 per cent over 1967 prices. It also went a step further and figured that, allowing for year-to-year equipment changes and deletions, the 1968 prices were up $79.93, or 2.28 per cent, a car. Its survey covered about 300 of the 357 models in the 1968 line. Those 300 were comparable with the 1967 models.

The U.S. Bureau of Labor Statistics estimated that new car prices in the 1968 line were up 3.75 per cent, or $87.54 per car. It said $26.95 of the increase was due to safety improvements and $11.20 to design changes to reduce emission of exhaust pollutants. The bulk, $49.39, it said, was a pure price boost.

The 1968 Car Line was longer, lower, and wider than its 1967 shape. It dropped some convertible and station wagon offerings and increased the choices in two-door hardtops, the hottest sellers in the 1968 car line.

AMC introduced the only new 1968 car, the Javelin. It challenges the Barracuda, Camaro, and Mustang for a share of the sporty car market, estimated at 1,000,000 units a year. AMC also was the only manufacturer to drop a car line. It abandoned its Marlin after four years.

People were spending more money for their 1968 cars, even though they were not buying as many as in earlier years. AMC documented this trend with figures on the first five weeks of its Javelin sales. Purchasers spent an average of $3,053 on each Javelin, which had a basic price of $2,450. Customers were virtually tailoring their cars to fit their personal tastes and pocketbooks. Prices of all U.S. made cars ranged from $1,923 for the Rambler American Six to $10,598 for the Cadillac Fleetwood 75.

The Auto Safety Furor lost some of its heat in 1967 as the federal government went ahead with its program calling for 20 safety items to be added to 1968 cars. Some automakers grumbled but managed to meet the modified, 1968-model safety standards. They included such items as windshield washers and defoggers, dual-cylinder brake systems, impact-absorbing steering columns, and safe door latches.

And if anyone had any idea that the government interest in cutting down the nation's traffic death toll of 52,000 a year was only a momentary thing, it was dispelled in October when U.S. Department of Transportation Secretary Alan S. Boyd issued 47 additional proposed standards covering cars through 1971. Boyd, who with Dr. William J. Haddon, Jr., the first director of the National Highway Safety Bureau (NHSB), is charged with enforcing the federal safety program, commented, "We do not expect miracles overnight." See SAFETY.

Ford of Britain took the wraps off its electric car, the Comuta, in mid-1967. This stubby (80-inch), short-range (40 miles) prototype runs on ordinary wet batteries and is being tested for city use.

Auto recall campaigns, which requested customers to return their cars for inspection and repair of suspected mechanical defects, continued in 1967. The NHSB tabulated 1,882,050 recalls in the 12 months ended Sept. 9, 1967. The total for the first 11 months of 1967 was estimated at about 2,800,000 cars. Government and industry officials seemed to agree that relatively few defective cars were found.

Electric Car development was being pushed by most of the carmakers as well as newcomers. Ford, GM, and AMC all exhibited experimental, short-range models. There was general agreement that practical models for city use were still years away. Also, the same, if not less cheerful, verdict was given on the outlook for a turbine-powered car – despite the spectacular technical performance of a turbine racer at the Indianapolis 500. See AUTOMOBILE RACING.

On the corporate front, two of the Big Four auto firms got new head men. James M. Roche, president of GM, moved up to board chairman, and Edward N. Cole, a GM vice-president, became president. AMC named Roy D. Chapin, Jr., son of one of Detroit's auto pioneers, as chairman and William V. Luneburg as president, as AMC continued its efforts to attain a profit-making position in the nation's auto industry. [CHARLES C. CAIN III]

See also MANUFACTURING; TRANSPORTATION.

AUTOMOBILE RACING. Denis Hulme, a 32-year-old New Zealander who had never won a Formula I Grand Prix race, emerged as 1967's world champion driver. Racing a Brabham-Repco, Hulme won only two of the 11 Formula I races, but placed second in three and third in four others to amass 51 points. Hulme's closest competitor was his boss, defending champion Jack Brabham of Australia, who scored 48 points.

Third, with 41 points, was Jim Clark of Scotland, the 1963 and 1965 champion. Driving a Lotus-Ford that was faster but less durable than the Brabham cars, Clark won four races, but failed to finish in four others. Clark's victory in the final race of the year, the Grand Prix of Mexico, tied him with Juan Fangio of Argentina for the most career victories in Grand Prix races, a total of 24.

Hulme and fellow New Zealander, Bruce McLaren, dominated the Canadian-American Sports Car Series. Driving McLaren-Chevrolets developed by McLaren, Hulme won the first three races and McLaren the fourth and fifth. Between them, they won more than $190,000 in prize money.

In United States Auto Club (USAC) competition, A. J. Foyt of Houston, Tex., won the Indianapolis 500 for the third time. Foyt drove his self-designed Ford-Coyote racer to a record average speed of 151.207 mph.

But the sensation of this race was a turbine-powered car developed by Andy Granatelli and driven by Parnelli Jones. It ran with an almost-silent "whoosh" instead of the familiar roar of a conventional piston engine, and Jones led the race for nearly 197 of the 200 laps. The car's gearbox failed less than 10 miles from the finish, and he dropped to fifth place. Officials indicated they would probably ban the turbine engine from future races.

In the overall USAC driver competition, Foyt waged a year-long battle with the 1965 and 1966 winner, Mario Andretti. Foyt finally won the title in the last race of the season, at Riverside, Calif.

Foyt teamed with Dan Gurney to score an impressive victory in his first year of endurance racing, as the pair won the classic 24-hour race at Le Mans, France, in a Mark IV Ford. It was the first time that American drivers in an American car had won the race since its inception in 1923. But Ford had to share the year's endurance honors with Ferrari, which won the 1967 manufacturers' championship.

In National Association of Stock Car Racing (NASCAR) action, Richard Petty of Randleman, N.C., drove a Plymouth to his second straight driving title. Petty won a record 27 races during the year. He also set NASCAR records for the most races won in a career (75) and for the most money won in one year ($130,275). [James O. Dunaway]

A turbine-powered car, driven by Parnelli Jones, almost won the Indianapolis 500. Owner Andy Granatelli runs beside it as Jones pulls away from pit stop.

AVIATION. The problem of congestion–in, on, and around airports–became acute in 1967. It was created in large part by the doubling of the nation's airport traffic since 1962. The industry was adopting the "systems" concept in its attempt to cope with the problem. Under this concept, all the components of air transportation–terminals, ground transport, runways, aircraft, and air traffic control facilities–are grouped together for consideration in planning and problem solving.

Large airports are faced with overcoming the "ground barrier," or the delays in getting to and from the airport. New and projected systems of rapid transit from the central city to the airport have been approved for Cleveland, Ohio, and London, England. Other cities were planning downtown check-ins, helicopter passenger transportation to planeside, and use of the "Sky Lounge," which operates as a conventional bus in the city and is airlifted with its passengers to the airport.

Some major airports added new runways to speed the receiving of aircraft while others provided shorter runways for general aviation aircraft in an effort to relieve congestion. Other airports specialized in handling cargo, long-haul passengers, flight training, or small aircraft. To relieve congestion further, airports were located above or beside freeways or on the outskirts of metropolitan areas as satellite airports, mostly for private or nonairline traffic.

The satellite Opa Locka Airport, 10 miles northwest of Miami, Fla., succeeded Chicago's O'Hare International Airport as the world's busiest. In the year ended June 30, 1967, its control tower handled 596,949 landings and take-offs, 8,422 more than at O'Hare. Only one other predominantly airline field, John F. Kennedy International, in New York City, was among the top six. It had 451,533 operations, trailing Van Nuys, Calif. (543,324); Long Beach, Calif. (499,724); and Ft. Lauderdale, Fla. (451,910).

The Federal Airport Aid Program for the fiscal year ending June 30, 1968, provided $70,200,000 in matching funds. Of this, $64,100,000 was allocated to improve 348 existing airports and $6,100,000 to help construct 38 new public airports. The government estimated an additional $2,500,000,000 would be needed for airport facilities before 1971. The number of civil aircraft landing facilities exceeded 10,000 for the first time with a total of 10,015, as of Aug. 1, 1967.

Airlines continued to set new records during the year. Domestic carriers logged more revenue passenger-miles (7,727,468,000) in August than in any previous one-month period. Air freight operations surged to new highs (see chart). Encouraged by the

Aviation's "ground barrier"–the crowded parking lots and airliner piers–is clearly demonstrated in this view of Kennedy International Airport.

Civil Aeronautics Board (CAB), there was little in the realm of experimental fares and promotional devices that was not, at least, suggested.

The "stretched" DC-8-62 transport of the McDonnell Douglas Corporation, also known as the Super-62, began its first U.S. service on Braniff International in September. Earlier, it had started runs on Scandinavian Airlines System (SAS). The wing-hugging engine pods and larger fuel capacity allow an ultra-long range of 6,478 miles for the fully loaded craft.

The airlines progressed rapidly toward becoming all-jet equipped. Trans World Airlines (TWA) retired its last propeller-driven airliner on April 6, 1967, becoming the first major U.S. line to have an all-jet fleet. Since 1957, 1,000 jet aircraft have been put into service by the nation's airlines, which are expecting a doubling of passenger traffic and a tripling of air freight by 1971.

Frontier Airlines absorbed Central Airlines in a merger approved by the CAB on Sept. 1, 1967. Pending mergers included Pacific Air Lines with Bonanza Air Lines and West Coast Airlines; Allegheny and Lake Central; Alaska, Alaska Coastal, and Cordova; and Northern Consolidated and Wien Air Alaska.

Government Activities. The Federal Aviation Agency took on its new role in the Department of Transportation as the Federal Aviation Administra-

The Rising Tide of Air Freight

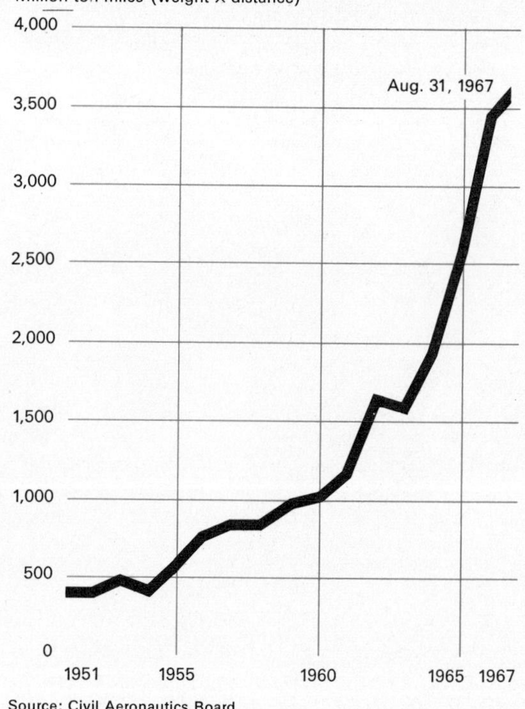

Source: Civil Aeronautics Board

The world's first supersonic airliner, the *Concorde,* made its debut in Toulouse, France, on Dec. 11, 1967. A British version of the *Concorde* also is underway.

tion (FAA) on April 1, 1967. The Bureau of Safety of the CAB also went to the new National Transportation Safety Board, and became the Bureau of Aviation Safety.

Air traffic control made progress. As the year ended, five of the 21 continental U.S. FAA Air Route Traffic Control Centers (ARTCCs) had been equipped with computers for processing flight data, calculating flight progress, and other tasks. The five ARTCCs serve Boston, Cleveland, Indianapolis, New York City, and Washington, D.C.

On Feb. 13, 1967, the first fully operational "three-dimensional" radar screens for air traffic control were put into use at the New York City ARTCC at Bohemia, Long Island. Transponders aboard aircraft automatically relay their altitude to the controllers' radar screens.

The FAA extended its positive control airspace downward from 24,000 feet to 18,000 feet above northeastern and north central United States, effective Nov. 9, 1967. To fly in such high-altitude airspace, an aircraft must operate under instrument flight rules and follow air traffic instructions.

Aircraft Industry. The progress of the first U.S. supersonic transport (SST) was slowed down by financing as well as engineering problems, but the redesigned Boeing 2707 was expected to be in service by late 1974. The British-French *Concorde,* while smaller (132 versus 277 passengers) and slower (1,450 versus 1,800 mph), was expected to be in production in 1971. Test flights of the *Concorde* were to start Feb. 28, 1968.

In the meantime, the Boeing 737, a competitor of the McDonnell Douglas DC-9 for the short-haul market, went into production, with limited deliveries scheduled for late in 1967. Boeing's jumbo jet, the 747, had reached the mock-up stage during the year. Five of the 747s, which could carry up to 490 passengers each, were expected to begin flight tests in late 1968, with delivery about three years away.

The Lockheed Aircraft Corporation announced its re-entry into the passenger air transport business with its L-1011, a three-engine, 227-to-300-seat airbus. It is designed for 800-to-2,000-mile flights at 595 mph. Lockheed aimed to have the L-1011 in service by 1972.

The civil aircraft order backlog, which was about $7,100,000,000 at midyear, caused employment in the aerospace manufacturing industry to increase. By March, 1968, payrolls were expected to reach 1,409,000. About 67 per cent of aerospace workers were producing aircraft; about 40 per cent of the total was employed on the Pacific Coast.

Two major aerospace industry mergers occurred in 1967. McDonnell Company and Douglas Aircraft Company combined on May 1, 1967, to form the McDonnell Douglas Corporation. And on Sept. 12, 1967, North American Aviation and Rockwell-Standard combined to form the North American Rockwell Corporation.

General Aviation production continued at about the same rate as in 1966. The total of new units – other than military craft or airliners – totaled about 15,000. Cessna produced its 75,000th aircraft in August, making it the world's leading general aviation manufacturer.

Business aircraft – those used in company operations – flew more hours than any other segment of general aviation. The FAA estimated their use would increase from the 6,500,000 hours in fiscal 1967 to 10,400,000 hours in 1977. Of approximately 22,000 aircraft currently in the business fleet, about 950 were turbine-powered. The turbine fleet is expected to increase to about 8,000 in the next 10 years. About half of all intercity air passengers fly on nonairline aircraft. The total number of persons served by general aviation approximates the number served by the scheduled airlines.

International Air Transportation. On Oct. 1, 1967, passenger fares were reduced as much as 6.5 per cent on transpacific routes between the U.S. West Coast and Asia. This was the final step, except for long-haul fares between North and South Ameri-

A Headache Ball

ca, in "closing" world-wide fares. Fares are "closed" when fixed by agreement and "open" when fixed by unrestricted competition.

Russia's newest long-range jet airliner, the Il-62, began service on the 6,000-mile Moscow-to-Montreal run in July.

Noteworthy Flights. An X-15 rocket aircraft set a winged-craft record on Oct. 3, 1967, with a speed of 4,534 mph at Edwards Air Force Base, California. It was flown by Major William J. Knight, USAF.

The 21st Annual All-Woman's Transcontinental Air Race (Powder Puff Derby) was won by Judy Wagner of Palos Verdes Estates, Calif.

Aviation Trophy and Award Winners in 1967:

Frank G. Brewer Trophy, to Dr. Mervin K. Strickler, Jr., for his work in aviation education.

Robert J. Collier Trophy, to James S. McDonnell, chairman of McDonnell Douglas Corporation, for his long leadership in the manufacturing of aircraft and spacecraft.

Harmon International Aviation Trophies went to Alvin S. White for test flight work with the XB-70: to astronauts Captain James A. Lovell, Jr., of the U.S. Navy and Lieutenant Colonel Edwin E. Aldrin, Jr., USAF, for their Gemini XII mission in November, 1966; and to Sheila Scott, of London, England, for her round-the-world speed records in a single-engine plane.

Wright Brothers Memorial Trophy for public service to aviation to Igor I. Sikorsky. [Leslie A. Bryan]

See also Armed Forces of the World; Disasters; National Defense; Space Exploration; Transportation.

AWARDS AND PRIZES presented in 1967 included the following:

General Awards

Academy of American Poets Awards. *Fellowship*, for distinguished poetic achievement, to John Berryman, also noted as a writer of criticism, fiction, and biography. *Lamont Award* to James Scully, assistant professor of English, University of Connecticut, for his first book of poems, *The Marches* (1967).

American Academy of Arts and Letters and National Institute of Arts and Letters Awards. *Gold Medals* to Katherine Anne Porter for fiction, and Arthur M. Schlesinger, Jr., for history and biography. *Marjorie Peabody Waite Award*, for continuing achievement and integrity in his work, to Stringfellow Barr, historian, critic, and essayist. *Rosenthal Foundation Awards* to painter Robert D'Arista and novelist Thomas Pynchon. *Awards in Art* to Bryon Burford, Jared French, Stephen Greene, Leo Kenney, Dennis Leon, Hugh Townley, and Louis Tytell. *Awards in Literature* to poet Philip Booth, novelist and short-story writer Hortense Calisher, poet and essayist Daniel Hoffman, critic Stanley Edgar Hyman, critic and historian Bernard M. W. Knox, novelist Walker Percy, and novelist David Wagoner. *Awards in Music* to composers George H. Crumb, Donald Martino, Julian Orbon, and Charles Wuorinen. *Award of Merit* in painting to John Heliker, assistant professor of painting, Columbia University. *Traveling Fellowship in Literature* to A. R. Ammons, poet.

American Academy of Arts and Sciences Emerson-Thoreau Award to Joseph Wood Krutch, literary and dramatic critic, and conservationist.

Anisfield-Wolf Awards by the *Saturday Review*, for books that deal most creditably with race-relations problems, to Oscar Lewis, author of *La Vida*, on slum life in New York and Puerto Rico, and David Brion Davis for *The Problem of Slavery in Western Culture*.

Aspen Institute of Humanistic Studies Award to Gilberto Freyre, noted Brazilian anthropologist, sociologist, and author of *The Mansions and the Shanties: The Making of Modern Brazil* and other books.

Australian Society of Writers Sir Thomas White Memorial Prize, for the best Australian book of the year, to Hugh Edwards for *Islands of Angry Ghosts*.

B'nai B'rith Jewish Heritage Award to Maurice Samuel, author and lecturer, for "positive contributions to contemporary literature by his authentic interpretation of Jewish life and values."

Brandeis University Creative Arts Awards to architects Kevin Roche and Ludwig Mies van der Rohe, composers Ross Lee Finney and Claudio Spies, poets Conrad Aiken and May Swenson, choreographer and director Jerome Robbins, theatrical producer Ellen Stewart, and literary critic Kenneth Burke.

Columbia University Frederic Bancroft Prizes, for studies in American diplomacy, history, or international relations, to William W. Freehling for *Prelude to Civil War: The Nullification Controversy in South Carolina, 1816-1836;* Charles Sellers for *James K. Polk, Continentalist: 1843-1846;* and James Sterling Young for *The Washington Community, 1800-1828*.

Dag Hammarskjöld Awards: *Artistic Prize* to Leonard Bernstein, music director, New York Philharmonic. *Cultural Prize* to Clare Boothe Luce, former U.S. ambassador to Italy. *Literary Prize* to William Manchester, author of *The Death of a President*.

Freedom House Freedom Award to Roy Wilkins, executive director of the National Association for the Advancement of Colored People, for outstanding contributions to the cause of human liberty.

Freedoms Foundation Awards. *George Washington Award* to Pfc. Hiram D. Strickland of Graham, N.C., killed in Vietnam on Feb. 1, 1966. In his last letter home, the young soldier said, "I'm writing this letter as my last one. . . . Believe me, I didn't want to die, but I know it was part of my job. . . . Don't mourn me, Mother, for I'm happy I died fighting my country's enemies. . . . I died a soldier of the United States of America." *Defender of Freedom Award* to Spec. 5 Carol A. Howland, U.S. Army WAC from Panorama City, Calif., for her letter entitled "Defending Freedom Safeguards America." *National Service Medal*, presented for the first time in 1967, to comedian Bob Hope, who for years has entertained American troops. *National Recognition Award* to actor Raymond Burr, who also has entertained American troops. *Freedom Leadership Medal* to Milton Caniff for "his continued creative editorials and cartoons which brilliantly espouse the precepts of human freedom."

Italian National Academy of the Lynxes Antonio Feltrinelli Prize for Fiction to John R. Dos Passos, journalist and novelist, who wrote *U.S.A.* (1938), *The Ground We Stand On* (1941), and other books.

National Association for the Advancement of Colored People Spingarn Medal, honoring an American Negro for distinguished achievement, to Edward W. Brooke, Massachusetts Republican and the first Negro elected to the U.S. Senate (1966) since Reconstruction days.

National Book Committee Awards. *National Book Awards: Arts and Letters Award* to Justin Kaplan for *Mr. Clemens and Mark Twain* (see KAPLAN, JUSTIN). *Fiction Award* to Bernard Malamud for *The Fixer* (see MALAMUD, BERNARD). *History and Biography Award* to Peter Gay for *The Enlightenment: An Interpretation: The Rise of Modern Paganism*. *Poetry Award* to James Merrill for *Nights and Days*. *Science, Philosophy, and Religion Award* to Oscar Lewis for *La Vida*. *Translations Awards*, presented for the first time in 1967: *Translation of a Contemporary Work Award* to Gregory Rabassa for his translation from the Spanish of *Hopscotch* by Julio Cortázar. *Translation of a Classic Award* to Willard Trask for his translation from the Italian of *History of My Life* by Giacomo Casanova. *National Medal for Literature*, for a lifetime of work to a living author, to British poet Wystan Hugh Auden.

National Endowment for the Arts Awards, to writers who have not heretofore received all the recognition due them, and presented for the first time in 1967, to poets Louise Bogan, Malcolm Cowley, Kenneth Patchen, John Crowe Ransom, and Yvor Winters.

Poetry Society of America Awards. *Gold Medal for Distinguished Service* to Marianne Moore. *Alice Fay di Castagnola Award* to Gustav Davidson for *The Poets and Their Angels* (yet unpublished). *Shelley Award* to Anne Sexton (see SEXTON, ANNE). *Melville Cane Award* to Lawrance R. Thompson for *Robert Frost: The Early Years, 1874-1915*.

Royal Institute of British Architects Gold Medal to German-born Nikolaus Pevsner, history of art professor at the University of London (Birkbeck College), and editor and author of nearly all of the *Buildings of England* series of architectural county guides (27 volumes) and books on European architecture.

Society of Architectural Historians Alice Davis Hitchcock Award for the most distinguished work of scholarship on the history of architecture published in 1966, to Jayne Wrightsman (pen name Richard Krautheimer), author of *Early Christian and Byzantine Architecture*.

United Nations Fridtjof Nansen Medal, for services to refugees, to Prince Bernhard of the Netherlands, who, as director of a campaign, raised $18,000,000 in 1966 for refugees in Africa and Asia.

West German Publishers and Booksellers Association International Peace Prize to Ernst Bloch, German philosopher and author of *Das Prinzip Hoffnung* (*Hope as a Principle*), a critical study of social utopias.

Yale University Awards. *Bollingen Poetry Prize*, presented every two years, to Robert Penn Warren. *Yale Series of Younger Poets Award* to Helen Chasin for *Coming Close*, to be published in early 1968.

Science and Industry

Acoustical Society of America Gold Medal to Vern O. Knudsen, chancellor emeritus of the University of California, Los Angeles, "for research into the propagation of acoustical waves through air and the sea."

Albert and Mary Lasker Foundation Awards. *Medical Journalism Awards: Magazine Award* to Lawrence Lessing for his series "The Biology Revolution" in *Fortune* and Albert Rosenfeld, *Life* medical and science editor, "for the consistent excellence of the magazine's medical articles in recent years." *Newspaper Award* to Barbara Yuncker for her series "The Pill" in *The New York Post*. *Television Award* to the American Broadcasting Company for its program "The Long Childhood of Timmy" on mental retardation, and Station WXYZ-TV, Detroit, Mich., for "Red Measles Sunday," a program promoting a mass inoculation drive. *Medical Research Awards: Basic Research Award* to Bernard B. Brodie, director of the National Heart Institute Chemical Pharmacology Laboratory, "for 30 years of research into what happens to drugs taken into the body." *Clinical Research Award* to Robert A. Phillips, director of the Pakistan-Southeast Asia Treaty Organization (SEATO) Cholera Research Laboratory in Dacca, East Pakistan, who developed a technique of intravenously feeding sodium bicarbonate and saline solutions to cholera patients to replace the body fluids. *Public Service Health Award* to Democratic U.S. Representative Claude Pepper of Florida for his interest in medical legislation in Congress (Senate 1936-1951, and House since Jan. 3, 1963).

American Chemical Society Awards. *Priestley Medal* to Ralph A. Connor, educator and manufacturing executive, for his achievements as a teacher, research chemist, and administrator. *Award for Creative Work in Synthetic Organic Chemistry* to Columbia University Professor Gilbert J. Stork, known for his achievements in the synthesis of terpenes (class of vegetable compounds of hydrogen and carbon) and techniques for preparing organic compounds.

American Physical Society Awards: *Oliver E. Buckley Solid State Physics Prize* to Professor Harry G. Drickamer of the University of Illinois for work on the effects of extreme pressures on the electronic and molecular structures of solids. *High Polymer Physics Prize* to Julian H. Gibbs, chairman of the Chemistry Department at Brown University, and E. A. Di Marzio for their theory of the glass transition and their contribution to the theory of the helix-coil transition in biological macromolecules. *Irving Langmuir Prize* to University of Florida Professor John Clarke Slater for his analysis of the mechanics which bond in molecules and solids.

American Psychological Foundation Distinguished Science Writers Award to Gay Gaer Luce and Julius Siegal for their book *Sleep*.

American Society of Plant Physiologists Kettering Award to University of Illinois Professor Eugene I. Rabinowitch for his scientific contributions on photosynthesis.

British Royal Astronomical Society Awards. *Gold Medals* to Professor Hannes Alfvén of the Swedish Royal Institute of Technology for fundamental research on cosmical electrodynamics, and Allan Rex Sandage of the Mount Wilson and Palomar Observatories in California for the history of the galaxy, optical data basic to modern cosmology, and fundamental work on stellar evolution. *Eddington Medal* to Robert F. Christy, physics professor, California Institute of Technology, for work on the nonlinear theory of pulsating stars.

AWARDS AND PRIZES

Columbia University Louisa Gross Horwitz Prize, awarded for the first time in 1967, to Luis F. Leloir, biochemistry professor, Buenos Aires University, for his discovery (1950s) of the nucleoside diphosphate sugars and the importance of these compounds in the biochemical production of carbohydrates. He and others have since discovered 54 such sugars and the part each plays in the interactions of chemicals within animals and plants.

Dickinson College Joseph Priestley Memorial Award to George W. Beadle, chancellor of the University of Chicago and Nobel medicine laureate (1958), for his "contributions to mankind through research in biochemistry."

Franklin Institute Franklin Medal to Britton Chance, chairman of the Biophysics and Physical Biochemistry Department, University of Pennsylvania Medical School, whose achievements include the development of extremely sensitive electronic and optical techniques for observing biochemical reactions in living tissues.

National Academy of Sciences Awards. *Charles Doolittle Walcott Medal* to Allison R. Palmer, professor, State University of New York, for work in Cambrian geology and paleontology. *Gibbs Brothers Medal* to A. A. H. Keil, head of the Department of Naval Architecture and Marine Engineering, Massachusetts Institute of Technology, for work in the physics of underwater explosions and their effect on ship structures. *Daniel Giraud Elliot Medal* to Ernst Mayr, director, Museum of Comparative Zoology at Harvard University, for his treatise "Animal Species and Evolution." *Kimber Genetics Medal* to Barbara McClintock of the Carnegie Institution Genetics Research Unit, Cold Spring Harbor, N.Y., for studies on chromosome structure and function.

National Medal of Science, presented by President Johnson, to the following distinguished scientists: Jacob A. B. Bjerknes, meteorology professor, University of California, Los Angeles, for discovering the cyclone-making waves of the air and the climate-controlling changes of the sea. Subrahmanyan Chandrasekhar, astrophysics professor, University of Chicago, for work in stellar astronomy, physics, and applied mathematics. Henry Eyring, retired dean, University of Utah Graduate School, for research on the structure and properties of matter and for his creation of absolute rate theory. Edward F. Knipling, director, Entomology Research Division of the U.S. Department of Agriculture, for unique biological approaches to the control of insect vectors responsible for diseases of humans, domesticated animals, and plants. Fritz Albert Lipmann, Nobel medicine laureate (1953) and professor of biochemistry, Rockefeller University, for discoveries of molecular mechanisms for transferring and transforming energy in cells and other work in biochemistry. John Willard Milnor, professor of mathematics, Princeton University, for work in topology, which solved long-outstanding problems and opened new areas in this field of mathematics.

William C. Rose, professor emeritus of biochemistry research, University of Illinois, for discovering the essential amino acid threonine. Claude E. Shannon, Donner professor of science, Massachusetts Institute of Technology, for research in mathematical theories of communications and information processing. John H. Van Vleck, Hollis professor of mathematics and natural philosophy, Harvard University, for contributions to the theories of molecular structure and the magnetic and dielectric properties of materials. Sewall Wright, professor emeritus of genetics, University of Wisconsin, for work in the mathematical foundations of the theory of evolution and contributions to genetics. Vladimir K. Zworykin, honorary vice-president, Radio Corporation of America, for major contributions to the instruments of science, engineering, and television, and for encouraging the application of engineering in medicine.

Pacific Science Center Arches of Science Award to James B. Conant, former professor of organic chemistry (1919-1933) and president (1933-1953) of Harvard University. He wrote organic chemistry textbooks, and such volumes as *On Understanding Science* (1947), *Science and Common Sense* (1951), *Modern Science and Modern Man* (1952), *The Citadel of Learning* (1956), and *The American High School Today* (1959). Conant, in recent years, also made studies of schools and teacher education.

Royal Canadian Geographical Society Massey Medal to John R. Mackay, geography professor, University of British Columbia, internationally known for his work in physical geography.

United Nations Educational, Scientific, and Cultural Organization Kalinga Prize, for the popularization of science, to Paul Couderc, French astronomer and author of *The Expansion of the Universe* (1952), *The Wider Universe* (1960), and other popular volumes.

U.S. Atomic Energy Commission Ernest O. Lawrence Memorial Award to: Mortimer M. Elkind, National Institutes of Health, "for his discovery that mammalian cells are capable of recovering in large measure from the damaging effects of radiation." John Melvin Googin, Y-12 Plant, Oak Ridge, Tenn., "for his many contributions to the development of production processes involving the separation of materials important to the nuclear energy program." Allan F. Henry, Bettis Atomic Power Laboratory in Pennsylvania, "for developing the first comprehensive theoretical description of the reactor kinetics of a pressurized water nuclear plant." Robert Thorn of the Los Alamos Scientific Laboratory, N.Mex., for work on the essential calculations for weapon designs. John O. Rasmussen, senior staff member of the Lawrence Radiation Laboratory, Berkeley, Calif., an authority in nuclear chemistry and physics, including the microscopic model of nuclear structure.

U.S. Atoms for Peace Award, established by the Ford Motor Company Fund in 1955 and presented for the first time since 1963 to: Bertrand L. Goldschmidt, director of the French Atomic Energy Commission and his country's permanent representative on the International Atomic Energy Agency Counsel of Governors; W. Bennett Lewis, senior vice-president, Atomic Energy of Canada, Ltd., and Canadian representative, United Nations Scientific Advisory Committee since 1955; Isidor I. Rabi, professor, Columbia University, credited as the originator of the first international nuclear research laboratory. He is a Nobel physics medalist (1944).

Vernon Stouffer Foundation Medical Award to four European scientists: Peter Holtz, West German pharmacologist, discovered the precursors of norepinephrine and later found that it is synthesized in the nerve tissue and in the adrenal glands. Ulf S. von Euler, Swedish physiologist, found norepinephrine to be the substance that relays nerve impulses to blood vessel walls, causing the blood vessels to contract. Prostaglandins, which affect arterial pressure, also were discovered by Von Euler. John W. Cornforth and George J. Popjak, London, codirectors of Shell Research Milstead Laboratory of Chemical Enzymology, contributed to the clarification of the means by which such fatty substances as cholesterol are produced and broken down in the body.

BAHAMAS. See West Indies.

BALLET. See Dancing.

BALLOONS. See Astronomy; Weather.

Lights burn far into the night at the Bank of England in preparation for the devaluation of the pound sterling from $2.79 to $2.40, announced on November 18.

BANKS AND BANKING. Short-term interest rates eased during the first half of 1967 from the high levels caused by the previous year's "credit crunch." But later in the year, they rose to new highs. Short-term business loan rates dropped moderately, to average less than 6 per cent about midyear. But after British devaluation of the pound on November 18, the *prime rate* (what banks charge on least-risk loans) was increased from 5 1/2 per cent to 6 per cent. This gave an added spurt to all business loan rates, which had been rising since midsummer.

Total bank credit increased at an unsustainable annual rate of over 20 per cent during much of the year. This was fueled largely by the growth of time deposits at commercial banks. Rates as high as 5 1/2 per cent were marginally attractive in the competition for savings. But by year-end such rates looked low relative to alternatives overseas.

The *money supply* (demand deposits and currency) also was rising. Over the first nine months of 1967, it grew at an annual rate of 7 per cent, in comparison with only 2.4 per cent yearly from 1957 to 1966. But it held at 23 per cent of the gross national product (GNP), about the same as in 1966 but down significantly from 30 per cent 10 years earlier. It was well below the approximately 35 per cent ratio in Great Britain, but above the 18 per cent in Canada.

U.S. commercial banks generally were able to meet demands for credit comfortably. Their loan-to-deposit ratio was 66 per cent in September, down slightly from a year earlier and lower than 1929's 73 per cent. The comparable ratios in Great Britain and in Canada were about 65 per cent and 53 per cent, respectively.

An Easy-Money Policy was maintained during much of the year by the Federal Reserve Board (FRB). In March, it acted to increase the availability of credit by reducing member banks' required reserve ratios on savings deposits, and on time deposits up to $5,000,000 per bank, from 4 per cent to 3 per cent. In April, the FRB decreased its *discount rate* from 4 1/2 per cent to 4 per cent. (The discount rate is what a member bank must pay for borrowing from Federal Reserve banks.)

Federal Reserve open-market purchases of securities also pumped substantial amounts of new money into the banking system during the first three quarters of 1967. During that period, member bank reserves available to meet the minimum required to be held against private demand deposits increased at an annual rate of over 6 per cent. In contrast, they had declined a year earlier.

Repercussions from Britain's devaluation of the pound from a value of $2.79 to $2.40, or by 14.3 per cent, were world-wide. Most, but not all, Commonwealth countries followed with devaluations.

To defend the new value of the pound, Britain borrowed $1,400,000,000 from the International Monetary Fund (IMF) and arranged for $1,600,000,000 more, if needed, from other sources. The Bank of England raised the *bank rate* (similar to the U.S. discount rate) to an unprecedented 8 per cent. Earlier, as pressure on the pound developed, the bank had raised the rate–first, from 5 1/2 per cent to 6 per cent on October 19, then to 6 1/2 per cent on November 9. See GREAT BRITAIN; INTERNATIONAL TRADE AND FINANCE; MONEY.

In the United States, the Federal Reserve made a token 1/2 point increase in its discount rate to 4 1/2 per cent and tightened open market operations to constrain inflation. The Bank of Canada also raised its bank rate, from 5 per cent to 6 per cent. In the wake of devaluation, gold worth about $300,000,000 was pumped into bullion markets to maintain its $35-an-ounce price, an avowed aim of the United States and its major trading partners.

Cash Positions, which had deteriorated in 1966, were bolstered by many U.S. businesses during 1967. Predictions of a growing federal deficit and related fears of renewed inflation and tight money spurred the cash build-up. Some corporations borrowed long to add to cash and short-term security holdings. Others issued *commercial paper* (negotiable, unsecured notes, bills, and drafts) for the first time to establish an alternative to bank credit. The amount of commercial paper placed through dealers nearly doubled in the year ended August 31. Corporations increased bond and note indebtedness during the first half of 1967, even beyond records of a year earlier. At the same time, they substantially reduced holdings of government securities.

Individuals added to their liquid assets and cut down on their additions to installment debt. Member banks reduced borrowings from the Federal Reserve System, as individual savings poured in. But the rising demand for loans kept bankers mindful of liquidity needs.

Liquid Assets Held by the Public

	(billions of dollars) Sept. 30, 1967	12-Month Change
Demand deposits, currency	$176.7	6.4%
Time deposits	236.9	12.3%
Savings and loan shares	122.5	9.1%
U.S. Savings Bonds	51.4	1.8%
U.S. government securities due within one year	48.5	−11.0%
Total	$636.0	7.0%

Source: *Economic Indicators*

Savings and Loan Associations (SLAs) generally made a particularly strong recovery from the liquidity crisis of 1966. SLAs enjoyed an increase in total savings capital of nearly 9 per cent. Their net gain in savings for the first nine months reached a record $8,200,000,000, more than five times the $1,373,000,000 increase for the 1966 period. SLAs also reduced indebtedness to Federal Home Loan Banks (FHLBs) to $4,153,000,000 in August; it was $7,226,000,000 a year earlier.

Fearful that SLAs would be hard-hit again by tight money, the FHLBs borrowed enough to triple holdings of liquid assets. Thus, SLAs would be able to obtain funds for loans quickly without having to borrow first, possibly on unfavorable terms. The FHLBs also were authorized to sell bonds, if necessary, directly to the Federal Reserve banks.

Housing Starts advanced to an annual rate of 1,400,000 in September, well above the tight-money low of 845,000 in October, 1966. Of this new construction, banks were financing an increasing share. Their mortgage portfolios grew 6 1/2 per cent over the 12 months ended Aug. 31, 1967. This topped the 4 per cent growth recorded by SLAs and life insurance companies–the traditional pacesetters. Mortgage rates remained high–more than 6 1/2 per cent for a 24-year maturity on the average new house. There were indications that the rates might be headed higher yet. Offerings of mortgages to the Federal National Mortgage Association came to almost $500,000,000 in the third quarter of 1967, six times the second quarter's total.

The reasons behind the long slump in building were reported in a study of the 1966 credit crunch undertaken by the U.S. Department of Commerce. The report criticized Federal Reserve credit constraints as ineffective in reducing business and industrial capital outlays. In contrast, the credit curbs

Jubilation follows the St. Louis Cardinals' victory over Boston in the seventh game of the World Series as Umpire Augie Donatelli escapes with two souvenir caps.

were all too effective in reducing the availability of funds for housing. See HOUSING.

Bank Mergers were ruled subject to prosecution under the Clayton Antitrust Act, according to a 8-to-0 decision of the Supreme Court of the United States on March 27, 1967. The Court ruled that the Bank Merger Act of 1966 placed the burden on banks – the same as did the Clayton Act on business in general – to prove that a merger would not cause anticompetitive effects that outweigh gains in service.

In September, a federal district judge in Washington, D.C., ruled that banks cannot manage mutual fund-type investment plans as part of their trust department operations. First National City Bank in New York City had such a plan operating.

The Number of Banks declined slightly in the first eight months of 1967. The pace of mergers and establishment of new banks remained comparatively slow in 1967. There were 13,742 commercial banks in the United States at the end of August, against 13,770 on Dec. 31, 1966. SLAs held about even at 6,200. Mutual savings banks declined from 504 to 501. Mutual savings banks – confined to 18 states, mostly in the Northeast – would be authorized under national charters in legislation approved by the Banking Committee of the U.S. House of Representatives. [WILLIAM G. DEWALD]

See also ECONOMY, THE; MONEY; Section One, SYLVIA PORTER: FOCUS ON THE ECONOMY.

BASEBALL. It was surprising enough that the St. Louis Cardinals soared from a sixth-place finish the year before to run away with the National League pennant. But what made the 1967 campaign particularly memorable was the amazing leap by their World Series rivals, the Boston Red Sox, who had finished ninth a year earlier.

Under a new manager, disciplinarian Dick Williams, the Red Sox battled their way to the American League championship in an unprecedented four-team contest that was not settled until the final day of the season. The Red Sox resurgence – they had finished 26 games out in 1966 – was sparked by left fielder Carl Yastrzemski and pitcher Jim Lonborg. Undismayed by his demotion from the team captaincy, Yastrzemski led his team by example and inspiration. He also led the league in batting (.326) and runs batted in (121), and tied Minnesota's Harmon Killebrew for the home run title (44). No left-handed Red Sox hitter had ever accomplished as much. Naturally, Yastrzemski was voted the most valuable player in the league.

The Cardinals, who had breezed to the pennant by 10 1/2 games over second-place San Francisco, took the World Series, four games to three. Right-handed pitcher Bob Gibson scored three of their victories, including the seventh game.

Lonborg, who had pitched Boston's pennant-clincher three days before the series opener, did not have sufficient rest to oppose Gibson in the first game. The Cardinal ace struck out 10 men and pitched a six-hitter to win, 2-1. Speedy Cardinal center fielder Lou Brock made four hits, stole two bases, and scored both his team's runs. The following day, however, Lonborg evened the score by firing a one-hitter, and the Red Sox won, 5-0. Yastrzemski contributed two home runs.

The series moved to St. Louis for the next three games. Brock again scored twice as Nelson Briles' seven-hitter enabled the Cards to win, 5-2. The Cardinals pushed the Red Sox to the brink in the fourth game when Gibson pitched a five-hit shutout, 6-0, but Lonborg kept Boston's chances alive with a 3-1 win in the fifth game.

Back in Boston's Fenway Park, the Red Sox rallied to tie the series at three games apiece, with Yastrzemski getting another home run in their 8-4 victory. The Cardinals had a slight edge in the deciding game, a confrontation of the star pitchers, because Gibson had rested three days and Lonborg only two. The 31-year-old Gibson, who was also the outstanding player in the Cards' 1964 series victory over the New York Yankees, pitched a three-hitter, while his teammates treated the weary Lonborg roughly and coasted to a 7-2 victory and the world championship. Brock set a series record by stealing seven bases.

The National League. Two newly acquired players, first baseman Orlando Cepeda and right fielder Roger Maris, helped the Cardinals establish a lead of four games as early as July 15. On that day, Gibson's right leg was fractured by a line drive slammed by Pittsburgh's Roberto Clemente. Gibson did not return until September. Instead of slumping during Gibson's absence, however, the Cards streaked to a big lead. Relief pitcher Briles replaced Gibson in the starting rotation and performed so well the Cards were able to capture the pennant almost two weeks before the end of the season. Cepeda, despite a late-season slump, batted .325 and drove in 111 runs. The former San Francisco Giant was voted his league's most valuable player.

The American League. Manager Eddie Stanky's Chicago White Sox batted so feebly that they averaged only .224 as a team, but strong pitching enabled them to lead the league most of the season. When they weakened, the Red Sox, the Minnesota Twins, and the Detroit Tigers moved into contention, and all four clubs struggled into the last weekend with good chances to win the pennant.

The White Sox were then beaten twice in a row by the Washington Senators, ending their hopes. On the next-to-last day of the season, Yastrzemski's three-run homer gave the Red Sox a 6-4 victory over the Twins. This left Boston and Minnesota

Final Standings in Major League Baseball

American League

	W.	L.	PCT.	GB.
Boston	92	70	.568	—
Minnesota	91	71	.562	1
Detroit	91	71	.562	1
Chicago	89	73	.549	3
California	84	77	.522	7½
Baltimore	76	85	.472	15½
Washington	76	85	.472	15½
Cleveland	75	87	.463	17
New York	72	90	.444	20
Kansas City	62	99	.385	29½

Leading Batters

Batting Average–Carl Yastrzemski, Boston	.326
Home Runs–Carl Yastrzemski, Boston, and Harmon Killebrew, Minnesota	44
Runs Batted In–Carl Yastrzemski, Boston	121
Hits–Carl Yastrzemski, Boston	189
Runs–Carl Yastrzemski, Boston	112

Leading Pitchers

Games Won–Jim Lonborg, Boston, and Earl Wilson, Detroit	22
Win Average–Jose Santiago, Boston (12-4)	.750
Earned Run Average–Hoyt Wilhelm, Chicago	1.31
Strikeouts–Jim Lonborg, Boston	246

National League

	W.	L.	PCT.	GB.
St. Louis	101	60	.627	—
San Francisco	91	71	.562	10½
Chicago	87	74	.540	14
Cincinnati	87	75	.537	14½
Philadelphia	82	80	.506	19½
Pittsburgh	81	81	.500	20½
Atlanta	77	85	.475	24½
Los Angeles	73	89	.451	28½
Houston	69	93	.426	32½
New York	61	101	.377	40½

Leading Batters

Batting Average–Roberto Clemente, Pittsburgh	.357
Home Runs–Henry Aaron, Atlanta	39
Runs Batted In–Orlando Cepeda, St. Louis	111
Hits–Roberto Clemente, Pittsburgh	209
Runs–Lou Brock, St. Louis, and Henry Aaron, Atlanta	113

Leading Pitchers

Games Won–Mike McCormick, San Francisco	22
Win Average–Nelson Briles, St. Louis (14-5)	.737
Earned Run Average–Frank Linzy, San Francisco	1.51
Strikeouts–Jim Bunning, Philadelphia	253

tied for first place. The Tigers then split a doubleheader with the California Angels and went into the final day trailing by half a game, and could still tie.

Boston clinched its first title in 21 years by beating the Twins, 5-3, as Lonborg gained his 22nd victory and Yastrzemski made four hits. The losing pitcher was Dean Chance, a 20-game winner, who earlier in the season had pitched both a nine-inning no-hit game and a five-inning no-hitter that was called off on account of rain.

Detroit kept alive its chances to tie the Boston-Minnesota winner and force a pennant play-off when it won the first game of another doubleheader over the Angels, 6-4. But the Tigers' relief pitching failed and they lost the second game, 8-5, to finish in a second-place tie with the Twins.

All-Star Game. The National League won the All-Star game, longest on record, when Tony Perez of Cincinnati hit a home run in the 15th inning for a 2-1 triumph at Anaheim, Calif. That marked the National League's fifth straight All-Star victory and the 16th of the last 21. Altogether, the National League leads 20 games to 17, with one tie.

Front Office. After the season, owner Charles Finley of the Kansas City Athletics was given permission by the American League to move his franchise to Oakland, Calif. Finley promptly hired former baseball star Joe DiMaggio, a native Californian, as executive vice-president. At the same time, the league voted to expand from 10 to 12 teams, by installing a new club in Kansas City and adding Seattle no later than 1971. The National League later made the same decision–to add two teams by 1971–but did not specify the cities. Despite the exciting pennant races, total 1967 attendance in the majors dropped 1,404,343.

Amateurs. In college baseball, Arizona State won its second National Collegiate Athletic Association (NCAA) title in three years, beating Houston in the final game of a double-elimination tournament, 11-2. The game was played at Omaha, Nebr. Japan won the Little League World Series in Williamsport, Pa., on August 26. The pitcher for the Japanese team was Masahara Miyahara, a righthander who weighed 104 pounds. [JOHN LAKE]

Award Winners in the major leagues were:

National League Most Valuable Player–Orlando Cepeda of the St. Louis Cardinals.

American League Most Valuable Player–Carl Yastrzemski of the Boston Red Sox.

National League Cy Young Award–Mike McCormick of the San Francisco Giants.

American League Cy Young Award–Jim Lonborg of the Boston Red Sox.

National League Rookie of the Year–Lee May of the Cincinnati Reds.

American League Rookie of the Year–Rod Carew of the Minnesota Twins.

National League Manager of the Year–Leo Durocher of the Chicago Cubs.

American League Manager of the Year–Dick Williams of the Boston Red Sox.

BASKETBALL. The 1966-1967 season marked the end of a long dynasty for the Boston Celtics in professional basketball, and the probable beginning of one for the University of California at Los Angeles (UCLA) in the college ranks. Important changes were made in the college rules, and a new, well-financed professional league emerged to challenge the dominant National Basketball Association (NBA).

Collegiate. The player of the year was Lew Alcindor, UCLA's 7-foot 1 3/8-inch center. Alcindor, a sophomore, started the season by scoring 56 points in his first varsity game. He went on to lead the UCLA Bruins to an undefeated season and the National Collegiate Athletic Association (NCAA) championship. Both major polls voted the UCLA team top national ranking.

UCLA won all 26 of its regular season games, becoming the sixth major college team ever to do so. In the NCAA regional play-offs, the Bruins beat Wyoming, 109-60, and Pacific, 80-64. Then, in the semifinals, they beat Houston, 73-58, and watched Dayton upset North Carolina, 76-62. UCLA then beat Dayton easily, 79-64, to win its third NCAA title in the last four years.

Alcindor finished the season second in scoring among all the major college players. He averaged 29 points per game, and set a record with a field goal accuracy of .667. On defense, his height and mobility made it almost impossible for opponents to take advantage of inside shooting. Some teams stationed two or three men around him to cut down his scoring, but he merely passed to teammates for easy shots. Southern California tried stalling to hold down UCLA's scoring power, and forced their game into overtime before UCLA won, 40-35.

None of these tactics really worked, partly because UCLA was more than a one-man team. Alcindor had strong support from three other sophomores, Lucius Allen, Ken Heitz, and Lynn Shackleford, as well as junior Mike Warren. Rival coaches gloomily agreed that UCLA, under coach of the year John Wooden, could be expected to remain in first place for the next two years.

The leading collegiate scorer was Jim Walker of Providence, who averaged 30.4 points per game. After Alcindor came Mal Graham of New York University (28.7), Elvin Hayes of Houston (28.4), Wes Bialosukna of Connecticut (28), and Bob Lloyd of Rutgers (27.9).

All-American. Alcindor, Hayes, and Walker were unanimous All-American choices. Others prominently mentioned in the various polls were Clem Haskins of Western Kentucky, Lloyd of Rutgers, Earl Monroe of Winston-Salem, and Westley Unseld of Louisville. Monroe had a record scoring average of 41.5 in leading Winston-Salem to the NCAA small-college title.

College coaches made two rule changes, partly in reaction to Alcindor. One outlawed the "dunk"

Lew Alcindor (33) dominated college basketball as few other players have done, leading UCLA to a third National Collegiate title in four years.

shot, in which a player drops the ball into the hoop from above. The second was designed to eliminate excessive stalling.

Professional. Wilt Chamberlain led the Philadelphia 76ers to the NBA championship, ending the Boston Celtics' string of eight consecutive titles. The Celtics played well enough to have won the Eastern Division in most other years, but their 60 to 21 season mark was eight games behind the Philadelphia team.

The San Francisco Warriors led the Western Division. So great was the strength of the 76ers, Celtics, and Warriors that the other seven teams in the league finished with season records under .500.

In the play-offs, Philadelphia beat Cincinnati and Boston to represent the East, while San Francisco eliminated Los Angeles and St. Louis to represent the West. In a seesaw final series, marked by brilliant but erratic play, the 76ers captured the title, 4 games to 2.

Chamberlain won the NBA's most valuable player award for the second year in a row. Although he fell to fifth in scoring, his strong playmaking and defensive abilities were the big factors in the 76ers' success. Rick Barry of the Warriors, 1966 rookie of the year, led all scorers with 2,775 points and a 35.6 average.

New League Problems. Barry was also involved in the noisiest sports litigation of the year. The Warrior star signed a reported $500,000, three-year contract with the Oakland Oaks of the new American Basketball Association (ABA), in apparent violation of the option clause of his NBA contract. Frank Mieuli, owner of the Warriors, won a court injunction forbidding Barry to play for the Oaks in the 1967-1968 season. Mieuli then sued singer Pat Boone, owner of the Oaks, for $4,500,000 in damages. Meanwhile, Barry announced he would sit out the season rather than play any more for the San Francisco Warriors.

The two leagues staged a brief "signing war" in May over the top college players, with the NBA taking the major honors. No. 1 draft choice was Jim Walker, who signed with the NBA's Detroit Pistons for about $300,000. He will join Dave Bing, the 1965 rookie of the year, in the Pistons' back court.

Another prominent recruit was Bill Bradley, the 1965 Princeton star who returned to the United States after two years as a Rhodes scholar at Oxford University. Bradley signed with the New York Knickerbockers of the NBA for a long-term contract estimated at $500,000.

Despite the challenge of the ABA, the NBA continued its gradual expansion, adding teams in San Diego (the Rockets) and Seattle (the SuperSonics) to bring its size to 12 teams. The goal is 18 teams by 1971. [James O. Dunaway]

BASUTOLAND. See Africa.

BECHUANALAND. See Africa.

BELGIUM. A trade recession, caused chiefly by a drop in exports to the Federal Republic of (West) Germany and the Netherlands, brought increased taxes to the nation and emergency powers to the government in January, 1967.

Acting under its emergency powers, the government authorized the financing of a $105,000,000 redevelopment program for the depressed mining and steel industries. On July 14, legislation was passed promising interest rebates, government guarantees, and tax exemptions to further encourage investment in these areas.

Congo (Kinshasa), Belgium's former colony, remained a continuing source of frustration to the government. In August, the government announced it would withhold most of its technical assistance to the African nation until it had received adequate guarantees for the safety of Belgians living there.

On the domestic scene, a fire destroyed L'Innovation, the second largest department store in Brussels in May (see DISASTERS). [KENNETH BROWN]

Facts in Brief. Population: 9,615,000. Government: King Baudouin I; Prime Minister Paul Vanden Boeynants. Monetary Unit: franc (49.63=U.S. $1). Foreign Trade: (including Luxembourg): exports, $6,829,000,000; imports, $7,174,000,000. Principal Exports: iron and steel, machinery, textiles.

BETHE, HANS ALBRECHT. See NOBEL PRIZES.

BIAFRA. See NIGERIA.

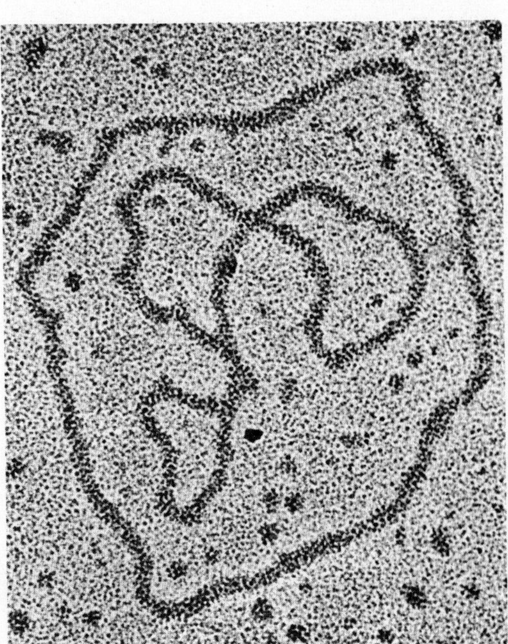

DNA, which controls growth and heredity of all living things, was synthesized at Stanford University. Picture was taken through an electron microscope.

BIOCHEMISTRY. A team of biochemists at Stanford University's School of Medicine announced, on Dec. 15, 1967, that they had made a synthetic version of the basic chemical that controls growth and heredity in living things. Nearly 11 years of research went into the historic achievement. The research team was directed by Arthur Kornberg, a 1959 Nobel prize winner, and Mehran Goulian.

The biochemists synthesized a type of deoxyribonucleic acid (DNA). This complex chemical is found in all living cells. It consists of thousands of molecules strung together into two parallel strands, which act as templates or molds for the formation of other chemicals that ultimately compose and carry out the functions of the cell. The arrangement and sequence of the molecules of the DNA strand determine what the cell is to be, whether it is human, animal, or plant, and what function it is to carry out.

The DNA that the Stanford team manufactured is the DNA of a simple pigmy virus (PHI X 174) which infects and destroys bacteria that inhabit the human intestinal tract. Kornberg previously had made a synthetic DNA, but the substance was biologically inactive. The DNA that his team has now created is biologically active. In other words, it can reproduce itself and generate new viruses.

President Lyndon B. Johnson immediately hailed the biochemists for having "unlocked a fundamental secret of life."

Oxygen Release. An important mechanism in controlling the flow of oxygen from the blood into surrounding tissues was reported, in March, 1967, by Reinhold Benesch and his wife Ruth, of Columbia University's College of Physicians and Surgeons. They discovered that diphosphoglyceric acid (DPG), normally present in blood and tissues, apparently regulates the way in which hemoglobin unloads the oxygen it carries into the body's cells. In the absence of DPG, oxygen is not released or is released very slowly. The higher the concentration of DPG, the Benesches found, the more readily hemoglobin gives up its oxygen.

Their work may prove of great importance in the treatment of vascular diseases, such as Buerger's disease, in which the oxygen supply to peripheral tissues is a critical factor.

Genetic Control Mechanism. Two cell substances that turn genes "on" and "off" were isolated and identified for the first time by three Harvard University scientists, Walter Gilbert, Benno Müller-Hill, and Mark Ptashne. Their work was reported in the "Proceedings of the National Academy of Sciences," published in March.

Genes are believed to control the development of cells by directing enzyme syntheses within them. Each cell in an organism contains an exact replica of every gene that was originally present in cells in the early embryo. Whether an embryonic cell becomes a kidney cell or a nerve cell may depend upon which of its genes are turned on or off.

A model designed to explain mechanisms for controlling enzyme synthesis in bacteria had been reported in 1961 by André Lwoff, Jacques Monod, and François Jacob of the Pasteur Institute in Paris, France. For this work, they received the 1965 Nobel prize. According to the French scientists, the control mechanism is a negative one. That is, a regulator gene sends out a substance that represses an operator gene. If the repressor substance is not formed or its action is blocked, the operator gene will activate other genes that determine cell structure.

The two cellular substances found by the Harvard scientists are believed to be repressors. One is a large protein molecule that prevents the common intestinal bacteria *E. coli* from using lactose for energy. The other is a small protein molecule that prevents the rupture of *E. coli* when it is attacked by infecting viruses.

While this research dealt with bacterial cells, the findings may aid biochemists' understanding of control mechanisms in higher organisms, even in man. Geneticists hope that an understanding of these processes will eventually lead to the control of hereditary diseases that involve the malfunctioning of genes.

Synthetic Antigens. Antibodies are produced in the tissues of all animals to defend against the invasion of certain foreign substances, known collectively as antigens. There are many types of antigens, but the most active are large molecules such as proteins. The interaction of antibodies and antigens is the basis of the immune response that underlies the body's defense against bacterial invasion and allergy, as well as its rejection of grafted tissues. The basic biochemical reactions involved in the antibody-antigen process have been better understood by the creation of a number of synthetic antigens of known chemical composition.

Michael Sela of the Weizmann Institute in Israel succeeded in creating a variety of synthetic antigens in 1967 that did not have to be attached to proteins, such as gelatin, as did all previous synthetic antigens. Since the earlier synthetic antigens required protein as part of their structure, there was always the possibility that the antibody reaction was directed toward the protein rather than toward the synthetic antibody. The antigens Sela developed have a synthetic polyalanine compound rather than a natural gelatin as their "backbone."

Some of the important findings made with the new antigens include the discovery that the surface of the antigen, rather than the amino acid composition, determines its characteristics. Thus, antigens with the same amino acid composition, but arranged in a different configuration, will evoke different antibodies. [HAROLD FEINBERG]

See also BIOLOGY; BOTANY; CHEMISTRY.

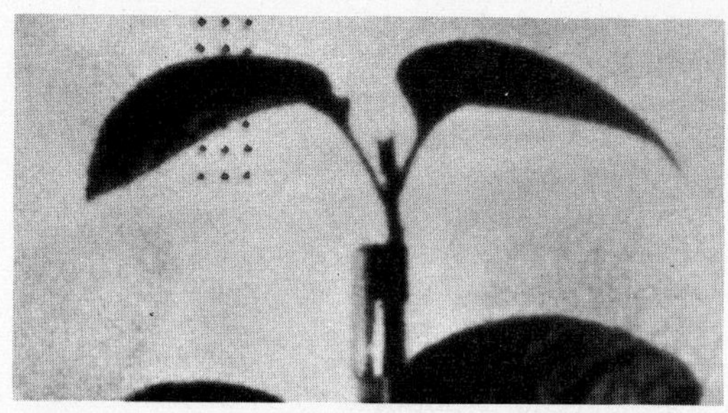

A pepper plant was launched into space aboard Biosatellite II on September 7. Before launch, the plant, *top*, grew normally. After 18 hours in space, the leaves drooped all the way to the stem.

BIOLOGY. Professor Sol Spiegelman, the University of Illinois microbiologist who synthesized the first self-reproducing virus in 1965, reported in April, 1967, that he and his associates had shaped what may be the smallest self-duplicating entity that ever existed. The new life-form, which he called the "little monster," is an abbreviated virus. While it probably has never existed naturally, it may be similar to living material at an early stage of evolution. It was developed by reducing the size of synthetic viruses by 83 per cent.

Spiegelman explained that he and the other researchers had subjected a self-duplicating molecule of ribonucleic acid (RNA) to a test-tube environment in which "selection pressure" tended to favor the molecular species that could replicate most quickly. It took comparatively few transfers (74) from one test tube to another to produce the "little monster," which replicated 15 times faster than the parent RNA. The new substance was no longer infectious. The only function it was able to perform was to reproduce itself.

Biological Clocks. Every organism appears to have a built-in clock regulating biochemical and, ultimately, all other behavior. Rhythmic fluctuations have been noted in body temperature, excretion of water and salts, hormone levels, and other biological activities. The study of these *circadian* (daily) rhythms has long fascinated biologists, who have noted that they are related to changes in the physical environment, such as the tides, the dark and light cycle, and temperature changes. Circadian rhythms are intrinsic, however, continuing after the environment is changed and occurring even in newly produced cells.

In 1967, T. Vanden Driessche, working at the University of Brussels, found what seems to be the pacemaker, or controller, of the circadian rhythms. He utilized Acetabularia, an alga, as his tool in tracing the origin of these rhythmic changes. Algae are capable of photosynthesis, and their circadian rhythms are associated with changes in chloroplast shape and photosynthetic oxygen production. The chloroplasts continue to display circadian rhythms even when the Acetabularia cell nuclei has been removed. The organism itself survives long after this has occurred.

It had been suggested that the pacemaker resided in the chloroplast and was somehow associated with chloroplast deoxyribonucleic acid (DNA). However, chemicals that prevent nuclear DNA transfer abolished the circadian rhythms. This apparent contradiction has now been resolved by Vanden Driessche, who has shown that messenger-RNA from the nucleus may persist for long periods after the nucleus is lost and permit the chloroplast to continue circadian rhythms. If the messenger-RNA transfer process is prevented, as it can be by special chemicals, then the rhythmic changes will stop.

International Biological Program. The International Biological Program (IBP) officially began in July, 1967. It is a five-year study aimed at obtaining information that will help man improve the management of his environment. The program was approved in 1961 by the International Union of Biological Sciences.

The IBP program, in which more than 40 countries are participating, calls for a comparative study of the various living communities – on land, in the sea, and in fresh water – under a whole range of contrasting environments. The environments are under both natural and artificially created conditions. The U.S. organization assigned to this program, the National Committee for the IBP, is headed by Roger Revelle, director of the Center for Population Studies at Harvard University. It is sponsored by the National Academy of Sciences.

Among the topics to be studied by the U.S. organization are:

- Airborne troublemakers – ranging from the pollen grains that make man sneeze to insects that damage various crops.
- Eskimo adaptation – investigating three Eskimo groups to understand the mechanisms of man's adaptation to his environment.
- Evolution in Hawaii – studying the unique plant and animal life of these islands. [HAROLD FEINBERG]

See also BIOCHEMISTRY; BOTANY; ZOOLOGY.

BLINDNESS. The most significant development in aid for the blind in 1967 was the enactment of federal legislation to establish a National Center for Deaf-Blind Youth and Adults. The bill, signed by President Lyndon B. Johnson on October 3, also authorized a five-year budget of $4,000,000 for the project. A bill authorizing a similar facility for deaf-blind children was expected to come before the Congress of the United States in 1968.

The need for national training of the deaf-blind became urgent in 1967 in the wake of *rubella* (German measles) epidemics in 1963 and 1965 that caused deafness, blindness, and other severe handicaps in at least 30,000 children. Although it was difficult to determine the number of children made deaf and blind by the epidemics, conservative estimates made in July, 1967, indicated special school facilities would be needed for more than 1,000 afflicted children by 1970. It was determined that professional staffs in the seven deaf-blind schools throughout the country could care for only one-tenth of that number.

The value of educating blind children in public schools was illustrated in statistics published by the American Printing House for the Blind. They showed that over 2,000 blind students attend colleges and universities each year – a reflection of the improved education being offered to the blind in public schools. In January, 1967, 8,312 blind children in the United States were attending residential schools as compared to 11,262 in public schools.

Programs. The American Foundation for Overseas Blind established a team to train rehabilitation and vocational instructors in the Far East. Its programs of integrated education continued to spread throughout the area, and, in 1967, Ceylon became the latest nation to adopt the method. The foundation expanded its services to former French possessions in Africa by establishing a rural training center in Cameroon. The Commonwealth Society for the Blind continued to expand its program in the English-speaking countries of Africa.

The World Rehabilitation Fund, Inc., initiated a special program to provide mobility instruction and vocational training to blinded South Vietnamese. The program will train local personnel in rehabilitation techniques for the blind as part of a larger rehabilitation program directed by Dr. Howard A. Rusk, professor and chairman of the department of physical medicine and rehabilitation, New York University Medical School.

International Conferences. The executive committee of the World Council for the Welfare of the Blind met in Belgrade, Yugoslavia, in May, to plan the World Council meeting in New Delhi, India, in November, 1969. In August, the International Conference for Education of Blind Youth convened at the Perkins School for the Blind in Watertown, Mass. [DOUGLAS C. MACFARLAND]

Intrepid, with Emil "Bus" Mosbacher, Jr., at the helm, defeated the Australian entry, *Dame Pattie*, four times in a row to decisively win the America's Cup race.

BOATS AND BOATING. Boating sales rose to a record level of slightly more than $3,000,000,000, some 7 per cent more than in 1966. At the New York City National Boat Show, bellwether of the industry, sales increased from $46,600,000 in 1966 to $48,900,000 in 1967.

Among the major trends were the increasing use of fiberglass for hulls, the growing number of boat manufacturers (692 as against 674 in 1966) despite a number of mergers, and an increasing volume of charter, rental, and leasing business.

Another trend, though a disturbing one, was the large increase in boat thefts. Studies by police indicated that many thefts were carried out by well-organized professional rings.

Motor Racing. In ocean power boat racing, Don Aronow of Coral Gables, Fla., won the world driving championship, as well as the U.S. offshore title. It was the first time one man had won both. The unlimited hydroplane championship was won by Bill Schumacher, a 24-year-old Seattle, Wash., bakery executive, driving *Miss Bardahl.*

Donald Campbell, holder of the world water speed record of 276.33 mph, died in January while attempting to better it. While traveling at an estimated 310 mph at Coniston Water, England, his $2,800,000 speedboat turned over and split in two. Six months later, Lee Taylor, Jr., of Downey, Calif., captured the record with a speed of 285.21 mph on Guntersville Lake, Alabama.

Sailing. For the 20th time since the yacht *America* won a silver cup by defeating England's best yachts in 1851, U.S. sailors successfully defended the America's Cup. The cup races were held off Newport, R.I., in September.

The defender was *Intrepid,* which won the right to represent the United States after outsailing *American Eagle, Columbia,* and *Constellation* in a series of elimination races. *Intrepid* was designed by Olin Stephens, the designer of three previous defenders, including the *Columbia* (1958) and the *Constellation* (1964). The craft was skippered by Emil "Bus" Mosbacher, Jr., who had steered *Weatherly* to a successful 4 to 1 defense over the Australian yacht *Gretel* in 1962.

The challenger was *Dame Pattie,* a new Australian craft, which qualified for the series by beating *Gretel* consistently in Australia earlier in the year. *Dame Pattie* was designed by Warwick Hood and skippered by Jock Sturrock, *Gretel's* helmsman in 1962.

Australian hopes were high for *Dame Pattie,* named for the wife of former Prime Minister Robert C. Menzies. But *Intrepid* doused them quickly with four decisive wins in a row. The smallest margin of victory was a sizable 3 minutes 35 seconds, equal to about half a mile.

The chief reason behind the 4 to 0 sweep was the fact that *Intrepid* was simply a better boat. Working within the narrow limitations of the 12-meter rule, designer Stephens produced a number of significant innovations. Most notable were double rudders, which improved steering ability, and the lowering of the boat's center of gravity by placing most of the crew and all heavy winches below decks.

Within a month after *Intrepid's* victory, new challenges for the cup came from Australia, England, France, and Greece. An elimination series was proposed to determine which nation would make the next attempt to win the cup in 1970.

Other Results. The winners of other major sailing competitions included:

Bud Friederichs of New Orleans, La., who won his third straight North American Dragon Class title in August. A week later, he won the world championship.

Lady Helmsman, a British catamaran, beat *Quest* of Australia, 4 to 1, in September to retain the Little America's Cup for Britain.

Bernard Moret and René Morch of France won the world 5-0-5 class title in August at La Paule, France.

William Witnall of Marblehead, Mass., won the world One-Design Class title at Hankoe, Norway, in July.

Paul Elvstrom of Denmark retained his world Star Class championship in August at Skovshoved, Denmark.

Clifford Campbell of Beechwood, N.J., won the North American senior sailing title, and the Mallory Cup, at Montreal in August. [James O. Dunaway]

BOLIVIA maintained a climate of relative political stability in 1967. It did so despite violence in the tin-mining industry and guerrilla warfare.

The tin-mine disturbances, which occurred in July near Oruro, stemmed from miners' demands for a return to pre-1965 wages. The student demonstrations, which were carried out in La Paz, erupted over dissatisfaction with the educational system. Swift action by the army quelled the disturbances.

The mine leaders and the students had apparently been spurred to antigovernment action by a small band of Cuban-inspired guerrillas. By October, however, government troops had reduced the guerrillas to a remnant force. One guerrilla leader, Cuba's Ernesto "Che" Guevara, was killed.

The economy continued to score gains in 1967. The gross national product rose to an estimated 5,049,000,000 peso bolivianos, up 6.3 per cent from 4,750,000,000 in 1966. Oil became a major export in 1967 as a pipeline running from Santa Cruz to the Chilean port of Arrica marked its first full year of operation. [Mary C. Webster]

Facts in Brief. Population: 3,815,000. Government: President René Barrientos Ortuño. Monetary Unit: peso boliviano (11.88=U.S. $1). Foreign Trade: exports, $126,000,000; imports, $131,000,000. Principal Exports: tin, silver, lead.

BOOKS. See Canadian Literature; Literature; Literature for Children.

BOSTON voters elected a new mayor, Kevin H. White, 38, by 11,000 votes over Mrs. Louise Day Hicks, 48, after a campaign that drew national attention in 1967. Mrs. Hicks, an opponent of school integration, gained a surprising 47 per cent of the ballots. See Civil Rights; Elections.

Outgoing Mayor John F. Collins, who declined to seek a third four-year term, threw his support to urban renewal expert Edward J. Logue. Finishing fourth in the September primary, Logue failed to make the run-off election.

Boston's physical renaissance seemed assured despite the change of administration in city hall. Federal aid commitments of $202,000,000 for existing projects were considered firm. In housing, the Boston Redevelopment Authority was committed to the rehabilitation of 30,000 dwelling units by 1975.

Two massive development plans were announced during the year. One proposed that 245 acres in the central business district be used to provide auto-free streets, arcades, and cultural and sports facilities. Architect Victor Gruen, who developed the plan, said it would liberate streets of traffic jams, noise, and pollution.

The second plan, announced in August, detailed a huge 300-acre redevelopment program for the Back Bay area. To cost $325,000,000, nearly all in private investment, the sweeping proposal is expected to be completed in a decade. [Donald W. Lief]

BOTANY. The function and nature of phytochrome, an important, light-sensitive pigment in plant cells, was the subject of many studies in 1967. The complex phytochrome molecules regulate such plant processes as germination, growth, and flowering, turning these functions on and off in response to the lengths of days and nights. William Hillman and Willard Koukkari of Brookhaven National Laboratory, near Upton, N.Y., reported in May, that "sleep movements" of many bean and pea plants are regulated by phytochrome. Sleep movement refers to the folding or closing of plant leaflets at sundown. Since this action is much more frequent than other phytochrome-controlled functions, such as flowering, it may provide a rapid means of detecting the presence of phytochrome in plants.

Abscisin, a recently discovered plant hormone, was assigned a role in plant growth regulation by its discoverer, Frederick T. Addicott of the University of California at Davis. He reported to a seminar on Plant Growth Regulation held in March in Kyoto, Japan, that abscisin helped cause dormant conditions in plants and helped cause aging portions of plants to drop off.

Ancient Seeds. Seeds frozen in Alaskan soil for at least 10,000 years were reported to have sprouted in the laboratory, and produced healthy plants. In October, Alf E. Porsild and Charles R. Harington of the National Museum of Canada, in Ottawa, told of planting arctic tundra lupine seeds, recovered in 1954 from frozen silt in a lemming burrow in the Yukon Territory. The previous record for revival of long-dormant seeds is thought to be that of 2,000-year-old lotus seeds, which were recovered from an Asian peat bog.

Biosatellite. In August, the National Aeronautics and Space Administration (NASA) launched the unmanned spacecraft Biosatellite II. Its contents included, among other fast-growing organisms, wild flowers and wheat seedlings. The satellite was recovered 45 hours after launch. The wheat seedlings, the first plants ever grown in space, were found to have sprouted roots that curved up toward the shoots and then outward. Though the results of this flight experiment will not be fully analyzed for another year, the seedling growth suggests that gravity and the absence of gravity have a distinct effect on plant growth.

Rabbage. A hybrid vegetable created by crossing a radish with a cabbage was reported by Professor Boris S. Moshchov, head of the Institute of Light Physiology in Leningrad, U.S.S.R. Both the roots of the new plant, which are similar to those of a radish, and the leaves, which are similar to those of a cabbage, are edible and rich in vitamin D. The institute harvested 20 crops of the hybrid in 12 months. The plants were raised indoors under artificial light. [JAMES A. PEARRE]

BOTSWANA. See AFRICA.

BOWLING. Dave Davis of Phoenix, Ariz., led the professionals in earnings with $54,115 and topped old pro Dick Weber's record of five victories in the Professional Bowlers Association (PBA) schedule. Davis, who also won the $70,000 PBA championship, December 3 to 9, in New York City, was named bowler of the year.

The top prize in the All-Star tournament at St. Louis, Mo., went to Les Schissler of Denver, Colo., who defeated Pete Tountas of Tucson, Ariz., in the final by a narrow margin of 613 pins to 610. The women's winner, Gloria Bouvia of Portland, Ore., upset Shirley Garms of Chicago, 558 to 516. Jim Stefanich of Joliet, Ill., was the winner of the Firestone Tournament of Champions at Akron, Ohio.

The 64th American Bowling Congress (ABC) tournament drew 18,000 contestants to Miami Beach, Fla., where the Balancer Glove team of Fort Worth, Tex., totaled 6,298 for six games and won the classic team division title. Pinky's Bowl team of Miami, Fla., with a series of 3,327, won the regular team division. In other ABC classic-division competition, Louis Mandragona of Miami won the singles competition, Bob Strampe of Detroit, Mich., took the all-events title, and Norman Meyers and Harry Smith of Atherton, Calif., won the doubles.

The Los Angeles Orphans won the Woman's International Bowling Congress (WIBC) title at Rochester, N.Y. [JOHN LAKE]

BOXING. Heavyweight champion Muhammad Ali, born Cassius Clay, again made the headlines, both in and out of the ring in 1967. In January, his pleas for deferment as a conscientious objector and as a Black Muslim minister were rejected by Kentucky Selective Service officials. In the ring, he successfully defended his title for the eighth and ninth times. In Houston, Tex., on February 6, he scored a lopsided 15-round decision over Ernie Terrell. On March 22, in New York City, he knocked out Zora Folley in seven rounds, thus scoring his 29th victory in 29 professional fights, 22 of them by knockouts.

Then, on April 28, in Houston, Ali refused to step forward and take the army induction oath, and federal marshals arrested him. By the next morning, the World Boxing Association, the British Board of

World Champion Boxers

Division	Champion	Where Fought	Year Won
Heavyweight	Muhammad Ali	Miami	1964
Light-heavyweight	Dick Tiger	New York	1966
Middleweight	Emile Griffith	New York	1967
Welterweight	Curtis Cokes	New Orleans	1966
Lightweight	Carlos Ortiz	San Juan	1965
Featherweight			Vacant
Bantamweight	Masahiko Harada	Nagoya	1965
Flyweight	Horacio Accavallo	Tokyo	1966
(disputed)	Chartchai Chionoi	Bangkok	1966

Boxing Control, and most American state boxing commissions issued statements stripping Ali of his title. However, he is still recognized as the champion in much of the world. In June, Ali was tried in Houston for refusing to be inducted, and found guilty. He was given five years in prison and a $10,000 fine. Ali remained at liberty pending appeals, but he was prevented from further bouts.

Tournament. Even before Ali's sentencing, the American boxing establishment was making plans to select a new champion. An eight-man tournament was arranged; it began on August 5 in Houston.

In the quarterfinal matches Oscar Bonavena of Argentina beat Karl Mildenberger of West Germany; Jerry Quarry of Los Angeles beat Floyd Patterson of New York City; Thad Spencer of San Francisco beat Ernie Terrell; and Jimmy Ellis of Louisville beat Leotis Martin of Philadelphia. Ellis then scored a unanimous 12-round decision over Bonavena in the first semifinal, on Dec. 3, 1967.

Only one major title changed hands, and that one for less than six months. On April 17, in New York City, Nino Benvenuti of Italy won the world middleweight crown, on a decision, from Emile Griffith of New York. On September 29, again in New York, Griffith regained the title. [JAMES O. DUNAWAY]

BOY SCOUTS OF AMERICA. See YOUTH ORGANIZATIONS.

BRAZIL. A new constitution was approved by the congress in January, 1967. Under its provisions, strong executive controls were established over congressional legislation and finance, as well as over the states. All taxes except real estate levies were to be collected by the federal government, then distributed to the states and municipalities.

The president was empowered to appoint state governors and to suspend individual political rights. In crimes against national security, military courts were given jurisdiction over civilians.

A new press law was passed upon the adoption of the constitution. It established stiff penalties for news considered damaging to the national security or to the country's financial situation. The congress also adopted a national security law which provided strong jail terms for any one promoting strikes or lockouts, or for committing offenses against the honor of the office of the president.

Inaugural Promises. Arthur da Costa e Silva was inaugurated as president on March 15, the day the new constitution went into effect (see COSTA E SILVA, ARTHUR DA). He promised a government of "social humanism," one that would be responsive to the needs and aspirations of the nation's poor and of its disgruntled youth. He also pledged his government to improve economic and social conditions and to seek new markets for Brazilian products.

Zora Folley, *left*, moves in on Muhammad Ali in the first round of a title bout. Folley was knocked out, but Ali was stripped of the title for refusing induction.

To back his words with actions, the president abolished the ban on student demonstrations. He also made it plain that he did not intend to enforce the press law, which had been enacted by the regime of outgoing president Humberto de Alencar Castelo Branco. Costa e Silva moved quickly to stem a sharp rise in rents, countermanded planned hikes in bus and commuter train fares, and boosted the take-home pay of a majority of Brazilians by increasing tax exemptions.

Boosting the Economy. During the succeeding months, President Costa e Silva devoted most of the government's energies to curing the nation's chronic economic ills. Planned public investments for 1967 were set 16 per cent higher than in the preceding year to help achieve Brazil's annual gross national product growth-rate target of 6 per cent–versus 4.3 per cent in 1966. Through a $100,000,000 loan negotiated with the Agency for International Development, businessmen were enabled to import U.S. machinery, capital goods, and raw materials, all of which would help boost industrial output. The agency also authorized loans totaling $76,100,000 for farm, power, and road projects.

The Inter-American Development Bank granted a loan of $34,000,000 to help finance the first stage of a giant hydroelectric project on the Paraná River. The project would have an initial capacity of 1,760,000 kilowatts (kw).

Agriculture received special attention during the year. A Fund for Farming Development was set up with a working capital of 216,000,000 new cruzeiros to provide financing for livestock breeders. From the World Bank, Brazil received a $40,000,000 loan to implement an $80,000,000 project whose aim was to hike beef, mutton, and wool output. Substantial increases in crops such as beans, coffee, corn, and rice, as well as peanuts and other oilseeds, were forecast. In September, the government reported that coffee exports had passed the 3,000,000-sack level, breaking all monthly records since 1905.

Currency Reform. Inasmuch as the government considered stabilized prices crucial to all its planning, it continued to fight inflation. Earlier in the year, Brazil decreed a surprise two-day bank holiday in order to effect a currency reform and, at the same time, carry out a devaluation. The cruzeiro was downgraded by 23 per cent–from 2.20 to the U.S. dollar, to 2.72 to the U.S. dollar. A few days later, a "new" cruzeiro worth 1,000 of the old units was placed in circulation. The devaluation was expected to stimulate Brazilian exports. [MARY C. WEBSTER]

Facts in Brief. Population: 87,695,000. Government: President Arthur da Costa e Silva. Monetary Unit: cruzeiro nóvo (2.72=U.S. $1). Foreign Trade: exports, $1,741,000,000; imports, $1,496,000,000. Principal Exports: coffee, iron ore, cotton.

BRIDGE AND TUNNEL. See BUILDING AND CONSTRUCTION.

BRIDGE, CONTRACT. Italy's magnificent Blue Team won its ninth consecutive world contract bridge championship at Miami Beach, Fla., in June, when it crushed the North American team on the last day of play. The final score in the competition for the Bermuda Bowl was 338-227.

In September, at Atlantic City, N.J., Robert Jordan and Arthur Robinson of Philadelphia, Pa., won the international team trials that selected U.S. representatives in the 1968 world championships in Deauville, France. Also selected were Edgar Kaplan, William Root, and Alvin Roth of New York City, and Norman Kay of Philadelphia.

At the spring tournament of the American Contract Bridge League (ACBL) at Seattle, Wash., in March, the Harold S. Vanderbilt trophy was won by Michael Lawrence of San Francisco, Calif.; Lew Mathe of Los Angeles, Calif.; Lew Stansby, and Ron Von der Porten all of San Francisco, Calif.; Jim Jacoby of Dallas, Tex.; and G. Robert Nail of Houston, Tex.

Winners of the Spingold trophy at the ACBL summer tournament at Montreal were Kaplan, Kay, Root, and Roth. [THEODORE M. O'LEARY]

BRITISH COLUMBIA. See CANADA.

BRITISH COMMONWEALTH OF NATIONS. See GREAT BRITAIN; and articles on various countries of the Commonwealth.

BRITISH GUIANA. See GUYANA.

BUILDING AND CONSTRUCTION spending reached an estimated high of $78,700,000,000 in 1967, for an increase of 5 per cent over expenditures of $75,300,000,000 in 1966, according to the U.S. Bureau of the Census. The F. W. Dodge Company expected the industry to rebound with a 10 per cent increase in construction spending. In terms of brick and mortar, not dollars and cents, the National Industrial Conference Board (NICB) predicted an actual growth rate of only about 1.5 per cent in 1968 construction.

Both the NICB and the Associated General Contractors of America saw soaring labor costs as the industry's primary problem. On Sept. 30, 1967, average wage rates for common labor in the 20 major construction centers covered in the *Engineering News-Record* cost indexes had risen an average of 26 cents per hour in 12 months. Skilled labor rates were still higher, up 29 cents from the December, 1966, level. Built-in contractural wage increases would push 1968 costs even higher, the magazine predicted.

Contributing also to rising construction costs were spiraling prices of materials, notably lumber and plywood and some metals. Demand for lumber and plywood picked up with the rise in housing starts, which reached an annual rate of 1,496,000 in October, compared with 875,000 in the 1966 month.

Financing of projects continued to become more expensive, with long-term borrowing costs reaching

Tokyo's 36-story Kasumigaseki Building, the tallest in Japan, neared completion in late 1967. Reinforced concrete-and-steel design resists earthquake damage.

the highest level in 40 years. State and local governments also felt the credit pinch in the interest they had to pay on their borrowings. See BANKS AND BANKING; MONEY.

A New Building Technique–building from the top down–was introduced on construction of two high-rise dormitories at Central Washington State College, Ellensburg, Wash. Each building has a central reinforced-concrete core, from which three wings fan out. Near the end of each wing, two columns support a heavy girder spanning out from the core, forming sort of a ridgepole. The girder, in turn, supports outriggers, or rafter assembly, from which high-tensile steel is dropped to the ground, where it is securely fastened. Plant-cast structural floor panels are then connected to this vertical steel.

Building Codes. A step toward the creation of a model national building code was made in January, 1967, with President Lyndon B. Johnson's appointment of a Temporary Commission on Codes, Zoning, Taxation, and Development Standards. The objective of the study was to recommend ways to modernize and standardize the nation's 5,000 or more building codes.

As a result of the disastrous fire that destroyed Chicago's McCormick Place exhibition hall on Jan. 16, 1967, the city of Chicago undertook revisions of its building code, particularly for providing for insulating coating of large-span girders and for better sprinkling systems. Early in the year, the National Building Code of the American Insurance Association was revised to tighten sprinkler installations and to provide for fire fighting access openings on each floor of a windowless building, if the ground-floor area exceeds 7,500 square feet. About 750 cities have adopted the code.

Outstanding Projects of 1967 included Chicago's 70-story Lake Point Tower, completed in December. The 645-foot skyscraper is the world's tallest reinforced-concrete structure. It will also continue to serve as a laboratory for structural research. Engineers have incorporated $250,000 worth of measuring and recording devices in its foundations and superstructure to measure various stresses and compression factors.

In New York City, the new Madison Square Garden Sports and Entertainment Center was also completed in December. The cable-supported roof, 404 feet in diameter, was the city's first permanent suspension roof and one of the largest in the United States. By eliminating interior columns, it affords an unobstructed view of the arena floor from all of the center's 20,234 seats. The center is part of a $116,000,000 project that also includes a 29-story office building, Two Pennsylvania Plaza, and the redevelopment of the Pennsylvania Station, with all of the railroad and terminal facilities being placed in underground locations.

BUILDING AND CONSTRUCTION

The American Society of Civil Engineers' Outstanding Civil Engineering Achievement Award for 1967 went to the St. Louis Gateway Arch, a spectacular stainless steel monument symbolizing the role of St. Louis as the gateway to the West during the nation's expansion. An elevator–half train, half ferris wheel–within the 630-foot-high arch carries sightseers to an observation room at the top.

Bridges. Venezuela opened its Angostura Bridge over the Orinoco River on Jan. 6, 1967, nearly six months ahead of schedule. The 5,507-foot-long suspension bridge has a central span of 2,336 feet, the longest clear suspension span in South America and the ninth longest in the world.

The first contracts for addition of a six-lane lower level to the Verrazano-Narrows Bridge were awarded in November. The $20,000,000 work on the Brooklyn-Staten Island crossing across lower New York harbor was being undertaken 10 years ahead of schedule because of the unexpected heavy volume of traffic in the three years since the bridge opened Nov. 21, 1964.

The Cowlitz River Bridge became the longest concrete arch span in the United States with its completion in December, 1967. The spectacular crossing, 250 feet above Mayfield Lake near Mossyrock, Wash., has an overall length of 1,136 feet and measures 520 feet between its arch spring lines.

The world's longest orthotropic span, the $70,000,000 San Mateo-Hayward Bridge across lower San Francisco Bay, was opened to traffic Oct. 31, 1967. The 7.4-mile crossing includes a 5,500-foot orthotropic section, which incorporates the flanged top of the girders into the road deck.

Dams. The United States took the honors as the No. 1 dam builder during the years 1963 through 1965, according to tabulations in the 1967 edition of the *World Register of Dams*. During the three years, 757 dams over 50 feet high were built, 298 of them in the United States. Japan, the runner-up, built 91. Of the 757 new dams, 640 were less than 200 feet high. Only 22 were more than 400 feet high.

In August, concrete crews topped out Hells Canyon Dam on the Snake River between Oregon and Idaho. The $70,000,000, 320-foot-high concrete-gravity structure has a generating capacity of 425,000 kilowatts (kw). It is the last of three dams the Idaho Power Company has built on the Hells Canyon reach of the Snake River.

The most important topping-out ceremony of the year took place in California on October 6, when workmen completed Oroville Dam, the world's highest earth-fill dam, and the highest U.S. dam of any type. The mile-wide, 770-foot-high dam tops Hoover Dam by 44 feet and contains 80,600,000 cubic yards of fill. The $133,500,000 structure is a key element in the $2,800,000,000 California water plan. It will impound 3,500,000 acre-feet of water, 59 per cent of which will flow annually through the 444-mile California aqueduct to arid counties in southern California.

Pakistan's huge Mangla Dam was opened on Nov. 23, 1967, a year ahead of schedule. President Ayub Khan pressed a button that opened the nine gates of the $644,000,000 dam, releasing a flow of water four times greater than that of Niagara Falls. This key structure in the Indus basin project will generate 1,000,000 kilowatts of power, as well as provide water for irrigation.

New Tunnels. The second of the $31,000,000 twin bore Berkeley Hills tunnels, a key project in the Bay Area Rapid Transit District development now under construction, was holed through on March 4. The 3 1/2-mile tunnels, extending from the Chabot Canyon area of Oakland in Alameda County to Orinda in Contra Costa County, will be the fourth longest vehicular tunnel in the United States.

Twin vehicular tunnels, 80 feet beneath the bed of the St. Lawrence River, were the outstanding components of that river's $85,000,000 bridge-tunnel crossing dedicated in March, 1967. Located just east of Montreal, the project connects north-south Route 15 with the east-west Trans-Canada Highway.

In April, the Maryland legislature authorized the State Roads Commission to build a second tunnel under Baltimore harbor. The tunnel was in the planning stage at year's end. [MARY E. JESSUP]

See also ARCHITECTURE; TRANSPORTATION.

BULGARIA remained one of the most loyal allies of the Soviet Union. Premier Todor Zhivkov paid two visits to Moscow early in 1967. During a subsequent visit of Communist Party General Secretary Leonid I. Brezhnev to Sofia in April, the two countries signed a new 20-year alliance. Similar pacts were concluded with Poland and East Germany. Zhivkov also visited Romania, Yugoslavia, and Outer Mongolia, and attended Communist-bloc conferences in Budapest, Karlsbad in Czechoslovakia, and also in Moscow, where he urged strong support for the Soviet positions on Vietnam, Communist China, and the Middle East.

In June, the Bulgarian government broke diplomatic relations with Israel over the Arab-Israeli war in the Middle East. It also delivered a sharp protest for an attack on its embassy in Peking.

This solidarity with the Soviet Union and its allies did not keep Bulgaria from practicing a more flexible diplomacy toward non-Communist nations. Exchanges of high-ranking delegations occurred with Austria, Denmark, Finland, India, and Norway. Bulgaria also concluded a new wheat agreement with Canada. [H. GORDON SKILLING]

Facts in Brief. Population: 8,385,000. Government: Premier and Communist Party First General Secretary Todor Zhivkov. Monetary Unit: lev (2=U.S. $1). Foreign Trade: exports, $1,305,000,000; imports, $1,474,000,000. Principal Exports: tobacco, clothing, fruit.

BURMA enjoyed a relatively stable year on the domestic front. With the approval of Union Revolutionary Council Chairman Ne Win, some of the more burdensome restrictions on the civilian population were relaxed, and a number of political prisoners were released from jail. Progress was also made toward settling a border dispute with India. Guerrilla activity in Karen province remained small.

Relations between Burma and Communist China were strained by violent anti-Chinese rioting in Rangoon and other Burmese cities from June 27 to 29. The riots were touched off when Chinese students in Rangoon attacked several Burmese teachers who had attempted to end a sit-in at a Chinese school. Burmese demonstrators retaliated by attacking the Chinese quarter.

Communist China, protesting the actions as anti-Chinese, withdrew its ambassador. Burma, in turn, closed its embassy in Peking. By year's end, relations between the two countries had reached an all-time low. [JOHN N. STALKER]

Facts in Brief. Population: 26,116,000. Government: Union Revolutionary Council Chairman Ne Win. Monetary Unit: kyat (4.81 = U.S. $1). Foreign Trade: exports, $189,000,000; imports, $153,000,000. Principal Exports: rice, oilseed cake and meal, cotton.

BURUNDI. See AFRICA.

BUS. See TRANSPORTATION.

BUSINESS. See ECONOMY, THE.

CABINET. Early in December, 1967, an announcement that U.S. Secretary of Defense Robert S. McNamara would leave his post touched off a national uproar with world-wide repercussions. McNamara, head of the Department of Defense since 1961, announced he was resigning to accept the presidency of the World Bank. There was widespread speculation, however, that McNamara's resignation had been requested by President Lyndon B. Johnson as a prelude to a change in the administration's policy toward the war in Vietnam. See NATIONAL DEFENSE; PRESIDENT OF THE UNITED STATES; VIETNAM.

U.S. Cabinet as of Dec. 31, 1967

(in order of succession to the presidency)

Secretary of State	Dean Rusk
Secretary of the Treasury	Henry H. Fowler
Secretary of Defense	Robert S. McNamara
Attorney General	Ramsey Clark
Postmaster General	Lawrence F. O'Brien
Secretary of the Interior	Stewart L. Udall
Secretary of Agriculture	Orville L. Freeman
Secretary of Commerce	Alexander B. Trowbridge
Secretary of Labor	W. Willard Wirtz
Secretary of Health, Education, and Welfare	John W. Gardner
Secretary of Housing and Urban Development	Robert C. Weaver
Secretary of Transportation	Alan S. Boyd

Three other cabinet changes were made during the year. In February, President Johnson named Acting Attorney General Ramsey Clark to the post of Attorney General (see CLARK, RAMSEY). Clark had been Acting Attorney General for nearly five months following the resignation of Nicholas deB. Katzenbach in October, 1966. Katzenbach had resigned to accept a post in the Department of State. Hours after Clark's appointment, his father, Tom C. Clark, retired as Associate Justice of the Supreme Court of the United States.

On May 22, Alexander B. Trowbridge, a 37-year-old business executive, was nominated to succeed John T. Connor as Secretary of Commerce (see TROWBRIDGE, ALEXANDER B.). Connor had announced his plans to resign in January. In August, President Johnson nominated Paul R. Ignatius, an assistant Secretary of Defense, to take over the post of Secretary of the Navy. Ignatius, a native of Los Angeles, Calif., and a graduate of the University of Southern California, had joined the Department of Defense on May 2, 1961.

Ignatius replaced John T. McNaughton, who was killed in an airplane crash in North Carolina on June 19. McNaughton, who had been confirmed by the Senate but had not taken office, had been scheduled to replace Paul H. Nitze.

CALDECOTT MEDAL. See LITERATURE FOR CHILDREN.

CAMBODIA shifted stance on its long-standing pro-Communist Chinese policy in 1967. Prince Norodom Sihanouk, alarmed by a rapid build-up of Maoist fervor in the country, clamped down on pro-Peking elements within and outside the government.

Sihanouk's concern stemmed from guerrilla efforts to disrupt his government's relations with the Khmer tribes along the Thai border. Pro-Maoist activities within Phnom Penh also increased his alarm. He abruptly dismissed his cabinet in April and organized one under his own supervision. In September, still disturbed by continuing Communist infiltration, he dismissed two pro-Communist cabinet ministers and quickly realigned his government to the right.

Yet, as Cambodia began to look for a political counterweight to Communist China, it continued suspicious of the West. It continued to rely on the Soviet Union for military support and on France for economic aid. Overtures were made to the United States, most notably after a visit late in the year by Mrs. John F. Kennedy. These moves, however, were generally viewed with skepticism. [JOHN N. STALKER]

Facts in Brief. Population: 6,750,000. Government: Chief of State Norodom Sihanouk. Monetary Unit: riel (35=U.S. $1). Foreign Trade: exports, $67,000,000; imports, $111,000,000. Principal Exports: rice, rubber.

CAMEROON. See AFRICA.

CAMP FIRE GIRLS. See YOUTH ORGANIZATIONS.

CANADA

"Canada's year in history." This was the theme as the Dominion of Canada celebrated its 100th birthday in 1967. On July 1, the centennial of the proclamation of the British North America Act that had united Britain's colonies, the roar of 100 guns echoed through the Parliament buildings in Ottawa. Elizabeth II, Queen of Canada; her consort, Prince Philip; Prime Minister Lester B. Pearson; and scores of prominent Canadians were among the throng of celebrants. The week-long visit by the Queen and Prince Philip highlighted centennial visits by more than 60 heads of state or their representatives.

The centennial observance began, however, with the dawn of the New Year (see Close-Up). The eyes of tourists from throughout the world turned toward Montreal on April 28 with the opening of the 1967 Universal and International Exhibition, Expo 67 (see FAIRS AND EXHIBITIONS). By year's end, the great success of the centennial observances had strengthened the pride of Canadians in their achievements. In its renewed mood of unity, the country rallied behind Prime Minister Pearson when he repudiated an attempt by French President Charles de Gaulle in July to interfere in Canada's domestic affairs by encouraging Quebec separatism.

Pearson called upon Canadians to ask themselves what they were prepared to do for the sake of unity. This meant, he said, making the whole country, and not just Quebec, "a homeland for all French Canadians." "The future of Canada, indeed its very survival," declared Pearson, "depends on our success in building a society where diverse races and languages, diverse talents and capacities, diverse energies and interests are not only permitted, but are encouraged to grow and develop side by side."

Thus dedicated, the government embarked upon "a battle for Canada," attacking the Quebec separatists, on the one hand, and the English-speaking Canadians who refused to accept the "French fact," on the other. At the end of 1967, crucial engagements in the campaign still lay ahead. Yet, there was a new mood of confidence in a united Canada, a confidence bolstered by the stirring experience of a memorable centennial year.

In December, Pearson announced his intention to resign as leader of his party and as prime minister, but would continue until a convention could select his successor.

Death of Vanier. Canada lost a beloved Governor-General on the eve of the centennial celebrations. On March 5, Major General Georges P. Vanier, 78, the 19th representative of the Crown in Canada, died after a heart attack. Vanier was the second native Canadian to hold the post.

Immensely popular, Vanier was given a state funeral and laid to rest in the military chapel of the Citadel at Quebec, a vice-regal residence. The Queen appointed Roland D. Michener, 67, a Toronto lawyer, former speaker of the House of Commons, and, since 1964, high commissioner to India, as Vanier's successor. He was sworn in on April 17, in time to assume the heavy burden of state duties accompanying the centennial observances. See MICHENER, ROLAND D.

Pearson's Liberal Government freshened its image in April. A leading Quebec intellectual, Pierre Elliot Trudeau, was named minister of justice to replace Lucien Cardin, who retired from Parliament. Associated with Quebec's "quiet revolution"

Prime Minister Pearson lit the centennial flame in the first seconds of 1967, touching off a year-long celebration of Canada's century of unity.

and an articulate exponent of constitutional change, Trudeau supported reform in divorce and birth control laws. John Turner, another representative of the new generation in Quebec politics, was promoted to cabinet status when he was made registrar-general, with responsibility for consumer affairs. Walter Gordon, who resigned as minister of finance in 1965, re-entered the inner circle of the cabinet as president of the Privy Council, to study foreign investments in Canada. Guy Favreau, former minister of justice and leader of Quebec's Liberal party, resigned from Parliament to become a judge of the Quebec Superior Court. Favreau died suddenly in Montreal on July 11. In September, Paul Hellyer, the author of a controversial armed forces unification bill, moved from the Department of National Defense to the Department of Transport. In the move, Hellyer replaced veteran minister John W. Pickersgill, who then became president of the new Canadian Transport Commission.

Political Changes. The Pearson government again held a minority position in 1967. It lost a seat in a by-election in May. As a result, the Liberals held 132 seats in the 265-seat House of Commons; Conservatives, 95 seats; New Democratic party, 22;

Créditistes, 8; Social Credit, 4; and independents, 3. One seat remained vacant.

The Progressive Conservative party held a leadership convention in Toronto from September 6 to 10. John G. Diefenbaker, who had led the party to office in 1957, sought to retain party leadership. But after five ballots, the delegates chose Robert L. Stanfield, premier of Nova Scotia, as their national leader. Stanfield edged out another provincial premier, Dufferin Roblin of Manitoba, 1,150 votes to 969. The 53-year-old Stanfield resigned his premiership, and later won a federal seat from that province. In November, Roblin, too, resigned, and planned to enter federal politics. The two were expected to bring new direction and vigor to the Conservative party's onslaught on the Liberal government.

The first session of Canada's 27th Parliament ended May 8, after a record session of 250 days. The Pearson government, gaining in confidence throughout the session, was strong enough at the end to destroy a Conservative filibuster over the controversial bill to unify the armed forces.

Its principal achievement, however, was the adoption of measures aimed at establishing a basic social welfare structure that would provide a minimum standard of life for all Canadians, even if sick, unemployed, elderly, poor, or disabled. The Pearson government then moved on to sponsor progressive legislation on air and water pollution, birth control, divorce, housing, and penal and parole codes.

The second session began on May 8, only a few hours after the first session ended. After the summer recess, the session resumed on September 25. Pearson designated 25 bills as essential to his legislative program. One, a proposal to abolish the death penalty except for murder of police officers or prison guards, was passed by the Commons in November. Among the other important legislative items passed in the second session was a measure establishing a new adult training program to combat unemployment, and one creating the Canada Deposit Insurance Corporation to insure deposits in banks and trust and loan companies. A new broadcasting act replaced the Board of Broadcast Governors with a more powerful regulatory body, and a complex statute brought all forms of transportation under a new agency, the Canadian Transport Commission.

The most controversial legislation, a new Bank Act and a bill to unify the armed forces, were also the most far-reaching in their effects. The Bank Act was designed to stimulate competition and add flexibility to Canada's banking system. After two years of heated debate, it emerged from its legislative passage almost unchanged. Under the act, chartered banks acquired a new range of powers, and could compete more effectively with the fast-growing trust and loan companies. The act replaced the 6 per cent interest ceiling on bank loans with a formula that gave a 7 1/4 per cent ceiling for 1967 and would thereafter tie the ceiling to the average yield on short-term government bonds.

"Long live free Quebec!" cried visiting French President Charles de Gaulle, awed by French Canada's enthusiastic welcome for him in July.

Foreign Affairs. Canada's centennial year was highlighted when, on a sensational state visit, President Charles de Gaulle of France gave open encouragement to the separatist movement in Quebec. Traveling aboard the French cruiser *Colbert*, he arrived in the city of Quebec on July 23, after a short visit to the tiny French islands of St. Pierre and Miquelon lying south of Newfoundland. He received a warm welcome in Quebec, and the next day drove to Montreal along the north shore of the St. Lawrence River. He remarked that his reception along the way reminded him of nothing so much as the liberation of France during World War II. In Montreal, he addressed a number of gatherings, offering traditional salutes to Quebec, the French Canadians, New France, and France. At one affair, he added the rallying cry of the Quebec separatists, "Vive le Québec libre!" ("Long live free Quebec!"). DeGaulle's use of this phrase startled the country.

Pearson called his cabinet into session on July 25, and it deplored the French president's attempt "to encourage the small minority of our population whose aim is to destroy Canada." The cabinet's statement went on to say, "The people of Canada are free. Every province of Canada is free. Canadians do not need to be liberated. Indeed, many thousands of Canadians gave their lives in two world wars in the liberation of France and other European countries." De Gaulle's remarks were "unacceptable to the Canadian people and its government."

Hearing this stinging rebuke, De Gaulle canceled his visit to Ottawa and flew home from Montreal on July 26.

Even the French press was critical of the general, but he remained unrepentant. In a statement issued on July 31, he stated that the confederation of Canada had not assured French Canadians of "liberty, equality, and fraternity in their own country." He applauded the determination of French Canadians "to become masters of their own progress," and stated France's intention to help them "realize the freedom aims that they have set themselves."

De Gaulle's statements proved embarrassing to Quebec's premier, Daniel Johnson, a nonseparatist, who said, "I think we can solve Canada's political problems in Canada." Mayor Jean Drapeau of Montreal told the departing general that Canada could find its own way without the help of France.

Later, speaking in London on November 27, Pearson declared firmly that while France has a right to develop cultural links with Quebec, Canada's problems of unity are "to be solved by us, and not by the intervention of any other country." A day later, in Paris, De Gaulle called for a complete change in Canada's governmental structure and for the solidarity of Frenchmen on both sides of the Atlantic. The general doubtlessly was making a difficult situation more difficult.

U.S. President Lyndon B. Johnson briefly visited Expo 67 on May 25, the U.S. National Day at the exhibition. He then stopped at Ottawa to discuss the Vietnam and Middle East situations with Prime Minister Pearson. The two leaders talked over the possibility of a conference of the Big Four powers (France, Great Britain, Russia, and the United States) on these subjects. Pearson reportedly urged the President to halt the bombing of North Vietnam in an effort to open negotiations with the Hanoi government. External Affairs Minister Paul Martin repeated this theme in presenting a Vietnam peace plan to the United Nations General Assembly in September. "It seems clear," he said, "that all attempts to bring about talks are doomed to failure unless the bombing is stopped. This is a matter of first priority if we are . . . to open the door to the conference room." See UNITED NATIONS.

Canada-U.S. Relations. A sharp clash of interests blurred the future of the U.S. controlled Mercantile Bank in Canada. It reflected the fear of American domination of Canada's economy. The dispute began in 1963 when the First National City Bank of New York (Citibank) bought the Dutch-owned Mercantile Bank despite warnings that the Canadian government would reject the transaction. At the time, Finance Minister Walter Gordon proposed that the Mercantile Bank be prevented from expanding its operations until Citibank sold 75 per cent of its shares to residents of Canada.

The U.S. government protested, and James S. Rockefeller, chairman of Citibank, had appeared before the Commons Finance Committee to ask that the legislation not be enacted. At the same time, he stated that shares in Mercantile would not be sold to Canadians. When Gordon's successor, Mitchell Sharp, also stood firm, Citibank was obliged to change its position.

In February, 1967, the Mercantile Bank stated its readiness to seek share participation by Canadian residents at an appropriate time. The Commons committee thereupon recommended that Mercantile be allowed to operate without restriction until the end of 1972, in order to reach a profitable position before selling its shares. By then, however, if it has not sold 75 per cent of its shares to Canadians, it must reduce its liabilities to 20 times its capital, which would substantially restrict its operations. This compromise was later inserted in the Bank Act.

Defense. A single military service, the Canadian Armed Forces, was established in 1967. A personal project of Defense Minister Paul Hellyer, unification encountered fierce opposition in the Commons and in its Defense Committee. After 59 days of argument, however, the Commons passed the measure in April by a vote of 127 to 73. The one uniform to be worn by the three services was first displayed by the military guard turned out at Expo 67.

Unification did not mean the end of the army, navy, and air force; land, sea, and air elements will continue their same tasks. The real value of unification is behind the scenes, in the merging of administrative and support functions. There was no hint it would affect Canada's military commitments.

The Federal Budget, brought down on June 1 by Finance Minister Sharp, appeared designed to stabilize a delicately balanced economy. It followed a supplementary budget of December, 1966, which increased taxes $290,000,000 to pay for improved old age pensions. The budget cut taxes on drugs and production machinery, but made no major change in the tax system. Inflationary pressures, Sharp warned, were still at work, and productivity was

Canada's Century Of Unity

When General Robert E. Lee surrendered his forces at Appomattox Court House, Va., more than a century ago, the Union Army was free to retaliate against Great Britain for its active support of the South.

Would it sweep north and seize Brittain's Canadian provinces? So fearful were four provinces – New Brunswick, Nova Scotia, Ontario, and Quebec – they banded together in 1867 as the Dominion of Canada.

The invasion never came, and Canada's century of unity has been marked, instead, by quiet compromise with its southern neighbor.

Now a prospering federation of 10 provinces and two territories, Canada marked the centennial of its Confederation with a year-long celebration in 1967. The festive centennial was to be a "catalyst in the process of developing and maturing our national personality." It was to be an occasion for Canadians to take the time to find out what Canada was all about, to help them build deep feelings of unity and purpose. It was to tell the world about modern Canada and its history.

The centennial celebration took five years to plan. As a first step, the Parliament at Ottawa passed "an Act Respecting the Observance of the Centennial of Confederation." The act received royal assent from Queen Elizabeth II in 1961, and a Canadian Centennial Commission was created to oversee special events, with a well-known Canadian radio personality, John Fisher, as commissioner. In 1963, his 80-member staff began to develop a master plan for the Centennial year. The budget for the entire national program was set at $100,000,000.

Planning and organizing the celebration brought many groups, government and private, together. The National Conference on the centennial of Confederation became the main steering committee. Its 60 members, from throughout Canada, were selected by Secretary of State Maurice Lamontagne. Other participating groups included the National Centennial Committee, a government agency; a provincial centennial organization in each province; and the private Canadian Centenary Council.

There was no shortage of ideas. By 1965, some 600 projects had been proposed. Of these, the Centennial Commission chose 19, which it grouped under the headings of cultural, historical, and ceremonial projects.

Despite the government planning, however, there was fear that Canadians themselves might not participate with enthusiasm. The Province of Quebec, where many citizens want self-determination, refused to participate officially, contending that the terms of confederation should be reshaped to give French Canadians a greater voice in Canadian affairs. And, as Prime Minister Lester B. Pearson said, "Average Canadians have always been rather shy and at times more than a little uncertain about soul-searching."

At midnight, Dec. 31, 1966, the centennial planners called for the final ingredient – the people. They came. In Newfoundland's provincial capital at St. John's, they gathered around a huge "fire of friendship" to welcome Canada's 101st year. Across thousands of miles to the westernmost provincial capital at Whitehorse, Yukon, church bells rang in celebration after celebration as midnight crossed seven time zones.

Many of the festivities had an innocent merriment. In London, Ont., a centennial rocket, designed to ascend to 1,000 feet in the air and then release a Canadian flag, misfired and stuck in a tree. It was knocked down by young girls throwing snowballs.

There were well-balanced, colorful, and significant events across the country during the year. A highlight was the 15-car confederation train, which left Victoria, B.C., in January, 1967. It visited 83 historical sites in every Canadian province and territory except Newfoundland, which still has narrow-gauge tracks.

The $1,000,000 train contained a lively panorama of Canadian history. Main exhibits showed the untamed country that confronted early French and English explorers and settlers. Visitors passed from car to car, first experiencing the discomfort of traveling steerage to Canada, then pausing for reflection inside a replica of Quebec's Chamber of Confederation be-

Confederation Train, *above,* rolled from British Columbia on Jan. 1, 1967, to spread the meaning of Canada's centennial across the land. Crowds, *below,* queued up to see the exhibit-packed train.

fore passing through period rooms of the past 100 years.

Truck caravans, each made up of eight 73-foot tractor trailers, stopped at towns not visited by the train. The rigs were arranged into a quadrangle to give the impression of a miniature fair. In many towns, celebrations were timed to welcome the caravan.

The centennial also allowed many Canadians to see their country for themselves. Groups of young people went to all parts of Canada on exchange visits sponsored by the Centennial Commission under two youth travel programs.

Some journeys were unusual. Teams of voyageurs took part in a 110-day canoe pageant along the old fur trade waterways from the western plains to Montreal and Expo 67. A Vancouver teen-ager celebrated the centennial in his own unique way. He roller-skated 2,500 miles to Montreal.

For 3,500 less-ambitious athletes, the Fifth Pan American Games were held at Winnipeg in July, making Manitoba's provincial capital the center of the sports world during the centennial year.

The arts were heavily stressed. Festival Canada, budgeted at $3,300,000, sponsored newly commissioned ballets, operas, plays, and symphonies. Canadian authors received grants for centennial books. Painters and sculptors vied for centennial prizes.

A wide-screen film, *Helicopter Canada,* was prepared for showing in theaters across the country. Another film, *The Hundredth Summer,* depicted three Prince Edward Island villages celebrating the 100th anniversary of the visit of the Fathers of Confederation to Charlottetown in 1864, three years before the final agreement to form a united Canada.

Traditional works were not neglected. Performances were given everywhere. Sir Laurence Olivier toured the country. Italian grand opera was performed in Yellowknife, Northwest Territories, and an Eskimo choir sang in Newfoundland.

There were numerous grants by the Centennial Commission for centennial structures such as community centers, libraries, municipal buildings, museums, and swimming pools. Virtually no Canadian city, town, or village was without its special centennial project–a new park, a new town square, or its own festival. There was church participation, aid to the Canadian Folk Arts Council, and historical pageants.

There was a do-it-yourself approach to many observances. A housewife in Woodstock, Ont., wrote 40 letters to persons in isolated settlements in the Northwest Territories as her project. The Hustler Young Men's Bible Class of Grace United Church, Toronto, Ont., raised almost $1,000,000 selling Canadian flag kits, and donated the money to children in underdeveloped countries. In Ottawa, 4,000 people marched in a "Miles for Millions" marathon that raised $81,000 to send well-drilling equipment to India.

During the year of celebration, the Prime Minister seemed well pleased. In a major speech, he said, "A national and noble purpose has been evolving during our first 100 years of confederation which is uniquely Canadian: the deliberate and willing choice of social and cultural diversity over conformity." Then, he added, "It is for us to ensure that the national purposes we pursue are founded upon human principles that have universal and permanent value. Then we can be as certain as any people that our nation will endure because it deserves to endure." [Jon Anderson] lagging. On prices, he said that the Canadian record had deteriorated over the previous two years. Unless checked, he said, inflation would worsen Canada's competitive position in respect to the United States, leading to reduced employment and profit. Later, in October, Sharp urged both business and labor to unite with provincial governments to hold down costs and prices. If voluntary action failed, he warned, the federal government would act, choking off production and income.

On November 30, Sharp announced a 5 per cent surcharge on 1968 personal income taxes, plus higher taxes on liquor and tobacco. Despite his action, the estimated budget deficit was $785,000,000, Canada's second largest in peacetime.

The Domestic Economy sluggishly continued its unspectacular growth since the first quarter of 1966. The estimated gross national product for 1967 was $60,152,000,000. This was about 6.7 per cent above 1966, but inflation disguised the unsatisfactory growth. Unemployment was somewhat higher than in 1966, averaging 4.3 per cent for the year.

Personal spending remained high in 1967, and was a powerful factor in sustaining the economy. Business capital investment was only about 2 per cent above 1966, responding to rising interest rates and tightened capital. Exports held up well in 1967, especially shipments of automotive products under the Canada-U.S. auto trade pact. During the first eight months, exports rose $7,497,400,000, about 13 per cent above the period in 1966. Two traditional exports–newsprint and wheat–showed little gain.

The Provinces

Alberta's provincial election in May saw the Social Credit party win its ninth successive term since 1935. Social Credit retained 55 of the 58 seats it held at dissolution, but was faced by more vigorous opposition from six young Conservatives elected from urban ridings. The Liberals kept the three seats they previously held. One Independent was elected.

Premiers of Canadian Provinces

Province	Premier	Political Party
Alberta	Ernest C. Manning	Social Credit
British Columbia	William A. C. Bennett	Social Credit
Manitoba	Walter Weir	Conservative
New Brunswick	Louis J. Robichaud	Liberal
Newfoundland	Joseph R. Smallwood	Liberal
Nova Scotia	George I. Smith	Conservative
Ontario	John P. Robarts	Conservative
Prince Edward Is.	Alexander B. Campbell	Liberal
Quebec	Daniel Johnson	Union Nationale
Saskatchewan	Ross Thatcher	Liberal

Alberta appointed Canada's first ombudsman, an official who investigates grievances against the provincial government's actions. The ombuds-

Queen Elizabeth II presents the colors before the parliament buildings in Ottawa during her one-week centennial visit in midsummer, 1967.

**Canada's Prairies–
Where Vast Resources
Are Being Tapped**

✦ Copper
⊙ Uranium
+ Nickel
× Zinc
▼ Sulfur plant (recovery from natural gas)
■ Potash mine
□ Potash mine (under construction)
❖ Coal field
⊡ Pulp and paper mill

Electric power plant exceeding 100,000 kw capacity:
* Thermal
Hydro

0 Miles 200 400

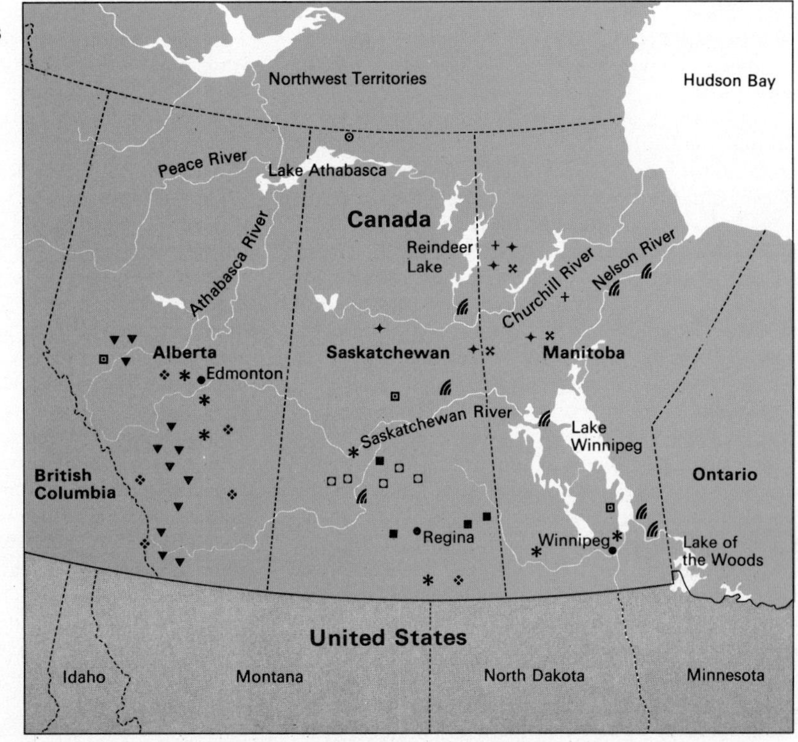

man is retired Royal Canadian Mounted Police Commissioner George B. McClellan.

British Columbia. The William A. C. Bennett Dam, on the Peace River, was completed in September. One mile long and 600 feet high, it is an important stage in the development of a power system in the northern part of the province.

Six explosions rocked a coal mine at Nanaimo, killing 15 miners and injuring nine on April 3. It was one of the province's worst mining disasters.

Manitoba adjourned its legislature in May, after a record-breaking session of 78 sitting days. It introduced a retail sales tax of 5 per cent, leaving only one province, Alberta, without a sales tax. The legislature also approved the principle of restoring French as a language of instruction in the schools. Bilingual schools had been banned in 1916. In March, 19 of 33 school divisions rejected a plan to place elementary education under the control of larger school boards. This was to have been a first step in modernizing rural education.

Premier Dufferin Roblin, runner-up in the race for Progressive Conservative party leadership retired from provincial politics. In late November, the party elected Highways Minister Walter Weir to succeed Roblin.

New Brunswick implemented a widely discussed municipal reform program, which gave the provincial government control of such major services as assessment, education, health, justice, and welfare. To help defray the cost, the provincial sales tax was doubled to 6 per cent. Expenditures for the year were forecast at $313,500,000, and revenues at just over $300,000,000.

In a bitterly fought election on October 23, the Liberal government of Louis J. Robichaud won a third term, retaining 32 seats in the 58-seat legislature. It was challenged by the Conservatives, under a colorful new leader, Charles Van Horne, who captured 26 seats. But Van Horne lost his own seat, as did three members of Robichaud's cabinet.

Newfoundland. One of North America's largest power projects was begun in July when Premier Joseph R. Smallwood set off the blasting of a new channel for the Churchill River in Labrador. The $800,000,000 Churchill Falls project, to be 10 years in construction, will generate 4,500,000 kilowatts (versus 2,190,000 kilowatts at Niagara Falls) for cities in Quebec and the eastern United States. The project's 7,000 workers signed an eight-year contract that bars strikes and provides periodic wage increases, plus guaranteed holidays and paid trips home every six months.

Nova Scotia. Premier Robert L. Stanfield won a fourth consecutive mandate from the voters on May 30. The Conservatives, in office since 1956, won 40 of the 46 seats in the legislature. The Liberals took the remainder, slightly increasing their share of the vote. Stanfield resigned in September, however, when he was elected leader of the national Conservative party. He was succeeded by George I. Smith, who was finance minister.

Coal mining and iron manufacturing on Cape Breton was badly hit during 1967. Following the news that the depressed mining industry would be phased out, the Dominion Steel and Coal Corporation, Ltd., announced in October that its steel mill at Sydney, employing 3,200 men, would be closed on April 30, 1968. The provincial government bought the mill, and announced it would operate at least one more year. One economic bright spot – a new $83,000,000 heavy-water plant that opened at Glace Bay, a coal mining town.

Ontario, one of five provinces to hold elections in 1967, gave another vote of confidence on October 17 to Premier John P. Robarts and his Progressive Conservative party. It was the eighth straight victory for the Conservatives, in office since 1943. Of 117 seats, the Conservatives took 69, the Liberals 28, and the New Democratic Party (N.D.P.) 20. The Conservatives lost ground in the popular vote, however, as the N.D.P. was up from 16 to 26 per cent. Two members of Robarts' cabinet were defeated.

In February, Provincial Treasurer Charles S. MacNaughton's first budget forecast revenues of $2,030,700,000 and a record deficit of $162,600,000.

Prince Edward Island. The Liberal government of 33-year-old Alexander B. Campbell submitted a record budget of $41,800,000 in expenditures and $42,100,000 in revenues for Canada's smallest province. The government announced the implementation of a new economic planning scheme to raise income and living standards in the island province.

Canada's newest university opened its doors in Charlottetown in September when the 133-year-old Prince of Wales College, for much of its life a junior college, was elevated to full university status.

Quebec. The debate over nationalism versus separatism continued unabated in 1967. Separatism gained a strong convert in René Lévesque, a member of Jean Lesage's former Liberal government. Lévesque later left the Liberal party in October when it refused to follow his lead; the party asserted that capital was fleeing Quebec out of fear of the separatist movement. Premier Daniel Johnson of the Union Nationale party also backed away from separatism, saying that it might build "a Great Wall of China" around Quebec.

After President De Gaulle's controversial visit to Quebec in July, France substantially increased its economic and technical aid to the province. For instance, scholarships to Quebec students for study in France were to be increased from 90 to 1,000. During a trip to France in May, Premier Johnson had arranged for more educational television programs, for training nuclear scientists, and for cooperation in economic planning.

Strikes plagued Quebec. Early in 1967, more than 10,000 elementary and secondary school teachers walked out for more than 20 days. They were forced back to work by an act of the legislature barring strikes by teachers for 18 months. Municipal workers in Montreal also went on strike in February in an effort to gain higher wages. In October, the bus drivers of Montreal also went on strike, but they, like the others, were forced to return to their jobs by legislative action.

Saskatchewan. In a provincial election on October 11, Premier Ross Thatcher's Liberal government emerged with 36 seats, increasing its margin over the Cooperative Commonwealth Federation to 13 seats. The victory was narrow in many ridings; seven seats were won by less than 50 votes. It was Thatcher's second electoral victory.

The largest body of water in Saskatchewan, the 150-mile-long lake filling behind the Gardiner Dam on the South Saskatchewan River, was named Lake Diefenbaker for the province's native son who became Conservative prime minister of Canada in 1957. [David M. L. Farr]

Facts in Brief. Population: 20,453,000. Government: Governor-General Roland Michener; Prime Minister Lester B. Pearson. Monetary Unit: dollar (1.08=U.S. $1). Foreign Trade: exports, $9,988,000,000; imports, $9,963,000,000. Principal Exports: paper and pulp, nonferrous metals, wheat.

CANADIAN LIBRARY ASSOCIATION (CLA) held its 22nd annual conference in Ottawa, Ont., in June, 1967, with "The Library and the Citizen" as its theme. The conference was marked by three important events: the official opening of the National Library of Canada, the CLA's observance of Canada's centennial, and the self-examination of the CLA by a conference within a conference.

When the CLA was formed in 1946, one of its primary purposes was the creation of a national library. In 1967, the library became a fact as members of the association attended the official opening of the new building in Ottawa.

CLA Events during the centennial year included a conference birthday party, the publication of various specialized indexes and catalogs, and the microfilming of all Canadian newspapers in existence from 1862 to 1873.

In cooperation with other library groups, the CLA organized two international conferences. The first, held in August in Toronto, Ont., was the 33rd Council of the International Federation of Library Associations. The second conference, in September, took the form of a Swedish-Canadian tour of parts of Ontario and Quebec.

New Library Facilities. In 1967, nearly 100 new library buildings and extensions were erected. The most distinguished of these was the Edmonton Public Library, which was opened on September 30.

The Red Deer, Alta., Public Library, opened in October, was a fine example of a library building designed to service a medium-sized city. The County Regional Library for Middlesex, Ont., was considered an outstanding building that would influence regional library architecture. New university library buildings included the Harriet Irving Library of the University of New Brunswick in Fredericton, and the University of Saskatchewan Library, Regina campus. The library that received the most attention and the most visitors was the Canadiana Library in the Canadian Pavilion at Expo 67. It held 5,000 books on Canada or by Canadians.

Young Canada's Book Week was celebrated from Nov. 15 to 22, 1967, under the patronage of Mrs. Dorothy Reid, a popular writer of Canadian Indian legends. In April, the CLA was one of several sponsors of Canadian Library Week, the theme of which was "Libraries and Man and His World."

Regional Library Service in the Northwest Territories was begun in 1967 and one of the three headquarters buildings was scheduled to open in December. The ordinance establishing this service had been passed in November, 1966. Canada thus had organized library service in all its provinces and its two territories. Two new library schools were established at the University of Western Ontario, London, Ont.; and at the University of Alberta, Edmonton, Alta. [Elizabeth Homer Morton]

CANADIAN LITERATURE. The centennial of Canadian Confederation encouraged Canadian authors, book illustrators, librarians, photographers, and publishers to produce an impressive variety of volumes and bibliographies. Credit for much of this was due to the Canadian Centennial Commission that made funds available for literary competitions. It also assisted research, freed authors to write, and aided in the publication of new works and the reprinting of Canadian classics. Categories covered were the following:

Biography. *The Clear Spirit; Twenty Canadian Women and Their Times* edited by Mary E. (Quayle) Innis; *Louis St. Laurent Canadian* by Dale C. Thomson; *Macdonald to Pearson, the Prime Ministers of Canada* by Bruce H. Hutchison; *Mitch Hepburn* by Neil McKenty; *My First Seventy-Five Years* by Arthur R. M. Lower; and *Mazo de la Roche of Jalna* by Ronald Hambleton, an interesting story of a strange and successful author.

Current Scene. *The Family That Stays Together—a Thing of the Past?* by Wilder Penfield analyzes every aspect of family life from religion to the bearded set. *The Challenge of Confidence;* written by Eric W. Kierans, is a novel discussion from the national point of view of an economist and sociologist. *The Modern Century* by Northrop Frye discusses the states of mind and quality of life that have created the modern world with lucid, sane, and original insight.

History and Literature. *The Oxford Companion to Canadian History and Literature* by Norah Story describes the range of Canadian literature and the background against which it has been written. *A Century of Canadian Literature,* compiled by H. Gordon Green and Guy Sylvestre, is an irreverent anthology by writers with a special ability to tell Canadians what manner of people they are. *A Century of Reporting* contains the writings of ace reporters.

House Decoration books include *A Guide to Pre-Confederation Furniture of English Canada* by Don R. Stewart; *A Heritage of Canadian Handicrafts* edited by Gordon Green; and *Nineteenth Century Pottery and Porcelain in Canada* by Elizabeth Collard.

Humor. *Marchbank's Almanack* by Robertson Davies brings back the curmudgeon of Marchbanks' Towers, that perpetual warrior against woolly thinking. *More Tales from Barrett's Landing* by Helen Dacey Wilson is a blend of honest humor and unsentimental wisdom.

Legends. *The Day Tuk Became a Hunter and Other Eskimo Stories* by Ronald Melzack captures the glamour of Eskimo life. *Willows Revisited* by Paul Hiebert is a successor to his popular *Sarah Binks.*

Local History was treated in such books as *Leeds and Grenville: Their First Two-Hundred Years* by Ruth McKenzie; and *Toronto* by Bruce West.

Pictorial Works were often accompanied by imaginative writing. Among the books were: *Toronto,* photographed by Boris Spremo, text by Dorothy Jane Goulding; *A Year of the Land* compiled by the National Film Board of Canada; *Canada in Cartoon; A Pictorial History of the Confederation Years* compiled by W. C. Werthman, with the text by W. S. MacNutt; *Nature's Heritage; Canada's National Parks* by David Baird; *The Polar Passion; the Quest for the North Pole* with selections from Arctic journals by Farley Mowat; and *Stones of History; Canada's Houses of Parliament* issued by the Queen's Printer.

Poetry included such works as *Modern Canadian Verse in English and French,* edited by A. J. M. Smith; *North of Summer* by Alfred Purdy, with paintings by A. Y. Jackson, revealing new aspects of the Arctic; and *Periods of the Moon* by Irving Layton.

The Governor-General's Literary Awards for 1967 went to Mrs. Margaret Laurence for *Jest of God* (English fiction); Margaret Atwood for *The Circle Game* (English poetry); and George Woodcock for *The Crystal Spirit: A Study of George Orwell* (English nonfiction); to Claire Martin for *La Joue Droite,* the second volume for her autobiographical work, *Dans un Gant de Fer* (French fiction); to Rejean Ducharme for his *L'Avalée des Avalés* (French poetry and theater); to Marcel Trudel for *Le Comptoir,* the second volume of *Histoire de la Nouvelle France* (French nonfiction).

The Stephen Leacock Memorial Award for Humor went to Richard Needham for his book *Needham's Inferno.* [Elizabeth Homer Morton]

CARMICHAEL, STOKELY (1941-), a leading advocate of black power, resigned May 12, 1967, as chairman of the Student Nonviolent Coordinating Committee (SNCC), after serving for a year. He then traveled throughout Europe, Africa, and Asia, making strong statements about racial prejudice in the United States. At Hanoi, capital of North Vietnam, he was quoted as saying, on August 31, that he was a revolutionary. Earlier, in Havana, Cuba, he predicted that Negroes in American cities would wage "a guerrilla fight to the death." In December, he returned to the United States.

Carmichael was born at Port-of-Spain, Trinidad, on June 21, 1941. He came to New York City with his parents in 1952. Carmichael was an outstanding student at the Bronx High School of Science, and was graduated from Howard University in 1964.

His involvement in civil rights demonstrations began when he was in high school. He was an early leader in the freedom marches, and was often jailed. As senior field secretary for SNCC in Alabama in 1965, he helped hundreds of Negroes register to vote for the first time in their lives.

Carmichael is coauthor, with Charles V. Hamilton, of *Black Power, the Politics of Liberation* (1967). H. Rap Brown, 23, of Baton Rouge, La., succeeded Carmichael as chairman of SNCC. [WALTER F. MORSE]

CARNEGIE MEDAL. See LITERATURE FOR CHILDREN.

CELEBRATIONS and anniversaries observed in 1967 included the following:

Year-Long Celebrations

Alaska Purchase Centennial commemorated the purchase of Alaska from Russia. U.S. Secretary of State William H. Seward signed the Treaty of Cession on March 30, 1867. Formal transfer of the territory took place the following October 18, when the United States flag was raised at Sitka. Major observances in 1967 included the Alaska 67 Centennial Exposition at Fairbanks, May 27 to September 10.

Arturo Toscanini Centennial commemorated the birth, March 25, 1867, of the famous operatic and symphonic conductor. His birthplace, a small house in Parma, Italy, was dedicated as a national shrine. Toscanini died in New York City on Jan. 16, 1957.

Canadian Confederation Centennial. Commemoration of the founding of the Dominion of Canada in 1867 began at midnight, Dec. 31, 1966. Prime Minister Lester B. Pearson lighted a symbolic centennial flame on Parliament Hill in the national capital at Ottawa. See ARCHITECTURE; CANADA (CLOSE-UP); FAIRS AND EXHIBITIONS; MUSIC.

Caracas Fourth Centennial commemorated the founding of Venezuela's capital city on July 25, 1567, by Spanish conquistador Diego de Losado. Caracas has been the national capital since 1829.

Chisholm Trail Centennial celebrations included the dedication of many historical markers along the trail over which cattle were driven from Texas to railroad centers in Kansas. The main part of the trail followed the one used by the half-breed Cherokee Indian trader Jesse Chisholm through Indian Territory (now Oklahoma) into Kansas. Illinois livestock buyer Joseph G. McCoy opened a cattle-shipping center at Abilene, Kans., and on Sept. 5, 1867, the first load of Texas longhorns was sent to Chicago.

Claudio Monteverdi Quadricentennial commemorated the birth of the first great composer of opera. He was born on May 14, 1567, at Cremona, Italy, and died in 1643. Monteverdi's opera, *Orfeo*, was first performed in 1607.

Copenhagen Octocentenary. Denmark's capital and largest city (official name Kobenhavn) probably began as a fishing village some 6,000 years ago. The 1967 celebration commemorated the building of a castle there in 1167 by Bishop Absalon of Roskilde. Because of its fine natural harbor, the village was called Kobmandehavn (Merchant's Harbor). It was chartered as a city in 1254, and became the capital of Denmark in 1416.

The Illustrated London News 125th Anniversary. Herbert Ingram, printer, bookseller, and news agent, founded the world's first illustrated weekly newspaper in 1842. The first issue, May 14, featured the Bal Masque at Buckingham Palace. Queen Victoria, then 23 years old, was in the fifth year of her reign.

Johann Strauss Waltz Year was celebrated in Austria, commemorating the centennial of "The Blue Danube" waltz. Waltz King Strauss wrote and introduced his most famous composition in 1867.

Kentucky 175th Anniversary commemorated its admission to the Union as the 15th state on June 1, 1792.

Mississippi Sesquicentennial commemorated the admission of Mississippi Territory to the Union as the 20th state on Dec. 10, 1817.

Nautical Almanac Bicentenary. The first issue of this publication, used by seamen of many countries, was for the year 1767. Astronomer Royal Nevil Maskelyne, director of England's Royal Greenwich Observatory, founded the almanac.

Nebraska Centennial commemorated the admission of Nebraska Territory to the Union as the 37th state on March 1, 1867.

New York Philharmonic 125th Anniversary Year began in the summer with the first Lincoln Center Festival, and is to continue throughout the 1967-1968 season. The Philharmonic, formerly known as the New York Philharmonic Symphony Orchestra, dates to the founding of the Philharmonic Society of New York (city), which gave its first concert on Dec. 7, 1842.

Protestant Reformation 450th Anniversary commemorated Oct. 31, 1517, when Martin Luther, a priest, nailed his Ninety-Five Theses to the door of All Saints' Church in Wittenberg, now in East Germany. His protest against certain practices of the Roman Catholic Church was the first of many events that culminated in the reformation.

Rugby School Quadricentenary. The school where many Englishmen received their secondary education before attaining fame and distinction was founded at Rugby, England, in 1567, through a bequest of Laurence Sheriffe. Rugby and its most distinguished headmaster Thomas Arnold were memorialized in *Tom Brown's School Days* (1857) by Thomas Hughes. Rugby football was first played at Rugby in 1823.

Virgin Islands Half-Century Celebration commemorated their 50 years as a U.S. possession. St. Croix, St. John, St. Thomas, and many nearby islands were purchased from Denmark. Formal transfer was on March 31, 1917. The 1967 celebration included an exhibit entitled "The Danish West Indies Through 250 Years."

Shorter Celebrations

April 17-10—Bataan and Corregidor 25th Anniversary was observed in the Philippines by Filipino and American veterans of World War II. Bataan defenders fought the Japanese invaders from Jan. 2 to April 9, 1942. Corregidor surrendered on May 6, 1942. Philippines

A replica of the *Spirit of St. Louis* was flown to France to help mark the 40th anniversary of Charles Lindbergh's historic flight across the Atlantic in 1927.

President Ferdinand E. Marcos, a survivor of the "Bataan Death March," was among the veterans attending the commemoration.

April 28-29—Rush-Bagot Agreement Sesquicentennial commemorated the signing on April 28-29, 1817, of what probably is the oldest arms limitation treaty in existence. It provided for disarmament of Canadian and U.S. navies on the Great Lakes. Treaty signers were U.S. Acting Secretary of State Richard Rush and Sir Charles Bagot, the British minister to the United States.

May 13—Our Lady of Fatima 50th Anniversary. Pope Paul VI visited this famous Roman Catholic shrine near Fatima, Portugal, to commemorate the day in 1917 when three peasant children reported having seen a vision of a lady in a cove while they were tending their sheep. Lúcia dos Santos, then 10 years old, her cousins, Francisco, who died in 1919, and his sister Jacinta Marto, who died in 1920, said she told them to return there on the 13th day of each month until October. On October 13, the lady identified herself as Our Lady of the Rosary. She told the children to say the rosary every day, and asked that a shrine be built in her honor. The Roman Catholic Church built the shrine, and in 1932 authorized devotion to Our Lady of Fatima as Our Lady of the Rosary. Lúcia dos Santos, now a Carmelite nun, appeared with Pope Paul VI at the 1967 observance.

May 17—New York Stock Exchange 175th Anniversary commemorated the signing of the Buttonwood Agreement on May 17, 1792. On that day, 24 businessmen agreed to meet daily under a buttonwood tree in Wall Street to buy and sell securities, and founded what is today the world's largest securities market place.

June 19—Tahiti Discovery Bicentennial commemorated the day in 1767 when the first white men stepped ashore on this tropical paradise in the South Pacific. Captain Samuel Wallis claimed the island for Great Britain. French control was established in 1842.

July 1-4—Erie Canal Sesquicentennial. Construction of the first important man-made waterway in the United States was started on July 4, 1817, and completed in 1825. Extending from Buffalo, on Lake Erie, to Albany and Troy on the Hudson River, the Erie Canal is now part of the New York State Barge Canal System.

July 1-September 14—Cheyenne Centennial. This historic town of the Old West was founded in 1867 as a Union Pacific Railroad division point. Cheyenne has been the capital of Wyoming since 1869.

July 11—John Quincy Adams Bicentennial commemorated the birth on July 11, 1767, of the 6th President of the United States (1825-1829) in Braintree (now Quincy), Mass. Adams died on Feb. 23, 1848, in Washington, D.C., having served as a U.S. Representative from Massachusetts since 1830.

July 12—Henry David Thoreau Sesquicentennial. The poetic naturalist, essayist, and philosopher was born in Concord, Mass., on July 12, 1817. *Walden* (1854), an American literary classic, is an account of his experiment in living. Thoreau died in 1862.

October 12—Discovery of America 475th Anniversary commemorated the arrival of Christopher Columbus in the New World on Oct. 12, 1492. He landed on what is now Watling Island in the Bahamas, and named it San Salvador. Columbus Day has been celebrated annually in the United States since 1920.

November 30—Jonathan Swift Tercentennary commemorated the birth of the greatest English satirist. The author of *Gulliver's Travels* (1726) was born in Dublin, Ireland, on Nov. 30, 1667. He died in 1745.

See also MEMORIALS.

CENSUS. At 11:03 A.M. Monday, Nov. 20, 1967, the population census clock in the lobby of the Department of Commerce Building in Washington, D.C., ticked off 200,000,000. Only Communist China, India, and the Soviet Union have larger populations. This represented an increase of 5 per cent over the 1960 figure.

At year's end, the Bureau of the Census estimated the population in the 50 states, the District of Columbia, and the armed forces abroad at 200,271,231 compared to the 1966 estimate of 198,000,000. The increase of 1.1 per cent approximated that of 1966. Both figures reflected the decreasing rate of population growth that has taken place since 1960, when the rate of increase was 1.6 per cent.

According to estimates in mid-1967, the states showing the greatest increase since the 1960 census were: Nevada, up 55.8 per cent; Arizona, 25.5 per cent; and California, 21.9 per cent. States showing population decreases were: Wyoming, down 4.6 per cent; West Virginia, 3.4 per cent; South Dakota, 1 per cent; and Iowa, .2 per cent.

Nonwhite Population. Nonwhite and Negro population figures, released in 1967, showed that:

- In mid-1967, Negroes numbered 21,983,000 persons or 11 per cent of the U.S. population, compared with 10 per cent in 1950 and 10.5 per cent in 1960.
- About 55 per cent of the nonwhite population, 92 per cent of it Negro, was living in central cities of the nation's 212 largest metropolitan areas.
- The number of nonwhite persons below the poverty income level declined from 10,700,000 in 1959 to 9,600,000 in 1966, a decrease of 13.2 per cent.

Special Censuses. During the first eight months of 1967, the bureau conducted 187 special federal censuses at the request of local authorities. These projects ranged from Memphis, Tenn., a city with a population of 536,585, to Guy, Ark., with only 190 persons. In addition, two special censuses were taken in New Haven, Conn., and in a section of North Philadelphia, Pa., to test methods for conducting the 19th Decennial Census of Population and Housing in 1970.

The County and City Data Book 1967 was published for the first time in five years. Another publication, *The Pocket Data Book USA 1967*, contained national and international statistics and charts compiled by the bureau, other government agencies, and private sources. Paperback editions will be made available every two years.

The 1967 census of business will be published early in 1968. For the first time, it will include architects, construction companies, lawyers, and travel agencies–all service businesses. Other censuses scheduled for 1968 include commercial fisheries, manufacturers, mineral industries, and transportation. [JOHN C. BAKER]

CENTRAL AFRICAN REPUBLIC. See AFRICA.

CENTRAL AMERICA. See LATIN AMERICA.

CEYLON was beset by labor and political problems and the declining production of tea, which accounts for about 65 per cent of the nation's foreign exchange, in 1967.

Tea production was down about $60,000,000 from the 1966 figure. So serious was the import-export imbalance the government was forced to halve domestic rice rations in order to reduce expenditures for food imports. The stringent measure, however, touched off further disruptions in the economy. The Bank Employees Union of Ceylon went on strike for about two months, tying up operations in 11 major banks. Tea and rubber workers forced wage concessions despite government efforts to hold the line on wages.

In September, Ceylon took steps to implement an Indo-Ceylonese citizenship agreement passed in 1964. Under it, the status of persons of Indian origin living in Ceylon was to be clarified; those accepted for Indian citizenship could be repatriated. Late in the year, Ceylon also cracked down on Chinese Communists after police reports indicated the presence of a vast spy ring. [JOHN N. STALKER]

Facts in Brief. Population: 11,976,000. Government: Governor-General William Gopallawa; Prime Minister Dudley Senanayake. Monetary Unit: repuee (5.95= U.S. $1). Foreign Trade: exports, $357,000,000; imports, $426,000,000. Principal Exports: tea, rubber, coconut oil.

CHAD. See AFRICA.

CHEMICAL INDUSTRY growth in 1967 was less than half that averaged during the previous five years, a scant 5 per cent compared to 11 per cent annually from 1962 through 1966. Shipments of chemical products moved up to a value of about $40,500,000,000 from $38,700,000,000 in 1966.

Inorganic chemicals fared much better than the organics–largely due to a big demand for fertilizers containing ammonia, phosphates, and nitrates.

The plastics sector of the chemical industry was particularly hard-hit. Historically, its production has risen at a rate of 15 per cent a year. In 1967, however, plastics managed to show a gain of only 6.5 per cent. Production ran to around 14,000,000,000 pounds, against 13,500,000,000 pounds in 1967. Synthetic fibers made little headway, while synthetic rubber output slid.

Industry capacity grew at about the 1966 pace, with just under $3,000,000,000 spent on new plants and the upgrading of older facilities. Formaldehyde supplies, tight in 1966, loosened in 1967 with the start-up of new units. The shortage of ethylene disappeared as capacity soared to 14,500,000,000 pounds. A heavy build-up was underway in ethylene oxide, which would push capacity to 5,000,000,000 pounds by 1970.

Prices. A wide range of chemicals rose in price in 1967. The price of sulfur, which was expected to remain scarce for five more years, was increased twice, as were chlorine and naphthalene prices. Also up during the year were such workhorse chemicals as caustic potash, caustic soda, phthalic anhydride, sulfuric acid, toluene, and xylene.

One notable exception to the higher price trend was methanol, used to make formaldehyde and a wide range of industrial products. The Du Pont Company cut its methanol price 2 cents in the East, to 25 cents a gallon in bulk quantities, on Nov. 1, 1967. Other producers made similar cuts.

Production of Leading Chemicals

Inorganics (1,000 tons)	**1965**	**1966**	**1967***
Ammonia	8,711	10,611	12,045
Chlorine	6,479	6,946	7,505
Hydrochloric acid	1,368	1,505	1,585
Nitric acid	4,890	5,337	6,130
Phosphoric acid	3,905	4,525	4,820
Sodium carbonate	4,928	5,073	4,835
Sodium hydroxide	6,796	7,342	7,740
Sulfuric acid	24,790	27,169	28,500
Organics (million pounds)			
Acetic anhydride	1,534	1,601	1,535
Acetone	1,114	1,291	1,220
Ethylene oxide	2,190	2,304	2,240
Formaldehyde	3,086	3,627	3,625
Methanol	2,869	3,219	3,440
Orthoxylene	351	333	380
Phenol	1,174	1,289	1,180
Phthalic anhydride	608	675	685
Styrene	2,875	3,192	3,210
Vinyl chloride	2,000	2,498	2,320
Plastics (million pounds)			
Phenolics	922	983	950
Polyethylene	3,048	3,559	3,755
Polypropylene	374	551	640
Polystyrene	1,369	1,614	1,575
Polyvinyl chloride	1,820	2,178	2,010

*Estimated. Other years, latest revised figures.

Sources: U.S. Department of Commerce (Inorganics); U.S. Tariff Commission (Organics and Plastics).

The government kept close watch on the industry for possible antitrust violations. A broad-scale investigation of chemical patents was launched and joint ventures in urethane foams and vinyl chloride were dissolved. However, the Supreme Court of the United States, in a 4-to-4 decision, permitted a joint venture in sodium chlorate to stand. Nevertheless, it ruled that a 1957 acquisition of a maker of household liquid bleaches was unlawful. Industry pricing practices were changed following the December, 1966, settlement of a price-fixing suit against major producers of chlor-alkali.

Petrochemical Feedstocks. With profits off and foreign competition more intense, chemical manufacturers called upon the government to help them cut their petroleum feedstock costs. They said they needed a relaxation of oil import controls to allow them a larger share of the lower-priced foreign crude oil or naphtha. Otherwise, they said, they could not keep competitive with overseas chemical companies. Domestic petroleum refiners strongly opposed the idea, arguing that the controls had been established for reasons of national security, not for cheaper chemical raw materials.

The chemical makers sought this cheaper foreign oil in three ways. First, they pushed for larger quotas for inland plants. Second, some firms asked for permission to set up foreign trade zones, or special-privilege areas. By far the most popular idea was the offer to establish huge petrochemical complexes in Puerto Rico and the Virgin Islands on the condition that these installations receive special oil quotas. At least a half dozen such proposals were made. All three schemes were argued back and forth at a series of government hearings.

Kennedy Round. The chemical industry was, perhaps, most aroused by the Kennedy Round tariff agreement (see INTERNATIONAL TRADE AND FINANCE). Under the two-step pact, the United States agreed to cut its chemical tariffs about 50 per cent in exchange for a 20 per cent reduction in European chemical duties.

A so-called "separate package" called for a further lowering of chemical tariffs by the Europeans in return for the elimination of the American Selling Price (ASP), a method of customs valuation that has protected U.S. dyestuffs firms since the 1920s. The dye makers protested against the 50-20 agreement, contending they would be forced out of business if the ASP were abandoned. [ARTHUR R. KAVALER]

See also MANUFACTURING; PETROLEUM AND GAS.

CHEMISTRY. Albert D. Allen and Caesar V. Senoff at the University of Toronto and James Collman at Stanford University combined, for the first time in the laboratory, molecular nitrogen directly with transition metal ions. The process is of prime importance in understanding the mechanism of nitrogen fixation, the process by which living organisms use nitrogen to produce protein. In the nitrogen fixation cycle, molecular nitrogen is transformed into ammonia and amino acids, which are more useful forms of nitrogen for utilization by living systems.

In these experiments, molecular nitrogen was combined with metal ions through the use of a hydrazine and an azide intermediate. No one previously had been able to achieve the direct interaction. The new process interacts reduced organometallic compounds with molecular nitrogen dissolved in nonaqueous solvents.

Technical Advances. The idea that a chemical reaction occurs "instantaneously" is no longer valid since new measuring techniques have made it possible to check the step-by-step pathway molecules follow in a reaction. Chemical reactions, even when they are extremely rapid, can now be measured by stopped-flow apparatus and temperature-jump apparatus. This has resulted in a more complete understanding of the patterns of behavior of molecules.

Stopped-flow apparatus can measure reaction times as low as two milliseconds. A millisecond is equal to one-thousandth of a second. The apparatus makes use of two special syringes that can squeeze chemical substances through a mixing chamber at a controlled rate. Temperature-jump apparatus now measures reactions that take place in only a microsecond, or one-millionth of a second. The basic element of this type of apparatus is a capacitor to which high voltages of electricity are applied. A sensor measures and analyzes the light that is produced as the voltage is then discharged through the chemical substance. These newer techniques for measuring chemical reactions allow the whole time span of chemical reactivity to be followed.

X-Ray Diffraction, the most definitive method of determining structure of complicated molecules, has been automated by the addition of a digital computer. The process involves passing X rays through a single crystal of the material under study. The relative positions of all the atoms in a molecule with respect to each other can be determined from the diffraction pattern the X rays make on a photographic plate. The process is simple, but the mathematical calculations necessary to interpret the diffraction patterns are highly complex and time-consuming. This technique has, however, unraveled the structure of some of the most complex molecules, such as those of the nucleic acids, such as DNA and RNA.

Each diffraction pattern appears on the photographic plate as a series of dots, or points. Both the intensity and the geometric distribution of these points are important in determining the structure of the molecular crystal. Equipment that automatically collects intensity data for a single crystal diffraction experiment now carries out structural determinations in a much more routine fashion than was previously possible. This, coupled with the digital computer, results in a relatively easy method for obtaining a final set of coordinates for a molecular crystal. The determination of the structure of molecules by X-ray diffraction will soon be completely automated. Thus, the chemist may devote more of his time to the study of the chemistry of molecules rather than their structure.

Recent developments have also advanced the techniques for determining various chemical and physical properties of matter. Such techniques as visible and infrared spectroscopy, various magnetic spectroscopies, mass spectroscopy, and a host of other tools permit modern chemists to probe ever deeper into the nature of chemical phenomena.

Nobel Prize. The Nobel prize for chemistry was shared by George Porter and Ronald G. W. Norrish of Britain and Manfred Eigen of Germany "for their studies of extremely fast chemical reactions." Norrish and Porter developed the technique of flash photolysis for analyzing chemical reactions, and Eigen devised the temperature jump method for analyzing highspeed reactions. [EVERLY B. FLEISCHER]

CHESS. Bobby Fischer of Brooklyn, N.Y., eight times U.S. chess champion, won two of the major international tournaments played in 1967. In April, he captured the 10-man Grand Prix at Monte Carlo, scoring seven points compared to six and one-half posted by runner-up Vassily Smyslov of the Soviet Union. In August, Fischer triumphed in the Tournament of Solidarity at Skopje, Yugoslavia. Fischer's record of 12 victories, three draws, and two losses left him one-half point ahead of Evfim Geller of the Soviet Union and the Yugoslav champion, Milan Matulovic, who tied for second.

In November, at Sousse, Tunisia, Fischer, who was leading in the Interzonal qualifying tournament, was dropped from the event after a dispute with officials. Bent Larsen of Denmark won.

Pal Benko of New York City, the defending co-champion, won the U.S. Open championship at Atlanta, Ga., in August, with a record of 11 victories and one loss. The second- and third-place winners were Anthony Saidy and Robert Byrne.

At New York City in May, Mrs. Gisela Kahn Gresser of New York City, with an 8 to 2 record, won her eighth U.S. women's championship. Mrs. Mona May Karff, also of New York, was second.

Winners of the U.S. men's and women's amateur championships, held in Philadelphia, Pa., in June, were Ronald Lohrman of Penfield, N.Y., and Mrs. Rachel Guinan of Philadelphia. [THEODORE M. O'LEARY]

CHICAGO had more than its share of misfortune in 1967, experiencing a disastrous fire, a paralyzing blizzard, and devastating tornadoes.

McCormick Place, the nation's largest convention center, burned to the ground in January. The spectacular $30,000,000 blaze along Lake Michigan occurred scant hours before the year's biggest trade show was scheduled to open. Various plans for a new center were quickly drawn; the latest design, tentatively approved in November, provided over 600,000 square feet of exhibition space.

On January 26, Chicago was paralyzed by a blizzard that dumped a record 23 inches of snow in 24 hours. Four more days of snow brought the total to 33 inches. Traffic came to a standstill, stores ran out of milk and bread, and sporadic looting broke out throughout the city. A vast digging-out enlisted thousands of men and machines, with some equipment borrowed from neighboring Indiana and Wisconsin communities. Mayor Richard J. Daley estimated snow-removal costs at $7,000,000.

Politics. Mayor Daley erased doubts of his political strength with a lopsided 500,000-vote majority as he gained an unprecedented fourth four-year term. The mayor swept every ward in the city in crushing Republican candidate John L. Waner. Elections in 1966 had indicated the mayor's support was slipping, but with 74 per cent of the 1967 vote, he restored his position among the nation's political

The controversial *Chicago Picasso*, a 50-foot-high, 163-ton steel sculpture, was unveiled in August. The design was a gift to the city from Picasso.

elite. Of 50 aldermen that were elected in April, 10 were Negroes, a net gain of one.

Orlando W. Wilson, 67, nationally famous police reformer and former university professor, announced his retirement as superintendent of police, a post he had held for seven years, in May. Wilson was widely recognized for reorganizing Chicago's once scandal-ridden police department.

Renewal. Mayor Daley announced on September 28 that federal aid, under revised financial techniques, would help rehabilitate 1,000 slum dwelling units without increasing rents or displacing families. It was to be the largest such effort in the nation, and was seen by officials as a promising prototype for further extensive renovation in slum areas.

Culture made news with the opening of the new Museum of Contemporary Art in October, and with the grand reopening, also in October, of the Auditorium Theatre. Chicagoans had raised $2,000,000 to restore the long-neglected architectural gem, designed in the 1880s by Louis Sullivan and Dankmar Adler. During the year, Chicago dedicated two works of sculpture by world-famous artists: an abstract five-story steel sculpture designed by Pablo Picasso, and a sculpture by British artist Henry Moore titled *Nuclear Energy*, commissioned for the 25th anniversary, in December, of the world's first self-sustaining nuclear chain reaction at the University of Chicago (see ENERGY). [DONALD W. LIEF]

CHILD GUIDANCE. An estimated 9,000,000 disadvantaged children profited during the 1966-1967 school year from enriched educational experiences and guidance provided through the Elementary and Secondary School Improvement Act of 1965. As of July, 286 community mental health centers were under construction or in operation with federal assistance, and approximately 140 mental retardation clinics were supported by federal funds.

A conspicuous trend was the emphasis on prevention of emotional problems rather than on their treatment. Psychiatrists and other child guidance professionals were increasingly active as consultants to anti-poverty programs, community projects, and schools in an effort to lessen the numbers of emotionally disturbed children and adults.

School guidance programs, traditionally centered in secondary schools, were also giving increasing attention to the younger child.

A possible breakthrough in the task of combating familial mental retardation was reported in 1967 by Dr. Robert Kugel. His studies showed that by bringing a wide range of services to underprivileged families in which retardation had appeared over several generations, it was possible to alter the unfavorable course of the children's development. This, he found, was especially true when he worked with the entire family as a unit, giving service and attention to all its members. [FRANCES A. MULLEN]

CHILD WELFARE. Proposals for improved federal support of services to children provoked a storm of protest in 1967. President Lyndon B. Johnson opened the battle with a message to Congress recommending support for child and parent centers in poverty-stricken areas, and increased Social Security payments for dependent children. See CONGRESS OF THE UNITED STATES; SOCIAL SECURITY.

Doubts about welfare programs and their costs sparked opposition to proposals designed to cut relief roles. Economy measures passed in several states and by the U.S. House of Representatives were denounced by many as, in effect, punishing infants for the "sins" of their mothers.

Attention was directed during the year to the need to expand the nation's facilities for day care of children outside their homes. Although virtually all states and territories included day-care services in their officially drawn child welfare services plans, actual expansion of services remained slow. This perhaps reflected the conflicting views toward the working mother. Two federal agencies called a major conference in June to speed solutions.

Concern over child abuse, first disclosed in 1961 as a major health problem, continued to grow rapidly. By the end of 1967, all 50 states had enacted statutes requiring physicians to report cases of suspected abuse. Studies showed that child abuse was widespread, and that battered children were no more evident in one ethnic, social, or economic group than in another. A U.S. Department of Health, Education, and Welfare official estimated that the 10,000 cases reported in 1967 actually represented 1,000,000 battered children.

Large numbers of families seeking to adopt children were unable to find a "suitable" child, while far larger numbers of children from minority groups or with handicaps were found to be in need of adoption. The Indian Adoption Program achieved adoptions of 67 Indian children in 1966 but reported 400 were still waiting. A Minnesota agency reported 20 Negro children were successfully placed with white families. Public interest mounted over cases in which foster parents were denied permission to adopt a child because of agency rules. In New York City and Los Angeles, Calif., experimental programs to allow single women to adopt children were being studied.

New York City had previously abandoned many of its requirements for adoption. Under revised and more liberal requirements, parents no longer had to be under 35 years old, nor have specified levels of income. In addition, families with working mothers were made eligible to adopt. Adoption agencies began to restudy their traditional policies of matching religions and races, and of recommending only "normal" children. [FRANCES A. MULLEN]

CHILDREN'S BOOKS. See LITERATURE FOR CHILDREN.

CHILE. On July 16, 1967, President Eduardo Frei Montalva signed one of the most ambitious agrarian reform laws in the history of Latin America. Under it, some 100,000 landless Chilean farmworkers were to become owners of small plots within five years. To accomplish this, nearly 15,000,000 acres of private property were to be expropriated–with compensation. The law would help raise living standards as well as increase agricultural productivity.

Early in the year, Chile signed agreements with three U.S. companies, Anaconda, Cerro, and Kennecott, which became partners with the government to spur copper output. Chile joined Congo (Kinshasa), Peru, and Zambia to set up a permanent joint council to coordinate and propose measures to obtain "legitimate, increased revenues derived from copper export."

During the year, the Cia Acero del Pacifico began a $130,000,000 program to expand its annual steel output to about 1,000,000 ingot tons versus the current production of 650,000 tons per year. Plans were also announced for the building of a $50,000,000 petrochemical complex near Punta Arenas. [MARY C. WEBSTER]

Facts in Brief. Population: 9,243,000. Government: President Eduardo Frei Montalva. Monetary Unit: escudo (4.85=U.S. $1). Foreign Trade: exports, $878,000,000; imports, $683,000,000. Principal Exports: copper, iron ore, sodium nitrate.

CHINA

The *People's Daily*, the Chinese Communist party newspaper, observed New Year's Day, 1967, with ebullient prophecy. The year ahead, it said, "will be a year in which the proletariat . . . will launch a general attack . . . on monsters and demons anywhere in society. . . . It will be a year of decisive victory . . ."

Like most predictions, it was only half right. If the sound of battle did echo throughout 1967, victory remained elusive. Most of the "monsters and demons," including Chairman of the Republic Liu Shao-chi, had been forced out of power in 1966, and Peking was in Mao Tse-tung's hands. But now the battlefield had moved to the provinces, and the struggle had become complex and indecisive. This, the second year of the Cultural Revolution, turned out to be a year of bloodshed and recurring crises.

Shanghai Incident. The first crisis came in the opening week of 1967, in Shanghai. Local party bosses had been fighting for survival against groups of Maoist extremists since September, 1966. Party offices were besieged and wrecked by bands of Red Guard "rebels." In factories, the "royalist" workers' militia fought battles with Maoist Red Guards, come to "make revolution."

For the first time since the establishment of Communism in China, factory and dock workers began to demand better pay, housing, and fringe benefits, and backed their demands with strikes. Local party officials gave in, partly because they had little choice, but also because concession looked like a good way to win friends. Peasants in the Shanghai area dipped into commune reserves to pay themselves an unauthorized year-end bonus. Some peasants even pitched camp in Shanghai's main streets in an unprecedented sit-down strike.

In the face of this anarchy, Mao and his associates had to act. Their supporters in Shanghai–11 "revolutionary mass organizations," some of them nothing more than a few youngsters–issued a proclamation on January 4. It urged the people to "smash thoroughly the new counterattack launched by the bourgeois reactionary line." Five days later, the appeal was repeated in the *People's Daily*, and was given Mao's official blessings. Almost overnight, the Maoists took power from the local party machine, and the Red Guards began to display the deposed leaders with dunce caps on their heads and abusive posters on their chests. The coup represented a major victory for Mao. All the concessions previously made

Red Guards displayed "antirevolutionaries" from the back of a truck in January. They forced victims to wear dunce caps that described their "crimes."

中国共产党万岁

to the workers were denounced as examples of the sin of "Economism," and the workers and peasants were ordered to return all the money paid to them, in installments if necessary.

Triple Alliance. Shanghai was only one of many places touched by anarchy. In mid-January, Mao turned for help to the army, largely reluctant to become involved in the civil conflict. With the army's aid, the Maoists "seized power" in four strategically placed provinces–Shantung in the east, Shansi in the west, Heilungkiang in the far north, and Kweichow in the deep south. In each province, a new "revolutionary rebel committee" was established. It represented what became known as the "triple alliance" of the army, the old party leaders who had vowed loyalty to Mao, and the Red Guards.

Leadership Debate. Mao's own circle of intimates disagreed on what to do in the midst of the growing anarchy. Premier Chou En-lai pleaded for an end to violence so that factories could resume normal production, crops be gathered, and the people fed. Ranged against him were the members of the Cultural Revolution Group, which has been trying, in Mao's name, to win control of the nation. The group included Mrs. Mao, better known as Chiang Ching. It argued that violence should continue until all opposition was crushed. It also wanted the army's help, but it objected to the zest with which the military was cracking the heads of the Red Guards, who, after all, were considered to be Mao's truest legions.

The debate in the inner circle led to strange happenings in Peking. All of Mao's intimates echoed Premier Chou's call for an end to the turmoil. At the same time, Red Guard bands controlled by the Cultural Revolution Group staged huge demonstrations against Premier Chou's vice-premiers. No ministry was immune; the ministry of agriculture was raided, and the minister of railways was dragged away before Chou En-lai's eyes. The foreign ministry was besieged for days, and finally ransacked.

In March and April, middle school and university students were ordered to return to their classrooms from wherever they were making revolution. Only some of them obeyed, and the incredible holiday from education, which began in May, 1966, continued for another six months.

It was difficult to tell who was really in control. Chou En-lai still directed the immense state bureaucracy, but its powers had been greatly abridged. In some ways, the Cultural Revolution Group became the shadow government of China. The army remained the most powerful single force in the land, but it, too, was disunited. So were the Red Guards, young, quick to explode in violence, and exploited by the rival pressure groups.

Swimming with the current, 50,000 Chinese soldiers cross the Yangtze River to commemorate the much heralded 1966 crossing of their leader, Mao Tse-tung.

Hydrogen Bomb. In most of the provinces, the governors, party bosses, and army commanders sought to preserve as much autonomy as they could. Thus, China's first hydrogen bomb test was held in Sinkiang province, where the army chief remained at odds with Peking. The test, which had an explosive force of several million tons of TNT, took place in June. U.S. officials and nuclear experts saw in it fresh evidence of the rapid progress being made by China in developing a nuclear arsenal.

Wuhan Crisis. A major crisis occurred in the Yangtze River port city of Wuhan on July 20, when two of Mao's lieutenants, including Public Security Minister Hsieh Fu-chih, were kidnaped by the commanding general. After the captives had been displayed in disgrace, they were allowed to return to Peking with a demand for the autonomy of Wuhan. This was a dangerous challenge. If the Wuhan general could get away with it, other regional leaders would be encouraged to break from Peking. Once again, Mao rose to the challenge. With the use of outside troops and of Maoist Red Guards in Wuhan, the general was deposed.

The crisis in Wuhan, however, rocked Peking. The disturbances there had come perilously close to civil war, and urgent steps were needed to repair the weakened state structure. On September 1, all the members of the Maoist regime joined in an appeal for order. The army was given sole responsibility for keeping the peace, and civilians were ordered to turn in their arms at once. Once again, students were told to return to their schools. The workers were ordered to stay on the job and "fight for production." The peasants were barred from making revolution in towns. To emphasize the new turn, Mao toured five provinces, and a number of "anti-Maoists" were executed.

In effect, the season when the masses were told that "to rebel is justified" was ended. Now the stress was on hard work and moral reform. The new slogan was, "Fight selfishness and combat revisionism." Through compromise, "revolutionary committees" were created in a dozen additional provinces and cities. And the generals took on the task of keeping the order. As 1967 ended, however, violence and disorders were bubbling over once again in several of the provinces.

Increasing Isolation. The year also saw China's growing isolation from the rest of the world. Many embassies in Peking were the objects of hostile demonstrations by vast crowds. More than a million Red Guards demonstrated before the Soviet embassy for 12 days in January and February. Relations were strained to a near breaking point with Burma, Great Britain, India, Indonesia, Outer Mongolia, the Soviet Union, and Yugoslavia. At the same time, Peking engaged in bitter exchanges with Ceylon, France, Italy, Japan, Kenya, Norway, Switzerland, and Tunisia. The diatribes against

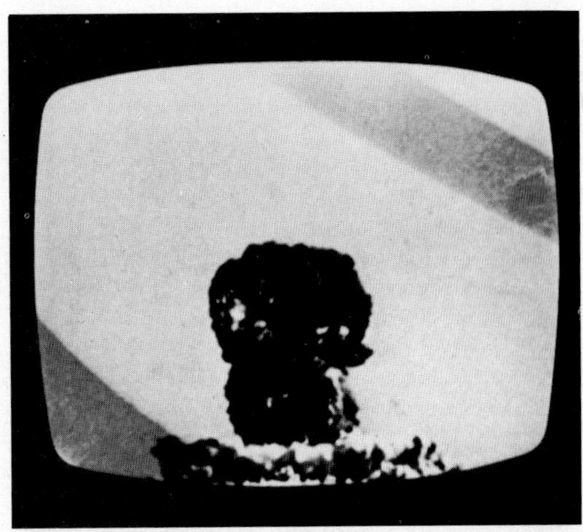

China's atomic bomb test was shown on Tokyo television in March. China followed this in June with its first explosion of a H-bomb.

Britain had repercussions in Hong Kong, where Chinese Communists tried to bring the British colonial authorities to their knees with strikes, riots, and do-it-yourself bombs. The reciprocal sieges of embassies in Peking and New Delhi, India, were followed in September with clashes on the border between Chinese Tibet and the Indian-protected state of Sikkim.

The blame for the disruption of China's contacts with other countries did not always rest entirely with Peking. The brutal persecution of the Chinese minority by Indonesia's military rulers made its break with China inevitable. So did Burma's decision to tighten controls over its Chinese community, which resulted in anti-Chinese riots.

Economy Disrupted. Inescapably, the turmoil had a severe impact on the economy. With industry working in spurts and with transportation badly disorganized, China's exports in 1967 took a sharp drop. Orders for delivery were not met; the shipments of food to Hong Kong declined in midsummer to a small fraction of the amounts sent in 1966. Ships unloading or taking on cargo in China's ports found themselves badly delayed, and their crew members were often subjected to indignities by the Red Guards. The 1967 wheat and rice crops appeared to be a little better than average.

At year's end, it was difficult to identify the ruling hierarchy. Of the seven members of the once all-powerful Standing Committee of the Communist Party's Politburo, four had been ousted. Of the 17 members of the Politburo, 12 were either out of office or under attack. Of the 10 secretaries of the party's Central Committee, seven had been forced out of office. On paper, Liu Shao-chi remained Chairman of the Republic and Teng Hsiao-ping was still general secretary of the party, but both had long been removed from power. The three men at the top were Mao Tse-tung, chairman of the party; Lin Piao, defense minister and the party's deputy chairman; and Premier Chou En-lai. Under them apparently was the "shadow government," or the Cultural Revolution Group, headed by Mao's former political secretary, Chen Po-ta, with Mrs. Mao as his first deputy. A consultant to the group, Kang Sheng, played an increasingly important role in Peking. In the past, he had been the party's specialist on purges and public security. [MARK GAYN]

Facts in Brief. Population: 723,000,000. Government: Communist Party Chairman Mao Tse-tung; Chairman of the Republic Liu Shao-chi; Premier Chou En-lai. Monetary Unit: yuan (2.46=U.S. $1). Foreign Trade: exports, $1,955,000,000; imports, $1,740,000,000. Principal Exports: rice, vegetables, textiles.

See also COMMUNISM; Section Two: MAO'S LAST REVOLUTION.

CHRONOLOGY. See pages 8 to 12.

CHURCHES. See EASTERN ORTHODOX; JEWS AND JUDAISM; PROTESTANT; RELIGION; ROMAN CATHOLIC.

CITY. A tragic chapter in the history of America's cities was written as racial violence in the slum areas of at least 68 large and small cities claimed 85 lives, injured more than 3,200 persons, and destroyed an estimated $300,000,000 in property. Almost all the riots broke out during the summer, but lesser outbreaks continued into the fall. By far the worst rioting occurred in Detroit, Mich. During five days of virtual guerrilla warfare in late July, 43 lives were lost, 386 persons were injured, and about $250,000,000 worth of property was damaged in predominatly Negro neighborhoods (see DETROIT).

A few weeks earlier, smaller-scale but similar violence engulfed Newark, N.J., where National Guardsmen helped restore order. More than $12,000,000 in damage was reported in Newark. Other cities with more than $1,000,000 in damage included Boston, Mass.; Cincinnati, Ohio; Milwaukee, Wis.; New Haven, Conn.; and Tampa, Fla.

While Detroit's ashes still smoldered, President Lyndon B. Johnson named a blue-ribbon commission, headed by Illinois Governor Otto Kerner, to investigate the causes of the civil disorders. In Congress, extended hearings on the riots were held by a permanent Senate subcommittee. Despite charges that the rioting had been planned, the Federal Bureau of Investigation (FBI) and various other agencies could find no clear evidence of conspiracies to create conflicts in the cities.

The outbreaks in Detroit and New Haven were regarded as especially shocking because they occurred in cities that had made extensive use of federal urban aid programs and that had been considered outstanding examples of local governments working hard to solve the problems of slum dwellers.

Reaction. The nation responded to the riots with little general agreement beyond the necessity of strengthening the ability of local and state police forces and the National Guard to maintain order. Elections in November of Negro mayors in Cleveland, Ohio, and Gary, Ind., added a note of optimism that the traditional political system could meet Negro hopes. See CIVIL RIGHTS; ELECTIONS.

The administration's legislative program for cities collided with an economy-minded House of Representatives, which, at first, refused to consider even rat control in large cities. Following public protests, the House approved a $40,000,000 rat control program. Funds for the already-authorized model cities program and for rent supplements were substantially less than the amounts sought by President Johnson. The administration, in turn, introduced no new legislation in the housing field, leaving it to the Senate to fashion a bipartisan measure to encourage home ownership by low-income families (see CONGRESS OF THE UNITED STATES; HOUSING). The war on poverty was extended at about the same level as the previous year, but with diluted control by the poor (see POVERTY).

The Death Of Hip

Through San Francisco's Golden Gate Park, the procession of mourners came, in beads and ponchos, furs and velvet, and raggedy skirts. There were shuffling sounds from sandaled feet and the faint odor of marijuana. The faces were mostly adolescent; some bearded, some smeared with red, yellow, and purple paint. The 15-foot casket, obligingly paraded before the TV cameras, was filled with orange peels and peacock feathers and bore the sign, "Summer of Love." Behind it came the "corpse" with a zinnia on its breast.

Then, as the casket was set afire and the strains of *Hari Krishna* echoed along the slopes of Hashbury (slang for San Francisco's Haight-Ashbury District), the mourners managed to shout almost in unison, "Hippies are dead! Now the free men will come through!"

It was the hippiedom funeral of the "Death of Hip." The hippies have been a source of puzzlement, anger, curiosity, and despair to most of our large cities. In the beginning, they were mostly middle-class adolescents or college drop-outs, who had withdrawn into their big-city "caves" as a protest against their parents' worship of money and material possessions. But their "differentness," their proclivities for the bizarre, ranging from LSD to unorthodox modes of dress, had brought them fame. And that fame had inevitably thrust them into contact with other people and back into the clutches of the affluent society. Like the "beats" of the previous generations, they had fallen prey to the pressures of commercialism and publicity.

Hippie bands traveled first class across the continent. Owners of hippie dance halls became wealthy, as did the drug pushers. The hippies found that there were not only "high" trips with LSD, but also dangerously "low" trips. They found their ranks thinned by the "plastic" hippies from uptown, the gainfully employed who became "hip" only on weekends. No longer was there a sanctuary in hippiedom. Indeed, hippie hovels were being increasingly invaded by runaway teen-agers, as well as distraught parents and the police.

The hippies were corrupted by the gray-haired ladies who bought their psychedelic posters and by the crowds of tourists who purchased various hippie paraphernalia–much of it bogus–behind drab storefronts. In the end, hippie authors of underground novels talked hopefully of having their mimeographed books reviewed in the San Francisco *Chronicle*. And, in fact, there was as much talk about money on San Francisco's Haight Street as there was on New York City's Wall Street. Mostly, the talk centered around how money could buy drugs and how drugs required more money. Life was viewed by many of the hippies as a sort of dizzy merry-go-round that required money to keep it moving.

In 1967, the hippies lost the philosophical glue that supposedly had held them together. For a time, it seemed as if a concept of "love" and some of the "nonviolence" tenets of Oriental civilizations might be unifying these drop-outs from society. Yet, instead of turning their flowered cheeks when attacked by the motorcycle gangs of Los Angeles or the junkies of New York City, the hippies grabbed knives and chains. In due course, any pretense toward nonviolence was largely destroyed by ample evidence to the contrary collected by the Federal Bureau of Investigation, federal narcotics agents, investigators of the Food and Drug Administration, and numerous police departments.

Some of the crimes were particularly hideous. "Superspade," who sold drugs to hippies in San Francisco, was thrown over a cliff. Linda Rea Fitzpatrick, daughter of a prosperous Connecticut importer, was brutally murdered in a dirty, East Village, New York City, boiler room, allegedly by "Groovy," a high-spirited harmonica player who peddled *acid* (LSD).

In 1968 and beyond, there will, of course, be beards and painted faces and all the other trappings of what was once considered hippiedom. There probably will even be some people who will call themselves "hippies."

Hippiedom, however, is dead. The hippies not only said so, they also gave it a funeral. [E. KENNETH FROSLID]

Rioting during the summer built up to widespread destruction, most dramatically demonstrated in the arson, gunfire, and looting in Detroit, Mich.

Model Cities. The model cities program took its first steps November 16 when the Department of Housing and Urban Development selected 63 cities and towns to receive planning grants. Of the largest U.S. cities, only Los Angeles, Calif., and Cleveland failed in their bid for planning funds. San Francisco, Calif., and Milwaukee did not apply. Of the grants, totaling $312,000,000, 17 went to communities of less than 100,000 population.

An Urban Coalition was formed on July 31 to mobilize the broad resources of the nation in behalf of cities. It called for massive public and private efforts to provide better housing and more jobs in slum areas. The movement spread, and, by November, about 50 cities had organized or had planned local counterparts.

The participation of business in the Urban Coalition suggested a hopeful development when the Federal Housing Administration announced on September 13 that it would guarantee mortgages in high-risk slum areas, the life insurance industry raised a $1,000,000,000 fund for investment in slum neighborhoods for both housing and job opportunities. [DONALD W. LIEF]

CITY AND REGIONAL PLANNING. Senator Abraham A. Ribicoff (D., Conn.) introduced a bill late in the 1967 session of Congress to create a federal, low-interest loan fund to encourage construction of planned towns and communities. Senator Ribicoff proposed the legislation after conducting a series of hearings during the year on the government's role in urban affairs. The federal loans would be made to states to enable them to acquire land areas and to construct the new communities.

New Towns. Financiers lost some of their enthusiasm for the development of new towns when Reston, Va., which seemed to be off to a good start in 1966, lost its momentum in 1967. Its developer, Gulf Oil Corporation, experienced a threat to its $15,000,000 investment due to the unanticipated financing required for completion of the city. Several observers concluded that plans of the magnitude and quality of Reston's could be implemented only with help from the federal government. Prospects for the enactment of a congressional bill appeared to be excellent in 1968 as developers increased pressures for federal subsidies.

An especially significant development during the year signaled the introduction of federal resources into planning and construction of new towns. In November, the Department of Housing and Urban Development (HUD) granted $877,140 to Washington, D.C., to plan a community on a 335-acre tract

of land owned by the federal government; the city was also assured an additional $12,800,000 to help finance construction of public facilities on the site. The action was the first step in a plan, announced by President Lyndon B. Johnson, to turn over unused, federally held land in metropolitan areas for the development of new communities.

Urban Planners. After a three-year wait, HUD received a $3,000,000 appropriation to conduct preservice and in-service training for public employees in the fields of housing, planning, urban renewal, and related community development programs. The program of federal assistance to increase the skills of urban planners was authorized by Congress in the Housing Act of 1964, but the legislature neglected to fund the program until 1967.

According to a 1967 survey released in June by the American Institute of Planners (AIP), the demand for city planners exceeds the supply by 300 annually. The AIP reported that there were approximately 7,000 professional-level planners in the field as of mid-1967.

Dennis O'Harrow, executive director of the American Society of Planning Officials since 1954, died suddenly on August 29 in Berlin, Germany, where he was presiding over a seven-day congress of the International Federation for Housing and Planning. [J. ROBERT DUMOUCHEL]

See also ARCHITECTURE; CITY.

CIVIL RIGHTS. "It looks like Berlin in 1945," said Mayor Jerome P. Cavanagh when the waves of summer rioting that rolled across the nation engulfed his city, Detroit, Mich., in 1967. In a six-mile area of the Negro ghetto, flames shot high against the dark sky, illuminating skeletons of burned homes and stores. Looters and arsonists raced through the shadows, grabbing goods and putting shops to the torch. The gunfire of snipers, policemen, National Guardsmen, and the regular army beat a steady staccato in the background.

Riots in the Cities. What happened in Detroit had happened earlier in the year in Newark, N.J., and it attacked with milder violence in some 50 cities, from New Haven, Conn., to Fresno, Calif. A mystifying aspect of the rioting was that it fell upon two cities with the most advanced programs for dealing with urban poverty and Negro civil rights—Detroit and New Haven. Various explanations were offered of the rioting. Most observers agreed hoodlumism played a large role. A survey of the Detroit riot area showed that 95 per cent of the Negro population took no part in the upheaval. Some attributed the rioting to frustrated expectations raised by past civil rights legislation, court decisions, and the Great Society program.

Racial strife in the cities galvanized public leaders into action. President Lyndon B. Johnson, in a nationwide televised address in July, stated that rioting was exacting the severest price from the Negro himself. The President established a day of prayer to bring reconciliation to the cities and appointed a commission, headed by Governor Otto Kerner of Illinois, to study measures to prevent future riots, but took no immediate action. In October, the President recommended a $40,000,000 pilot program to persuade private industry to build new businesses and to create new jobs in urban ghettos. The President's modest action was attributed to a balky Congress, especially in the House of Representatives, where a growing desire to economize held sway.

With such limited responses coming from Washington, D.C., increasing burdens fell upon the nation's mayors. Mayor John V. Lindsay steered New York City through the summer without a major upheaval, an achievement that was aided by his walks through ghetto streets to show his concern, and by his tapping of industry for summer job and recreation programs. In Chicago, Ill., Mayor Richard J. Daley conducted a "summer celebration," featuring "splash parties" provided by fire hoses. Many cities conducted job programs, but applications far outstripped opportunities.

Urban Coalition. A newly formed national Urban Coalition of 22 business, civil rights, labor, municipal, and religious leaders, announced in August that it planned to call for an immediate public-private effort to find 1,000,000 jobs and to build at least 1,000,000 housing units a year for low-income families. In September, 350 life insurance companies formulated a program to invest $1,000,000,000 in slum redevelopment.

Housing was at the forefront of civil rights concerns in 1967. President Johnson's most ambitious objective in new civil rights legislation was an open housing bill, but it remained stalled in Congress. Louisville, Ky., possessor of a progressive record on civil rights, was the scene of a resolute drive to break down patterns of residential segregation. During the summer and the winter, Milwaukee, Wis., was also the scene of demonstrations and confrontations for fair housing.

Education continued high on the list of Negro civil rights concerns. The discouraging character of its present state was underscored in a study by the U.S. Civil Rights Commission. The study showed that more Negroes attended segregated schools in the South in 1967 than when the Supreme Court ruled against school segregation in 1954. William L. Taylor, the commission's staff director, noted that the vast majority of Negroes who entered the first grade in 1955 graduated from high school in 1967 "without ever having attended a single class with a single white student."

One good sign, however, was the growing rate of admission of Negroes to southern colleges. The Southern Regional Education Board adopted a report calling for the immediate strengthening of Negro colleges and the eventual development of a unified, integrated system of higher education. In a historic turnabout, some 10 years after the school crisis in Little Rock, Ark., the school board appointed William Henry Fowler, a Negro, as assistant superintendent for personnel.

Comedian Dick Gregory joined Father James E. Groppi in civil rights march through downtown Milwaukee, Wis., in effort to force open housing.

Elections. Negroes made themselves felt as a local political force, even in the deep South, in 1967. Having finally registered under the Voting Rights Act of 1965, they turned out in large numbers for the Democratic primaries. In Mississippi, the scene of the most obdurate white resistance, Negroes captured nominations for such posts as chancery-court clerk, constable, coroner, county supervisor, and justice of the peace. Negroes also entered into the nation's mayoralty picture. In Cleveland, Ohio, and Gary, Ind., Negro candidates captured the Democratic mayoralty primaries and both won in the November elections. In Boston, Mass., Louise Day Hicks, mayoral candidate running on a platform opposing school integration, was defeated. See ELECTIONS. In Washington, D.C., President Johnson appointed Walter E. Washington, 52, a Negro, as commissioner, or mayor, of the nation's capital.

The Black Power Wing of the Negro civil rights leadership remained in the spotlight. A Black Power conference at Newark, in July, adopted a resolution calling for the possible separation of the United States into black and white countries. H. Rap Brown, 23-year-old chairman of the Student Nonviolent Coordinating Committee (SNCC), voiced the more violent black power theme: "If America don't come around, we've got to burn America down, brother."

Church and State. A growing issue on the civil liberties scene centered upon the relationship of church and state. In a dozen states, bills were introduced to begin or to expand tax support for parochial schools. In New York state, a constitutional convention framed a draft constitution which dropped the so-called "Blaine amendment," which barred state funds for private or parochial schools, and substituted provisions that could open the way for extensive state aid to those schools. New York voters, however, defeated the plan in the November elections. See EDUCATION.

Wiretapping and electronic "bugging" by federal authorities were sharply curtailed by order of Attorney General Ramsey Clark. The order exceeded restrictions previously set by President Johnson and the Supreme Court of the United States. In 1961, the Court ruled that "bugs" planted inside a room violated constitutional protections against trespassing. The decision prompted federal investigators to place microphones on walls outside rooms or on window sills. Under the order, use of bugging devices must have the Attorney General's approval. National security cases were excepted.

The President's commission to investigate city riots met at the White House in August. The chairman, Illinois Governor Otto Kerner, is seated at President's right.

The Courts were, as usual, busy forums for further refinement and definition of civil rights and civil liberties. A U.S. Circuit Court of Appeals ruled *de facto*, as well as actual school segregation unconstitutional. The *de facto* segregation referred to segregated housing patterns and a policy of neighborhood schools in Washington, D.C., which had concentrated Negro pupils in Negro schools, and white pupils in white schools. The decision, imposed by law, could affect northern school systems, in both cities and suburbs. In May, the U.S. Court of Appeals for the Fifth Circuit affirmed a ruling by a federal judge who had ordered complete desegregation of all Alabama schools. This was the first order, with state-wide coverage, ever issued by a court.

The courts also struck at discrimination in housing. In a 5 to 4 ruling in May, the Supreme Court upheld the California supreme court in holding unconstitutional a 1964 referendum that rejected the state's fair housing code. The Court found that the referendum, known as Proposition 14, violated Amendment 14 of the U.S. Constitution by creating, in effect, "a constitutional right to discriminate on racial grounds in the sale and leasing of real property." California and Michigan courts struck down laws giving homeowners the right to sell or rent to whomever they wished. Illinois and New York courts permitted their states to punish real estate brokers for discriminatory actions.

In Other Rulings, the Supreme Court also declared that the Fifth Amendment to the Constitution covers a government employee who refuses to testify in an investigation concerning his job. The Court also ruled that Congress lacks authority to strip Americans of citizenship without their consent. Previously, the Court had held that citizenship could be taken away if an American citizen voted in a foreign election. A circuit court of appeals held that the draft cannot be used to silence students who had demonstrated against it.

Abroad, probably the most sensational assault of the year on civil rights and civil liberties transpired in Greece where a junta seized power and installed rule by decree in April. Waves of arrests and repressions followed. Trade unions and social and political clubs were outlawed. Youth organizations of all parties were disbanded, unreliable mayors dismissed, and youths were arrested for scrawling slogans on walls. Blacklists of Greek and foreign authors were issued, and special courts-martial were established throughout the country for those offending church, king, or junta. An attempt in December by King Constantine II to reverse the April coup and depose the junta failed, thereby forcing the royal ruler and his family to flee the country to Rome, Italy (see GREECE). [LOUIS W. KOENIG]

See also CITY; DEMOCRACY; DETROIT; SUPREME COURT OF THE UNITED STATES.

CLARK, RAMSEY (1927-), took the oath of office as the 66th Attorney General of the United States on March 10, 1967. On the same day, his father, Supreme Court Justice Tom C. Clark, 67, announced his retirement. Ramsey Clark, a lanky 6-footer, had been acting Attorney General since October, 1965.

Clark, in the six years he had been in the Department of Justice–first as an assistant Attorney General and later as deputy Attorney General–had gained a reputation for candor and a deep concern for the legal rights of the individual.

Clark was born in Dallas, Tex., on Dec. 18, 1927. Much of his youth was spent in Washington, D.C.

In 1949, he earned his B.A. degree at the University of Texas, where he had met and married Georgia Welch on April 16, 1949. In one more year, he received an M.A. degree in history and a J.D. degree, both at the University of Chicago. He practiced law in Dallas until he was called to the nation's capitol in 1961.

Clark is an avid reader and has succeeded in avoiding the capital's social whirl. The Clarks live in suburban Falls Church, Va., with their two teenage children, Ronda and Tom.

CLUBS, BOYS' AND GIRLS'. See YOUTH ORGANIZATIONS.

COAL. See MINES AND MINING.

COIN COLLECTING. See HOBBIES.

COLOMBIA passed a foreign exchange and trade law in March, 1967, to keep imports in check, encourage exports, and thus narrow the republic's chronic balance of payments gap. Although the law established a fluctuating exchange rate based on supply and demand, it pegged the minimum rate at 13.50 pesos per U.S. $1, and the maximum rate at 16.30.

In April, the International Monetary Fund authorized a $60,000,000 stand-by loan to help the nation meet its international payments difficulties and maintain financial stability. In May, Colombia received a $40,000,000 loan from the Agency for International Development, with a pledge of another $60,000,000 to finance imports from the United States. Meanwhile, the government substantially cut budgetary and coffee deficit financing and eased the restrictions on imports so as not to hurt industry.

Early in the year, guerrilla terrorism was rampant in the interior. Martial law was declared, and about 25 Communist leaders were arrested. In February, an earthquake caused at least 100 deaths (see DISASTERS). [MARY C. WEBSTER]

Facts in Brief. Population: 19,555,000. Government: President Carlos Lleras Restrepo. Monetary Unit: peso (14.72=U.S. $1). Foreign Trade: exports, $506,500,000; imports, $674,300,000. Principal Exports: coffee, petroleum, bananas.

COMMUNICATIONS. Man's ability to be in instant communication with others, no matter how far removed or dispersed, made impressive progress in 1967. Two more communications satellites, each with a capacity of 240 voice circuits, joined the pioneer Early Bird and Lani Bird in the program of the International Telecommunications Satellite (Intelsat) consortium–an organization of 57 nations–to build a global satellite communications system.

One of the satellites launched in January, 1967, brought commercial service via satellite to the Pacific area for the first time, while the second, in April, 1967, doubled the space circuitry across the Atlantic Ocean. Ten new ground facilities for these satellites went into service in 1967 at Brewster Flat, Wash., and Paumalu, Hawaii, and overseas on Ascension Island, Australia, and the Canary Islands, and in Japan and Spain. Additional surface facilities for satellite service were provided on three ships used in the National Aeronautics and Space Administration (NASA) program.

Aside from the Intelsat program for the development of a global commercial system, Russia continued its own separate communications satellite program. The sixth and seventh *Molniya* (Lightning) satellites were launched in October, mainly for transmitting television programs across Russia.

The U.S. Department of Defense launched two more clusters of communications satellites, in January and July, to join seven in orbit since June, 1966. At the end of 1967, it had 19 communications satellites in operation.

The Submarine Cable Network continued to expand in pace with the growth of satellite communications. The Southeast Asia Commonwealth (SEACOM) formally opened a cable from Guam to Australia on March 30, 1967. This joined the transatlantic (CANTAT) and transpacific (COMPAC) cables in the British Commonwealth's 23,000-mile coaxial submarine cable network. Another milestone was the inauguration of service Oct. 9, 1967, over the world's first wideband submarine telephone cable. The 80-mile link, between Norway and Denmark, provides 480 circuits.

At the end of 1967, there were approximately 75,000 nautical miles of telephone cable linking the nations of the world. Of this total, about 9,000 miles had been added to the underseas system during 1966 and 1967.

Russia and Japan marked the opening of commercial air service between their capitals with a historic television program on April 20, 1967. It was another demonstration of the expansion of communications facilities around the world. The "live" telecast from Moscow was transmitted about two-thirds the way around the world, traversing seven European countries and the United States by land, and two oceans by satellite before being shown on television screens throughout Japan.

Telephones in Service throughout the world totaled an estimated 208,543,200 on Jan. 1, 1967, an increase of about 13,200,000 over the previous year. At least that many more were expected to be added by the end of 1967.

A landmark was reached in the United States in May, when the 100,000,000th telephone was put into service. By the end of 1967, the total number had reached about 103,400,000 telephones. Of these, some 17,100,000 were owned and operated by independent companies, and the remainder were a part of the Bell System.

Many of these telephones will be tied even more closely to those in other nations overseas by the early 1970s. The Bell System reported that a four-month trial of customer direct dialing of calls between New York City, London, and Paris showed that the selected customers, all heavy users of overseas service, had increased calling volumes nearly 35 per cent. Code numbers already have been assigned for direct dialing to each of the world's nine zones.

The cost of long-distance service in the United States also was lowered during the year. Partly as an outgrowth of the Federal Communications Commission's general telephone rate investigation, charges for interstate calls were reduced a total of $100,000,000 on Nov. 1, 1967. [THOMAS M. MALIA]

See also ELECTRONICS; RADIO; TELEVISION.

Chinese Communists, members of the Red Guard, burn effigies of Russian leaders outside Soviet embassy in Peking during anti-Soviet rioting.

COMMUNISM. The 50th anniversary of the Bolshevik revolution and the beginning of Soviet rule in Russia was celebrated in Moscow in 1967. Conspicuous by their absence from the Moscow observance on November 10 were representatives of Chinese Communism. The Central Committee, in a set of theses issued for the 50th anniversary, had hailed the revolution as the birth of international Communism but it had also warned of the threat to unity represented by Chinese nationalism and its deviation from Marxism-Leninism.

Throughout the year, both Communist countries had traded insults and denunciations, testifying to a total breakdown of unity of action and of thought. Although tenuous diplomatic bonds were miraculously maintained, the links between the parties had been almost completely severed. See CHINA; RUSSIA.

Discord Continues. The basic standpoints of the two leading Communist powers remained unchanged. Soviet spokesmen were severely critical of the excesses of Communist China's Cultural Revolution and then openly attacked the Party Chairman Mao Tse-tung and his followers for their "criminal actions." The Chinese leaders, on the other hand, repeatedly denounced the "revisionist" tendencies of the Soviet Union's domestic policy and its "conciliation" of world imperialism.

The war in Vietnam persisted as a focal point of discord between the two Communist powers. The Chinese, condemning even the slightest tendency on the part of Hanoi to move toward a peaceful settlement, also attacked the Soviet Union for conspiring with the United States to end the war. The Soviet Union in turn accused the Chinese of hindering joint aid to North Vietnam by their intractable attitude. Caught between two fires, the North Vietnamese Communists sought to maintain friendship with both Moscow and Peking.

Isolating Communist China. Meanwhile, China remained isolated in the world Communist movement. Its main supporters were Albania, in Europe, and the relatively insignificant Communist party of New Zealand. Otherwise, the Chinese camp was made up almost entirely of splinter groups and parties. Apart from Albania, not a single ruling party was openly and definitely pro-Chinese.

Nevertheless, the powerful Soviet Communist party failed in its steady efforts to convene an international conference to exclude or to isolate the Chinese. An agreement was finally reached between the Soviet Communist party and 17 others to convene a meeting in Budapest in early 1968 to prepare for a world Communist conference at a later date. No reference was made to the Chinese party and neither the Romanians nor the Yugoslavs associated themselves with this move.

New rifts appeared in the European Communist camp. Romania's decision to establish diplomatic relations with West Germany led to an open protest by the East Germans against this breach of solidarity (see ROMANIA). A hastily convened conference of the foreign ministers of the Warsaw Pact nations, with Romania represented only by a deputy foreign minister, disbanded without issuing a communiqué. Although other Eastern European Communist states were already engaged in discussions with Bonn, they yielded to the pressure of their East German ally, and abandoned any intentions of following Romania's course. In March, three bilateral pacts negotiated between Czechoslovakia, Poland, and East Germany, placated the latter by forming a kind of "iron triangle" in the north. The regime of East Germany's Walter Ulbricht later followed up this success with similar long-term treaties with Bulgaria and Hungary. See BULGARIA; HUNGARY.

Conference Fails. In April, a conference of European Communist parties was held in Karlsbad, Czechoslovakia. What was intended to be a demonstration of Communist unity and a regional substitute for a world conference proved a fiasco. Representatives of only 25 parties were present, and of these only 24 signed the declaration on European security. This document repeated the 1966 Bucharest proposal for a European security system to replace existing military alliances.

Romanian Intransigence. In May, the independent viewpoint of the Romanian Communist party was set forth in a statement affirming Communist unity, but asserting the right of each party to shape its own political line and to participate or not to participate in Communist conferences.

The war in the Middle East provided a new opportunity for Romania to adopt a distinctive course; it also provided further evidence of Communist disunity (see MIDDLE EAST). A summit conference held in Moscow in June condemned Israel as an aggressor and called for sanctions. Romania was represented but did not sign the declaration. Nor did it break diplomatic relations with Israel, as did Bulgaria, Czechoslovakia, Hungary, Poland, and the Soviet Union. Romania later called for direct Arab-Israeli negotiations. Paradoxically, Yugoslavia took part in this bloc conference, signed the declaration, and broke off relations with Israel. A subsequent top-level conference in Budapest, which included Yugoslavian but not Romanian delegates, pledged to supply economic and military assistance to the Arab countries.

A meeting of deputy premiers in Belgrade, in September, was confined to the discussion of economic aid by individual countries and was attended by Romania. China adopted a strongly pro-Arab position but severely criticized the stand of the Soviet Union and its allies. In Israel itself, the Communist party split into two separate parties, both pro-Soviet, but one faction was pro-Israel, and the other was pro-Arab. [H. GORDON SKILLING]

COMPUTERS. Spokesmen for the computer industry expressed hopes that technological developments would settle down enough to permit the industry to reduce development costs and retain more of their rental revenue. New developments in integrated circuits and memory design continued to spur investment in advanced hardware engineering in 1967.

Large-Scale Integration (LSI), the latest extension of integrated circuit technology, was utilized in advanced computer design by many firms, including the industry giant, International Business Machines Corporation. LSI involves the fabrication of as many as 100 circuits on a single chip of silicon in a space that previously held only 5 to 10. The increased density of the circuits also results in increased computing speed. LSI is expected to provide lower cost, higher reliability, and greater flexibility of designs than that available in the previous generation of integrated circuits.

Efforts also were made to transfer some of the functions of software – the programs of instructions to computers – to small, high-speed memories, which could operate as "assistants" to computer processing circuitry. Both magnetic and LSI memories were investigated for this function, which was given the new label "firmware." Firmware is expected to appear first in military computers where high speed and small size are important. It is hoped that firm-

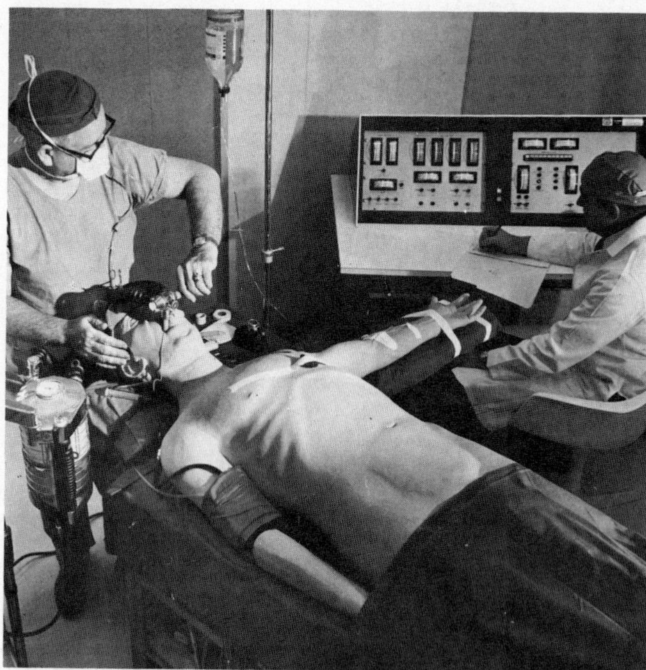

Sim One, a computer-controlled robot that breathes, coughs, and has blood pressure, was developed in 1967 for training doctors.

ware will also eventually reduce the high costs of nonmilitary computer use. General Electric Company estimated that computer users now spend 75 cents of every computer dollar on software and operation, and only 25 cents on rental.

Computer Memories, constructed of plated wires, were used in 1967, in the Univac 9000 computer series, made by the Univac Division of Sperry Rand Corporation in New York City. In such memories, information is stored by magnetization of thin wires in paths which encircle the wires at regular intervals. Wide use of plated-wire memory systems was possible because they were now comparable in cost, size, and speed to ferrite-core memories.

Time-Sharing, a trend in computer use which came of age in 1965, was advanced a step further in 1967. Small computers were marketed which, in addition to performing low-level, on-the-spot, computation, also served as terminals for communication with larger, remote computers, which could handle tasks beyond the local units' capacity. An experimental network of 35 large computers to be shared by many users was discussed at a meeting of the Department of Defense's Advanced Research Projects Agency in July. Before the network can become a reality, means must be developed for communication between computers that use different programming languages. [JAMES A. PEARRE]

CONGO (BRAZZAVILLE.) See AFRICA.

Former Congolese Premier Moise Tshombe, imprisoned in Algeria and condemned to death by the Congo regime, glowers over his future.

CONGO (KINSHASA). A military court met in Kinshasa from March 6 to 13, 1967, and sentenced Moise Tshombe, who was in exile in Europe, to death for treason. The former premier's older brother Thomas, also in exile, received 15 years' imprisonment for complicity. On July 1, a gunman hijacked Moise Tshombe's chartered plane over the Mediterranean Sea and forced the pilot to fly the plane to Algeria. The Congo immediately requested that Tshombe be returned for execution, but Algeria refused because of foreign pressures and a desire to use Tshombe for political bargaining. See ALGERIA.

On July 5, Major Jean Schramme led a rebellion in the eastern Congo by 170 white mercenaries and 1,500 gendarmes from Katanga, Tshombe's home province. They defeated local Congolese troops and demanded freedom for Tshombe and the overthrow of President Joseph Mobutu. African mobs, embittered by the mercenaries' action, attacked white civilians and the Belgian embassy in Kinshasa. Mobutu asked the United States for aid against the rebels, and received three army transport planes, which flew Congolese paratroopers to the town of Bukavu. By November, they had forced the rebels into neighboring Rwanda and ended the revolt.

The Congo nationalized the Belgian copper mining company, the Union Minière du Haut Katanga, in January, and a new government company was set up to administer its $800,000,000 assets. Belgium protested the seizure, and 1,500 essential Belgian technicians threatened to leave the Congo. The crisis ended on February 17 with a new three-year agreement for technical cooperation.

Foreign Affairs. Heads of state from east and central Africa met in Kinshasa from February 12 to 14, with President Mobutu as chairman. The meeting resulted in the "Kinshasa Declaration," which backed the Congo in its dispute with Union Minière, supported freeing South African and Portuguese areas from white control, and demanded that Great Britain use force to end white rule in Rhodesia.

The Organization of African Unity (OAU) met in Kinshasa from September 11 to 14. United Nations Secretary-General U Thant and representatives of 37 African nations attended.

New Constitution. A referendum in June gave Mobutu 97.8 per cent of the vote. A new constitution made the president commander in chief of military and police forces, enlarged the national assembly to 300 members, and gave voting rights to all Congolese over 18 years of age. Elections for the assembly, now suspended, were planned for 1968, and a presidential election for 1970. [BENJAMIN E. THOMAS]

Facts in Brief. Population: 16,508,000. Government: President Joseph Mobutu. Monetary Unit: zaire (1 = U.S. $2.00). Foreign Trade: exports, $329,000,000; imports, $320,000,000. Principal Exports: copper, vegetable oils, diamonds.

CONGRESS OF THE UNITED STATES

The first session of the 90th Congress ignored many of President Lyndon B. Johnson's programs and distorted others. Its meager legislative record reflected the nation's dissatisfaction with the mounting costs of the war in Vietnam, rising prices, and the expense of the President's Great Society and War on Poverty programs.

Among major measures carried over for action in the second session when Congress adjourned on Dec. 15, 1967, were the President's request for a 10 per cent surcharge on personal and corporate income taxes, civil rights and anticrime legislation, wiretapping curbs, firearms control, election campaign reform and campaign financing, and various measures designed to protect consumers.

Ethics charges hit Adam Clayton Powell, *left*, a Democrat who was denied his House seat from New York City's Harlem district, and Senator Edward V. Long, *below*, who was investigated on charges of misusing his office.

From the beginning, the mood of the 90th was critical of the administration. When Congress convened Jan. 10, 1967, there were 64 Democrats and 36 Republicans in the Senate and 247 Democrats and 187 Republicans in the House (with one vacancy). The Republicans, with 47 new members in the House and three in the Senate, allied with conservative Southern Democrats in opposition to the administration. As soon as it convened, the House voted to eliminate the 21-day rule, which had been adopted in 1965 to make it impossible for the Rules Committee to delay legislation more than 21 days.

In his State of the Union Message on the same day, President Johnson appealed for national support for the war in Vietnam and asked Congress to pass a 6 per cent surcharge on personal and corporate income taxes to pay for the war. He also requested increased Social Security benefits and a strong federal anticrime program.

In the weeks that followed, the President also asked for:

- A merger of the Labor and Commerce departments.
- An Air Quality Act to encourage states to develop regional programs to counter air pollution.
- Support of his anti-poverty program.
- Increased veterans' benefits.
- A fair housing law.
- A $350,000,000,000 program to stimulate local and state law enforcement and crime prevention.

Senator Thomas J. Dodd (D., Conn.), *above*, was censured by the Senate for personal use of campaign funds. Robert "Bobby" Baker, *right*, former secretary to Senate Democrats, was convicted and sentenced to prison for 1 to 3 years on conspiracy, tax evasion, and other charges.

The Budget was presented to Congress by the President on January 24. The estimated expenses of the national income accounts budget for fiscal 1968 totaled a record $169,200,000,000, an increase of $15,600,000,000 from the 1967 budget. This type of budget includes all federal receipts and expenditures that affect the current flow of the nation's income or output. Estimated receipts were calculated at $167,-100,000,000, a rise of $17,300,000,000. Of the total, estimated defense spending accounted for $73,100,-000,000, the nation's third highest defense budget ever. Congress voted a total of about $157,000,000,-000 in new appropriations during the first session, some $15,000,000,000 of it for fiscal 1967 spending. See PRESIDENT OF THE UNITED STATES; TAXATION.

On September 13, Congress approved a $69,936,-620,000 defense-spending bill for fiscal 1968, the largest single appropriation bill ever passed. Some $20,000,000,000 went for the war in Vietnam. An amendment, however, provided that all U.S. naval vessels were to be built in U.S. shipyards, nullifying an administration agreement to allow Britain to bid on the construction of seven wooden-hulled minesweepers worth $60,700,000. Earlier, Britain had agreed to buy $2,600,000,000 worth of U.S. military equipment and the United States was committed to buy $325,000,000 in British arms. When the President signed the bill on September 30, he declared he would find a way to allow British bids on the minesweepers. See NATIONAL DEFENSE.

The Vietnam Issue. While most Congressmen somewhat reluctantly approved the President's conduct of the war in Vietnam, there were increasing defections from the President's policy as the session wore on. In March, Congress stated its support for the 1954 Geneva accords and urged an international meeting to effect an "honorable conclusion" to the war. It was its first policy statement since the 1964 Gulf of Tonkin resolution. At the same time, it authorized $4,548,200,000 in additional funds for the war. On April 4, the President signed a $12,200,-000,000 supplemental appropriations bill for war expenses for fiscal 1967.

As dissent in Congress grew, the administration called General William C. Westmoreland, commander of U.S. forces in Vietnam, to Washington, where he addressed a joint session on April 28. This was the first time in history that a U.S. battle commander had been called home from the front to defend the conduct of a war. Nevertheless, the questioning of the administration's war policy continued. Some of the critics – the "doves" – asked the President to stop the bombing of North Vietnam and questioned his power to continue fighting without a declaration of war from Congress. His other critics – the "hawks" – urged more escalation of the war. The President answered the doves by pointing to the power Congress had given him in the Gulf of Tonkin resolution. If Congress wanted to reverse itself, the President said at a news conference on August 18, it could vote to rescind the resolution.

In November, the Senate Foreign Relations Committee adopted a resolution calling on the President to get "affirmative action by Congress" before he makes any future "commitment of the armed forces . . . on foreign territory." In another 14-to-0 vote, it urged the President to take the initiative in placing the issue of ending the war in Vietnam before the United Nations Security Council. This was adopted by the full Senate on November 30 by an 82-to-0 vote.

Foreign Aid. In signing the Foreign Assistance Act of 1967 on November 15, the President said "the money cuts and other restrictions . . . will seriously inhibit this government's effort to assure and enlarge the security of the Free World." The bill had reduced his request for $3,250,000,000 to an authorization of $2,860,000,000. And the appropriations measure – passed in the final hours of the first session – reduced the amount of money available for fiscal 1968 to $2,290,000,000. It was the smallest amount in the 20-year history of the program.

Inflation and Taxes – the danger of the first and the need for the latter – pitted the Congress and the administration against one another throughout 1967. On May 31, Congress restored the major business tax incentives that it had suspended in October, 1966, to help stem inflation. One was the 7 per cent investment credit for new capital equipment; the other, the system of accelerated depreciation allowances on buildings. Although the administration supported the bill, it wanted the effective date, made retroactive for some parts of the bill, delayed. The bill suspended provisions of the 1966 tax law that provided funds for presidential campaigns.

In July, President Johnson again urged Congress to approve a 6 per cent surcharge on personal and corporate income taxes. Otherwise, he said, the 1968 federal deficit might reach $20,000,000,000. As inflationary pressures mounted, he raised his request in August to 10 per cent.

Despite the President's often-repeated plea, Chairman Wilbur Mills (D., Ark.) refused to let his House Ways and Means Committee consider the tax rise until the administration scaled down its spending plans and submitted data on the 1969 budget. Mills said his committee would take another look when it reconvened in January, 1968.

The War on Poverty suffered in the economy-minded Congress. At the end of the session, the administration's request was cut by $287,000,000 when a $1,773,000,000 appropriation was voted.

On June 29, the President signed a $1,200,000,-000 aid-to-education bill, authorizing extension of the Teacher Corps for three years. But Congress voted a two-thirds cut in funds for the corps to $13,-500,000 in fiscal 1968. At the session's end, a total of $9,300,000,000 was authorized in aid to schools for fiscal 1969 and 1970 (see EDUCATION).

Members of the United States House

The House of Representatives of the 90th Congress consists of 248 Democrats and 187 Republicans, compared with 295 Democrats and 140 Republicans for the 89th Congress. Table shows congressional districts, winner, and party affiliation. Asterisk denotes those who served in the 89th Congress. AL denotes "At Large."

Alabama

1. Jack Edwards, R.*
2. William L. Dickinson, R.*
3. George W. Andrews, D.*
4. William Nichols, D.
5. Armistead I. Selden, Jr., D.*
6. John H. Buchanan, Jr., R.*
7. Tom Bevill, D.
8. Robert E. Jones, D.*

Alaska

(AL) Howard W. Pollock, R.

Arizona

1. John J. Rhodes, R.*
2. Morris K. Udall, D.*
3. Sam Steiger, R.

Arkansas

1. E. C. Gathings, D.*
2. Wilbur D. Mills, D.*
3. J. P. Hammerschmidt, R.
4. David Pryor, D.

California

1. Don H. Clausen, R.*
2. Harold T. Johnson, D.*
3. John E. Moss, D.*
4. Robert L. Leggett, D.*
5. Phillip Burton, D.*
6. William S. Mailliard, R.*
7. Jeffery Cohelan, D.*
8. George P. Miller, D.*
9. Don Edwards, D.*
10. Charles S. Gubser, R.*
11. Paul N. McCloskey, R.
12. Burt L. Talcott, R.*
13. Charles M. Teaque, R.*
14. Jerome R. Waldie, D.*
15. John J. McFall, D.*
16. B. F. Sisk, D.*
17. Cecil R. King, D.*
18. Robert B. Mathias, R.
19. Chet Holifield, D.*
20. H. Allen Smith, R.*
21. Augustus F. Hawkins, D.*
22. James C. Corman, D.*
23. Del M. Clawson, R.*
24. Glenard P. Lipscomb, R.*
25. Charles E. Wiggins, R.
26. Thomas M. Rees, D.*
27. Ed Reinecke, R.*
28. Alphonzo Bell, R.*
29. George E. Brown, Jr., D.*
30. Edward R. Roybal, D.*
31. Charles H. Wilson, D.*
32. Craig Hosmer, R.*
33. Jerry L. Pettis, R.
34. Richard T. Hanna, D.*
35. James B. Utt, R.*
36. Bob Wilson, R.*
37. Lionel Van Deerlin, D.*
38. John V. Tunney, D.*

Colorado

1. Byron G. Rogers, D.*
2. Donald G. Brotzman, R.
3. Frank E. Evans, D.*
4. Wayne N. Aspinall, D.*

Connecticut

1. Emilio Q. Daddario, D.*
2. William L. St. Onge, D.*
3. Robert N. Giaimo, D.*
4. Donald J. Irwin, D.*
5. John S. Monagan, D.*
6. Thomas J. Meskill, R.

Delaware

(AL) William V. Roth, Jr., R.

Florida

1. Robert L. F. Sikes, D.*
2. Don Fuqua, D.*
3. Charles E. Bennett, D.*
4. A. Sydney Herlong, Jr., D.*
5. Edward J. Gurney, R.*
6. Sam M. Gibbons, D.*
7. James A. Haley, D.*
8. William C. Cramer, R.*
9. Paul G. Rogers, D.*
10. J. Herbert Burke, R.
11. Claude D. Pepper, D.*
12. Dante B. Fascell, D.*

Georgia

1. G. Elliott Hagen, D.*
2. Maston E. O'Neal, Jr., D.*
3. Jack T. Brinkley, D.
4. Ben B. Blackburn, R.
5. Fletcher Thompson, R.
6. John J. Flynt, Jr., D.*
7. John W. Davis, D.*
8. Williamson S. Stuckey, Jr., D.
9. Phillip M. Landrum, D.*
10. Robert G. Stephens, Jr., D.*

Hawaii

(AL) Spark M. Matsunaga, D.*
(AL) Patsy T. Mink, D.*

Idaho

1. James A. McClure, R.
2. George V. Hansen, R.*

Illinois

1. William L. Dawson, D.*
2. Barratt O'Hara, D.*
3. William T. Murphy, D.*
4. Edward J. Derwinski, R.*
5. John C. Kluczynski, D.*
6. Daniel J. Ronan, D.*
7. Frank Annunzio, D.*
8. Daniel D. Rostenkowski, D.*
9. Sidney R. Yates, D.*
10. Harold R. Collier, R.*
11. Roman C. Pucinski, D.*
12. Robert McClory, R.*
13. Donald Rumsfeld, R.*
14. John N. Erlenborn, R.*
15. Charlotte T. Reid, R.*
16. John B. Anderson, R.*
17. Leslie C. Arends, R.*
18. Robert H. Michel, R.*
19. Thomas F. Railsback, R.
20. Paul Findley, R.*
21. Kenneth J. Gray, D.*
22. William L. Springer, R.*
23. George E. Shipley, D.*
24. Charles Melvin Price, D.*

Indiana

1. Ray J. Madden, D.*
2. Charles A. Halleck, R.*
3. John Brademas, D.*
4. E. Ross Adair, R.*
5. J. Edward Roush, D.*
6. William G. Bray, R.*
7. John T. Meyers, R.
8. Roger H. Zion, R.
9. Lee H. Hamilton, D.*
10. Richard L. Roudebush, R.*
11. Andrew Jacobs, Jr., D.*

Iowa

1. Fred Schwengel, R.
2. John C. Culver, D.*
3. H. R. Gross, R.*
4. John H. Kyl, R.
5. Neal Smith, D.*
6. Wiley Mayne, R.
7. William J. Scherle, R.

Kansas

1. Robert J. Dole, R.*
2. Chester L. Mize, R.*
3. Larry Winn, Jr., R.
4. Garner E. Shriver, R.*
5. Joe Skubitz, R.*

Kentucky

1. Frank A. Stubblefield, D.*
2. William H. Natcher, D.*
3. William O. Cowger, R.
4. Marion Gene Snyder, R.
5. Tim Lee Carter, R.*
6. John C. Watts, D.*
7. Carl D. Perkins, D.*

Louisiana

1. F. Edward Hébert, D.*
2. Hale Boggs, D.*
3. Edwin E. Willis, D.*
4. Joe D. Waggonner, Jr., D.*
5. Otto E. Passman, D.*
6. John R. Rarick, D.
7. Edwin W. Edwards, D.*
8. Speedy O. Long, D.*

Maine

1. Peter N. Kyros, D.
2. William D. Hathaway, D.*

Maryland

1. Rogers C. B. Morton, R.*
2. Clarence D. Long, D.*
3. Edward A. Garmatz, D.*
4. George H. Fallon, D.*
5. Hervey G. Machen, D.*
6. Charles McC. Mathias, Jr., R.*
7. Samuel N. Friedel, D.*
8. Gilbert Gude, R.

Massachusetts

1. Silvio O. Conte, R.*
2. Edward P. Boland, D.*
3. Philip J. Philbin, D.*
4. Harold D. Donohue, D.*
5. F. Bradford Morse, R.*
6. William H. Bates, R.*
7. Torbert H. Macdonald, D.*
8. Thomas P. O'Neill, Jr., D.*
9. John W. McCormack, D.*
10. Margaret M. Heckler, R.
11. James A. Burke, D.*
12. Hastings Keith, R.*

Michigan

1. John Conyers, Jr., D.*
2. Marvin L. Esch, R.
3. Gary Brown, R.
4. Edward Hutchinson, R.*
5. Gerald R. Ford, R.*
6. Charles E. Chamberlain, R.*
7. Donald W. Riegle, Jr., R.
8. James Harvey, R.*
9. Guy Vander Jagt, R.
10. Elford A. Cederberg, R.*
11. Philip E. Ruppe, R.
12. James G. O'Hara, D.*
13. Charles C. Diggs, Jr., D.*
14. Lucien N. Nedzi, D.*
15. William D. Ford, D.*
16. John D. Dingell, D.*
17. Martha W. Griffiths, D.*
18. William S. Broomfield, R.*
19. Jack H. McDonald, R.

Minnesota

1. Albert H. Quie, R.*
2. Ancher Nelsen, R.*
3. Clark MacGregor, R.*
4. Joseph E. Karth, D.*
5. Donald M. Fraser, D.*
6. John M. Zwach, R.
7. Odin Langen, R.*
8. John A. Blatnik, D.*

Mississippi

1. Thomas G. Abernethy, D.*
2. Jamie L. Whitten, D.*
3. John Bell Williams, D.*
4. G. V. Montgomery, D.
5. William M. Colmer, D.*

Missouri

1. Frank M. Karsten, D.*
2. Thomas B. Curtis, R.*
3. Leonor K. (Mrs. John B.) Sullivan, D.*
4. Wm. J. Randall, D.*
5. Richard Bolling, D.*
6. W. R. Hull, Jr., D.*
7. Durward G. Hall, R.*
8. Richard H. Ichord, D.*
9. William L. Hungate, D.*
10. Paul C. Jones, D.*

Montana

1. Arnold Olsen, D.*
2. James F. Battin, R.*

Nebraska

1. Robert V. Denney, R.
2. Glenn C. Cunningham, R.*
3. David T. Martin, R.*

Nevada

(AL) Walter S. Baring, D.*

New Hampshire

1. Louis C. Wyman, R.
2. James C. Cleveland, R.*

New Jersey

1. John E. Hunt, R.
2. Charles W. Sandman, Jr., R.
3. James J. Howard, D.*
4. Frank Thompson, Jr., D.*
5. Peter H. B. Frelinghuysen, R.*
6. William T. Cahill, R.*
7. William B. Widnall, R.*
8. Charles S. Joelson, D.*
9. Henry Helstoski, D.*
10. Peter W. Rodino, Jr., D.*
11. Joseph G. Minish, D.*
12. Florence P. Dwyer, R.*
13. Cornelius E. Gallagher, D.*
14. Dominick V. Daniels, D.*
15. Edward J. Patten, D.*

New Mexico

(AL) Thomas G. Morris, D.*
(AL) E. S. Johnny Walker, D.*

New York

1. Otis G. Pike, D.*
2. James R. Grover, Jr., R.*
3. Lester L. Wolff, D.*
4. John W. Wydler, R.*
5. Herbert Tenzer, D.*
6. Seymour Halpern, R.*
7. Joseph P. Addabbo, D.*
8. Benjamin S. Rosenthal, D.*
9. James J. Delaney, D.*
10. Emanuel Celler, D.*
11. Frank J. Brasco, D.
12. Edna F. Kelly, D.*
13. Abraham J. Multer, D.*
14. John J. Rooney, D.*
15. Hugh L. Carey, D.*
16. John M. Murphy, D.*
17. Theodore Kupferman, R.*
18. Adam C. Powell, D.*
19. Leonard Farbstein, D.*
20. William F. Ryan, D.*
21. James H. Scheuer, D.*
22. Jacob H. Gilbert, D.*
23. Jonathan B. Bingham, D.*
24. Paul A. Fino, R.*
25. Richard L. Ottinger, D.*
26. Ogden R. Reid, R.*
27. John G. Dow, D.*
28. Joseph Y. Resnick, D.*
29. Daniel E. Button, Jr., R.
30. Carleton J. King, R.*
31. Robert C. McEwen, R.*
32. Alexander Pirnie, R.*
33. Howard W. Robison, R.*
34. James M. Hanley, D.*
35. Samuel S. Stratton, D.*
36. Frank Horton, R.*
37. Barber B. Conable, Jr., R.*
38. Charles E. Goodell, R.*
39. Richard D. McCarthy, D.*
40. Henry P. Smith III, R.*
41. Thaddeus J. Dulski, D.*

North Carolina

1. Walter B. Jones, D.*
2. L. H. Fountain, D.*
3. David N. Henderson, D.*
4. James C. Gardner, R.
5. Nick Galifianakis, D.
6. Horace R. Kornegay, D.*
7. Alton Asa Lennon, D.*
8. Charles Raper Jonas, R.*
9. James T. Broyhill, R.*
10. Basil L. Whitener, D.*
11. Roy A. Taylor, D.*

North Dakota

1. Mark Andrews, R.*
2. Thomas S. Kleppe, R.

Ohio

1. Robert A. Taft, Jr., R.
2. Donald D. Clancy, R.*
3. Charles W. Whalen, Jr., R.
4. William M. McCulloch, R.*
5. Delbert L. Latta, R.*
6. William H. Harsha, R.*
7. Clarence J. Brown, Jr., R.*
8. Jackson E. Betts, R.*
9. Thomas L. Ashley, D.*
10. Clarence E. Miller, R.
11. J. William Stanton, R.*
12. Samuel L. Devine, R.*
13. Charles A. Mosher, R.*
14. William H. Ayres, R.*
15. Chalmers P. Wylie, R.
16. Frank T. Bow, R.*
17. John M. Ashbrook, R.*
18. Wayne L. Hays, D.*
19. Michael J. Kirwan, D.*
20. Michael A. Feighan, D.*
21. Charles A. Vanik, D.*
22. Frances P. Bolton, R.*
23. William E. Minshall, R.*
24. Donald E. Lukens, R.

Oklahoma

1. Page Belcher, R.*
2. Ed Edmondson, D.*
3. Carl B. Albert, D.*
4. Tom Steed, D.*
5. John Jarman, D.*
6. James V. Smith, R.

Oregon

1. Wendell Wyatt, R.*
2. Al Ullman, D.*
3. Edith Green, D.*
4. John R. Dellenback, R.

Pennsylvania

1. William A. Barrett, D.*
2. Robert N. C. Nix, D.*
3. James A. Byrne, D.*
4. Joshua Eilberg, D.
5. William J. Green III, D.*
6. George M. Rhodes, D.*
7. Lawrence G. Williams, R.
8. Edward G. Biester, Jr., R.
9. G. Robert Watkins, R.*
10. Joseph M. McDade, R.*
11. Daniel J. Flood, D.*
12. J. Irving Whalley, R.*
13. Richard S. Schweiker, R.*
14. William S. Moorhead, D.*
15. Fred B. Rooney, D.*
16. Edwin D. Eshleman, R.
17. Herman T. Schneebeli, R.*
18. Robert J. Corbett, R.*
19. George A. Goodling, R.
20. Elmer J. Holland, D.*
21. John H. Dent, D.*
22. John P. Saylor, R.*
23. Albert W. Johnson, R.*
24. Joseph P. Vigorito, D.*
25. Frank M. Clark, D.*
26. Thomas E. Morgan, D.*
27. James G. Fulton, R.*

Rhode Island

1. Fernand J. St. Germain, D.*
2. Robert O. Tiernan, D.

South Carolina

1. L. Mendel Rivers, D.*
2. Albert W. Watson, R.*
3. W. J. Bryan Dorn, D.*
4. Robert T. Ashmore, D.*
5. Thomas S. Gettys, D.*
6. John L. McMillan, D.*

South Dakota

1. Benjamin Reifel, R.*
2. E. Y. Berry, R.*

Tennessee

1. James H. (Jimmy) Quillen,. R*
2. John J. Duncan, R.*
3. W. E. (Bill) Brock III, R.*
4. Joe L. Evins, D.*
5. Richard H. Fulton, D.*
6. William R. Anderson, D.*
7. Leonard Ray Blanton, D.
8. Robert A. Everett, D.*
9. Dan H. Kuykendall, R.

Texas

1. Wright Patman, D.*
2. John Dowdy, D.*
3. Joe R. Pool, D.*
4. Ray Roberts, D.*
5. Earle Cabell, D.*
6. Olin E. Teague, D.*
7. George H. W. Bush, R.
8. Robert C. Eckhardt, D.
9. Jack Brooks, D.*
10. J. J. Pickle, D.*
11. W. R. Poage, D.*
12. James C. Wright, Jr., D.*
13. Graham Purcell, D.*
14. John Young, D.*
15. Eligio de la Garza, D.*
16. Richard C. White, D.*
17. Omar Burleson, D.*
18. Robert D. Price, R.
19. George H. Mahon, D.*
20. Henry B. Gonzalez, D.*
21. O. C. Fisher, D.*
22. Robert R. Casey, D.*
23. Abraham Kazen, D.*

Utah

1. Laurence J. Burton, R.*
2. Sherman P. Lloyd, R.

Vermont

(AL) Robert T. Stafford, R.*

Virginia

1. Thomas N. Downing, D.*
2. Porter Hardy, Jr., D.*
3. David E. Satterfield III, D.*
4. Watkins M. Abbitt, D.*
5. William M. Tuck, D.*
6. Richard H. Poff, R.*
7. John O. Marsh, Jr., D.*
8. William L. Scott, R.
9. William C. Wampler, R.
10. Joel T. Broyhill, R.*

Washington

1. Thomas M. Pelly, R.*
2. Lloyd Meeds, D.*
3. Julia Butler Hansen, D.*
4. Catherine May, R.*
5. Thomas S. Foley, D.*
6. Floyd V. Hicks, D.*
7. Brock Adams, D.*

West Virginia

1. Arch A. Moore, Jr., R.*
2. Harley O. Staggers, D.*
3. John M. Slack, Jr., D.*
4. Ken Hechler, D.*
5. James Kee, D.*

Wisconsin

1. Henry C. Schadeberg, R.
2. Robert W. Kastenmeier, D.*
3. Vernon W. Thomson, R.*
4. Clement J. Zablocki, D.*
5. Henry S. Reuss, D.*
6. William A. Steiger, R.
7. Melvin R. Laird, R.*
8. John W. Byrnes, R.*
9. Glenn R. Davis, R.*
10. Alvin E. O'Konski, R.*

Wyoming

(AL) William Henry Harrison, R.

Puerto Rico

Resident Commissioner
Santiago Polanco-Abreu, D.*

Members of the United States Senate

The Senate of the 90th Congress consists of 64 Democrats and 36 Republicans, compared with 67 Democrats and 33 Republicans for the 89th Congress. Senators shown starting their terms in 1967 were elected for the first time in the Nov. 8, 1966, elections. Those shown ending their current terms in 1973 were re-elected to the Senate in the same balloting. The second date in each listing shows when the term of a previously elected Senator expires.

State	Term
Alabama	
Lister Hill, D.	1938–1969
John J. Sparkman, D.	1946–1973
Alaska	
E. L. "Bob" Bartlett, D.	1959–1973
Ernest Gruening, D.	1959–1969
Arizona	
Carl T. Hayden, D.	1927–1969
Paul J. Fannin, R.	1965–1971
Arkansas	
John L. McClellan, D.	1943–1973
J. William Fullbright, D.	1945–1969
California	
Thomas H. Kuchel, R.	1953–1969
George L. Murphy, R.	1965–1971
Colorado	
Gordon L. Allott, R.	1955–1973
Peter H. Dominick, R.	1963–1969
Connecticut	
Thomas J. Dodd, D.	1959–1971
Abraham A. Ribicoff, D.	1963–1969
Delaware	
John J. Williams, R.	1947–1971
J. Caleb Boggs, R.	1961–1973
Florida	
Spessard L. Holland, D.	1946–1971
George A. Smathers, D.	1951–1969
Georgia	
Richard B. Russell, D.	1933–1973
Herman E. Talmadge, D.	1957–1969
Hawaii	
Hiram L. Fong, R.	1959–1971
Daniel Ken Inouye, D.	1963–1969
Idaho	
Frank Church, D.	1957–1969
Len B. Jordan, R.	1962–1973
Illinois	
Everett M. Dirksen, R.	1951–1969
Charles H. Percy, R.	1967–1973
Indiana	
R. Vance Hartke, D.	1959–1971
Birch E. Bayh, D.	1963–1969
Iowa	
Bourke B. Hickenlooper, R.	1945–1969
Jack R. Miller, R.	1961–1973
Kansas	
Frank Carlson, R.	1950–1969
James B. Pearson, R.	1962–1973
Kentucky	
John Sherman Cooper, R.	1956–1973
Thruston B. Morton, R.	1957–1969

State	Term
Louisiana	
Allen J. Ellender, Sr., D.	1937–1973
Russell B. Long, D.	1948–1969
Maine	
Margaret Chase Smith, R.	1949–1973
Edmund S. Muskie, D.	1959–1971
Maryland	
Daniel B. Brewster, D.	1963–1969
Joseph D. Tydings, D.	1965–1971
Massachusetts	
Edward M. Kennedy, D.	1962–1971
Edward W. Brooke, R.	1967–1973
Michigan	
Philip A. Hart, D.	1959–1971
Robert P. Griffin, R.	1966–1973
Minnesota	
Eugene J. McCarthy, D.	1959–1971
Walter F. Mondale, D.	1964–1973
Mississippi	
James O. Eastland, D.	1943–1973
John Cornelius Stennis, D.	1947–1971
Missouri	
Stuart Symington, D.	1953–1971
Edward V. Long, D.	1960–1969
Montana	
Mike J. Mansfield, D.	1953–1971
Lee Metcalf, D.	1961–1973
Nebraska	
Roman Lee Hruska, R.	1954–1971
Carl T. Curtis, R.	1955–1973
Nevada	
Alan Bible, D.	1954–1969
Howard W. Cannon, D.	1959–1971
New Hampshire	
Norris Cotton, R.	1954–1969
Thomas J. McIntyre, D.	1962–1973
New Jersey	
Clifford P. Case, R.	1955–1973
Harrison A. Williams, Jr., D.	1959–1971
New Mexico	
Clinton P. Anderson, D.	1949–1973
Joseph M. Montoya, D.	1965–1971
New York	
Jacob K. Javits, R.	1957–1969
Robert F. Kennedy, D.	1965–1971
North Carolina	
Sam J. Ervin, Jr., D.	1954–1969
B. Everett Jordan, D.	1958–1973
North Dakota	
Milton R. Young, R.	1945–1969
Quentin N. Burdick, D.	1960–1971

State	Term
Ohio	
Frank J. Lausche, D.	1957–1969
Stephen M. Young, D.	1959–1971
Oklahoma	
A. S. Mike Monroney, D.	1951–1969
Fred R. Harris, D.	1965–1973
Oregon	
Wayne L. Morse, D.	1945–1969
Mark O. Hatfield, R.	1967–1973
Pennsylvania	
Joseph S. Clark, Jr., D.	1957–1969
Hugh D. Scott, Jr., R.	1959–1971
Rhode Island	
John O. Pastore, D.	1950–1971
Claiborne de Borda Pell, D.	1961–1973
South Carolina	
Strom Thurmond, R.	1956–1973
Ernest F. Hollings, D.	1967–1969
South Dakota	
Karl E. Mundt, R.	1948–1973
George S. McGovern, D.	1963–1969
Tennessee	
Albert A. Gore, D.	1953–1971
Howard Baker, Jr., R.	1967–1973
Texas	
Ralph W. Yarborough, D.	1957–1971
John G. Tower, R.	1961–1973
Utah	
Wallace F. Bennett, R.	1951–1969
Frank E. Moss, D.	1959–1971
Vermont	
George D. Aiken, R.	1941–1969
Winston L. Prouty, R.	1959–1971
Virginia	
Harry F. Byrd, Jr., D.	1966–1971
William B. Spong, Jr., D.	1967–1973
Washington	
Warren G. Magnuson, D.	1944–1969
Henry M. Jackson, D.	1953–1971
West Virginia	
Jennings Randolph, D.	1958–1973
Robert C. Byrd, D.	1959–1971
Wisconsin	
William Proxmire, D.	1957–1971
Gaylord A. Nelson, D.	1963–1969
Wyoming	
Gale W. McGee, D.	1959–1971
Clifford P. Hansen, R.	1967–1973

"Shine, Joe?"

In October, Congress authorized $170,000,000 for a two-year extension of aid to Appalachia, and in the same month, cut funds for rent subsidies and the model cities program in its $10,100,000,000 appropriation for the Department of Housing and Urban Development and 18 independent agencies. See CITY; HOUSING; POVERTY.

The Social Security proposals of the administration were adopted–with reductions and alterations. A request for a 15 per cent increase in benefits was reduced to 13 per cent, and stringent new controls on welfare payments were imposed in the final vote, which was taken on December 15. See SOCIAL SECURITY; SOCIAL WELFARE.

Other Legislation. In June, Congress authorized a four-year extension of the Selective Service Act in a compromise under which the President might draft 19-year-olds first but was not to institute a draft lottery without Congress's approval.

Emergency antistrike legislation was passed on three occasions at the President's request. On April 12 and again on May 2, the President signed joint resolutions of Congress delaying a nationwide railroad strike for 20 and 47 days, respectively. After the ban expired and after the six unions tired of waiting for a legislative solution, the nation's most extensive railroad strike since 1946 began. Two days later, on July 18, Congress passed and the President signed an emergency law ordering the strikers back to work for 90 days. A special board was to mediate the dispute and impose a settlement if no agreement could be reached. It was the first time that Congress had ordered a form of compulsory arbitration. See LABOR.

One of the President's consumer bills succeeded in passing in the final days of the session. The measure extended federal standards of inspection to all meat packing and processing plants selling entirely within states. The states were given two years to bring their systems in line with federal standards or have the U.S. Secretary of Agriculture impose federal inspection. See FOOD.

Among Other Bills approved were:

- The Air Quality Act of 1967, enacted on November 21. It authorized a three-year, $428,000,000 program to control air pollution. See CONSERVATION.
- Postal rate increases, to go into effect Jan. 8, 1968. First-class mail rates were raised from 5 cents to 6 cents, and air mail, from 8 cents to 10 cents. See POST OFFICE.
- Federal pay increases in three stages: Oct. 1, 1967; July 1, 1968; and July 1, 1969. The first year's increase would be about 5.6 per cent for 3,500,000 military personnel and between 4.5 per cent and 6 per cent for 2,000,000 civilian workers.
- A Vietnam veterans' Bill of Rights, extending a broad range of benefits to all veterans with at least 180 days of service since Jan. 31, 1955, the legal end of the Korean War. See VETERANS.
- Two measures to assure equal opportunity for women, both in federal civilian jobs and in the armed forces. See LABOR.
- The Public Broadcasting Act of 1967, enacted November 7. It established a nonprofit public corporation to aid noncommercial television and radio stations improve facilities, operations, and program quality. See RADIO; TELEVISION.
- The termination, on June 24, 1968, of the redemption of silver certificates for silver. See MONEY.

The First Veto of the 90th Congress came on August 12. President Johnson rejected a bill to raise life insurance for federal employees. It would have cost $61,000,000 the first year, against $13,000,000 in the administration's plan.

Problems of Ethics came to the fore in the 90th Congress. On March 1, the House voted 307 to 116 to exclude Adam Clayton Powell because of his alleged misuse of public funds. The Negro clergyman had represented the 18th District in New York City's Harlem since 1945. Powell swept a special congressional election in Harlem April 11 by a 7-to-1 margin, but he remained on the island of Bimini in the Caribbean, and his seat was left vacant throughout the first session of the 90th. On April 13, the House voted unanimously to set up an ethics committee to outline rules of acceptable conduct for its members and employees.

Similar problems arose in the Senate. In January, former Senate employee Robert "Bobby" Baker was convicted of larceny, conspiracy, and tax evasion and sentenced to 1 to 3 years in prison. In March, the Senate Ethics Committee opened its investigation of Senator Thomas J. Dodd (D., Conn.). On June 23, after lengthy hearings, the Senate voted 92 to 5 to censure Dodd for misuse of funds.

On October 25, the Ethics Committee cleared Senator Edward V. Long (D., Mo.) of charges of trying to use his committee's inquiry on wiretapping to help keep Teamsters Union chief James R. Hoffa out of jail. It said there had been no connection between Long's committee activities and payments from a Hoffa attorney. In November, the committee agreed to reopen the hearing because of new evidence. See Section Two, THE ECONOMICS OF POLITICS.

Leaders of the first session of the 90th Congress: *In the Senate:* Carl Hayden, Arizona, president *pro tempore*; Mike Mansfield, Montana, majority leader; Russell B. Long, Louisiana, majority whip. Everett M. Dirksen, Illinois, was minority leader; Thomas H. Kuchel, California, minority whip.

In the House, John W. McCormack, Massachusetts, was Speaker; Carl Albert, Oklahoma, majority leader; T. Hale Boggs, Louisiana, majority whip. Minority leader was Gerald R. Ford, Michigan; Leslie Arends, Illinois, minority whip. [CAROL L. THOMPSON]

See also DEMOCRATIC PARTY; REPUBLICAN PARTY; Section One, SYLVIA PORTER: FOCUS ON THE ECONOMY, JAMES B. RESTON: FOCUS ON THE NATION.

Where the Air Is Dirtiest

City	Ratings	City	Ratings
New York	457.5	Minneapolis-St. Paul	257
Chicago	422	Hartford	254.5
Philadelphia	404.5	Nashville	253
Los Angeles	393.5	San Francisco	253
Cleveland	390.5	Seattle	252.5
Pittsburgh	390	New Haven	246
Boston	389	York, Pa.	246
Newark	376.5	Springfield, Mass.	241
Detroit	370	Worcester	234.5
St. Louis	369	Houston	233.5
Akron	367.5	Memphis	232
Baltimore	355	Columbus, Ohio	231.5
Indianapolis	351	Richmond, Va.	230.5
Wilmington	342	San Jose	217.5
Louisville	338	Portland, Ore.	210.5
Jersey City	333.5	Syracuse	209
Washington	327.5	Atlanta	208
Cincinnati	325.5	Grand Rapids	204
Milwaukee*	301.5	Rochester, N.Y.	200.5
Canton	302	Reading, Pa.	196.5
Youngstown	294.5	Albany, N.Y.	187.5
Toledo	287	Dallas	178
Kansas City	285.5	New Orleans	160.5
Denver	280	Fort Worth	156.5
Bridgeport	261	San Diego	151.5
Providence	261	Miami	117
Buffalo	260	Wichita	102
Birmingham	259.5	Greensboro, N.C.	87

*Its air was judged dirtier than Canton's because of the inadequacy of sulfur dioxide data.

The U.S. Public Health Service ranked cities from 1 to 65 on each of eight air pollution factors. Maximum (worst) score possible: 520.

CONSERVATION in 1967 put increased emphasis on attacking the environmental problems of an urban society. President Lyndon B. Johnson keynoted this theme in his conservation message to Congress on Jan. 30, 1967. "The air and water grow heavier with the debris of our spectacular civilization," he said. Devoting the major part of his message to air pollution, he urged legislation to establish pollution limits that industrial plants could not exceed. Congress responded by enacting the Air Quality Act of 1967 in October. The legislation gives the federal government unprecedented power to cope with air pollution emergencies, even to the extent of halting traffic into cities and shutting down factories.

Most major conservation legislation, however, remained bogged down as the first session of the 90th Congress ended. Of President Johnson's four major new park proposals, a Redwood National Park in northern California, a North Cascades National Park in the state of Washington, and the Apostle Islands National Lakeshore in Wisconsin had been approved only by the Senate. Plans for a Potomac Valley National Park in Maryland, Virginia, and West Virginia had not been acted upon by either house. Approval of all four of these proposals was expected in the 1968 session.

Water

The growing world-wide concern with water use and conservation problems was demonstrated at the International Conference on Water for Peace in Washington, D.C., May 23 to 31. It was the largest international meeting ever held in the nation's capital. There were approximately 6,000 official delegates, water experts, and observers from 99 nations, including the United States. The conference was the first to cover all aspects of water resource conservation and development.

The administration dropped its support of the controversial Hualapai (formerly Bridge Canyon) and Marble Canyon dams on the Colorado River early in 1967. Conservationists had contended such dams would threaten the Grand Canyon. The Senate approved a damless Central Arizona Project, with power for pumping water out of the Colorado River to be supplied by a steam generating plant. The bill was pigeonholed by the House, however, largely as the result of opposition by California and Colorado Congressmen.

Later, in June, the administration appeared to have scuttled plans for another huge dam, the $2,000,000 Rampart Dam on the Yukon River in Alaska. The reservoir would have covered a wilderness area the size of the state of New Jersey. It had aroused strong opposition from conservation and fish and wildlife groups. Secretary of the Interior Stewart L. Udall proposed an Alaska Power Administration, which would develop lower cost hydro and thermal power projects.

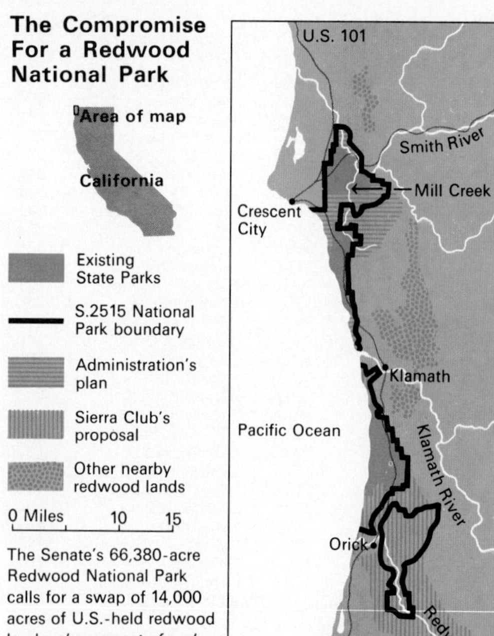

The Senate's 66,380-acre Redwood National Park calls for a swap of 14,000 acres of U.S.-held redwood lands, *shown east of park.* S.2515 was a compromise between the 43,434 acres in the administration's bill and the 90,000 acres of the Sierra Club's plan.

Antipollution Efforts were stepped-up under the Water Quality Act of 1965. By mid-year all 50 states had submitted proposals for water quality standards for their interstate and coastal waters to the Federal Water Pollution Control Administration. After review, standards for most of the states were approved.

Notable among water pollution enforcement actions in 1967, was a conference held at Buffalo, N.Y. The conference resulted in a far-reaching agreement among 54 municipalities and 80 industries on remedial action to save Lake Erie. See Section Two, THE KILLING OF A GREAT LAKE.

Desalination. On May 19, President Johnson signed a bill to authorize construction of the world's largest seawater desalting plant on a man-made island off southern California's Bolsa Chica State Park. The plant will use two nuclear reactors to produce 1,800,000 kilowatts of power and 150,000,000 gallons of fresh water per day. When the plant reaches full production, engineering estimates indicate the cost of desalting water will be 22 cents per thousand gallons.

On July 20, 1967, Key West, Fla., became the first U.S. city to get its fresh water from the sea. The $3,300,000 multistage, flash distillation plant can produce up to 2,620,000 gallons of fresh water a day at a cost of 85 cents per thousand gallons.

Losses from Floods in the United States increased substantially over 1966. There were four of

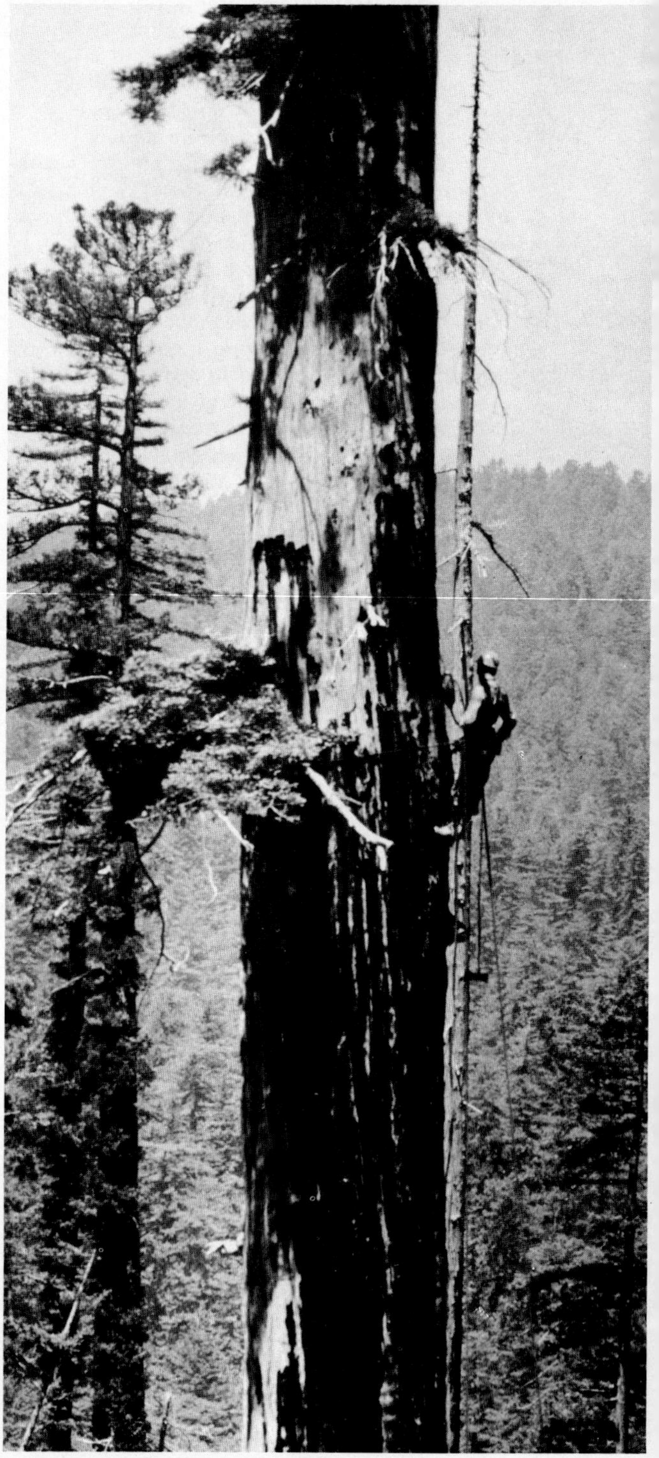

Redwood logging goes on outside the proposed National Park. Lumberman is rigging a pulley line to guide huge redwood's fall when it is cut.

Chicagoans got a breath of foul air after millions of dead alewives washed ashore.
Park district clean-up crews worked for days to rid the beaches of the fish.

such severity that they were declared major disaster areas by the President and received federal emergency relief. They occurred in the Ohio River basin in March, with damage of $35,000,000; in the Missouri River basin in June, with damage of $110,000,000; in the Fairbanks, Alaska, area in August, with damage of $178,000,000; and in southern Texas in September, caused by heavy rains from Hurricane *Beulah*. The rainfall exceeded 20 inches in several locations. The flooding caused damage estimated as high as $1,000,000,000. See DISASTERS.

Except for a few isolated pockets, streams and ground water levels in the Northeast returned to normal, and water experts declared that the drought of 1961 to 1965 was broken. Stream levels dropped to record lows in the Northwest, however.

Parks and Outdoor Recreation

The rising demand for outdoor recreation was demonstrated by the continuing increase in visitors to areas under the direction of the National Park Service. The record estimated total of 140,000,000 visits was an increase of almost 7,000,000 more than the revised 1966 total of 133,081,000. The Bureau of Outdoor Recreation reported that public participation in major outdoor recreation activities had increased by 51 per cent since 1960 and said the trend was accelerating. Congressional approval of new park and recreational facilities lagged, however. Proposals for nationwide systems of hiking trails and scenic rivers failed to be enacted (see FORESTRY AND FOREST PRODUCTS). Budgetary pressures created by the war in Vietnam were part of the reason.

To meet the challenges of the impact of our burgeoning population on conservation values, the National Audubon Society in October proposed an "environmental defense fund." The fund would be used to pay for conservation court battles whenever natural resources were threatened with permanent damage.

The Land and Water Conservation Fund, which provides money for federal and state acquisition of recreation lands, received about $235,000,000 from the sale of $7 "Golden Eagle" entrance permits and other fees in federal recreation areas and other sources in 1967. For the year started July 1, 1967, the fund apportioned $61,750,000 to states and territories to be used on a 50-50 matching basis for outdoor recreation projects.

Forests

The National Forest Service has reviewed about one-third of existing National Forest primitive areas and proposed their reclassification as Wilderness Areas under the Wilderness Act of 1964. One proposal, for a 142,722-acre San Rafael Wilderness in the Los Padres National Forest, in southern California, was transmitted to Congress Feb. 1, 1967.

Secretary of Agriculture Orville L. Freeman ordered a halt in logging June 1, 1967, in the 173,000-

acre Magruder Corridor, which lies between the Selway-Bitterroot Wilderness and Salmon River Breaks Primitive Area on the Montana-Idaho border. Altogether, these areas make up one of the vastest stretches of wilderness in the country. Conservationists had opposed logging operations because of fragile soil conditions on the steep slopes and the danger of silting of the clear waters of the Selway River. The Forest Service was to prepare a new integrated development plan that would protect all the values of the watershed.

Wildlife

A number of noteworthy efforts were made to protect rare and endangered animal species in 1967. The United States and Canada, for instance, took six whooping crane eggs from the wilds of northern Canada in early June for hatching at the Patuxent Wildlife Research Center near Laurel, Md. Four chicks survived in the experiment. The center is conducting pioneering research into how to raise and condition the cranes in captivity so that they can later be released into the wild and survive.

In March, 1967, Secretary Udall designated 78 species of U.S. wildlife as under the threat of extinction. It was the first list to be issued under the Endangered Species Preservation Act of 1966. It listed 36 birds, 22 fishes, 14 mammals, and 6 reptiles and amphibians. The ivory-billed woodpecker, which had been believed extinct, was added to the list. Three pairs of the large, showy birds had been sighted since December, 1966, in eastern Texas.

Federal Aid in Wildlife Restoration apportionments to states and territories totaled $23,533,000 for the year ending June 30, 1968. The projects included acquisition and development of land and water for wildlife refuges, sportsmen facilities, and research. Another $7,535,000 was apportioned for Federal Aid in Fish Restoration projects.

A nationwide program of monitoring pesticides in fish began in May. Samples, taken twice a year at 50 stations, will determine levels of chlorinated hydrocarbon insecticides in the fish. The program is one phase of a national program to determine levels in air, man, soil, water, and wildlife.

Soil Conservation

Organized soil conservation districts numbered 3,010 on June 30, 1967, a gain of 15 for the year. They covered 99 per cent of U.S. farms and ranches. Nearly 1,200,000 landowners were engaged in soil conservation practices.

Soil scientists report erosion can be greatly reduced in formerly tilled fields by halting the plowing, killing weeds with herbicides, and drilling seeds directly into the sod. Experiments in Ohio showed untilled plots yielded as much corn as plowed areas and reduced erosion 2.7 tons per acre.

Minerals and Fuels

For years, oil companies and others have had their eyes on the rich oil-bearing shale deposits in Colorado, Wyoming, and Utah. The 16,000-square-mile area is estimated to contain 2,000,000,000 barrels of oil, 70 times United States proved reserves. More than 80 per cent of the land is government-owned. The deposits are estimated to be worth five trillion dollars, once an economic means is found to extract the oil. In May, Udall proposed to lease 30,000 acres to private firms, with a limit of 5,120 acres to any one company, to encourage research and development. The proposal was hedged with restrictions to prevent windfall profits or land grabs.

Don Quixote

A long-term, nationwide program to restore lands "looted and ravished" by strip and surface mining was proposed in a report to Congress in July. The two-year study, "Surface Mining and Our Environment," submitted by Udall found that of the 3,200,000 acres affected by mining, 2,000,000 acres needed remedial treatment. West Virginia enacted one of the strictest strip-mining control laws in the nation in March. Effective July 1, 1967, it gave the state's director of natural resources sweeping power over all stripping operations and established a scale of stringent requirements. [ANDREW L. NEWMAN]

See also AGRICULTURE; FISHERY; HUNTING AND FISHING; MINES AND MINING; PETROLEUM AND GAS.

CONSTITUTION OF THE UNITED STATES. See CONGRESS OF THE UNITED STATES; PRESIDENT OF THE UNITED STATES; SUPREME COURT OF THE U.S.

COSTA RICA. See LATIN AMERICA.

COSTA E SILVA, ARTHUR DA (1902-), was inaugurated on March 15, 1967, as the 22nd president of Brazil. A retired army marshal and former minister of war, he was a leader in the 1964 military coup that ousted President João Goulart. He was elected without opposition by the Brazilian congress on Oct. 3, 1967, succeeding fellow army officer, General Humberto de Alencar Castelo Branco. Though Costa e Silva conducted a military government, he was more liberal than his predecessor. He continued the economic development program, and said he hoped, someday, to fully restore democracy.

The new president took on, with the cheerfulness that has been his nature throughout life, the problems of a land long plagued by dizzying inflation and widespread illiteracy.

Costa e Silva was born Oct. 3, 1902, in the small town of Taquara, where his father owned a general store. He was one of nine children. He attended his nation's military academy, Escola Militar do Realengo, graduating at the head of his class. He was an officer in the Brazilian Expeditionary Force in Italy in World War II, and was advanced to brigadier general in 1952, rising thereafter to major general and then to general.

A lifelong outdoorsman, the president is an accomplished swimmer and hiker. He and his wife Dona Iolanda have one son, Alcio, an army colonel, and four grandchildren. [WALTER F. MORSE]

COURTS AND LAWS. In a landmark decision in May, 1967, the Supreme Court of the United States ruled 8 to 1 that juvenile offenders were entitled to the same constitutional protection afforded adults. A 58-page opinion written by Associate Justice Abe Fortas, ruled that juveniles involved in delinquency cases had the right to: (1) notice of the charge against them; (2) adequate warning against self-incrimination and of the right to remain silent; (3) a lawyer, appointed by the court, if necessary, in any case in which incarceration might result; (4) cross-examination of complainants and witnesses; (5) a transcript of the proceedings; and (6) retrial in a higher court.

In another far-reaching decision, the Supreme Court ruled 7 to 1 on December 18 that electronic eavesdropping may improperly invade a person's right to privacy even if there is no form of physical trespass. Specifically, the evidence obtained from incriminating telephone calls made by a gambler from a "bugged" public telephone booth was held by the Court to be inadmissable.

In a key case, an all-white jury in a Mississippi federal court convicted seven out of 15 defendants accused of participating in a Ku Klux Klan plot that resulted in the slaying of two New York City civil rights workers and a Meridian, Miss., Negro in 1964. A Mississippi federal judge, W. Harold Cox, presided over the trial, held in October, and approved the verdicts, said to be the first for a civil rights slaying in Mississippi.

Significant Acts and Laws of 1967 included the announcement by Attorney General Ramsey Clark of a $99,177 federal grant under the Law Enforcement Assistance Act of 1965 to the Vera Institute of Justice of New York City for a demonstration project in which destitute alcoholics in New York City would be treated rather than prosecuted.

In addition, Congress passed a Narcotic Addict Rehabilitation Act which provided for civil commitment of people charged with narcotic addiction. An earlier state law, New York's narcotic Addiction Control Law, which became effective April 1, provided for involuntary civil commitment and treatment of addicts who use opium or similar drugs.

In the case of Paul James, which came before the New York state supreme court in August, the court held portions of the law violated the principle in the *Miranda vs. Arizona* case, which limited police questioning of accused persons, and deprived a sick addict of his constitutional rights. In December, the appellate division reversed the case, and it went to New York's highest court, the Court of Appeals.

Legal Advice for the Poor. In March, 1967, President Lyndon B. Johnson expressed his intention to establish a Legal Service Center in every indigent community to prosecute those guilty of charging excessive prices and dealing in unfair credit practices.

Supreme Court Appointment. The appointment on June 13 of U.S. Solicitor General Thurgood Marshall, 59, as an Associate Justice of the Supreme Court of the United States to fill the vacancy left by the retirement of Tom C. Clark, placed the first Negro on the highest court in the land. See MARSHALL, THURGOOD.

The American Bar Association (ABA) held its annual meeting in Honolulu, Hawaii, in August. Resolutions passed by some 6,000 lawyers at the meeting called for massive policing to stop and prevent rioting, and for a policy of firmness but not of vindictiveness in dealing with those arrested. The ABA also approved a new New York law, which authorized supervised law students to appear in court on behalf of indigent criminal defendants. A panel of lawyers, judges, and law professors was appointed by the ABA to formulate guidelines for law enforcement authorities in dealing with legal problems resulting when hundreds or thousands are arrested within a few hours for acts of civil disobedience.

World Law. The third World Peace Through Law Conference, held in Geneva, Switzerland, in July, brought together 16,000 high court judges and leading officers from more than 100 nations. They approved 30 resolutions designed to develop international law for world peace. [FANNIE J. KLEIN]

See also CIVIL RIGHTS; CONGRESS OF THE UNITED STATES; MENTAL HEALTH; STATE GOVERNMENT; SUPREME COURT OF THE UNITED STATES.

CRIME. The official report of the President's 19-member Commission on Law Enforcement and Administration of Justice, published on Feb. 6, 1967, revealed the results of an 18-month study of crime in the United States. Titled *The Challenge of Crime in a Free Society*, the 308-page report called for "sweeping and costly changes in the administration" of corrective institutions throughout the country.

The commission concluded that crime could be reduced only if seven objectives were vigorously pursued: (1) emphasis on crime prevention, (2) development of new ways of dealing with offenders, (3) elimination of unfairness and existing injustices in the courts, (4) attracting more effective personnel, (5) more research, (6) more money, and (7) the acceptance by all Americans of the responsibility for change.

In all, the commission made more than 200 specific recommendations, ranging from general positions on capital punishment and the invasion of privacy to controversial demands for birth control programs and a guaranteed annual family income.

Increase in Crime. In August, the Federal Bureau of Investigation (FBI) reported an 11 per cent increase in serious crimes in the United States from 1965 to 1966. The risk of becoming a victim of a serious crime increased 10 per cent in 1966, reaching almost two victims for every 100 persons. Arrests of juveniles for serious crimes had increased more than 50 per cent since 1960. The greatest increases in juvenile crimes were: aggravated assault, 115 per cent; larceny, 66 per cent; robbery, 55 per cent; and auto theft, 48 per cent. Of persons arrested for serious crimes during 1967, nearly half were under 18 years of age. The problem of the juvenile offender, said the FBI and the President's National Crime Commission, had reached staggering proportions. Further, in an epoch-making decision, the Supreme Court of the United States ruled, in May, that juveniles are protected by the Bill of Rights of the U.S. Constitution and have the same rights, when arrested, or as defendants in juvenile proceedings, as adults (see COURTS AND LAWS; SUPREME COURT OF THE UNITED STATES).

Arrests and Convictions. Albert DeSalvo, 35, the self-confessed "Boston Strangler," escaped from the Bridgewater State Hospital in February, a month after he was sentenced to life imprisonment. His escape triggered an enormous manhunt, and DeSalvo was quietly recaptured several days later.

Robert "Bobby" G. Baker, 38, one-time secretary to the Democratic majority in the Senate, was convicted in January on seven counts of conspiracy to defraud the government, income tax evasion, and theft in the federal courts in Washington, D.C. He was sentenced in April to seven 1-to-3 year terms, to run concurrently.

Edgar Labat, 44, and Clifton Poret, 38, were ordered released from a Louisiana prison in May by a federal court after spending 14 years in "death row." The court ruled that the men, both Negroes, were denied a fair trial due to exclusion of Negroes from the Louisiana jury system. Labat and Poret, convicted in 1953 of a 1950 rape of a white woman, were immediately rearrested, however, on an indictment stemming from the original charge.

In California, the execution in April of Aaron Mitchell for the 1963 slaying of a Sacramento, Calif., policeman was the first use of the gas chamber since January, 1963.

Art Treasures worth $6,000,000 were stolen in January from the Gallery of Durwich College in South London, England. The theft was believed to be the largest in history. It included three paintings by Rembrandt and three by Rubens. The police, acting on an anonymous telephone call, recovered the works of art within a week.

Major Crimes. Nearly $1,000,000 was taken from the Venezuela International Airways in April. In May, in Curaçao, Netherlands Antilles, four men were arrested for possessing 14 1/2 gold bars believed to be part of the airlines theft. Also in May, three masked men with machine guns had waited inside a closed bank in Brockton, Mass., for the arrival of a Brinks armored car. Ambushing the crew, they escaped with $630,000 in cash. In nearby Quincy, a month earlier, another armored car had been looted of some $200,000 in cash and $400,000 in checks.

In Montreal, Que., four gunmen waylaid employees of Brinks, Inc., who were collecting department store receipts. They escaped with $400,000, $300,000 of which was recovered a week later. In London, England, in May, a gang hijacked an armored car belonging to N. M. Rothschild & Sons and stole 144 gold bars worth over $2,000,000.

Mass Slayings. Richard Franklin Speck, arrested in 1966 for the Chicago slayings of eight student nurses, was sentenced, in June, to die in the electric chair.

In August, at Shell Lake, Saskatchewan, nine members of the Peterson family were found murdered. The killer spared only a 4-year-old girl.

In Lock Haven, Penn., in October, Leo Held, 39, and the father of four, was killed by police after he had killed six friends and wounded six others at a paper mill where he worked.

An Arizona county superior court, in October, found Robert Benjamin Smith, 19, guilty of five counts of murder in the November, 1966, slaying of four women and a child in a Mesa, Ariz., beauty school. Smith was sentenced to death after a 32-day trial.

In November, a New York City grand jury indicted Donald Ramsey, a 26-year-old black nationalist, and Thomas Dennis, 26, an East Village hippie known to his friends as "Groovy," on charges of slaying a teen-aged Connecticut girl and her boy friend at an East Village party. [JOSEPH D. LOHMAN]

Cuba's Fidel Castro and Soviet Premier Aleksei Kosygin converse through an interpreter, *left*, during a meeting of the two Communist leaders in Havana.

CUBA. Premier Fidel Castro marked his ninth year in power more firmly in command than ever before. Through trade with various U.S. allies, Cuba was able to buy bulldozers, graders, heavy-duty trucks, and a multimillion-dollar fertilizer plant, as well as ships, cattle breeding stock, and other items important to the economy. They were purchased largely on credit, the suppliers apparently believing that the Soviet Union would underwrite Cuba's debts.

Meanwhile, the sugar crop reached 6,128,287 tons in 1967. Although it was the third largest harvest in the island's history, it fell far short of the 7,500,000 projected total. The Latin-American Solidarity Organization met in Havana from July 28 to August 5. Attended by delegates from Latin-American Communist parties and guerrilla movements, it called for the seizure of power through armed struggle in the Western Hemisphere. The meeting was rocked, however, by a Cuban proposal condemning the Soviet Union's economic policy in the Western Hemisphere, thus disclosing a split between the Soviet-oriented revolutionary parties in Latin America and advocates of the Cuban-supported revolutionary movements. [MARY C. WEBSTER]

Facts in Brief. Population: 8,060,000. Government: President Osvaldo Dorticos Torrado; Premier Fidel Castro. Monetary Unit: peso (1 = U.S. $1). Foreign Trade: exports, $686,000,000; imports, $865,000,000. Principal Exports: sugar, chemicals, tobacco.

CYPRUS. An uneasy peace between Greek and Turkish Cypriots was shattered by a bitter clash in November. As a result, the neighboring nations of Greece and Turkey–each a determined protector of its ethnic groups on the island–nearly plunged the Middle East into war. See GREECE; TURKEY.

The primary cause of the confrontation was the presence in Cyprus of Greek and Turkish troops in numbers beyond those authorized under a United Nations (UN)-sponsored truce of 1964. Tension mounted over the succeeding years as the clandestine troop build-ups progressed. On Nov. 15, 1967, it reached a climax in the village of Aghia Theodoros where a clash resulted in the death of 24 Turkish and two Greek Cypriots. The fighting quickly spread.

Turkey immediately threatened to intervene militarily unless the shooting ceased and Greece agreed to a bilateral reduction of troop strength on the island. Turkish air and ground forces were alerted and naval units were prepared for an invasion of Cyprus. War was averted, however, by the diplomatic intercessions of the United States, the UN, and the North Atlantic Treaty Organization. See NORTH ATLANTIC TREATY ORGANIZATION (NATO).

Facts in Brief. Population: 604,000. Government: President Archbishop Makarios. Monetary Unit: pound (1 = U.S. $2.40). Foreign Trade: exports, $77,000,000; imports, $158,000,000. Principal Exports: copper, fruits and nuts, potatoes.

CZECHOSLOVAKIA. Tensions between the regime and the intellectuals increased following a writers congress held in July, 1967. The prominent novelist, Ludwick Vaculik, denounced the regime's abuse of power and criticized its failures. Other writers censured Czech propaganda against Israel during the war in the Middle East (see MIDDLE EAST). The final resolution called for reduction of censorship and a modification of the new press law.

Government Crackdown. Repeated speeches by President Antonín Novotny and party ideologist Jiri Hendrych both criticized the dissidents and defended the party's leadership. The weekly journal of the writers union, *Literarni Noviny*–which had become an organ of dissent–was placed under the ministry of culture and information. Vaculik and others were expelled from the party. Another writer, Jan Procházka, lost his seat on the Central Committee after writing a tribute to Thomas G. Masaryk, who died mysteriously in 1948. Jan Benes, another author, was charged with providing information to émigrés in Paris. He was sentenced to serve five years in prison.

The so-called "new economic model" went into effect on January 1, but with serious modifications that reduced its radical character and caused misgivings among its most ardent supporters. The reform was hampered by the general weakness of the economy and its success or failure could only be determined later. Meanwhile, Central Committee meetings were devoted to such specific problems as inflation and living standards. A reorganization of agriculture was effected through the establishment of district associations that united collective and state farms and other agricultural enterprises.

Loyal to Moscow. In foreign policy, Czechoslovakia continued a loyal partner of the Soviet Union, supporting its attitude toward Chinese Communism, Vietnam, and the war in the Middle East. The Czechoslovak regime outdid itself in propaganda against Israeli "aggression" and severed diplomatic relations with Israel. President Novotny made his usual trip to the Soviet Union and also visited Yugosolvia, Poland, and Canada.

During the year, Czech relations with West Germany improved with the creation of trade missions. Yielding to East German pressure, Prague did not establish diplomatic relations with Bonn. It did, however, conclude a 20-year alliance with Poland and East Germany. [H. GORDON SKILLING]

Facts in Brief. Population: 14,412,000. Government: President and Communist Party First Secretary Antonín Novotny; Premier Josef Lenart. Monetary Unit: koruna (16.20=U.S. $1). Foreign Trade: exports, $2,745,000,000; imports, $2,729,000,000. Principal Exports: machinery, fuels, consumer goods.

DAHOMEY. See AFRICA.

DAIRYING. See AGRICULTURE.

DALLAS gave the country an example of democracy in 1966 and 1967, when 6,380 persons attended 33 meetings to discuss a citywide "Goals for Dallas" program. The goals were listed by Mayor John Erik Jonsson in February. Under the urging of a 1,000-member citizens committee, voters approved a massive $175,000,000 bond program in August. Divided into 14 separate issues, most of the bond program passed by 2-to-1 margins.

Of the sum, $38,000,000 will go for a new city hall, a plaza and underground garage, and a needed expansion of the Memorial Auditorium. The most controversial issue–that allowing land purchase for the huge regional airport to serve both Dallas and Fort Worth–passed easily. Final plans for the jetport, to cost an eventual $250,000,000, were publicly announced in October.

Growth and prosperity were shown in the city's rising employment figures. In May, the Dallas area work force exceeded 600,000 for the first time. A shortage of office space pushed up the schedule of the $41,000,000 One Main Plaza, the largest part of Main Place, a privately financed, multilevel $120,000,000 project. In August, work began on a $19,000,000 federal center. Construction started in September on an $8,500,000 building to contain offices, a motel, and a theater, to be built next to Main Place. [DONALD W. LIEF]

DAM. See BUILDING AND CONSTRUCTION.

DANCING. The outstanding feature of 1967 was New York City's spring season. New York City Ballet and American Ballet Theatre appeared at New York State Theater, overlapping the six-week stay of Britain's Royal Ballet next door, at the Metropolitan Opera House. All three companies won high critical acclaim–and did excellent business–in a season that lasted from March 28 to June 4.

New York City Ballet enjoyed its greatest success in years with George Balanchine's *Jewels.* American Ballet Theatre became the first U.S. company to perform the full-length Petipa-Ivanov *Swan Lake,* staged by David Blair, premier danseur of the Royal Ballet. From the Ballet Theatre's own ranks came a promising new choreographer, Eliot Feld, who was acclaimed for his first ballet, *Harbinger.* Feld's second ballet, to Gustav Mahler's *Rückert Songs,* was given its world première during the company's fall season at New York City Center. The Rockefeller Foundation granted $5,000 to pay for rehearsals. The National Council on the Arts and Humanities gave a matching grant of $195,000 to help support the company's tour during the year.

Guest Artists. Carla Fracci, prima ballerina of La Scala Theater, Milan, Italy, made her New York debut, dancing *Giselle, La Sylphide,* and *Romeo and Juliet pas de deux* as guest artist of the American Ballet Theatre. The choreographer for *Romeo and Juliet* was the great Danish star, Erik Bruhn, who was her partner in all three works.

Dame Margot Fonteyn and Rudolf Nureyev proved as potent box office magic as ever during the transcontinental tour of the Royal Ballet. In July, they created a sensation off-stage when they were held in a police station overnight following their arrest in a raid on a hippie pad in San Francisco's Haight-Ashbury district. The Royal Ballet proved itself a great company, however, even without its glamour stars. Anthony Dowell, especially, became a new favorite, scoring in *Shadowplay,* Antony Tudor's first important ballet in many years.

New York City Ballet performed two separate short seasons at the Wilfrid Pelletier Theatre in Montreal, Que., as part of Expo 67. The second season substituted for the Russian Festival, which was canceled by the Soviet government as a political gesture following the Arab-Israeli war. In August, New York City Ballet also sent 24 dancers to the Edinburgh Festival in a repertoire selected to emphasize its choreography to Igor Stravinsky's music. It was the hit of the festival.

City Center Joffrey Ballet had spring and fall seasons at New York City Center. The spring season was distinguished by the company's remarkable revival of the 1932 Kurt Jooss antiwar ballet, *The Green Table,* and the fall season by Robert Joffrey's *Astarte,* the first mixed-media ballet. Performed with pulsating lights, mod music, and a wild film, *Astarte* was a psychedelic *pas de deux.* The company appeared

Margot Fonteyn and Rudolf Nureyev were the star-crossed lovers in Kenneth MacMillan's *Romeo and Juliet* during the Royal Ballet's tour of the United States.

from June 27 to July 2 at Stanford University's summer Festival of the Arts, and was asked to return in 1968. It also had a two-month summer residence in Tacoma, Wash., sponsored by Pacific Northwest Ballet Association, which received a $25,000 matching grant from the National Foundation on the Arts and Humanities. Its stay at Tacoma was the first in a five-year plan that called for rehearsal periods, scholarship programs, and performances, including a week at the Seattle Opera House.

Manhattan Festival Ballet established its headquarters off Broadway at the Theatre 80 St. Marks, where it danced each Monday from Nov. 21, 1966, through 1967. It is a pleasant but not yet distinguished group. Ron Sequoio, artistic director, is its principal choreographer and a leading dancer.

The Martha Graham Dance Company appeared at the Mark Hellinger Theatre on Broadway from February 21 to March 12. The program included the première of Miss Graham's latest work, *Hecuba*.

After three years of extensive touring in the United States and abroad, the Harkness Ballet made its New York debut with a three-week season at the Broadway Theatre in November. It displayed a dazzlingly talented group of dancers.

Festivals. Jacob's Pillow held its 35th annual summer Dance Festival at Lee, Mass. The American Dance Festival, at Connecticut College, New London, Conn., celebrated its 20th anniversary with performances by the Martha Graham and the José Limón companies. For the occasion, Miss Graham repeated her *Diversion of Angels*, which was given its première at the first festival in 1948. Limón followed suit with his *Moor's Pavane*, which was first offered at the second festival.

Donald McKayle's evening-length *Black New World*, first presented at the 92nd Street YM-YWHA in New York City on February 8, was triumphantly performed at the Edinburgh Festival and then for a three-week season in London.

Awards. Paul Taylor, modern dancer and choreographer, won the 1967 Capezio Award. Alvin Ailey won the Grand Prix Italia, considered Europe's most important television award. He created a ballet, *Riedaiglia*, for Swedish television. The ballet got its title from the names of composer Georg Riedel, producer Lars Egler, and Ailey. Both Taylor and Ailey toured with their companies abroad. They were sponsored by the Cultural Presentations Program of the U.S. Department of State. Maria Tallchief of the New York City Ballet received the 1967 Indian Achievement Award.

Two important books were published in 1967. These were Walter Sorell's *Dance Through the Ages* (Grosset & Dunlap) and Anatole Chujoy's and P. W. Manchester's *Dance Encyclopedia* (Simon and Schuster). Lillian Moore, considered America's leading dance historian, died of cancer in New York City on July 28. [P. W. MANCHESTER]

DAVIS, DAVID BRION (1927-), American historian and teacher, won the 1967 Pulitzer prize in general nonfiction for his book, *The Problem of Slavery in Western Culture*, an introduction to a projected multivolume history of antislavery movements. The initial volume dealt with the slavery controversy in Western society from ancient times to the 1770s. Professor Davis' broad conclusion was that slavery created prejudice in society, rather than vice versa. He also noted that, throughout history, slavery stemmed more from a need for cheap labor than from racial feelings.

David Davis was born in Denver, Colo., the only son of the late Clyde Brion Davis, a novelist, and Martha Wirt Davis, a well-known mystery writer. He received a B.A. degree from Dartmouth College, where he was Phi Beta Kappa, in 1950; and M.A. and Ph.D. degrees from Harvard University in 1953 and 1956.

Davis taught a year at Dartmouth College before joining the faculty of Cornell University as an assistant professor in 1954. He was a Guggenheim fellow in 1958 and 1959, and became a full professor of history at Cornell in 1963.

His previous works include *Homicide in American Fiction, 1798-1860* (1957), and an article, "The Movement to Abolish Capital Punishment," which appeared in the *American Historical Review*. In 1967, he taught in India on a Fulbright grant.

DAYAN, MOSHE (1915-), a native Israeli, was appointed his nation's defense minister on June 1, 1967, after offering an elaborate plan to meet looming hostilities with neighboring Arab states. He then led his forces to military victory in the six-day war, from June 5 through 10.

Dayan insisted that Israel hold most of the conquered territory as vital to national security. For the 1,000,000 Arabs suddenly placed under Israeli rule, he set up an "occupation without administration," with Arab officials retaining their jobs.

Dayan was born May 20, 1915, in Deganiya, a communal farm in the Jordan Valley. He attended the agricultural high school at Nahalal. At the age of 12, he became a village guard. The black plastic eyepatch that distinguishes him dates from 1942, in World War II, when gunfire slammed his field glasses into his eye. By 1948, in Israel's war for independence, Dayan had risen to lieutenant colonel. He was army chief of staff from 1953 to 1958, leading Israeli forces in the Sinai war of 1957.

His interests range beyond the military to agriculture and archaeology. From 1959 to 1964, he was minister of agriculture, and his home is crowded with artifacts from bygone eras.

Dayan and his wife, the former Ruth Schwarz, have a daughter, Mrs. Yael Sion, 28, an author; and two sons, Ehod, 25, and Assaf, 21. Both sons and the son-in-law are army officers. [WALTER F. MORSE]

Konrad Adenauer, chancellor of West Germany until 1963, died at the age of 91.

Francis Cardinal Spellman, Archbishop of New York, died in New York, Dec. 2.

Paul Muni, who was the s ır of a movie about Pasteur, won many screen awards.

DEATHS OF NOTABLE PERSONS in 1967 included those listed below. An asterisk (*) means the person has a biography in *The World Book Encyclopedia*. Persons listed were Americans unless otherwise indicated.

***Adenauer, Konrad** (1876-Apr. 19), first Chancellor of the West German Federal Republic (1949-1963), led his country through reconstruction after World War II to economic prosperity. See GERMANY.

Andrews, La Verne (1915-May 8), was the oldest member of the Andrews Sisters singing trio. She, Maxene, and Patty came to fame with their recording of the Yiddish song "Bie Mir Bist du Schoen" in 1937. They appeared in films, and on radio and television.

***Angell, Sir Norman** (1872-Oct. 7), English author of *The Great Illusion*, on the futility of war, was awarded the Nobel peace prize for 1933.

***Attlee, Clement Richard** (1883-Oct. 8), EARL ATTLEE, British Labour party leader (1935-1955), served as prime minister of Great Britain (1945-1951). His government nationalized various industries, and established extensive health and welfare services.

Auer, Misha (1905-Mar. 5), Russian-born character actor and comedian, came to fame in *My Man Godfrey* (1935). His other film successes include *You Can't Take It With You*, *Destry Rides Again*, and *Brewster's Millions*.

Aymé, Marcel (1902-Oct. 14), French novelist and playwright, also wrote essays and short stories. *La Tableaux-Crevés* (1929), about peasant life, established his literary reputation. *The Green Mare* novel was filmed. *The Transient Hour* is about Paris under the Germans, *The Barkeep of Blémont*, about a postwar village, and *The Miraculous Barber*, a satire on modern French life. Aymé's plays include *Clérambard* (Paris, 1950, New York, 1957) and *Moonbirds* (1959).

Barnes, Margaret Ayer (1886-Oct. 25), was awarded the Pulitzer fiction prize (1931) for *Years of Grace*. Her other novels include *Within This Present* and *Edna. His Wife. Jenny*, *Dishonored Lady* (plays written with Edward Sheldon), and *The Age of Innocence* were produced on Broadway.

***Barton, Bruce** (1886-July 5), a founder and executive of Batten, Barton, Durstine & Osborne advertising agency, was known for *The Man Nobody Knows* and other books on religious faith. He was a Republican U.S. Representative from New York (1937-1941).

Bickford, Charles A. (1889-Nov. 9), ranch master in "The Virginian" television series for the past several years, was a Broadway actor before going to Hollywood. He starred in the film *Dynamite* (1929). Movies in which he played outstanding supporting roles include *Johnny Belinda*, *The Farmer's Daughter*, and *The Song of Bernadette*.

Bracci, Francesco Cardinal (1879-Mar. 24), a Vatican authority on canon law, was elevated to the Sacred College of Cardinals in 1958.

Bullitt, William Christian (1891-Feb. 15), the first U.S. Ambassador to Soviet Russia (1933-1936), was U.S. Ambassador to France (1936-1940). Bullitt, had also attended the Versailles peace conference as an ad viser to President Woodrow Wilson.

***Burchfield, Charles Ephraim** (1893-Jan. 10), watercolorist, painted nature, rural, small-town, and industrial scenes. *The Sphinx and the Milky Way* represents his later paintings of the seasons.

Burlingame, (William) Roger (1889-Mar. 19), author of such books as *Benjamin Franklin: The First Mr. America*, *Whittling Boy: The Story of Eli Whitney*, *Henry Ford*, and *Backgrounds of Power*, also wrote short stories, verse, and novels.

Burliuk, David (1882-Jan. 15), a founder of the Futurist art movement in Russia (1911) and the De Blaue Reiter movement (with Picasso and others) in Germany, produced numerous oil, water-color, and pastel paintings in the United States.

Burnette, "Smiley" Lester Alvin (1911-Feb. 16), who appeared in Western pictures with Gene Autry, also made films with Roy Rogers. He wrote "Mama Don't Allow No Music Played Here," and many other songs, and appeared on radio and television.

Cardijin, Joseph Cardinal (1882-July 25), founder of the international Young Christian Workers (Jeunesse Ouvrièce Chrêtienne, 1925, in his native Belgium), was elevated to the Sacred College of Cardinals in 1965.

Carnera, Primo (1906-June 29), Italian-born boxer, won the world heavyweight championship title from Jack Sharkey on June 29, 1933, and lost it to Max Baer on June 14, 1934.

Cellini, Renato (1912-Mar. 25), Italian-born conductor and general director of the New Orleans (La.) Opera Association since 1954, founded the Experimental Opera Theatre of America in 1955.

Charoux, Siegfried Joseph (1896-Apr. 26), Austrian-born sculptor, worked in stone, terra cotta, and bronze. His work includes *The Islanders* for the Festival of Britain (1950-1951), stone carvings (two groups) on Liverpool's Exchange Buildings, and *Civilization: The Judge* in London's Tate Gallery, and many memorials and other works in Vienna.

Christophoros II (1876-July 23), Eastern Orthodox Patriarch and Pope of Alexandria and All Africa since 1939, was ordained in 1905. He was born in Greece.

Cluytens, André (1905-June 3), Belgian-born opera and symphony conductor, was opera conductor at Antwerp's Theátre Royal Français (1927-1932). He later conducted at the Opéra-Comique and was musical director of the Paris Opéra. Cluytens appeared with major European orchestras.

Clyde, Andy (1892-May 18), Scottish-born actor, starred in silent comedies and later played in such films as *McFadden's Flats*, *Annie Oakley*, *Abe Lincoln in Illinois*, and the early Hopalong Cassidy pictures.

***Cockcroft, Sir John Douglas** (1897-Sept. 18), English nuclear physicist, shared the 1951 Nobel physics prize with Ernest T. S. Walton. They were cited as the first to split atoms artificially.

Copello, James Louis Cardinal (1880-Feb. 9), Chancellor of the Roman Catholic Church since 1959 and former Archbishop of Buenos Aires, was the first Argentine prelate elevated (1935) to the Sacred College of Cardinals.

Dante, Enrico Cardinal (1884-Apr. 24), Vatican Prefect of Pontifical Ceremonies, was elevated to the Sacred College of Cardinals in 1965.

Darwell, Jane (1880?-Aug. 13), who played mother, grandmother, and housekeeper roles in many films, won a Motion Picture Academy award (1940) for her role as Ma Joad in *The Grapes of Wrath*. She last played the Bird Woman in *Mary Poppins* (1963).

Davis, Watson (1896-June 27), pioneered in the popularization of science. He served with Science Service news agency as managing editor (1921-1933) and director (1933-1966). Davis was editor of the agency's *Science News Letter* magazine (1922-1966), and director of Science Clubs of America since 1941, of Westinghouse Science Talent Search since 1942, and of National Science Fair International since 1949.

Denny, Reginald (1891-June 16), English actor, played Colonel Pickering in *My Fair Lady* (Broadway, 1958-1959). His many films include the *Bulldog Drummond* pictures, *Around the World in 80 Days*, and *Mr. Blandings Builds His Dream House*.

Dibelius, Otto Friedrich Karl (1880-Jan. 31), known for his defiance of the Nazis and the Communists, was Lutheran Bishop of Berlin and Brandenburg (1945-1966) and a founder and head of the All-German Evangelical Church Council (1949-1961).

Donath, Ludwig (1900?-Sept. 29), Austrian-born actor, played the cantor-father in *The Al Jolson Story* and *Jolson Sings Again*; Hitler's double in *The Strange Death of Adolf Hitler*; and a Gestapo agent in *Hostages*, all films. He also was a stage and television actor.

Dunn, James (1905-Sept. 3), came to fame in *Bad Girl* (1931), played in *Stand Up and Cheer* (1934) and other Shirley Temple pictures, and won the Motion Picture Academy best supporting-actor award as Johnny Nolan in *A Tree Grows in Brooklyn* (1946). He also appeared in many stage and television plays.

***Duryea, J. Frank** (1869-Feb. 15), with his brother Charles E. (1861-1938), built the first successful gasoline-powered automobile in America. Their one-cylinder model made a trial run in 1893 in Springfield, Mass. Their second model car won the Chicago-Evanston, Ill., Thanksgiving Day race in 1895, the first such race in the United States.

Duvivier, Julien (1896-Oct. 29), French film director, had among his international successes *The Little World of Don Camillo*, *Pépé le Moko*, and *The End of a Day*. His British film, *Anna Karenina*, starred the late Vivien Leigh. American pictures include *The Great Waltz* and *Tales of Manhattan*.

***Eddy, Nelson** (1901-Mar. 6), baritone, with the late Jeanette MacDonald, won fame in such films as *Naughty Marietta* and *I Married an Angel*. He also did concert work and sang on radio.

Ehrenburg, Ilya G. (1891-Sept. 1), Russian author of novels, stories, and essays, wrote mostly about life in Russia. His early books include *The Self-Seeker* and *A Street in Moscow*. He received his first Stalin prize for *The Fall of Paris*. *The Thaw* and *The Spring* were published during the 1950s.

***Elman, Mischa** (1891-Apr. 5), Russian-born concert violinist, was an immediate success when he made his first public appearance in St. Petersburg (now Leningrad) in 1904. He toured Germany, and gave his first concert in the United States in 1908. Elman returned from a European tour in January, 1967.

Erwin, Stuart (1903-Dec. 21), starred in the television series "The Trouble with Father," later entitled "The Stu Erwin Show." His films include *Dangerous Dan McGrew*, *Great Mike*, *Pillow to Post*, *Heaven Only Knows*, and *Strike It Rich*.

Evelyn, Judith (1913-May 7), starred as Mrs. Manningham in *Gaslight* (film, 1941) and in *Angel Street* (Broadway, 1941-1944). She played Ann Downs in *The Shrike* (stage) and Irina Arkadina in *The Sea Gull* (stage and screen).

***Farrar, Geraldine** (1882-Mar. 11), opera and concert soprano, made her debut in Berlin in 1901 as Marguerite in *Faust*. At the New York Metropolitan Opera Company (1906-1922), she sang such title roles as *Madame Butterfly* (95 times), *Carmen*, *Manon*, and *Tosca*. *Joan of Arc* and *Carmen* were among the films she made during her singing career.

***Forbes, Esther** (1894-Aug. 12), novelist of the Revolutionary War period, was awarded the Pulitzer history prize (1943) for *Paul Revere and the World He Lived In* and the Newbery medal (1944) for *Johnny Tremain: A Novel for Young and Old* (filmed by Walt Disney). *The Running of the Tide* also was filmed. Her other books include *A Mirror for Witches*, *The General's Lady*, and *Rainbow on the Road*.

Fogarty, John E. (1913-Jan. 10), Democratic U.S. Representative from Rhode Island, had served in Congress since 1941.

Foxx, James E. (1907-July 21), National Baseball Hall of Fame member since 1951, retired in 1945 with a lifetime total of 534 home runs, second at that time to Babe Ruth's total of 714.

Frankau, Pamela (1908-June 8), English novelist, wrote such well-known books as *The Willow Cabin* and *To the Monument of Triumph*. *Over the Mountains*, the third volume of her trilogy, *The Clothes of a King's Son*, was published in 1967.

Funk, Casimir (1884-Nov. 19), Polish-born biochemist and discoverer of vitamins, found a small crystalline substance in rice bran capable of curing a form of beriberi in pigeons (reported in 1912). He thought it belonged to a class of chemical compounds called amines, which he combined with *vita*, Latin for life, coining the word *vitamine*. Later the "e" was dropped.

***Garden, Mary** (1874-Jan. 3), operatic soprano and singing actress, made her debut in Gustave Charpentier's *Louise* (1900) in Paris. She created the role of Mélisande in Claude Debussy's *Pelléas and Mélisande* (1902), made her American debut at New York's Manhattan Opera House in the title role of *Thaïs* (1907), and appeared with the Chicago Grand Opera Company (1910-1931). The singer spent her last years in her native Aberdeen, Scotland.

***Garner, John Nance** (1868-Nov. 7), Vice-President of the United States during the first two terms of the late President Franklin D. Roosevelt (1933-1941), opposed a third term for Mr. Roosevelt. He ran against him unsuccessfully at the 1940 Democratic National

A Poet's Voice Is Stilled

Poet, novelist, biographer of Lincoln, and balladeer, Carl Sandburg died after a heart attack in Flat Rock, N.C., at the age of 89. President Lyndon B. Johnson spoke of Sandburg as "the bard of democracy, the echo of the people." In this tribute, Pulitzer prize-winning poet Gwendolyn Brooks tells of the "twinkling-eyed preacher-on-the-run."

Carl Sandburg, the people you celebrated are saying Yes today as they never said Yes before. Even their varieties of No are materials for an ultimate Yes.

That could be said to Carl Sandburg, the troubadour so raucous and so hoarse that his searches and syntheses offended the gentler readers of 1915. *Chicago Poems* put together "hyacinths and biscuits," steel and star and stench.

It was always the unsung he sang, and the songless. He believed in the "little" people. The people, he said, make mistakes–but they learn. They are tricked, they are sold–but they bridle and they return. They eat earth for strength, for revival. They are in tune with the universal. And they do somewhat love each other: "brother may yet line up with brother." Man is "color poems," "console organ of changing themes," wind that cannot be hindered from blowing, at once holder-to-the-humdrum and stretcher-toward-the-light. Man is hero, hoodlum.

Bernard Hoffman, *Life* © Time Inc.

Carl Sandburg (1878-1967)

To imitate Sandburg is a foolish thing. The imitation will not come off well. The Sandburg voice is distinct, unmistakable. Sandburg poetry is curious: sonorous, but dotted with pieces of journalism; sweet, but threaded through with mischievous acid; tender, but affording thick needles and nails.

Carl Sandburg was a colloquial boxer, a twinkling-eyed preacher-on-the-run, a twitching handholder, a rough and sometimes absent-minded patter of puzzled heads.

From *The People, Yes:*
In the darkness with a
great bundle of grief
the people march.
In the night, and overhead
a shovel of stars for
keeps, the people march:
"Where to? What next?"

From "Timesweep" in *Honey and Salt:*
There are hungers
for a nameless bread
out of the dust
of the hard earth,
out of the blaze
of the calm sun.

And wry sarcasm from "Call the Next Witness" in *Honey and Salt:*
there will be people left over
enough inhabitants among the
Eskimos
among jungle folk
denizens of plains and plateaus
cities and towns synthetic
miasma missed
enough for a census
enough to call it still a
world
though definitely my friends
my good friends
definitely not the same old
world
the vanquished saying, "What
happened?"
the victors saying "We
planned it so."

Chicago Poems was Sandburg's most influential and "reforming" work, but there have been nine other volumes of his poetry. There is a six-volume Lincoln biography, *Abraham Lincoln* (*The Prairie Years*, 2 vols., 1926, and *The War Years*, 4 vols., 1939, with a one-volume edition in 1954). There is one novel, *Remembrance Rock* (1948). There are six books "for young folks" –including the distinctive *Rootabaga Stories* (1922). There is an autobiography, *Always the Young Strangers* (1953).

And there are 10 books of miscellaneous testimony to his direct interest in race relations, American aphorism and song, photography, prairie men and farmers, and the simultaneously tall-and-small of cities and towns. At 85, he published *Honey and Salt.*

This drawling, guitar-playing rover, his hair a careful wildness, his eyes a slow rhapsody, made free music of dinginess and frailty, but always remembered to look at the world's embroidery.

"I shall always sing a little in tough weather."

John Masefield, 16th poet laureate of England, died at his home on May 12.

© Philippe Halsman

J. Robert Oppenheimer, who won fame as a theoretical physicist, died at age 63.

Barney Ross, lightweight champion boxer in 1933 and 1934, died at age of 58.

Convention. Garner served as a Democratic U.S. Representative from Texas (1903-1933), and was Speaker of the House (1931-1933).

Gassner, John W. (1903-Apr. 2), Hungarian-born Yale University Sterling Professor of Playwriting and Dramatic Literature and noted drama critic, wrote *Directions in Modern Theatre and Drama* and other books.

Griffin, Gwyn (1925?-Oct. 12), British veteran of World War II and author of the best-selling novel *An Operational Necessity* (1967), also wrote *Master of This Vessel*, both about the sea. *By the North Gate* and other books are set in Africa, where he was born (Egypt) and worked before the war.

Guinness, Rupert Edward Cecil Lee (1874-Sept. 14), EARL OF IVEAGH, was board chairman of Arthur Guinness, Son & Company (1927-1962). He used his wealth to improve Guinness slum property in London, fought for better housing in the House of Commons (1908-1910, 1912-1927), and was responsible for the sanitation of milk and the elimination of tuberculosis from cattle herds in England.

Guthrie, "Woody," Woodrow Wilson (1912-Oct. 3), folk singer and composer of many songs about American life such as "This Land Is Your Land," also wrote *Bound for Glory* about his life. *American Folksong* is a volume of his songs and sketches.

***Heyrovsky, Jaroslav** (1890-Mar. 27), Czechoslovak scientist, was the first in his country to be honored with a Nobel prize. He was awarded the chemistry prize (1959) for the origin and development of polarography, an electrochemical method of analyzing complicated chemical solutions.

***Hinshelwood, Sir Cyril** (1897-Oct. 9), English scientist, was awarded (with Nikolai N. Semenov of Russia) the Nobel chemistry prize in 1956 for his research in chemical kinetics and for its application to bacterial cells.

Hobart, Alice Tisdale (1882-Mar. 14), author of the best-selling novel *Oil for the Lamps of China* (1933, filmed, 1935), also wrote *Venture into Darkness*, *The Innocent Dreamers*, and *Within the Walls of Nanking* (nonfiction) about China where she once lived. *The Cup and the Sword* (1942) was filmed as *This Earth Is Mine* (1959).

Holt, Harold E. (1908-Dec. 17), was Prime Minister of Australia. See AUSTRALIA.

***Hopper, Edward** (1882-May 15), realist painter and etcher, depicted rural, city, and industrial scenes. *Early Sunday Morning* and *Night Hawks* (now considered an American classic) are examples of the deserted, lonely scenes he often produced. *Cat Boat*, *Lonely House*, and *Girl on Bridge* are etchings.

Howe, Mark De Wolfe (1906-Feb. 28), Harvard University's first Charles Warren Professor in the History of American Law, wrote *Mr. Justice Holmes: The Shaping Years, 1841-1870* (1957) and *The Proving Years, 1870-1882* (1963).

***Hughes, Langston** (1902-May 22), poet, playwright, and novelist, wrote mostly about Negro life. *The Weary Blues* (1926) was the first of his many books of verse. His other works include *Not Without Laughter* (novel), *Laughing to Keep from Crying* (stories), and anthologies, *Simply Heavenly* (musical), *Mulatto* (play), *Black Nativity* (song play), and lyrics for *Street Scene* (musical).

***Hyderabad, Nizam of** (1886-Feb. 24), SIR USMAN ALI, ruler of Hyderabad in India (1911-1948), was once one of the world's wealthiest men. He continued as *Rajpramukh* (symbolic head of government) after the princely state was forced to join independent India (1950). He retired when Hyderabad was dissolved as a state (1956).

Isaacs, Alick (1922?-Jan. 26), Scottish virologist, discovered a large protein molecule of cells in man and other mammals and named it interferon, reported in 1957). It controls the production of adenosine triphosphate (ATP), a high energy substance necessary for cell and virus growth.

Juin, Alphonse Pierre (1888-Jan. 27), Marshal of France, commanded French forces in North Africa and Italy in World War II. He openly opposed President Charles de Gaulle's Algerian policy, and was dismissed from the National Council in 1960.

***Kaiser, Henry John** (1882-Aug. 24), went from highway, dam, and pipeline construction to shipbuilding in World War II, and won international acclaim for his speedy assembly of ships. He entered other industries, and founded (1956) the Kaiser Industries Corporation with himself as chairman.

Kennedy, Margaret (1896-July 31), English author whose novel, *The Constant Nymph* (1924), was dramatized with Elisabeth Bergner as Tessa, also wrote *Escape Me Never* (1934) for the actress. Her other works include *The Mechanized Muse* (criticism, 1944), *Jane Austen* (1950), and *The Outlaws on Parnassus* (1958) on the art of fiction.

Kesselring, Joseph (1902-Nov. 5), wrote *Arsenic and Old Lace*, a hilarious murder play that ran on Broadway for more than three years, Jan. 10, 1941, through

Claude Rains, noted English actor of stage, screen and television, died on May 30.

Woodrow Wilson Guthrie, known to fans as "Woody," died after a long illness.

Sir Malcolm Sargent died after many years as chief conductor for the BBC.

June 17, 1944. It had an equally long run in London, and was filmed.

Kilgore, Bernard (1908-Nov. 14), Dow, Jones & Co. board chairman, was president of the financial publishing firm (1945-1966). He joined *The Wall Street Journal* staff in 1929 and advanced to managing editor by 1941. In 1962, he founded *The National Observer*, a weekly newspaper.

Kiplinger, Willard Monroe (1891-Aug. 6), founder and editor of the *Kiplinger Washington* (D.C.) *Letter* (1923) and *Changing Times* (first appeared as Kiplinger *Magazine*, 1947), also published the *Kiplinger Foreign Trade Letter* (founded as Overseas Postscript, 1953). His books include *Washington Is Like That* (1942) and *Your Guide to a Higher Income* (1959).

***Kodály, Zoltán** (1882-Mar. 6), Hungarian composer and teacher, won international acclaim as a creator of rhapsodies based on folk material. *Psalmus Hungaricus*, a choral work, and *Háry János*, an opera from which he made a popular suite, are among the most famous of his works.

***Köhler, Wolfgang** (1887-June 11), German psychologist and author of *Gestalt Psychology* (1929, now considered a classic), pioneered in the study of the mentality of apes.

***Krupp von Bohlen und Halbach, Alfried** (1907-July 30), the fifth head of the great Krupp industrial empire in West Germany, had served as chairman since 1943. Sentenced to 12 years in prison after World War II and freed in 1951, he rebuilt the concern, no longer manufactured arms.

***Kuhn, Richard** (1900-Aug. 1), Hungarian-born German chemist, was prevented from accepting the Nobel chemistry prize by the Nazi government in 1938. He did notable vitamin research, especially on the carotenelike substances, and isolated riboflavin from egg albumin.

Lahr, Bert (1895-Dec. 4), stage, screen, and television comic actor, is remembered as the Cowardly Lion in *The Wizard of Oz* (film, 1939). He starred in such Broadway musical comedies as *Hold Everything* (1928), *Life Begins at 8:40* (1934), and *DuBarry Was a Lady* (1939). He also won acclaim as Estragon in *Waiting for Godot* (Broadway, 1956).

Leigh, Vivien (1913-July 8), English actress whose role as Scarlett O'Hara in *Gone with the Wind* won her the Motion Picture Academy best actress award in 1939, also won the award as Blanche DuBois in *A Streetcar Named Desire* (1951). She costarred with Sir Laurence Olivier in *Caesar and Cleopatra* and in *Antony and Cleopatra*, and had many other stage successes.

***Luce, Henry Robinson** (1898-Feb. 28). See Close-Up.

***Luthuli, Albert John** (1898-July 21), former Zulu chief, was awarded the Nobel peace prize in 1960 for his nonviolent methods of opposing segregation of the races in South Africa.

Macken, Walter (1915-Apr. 22), Irish playwright, actor, and novelist, starred as the Irish father in his play *Home Is the Hero*. His best-known literary work is the historical trilogy about Ireland: *Seek the Fair Land* (1959), *The Silent People* (1963), and *The Scorching Wind* (1964).

Magritte, René (1898-Aug. 15), Belgian surrealist painter, was given retrospective exhibits at New York's Museum of Modern Art in 1965 and at Rotterdam's (Netherlands) Boymans Museum in 1967. His paintings include *The Wind and the Song*, *Ladder of Fire*, and *The Castle of the Pyrenees*.

Mansfield, Jayne (1937-June 29), actress, appeared in the Broadway comedy *Will Success Spoil Rock Hunter* (also film), and such films as *The Wayward Bus*, *The Girl Can't Help It*, and *Kiss Them for Me*.

Marshall, Edison (1894-Oct. 29), wrote *Benjamin Blake* (his first, 1941, filmed as *Son of Fury* with Tyrone Power), *Yankee Pasha*, *Gypsy Sixpence*, *The Heart of the Hunter*, and other historical novels. *The Viking* (1951) also was filmed.

Martínez Ruiz, José (1873-Mar. 2), Spanish literary figure, wrote under the pseudonym Azorin. His greatest work was in the field of criticism. *Antonio Azorín* is an autobiographical novel, and *Brandy, Mucho Brandy*, a well-known play.

***Masefield, John** (1878-May 12), poet laureate of England since 1930, also wrote fiction and drama. *Salt-Water Ballads* (1902) was his first book of poems. *Sard Harker*, *Odua*, *The Bird of Dawning* (about China clippers), and *Victorious Troy* are novels of the sea. "The Everlasting Mercy," "Dauber," "Reynard the Fox," and "The Widow in the Bye Street" are well-known long poems. Masefield dramas include *The Tragedy of Pompey the Great* and *End and Beginning*.

***Massey, Vincent** (1887-Dec. 30), the first Canadian-born governor-general of Canada (1952-1959), served as high commissioner for Canada in Great Britain (1935-1946). The noted statesman was a brother of Raymond Massey, the actor.

***Maurois, André** (1885-Oct. 9), French man of letters, was born Emile Herzog. His first success came as

The Man Who Made *Time*

Many historians call them "personal journalists." For they–in their own way and in their own time–imprinted their own brand of journalism on the American scene.

Among the personal journalists of other eras were such men as Ben Franklin, James Gordon Bennett, Horace Greeley, Joseph Pulitzer, and William Randolph Hearst.

Few can deny that Henry Robinson Luce, who built a magazine publishing empire, belongs among the great "personal journalists." Like all the others, he brought a methodology to journalism that in many ways was a reflection of himself. Like the others, Henry Luce was a man of controversy. The object of admiration and criticism, his power as an opinion molder was respected and feared.

On Feb. 28, 1967, while vacationing at Phoenix, Ariz., Henry Luce died of a heart attack at the age of 68, ending a journalistic career that began in 1923 with the founding of *Time, The Weekly News Magazine*. At the time of his death, the communications empire that he helped found had sales totaling nearly $500,000,000 a year. It included not only *Time*, *Life*, *Fortune*, and *Sports Illustrated*, but also television stations, book publishers, a paper company, and subsidiaries that operated in most of the industrialized countries of the Free World.

Drawing by Robert Vickrey, *Time* © Time Inc. 1967

Henry R. Luce (1898-1967)

Luce, his friends were to call him "Harry," was born April 3, 1898, in Tengchow, China, the son of Presbyterian missionaries. He attended a strict boarding school at Chefoo, China, where caning was the practice. At the age of 15 he went on to Hotchkiss School in Lakeville, Conn., and in 1916 enrolled at Yale University, where he compiled a brilliant academic record, wrote verse, and was an editor of the campus newspaper, the *Yale Daily News*.

After graduation, interrupted by army service at Camp Jackson, S.C., and by studies at Oxford University, England, he returned to the United States in 1921, and became a *legman* (information gatherer) for author-columnist Ben Hecht of the *Chicago Daily News*. Later, he joined a former Yale classmate, Briton Hadden, of the Baltimore (Md.) *Evening News*.

Luce and Hadden had an idea for a new magazine which they first called *Fact*, later changed to *Time*. In their spare time, they developed a format. Backed by $86,000 from 72 investors, they made their plunge in 1923 into the world of publishing.

From the beginning, the two young journalists challenged a basic premise upon which American journalism was based. They challenged the notion of "objective reporting," under which reporters and editors "objectively" chose the facts, attempting to maintain a balance between different points of view.

Time took a stand on many stories it published. Organized into departments, such as national affairs, medicine, and art, its goal was to tell the hurried business or professional man only what he needed to know. As a result of its twin policies of "economy in words" and "liveliness," the magazine developed a unique style. Descriptive adjectives were put before the names of people. Sentences were inverted, and a premium was placed on action verbs. By contracting words whenever possible, *Time* contributed many words to the language, among them "socialite," "newsman," and "cinemaddict." The magazine also popularized such words as "tycoon," "moppet," and "OpArt."

In his time, Henry Robinson Luce's influence went far beyond his magazines or his readers. He was one of those most responsible in persuading Dwight D. Eisenhower to run for the presidency in 1952. He was an adviser to his wife, Clare Booth Luce, when she was U.S. ambassador to Rome during the Eisenhower administration. He helped influence China policy, the Marshall Plan, the Republican party, and the ecumenical movement. He also played an important role in popularizing the arts. These represented only a few of his many interests.

Said President Lyndon B. Johnson, on Luce's death: "The magazines that bear his stamp are an authentic part of life in America. They are living memorials to a man of great courage, far-sighted vision, and strong convictions."

Even his foes would agree with that. [E. KENNETH FROSLID]

Thomas MacAvoy, *Life* © Time Inc.

John Nance Garner, left, was Vice-President under Franklin Roosevelt.

Spencer Tracy died in Hollywood after a 37-year career in motion pictures.

Bert Lahr, who played the lion in *The Wizard of Oz,* died at the age of 72.

a novelist. He also wrote essays and histories, but excelled as a biographer. Volumes on Shelley, Disraeli, Victor Hugo, Proust, the Dumas, George Sand, and others were followed by *Prometheus: The Life of Balzac* (1965), considered his masterpiece.

McAdoo, Eleanor Wilson (1889-Apr. 5), the last surviving daughter of President Woodrow Wilson, was married in the White House on May 7, 1914, to William Gibbs McAdoo, her father's Secretary of the Treasury.

***McCollum, Elmer Verner** (1879-Nov. 15), biochemist, originated the letter system of naming vitamins. He, with associates, cited evidence (1915) that more than one vitamin existed. McCollum classified these substances as "fat-soluble A" and "water-soluble B" vitamins.

***McCullers, Carson** (1917-Sept. 29), novelist, wrote *The Heart Is a Lonely Hunter* (1940). *The Member of the Wedding* (1946), produced on Broadway, won the New York Drama Critics Circle award in 1950, and was filmed in 1952. Later novels included *The Ballad of the Sad Cafe* (1951, dramatized, 1963) and *Clock Without Hands* (1961).

***Morgenthau, Henry, Jr.** (1891-Feb. 6), U.S. Secretary of the Treasury (1934-1945), played a leading part in the Bretton Woods (N.H.) international monetary conference in 1944.

***Muller, Hermann Joseph** (1890-Apr. 5), geneticist, was awarded the Nobel medicine prize (1946) for discovering that X rays produce mutations, sudden changes in genes, and thus affect heredity.

Muni, Paul (1895-Aug. 25), Austrian-born actor, famous for biographical roles, starred in *The Story of Louis Pasteur* (won the Motion Picture Academy best actor award in 1936), *The Story of Emile Zola*, and *Juárez*. Earlier films in which he won acclaim include *I'm a Fugitive from a Chain Gang* and *Scarface*. His Broadway successes include *Counsellor-at-Law*, *Key Largo*, and *Inherit the Wind*.

Murch, Walter Tandy (1907-Dec. 11), Canadian-born artist known for his paintings of machines, taught at several universities. An exhibit of his art opened at the Brooklyn Museum in December, 1967.

***Oppenheimer, J. Robert** (1904-Feb. 18), theoretical physicist famous as director of the Los Alamos (N.Mex.) Laboratory (1943-1945, where first atom bomb was developed), also served with the Atomic Energy Commission (1947-1954) and received its Fermi award in 1963. He was director of the Institute for Advanced Study at Princeton, N.J., from 1947 through 1966.

Orr, Carey Cassius (1890-May 16), whose front-page cartoons were a daily feature of the *Chicago Tribune* for years, was awarded the Pulitzer cartoon prize in 1961.

Orsborn, Albert W. T. (1886-Feb. 4), general of the International Salvation Army (1946-1954) and British commissioner (1940-1946), wrote more than 250 songs and hymns for the Salvation Army.

Pacini, Alfredo Cardinal (1888-Dec. 23), an Italian member of the Roman Curia, served for years in the Vatican's diplomatic service. He was elevated to the Sacred College of Cardinals in June, 1967.

Parker, Dorothy Rothschild (1893-Jan. 7), humorist, critic, and short-story writer, established her literary reputation with *Enough Rope* (1926) and other books of poetry. She also wrote several plays.

Pendleton, "Nat," Nathaniel Greene (1899-Oct. 11), character actor, appeared in such films as *Northwest Passage*, *The Sea Wolf*, *The Star Witness*, and *Attorney for the Defense*, and was the ambulance driver in the *Dr. Kildare* films of the 1930s.

Rains, Claude (1889-May 30), English actor, after numerous stage successes at home and in the United States, launched an equally successful film career as the scientist-hero in *The Invisible Man* (1933). *Anthony Adverse*, *Caesar and Cleopatra*, *Mr. Smith Goes to Washington*, *Casablanca*, *Mr. Skeffington*, and *Notorious* were among his memorable pictures. His Broadway role in *Darkness at Noon* (1951) won him the New York Drama Critics Circle best-actor and other awards.

***Randall, Clarence Belden** (1891-Aug. 4), Inland Steel Company president (1949-1953) and board chairman (1953-1956), served as economic adviser to the United States government and as a special adviser to the President on foreign economic policy matters.

***Ransome, Arthur** (1884-June 3), English novelist for children, was awarded the British Library's first Carnegie medal for *Pigeon Post* (1936). His many other delightful books include *Old Peter's Russian Tales* (1916), *Peter Duck* (1932), *Coot Club* (1935), and *We Didn't Mean to Go to Sea* (1938).

Rathbone, Basil (1892-July 21), English actor, is best remembered, perhaps, for his Sherlock Holmes films and radio series of the 1940s-1950s. *The Last of Mrs. Cheyney* (1929) was his first sound picture. He played character roles in *A Notorious Affair*, *The Bishop Murder Case*, *A Tale of Two Cities*, *Anna Karenina*, and *David Copperfield*, and starred in *Son of Frankenstein*. Broadway roles include *The Barretts of Wimpole Street*, *The Heiress*, and *Obsession*.

Riberi, Antonio Cardinal (1897-Dec. 16), who was elevated to the Sacred College of Cardinals in June, 1967, was the first Apostolic Internuncio to China (1946). He was expelled from there in 1951.

***Rice, Elmer** (1892-May 8), author of books about the theater and 50 or more plays, wrote the Pulitzer prize (1929) play *Street Scene* (also filmed and produced as a musical). *On Trial* (1914, his first), *The Adding Machine* (1923), and *Counsellor-at-Law* (1931) were also great successes.

Riggs, Tommy (1910?-May 21), radio, television, and night club entertainer, created the little girl voice of Betty Lou. He appeared many times with such personalities as Rudy Vallee and Edgar Bergen.

***Ritter, Joseph Cardinal** (1892-June 10), Archbishop of St. Louis since 1946, was elevated to the Sacred College of Cardinals in 1961.

Ross, Barney (1909-Jan. 18), world lightweight boxing champion, won the title from Tony Canzoneri in June, 1933, and lost it to the same boxer in 1935. He won the welterweight title from Jimmy McLarnin in 1934, lost it to him the same year, won it again in 1935 from McLarnin, and in May, 1938, lost it to Henry Armstrong. Ross tells his story in *No Man Stands Alone*. *Monkey on My Back* (film) was based on his life.

Ruffini, Ernesto Cardinal (1888-June 11), Archbishop of Palermo, Italy, since 1945, was elevated to the Sacred College of Cardinals in 1946.

Ruman, "Sig," Siegfried Albon (1885?-Feb. 14), German-born character actor, played in 150 or more films. He is remembered for such roles as Sergeant Schultz in *Stalag 17* and a Soviet envoy in *Ninotchka*. Ruman made his Broadway debut in 1928 as the German officer in *The War Song*. In *Grand Hotel* (1930), he played the industrialist Preysing, and Katharine Cornell's professor-father in *Alien Corn* (1933).

Sabata, Victor de (1892-Dec. 11), Italian conductor and composer, for years was musical director at La Scala Opera House, Milan, and appeared with major European and American musical groups.

Saigh, Maximos IV Cardinal (1878-Nov. 5), Roman Catholic Melchite Patriarch of Antioch and All the Orient since 1947, was elevated to the Sacred College of Cardinals in 1965. He was born in Aleppo, Syria.

***Sandburg, Carl** (1878-July 22). See Close-Up.

***Sargent, Sir Malcolm** (1895-Oct. 3), was one of the most popular English conductors of his time. He was conductor in chief of the British Broadcasting Corporation Symphony Orchestra (1950-1957), and for years conducted its Promenade Concerts.

***Sassoon, Siegfried** (1886-Sept. 1), English author, was a soldier poet of World War I. *The Old Huntsman* (1917), *Counter-Attack* (1918), and *Collected War Poems* (1919) won him recognition. *The Memoirs of a Fox-Hunting Man* (1928), about country life in England before World War I, is his most notable work.

Savage, John Lucian (1879-Dec. 28), internationally noted engineer, designed such projects as the Grand Coulee, Hoover, and Shasta dams.

***Schick, Béla** (1877-Dec. 6), Hungarian-born pediatrician, developed the widely used Schick test for diphtheria, announced in 1913. He and Clemens von Pirquet in 1902 described serum sickness, and disclosed fundamental knowledge about, and coined the word, allergy.

Schuyler, Philippa Duke (1932?-May 9), pianist-composer, made her debut at 14 with the New York Philharmonic Symphony Orchestra. Her compositions include *Sanga*, an Ethiopian hero dance, and *White Nile Suite*. She also was a journalist.

Sevitzky, Fabien (1893-Feb. 2), Russian-born musical director and conductor of the Greater Miami Philharmonic Society since 1965 and musical director and conductor of the Indianapolis Symphony Orchestra (1937-1955), conducted the University of Miami Symphony Orchestra (1959-1965).

Shepard, Odell (1884-July 19), was awarded the Pulitzer biography prize (1938) for *Pedlar's Progress: The Life of Bronson Alcott*. His other books include *Bliss Carman: A Study of His Poetry*, *The Lore of the Unicorn*, and *Jenkin's Ear* (coauthor).

Sheridan, Ann (1915-Jan. 21), once known as the "oomph girl," starred in *The Man Who Came to Dinner*, *George Washington Slept Here*, *Angels with Dirty Faces*, *Male War Bride*, and *Kings Row*.

***Smith, Holland Mctyeire** (1882-Jan. 12), United States Marine Corps general, fought in the Pacific during World War II. His toughness in combat won him the nickname "Howlin' Mad."

***Spellman, Francis Cardinal** (1889-Dec. 2), Archbishop of New York since 1939, was elevated to the Sacred College of Cardinals in 1946. The widely traveled prelate was an outspoken foe of Communism, and an influential figure in ecclesiastical affairs.

Steenbock, Harry (1886-Dec. 25), biochemist, in the early 1920s discovered a process of increasing the vitamin D content of food by irradiation.

Strayhorn, William Thomas (1915-May 31), jazz composer, pianist, and lyricist, had worked for Duke Ellington since 1939. He composed and arranged "Take the A Train," and numerous other songs, and collaborated with Ellington on such major works as *Such Sweet Thunder* for the Stratford (Ont.) Shakespeare Festival and *Far East Suite*.

Tatum, "Goose," Reese (1921-Jan. 18), famed as the Clown Prince of Basketball, played with the Harlem Globetrotters (1946-1955) before organizing his own team, the Harlem Road Kings. Tatum, an outstanding player, loved to entertain the spectators. He said, "My goal in life is to make people laugh."

***Tedder, Arthur William** (1890-June 3), BARON TEDDER OF GLENGUIN, chief of the British Air Staff (1946-1950), held commands in North Africa and the Mediterranean in World War II before serving as deputy supreme commander (1943-1945) to the supreme Allied commander in Europe General Dwight D. Eisenhower. The Tedder memoirs, *With Prejudice*, appeared in 1966.

Tien, Thomas Cardinal (1890-July 14), the only Chinese elevated to the Sacred College of Cardinals (1946) and the only Roman Catholic Archbishop of Peking (1946), had lived in exile since the Communists seized control in China in 1949.

Toklas, Alice B. (1877-Mar. 7), was internationally known, with the late writer Gertrude Stein, for a celebrated literary salon in Paris. Miss Toklas wrote of their association (1907-1946) in *What Is Remembered*. *The Autobiography of Alice B. Toklas* (1933), by Miss Stein, is a Stein autobiography.

Tracy, Spencer (1900-June 10), film star for 37 years, was awarded Motion Picture Academy best-actor awards as the Portuguese fisherman in *Captains Courageous* (1937) and as Father Flanagan in *Boys' Town* (1938). His other memorable films include *The Old Man and the Sea*, *Father of the Bride*, *Inherit the Wind*, and *Judgment at Nuremberg*. Films with Katharine Hepburn include *Keeper of the Flame* and *State of the Union*.

Valletta, Vittorio (1883-Aug. 9), board chairman and managing director (1945-1966) of the Italian complex Fiat (Fabbrica Italiana Automobili Torino), joined the manufacturing concern in 1920, and directed its reconstruction after World Wars I and II.

Van de Graaff, Robert J. (1901-Jan. 16), pioneered in the development of nuclear accelerators. The Van de Graaff generator was first tested in 1933.

***Vanier, Georges Philias** (1888-Mar. 5), Governor-General of Canada since 1959, was the first French Canadian and the first Roman Catholic to serve in this office. He was a noted soldier and diplomat.

Walbrook, Anton (1900-Aug. 9), Austrian-born English actor, came to fame in Germany, and then appeared in Britain in such roles as Otto in *Design for Living* (1939) and Kurt Müller in *Watch on the Rhine* (1942). His many films include *Victoria the Great, Sixty Glorious Years, Colonel Blimp, La Ronde, The Red Shoes,* and *Saint Joan.*

Warner, Albert (1883?-Nov. 26), retired vice-president and treasurer of Warner Bros. Pictures, Inc., with his three brothers pioneered in the exhibition, distribution, and production of films.

Waxman, Franz (1906-Feb. 24), German-born composer and conductor, was awarded Motion Picture Academy awards for the scores for *Sunset Boulevard* (1950), and *A Place in the Sun* (1951). He wrote the music for *The Nun's Story* and many other films.

***Whiteman, Paul** (1890-Dec. 29), orchestra conductor, introduced the first "symphonic jazz." He conducted the first performance of George Gershwin's *Rhapsody in Blue* (1924).

Xceron, Jean (1890-Mar.29), Greek-born artist, won acclaim with his first one-man show (1931) in Paris. He pioneered nonobjective art in the United States. *Two Circles* is a tempera painting, and *Painting $432*, an oil.

Yoshida, Shigeru (1878-Oct. 20), as Prime Minister of Japan (1946-1947, 1948-1954), worked with the late General Douglas MacArthur during the Allied occupation, signed a peace treaty and a security pact with the United States.

Younger, J. Arthur (1893-June 20), Republican U.S. Representative from California, was elected in 1952.

Youssoupoff, Prince Felix (1887-Sept. 27), was one of a group of Russian noblemen who assassinated the Mad Monk Rasputin in December, 1916. He wrote about it in *Rasputin: His Malignant Influence and His Assassination* and *Lost Splendor.*

DEMOCRACY. A few young men burned their draft cards; others carried Viet Cong flags, "peace balloons," and banners and placards emblazoned with biting messages. Mostly, the marchers were young and of varied religious faiths. Many of them were college students.

Some 125,000 of these demonstrators moved down New York City's Madison Avenue on April 16, singing and chanting. It was a demonstration sponsored by the Spring Mobilization Committee to End the War in Vietnam, and there was a parallel rally of 50,000 in San Francisco, Calif. Occasionally, the marchers were pelted with eggs and cans, but the demonstrations came off with little trouble.

In October, in Washington, D.C., a less orderly demonstration involving an estimated 50,000 war protesters centered around the Pentagon. A reported 683 demonstrators were arrested. Of these, 580 were convicted, mostly for disorderly conduct. The Pentagon disclosed spending more than $1,000,000 on troops and equipment to repulse the protest. The nation's ability to tolerate dissent; the strength, therefore, of its democratic commitment, was being severely tested.

American democracy showed its vitality in the nomination on June 13 of Thurgood Marshall to the Supreme Court of the United States. Marshall was the first Negro to sit on the Court (see MARSHALL, THURGOOD).

In what the Reverend Martin Luther King, Jr. called the "one-two-three punch against backlash and bigotry," voters in November elected Negro mayors in Cleveland, Ohio, and Gary, Ind. In Boston, Mass., the electorate defeated mayoral candidate Louise Day Hicks, who was considered an opponent of school integration. See CITIES; CIVIL RIGHTS. Julian Bond, a Negro, elected in 1966 to Georgia's lower legislative house, was denied a seat because he publicly advocated the burning of draft cards. In response to a Supreme Court ruling in January, 1967, Bond was seated. Off-Broadway theater pushed freedom of expression to far limits in the play *MacBird!* Employing innuendo and the theme of Shakespeare's *Macbeth*, and with characters resembling Presidents Lyndon B. Johnson and John F. Kennedy and Senator Robert F. Kennedy, the play told how the assassin of the president in turn became president (see THEATER).

Abroad, democracy continued to gain in several countries unaccustomed to its traditions. In West Germany, Chancellor Kurt Georg Kiesinger, little known before he assumed his post in 1966, provided confident new leadership at home and freshness of view in foreign affairs. In Japan, Prime Minister Eisaku Sato successfully conducted an election campaign on a platform calling for the retention of freedoms in Japan.

Many countries struggling to establish the essentials of democracy conducted ambitious but blemished elections. Jamaica held an election in March within three weeks after the government dissolved, thus failing to allow adequate time for campaigning. However, the terror that had been feared did not materialize.

In South Vietnam, elections on September 3 produced mixed results for democratic processes. An eligibility committee of the provisional assembly eliminated five tickets most opposed to the existing administration, and poll watchers were unavailable in outlying areas. As the elections approached, the Viet Cong intensified their attacks, but an impressive 83 per cent of the eligible voters went to the polls. The victorious government ticket did not win massively, receiving only 34.8 per cent of the vote, a testimonial to the poll's essential fairness.

In Africa, new nations provided no exception to a familiar pattern—the overthrow of governments by coups or force. Sierra Leone seemed about to break this pattern when, following an election in March, the leader of the opposition was sworn in as prime minister. An army coup, however, deposed him. The year's most dramatic coup occurred in Greece in April when a junta took over and quickly displaced elementary democratic freedoms with martial law. See GREECE. [LOUIS W. KOENIG]

See also CITIES; CIVIL RIGHTS; COURTS AND LAWS; SUPREME COURT OF THE UNITED STATES; and articles on the various countries.

DEMOCRATIC PARTY leaders were worried, unhappy, and divided in 1967, the last year before the 1968 presidential election campaign. President Lyndon B. Johnson appeared to be in deep trouble with his fellow Democrats, chiefly because of the way he had handled the war in Vietnam. Despite his 1964 landslide election, his popularity had dropped to an all-time low by November, 1967. A public opinion poll published by Louis Harris showed Johnson running behind any one of the six top Republican contenders for the 1968 nomination.

The Iowa Poll conducted by the *Des Moines Register and Tribune* showed that 65 per cent of Iowa Democrats favored Senator Robert F. Kennedy (D., N.Y.) over Johnson as the party's 1968 nominee. Kennedy, however, continued to discourage all talk of his replacing the President on the 1968 ticket and pledged his support in the election. But another liberal Democratic Senator, Eugene J. McCarthy (Minn.), announced on November 30 that he would enter some of the 1968 presidential preference primaries. His principal purpose would be, he said, to try to force the President to de-escalate the Vietnam conflict. See McCarthy, Eugene J.

A Rebellious Congress revealed the divisions within the Democratic party. Some weakening of the party was inevitable after the 1966 elections in which the Republicans gained 47 seats in the House of Representatives. In the new Congress, the President's reputation as a legislative wizard suffered severely. The "fabulous" 89th Congress had given way to the nay-saying 90th.

Nowhere was the party's chief in more trouble than in the new Congress. The staggering cost of the war in Vietnam, estimated at $30,000,000,000 a year, plunged the House into an economy mood. It slashed spending for the Great Society, refusing to agree with the President that the nation could afford both guns and butter. His leadership was further thwarted in the House by the revival of the conservative coalition consisting of Republicans and Southern Democrats.

The party's weak leadership on both sides of Capitol Hill sapped the President's program. Giving voice to a sentiment widely held by House Democrats, Representative Richard Bolling (D., Mo.) openly called for the resignation of the House Speaker, 76-year-old Representative John W. McCormack (D., Mass.). In the Senate, Majority Leader Mike Mansfield (D., Mont.) gave only half-hearted support to Johnson's domestic program, and Mansfield's easy-going leadership left a power vacuum. See Congress of the United States.

Rebuff by Governors. In October, the annual Governors Conference failed to approve a Democratic resolution – as it had done the year before –

Delegates to a Conference of Concerned Democrats demonstrate for Senator Eugene McCarthy (D. Minn.), center. He was their choice for the presidential nomination.

Senator Robert F. Kennedy of New York and President Lyndon B. Johnson were at odds throughout the year, especially after the Senator challenged U.S. policy in Vietnam.

supporting the administration's war effort in Vietnam. The Republican governors declined to join the Democrats in voting for the resolution after California Governor Ronald Reagan had made public the copy of a secret White House cable, which contained instructions on how to pressure two Republican governors. The Republicans promptly noted that it proved White House intervention in the conference. See President of the United States.

Off-Year elections gave a little solace to the Democrats. Mayor Richard J. Daley of Chicago, Ill., who heads the nation's most powerful Democratic city organization, won re-election to a fourth term in April. He received a record-breaking 74 per cent of the vote. See Chicago.

In November, Negro Democrats defeated white Republicans to retain Democratic control of the mayorships of Cleveland, Ohio, and Gary, Ind. The nonpartisan contest for mayor of Boston, Mass., was won by Kevin H. White, the racial moderate of the two Democratic candidates (see Boston). Carl B. Stokes in Cleveland and Richard G. Hatcher in Gary overcame the white backlash vote. The two Democratic strongholds were the first large U.S. cities ever to elect Negro mayors. But the narrow margins in both contests reflected a heavy defection of white Democratic voters and a strained relationship in the local Democratic organizations. Nevertheless, Democratic strategists read encouraging

Under a picture of his party's chief, Speaker of the House John W. McCormack exhorts fellow Democrats at a $250-a-plate dinner in Washington.

"Can I help it if a peace feeler followed me home?"

signs into the three victories. The results, according to Democratic National Chairman John M. Bailey, "put the so-called white backlash in its place," and marked a "big step toward uniting the Democratic party behind Lyndon Johnson in 1968." See CITY; CIVIL RIGHTS.

The election results contained some significant setbacks for them, however. The Democrats lost the Kentucky governorship to the Republicans for the first time in 24 years. That loss could mean trouble in the 1968 campaign, since it gave the Republicans a 26-to-24 majority of the nation's governors. The Democrats also lost control of both houses of the New Jersey legislature. See ELECTIONS.

Finances. As the troubled Democrats looked ahead to the 1968 testing time, they could, at least, breathe easily over party finances. The Democratic National Committee reported that the debt of more than $4,000,000 left over from the 1964 campaign had been wiped out, and a healthy start made on a war chest for the coming battle.

There were some Democrats, however, who wished their party would follow the Republicans into Miami Beach, Fla., in August, 1968, for their nominating convention. The Chicago site, they said, could embarrass the party, if riots erupted during the convention. But the President was confident that his friend, Mayor Daley, could keep things under control. [WILLIAM McGAFFIN]

DENMARK suffered from rising inflation and a serious trade deficit in 1967. Due partly to an anti-inflationary measure proposed by Prime Minister Jens Otto Krag, his government fell in December.

In July, the nation's already serious trade deficit and a slowdown in economic expansion prompted the Social Democrats and the People's Socialist parties to combine forces and work out a joint program of action. As a result, legislation was passed to bring in direct "pay-as-you-earn" taxation.

Labor unrest also plagued the nation during the year. Disagreement arose in the spring between trade unions and employers over wage agreements. A mediator was appointed when negotiations broke down and strikes were threatened. He recommended reduction of the work week from 44 1/2 hours to 42 1/2, increased social benefits, and a 2 per cent wage increase.

In December, Krag proposed the postponement of the wage increase scheduled for 1968. His proposal, which was tied to a vote of confidence, was defeated 92 to 85 with two members abstaining. Krag resigned and scheduled new elections for January, 1968. [KENNETH BROWN]

Facts in Brief. Population: 4,840,000. Government: King Frederik IX; Prime Minister Jens Otto Krag. Monetary Unit: krone (7.5 = U.S. $1). Foreign Trade: exports, $2,454,000,000; imports, $3,003,000,000. Principal Exports: machinery, bacon and ham, butter.

DENTISTRY. Dental scientists, in 1967, were developing vaccines against tooth decay. One study was described by Irving L. Shklair, a microbiologist at Naval Dental Research Institute at Great Lakes, Ill., at the 45th general meeting of the International Association for Dental Research. The U.S. Navy research team found that blood specimens from sailors with decay-resistant teeth had more antibody to the cavity-causing streptococcus than any of the other men tested.

Research on decay bacteria occupied at least 10 other laboratories in the United States and Sweden. Several strains of decay bacteria were found, and researchers at the University of Notre Dame immunized rats against one type. The Notre Dame team prepared a vaccine using a killed suspension of *Streptococcus saelalis*, a type of bacteria known to cause tooth decay in animals. After receiving injections of the vaccine, the rats became immune to tooth decay. About 24 strains of Streptococci and Lactobacilli are known to cause cavities in animals. Some of these may also cause tooth decay in human beings. Researchers indicated that many of the strains are so similar that only five or six vaccines will be needed to deal with all 24 organisms.

Children's Dental Health Program. Congress considered a children's dental health program that was proposed by the American Dental Association (ADA) at its annual meeting in Dallas, Tex., in

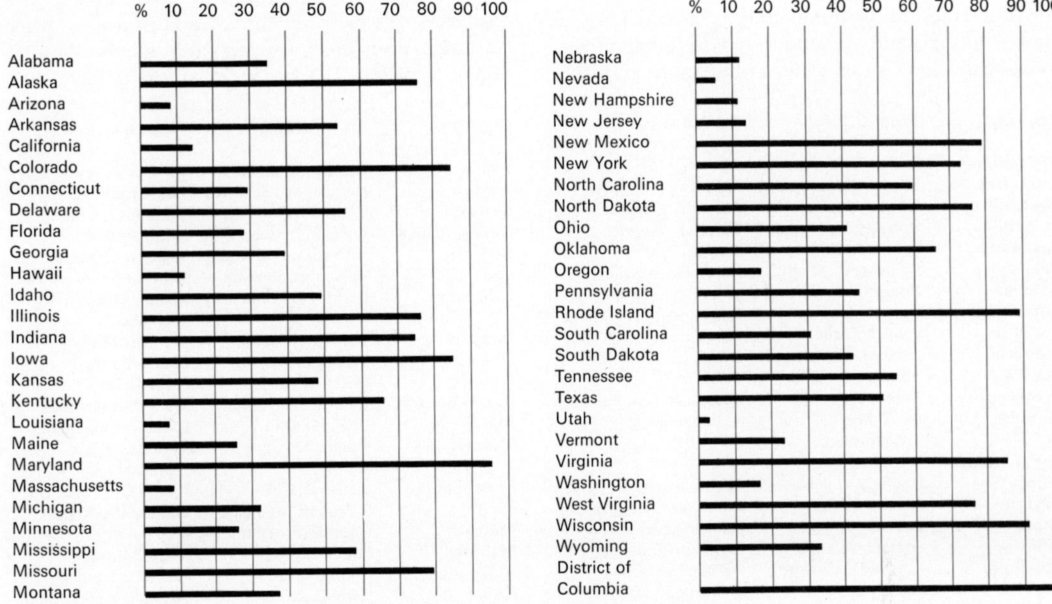

The states and the District of Columbia show wide variations in the percentage of population having access to fluoridated water, either natural or controlled.

November, 1966. A bill that would provide grants "of a comprehensive nature for dental care and services for children" in low-income areas was passed by the House of Representatives on August 17, with the funds to be appropriated in July, 1968. The Senate was expected to act on the bill before the end of the year.

Dental Research. A University of Pennsylvania scientist, Edward P. Henefer, developed a new acrylic sponge which he used successfully to replace lost sections of jawbones in monkeys. He reported that rapid bone growth, without significant inflammation during healing, encourages the use of this "acrylate amide elastomer" in treating human beings. It would be used to replace jawbone lost because of oral disease. Henefer and his co-workers created bone defects next to the teeth roots of 20 monkeys. They then inserted the acrylic sponge into the defective areas. The sponge prevented the collapse of overlying gum tissues and promoted bone growth within two months.

International Dentistry. The Féderation Dentaire Internationale (FDI), at its 55th annual session held in conjunction with the 14th World Dental Congress in Paris, unanimously adopted a policy statement supporting water fluoridation. The FDI also established an advisory board to help member national associations conduct broad-scale education programs in dental health. [Lou Joseph]

DETROIT suffered the worst American race riot since 1943. On Sunday morning, July 23, 1967, a routine telephone call to the police triggered five days and nights of rampaging mobs. Hundreds of stores were looted and burned; 43 persons were killed, 386 injured, and 7,231 arrested. Nearly half those arrested were released without being charged, but it took thousands of federal troops, National Guardsmen, and state and local police to tame the seething slum areas. See City; Civil Rights.

Mayor Jerome P. Cavanagh acted promptly to restore the city's shattered image. He named a 39-member New Detroit Committee. The committee took steps to encourage the hiring of unskilled Negroes and to improve educational programs and housing. Mayor Cavanagh also appointed a task force of experts to review the operations of the city government. Its report of October 28 called for a sweeping overhaul of the city hall administration.

Labor Unrest ran high during the year. In June, hundreds of policemen stayed off the job on sick leave in an effort to win higher wages. In September, public school teachers went on strike for two weeks at the start of the school term. The United Auto Workers went on strike at the Ford Motor Company from September 6 to October 20 (see Automobile; Labor). [Donald W. Lief]

DICTIONARY. See Section Five: Dictionary Supplement.

DIPLOMAT. After the outbreak of fighting between Israel and several Arab countries in June, 1967, Algeria, Iraq, Mauritania, Sudan, Syria, United Arab Republic, and Yemen severed diplomatic relations with the United States. Lebanon and the United States withdrew their respective ambassadors for a short period during the war crisis. Ambassadors representing the United States in other countries and their counterparts to the United States, as of Jan. 1, 1968, included the following:

Country	From U.S.A.	To U.S.A.
Afghanistan	Robert G. Neumann	Abdullah Malikyar
Argentina	Edwin M. Martin	Alvaro C. Alsogaray
Australia	Edward W. Clark	John Keith Waller
Austria	Douglas MacArthur II	Ernst Lemberger
Barbados	Fredric R. Mann	Sir John Carter
Belgium	Ridgway B. Knight	Baron Louis Scheyven
Bolivia	Douglas Henderson	Julio Sanjines-Goytia
Botswana	Vacant	Zachariah K. Matthews
Brazil	John W. Tuthill	Vasco Leitão da Cunha
Bulgaria	John M. McSweeney	Luben Guerassimov
Burma	Henry A. Byroade	U Tun Win
Cameroon	Robert L. Payton	Joseph N. Owono
Canada	W. Walton Butterworth	A. Edgar Ritchie
Cen. African Rep.	Geoffery W. Lewis	Michel Gallin-Douathe
Ceylon	Andrew V. Corry	Oliver Weerasinghe
Chad	Sheldon B. Vance	Boukar Abdoul
Chile	Edward M. Korry	Radomiro Tomic
Colombia	Reynold E. Carlson	Hernán Echavarria Olózaga
Congo (Kinshasa)	Robert H. McBride	Cyrille Adoula
Costa Rica	Clarence A. Boonstra	Fernando Ortuño
Cyprus	Taylor G. Belcher	Zenon Rossides
Czechoslovakia	Jacob D. Beam	Karel Duda
Dahomey	Clinton E. Knox	Maxime-Leopold Zollner
Denmark	Katharine Elkus White	Torben Ronne
Dominican Rep.	John Hugh Crimmins	Héctor Frederico Garcia-Godoy
Ecuador	Vacant	Carlos Mantilla-Ortega
El Salvador	Raul H. Castro	Ramon de Clairmont-Duenas
Ethiopia	William O. Hall	Vacant
Finland	Tyler Thompson	Olavi Munkki
Formosa	W. P. McConaughy	Chow Shu-kai
France	Vacant	Charles E. Lucet
Gabon	David M. Bane	Louis Owanga
Gambia	L. Dean Brown	Vacant
Germany, West	George C. McGhee	Heinrich Knappstein
Ghana	Franklin H. Williams	Ebenezer Moses Debrah
Great Britain	David K. E. Bruce	Sir Patrick Dean
Greece	Phillips Talbot	Christian Xanthopoulos-Palamas
Guatemala	John Gordon Mein	Francisco Javier Linares Aranda
Guinea	Robinson McIlvaine	Karim Bangoura
Guyana	Delmar R. Carlson	Sir John Carter
Haiti	Claude G. Ross	Arthur Bonhomme
Honduras	Joseph J. Jova	Ricardo Midence Soto
Hungary	Martin J. Hillenbrand	Vacant
Iceland	Karl F. Rolvaag	Petur Thorsteinsson
India	Chester Bowles	Braj Kumar Nehru
Indonesia	Marshall Green	Suwito Kusumowidagdo
Iran	Armin H. Meyer	Hushang Ansary
Ireland	Raymond R. Guest	William P. Fay
Israel	Walworth Barbour	Avraham Harman
Italy	Vacant	Egidio Ortona
Ivory Coast	George A. Morgan	Timothée n'Guetta Ahoua
Jamaica	Walter N. Tobriner	Egerton R. Richardson
Japan	U. Alexis Johnson	Takeso Shimoda
Jordan	Harrison M. Symmes	Abdul Hamid Sharaf
Kenya	Glenn W. Ferguson	Burudi Nabwera
Korea, South	William J. Porter	Dong Jo Kim
Kuwait	Howard Rex Cottam	Talat Al-Ghoussein
Laos	William H. Sullivan	Khamking Souvanlasy
Lebanon	Dwight J. Porter	Ibrahim Hussein El-Ahdab
Lesotho	Vacant	Albert S. Mohale
Liberia	Ben H. Brown, Jr.	S. Edward Peal
Libya	David D. Newsom	Fathi Abidia
Luxembourg	George J. Feldman	Maurice Steinmetz
Malagasy	David S. King	Louis Rakotomalala
Malawi	Marshall P. Jones	Nyemba Wales Mbekeani
Malaysia	James D. Bell	Tan Sri Ong Yoke Lin
Mali	C. Robert Moore	Moussa Léo Keita
Malta	Hugh H. Smythe	Arvil Pardo
Mexico	Fulton Freeman	Hugo B. Margáin
Morocco	Henry J. Tasca	Ahmed Osman
Nepal	Carol C. Laise	Padma Bahadur Khatri
Netherlands	William R. Tyler	Carl W. A. Schurmann
New Zealand	John F. Henning	Frank H. Corner
Nicaragua	Kennedy M. Crockett	G. Sevilla-Sacasa
Niger	Robert J. Ryan	Adamou Mayaki
Nigeria	Elbert G. Mathews	N. Ade Martins
Norway	Margaret Joy Tibbetts	Arne Gunneng
Pakistan	Benjamin H. Oehlert, Jr.	Agha Hilaly
Panama	Charles W. Adair, Jr.	Ricardo M. Arias E.
Paraguay	Benigno C. Hernandez	Juan Plate
Peru	J. Wesley Jones	Celso Pastor
Philippines	Vacant	Vacant
Poland	John A. Gronouski, Jr.	Jerzy Michalowski
Portugal	W. Tapley Bennett, Jr.	Vasco Vieira Garin
Romania	Richard H. Davis	Corneliu Bogdan
Russia	L. E. Thompson, Jr.	Anatoliy F. Dobrynin
Rwanda	Leo G. Cyr	Celestin Kabanda
Saudi Arabia	Hermann F. Eilts	Ibrahim Al-Sowayel
Senegal	L. Dean Brown	Ousmane Socé Diop
Sierra Leone	Robert G. Miner	Christopher O. E. Cole
Singapore	Francis J. Galbraith	Wong Lin Ken
Somalia	Raymond L. Thurston	Ahmed Mohamed Adan
So. Africa, Rep. of	William M. Rountree	H. L. T. Taswell
Spain	Angier Biddle Duke	The Marquis de Merry Del Val
Sweden	William W. Heath	Hubert de Besche
Switzerland	John S. Hayes	Felix Schnyder
Tanzania	John H. Burns	Chief Michael Lukumbuzya
Thailand	Leonard Unger	Vacant
Togo	Albert W. Sherer, Jr.	Alexandre Ohin
Trinidad and Tobago	William A. Costello	Sir Ellis E. I. Clarke
Tunisia	Francis H. Russell	Rachid Driss
Turkey	Parker T. Hart	Melih Esenbel
Uganda	Henry E. Stebbins	E. Otema Allimadi
Uruguay	Vacant	Juan Felipe Yriart
Venezuela	Maurice M. Bernbaum	E. Tejera-Paris
Vietnam, So.	Ellsworth Bunker	Bui Diem
Yugoslavia	C. Burke Elbrick	Bogdan Crnobrnja
Zambia	Robert C. Good	Rupiah B. Banda

DISARMAMENT. The United States and the Soviet Union agreed in 1967 on the terms of a treaty that would forbid the transfer of nuclear weapons to "any recipient whatsoever." Other proposals would permit nuclear explosions for peaceful purposes, but would allow signatory countries to withdraw if they felt it was not working effectively.

Final action on the treaty was held up primarily by objections from some West European nations concerning inspection proposals. The United States and the Soviet Union proposed that the nonnuclear power nations be inspected by officials of the United Nations (UN)-affiliated International Atomic Energy Agency (IAEA). The West Europeans, however, preferred that inspection be carried out by their own international agency, the European Atomic Energy Community (Euratom), because, they contended, the Communist members of the IAEA inspection teams could easily steal their industrial secrets.

Other Progress. A treaty to create a nuclear-free zone in Central and South America and the Caribbean was signed on February 14 by Bolivia, Chile, Colombia, Costa Rica, Ecuador, El Salvador, Guatemala, Haiti, Honduras, Mexico, Panama, Peru, Uruguay, and Venezuela. Later, Brazil added its signature, and Great Britain agreed on behalf of its possessions in the Western Hemisphere. It would take effect when ratified by 11 countries.

Space Treaty. The treaty that had been negotiated in 1966 to ban nuclear weapons in outer space and military bases on the moon went into effect Oct. 10, 1967, upon its ratification by the United States, the Soviet Union, Great Britain, and 10 other nations. Altogether, more than 70 nations had signed it; only Communist China had scorned the pact.

Doubts about the treaty's effectiveness were raised on November 3, however, when U.S. Secretary of Defense Robert S. McNamara disclosed that the Soviet Union was developing a Fractional Orbital Bombardment System (FOBS). Nuclear weapons in this system, which McNamara said might be operational as early as 1968, could be sent into "very low orbit about 100 miles above the earth." They could be brought down on a target at any time, he pointed out, by firing a retrorocket before the first orbit was complete.

The Arms Race escalated another notch in 1967 as the Soviet Union declined to discuss a ban on Antiballistic Missiles (ABMs), and began installing ABMs around major Russian cities on an experimental basis. On September 18, Secretary McNamara announced that the United States would build a $5,000,000,000 "limited" ABM system. Both the Americans and the Russians contended they were preparing a defense against a possible surprise attack by Communist China. [MILT FREUDENHEIM]

See also ARMED FORCES OF THE WORLD; NATIONAL DEFENSE; UNITED NATIONS (UN).

DISASTERS. Floods in 1967 were among the worst natural disasters. Brazil was especially hard-hit during the early months of the year. Turkey and Venezuela were the scenes of the worst earthquakes. The most disastrous fire was in a department store in Brussels, Belgium.

Major disasters included the following:

Aircraft Crashes

Feb. 2–Manado, Celebes, Indonesia. A Garuda State Airlines Electra jet burst into flames and exploded, killing 21 persons.

Mar. 5–Near Kenton, Ohio. A Lake Central Airlines Convair 580 crashed and killed 38 of the 89 persons aboard the plane.

Mar. 5–Monrovia, Liberia. A Varig Airlines DC-8 crashed into a house, killing 48 persons in the plane and five in the house.

Mar. 9–Near Urbana, Ohio. A Trans World Airlines DC-9 and a twin-engine Beechcraft burst into flames in the air; 26 persons, including the Beechcraft pilot, were killed.

Mar. 30–New Orleans, La. A Delta DC-4 crashed through two houses and into a motel. Among the 19 persons killed were six in the plane and nine high school senior girls from Juda, Wis., who were staying in the motel.

Apr. 8–Seoul, South Korea. A South Korean Air Force plane crashed, killing 55 persons.

Apr. 11–Ouargla, Algeria. An Algerian National Airline DC-4 hit a peak of the Hoggar Mountains, killing 35 persons.

Apr. 20–Near Nicosia, Cyprus. A Swiss-owned Britannia crashed during a storm, killing 126 persons.

Rescue workers search for victims in the rubble of a demolished building in Adapazari, Turkey, center of earthquakes that struck the country in July.

Dazed and frightened schoolchildren make their way home from Belvidere High School after twisters caused widespread death and destruction over much of northern Illinois in April.

June 3–Pyrenees Mountains, France. A chartered British airliner crashed into Mount Canigou, killing 88.

June 4–Stockport, England. A British Midland Airways plane crashed into the center of the town; 72 persons on the plane were killed.

June 23–Camp LeJeune, N.C. Two Marine helicopters collided, killing 22 men.

June 23–Near Blossburg, Pa. A Mohawk Airlines plane crashed, killing all 34 persons aboard.

June 30–Hong Kong. A Thai International Airways jetliner crashed into the harbor; 21 of the 80 persons aboard were killed.

July 6–Negros Island, Philippines. A Philippines Airline plane hit a mountain, killing 21 persons.

July 19–Near Hendersonville, N.C. A Piedmont Airlines Boeing 727 and an off-course private plane collided, killing 82 persons (3 in private plane).

Sept. 5–Gander, Newfoundland. A Czechoslovak Ilyushin 18 airliner crashed and burned, killing 34 persons.

Oct. 12–Off Southwest Coast of Turkey. A British European Airways Comet airliner crashed. All 66 persons aboard were killed.

Nov. 3–Near Curitiba, Brazil. A Sadia Airlines plane crashed on a mountain peak, killing 20 persons.

Nov. 4–Near Fernhurst, England. An Iberia Airlines Caravelle crashed and killed 37 persons.

Nov. 20–Near Constance, Ky. A Trans World Airlines Convair 880 jet plane crashed as it was nearing the Greater Cincinnati (Ohio) Airport; 69 of the 82 persons aboard were killed.

Dec. 8–Peru. A Fawcett Airlines DC-4 crashed after leaving Huánuco, killing 67 persons.

Blizzards and Storms

Jan. 26-27–Midwest United States. Snow and cold weather killed more than 20 persons. Among the worst hit areas were Chicago and several of its suburbs.

Feb. 7-8–New England. Snow and subzero weather killed at least 18 persons.

Feb. 23-24–Northern Europe. Driving winds and rain killed more than 40 persons.

Dec. 13-20–Southwest United States. Heavy snow in some areas, and sleet and freezing rain in others, took the lives of at least 37 persons. They also brought great suffering to Indian reservations in the area.

Bus and Truck Wrecks

Jan. 6–Philippines. Two buses collided on a narrow mountain road and fell into a deep gorge. 87 persons were killed.

Aug. 13–Iran. Two buses collided southeast of Teheran, killing 40 persons.

Oct. 15–Catarman, Philippines. A bus plunged off a bridge into a river, drowning 20 persons.

Nov. 12–Mae Sarieng District, Thailand. A truck carrying villagers to a festival ran out of control and killed 25 persons.

Earthquakes

Feb. 9–Colombia. An earthquake caused damage in Bogotá and other areas, and killed 100 persons.

Feb. 20–Indonesia. An earthquake in East Java killed 26 persons.

Apr. 11–Madjene, Celebes, Indonesia. An earthquake killed 37 persons.

May 1–Northwestern Greece. An earthquake killed 9 persons.

July 22–Northwestern Anatolia, Turkey. An earthquake killed at least 86 persons.

July 27–Erzincan and Tunceli, Turkey. An earthquake killed 126 persons in 65 villages.

July 29–Venezuela. Three earthquakes shook Caracas and surrounding areas, killing 277 persons.

Nov. 30–Yugoslavia and Albania. An earthquake in the border area killed at least 20 persons.

Dec. 11–India. An earthquake shook the west coast from Bombay to Bangalore, killing 172 persons.

Explosions and Fires

Feb. 7–Tasmania. Brush fires in the southern part of this island state of Australia killed 57 persons.

Feb. 7–Montgomery, Ala. Fire in a restaurant atop the Walter Bragg Smith apartment building killed 25 persons.

Feb. 11–Joliet, Ill. Fire in the Grand Hotel killed eight persons.

Feb. 13–Near Brussels, Belgium. Fire destroyed an elderly people's rest home and killed 21 persons.

Feb. 17–Hawthorne, N.J. Explosions in a chemical plant killed at least four persons.

Feb. 18–Southeast Brazil. A dynamite explosion in a hydroelectric tunnel killed 18 workers.

Mar. 6–Near Taninges, France. Fire nearly destroyed an orphanage, and killed 18 children, ages eight to 18 years.

Apr. 5–Ithaca, N.Y. Fire in a Cornell University residence hall killed eight students and a member of the university faculty.

May 22–Brussels, Belgium. Fire destroyed L'Innovation department store and killed 322 persons.

June 22–Near Burlington, Iowa. An explosion in an Army Ordnance plant killed four women employees.

Aug. 15–Guijuelo, Spain. An explosion in a meat warehouse, caused by a gas leak, killed 15 persons.

Sept. 11–Muscle Shoals, Ala. An explosion in a smelting furnace killed four persons.

Oct. 15–Cliffside Park, N.J. A block of wall fell, killing five firemen as they fought a bowling alley blaze.

Nov. 8–Central Peru. Gas fumes from a dynamite explosion at a hydroelectric project killed 15 workers.

Floating derrick recovers part of Silver Bridge which collapsed into the icy waters of the Ohio River during pre-Christmas rush-hour traffic.

The overflowing Chena River swept through the downtown section of Fairbanks, Alaska, in August and forced half the city's 30,000 residents to flee.

Floods

Jan. 23-26–Brazil. Heavy rains in Rio de Janeiro and São Paulo states killed 800 or more persons.

Feb. 17-20–Rio de Janeiro, Brazil. Rains and landslides killed at least 224 persons in the surrounding area and in Niterói.

Mar. 19–Brazil. Floods and a landslide killed at least 120 persons in Caraguatatuba, and 40 persons in Paraibuna.

Aug. 28-31–Japan. Floods in Niigata and Yamagata prefectures killed 34 persons.

Sept. 5–Northern and Central India. Floods killed at least 93 persons.

Sept. 8–India. The Nanaksagar Dam in the Himalayan foothills burst, killing 75 persons.

Oct. 13–Buenos Aires, Argentina. Rain and floods in the area killed at least 26 persons.

Nov. 21–Southern California. Rains and floods were reported to have killed 12 persons.

Nov. 25-26–Lisbon, Portugal. Rain and floods in the area killed at least 464 persons.

Nov. 30–Central Java, Indonesia. An irrigation dam broke, killing 160 persons.

Hurricanes and Typhoons

July 9–Japan. *Billie*, the season's first typhoon killed at least 260 persons.

Sept. 7-12–Caribbean Sea. Hurricane *Beulah* hit Martinique, St. Vincent, Puerto Rico, St. Lucia, the Dominican Republic, and Haiti, killing 18 persons.

Sept. 17-27–Mexico and Texas. Hurricane *Beulah* lashed the Yucatán Peninsula and swept up the Gulf of Mexico. The Rio Grande overflowed its banks in Texas and Mexico, causing at least 16 deaths.

Oct. 17-18–Formosa. Typhoon *Carla* lashed the island, collapsed houses, and flooded large areas. About 36 persons were killed.

Richard Swanson, *Life* © Time Inc.

Fire on the U.S.S. *Forrestal* killed 134 men on July 29 off North Vietnam, when a fuel tank fell from an A-4 Skyhawk warming up on the carrier's flight deck.

Oct. 28–Central Japan. Typhoon *Dinah* set off landslides and floods, causing 27 deaths.

Nov. 4–Central Philippines. Typhoon *Emma* caused the deaths of 67 persons.

Mine Disasters

Jan. 16–Orange Free State, South Africa. A gas explosion in the Virginia mine killed 17 men.

Jan. 19–Near Greymouth, New Zealand. An explosion in a coal mine killed 19 men.

Apr. 3–Natal, British Colombia. An explosion in a coal mine killed 11 men.

July 25–Carletonville, South Africa. Some Negro workers lost their footing on a stairway in a mine. Screams set off a panic, and 50 workers were killed.

Sept. 5–Chile. An explosion in the Chuquicamata copper mine killed at least 21 workers, some 40 miles northeast of Antofagasta.

Oct. 13–Near Carletonville, South Africa. An explosion in a gold mine killed 14 workers.

Shipwrecks

Jan. 14–Off South Korea. The coastal ferryboat *Hannil-Ho* collided with the navy destroyer *Chungnam-Ho*, and sank; 62 persons were reported missing.

Feb. 28–North Sea. A Russian fish-processing ship sank off Denmark's Jutland peninsula, drowning 52 members of the crew.

Mar. 25–North of Bombay, India. A boat sank in the storm-lashed Par River, drowning 35 persons.

May 3–Near Singa, Sudan. A river boat capsized on the Blue Nile (Bahr el Azraq), drowning 60 persons.

May 24–Off Toulon, France. The Greek oil tanker *Circe* was split in two by an explosion: only one of the 39 men aboard survived.

Oct. 18–Off Western Denmark. The coal freighter *Naugusena* sank in a storm with a crew of 25 men.

Tornadoes

Apr. 21–Northern Illinois. Tornadoes in the Chicago area and in Belvidere killed 57 persons.

Earthquake debris blocks street in Bogotá, Colombia. Store signs dangle from their hangings, and falling walls wreck a parked automobile.

Apr. 30–Southern Minnesota. Tornadoes caused the death of 16 persons in such places as Albert Lea, Alden, and Waseca.

Oct. 30–Mississippi. Two tornadoes battered Gulfport and Mississippi City, killing three persons.

Dec. 18-19–Alabama. Tornadoes killed four persons in the northeastern part of the state.

Dec. 21–Potosi, Mo. A tornado killed three persons.

Train Wrecks

July 6–Nakhon Ratchasima, Thailand. An express train hit a bus, killing 43 bus passengers.

July 6–Near Magdeburg, East Germany. A commuter train and a truck collided at a grade crossing; 44 of the 83 persons killed were children.

Aug. 10–Near Odense, Denmark. One passenger train ran into another one, which had stopped on an overpass; 14 persons were killed.

Oct. 4–Fexhe-le-haut-Clocher, Belgium. The engine of a train hit from behind by a second train was hurled into the path of a Brussels express; 12 persons were killed in the triple crash.

Sept. 16–Mount Washington, New Hampshire. The train of the historic cog railway fell off the track into a gorge; eight persons were killed.

Nov. 5–Near London, England. A Hastings-to-London train was derailed, killing 53 persons.

Nov. 9–Near Salerno, Italy. Buffalo on the tracks derailed the engine of a commuter train. The engine was hit by another train; 12 persons were killed.

Other Disasters

Dec. 15–Kanauga, Ohio-Point Pleasant, W. Va. A suspension bridge collapsed during the evening rush hour and fell into the Ohio River, taking with it pedestrians, automobiles, and trucks; 36 persons were known to have drowned and 10 others were missing.

DOMINICAN REPUBLIC. See LATIN AMERICA.

DRUGS. Prescription drugmakers were still under siege in 1967. In Congress, there were continued charges that drug prices were too high. The Food and Drug Administration (FDA) pursued its strict regulatory policy, and its chief, Dr. James L. Goddard, said he thought industry research was both expensive and inefficient.

Three major congressional investigations were held during the year. In May, the monopoly subcommittee of the Senate's Select Committee on Small Business began hearings on the industry's pricing practices under the chairmanship of Senator Gaylord Nelson (D., Wis.). One witness, U.S. Comptroller General Elmer B. Staats, testified that millions of tax dollars could be saved if welfare prescriptions were filled with *generic* (chemical name) rather than brand-name drugs. Senator Russell B. Long (D., La.) – whose Finance Committee was investigating costs of drugs used under Medicare and Social Security – unsuccessfully urged such legislation for all federal programs.

In the House, Chairman John D. Dingell (D., Mich.) had his Small Business subcommittee look into the matter of drug price discrimination and its impact on the small businessman. Ammunition for all three of these inquiries was provided in a book, *The Handbook of Prescription Drugs*, by Dr. Richard Burack, an affiliate of pharmacology at Harvard Medical School. It lists 162 drugs and compares the prices of the generic and brand names of each. For digitalis, for example, the price range was from $1.36 to $18.40 per 1,000 tablets.

FDA and Drug Industry relations were no more friendly than those between drugmakers and lawmakers. Early in 1967, an FDA study maintained that generic drugs were equal to, if not better than, brand-name products in potency.

Meanwhile, in October, members of the Pharmaceutical Manufacturers Association managed to reach an out-of-court settlement of a four-year dispute with the FDA. Regulations henceforth would require that a drug's generic name always be given only when the brand name appeared prominently on a label or in an ad – not each time the brand name appeared in the text. Paving the way for the settlement was a Supreme Court decision on May 22 that such FDA rules could be challenged in lower courts.

New Drugs. The pace of new drug introductions picked up in 1967. For the eight months through August, some 18 new single chemical products were cleared through the FDA and marketed, against 12 in all of 1966.

World-wide prescription drug sales by U.S. firms totaled $5,100,000,000 in 1967, compared with $4,700,000,000 in 1966. The global outlay on research totaled about $460,000,000. [ARTHUR R. KAVALER]

See also HEALTH; HOSPITAL; MEDICARE; MEDICINE; MENTAL HEALTH; SOCIAL SECURITY.

EARTHQUAKES. See DISASTERS; GEOLOGY.

EASTERN ORTHODOX. Theodosius (Lazor) became the third American-born bishop of the Russian Orthodox Church in America. Consecrated on May 6, he was assigned the Alaska diocese, the oldest in North America.

The Standing Conference of Canonical Orthodox Bishops in the Americas issued a statement in support of the U.S. policy in Vietnam on March 12. A dissenting opinion was expressed by Metropolitan John (Wendland), Exarch of the Patriarchate of Moscow in New York City.

A statement by Archbishop Iakovos, head of the Greek Archdiocese of North and South America, provoked a lengthy controversy in the Greek-American community in September when he called for "de-Hellenizing" the church's theology.

On October 1, a new Exarch, Archbishop Jonathan, was appointed to head the parishes of the Muscovite jurisdiction in America, while Metropolitan John was recalled to the Soviet Union and appointed to the Metropolitan See of Yaroslavl.

The 13th All American Church Convention of the autonomous Russian Church in America, held on November 16, voted to discuss a change of its name to "The Orthodox Church in America" at its 1969 convention. The decision revealed the growing tendency on the part of the Orthodox communities in America toward the establishment of an American Orthodox Church.

It is estimated that there are between 2,000,000 and 3,000,000 Orthodox communicants in the United States, all members of ecclesiastical organizations that still follow the ethnical patterns of the Old World.

Outside the United States, on October 16, for the first time since the separation of the Eastern and Western Churches in 1054, the Patriarch of Constantinople, Athenagoras I, "first among the equal" Orthodox bishops, was received by Pope Paul VI in St. Peter's Basilica in Rome and joined the pope in a service for Christian unity. During the same trip, the Patriarch also visited the Orthodox primates in Bulgaria, Romania, and Yugoslavia, as well as the Archbishop of Canterbury in London, England, and the headquarters of the World Council of Churches in Geneva, Switzerland.

Following the seizure of power by the military junta in Athens, Greece, on April 21, the violently anti-ecumenical Bishop of Athens, Chrysostom, was replaced by the former chaplain to the king, Geronimos (Kotsonis), who initiated several reforms within the Church of Greece. See DEMOCRACY; GREECE.

A group of dioceses in eastern Yugoslavia proclaimed their independence from the Patriarchate of Belgrade and established an "autocephalous" Macedonian Orthodox Church. This act, however, was not recognized by the Church of Yugoslavia and other Orthodox Patriarchates. [ALEXANDER SCHMEMANN]

See also ROMAN CATHOLIC.

ECONOMY, THE

The year 1967 might well be called "the year of anxiety." It began with widely expressed U.S. concern that an economic slowdown was in prospect and ended with an even more widely expressed fear that inflation might get out of hand. In Europe, the opening months saw Britain desperately battling to protect the value of the pound sterling and the whole continent concerned about the outcome of the Kennedy Round of tariff negotiations. The year ended uneasily, with the need to meet new problems: the

devaluation of the pound, speculation in gold, and France's renewed veto of Britain's entry into the Common Market.

U.S. expectations of early sluggishness were basically confirmed. Gross national product (GNP) struggled slowly upward during the first half of the year, helped by rapidly climbing prices. Then, in the last half of the year, GNP picked up speed to end 1967 with an estimated total output of nearly $785,000,000,000. This was more than 5 per cent above the level of 1966. But since prices rose approximately 3 per cent, real growth amounted to only slightly more than 2 per cent. It was the lowest net increase since 1961, but it also was the 13th successive year of gain in real GNP.

This good news, however, failed to dispel the concern that further price increases might result in an actual decline in per capita purchasing power in 1968. To cool off the economy, President Lyndon B. Johnson had called on Congress to enact a 10 per cent increase in income taxes. Opponents of the tax boost argued that the way to halt inflation was to eliminate excessive governmental expenditures. At year's end, the debate was still raging. See PRESIDENT OF THE UNITED STATES.

Conferring on new tax bill are, left to right, Henry Fowler, William McC. Martin, Joseph Califano, Jr., Gardner Ackley, Charles Schultze, and the President.

City Workers' Family Budgets (1959 vs. 1966)

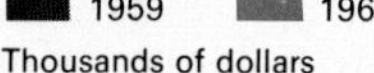

Thousands of dollars

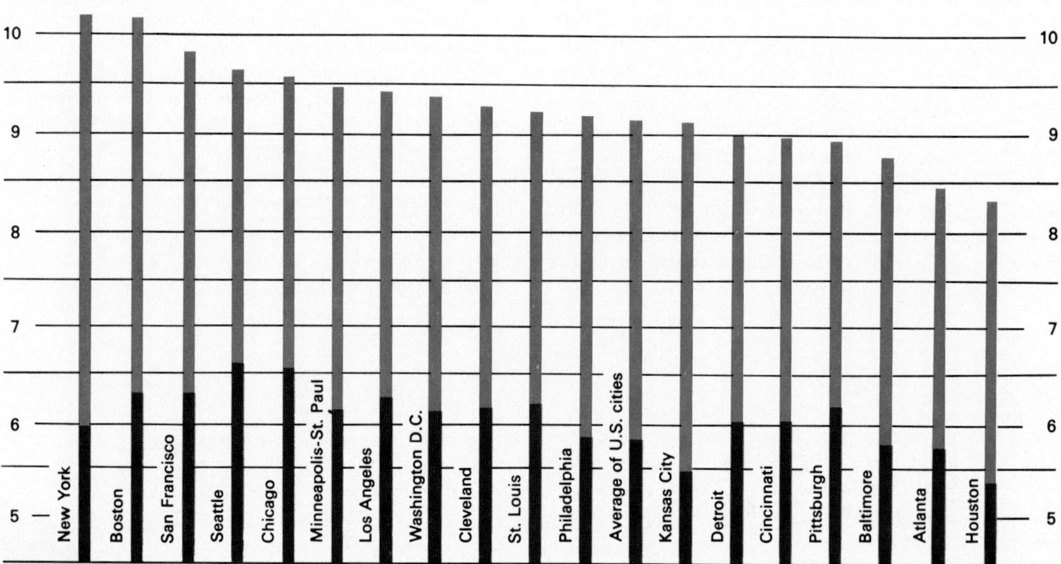

In the fall of 1966, it cost an average of $9,200 for an urban family of four—renters and homeowners—to live "moderately." In 1959, the cost was estimated at $5,800.

The economy of Western Europe, with the exception of Italy, experienced its most dismal year since 1958. Britain's growing balance of payments, dock strikes, unemployment at highest levels since World War II, and other effects of a severe austerity program forced the devaluation of the pound sterling by 14.3 per cent, from $2.80 to $2.40 in terms of the dollar, on November 18 (see GREAT BRITAIN). On the continent, the Common Market nations showed an estimated real growth of only 2 1/2 per cent. West Germany's real GNP declined 1 per cent. Italy was the only member managing to maintain a high rate of growth, 6 per cent. The successful conclusion of the Kennedy Round of tariff revisions gave hope of a sounder base for the European economy in years to come. The United States and most other countries of the Free World agreed on reductions in tariffs of up to 50 per cent, to go into effect over a five-year period (see INTERNATIONAL TRADE AND FINANCE). Elsewhere, Russia continued to boost its output of consumer goods at a record pace–14 per cent above 1966 levels for the first half of 1967. For Soviet industry as a whole, the gain was only 10.6 per cent. Japan's soaring economy continued to grow at about a 9 per cent rate. In 1967, its GNP passed the $100,000,000,000 mark, thus making Japan the world's fourth largest economy, ranking after the United States, the Soviet Union, and West Germany.

The U.S. Economy. All government expenditures, especially those for defense, continued to contribute a major share of the GNP. They rose from $154,000,000,000 in 1966 to an estimated $177,000,000,000 in 1967. The federal government–for the first time since 1964–accounted for slightly more than the state and local governments' purchases of goods and services. National defense expenditures accounted for more than $13,000,000,000 of the total $23,000,000,000 increase. Nondefense federal expenditures rose less than $1,000,000,000.

While the public sector of the economy was expanding, gross private domestic investment dropped from a level of $118,000,000,000 in 1966 to less than $110,000,000,000 in 1967. The greater portion of this decline was accounted for by a drop in inventory accumulation. Total expenditures on new plant and equipment were slightly higher than the year before, and housing starts made a substantial comeback from the low levels of 1966. Total construction expenditures gained less than 1 per cent from the $74,400,000,000 of 1966. See BUILDING AND CONSTRUCTION; HOUSING.

Industrial Production failed to make headway in 1967. The Federal Reserve index of output (1957-1959=100) hovered around the levels of 1966, but was down from the 159.5 mark achieved in December of that year. The 1965 to 1966 rise in the index had been 12.9 points–from 143.4 to 156.3. The usual fall pickup in industrial production was hobbled by the 49-day strike at the Ford Motor Company. After it was settled late in October, industrial output began to rise near the August peak for the year, 158.2. The settlement called for wage and fringe benefit increases over the next three years of from 6 to 6 1/2 per cent a year–about double the former wage-price guidelines of 3.2 per cent. Its full effect on the economy would not be felt until well into 1968, although it quite clearly set an inflationary wage pattern. See LABOR.

Average hourly earnings of all workers in manufacturing industries rose from $2.77 per hour in December, 1966, to $2.85 per hour in October, 1967. A somewhat shorter workweek and rising prices, however, reduced the average weekly earnings in real purchasing power for those two months from $99.74 to $98.18. Despite this slight drop in real weekly earnings, consumers as a whole continued to spend, and save, at a record clip.

The Consumer continued to rule, by far, the largest sector of the economy. Personal consumption expenditures totaled about $493,000,000,000 for the year, against $465,900,000,000 for 1966. Jobs were plentiful, with total civilian employment averaging nearly 74,500,000 for the year. Unemployment was low, as it had been in 1966, averaging only 3.8 per cent of the civilian labor force. The big payrolls put enormous amounts of cash into consumers' pocketbooks, yet their purchases of durable goods rose only slightly during the year, from $70,300,000,000 to $72,500,000,000. Their expenditures on services, however, rose to $202,000,000,000–a whopping 7.8 per cent. Purchases of nondurables grew by more than 4 per cent. This state of affairs has become increasingly typical of our affluent society. Ten years ago expenditures on services made up 38 per cent of personal outlays. Today they average 40 per cent, the percentage having grown in every year of the decade.

U.S. Consumer Income and Outgo

	Calendar Year			3d Quarter Rate		
	1961	1966	Change	1966	1967	Change
	($ billions)		%	($ billions)		%
Personal Income	416.8	584.0	40.1	589.3	631.0	7.0
Less Taxes	52.4	75.2	43.5	76.9	82.8	7.7
Disposable Income	364.4	508.8	39.6	512.4	548.2	7.0
In 1958 dollars	350.7	446.7	27.4	451.0	465.8	32.8
Personal Outlays	343.2	479.0	39.6	483.2	509.6	5.5
Savings	21.2	29.8	40.6	29.2	38.5	31.8
Nonmortgage Debt	57.7	94.8	64.3	91.6	95.9	4.7
Prices and Jobs						
Consumer Price Index	104.2	113.1	8.5	114.1	117.1	2.6
Employed (millions)	66.8	72.9	9.1	73.2	74.6	1.9
Unemployed (millions)	4.8	2.9	−39.6	2.8	3.2	14.3

Despite these record expenditures, personal savings also rose. In 1966, savings amounted to only 5.9 per cent of *disposable* (after-tax) personal income, but for the third quarter of 1967, the rate had reached 7 per cent, the highest in 10 years. For the entire year, it was estimated personal savings would exceed $37,500,000,000. Total disposable personal income had risen to an annual rate of $548,200,000,000 on Sept. 30, 1967–a rise of nearly 7 per cent in 12 months. While the affluent consumer was saving more, he was also borrowing less. Total consumer credit grew much less rapidly in 1967 than in 1966. From September, 1965, to September, 1966, the total outstanding credit rose $7,800,000,000; in the 1966-1967 period the gain was down to $4,300,000,000, for a total of $95,886,000,000. Almost all of the increase was in the form of installment credit.

Prices, under pressure of increased spending by both government and consumers, continued to climb in 1967. The U.S. Bureau of Labor Statistics index of consumer prices (1957-1959=100) rose from 114.7 in December, 1966, to 117.8 in November, 1967. Prices of services rose more rapidly than other items. The cost of medical care led the procession, with a rise of nearly 8 percentage points.

Wholesale prices leveled out during the year, in contrast to their marked jump during 1966 from 102.5 to 105.9. This index closed the year barely changed at about 106. To everyone but the farmer this was welcome news. It promised to limit consumer price rises and suggested a period of price stability. Prices farmers received fell about 6 per cent, while the prices they paid rose about 3 per cent. As a result, total net farm income dropped about 10 per cent from the 1966 total of $16,400,000,000.

The most comprehensive of all price indexes, the implicit price deflator for total GNP jumped more than 3 points in the 12 months from the end of the third quarter of 1966. The deflator is figured by dividing GNP, in current prices, by GNP, in 1958 prices. For the calendar year, the index was expected to rise to about 117, versus 113.9 in 1966.

As 1967 closed, there was a continuing anxiety about the future course of prices. Would the auto industry push its prices higher after the substantial wage boosts of late 1967? As the pay increase pattern spread to other industries, would their prices also rise? What would be the effect of the 10 per cent surtax–if it should be enacted? And if the U.S. balance of payments should go deeper into deficit, would the dollar go the way of the pound? These were the questions facing the economy as the United States rounded out its 82nd month of boom–the longest on record, in war or peace.

Easy Money. The record boom seemed to have proved the validity of the "new economics"–that dexterous fiscal and monetary manipulation could assure prosperity. But in the most recent year of the boom, a new phenomenon appeared that seemed to repeal the law of supply and demand.

For most of 1967, the Federal Reserve Board (FRB) eased its restraints on credit, adopting a policy of easy money (see BANKS AND BANKING). The supply of money was allowed to rise by almost $12,000,000,000, on a seasonally adjusted basis, to more than $180,000,000,000. At the same time, interest rates began to climb. Rates on corporate bonds reached the highest levels since just after the Civil War. The cost of borrowing money had gone up, despite the fact that there was more of it around–in pocketbooks, checking accounts, and savings.

It was once thought that raising interest rates–the price of money–would have a substantial effect on pricing decisions and consumer spending. But in the face of greater supplies of money and expansionary fiscal policy–federal borrowing–this anti-inflationary weapon was largely nullified. In an expansionist, inflationary economy, the demand for money rises. The guiding philosophy seems to be: "Borrow now and forget the high rates; tomorrow they will be all the higher."

The Wall Street Journal in late December quoted bond research specialist Sidney Homer's explanation of the paradox of high interest amidst a money glut: "On the one hand, we have the government waging a costly war without raising taxes. On the other hand, we have corporations and cities, counties, and states (also) borrowing money for expansion and improvement at a record pace. The money market can handle one or the other easily. It has never been called on to handle both."

University of Chicago economist Milton Friedman, who is a consultant to the FRB, has maintained that "over the long run, acceleration of monetary growth raises interest rates," and that in time this "is bound to sink in" at the FRB. Perhaps it had. For in the last 10 days of the year, a tightening of Federal Reserve credit policy was noted. Both the money supply and the net reserve surplus of Federal Reserve member banks had contracted sharply and total reserves in member banks had shrunken below the high levels of the two previous months.

Balance of Payments. If the high interest rates were failing to slow the urge to borrow in the United States, they were still effective in persuading foreigners to keep their dollar holdings invested in this country rather than converting them into gold for investment elsewhere in the world. Nevertheless, the "rush to gold" after the devaluation of the pound brought the U.S. gold stock down to $12,432,000,000 on Dec. 20, 1967, from $13,159,000,000 at the end of 1966. After the initial rush, the seven leading Western industrial countries, with France refusing

Profile of the Longest U.S. Boom on Record

Billions of dollars

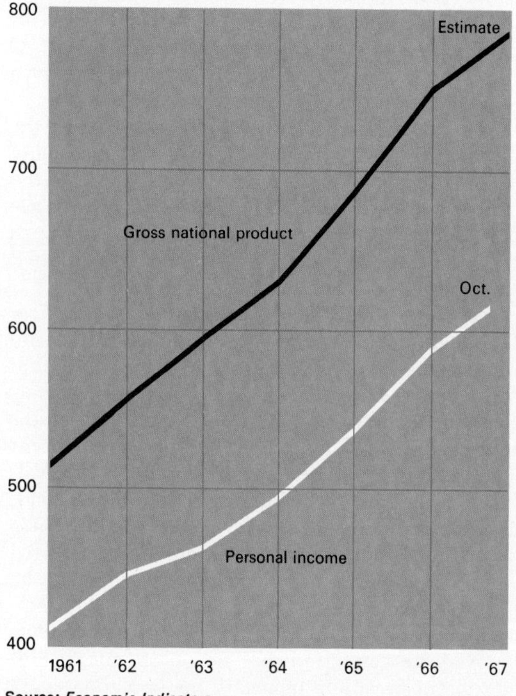

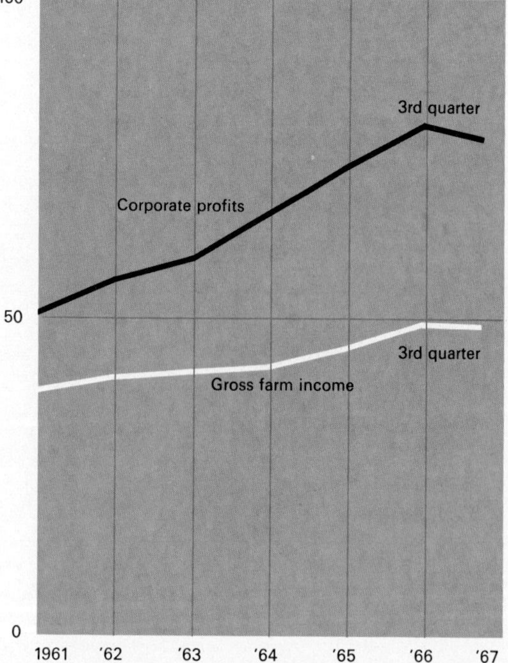

Source: *Economic Indicators*

The Asphalt Jungle

to participate, pooled their efforts on the London gold market to discourage speculators and hold the price of gold at $35 an ounce. Raising the price of gold from $35 would be the same as devaluing the dollar unless all nations did so simultaneously.

Despite a nearly $1,000,000,000 widening in the excess of U.S. merchandise exports (about $31,000,000,000) over imports (about $26,500,000,000), the unfavorable balance of payments gap grew by about as much. Our deficit for 1967 was estimated at $2,400,000,000, compared to $1,357,000,000 in 1966. Here again the heavy expenditures on the war in Vietnam appeared to be a major contributing cause. See INTERNATIONAL TRADE AND FINANCE.

The Stock Market in 1967 tended to confirm the belief that it predicts rather than reflects the course of the economy. The sharp upswing at the start of the year occurred when economic growth was the lowest and thus appeared to be forecasting a strong last six months. The upturn, of course, did occur marred only by a so-so level of industrial output caused largely by the automotive strike.

The Dow-Jones Industrial average began 1967 at 785 and closed the year at about 120 points higher. But this modest gain concealed some intermediate roller-coaster movements. The averages reached 918 in May, fell back into the 860s during the summer, and then hit 940 on September 22. A sharp decline followed until early November, when a recovery to the end of the year got underway. The more comprehensive 500-stock index of Standard and Poor Corporation rose from 81.33 at the start of the year to 105.11 at year end. See STOCKS AND BONDS.

Corporate Profits declined in 1967—not unexpectedly in the face of rising costs and a slower rate of growth than had been anticipated. Before-tax earnings, which had hit $83,800,000,000 in 1966, failed to reach the $80,000,000,000 mark for the entire year 1967. After-tax returns showed a decline of nearly $2,700,000,000 to $46,600,000,000 for the year.

These were declines of less than 6 per cent, but the overall drop masked the many wide fluctuations from industry to industry. For example, after-tax earnings of rubber and allied products firms dropped 41 per cent; steel and iron, 30 per cent; and automobiles and parts 26 per cent in the first nine months, compared with the similar period of 1966. On the other hand, office and computing equipment firms increased their earnings by 20 per cent, and the airlines, by 14 per cent during the same period.

With business picking up late in the year, the full returns may cause some happier faces in corporate board rooms. The fact remains, however, that while 1967 was not as good for the corporate sector as 1966, it was still, by a narrow margin, the second most profitable year on record. Total profits, however, must rise and continue to rise if the owners of businesses are to continue to receive even the same

Gross National Product
By Sectors of the Economy

	Calendar Years			3d Quarter Annual Rate		
	1961	1966	Change	1966	1967	Change
	($ billions)		%	($ billions)		%
Consumer	**335.2**	**465.9**	**38.9**	**470.1**	**495.3**	**5.4**
Durables	44.2	70.3	59.0	70.9	72.7	2.5
Nondurables	155.9	207.5	33.0	209.5	218.5	4.3
Services	135.1	188.1	39.2	189.8	204.1	7.5
Business	**71.7**	**118.0**	**64.6**	**116.4**	**112.2**	**−3.6**
Fixed Capital	69.7	104.6	50.0	104.9	108.4	2.4
Housing	22.6	24.4	8.0	23.7	25.6	8.0
Other Bldg.	18.4	27.9	51.6	28.2	26.6	−5.7
Equipment	28.6	52.3	82.9	53.1	56.2	5.8
Inventory change	2.0	13.4	*	11.4	3.8	*
Net Exports	**5.6**	**5.1**	**−8.9**	**4.6**	**5.4**	**17.4**
Government	**107.6**	**154.3**	**43.4**	**157.7**	**178.2**	**12.9**
Federal	57.4	77.0	34.1	79.5	90.9	14.3
State, Local	50.2	77.2	39.4	78.1	87.4	11.9
Total	**520.1**	**743.3**	**42.9**	**748.8**	**791.2**	**5.7**
In 1958 prices	497.2	652.6	31.3	654.8	672.0	2.6

*Not applicable
Source: U.S. Department of Commerce.

rate of return on their growing investment in the productive equipment of our society.

One thing appeared certain as the United States headed into 1968: that another record-breaking year was in prospect. With a steadily increasing

The Pulse of Business

	Bottom of the 1961 Recession (Feb., 1961 or 1st quarter)	1966 (October or 3rd quarter)	1967*
Total output (GPN, billion, annual rate)	$503.6	$748.8	$791.2
Outputs of industry (1957=100)	102.1	159.4	156.2
Autos, other hard goods	94.3	168.9	160.3
Clothing, other soft goods	110.8	152.8	154.3
Unemployment (per cent of civilian labor force)	6.8	3.8	4.3
Farm net income (billions, annual rate)	$ 12.8	$ 15.0	$ 15.1
Retail trade (billions, monthly)	$ 17.8	$ 25.6	$ 26.2
New construction (billions, annual rate)	$ 54.6	$ 72.3	$ 78.7
Housing starts, private (millions annual rate)	1.2	0.8	1.5
Business inventories (billions)	$ 93.4	$132.4	$138.5
Factories' new orders (billions, monthly)	$ 29.1	$ 45.2	$ 45.5
Unfilled orders (hard goods, end of month)	$ 42.8	$ 79.9	$ 81.6
Factory workweek (average hours)	39.3	41.3	40.7
Corporation profits (billions, annual rate)			
Before taxes	$ 45.0	$ 81.9	$ 49.4
After taxes	$ 24.0	$ 79.3	$ 47.2
Spending for plant and equipment (billions, annual rate, December)	$ 33.8	$ 62.8	$ 62.7
Exports of goods (billions monthly)	$ 1.7	$ 2.6	$ 2.4
Imports of goods (billions monthly)	$ 1.1	$ 2.3	$ 2.2

*Preliminary

population, having passed the 200,000,000 mark in late November, a growing backlog of domestic needs – the rebuilding of cities, improving of streets and highways, clearing of streams and pollution of air, expanding and upgrading of education – and with a confident, almost fully employed labor force, with all these expansive forces at work nothing is likely to stop the economy's momentum. Even the unexpected ending of the war in Vietnam could only slow, not reverse, the pace of the society.

As the United States pushed toward the predicted trillion-dollar GNP in 1975, most economists were expecting that 1968 would bring the GNP to the $840,000,000,000 to $850,000,000,000 range. This would mean a rate of growth ranging from almost 7 per cent to slightly more than 8 per cent. Of that growth, perhaps 3 per cent would be the result of higher prices rather than a rise in output. Nevertheless, a net growth rate of 4 per cent or 5 per cent would be much better than the 1967 achievement.

See also Section One, SYLVIA PORTER: FOCUS ON THE ECONOMY; and articles on the various countries.

ECUADOR. See LATIN AMERICA.

Fred Devan, *Life* © Time Inc.

EDUCATION in 1967 was marked by a growing militancy among teachers, increasing debate over the relationship between church and state, and by mounting concern over skyrocketing costs of financing higher education. The focus of public attention was again the question of how to make city school systems more responsive to the needs of children, especially in urban slums.

Costs and Expenditures. The nation's education expenditure in 1967 was estimated at about $52,000,000,000, or almost 7 per cent of the gross national product. This represented an increase of almost $3,000,000,000 over the previous year. The annual cost of operating the public elementary and secondary schools came to about $30,000,000,000 and that of the nonpublic schools to about $4,000,000,000. Private higher education cost $7,600,000,000. While most public education continued to be financed by local and state budgets, federal contributions grew to about 8 per cent.

Enrollments. Total 1967 enrollment in all types of institutions, public and private, reached a record 57,200,000. The largest increase, 8.3 per cent, was registered in higher education, with 6,500,000 students, compared with 6,000,000 for 1966. These totals included the most rapidly growing sector, the 1,500,000 students in two-year community colleges. High school enrollments, in grades 9 through 12, increased 3 per cent, from 13,300,000 to 13,700,000.

The growing militancy of the nation's teachers was reflected in a New York City rally of some 8,000 striking union members on the opening day of school.

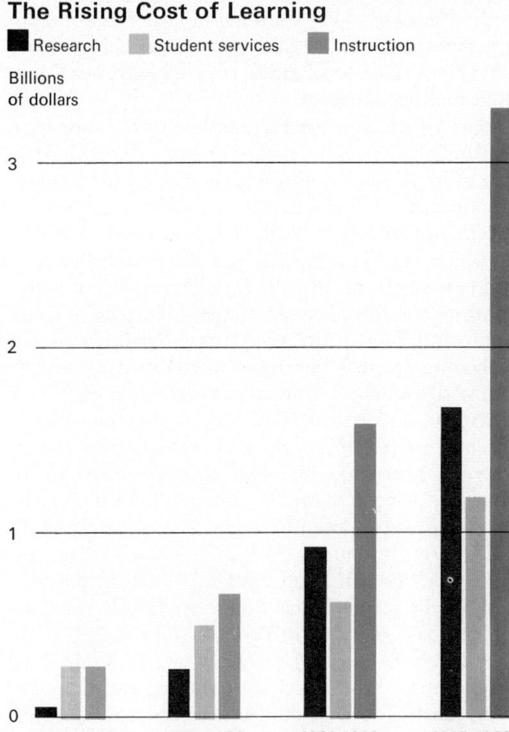

Of this total, the largest nonpublic sector was that of the Roman Catholic parochial schools, with enrollments of 100,000 students.

The declining birth rate, evident since 1961, had for the first time begun to slow the growth of elementary school rolls. In 1967, there was a slight gain of only 1.4 per cent, from 36,500,000 to 37,000,000. Of this total, Roman Catholic parochial schools accounted for about 4,300,000, a decline of about 100,000 over the previous year. However, the U.S. Office of Education reported that the full impact of these lower birth figures will not be felt until the early 1970s, when there may be, for the first time, an actual, though small, reduction in the total number of children in the public elementary schools.

In 1967, nearly 2,700,000 students, or about 75 per cent of the age group, graduated from high school, and 40 per cent of these high school graduates continued on to college. Universities and colleges conferred about 673,000 bachelor's and first professional degrees, 135,000 master's degrees, and 21,000 doctorates. The most substantial increase was in bachelor's degrees, a startling 18 per cent. The reason was the high birth rate of the postwar era.

Teacher Supply. The number of teachers in 1967 reached an all-time high of 2,600,000, and yet there was still a serious shortage. In analyzing the teacher shortage, it was difficult to estimate the exact demand for teachers, however, because of the diverse standards of certification and the number of overloaded classrooms. Nevertheless, it was clear that the shortage had taken on serious proportions.

The National Education Association (NEA) estimated that the nation's schools lacked at least 170,000 qualified teachers in 1967.

Teacher Militancy was closely related to the teacher shortage. Many factors contributed to dissatisfaction within the profession, but the most generally recognized causes were the competition between the NEA and the American Federation of Teachers (AFT); the inflationary economy which has given other professions increased pay and other benefits, the difficult working conditions in the urban slums, and the general air of militancy in American society, with vocal protests often replacing more traditional negotiations.

The contest between the NEA, traditionally a professional rather than trade union organization, and the AFT, with its more militant trade union background, was underlined by several conflicts. The AFT achieved a highly favorable contract in Detroit, Mich., after closing the schools in a start-of-the-year strike, with beginning salaries being raised to $7,500 in the second year of the contract. In Florida, the NEA achieved gains in a battle of strength with the state government and several local communities. In New York City, the flagship local of the AFT, the United Federation of Teachers (UFT), paralyzed the city's schools by getting its members to submit mass resignations in defiance of a new law that prohibited strikes by public employees. After almost three weeks of the walkout, the UFT and the city signed a contract which, in its second year, will give the teachers a scale of from $6,750 to a maximum of $13,900. With 49,000 members, the UFT constituted a powerful segment of the AFT's total membership of 143,000. As the largest single union local in the country, the UFT was widely considered the spearhead of the drive to speed unionization of white-collar workers and professionals. In apparent recognition of this drive, the NEA, which has a membership of more than 1,000,000 teachers and administrators, and which was traditionally opposed to teacher strikes as nonprofessional, reversed its stand. At its annual convention in Minneapolis, Minn., the NEA promised support to each local chapter that considered strike action essential to achieving its goals.

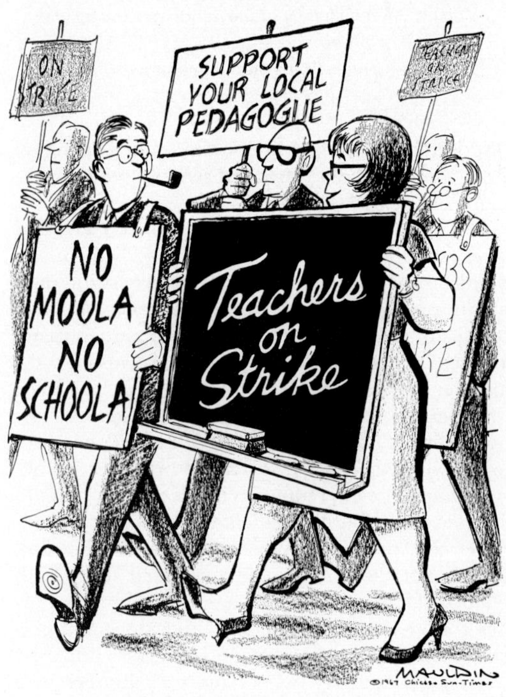

"It seemed more appropriate, somehow."

Urban Schools. While teachers demanded higher salaries, they also increasingly stressed the need for better schools. The AFT made the More Effective Schools Project (MESP), which it had cosponsored in the New York City slum neighborhoods, a major contract issue. The MESP, which was being introduced in a number of cities, stressed extra teaching staffs and small classes.

New York City, under a mandate by the state legislature, was moving toward greater decentralization of its school system, with a specific plan being prepared by a blue-ribbon committee headed by McGeorge Bundy, president of the Ford Foundation. The Ford Foundation had also established several experimental projects in which informal community governing boards, made up largely of local Negro and Puerto Rican parents and neighborhood spokesmen, were being urged to establish a partnership with school administrators and teachers.

Church and State. The debate over the separation of church and state became more prominent in 1967. In Maryland, the state supreme court ruled that two Roman Catholic colleges were ineligible for public funds because they were directly controlled by the church, but that Hood College in Frederick, though Protestant in its basic sponsorship, could receive such funds because it was not subject to religious control.

Not only because of recent court decisions, but also because of the search for a more general role in the mainstream of higher education, a number of Roman Catholic universities, notably Notre Dame, St. Louis, Detroit, and Fordham, moved to virtual

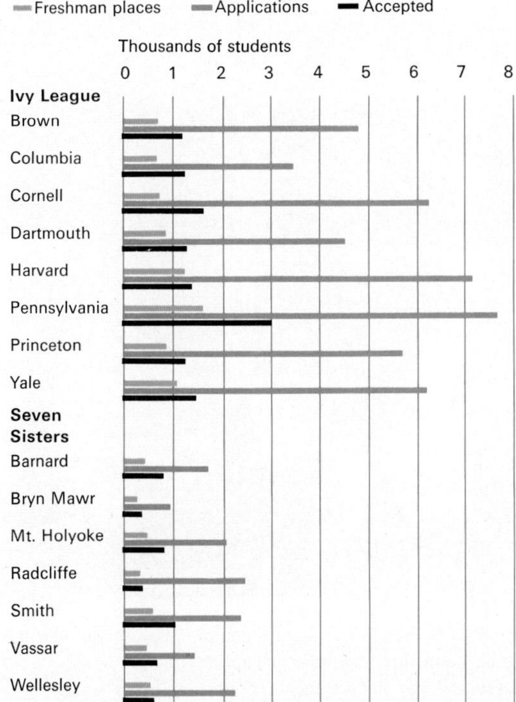

lay control of their boards of trustees. In a startling move, Sister Jacqueline Grennan, president of Webster College in St. Louis, Mo., left the order of the Sisters of Loretto and, with church permission, became the first lay president of the college.

The church-state issue also assumed new importance in New York's constitutional convention which recommended the repeal of a 113-year-old ban on the expenditure of public funds, either directly or indirectly, for the support of church-related institutions. The convention substituted for the existing article, popularly known as the Blaine amendment, the language of Amendment 1 to the U.S. Constitution, adding a "judicial review" clause giving citizens the right to bring suit against the state and its officials in efforts to test the constitutionality of such aid. In November, however, New York state voters defeated the new state constitution.

Campus Unrest. In the aftermath of the student rebellion of 1964 at Berkeley, the huge University of California system was shaken when the board of regents, newly joined by Governor Ronald Reagan as an ex-officio member, dismissed Clark Kerr, the university's president. Kerr had held the post since 1958. As Berkeley's chancellor, Kerr had defended faculty members who had been fired for refusing to sign loyalty oaths during the 1950s. The final controversy over Kerr erupted over the governor's proposal to cut the university's budget and impose tuition fees. However, after Kerr's dismissal, the trustees themselves refused to agree to the imposition of tuition, although they agreed to an increase of the $220 annual fee. Kerr remained at Berkeley as a full professor and also accepted the chairmanship of a newly formed Commission on Higher Education, financed by the Carnegie Corporation of New York.

Higher Education Costs. As costs mounted, experts expressed increasing concern over the inability of many families to pay for their children's college years. Surveys indicated that even at free or low-tuition public universities the cost of subsistence alone totaled between $1,000 and $1,500 annually. The total annual cost of many private institutions was more than $3,500 a year.

Among proposals advanced was a plan by the New York State Board of Regents to give some measure of public subsidy to all students on a declining scale according to need, provided their families' taxable income was not above $15,000. In another proposal, a panel of White House advisers, headed by physicist Jerrold Zacharias of the Massachusetts Institute of Technology, called for the establishment of a federally organized Educational Opportunity Bank. The bank would permit any student to borrow up to the full cost of his undergraduate education, with the understanding that he would repay the debt after graduation on the basis of a fixed percentage of his annual taxable income.

Conant Report. James B. Conant marked the 10th anniversary of his influential report, *The American High School Today*, with the publication of a follow-up report, *The Comprehensive High School*, in which he charged that the financing of public education remains "chaotic." He urged a greater shift from local to state financing.

Foundation Activities. The Ford Foundation announced that it would reduce its direct support of specific colleges and universities and urged those institutions to invest their funds more effectively and to present their financial dilemma to the public and the federal government with greater honesty and clarity. During the year, the foundation concentrated more of its funds on the support of the nation's Negro colleges. It also gave an initial $41,500,000 for a project to improve the quality of Ph.D. studies, as part of a joint program with more than 20 participating universities.

The Alfred P. Sloan Foundation made a $7,500,000 grant – the largest in its history – to 20 small liberal arts colleges in order to help them improve science instruction. [FRED M. HECHINGER]

See also Section One, LAWRENCE A. CREMIN: FOCUS ON EDUCATION.

EDUCATIONAL FOUNDATIONS. See FOUNDATIONS.

EGYPT. See UNITED ARAB REPUBLIC (U.A.R.).

EIGEN, MANFRED. See NOBEL PRIZES.

EIRE. See IRELAND.

EISENHOWER, DWIGHT D. (1890-), former President of the United States and five-star general in World War II, received the distinguished service citation of the Centennial Legion of Historic Military Commands in October as "the outstanding figure in peace and war of our generation."

Throughout 1967, he continued to support the administration's war effort. During an April visit from General William C. Westmoreland, U.S. commander in Vietnam, Eisenhower said he hoped "America will wake up to the fact that our soldiers are dying for something we believe in." In October, he joined the new nonpartisan Citizens Committee for Peace with Freedom in Vietnam. In a taped television interview at his Gettysburg, Pa., farm in November, he urged that U.S. troops be allowed to "make end runs" around the demilitarized zone in Vietnam "either from the sea or from the hills." He also urged that troops be allowed to pursue attackers into Laos or Cambodia.

On Nov. 27, 1967, General and Mrs. Eisenhower deeded their Gettysburg farm to the government as a national historic site. The general will have life tenancy. If Mrs. Eisenhower is the survivor, she will be allowed occupancy for six more months.

His book *At Ease: Stories I Tell to Friends* was published in June. Late in the year, he was reported to be working on another book. [CAROL L. THOMPSON]

See also PERSONALITIES.

Richard G. Hatcher, at a pre-election press conference at his campaign headquarters, confidently predicted he would win election as mayor of Gary, Ind. He did.

ELECTIONS. Negroes scored a historic advance, and the Republicans made scattered gains in off-year elections of mayors, governors, and state legislators. Negroes broke the color bar in city hall for the first time on Nov. 7, 1967, in two large U.S. cities. In Cleveland, Ohio, Democrat Carl B. Stokes, whose great-grandfather was a slave, defeated Republican Seth C. Taft, whose grandfather was President William Howard Taft. In Gary, Ind., Democrat Richard G. Hatcher won over Republican Joseph B. Radigan.

The election of two Negro mayors who are both moderates on civil rights issues was hailed as a setback to black militant leaders. Although Cleveland and Gary are heavily Democratic cities, strong white backlash produced extremely thin vote margins. Stokes won by only 1,679 votes and Hatcher by 1,871, indicating the defection of many white Democratic voters. The white backlash was also overcome in Boston's nonpartisan election for mayor. Kevin H. White, the Massachusetts secretary of state, defeated Louise Day Hicks by 12,429 votes. Mrs. Hicks, who had headed the Boston School Committee, was an outspoken opponent of busing for school integration. Her campaign slogan was, "You know where I stand" (see BOSTON; CITY).

In the South, as well, the Negro vote had grown in importance. In Mississippi, Robert G. Clark was the first Negro since Reconstruction days to win a seat in the state house of representatives; and in Virginia, Dr. William Ferguson Reid performed the same feat in the general assembly. A Negro, James M. Bradby, was also elected sheriff for the first time within memory in rural Charles City County. His opponent had been sheriff for 43 years.

The Republicans made strong gains in two states. In Kentucky, they won control of the statehouse in the upset victory of Louie B. Nunn over Democrat Henry Ward in the governor's race. It was the first time in more than 20 years that Kentucky had chosen a Republican as governor. Nunn's triumph also gave the Republicans 26 out of the 50 governorships in the nation – the first Republican majority of governorships since 1955. In New Jersey, the Republicans regained control of both houses of the state legislature, which they had held from 1913 until 1965. In that year, they were swept out of office in the Democratic landslide that re-elected Governor Richard J. Hughes for a second four-year term.

Were these successes a "continuing Republican trend"? Republican National Chairman Ray C. Bliss thought that they were, while Democratic National Chairman John M. Bailey said he could see "no particular trend." See REPUBLICAN PARTY.

The Democrats retained their hold on the mayorships of Chicago, Ill.; Cleveland; Gary; Philadelphia, Pa.; and San Francisco, Calif. They regained Baltimore, Md., and elected governors, as expected, in Mississippi and Louisiana.

In Chicago, Democrat Richard J. Daley set a personal, all-time vote-getting record on April 4, when he won re-election to a fourth term as mayor of the second largest city in the United States. Carrying all 50 wards of Chicago, he overwhelmed his Republican opponent, John L. Waner, by amassing 74 per cent of the votes. Daley's personal popularity had slipped at the end of 1966, particularly in Negro neighborhoods and in white communities that had been affected by the riots in the summer of 1966. But his victory reaffirmed his position as head of the nation's top Democratic city organization (see CHICAGO). In November, the Democrats were heartened by the re-election of Mayor James H. Tate in Philadelphia who turned back a major challenge from District Attorney Arlen Specter, a Democrat-turned-Republican, who was a slight favorite in the race (see PHILADELPHIA). In Baltimore, Thomas J. D'Alesandro III, son of a former mayor, recaptured city hall for the Democrats with a landslide victory for the seat of retiring Republican Mayor Theodore R. McKeldin. In San Francisco, Democrat Joseph Alioto won over Republican Harold Dobbs for the post vacated by John Shelley (see SAN FRANCISCO).

In Mississippi, the governor's contest was easily won by Representative John Bell Williams, a segregationist Democrat who bolted the party in 1964 to back Barry Goldwater for President. His Republican opponent, Rubel L. Phillips, who had run for governor in 1963 as a segregationist, campaigned as a racial moderate – and got a smaller percentage of the vote than before. In Louisiana, where the Republicans did not field a candidate, the election was decided in the Democratic primary won by the incumbent governor, John J. McKeithen.

Other Issues. In New York state, a new constitution that would have opened the way for public aid to parochial schools was defeated by a 5-to-2 margin. The war in Vietnam was a direct issue on the ballots in two cities. San Francisco voters rejected, 132,000 to 76,600, a proposal for a cease-fire and a U.S. withdrawal from Vietnam. A Cambridge, Mass., referendum urging the "prompt return home of American soldiers from Vietnam" was defeated by a vote of 17,700 to 11,300.

Voters supported more than 90 per cent of state and local bond propositions, for a total of slightly more than $3,000,000,000. New York state's $2,500,000,000 in airport, highway, and mass transit bonds accounted for the overwhelming bulk of the issues. New Yorkers, however, rejected another $150,000,000 in state industrial development bonds. Nationwide, school construction proposals fared poorly; only 53 per cent of the $221,800,000 worth of such bonds won approval. [WILLIAM MCGAFFIN]

See also CIVIL RIGHTS; STATE GOVERNMENT; TAXATION.

ELECTRIC EQUIPMENT. See ELECTRIC POWER AND EQUIPMENT; MANUFACTURING.

ELECTRIC POWER AND EQUIPMENT. Electric utilities faced their greatest challenges in 1967 in their efforts to meet ever-growing loads, higher equipment costs, and industrial demands for greater service reliability. Load growth stemmed, in part, from an upsurge in electric heating and from the increasing demand for air conditioning. Most of the growth, however, was traceable to the continuing efforts of the industry to satisfy the needs and the whims of an affluent society.

Generating costs dropped about 1 mill per kilowatt-hour (kwh) during the year, reaching an impressive 5.84 mills, based on a recent survey of fossil-fueled central stations. Nevertheless, the capital costs of building more reliable systems continued to climb. The reduction in generating costs could be traced to the basic economies in using large units plus higher efficiencies from improved operating practices. The number of operating and maintenance persons per 100,000 kilowatt (kw) of generating capacity had dropped from 30.6 men in 1960 to about 17.5 men in 1967.

The utility industry had a good year, in revenue, profit, and kwh output. Industry figures for the year ending December 31 were:

	1966	1967	% Gain
	(in millions)		
Total generation (kw)	265	286	7.9
Total production (kwh)	1,248,000	1,315,000	5.4
Utilities' output (kwh)	1,144,000	1,212,000	6.0
Utilities' revenues*	$13,800	$14,570	5.8

*for investor-owned companies

Even with these gains, some within the industry believed the selling price of their product – the kilowatt-hour – should be increased, and that rates should be linked to reliability – minimum rates for those systems, or portions of systems, offering the least in service reliability.

The Quest for Reliability in 1967 was expensive. Utilities spent lavishly in improving their generating and transmitting facilities to prevent a recurrence of the November, 1965, Northeast blackout. Despite these steps, the Pennsylvania-New Jersey-Maryland power pool failed on the morning of June 5, 1967, throwing a 15,000-square-mile area of the heavy-industry states on emergency stand-by, where such stand-by existed. Restoration of power took from 30 minutes to as long as 10 hours. Costs in business losses were an estimated $30,000,000 to $40,000,000.

On July 26, 1967, following 20 months of study, the Federal Power Commission released a three-volume report to the President titled *Prevention of Power Failures.* It urged the strengthening of interconnections between electric systems, the provision of emergency power in central stations, and the further development of instrumentation and control techniques. Each step, it said, was geared to improving the reliability of utility systems, and would decrease, but not altogether eliminate, the probability of blackouts.

Thermal Pollution of rivers and lakes became a critical problem for utilities as their generating units approached the 1,000,000-kw capacity size. Such units use enormous amounts of water for cooling. The heated discharge may cause an explosive growth of algae and injure fish and other aquatic life. Some utilities are leaning toward use of cooling towers for disposal of unwanted heat.

The old battle against air pollution made measurable gains. Research efforts centered on (1) removing sulfur from fuel before burning and (2) collecting sulfur from stack gases after combustion. These steps would, of course, add to costs.

Capital Costs of generating plants were rising. For example, in 1966, the Tennessee Valley Authority (TVA) estimated energy costs of 2.39 mills per kwh for two nuclear units. In 1967, the TVA predicted a cost of 2.75 mills per kwh for a similar newly ordered nuclear plant.

The locating of a nuclear power plant in urban areas adds complications that add to costs. New York City's Consolidated Edison Company was studying the feasibility of locating a nuclear power plant within city limits, but underground. Such a location would meet the twin challenges of safety and load growth. A nuclear plant built underground would also meet New York's tough air pollution controls. [JAMES J. O'CONNOR]

See also ENERGY; MANUFACTURING.

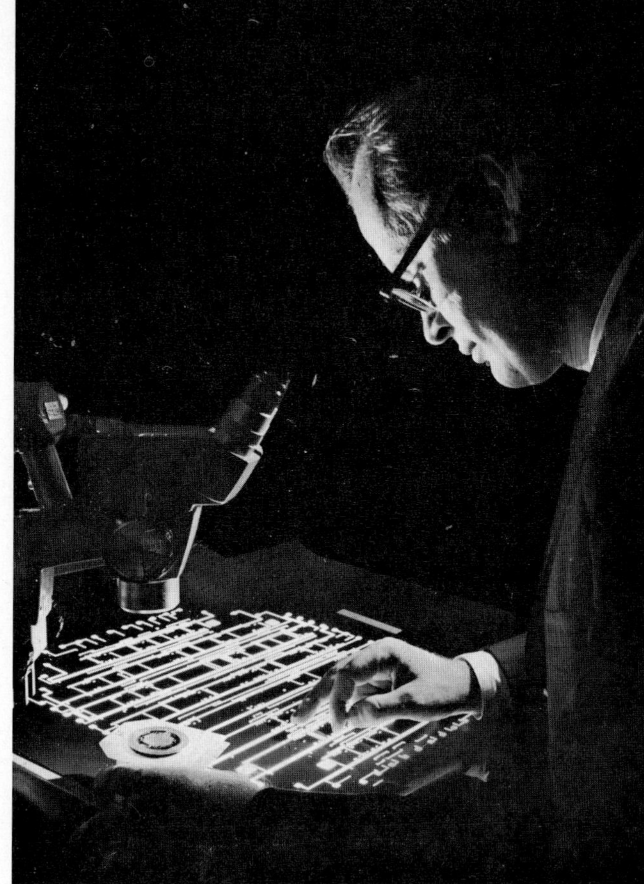

Laboratory technician holds tiny circuit array in his hand, *above*, as he examines it with enlargement. Another integrated component, *below*, is only 2½ inches square, yet has 32 leads on each side.

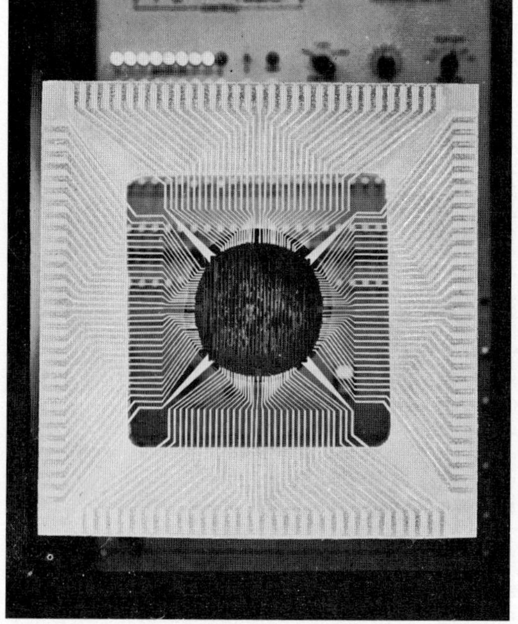

ELECTRONICS. Solid state diodes were used, in 1967, in experimental microwave transmitters instead of klystron tubes. These tubes have always been the most expensive and bulkiest component of such transmitters, but they could not be replaced by solid state diodes until a way could be found that would allow the thin diodes to withstand high voltages.

This is now possible as a result of a discovery, by John A. Copeland of Bell Telephone Laboratories, of a new kind of electronic oscillator, or frequency generator. Called the limited space-charge accumulation (LSA) diode, the device can produce more power at high frequencies than any other solid state oscillator built so far. In LSA diodes, frequency is independent of thickness. A research group at Cornell University used an LSA diode to generate microwave pulses of 8,000,000,000 cycles per second at 615 watts power, a record for solid state microwave generation.

Speaking at a summer conference at Cornell University, Copeland predicted that LSA devices would be used commercially first in communications satellites transmitting between cities on frequencies from 30 gigahertz (GHz) to 300 GHz. One GHz equals 1,000,000,000 cycles per second. Such links will make increasing use of the high end of the microwave spectrum, which permits wider bandwidths and a larger number of channels than the crowded, lower frequency regions. The high cost of present microwave sources has been a major factor in limiting use of microwaves to military or critical industrial applications.

Integrated Circuits. An experimental radio displayed in Chicago, Ill., in June, contained two of the most complex integrated circuits (ICs) yet built. Each IC performed five separate functions. They were built by the Philco-Ford Corporation. The radio outperformed standard transistor radios in all respects. ICs were first introduced to the high fidelity field in December, 1966, when H. H. Scott, Incorporated, began to market three FM tuner-amplifier models containing ICs. Four major semiconductor manufacturers displayed other ICs designed for use in consumer electronic products at a Chicago conference in June, 1967. The devices were priced to compete with the vacuum tube and transistor circuits in radios and in television sets, which they were designed to replace.

General Motors Corporation began installing IC voltage regulators on some of the models in their 1968 Pontiac line.

Lasers. Sales of lasers during 1967 were expected to reach $29,000,000. More than 20 companies were manufacturing lasers ranging in price from about $300 to $250,000.

A laser-driven, tunable light source was developed by Stephen Harris, professor of electrical engineering at Stanford University. Harris passed the beam of an argon laser through a crystal of lithium niobate and tuned the frequency of the emerging beam from infrared to deep green-blue by changing the temperature of the crystal from 75°C. to 350°C. Though previous lasers could generate more than one discrete wave length, none could be tuned "up and down the scale," so to speak, as can the one developed by Harris.

International Business Machines Corporation developed a versatile laser that could use almost any gas. It produced beams at frequencies ranging from infrared to ultraviolet, and was pumped inductively with a low-cost, compact power supply. The laser fulfilled many of the requirements needed to develop laser systems for projecting wall-sized displays and for high-speed photographic printing.

Recording. Siegfried S. Meyers, physics professor at Madison College, Harrisonburg, Va., announced that he had developed a magnetic recording tape that could record on both sides without any loss in recording quality. The double-duty tape had a ferrite middle layer placed between two conventional Mylar layers. The ferrite, serving as a barrier, kept magnetic flux from one side from interfering with the signals on the opposite side. [James A. Pearre]

EL SALVADOR. See Latin America.

EMPLOYMENT. See Automation; Economy, The; Education; Labor; Social Security; Social Welfare; Section One, Sylvia Porter: Focus on The Economy; Section Two, Where The Jobs Will Be.

ENERGY. The adoption of nuclear power for commercial generation of electricity increased in 1967. In the first 10 months, plans for 26 new nuclear power station units were announced. This brought the number of domestic nuclear power station units in operation, under construction, or committed to 84. The Atomic Energy Commission (AEC) reported to President Lyndon B. Johnson, in March, that 23 to 30 per cent of U.S. electric generating capacity will be nuclear by 1980 and 50 per cent by the year 2000.

The AEC, in the same report, revised its estimate of the amount of reactor fuel, slightly enriched U-238, that will be needed by 1980. The present annual consumption is less than 30 metric tons. The AEC estimated that between 3,000 and 4,000 metric tons per year will be required by 1980. Though government-owned gaseous diffusion plants can supply fuel to the power industry until at least that date, AEC representatives reported that they were presently negotiating with interested industrial firms to transfer fuel production to private industry.

Gas Centrifuge Research. The AEC then announced, however, that private development of the gas centrifuge process for separating fissionable U-235 from U-238 would be halted for national security reasons. The move was prompted by concern that unauthorized knowledge of the process, which lends itself to small, easy-to-conceal plants, could contribute to nuclear weapon proliferation. United States work on the process was being conducted by four firms, Allied Chemical Corporation, Electro-Nucleonics Incorporated, General Electric Company, and W. R. Grace and Company. In the case of Electro-Nucleonics, gas centrifuge research was its sole business. The AEC agreed to review each company's research program to determine if it could be useful to the AEC's own classified program on a contract basis.

Though the move was aimed at keeping gas centrifuge technology within the United States, critics pointed out that China reportedly had been operating such a plant since 1966, and that Great Britain, Japan, the Netherlands, and West Germany were all working on the process.

World-Wide Developments. Canada's first full-scale nuclear power plant went into trial service in January, 1968. The 200-kilowatt station is located at Douglas Point, Ont.

The Soviet Union announced in October that the 76 billion electron volt (bev) accelerator at Serpukhov, south of Moscow, had begun operation. This is the most powerful accelerator in the world, more than doubling the energy output of the accelerator at Brookhaven National Laboratory on Long Island. The machine to be built at Weston, Ill., however, is expected to achieve 200 bev, or more.

On June 17, Communist China exploded its first hydrogen bomb. The blast had a yield estimated at

World Notes Birth of the Atomic Age

At 3:25 P.M. Wednesday, Dec. 2, 1942, the late Italian physicist Enrico Fermi ordered a cadmium-plated rod slowly lifted from deep within the first atomic pile at the University of Chicago. The pile was beneath the now demolished west stands of Stagg Field, the university's athletic stadium. For 28 minutes, the fires of nuclear fission burned within the depths of the pile, and man thus achieved the first self-sustaining nuclear chain reaction.

The power produced by the pile was only half a watt, but enough to alter the course of history. Later that afternoon, after the pile was turned off, the late Arthur Holly Compton, who was in charge of Manhattan Project operations at the university, telephoned the project's overall scientific chief, James B. Conant, president of Harvard University.

"The Italian navigator has landed in the New World," he told Conant.

"How were the natives?" Conant asked.

"Very friendly," replied Compton.

This improvised exchange has since become perhaps the best-known secret code of the 20th century. The event marked the beginning of the "Atomic Age." The energy produced by the atom has become the world's greatest hope for an almost unlimited source of energy for creating useful power. It also threatens man's very existence through the possibility of almost complete destruction in atomic warfare.

Moore bronze commemorates control of nuclear energy.

The output of the Chicago pile was raised to 200 watts on Dec. 12, 1942. It could have been increased still further, but it was decided not to do so because of the possible health hazard to personnel by the radiation emitted. For this reason, the first chain-reacting pile was dismantled early in 1943 and reconstructed at Palos Park, outside Chicago. The rebuilt pile, in the form of a cube, was provided with adequate radiation shielding and improved safety devices.

In honor of the 25th anniversary of the first chain reaction, a special observance was held on the campus of the University of Chicago, Dec. 1 and 2, 1967. Six Nobel laureates were among the speakers. They were Melvin Calvin, University of California, Berkeley (chemistry, 1961); Sir John Cockcroft, Churchill College, Cambridge, England (physics, 1951); Willard F. Libby, University of California, Los Angeles (chemistry, 1960); Glenn T. Seaborg, chairman of the U.S. Atomic Energy Commission (chemistry, 1951); Emilio Segrè, University of California, Berkeley (physics, 1959); and Eugene P. Wigner, Princeton University (physics, 1963).

One account of the first chain reaction related at the meeting was that of the only woman present at the historic start. She is Leona Marshall, now Mrs. Willard Libby.

Immediately after the reaction was stopped, she said, "There was absolutely dead silence." Finally, Eugene Wigner produced a bottle of chianti in honor of their Italian boss, Fermi. "Everyone drank it very quietly," added Mrs. Libby. "There was no toast–nothing. I am sure everyone was thinking immediately ahead to the bomb from that minute on."

Walter H. Zinn, another scientist, told of fighting cold in the unheated building by installing gas-fueled devices that produced intolerable fumes. The group finally was able to solve their temperature problem by donning old raccoon coats that they found in a locker. The coats were left by a university football team.

A highlight of the observance was the dedication of *Nuclear Energy*, a major work by the British sculptor Henry Moore, which had been commissioned for the occasion. The 12-foot sculpture was cast in bronze by Hermann Noack in Hamburg, Germany, and shipped to Chicago through the St. Lawrence Seaway. It was unveiled by Mrs. Enrico Fermi.

Moore's symbolic bronze now rests on the exact site where Nobel laureate Fermi and his 29 assistants first unleashed the power of the atom. Scholars and statesmen from many nations took part in seminars that were held during the observance.

The year 1967 was also the 25th anniversary of the first isolation and weighing of the radioactive element plutonium. One microgram of plutonium was isolated at the University of Chicago on Sept. 10, 1942. The event was observed at the university in September. [FOSTER P. STOCKWELL]

In budget-cutting drive, President Johnson decided to drydock the nuclear-powered ship *Savannah*, but protests led to a reprieve in June, and the ship sailed again.

three megatons. The achievement prompted the U.S. congressional Joint Committee on Atomic Energy to state that Chinese progress in nuclear weapons development had been more rapid and effective than predicted. China's first atomic bomb was exploded in October, 1964. See CHINA.

Irradiation. After many years of research and development of processes for irradiating food to preserve it without refrigeration, the AEC entered the pilot plant stage in 1967. Irradiated Foods, Incorporated, of Allentown, Pa., was awarded a contract to build a plant capable of irradiating 1,000,000 pounds of meat per year. The meat will be purchased by the Department of Defense for feeding U.S. soldiers. Commercial marketing of irradiated meats for public consumption awaited approval by the Food and Drug Administration (FDA). The FDA did approve three other radiation-processed foods, however, in 1967–bacon, potatoes, and wheat.

Plowshare, the AEC's program for the peaceful use of nuclear explosives, reached the testing stage in one of three projects under development. The program is designed to recover minerals from deposits which defy conventional mining procedures. On December 10, a nuclear device was exploded in a deposit of gas-bearing rock 4,000 feet underground in the San Juan Basin, 55 miles east of Farmington, N. Mex. It was the first test shot in Project Gasbuggy, an experiment in using nuclear charges to fracture low permeability, gas-bearing rock, permitting gas to exit through well shafts. See PETROLEUM AND GAS.

The two other projects in the Plowshare program are Project Sloop and Project Bronco. Sloop will test the feasibility of using a nuclear charge to fracture copper ore, permitting copper extraction via acid pumped into the deposit and back to the surface for copper recovery. Bronco will test the feasibility of using nuclear explosives to release large quantities of oil held in underground shale deposits.

Fusion Research scored an important gain with the successful operation of a device that held deuterium plasma stable for a significant length of time. Control of plasma, a super-hot form of matter like that within an exploding hydrogen bomb, is the key to harnessing thermonuclear fusion which could provide an inexhaustible source of power in the future. Tihiro Ohkawa, a nuclear physicist at General Dynamics' General Atomic Division, used a doughnut-shaped magnetic "bottle" to keep the deuterium plasma stable for about one-thousandth of a second. This is one hundred times longer than any previous experiment in plasma control had achieved.

The MHD Generators. Magnetohydrodynamics (MHD) received increasing attention as encouraging results were reported for various experimental MHD systems. Unlike conventional electric generators that move a solid conductor, usually copper wire, through a magnetic field, MHD generators develop a current by sending a high speed conducting fluid, either molten metal or plasma, through a strong magnetic field. When perfected, MHD generators are expected to offer greater efficiencies than conventional dynamos.

A MHD generator installed at the U.S. Air Force's Arnold Engineering and Development Center in Tennessee will go into regular service early in 1968. It will power a hypersonic wind tunnel. According to the developer, Avco-Everett Research Laboratory, it is the first known practical application of MHD power in the United States. Many research groups expect that MHD eventually will be used in tandem with steam driven central power station dynamos. This should boost overall station efficiencies 5 to 10 per cent above the present limit of about 40 per cent.

Members of the Soviet Academy of Sciences, attending the Eighth Symposium on Engineering Aspects of Magnetohydrodynamics at Palo Alto, Calif., in March, described plans for a 10,000,000 watt experimental MHD generating plant in Moscow.

The U.S. Army is studying MHD generators as a possible source of high power for portable high energy lasers. The AEC and the National Aeronautics and Space Administration's Jet Propulsion Laboratory were also working on designs for MHD systems that might provide power in space.

Fuel Cells. A large research and development program on fuel cells to provide the total energy for household needs was announced in February. Companies in the United States and England will jointly participate in the $19,000,000 research program, initiated by the Natural Gas Pipeline Company of America and the Pratt & Whitney Division of United Aircraft Corporation. They hope to develop a natural gas-powered fuel cell system that would meet all the heating, air-conditioning, and electric power needs of a home at a cost competitive with that of electric power companies. The results of U.S. research will be made available to a British industrial coalition.

Electric Automobile. Though several firms began low volume production of small electric passenger cars in 1967, there was little agreement among the experts as to when advanced batteries could be developed to power larger electric cars for high speed, intercity driving. Estimates ranged from 2 to 10 years. One group maintained that a series of hybrid stages would be involved before large, totally electric cars could come into widespread use.

The hybrids would combine internal combustion engines with alternator-generators and batteries to power electric drives, with batteries playing an increasingly important role as practical, high energy-density versions are developed. Others predicted that rechargeable fuel cells would power cars late in the century. Experimental versions of all of these concepts were under investigation. [James A. Pearre]

ENGINEERING. Air and water pollution, solid-waste disposal, and urban transportation were the subjects given top priority at meetings held by professional engineering societies in 1967. Wide interest was also expressed in the relatively new field of deep-ocean engineering, and several of the societies sponsored conferences devoted to the subject.

Training Young Engineers. The special problems involved in training young engineers in the developing countries of Africa were studied at a week-long conference, held at Kumasi, Ghana, in July. The Ford Foundation was the sponsor of the conference, which brought together engineering educators, government officials, and practicing engineers from nine central African countries. The training of young engineers also was a primary concern at the 10th plenary assembly of the Conference of Engineering Societies of Western Europe and the United States, held in Zurich, Switzerland, in September. Representatives from 25 engineering societies in 17 countries agreed to help develop improved training programs in their homelands.

In the United States, the professional engineering societies urged more use of technicians – for drafting, surveying, and other work not requiring professional engineering services – as a means of alleviating the shortage of engineers. Through the Engineers' Council for Professional Development, steps were taken to upgrade curricula in engineering technology in order to prepare young technicians for greater responsibility. A report of the National Science Foundation showed that over 45 per cent of those employed as engineers do not hold college degrees.

Engineer Shortage. Although the U.S. supply of engineers is augmented 10 to 20 per cent each year through the immigration of European engineering graduates, the Engineering Manpower Commission of the Engineers' Joint Council predicted that the demand for qualified graduates will greatly exceed the supply in the next decade. Based on replies from 490 employers, the commission's annual survey showed that there will be a need for 830,000 graduate engineers in the next 10 years but that there will be only 500,000 graduates to meet that demand.

In keeping with this forecast, a survey of 1,289 engineering schools, conducted by the Engineering Manpower Commission, showed that about 28,800 bachelor's degrees in engineering were awarded in June, 1967 – a decline of 2.5 per cent from the number awarded in 1966. Most of these degrees, 8,183, were in the electrical-electronic field. Mechanical engineering had the second highest number, 6,218, and civil engineering the third highest 4,135.

Starting salaries were the highest ever. The College Placement Council found that offers to engineering students graduating in June averaged $713 a month, up 6.3 per cent from 1966 offers. Technical graduates at the master's level started at about $849 a month. [Mary E. Jessup]

ESPIONAGE. The old-fashioned methods of spying continued to thrive despite the growing sophistication of electronic eavesdropping, cryptography, and "spy in-the-sky" photo satellites. Scores of spies disguised as diplomats, journalists, businessmen, military personnel, students, and travelers were unmasked by counter-intelligence agencies in 1967.

A huge spy ring, operated by the Soviet military intelligence, was uncovered by the Italian intelligence agency Servizio Informazione Difesa (SID). More than 30 suspects were seized and five Soviet diplomats were expelled by European countries as the network was unraveled.

It was learned that Soviet espionage operations had penetrated the North Atlantic Treaty Organization (NATO) since 1960 to obtain details of bases in the Mediterranean and in Europe. The spies were tracked down after SID caught a courier with 19 rolls of microfilm at the French-Italian border on March 15.

On March 19, the Italian police arrested Giorgio Rinaldi, 39, an amateur sky diver and stunt man; his wife; his chauffeur; and Yuri K. Pavlenko, 35, a Soviet officer listed as an attaché in the Soviet embassy in Rome. Rinaldi disclosed the key to coded messages from Moscow and the drop points he used for delivering his reports.

More Soviet Spy Rings. Within weeks of the Rinaldi arrest, the Netherlands arrested a Soviet airline official for spying, Cyprus expelled a Soviet diplomat and an airline officer, Greece ousted two Soviet diplomats, Austria arrested a suspected spy, Norway uncovered a Soviet spy ring, and Belgium expelled a Soviet Tass reporter in Brussels.

In mid-October, Bonn reported the smashing of five Communist spy rings and the arrest of 12 key agents. There were reports that some 16,000 Communist spies still were operating in West Germany.

The breakup of the German spy rings was linked to the U.S.-announced defection of Soviet army Lieutenant Colonel Yevgeniy Y. Runge of the Soviet Union's Committee on State Security (KGB) in Germany. Captured agents were traced to the German foreign office and the French embassy in Bonn. One of them, a messenger, was accused of using a special camera, hidden in a cigaret case, that photographed documents as it was passed over the sheet.

The extent of these Soviet spy operations was documented in a book, *The Espionage Establishment*, by Washington, D.C., newsmen David Wise and Thomas Ross. The authors estimated the Soviet KGB has 20,000 to 25,000 employees.

Soviet intelligence appeared to be concentrating upon U.S. communications. Two army sergeants with long experience in military communications were arrested in August and accused of conspiring to pass secrets to the Russians. Army Staff Sergeant Leonard J. Safford and Sergeant 1st Class Ullysses L. Harris were linked to Nikolai F. Popov, a first secretary of the Soviet embassy, and to Anotoliy T. Kireyev of the Soviet mission to the United Nations, both of whom had left the country. Safford was convicted in November and received a 25-year prison sentence. Harris' court-martial was pending.

The long-range preparations and planning of Soviet intelligence were dramatized in London reports about George Blake and Harold A. R. (Kim) Philby. Blake, a former British diplomat who had broken out of a London prison in 1966 where he had been sentenced in 1961 as a Soviet spy, turned up in Moscow. Soviet agents reportedly had engineered his escape. Philby, once a high-ranking British intelligence agent, was revealed by his son to have joined Soviet intelligence in 1933 only a few months after graduation from Cambridge University. Philby's astounding feat of penetrating British M16, as counter-intelligence is known, was recounted by his son John, who had talked with him in Moscow. Suave and dashing, Kim Philby had defected to the Soviet Union in 1963 while posing as a journalist.

Industry. In the United States, industrial spying –from recording telephone calls and "bugging" hotel and conference rooms to planting agents and "observing" competitors' equipment and operations –was estimated to cost U.S. industry some $2,000,000,000 in 1967. [LLOYD NORMAN]

See also ANTHROPOLOGY.

ETHIOPIA. The tense border dispute between Ethiopia and neighboring Sudan continued in 1967. Ethiopia accused Sudan of harassing Ethiopian farmers along the border, insisting on an unacceptable 1902 border agreement, and supporting the rebel Eritrean Liberation Front (ELF), which sought to detach Moslem Eritrea from Christian Ethiopia. In July, however, Sudan permitted the farmers to resume cultivation along the border. The Ethiopian army launched a major campaign against the ELF in August after its support was crippled by Israel's victory over the Arabs in June.

Emperor Haile Selassie I traveled widely. He received an honorary degree from the University of California, Los Angeles, dedicated Ethiopia's exhibit at Expo 67, and conferred with President Tito of Yugoslavia on the Middle East crisis.

The Soviet-built Assab oil refinery opened in April. The International Finance Corporation committed $9,000,000 toward a $22,500,000 sugar mill in the Awash Valley, to produce 47,000 tons of sugar annually by 1970. The United States loaned Ethiopia $5,800,000 to finance a malaria eradication program. [WILLIAM SPENCER]

Facts in Brief. Population: 23,600,000. Government: Emperor Haile Selassie I; Prime Minister T. T. Aklilou Abte-Wold. Monetary Unit: dollar (2.5 = U.S. $1). Foreign Trade: exports, $111,000,000; imports, $162,000,000. Principal Exports: coffee, hides and skins, oilseeds.

EUROPE

Progress toward the unification of Europe at various levels—political as well as economic—made steady gains in 1967. An East-West dialogue, though slow and cautious, gave renewed hope of some future understanding that would bridge the gap between the two Germanys. In Geneva, Switzerland, a treaty for preventing the spread of nuclear weapons came a step nearer fulfillment. Denmark, Great Britain, Ireland, and Norway applied for membership in the European Economic Community (EEC, or Common Market), but their hopes were slashed by what amounted to a French veto in December.

Community Actions. The Kennedy Round of tariff-cutting talks ended in success (see INTERNATIONAL TRADE AND FINANCE). The long-awaited merger of the executive bodies of the three European communities took place on July 1, resulting in the formation of a single, 14-member European Economic Community Commission (EECC). The bodies that merged were: the Executive Commission of the EEC; the High Authority of the European Coal and Steel Community (ECSC); and the Executive Commission of the European Atomic Energy Community (Euratom). The new EECC was headed by Jean Rey, who had succeeded Walter Hallstein as president of the EEC Executive Commission on January 5. Hallstein, it was said, had "sacrificed himself on the altar of a united Europe" when he withdrew his candidacy for the EECC presidency. He had clung to the belief that economic decisions progressively involved political decisions. The dislike by French President Charles de Gaulle for Hallstein's supranational tendencies had led to a struggle between the two men, and Hallstein's decision had been made largely to end the impasse.

Nevertheless, there were setbacks to this process of reunification and liberalization. Western Europe was shocked when a military junta took over in Greece, long regarded as the home of democracy. The familiar pattern of suppression of the press and free speech, mass arrests, and curfews led to protests in the Council of Europe and a request that the United Nations (UN) Commission on Human Rights consider whether or not there had been a breach of the European Convention on Human Rights. See GREECE.

Other Problems. Austria declared itself anxious to enter the Common Market, but its way was blocked by Italy because of Austro-Italian border

Overproduction, and a sharp drop in exports in 1967, resulted in temporary overstocking in many European factories, such as the Opel plant in West Germany.

OPEL

incidents, which continued during the year in the mainly German-speaking South Tyrol. Other disruptions were caused by economic recessions in Great Britain, the Netherlands, and West Germany; because of them, the economic equilibrium of most of the other countries trading in Western Europe was upset. The devaluation of the British pound in November did little to ease the situation. See BANKS AND BANKING; GREAT BRITAIN; MONEY.

The big question mark in Europe in 1967 was again President De Gaulle. Would he veto Britain's application to join the Common Market, as he had done in 1963? There was a great deal of lobbying by British ministers and by those of other countries – notably Italy, the Netherlands, and West Germany in the capitals of Europe. In November, the aging French president warned at a press conference in Paris that France would not negotiate on this issue, and a month later France voted against British membership in the Common Market. See FRANCE.

The Common Market's external trade balance improved from a deficit of $1,200,000,000 for the first six months of 1966 to a surplus of $317,000,000 at the end of the corresponding period in 1967. Much of the improvement was accounted for by West Germany's surplus, which rose from $540,000,000 to $1,619,000,000.

Meanwhile, other Common Market countries reduced their deficits on external trade as follows: Italy, from $558,000,000 to $423,000,000; France, from $448,000,000 to $302,000,000; and the Netherlands, from $429,000,000 to $293,000,000. Common Market exports to Russia were $134,000,000, a rise of 81 per cent, while those to the United States went up 10 per cent to a total of $2,074,000,000.

British Membership. Britain's efforts to enter the Common Market had first to be approved by the European Free Trade Association (EFTA). Once this was granted, in April, high-ranking British statesmen visited the capitals and community centers of Europe. One of the chief concerns of Britain's Prime Minister Harold Wilson was the reaction of President De Gaulle. Britain had the support of the western European Union – the "Six" plus Britain – but this was with French abstention. The move was also favored by the Action Committee for the United States of Europe under the chairmanship of Jean Monnet. On June 27, the new EECC came out in favor of opening negotiations allowing for the entry of Great Britain, Denmark, Ireland, and Norway into the Common Market.

George Brown, Britain's foreign secretary, told the Six in The Hague, in July, that Britain would accept the free movement of capital and that the role of the pound sterling, a reserve "world" currency in Europe, would not be an obstacle to British membership in the Common Market. He forecast that Britain's entry would mean "a greater political purpose for Western Europe."

French Resistance. France, however, made known its views a few days later. British membership, according to France's Foreign Secretary Maurice Couve de Murville, will mean the transformation of the European Community into an Atlantic trading system.

Paul-Henri Spaak, a former foreign minister of Belgium and one of the founders of the European Economic Community, strongly supported Britain's entry because it "would be the stimulus for Europe to recover its former role in world affairs." The impression gained by Lord Chalfont, Britain's minister of state in charge of European affairs, was that France, while not wishing to veto Britain's application, would try to drag out negotiations and delay a decision by the Six. Lord Chalfont had been appointed by Prime Minister Harold Wilson to mastermind the negotiations.

On September 20, Jean Rey told the European Parliament meeting in Strasbourg, France, that the Common Market members had recommended the opening of negotiations with Britain and the other applicants. "Now that Britain and other EFTA members are knocking on our door," he said, "it would be unforgivable if we did not find the means of opening it."

At their meeting in Luxembourg on October 27, the Common Market Council of Ministers adjourned their debate on the British application. The bone of contention was the role of the pound sterling. France emphasized all the difficulties, including those of the British economy. In November, these difficulties were spotlighted by Britain's devaluation of the pound. Because of it, British membership in the supranational organization remained as uncertain as ever as the year ended. See GREAT BRITAIN.

EFTA Successes. Entering its eighth year, EFTA continued to encourage European economic integration. It also continued to chalk up new economic successes among its member countries. Total exports of EFTA countries in the first six months of 1967, totaling about $15,656,000,000, were 7.7 per cent higher than the preceding year. Total imports, set at $18,855,000,000, were up by 6.2 per cent for the same period. Trade between EFTA countries, valued at $4,175,000,000, was up 14.4 per cent; but EFTA exports to the Common Market countries, at $3,790,000,000, were down 1.8 per cent from a year earlier. Only Britain, Norway, and Switzerland increased their sales to Common Market countries.

In trade with the rest of the world, EFTA exports totaled about $6,201,000,000 in the first half of 1967, 11.1 per cent higher; imports, at $6,947,000,000, were up by 5.4 per cent.

Historic Tariff Cuts. A dramatic make-or-break night session of the Kennedy Round of tariff-cutting talks in Geneva ended in success in 1967. Shortly before midnight on May 15, 53 countries, working within the framework of the General Agreement on

French President Charles de Gaulle, gesturing to make his point in the Elysée Palace in Paris, tells a press conference that Great Britain must wait for EEC membership.

Tariffs and Trade (GATT), agreed to slash import duties on thousands of each other's goods. The agreement, which had been reached after four years of tedious haggling, was described as the most far-reaching trade agreement ever negotiated. Under it, international trade–in products totaling an estimated $40,000,000,000 annually–would be freed of high tariff barriers. In general, the tariff cuts would be gradually applied between Jan. 1, 1968, and Jan. 1, 1971.

World Disarmament. The United States and the Soviet Union agreed early in the year on a draft text for a treaty to stop the spread of nuclear weapons. It excluded any possibility of West Germany joining a consortium in possession of its own nuclear weapons, thereby ruling out proposals such as the Multilateral Nuclear Force (MLF) or Atlantic Nuclear Force (ANF). These ideas were thus dropped in favor of a purely consultative role for a North Atlantic Treaty Organization (NATO) nuclear planning group, of which West Germany was a member. See DISARMAMENT.

East-West Relations. The establishing of a trade link between Bonn and Bucharest in February resulted in the switching of a conference of the East European Communist nations from Bucharest to Warsaw. West Germany's accord with Romania was regarded as an important piece of East-West diplomatic "bridge-building" that could lead to a change in the political balance in Central and Eastern Europe. See ROMANIA.

A conference of 24 Communist parties from East and West Europe was held in Czechoslovakia in April. Apart from the usual calls for mutual allegiances between the Soviet Union and the East European countries, the conferees did have something new to offer–a suggestion that all the European states, East as well as West, sign a treaty renouncing the use of force in relations with one another as well as pledge noninterference in internal affairs. Meanwhile, a formal exchange of letters between East and West Germany was seen as an indication of a possible rapprochement between the two countries. See GERMANY.

Defense Alliance. NATO closed its operations in France on October 12 and moved to temporary headquarters in Brussels, Belgium. The move followed that of Supreme Allied Headquarters from Rocquenfort, near Paris, to Casteau, near Mons, Belgium. The NATO Defense College was transferred to Rome. By March 31–the last day of the 12-month period set for NATO's removal from France by President De Gaulle–all NATO operational elements had been evacuated from French locations. See NORTH ATLANTIC TREATY ORGANIZATION (NATO). [KENNETH BROWN]

EXPLORATION. See OCEAN; SPACE EXPLORATION.

EXPLOSION. See DISASTERS.

Panoramic view of Expo 67 captures the dazzling diversity of structural designs used for the pavilions. Canada's inverted pyramid is at left. *Below,* is the United States' geodesic dome.

A setting sun on Ile Notre Dame fails to dim the glow of excitement at Expo 67.

FAIRS AND EXHIBITIONS. Expo 67, Canada's record-breaking World's Fair, enjoyed universal praise from critics, participants, and visitors. A highlight of the year-long Canadian centennial celebration, the fair, held in Montreal, Que., from April 28 to October 27, attracted 50,306,648 paid visitors and sold more than $71,000,000 worth of tickets. It became the greatest box-office success in the history of international fairs and exhibitions. By comparison, the 1958 Brussels World's Fair had attracted about 42,000,000 paid visitors; the Seattle World's Fair in 1962 had been visited by 12,000,000 people. Although the 1964-1965 New York World's Fair had 51,607,037 paid admissions, the figure was not comparable, because the Fair had run two years.

Altogether, 59 foreign governments participated in Expo 67. Its 105 buildings and pavilions cost more than $200,000,000, and the total cost of the fair, including site preparation, roads and bridges, public improvements, promotion, administration, and restoration of site, was estimated at well over $500,000,000. The final deficit was expected to run to about $250,000,000, or approximately $47,500,000 more than the original forecast. Because public satisfaction with the enormous success of the fair as an outstanding and prestigious Canadian achievement ran so high, there was no controversy over the huge deficit. Indeed, the fair was regarded as a mark of Canada's maturity, of the nation's ability and willingness to think, plan, and achieve on a large

A monumental hammer and sickle dominated the approaches to the Russian pavilion at Expo 67.

scale. This attitude was reinforced by the knowledge that visitors from the United States and dozens of other countries had helped Canada's foreign travel earnings reach a peak of $1,250,000,000. It was by far the highest such total ever recorded in the history of Canadian tourism.

The three most popular pavilions at the fair were the Soviet Union's vast $12,000,000 structure, which attracted 13,000,000 visitors; the Canadian pavilion, which drew 11,000,000 visitors, and the United States' spectacular geodesic dome, which had an attendance of 9,000,000. About 53 per cent of all visitors to the fair were Canadians (26,662,523); 45 per cent were from the United States (22,637,991); and 2 per cent were from other countries.

The Canadian prime minister, Lester B. Pearson, summed up the fair on its closing day as a Canadian dream come true: "This is a moment of triumph and sadness," he said. "Triumph because the success of Expo has been complete, the dream has been fulfilled. Sadness because the short, glorious season of Expo has ended. We have discovered that we do have a character and quality of our own, rich and diverse, but Canadian."

Other Fairs. The normal array of trade, industrial, scientific, and cultural fairs held in 57 other nations in 1967 offered nothing comparable in scale or spectacle to that of Expo 67, nor did the 4,000 trade fairs or 2,000 state and county fairs held in the United States.

State fairs that attracted more than 1,000,000 visitors in 1967 were those of Illinois, Indiana, Michigan, Minnesota, North Carolina, Oklahoma, Texas, and Wisconsin. Total attendance at all 6,000 U.S. fairs was an estimated 1,500,000,000. It was a measure not only of the importance these exhibitions held in the American way of life generally, but also of their roles as educational and recreational attractions and as sales events.

Looking Ahead. On the horizon, three major fairs loomed large, HemisFair '68, scheduled to run from April 6 to Oct. 6, 1968, in San Antonio, Tex., was moving well ahead of schedule. Dedicated in theme to "The Confluence of Civilizations in the Americas," and enjoying the strong support of President Lyndon B. Johnson, the fair has already attracted the participation of 17 nations from Asia, Europe, and the Western Hemisphere. There will be at least 17 major exhibits. Among them will be Texas' $10,000,000 pavilion and the $6,500,000 U.S. exhibit building.

The dominant structure of the fair will be the 622-foot Tower of the Americas. Topped by a revolving restaurant, it will stand 22 feet higher than the famous Space Needle at the Seattle World's Fair and 67 feet higher than the Washington Monument.

Osaka, Japan's second largest city, is to be the site of Asia's first World's Fair, from March 15 through Sept. 13, 1970. It is expected to attract 30,000,000 visitors – 29,000,000 Japanese and 1,000,000 foreigners. Its central theme, "Human Progress in Harmony" will mark 1,000 years of Japanese history and human achievement.

In 1976, the U.S. will observe the 200th anniversary of its independence. Tentative plans call for a bicentennial celebration and World's Fair. Boston, Detroit, Los Angeles, Philadelphia, and Washington, D.C., were being mentioned as possible fair sites. The U.S. Secretary of the Interior, Stewart L. Udall, suggested, however, that the entire nation be committed now to transforming itself into a transcontinental showcase of permanent, positive accomplishment. [William D. Patterson]

FARM EQUIPMENT. See Manufacturing.

FASHION

FASHION focused on the look of the leg in 1967. Short skirts worn still higher above the knee gave legs exposure they had not had in years. Women took advantage of this fashionable trend by cloaking their legs in a wild assortment of textured and colored hose, both sheer and opaque. Showing from beneath flippy, brief skirts, the stockings gave fashions a mod mood of youthful spirit. Mini-skirts made pantie hose, in complexion sheerness as well as color and texture, increasingly popular because they not only gave the leg a hip-to-toe smoothness, but eliminated the possibility of garter-show.

Women showed off their legs in peekaboo fishnets, wide windowpane effects, spidery weaves, and delicate lacy looks. As the year progressed, stockings tended toward bold zigzag and striped patterns and whimsical floral designs. The nurses' "white leg" look was popular in the spring, but black and dark shades of brown and gray became predominant for fall. The entire color spectrum, hot to pale, including blue, lime, orange, pink, and yellow, were worn to match or clash with dresses and suits. For evenings, legs sparkled in glittery copper, gold, and silver, completing the metallic mood of dazzling evening costumes.

Women also fancied high boots as a fashionable means of covering their new length of leg. High-rise stretch vinyl or patent leather provided glovelike sleekness to complement winter fashions. Women donned boots in shiny black and brown as well as other high-gloss colors. Boots stretched to the knees, to the thighs, or even to cover the entire leg like fisherman's hip boots.

Fit and Flare. Youth continued to set the pace for fashion, but the return of the belt gave the mood a refreshing change. From freewheeling tents came dresses and suits with a more shapely pinch from the belt. The belt did not simply define the waist; unlike styles in the past, it created a new "fit and flare" attitude. From belts–worn high and wide, or loosely at the waist–came skirts that moved away from the body in swinging shapes. Movement and freedom keynoted these skirts that widened into A-lines or soft dirndl effects. With colorful and textured legs showing from beneath brief and breezy silhouettes,

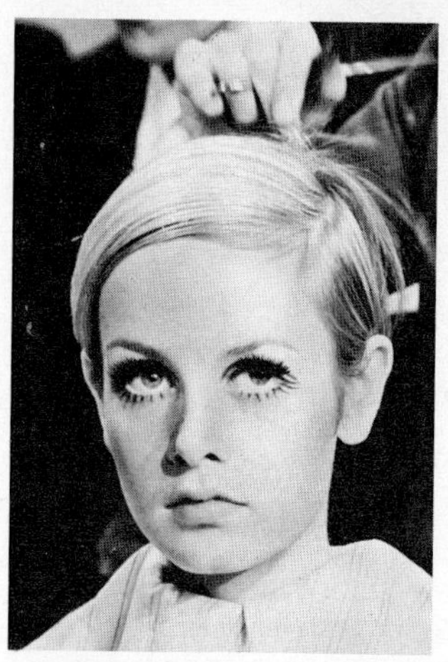

Maxi-model of the mod world, Twiggy provided the one-dimensional look of the year, posing a challenge to fashion-conscious women.

U.S. Consumer Spending on Fashion Goods

Billions of dollars

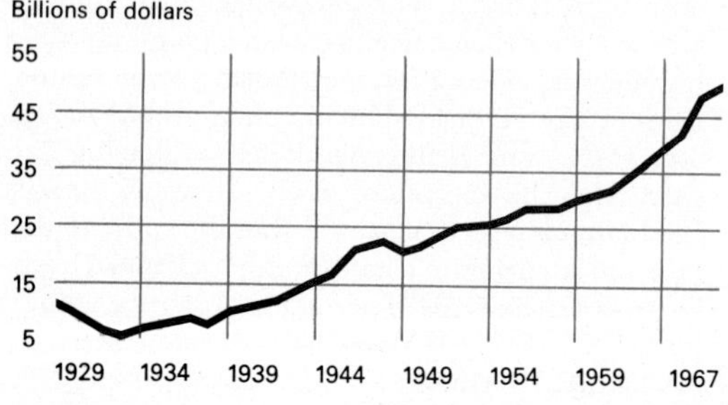

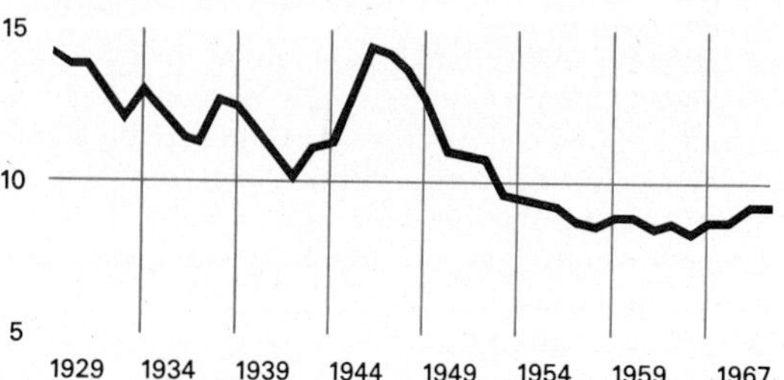

The Fragile Silhouette Of Fashion

Twiggy, the skinny-mini, 17-year-old British model, was the fashion image of 1967. She burst upon a news-seeking world, blossomed on the pages of nearly every major magazine, and brought the age of the mini-mod to full fashion flowering. Not only did she become the idol of the 13- to 15-year-old group, but within six months, this Cockney Cinderella was also the epitome of the youth-oriented, nervily amusing style of dressing that had originated on the streets of London, seeped up to influence *haute couture*, and was copied by women of all ages everywhere.

The girl of the year was the youngest top model in history. She was stick-straight and knock-kneed, had a magical spritelike face switchable from that of an innocently incomplete teen-ager on the cover of *Seventeen* to that of a wickedly worldly young woman wearing a Paris original in *Vogue*. Her image was the center of high controversy. To some, she was an insult to femininity, a vicious joke played on a pop-twisted world, the ultimate word in a life-style that blurred the outward differences between boys and girls. Others lavished her fresh, new look with rivers of perfumed prose.

Indeed, Twiggy–who was born Lesley Hornby on Sept. 19, 1949–brought a never-before look to the fashion world. With her emaciated, 5-foot 6-inch frame and meager 31-22-32 proportions, she made assets out of all the miseries of awkward adolescence. Her enormous, haunting gray eyes were emphasized by three layers of pasted and painted eyelashes. Her lips were almost old-fashioned–moist, curving like a newborn babe's, glossed with the slightest hint of color. Freckles speckled the porcelain-delicate face that was framed by sunny hair, clipped away like a boy's, with silken sideburns.

Twiggy entered the international fashion scene at the right, ripe moment. For several years, fashion leaders had exalted the property of youth and had increasingly erased the boundaries between children and adults. More and more, grown-up women wore shoes without heels, hems that exposed not only the knee but also part of the thigh, dresses without waistlines or bust seams. Twiggy suddenly represented the child-woman born to model these fashions.

The youth kick reached its zenith with Twiggy. And women accommodated themselves to the new kind of clothes. They dieted with uncommon discipline to shrink themselves into the "little-nothing" dresses. They exercised to narrow their knees, chose lighter shades of lipsticks; in short, they did everything they could to turn back the years.

Twiggy's influence was most felt by the beauty salons. Not since the 1920s, when Gibson girls became flappers, was there such a loud click of scissors heard across the land. Rich, attractive women took magazine pictures to their favorite hairdressers and asked to have their shoulder-length tresses shorn a la Twiggy. Three-tiered eyelashes named for Twiggy and manufactured by Yardley became a sensation. Pant-suits, prance-suits, and other mini-clothes, designed in London with Twiggy's approval, were swooped up by teen-agers. Window displays used life-size magazine covers of Twiggy's face to sell sunglasses; store mannequins were fashioned and sculptured to represent her unusually fragile silhouette.

Television specials recorded her first trip to America. Curious crowds had to be kept away by a guardian attack dog and her chesty bodyguard, Mr. Universe.

Photographers hailed her natural rapport with the camera. She seemed to know how to become what she wanted to be as she went along. Thinking she was exploited, the public gave her added interest and sympathy as a personality. Yet Twiggy avoided explaining herself. Occasionally, she admitted being dazzled by her sudden success.

Although she had dined with celebrities such as Princess Margaret, she avoided the big social rush of jet-set living. When not on tour, she returned to live with her parents among her stuffed or live animal pets. Somehow public feeling, on the whole, was on her side, as if foreknowing the short-lived splendor of what it meant to be an international symbol of youth and beauty in 1967. [KATHRYN ZAHONY] the look was indeed young and demure, giving 1967 fashions a witty and clever romantic spirit. Most important advocates of this look were Paris designers Pierre Cardin, the House of Dior, Yves Saint Laurent, and Emanuel Ungaro.

At the beginning of the year, pants-dresses were extremely popular. Although they looked like dresses, they were cut into easy-to-wear flaring pants. Women wore them short and shift-shaped, usually for casual day wear.

Hardware. The glint of metal on fall and winter fashions and accessories created a brazen, brave, and bold mood. Composing the high-voltage look were gleaming metal squares, nailheads, rattling chains, galosh hooks, zippy industrial zippers, brass buttons and clamps, all giving an electric charge to dresses, shoes, belts, and even gloves. An important element of the look was the chain belt, formed of interlocking circles or squares, and worn around the waist or casually about the hip.

In proportion to 1967's scaled-down silhouettes, shoes were set on low, chunky heels, with toes newly rounded or squared. These styles, based on a wall-to-wall flatness, attracted ornamentation: frivolous bows and poufs, ties, and straps. They also took to hardware and alligator, lizard, snake, and tortoise ornament, all of which were significant fashion trends. Autumn gave new luster to shoes and handbags of patent leather, which is usually reserved for spring wear. Women chose these fall patents in a wide array of colors.

Also scaled to the small shape of the day was the mini bag, tiny in design but unusually roomy inside due to its accordion compartments. It was striking when hung from a swinging chain handle.

Awards. Five American designers, Donald Brooks, Oscar de la Renta, Rudi Gernreich, and Beth and Herbert Levine, received Coty American Fashion Critics Awards for 1967. The top award, a bronze statuette called a Winnie, went to De la Renta. Gernreich, who originated the daring topless swimsuit, automatically became a member of the Coty Hall of Fame by winning the award for the third time. Shoe designer-producers Beth and Herbert Levine received a special award for making 1967 "the look of the leg."

Men's Fashions in 1967 tended toward a more shaped silhouette, with emphasis on the double-breasted look and the high-cut jacket. Shoulders and lapels were wider, waists were nipped in, and deep vents at the side or center back were the rule. Although the mood departed somewhat from the mod of Carnaby Street, the British look was still evident. Plaid and tweed suits and colorful and lively accessories predominated. Turtleneck sweaters and shirts worn with blazers and sports coats became an important trend, eliminating the need for a tie. The most daring sported the turtleneck under dinner jackets for a more casual elegance. [Rachelle Hasson]

FINLAND, in a surprise move, devalued its currency by 31 1/4 per cent in 1967. It was a move that the government hoped would keep imports in check and encourage exports. By year's end, the balance of payments gap had been reduced considerably.

On December 6, President Urho K. Kekkonen, in a speech celebrating 50 years of Finnish independence, stressed that Finland would guard its neutrality between the East and the West. He also reminded the Finns that their nation was among the 15 wealthiest in the world on the basis of per capita income.

In March, the International Monetary Fund (IMF) approved a stand-by credit of $93,750,000 to strengthen Finland's foreign reserves and restore equilibrium in the balance of payments. The Socialist government enacted strict measures to help curb an inflationary trend in the economy.

Industrial expansion continued to bolster the economy. Finland's newest industries–textiles and footwear–nearly doubled their export figures during the year. [Kenneth Brown]

Facts in Brief. Population: 4,705,000. Government: President Urho K. Kekkonen; Prime Minister Rafael Paasio. Monetary Unit: markka (4.20 =U.S. $1). Foreign Trade: exports, $1,506,000,000; imports, $1,726,000,000. Principal Exports: paper and pulp, lumber, ships and boats.

FIRE. See Disasters; Forestry; Safety.

FISHERY. Although the 1967 world fish catch was expected to reach a record 120,000,000,000 pounds, the U.S. catch was dropping to an estimated 4,100,000,000 pounds, the lowest since 1943. Among reasons were the low salmon run, reduction of certain New England species, and the decline of menhaden in the Gulf of Mexico and the South Atlantic Ocean.

The U.S. Food and Drug Administration on Feb. 2, 1967, approved the use of fish protein concentrate (FPC) for human use. The "fish flour" is manufactured from ground whole fish and contains over 80 per cent animal protein. See Food.

Also in February, the United States reached separate agreements with the Soviet Union and Japan on the extension of U.S. fishing jurisdiction from 3 to 12 miles. The two countries were allowed to carry on certain fishing operations within the U.S. 12-mile zone in return for limiting their activities beyond the zone. In late November, a similar U.S.-Soviet agreement was reached, effective Jan. 1, 1968, on fishing along the Middle Atlantic coast.

The war against sea lampreys, which had imperiled Great Lakes fisheries, made progress. Lake Superior's lampreys declined 29 per cent and as a result its lake trout population rose sharply in the year. [Andrew L. Newman]

FISHING. See Hunting and Fishing.

FLOOD. See Disasters; Conservation.

FLOWER. See Garden and Lawn.

FOOD. The feeding of a hungry world remained a pressing problem as human demand for food continued to exceed production in 1967. While population persistently grew larger in the developing countries, the pressure on world food supplies was somewhat alleviated by more abundant crops in areas long deficient in grain. India, for example, has been dependent upon grain imports for survival. As the result of better crops in 1967, India was expected to be able to meet more of its basic grain needs in 1968. Still, the United States was expected to dispatch 6,000,000 tons of grain to India during 1968, half of which the Indian government hoped to stockpile against possible crop failures in the future. See INDIA; POPULATION, WORLD.

The U.S. government, meanwhile, opened a new War on Hunger office within the Agency for International Development (AID). In May, the Chicago Board of Trade organized the First International Agri-Business Conference at which the U.S. food industry was urged to lend its technical capabilities and capital to the developing countries. See Section One, HARRISON BROWN: FOCUS ON SCIENCE.

New Protein Sources. Great advances were made in 1967, by both private businesses and governments, in the search for new and cheaper natural and synthetic sources of high quality protein. Agricultural scientists discovered that a wild oat that grows in Israel and other Mediterranean countries contained 30 per cent protein, or 10 per cent more than varieties commonly in use. It was hoped that a new type of oats, more resistant to crown rust and higher in protein content, could be produced by crossing the Mediterranean and some of the other common varieties.

Whole Fish Protein concentrate, long under study by the Food and Drug Administration (FDA), was approved for home consumption. Manufactured from whole hake or hakelike fish, the new concentrate is comparable to milk in protein content. See FISHERY.

A textured vegetable protein (TVP) was in commercial production. It reportedly tastes and chews like meat. It was possibly of great importance to developing countries because in its dry state no refrigeration is required. Soybeans and vegetable proteins continued to sell commercially for about 12 cents a pound, a fact of great importance to developing countries.

The most dramatic revelation in the search for new protein sources came as a result of petroleum research. It was found that through petroleum fermentation, or biosynthesis, the hydrocarbons in petroleum and natural gas could be converted by bacteria into a yeasty protein. Pilot plants were set up in France, India, and the United States to begin converting oil and gas into edible proteins.

Government and Industry. Dr. James L. Goddard, chief of the FDA, continued vigilant policing of the preparation, distribution, advertising, and packaging of food in the United States. While questioning the wide use of additives, Goddard reminded food processors to comply with the FDA requirement for providing the agency with basic usage data on the additives actually contained in the products being marketed. He criticized the frozen food industry by asking that greater care be used in safeguarding frozen foods during distribution.

Tainted Foods. Food processors, distributors, and consumers were concerned during the year over the "salmonella question." The salmonella bacteria, which can cause food poisoning, may not be present in food ingredients or in final products, according to FDA regulations. In 1967, certain nonfat dry milk products, dried and frozen egg products, debittered and dried brewers yeast, dried drink mixes, and carmine red coloring used in candies came under attack for allegedly being contaminated with salmonella. Spurred by seizures and threats of seizure by the government, a number of food processors voluntarily recalled their products.

A problem of far graver import for consumers was made public on November 9, when a team of U.S. investigators, testifying before a Senate subcommittee, reported finding filthy conditions in meat packing plants not covered by federal inspection. Their testimony came during congressional hearings on a bill that would extend federal meat inspection, or help, to states without adequate inspection facilities.

As a result of conditions revealed in the report, President Lyndon B. Johnson, on December 15, signed into law a bill requiring meat packing plants engaged in intrastate commerce to observe the same standards as federally inspected plants. About 15,000 plants were affected.

Labeling and Packaging. A number of new labeling proposals were set forth by the FDA in 1967. According to the FDA, packages weighing less than four pounds should indicate the weight in ounces, that is, 24 ounces or 1 lb. 8 oz. This information would have to be placed in the lower 20 per cent of the main display panel on every package of food, and no other information could appear below or to either side of it. The package, according to the FDA proposals, should also state whether the contents were diced, sliced, whole, minced, or strained. Words commonly used in advertising, such as "giant," "jumbo," "full quart," and so forth, were to be banned from the label. When the number of servings was given, the weight of each serving should also appear.

Litter Program. *National Bottler's Gazette*, to forestall possible restrictive ordinances by the government, urged its subscribers to concern themselves with the national litter problem created by the 6,000,000,000 disposable cans and 23,000,000,000 disposable bottles sold in 1967. More cans topped with peel-open closures and bottles with caps that could be screwed back on after once being opened were available. Plastic milk bottles in gallon and half-gallon sizes made their appearance during the year. Some had cartoon characters stamped on them for youngsters in the family to color.

Technical Advances. Liquid nitrogen, commonly used to keep foods at low temperatures, was injected into trailer trucks to cool milk rapidly and to help keep it at a low temperature over long, hot hauls. The FDA approved irradiated canned bacon, potatoes, wheat, and wheat flour for human consumption. Irradiated meats are reportedly more tender than fresh cuts. They are also reported to require no refrigeration.

The Atomic Energy Commission planned to build and operate a plant designed to preserve meat by radiation (see ENERGY). A heavy dose of radiation kills the bacteria that normally cause spoilage.

New Products in 1967 were more basic than gimmicky. Synthetic flavorings, using soybean protein for a base, managed to capture artificially the elusive flavors of mushrooms and butter. As a result, fewer mushrooms are now required for flavoring soups and other dishes. Synthetic butter, called Butter-Aid, also appeared in both powdered and liquid form. It was to be used for the enrichment in butter flavor of sauces, gravies, candies, and a host of other foods. [ALMA LACH]

FOOTBALL. Only one major college football team, Wyoming, managed to make its way through the regular 1967 season unbeaten and untied. The Cowboys' 65-man roster included players from 21 states, but only three from Wyoming itself. They finally met defeat in the Sugar Bowl.

The MacArthur Bowl, symbolic of the national championship, was voted to once-beaten Southern California at the end of the regular campaign. The Trojans scraped past their cross-town rival, top-ranked UCLA, in a 21 to 20 battle, with the big play of the game a 64-yard touchdown run by the Trojans' All-America halfback, Orenthal James Simpson. Southern Cal's defense blocked two field-goal tries by UCLA'S soccer-style place-kicker, Zenon Andrusyshyn, then rushed him so hard he missed his final extra-point try.

1967 Conference Champions

Conference	School
Big Ten	Indiana, Purdue, Minnesota (tie)
Southeastern	Tennessee
Southwest	Texas A&M
Big Eight	Oklahoma
Atlantic Coast	Clemson
Ivy League	Yale
Middle Atlantic	Temple
Southern	West Virginia
Missouri Valley	North Texas State
Western Athletic	Wyoming
Yankee	Massachusetts
Pacific Eight	Southern California
Mid-American	Ohio, Toledo (tie)

To confuse the college picture, neither Southern California nor UCLA could beat Oregon State, an also-ran in the same conference, which tied the UCLA Bruins, 16 to 16, and nipped the Trojans, 3 to 0, on a field goal by Mike Haggard.

Season of Reversals. Notre Dame, which topped the preseason polls, was thrashed by both Southern California and Purdue, in a season replete with reversals. And Purdue itself, sparked by sophomore quarterback Mike Phipps and a junior triple-threat, Leroy Keyes, managed no better than a three-way tie for first place in the Big Ten, although Keyes led the nation in scoring with 114 points. Going into their traditional final game against unranked Indiana, the Purdue Boilermakers were favored to take the conference title. But the Hoosiers sprang a 19 to 14 upset and were selected to go to the Rose Bowl to face Southern California.

The Bowl Games

Bowl	Winner	Loser
Liberty	North Carolina, 14	Georgia, 7
Bluebonnet	Colorado, 31	Miami, 21
Sun	Texas, 14	Mississippi, 7
Gator	Florida State, 17	Penn State, 17
Cotton	Texas A&M, 20	Alabama, 16
Sugar	Louisiana State, 20	Wyoming, 13
Rose	Southern California, 14	Indiana, 3
Orange	Oklahoma, 26	Tennessee, 24

All-America Team

Offense

Ends–Dennis Homan, Alabama; and Kenneth Hebert, Houston.
Tackles–Ron Yary, USC; and Edgar Chandler, Georgia.
Guards–Gary Cassells, Indiana; and Harry Olszewski, Clemson.
Center–Bob Johnson, Tennessee.
Quarterback–Gary Beban, UCLA.
Halfbacks–O. J. Simpson, USC; and Leroy Keyes, Purdue.
Fullback–Larry Csonka, Syracuse.

Defense

Ends–Ted Hendricks, Miami (Fla.); and Bob Stein, Minnesota.
Tackles–Dennis Byrd, North Carolina State; and Mike Dirks, Wyoming.
Guards–Wayne Meylan, Nebraska; and Granville Liggins, Oklahoma.
Linebackers–Adrian Young, USC; and Corby Robertson, Texas.
Halfbacks–Fred Combs, North Carolina State; Frank Loria, Virginia Tech; and Tom Schoen, Notre Dame.

Indiana provided thrills and chills for its followers all season long, frequently falling behind and winning by such harum-scarum margins as 1, 2, 3, 4, and 5 points. There was no question about its only defeat, however. Minnesota mauled them, 33 to 7.

Tennessee lost its opener to UCLA, and then reeled off nine straight victories. Among its victims were the defending champions of the Southeastern Conference, Alabama.

Southern California halfback O. J. Simpson dived over Oregon players for a first down on October 28. Simpson was credited with leading his team to national championship.

Early-season foibles also afflicted Penn State, which lost to Navy, 23 to 22, and to UCLA, 17 to 15, but won all other games and the Lambert Trophy.

The Heisman Trophy, awarded to the outstanding college player, was won by UCLA's senior quarterback, Gary Beban.

Professional. Interest in the professional football scene was more commanding than ever as game attendance reached new highs in both the National Football League (NFL) and in the American Football League (AFL). Attendance in the NFL rose to 6,160,000, or 90 per cent of stadium capacity. The AFL figures went from 2,160,369 to 2,272,124, as every franchise except Boston and Buffalo showed gains. Television ratings were up, too.

Superbowl. The first Superbowl, or NFL-AFL World Championship, was held at Los Angeles in January, 1967. It marked the first confrontation of teams in the newly merged leagues. But the games in which the 1966 NFL champion Green Bay Packers defeated the Kansas City Chiefs, 35 to 10, failed to match the publicity that preceded it.

League Expansions. The NFL expanded during the year to 16 teams with the addition of the New Orleans Saints, and then divided for the first time into four divisions within two conferences (Eastern and Western). The AFL also agreed to expand, but in the 1968 season. It granted a franchise to Cincinnati. The new club, the Bengals, will be directed by Paul Brown, formerly of the Cleveland Browns.

The Packers captured the 1967 NFL championship by beating the Dallas Cowboys 21 to 17. In the games leading up to the championship rounds, the Packers crushed the Los Angeles Rams 28 to 7, and the Cowboys routed Cleveland 52 to 14. Jim Bakken of the St. Louis Cardinals set the NFL season record in scoring with 117 points, while Leroy Kelley of Cleveland was the league's leading rusher, covering a total of 1,205 yards. Sonny Jurgensen of the Washington Redskins was the best passer, with a record of 288 completions out of 508 attempts. Charley Taylor of Washington again won pass receiving honors with 70 catches for 990 yards.

Standings in National Football League

Century Division	W.	L.	T.	Pc.
Cleveland	9	5	0	.643
New York	7	7	0	.500
St. Louis	6	7	1	.462
Pittsburgh	4	9	1	.308
Capitol Division	**W.**	**L.**	**T.**	**Pc.**
Dallas	9	5	0	.643
Philadelphia	6	7	1	.462
Washington	5	6	3	.455
New Orleans	3	11	0	.214
Central Division	**W.**	**L.**	**T.**	**Pc.**
Green Bay	9	4	1	.692
Chicago	7	6	1	.538
Detroit	5	7	2	.417
Minnesota	3	8	3	.273
Coastal Division	**W.**	**L.**	**T.**	**Pc.**
Los Angeles*	11	1	2	.917
Baltimore	11	1	2	.917
San Francisco	7	7	0	.500
Atlanta	1	12	1	.077

*Won division title on points vs. Baltimore

Standings in American Football League

Eastern Division	W.	L.	T.	Pc.
Houston	9	4	1	.692
New York	8	5	1	.615
Buffalo	4	10	0	.286
Miami	4	10	0	.286
Boston	3	10	1	.231
Western Division	**W.**	**L.**	**T.**	**Pc.**
Oakland	13	1	0	.929
Kansas City	9	5	0	.643
San Diego	8	5	1	.615
Denver	3	11	0	.214

The AFL play-off between the Houston Oilers, winners of the Eastern crown, and the Oakland Raiders, holders of the Western title, was won by Oakland, 40 to 7. Daryle Lamonica of the Raiders was voted the most valuable player in the league. He also was the best passer with 220 completions out of 425 attempts for 3,228 yards and 30 touchdowns. Teammate George Blanda had the season record in scoring with 116 points, and Jim Nance of the Boston Patriots was the best rusher, totaling 1,216 yards. George Sauer of the New York Jets was top pass receiver with 75 catches for 1,189 yards. [JOHN LAKE]

FOREST PRODUCTS. The conflict between the interests of the lumber and forest products industry and the goals of land and forest conservation intensified in 1967. At the annual meeting of the National Forest Products Association in May, industry spokesmen attacked several bills asked for by the federal administration as threatening a "catastrophic" impact on commercial timberlands. They particularly opposed legislation for establishing a National Trails System, national parks in California's redwood region and in the North Cascades, and for protecting scenic and wild rivers. Each of these bills was vigorously backed by conservationists.

Production of logs in the United States in 1967 was estimated at 11,600,000,000 cubic feet, up slightly from 1966. Domestic lumber output was estimated at 35,900,000,000 board feet, down from the 36,400,000,000 board feet in 1966. However, at year's end industry sources reported they expected a further drop of up to 1,500,000,000 board feet to be reflected in final 1967 figures, despite an increase in lumber use in housing construction.

Industry protests that rapidly increasing log exports to Japan were causing higher prices led congressional delegations from states in the Northwest to urge, in December, that the United States restrict federal timber exports to the 1966 level of 350,000,000 board feet.

Forest Fires. By the time the fire emergency in the Northwest had ended in early September, 3,500 fires had burned over 200,000 acres of forests in California, Idaho, Montana, Oregon, and Washington. To combat the blazes, which hit national forests in Montana and northern Idaho the hardest, 4,100 fire fighters and 226 tons of equipment were flown into critical areas.

More than 469,000,000 acres of state and private forest land were protected under the Forest Service's cooperative fire control program in 1967. Another 47,000,000 acres remain unprotected.

Redwood Moratorium. Four lumber companies agreed in September to extend an agreement not to cut timber in areas proposed for a Redwood National Park in California. Compromise legislation (S. 2515) to create a 64,000-acre park was approved by the Senate on Nov. 1, 1967. Action was expected in the House of Representatives in early 1968. See CONSERVATION (map).

Pest Control efforts were intensified by the Forest Service, which sprayed 102,000 acres of forest by aircraft to suppress epidemics, and treated 1,100,000 trees to control bark beetles and 700,000 to contain white pine blister rust. Research was pressed to find substitutes for DDT in pest control to avoid harmful effects on wildlife. One approach was biological control to combat insects. A wasp that attacks the European elm bark beetle and insects that prey on the balsam woolly aphid are being raised and studied for use against tree pests. [ANDREW L. NEWMAN]

FORMOSA, or **TAIWAN,** the island stronghold of the Chinese Nationalist government, continued to keep a close watch on developments in Communist China. Throughout the year, it remained one of the West's primary listening posts on the Peking regime and its political problems. See CHINA.

Unlike mainland China, Formosa enjoyed political stability and economic prosperity in 1967. Its gross national product was 7 per cent higher than it was in 1966. Capital investments continued to pour in, not only from individual corporations abroad but also from such international organizations as the United States Export-Import Bank and the International Bank for Reconstruction and Development, or World Bank. In August, the World Bank approved a $15,000,000 loan to help industrialists expand and modernize factories.

Plans were made in 1967 to expand Formosa's free school system from six to nine years. The goverment appropriated $90,000,000 to implement the program, which called for 95 new school buildings, 2,000 new classrooms, and the recruiting of about 5,000 teachers.

Facts in Brief. Population: 13,215,000. Government: President Chiang Kai-shek; Vice-President and Prime Minister Yen Chia-kan. Monetary Unit: dollar (40.1 = U.S. $1). Foreign Trade: exports, $536,300,000; imports, $622,400,000. Principal Exports: sugar, bananas, textiles.

FOUNDATIONS in the United States now distribute about $1,200,000,000 in grants annually, according to a report by the Foundation Library Center. Assets of philanthropic foundations were estimated to be $20,300,000,000, an increase of nearly $6,000,000,000 over the amount reported in the 1964 edition of the center's *Foundation Directory*.

Education continued to be the most favored field of foundation activity in 1966. Direct grants by major foundations in this area came to $418,000,000. Welfare ranked second, and received $196,000,000. International activities received $170,000,000; health, $167,000,000; the sciences, $120,000,000; and religion, $107,000,000. The humanities received a total of $67,000,000.

Major educational foundations reporting on their activities in 1967 included the following:

Alfred P. Sloan Foundation, New York City, reported assets of $195,557,709 as of Dec. 31, 1966. Income totaled $13,230,647. Grants authorized came to $20,593,809. The Sloan College Science Program received a $7,500,000 appropriation, the largest for a single purpose in the foundation's 32-year history. These grants, ranging from $250,000 to $500,000 over a five-year period, go to 20 private, four-year liberal arts colleges in support of their mathematics and science departments. The Sloan Program for Basic Research in the Physical Sciences received $1,400,000, and the Sloan National Scholarship Program, $1,200,000. The Sloan Educational Opportunity Awards Program, now in its second year of operation and designed to assist 10 predominantly Negro colleges in the South, received a $275,000 appropriation. A special grant of $3,000,000 was made to the Sloan-Kettering Institute for Cancer Research for the reconstruction of its original laboratory building, and also a $250,000 grant for a new biomathematics facility. The Council for Research in Glaucoma and Allied Diseases received $200,000, and the Deafness Research Foundation, $316,250.

Carnegie Corporation of New York announced a grant of $160,000 for a Yale-Vassar study on possible cooperative arrangements. A $400,000 grant went to Columbia, Harvard, and Yale universities to help students, mainly Negroes, go on to graduate school. Yale University received a grant of $35,800 to continue a language program through 1968.

The Commonwealth Fund, New York City, reported assets of $94,845,882 as of June 30, 1967. Its income totaled $6,346,431, and appropriations, $7,059,190. Major grants included $5,401,190 for medical education and community health; $60,000 to the Commonwealth Fund book program; and $1,068,000 for its Division of International Fellowships.

Ford Foundation, New York City, reported assets of $3,033,546,956 as of Sept. 30, 1966, and an income of $157,440,736. New appropriations totaled $139,914,792, and included $2,135,356 for economic development and administration; $3,993,812 for education; $2,923,225 for humanities and the arts; $816,823 for science and engineering; $1,500,000 for population; $8,612,722 for public affairs; $5,515,000 for international affairs; $4,064,363 for international training and research; and $54,430,063 for overseas development. Special programs, which included assistance for urban university development and the development of noncommercial television, received an appropriation of $55,000,000 (see TELEVISION).

John A. Hartford Foundation, New York City, reported assets of $184,287,495 as of Dec. 31, 1966, and an income of $14,643,317. Appropriations for medical sciences and clinical and other programs came to $14,462,862. The Hartford Foundation now supports 232 active research and clinical projects through grants to 136 hospitals, medical schools, and other research facilities in 69 communities in the United States and Canada. An appropriation of $41,400 was made to religious, health, charitable, and welfare organizations.

John and Mary R. Markle Foundation, New York City, reported assets of $33,433,899 as of June 30, 1967. Income totaled $1,711,472. The Markle Foundation observed its 40th anniversary in 1967, and reported the distribution of approximately $31,000,000 in grants since its founding in 1927. Of this amount, $14,000,000 has been used to aid 456 Markle scholars, a program instituted in 1947. Appropriations in 1967 included $750,000 to aid 25 new Markle scholars in academic medicine. The Association of American Medical Colleges received two grants: $46,000 for an executive development program in medical education, and $195,000 for the development of a computer program.

John Simon Guggenheim Memorial Foundation announced fellowship awards of $2,196,100 to 294 scholars, scientists, and artists.

Rockefeller Foundation, New York City, reported an income of $30,800,000 for the year ending Dec. 31, 1966. Appropriations approved came to $41,800,000. Grants amounting to $31,900,000 to the foundation's five major world-wide areas of interest were allocated as follows; $8,600,000 toward the conquest of hunger, $7,800,000 for university development, $3,800,000 for problems of population, $4,900,000 toward equal opportunity, $3,300,000 for aiding cultural development in the United States, and $3,500,000 for projects closely related to the above programs.

FOUR-H CLUBS. See YOUTH ORGANIZATIONS.

FRANCE

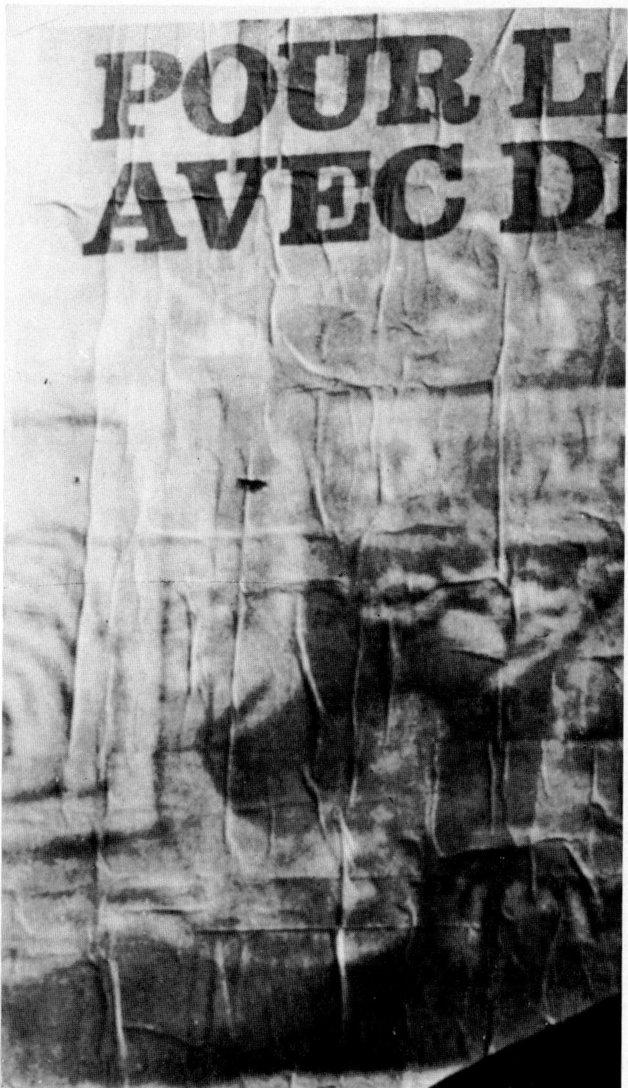

It was not a vintage year for 77-year-old President Charles de Gaulle either at home or on the international scene. In the French parliamentary elections held in the spring, his adherents barely held their majority and were soon defending themselves against a vote of confidence. A series of domestic strikes and demonstrations further showed that De Gaulle's administration lacked even the full support of the workers in his country.

Abroad, De Gaulle fared little better. His Arab-oriented "neutrality" in the Middle East conflict, his interference in Canadian internal affairs, and his "brinkmanship" in dealings with Germany, earned him not only the condemnation of a large segment of the French press but also lost him political support at home and abroad. See CANADA; MIDDLE EAST.

The big question in the embassies and economic communities of Europe, however, was whether De Gaulle–with his eyes fixed on a Third World force, and his suspicion of Britain's ties with the United States–would again veto Britain's bid to enter the European Economic Community (EEC, or Common Market). Eleven days before the end of the year, France voted against negotiations for British membership in the Common Market. Its five partners in the EEC protested, but were powerless in the face of what amounted to a French veto on the question of the recovery of the British economy.

In March, as the last of the North Atlantic Treaty Organization (NATO) forces left France, French Foreign Minister Maurice Couve de Murville assured Manlio Brosio, the secretary-general of NATO, that he stood by De Gaulle's letter of March 7, 1966, to U.S. President Lyndon B. Johnson. In it, De Gaulle had informed Mr. Johnson of France's intention to withdraw from NATO's unified command. He had also written that France would remain in the alliance even after it became permissible, under the NATO treaty, for any member country to withdraw in 1969. All things considered, however, it was felt that De Gaulle would let nothing interfere with one of the basics of his foreign policy–the reconciliation between East and West "from the Atlantic to the Urals."

France became a nuclear power at sea in 1967, as well as on land and in the air, when a 5,000-ton nuclear powered submarine, the *Redoutable*, was launched at Cherbourg in March. The submarine, which was the first of a series of three scheduled for completion by 1972, would be armed with Polaris-type missiles.

Election Results. The Gaullists were jolted by the results of a two-day national assembly election held in March. Candidates pledged to support President De Gaulle won 244 of the assembly's 487 seats; the combined opposition won 241 seats. The big winners were the French Communist Party (PFC) and the non-Communist Federation of the Democratic and Socialist Left. The PFC won 73 seats, a gain of 32; the federation won 116 seats, a gain of 25. The resulting reduction of the Gaullist majority in the assembly to a bare minimum promised stormy political weather ahead.

Premier Georges Pompidou handed in his government's resignation on April 1 but he was immediately entrusted with forming a new one. The new government quickly aroused a storm of criticism when it decided to press for special powers to decree

French opposition to President Charles de Gaulle, as symbolized in a defaced campaign poster, ran high during parliamentary elections in March, 1967.

social and economic legislation. The opposition in the assembly made it the excuse for an issue of no confidence; the trade unions called a nationwide one-day strike on May 17, the day the bill went before the assembly. A mere eight votes saved the government from censure, and the bill was defeated. Another nationwide strike was held on December 13 as a protest against lowered living conditions.

Record Budget. The proposed budget for 1968, presented in August, mirrored the struggle to stabilize prices while increasing public expenditures. Total expenditures for the year were the highest ever. At $25,700,000,000, they represented a 9.26 per cent increase over 1967. The government, however, refused to raise taxes proportionately, arguing that this would raise costs and weaken competition within the Common Market. Instead, it planned an estimated deficit of $1,400,000,000.

Foreign Visits. President De Gaulle visited Canada in July and caused an international uproar. In a speech delivered in Montreal, Que., he endorsed a "free Quebec." His overt support for those French Canadians who were advocating "separatism" was regarded by Canadians as an intrusion into domestic affairs. See CANADA.

Caught in the center of the controversy, which provoked an emergency session of the Canadian cabinet, De Gaulle cut short his visit, canceled a visit to Ottawa, and flew home.

A visit made by De Gaulle to Poland in September was carried out more tactfully. But De Gaulle's advice to Poland to integrate itself more closely with Europe brought the reply from First Secretary Wladyslaw Gomulka that the Russian alliance was the "cornerstone of Poland's policy."

Joint Projects. An Anglo-French project for a swing-wing military aircraft was canceled in 1967. Original estimates made in January placed costs of the project at $5,100,000,000. By May, however, $150,000,000 had been added to its cost, and the French began to have doubts about the program. In June, France decided to drop the project in favor of a variable geometry aircraft. Though France pleaded budgetary reasons as its excuse, one of the difficulties was that it wanted an interceptor-type plane, while Britain's aim was a strike aircraft. In September, France said that it would go ahead with its own version of the swing-wing aircraft.

This left three joint projects in the works–the *Concorde*, a supersonic jetliner, due for a test flight early in 1968; the air bus, a tripartite effort with Britain and West Germany; and the Jaguar tactical fighter. See AVIATION.

Farmers in Revolt. A wind of revolt swept through the French farming community, including the Breton artichoke growers, the Midi wine producers, and the poultry farmers and small stock and pig breeders of western France. They held "national protest days," blocked roads and rail lines leading into the nation's principal cities, and clashed with the police. The farmers complained that they could not compete at Common Market prices.

In April, 3,000 marines and 10,000 volunteers were mobilized to help fight the tide of oil reaching the channel coastline from the sunken *Torrey Canyon* tanker. Holiday resorts in Britanny and Normandy suffered because of a drop in tourism. See CONSERVATION; GREAT BRITAIN.

French Somaliland held a referendum in March to decide whether it would keep its ties with France or become independent. Results showed that 60 per cent of the population desired continuing links with France. At least 12 persons were killed in rioting that followed the announcement of the results. See AFRICA. [KENNETH BROWN]

Facts in Brief. Population: 50,488,000. Government: President Charles de Gaulle; Premier Georges Pompidou. Monetary Unit: franc (4.9=U.S. $1.) Foreign Trade: exports, $10,890,000,000; imports, $11,843,000,000. Principal Exports: chemicals, iron and steel, machinery, wine.

Members of the French cabinet turn out at 4 A.M. to welcome President Charles de Gaulle on his return to Paris from a controversial state visit to Canada.

FURNESS, BETTY (1916-), actress and television personality, was named special assistant for consumer affairs to President Lyndon B. Johnson on March 4, 1967. Some eyebrows were raised when she said she had not been in a supermarket in six years and that her housekeeper knew more about prices than she did.

Miss Furness, however, plunged energetically into her job, pledging to learn as she went. The consumer's greatest complaint, she reported in early October, is inability to get proper service for the products he buys. Later, she gave vigorous testimony before the House Agriculture Committee for the extension of federal meat inspection. See FOOD.

She was born in New York City on Jan. 3, 1916. Beginning her career as a model, she moved to Hollywood in 1932. After appearing in several films, she conducted her own radio and television shows.

Miss Furness was married to Leslie Midgley, 52, a television producer for the Columbia Broadcasting System, on Aug. 15, 1967. Her first marriage, to John W. Green, ended in divorce. Her second husband, Hugh B. Ernst, Jr., died in 1950.

FUTURE FARMERS OF AMERICA (FFA). See YOUTH ORGANIZATIONS.

FUTURE HOMEMAKERS OF AMERICA (FHA). See YOUTH ORGANIZATIONS.

GABON. See AFRICA.

GAMBIA. See AFRICA.

Dozens of frightfully delicious "Incredible Edibles" could be molded with a special heating unit and a sugarless liquid in a new and popular toy kit.

GAMES, MODELS, AND TOYS. A craze dormant for nine years was revived in 1967, as children throughout the United States cavorted in hula hoops. The hoops had the added feature of small metal pellets inside the plastic tubing to provide what the maker called a "hooplet sound."

Toys inspired by space exploration supplanted Batman and secret agents. Capsules, space platforms, and figures clad in space suits were available individually or in elaborate kits. The sobering effect of Vietnam put a damper on military toys.

The trend toward realism in dolls increased. One doll seemed to chew and eat food. Another sat in a bathtub and splashed water. Most controversial was an anatomically realistic boy doll.

Also popular was a device that turned peanuts into peanut butter by the turn of a crank. One kit contained molds in the shapes of bugs, snakes, frogs, etc., and a licorice-flavored liquid which, when poured into the mold and cooked, produced "incredible edibles."

Action games edged out board games in popularity. In one, Tie and Tangle, players tied each other with a cord according to written instructions selected at random by a spinning pointer. The winner was the player with the most unused cord.

Model Making. Reid Simpson of Des Moines, Iowa, won both the Grand National and the Open National championships at the National Model Airplane contest at Los Alamitos, Calif., in July. Bill Hunter of Pacoima, Calif., won the senior championship, while junior honors went to Dan Wakerly of Napa, Calif. The Oakland Cloud Dusters took the national club championship and the U.S. Air Force won the team title.

In what some regarded as a giant put-on, the *Scientific American* sponsored an international paper airplane contest which drew 11,000 entries and culminated in a fly-off in New York City in February. Publisher Gerald Piel said the contest was held "to help remind people that science is done by people and not machines." The winners were: *Duration Aloft*, Frederick J. Hooven, Bloomfield Hill, Mich.; *Distance Flown*, Robert Meuser, Oakland, Calif,; *Aerobatics*, Edward Ralston, Urbana, Ill.; and *Origami* (ancient Japanese paper folding), James Sakoda, Providence, R.I.

Craftsman's Guild Winners. In the annual Fisher Body Craftsman's model car building competition, university scholarships went to: *Senior Division* –David C. Goelz, Burbank, Calif., $5,000; Stephen Paulson, Upton, Mass., $4,000; Jerome A. Svitek, Whiting, Ind., $3,000; and Ronald E. Pietruska, Stamford, Conn., $2,000. *Junior Division*–John F. Faust, Anderson, Ind., $5,000; Roger F. Bartlett, Mansfield, Ohio, $4,000; Jerry W. Weber, Wichita, Kans., $3,000; and David G. Catalano, Buffalo, N.Y., $2,000. [THEODORE M. O'LEARY]

GARDEN AND LAWN. Despite a valiant effort by Illinois Senator Everett M. Dirksen to get the marigold designated as the national flower, the United States remained the only country in the world without a national floral emblem. Early in 1967, Senator Dirksen introduced Joint Resolution 73 into Congress to designate the marigold as the national flower. In doing so, he told his fellow Senators that the "marigold is as sprightly as the daffodil, as colorful as the rose, as resolute as the zinnia, as delicate as the carnation, as haughty as the chrysanthemum, as aggressive as the petunia, as ubiquitous as the violet, and as stately as the snapdragon." He found little support, however, and one of his colleagues even called the marigold un-American. Television newscaster David Brinkley suggested that "the trouble with the marigold as the American national flower is that its texture is coarse, its colors harsh, and it smells bad."

Increasing Growth. A new method of long-time feeding for plants was announced by the Wisconsin Alumni Research Foundation. The method consists of placing soluble fertilizer in a polyethylene envelope pierced with a predetermined number of tiny holes. The bag is put into the soil under woody plants, and the food is released through the tiny holes in proper amounts by the general conditions of moisture in the soil. The bag of fertilizer continues to feed the plant for as long as five years.

Both the Michigan and Delaware agricultural experiment stations released data showing that crop production in sandy soils could be greatly increased by placing a 1/8-inch layer of asphalt two feet underground. This prevents the loss of water and nutrients through downward leaching.

New Plants. Among the new and improved flowers introduced in 1967 were three All-America Selections: the silver medal winner, a foxglove named "Foxy," in mixed colors; a double yellow marigold called "Golden Jubilee"; and a salmon, cream, and pink sweet pea, "San Francisco." The new vegetables included the sweet, green pepper, "Bell Boy," and a fusarium- and verticillium-resistant tomato, "Spring Giant." Both won All-America recognition.

All-America Rose Selections for 1967 were: "Miss All-American Beauty," a pink hybrid tea; "Scarlet Knight," a grandiflora; and "Europeana," a cardinal-red floribunda. The first two were bred by the House of Meilland in France, and the other was developed by the late Gerrit deRuiter of the Netherlands. The All-America gladioli for the year were the miniature yellow "Kon-Tiki" and a large-flowered, luminous "American Beauty."

Clubs and Shows. The Men's Garden Clubs of America moved its national headquarters to Des Moines, Iowa, where it will occupy a new building. Its headquarters was formerly at Morrisville, N.Y.

The Massachusetts Horticultural Society in Boston, Mass., returned its famed Fall Flower Show, the oldest horticultural exhibition in America, to tents on Boston Common, something it had not done in more than 100 years. Previously it held the show in Boston's Horticultural Hall. The society advocated the use of horticultural-botanical stamps by the U.S. Post Office to commemorate the 11th International Botanical Congress, scheduled to be held in Seattle, Wash., in August, 1969. The United States is one of the few countries of the world that does not issue stamps to commemorate horticultural events.

Awards. At its 22nd annual congress, held in Cleveland, Ohio, from September 20 to 23, the American Horticultural Society awarded its Liberty Hyde Bailey Medal to Harold B. Tukey, Sr., for 40 years of research. Tukey was also awarded the Gold Medal of the Garden Club of America.

The award of the Arthur Hoytt Scott Horticultural Foundation at Swarthmore College, Pennsylvania, for the greatest and most sustained contribution to horticulture was given to Frederic Heutte, founder of the Norfolk, Va., Botanical Garden.

The Horticultural Society of New York cited Mrs. Albert D. Lasker, who established the first garden for the blind in Rockland County, for distinguished service. They also honored Martin Flayter, executive director of the Queens Botanical Garden and the Boyce Thompson Institute for Plant Research in Yonkers, N.Y. [EDWIN F. STEFFEK]

See also AGRICULTURE; BOTANY.

GARRISON, JIM C. (1921-   ), New Orleans district attorney since 1962, announced on Feb. 18, 1967, that he had gathered evidence proving that the assassination of President John F. Kennedy on Nov. 23, 1963, was the result of a conspiracy. Later, Garrison stated that the slayers were five anti-Castro Cubans enraged by Kennedy's handling of the Bay of Pigs invasion. Of Lee Harvey Oswald, who was named as Kennedy's assassin by the Warren Commission, Garrison said, "It's my personal belief that Oswald did not kill anyone that day."

Garrison obtained indictments against persons he declared were involved in the plot and issued many accusations. But other law-enforcement agencies refused to accept Garrison's conclusions. His case was widely considered to be deliberate fakery. It also created international controversy.

Garrison was born in Dennison, Iowa, Nov. 20, 1921. After serving as a fighter pilot in World War II, he attended Tulane University. Except for service in the Korean War, he lived in New Orleans and practiced law throughout the 1950s. He became an assistant city attorney and, in 1962, he was elected district attorney.

As district attorney, Garrison launched a crackdown on vice and on public officials accused of abetting crime. He was credited with pushing the Louisiana legislature into improving bail-bond laws and with reducing vice in New Orleans. [WALTER F. MORSE]

Breakup of a Supercontinent

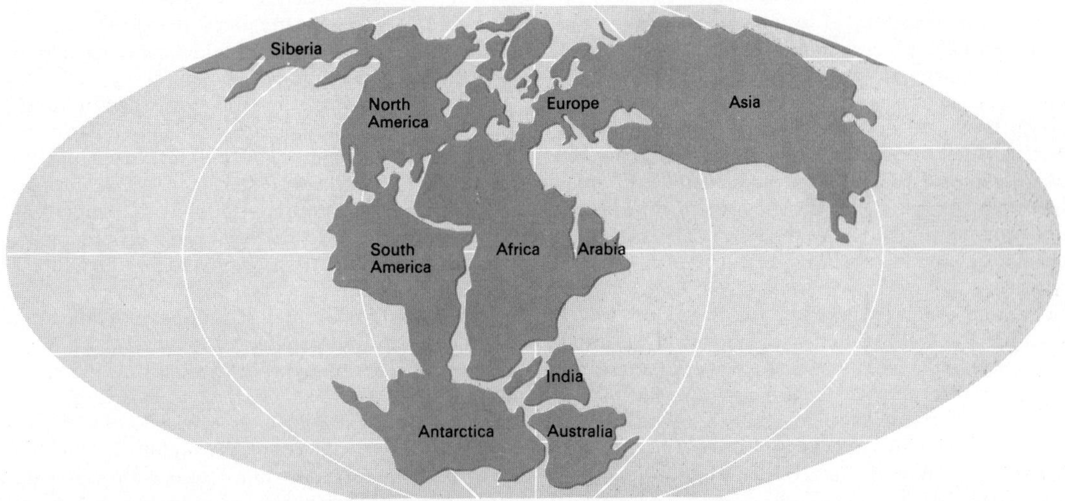

A single supercontinent, presumed to have existed some 150,000,000 years ago, would probably have resembled the continent depicted here. According to the continental drift theory, which is more than 50 years old but has only recently received wide acceptance, convection currents in the earth's underlying mantle cause the ocean floor to expand away from mid-ocean ridges, which are composed of upwelling mantle material. The theory was reformulated by Harry Hess in 1962.

GEOLOGY. New evidence was submitted in 1967 to support the theory of continental drift. The theory is more than 50 years old but has not been generally accepted until the last few years. It states that the continents were once part of a supercontinent that separated and began drifting apart at some time in the remote past. A more recent but closely related theory states that convection currents in the earth's mantle cause mantle material to well up and spread out. Evidence for such spreading is found in mid-oceanic volcanic ridges. This ocean floor spreading is believed to have pushed the land masses apart.

Professor J. Tuzo Wilson of the University of Toronto summarized the data that has been collected regarding continental drift at the American Geophysical Union meeting in April. He said that the evidence indicated that Atlantic Ocean floor spreading has undergone several reversals, first spreading the continents apart and then rejoining them. He suggested that Africa, the Americas, and Europe may have been joined 450,000,000 years ago, then may have drifted apart and rejoined 120,000,000 years ago, only to separate again. The Geophysical Union also discussed a theory of heat and mass transfer within the earth's mantle that was developed by Donald L. Turcotte of Cornell University and E. Ronald Oxburgh of Oxford University, England, to explain the convection currents that cause upwelling and movement of the earth's crust.

Lynn R. Sykes of Columbia University's Lamont Geological Observatory reported, in April, that a study of the seismograph records and analysis of 17 earthquakes had confirmed some aspects of the continental drift theory. The study showed that the earth movements were about what might be expected if the continents slowly shift as a result of an upwelling of the earth's mantle material along mid-oceanic ridges.

Age of Rocks. U.S. and Brazilian geologists engaged in a joint effort to test the continental drift theory. They reported their results in August. The geologists reasoned that since rock formations of two highly distinctive geological ages were known to exist in Africa, rocks of similar ages should exist in South America, if the two continents were once one. The rock formations are found on the west coast of Africa, near Accra, Ghana, and are about 550,000,000 years old and about 2,000,000,000 years old. Using radioactive dating methods, the geologists found rock formations of identical age in Brazil, exactly where they should be if Africa and South America were once joined together. Massachusetts Institute of Technology geology professor Patrick M. Hurley, who headed the U.S. team in the project, said the investigation had been undertaken to disprove the theory of continental drift, but that the findings made it more difficult than ever to argue against the theory.

Geomagnetic Studies conducted in 1966 and 1967 permitted geologists to calculate the rates of ocean floor spreading. It is known that the earth's magnetic field has undergone a series of reversals in polarity. Volcanic rocks can be dated by these polarity "epochs," since they retain the polarity of the epoch in which they were formed. In 1963, Frederick J. Vine of Princeton University and Douglas H. Matthews of the Cambridge University, England, theorized that parallel bands of alternating polarity found on ocean floors were the result of mantle material retaining the polarity of the epoch during which it solidified as it emerged from mid-oceanic ridges and began to spread.

Magnetometer readings taken from oceanographic vessels during 1966 and 1967 revealed bands lying in a mirror image fashion on either side of active mid-oceanic ridges. Since each set of bands could be related to a known polarity epoch, the rate of spread could be calculated by measuring the distance of the bands from the ridge of origin. Vine and his co-workers calculated rates of spread varying from one-half a centimeter per year southwest of Iceland to four-and-one-half centimeters per year in the South Pacific.

Surveyor V, which soft-landed on the moon September 10, collected chemical data indicating that the moon's crust is geologically similar to the earth's crust. [JAMES A. PEARRE]

GERMANY. An exchange of letters between the heads of the (East) German Democratic Republic and the Federal Republic of (West) Germany in 1967 was considered a hopeful sign that diplomatic relations between the two states might be restored. The fact that each government acknowledged the messages it received from the other implied a kind of recognition that had not existed since the end of World War II.

The letters were prompted by proposals that West Germany had made calling for expanded cooperation between the two Germanys. The proposals had first been presented in April in a 16-point program submitted to the Bundestag by Chancellor Kurt Georg Kiesinger and then transmitted to the East German government. The programs urged that steps be taken to lessen tensions between the two states and to improve social and economic contacts between their citizens. Specifically, the proposals had called for an easing of travel restrictions along the common frontier, restoration of totally free civilian movement throughout Berlin, and measures to increase intra-German trade, communication, and transportation.

On May 10, East Germany replied to the Bonn proposals in a letter in which its premier, Willi Stoph, invited Chancellor Kiesinger to come to East Berlin for direct talks. Stoph also called for full diplomatic recognition between the two governments, recognition of Europe's existing borders, including the controversial Oder-Niesse boundary between East and West Germany, and the creation of a nuclear-free zone in Germany and other nations of Central Europe.

Although Kiesinger's reply–disclosed in mid-June–rejected an immediate meeting of the two top leaders, he did propose that both sides appoint representatives from lower government levels to open talks on matters of common interest. Kiesinger followed the proposal with a declaration, in September, that his government was ready to conduct direct negotiations with East Germany. By year's end, however, the East German regime had not indicated whether it would accept the proposal.

Economic Problems. For the first time in nearly two decades, the West German economic growth rate slowed down and the long post-World War II boom appeared to be coming to a close. By the end of April, there were more than 500,000 unemployed, compared with 120,000 the previous year–or 2.3 per cent of the labor force versus 0.5 per cent. Industry generally was working at only 80 per cent capacity, and industrial production, which had leveled off drastically toward the end of 1966, declined by 5 per cent in the first three months of 1967.

A large part of the responsibility for the economic slowdown in 1967 was placed on the financial policies pursued by the previous government of Chancellor Ludwig Erhard and by the Bundesbank, West Germany's central bank. Fearful of inflation, the Erhard government and the bank had tightened the supply of money in 1966. By the beginning of 1967, credit was in scarce supply except at extremely high interest rates or from foreign investors. As a result, industry could not get funds for expansion and state and local governments could not raise the money for planned public spending. Industry and government in turn had to cut back their orders to suppliers. Consumer confidence waned and the downward spiral gathered momentum.

To remedy the situation, the Bundesbank made four consecutive reductions in the discount rate–the basic lending rate–between January and June of 1967. The federal government introduced a $625,000,000 contingency budget, over and above the regular $19,000,000,000 budget, to throw still more money into pump-priming. In June, the Bundestag passed an "economic stabilization" law that it hoped would renew business confidence. These measures, however, did little to boost the economy and by the year's end the government was still seeking ways to regain the 4 per cent growth rate that had prevailed in previous years.

The economic gloom was lightened, however, by one bright spot: the import-export ratio. With demand on the decline at home, German manufacturers focused their attention on selling abroad. As a result, they met with notable success, especially in

West Germany's coalition government leaders include: Chancellor Kurt Georg Kiesinger, at rostrum, Willy Brandt, first row right, and beside him, Franz Josef Strauss.

the United States. Simultaneously, imports declined sharply, resulting in a healthy trade and payments surplus by December.

Defense Spending Cuts. Bonn's domestic economic difficulties led to a reappraisal of the government's defense spending. In September, it was announced that allocations for defense spending in 1968 would be cut to $4,500,000,000, or approximately $350,000,000 less than that allocated for 1967. The government stressed, however, that the proposed cut would not reduce the strength of the armed forces but would result in a slowing down of orders for arms and equipment.

Earlier in the year, after lengthy negotiations that included high-level talks in London and Washington, D.C., between West Germany, Great Britain, and the United States, it was announced that agreement had been reached on reducing allied troop strength in West Germany. Under the agreement, about 35,000 U.S. military personnel, of both ground and air units, would be redeployed from West Germany to the United States. Similarly, about 5,000 British Troops would return to Great Britain.

East Germany's economy expanded steadily during the year, due primarily to a lessening of central government "control." Despite an acute labor shortage, industrial production rose by 7.6 per cent during the first seven months of 1967 compared to the same period of the preceding year. Most of the gain was achieved through an increase in individual workers' productivity. To remedy the labor shortage, East Germany entered into agreements with other European Communist countries to import labor on a major scale.

In December, Walter Ulbricht proposed in the East German parliament that the nation's present constitution be replaced with a new one designed to establish the country as a "sovereign socialist state." His proposal was unanimously adopted and a 40-man committee, assisted by 22 legal experts, was appointed to draw up the terms of a new constitution.

Former Chancellor Dies. In April, the world mourned the death of Konrad Adenauer, chancellor of West Germany from 1949 to 1963. See Deaths of Notable Persons. [Kenneth Brown]

Facts in Brief. Germany (East). Population: 17,147,000. Government: Council of State Chairman and Communist Party First Secretary Walter Ulbricht; Prime Minister Willi Stoph. Monetary Unit: mark (4.2 = U.S. $1). Foreign Trade: exports, $3,067,000,000; imports, $2,802,000,000. Principal Exports: machinery, fuel, clothing.

Germany (West). Population: 60,851,000. Government: President Heinrich Luebke; Chancellor Kurt Georg Kiesinger. Monetary Unit: deutsche mark (4 = U.S. $1.) Foreign Trade: exports, $20,145,000,000; imports, $18,036,000,000. Principal Exports: machinery, motor vehicles, chemicals.

GHANA crushed two attempted coups in 1967. In January, a plot was exposed before it reached the stage at which government leaders were to be assassinated. It involved two army lieutenants, two other Ghanaians, and a Nigerian. Then, on April 17, three army lieutenants and one squadron of troops attempted to wrest control of the government from Lieutenant General Joseph A. Ankrah. The rebels seized Christiansborg Castle, Ankrah's residence; the state radio station; and the airport at the capital city of Accra. Lieutenant General E. K. Kotoka, commander of Ghana's armed forces, and three other loyal leaders were killed. For four hours, the rebels broadcast reports of the creation of a new government. But there was no popular support, and General Ankrah crushed the revolt within a day.

The former governor of the Bank of Ghana, the economic adviser, and eight cabinet ministers under exiled former president Kwame Nkrumah were charged with misuse of public funds. The ministers were acquitted in April, but the others were given prison terms. Kwesi Armah, former high commissioner to Britain, remained in London, and Britain refused extradition on the grounds that the charges against him were partly political.

Representatives of Ghana, Great Britain, the United States, the World Bank, and six other Western creditor nations met with officials of the International Monetary Fund at Paris in April. They relieved financial pressure on Ghana, so that the country could develop a sound economic base. Earlier, in March, Ghana obtained a postponement of payment on debts owed the Soviet Union. New trade and payment agreements also were signed with Czechoslovakia, Hungary, Poland, and Yugoslavia.

Ghana signed agreements with the U.S. Department of Agriculture for $5,500,000 under the Food for Peace program. An agreement with the U.S. Agency for International Development guaranteed American investors against losses that might be caused by war or revolution.

The International Hotel Corporation of New York, a subsidiary of Pan American World Airways, agreed to operate three major hotels for the Ghanaian government. These included the Ambassador Hotel in Accra, one of the most luxurious in Africa. On February 3, Ghana, assisted by a French firm, opened an $8,000,000 state textiles factory at the coastal city of Tema. [Benjamin E. Thomas]

Facts in Brief. Population: 8,274,000. Government: National Liberation Council Chairman Joseph A. Ankrah. Monetary Unit: new cedi (1.02=U.S. $1). Foreign Trade: exports, $244,000,000; imports, $352,000,000. Principal Exports: cocoa beans, lumber, diamonds, manganese.

GIBRALTAR. See Great Britain; Spain.

GIRL SCOUTS. See Youth Organizations.

GIRLS CLUBS OF AMERICA. See Youth Organizations.

GLASS. See Manufacturing.

GOETZMANN, WILLIAM H. (1930-   ), historian and author, was awarded the 1967 Pulitzer prize in history. He is head of the American studies department at the University of Texas. His prize-winning work, *Exploration and Empire: The Explorer and The Scientist in the Winning of the American West,* has been called a "staggeringly complete record of Western discovery." He worked on it for more than 10 years, beginning the project as his doctoral dissertation at Yale University.

The book starts with the return of Lewis and Clark from their journey of exploration and ends with the retirement of John Wesley Powell from the U.S. Geological Survey. Throughout, the author focuses on exploration as an important cultural activity and seeks to relate the works of explorers to the intellectual, social, economic, and political development of America as a whole.

Goetzmann was born in Washington, D.C., in 1930. He received his bachelor's degree from Yale in 1952 and his Ph.D. degree in 1957. He taught history there from 1955 to 1964, when he moved to the University of Texas. He completed his book on the history of exploration with the financial assistance of the Executive Committee of American Studies at Yale and the Social Science Research Council. He also had a Susan B. Morse fellowship. Goetzmann is married and has three children. He lives near the university, at Austin.

GOLF. Jack Nicklaus and Arnold Palmer, two of golf's friendliest but most spirited rivals, maintained a wide lead over all other players in the Professional Golfers Association (PGA) tour in 1967. It was the richest year ever, with the PGA offering more than $4,500,000 in prize money. By contrast, the total prize pot on the 1957 tour amounted to $987,632. The 1967 schedule included three tournaments paying $200,000 or more and no fewer than 25 others where the total prize money was at least $100,000.

The richest of all, the $250,000 Westchester Classic at Rye, N.Y., on August 30, was won by the 27-year-old Nicklaus. He took first prize in the World Series of Golf at Akron, Ohio, 12 days later. By the end of the season, Nicklaus had won six tournaments and Palmer four. Together, they made up the winning two-man team for the international World Cup matches at Mexico City, November 9 to 12. Major individual titles eluded Palmer, however.

In the first big event of the year, the Masters Tournament at Augusta, Ga., in April, defending champion Nicklaus found himself in such a slump that he failed to qualify. Gay Brewer of Dallas, Tex., shot 280 to take the title, winning by one stroke over Bobby Nichols.

Two months later, however, in June, Nicklaus not only won the U.S. Open at Baltusrol in Springfield, N.J., but also carded 275, which broke Ben Hogan's 19-year-old Open record by one stroke. A senti-

With a sharp knee bend and a smile, Jack Nicklaus dropped a putt for a birdie on his way to winning the U.S. Open at the Baltusrol Golf Club in Springfield, N.J.

mental favorite of the crowd, 23-year-old amateur Marty Fleckman of Port Arthur, Tex., led the entire field going into the fourth and final round. But on the final day, Nicklaus shot a 65 to take the prize, while Fleckman had a disastrous 80 that left him in a tie for 18th place.

Other Winners. In the prestigious British Open, in July, Roberto de Vicenzo of Argentina, a 44-year-old who plays few tournaments in the United States, shot 278 to defeat Nicklaus by two strokes and take first prize. The PGA championship, at Columbine Country Club, near Denver, Colo., was won by Don January, of Dallas, who outshot his fellow Texan, Don Massengale, of Jacksboro, to take the title by two strokes.

Robert Dickson, a U.S. Army private from McAlester, Okla., won both the U.S. and British amateur championships. Only three other golfers have won both titles in the same year – and none since Lawson Little, in 1935. In the competition for the Walker Cup, in May, U.S. amateurs scored their 19th triumph in 21 competitions against the British since 1922. The score was 13 to 7, at the Royal St. George course in England.

Rule Change. Undoubtedly the most controversial rule change of the year was the decision by the U.S. Golf Association and Britain's ruling body, the Royal and Ancient Golf Club of St. Andrews, Scotland, to forbid the use of increasingly popular croquet-style putters. The ban stated that no "astride" stroke could be considered a true golf shot.

Women's Play. Among the women professionals on the U.S. circuit, Kathy Whitworth of San Antonio, Tex., was again the leading money winner. She also won the Women's World Series.

The most surprising showing, however, was provided by a 22-year-old French player, Catherine Lacoste, whose father, René, was once well known for his prowess as a tennis champion. He is now 63. Miss Lacoste became the first foreign, the first amateur, and the youngest winner of the U.S. Women's Open. In the tournament held in July at Hot Springs, Va., the 5-foot 3-inch French girl entered the final round of the 72-hole event leading by five strokes. She held on to win by two strokes, with a score of 294, over Beth Stone and Susie Maxwell.

Amateur Golf. Youth also did well in the U.S. Women's Amateur final at Pasadena, Calif., in August. Lou Dill of Deer Park, Tex., a 19-year-old, upset former champion Jean Ashley, 28, in their scheduled 36-hole final.

In college golf, the University of Houston scored its 10th team triumph in 12 years in winning the National Collegiate Athletic Association (NCAA) championship. Individual honors, however, went to Hale Irwin, a University of Colorado football player, whose 286 score set a course record at Shawnee-on-Delaware, Pa., in June. [John Lake]

GOVERNORS OF THE STATES holding office in 1968 are listed below, with their political affiliations and their years in office. Governors were elected in two states on Nov. 7, 1967. The Republicans won the governorship in Kentucky for the first time since 1943, and, with 25 incumbents, now have a total of 26. The Democrats won in Mississippi. With 23 incumbents, they hold a total of 24 governorships. See ELECTIONS.

Governors of the 50 States

State	Governor	Terms
Ala.	Lurleen Wallace, D.	1967-1971
Alaska	Walter J. Hickel, R.	1966-1970
Ariz.	John R. Williams, R.	1967-1969
Ark.	Winthrop Rockefeller, R.	1967-1969
Calif.	Ronald Reagan, R.	1967-1971
Colo.	John A. Love, R.	1963-1971
Conn.	John N. Dempsey, D.	1961-1971
Del.	Charles L. Terry, Jr., D.	1965-1969
Fla.	Claude R. Kirk, Jr., R.	1967-1971
Ga.	Lester G. Maddox, D.	1967-1971
Hawaii	John A. Burns, D.	1963-1971
Idaho	Don W. Samuelson, R.	1967-1971
Ill.	Otto J. Kerner, Jr., D.	1961-1969
Ind.	Roger D. Branigin, D.	1965-1969
Iowa	Harold E. Hughes, D.	1963-1969
Kans.	Robert Docking, D.	1967-1969
Ky.	Louie B. Nunn, R.	1967-1971
La.	John J. McKeithen, D.	1964-1968
Me.	Kenneth M. Curtis, D.	1967-1971
Md.	Spiro T. Agnew, R.	1967-1971
Mass.	John A. Volpe, R.	*1965-1971
Mich.	George W. Romney, R.	1963-1971
Minn.	Harold E. Le Vander, R.	1967-1971
Miss.	John Bell Williams, D.	1968-1972
Mo.	Warren E. Hearnes, D.	1965-1969
Mont.	Tim M. Babcock, R.	1962-1969
Nebr.	Norbert T. Tiemann, R.	1967-1971
Nev.	Paul Laxalt, R.	1967-1971
N.H.	John W. King, D.	1963-1969
N.J.	Richard J. Hughes, D.	1962-1970
N.Mex.	David F. Cargo, R.	1967-1969
N.Y.	Nelson A. Rockefeller, R.	1959-1971
N.C.	Daniel K. Moore, D.	1965-1969
N.Dak.	William L. Guy, D.	1961-1969
Ohio	James A. Rhodes, R.	1963-1971
Okla.	Dewey Bartlett, R.	1967-1971
Ore.	Tom McCall, R.	1967-1971
Pa.	Raymond P. Shafer, R.	1967-1971
R.I.	John H. Chafee, R.	1963-1969
S.C.	Robert E. McNair, D.	1965-1971
S.Dak.	Nils A. Boe, R.	1965-1969
Tenn.	Buford Ellington, D.	†1967-1971
Tex.	John B. Connally, Jr., D.	1963-1969
Utah	Calvin L. Rampton, D.	1965-1969
Vt.	Philip H. Hoff, D.	1963-1969
Va.	Mills E. Godwin, Jr., D.	1966-1970
Wash.	Daniel J. Evans, R.	1965-1969
W.Va.	Hulett C. Smith, D.	1965-1969
Wis.	Warren P. Knowles, R.	1965-1969
Wyo.	Stanley K. Hathaway, R.	1967-1971

*Served previous term (1961-1963).
†Served previous term (1959-1963).

GRANITE, RAGNAR ARTHUR. See NOBEL PRIZES.

GREAT BRITAIN

The value of the pound sterling was cut approximately 14 per cent on November 18 by Prime Minister Harold Wilson's Labour party government. Its value in U.S. dollars fell from $2.79 to $2.40. Sterling was supported at its new level by large international loans, and the bank rate, the key interest rate on loans, was promptly increased to 8 per cent to hold down inflation.

Devaluation was the outcome of Britain's chronic economic troubles. The Treasury had earlier warned Chancellor of the Exchequer James Callaghan that the country faced a balance of payments deficit with the outside world for the fifth straight year. Sterling was weakened still further by the shock of the Arab-Israeli war and the closing of the Suez Canal in June, and by crippling dock strikes at home. From midsummer onward, speculators anticipated collapse and were selling pounds, undermining further the pound's already unstable position on the international market.

Meanwhile, Britain's stagnant industrial production and rising unemployment, produced by the save-the-pound deflationary measures of July, 1966, added to the discontent of the trade unions and the electorate. The United States headed efforts to raise a $5,000,000,000 international loan to rescue the pound again, but only West Germany agreed to join in. France was openly critical. Wilson thereupon resolved to devalue, in hopes that lower prices for British goods would spark an export-led boom.

Only those countries closely tied to the British economy (Denmark, Iceland, Ireland, and New Zealand) or in economic troubles of their own (Israel and Spain) devalued their currencies along with Britain. See BANKS AND BANKING; INTERNATIONAL TRADE AND FINANCE; MONEY.

After Devaluation. Most economists applauded Wilson's decision. Some questioned, however, whether his 14 per cent cut in the exchange rate would be enough, especially since the government had simultaneously increased the corporate tax, removed the payroll tax premium hitherto awarded to manufacturers, and, to satisfy the United States, removed a minor tax rebate to exporters. British exporters, burdened with these extra costs, were complaining that the devaluation really amounted to less than 10 per cent. Other doubts hinged on the government's apparent unreadiness to keep wages down, which would be essential to maintain competitive British prices overseas and to deflate

For Labour Prime Minister Harold Wilson, the year 1967 was indeed painful—in the pocketbook, at the polls, and in devaluating his own political future.

the consumer market at home. A further major concern after devaluation was the attack launched on the U.S. dollar by the gold-minded French.

Wilson Under Fire. Because Wilson had been personally committed to the old exchange rate, the Conservative opposition in Parliament loudly demanded his resignation. The Tories irately recalled that Britain had had only three Labour prime ministers–Ramsey MacDonald, Clement Attlee, and Wilson–and each had devalued the pound–in 1931, 1949, and 1967. Wilson hung on, however, reminding critical Labour members of Parliament that they, too, would be thrown out if he were forced to call a general election. Callaghan, although equally responsible, received kinder public treatment. He indicated a wish to leave the Treasury once his "immediate responsibility" was over. He resigned in December, and was replaced as chancellor by Home Secretary Roy Jenkins.

European Failure. By the end of the year, Wilson's bid to secure British entry into the European Economic Community (EEC, or Common Market) looked as if it could be written off, at least for as long as French President Charles de Gaulle was alive.

Once an opponent of entry, Wilson had undergone a personal conversion, encouraged by the sad experience of the British economy outside the Common Market. He was hopeful that the French would consider Britain's growing technology a useful EEC counterweight to U.S. competition. Thus, the British application for membership in the EEC was submitted on May 12. Although it was officially welcomed by the five other member nations, France remained hostile. De Gaulle suggested an "associate" status for Britain, but this had previously been rejected by Wilson. Neither side altered its views when Wilson visited Paris in June.

At French insistence, an EEC report on the problems likely to arise from Britain's application was reworded to emphasize Britain's own economic problems. Details of this criticism, reaching British cabinet ministers during the Labour party conference in early October, plunged even the most pro-EEC ministers into profound gloom. British attempts to threaten political and even military reprisals fell flat. It seemed negotiations could not even begin.

The Irrepressible George. Light relief for the country, although another embarrassment for Wilson, came from the public behavior of Foreign Secretary George Brown. Openly admitting his liking for a sociable drink, Brown clambered from headline to headline in a series of brushes with diplomats, miners' leaders, newspaper baron Lord Thomson, press photographers, and television interviewers. While proper Britons were censorious, Brown could still get an attentive ear from U.S. President Lyndon

The Duke and Duchess of Windsor, *right,* help unveil a memorial to his mother, Queen Mary, in June. It was the duke's first public reunion with the royal family since 1936.

In a London street fight, Chinese embassy personnel swung everything but Mao's red book at the bobbies, following trouble in Hong Kong.

B. Johnson and Russian Premier Aleksei N. Kosygin. And when he was caught taking time off from the United Nations (UN) to dance the frug aboard the *Queen Mary*, it was, after all, the liner's last, sentimental crossing to New York. But it was a difficult year for his friends, and Brown's political claim to be an alternative to Wilson was laughed away.

Electoral Disaster. Labour's failures had brought electoral humiliation to the party long before the devaluation of the pound in November. In local elections in April and May, the Conservatives won control of almost all the major cities. The Tory capture of London was the first since 1933. In a series of parliamentary by-elections, the Labour party lost seats to the Conservatives in Cambridge, Glasgow, Leicester, and northeast London. It barely held a "safe" Manchester seat against a Tory named Winston Churchill, grandson of the great statesman. Labour voters were not just staying at home, they were switching to the other side.

In one of the biggest upsets since the war, Labour lost Hamilton, in Scotland, to Mrs. Winifred Ewing, a vivacious Scottish Nationalist and the mother of three children. The Nationalists, demanding full independence–up to "a UN seat between Saudi Arabia and Senegal"–had only once before captured a Scottish parliamentary division. With both a Welsh Nationalist and a Scottish Nationalist at Westminster, Celtic Britain was showing its teeth.

Ted's Troubles. Conservative electoral success came in the nick of time to save Tory leader Ted Heath from internal revolt. Heath, socially distinct from earlier leaders with his middle-class background and grammar school education, had difficulty in personal politicking and appeared uneasy with local leaders. His appointment of a new Conservative party chairman, the waspish-tongued Tony Barber, was criticized as inept. Until October, Heath fell steadily in the opinion polls while his party's fortunes rose. The Conservative party conference gave him a lengthy ovation on October 21, however, signaling that it would keep him at least until the next general election.

In January, the Liberal leader, Jo Grimond, retired after 10 years' effort to restore his radical party to major political status. With fewer than 3,000,000 votes nationally and only 12 seats in the Commons, he had not quite brought it off. He was succeeded by Jeremy Thorpe, a witty, 38-year-old barrister who, like Ted Heath, is still a bachelor.

Foot and Mouth Disease, detected first in late October in two pigs on a Shropshire farm, erupted across England's West Midlands. It was the worst animal epidemic on record. By December, rigid controls, including a ban on horseracing, had eased the situation, but a quarter of a million cattle, pigs, and sheep–some of Britain's finest herds–had to be killed, then burned or buried, under the government's slaughter policy. Meat prices rose, and restrictions on meat imports were imposed by the government to prevent further outbreaks.

Aden Handover. British troops left Aden on November 29, handing over power to the National Liberation Front (NLF) government. The troops had for months maintained internal security while the NLF and its rival Front for the Liberation of Occupied South Yemen (FLOSY) tried to wipe each other out, indicating the breakdown of political authority during the last period of colonial rule. The federal government of South Arabia, to whom power was to have gone under the Conservatives' program of 1964, did not win the full confidence of Labour ministers. By the end of August, the NLF had seized control in many of the sheikdoms, the federal army refused to take over, and confusion reigned. The evacuation of Egyptian forces from neighboring Yemen helped the NLF overcome the pro-Egyptian FLOSY throughout the country. While majority opinion in Britain was only too glad to be rid of the problem, the belief remained that violence, not political foresight, had won the day. See South Arabia, Federation of; Yemen.

Hong Kong. From May onward, Communist attempts to subvert British rule in Hong Kong persisted. Strikes, riots, and bomb-throwing inside the colony were accompanied by minor incidents on the border with mainland China, including the kidnaping of a British police officer. When Britain retaliated in August by arresting the colony's Communist editors, Red Guards burned down the British legation in Peking and subjected the staff to petty humiliations. In London, the staff of the Chinese embassy charged onto the streets with pikes, baseball bats, and a revolver to join battle with police and bystanders.

Smith of Rhodesia. A deadlock continued between Britain and the illegal white government of Prime Minister Ian Smith in Rhodesia. Wilson kept up economic sanctions, with UN backing, and continued publicly to insist on NIBMAR (no independence before majority African rule). Smith asserted that he would never give up independence. Lord Alport, a former high commissioner to Rhodesia, went to Salisbury, Rhodesia, semiofficially in June, and concluded that "Smithy" wanted talks at government level. Commonwealth Secretary George Thomson duly turned up in November. But if anything constructive happened, neither Smith nor Thomson would admit it.

Reforming the Lords. In a speech read by the Queen to Parliament on October 31, the government said it meant "to reduce the powers of the House of Lords and to eliminate its present hereditary basis." Of more than 1,000 peers (including the four royal dukes: Edinburgh, Gloucester, Kent, and Windsor) eligible for summons to Westminster, nine-tenths hold hereditary titles, and the others are life peers created since 1958. Only 200 of their lordships could be said to be active parliamentarians. The lords do useful work tidying up government bills, but they can delay legislation for months. The Labour government has not been noticeably hindered by being in a permanent minority in the House of Lords, but its few left-wing members have favored drastic changes.

Pop Go the Pirates. Britain firmly declared illegal the fleet of shipborne commercial radio stations broadcasting pop tunes and ads just outside the three-mile limit. All the pirates gave in, except one, sheltering off the coast of the Isle of Man. In their place, the British Broadcasting Corporation, rejecting its "auntie" image, set up a new network to broadcast pop–but no commercials, as yet.

Free Anguilla. The people of the tiny British West Indies island of Anguilla (population 6,000) expelled their 27 policemen on May 31 and declared themselves independent of the neighboring island of St. Kitts. They also applied to join the United States and the United Nations. Wearily, the British government refused St. Kitts' request to send a gunboat, but sent a junior minister to take up the imperial burden again. [Alastair Burnet]

Facts in Brief. Population: 55,684,000. Government: Queen Elizabeth II; Prime Minister Harold Wilson. Monetary Unit: pound (1=U.S. $2.40). Foreign Trade: exports, $14,661,000,000; imports, $16,671,000,000. Principal Exports: machinery, motor vehicles, chemicals.

GREECE suffered two major crises in 1967. One stemmed from a military coup that ended democratic rule and resulted in King Constantine II fleeing the country. The other erupted over Cyprus and nearly resulted in a war with Turkey (see Cyprus).

The government crisis began on March 13 when the caretaker government of Premier Ioannis Paraskevopoulos fell after 14 weeks in office. The immediate cause had been a deadlock in parliament over an amendment that would have extended legal immunity to members of parliament in an interim period between parliament's dissolution and the holding of general elections in May.

King Constantine, in an attempt to establish a new coalition government, asked Payanotis Kanelopoulos, leader of the National Radical Union, to form a new cabinet. Announcement of the new cabinet, however, was followed by street demonstrations in Athens and Salonika. Under pressure, the king dismissed the Greek parliament and promised a general election on May 28.

The Greek army, meanwhile, had grown restive at the turn of events. On April 21, it moved to end what it called "political disorder." Acting on orders of Colonel George Papadopoulos, army units equipped with tanks and armored cars, seized the palace, government offices, and the nation's radio and telecommunications centers. Premier Kanelopoulos and other leaders were arrested. Also, 11 articles of the constitution were suspended "because of danger to public security." With army approval, Constantine Kollias was named premier. General Grigorios Spandidakis, chief of the army general staff, was named his deputy.

King Constantine made no secret of the fact that he disapproved of the coup which, although it was carried out in his name, had in fact been executed without his knowledge or consent. On December 13, the king attempted to reverse the April coup by publicly repudiating the junta. Addressing the nation from Larissa and, later, Salonika, he called on the people and army units loyal to the Crown to join in ousting the military regime.

The countercoup failed, however, and on December 14 the king fled the country, together with his wife, his children, and Queen Mother Frederika. The royal party was accompanied by Premier Kollias, whose sympathies had cooled toward the military regime. Colonel Papadopoulos took over Kollias' post. Lieutenant General George Zoitakis was named regent in place of the king. [Kenneth Brown]

Facts in Brief. Population: 8,690,000. Government: Regent: Lieutenant General George Zoitakis; Premier George Papadopoulos. Monetary Unit: drachma (30=U.S. $1). Foreign Trade: exports, $406,000,000; imports, $1,223,000,000. Principal Exports: tobacco, dried fruit, cotton.

GUATEMALA. See Latin America.
GUINEA. See Africa.

GUYANA was stirred in November by a bitter debate over a proposed bill that would require all males 14 years of age and over to register at government-established centers. The bill's chief supporter was the Negro-dominated People's National Congress party. It argued that the bill sought only to determine the number of voters in the country. Opponents of the bill, led by the East Indian-dominated People's Congress party, felt it was part of a plot to by-pass the country's election commission and set up machinery to rig forthcoming elections.

Despite the political bickering and continuing racial unrest, the country's bauxite mining industry continued to expand, with annual production nearing the 3,000,000-ton mark. In July, the government announced it had received a $7,500,000 loan from the United States for an $11,000,000 road construction program. The road, when completed, would run from Mackenzie, the fastest growing city in Guyana, to Georgetown, the capital. It would open up part of the long-isolated interior, which is rich in mineral deposits. Another project was one designed to protect coastal areas from the high tides that periodically submerged them.

Facts in Brief. Population: 694,000. Government: Governor-General Sir David Rose; Prime Minister L. F. S. Burnham. Monetary Unit: dollar (2=U.S. $1). Foreign Trade: exports, $109,000,000; imports, $118,000,000. Principal Exports: bauxite, cane sugar, rice.

HAACK, ROBERT W., a former investment banker, was named president of the New York Stock Exchange in 1967. He was the first new president in 16 years, succeeding G. Keith Funston, who resigned on September 9 when his contract expired.

Haack had spent his entire business career in the securities industry. Born in 1917 in Milwaukee, Wis., he was educated in the city's public schools. Following his graduation from Hope College in Holland, Mich., in 1938, he attended Harvard University's Graduate School of Business Administration on an alumni scholarship and won a master's degree.

After leaving Harvard, Haack took a job with The Wisconsin Company, a brokerage firm in Milwaukee. In 1942, he enlisted in the U.S. Navy and saw action in the South Pacific. Discharged with the rank of a lieutenant, Haack returned to The Wisconsin Company, which later became Robert W. Baird and Company.

By 1950, he had become a general partner. In 1959, he became associated with the National Association of Securities Dealers, Inc., an association of some 3,700 brokers and dealers in the over-the-counter securities business. In 1964, he became president of the association, a position he was holding at the time he was named president of the New York Stock Exchange. Haack lives with his wife and four children in Potomac, Md.

HAITI. See LATIN AMERICA.

HANDICAPPED, THE. The President's Committee on Employment of the Handicapped observed its 20th anniversary in 1967. Created by President Harry S. Truman in 1947 to increase employment opportunities for the physically handicapped, the committee shortened its name and expanded its functions in 1962. At that time, President John F. Kennedy requested that the word "physically" be dropped from its title in order to bring the mentally retarded and mentally ill into the scope of its work.

With the cooperation of business, civic and industrial, and labor and professional groups, the committee approaches employers who, either from fear or lack of information, are prejudiced against hiring the physically or mentally disabled. The progress made by the committee in the two decades of its existence was hailed by 3,500 national and international delegates who attended the 1967 annual meeting, held April 27 and 28, in Washington, D.C.

Progress Report. The Vocational Rehabilitation Administration (VRA) reported that 173,594 handicapped persons were returned to useful employment in the year ended June 30, 1967. For the sixth year in succession, Pennsylvania, with 13,112 persons rehabilitated, led the states. Illinois with 9,712 ranked second, followed by North Carolina, 9,531; Georgia, 8,751; New York, 8,187; and Florida, 8,086. In addition to the basic services provided to individuals with physical or mental disabilities, the VRA and cooperating state agencies gave special attention to alcoholics, narcotics addicts, and others requiring specially designed programs of service.

The VRA and the Small Business Administration (SBA) began a joint program to help disabled persons establish their own business enterprises. The SBA administers loans under Title IV of the Economic Opportunity Act of 1964. It also provides a free counseling service for persons who are interested in establishing small private businesses.

Permobil. The wheel chair of the future may be an electrically driven, cross-country wheel chair that won the Grand Prix at the International Inventors Exhibit in Brussels, Belgium, in March, 1967. Named Permobil, it was built by a Swedish inventor and physician, Dr. Per Udden of the Timra Medical Center, Timra, Sweden. Udden says that it will permit a handicapped person to "visit a park or a beach, drive on gravel paths and pavements, go to church or visit his old friends, and he can do all this on his own and when it suits him. It can surmount curbs and doorsteps six inches high, and climb some steps that are low and wide. It can climb rough terrain, and can descend safely on steep slopes." Several models have been tested in actual use and, the Swedish parliament permitting, 2,000 Permobils will be distributed to severely handicapped persons in that country. [JOSEPH P. ANDERSON]

HARNESS RACING. See HORSE RACING.

HARTLINE, HALDAN KEFFER. See NOBEL PRIZES.

HEALTH AND DISEASE. The cost of medical care in the United States continued to rise in 1967, and the increased demand for improved and expanded health care was expected to push prices still further upward. This was the bleak report released in March by John W. Gardner, Secretary of Health, Education, and Welfare. The study, made at the direction of President Lyndon B. Johnson, showed that the price of medical care had risen faster than consumer prices generally since World War II.

In submitting the report, Gardner said that the primary challenge of this problem was up to the health professions. "The search," he said, "for new, better, and less expensive ways of doing things must be carried on by hospitals, medical schools, community agencies, and by the thousands of individual physicians serving the health needs of the people."

Regional Plans. The national campaign against heart disease, cancer, and stroke began in April, 1967, with the approval of the first regional plan, centered in Albany, N.Y. By November, comprehensive medical programs were operating in five regions with the help of $7,300,000 in federal grants. Besides the Albany region plan, covering northeastern New York and portions of southern Vermont and western Massachusetts, plans were in operation in the Intermountain region, covering Utah and parts of Colorado, Idaho, Montana, Nevada, and Wyoming; and in the Kansas, Missouri, and Wisconsin regions.

Though the funds come from the U.S. Public Health Service, these plans are initiated in the regions. In the plans, the emphasis was on continuing education in advanced techniques for doctors, nurses, and other medical professionals. There was also an attempt under the plan to educate the general public in health matters.

Disease Eradication. Since a vaccine against rubeola, or common measles, was first licensed and made available in 1963, the number of recorded cases is said to have been cut in half. It was hoped that a major campaign in 1967, underwritten by $7,000,000 in federal grants to the states, would virtually eliminate the disease from the United States. By March, the U.S. Public Health Service's National Communicable Disease Center in Atlanta, Ga., had helped 42 state-wide and 61 city and county campaigns against the disease.

Three Monsanto Company chemists reported, in February, that they had discovered a resinlike substance that can remove the infectious hepatitis virus from water supplies. The material is used as a water filter. [THEODORE F. TREUTING]

See also DENTISTRY; HOSPITAL; MEDICINE; MENTAL HEALTH.

HIGHWAY. See TRANSPORTATION.

Cigarette Smoking–Effects on Health

Death rate per 100,000 population

	Men cigarette smokers	Men nonsmokers	Women cigarette smokers	Women nonsmokers
Cause of death:				
Heart disease				
Age				
45-54	422	150	66	33
55-64	996	542	275	163
65-74	2,025	1,400	941	653
Stroke				
Age				
45-54	42	28	38	18
55-64	130	92	88	57
65-74	477	349	315	228
Lung cancer				
Age				
45-64	87	11	15	7
65-79	262	23	30	17

Source: U.S. Public Health Service

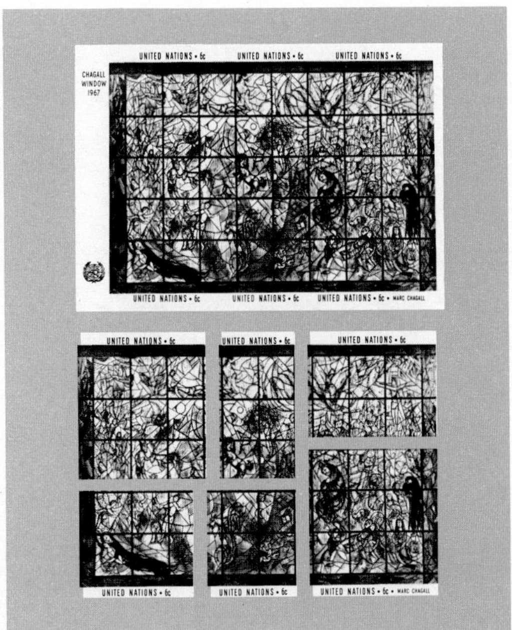

The United Nations Postal Administration issued a miniature art sheet of six stamps that reproduced the Chagall stained-glass panel at the UN Building.

HOBBIES. Controversy–political, aesthetic, and religious–enlivened the stamp world in a year that was also marked by the retirement of a self-acknowledged forger who had defrauded stamp collectors out of millions of dollars.

On June 22, just after the brief Arab-Israeli war, the United Arab Republic issued a stamp depicting President Gamal Abdel Nasser, a cheering crowd, and a map of the prewar Israeli border in flames. Abba Eban, the Israeli foreign minister, charged the stamp's symbolism indicated premeditated aggression, since it was obviously produced before the war started. Israel issued three stamps commemorating its victory in the war. Immediately, Poland barred all mail bearing them.

Widespread criticism of the portrait on the 1966 version of the Washington 5-cent stamp led Postmaster General Lawrence O'Brien to commission artist Steven Dohanos to remove shading and harsh lines from the reproduction. The portrait of Washington was originally painted by Rembrandt Peale in 1823. Complaints, which had continued into 1967, contended that Washington appeared to need a shave and looked like "a sour and disagreeable old man." The redesigned stamp was issued by the Post Office November 17.

After it was announced that the 1967 Christmas stamp would be based on *Madonna and Child with Angels*, by the 15th century Flemish artist Hans Memling, Protestants and Other Americans United for Separation of Church and State asked for but did not obtain a court ruling banning the stamp on the ground it favored the Roman Catholic Church and was a form of proselytizing.

In January, the American Philatelic Society revealed that it had bought out the stock and equipment of Raul de Thuin, 76, of Merida, Mexico, who for more than 30 years had been imitating valuable stamps and other postal rarities for sale to collectors. His forgeries were mainly of postal markings, overprints, surcharges, and cancellations which he applied to stamps of many countries but mostly to those of Latin America. In selling out, Thuin bound himself to quit the stamp business forever. Fraud orders brought against him by the U.S. government proved ineffective.

In February, part of the stamp collection of the late Josiah K. Lilly, pharmaceutical manufacturer, was auctioned in New York City, bringing $493,550, a record high for a single auction. Raymond Weill, New Orleans, La., stamp dealer, paid the highest price yet recorded for a U.S. stamp when he bid $35,000 for an inverted center 15-cent stamp issued in 1869.

The United Nations put out one of the most unusual issues of the year, a multicolored sheet of six stamps which together depicted Marc Chagall's stained glass window in the Secretariat Building. The sheet was perforated to produce six 6-cent stamps, only two of which, the upper left and the lower right, were the same size.

Coins. Despite opposition by some coin dealers, the New York Mercantile Exchange, best known as a center for potato trading, and the Commodity Exchange, Inc., began spot trading in silver dollars in August with bags of 1,000 as the basic unit. Several coin dealers joined the exchanges. Bags, which in March had brought $1,500, soared to as much as $2,500, reflecting the sharp increase in the price of silver after the government abandoned its price of $1.29.3 an ounce and began auctioning its silver supply to commercial users.

Even though more than 200,000,000 of the 40 per cent silver Kennedy half dollars had been minted between January, 1966, and April, 1967, virtually none were appearing in normal channels. This indicated they were being hoarded as much as previous issues. A record 40,300,000 halves were minted in March alone. Because of the silver shortage and the fact that the Kennedy halves were not circulating, strong sentiment arose to completely eliminate silver from half dollars. [THEODORE M. O'LEARY]

HOME ECONOMICS. See FASHION; FOOD; INTERIOR DESIGN; MONEY; YOUTH ORGANIZATIONS (Future Homemakers of America).

HOME FURNISHINGS. See INTERIOR DESIGN.

HONDURAS. See LATIN AMERICA.

HONG KONG. See GREAT BRITAIN.

Jerry Cooke, *Sports Illustrated* © Time Inc.

Damascus, ridden by Willie Shoemaker, pushed ahead with a burst of speed in the home stretch to win the Woodward Stakes and horse of the year honors.

HORSE RACING. Damascus, a three-year-old son of Sword Dancer and Kerala, was the horse of the year. Owned by Edith W. Bancroft and trained by Frank Whitely, Jr., Damascus won 12 of 16 races, setting a one-year earnings mark of $817,941.

Ironically, Damascus ran his only poor race in the Kentucky Derby. Apparently frightened by the Derby Day uproar at Churchill Downs, he behaved nervously at the start. Although well-placed throughout the race, he lacked his usual finishing burst of speed and came in third, four lengths behind the winner, Proud Clarion.

Damascus came back, however, to win the final two-thirds of the Triple Crown, the Preakness and Belmont Stakes, with strong stretch runs. By then, his challengers among the three-year-olds were narrowed down to one, Dr. Fager, a speedy front-runner who had beaten Damascus in the Gotham Mile earlier in the season.

On September 30, in the Woodward Stakes at New York's Aqueduct track, Damascus and Dr. Fager met for the second time. Adding spice to the race was the 1966 horse of the year, Buckpasser, who, despite recurring hoof trouble was running strongly. The event was billed as "The Race of the Decade." Even the outsider in the betting, Handsome Boy, had won three $100,000 races in his last four starts.

After Dr. Fager set a quick early pace, Damascus made his move on the final turn and galloped to a stunning 10-length victory. Buckpasser barely managed to pass Dr. Fager to come in second.

Buckpasser's owner, Ogden Phipps, retired his four-year-old colt after the Woodward Stakes race. Buckpasser concluded his career with 25 victories in 31 starts. His earnings placed him third in all-time winnings, behind Kelso and Round Table.

Major U.S. Races of 1967

Race	Winner	Value to Winner
Arlington Classic	Dr. Fager	$ 61,000
Arlington-Washington Futurity	Vitriolic	105,875
Belmont Stakes	Damascus	104,950
Brooklyn Handicap	Handsome Boy	69,355
Champagne Stakes	Vitriolic	119,500
Delaware Handicap	Straight Deal	76,879
Flamingo Stakes	Reflected Glory	93,990
Garden State Stakes	Bugged	188,721
Gardenia Stakes	Gay Matelda	112,722
Gulfstream Handicap	Pretense	97,600
Hollywood Derby	Tumble Wind	72,900
Jockey Club Gold Cup	Damascus	69,290
Kentucky Derby	Proud Clarion	119,700
Metropolitan Handicap	Buckpasser	70,980
New Hampshire Sweepstakes	Dr. Fager	167,517
Preakness	Damascus	141,500
Santa Anita Derby	Ruken	94,900
Santa Anita Handicap	Pretense	100,000
Suburban Handicap	Buckpasser	71,370
Washington, D.C., International	Fort Marcy	90,000
Widener Handicap	Ring Twice	81,640
Woodward Stakes	Damascus	70,070

Major Foreign Races of 1967

Race	Winner	Value to Winner
Epsom Derby	Royal Palace	$173,370
Grand National Steeplechase	Foinavon	49,364
Grand Prix de Paris	Phaeton	152,620
Irish Derby	Ribocco	161,308
Prix de l'Arc de Triomphe	Topyo	203,958

Besides Damascus, other divisional leaders were: best two-year-old, Vitriolic; best two-year-old filly, Queen of the Stage; best three-year-old filly, Furl Sail; best older horse, Buckpasser; best mare, Straight Deal; best sprinter, Dr. Fager; and best grass horse, Fort Marcy.

Harness Racing. In a reaction to a series of scandals involving betting frauds and possible underworld influence, the 38 member tracks of the Harness Tracks of America set up a protective bureau to police the sport.

On the track, four-year-old pacer Romeo Hanover ran his string of victories up to 21 in a row before being beaten, and Speedy Streak won the classic Hambletonian trot for three-year-olds.

The sensation of the year was Nevele Pride, a two-year-old trotter. At one point he won 17 races in a row. He also set a record for earnings by a two-year-old and established a new world record for the mile among juveniles with a time of 1 minute 58 2/5 seconds. [JAMES O. DUNAWAY]

HOSPITAL. The demand for more hospital services reached crisis proportions in 1967, and doctors themselves recognized that facilities were inadequate for the computer age. Some experts pointed out that virtually all hospitals built in the past 30 years were geared to a system of medicine that no longer exists for millions of Americans, a system that depended upon the availability of the family doctor as the first recourse in a medical emergency. Many people today have no family doctor and turn to hospitals in any emergency.

One approach to the problem involved rebuilding or replacing most hospitals, at a cost of billions of dollars. New designs included (1) buildings with pneumatic chutes and conveyor systems for removing wastes and delivering drugs, instruments, linens, and prepackaged food; (2) a return to "skyscraper" design, with computer-controlled self-service elevators; and (3) one-bed and two-bed suites with individual oxygen lines, and individual controls for air conditioning, heat, light, and water.

Hospitals were also closing their nursing schools, having reached the conclusion that the cost of training their own nurses had become prohibitive. As a result, the National League for Nursing declared that the shortage of nurses might be more than twice as serious by 1970. [THEODORE F. TREUTING]

See also HEALTH AND DISEASE; MEDICARE.

HOTEL. See TRAVEL.

HOUSING generally got short shrift from Congress in 1967. It chopped in half President Lyndon B. Johnson's request for $40,000,000 to continue the rent supplement program. It cut $613,391,000 out of the entire Department of Housing and Urban Development (HUD) budget, leaving the department with $1,898,000,000 to finance the nation's major community housing and development programs in fiscal 1968. The Congress failed to enact any of some 30 urban bills, including several that would have provided federal assistance to stimulate home ownership by low-income families.

The National Association of Housing and Redevelopment officials, representing local, state, and federal administrators of housing and urban renewal programs, in its biennial Program Policy Resolution stated that it was "dismayed and frustrated over the lack of a sense of urgency" in the administration's and Congress' dealing with urban affairs. It condemned " 'action by press release' at every level of government."

In October, Representative William B. Widnall (R., N.J.), ranking minority member of the housing subcommittee of the House Committee on Banking and Currency, attacked Congress' failure to produce major housing legislation during the 1967 session.

Model Cities. Of the 193 cities that had submitted applications in the model cities program enacted in the 1966 session of Congress, 63 received

Engineering News-Record © McGraw-Hill, Inc.

A slum renovating experiment in New York City, using boxlike prefabricated units, proved highly successful in 1967. *At top*, a boy views dwelling to be renovated. As work begins, *center*, workmen lower a "drop-in" core containing kitchen and bath through roof; 48 hours later, the core, *bottom*, is in place.

grants in the first round of approvals by HUD. The 63 will share $11,000,000 in planning funds and–after they have drawn up detailed plans–will be eligible for funds for actual construction. In October, Congress appropriated $300,000,000 to finance up to 80 per cent of the costs of the projects to rebuild slum neighborhoods. In this program, too, Congress had chopped deeply. The administration had asked for $662,000,000. See CITY.

Housing Starts inched upward to an annual rate of slightly more than 1,200,000 by midyear from the late 1966 rate of fewer than 1,000,000 units. But by October, the private nonfarm rate had climbed to 1,477,000. For the year 1967 as a whole, the total was estimated at about 1,300,000. The demand for housing held at the 1966 level of 1,600,000 units.

The value of new private, nonfarm housing units constructed in 1967 was about $18,250,000,000, just $500,000 above the total for the previous year. The low rate of rental vacancies, 6.7 per cent for the year, confirmed the increasing demand for new apartment construction.

Both federal and private-sector economists predicted 1968 housing starts at 1,500,000, or about 15 per cent higher than the 1967 level. They made this forecast despite indications that there will be additional increases in land and construction costs. There was some hedging, however, on the effect higher interest rates would have on the mortgage markets and therefore on new building. Builders, mortgage lenders, and real estate dealers were asking for a rise in the 6 per cent limit on home loans backed by the Federal Housing Administration (FHA) and Veterans Administration (VA). Raymond H. Lapin, president of the Federal National Mortgage Association, supported the proposal. He said such action would slow the trend toward increasing the "discount points," or premiums, that home buyers and sellers have to pay when FHA or VA mortgages are used to finance purchases.

The Life Insurance Industry pledged $1,000,000,000 to finance projects to restore slum areas, mostly by the construction of rent-supplement housing. Most of the industry's 348 firms agreed to invest in proportion to their assets. The September 13 announcement came after representatives of such corporate giants as Metropolitan Life Insurance Company and Prudential Insurance Company of America met with President Johnson, three Cabinet members, two governors, and a host of other officials in the White House.

The FHA measured its housing for minority groups and found it wanting in 1967. It surveyed all FHA-insured subdivision housing put up since the 1962 executive order that forbade discrimination in federally insured housing. Of the 410,574 such houses sold, only a total of 13,832 had gone to Negro families. [J. ROBERT DUMOUCHEL]

HOUSTON. By a smashing vote of 71,544 to 23,614, voters approved a sales tax on December 5. The tax was expected to relieve the municipal revenue crisis that prevented salary increases for police and firemen. A strong supporter of the tax, Mayor Louie B. Welch, earlier won a third term by defeating former Mayor Lewis Cutrer.

Construction. Economic growth in petrochemicals and aerospace activity spurred demand for additional office space. Still rising was One Shell Plaza which, at 700 feet, will be the tallest building in Texas. Under construction near the 50-story tower were the Houston Lighting and Power Company building, the Space Hall of Fame, and the Houston Convention Center. Designed to increase the city's first-class tourist facilities by 50 per cent within a year, 19 hotel and motel projects were ready to go into construction. A 32-day bricklayers' strike ended October 3; the work stoppage halted $100,000,000 worth of construction.

Downtown. The city council voted $50,000 to study the first phase of the "Blueprint for the Future," advanced by the local chapter of the American Institute of Architects (AIA). The initial stage, a $2,000,000 underground mall, would be part of a full-scale downtown rejuvenation. The city council also encouraged plans for a 14-block air-conditioned mall surrounding Houston's busiest intersection. [DONALD W. LIEF]

HUMPHREY, HUBERT HORATIO (1911-), traveled widely at home and abroad in 1967 to broaden support for the United States position in Vietnam. From March 26 to April 10, he visited seven European nations: Belgium, Britain, France, Italy, the Netherlands, Switzerland, and West Germany. At the Vatican, he met with Pope Paul VI and, in London, with 200 members of the British Parliament. Almost everywhere he went, Humphrey was met by antiwar demonstrators.

On October 29, Humphrey arrived in Saigon to attend the inauguration of South Vietnamese President Nguyen Van Thieu; later, he visited Malaysia and Indonesia before returning to Washington, D.C., on November 7.

Humphrey campaigned tirelessly for the Vietnam cause at home. In February, he addressed a joint session of the Texas legislature, and was jeered by antiwar picketers. In October, on a trip to Minnesota and California, the Vice-President again asked for public support for the war.

The Vice-President continued to speak out on urban problems. Addressing a meeting of the 44th Congress of Cities in Boston, Mass., in July, he called "slumism" the No. 1 challenge for America. The following month, at the meeting of the National Association of Counties in Detroit, Mich., he suggested a "Marshall Plan" to aid the impoverished areas of the United States. [CAROL L. THOMPSON]

HUNGARY held elections for the national assembly on March 19, 1967. For the first time since 1947, when the Communists came to power, the voters had an opportunity to choose between two rival candidates for 9 of the 349 parliamentary seats at stake and about 750 of the 84,635 seats on county, district, and local councils. A law permitting the inclusion of more than one name on an election ballot had been enacted in 1966.

Shortly after the elections, Jenö Fock was named premier in a government shuffle that included the resignation of President Istvan Dobi. President Dobi was succeeded by Pal Losonczi. Fock, in his first address to the national assembly, promised "a complete change in the economic affairs management."

During the year, visits were exchanged by Hungary's Communist leader, Janos Kadar, and the Soviet Union's Leonid I. Brezhnev. Hungary's pro-Soviet policy, however, did not prevent the Hungarian government from maintaining good relations with Romania and Yugoslavia–both Communist dissidents–and with non-Communist countries as well. [H. GORDON SKILLING]

Facts in Brief. Population: 10,242,000. Government: Communist Party First Secretary Janos Kadar; President Pal Losonczi; Premier Jenö Fock. Monetary Unit: forint (23.48=U.S. $1). Foreign Trade: exports, $1,593,000,000; imports, $1,565,000,000. Principal Exports: machinery, transportation equipment, chemicals.

HUNTING AND FISHING. The biggest fishing news in 1967 was the growth of coho (also called silver) salmon in Lake Michigan. Nearly 800,000 cohoes were placed in rivers and streams that flow into the lake in 1966. These original plantings were 7-inch fish from West Coast stock. In September, 1967, many of these fish returned to the streams where they were first planted to spawn, but they had grown so much that 5- to 15-pound fish were commonplace. Salmon weighing over 20 pounds were also reported.

The growth rate of the Lake Michigan coho is rapid because they eat alewives, small forage fish that have crowded into the lake. It is hoped that the salmon will eventually reduce the overabundance of alewives.

Hunters and fishermen in the United States spent more than $139,000,000 for 42,103,510 hunting and fishing licenses and permits in 1966–the latest period for which U.S. Department of the Interior figures are available.

Big Game. The take of big game in 1966, most recent year for which Bureau of Sport Fisheries and Wildlife figures were available, showed an overall increase of 6.4 per cent. The bag for the following species was up: white-tailed deer, 8.8 per cent; black-tailed deer, 14.3 per cent; elk, 11.1 per cent; caribou, 16.7 per cent; grizzly bear, 36.7 per cent; and polar bear, 5.8 per cent.

About 2,020,000 deer of all kinds were bagged in the United States in 1966, with Texas reporting the biggest take in white-tails, 262,500. In other big game, Alaska reported the biggest bags in moose, 7,100; grizzly bear, 865; mountain goat, 600; polar bear, 399; and caribou, 36,000.

Fishing Records. A 54-year-old salt-water fishing record, which many persons thought could never be matched, was tied in 1967. On June 16, Charles Cinto landed a 73-pound striped bass–exactly the same size as one taken by Charles Church in 1913. Both stripers came from the Vineyard Sound off Massachusetts. The Cinto striper, however, will not be officially listed in the salt-water records kept by the International Game Fish Association because he used a wire line and a lure with multiple hooks.

One tie did make the salt-water records, however. A Pacific blue marlin weighing 1,100 pounds was taken off Hawaii on May 23 by Hale L. Erickson. Another record was set by Joseph Chesla for an 81-pound cod caught March 15 off New Jersey.

In the official fresh-water world records kept by *Field & Stream* magazine only one new entry was made. A subspecies of the black bass family, the redeye bass, was added to the records list. The largest redeye reported was a 6-pound 1/2-ounce bass caught in Alabama, on March 24, by Thomas L. Sharpe. [CLARE CONLEY]

ICE HOCKEY. The high-scoring Chicago Black Hawks, playing strongly over the last half of the season, won the 1967 National Hockey League championship by a wide margin. But in the post-season play-offs, the Toronto Maple Leafs captured the Stanley Cup.

The Black Hawks set two scoring records. Their 264 goals broke the mark of 259 set by Montreal in 1961-1962, and their line of Stan Mikita, Doug Mohns, and Ken Wharram scored 228 points to top the 226 scored by Detroit's Gordie Howe, Ted Lindsay, and Norm Ullman in 1956-1957.

Mikita broke his own league record for assists with 62, and his 97 points (goals plus assists) tied the league record set by Bobby Hull, a teammate, in the previous season. Hull led in goals with 52, a record second only to his score of 54 the previous year. Another scoring record was set by Detroit veteran Gordie Howe, whose 25 goals raised his career total to 649.

Play-Offs. In the first round of the Stanley Cup play-offs, Toronto eliminated the Black Hawks, 4-2, while the Canadiens won four straight from the Rangers. In the final round, the first four games were split, with Toronto winning two in a row to take the cup, 4-2.

Four Black Hawks were named to the league's all-star team. They were Hull, Mikita, Wharram, and Pierre Pilote, a defenseman. The other two all-stars were goalie Ed Giacomin and defenseman Harry Howell, both of the Rangers. Hull, Mikita, and Pilote were repeaters from the 1965-1966 team.

Expansion. The league doubled its size for the 1967-1968 season. Six new teams made up the Western Division, with the six older teams playing as the Eastern Division. The Western teams are the Los Angeles Kings, the Minneapolis-St. Paul North Stars, the Philadelphia Flyers, the Pittsburgh Penguins, St. Louis Blues, and the San Francisco-Oakland Seals.

Amateur Hockey. Russia won its fifth consecutive amateur world title at Vienna, Austria, in March. The undefeated Russians scored 58 goals and yielded only 9 in seven games. Sweden was second, followed by Canada, Czechoslovakia, the United States, and Finland. The National Collegiate Athletic Association (NCAA) championship was won at Syracuse, N.Y., by Cornell.

Awards in the National Hockey League:

Calder Trophy (best rookie), Bobby Orr, Boston.

Hart Trophy (most valuable player), Stan Mikita, Chicago.

Lady Byng Trophy (sportsmanship), Mikita, Chicago.

Norris Trophy (best defenseman), Harry Howell, New York.

Ross Trophy (leading scorer), Mikita, Chicago.

Smythe Trophy (most valuable in Stanley Cup play), Dave Keon, Toronto.

Vezina Trophy (leading goalie), Glenn Hall and Denis DeJordy, Chicago. [JAMES O. DUNAWAY]

ICE SKATING. It was a good year for defending title-holders in the World Figure Skating Championships, held at Zurich, Switzerland, in March. For the second straight year, Peggy Fleming, 18, of Colorado Springs, Colo., won the women's world championship. European champion Gabriele Seyfert of East Germany, the 1966 runner-up, was again second. Miss Fleming piled up a wide margin in the compulsory figures to win easily despite a fall at the start of her free skating routine.

In the men's competition, European champion Emmerich Danzer of Austria came from behind with a brilliant free skating exhibition to win his second straight title. His countryman, Wolfgang Schwartz, was next, and Gary Visconti of Detroit, Mich., was third, just as in 1966.

The pairs title was won for the fourth time in a row by the Russian husband-and-wife team, Lyudmilla Belousova Protopopov and Oleg Protopopov. West Germany's Margot Glockshuber and Wolfgang Danne were second, and Cynthia and Ronald Kauffmann of Seattle, Wash., third. Completing the list of successful defenders were Diana Towler and Bernard Ford of Great Britain, who won the ice dance championship for the second time, with Lorna Dyer and John Carrell of Seattle, Wash., as runners-up.

In January, Miss Fleming won her fourth straight U.S. title. Visconti, who had won the U.S. men's

Cees Verkerk of the Netherlands set a world record in the 10,000-meter speed-skating race at Oslo, Norway. He also won the 5,000-meter race.

crown in 1965, regained it from Scott Allen of Smoke Rise, N.J., the winner in 1964 and 1966. The Kauffmanns retained their pairs championship, and Miss Dyer and Carrell won the dance championship. All except Visconti went on to win the North American championships in Montreal. The men's victor was Donald Knight of Canada.

In addition to Danzer and Miss Seyfert, the European titles were won by the Protopopovs in the pairs, and Ford and Miss Towler in the dance.

Speed Skating found the men's championship also a rerun of 1966. Cees Verkerk of the Netherlands won his second straight world title, setting a new record low score of 178.058 points. Verkerk swept the 5,000- and 10,000-meter races to win easily from Ard Schenk, also of the Netherlands and also second in 1966. Schenk won the 1,500 meters, while in the 500 meters, Keiichi Suzuki of Japan defeated the 1966 winner, Tom Gray of Minneapolis, Minn.

The Netherlands also produced the winner in the women's world championship, a stunning upset. Stien Kaiser, a 28-year-old Dutch police clerk, won the 1,000, 1,500, and 3,000 meters events and the overall title. Second was Lasma Kauniste of Russia, with Dianne Holum, a 15-year-old high school student from Northbrook, Ill., a surprising third. The 500 meters was taken by Mary Meyers of St. Paul, Minn. [James O. Dunaway]

IGNATIUS, PAUL ROBERT (1920-), an assistant Secretary of Defense since 1964, was sworn in Sept. 1, 1967, as Secretary of the Navy. He was appointed to the navy's top civilian post after the death of John T. McNaughton, who was killed in an airplane crash, on July 19, before taking office.

Ignatius is known as a nonstop worker of great ability in surmounting administrative problems. Secretary of Defense Robert McNamara praised his new Secretary of the Navy as "one of my most trusted and valuable associates."

Before becoming Secretary of the Navy, Ignatius had been with the Department of Defense since 1961, when he was appointed assistant Secretary of Defense for installation and logistics. He entered government service after 11 years as vice-president and director of Harbridge House, Incorporated, a Boston management and consultant firm.

Ignatius was born Nov. 11, 1920, at Los Angeles, Calif. He was a Phi Beta Kappa graduate of the University of Southern California in 1942. During World War II, he was a navy ordnance specialist aboard aircraft carriers in the Pacific. After the war, he earned a M.B.A. degree from Harvard in 1947 and then taught business administration at the Harvard Business School until 1950.

Ignatius and his wife, the former Nancy S. Weiser, have four children, David, 17; Sarah, 15; Amy, 11, and Alan, 8. [Walter F. Morse]

IMMIGRATION AND EMIGRATION. Legislation to amend the 1965 immigration reform law was introduced in Congress on Oct. 11, 1967, by Senator Edward M. Kennedy (D., Mass.) and Representative Emanuel Celler (D., N.Y.). Designed to remove "inequities" remaining in the nation's immigration policies, it would provide a new "policy of asylum" for refugees, authorizing the issuance of 12,000 immigrant visas annually to qualified refugees throughout the world. The bill would also clean up a backlog of applicants that had accumulated under the original national origin quota system. Other reforms of a more controversial nature were to be postponed until recommendations could be made.

Cuban refugees benefited from a bill passed by Congress on Nov. 2, 1966. The bill applied to about 150,000 cuban refugees who were in the United States as "parolees." Since they had been admitted under emergency procedures, they were without visas and could not, therefore, apply for citizenship. In fiscal 1967, 27,792 took advantage of the new law to become permanent resident aliens, a first step to achieving naturalized citizenship.

Immigrants admitted to the United States in fiscal 1967 totaled 361,972, compared to 323,040 the previous year. In the same period, 104,902 aliens became citizens of the United States and 9,260 were deported. [William McGaffin]

INCOME TAX. See Taxation.

INDIA

India marked the 20th anniversary of its independence, with little to celebrate in 1967. A shaky federal government, a number of unstable state governments, irresponsible labor lockouts, food riots, and an economic recession all reflected the nation's many problems.

A Crippled Party. In February, India held its fourth national election. Although the Congress party again led at the polls, its legislative plurality was reduced from 238 seats to 50. Three of the party's most powerful leaders, including Kumaraswami Kamaraj, its president, lost their legislative seats. They had become disenchanted with Prime Minister Indira Gandhi's leadership and their personal defeat was a primary factor in helping Mrs. Gandhi retain the prime ministership. Another factor was the fact that Morarji R. Desai, her principal rival for the post, accepted the deputy prime ministership. Meanwhile, the Freedom party, which endorses free enterprise, emerged as the largest opposition party. It increased its seats from 22 to 42. The Jan Sangh, a militant Hindu party, went from 12 to 33 seats.

State Governments. The Congress party lost even more ground at state levels. Coalitions formed between non-Congress party candidates won in 7 of the 16 states. In the state of West Bengal, the 14-party coalition government was dominated by Communists who fomented agrarian and labor unrest. At Naxalbari, a sensitive border area adjoining Communist Chinese-occupied Tibet, pro-Peking Communists encouraged Santhal tribesmen to commit terrorist acts and simultaneously establish "liberated" areas. Peking called such actions "the front paw of the Great Indian Revolution." Yet the state government did not move against the marauders until federal intervention was threatened. In Calcutta, while workers surrounded factories and kept managers captive for as long as 160 hours, the state police professed neutrality. Finally, the central government dismissed the state government and imposed "president's rule" over the unruly province. Other states were similarly placed under "president's rule" during the year.

Government Hesitant. Indecision characterized the newly elected government. Although the country desperately needed fertilizer plants, negotiations with foreign companies dragged on in mutual suspicion. A long-standing controversy over replacing English as the basic language in the universities

Pilfering pigeons raid a truckload of wheat, part of a shipment imported by India in 1967 to stave off a threatened famine in Gaya, a village in Bihar state.

TONNES

India's Prime Minister Indira Gandhi, campaigning for re-election to parliament, drapes a garland of flowers on a village boy who came to hear her speak.

broke out again. A bill to make English an associate official language, however, was finally approved.

Two new words, one meaning labor lock-in of management and the other meaning strikes, entered the political lexicon of India in 1967, causing endless labor strife, disruption of production, and in some cases, outright labor blackmail. But the central government did little to curb such lawlessness. No firm conclusions were reached on proposals calling for the abolishment of the huge government-paid allowances to India's 350 princes and maharajas. Even a decision to nationalize all banks, long a part of the Congress party's platform, was watered down in favor of tightening controls only.

Industrial Recession. As a result of agricultural priorities, industrial development expenditures were scaled down 10 per cent during the year. Strikes, inflation, and inefficient industries created a recession. Several plants operated at only half capacity. The priorities given to agriculture, however, seemed to be paying dividends. Total food production for 1967 was expected to reach 95,000,000 tons, about 6 per cent higher than the 1964 high-water mark. A providential monsoon contributed to this success, but so did such wise governmental policies as a 40 per cent increase in agricultural investment, the use of more high-yielding seeds, a step-up in fertilizer production, wider use of irrigation, and farm credits. Despite the bumper yield, famine threatened a number of areas in 1967, notably in the state of Bihar, where two districts and several regions affected by drought were declared disaster areas in April. To ease the threat of starvation among the state's approximately 12,000,000 inhabitants, the government began shipping in about 175,000 tons of grain per month, most of it from the United States. Late in July, rains soaked the parched fields of Bihar as well as Uttar, where famine had also threatened. Government agricultural experts immediately moved in with aid for the distressed farmers. This included a mass distribution of seed on credit and the launching of an extensive irrigation system.

Foreign Policy. The year saw a further decline in the prestige of India's foreign policy. Its apparently uncritical and hasty support of the Arab bloc in the Middle East crisis was labeled unimaginative and against India's own interests by a number of critics. Its repeated pleas for a cessation of the U.S. bombing of North Vietnam were ignored even by pro-Soviet, Afro-Asian leaders. Only against China and its alleged military probes at Nathu La and Cho La in the Himalayas did Indian foreign policy appear resolute. [Keki R. Bhote]

Facts in Brief. Population: 515,768,000. Government: President Zakir Husain; Prime Minister Indira Gandhi. Monetary Unit: rupee (7.58=U.S. $1). Foreign Trade: exports, $1,608,000,000; imports, $2,753,000,000. Principal exports: textiles, tea, iron ore.

INDIAN, AMERICAN. The Bureau of Indian Affairs moved to give Indians increasing leadership in the development of Indian programs in 1967. In line with this policy, the Indian Resources and Development Act was introduced in Congress in May to provide up to $5,000,000 in working capital for commercial, community, and industrial development in Indian areas.

Assistance was also planned for Indians who choose to relocate. As a pilot program, the Madera, Calif., Employment Training Center was opened on a deactivated radar base to provide a complete "community" to teach Indians job skills. It was also to provide experience for a successful adjustment to modern urban life. A similar program was underway on the Choctaw Reservation in Mississippi.

During the year, more than 10,000 Indians were assisted in acquiring skills and finding jobs through programs near reservations and at seven relocation centers in major U.S. cities.

In June, the U.S. Court of Claims ruled that the Seminole Indians had established the fact that they held title to most of Florida in 1823. The Indian Claims Commission then took over the task of determining the value of the acreage involved at the time of the Treaty of Moultrie ceding the land to the United States. Congress will then be asked to appropriate funds to be distributed among descendants of the Seminoles. [A. L. NEWMAN]

INDONESIA gained steadily in its efforts to restore political order, introduce a sense of fiscal responsibility, and reconstitute its image abroad as a responsible nation.

Politically, the power of deposed President Sukarno was still in evidence as the year began. Accordingly, General Suharto, who had replaced Sukarno, moved with great care and caution as he began to strip Sukarno and his supporters of their remaining power. The moves were made on several fronts. First, the government continued its purge of the Indonesian Communist party. Second, key Sukarno supporters–both in the armed forces as well as civilians –were arrested on various capital charges and brought to trial before a special national court. Some were executed. Finally, after carefully winning support of various student and Moslem organizations, Suharto's group began to ease Sukarno into a controlled oblivion.

By February, Sukarno had been placed under such intense pressure that he agreed to surrender his executive powers to Suharto. The political tug-of-war between Sukarno and Suharto continued, however, behind the scenes. The arrests of a number of high-ranking military leaders on charges ranging from corruption to treason implicated Sukarno still further while simultaneously reducing his power in military circles. Sukarno's stature was further diminished as the new government revealed that he was linked, if only as a figurehead, to antigovernment Communist plots planned with the help of Communist China. At year's end, Sukarno had been stripped of his powers and confined to his residence outside Djakarta.

The effects of years of economic mismanagement threatened to take the toll of the nation in 1967. To offset them, Suharto acted simultaneously on several fronts. He first acted to re-establish the nation's international credit. A major achievement was seen in the readmission of Indonesia to membership in the World Bank. Through a series of agreements, creditors agreed to postpone, re-fund, or extend additional credits to the nearly bankrupt country. A second, and even more important step, was the securing of additional development funds to shore up the total economic picture. These were forthcoming from American, Dutch, Japanese, and West German interests. They were partly tied to agreements by which Indonesia promised to pay compensation for all previously seized, foreign-owned interests.

Economic Aid as well as credits from other countries began to open the way for an Indonesian economic revival. In August, some 100 industrialists from both Asia and the West gathered in Djakarta to discuss long-term investments in the nation. To further speed foreign investment, previously nationalized industries such as mining, oil, rubber, and tea, were denationalized and turned back to foreign managements. At the year's end, Indonesia appeared likely to regain its economic balance.

In its international relations, the swing away from the Communist world continued. Indonesian relations with Communist China were to all intents and purposes permanently suspended as trade relations were broken, diplomatic channels closed, and resident Chinese expelled from the country. Concurrently, there was a determined effort to re-establish cordial relations with other Southeast Asian nations. Singapore and Malaysia formally established such contacts, and the Indonesian-sponsored guerrilla movement in Borneo was withdrawn. Indonesia continued to take a more or less neutral stand toward the struggle in Vietnam but its very refusal to follow the Chinese Communist lead indicated a growing alignment with the rest of non-Communist Asia.

In December, General Suharto announced plans to divert some of the army's extra manpower out of the barracks and into road building and other civic action projects in areas that were formerly Indonesian Communist strongholds. Most of the funds needed to carry out the projects were supplied by the International Monetary Fund and other international agencies. [JOHN N. STALKER]

Facts in Brief. Population: 111,315,000. Government: Acting President Suharto. Monetary Unit: rupiah (100 = U.S. $1). Foreign Trade: exports, $707,000,000; imports, $622,000,000. Principal Exports: petroleum, rubber, tin.

The oldest fossil ant ever found, more than 100,000,000 years old, was discovered in a piece of amber in New Jersey.

INSECT. Two 100,000,000-year-old ants, preserved in amber, were identified in 1967. They had been found in New Jersey by amateur rock collectors, Mr. and Mrs. Edmund Frey. Entomologists reported that the specimens have characteristics of both ants and wasps. The find almost doubles the time period of the recorded ancestry for ants, and is the first example of social insects, a category that also includes termites and bees, living during the Mesozoic era. Prior to the discovery, the oldest ant specimen known was 60,000,000 years old. The Mesozoic ants are probably a link between ants and the more ancient solitary wasp, from which entomologists suspect all social insects descended.

Caribbean Fruit Flies were threatening to cause heavy losses to Florida agriculture in 1967. It was believed they had entered the United States in 1965. Eradication efforts so far have failed to rid Florida of the fast-breeding pest, which had spread to 24 counties by mid-1967.

Bees. Otto Mackensen of the U.S. Department of Agriculture reported at the 21st International Apicultural Congress, in August, that bees now can be bred with a preference for particular plants. The development is of importance in agriculture, since bees are believed to be responsible for at least 80 per cent of insect pollinating activity. Pollen preferences among bees can spell success or failure for crops such as alfalfa or clover. [James A. Pearre]

INSURANCE. In recent years, extraordinary natural disasters–floods, hurricanes, and tornadoes–caused huge claims against the fire and casualty insurance companies. In 1967, the catastrophes were man-made–the urban riots. A final tabulation put the insured losses in the Detroit riots alone at $32,000,000, according to Michigan's insurance commissioner, David Dykhouse.

As a consequence of the riots, the fire and casualty insurance firms could not be expected to provide new insurance in the urban ghettos at standard rates–or at any rate. But without fire and damage insurance for businesses, ghetto and fringe neighborhoods were in danger of losing vital services.

In September, a presidential advisory panel on insurance in riot-affected areas urged the industry to "make insurance available to all persons whose properties meet reasonable standards of insurability" regardless of their location. This was a plan that has been followed for residential properties in Boston, Mass., since 1960. Under another plan, all insurance firms in a state would contribute money to form a special pool to underwrite policies for ghetto areas and thus share the risks.

Life Insurance companies, also in September, pledged to invest $1,000,000,000 in ghetto real estate, mostly in housing. By late November, 153 of the 348 U.S. life firms had committed themselves to participate. They represented 90 per cent of the industry's $170,000,000,000 in assets. See Housing.

Total life insurance in force, having achieved the amazing mark of a trillion dollars in 1966, continued its growth in 1967 with a sales increase of 7 per cent. Benefits paid to policyholders and beneficiaries rose more than 7 per cent above the revised 1966 total of $12,342,200,000.

Auto Insurance companies continued to be beset by rising claims growing out of the steadily increasing numbers of cars and ever more costly accidents. A solution, dating back to a Columbia University study during the 1930s, came to the fore: Simply eliminate the issue of who is to blame for an accident by issuing policies that would pay off immediately on any damages up to a fixed dollar amount. It would do away with most long, costly court battles–at savings to both the insured and the insurer. A somewhat similar "no-fault" insurance plan has been operating successfully in Saskatchewan, Canada, since 1946. The insurance is compulsory and is sold only by the province. If the payments, which are made under a set schedule, seem inadequate to a victim, he may sue for additional damages.

Throughout 1967, pressure was mounting for adoption of some similar system in the United States. In November, a *Fortune* magazine article argued that "there is a powerful case for scrapping" the U.S. car insurance system "altogether and replacing it" with no-fault coverage. [Edwin W. Darby]

See also Medicare; Social Security.

INTERIOR DESIGN. Contemporary-style furniture and accessories remained extremely popular in 1967 because of their adaptability to both modern and traditional settings. Functional and colorful, they reflected the influences of the "Mod" trend in art, fashion, and music. Upholstered furniture, however, featuring rich velvet and fur–both real and artificial–remained a favorite among many decorators. Styles such as rural English, Early American, French, and Italian were prominently displayed at the merchandise markets as well as in the retail stores. Spanish designs also continued to be favorites with designers. Manufacturers emphasized grains, light finishes, and warmth of tone in the wood trims.

See-Through Furnishings. The use of flexible materials such as plastic, paper, vinyl, synthetic fibers, steel, and aluminum created radically changed interiors in 1967. Designers used plastics and lucites to develop new forms for tables, chairs, and stools. The use of chromed tubular steel or heavy aluminum tubing for frames and legs gave furniture a "floating" appearance. Inflatable pillows, in either sheer or colored plastic, were used for seats and backs. Exciting in appearance, the see-through furniture allowed for wider individualism in decorating.

By using advanced methods of embossing, lamination, and chemically treated wood pulp, the paper industry created a vast selection of durable, colorful, yet inexpensive disposable furnishings for every room. High-style paper chairs, tables, bookshelves, children's furniture, and even draperies, bedspreads, and rugs had universal appeal.

Vivid Colors. The uninhibited use of color in fabrics remained popular with such vivid combinations as pink, purple, and red, or blue, green, lime, and lavender. Nearly all fabrics used for upholstery or drapery were chemically treated for spot and stain resistance by manufacturers.

Floor coverings also came in bright, radiant colors and a variety of textures, ranging from plain to sculptured surfaces. Soft floor coverings, including artificial furs, were used in all rooms, including bathrooms and kitchens.

Although swirls of color and oriental patterns were the two leading trends in patterned rugs in 1967, secondary trends included a continuing interest in geometric designs, in plaids and paisleys, and in floral and medallionlike patterns.

Home Brighteners. Lighting, with the emphasis on bare bulbs, was making a comeback in some circles, bringing with it spaghettilike tangles of exposed wiring. The trend was particularly apparent at the National Lighting Exposition held in the Coliseum in New York City in May. Many fixtures sprouted bulbs, sockets, and wiring like blossoms on a tree. One of the hits of the show was a table lamp that looked like a miniature tree with bulbs instead of buds decorating its twiglike arms. Other designs included a lamp that looked like a giant light bulb, and one made of neon tubing that had been twisted into a pretzel-like design.

"Le Mistral," a deep-pile, sculptured-look rug, won the international design award given by the American Institute of Interior Designers in 1967.

In the fall, the International Home Furnishings Market was held in Chicago. One of the displays featured a Plexiglas screen called Luminor, on which ever-changing abstract color pictures appeared when the screen was plugged into a hi-fi sound system. Luminor was the creation of Earl M. Reiback, a nuclear physicist, inventor, and artist.

Award Winners announced by the American Institute of Interior Designers in 1967 included: *traditional furniture*, Don Ruseau and Fredrick P. Victoria; *contemporary furniture*, Warren Platner; *outdoor furniture*, Richard Schultz; *institutional furniture*, Hans Wegner; *traditional fabrics*, James H. W. Thompson; *contemporary fabrics*, Frances Louise Richardson-Jones and Boris Kroll; *traditional wallpaper*, Flora Scalamandre; *contemporary wallpaper*, H. Crane Day; *wall coverings other than paper*, Jack Denst and Clarence Hawking; *hard surface flooring*, Elliot Fields; *soft surface flooring*, Keith E. Wells; *traditional lamps*, Josef Head; *contemporary lamps*, Jonathan Lange and George H. P. Williams; *lighting fixtures*, the Nessen Company design staff; *traditional lighting fixtures*, Francis Mair; *window shades and blinds*, Paul H. Krause; *china*, Niels Refsgaard; *glass*, Sven Palmquist; *traditional decorative accessories*, Carter L. Ormsby; *contemporary decorative accessories*, Hugh M. Hirth; and *domestic linens*, Tony Ziernicki. [HELEN C. SCHUBERT]

INTERNATIONAL TRADE AND FINANCE made history in 1967. The year included three events whose consequences will affect the course of world commerce for years to come.

The first was the successful conclusion on May 15 –after four years of negotiation and a dramatic final confrontation among the leading trading countries –of the "Kennedy Round" of trade negotiations. The final agreement in Geneva, Switzerland, produced the most extensive tariff reductions ever negotiated in the 20-year history of the General Agreement on Tariffs and Trade, under which the negotiations were conducted.

The second was the agreement, negotiated by the 10 leading financial powers known as the "Group of Ten" and finally approved by the 107 member nations of the International Monetary Fund (IMF) at Rio de Janeiro, on September 29, for the creation of "paper gold," or, more precisely, credits called special drawing rights (SDRs). The legal terms of the SDRs were still to be worked out and ratified by the members' parliaments. The SDRs will be a new type of asset to go into nations' monetary reserves alongside gold and dollars, with the aim of assuring a continued freedom of exchange between currencies and a continued growth of world trade.

The third event was more disturbing. It was the devaluation of the British pound by 14.3 per cent on November 18, marking the failure of three years of strenuous effort by the British government to head off just such a step. The devaluation set off a wave of turbulence in the world's money markets, including a rush to buy gold without precedent since World War II. It raised the serious question of whether other key currencies–including the U.S. dollar–could hold.

As the year ended, the question was whether international cooperation–in this case, without France–could head off a financial crisis and allow time for the Kennedy Round and Rio agreements to work their longer-term benefits. Much of the answer would be up to the United States, whose currency plays a major role in world trade and finance.

World Trade performance in the year reflected the market forces at work in the world economy, not the success of international negotiations. Those consequences could not be immediate. For the first time in many years, a slowdown occurred in the familiar, and almost spectacular, growth of exchange of goods among nations.

With the U.S. economy slack for much of the year and the West German and British economies sluggish for nearly all of it, world trade grew less than in any year since 1958. By the third quarter of 1967, world exports were at an annual rate of $178,900,-000,000, little more than the $176,900,000,000 of the

Countries Participating in the General Agreement on Tariffs and Trade

Members	Members	Members	Provisional members
Australia	Germany, West	Niger	Argentina
Austria	Ghana	Nigeria	Iceland
Barbados	Greece	Norway	Tunisia
Belgium	Guyana	Pakistan	United Arab Republic
Brazil	Haiti	Peru	
Burma	India	Portugal	
Burundi	Indonesia	Rhodesia	
Cameroon	Israel	Rwanda	
Canada	Italy	Senegal	**Special members**
Central African Republic	Ivory Coast	Sierra Leone	Cambodia
Ceylon	Jamaica	South Africa	Poland
Chad	Japan	Spain	
Chile	Kenya	Sweden	
Congo (Brazzaville)	Korea	Switzerland	
Cuba	Kuwait	Tanzania	
Cyprus	Luxembourg	Togo	**Membership pending**
Czechoslovakia	Madagascar	Trinidad and Tobago	Algeria
Dahomey	Malawi	Turkey	Botswana
Denmark	Malaysia	Uganda	Congo (Kinshasa)
Dominican Republic	Malta	United Kingdom	Lesotho
Finland	Mauritania	United States	Maldive Islands
France	Netherlands	Upper Volta	Mali
Gabon	New Zealand	Uruguay	Singapore
Gambia	Nicaragua	Yugoslavia	Zambia

same quarter a year earlier—scarcely more than a 1 per cent gain, as against about 10 per cent in 1966.

Exports from the less developed countries, as usual, had suffered the most from the "mini-recession" in much of the industrial world. These nations also fared badly in the Kennedy Round, which was called "a rich man's club." Although the poorer nations got tariff cuts on some raw materials, they failed to win the sweeping reductions they wanted on processed goods and manufactures.

For U.S. Trade, it was a year of some disappointment. Exports rose, but only about 5 per cent—largely because of the slowdown in some of the main markets for U.S. goods. Imports, reflecting the sluggish domestic economy, rose only about 3 per cent. As a result, the trade surplus rose to about $4,500,000,000, less than had been hoped for.

For the overall U.S. balance of payments, there was a major deterioration. Tourism, foreign aid, the war in Vietnam, other military expenditures abroad, and lending and investing abroad by banks and corporations continued to pump dollars to the rest of the world. The balance of payments not only continued in deficit for the 10th consecutive year, but it also deteriorated to a deficit of probably about $3,800,000,000, compared with $1,357,000,000 in 1966. It would have been worse but for some special devices to make it look better statistically. The worsening U.S. balance of payments gave impetus to the rush to gold at the end of the year. The gold speculators, however, appeared to have little hope of winning their bet that the dollar, like the pound, might have to be devalued, thereby increasing the price of gold above the official $35 an ounce.

Kennedy Round Benefits were certain to accrue to the United States in the years ahead—assuming that the world-wide uneasiness over the cheaper pound could be calmed and that a potentially chaotic wave of currency devaluations could be avoided. Some difficulties might result for a few domestic industries. The reductions in tariffs on industrial goods by the leading nations averaged 35 per cent, and on thousands of products they were 50 per cent.

Some quotas and other nontariff trade barriers remained, and restraints on trade in farm products were not significantly diminished. Nevertheless, the agreement meant that the tariff wall around the United States, Britain, and the European Economic Community (EEC, or Common Market) will be reduced to a low fence after the reductions are fully in effect in 1973. Equally important, the agreements headed off the threat of a reversion to world trading blocs sheltered by high tariffs—a distinct possibility if the Kennedy Round had failed. A drive to curb specific imports, such as steel and textiles, was turned back in the Congress of the United States late in the session. Its strength revealed, however, that the issues of freer trade versus protection will remain.

Shooting for a Double

The Monetary Agreement in Rio may have laid the groundwork for the eventual disappearance of gold as a monetary metal with the IMF's creation of the SDRs. It is possible that future generations will be worrying about the SDR drain instead of the gold drain.

Under the plan, the IMF will simply enter credits—expected to total as much as $2,000,000,000 a year—on its books. These credits will be added to each member nation's gold and foreign currency reserves. Since only 30 per cent of the SDRs will have to be repaid, they will, in effect, become new money. As such they will help finance ever-expanding world trade. Each member nation will be able to draw on the pool of SDRs according to its proportion of gold and currency contributions to the fund. The SDRs can be exchanged for the currency needed in any trade transaction.

For the first time, the nations will have a device to make monetary reserves grow in an orderly fashion—regardless of whether gold loses its monetary status. No longer will they have to depend on such a factor as how much gold is mined in South Africa. The first SDRs were yet to be created. But when they are, it will be by an 85 per cent weighted vote of IMF members. It will be something that history has never before recorded. [EDWIN L. DALE, JR.]

See also BANKS AND BANKING; ECONOMY, THE; EUROPE; MONEY; STOCKS AND BONDS.

INVENTION

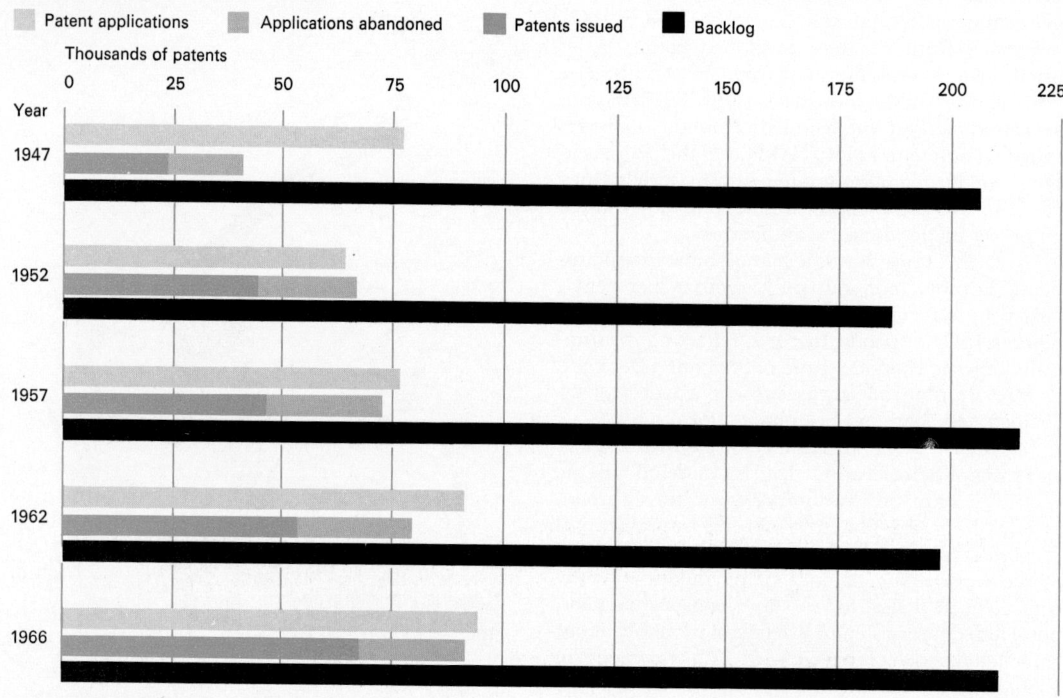

INVENTION. A major step toward United States participation in an international patent filing system was taken in October, 1967, by a committee of patent experts meeting in Geneva, Switzerland. They agreed not to require the United States to change its patent philosophy from a "first-to-invent" criterion to a "first-to-file" criterion, which had been a block to U.S. involvement. The committee met to review the first draft of a Patent Cooperation Treaty prepared by a working group of the 77-member United International Bureau for the Protection of Intellectual Property. Of the 77 members, only the United States, Canada, and the Philippines base priority of invention on the "first-to-invent" criterion. All others make the filing date the criterion in settling disputes between inventors.

The treaty provides for a single filing, search, and examination procedure for international patents. It is aimed at reducing the large duplication of effort existing today in international patent filing. Edward J. Brenner, U.S. commissioner of patents, estimated that more than half of the 650,000 patent applications filed world-wide are duplicates of others.

The next step in adoption of the treaty will be approval of the draft by an executive committee. Each member nation can then expand the treaty in more detail before sending delegates to a conference to negotiate the final version. It is hoped that the treaty will be adopted by 1970.

The Rolamite–A Revolutionary Invention

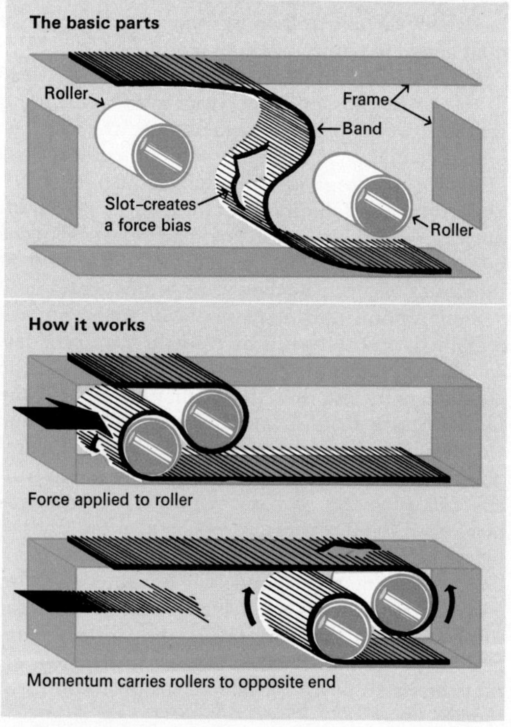

Rolamite. Wide publicity was accorded a new mechanical device announced in October by the Atomic Energy Commission's (AEC) Sandia Corporation at Albuquerque, N.Mex. Called rolamite, this device virtually abolishes friction when used as a bearing in applications not involving large loading, pressures of less than 3,000 pounds per square inch. Rolamite consists of two or more cylindrical rollers inside parallel guides with a thin, flexible metal band looped around them in figure "S" fashion. When the rollers turn, there is no sliding friction. The AEC filed a patent application in the name of the inventor, Donald F. Wilkes. The new bearing concept may eventually replace conventional bearings in devices such as dampers, firing pins, hinges, locks, pumps, relays, shock absorbers, speed changers, switches, and thermostats, according to inventor Wilkes.

Novel Inventions awarded patents during the year included a mechanical calf that is used in training ranch horses to herd cattle. The device moves about on three wheels in response to radio commands. It resembles a calf, weighs 600 pounds, and was patented by Lee R. Harris of Brenham, Tex.

A harvester that knocks citrus fruit from trees with blasts of air was patented by Lee W. Winninger, with rights assigned to the FMC Corporation, San Jose, Calif. The device can pass through crowded fruit groves without damaging trees. [James A. Pearre]

IRAN signed military aid agreements with the Soviet Union amounting to $110,000,000. Previously, all of Iran's arms, nearly $1,000,000,000 worth, had come from the United States. Mohammed Riza Pahlevi explained that Russia had offered eight-year loans at 2.5 per cent interest, payable in Iranian products, while the United States insisted on cash.

The Soviet Union also loaned Iran $280,000,000 to build a steel mill at Isfahan, payable in natural gas. In turn, the National Iranian Oil Company gave the Soviet Union an oil concession in northern Iran. Bulgaria, Romania, and Czechoslovakia also extended credits to Iran for industrial expansion.

The shah's reform program reaped a bonus from the Arab-Israeli war. Oil production was increased 20 per cent to meet the demand created by the withdrawal of much of the Arab oil from world markets. The shah nationalized all water resources in order to break down a custom that required well-users to pay owners a percentage of their crops. Another law abolished the ownership of villages by landlords. On October 26, the shah officially crowned himself hereditary ruler of Iran. [William Spencer]

Facts in Brief. Population: 24,873,000. Government: Shah Mohammed Riza Pahlevi; Premier Amir Abbas Hoveida. Monetary Unit: rial (75.75 = U.S. $1). Foreign Trade: exports, $1,309,000,000; imports, $930,000,000. Principal Exports: petroleum and petroleum products, cotton, carpets.

Before the splendor of the Peacock Throne the Shah of Iran crowned his empress, Farah Diba, and himself on his 48th birthday in October.

IRAQ arranged a financial settlement with the foreign-owned Iraq Petroleum Company (IPC) over disputed royalties. IPC paid $39,200,000 as an advance against future production. Syria's continuing dispute with IPC over royalties for shipments across Syrian territory kept that outlet closed, and the Arab-Israeli war plus Iraq's adherence to the Arab oil embargo reduced Iraqi oil exports 25 per cent (see MIDDLE EAST). In August, the remaining IPC concession areas were nationalized. Subsequently, France signed an agreement with the state-owned oil company to exploit them despite IPC protests, while a Soviet-Iraqi pact granted Russia concession rights in northern Iraq.

There was less disorder than usual in internal politics. President Abdul Rahman Arif formed a national coalition cabinet, with himself as prime minister. In July, Arif turned the prime ministership over to Lieutenant General Taher Yahya.

A draft election law, voted by the cabinet in February, provided for single-stage elections to re-establish the national assembly no later than November, 1968. It set a minimum voting age of 18, and permitted women to vote. [WILLIAM SPENCER]

Facts in Brief. Population: 8,899,000. Government: President Abdul Rahman Arif; Prime Minister Taher Yahya. Monetary Unit: dinar (1 = U.S. $2.80). Foreign Trade: exports, $935,000,000; imports, $493,000,000. Principal Exports: crude petroleum, dates, cement.

IRELAND held local elections for 108 county and county borough council seats on June 28, 1967. They were the first such elections in seven years. About 41 per cent of the votes were cast for Fianna Fáil party candidates, 33 per cent for those allied with Fine Gael, about 16 per cent for Labour party adherents, and 10 per cent for others, including independent candidates.

Minister of Finance Charles Haughey presented a 1967-1968 budget of $826,600,000 to parliament in April. It featured small increases in beer and cigarette taxes and small but wide-ranging increases in welfare benefits. Among the welfare benefits were provisions to: (1) raise old-age and widow's pensions, (2) give free electricity and travel on public transport for old-age pensioners and blind pensioners, and (3) increase the term that unemployment benefits could be paid from 6 to 12 months.

In April, Ireland formally requested that its applications be reactivated for full membership in the European Economic Community, the European Coal and Steel Community, and Euratom. By year's end, however, its application was still pending because of a merger of the three communities.

Facts in Brief. Population: 2,902,000. Government: President Éamon de Valéra; Prime Minister John Lynch. Monetary Unit: pound (1 = U.S. $2.40). Foreign Trade: exports, $680,000,000; imports, $1,043,000,000. Principal Exports: cattle, meat, dairy products.

ISRAEL nearly doubled its responsibilities in its sudden victory over the combined Arab armies in June. It also added many new headaches. Israeli forces seized Jerusalem and occupied the entire west bank of the River Jordan, the Gaza Strip, the Sinai Peninsula, and the Syrian heights above the Sea of Galilee. See MIDDLE EAST.

The cost of victory was high, although Israel suffered relatively few casualties – 679 killed, 2,563 wounded. Costs of mobilization, the loss of industrial manpower to the army, and equipment were $13,000,000 a day for the six-day war. World Jewry raised $500,000,000, however, and $171,200,000 from State of Israel Bond sales met the deficit.

The government took steps, ignoring severe foreign criticism, to secure its triumph. The *Knesset* (parliament) formally annexed Arab Jerusalem. The Mandelbaum Gate was torn down and the halves of Jerusalem it had divided were united under Israeli currency, Israeli laws, and Israeli supervision of the schools. Israel pumped oil for its own use from wells in occupied Sinai and widened the channel of the Jordan to increase its water supply.

Economic Struggles with a serious recession were not as successful. Unemployment reached 10 per cent as Israel's traditionally booming economy felt the effects of war. There were 38,000 unemployed workers registered at labor exchanges, and,

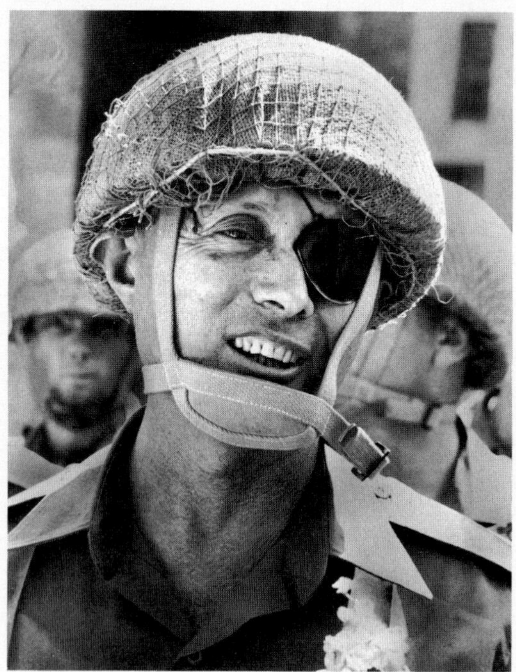

At a critical hour, Moshe Dayan became Israel's defense minister, bringing added confidence and strategic genius to his army.

for the first time in history, the government issued unemployment compensation grants. The 1966 growth rate of 3.5 per cent fell below the 6 per cent the World Bank considered necessary to help deter inflation in Israel.

The United States granted $27,500,000 in agricultural products. Romania extended a $35,000,000 credit in April for Israeli textiles in exchange for Romanian beef and timber.

A continuing decline of immigration caused concern. In 1966, there were 25,000 immigrants compared to 30,000 in 1965, far short of the 40,000 required yearly to sustain economic growth.

Politics. The war produced a partial realignment in Israel's internal politics. Three labor parties planned to merge: Mapai, the dominant party in the Knesset; Rafi, headed by war hero Moshe Dayan; and Achdut Ha'avoda, the party of former defense minister Yigal Allon. The combined party would have had a clear majority in the Knesset. But negotiations broke down over Rafi's insistence that Dayan replace Mapai's Levi Eshkol as prime minister. [WILLIAM SPENCER]

Facts in Brief. Population: 2,768,000. Government: President Shneor Zalman Shazar; Prime Minister Levi Eshkol. Monetary Unit: pound (3.5=U.S. $1). Foreign Trade: exports, $503,300,000; imports, $833,000,000. Principal Exports: diamonds, fruits, textiles.

See also JEWS AND JUDAISM.

ITALY. With the disastrous floods of 1966 in mind, the Italian parliament approved a record budget in August, 1967, that included allocations of $597,000,000 for land reclamation, reforestation, and flood control. The total budget of $16,758,000,000 was 9.6 per cent higher than 1966 and the largest in Italian history. The biggest single item was a 21 per cent allocation for public education.

Trade Deficit. Production generally, and industrial production in particular, was on the upsurge. Economic expansion, measured in terms of increase in national income, rose by 5.5 per cent in 1967. A serious balance of payments deficit, however, was cause for alarm. In the first half of 1967, the deficit was $235,800,000 compared with a surplus of $474,000,000 for the corresponding period of 1966. Exports had increased by 10 per cent, but imports had risen 13.7 per cent. The deficit was attributed to falling tourism revenues, a poor harvest following the floods, and recession in Germany–one of Italy's principal trading partners.

A Medical Crisis involving physicians and chemists arose in the spring when members of both professions ceased work because of governmental delay in paying the fees due them under the national health insurance program. The physicians said they were due $360,000,000; the chemists placed the money due them at $126,000,000. Swift government intervention ended the crisis as it did in August, when Mayor Amerigo Petrucci of Rome advised the treasury that unless it immediately paid the city $22,100,000 due for government-sponsored social services, all such activities in Rome would stop.

Foreign Relations. Despite an appeal by Austrian Chancellor Josef Klaus, Italy refused to approve Austrian membership in the European Economic Community late in the year. Italy's refusal was the consequence of continuing terrorism in the Alto Adige region where terrorists, whom Italy contended were Austrian "separatists," had taken the lives of four Italian soldiers in March. See AUSTRIA.

More harmonious relations were established between Italy and the Soviet Union in May, however, when Italian Foreign Minister Amintore Fanfani visited Soviet Foreign Minister Andrei Gromyko in Moscow. At the conclusion of their talks, the two ministers signed a pact that had been initialed earlier by Soviet President Nikolai Podgorny during a visit to Italy. Under the pact, both nations agreed to cooperate in matters pertaining to tourism and in agriculture. [KENNETH BROWN]

Facts in Brief. Population: 52,510,000. Government: President Giuseppe Saragat; Prime Minister Aldo Moro. Monetary Unit: lira (623.8=U.S. $1). Foreign Trade: exports, $8,032,000,000; imports, $8,571,000,000. Principal Exports: machinery, textiles, chemicals.

IVORY COAST. See AFRICA.

JAMAICA. See WEST INDIES.

JAPAN held general elections for its house of representatives on Jan. 29, 1967. The results indicated that the conservative Liberal-Democratic party had won less than a majority of the popular vote. It had captured only 48.8 per cent of the total cast as compared to 55 per cent in the 1963 elections. By winning 277 of the 486 seats in the house–a loss of only six from its holdings in the previous session–it retained its parliamentary majority.

Rival Parties. The Socialist party, with 27.9 per cent of the total vote, won 140 seats. The Democratic Socialists won 30 seats. Kōmeitō, the "Clean Government Party" that serves as the political arm of the Soka Gakkai Buddhist sect, took 25 seats. Detailed election returns showed that Kōmeitō, participating in its first national election, had run candidates only where its followers were most numerous. The Communist party won 5 seats and 4.8 per cent of the vote, an increase of less than 1 per cent.

On February 17, Eisaku Sato was formally reelected prime minister for his second successive term. He received 279 votes; his chief rival for the post, Socialist party leader Kozo Sasaki, got 131 votes.

Island Negotiations. In November, Prime Minister Sato visited the United States to confer with President Lyndon B. Johnson on a number of issues involving American-Japanese relations. Included among them was the status of Okinawa and other Pacific Islands won from Japan by U.S. forces dur-

Prime Minister Eisaku Sato, indulging in Japanese superstition, paints in a Daruma doll's missing eye as a symbol of gratitude for his re-election.

ing World War II. Public opinion in Japan was becoming increasingly insistent that the islands be returned to Japanese control. On his return to Japan, Prime Minister Sato announced that the United States had promised the "early" return of the Bonin Island group, a string of sparsely settled islands of which the best known is Iwo Jima. On the question of U.S.-occupied Okinawa, the island home of nearly 1,000,000 Japanese, Sato fared less well. Although the United States was sympathetic to his request for the island's return, it indicated that for "the near future" it would keep control of Okinawa as well as other Ryukyu Islands.

Anti-Chinese Feelings. Japanese public opinion turned increasingly against Communist China in 1967, because of the political turmoil created there by the Cultural Revolution of Mao Tse-tung. A no less important reason was China's explosion of a hydrogen bomb on June 17 (see China). The Communist party of Japan voluntarily cut its ties with Peking; in August, Kozo Sasaki, the pro-Chinese head of the Socialist party, resigned his post. His successor, Seiichi Katsumata, was considered more of a political moderate. A poll of Japanese high school students revealed that 70 per cent of them were strongly critical of the Red Guard movement in Communist China.

Economic Growth continued at a high level in 1967, indicating that the country had recovered from the mild recession it had experienced in 1964. The gross national product (GNP), which had averaged an annual growth rate of 10 per cent for the past 20 years, was expected to maintain that pace in 1967. With the GNP thus standing at about $100,000,000,000 per year, Japan ranked as the fourth largest economic power in the world after the United States, the Soviet Union, and the Federal Republic of (West) Germany.

On October 20, former Prime Minister Shigeru Yoshida died at his seaside residence at Oiso, Kanagawa Prefecture. Shigeru had held the post almost uninterruptedly from 1946 to 1954.

A 12-nation study conducted under the auspices of the United Nations Educational, Scientific, and Cultural Organization showed that 31 per cent of Japan's 13-year-old mathematics students placed in the upper tenth in a mathematics achievement test, as compared with only 2 per cent of U.S. students. The international study, published in 1967, also indicated that the Japanese public schools were doing by far the "best overall job" in mathematics instruction. [John M. Maki]

Facts in Brief. Population: 100,360,000. Government: Emperor Hirohito; Prime Minister Eisaku Sato. Monetary Unit: yen (362=U.S. $1). Foreign Trade: exports, $9,777,000,000; imports, $9,523,000,000. Principal Exports: machinery, iron and steel, transportation equipment, textiles.

JEWS AND JUDAISM. The war between Israel and the Arab states in June, 1967, had a powerful effect upon American Jews. It effectively recast their self-image and thus conditioned their relationships to other religious groups in the United States and abroad. The debate within the Jewish community concerning the propriety and wisdom of ecumenical engagement with Christianity, both Roman Catholic and Protestant, ground to an abrupt stop with the outbreak of hostilities in the Middle East.

Public Reaction. The open threat of extermination voiced repeatedly by the radios of Cairo, Egypt, and Damascus, Syria, roused the dormant memories of Nazi concentration camps to fresh life. In June, 1967, American Jews bolstered the domestic economy of Israel, which had been upset by the war, with cash and pledges of more than $200,000,000.

Hundreds of young American Jewish collegians besieged the offices of the Jewish Agency headquarters in New York City and Israeli consulates in the United States for an opportunity to work on Israel's farms and collective settlements so that Israelis could be released for military service. A similar reaction was noted in major European capitals. In Paris, France; Bonn, West Germany; Stockholm, Sweden; Geneva, Switzerland; Rome, Italy; and London, England, street demonstrations were held, some of them in protest of their governments' foreign policy. Declarations of support were drawn from the major economic, political, professional, religious, and social groups of each of the nations involved.

Church Reaction. The dominant position taken by the ecumenical leadership of the Christian churches was considered by many Jews to be either one of benevolent neutrality or Arab partisanship.

Though some Catholic bishops and Protestant ministers supported the stand of the American Jewish community, the position taken by the National Council of Churches on July 7 toward the Middle Eastern crisis was unsatisfactory to most U.S. Jews. Despite the urgent requests of the American Jewish Committee and the Synagogue Council, Roman Catholic bishops and cardinals were, in the main, wary of committing themselves, as a group, to the Jewish view of the conflict.

In the Theological Realm, the brief flurry of excitement occasioned by a Jewish version of the "God-is-dead" theme of radical Protestantism all but disappeared. The various rabbinical associations also spent energy in seeking closer relations with organizations in Israel. The most notable success was that of the Conservative Rabbinical Assembly, which opened a forum in Israel in cooperation with the Histadrut, the Israeli labor organization.

People. John Slawson, for 40 years the directorial head of the powerful American Jewish Committee, retired in 1967. He was succeeded by Bertram Gold of San Francisco, Calif. The general trend of committee policy had been toward the understanding and promotion of intergroup cooperation, but a slow but noticeable shift had occurred. The research of the committee became increasingly oriented toward the problem of Jewish identity in the United States. Both of these emphases were seen in the two-volume *Lakeville Studies*, sponsored by the committee and edited by sociologists Joseph Greenblum, Benjamin Ringer, and Marshall Sklare. The researchers documented the relative disquiet and ambivalence of the Jews of Lakeville, a fictitious name for the community of Highland Park, Ill., toward their Jewish heritage, and their Gentile neighbors. The second volume was generally hopeful, holding to the possibility that Jews and Gentiles would move from the "edges of friendliness" to true pluralism.

In October, the Jewish Museum in New York City, in cooperation with Israeli archaeologist Yigael Yadin, opened its Masada exhibition. The artifacts, exhumed between 1963 and 1965, were visible evidence of the desperate heroism of the fortress' defenders who had committed suicide rather than surrender to the Romans who overran and razed the outpost in A.D. 73. The exhibit was a great success in terms of attendance, opening as it did in the wake of the Arab-Israeli war. It also generated scholarly controversies with respect to the validity of Yadin's contention that his "find" substantiated the story of Masada as told by Josephus in *The Jewish War*. [DAVID WOLF SILVERMAN]

David Rubinger, *Life* © Time Inc.

After Israel seized control of Arab Jerusalem, its army's chief rabbi, Shlomo Goren, *above*, led victorious soldiers in prayer at the Wailing Wall, to which Israeli pilgrims later flocked, *below*.

President Lyndon B. Johnson enjoys his baby-sitter role as he shows off his first grandchild, Patrick Lyndon Nugent, at a summertime gathering at the White House.

JOHNSON, LYNDON BAINES. The frustrating war in Vietnam and his further declining popularity bedeviled President Johnson throughout 1967. His critics were saying he was not to be trusted and that he was building a "credibility gap" between himself and the American people. Public opinion polls reflected the national discontent. In November, the Gallup Poll reported that only 38 per cent of those questioned approved the way Mr. Johnson was handling his job.

On the home front, he was criticized for neglecting the war against poverty as the costs of the war in Vietnam continued to rise. Urban riots stirred middle-class opposition to any more social benefits for the nation's poor. But Mr. Johnson maintained that he would support his commitments to South Vietnam and to America's urban and rural poor. Opposition in Congress prevailed in curtailing his programs and the progress of the Great Society.

The Wedding of their elder daughter Lynda Bird on December 9 was the highlight of the Johnson family's social calendar in 1967. Lynda, 23, and 28-year-old Marine Captain Charles Spittal Robb of Milwaukee, Wis., exchanged vows before 500 guests in the East Room of the White House. She was the first daughter of a President to marry in the White House since Woodrow Wilson's daughter Eleanor married William Gibbs McAdoo in 1914.

The President became a grandfather on June 21, 1967, when 8-pound 10-ounce Patrick Lyndon Nugent was born to his daughter Luci, in Austin, Tex. Between sessions of talks with Soviet Premier Aleksei N. Kosygin at Glassboro, N.J., June 23 and 25, the President flew to Los Angeles, Calif., to make a speech and then to Texas to see the baby. After the Glassboro meetings, he returned to the LBJ Ranch to celebrate Luci's 20th birthday, and attended his grandson's christening at St. Francis Xavier Roman Catholic Church in Stonewall, Tex.

Trips and Entertainment. President Johnson left the country six times in 1967, flying to Guam, Uruguay, West Germany, Canada, Mexico, and Australia. In April, before the Western Hemisphere summit conference at Punta del Este, Uruguay, the President flew 29 Latin American ambassadors and their wives from Washington to the LBJ Ranch in Air Force One. After the Punta del Este meeting, the President flew to West Germany to attend the state funeral of former West German Chancellor Konrad Adenauer.

On May 25, the President flew to Montreal, Canada, to visit Expo 67. He lunched with Canadian Prime Minister Lester B. Pearson and conferred with him on the Arab-Israeli crisis. On October 28, Johnson went to the border city of Ciudad Juárez to formally transfer 437 disputed acres to Mexico. In late December, he flew to Australia to attend memorial services for Prime Minister Harold Holt, stopping off on the way back to visit American military men in Vietnam and Pope Paul VI in Rome.

Marine Captain Charles Robb slices into a towering wedding cake while his bride Lynda Bird and her father, the President, study his technique.

A Book and a Picture. Amid the clamor over the April publication of William Manchester's book, *Death of a President*, Mr. Johnson remained calm. His differences with Senator Robert F. Kennedy (D., N.Y.) over the war in Vietnam sharpened, but his relations with the Kennedy family in general remained friendly.

In January, it was disclosed that Mr. Johnson had told artist Peter Hurd that the officially commissioned, 40-by-48-inch presidential portrait was "the ugliest thing I ever saw." Hurd said what irked him the most was Johnson's preference for a portrait by Norman Rockwell.

Mrs. Johnson's interest in preserving America's natural beauty continued in 1967. In June, she visited historic and scenic spots in New England. On June 12, she addressed the graduating class and received an honorary degree from Middlebury College in Vermont. In September, the First Lady took a four-day Midwestern tour. Its purpose was to foster a renaissance of rural life and values. In October, when she went to Williams College, Williamstown, Mass., to receive an honorary degree, about 75 students walked out to protest the President's Vietnam policy. [CAROL L. THOMPSON]

See also DEMOCRATIC PARTY; PRESIDENT OF THE UNITED STATES; VIETNAM.

JORDAN was the hardest hit of the Arab states during Israel's "preventive attack" in June, 1967. The loss of territory and the heavy influx of refugees were most painful because Jordan had been marking modest gains in many areas of its economy. Before the war, the United States furnished $27,000,000 in aid and Great Britain loaned $5,600,000 to improve the national electricity network.

Militarily, Jordan purchased heavy artillery and 36 used Starfighter jets from the United States. The defeat by Israel–losses included 6,094 killed or missing, 762 wounded, 463 prisoners, 300,000 refugees, and destruction of all but two air force planes–was indeed a bitter postscript to a speech by King Hussein I in January. Jordan, he said, could defend itself against any attack. See MIDDLE EAST.

April elections for 60 seats in the chamber of deputies returned 32 incumbents. Five members of the anti-Hussein Muslim Brotherhood were elected. Hussein named former diplomat Saad Jumma to head a new cabinet. But in October, Hussein took command of the armed forces and named Bahjat Talhouni to replace Jumma. [WILLIAM SPENCER]

Facts in Brief. Population: 2,140,000. Government: King Hussein I; Premier Bahjat Talhouni. Monetary Unit: dinar (1=U.S. $2.79). Foreign Trade: exports, $35,000,000; imports, $184,000,000. Principal Exports: phosphates, fruits, and vegetables.

JUNIOR ACHIEVEMENT (JA) reported that more than 130,000 high school students formed 6,302 companies in 450 communities in the United States and Canada during the 1966-1967 program year.

Junior Achievement alumni were invited to evaluate their experience in JA in a survey conducted by Opinion Research Corporation. The aim of the study was to determine the effectiveness of the JA program and its long-term value to the achiever, the business community, and the nation. The survey, conducted in 23 cities, included 552 men and women who were in JA from four to eight years ago. Of those interviewed, 91 per cent found JA helpful in giving them a better understanding of the role of business in the economy and 87 per cent indicated that the program gave them an accurate picture of the business world.

The 24th National Junior Achievers Conference was held Aug. 20 to 25, 1967, at Indiana University in Bloomington. Teen-age JA executives from 48 states and five Canadian provinces attended. Also present were guest achievers from JA programs in England and Venezuela.

Jerry Johnston, 18, from San Francisco, Calif., was awarded the title of "JA President of the Year." Donna Stone, 17, from Atlanta, Ga., was named "Miss Junior Achievement."

JUVENILE DELINQUENCY. See CRIME.

Trudging single file across the River Jordan, Jordanian refugees leave the Israeli-occupied west bank for an uncertain future in their defeated homeland.

KAPLAN, JUSTIN (1925-), journalist and free-lance writer, was winner of the 1967 Pulitzer prize in biography for his study *Mr. Clemens and Mark Twain.* He also won the National Book Award for the same work. Until 1959, when he resigned to write the prizewinning biography, Kaplan had been a senior editor for book publishers Simon and Schuster. He has also compiled popular anthologies of the works of Plato and Aristotle.

In composing the biography of Mark Twain, Kaplan used material and correspondence that has become available only in recent years. The book begins Twain's life when he was 31 years old, and, according to the publishers, shows him as both a triumphant and a tragic man rather than the somewhat bland personality often found in textbooks.

Kaplan was born in New York City in 1925, attended Horace Mann School there, and later graduated from Harvard University. He is married to novelist Ann Bernays. The couple and their three daughters live in Cambridge, Mass.

When he was told of the Pulitzer award, Kaplan responded by voicing his "distress over the course we are following in Vietnam," and urged that the United States take a "positive alternative." He said he would donate the $500 in prize money to the American Friends Service Committee, a group that supports programs to build peace.

KASHMIR. See India; Pakistan.

KENYA struggled against Somali guerrillas who demanded that their region be made part of neighboring Somalia. Kenya police reported on Jan. 8, 1967, that six members of a bandit gang they had killed in the northeast region were actually Somali soldiers. Then, in April, Minister of Defense Njoroge Mungoi accused Somali soldiers of supplying the Somali insurgents with land mines, of firing mortars into Kenya from Somalia, and of twice crossing the border into Kenya. Mungoi said that 1,200 Somali insurgents had been killed since 1964, and that 1,800 had been wounded, captured, or allowed to surrender. He added that Kenya losses were slight.

In May, Kenya-Somali relations reached a crisis. Kenya threatened war unless Somalia stopped aiding the guerrillas. Vice-President Daniel Arap Moi went to Cairo to protest the United Arab Republic (U.A.R.) furnishing of weapons to Somalia. He charged that Somali insurgents had used them against Kenya. On May 15, Moi reported that the U.A.R. was no longer supplying arms to Somalia. Kenya President Jomo Kenyatta offered an amnesty to Somali insurgents in June and July. During the amnesty, 340 guerrillas surrendered, but others continued terrorist attacks. Discussions between Kenya and Somalia averted war and led to a renewal of diplomatic relations in October, but they did not reach a final solution on Kenya's control of the land that is inhabited by Somalis.

Kenya was critical of the visit of U.S. Undersecretary of State Nicholas deB. Katzenbach in May. The ruling party said that U.S. African policy was "naive" and that, in Vietnam, the United States fought to make the Far East "safe for Coca-Cola."

In a debate before the national assembly on May 26, Tom Mboya, minister of planning, warned of spying by Britain, Communist China, France, the Soviet Union, and the United States. China angrily protested. A series of sharp notes led to a break in relations between Kenya and China.

Kenya, Tanzania, and Uganda arranged for closer trade relations and discussed steps toward a customs union. They postponed plans to dissolve the University of East Africa, which has colleges in the three countries. The East African Development Bank, supported by all three, opened in June.

The International Development Association loaned almost $9,000,000 to improve Kenya's small farms and sugar cane production. The U.S. Agency for International Development and the East African Development Bank loaned $3,000,000 to hard-surface the road connecting the capitals of Uganda and Tanzania with Nairobi. [Benjamin E. Thomas]

Facts in Brief. Population: 9,911,000. Government: President Jomo Kenyatta. Monetary Unit: shilling (7.14=U.S. $1). Foreign Trade: exports, $174,000,000; imports, $314,000,000. Principal Exports: coffee, tea, petroleum products.

KERNER, OTTO (1908-), governor of Illinois, was appointed chairman of a Special Advisory Commission on Civil Disorders by President Lyndon B. Johnson in July, 1967. The commission was set up in the wake of riots in Detroit, Mich.; Newark, N.J.; and other cities to study the causes of such riots and to make recommendations to federal, state, and city officials. Kerner, a Democrat, was elected governor in 1960 and is serving his second term.

Kerner was born in Chicago, where his late father served as judge in the U.S. Court of Appeals. He was graduated from Brown University in 1930, studied a year at Cambridge University in England, and received his law degree from Northwestern University in 1934. Following several years in private practice, Kerner served as U.S. attorney for the judicial district of northern Illinois from 1947 to 1954. From 1954 to 1961 he was county court judge of Cook County, which includes Chicago.

Kerner's service record began with his entry into the Illinois National Guard in 1934. He was called to active duty in 1941, and served in World War II in Africa, Sicily, the Philippines, and Japan. He retired from the National Guard in 1954 with the rank of major general.

Kerner's wife, Helena, is the daughter of Anton J. Cermak, the Chicago mayor who was killed in an apparent attempt on the life of President Franklin D. Roosevelt in 1933. [Walter F. Morse]

Fists fly and a scuffle breaks out between an American MP and a North Korean guard. Both were on duty at an armistice meeting being held in Panmunjom, Korea.

KIRCHNER, LEON (1919-   ), composer and pianist, was awarded the 1967 Pulitzer prize in music in May. The award honored his *String Quartet No. 3*, a work combining a string quartet and a taped electronic sound score. His first work to be publicly recognized, *Piano Sonata*, was performed in 1949. Kirchner composes primarily for the piano and for stringed instruments. His work is generally conceded to be highly individual and complex. His early work won several major awards, including the New York Music Critics Circle Award in 1950. A critic wrote of Kirchner, "Obviously (he) is not afraid of unmasking himself in his music."

The son of a Russian emigrant embroidery manufacturer, Kirchner was born in Brooklyn, N.Y. As a child, he showed remarkable music ability, and he was performing publicly at the age of 14. He received the B.A. degree from the University of California, Berkeley, in 1940 and was a Guggenheim fellow in the late 1940s. In 1961, he joined the faculty of Harvard University after 10 years on the faculties of the University of Southern California and Mills College in Oakland, Calif. In 1966, he was appointed professor of music at Harvard.

Among Kirchner's works in progress is an opera based on Saul Bellow's novel, *Henderson the Rain King*. He and his wife, the former Gertrude Schoenberg, have two children, Paul and Lisa. [Walter F. Morse]

KIWANIS INTERNATIONAL See Service Clubs.

KOREA. South Korea's President Chung Hee Park was sworn in to a second four-year term on July 1, 1967. His inauguration followed a general election in May that had been accompanied by widespread violence and subsequent charges by the opposition party that President Park's Democratic Republican party had rigged the voting. When the new national assembly convened formally on July 10, 44 opposition members boycotted it. In November, however, the opposition ended the boycott and assumed their seats in the assembly.

The 2 1/2-mile-wide demilitarized zone separating North Korea from South Korea saw an intensification of border incidents during the year. By October, 250 North Korean troops and infiltrators had been killed or captured by the South Korean forces guarding the border. About 80 South Korean troops and 20 U.S. soldiers had lost their lives in that period.

Facts in Brief. Korea (North). Population: 12,784,000; Government: Chairman of the Presidium Choe Yong Kun; Prime Minister Kim Il-sung. Monetary unit: won (1.20=U.S. $1). Foreign Trade: no statistics available. Principal Exports: agricultural products, metals, minerals.

Korea (South). Population: 30,360,000. Government: President Chung Hee Park; Prime Minister Il Kwon Chung. Monetary Unit: won (268=U.S. $1). Foreign Trade: exports, $250,300,000; imports, $716,400,000. Principal Exports: textiles, clothing, plywood.

KUWAIT held its first elections since 1963 in January, 1967. At stake were 50 seats in the national assembly. A new election bill, which divided the country into 10 constituencies, was the basis for voting; each constituency returned five deputies. Since political parties were banned, candidates ran on their position, prestige, or relationship to the royal family. Three deputies were elected from a faction pledged to total Arab unity. But the other 47 seats went to royalist candidates who supported independence. Nine deputies boycotted the assembly's first session, however, claiming election frauds. A new cabinet took office after the elections.

Kuwait cautiously joined the short-lived Arab embargo on oil shipments to the West during the Arab-Israeli war in June, but did not break diplomatic relations with Western nations.

The Kuwait Fund for Arab Economic Development loaned Sudan $14,000,000 for land reclamation. Despite protests from the Kuwait Oil Company, the government signed a concession for exploitation of 3,500 square miles by the Spanish state oil company, Hispanoil. [WILLIAM SPENCER]

Facts in Brief. Population: 624,000. Government: Sheik Sabah al-Salim al-Sabah; Premier Jabr al-Ahmad al-Sabah. Monetary Unit: dinar (1 = U.S. $2.79). Foreign Trade: exports, $1,304,000,000; imports, $463,000,000. Principal Exports: crude petroleum and petroleum products.

LABOR force changes in 1967 reflected the continued expansion of the economy. Despite the addition of almost 2,000,000 workers to the total labor force, the unemployment rate stabilized at slightly under 4 per cent. Figures below are based on preliminary Bureau of Labor Statistics estimates:

	1966	1967
	(in thousands)	
Total Labor Force	**78,893**	**80,793**
Civilian employment	72,895	74,371
Armed forces	3,123	3,447
Unemployment	2,875	2,975
Unemployment rate	3.8%	3.8%

With the rise in employment, average hourly earnings of production workers on private nonagricultural payrolls increased by about 10 cents, the same amount as in 1966. Weekly hours declined slightly, so that gross weekly wages rose by only $3.53 a week to $103.41 at the end of September, 1967.

Union wage settlements during the first nine months of 1967 increased substantially. The median wage and benefit package increase came to almost 5 per cent, compared with 4.5 per cent for all of 1966. In the 12 months, however, prices had gone up 2.6 per cent, as measured by the consumer price index (CPI). Therefore, the real after-tax (spendable) weekly pay of the typical industrial production worker with three dependents increased very little from the 1965-1966 level. The CPI in November, 1967, was 117.8, which meant that it took $11.78 to buy goods and services that had cost only $10 in the 1957-1959 period.

Collective Bargaining. Industrial unrest heightened during the year for several reasons, including the large number of pattern-setting contracts that were open, the pressures for substantial wage increases stemming from tight labor markets and rising prices, stiffened management resistance because of profit uncertainty, and the greater use of collective bargaining by public employees, especially by schoolteachers.

In major cities, teachers turned aggressively to militant bargaining. Led by American Federation of Teachers (AFT) affiliates in New York City and Detroit, Mich., the teachers delayed school openings in the fall by at least two weeks in their successful fights for higher pay. In New York, the yearly salary range was raised from $5,400-$9,950 to $6,200-$10,350. The National Education Association (NEA), the million-member organization of teachers and other professional school employees, became more militant as it competed with the AFT for teacher support. It applied sanctions in Florida, endorsed strikes by teachers, and elected a Negro president. The AFT, however, continued to win recognition elections in major cities. The NEA dominated other areas. See EDUCATION; Section One, LAWRENCE A. CREMIN: FOCUS ON EDUCATION.

A Peaceful Settlement reached in the meat-packing industry provided a novel change. Armour and Company and the two meat packing unions agreed on a new three-year contract six months before the expiration of the old agreement. It was accomplished without the traditional threat of strike and familiar last-minute, crisis bargaining.

The settlement was representative of the increased 1967 gains in large-scale industry. Among the benefits were: hourly increases of 12 cents, 11 cents, and 11 cents each year of the agreement plus additional boosts for the more skilled workers, a narrowing of the wage differential at Southern plants, a continuation of the cost-of-living clause, a ninth paid holiday, four weeks vacation after 15 years, an increase in pension benefits from $3.25 to $5 per month for each year of service, and retirement starting age at 62, instead of 65.

A Railroad Strike by 137,000 members of six shopcraft unions was barred by a variety of government actions extending from late January until the middle of July. After a two-day strike that idled 600,000 railroad employees and 90 per cent of the U.S. rail mileage, Congress passed a joint resolution. It provided for extended mediation and mandatory acceptance of the recommendations, which were greeted more favorably by the unions than the rail managements. They provided for a two-year agreement with a 6 per cent general wage increase retroactive to Jan. 1, 1967, a 5 per cent increase on July 1, 1968, and an additional 20 cents an hour for skilled workers in four 5-cent increments during the completion of the life of the agreement.

The Auto Industry settlements were patterned on the agreement reached with Ford Motor Company after a 49-day strike. Production workers received hourly wage boosts of 20 cents immediately and 3 per cent annual increases in addition to cost-of-living adjustments. Skilled workers received an additional 30 cents an hour. Pension and insurance benefits were improved, an additional holiday was gained, and assembly-line relief periods were increased by 12 minutes to a total of 48 minutes a day.

The United Automobile Workers (UAW) was not successful in its demand to win salaried status for hourly paid production workers. The union did, however, obtain an annual income plan that provided experienced workers with a guarantee of a year's layoff pay of approximately 90 per cent of normal take-home pay. The Chrysler Corporation settlement also raised its Canadian wages to parity with those paid its U.S. workers, eliminating a 40-cent-an-hour gap.

Other Settlements. In the trucking industry, a three-year national master freight handling agreement was reached April 12, after a short nationwide lockout – the industry's first. The agreement provided for a 23-cent increase in the first year – 11 cents of it from the cost-of-living clause – and 12 cents and 13 cents an hour, respectively, in the second year and third year.

At plants of the five major rubber producers, strikes extended over a three-month period beginning April 21. As many as 76,000 workers were idle at one point. Settlements provided for three annual increases of 15, 15, and 13 cents plus 10 cents for skilled workers. Fringe benefits included an increase in layoff benefits to 80 per cent of straight-time hourly earnings.

Construction industry agreements generally provided increases in wages and benefits of $1 an hour or more over three years. For 80,000 apparel industry workers, with earnings averaging $77 per 35-hour week, new contracts provided increases of 9 per cent effective February, 1967, and 6 per cent a year after that.

Strikes. Man-days lost through labor disputes in the first half of 1967 increased substantially over the 1965 and 1966 periods. Man-days lost by strikes between 1960 and 1966 had ranged from .13 to .19 per cent of total working days. It appeared that time lost in 1967 would be almost twice that amount. The number of strikes also was on the increase. From 1956 through 1965 there had been fewer than 4,000 strikes per year. In 1966, they rose to 4,400. Prelimi-

Striking members of the United Auto Workers union, placards aloft, man the picket line outside the Ford Motor Company's River Rouge plant near Detroit, Mich.

FORD MOTOR COMPANY
UAW ON STRIKE FOR JUSTICE
UAW ON STRIKE FOR BETTER REPRESENTATION
UAW ON STRIKE FOR ANNUAL INCOME
Ford
Rouge Area
Gate 4
STOP

LATIN AMERICA

Latin America pursued its goal of creating a hemispheric common market. It did so despite disruptive guerrilla activities in a number of its republics, trade barriers that would hamper Latin-American exports, and the constantly present problems of exploding populations, unemployment and the lack of job opportunities, hunger, poverty, illiteracy, one-crop economies, and social and fiscal inequities. The region's per capita growth rate for 1967 was forecast at 1.2 per cent. Although it was above the 1 per cent figure for 1966, it was still below the Alliance for Progress target of 2.5 per cent. The signs were encouraging but obviously much more remained to be done.

Punta del Este Conference. In April, top-level representatives of all the Latin-American nations except Bolivia met in Punta del Este, Uruguay. Bolivia boycotted the meeting because the agenda did not include a question it had asked be placed there. After several sessions, in which the United States also participated, they agreed in principle to create a fully functioning Latin-American common market by 1985. To accomplish this, the nations planned to gradually merge the five-nation Central American Common Market (CACM) and the 11-nation Latin-American Free Trade Association (LAFTA) into one unit, with provisions being made for the eventual admission of other Latin republics. Of all the countries only Ecuador refused to sign the plan-of-action document.

U.S. President Lyndon B. Johnson, in a speech at the conference on April 13, stressed the need for the Latin Americans to take the lead in their own economic development and political salvation. He refused to court their favor with lavish new promises of aid, but he did make a firm offer to help those who were ready to help themselves, even if it required their adoption of difficult and perhaps unpopular measures at home. Creating the common market was expected to cost between $600,000,000 and $700,000,000 in intranational compensations for trade adjustments, industrial dislocation, and other factors. The United States was expected to supply at least 50 per cent of the required sum in the form of credits, beginning about 1970. The rest would come from the Latin-American countries.

The presidents of 19 Western Hemisphere nations gather around a table during a historic inter-American conference in Punta del Este, Uruguay.

Mutual Cooperation. A number of Latin-American nations had formulated jointly sponsored economic plans prior to the Punta del Este Conference. In February, Argentina, Bolivia, Brazil, Paraguay, and Uruguay had initiated programs to develop the Rio de la Plata basin, programs that would involve 1,600,000 square miles and the major waterways of the La Plata, Paraná, Paraguay, and Uruguay rivers. A survey team of the Organization of American States (OAS) began taking an inventory of the region's hydrologic and climatologic data. In June, the so-called Bogotá group (Chile, Colombia, Ecuador, Peru, Venezuela, and, later Bolivia) signed an agreement covering various economic integration measures, including the formation of the Andean Development Corporation that would develop multinational projects. Venezuela also made plans with Colombia and Puerto Rico to spur petrochemical projects among the three countries.

Much of the capital needed to finance these projects was advanced by the United States and other international agencies such as the Inter-American Development Bank (IADB), and CACM. The IADB planned a major expansion of its role as a lending agency in Latin America by boosting its resources to a total of $5,500,000,000, with the United States supplying $1,312,000,000.

Further Aid. The CACM bank subsequently announced plans to provide $70,300,000 in industrial credit in the region over the next four years, with the IADB contributing $10,000,000 of the amount. Since its formation in 1960, the CACM had lifted tariffs on 93.6 per cent of the interzonal trade between members and it had set up uniform tariffs on 97.5 per cent of the external trade.

A number of Mexican industries announced plans to supply technical and financial aid to the Central American nations to help them build and operate 12 basic industrial projects involving, among others, chemical, pharmaceutical, and steel industries. Mexico also arranged to grant $36,000,000 in aid to Costa Rica for development projects, and signed a $5,000,000 reciprocal credit agreement with Brazil. This would serve as a backdrop in credit and payment agreements on trade between the two nations. In effect, the latter agreement meant that Mexico now has reciprocal compensation accords with all the countries of the CACM and the LAFTA.

Steps Toward a Common Market. On August 28, the foreign ministers of the 11 nations belonging to LAFTA met in Asunción, Paraguay, to take the first steps toward creating a hemisphere-wide common market. Although the results were "limited," they were also an important "step" in an integration process that most observers believed would require a long period of time before achievement. At the meeting, the delegates (1) approved the concept of subregional groupings within LAFTA; (2) classified Uruguay, along with Bolivia, Ecuador, and

Paraguay, as an undeveloped nation so that special tariff concessions could be made; (3) voted for the creation of a CACM-LAFTA coordinating committee; (4) initialed a protocol for peaceful settlements of disputes among themselves; (5) approved tariff preferences for Panama and the Central American countries without requiring reciprocity; and (6) approved an increase of funds for technical studies as well as for the establishment of a unit within the LAFTA secretariat that would help the less developed nations with their problems. The meeting, however, tabled for further discussion such projects as the replacing of product-by-product tariff negotiation with a system of programed tariff reduction, the freezing of present tariff levels, and the inclusion in the national lists of all products included in the common list as of 1969.

The OAS agreed in January to admit Trinidad and Tobago and Barbados as members of the organization. On February 27, hemisphere foreign ministers signed the important Protocol of Buenos Aires, updating and streamlining the 16-year-old OAS charter. In it, the Inter-American Economic and Social Council was upgraded to the same level as the OAS Political Council, and an annual foreign ministers' conference, to be called the General Assembly, was created.

Population Problems. On September 11, over 100 representatives and observers from 16 Latin-American governments and the United States met in Caracas, Venezuela, to discuss ways in which to curb population growth. It was the first time that an international conference had been held under government auspices to consider a problem that is a religiously sensitive one in Latin America.

The sponsors of the meeting were the OAS, the Pan American Health Organization, the Population Council in New York City, and the Aspen Institute for Humanistic Studies.

At the conclusion of its meetings, the conference issued a report recommending that all Latin-American nations support "to the extent of their capabilities" the development of clinical programs for family planning. It suggested that family planning information and medical services be conducted in health centers, hospitals, and maternity clinics. It also called on individual governments and social security systems to support the programs "to the extent of their capabilities and in accordance with the particular conditions in each country." See POPULATION, WORLD.

Central America

Costa Rica. Disagreements between President José Joaquín Trejos Fernández and the national assembly complicated the republic's efforts to solve a serious financial crisis in 1967. In August, the International Monetary Fund (IMF) approved a 12-month, $15,500,000 stand-by agreement to support the government's efforts to restore equilibrium to the country's balance of payments. The assembly killed a government-sponsored bill aimed at the reestablishment of private banking in the republic, while the central bank authorized all banks to participate directly in the free market.

El Salvador. Confronted by a balance of payments deficit and a deteriorating economy, the government took drastic action. It raised the percentage of commercial bank legal reserves, reduced the amount of commercial loans allowed by such banks, put a 100 per cent prior deposit on certain nonessential imports, and made plans to overhaul the tax system in order to raise revenues. Part of the nation's problems were caused by a 50 per cent drop in the production of cotton, its second most important crop, and low prices in the international coffee market.

On March 5, the nation chose a moderately liberal, semimilitary regime by electing Colonel Fidel Sánchez Hernández of the ruling National Conciliation party as president. He took office July 1, for a five-year term.

Guatemala. As of August, three congressmen had been murdered, while political extremists from the left as well as the right carried out sporadic terrorist activities. Under pressure from business and landowning interests, as well as political terrorism, the government postponed for one year a much needed tax reform, thus delaying the problem of acquiring

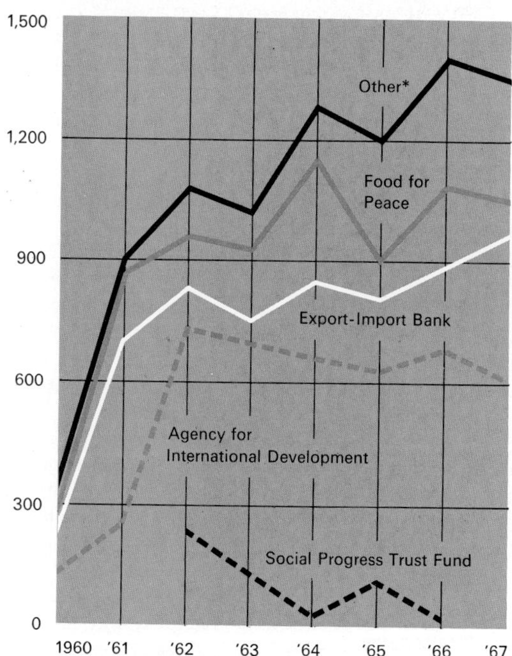

*Other: the Peace Corps, grants for the Inter-American Highway, and Inter-American Development Bank allocations.

Facts in Brief on the Latin-American Countries

Country	Population	Government	Monetary Unit	Foreign Trade (million U.S. $) Exports	Imports
Argentina*	23,266,000	President Juan Carlos Onganía	peso (350 = $1)	1,593.2	1,124.3
Bahamas	151,000	Governor Sir Ralph Grey; Prime Minister Lynden O. Pindling	dollar (1.04 = $1)	19	105
Barbados	251,000	Governor-General Sir Winston Arleigh Scott; Prime Minister Errol W. Barrow	East Caribbean dollar (2 = $1)	40	76
Bolivia*	3,815,000	President René Barrientos Ortuño	peso boliviano (11.88 = $1)	126	131
Brazil*	87,695,000	President Arthur da Costa e Silva	cruzeiro nôvo (3.2 = $1)	1,741	1,496
British Honduras	114,000	Governor Sir John Paul; Premier George Price	dollar (1.66 = $1)	12	24
Chile*	9,243,000	President Eduardo Frei Montalva	escudo (4.85 = $1)	878	683
Colombia*	19,555,000	President Carlos Lleras Restrepo	peso (14.72 = $1)	506.5	674.3
Costa Rica	1,587,000	President José Joaquín Trejos Fernández	colon (6.62 = $1)	138.7	178.5
Cuba*	8,060,000	President Osvaldo Dorticós Torrado; Premier Fidel Castro	peso (1 = $1)	686	865
Dominican Republic	3,953,000	President Joaquín Balaguer	peso (1 = $1)	137	184
Ecuador	5,506,000	Constitutional President Otto Arosemena Gómez	sucre (18.18 = $1)	148	171
El Salvador	3,182,000	President Fidel Sánchez Hernández	colon (2.50 = $1)	192	220
Guatemala	4,788,000	Chief of State Julio César Méndez Montenegro	quetzal (1 = $1)	228	207
Guyana*	694,000	Governor-General Sir David Rose; Prime Minister L. F. S. Burnham	dollar (2 = $1)	109	118
Haiti	4,931,000	President François Duvalier	gourde (5 = $1)	32	36
Honduras	2,475,000	President Oswaldo López Arellano	lempira (2 = $1)	145	149
Jamaica	1,850,000	Governor-General Sir Clifford Campbell; Prime Minister Hugh Shearer	pound (1 = $2.40)	225	321
Mexico*	45,012,000	President Gustavo Díaz Ordaz	peso (12.49 = $1)	1,228	1,605
Nicaragua*	1,789,000	President Anastasio Somoza Debayle	córdoba (7.05 = $1)	137.6	181.9
Panama*	1,338,000	President Marco Aurelio Robles	balboa (1 = $1)	89	253
Paraguay	2,181,000	President Alfredo Stroessner	guaraní (126 = $1)	49	58
Peru*	12,656,000	President Fernando Belaúnde Terry	sol (38.70 = $1)	763.2	817.2
Puerto Rico*	2,780,000	Governor Roberto Sánchez Vilella	dollar (U.S.)	1,136	1,735
Trinidad and Tobago	1,051,000	Governor-General Sir Solomon Hochoy; Prime Minister Eric Eustace Williams	dollar (2 = $1)	426	457
Uruguay*	2,806,000	President Jorge Pacheco Areco	peso (99.50 = $1)	186	164
Venezuela*	9,549,000	President Raúl Leoni	bolívar (4.5 = $1)	2,713	1,331

*Indicates countries that have separate articles.

financial resources for economic programs. In April, the IMF approved a $13,400,000 stand-by credit to help the republic adjust to a temporary decline in export earnings resulting mainly from lower world coffee prices and a 19 per cent cutback in acreage planted to cotton. The International Bank for Reconstruction and Development (World Bank) granted $15,000,000.

Honduras. Bad weather, which adversely affected coffee production, and a slowdown in banana exports, handicapped Honduras' chance of meeting its growth rate goal for 1967. Local businessmen complained about tight money conditions. However, a $22,400,000 loan from the World Bank and the IADB was expected to help bolster the economy.

Caribbean Islands

Dominican Republic. An austerity law, scheduled to expire on July 1, 1967, was extended indefinitely in order to "facilitate the continued rehabilitation of the economy." The republic's monetary board was empowered to restrict foreign exchange outlays and thus defend the peso and help reduce a balance of payments deficit.

President Joaquín Balaguer, despite sporadic outbreaks of terrorism, was able to maintain political and social stability. Under his leadership, the nation seemed more stable, united, and optimistic than at any time since the assassination of dictator Rafael Leonidas Trujillo y Molina in 1961.

Haiti. Economic conditions continued to deteriorate. High unemployment prevailed; defense expenditures, which accounted for about 25 per cent of the $28,000,000 national budget for the fiscal year ended September 30, were a further drain on the economy. The IMF agreed, in August, to allow Haiti to draw up to $1,300,000 in order that it meet payments difficulties caused by a drop in anticipated export earnings. In mid-April, Haiti celebrated the 60th birthday, and 10th anniversary in power, of François Duvalier, its president-for-life and renovator of the nation.

Trinidad and Tobago, which joined the OAS during the year, became that organization's first new member since it was formed in 1948. The islands established a Trade Promotion Advisory Council, its main goal being to shift the structure of the economy from its overdependence on petroleum. Following rising unemployment, the cabinet was shuffled, with Prime Minister Eric Eustace Williams taking over the finance ministry. In June, at the country's request, the United States relinquished its Chaquaramas naval base.

South America

Ecuador. A new constitution, which became effective on May 25, 1967, provided that a general election for the presidency and congress would be held June 2, 1968. Despite the austerity program and budget cuts, the 1967 budget deficit was forecast at

"Come, let us reason together."

$27,800,000, considered an excessive figure. However, the economy benefited from political calm, as evidenced by the fact that gross monetary holdings, which reached a record $55,400,000 on September 15, were up 75 per cent within a 12-month period.

In October, at the request of the Ecuadorean government, the United States recalled its ambassador, Wymberley DeR. Coerr, from his post in Quito. Ecuador charged he had assumed an "attitude of public, open criticism" of President Otto Arosemena Gómez. The latter had attacked the Alliance for Progress program – its red tape, high cost, and mandatory purchase of United States goods – and the U.S. diplomat had defended the scheme.

Paraguay. Economic growth stayed at a relatively low rate, mainly because bad weather cut agricultural output and external demand for primary products weakened. The IADB granted Paraguay a $14,500,000 loan to enable it to complete its 45,000 kilowatt (kw) Acaray River hydroelectric power station and expand the station's capacity to 90,000 kw.

In May, President Alfredo Stroessner and his Colorado party captured 68 per cent of the votes cast for a National Constitutional Convention, which, on August 25, approved a new constitution that would permit Stroessner to run for two more five-year terms. [MARY C. WEBSTER]

LAW. See COURTS AND LAWS; CIVIL RIGHTS; CRIME; SUPREME COURT OF THE UNITED STATES.

LEBANON continued to feel the aftereffects of the collapse of Intra Bank, the country's largest financial institution. Intra was declared bankrupt in January; its debt was given as $33,000,000. In October, the Boston, Mass., investment firm of Kidder Peabody assumed management of Intra's liquidation, and drew up an agreement between the administrators of the bank and its creditors that may enable Intra to resume business.

The government introduced new banking regulations. Commercial banks were required to deposit 25 per cent of demand deposits in the State Bank. Deposits under $15,000 were insured, and foreign banks had to show a minimum capital of $943,000.

Banking problems and the cut-off of tourism due to the Arab-Israeli war – there were 600,000 tourists in 1966 – clouded Lebanon's economic future. The Iraq Petroleum Company, however, increased its payments for Iraqi oil piped across Lebanon from $4,000,000 to $6,200,000, and Kuwait granted $6,700,000 to finance a power station. But without tourists, Beirut was a quiet place. [WILLIAM SPENCER]

Facts in Brief. Population: 2,470,000. Government: President Charles Helou; Premier Rachid Karamí. Monetary Unit: pound (3.2=U.S. $1). Foreign Trade: exports, $85,800,000; imports, $485,100,000. Principal Exports: fruits, dried beans, iron and steel.

LESOTHO. See AFRICA.

LIBERIA. See AFRICA.

LIBRARY. The United States Office of Education, on July 18, 1967, announced details of a $3,500,000 Library and Information Sciences Research Program. All types of libraries were expected to benefit from the program, which was funded under Title II-B of the Higher Education Act of 1965. The 38 projects commissioned under this program "to devise better ways to cope with the information explosion" include research in the use of library resources, development of library and information services, and training of librarians.

The National Union Catalog of publications with pre-1956 imprints will be published in book form, beginning in late 1968, by Mansell Information-Publishing, Limited. The catalog, which will list the location of important research books held in more than 700 libraries throughout the United States and Canada, now exists only as a file of more than 16,000,000 index cards at the Library of Congress in Washington, D.C. The largest single publication undertaken since the invention of printing, it will, when completed in 1977, consist of about 610 volumes of 704 pages each.

Preliminary plans for the Library of Congress James Madison Memorial Building, authorized in 1965, were announced in August. The urgently needed building will supplement the Library of Congress' 1897 Main Building and its 1939 Annex, and will cost an estimated $75,000,000.

In September, Secretary of Agriculture Orville L. Freeman laid the cornerstone of a new $7,000,000 building to house the National Agriculture Library at the Federal Agricultural Research Center in Beltsville, Md. The 1,250,000-volume library is the most extensive in its field.

Automation. The Library of Congress Project Machine-Readable-Catalog (MARC) for the distribution of computer tapes containing catalog data for current English-language monographs became operational in 1967. The 16 participating research libraries will continue to receive the MARC service on an experimental basis. Eventually, the entire catalog may be put on computer tape.

The practical and economically feasible aspects of systems were emphasized at a joint conference on "Mechanized Information Storage, Retrieval, and Dissemination" held in Rome, Italy, in July, and sponsored by the International Federation for Documentation and the International Federation for Information Processing. The conference exemplified the growing importance of automation in libraries.

The International Federation of Library Associations held its 33rd annual meeting in Toronto, Canada, in August. The theme of the meeting was "Library Service for a Nation of Large Geographical Area." About 300 delegates and observers from 26 countries attended. [ROBERT J. SHAW]

LIBYA supported the Arab cause against Israel in the Middle East war although it sent no troops to the front. Mobs rioted in Tripoli, causing damage to Jewish-owned property. On June 6, the government imposed an embargo on oil shipments to all European countries and the United States. Libyan stevedores in Tripoli even refused to unload foreign ships. When the embargo was lifted in July, the still-hostile Libyan Labor Federation called a general strike that paralyzed Tripoli. By September, though, oil flowed westward as plentifully as ever (see PETROLEUM AND GAS).

Occidental Petroleum made four new oil strikes. One, near the Idris field, brought in 75,000 barrels daily. Bulgaria agreed to build the first 476 of an eventual 100,000 low-cost houses envisaged in King Idris' housing program of 1965.

In April, the cabinet was enlarged to 23, with three new ministries: cabinet affairs, municipal affairs, and youth and sport. The Libyan University graduated its first lawyers and added faculties in agriculture and civil engineering. [WILLIAM SPENCER]

Facts in Brief. Population: 1,732,000. Government: King Idris; Premier Abd Al-Qadir Badri. Monetary Unit: pound (1=U.S. $2.79). Foreign Trade: exports, $995,000,000; imports, $405,000,000. Principal Export: crude petroleum.

LIONS INTERNATIONAL. See SERVICE CLUBS.

A $5,000 gold key presented to Libya's King Idris celebrated the opening of giant Marsa El Brega port, designed to load 1,000,000 barrels of Libyan oil a day.

An audience jammed the Sports Palace in Luzhniki, Russia, to hear the internationally known poet, Yevgeny Yevtushenko, read from his works.

LITERATURE. If trivia, sensational novels, and controversial headlines seemed to predominate in much of the news of book publishing in the United States in 1967, the serious book buyer could at least take comfort in the wide diversity of popular as well as scholarly fare offered by the booming industry. Of trivia there was more than enough. It ranged from such items as Morton Shulman's *Anyone Can Make a Million*, a nonfiction best seller, to Sally Luscomb's *The Collector's Encyclopedia of Buttons*. Of sensational novels, including many that would have been considered outright pornography a decade before, there also was a bountiful supply. They ranged from the purely commercial style of Henry Sutton's *The Exhibitionist*, which had nothing to recommend it except Hollywood sex scandals, to the quasi-literary mode of Norman Mailer's *Why Are We in Viet Nam?*, a curious tale that could be read as satire but whose only claim to distinction was that it probably set a record for the number of dirty words per page.

Fiction

A complaint heard frequently among students of the novel is that few writers in our affluent society will forego the comparatively easy route of commercially salable fiction to come to serious grips with major issues. One author who appeared to have done so in 1967 was William Styron, whose *The Confessions of Nat Turner* was the finest novel written by an American during the year. It told the story, in the slave Nat Turner's own words, of the bloody insurrection he led against his white masters in Southampton County, Va., in 1831. Although Styron observed that the idea for the novel was conceived long before the racial strife of the 1960s began, the final writing and the timing of its publication linked it inevitably to the contemporary scene.

A beautifully structured work, original in its execution, dramatic, powerful, and written with great skill, it was the finest book from Styron since his eloquent first novel, *Lie Down in Darkness* (1951). In a year that was singularly empty of major fiction efforts, it was an immediate success both with the critics and with the public. It seemed to assure the Virginia novelist a front-rank position among his contemporaries.

Other established novelists were predominant in the rest of the year's fiction list. Among them were such old hands as John O'Hara, Wallace Stegner, Philip Roth, Peter De Vries, Thornton Wilder, and Isaac Bashevis Singer. O'Hara's offering, *The Instrument*, was a short novel about a playwright and his love affairs, and it held together better than most O'Hara novels as a showcase for his unusual skill as a master of dialogue. Stegner evoked a contemporary dilemma in his amusing novel *All the Little Live Things* by portraying the older generation's efforts to cope with today's "hippies." Roth, most of whose previous fiction had been concerned with Jewish life, turned with surprising power and effectiveness to the Midwest for *When She Was Good*, about a paranoiac girl's deadly effect on several lives. De Vries' *The Vale of Laughter* was in the familiar vein of his other comic novels, and if it seemed redundant it still demonstrated his peerless capacity to amuse.

Of all the older novelists to publish during the year, perhaps the most had been expected from Thornton Wilder. His complex tale, *The Eighth Day*, won critical acclaim and a fair measure of popular support. It told the story of a strange murder and its effect upon the affairs of two American families. The Yiddish novelist Isaac Bashevis Singer once again proved his mastery of the novel in *The Manor*, the first volume of a family chronicle that takes place in 19th century Poland.

The "black humor" school of modern comic novelists was represented best by Stanley Elkin, whose *A Bad Man* was an unpleasant but technically skillful and impressive story of Feldman, an irrational and "bad" man. It shared honors on the shelf of off-beat fiction alongside such experimental novels, or bewildering put-ons, as Susan Sontag's *Death Kit*, called by one reviewer "an existential whodunit"; Donald Barthelmes' *Snow White*, a sex spoof that was called "an *avant-garde* fairy tale," and Mailer's unconventional *Why Are We in Viet Nam?*

A more orthodox approach to the novel was exhibited in two fresh talents whose satirical gifts attracted critical attention. One was Robert Stone, whose *A Hall of Mirrors* was a richly original tale of a musician turned drifter in modern New Orleans, La. The other was Robert Flynn, whose tale of a modern cattle drive, *North to Yesterday*, was marked by an uncommonly inventive approach to the Western theme.

Short Story collections that seemed most notable during the year were all from abroad, with the exception of Arthur Miller's *I Don't Need You Any More.* Miller's stories exhibited a skill with this form not commonly ascribed to the playwright. Of the English contributions, two were praiseworthy–Graham Greene's *May We Borrow Your Husband? And Other Comedies of the Sexual Life*, facile and witty excursions into the realm of domestic relations; and William Golding's *The Pyramid*, a series of three novellas of English life. Three collections of importance came from South America–the Argentinian tales of Enrique Anderson Imbert's *The Other Side of the Mirror*, which introduced a little-known master of fantasy; the Brazilian tales of Jorge Amado in *Shepherds of the Night* and of Julio Cortazar in *End of the Game and Other Stories*. The influx of Russian writers continued with a noteworthy collection of 15 short stories by Yevgeny Zamyatin entitled *The Dragon*.

Importations. Perhaps the outstanding novel from abroad to be published in the United States during the year was an almost 30-year-old Russian work that appeared in English for the first time in two different translations, Mikhail Bulgakov's *The Master and Margarita*. A satire on the Stalinist regime in Russia, its plot included the Devil, who turned Moscow into a lunatic asylum. The novel was not published in Moscow until 1966–and then in a somewhat censored version.

The 1967 Nobel prize winner, Miguel Angel Asturias, was represented in the novel lists with *Mulata*, a surrealistic retelling of an old Guatemalan folk tale. From Cuba came an exceptionally well-written novel of the revolutionary scene in Edmundo Desnoes' *Inconsolable Memories*. The author is an editor for Castro's state publishing house.

The supply of English novels, usually abundant in any year, was down to a trickle in 1967. However, the three that got attention in varying degrees were Angus Wilson's well-written but largely unexciting family chronicle, *No Laughing Matter;* Michael Frayn's highly amusing *Against Entropy*, which dealt with the troubles of a British newspaper staff; and Pamela Frankau's *Over the Mountains*.

Nonfiction

Autobiography, Biography, Diaries, and Letters. The first volume of *The Autobiography of Bertrand Russell*, dealing with the period 1872 to 1914, was heavily bid for in the United States. The large price obtained was to go to Lord Russell's peace foundation. The book was a chatty and frank memoir whose confessions sometimes revealed a childlike naivete within the mind and spirit of the celebrated philosopher. It was, nevertheless, a vastly absorbing account of Russell's rise to intellectual renown, covering his remarkable childhood in Victorian England, the writing of his masterwork *Principia Mathematica*, his disastrous marriages, and his indiscretions.

Another newsmaker in the autobiographical field was Svetlana Alliluyeva, the daughter of the Russian dictator Joseph Stalin, who told in her frank and vivid *Twenty Letters to a Friend* of her growing up in the Kremlin and of her final disillusionment with the Soviet system.

Another expatriate Russian, Vladimir Nabokov, who had left Russia much earlier, in 1940, published a new version of his autobiography in *Speak, Memory*, which was marked by his usual sardonic wit and stylistic grace. Nabokov was the subject also of an unusual and widely acclaimed critical biography, *Nabokov: His Life in Art*, by a young critic and admirer, Andrew Field, who parodied his hero's style.

Still another Russian writer, Ilya Ehrenburg, one who chose to remain in his own land through the Stalin regime and until his death in 1967, told his story in *Postwar Years, 1945-1954*, a final volume of memoirs.

The memoirs of growing up written by young men scored critical triumphs during the year and proved that worthwhile autobiography need not necessarily be the product of advanced age. In *North Toward Home*, Willie Morris, a Mississippian who became the editor of *Harper's* magazine at 33 told with spirit and candor of his journey to "home" (New York City) from a childhood in Yazoo City, Miss. In *Stop-Time,* the young American novelist Frank Conroy produced a memorable account of his early years.

Randolph S. Churchill published the second volume of his skillful and incisive biography of his father in *Winston S. Churchill: The Young Statesman, 1901-1914.* Another important English series was continued with the publication of Harold Nicholson's *Diaries and Letters: Volume II, the War Years, 1939-1945,* edited by Nigel Nicholson, which offered much revealing background on the war years in England.

In America, the publication of George F. Kennan's *Memoirs, 1925-1950,* attracted much attention for its revelations of pre-and post-war diplomacy, especially with regard to this career diplomat's role in shaping American policy toward the Russians.

One of the year's best biographical studies was W. A. Swanberg's *Pulitzer,* an exhaustive and revealing portrait of Joseph Pulitzer, the invalid genius who was the publisher of the *St. Louis Post-Dispatch* and the *New York World.*

Among the other outstanding biographies of the year were Cornelia Otis Skinner's *Madame Sarah,* a lively and often amusing portrait of the French actress Sarah Bernhardt; George Eeel's engaging portrait of the popular composer Cole Porter, *The Life That Late He Led;* Stanley Weintraub's admirable *Beardsley: A Biography,* fortunately timed for the current revival of interest in Aubrey Beardsley's work; Alan Villiers' well-researched *Captain James Cook;* Fawn M. Brodie's perceptive portrait of Sir Richard Burton, *The Devil Drives;* Robert Blake's exhaustive and long-needed fresh assessment of *Disraeli;* Richard Winston's majestic *Thomas Becket;* and Robert K. Massie's *Nicholas and Alexandra,* a colorful and illuminating dual biography of the last of the Romanovs.

In the strictly literary field, usually a crowded area, the crop was relatively thin in 1967. Henri Troyat's authoritative and colorful *Tolstoy* shed new light on the sometimes enigmatic Russian master and his strange life. Gay Wilson Allen, the author of a notable critical biography of Walt Whitman, turned to a distinguished but all too little-known 19th century American philosopher for his excellent biography *William James.*

Dylan Thomas' biographer, Constantine FitzGibbon, whose autobiography *Through the Minefield* was among 1967's little-noticed books, performed a signal service for the Thomas cult in publishing his skillfully edited *Selected Letters of Dylan Thomas,* in which the glories and the agonies of the Welsh poet's life is intimately reflected in his own words. Richard Ellmann, the biographer of James Joyce, performed a similarly admirable job in editing the second and third volumes of *Letters of James Joyce.*

History, War, and World Affairs. The year brought an end to a series of popular historical books that began some 40 years ago as Will and Ariel Durant published *Rousseau and Revolution,* the 10th and last volume in the Durants' *The Story of Civilization.*

The most publicized book of popular history was, of course, William Manchester's *The Death of a President: November 20 – November 25, 1963,* a journalistic and highly emotional account of the assassination of John F. Kennedy. Despite its unscholarly excesses and an excessive accumulation of detail, it seemed likely to remain a key sourcebook for any subsequent studies of the tragedy.

War and Foreign Policy were the concerns of many new books. In *The Korean War,* General Matthew B. Ridgway wrote with force and vigor of his role in that campaign and, at the same time, offered a spirited defense of limited warfare. The war in Vietnam continued to arouse dissent, and two of the more prominent dissenters who published books on the subject were Senator J. William Fulbright, whose *The Arrogance of Power* condemned American intervention, and Arthur M. Schlesinger, Jr., historian and former assistant to President Kennedy, whose *The Bitter Heritage* called the country's involvement "a triumph of the politics of inadvertence." Perhaps the best background studies of the conflict were offered in the French newspaperman Lucien Bodard's *The Quicksand War: Prelude to Viet Nam* and Joseph Buttinger's *Vietnam: A Dragon Embattled.* The former book described the French-Indochina war from 1946 to the French defeat at Dien Bien Phu in 1954, while the latter was a history of Vietnamese politics from the beginning of the century to the present conflict.

The American Scene. The civil rights struggle continued to provide a fertile field for writers. Among the more notable books related to the theme were Robert Coles' *Children of Crisis: A Study of Courage and Fear,* which was a psychiatric inquiry into the effects of school integration on 20 Southerners, both Negro and white; Jonathan Kozol's *Death at an Early Age,* a Boston substitute teacher's report on ghetto education as he witnessed it; and Martin Luther King's *Where Do We Go from Here: Chaos or Community?,* a reasoned criticism of the "Black Power" slogan and a call for "a meaningful interracial political coalition."

Jeanne R. Lowe's *Cities in a Race with Time* was a searching study of the urban renewal projects of five American cities – New York City; Philadelphia, Pa.; Pittsburgh, Pa.; Washington, D.C.; and New Haven, Conn. – and their problems and possible remedies.

In *The New Industrial State,* one of the year's most provocative books, the Harvard economist John Kenneth Galbraith offered the startling observation that economic planners, once the bane of corporate capital, are now the real power in many of the larger American business corporations. [Van Allen Bradley]

Elia Kazan, *center*, stage and screen director turned novelist, discusses his new book, *The Arrangement*, with playwrights Tennessee Williams, *left*, and Arthur Miller.

Poetry. American poetry, for generations the neglected sister of the arts, bid fair to steal all bouquets for popularity in 1967. Public readings by poets were as common as violin recitals had once been, while scarcely a college could not boast one "real live poet" on its staff. Indeed, because poets were deeply engaged in the protest movements of the day, they were willing, even eager, to give up the formalism that obsessed painters and composers and to instead write about social and political issues. Because of this, they found an ever-widening audience, especially of young people. At the same time, paradoxically, they won support from the very object of their attack–the Establishment. The federally financed National Endowment for the Arts, for example, granted $70,000 to the Academy of American Poets to support readings and workshops in the high schools of New York City; Detroit, Mich.; Pittsburgh, Pa.; Chicago, Ill.; Minneapolis, Minn.; and Los Angeles, Calif. It also sponsored, jointly with a private foundation, a plan to send teams of Negro and white poets to "developing colleges" in the South. Through these and scores of similar projects, poetry-in-the-making was brought to young Americans on a broad scale, not as a mere curiosity, but as a part of their lives.

But money appeared, too, for other than strictly educational purposes. For example, poet Stanley Kunitz, winner of a Pulitzer prize, was sent to Russia by the Department of State. Foreign poets were invited to the United States, including the Russian Andrei Voznesensky, whose gala New York reading was mysteriously canceled amid rumors of restrictions from Moscow. At a World Poetry Conference in Montreal, in September, where the United States was represented by Denise Levertov, Robert Lowell, and Robert Creeley, excited discussion of the poet's relation to society interrupted the set program of readings and lectures, sparked equally by renewed evidence of coercion among Soviet poets and by the emergence of a "poetry of engagement" in America.

Meanwhile, hints of stress appeared at home. Now that the elder poets were mostly gone–one of the last, Carl Sandburg, died in 1967–the question was openly asked: Who will succeed Robert Frost as the nation's unofficial poet laureate? It was an embarrassing question, which the poets ducked; yet there was obvious jockeying for position.

New Works. Two of the year's most important books were by poets with virtually unknown reputations. The first half of Louis Zukofsky's personal epic, called simply *A*, in progress since 1924, was published at last, first in England, and then in the United States. Charles Olson's *Selected Writings* assembled for the first time the scattered works of the leader of the Black Mountain poets. [HAYDEN CARRUTH]

LITERATURE, CANADIAN. See CANADIAN LIBRARY ASSOCIATION; CANADIAN LITERATURE.

LITERATURE FOR CHILDREN. In the year in which Carl Sandburg died, one of his ageless Rootabaga Stories, *The Wedding Procession of the Rag Doll and the Broom Handle and Who Was In It*, appears with illustrations by Harriet Pincus. *London Bridge Is Falling Down: The Song and the Game*, illustrated by Ed Emberley, and *London Bridge Is Falling Down!*, illustrated by Peter Spier, come just when the old bridge is really "falling down." A new London bridge is to be built soon. The present one is to be taken down piece by piece, and eventually located at a new site.

Translations of the year include two literary classics. Alan A. Milne's *Winnie-the-Pooh* has been translated into Russian by Boris Zakhoder as *Vinni-Pukh i Vse-Vse-Vse* (and All-All-All). For older boys and girls and adults, *Scarlet Sails*, by Alexander Green (Aleksandr S. Grinevskiu), has been translated from the Russian by Thomas P. Whitney and beautifully illustrated by Esta Nesbitt.

Ruth Sawyer, who has traveled and listened well, wrote for parents, teachers, and librarians *My Spain: A Storyteller's Year of Collecting*. Virginia Haviland of the Library of Congress collected *Children's Literature: A Guide to Reference Sources*. Now in paperback for parents and teachers is Lillian H. Smith's *The Unreluctant Years: A Critical Approach to Children's Literature*.

A trend toward more realism, shown in 1966, continued in 1967. *Darkness Over the Land*, by Martha B. Stiles, concerns a boy growing up in Germany under the Hitler regime, learning to keep alive and the way to feel inwardly about totalitarian government. Delightful fantasy also was published. Some had sinister notes, but often provided a way of coping with realism. Some was light and humorous.

From *Seashore Story*, written and illustrated by Taro Yashima. The fisherman in this tale from Japan "went away on a turtle's back." Publisher: Viking.

The importance of religion to the social life of the people is evident in *The Story of World Religions*, by Katharine Savage. Legend and reality are mingled in *Gautama Buddha in Life and Legend*, by Betty Kelen. *Gilgamesh: Man's First Story*, beautifully written and illustrated by Bernarda Bryson, also represents research in archaeology. *The Five Sons of King Pandu: The Story of the Mahabarata*, adapted and edited by Elizabeth Seeger, presents a great Hindu epic older than the Christian Bible. *Cross and Crescent: The Story of the Crusades*, by Richard Suskind, tells of feudal life in the Middle Ages. *David*, by Max Bolliger, the Bible story translated by Marion Koenig, won the National German Children's Book Award. *The Three Brothers of Ur*, by J. G. Fyson, is a Biblical tale of family life in ancient Sumeria, based on the story of Abraham. Heywood Broun's *A Shepherd* appears as a picture book and designed as a scroll by Gilbert Riswold. Madeleine L'Engle wrote *The Journey with Jonah*, a play for older students' performance. Louis Untermeyer edited *Songs of Joy from the Book of Psalms* to introduce the poetry of the Bible.

As to literature, parents and older children will enjoy *Jane Austen and Her World*, by Ivor Brown; or *Henry David Thoreau: A Man for Our Time*, with selections and drawings by James Daugherty. Parents and the younger ones will enjoy *Little Wide Awake: An Anthology of Victorian Children's Books and Periodicals*, edited by Leonard de Vries and containing many pictures.

Picture Books

John Burningham's ABC has capitals and lower case with familiar words and objects gaily pictured.

The Little Circle by Ann Atwood. Good color photography aids this fantasy, introducing a space concept.

I Love You Mary Jane by Lorna Balian. Never did a dog have such a birthday, giving as well as receiving presents.

Frederick by Leo Lionni. A childlike simplicity in art and verse about a field mouse.

Will I Have a Friend? by Miriam Cohen. Pictures by Lillian Hoban show the first day in an integrated primary class.

Drummer Hoff by Barbara Emberley. Brightly colored woodcuts of military action by Ed Emberley invite participation.

Peter's Chair by Ezra Jack Keats, pictures Peter's gradual acceptance of a baby sister.

Rabbit Garden by Miska Miles, has true-to-life pictures of small animals and birds by John Schoenherr.

The Little Woman Wanted Noise by Val Teale. Pictures by Robert Lawson. The humor in this farm story is as much fun to share as it ever was.

The Four Clever Brothers by the Brothers Grimm. Swiss artist Felix Hoffmann portrays the father, the sons, and the rescue of the princess from the dragon, in gay colored pages.

Rumpelstiltskin by the Brothers Grimm. Red, gold, and green pictures by Jacqueline Ayer portray the greedy king, bragging miller, and the daughter he contended could spin gold from straw.

Buford the Little Bighorn by Bill Peet. As a mountain climber he was an expert, as a skier he was a sensation.

Gunpowder Tower by Hans P. Schaad. Translated by Elizabeth D. Crawford. Two boys find adventure and a treasure in this tale of an ancient Swiss town.

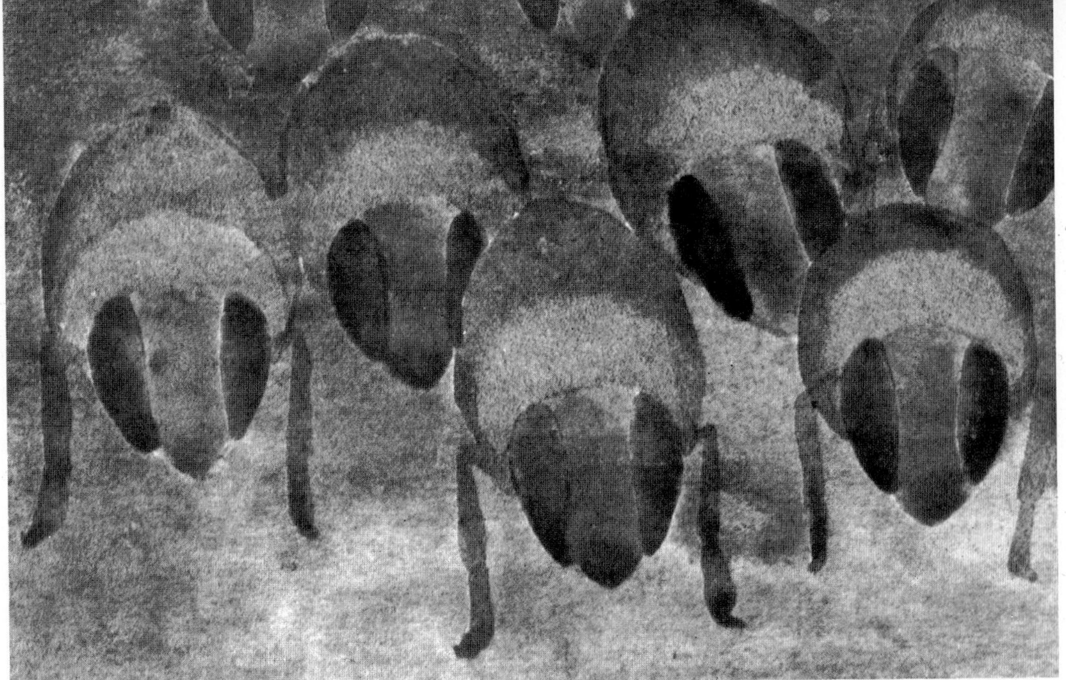

From *The Honeybees*, illustrated by Colette Portal. Franklin Russell begins in early spring, when "the hive of bees stirs, sleepy and warm," and describes the life cycle and the work in a honeybee colony. Publisher: Alfred A. Knopf.

The Last Free Bird by A. Harris Stone. Illustrated by Sheila Heins. A most beautiful and meaningful book for all ages shows the change in air, streams, and woods wrought by man's encroachment.

Collections for the Storyteller

How the People Sang the Mountains Up by Maria Leach. "Why and how stories" from all over the world include creation myths, and concern man, animals, birds, and plants.

Tricky Peik and Other Picture Tales, selected by Jeanne B. Hardendorff, introduce the humor of many lands.

Brer Rabbit and His Tricks by Ennis Rees. Three favorite tales in modern rhyme have attractive new pictures by Edward Gorey.

Tales Told Near a Crocodile: Stories from Nyanza, by Humphrey Harman, help children understand the land, the weather conditions, and the people on the shores of Lake Victoria.

The Beautiful Blue Jay and Other Tales of India, edited by John W. Spellman, are said to be "the tales that mothers actually tell their children . . . today" in India.

Russian Fairy Tales. Translated, chosen, and retold by Moura Budberg and Amabel Williams-Ellis. A total of 32 tales include "The Twelve Months" and "The Travelling Frog."

Tit for Tat and Other Latvian Folk Tales. Retold by Mae Durham. Translation from Skaidrite Rubene-Koo has valuable notes for storytellers.

A Gift from the Heart: Folk Tales from Bulgaria by Radhost Pridham. Line drawings accompany these short variant tales.

Tales, Fables, and Legends

Autun and the Bear: An Old Icelandic Legend retold by Anita Feagles. Illustrations portray well the hero's travels of Viking days.

Little Tuppen by Paul Galdone. Scandinavian version of a cumulative tale for the youngest.

William Tell and His Son, by Bettina Hürlimann, is dramatically and vividly told for story-hour and family sharing, with pictures by Paul Nussbaumer.

Mr. Miacca: An English Folk Tale by Joseph Jacobs. Illustrations by Evaline Ness interpret and create suspense in this tale of a bad boy.

The Monkey, the Lion, and the Snake by Kurt Werth. Retold from the Gesta Romanorum tales collected by monks of the Middle Ages. The ungrateful nobleman saved from the pit denies his rescuer and is banished.

The Hare and the Tortoise based on the fable by Jean de la Fontaine. Pictures by Brian Wildsmith.

The Tsar's Riddles or The Wise Little Girl. Retold from the Russian by Guy Daniels. Common sense spiced with humor. Illustrated by Paul Galdone.

The Fearsome Inn by Isaac Bashevis Singer. Illustrated by Nonny Hogrogian. Translated by the author and Elizabeth Shub. A witch and her half-devil husband hold three girls who are rescued by three handsome young men, one with a piece of magic chalk.

Stargazer to the Sultan by Barbara K. Walker and Mine Sümer. Illustrations by Joseph Low provide a rich setting for a well-constructed tale.

The Silkspinners by Jean Russell Larson. Li Po uses common sense to accomplish each task, and finally persuades the last silkspinners of China to return to civilization.

A Blue Seed by Ricko Nakagawa. Illustrated by Yuriko Omura. Yuji exchanges a toy for the blue seed and plants it, in this Japanese fable.

Taliesin by Robert Nye. This tale from the Mabinogion, a famous collection of Welsh folklore dating back to the Middle Ages, is for older children, or story hour.

Deirdre by Madeleine Polland. Beautiful Deirdre of the Sorrows is a romance for older girls.

Fantasies

One Monday Morning by Uri Shulevitz. A little city boy's imagination parallels his everyday activities as the king, queen, and others from the playing cards come to life and visit him.

Where the Wild Apples Grow by John Hawkinson. Fantasy of the wild girl with long brown hair and wild horse.

Zeely by Virginia Hamilton. An 11 year-old Negro girl lives in a fantasy world on a summer visit.

From Brian Wildsmith's *Birds*. "A sedge of herons" is one of various bird groups the artist pictures in gay colors. Publisher: Franklin Watts, Inc.

Jack of Dover by Richard Garnett. Literal-minded Jack is a very English "Don Quixote" in this fantasy.

The Moonball by Ursula Moray Williams. Real children have an impossible creature for a friend.

Octagon Magic by Andre Norton. Fantasy and historical fact are woven together in a delightful story about an ancient eight-sided house.

Moon Eyes by Josephine Poole. Whatever the supernatural powers of Aunt Rhoda and her strange dog, Moon Eyes, Kate fears they could bring only harm to her mute five-year-old brother.

Ivanov Seven by Elizabeth Janeway. A simple peasant conscript in the Russian army returns home with a howitzer, which helps him control the rain.

Taran Wanderer, by Lloyd Alexander, is the author's fourth book in a well-written series about the kingdom of Prydain. This volume concerns itself with failure, self-searching, and success.

The Moon of Gomrath by Alan Garner. A wizard and two children struggle with forces of good and evil.

The Great and Terrible Quest, by Margaret Lovett, is a breathless adventure tale of a boy, a man, a lost heir, and a faithful knight.

Earthfasts by William Mayne. A drummer boy of two centuries ago marches out of a hill, and meets two boys of the present.

The Whirling Shapes by Joan North. The world of fantasy invades and conquers the world of reality for a while in this gripping tale.

History and Historical Tales

Claymore and Kilt: Tales of Scottish Kings and Castles, by Sorche Nic Leodhas, covers events from A.D. 211 to 1611.

The Marsh King by C. Walter Hodges. England's King Alfred takes a stand against hatred and revenge.

The Spanish Letters by Mollie Hunter. Jamie joins the "caddies," an organized gang of porters and messengers, who help track down Scottish traitors to England in this Edinburgh mystery of the 1700s.

Early Thunder by Jean Fritz. Daniel West grows up in Salem in 1775, and changes from Tory to Whig.

Revolution! France 1789-1794 by Sarel Eimerle. By focusing on people, the reader perceives the lack of understanding various groups have for others.

Journey Toward Freedom: The Story of Sojourner Truth, by Jacqueline Bernard, is a researched, fictionized life of a slave, who championed rights of Negroes and women.

No Beat of Drum, by Hester Burton, is a powerful tale of plowmen and threshers starving in 1830 in England.

The Treeless Plains, by Glen Rounds, pictures sod houses and life on the western plains of the United States.

Katia by E. M. Almedingen. The whole world of czarist Russia comes to life in this fascinating biography of a children's author in the 1800s.

Fierce and Gentle Warriors: Three Stories by Mikhail Sholokhov. Translated by Miriam Morton. A Russian Nobel novelist writes of children and war in "The Colt," "The Rascal," and "The Fate of Man."

The Outsiders of Uskoken Castle by Kurt Held. Translated by Lynn Aubry from the German. Five war orphans band together for survival with outlaws in an old castle in Yugoslavia.

Horses of Anger, by James Forman, concerns World War II on the German battlefield and home front as seen by Hans, his former schoolmates, and his family.

And Miles to Go: The Biography of a Great Arabian Horse: Witz II, by Linell Smith, is the story of Poland's most famous Arabian stallion.

His Enemy, His Friend, by John R. Tunis, is a serious mature story of World War II and the relationships of a German sportsman with the French.

Stories for Middle Grades

My Brother Stevie by Eleanor Clymer. Annie tells about her grandmother, her brother, her favorite teacher, an important train ride, and a dog.

Isfendiar and the Wild Donkeys by Bronson Potter. An Iranian charcoal burner's son searches for the legendary donkeys and learns the things to be done to survive on the desert.

In-Between Miya by Yoshiko Uchida. Miya learns the real values in life after a visit to Tokyo.

From the Mixed-Up Files of Mrs. Basil E. Frankweiler, by E. L. Konigsburg, concerns the humorous adventures of Claudia and her brother, who live for a week in the Metropolitan Museum of Art.

Jennifer, Hecate, Macbeth, William McKinley, and Me, Elizabeth by E. L. Konigsburg. This suburban story concerns girls of different races.

A Matter of Miracles by Edward Fenton. Fatherless Gino finds few jobs in Sicily to help his mother and sisters until he acquires a dog and joins a company of puppeteers.

Richleighs of Tantamount by Barbara Willard. Four little rich children, deserted in a smuggler's castle, learn to fend for themselves.

Don't Take Teddy by Babbis Friis-Baastad. Translated from the Norwegian by Lise Somme McKinnon. The responsibility small Mikkel feels for his mentally retarded brother is at length resolved.

Teen Stories

The Blue Year by Bianca Bradbury. Jill matures to understand her parents' divorce.

Shadow on the Water by Robinson Barnwell. Self-pity overwhelms 13-year-old Cammie, whose parents are considering a divorce.

Too Bad About the Haines Girl by Zoa Sherburne. A girl in a "nice" family lets her emotions be her undoing.

Sam by Barbara Corcoran. Sam, who has spent all her life on an island, explores the confused world of high school and learns to understand adults.

Tides of Danger by Elizabeth Baldwin Hazelton. Trinidad Delgado struggles to replace the stolen pearl, and to pay for his family's freedom.

The Black Pearl, by Scott O'Dell, is a short novel concerning superstitions, a devilfish, tragedy, and a boy's growing up.

The Big Wheels by William E. Huntsberry. A real picture of six high school boys, and the corruption that results from gang control.

The Outsiders by S. E. Hinton. Ponyboy, the youngest of three orphaned brothers, tells of the fights between the Socs and the greasers, who are considered the outsiders.

Good-Bye to the Jungle by John Rowe Townsend. A new housing project gives an English slum family a chance.

Season of the Briar by H. F. Brinsmead. A weed-spraying team of four boys spend a summer in an isolated community in Tasmania.

Smoke by William Corbin. A teen-age boy gives a half-starved wild dog all his love and attention, although it means disobeying his stepfather.

Henry 3, by Joseph Krumgold, is a tale of a boy growing up in suburbia today.

The Wind Chasers by Esther Wier. Him as chases the wind don't catch nothin'!," is the philosophy of Jobidiah Klink, who has four motherless sons to rear.

Irving and Me by Syd Hoff. Humorous account of 13-year-old Artie's adjustment to living in Florida.

Music, Art, Drama, and Poetry

American Indians Sing, by Charles Hofmann, is well-illustrated, and includes dances, ceremonies, and a recording.

Cowboys & the Songs They Sang by Samuel J. Sackett. Music and words for songs of the trail, the range, and the cowboy's sorrows and dreams.

A Fiesta of Folk Songs from Spain and Latin America, edited by Henrietta Yurchenco. Spanish text enlivens language as well as music studies.

The Story of Smetana's The Bartered Bride. Narrative and pictures by Lisl Weil. A gay tale of mistaken identity may arouse interest in the Czech comedy.

What Is a Color? by Alice and Martin Provenson. Children are interested in yellow lions, blue policemen, and red fire engines. They like this easy-on-the-eyes typography.

Tormented Genius: The Struggles of Vincent Van Gogh, by Alan Honour, introduces the man, his unhappy life, and his drive to accomplishment.

Melissa Hayden, Ballerina by Rasa Gustaitis. A short, interesting picture of her persistence and her home life, with many photographs.

Higglety Pigglety Pop! or There Must be More to Life, written and illustrated by Maurice Sendak, is a small drama from Mother Goose for play-acting.

From King Boggen's Hall to Nothing-At-All: A Collection of Improbable Houses and Unusual Places Found in Traditional Rhymes and Limericks. Illustrated by Blair Lent.

The Bold Fisherman by Mark Taylor. Illustrated by Graham Booth. A tall tale about a whale and John Jonah Jones, with a folk song.

Miracles: Poems by Children of the English-Speaking World. Edited by Richard Lewis. "Without poetry our world would be locked within itself."

Reflections on a Gift of Watermelon Pickle, and Other Modern Verse. Compiled by Stephen Dunning and others. Because these were selected by students, they can see a poem "gradually unfolding." Exquisite photographs help visualization.

D. H. Lawrence: Poems Selected for Young People, by William Cole, is a handsome volume, illustrated by Ellen Raskin.

From *Knee-Deep in Thunder*, with drawings by Peter Parnall. Sheila Moon writes about a world of fantasy, adventure, and beauty. Publisher: Atheneum.

Awards in 1967 included;

American Library Association Children's Services Division Awards: *Caldecott Medal*, for the most distinguished American picture book in 1966, to Evaline Ness, author and illustrator of *Sam, Bangs & Moonshine. Newbery Medal*, for the most distinguished contribution to American literature for children in 1966, to Irene Hunt, Cicero, Ill., public schools consultant in language arts, for *Up a Road Slowly*.

Book Week Spring Children's Book Festival Awards: *Picture Books* to Tomi Ungerer, author and illustrator of *Moon Man. For Children 8 to 12* to Zilpha Keatley Snyder, author of *The Egypt Game. For Older Boys and Girls* to Erik Haugaard, author of *The Little Fishes.*

British Library Association Awards: *Carnegie Medal*, for an outstanding book for children, was not awarded in 1967, but highly recommended was *The Bayeux Tapestry* by Norman Denny and Josephine Filmer-Sankey. *Kate Greenaway Medal*, for the most distinguished work in the illustration of children's books in 1966, to Raymond Briggs, author and illustrator, for his illustrations in *The Mother Goose Treasury*.

Canadian Library Association Book of the Year for Children's Award. See CANADIAN LIBRARY ASSOCIATION.

Catholic Library Association Regina Medal, for a lifetime dedication to the highest standard of literature for children, to Bertha Mahony Miller, founder of *The Horn Book Magazine* (1924), editor until 1951, and chairman of the board since 1963.

Child Study Association of America Children's Book Award, for a distinguished book for young people which deals realistically and courageously with contemporary problems, to Robert Burch, author of *Queenie Peavy*.

Thomas Alva Edison Foundation National Mass Media Awards: *For the Best Children's Book on Natural Science* to S. Carl Hirsch, author of *The Living Community. For the Best Science Book for Youth* to George W. and Muriel Beadle for *The Language of Life: An Introduction to the Science of Genetics. For Excellence in Portraying America's Past* to Robert G. Abernethy for *Introduction to Tomorrow: The United States and the Wider World, 1945-1965. For Excellence in Contributing to the Character Development of Children* to Reginald Ottley for *Boy Alone.* [ELOISE RUE]

LIVESTOCK. See AGRICULTURE.

LIVESTOCK SHOW. Two Iowa girls shared $17,050 when their grand champion Aberdeen-Angus was sold at auction during the 1967 International Live Stock Exposition. Modern, a 1,100-pound black senior calf, brought $15.50 a pound to Marlene Wiseman, 20, and Anita Bulfer, 17, of Gilman. It was the sixth highest price ever paid for a grand champion at the show.

Calvin Wiseman, 16, brother of the co-winner, showed the junior grand champion, a 1,095-pound Angus named Finally. His steer brought a price of 70 cents a pound.

Mark Love, 17, of Hartford City, Ind., won the grand and junior championships of the swine show with a 205-pound Hampshire-Chester White named Mr. Hippie. The pig brought a record $26 a pound at auction. The Chicago Mercantile Exchange bought Mr. Hippie and Modern, the first time in the show's history that one buyer had purchased both of the champions.

The 68th annual exposition, held at the International Amphitheatre in Chicago November 17 to 26, drew a paid attendance of 225,000 and exhibitors from 40 states and Canada.

A 999-pound Angus was grand champion of the 69th American Royal Live Stock Show and Horse Show at Kansas City, Mo., in October. The steer's owner, Lyle Miller of Osceola, Iowa, received $5,144.85 for the Angus.

LOS ANGELES. The slow pace of development in the Bunker Hill urban renewal area aroused strong criticism in the city council. The 136-acre site adjacent both to downtown and the new Civic Center has been described as one of the nation's most strategically located pieces of real estate. At year's end, the project began moving: steel columns began to rise on November 27 for Bunker Hill Towers, a three-building $60,000,000 apartment complex consisting of one 30-story and two 17-story structures.

In December, agreement was reached for development of a key 3.55-acre site as a huge nine-level 4,000-automobile garage. Eventually, the area will attract $500,000,000 in construction activity, and is expected to have a working population of 25,000 along with 5,000 residents.

Despite its lagging pace, Bunker Hill's prospects were stimulating private activity near its boundaries. Across from the garage, twin 55-story office towers were planned. An investment of $120,000,000 was involved for the project, downtown Los Angeles' largest. When the plans were revealed on August 9, the 42-story Crocker-Citizens Plaza just a block away, was topped out. The $32,000,000 structure was the city's tallest building.

On the other side of Bunker Hill, the Music Center reached completion in mid-April with the opening of two new theaters. The 750-seat Mark Taper Forum and 2,100-seat Ahmonson Theater were fully financed by private sources. Combined with the Dorothy Chandler Pavilion, they constituted an impressive $33,500,000 complex for the performing arts.

Following nearly 25 years of controversy, the city council, on September 11, overwhelmingly approved construction of a convention center which will cost at least $38,500,000.

Transportation. According to a study commissioned by the city and announced in December, the growth of the downtown core will breed enormous parking problems. The current shortage of 5,100 spaces could grow to nearly 19,000 by 1980; more than 20,000 new spaces will be needed in the 237-block central business district. Demand for another 13,000 will be generated by Bunker Hill. The study showed that 59 per cent of the central business district is used for roads, sidewalks, and parking space. In response, officials and businessmen noted that the automobile could strangle the city's downtown growth in a dozen years unless public transportation improves. Yet efforts to finance a rapid transit system for the metropolitan area were defeated in the California state senate during the summer.

To help solve some of its problems through advanced management techniques and technology, the city created a nonprofit technical services corporation, patterned after the "think factories" of the space and defense programs. [DONALD W. LIEF]

LUMBER. See FOREST PRODUCTS.

LUXEMBOURG. Steps to end the use of Luxembourg as a tax haven for foreign firms were taken by the nation's partners in the European Economic Community (EEC, or Common Market) in 1967. At least 2,000 financial companies, many of them internationally known holding companies, have been established in the grand duchy since 1966. Belgium, France, and Germany pressed not only for unification of EEC tax laws, but also for an ending of the situation whereby, in Luxembourg, dividends, profits, and investments are tax free. Luxembourg's President Pierre Werner told a Common Market commission, set up to study the proposal, that the plan, if adopted, would cause transference of companies out of the Common Market to the Bahamas, Liechtenstein, and other tax havens.

The merging of two large companies in July made Luxembourg the third largest steel producer in the European Community, with an output of 5,000,000 tons of crude steel a year–representing 90 per cent of the total production. [KENNETH BROWN]

Facts in Brief. Population: 339,000. Government: Grand Duke Jean; Prime Minister and President Pierre Werner. Monetary Unit: franc (49.63=U.S. $1). Foreign Trade (including Belgium): exports, $6,829,000,000; imports, $7,174,000,000. Principal Exports: iron and steel, machinery, textiles.

MAGAZINE. See PUBLISHING.
MALAGASY REPUBLIC. See AFRICA.

MALAMUD, BERNARD (1914-), was awarded the 1967 Pulitzer prize in literature and the National Book Award for fiction for *The Fixer,* a novel about the persecution of an unemployed Jewish handyman. The novel tells the story of a fixer who is arrested in Kiev in 1911, charged with the ritual murder of a young Christian boy. As he is arrested, the fixer asks, "Why me?" But after awaiting sentence in prison for two years, he slowly learns to understand and endure his fate. The novel emphasizes Malamud's constant theme of the human spirit in a world that is "horrifying and unjust."

Malamud's works are far from being limited in historical setting or locale. His first published novel, *The Natural* (1952), was a mythical story of a contemporary American baseball superhero. He has written two other novels, *The Assistant* (1957), and *A New Life* (1961) and two books of short stories, *The Magic Barrel* (1958), winner of the 1959 National Book Award for fiction, and *Idiots First* (1963).

Malamud lives on a Vermont farm, a mile from Bennington College, where he has been on the faculty since 1961. Before that, he was associate professor of English for 12 years at Oregon State University. Before and after receiving his M.A. degree from Columbia University in 1942, Malamud taught evening high school classes in Brooklyn and in New York City's Harlem district. [WALTER F. MORSE]

MALAWI. See AFRICA.

MALAYSIA, FEDERATION OF, enjoying a relatively stable year, achieved steady political as well as economic progress in 1967. One of its most significant political gains was an agreement with Great Britain for the gradual withdrawal of all British defense forces from Malaysia by 1970. The first British contingent left Penang during the summer.

Some of the gaps in Malaysia's defense system were taken up by Australia and New Zealand, with whom Malaysia re-established firm ties. Similarly, Malaysia sought to establish new diplomatic and trade relations with the Soviet Union and Yugoslavia, as well as with Formosa. One of Malaysia's most promising negotiations in the diplomatic field involved Japan. After years of controversy over war claims made against Japan by Malaysia on behalf of its Chinese population, a settlement was reached in which Japan agreed to indemnify Malaysia. A further demonstration of closer ties was the opening of the Malayamata steel mill, a jointly owned Malay-Japanese industry located in Prai.

Malaysia's Economy made steady upward progress. Rubber, the nation's biggest export crop, continued to be so in 1967 with Malaysia producing close to 40 per cent of the world's natural rubber. In order to diversify the industrial base, however, and lessen such dependence on rubber, the government enacted several tax incentives to encourage other industries. One result was the growing of a double rice crop in Krian for the first time in the nation's history. Although declining world rubber prices in 1967 had a somewhat adverse effect on the nation's foreign exchange earnings, the year generally was a good one, with exports and imports nearly in balance.

In Domestic Politics, the year saw some progress in the gradual integration of Sabah and Sarawak into greater Malaysia. Orderly elections held in Sabah returned a substantial government majority to the legislature. In Sarawak, however, elections were postponed for a year because of continued guerrilla activity.

The government took a major step by passing a new law calling for Malay as the official language of the country, while permitting English to be used in parliament, the law courts, and a few other specified circumstances. Even these concessions aroused some resentment in a nation where racial strife was still a problem, especially between Malays and Chinese. A serious outbreak of violence between the two groups occurred in November. [JOHN N. STALKER]

Facts in Brief. Population: 10,136,000. Government: Paramount Ruler Ismail Nasiruddin Shah; Prime Minister Tunku Abdul Rahman. Monetary Unit: dollar (3.08=U.S. $1). Foreign Trade: exports, $1,256,000,000; imports, $1,104,000,000. Principal Exports: rubber, tin, timber.

MALI. See AFRICA.

MALTA. Talks on Great Britain's plans to cut its defense spending in Malta from $43,500,000 to $20,000,000 and its military forces there by two-thirds broke down at the end of January. Britain's Commonwealth Secretary Herbert Bowden refused to modify the cuts, and Prime Minister Giorgio Borg Olivier retaliated with a declaration that his government no longer considered the defense treaty between the two countries binding.

A bill to deprive British forces in Malta of their legal position was presented to the house of representatives. Discussion on the bill was postponed, however, when Britain made proposals designed to alleviate the economic effects of withdrawal. Prolonged talks followed in London, but several times they almost broke down. On March 12, a "package deal" was agreed upon. Under its terms, the two nations established a joint economic commission in Malta. In July, the commission recommended an action program involving a build-up of the island's industrial and tourist facilities.

In July, an agreement was signed between Malta and Italy, covering cultural, economic, and trade cooperation. [KENNETH BROWN]

Facts in Brief. Population: 321,800. Government: Governor-General Sir Maurice Dorman; Prime Minister Giorgio Borg Olivier. Monetary Unit: pound (2.40=U.S. $1). Foreign Trade: exports, $24,200,000; imports, $97,900,000. Principal Export: textiles.

MĂNESCU, CORNELIU (1916-), foreign minister of Romania, was elected president of the United Nations (UN) General Assembly's 22nd session when it convened on Sept. 19, 1967. The first delegate from a Communist nation to hold the office, Mănescu succeeded Abdul Rahman Pazhwak of Afghanistan. The vote for Mănescu was 112 to 0, with five abstentions. See UNITED NATIONS.

Mănescu was born Feb. 8, 1916, at Ploeşti. The son of a government clerk, he took degrees in law and economics at the University of Bucharest in 1940. A veteran Communist, Mănescu joined the party in 1936 and rose steadily in its ranks after it seized power in Romania a decade later. He has been head of the Romanian army's higher political division; deputy minister of the armed forces, with the rank of lieutenant general; vice-chairman of the State Planning Committee; and ambassador to Hungary. He was the head of the Romanian delegations to the UN from the time of his appointment as foreign minister in March, 1961.

Mănescu had been a member of the Romanian national assembly since 1965, where he was respected as a versatile negotiator. He worked toward increasing Romania's independence from Russia. Debonair, fluent in French, six feet two inches tall, and handsome, he has been called "the glamourboy diplomat of Eastern Europe." [WALTER F. MORSE]

MANITOBA. See CANADA.

MANUFACTURING generally reflected uncertainties in the economy during 1967–the war in Vietnam, the possibility of a 10 per cent corporate tax surcharge, the sluggish state of home building, a number of long strikes in basic industries, and the renewed talk of tight money. As a result, manufacturing output was held below the levels of 1966. The Federal Reserve index of manufacturing output (1957-1959=100) dipped from a seasonally adjusted 158.1 in the month of September, 1966, to 156.7 in September, 1967.

The pace of new orders at factories–a key to future output–slackened. In September, new orders dropped almost $1,000,000,000 to a seasonally adjusted $44,945,000,000, down 2.1 per cent from the August figure of $45,900,000,000. It was the lowest level since April.

Orders for durable goods were particularly sluggish from August through October. At a seasonally adjusted rate, they totaled $22,500,000,000 in October, down from September's $23,500,000,000 and the $24,200,000,000 of a year earlier. Statistics for September suggested that the drop would have been more severe if defense product orders had not risen from August's $2,841,000,000 to $3,549,000,000. See ECONOMY, THE.

Capital Expenditures and Excess Capacity. While the reinstatement of the 7 per cent investment tax credit helped stimulate record-breaking investments in manufacturing plant and equipment of $27,310,000,000 in 1967, the total was only $320,000,000 above the 1966 figure. The 1965 to 1966 increase had been $4,440,000,000.

Excess capacity in some lines brought the operating rate of factories to the lowest since 1963–down to 83.3 per cent of capacity in the third quarter, slightly below the 84.8 per cent of the second quarter, and sharply below the 90.6 per cent of the year before. It was the fifth consecutive quarterly decline in plant operating rate. During September alone, factory shipments sank 2.7 per cent to $44,448,000,000, the lowest since April.

Along with the decline in operating rate, there was relatively small growth in the productivity of factory workers. Gains in output per man-hour in manufacturing had fallen from the 1960 to 1965 rate of 3.9 per cent a year, to only 1.6 per cent in 1966. For the first nine months of 1967 the level remained virtually steady, while total man-hours worked lagged 4 per cent behind 1966 levels. Payrolls rose roughly 2 per cent, and unit labor costs, which had advanced steadily since early in 1966, hit a postwar high of 108.3 in November (1957-1959=100), about 5 per cent above the 103.1 of November, 1966.

The Shaw Process of precision casting of titanium was developed in 1967. It received impetus from the administration's decision to build two prototype supersonic airliners. Their all-titanium airframes must be able to withstand the 400 to 500° F. temperatures created by the 2,000-mph speed of the plane. This presented the need to find a technology capable of producing dies that could form titanium parts at temperatures of 1450° F. as well as dies that would require little or no machining. Machining the necessary 8,000 sets of dies would be prohibitive in terms of cost and time.

After a two-year study by the Illinois Institute of Technology Research Institute for the Boeing Company, it was reported that Shaw process molds gave the best results–showing good dimensional reproducibility, surface smoothness, and faithful replication of pattern details in excess of the quality needed. The Shaw process uses a dimensionally stable ceramic mold that produces castings in all ferrous and nonferrous alloys. The dies were to be delivered to Boeing and its subcontractors in 1968.

Machine Tool orders in September dropped to $87,100,000, lowest for any month since November, 1963, and down nearly 30 per cent from August. Buying in October improved, however. The September decline had resulted in part from a few extra-large orders from the aerospace industry, pushing August's order total to $122,550,000.

For the first nine months of 1967, shipments of cutting and forming tools totaled $1,173,750,000, up 10 per cent from the comparable 1966 period. They also were nearly 20 per cent higher than the $983,150,000 in net new orders, which declined steadily in

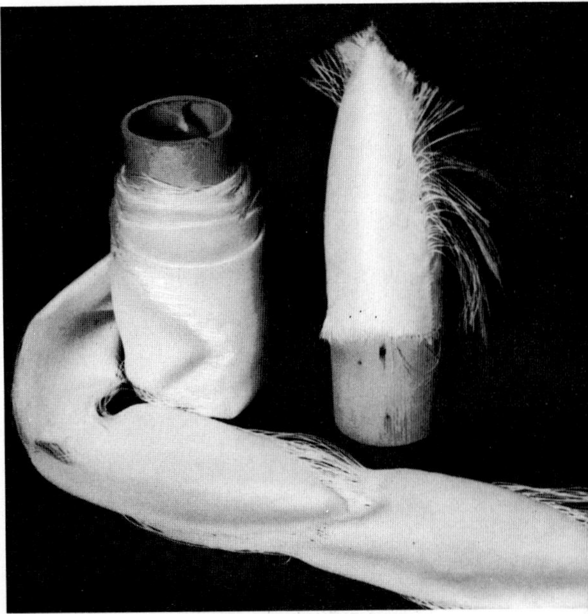

Old tools, such as the textile loom, *left*, are now being used to produce three-dimensional weaves from aluminum, plastic, and even steel. The fiberglass socks, *above*, were produced for a missile program.

1967. In the first nine months, machine tool orders fell 32 per cent from the 1966 period. The lower rate of production and unsettled labor conditions in many key machine tool-purchasing industries were cited as major deterrents to ordering.

While bookings slid, backlogs remained high. As of September 30, the industry average for metal-cutting machine tools stood at about 9 months of production. According to a *Wall Street Journal* report, this high backlog with long delivery times gave foreign tool builders an opportunity to boost their U.S. sales. Machine tool imports more than doubled during 1966; for the first seven months of 1967 they jumped to $106,900,000 from $56,800,000 in the 1966 period.

Throughout 1967, toolmakers were turning more and more to new electronic processes, such as electromechanical machining (ECM), which is the controlled removal of metal by electrolytic action. ECM is the newest of the electrical machining techniques. Electrical-discharge machining, the oldest of the methods, was improved by the availability of higher power supplies, which permit faster metal removal rates to a maximum of 12 cubic inches an hour.

Electrical Plants' total shipments in 1967 were expected to increase 4 1/2 per cent on a dollar value basis. The National Electrical Manufacturers Association (NEMA) said the total would reach $38,990,000,000 in 1967, against $37,300,000,000 in 1966.

New highs were established in all categories except consumer products and electrical insulating materials. Shipments of consumer products remained at the high 1966 level of $9,145,000,000. One segment, however, slumped noticeably. Through September 22, television sales were down 12.1 per cent, radio sales off 4.8 per cent, and phonograph sales down 7.5 per cent.

NEMA reported the highest increase for electric utility equipment, with the value of shipments likely to reach $3,656,000,000, up 15 per cent from the $3,100,000,000 for shipments in 1966. See ELECTRIC POWER AND EQUIPMENT.

The perennial leader in dollar volume, industrial electronics and communications equipment, had another outstanding year, with a rise of 8 per cent to $12,600,000,000, compared with $11,670,000,000 in 1966. See COMMUNICATIONS; ELECTRONICS.

An Electric Motor Breakthrough was scored by Reliance Electric Company of Reliance, Ohio, in 1967, when it introduced a series of adjustable-speed drives for direct current (d.c.) motors. While most plants operate on alternating current, d.c. motors drive machines for jobs requiring adjustable speeds and fine tolerances.

Little had been done to meet these needs until Reliance's development, considered to be the most significant advance in d.c. motors in 30 years. Such motors range from 1/8 horsepower (hp) for small business machinery, to 500 hp, for tubing mills, steel conveyors, and galvanizing lines. The new motors were said to eliminate d.c. problems of overheating and slowed motor response.

Apparel Industry sources estimated that sales for 1967 would reach $35,600,000,000, up from the record level of $34,100,000,000 in 1966.

A major technical advance in fabrics was the successful application of "permanent press" to woolens. The process had previously banished wrinkles from cotton and synthetic blend apparel. Three of the biggest textile makers introduced permanent press woolens and blends, which were used for slacks, skirts, and other tailored and sporty apparel. All take lasting creases or pleats at the factory, and require little ironing.

Millmaster Onyx Corporation introduced a post-cure, reactant system to achieve durable press on white, pastel, and brightly printed 100 per cent cotton fabrics and garments as well as on high-cotton content blends. Tests on the post-curing process encouraged the hope of widening markets for textile and garment manufacturing industries and retailers, and of offering a greater choice to consumers.

Rubber and Tire output was severely curtailed by prolonged strikes in 1967. Total consumption was estimated by the Rubber Manufacturers Association at 2,115,000 long tons, down 4 1/2 per cent from 1966. Synthetic rubber production accounted for 76.6 per cent of the total as against 74.9 per cent in 1966, despite the fact that natural rubber prices were at their lowest level in 18 years.

While 1967 passenger car tire shipments held close to the 1966 level of 151,000,000 units, production fell approximately 9 1/2 per cent. Shipments of replacement passenger tires rose 6 per cent to a record of 108,000,000 units. However, shipments of original equipment tires declined about 13 per cent from 47,000,000 to 41,000,000 units.

Nontire industrial products such as belting, hose, and molded and extruded goods remained at their 1966 levels. Consumer products such as rubber flooring, footwear, heels, soles, and sundries continued at a slight downward trend, because of imports and substitutions of materials competing with rubber.

With the push for tighter federal tire-safety standards, certain industry-wide trends became evident during 1967:

- The radial-ply tire concept, but not necessarily the radial-ply tire itself, is here to stay.
- The wide tire has become well established.
- Polyester and glass fiber were being used more in tire cords, nylon and rayon probably less.

Farm Machinery sales began 1967 exhibiting much of 1966's strength. However, sales dropped drastically as unseasonable weather and a downturn in farm prices reduced the expected 10 per cent gain in equipment sales to a mere 3 per cent gain over the 1966 volume of $3,000,000,000. See AGRICULTURE.

The use of highly mechanized and sophisticated farm machinery was spreading at a fast rate into crop harvesting. While not yet in the mass-production stage, many specially built units were being used during the year for the harvesting of beans, cherries, cucumbers, grapefruit, and tomatoes. A substantial portion of the 1967 tomato crop in California was picked by a special machine that has rubber "fingers."

This resulted in a massive inventory build-up at the factory, forcing cutbacks in production. Manufacturers trimmed prices in efforts to move their machinery. This came in the face of higher labor costs in union negotiations. It was expected that prices would be raised and that 1968 sales would hold at the 1967 level.

Significant advances were made during 1967 in wheel tractors, which make up 40.1 per cent of all farm machinery sold. The need for tractors to operate up to 12 hours a day has resulted in bigger units, powered by engines of greater horsepower, with all equipment on the tractor hydraulically operated. Transmissions on the 1967 tractor used as many as 14 forward speeds. [GEORGE J. BERKWITT]

See also AUTOMOBILE; AVIATION; CHEMICAL INDUSTRY; ECONOMY, THE; ENERGY; STEEL INDUSTRY; TRANSPORTATION.

MARINE CORPS, U.S. See ARMED FORCES OF THE WORLD; NATIONAL DEFENSE.

MARSHALL, THURGOOD (1908-   ), on June 13, 1967, became the first Negro to be appointed to the Supreme Court of the United States. In announcing his choice, President Lyndon B. Johnson said, "I believe it is the right thing to do, the right time to do it, the right man, and the right place."

Justice Marshall was born in Baltimore, Md., on July 2, 1908, the great-grandson of a Congo-born slave. After a shaky start at Lincoln University in Pennsylvania, Marshall was graduated with high honors in 1930.

His legal experience spans the 34 years since his graduation from Howard University's law school in Washington, D.C., in 1933. He served as counsel for the National Association for the Advancement of Colored People (NAACP). The most notable victory of his career was the school desegregation decision in 1954.

His NAACP service ended with his 1961 appointment to the U.S. Court of Appeals in New York. In August, 1965, he was named U.S. Solicitor General. By a 69-to-11 vote, the U.S. Senate confirmed Marshall as an Associate Justice on Aug. 30, 1967. He was sworn in on Oct. 2, 1967.

Marshall lives in an integrated Washington neighborhood with his second wife, Cecelia S. Suyat, and their two sons. His first wife was Vivian Burey, whom he married in 1929. She died in 1955.

MAURITANIA. See AFRICA.

McCARTHY, EUGENE JOSEPH (1916-), U.S. senator from Minnesota and critic of U.S. policy on Vietnam, announced Nov. 30, 1967, that he would enter several Democratic presidential primaries in 1968. McCarthy said he was "concerned that the administration seems to have set no limit to the price which it is willing to pay for a military victory" in Vietnam. McCarthy said his name would be listed in primaries in California, Massachusetts, Nebraska, Oregon, and Wisconsin. He opened his campaign at the Conference of Concerned Democrats in Chicago early in December.

McCarthy began his political career in 1947 when he aided Hubert H. Humphrey, now Vice-President, and Orville L. Freeman, now Secretary of Agriculture, in fighting Communist influence in Minnesota's Democratic-Farmer-Labor party. In 1948, McCarthy was elected to the House of Representatives and, in 1958, to the Senate. He has served on the Finance and Foreign Relations committees.

McCarthy, born at Watkins, Minn., was graduated from St. John's University at Collegeville, Minn., in 1935, and received an M.A. degree from the University of Minnesota in 1939. He saw civilian service in military intelligence during World War II and has taught in high school and college. McCarthy, known for his liberal views, has written several books, including *A Liberal Answer to the Conservative Challenge* (1964). [WALTER F. MORSE]

MEDICARE, the program of health care for persons age 65 and older, entered its second year of operation in 1967. The first 12 months – July 1, 1966, to June 30, 1967 – showed impressive accomplishments and highlighted serious problems in administration. Robert M. Ball, commissioner of Social Security, listed the following accomplishments:

- Older persons received from 15 per cent to 20 per cent more in-patient hospital service.
- There were over 5,000,000 admissions – involving 4,000,000 persons – for in-patient hospital care. This cost $2,400,000,000.
- More than $60,000,000 was paid for extended-care services for 200,000 persons.
- About $13,000,000 was paid for home health agency services for 200,000 persons.
- Some $12,000,000 was paid to hospitals for out-patient diagnostic and therapeutic services.
- About $640,000,000 was paid under the voluntary medical insurance program, of which 90 per cent was for physicians' services.

Medicare's civil rights requirements opened up many previously segregated hospitals and nursing homes. In many communities, minority groups had high-quality care for the first time.

Ball also identified two problem areas. The first was the delay in payment to doctors, hospitals, and patients. This was caused by the size and complexity of the program and by unnecessarily complicated procedures. By the end of the first year, however, corrective steps had reduced the processing of claims to an average of less than 21 days.

The second problem was caused by unwillingness on the part of some physicians to cooperate with the program. Under the present law, when a physician accepts Medicare assignments, he agrees to accept as full payment the reasonable charge determined by the insurance policy. About 57 per cent of the physicians were accepting assignments at least part of the time. The remaining 43 per cent refused to accept assignments from their Medicare patients under any circumstances. In some instances, the patient had to borrow money to pay the physician before being reimbursed.

Legislation was approved by Congress in 1967 to deal with this aspect of Medicare as well as with the complaint from doctors about an excess amount of paperwork. Under the new law, patients can submit itemized but unpaid bills to the government when their doctors decline to submit the bills themselves. To reduce paperwork, the new legislation eliminates the requirement that doctors must sign a certificate of necessity every time a Medicare patient is admitted to a hospital.

Other provisions of the 1967 Medicare amendments include the following:

- Each Medicare beneficiary will have a lifetime reserve of 60 extra days of hospital care beyond the 90 days now allowed for each illness. The patient will have to pay $20 of the cost for each of the additional 60 days.
- Reasonable charges for the services of radiologists and pathologists to in-hospital patients will be paid in full by the government.

Medicaid programs were established by 38 states by the end of 1967. Formerly, the states determined how much income a family could earn and still qualify as "medically indigent," with the federal government matching on a sliding scale the amount paid by the states. But, members of Congress concluded that the programs in some states went beyond what was intended when the Medicaid program was started. They adopted legislation that established maximum income levels.

Effective July 1, 1968, the federal government will pay no medical costs for a person earning more than 150 per cent of the income level that qualifies a person for cash public assistance in his state. In 1969, the income limit will drop to 140 per cent, and, in 1970, to 133 1/3 per cent, the permanent ceiling. States without Medicaid programs will use the 133 1/3 per cent ceiling when they begin the program.

New legislation passed in 1967 also requires that states place Medicaid patients only in nursing homes that meet fully adequate standards relating to environment, housekeeping, fire protection, and sanitation. [JOSEPH P. ANDERSON]

MEDICINE. The world's first successful human heart transplant occurred on Dec. 3, 1967, at Cape Town, South Africa. The five-hour operation was performed by a team of 30 surgeons, anesthesiologists, technicians, and nurses under the direction of Dr. Christian N. Barnard. The surgeons removed the heart of a young woman who died after an automobile crash and placed it in the chest of a 55-year-old man dying because his own heart was damaged. The transplanted heart functioned surprisingly well until December 21, when the patient, Louis Washkansky, died of pneumonia.

Physicians around the world hailed the achievement. The doctors had been able to overcome the crucial problem of the body's natural tendency to reject foreign tissue by the use of cobalt rays. Drugs prevented blood clots from developing.

The first known heart transplant attempt took place almost four years before, when surgeons at the University of Mississippi Medical Center in Jackson, Miss., transplanted the heart of a large chimpanzee into the body of a man dying of heart disease. The procedure failed primarily because the heart was not large enough to support the recipient. In 1966, Dr. Michael E. DeBakey of Houston, Tex., and Dr. Adrian Kantrowitz of New York City had installed artificial devices in human patients to assist the normal operation of their hearts.

Cholesterol Study. Researchers attending the annual meeting of the American Medical Association at Atlantic City, N.J., in June, proposed a massive study to determine once and for all whether the extraordinarily high death rate from heart disease is linked to the fats in the average American's diet. The proposed study would be one of the largest medical experiments ever attempted. It would cost $30,000,000 to $50,000,000, involve as many as 68,000 middle-aged American men, and last at least five years. A special committee was appointed to work out details for this cholesterol study.

Cancer. Although researchers are not optimistic about progress in the battle against cancer, there were advances, in 1967, in treatment by drug therapy, stimulation of natural body defenses, radiation, and surgery. Lung cancer, however, which is the principal cancer killer of males, was seen as an enduring health hazard by Dr. Kenneth M. Endicott, director of the National Cancer Institute, Bethesda, Md. While naming the members of a presidential Lung Cancer Task Force on August 17, Dr. Endicott noted that 50,000 Americans die from the disease each year. He also commented that 70 to 80 per cent of lung cancer could be eliminated if people would quit smoking, but he doubted this would happen.

Leukemia Treatment. A new drug, called L-asparaginase, is attracting wide interest. Used in

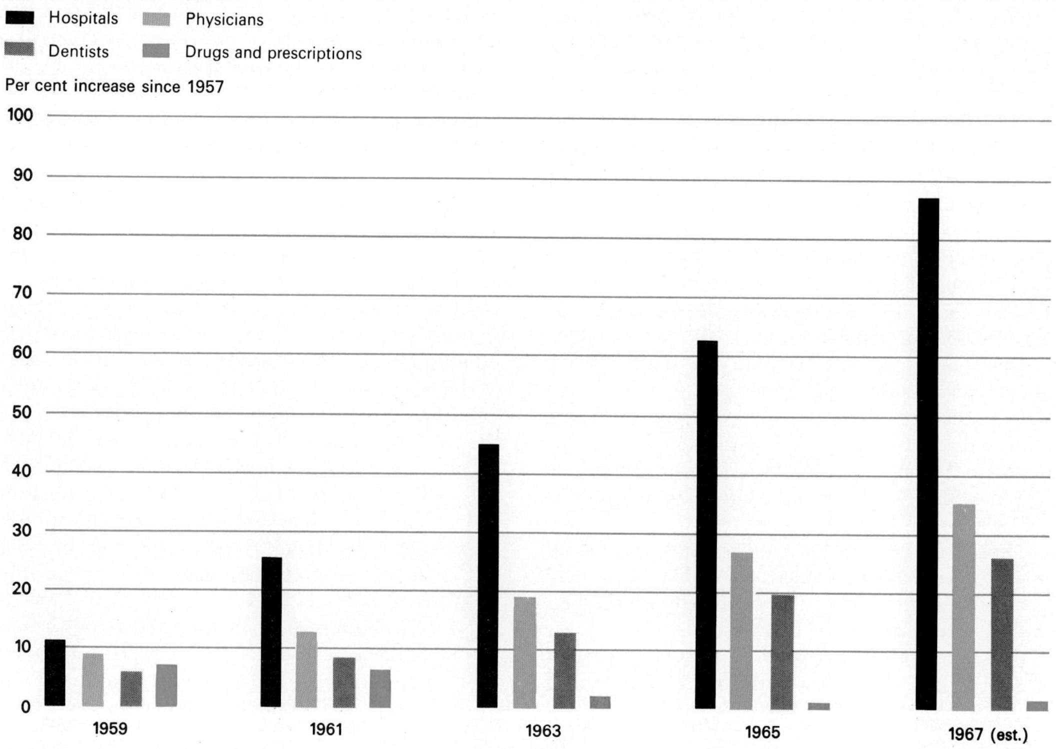

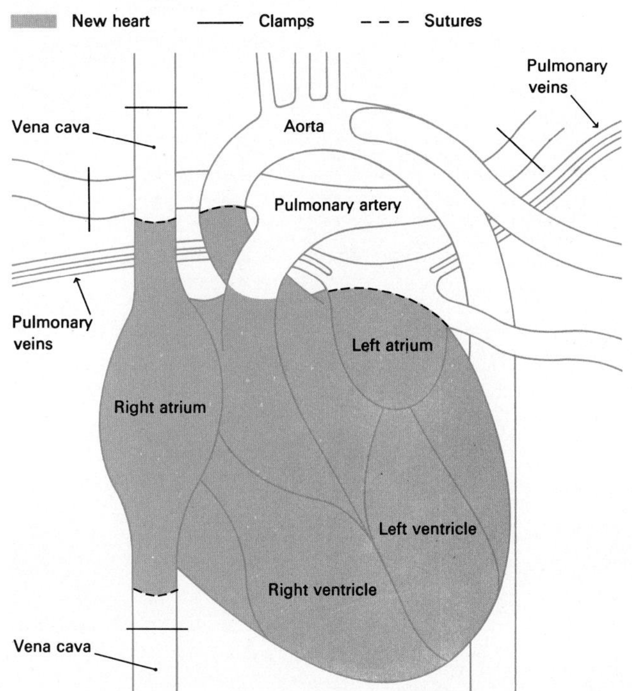

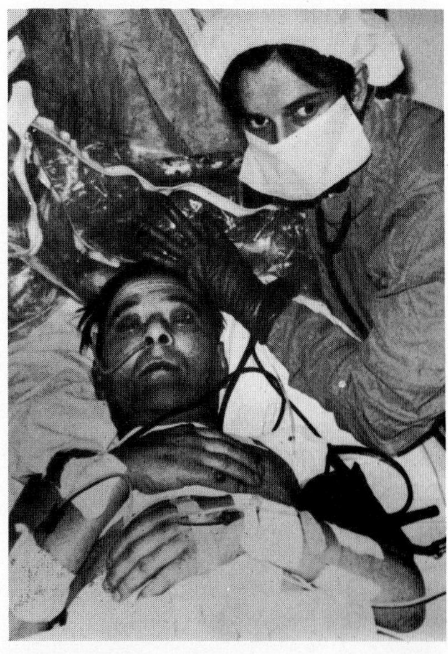

First successful heart transplant was performed in South Africa on Dec. 3, 1967. Diagram indicates how organ was attached to body. Nurse, *above*, checks patient.

mice, it appears to be highly effective against leukemia, and is active against the malignant cells only. Other antileukemia drugs attack not just leukemic cells but all cells, and this severely limits their use. Use of the drug for human leukemia victims will not be started until experiments have been completed to determine whether the drug has any serious side effects. The initial study was conducted at the University of Illinois Medical Center in Chicago.

In April, Dr. James T. Grace, Jr., director of Rosewell Park Memorial Institute, reported that he had found a fragment from the genetic machinery of living cells that has proved to be a powerful antagonist to one kind of human cancer tissue, myelocytic leukemia. The compound seems to embody a new principle in the drug treatment of cancers–that of affecting the basic control mechanisms of the cancer cells. Most anticancer drugs act by selectively poisoning cancer cells, and scientists have for years sought some means which might instead regulate their disorderly growth.

The substance has been found in the ribonucleic acid of calf liver, chick embryo, human cancer cells, peas, spinach, and yeast cells. Its chemical name is N6 (delta 2 isopentenyl) adenosine, usually abbreviated IPA. In plants it is a powerful stimulator of growth and development. In animal cells it may have the same effect, and thus prove to be of help in restraining the growth of cancer cells.

Treating Brain Damage. Glenn Doman, a physiotherapist, and Carl Delacato, a reading therapist, have reported notable success in treating persons with brain damage at their Institutes for the Achievement of Human Potential in Philadelphia, Pa. Established in 1955, the institutes' work has been based on the theory that the development of different functions of movement, speech, and higher faculties is related to successively higher centers of the brain. Brain injury at any of these levels, according to the theory, will impair performance at a higher brain level. Thus their treatment for children who are slow readers begins with crawling exercises and moves on to increasingly involved exercises.

The institutes' claims for success were questioned by some researchers in 1967. Writing in the *Journal of the American Medical Association*, Dr. Roger D. Freeman of Temple University Medical School noted that "many physicians observed children with severe brain damage who have achieved partial or apparently complete recoveries of function without either conventional physical therapy or the methods of the institutes." In another article in the same publication, Dr. Melvyn Robbins of the University of Toronto presented findings of a controlled study that showed the reading skill of a group of second-graders had no relationship whatsoever to their ability to crawl or creep. [THEODORE F. TREUTING]

See also BIOCHEMISTRY; DENTISTRY; HOSPITAL.

Bronze statue of Pope John XXIII is viewed by Italian villagers on its way to Sotto il Monte, boyhood home of the late pontiff revered as "John the Good."

MEMORIALS dedicated or announced in 1967 included the following:

Adlai Stevenson Institute of International Affairs opened its headquarters in Robie House, 5757 South Woodlawn Avenue, Chicago, on February 5. It was the 67th anniversary of the birth of the late United Nations ambassador. Adlai E. Stevenson served as U.S. Permanent Representative to the United Nations from January, 1961, until his death in London on July 14, 1965.

Auschwitz Memorial was dedicated on April 16. The monument, consisting of a series of granite stones, was designed by Polish and Italian sculptors. It is a memorial to Europeans, most of them Jews, who were destroyed in the gas chambers or starved to death at the Birkenau camp, Auschwitz (now Oswiecim, Poland). Plaques at the foot of the monument are inscribed in 18 languages as follows; "Four million people suffered at the hands of the Nazi murderers between the years 1940 and 1945."

Dachau Memorial was dedicated on May 7 to the Jewish victims who died or were executed at the first major Nazi concentration camp, established in 1933 near Dachau, Germany. A *Menorah* (ceremonial candelabra) is the only decoration on the memorial of rough stone. It was placed at the peak of the vault's slanted roof. More than 3,500 inmates underwent brutal medical experiments at Dachau. Many of them died. Thousands of others were executed, or died of diseases. Surviving inmates were freed by American forces on April 29, 1945.

Jan Sibelius Monument was unveiled on September 7 in Sibelius Park, Helsinki, in memory of Finland's famous composer. The 28-ton abstract sculpture is the work of Eila Hiltunen. It consists of 580 stainless steel pipes of varying lengths, decorated with rough high relief and grouped together at various lofty heights. Back of the monument are trees. Sibelius, remembered especially for his symphonies and tonal poems, died on Sept. 20, 1957.

John F. Kennedy Memorial was dedicated in Argentina on May 29, the 50th anniversary of his birth. The granite and marble monument stands at a crossroads near the village of Quemu Quemu in La Pampa province. The marble rectangle, 130 by 40 by 15 feet, has a triangular opening in the center, and rests on a black granite base. A marble triangle, the same size and shape as the opening in the rectangular section, rests horizontally across the base of the triangular opening. The memorial was designed by the Uruguayan architect and artist, Lincoln Presno.

Sir Winston Churchill Forest was dedicated in Israel on April 6 by the British statesman's son, Randolph S. Churchill. Some 300,000 trees have already been planted on historic Mount Kesalot, overlooking the valley of Jezreel in northern Israel. Most of the Churchill Forest has been planted with the Jerusalem pine. It is one of the few kinds of trees that grows well in that particular area.

Theodore Roosevelt Memorial on Theodore Roosevelt Island in the Potomac River, District of Columbia, was dedicated by President Lyndon Johnson, Oct. 27. It was the 109th anniversary of the birth of the 26th President of the United States (1901-1909). The 17-foot bronze Roosevelt statue, executed by the late Paul Manship, stands in front of a 30-foot high granite shaft and overlooks an oval terrace. There is also an outer surrounding terrace. It has a circular promenade, and is encircled by a water moat. Eric Gugler designed the memorial. Four 21-foot high granite slabs in the outer terrace are inscribed with Roosevelt quotations.

See also CELEBRATIONS.

MENTAL HEALTH. Research into the problem of schizophrenia, a baffling disease that afflicts nearly 500,000 Americans and hospitalizes 250,000, led to an exciting development in 1967. Investigators at the Tulane University School of Medicine reported, in January, that they had amassed evidence that some cases of schizophrenia involve a disorder of the body's immune system. The disease in these cases results in the production of antibodies against the patient's brain. The work of the Tulane research team, headed by Robert G. Heath, is the result of 10 years of studies that have produced consistent findings. Other laboratories have since obtained similar results.

Heath, who is chairman of Tulane's department of psychiatry and neurology, had discovered 10 years earlier that a mysterious substance found in the blood of schizophrenics was capable of inducing schizophrenia-like symptoms when injected into monkeys and healthy human volunteers. The research he presented in January supported his theory that schizophrenia is an immunologic disorder involving that substance. He demonstrated that the substance is most likely an antibody that attacks the nerve cells in those parts of the brain thought to be involved in schizophrenic disturbances. His findings may lead to a treatment for schizophrenia.

Suicide. More than 20,000 suicide deaths are recorded in the United States each year, but the actual number is believed to be far greater since many suicides are covered up for social and insurance reasons. According to prevailing psychiatric opinion, many or most suicides can be prevented, if the warning signs are heeded, by the use of antidepressant drugs, psychiatric consultation and treatment, and close observation.

Leston L. Havens, a Harvard psychiatrist, told physicians in a January issue of the *New England Journal of Medicine* how to recognize the suicidal risk through a psychological evaluation. He pointed out that suicide is often associated with such crises as the loss of a job or a loved one, or a personal, social, or financial failure. In the suicidal patient, the depression that accompanies the crisis leaves him feeling helpless and hopeless, and without enough reason to go on living. Also in danger, Dr. Havens noted, are "depressed people who recover suddenly, without obvious reason, and who assume a calm and settled purposefulness. Not a few have decided to die."

Mental Retardation. Massachusetts has established, under legislation enacted in August, 1966, a program that provides clinical nursery schools for mentally handicapped children from three to seven years of age. Begun as a volunteer effort by parent groups more than 10 years ago, the program now serves 440 children in 26 clinics throughout the state. [THEODORE F. TREUTING]

See also HANDICAPPED, THE; PSYCHOLOGY.

MERRICK, DAVID (1911-   ), is considered by many to be the most successful theatrical producer in the United States since David Belasco and Florenz Ziegfeld. In 1967, his production of *Hello, Dolly!* with an all-Negro cast was the smash hit of the season.

Merrick was born in St. Louis, Mo., the youngest of seven children. His parents were immigrants from Poland, and his name was David Margulois in those days. While in high school he fell under the spell of the theater and decided to make a career of it. He studied for a law degree, however, at Washington University in St. Louis. After he married Lenore Beck, he moved to New York in 1939 and began to produce plays. His first big success was *Fanny*, which he presented in 1954.

Major plays he produced were: *The Matchmaker* (1955), *Romanoff and Juliet* (1957), *Becket* (1960), *Oliver* (1962), *Stop the World–I Want to Get Off* (1962), and *Hello, Dolly!* (1963).

Merrick is noted for his tremendous drive. He not only manages the overall theatrical effect of each production, but also watches every tiny detail, from the footlight microphones to peeling paint on the sets. He even takes elaborate taxi tours of the city to inspect the billboard notices of a show. His publicity campaigns have made public relations history, and his running battles with the New York drama critics have enlivened newspaper pages for years.

METALLURGY. A new high-strength steel alloy was announced in 1967. It possesses extraordinary properties obtained by simple variations of steelmaking processes. Called TRIP (for Transformation-Induced Plasticity) steel, the alloy can be stretched from two to five times as much as earlier steel.

TRIP steels also are "self-healing." When a defect in the crystal structure of the steel permits a fracture to start forming because of stress, the TRIP steel will undergo a chemical reaction at the atomic level that blunts, halts, and fills the fracture. TRIP properties are obtained by subjecting the steel to deformation processes when it is heated to between 400° and 1200° F. TRIP steels remain ductile at pressures as high as 300,000 pounds per square inch. They were developed at the University of California's Lawrence Radiation Laboratory.

Basic research also resulted in a new metal-coating technique, developed at the General Electric Company's Research and Development Center. Called "metalliding," the process involves electrolytic deposition of a wide range of metals into the surface of a metal so that an alloy is formed. Metalliding units operate with an electrolyte of molten fluoride salts. The fluorides dissolve all oxides from the substrate metal and in this way ensure uniform coating. [JAMES A. PEARRE]

See also MINES AND MINING; STEEL INDUSTRY.

METEOROLOGY. See WEATHER.

MEXICO experienced unprecedented prosperity in 1967. The economy, as of the beginning of September, was growing at an annual rate of 7.5 per cent, which was similar to that of 1966. New construction was at record levels, due in part to the new hotels and motels being built in preparation for an influx of tourists expected for the 1968 Olympic Games in Mexico City. Work had also begun on the building of a $200,000,000 subway system for Mexico City, the capital.

Top Production Achieved. Bumper crops in corn, tomatoes, and wheat were forecast for the year. General manufacturing activity in the first quarter was strong, with most of the basic industries operating at virtually top capacity. Indications were that for the year as a whole manufacturing probably would be up at least 12 per cent, compared to an 11 per cent growth in 1966. In order to encourage higher-quality output, the government indicated it would reduce its high-duty protection for those manufacturers who were producing low-quality goods and selling them at high prices. Mexico was under heavy and immediate pressure to provide jobs for one of the fastest rising populations in the world, a 3.5 per cent growth rate a year. To keep up with population growth, it was estimated that the republic would have to create 500,000 new jobs a year for the next 10 years.

Presidential Message. President Gustavo Díaz Ordaz, in his third annual report to the nation on Sept. 1, 1967, coupled economic conservatism with revolutionary fervor. He indicated acceptance of public dissent, but intolerance for disorder. He opposed intervention in the affairs of other nations, and rejected intervention in Mexican life "from wherever it may come."

Behind the president's words were the same solid factors: (1) the stability of the peso was at a record high in recent years; (2) the Bank of Mexico's total reserves were at $1,179,000,000, representing gold and U.S. dollar holdings of $589,000,000 and standby and secondary lines of credit of $590,000,000; (3) government and private investments were at their highest levels in history, public projects alone initiated in the year involving $1,760,000,000; and (4) the republic's international credit standing was in highest esteem, primarily because of the nation's ability to finance about 90 per cent of its total investment needs from its own resources.

Internal Unrest. A rash of disturbances occurred during the year. In mid-May, the army was forced to take control of Sonora state following three days of violence which included gun battles between police and university students over the latter's opposition to the ruling political party's nominee for state governor. The nominee won anyway. In July, Mex-

A polished obelisk, unveiled at El Paso, Tex., by President Lyndon B. Johnson and Mexico's President Gustavo Días Ordaz, marks the new U.S.-Mexican border.

The campus of Mexico's famous university city form the backdrop for the 80,000-seat stadium in which the 1968 Olympic Games will be held in October.

ican agents smashed a Communist plot assertedly financed by Communist China. At least 13 persons were arrested and 20 tons of books, films, and printed materials were confiscated. A gunfight, in August, between rival factions of a copra growers union in Acapulco resulted in 32 deaths.

Prospects were bright for sulfur producers, as a world shortage grew more acute. Total output was estimated at over 2,000,000 tons, up from 1,670,000 in 1966. It represented about $100,000,000 in export sales. At least 12 Mexican-foreign venture companies tried to find deposits in the Isthmus of Tehuantepec. Mexican interests bought a 66 per cent interest in Azufrera Panamericana, the nation's biggest producer, for about $75,500,000.

Border Changed. On October 28, President Díaz Ordaz and U.S. President Lyndon B. Johnson met on the Mexican border to participate in ceremonies marking the formal transfer between the two countries of a strip of land, known as El Chamizal, along the Rio Grande. Mexico's net gain was 437 acres. The transfer marked the end of a land dispute that had begun shortly after 1848 when the Rio Grande had shifted its course. [MARY C. WEBSTER]

Facts in Brief. Population: 45,012,000. Government: President Gustavo Díaz Ordaz. Monetary Unit: peso (12.49=U.S. $1). Foreign Trade: exports, $1,228,000,000; imports, $1,605,000,000. Principal Exports: cotton, coffee, maize, sugar.

MICHENER, DANIEL ROLAND (1900-), Canadian high commissioner to India since 1964, was appointed Governor-General of Canada by Queen Elizabeth II on April 4, 1967. The post, as the personal representative of the Queen, has long been chiefly ceremonial. Indeed, many Canadian leaders and newspapers believe the governor-generalship has become obsolete with Canada's increasing independence from Great Britain. There have been 20 governors-general since the confederation of Canada 100 years ago, but Michener was only the third to be Canadian-born. He succeeded Major General Georges Philias Vanier, who died on March 5. See CANADA; DEATHS OF NOTABLE PERSONS.

Michener was born on April 19, 1900, at Lacombe, Alta. At the University of Alberta he won a Rhodes scholarship to Oxford University in England. He went on to study law at the Middle Temple, London, and, after serving in the Royal Air Force, practiced law in Toronto, Ont. Michener was a Progressive Conservative party member of the Canadian House of Commons from 1953 to 1962, serving two terms as speaker. He was respected for his impartiality and constant good humor, qualities that should serve him well in smoothing difficulties between French and English Canadians.

The new governor-general is a lifelong friend of Prime Minister Lester B. Pearson. He and his wife Norah have three daughters. [WALTER F. MORSE]

MIDDLE EAST

The third major clash of arms since Israel achieved its independence in 1948 erupted on June 5 between the Arab states and Israel. Heavily outnumbered, the citizen-soldiers of Israel again scored a swift military triumph, even more crushing than before. But stability in the Middle East seemed as improbable at the year's end as at its beginning.

Although a steady escalation of Arab attacks and Israeli reprisals triggered the war, the roots of the crisis lay, as before, in the Arab refusal to accept Israel's existence on the soil of Palestine.

The Mounting Tension was described by United Nations (UN) Secretary-General U Thant as the most menacing since the war of 1956. In April, harassment of Israeli farmers by Syrian artillery on the heights above Galilee–Syria claimed the farmers were violating the armistice line–provoked massive retaliation by Israel; six Syrian MIGs were shot down on April 7. Terrorism by Arab guerrillas and increasingly frequent incidents on the Syrian border caused Israeli Prime Minister Levi Eshkol to partially mobilize the armed forces in May, purportedly for the parade honoring the 19th anniversary of Israel's independence. On May 11, Israel stated it held Syria responsible for the border raids, and that it was ready to defend itself.

President Gamal Abdel Nasser of the United Arab Republic (U.A.R.), bound by a treaty to support Syria and informed that the signs pointed to an imminent Israeli attack, ordered his armies on a state of alert. Nasser demanded on May 18 that the 3,400-man UN Emergency Force (UNEF) withdraw from the Gaza Strip and Sinai Peninsula, in view of the danger of war. Unexpectedly, U Thant agreed.

With the withdrawal of the UNEF forces, U.A.R. troops occupied Sharm el-Sheikh and, on May 22, unilaterally closed the Gulf of Aqaba to Israeli or Israel-bound ships. The closure was called an act of war by Israeli Prime Minister Eshkol. U Thant, in Cairo, warned Nasser of the danger of his move.

The UN Security Council rushed into emergency session on May 24, but the UN–as it was to be throughout the crisis–found itself powerless to act. A new U.S. ambassador, Richard Nolte, arrived in Cairo on May 26 and urged the restoration of UNEF and the reopening of the gulf. But Nasser declared the Strait of Tiran was U.A.R. territory.

On May 29, the U.A.R. national assembly gave Nasser emergency powers to rule by decree. He

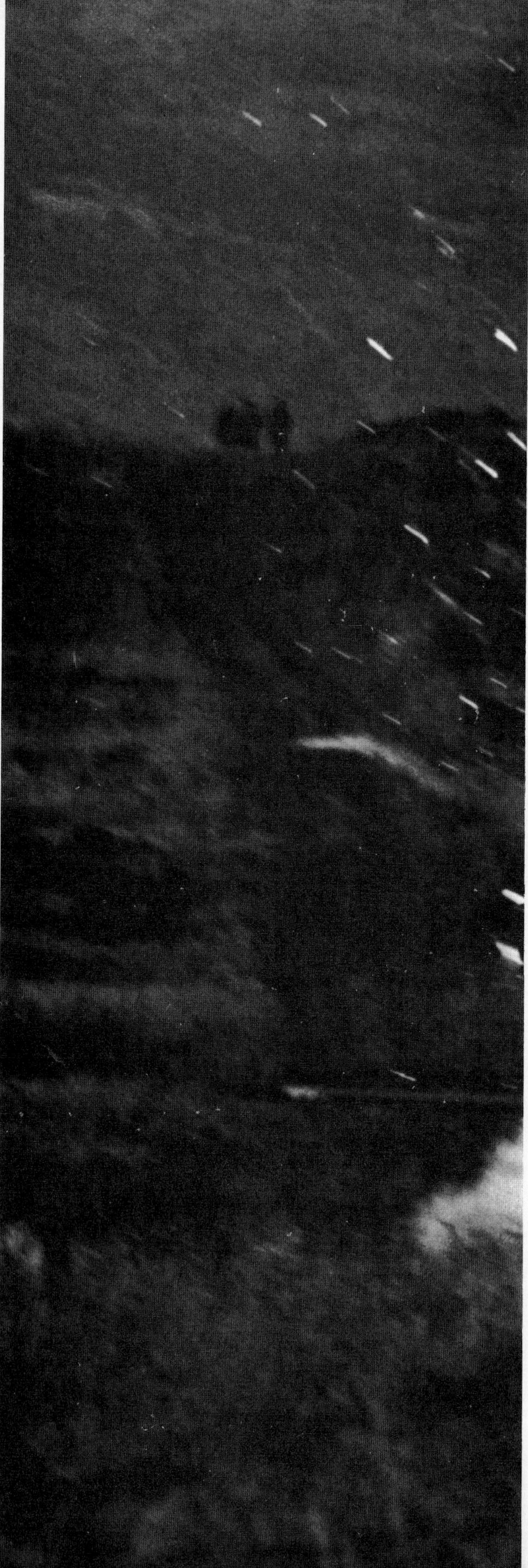

A Syrian tank caught a searing phosphorus shell during the Israeli charge up the Syrian heights that climaxed the six-day victory over the Arabs.

Civilians in May, a well-trained legion in June, Israel's soldiers chased Arab armies down the Gaza Strip, and toward the Suez Canal.

signed a mutual defense treaty with Jordan the next day, closing the ring around Israel. Turkey agreed to allow passage of Soviet warships through the Dardanelles. The scene was set for war.

Pre-Emptive Thrusts. Even as the Arab armies went on the alert, Israel fully mobilized. General Moshe Dayan, hero of Suez in 1956, returned to the cabinet as minister of defense (see DAYAN, MOSHE). On June 5, as the UN futilely struggled to preserve peace, Israel launched a lightning "preventive attack." In the first hours, Israeli planes bombed and strafed airfields in Iraq, Jordan, Syria, and the U.A.R. The Arab air forces were caught on the ground; more than 300 aircraft were destroyed.

Lacking air support, the Arab armies were quickly beaten. By June 8, Israeli ground forces had occupied Arab Jerusalem, the Gaza Strip, Sinai, the west bank of the River Jordan, and had opened the Gulf of Aqaba. Jordanian and U.A.R. ground forces had suffered catastrophic losses of men and equipment. Hostilities temporarily ceased on June 10, when both sides accepted a UN cease-fire, but only hours later, Israel attacked and seized the Syrian heights, where the trouble had started.

Israel's clear-cut military superiority was of slight value, however, in bringing the Arabs to the conference table or in achieving a permanent settlement. World-wide support for a tiny country fighting for its life gradually cooled as the Israeli occupation of Arab land assumed a permanent look. Israel unilaterally annexed Arab Jerusalem on June 28. In its determination to preserve its gains until the Arabs agreed to recognize Israel and begin direct negotiations, Israel rejected third-power proposals for mediation. Israel's banking systems, currency, laws, and taxes, even its teachers and textbooks, were introduced in the occupied territories.

Israeli Intransigence and Arab bitterness over defeat blocked effective action by emergency sessions of the UN Security Council. An emergency session of the General Assembly met on June 19. In mid-July, the UN sent truce observers led by General Odd Bull of Norway to the Suez Canal area after intermittent artillery duels across the waterway had broken the cease-fire. The General Assembly session closed on July 21 with but one resolution, the censure of Israel, 99-0, with 20 abstentions, for its annexation of Arab Jerusalem. See UNITED NATIONS.

Other than a tacit agreement between the United States and Russia to keep the conflict localized, the major powers neither displayed cooperation nor produced positive policies that might lead to a settlement. Although Israeli planes attacked the U.S. communications ship *Liberty* during the fighting and President Lyndon B. Johnson declared strict neutrality, the Arabs identified American and Israeli interests as synonymous. France's pro-Arab stand baffled Israel and many European countries but it pleased some of the Arab nations.

Background To the Six-Day War

The flash war that brought victory to Israel and disarray to the Arab world in June was sparked by a number of immediate, easily identifiable incidents. Commando-executed border raids and retaliatory attacks, aggressive statements and belligerent replies, and, finally, a sea blockade were all contributing factors. Fundamentally, however, the war sprang from a dispute, rooted in history, involving the ownership of a piece of land about the size of the state of New Jersey. That piece of land is known today as the State of Israel.

To the Arabs, who believe the land occupied by Israel belongs to them, the State of Israel is a fiction created out of former Arab territory by the Western powers. To recover it, they swore to destroy the Jewish state.

For the Jews, however, Israel is not only a state but a state of mind. For them, modern Israel is the fulfillment of a struggle that has pitted the Jew against the world at large, and the Arabs in particular, for centuries. It is the Biblical land of the Old Testament to which the Hebrew patriarch Abraham and his tribes were given divine title after they crossed the Arabian Desert from Mesopotamia in about 1900 B.C. It is the promised land toward which the prophet Moses led the Hebrews in the 1200's B.C. after their sojourn in Egypt.

Title to the land has indeed become clouded through the centuries. For hundreds of years after Moses brought the children of Israel home, it was the land of Zion, Judea, the homeland of the Jews. Then, in 721 B.C., Israel was conquered by the Assyrian Empire. In 165 B.C., the Greek rulers of Syria marched in. Roman legions cast their mailed shadows across the land in 63 B.C. But even when the Roman rulers expelled the Jews from Jerusalem in A.D. 135, the latter continued to look upon the land as rightfully theirs.

The Jews' claim to title, already grown murky, became even murkier as conqueror after conqueror took over. In succeeding centuries, the land that the Romans renamed Syria Palestina was overrun by the Arabs–fresh and zealous converts to Islam. Then Palestine–as it came to be called–together with other Arab provinces fell to the Seljuk Turks. Later, the Turks lost most of Palestine to the Crusaders, who came to free the Holy Land from the Moslems. The Crusaders were in turn driven out by the Mamelukes of Egypt. In 1517, Palestine was conquered by the Ottoman Turks.

For the next few centuries, Palestine was mostly in the hands of the Moslems; by the 1800s, only a comparative handful of poverty-stricken Jews hung on in a homeland that had been passed from Assyrian, Greek, and Roman rulers to Arabic, European, and Turkish rule.

In the late 19th century, however, the Jews began to look homeward. The immediate catalysts were the bloody, anti-Semitic pogroms in Czarist Russia and Poland during which the Jews were expelled from their ghettos. The hardier ones, to escape their persecutors, headed back to Palestine, their ancestral home. There, supported by money from the French branch of the Rothschild family and the World Zionist Organization, these early Jewish pioneers bought land from the Turks, organized themselves into kibbutzim, and began planning the revival of a Jewish nation located in what was to them their patrimony. The dream was encouraged by Theodor Herzl of Vienna who had founded modern Zionism at an international conference held at Basel, Switzerland, in 1897.

By 1914, there were nearly 90,000 Jews in Palestine. Their dream, however, of creating a Jewish homeland, was to prove an elusive one as World War I again turned Palestine into a battlefield. The gloom of the war was relieved, for the Jews, only by a statement the British government issued in 1917 favoring the establishment of a Jewish national homeland in Palestine. That statement, prompted by a British scientist-statesman named Chaim Weizmann, became known as the Balfour Declaration.

The British government was thus committed to honor the Balfour Declaration when the British forces in the Middle East drove out the Turks and occupied Palestine in 1918. Subsequently, the newly established

Background To the Six-Day War

Continued

League of Nations ratified the declaration; in 1922, it appointed the British to rule the country as a league mandate. The British government in turn appointed members of the Zionist movement to act as its advisers.

Statehood for the Jews, however, was still far from a reality. The British had promised Palestine to the Arabs in 1915. They had promised it to the Jews in 1917. Now they appeared unable to make a decision in favor of either.

In 1936, the Arabs in Palestine grew restive as Jewish immigrants continued to pour into the country. Determined to stop the inflow, and infected at the same time by an up-surge of pan-Arabism, the Palestinian Arabs resorted to guerrilla tactics to harass the Jews. Under increasing pressure, the British in 1939 yielded in a large measure to Arab demands; they agreed to ban further Jewish immigration. The Arabs were mollified; the Jews, however, bitterly resentful of what they considered the end of their hopes for a national home, adamantly opposed Britain's policy. Many Jewish immigrants were brought in illegally and trouble between the Jews and British grew steadily worse.

It was World War II and the Nazi persecution of the European Jews that swung the pendulum of world opinion in favor of the Jews. Appalled by the horrors of Dachau, of Belsen, and of Buchenwald, the Western world shuddered–and took up the Jewish cause as its own. When thousands of displaced Jews began flooding into Palestine illegally, in defiance of the British ban on immigration, the world looked the other way. But as illegal immigration increased, trouble between the British and the Jewish terrorists who were determined to establish a homeland in Palestine became steadily worse.

By 1947, the British administration had reached the limits of its endurance. Despairing of untangling the situation, the British turned the Palestine problem over to the United Nations (UN). Ten weeks after it had been given the problem, the UN General Assembly voted to partition the land into two independent states, a Jewish state and an Arab state. It also decided that the city of Jerusalem should be internationalized. The Jews were jubilant; the Arabs dour and determined to resist. At 4 o'clock on the afternoon of May 14, 1948, David Ben-Gurion read a 979-word pronouncement declaring Israel an independent Jewish state.

The Arabs, however, refusing to accept the partition, reacted immediately and violently. Charging that the Jews had usurped Arab land, Egypt, Iraq, Saudi Arabia, Lebanon, Syria, and Transjordan (now Jordan) and Yemen, who had formed an Arab League in 1945, invaded Israel.

A spirited conflict ensued and it was not until the end of 1948 that the United Nations was able to end most of the fighting. Early in 1949, Israel signed a series of armistice agreements with four Arab nations, Egypt, Lebanon, Syria, and Transjordan.

With the war won, Israel settled down to reap the fruits of its victory. Bolstered by massive aid from the United States, private donations from abroad, and, in time, reparations from the Federal Republic of (West) Germany, the nation soon became a modern-day miracle. Steel and concrete cities, such as Tel Aviv-Yafo, were built where once were only antiquated buildings. Ports and harbors were dredged. Telegraph and telephone communications lines began to crisscross the land.

The land itself became a miracle of 20th century ingenuity. Power and irrigation plants sprang up. New agricultural methods were introduced–mechanized equipment, chemical fertilizers, crop rotation, experimental seeds, collective farms and villages–and the results were incredible: the desert literally bloomed again.

Seldom, if ever before, in history, had a people worked with such energy to build a modern industrial nation on the ruins of the past.

The war that had supposedly ended, however, remained very much alive beneath the surface and in the years between 1949 and 1967 it repeatedly broke out along Israel's borders and the neighboring Arab states until, in June, it exploded into a full-scale war that shook the world. [Paul Tullier]

War in the Middle East– June, 1967

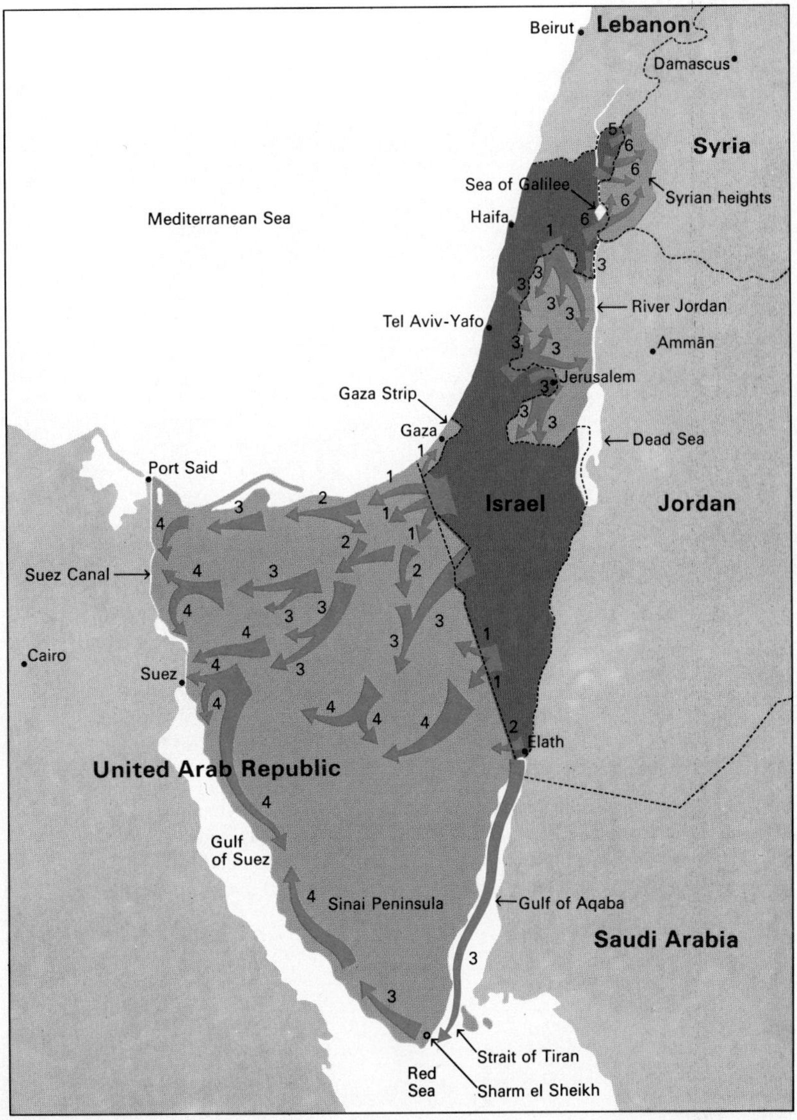

The big gains were scored by the Soviet Union. Russia sought to brand Israel as the aggressor and force it to pay indemnities. Soviet warships entered the eastern Mediterranean Sea in force and visited Alexandria, Egypt, even as renewed fighting broke out along the Suez Canal. The most startling evidence of Soviet support for the Arabs was the sinking of the Israeli destroyer *Elath* by a U.A.R. patrol boat using the new Soviet Styx missile. By October, Russia had replaced 80 per cent of the U.A.R. military equipment destroyed in the war. The United States, on the other hand, offered a five-point peace plan based on territorial integrity for all states, rights of innocent maritime passage, and an end to the arms race.

War's Aftermath. The festering refugee problem worsened after the war as 120,000 refugees fled into Jordan. Israel agreed to allow some to return, but an August cut-off date and Israel's stiff requirements for proof of status limited the returnees to about 12,-000. The United Nations Relief and Rehabilitation Administration continued to administer the refugee program, but anticipated a $4,000,000 deficit.

The Arabs had united briefly against Israel, but their defeat revealed not only their military weakness but also the continuing differences in the Arab world over domestic as well as foreign policy. Algeria, Iraq, Morocco, and Tunisia offered troops, but took no actual part in the war. There were severe anti-Jewish riots in Tripoli and Tunis, and these

Hubert Le Campion, *Life* © Time Inc.

In the first hours of the June war, a group of dazed and uncomprehending Arab prisoners stared up at their Israeli captors, *above*. Barely five days later, the vanguard of Israel's Sinai army had dashed across the desert and reached the Suez Canal, *below*. There they stopped, though they met little resistance.

What were supersonic MIG-21s lie in ashes—a scene repeated a hundredfold—after lightning Israeli air strikes on June 5 annihilated Arab air power.

also turned on U.S. and British property. The Arab summit conference in Khartoum, Sudan, early in August produced no common postwar policy against Israel. In private statements, Nasser and King Hussein I of Jordan expressed willingness to negotiate through a third power even as Algeria's President Houari Boumedienne called for a Muslim holy war of extermination. Nor could the Arabs follow through with their promised oil embargo; a ban on exports to the West would have involved too great a financial sacrifice.

One positive result of the Khartoum conference was a pact between Nasser and King Faisal of Saudi Arabia to settle the civil war in Yemen. Hopes for peace were imperiled, however, after the overthrow of President Abdullah al-Sallal, when fighting began again between the nationalist groups. Similarly, rival Arab nationalists in Aden, which agreed in September to cease fire and discuss a future government, began fighting again in November when Britain announced that its troops would withdraw by the end of the month (see GREAT BRITAIN). Instability remained the one consistent factor in Arab politics. [WILLIAM SPENCER]

See also IRAQ; ISRAEL; JORDAN; LEBANON; SOUTH ARABIA, FEDERATION OF; UNITED ARAB REPUBLIC (U.A.R.); YEMEN; and articles on related countries.

MINERALOGY. See GEOLOGY; METALLURGY; MINES AND MINING.

MINES AND MINING entered the Nuclear Age on Dec. 10, 1967, with the successful detonation of a nuclear device about a mile underground at Farmington, N. Mex. The blast was expected to free large quantities of natural gas from rock formations too dense to be tapped by normal drilling. Called Operation Gasbuggy, it was a joint experiment conducted by the El Paso Natural Gas Company, the Atomic Energy Commission, and the U.S. Bureau of Mines.

Although results will not be known until well into 1968, Gasbuggy was expected to revolutionize the mining industry. Kennecott Copper Corporation announced the possibility of using nuclear explosions to double the U.S. supply of copper. Major oil companies predicted that hydrogen blasting would eventually become the economical way to recover the estimated $3,500,000,000,000 store of oil in oil shale beds of the Rocky Mountains.

Major Discoveries of nickel and copper in West Australia helped offset a decrease in the country's agricultural exports, down because of a prolonged drought. A mining boom in Ireland more than quadrupled the $20,000,000 export of metal ores in 1965. The "sulfur rush of 1967" in Mexico, on the Texas Gulf coast, and in Ontario, Canada, helped to fill the various Free World needs for sulfur. See CHEMICAL INDUSTRY.

The importance of sea-floor mining came to the fore when the Wood's Hole Oceanographic Institute revealed the discovery of $1,500,000,000 worth of copper, gold, silver, and zinc underlying the bed of the Red Sea.

Underdeveloped Nations of the world intensified their search for hidden mineral resources to aid economic stability. Discovery of new sources was speeded up by the use of aerial geophysical surveys, encouraged by the United States through programs such as a 1967 grant of $7,000,000 for a geophysical survey in India.

Coal. The 1967 recovery of the coal industry continued to surprise many observers, with a steady climb to 548,000,000 tons mined, up from 534,000,000 tons in 1966 and 403,000,000, the low point in 1961. The rise was due to a growing use of coal by utility companies to generate electric power.

Aluminum achieved a balance of supply and demand in 1967. Customer stocks began declining in late 1966 and were reduced a total of 18 per cent by the end of 1967. But the import-export balance improved with imports dropping 20 per cent and exports rising 25 per cent above 1966 levels.

On the Labor Front, a nationwide copper strike involving 60,000 strikers went into effect on July 15 and was still in progress at year's end. In the past, contracts had been negotiated separately with individual unions, creating wage differences between the various work groups. In 1967, 22 unions within the industry united for collective bargaining seeking wage uniformity in contracts. [MEL F. BRDLIK]

MONACO. A long-standing controversy between Prince Rainier III and Greek shipping magnate Aristotle S. Onassis over control of the Société des Bains de Mer (SBM), ended in March, 1967. Prince Rainier had believed that the SBM, which controls the casino and other property in the principality, was blocking economic development of the country. Onassis' appeal against a new law that deprived him of SBM control was dismissed in the supreme court, and the treasury paid $15,000,000 into his account, the sum representing the redemption value of his shares.

A bid to attract American investment in Monaco began in October with the appointment of a New York banker, Marcel Palmaro, as president of SBM. It was a move designed to encourage the building of new hotels that would be needed if Monaco was to challenge the neighboring French Riviera resorts for the American tourist trade. Prince Rainier appointed William Groote as director-general of SBM.

SBM development plans for the principality called for the construction of two huge platforms in the eastern Le Larrotto area of the Mediterranean. The platforms, built on rock, will hold apartments, an auditorium, luxury hotels, sound and picture recording studios, and a theater. [Kenneth Brown]

Facts in Brief. Population: 23,000. Government: Prince Rainier III. Monetary Unit: franc (4.9=U.S. $1). Principal Sources of Income: shipping and tourism.

MONEY. As a result of the British devaluation of the pound in November from $2.79 to $2.40, in U.S. dollars, a number of countries were forced to devalue their own currency.

The U.S. money supply rose to about $180,000,000,000 on a seasonally adjusted basis in 1967. This consisted of public holdings of $40,000,000,000 in currency and coin and $140,000,000,000 in demand deposits with commercial banks. Each component of the money supply increased at a relatively high annual rate of 7 per cent.

Silver Certificates became a valuable asset in 1967, occasionally being offered at premiums of more than 30 per cent. In an unprecedented move, on May 18, the U.S. Treasury stopped offering silver to anyone except domestic industrial users at the monetary price of $1.293 per troy ounce. World silver prices jumped immediately. Industrial demand had risen so much in recent years that this price had been maintained only by continued sales of silver from U.S. Treasury stocks. Treasury free stocks dwindled to less than 60,000,000 ounces in 1967, well down from nearly 2,000,000,000 in 1960.

On July 14, the Treasury exercised its authority under the Currency Act of 1965 to halt silver sales altogether. The price of silver advanced subsequently to about $2 an ounce, a price at which pre-1966, 90 per cent silver coins were worth more as metal than as money.

Authority was granted to the Treasury under the Currency Act to ban the melting of coins for their bullion value. A problem the Treasury faced was whether to continue to mint the new 40 per cent silver half dollars or bow to the inevitable and either stop minting half dollars or ask Congress to eliminate their silver content. The United Kingdom stopped minting silver coins in 1947, and Australia, Canada, and South Africa were in the process of discontinuing the use of silver in coins. Canada announced a crash program in 1967 to shift from silver to nickel-alloy coins.

New Legislation in 1967 authorized the Secretary of the Treasury to write off up to $200,000,000 of silver certificates as either lost or in collections of notes not likely to be presented for silver. This authority adds about 150,000,000 ounces to Treasury reserves. Under the law, silver certificates lose their redeemability for silver June 14, 1968, but not their legal tender status. The Treasury was also directed to maintain a minimum of 165,000,000 ounces of silver for transfer to the strategic stockpile in June, 1968. Free stocks of silver actually fell below this level in 1967, but the Treasury began melting coins in late December to make up the deficit. In addition, no one expected that all of the outstanding silver certificates would be redeemed before the June, 1968, deadline.

The U.S. Mint output added almost $1,000,000,000 of fractional coins in the 12 months ended August 31. After nearly a decade of inadequate coin supply, there was clear evidence that no general coin shortage remained in 1967 in that about three-fifths of the 1967 mint output could be added to the coin stocks held by the Treasury and the Federal Reserve Banks. There was insufficient demand from the public to absorb such an enormous increase in coin volume. Coins accounted for 10.1 per cent of the currency in circulation in August, the same level as 1966 but well above the 6 to 7 per cent level during the 1950s. Despite growth in the availability of coins in the economy, the half dollar did not circulate effectively. People held on to newly minted "Kennedy heads" for sentimental reasons and in hopes that their 40 per cent silver content would increase their value in the future.

New World Currency. On September 29, at Rio de Janeiro, Brazil, 106 member nations of the International Monetary Fund approved a major reform of the world monetary system. The plan would establish new reserves in an account based on each country's quota. The reserves would be in the form of special drawing rights (SDRs) to be used in the place of gold. [William G. Dewald]

See also Banks and Banking; Great Britain; International Trade and Finance; Section One, Sylvia Porter: Focus on The Economy; and the various country articles and tables for other foreign exchange rates.

MONGOLIAN PEOPLE'S REPUBLIC became the focus in 1967 of urgent efforts by the Soviet Union to make it a bulwark of defense against hostile Communist Chinese. Mongolia, faced with an extensive difficult-to-defend border with China, made efforts to shore up its defenses on several fronts. A first step was to mobilize almost every male in the nation into a home guard.

Though divided geographically into special civil units, they could be mobilized instantly in the event of a major disturbance anywhere along the border. Far more important than the civil mobilization, however, was the setting up of major missile sites along the Mongolian-Chinese border.

Despite precautions, the Maoist controversy continued to spill into Mongolia. In particular, there were attempts to infiltrate the Chinese-speaking schools. This resulted in the wholesale expulsion of Chinese teachers from the schools by the government and a tightening of security regulations in the entire school system. To further assure Mongolian internal security, the government also began to strengthen its ties with other Soviet Union-oriented nations. [JOHN N. STALKER]

Facts in Brief. Population: 1,123,000. Government: Chairman of the Presidium of the Great People's Khural Jamsramgiyn Sambuu. Monetary Unit: tugrik (4=U.S. $1). Foreign Trade: exports, $72,000,000; imports, $97,000,000. Principal Exports: wool, cattle.

MOROCCO. King Hassan II supported Arab unity against Israel, but urged a peace settlement. His political opponents used his moderation and alleged pro-Americanism–shown by a state visit to the United States in February, which resulted in a $15,000,000 arms agreement–to embarrass the king. Anti-Jewish riots were provoked in several Moroccan cities following the June Arab-Israeli war. Hassan retaliated by closing opposition newspapers. In March, a cabinet reshuffle elevated the nonpolitical Mohammed Benhima, minister of education, to prime minister.

The end of the Ben Barka trial with the acquittal of Colonel Ahmed Dlimi, Morocco's deputy chief of security services, improved Franco-Moroccan relations. French influence, especially in Moroccan education, continued its decline. The U.S. Aerojet-General Corporation and Morocco agreed in May to open an American university at Tangier in 1968.

A poor wheat harvest forced Morocco to import 170,000 tons of U.S. wheat. Elsewhere, the economy brightened, as a stabilization program took effect. Morocco realized its first favorable trade balance since its independence in 1956. [WILLIAM SPENCER]

Facts in Brief. Population: 14,270,000. Government: King Hassan II; Prime Minister Mohammed Benhima. Monetary Unit: dirham (5.06=U.S. $1). Foreign Trade: exports, $428,000,000; imports, $477,000,000. Principal Exports: phosphates, citrus fruits, vegetables.

MOTION PICTURES. With its domestic grosses for 1967 estimated at about $1,000,000,000, the American motion picture industry enjoyed its most prosperous year in more than a decade. It also had other causes for rejoicing. Censorship, which had plagued the studios for half a century, was virtually a thing of the past; state censorship was completely gone, and only a handful of communities still had censor boards that maintained any kind of sniping action. In addition, the industry's own Production Code, liberalized late in 1966, proved not only enlightened, but also lenient. There was precious little that the major studios could not put on the screen if they so desired, provided that they did it in "good taste."

Violence. What the public got in 1967, and in great abundance, were films that featured violence. No Biblical spectaculars went into production, nor even the pseudo-historical pageants so beloved by the Italian film makers. For many, *Bonnie and Clyde* was the motion picture of the year, a zesty blend of sex and violence, nostalgia, and social comment. Attacked at the outset for what some critics considered an excess of gore, it was no less hotly defended by its admirers who saw in its story of two carefree killers of the 1930s, important parallels to the mindless violence of our own time. Similarly, Robert Aldrich's *The Dirty Dozen*, depicting the transformation of a squad of wartime criminals into an effective commando team, was both praised and criticized for its scenes of ruthless bloodletting. Less of a case could be made for such efforts as *Point Blank*, or the *St. Valentine's Day Massacre*. In both, the violence was injected for sheer sensationalism, but if the public objected, it certainly did not raise its objections at the box offices. Significantly, when Richard Brooks' skilled adaptation of *In Cold Blood* went into release at the end of the year, few critics, despite its gruesome theme, looked upon it merely as an exercise in sadism or a treatise on violence.

Sex and Nudity were even more in evidence in 1967, due in part to the greater permissiveness of the Production Code, but also due to the influx of foreign films that had won both critical and audience approval. Significantly, the year began with the release of *Blow-Up*, a film made in England for Metro-Goldwyn-Mayer (M-G-M) by the Italian director Michaelengelo Antonioni. It was promptly refused a code seal, and given a condemned (C) rating by the National Catholic Office for Motion Pictures. Yet *Blow-Up*, which dealt with London's "Mod" world of fashion, and included a scene in which two naked teen-agers tussle amorously with the film's photographer hero, went on to become one of the year's great successes. Its amoral characters and their enigmatic activities held a strong fascination for a new generation of moviegoers.

The New Trend. The result of all this was a series of films, among them some of the very best of the year, that were determinedly modern in tone, experimental in technique, and sexy *in extenso*. In many instances, their writers and directors were fresh, relatively untried talents imported from Broadway, television, or the European studios by producers who sensed the need for change. Thus, *Bonnie and Clyde* was a first script for writers Robert Benton and David Newman, as well as a first attempt at production for its star, Warren Beatty.

Cool Hand Luke was the first feature directed by Stuart Rosenberg, from television. *Point Blank* was the first American effort of John Boorman, a youthful British director. Francis Ford Coppola, who had made his directorial bow in "nudies," both wrote and directed *You're a Big Boy Now;* and Theodore J. Flicker, after one determinedly *avant-garde* effort in New York, was entrusted by Paramount with James Coburn and *The President's Analyst*.

Perhaps the best of the year's crop of off-beat pictures, however, was Mike Nichols' wild and witty *The Graduate*, which chortled over the sexual awakening of a somewhat timid post-teen-ager.

Inevitably, not all the movies, or the moviemakers, followed the new trend. Although Stanley Kramer's *Guess Who's Coming to Dinner* and Otto Preminger's *Hurry Sundown* dealt with the thoroughly contemporary problem of racism, they did so in completely conventional terms. The Kramer film had the further distinction of being the last, tragic pairing of Katharine Hepburn and Spencer Tracy; Tracy died after completing his role.

Motion pictures were big attractions at Expo 67. Czechoslovakia's pavilion featured the Diapolyecran, which produced stunning mosaics of colors and shapes from its 224 slide projectors inside 112 blocks that moved from side to side.

Robert Shaw, *left*, as Henry VIII and Paul Scofield as Sir Thomas More starred in *A Man for All Seasons*, which won six Academy Awards, including one for best feature film. Scofield won his first Oscar as best actor.

Sandy Dennis, one of the top stars in 1967, portrayed a teacher confronting the problems of her first school job in *Up the Down Staircase*.

The Imports of 1967 contributed further to the impression that lines are sharpening between the new and the old. Far and away the most successful at the box office was Claude Lelouch's stylistically exciting *A Man and a Woman* which, despite a familiar and sentimental story, earned more than $3,000,000. Sweden's Ingmar Bergman proved with *Persona* that he remained well in the forefront of the medium's most brilliant and imaginative technicians; while England's youthful Peter Watkins, in *The War Game* and *Privilege*, revealed a mastery in giving a documentary look to events in the future rivaled only by Italy's Gillo Pontecorvo who, in *The Battle of Algiers*, succeeded in giving an equally authentic appearance to his re-creation of a past event. Even Czechoslovakia seems to have fallen in with the modern trend, particularly as evidenced by Vera Chitylova's sprightly *Daisies*. [ARTHUR KNIGHT]

Awards in 1967 included:

Academy of Motion Picture Arts and Sciences Awards for 1966 to: *A Man for All Seasons*, best film; Elizabeth Taylor in *Who's Afraid of Virginia Woolf?*, best actress; Paul Scofield in *A Man for All Seasons*, best actor; Fred Zinnemann, *A Man for All Seasons*, best director; Sandy Dennis in *Who's Afraid of Virginia Woolf?*, best supporting actress; Walter Matthau in *The Fortune Cookie*, best supporting actor; *A Man and a Woman*, best foreign film.

MOTORBOAT RACING. See BOATS AND BOATING.

MUNICIPAL GOVERNMENT. See CITY.

MUSEUMS, like other public institutions, examined their role in troubled American cities in 1967. The Whitney Museum of American Art began an experimental storefront gallery in a neighborhood of disadvantaged New Yorkers. In an area of high tensions in Washington, D.C., the Smithsonian Institution transformed an abandoned movie theater into a small, active museum geared to the community's needs. Unemployed youths were hired to help clean up and remodel the building. They also gave advice on exhibits and programs that would interest them. The Carnegie Corporation of New York gave funds to support both projects.To assist in another trouble spot, American museums sent conservators to Florence and Venice, Italy, where they joined in an international effort to restore art treasures damaged by floods in 1966.

Traveling Museums. A train took exhibits of the story of Confederation to cities across Canada (see CANADA [Close-Up]). Caravans of exhibit trailer trucks visited communities not reached by rail. The New York State Council on the Arts equipped an exhibition barge and sent it along the Erie Canal. The exhibits pictured 150 years of canal history and showed what the canal had done for the economy of the state. A mobile art museum from the Minneapolis Institute of Arts carried an exhibition of American art to many sections of Minnesota. Visitors listened to music of American composers and viewed paintings by John Singer Sargent as well as works of American craftsmen and furniture makers.

New Museums. The Indianapolis City Hall became the new Indiana State Museum. It opened with temporary displays while a staff of curators worked on permanent exhibits. In Columbus, Ohio, contracts were let for the new $8,500,000 Ohio History Center.

Canada opened new museums to celebrate 100 years of Confederation. The National Museum of Science and Technology in Ottawa, Ont., installed its first exhibits in temporary quarters. It will become the largest in the country when completed. The province of Alberta completed its $6,000,000 Centennial Museum and Archives in Edmonton. Calgary built a $1,500,000 Centennial Planetarium.

Old Salem, the restored Moravian community at Winston-Salem, N.C., raised more than $2,000,000 to preserve 12 more structures and increase its endowment. Old Sturbridge Village in Massachusetts began a 10-year, $11,000,000 expansion campaign. The Boston Museum of Science started construction on an $8,000,000 enlargement program. The Metropolitan Museum of Art in New York City agreed to build a $2,500,000 wing to protect and exhibit the 2,000-year-old Egyptian Temple of Dendur. The United Arab Republic gave the ancient monument to the United States in return for American aid in saving the Temples of Abu Simbel. [RALPH H. LEWIS]

MUSIC

The special distinction of the American symphony orchestra, its collective virtuosity and polish, traditionally has been the result of exceptional musicians working for years with a highly skilled resident music director. A continuing tradition of excellence demands that there should be an orderly succession of distinguished leaders in the major posts, but in 1967 three major orchestras – the Boston Symphony, the Chicago Symphony, and the New York Philharmonic – were seeking new conductors.

The Boston Symphony's conductor for five years, Erich Leinsdorf, 55, resigned in December. Leinsdorf agreed to stay on until September, 1970, if a successor could not be found sooner.

The Chicago Symphony Orchestra, which Jean Martinon will lead until June, 1968, spent the year searching for a new chief conductor, but had found no one at year's end.

The Philharmonic temporarily solved its difficulties by deciding to share a conductor with another major orchestra. When the Philharmonic's chief conductor, Leonard Bernstein, steps down in 1969, George Szell of the Cleveland Orchestra will become chief artistic executive of the Philharmonic and share the orchestra with guest conductors until a new music director is named.

Anniversaries were marked by three great orchestras in 1967. The Vienna Philharmonic, which played its first concert in March, 1842, was 125 years old, the world's oldest symphonic orchestra with a record of continuous performance. The New York Philharmonic was close behind, reaching the century-and-a-quarter mark in December. The Viennese marked their birthday with an American tour, and joined the New York Philharmonic in the opening of its 1967 season. The Cleveland Orchestra, youngest of the great American ensembles, opened its 50th season with a festive European tour followed, unfortunately, by a strike. Negotiations were successfully completed.

Perhaps it was the anniversary spirit, but the New York Philharmonic, with minimal strife, negotiated a new contract that made it the highest paid orchestra in the United States. However, its weekly broadcasts, heard nationally since the early days of radio, came to a close in 1967.

André Previn, who, at age 38, insists he has "made the choice between Debbie Reynolds' movies and Gustav Mahler's music," became conductor of the Houston Symphony where his predecessors have included Sir John Barbirolli and Leopold Stokowski.

The memory of Arturo Toscanini was marked in 1967 by a series of concerts in March celebrating the 100th anniversary of his birth. Sir Malcolm Sargent, who died in October, appeared in Chicago during the summer at the Ravinia Festival with the Chicago Symphony, making his belated debut with the orchestra at age 72. André Cluytens, scheduled to join the conducting staff of the Metropolitan Opera Company, died in June at age 62, at the height of an international career.

World Tours. Following the brief war in the Middle East, in June, the Israel Philharmonic visited the United States for three weeks in July and August to raise emergency funds for its beleaguered homeland. The London Symphony was back at Daytona Beach, Fla., for a second year of the Florida International Music Festival. Zubin Mehta conducted as the Los Angeles Philharmonic made its first tour east of the continental divide, which was followed by the orchestra's initial overseas tour. The Philadelphia Orchestra went to Japan and Alaska in May and June, and the National Symphony traveled to Europe in October.

New Score. The most widely discussed new symphonic score was the *Passion According to St. Luke* by a 34-year-old Polish composer, Krzysztof Penderecki. Commissioned by the West German Radio in Cologne for the 700th anniversary of the Münster cathedral, the score was first heard in March, 1966. It reached London, England, in a production by the British Broadcasting Corporation in May, 1967. The symphony received its U.S. première by the Minneapolis Symphony in the autumn, by which time two recordings were available on the American market. A stark work, filled with distinctive sounds, it retold the trial of Christ in vividly contemporary terms.

Opera experienced an unfavorable year in 1967. The Metropolitan Opera Company's road company, the Metropolitan Opera National Company, a noble experiment, was declared dead after two seasons. Its place on the road was taken by the American National Opera Company, an adventurous group headed by Boston's Sarah Caldwell. The Lyric Opera of Chicago canceled its 14th scheduled season in 1967 due to an unresolved labor dispute. It was the first major company to suspend operations because of union troubles. However, a successful settlement for the 1968 season was reached in December.

The Lake Erie Opera Theater of Cleveland, Ohio, one of the best of the smaller companies, was also inactive because of a union problem. The Santa Fe Opera, noted for its lively innovations, lost its home when its theater was demolished by a fire in July.

There were some brighter aspects to the picture. The Met began a $3,000,000 fund drive in March to prevent its most serious financial problems in 35

A new production of Richard Wagner's *Die Walküre* at the Salzburg Easter Festival won acclaim for its magnificent sets as well as for the singing.

Fernando Turchi, *Time* © Time Inc.

English sculptor Henry Moore designed the stark stage settings for Mozart's opera *Don Giovanni*, which was presented at the Festival of Two Worlds in Spoleto, Italy.

years. By October, it had exceeded its goal by a total of nearly $500,000.

The Met completed its first season in New York City's Lincoln Center for the Performing Arts after 30 weeks of production and 214 performances. It was the longest season in its history. In June, the Met made its debut in a New York City park, with a series that drew 225,000 listeners to nine free programs. In August it went to Newport, R.I., for a new, 10-day Verdi festival that it hoped would become a regular summer attraction.

Perhaps the most surprising news was the Met's successful première of an American opera, Marvin David Levy's *Mourning Becomes Elektra*, based on Eugene O'Neill's retelling of the Greek tragedy. The 83rd season opened September 15 with Verdi's *La Traviata*. In November, it featured the American operatic debut of Herbert von Karajan as conductor-producer of a version of Wagner's *Die Walküre*, first staged at the Salzburg Easter Festival. The performance was the start of a new version of Wagner's *The Ring of the Nibelungs* cycle. The San Francisco Opera was also doing *The Ring*, one opera at a time, starting with *Das Rheingold*.

Few would deny that Expo 67 in Montreal, Canada, was the most cultured world's fair ever offered on the North American continent, and that opera was one of its special glories. Visiting groups included the Royal Opera of Sweden, which staged Blomdahl's *Aniara*, a work set in outer space; the Hamburg Opera with a dazzling group of contemporary scores later seen in New York; the Bolshoi Opera from Moscow; the Vienna State Opera; the English Opera Group; and LaScala of Milan, Italy.

Alberto Ginastera's *Bomarzo* received its world première in Washington, D.C., in May, and later caused an international debate when it was considered unsuitable for production in the composer's native Argentina. The Tanglewood, Mass., concerts of the Boston Symphony included the first American production of Beethoven's *Fidelio* in the original 1805 version.

Of the established composers, the most popular in 1967 seemed to be Gustav Mahler, whose works were featured in the fall seasons of nearly all the major orchestras. The nine Mahler symphonies, recorded by Leonard Bernstein and the New York Philharmonic, were issued in a 14-record album in October. It was a year for oversized editions, and even this album was modest when its size was compared with the 19-record set that offered Wagner's complete *Ring* cycle.

Recordings. Low-priced labels, after years in the shadows, were thriving, largely due to the issuance of some of the great recordings of the older catalogs. Tape was enjoying a big boom, too, with an ever growing segment of the market going to cartridge players. [ROBERT C. MARSH]

MUSIC, POPULAR. New stars, new ideas, and new instruments enlivened the pop scene in 1967. The trend toward innovation grew so powerful that it became difficult to classify any performance in a particular category.

A typical case was that of Bobbie Gentry, a 23-year-old dancer, singer, and composer from Mississippi. In her record debut, she accompanied herself on guitar, singing "Ode to Billie Joe." A somber story about a suicide, the song took the form of a scenariolike narrative. Appealing to fans of pop, rock, blues, country music, and jazz alike, it sold more than 2,000,000 records.

Other songs in an easy-listening style were introduced by such groups as the Electric Prune and Harpers Bizarre, both from California, and by The Fifth Dimension, whose "Up, Up, and Away" offered a rare example of Negro artists working in an idiom normally identified with white groups.

In ear-shattering contrast, the harder sound of the more conventional rock groups maintained its popularity through Big Brother and the Holding Company, the Jefferson Airplane, and Country Joe and the Fish.

Important New Faces of the year included the pretty 19-year-old English blonde known simply as Lulu. She was seen in the film *To Sir, With Love*, and her record of the title song became a hit. A fast-rising new British vocal combo, Procol Harum, came to the United States for in-person and television appearances.

In the rhythm and blues field, Aretha Franklin, a big star of the early 1960s, sang her way back to the top with "I Never Loved a Man the Way I Love You" and "Respect." Dionne Warwick, the Supremes, and the Four Tops extended their popularity in the rhythm and blues and general pop fields.

Top songs by leading vocal groups were the Turtles' "Happy Together," the Rolling Stones' "Ruby Tuesday," the Box Tops' "The Letter," and several new hits by the Beatles, among them "Sergeant Pepper's Lonely Hearts Club Band," "Strawberry Fields Forever," and "All You Need Is Love."

Vocal Duos, normally a rarity in pop music, became unusually popular. Outstanding were Sam & Dave, best known for "Soul Man," and Peaches & Herb with "Love Is Strange."

The tonal range of popular music was enlarged as Indian and other Far Eastern sounds expanded their influence. In addition to the sitar, instruments such as the dulcimer, harpsichord, and electric violin were introduced by experimental pop groups. The Beatles and others enhanced the sound of their recorded work through the use of multitracking tapes played backward and speeded up.

Festivals of popular music showed substantial signs of growth. Those held at Monterey, Calif., and Newport, R.I., proved even more successful than their jazz counterparts.

Jazz. Throughout 1967 there were many signs that jazz was losing ground in the United States. Many observers felt that the young fans who had constituted most of its audience found today's jazz too esoteric and now derived more satisfaction from rock and other pop forms. Acknowledging this trend, two leading American jazz magazines changed their policy to incorporate rock in their reportage.

Many night clubs found a waning audience for jazz. New York City's Eddie Condon's, famous for 22 years, closed its doors. A few musicians were offered encouragement to stay in the jazz field. In an unprecedented move, the Guggenheim Memorial Foundation offered a fellowship to saxophonist Ornette Coleman so that he could pursue his efforts as a jazz composer.

Jazz Festivals. The most provocative groups of the year were two small combos. Saxophonist Archie Shepp led a group that was described by critics as fierce and intense, expressing anger and other violent emotions in its "freedom sounds." The brilliant vibraphonist Gary Burton led a quartet that included a remarkable young guitarist named Larry Coryell, one of several young musicians who had prior experience in rock groups before taking up jazz.

Some students saw signs of a rapprochement between jazz and pop, and an overlapping of their audiences. Charles Lloyd and John Handy drew

Herb Alpert's 15-year-old handmade trumpet and his seven-man Tijuana Brass band made the "Ameriachi" sound popular with all age groups.

The Who, an English group, dropped smoke bombs and smashed instruments to end its performance at the Monterey International Pop Festival.

rock fans to their appearances in San Francisco, Calif. Lloyd, a saxophonist and composer, enjoyed triumphant festival appearances at Tallinn in the Soviet Union and at Antibes in France, but returned to the United States to play in half-empty night clubs. In the fall, he took his quartet back to Europe.

George Wein, the Newport, R.I., festival impresario, also found the most receptive audiences overseas. In October, he and 40 other musicians participated in a week-long series of jazz concerts in London, followed by four recitals in Berlin and a dozen more in seven other countries. The participants included Sarah Vaughan and the combos of Burton, Shepp, Miles Davis, and Thelonious Monk. Most of the performances played to full houses.

The only jazz artist to achieve mass popular recognition in the United States in 1967 was Julian "Cannonball" Adderley, the saxophonist whose "Mercy, Mercy, Mercy!" was a million-selling record. Also popular were the guitarists Wes Montgomery and Gabor Szabo. The latter, a Hungarian refugee, developed new ideas that incorporated tonal distortions and the use of Indian scales. His best album was "Jazz Raga."

The year 1967 saw the passing of many great jazz artists: Red Allen, Buster Bailey, Herman Chittison, John Coltrane, Sidney de Paris, Edmond Hall, Pete Johnson, Willie Smith, Muggsy Spanier, Rex Stewart, and Billy Strayhorn. [LEONARD G. FEATHER]

NATIONAL DEFENSE. New strategic decisions and growing requirements for the war in Vietnam bulged the U.S. defense program in 1967 to a record of more than $75,000,000,000. President Lyndon B. Johnson gave the go-ahead in September for production and installation of a $5,000,000,000 "thin" Nike-X defense called the Sentinel against a possible threat by the mid-1970s from Communist China's missiles. He also approved further development of the U.S. strategic missile force with advanced Minuteman III ICBMs and with submarine-launched Poseidon missiles carrying ingenious multiple warheads that could spew forth a dozen nuclear weapons at separate targets from a single missile. The Department of Defense favorably considered developing a new jet fighter plane for the Air Force called the "FX," but other major weapons systems under development were given little chance of approval because of the mounting costs of the war in Vietnam.

Approval of the limited deployment of the long-debated Nike-X system was the outstanding development of the year. Since 1955, the Nike-X antimissile system had been the subject of research at a total cost of some $4,000,000,000, but until 1967 President Johnson and his predecessors had kept it in the development stage. Pentagon studies showed that the Nike-X design could effectively intercept a small enemy ICBM attack, but would be overwhelmed by a hail of hundreds of sophisticated ICBM warheads. Even a complete antimissile system, covering major U.S. cities and costing an estimated $40,000,000,000, would still be swamped by an all-out Soviet missile attack, Secretary of Defense Robert S. McNamara said.

The "thin" sentinel antimissile defense that was finally agreed upon will consist of about 10 to 15 missile sites across the northern United States pointed toward China. Five to seven perimeter acquisition radar stations, each with a range of 1,200 miles, will detect and track any approaching enemy warheads. Missile site radars will pick up their tracks and, with the help of electronic computers, aim antimissile interceptors.

The Nike-X System will contain two missiles, the Spartan for long-range interception, and the Sprint for short-range defense against any warheads that get past the Spartan. The 54-foot Spartan has a range of 400 miles, reaching high into space to meet the glowing red-hot ICBMs hurtling downward at 15,000 mph from their 600-mile-high arc. The 27-foot cone-shaped Sprint zips out of its underground lair in a blur of last minute superspeed to meet the bomber or enemy nuclear warhead 10 to 15 miles above the earth.

Production of the antimissile system will start early in 1968 and is scheduled to provide a combat-ready net by 1973. The army had $529,000,000 in stand-by funds for fiscal 1968 to start production of

United States World-Wide Defense Pacts

NATO, SEATO, CENTO, OAS (Rio Pact), ANZUS, and bilateral treaties.

Countries that have U.S. defense pacts

Countries that do not have U.S. defense pacts

Communist and Communist-aligned countries

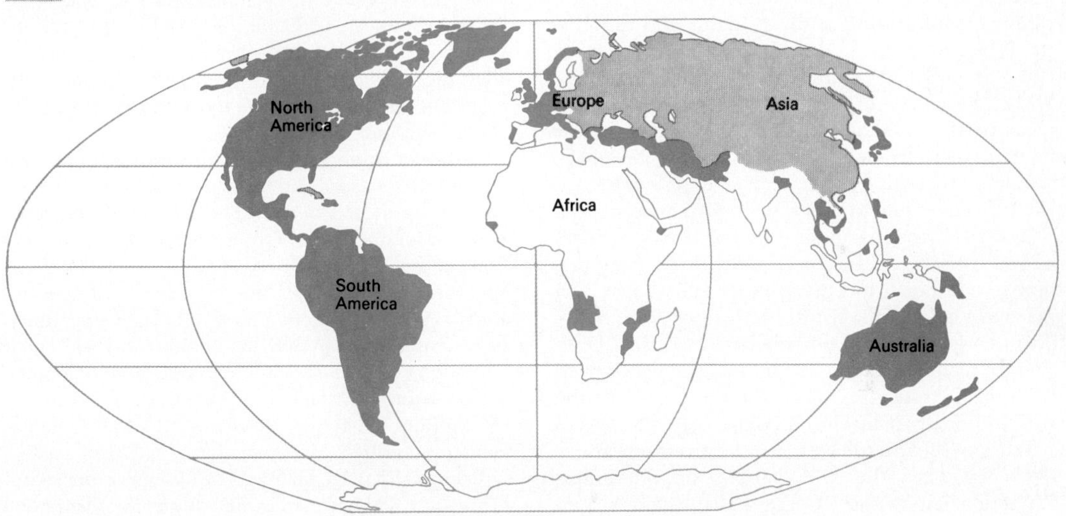

Nike-X in a complex of more than 90 firms under the prime contractor, the Western Electric Company. The Nike-X budget for fiscal 1969 was expected to run about $1,000,000,000 over and above the $500,000,000-a-year research program. The defensive shield may be so deployed to cover Minuteman ICBM launchers in the United States.

The outlook for other major new weapons systems was cloudy. Research on the Advanced Manned Strategic Aircraft (AMSA) bomber was continued at a cost of about $26,000,000 a year with $25,000,000 extra voted by Congress. But production of a new supersonic bomber force costing some $10,000,000,000 was postponed, as were other proposed jet fighter planes. The only advanced supersonic jet fighter, the swivel-winged F-111, is in production and a few will be sent to a base in Thailand for bombing runs against North Vietnam. The development of the navy's carrier-based version of the F-111, the F-111B, was slowed by technical difficulties.

Outlays for the war in Vietnam were estimated in President Johnson's budget in January, 1967, at $21,900,000,000 for the fiscal year ending June 30, 1968, compared with $19,419,000,000 in the preceding year. Actual war spending, however, was expected to be about $30,000,000,000 as more troops were deployed to Vietnam, more bombers were lost in the air war against North Vietnam, and the intensity of the war heightened.

U.S. Troop Strength in Vietnam had reached 475,000 men by the end of 1967, and was to be boosted to 525,000 by mid-1968. This was President Johnson's decision after conferring with General William C. Westmoreland, U.S. commander in Vietnam, and Secretary of Defense McNamara. General Harold K. Johnson, Army Chief of Staff, indicated this augmentation should be adequate without further major additions if Communist China and other Communist forces do not intervene. General Johnson said the progress of the war suggested the United States might consider a phased withdrawal of U.S. troops from Vietnam by the end of 1968. General Westmoreland indicated in November that a token withdrawal of U.S. troops might start by 1969. Other military and government officials were either not that sanguine or were unwilling to make such predictions.

Shift in War. The war in Vietnam in 1967 shifted in character and in geographical emphasis. After the Vietnam lunar year holiday pause in the fighting, the Viet Cong and North Vietnamese troops switched to mortar, rocket, and artillery attacks upon U.S. bases, particularly in the northern provinces near the so-called demilitarized zone (DMZ) dividing Vietnam. Heavier caliber weapons were used by the Viet Cong for the first time. The Communists appeared to abandon battalion-sized (about 500 men) attacks in the central highlands, the lowlands, and other southern provinces after their reverses against more powerful and highly mobile U.S. units. Instead, the Communists exploited their shorter supply lines and bases near the DMZ to assault the U.S. marine bases just below the line at Cam Lo, Camp Carroll, Con Thien, Dong Hoi, Gia Dinh, Khe Sanh, and the "Rockpile." Two or three North Vietnamese divisions, or some 25,000 men, reportedly operated above the DMZ, with several regiments infiltrating south to harass and dislodge the U.S. Marines.

To impede Communist infiltration across the DMZ, Secretary of Defense McNamara ordered construction of a defense line of obstacles, mine fields, and electronic detectors just below the DMZ.

Enemy pounding of the marine bases compelled the U.S. command to shift army troops to bolster the 75,000 to 80,000 marines in the northern provinces of South Vietnam. In April, 1967, three army brigades were flown to Quang Ngai and Quang Tri provinces and formed into "task force Oregon"–later reorganized and renamed the Americal Division. In October, an air cavalry brigade was moved up from the south to bolster the army units as the two and one-half marine divisions held the DMZ.

In the rest of South Vietnam the ground fighting slackened after the U.S. large-scale operations "Junction City" and "Cedar Falls" against Viet Cong hideouts in Tay Ninh forest and War Zones C and D near Saigon. During the spring of 1967, these operations encountered only sporadic and light actions with the Viet Cong main force. U.S. intelligence reports suggested that the Viet Cong and North Vietnamese battalions had been battered by the fast-striking U.S. and allied forces and some of these units had withdrawn to sanctuaries across the border into Laos and Cambodia.

Enemy Strength. Despite these losses, the Viet Cong and North Vietnamese forces were reported to have increased slightly in 1967 from 280,000 to 297,000 men. U.S. intelligence, however, restudied this estimate and lowered the numbers of the enemy's main force strength from 126,000 to 118,000 combat troops. Analysis of enemy infiltration from North Vietnam indicated the flow had declined in 1967 to an average of 3,000 troops a month compared with 4,500 a month in 1966. The U.S. command in Vietnam estimated that enemy losses through death, illness, and defections began to exceed the intake of new recruits and infiltrators.

Evaluation of the War's Progress was confusing. Critics of the government's war policy saw the fighting as a military stalemate. They urged a halt or limitation of the bombing of North Vietnam and a scaling-down of U.S. operations to reduce casualties. However, General Westmoreland and Pentagon leaders reassuringly reported "steady progress" in the conduct of the war.

The apparent enemy losses in the ground fighting and the intensified bombing campaign against North Vietnam did not budge the Hanoi government. President Johnson stepped-up the bombings, particularly against targets in the Hanoi-Haiphong area under pressure from military chiefs and from Congressmen who insisted this bombing would shorten the war.

After more than 200,000 bombing sorties since 1965, dropping about 500,000 tons of bombs on North Vietnam, U.S. bombing policy became the center of heated controversy in Congress and the Pentagon. Like the rest of the war in Vietnam, the results of the bombing were too ambiguous and elusive to evaluate precisely.

Defense Spending. With the progress of the war difficult to measure and the war's end still uncertain, its cost continued to rise. The war in Vietnam accounted for one-third of the more than $75,000,000,000 national defense budget. Of this total defense spending estimated in the President's budget for fiscal 1968, $72,300,000,000 was for the Department of Defense, up from $68,500,000,000 in fiscal 1967; $800,000,000 was for military aid; $2,330,000,000 was for atomic energy, and the rest was for strategic stockpiling, Selective Service, and other defense-related activities.

Congress cut Department of Defense requests totaling $71,584,000,000 in new funds for fiscal 1968 (not including construction, housing, military aid, and civil defense) to $69,936,620,000. This total was divided as follows: $22,614,503,000 to the army, $19,677,900,000 to the navy, $23,921,995,000 to the air force, and $3,722,222,000 for other defense agencies.

These funds provide for a military strength by mid-1968 of 3,465,000 men including 1,521,000 army, 762,000 navy, 295,000 marine corps, and 887,000 air force. This would mean a small increase from 3,411,833 men on Nov. 30, 1967.

Of these troops, some 475,000 were in South Vietnam, 42,000 with the Seventh Fleet off Vietnam, 41,000 in Thailand, 350,000 in Europe, 50,000 in South Korea, and 25,000 were with the Sixth Fleet in the Mediterranean.

U.S. Army

The army had 18 divisions, including the newly formed Americal Division. It was organizing another new division, the 6th Infantry Division, scheduled to be ready by September, 1968, to replace the U.S. units being deployed to Vietnam. Of the planned 19 army divisions, five will be in the United States, five in Europe, two in South Korea, and seven in South Vietnam.

In West Germany, as part of an economy effort to reduce dollar exchange outlays, the army pulled out two brigades, totaling some 30,000 men including support, of the 24th Infantry Division. The brigades will be held in readiness at a U.S. base for airlift in an emergency to Europe.

U.S. Navy

The Polaris missile submarine program was completed in April, 1967, with the commissioning of the *Will Rogers*, the 41st and last of the Polaris long-range missile-carrying subs. It will join six Polaris subs operating from Guam. The remaining 34 subs are in Spain, England, and the United States.

Besides this major participation in the U.S. strategic force, the navy operated 16 attack carriers and 7 antisubmarine carriers in its fleet of 940 warships. The navy recalled the World War II battleship *New Jersey* from mothballs, and refurbished it at a cost of $27,000,000 at the Philadelphia navy yard for deployment in the summer of 1968 to Vietnam.

Paul R. Ignatius, former Assistant Secretary of Defense, became Secretary of the Navy Sept. 1, 1967, replacing Paul H. Nitze, who was promoted to Deputy Secretary of Defense upon the resignation in June of Cyrus R. Vance. Admiral Thomas H. Moorer, former Atlantic commander, replaced Admiral David McDonald, retired, as Chief of Naval Operations, Aug. 1, 1967.

The marines had two and one-third divisions in South Vietnam, including a special landing force with the Seventh Fleet. The embattled marines, pounded by heavy enemy shelling of the bases near the DMZ, took the brunt of all the fighting in the latter half of 1967.

In a surprise move, President Lyndon B. Johnson nominated Robert S. McNamara, Secretary of Defense since 1961, to be president of the World Bank.

U.S. Defense Budgets

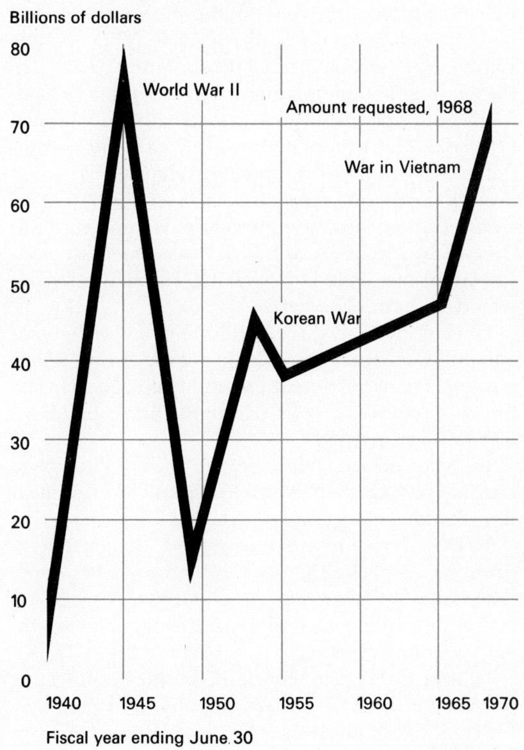

U.S. Air Force

With more than 1,400 planes including 1,000 fighter bombers in South Vietnam and Thailand, the air force accounted for more than one-half of the attack sorties against North Vietnam, and most of the supporting flights in South Vietnam. Highly effective electronic countermeasures, more accurately guided bombs, and special bombs against radars and gun batteries helped air force pilots improve their bombing raids over North Vietnam.

The air force B-52s, bombing Vietnam targets from Guam, extended their operations from a base in Thailand in April, 1967. Capable of carrying 30 tons of bombs each, the B-52s hammered Viet Cong base areas, supply routes in the southern end of North Vietnam, and in the DMZ. The air force's 14,000 planes included 600 B-52s and 70 B-58 jet bombers. In Europe, the air force withdrew four jet fighter squadrons as part of an economy move.

U.S. Coast Guard

The U.S. Coast Guard, with 361 vessels including 10 icebreakers, and 36,000 men in uniform, operated 31 ships in Vietnam. It had assigned 1,500 coast guardsmen to Vietnam and Thailand. During fiscal 1967, the coast guard saved 2,500 lives and ships or aircraft valued at $2,341,693,000. Its budget for fiscal 1968 totaled $363,283,000. [Lloyd Norman]

See also Armed Forces of the World; Civil Rights; Congress of the United States; Vietnam.

NEPAL continued to develop its ties with Communist China during 1967. It reaffirmed an agreement, made in 1966, that called for China to supply Nepal with 20,000 metric tons of rice. Nepal also signed a new agreement with China under which a 10,000 kilowatt hydroelectric power station and transmission line would be erected on the Sun Kosi River. China agreed to build a highway that would improve Katmandu's connection with a new 65-mile road leading to the Tibetan border.

Although these agreements seemed to indicate an increasing Nepalese reliance on China, there were signs that the Nepalese government was treating the relationship with guarded caution. This became especially apparent when Maoists and Nepalese conservatives clashed in open violence at the opening of the Chinese pavilion at Katmandu's international exhibition in the summer. The Nepalese government peremptorily closed the pavilion despite Chinese protests. The government then sought ties with France, Hungary, and the United States.

As the year closed, Nepal's Mahendra (King) Bir Bikram Shah Deva, and Queen Ratna paid a two-day state visit to the United States. [JOHN N. STALKER]

Facts in Brief. Population: 10,560,000. Government: Mahendra (King) Bir Bikram Shah Deva; Council of Ministers Chairman Surya Bahadur Thapa. Monetary Unit: rupee (10.1=U.S. $1). Foreign Trade: no statistics available. Principal Exports: rice, jute, timber.

NETHERLANDS, THE. National elections held in February saw a new party emerge–Democracy 1966. It won seven seats in an attempt to prove that the electorate was "sick and tired" of proportional representation. The Catholics lost seven seats, the Socialists, six. Premier Jelle Zijlstra attempted, without success, to form a coalition cabinet, and it was not until April that Petrus J. S. de Jong, a former defense minister, succeeded in forming a new one.

The new cabinet's first task was to counter inflation. A deficit was running an estimated $690,000,000 a year. In June, a number of taxes were increased by 20 per cent and house rents went up by 10 to 15 per cent. Big cutbacks were forecast on government spending for construction, defense, and education. The September budget showed a deficit of almost $900,000,000 on expenditures of $6,900,000,000.

Princess Margriet, 23, married a commoner, Pieter van Vollenhoven, 27, in January. Crown Princess Beatrix, married a year earlier to German diplomat Claus von Amsberg, bore a son, the first in the House of Orange for a century. [KENNETH BROWN]

Facts in Brief. Population: 12,655,000. Government: Queen Juliana; Premier Petrus J. S. de Jong. Monetary Unit: guilder (3.6=U.S. $1). Foreign Trade: exports, $6,751,000,000; imports, $8,017,000,000. Principal Exports: machinery, chemicals, textiles, petroleum products.

NEW BRUNSWICK. See CANADA.

NEW GUINEA, an island in the Pacific, continued under the joint control of Indonesia and Australia. The eastern portion, under the administration of Australia, consisted of a United Nations trusteeship over the northern part (West New Guinea) and the southern portion (Papua-New Guinea), a colony with limited self-government.

Throughout the year, Australia encouraged economic and social growth in the two areas under its control, with special emphasis on Papua-New Guinea. In January, it announced it was relaxing restrictions on Japanese investments in the area. Simultaneously, it instituted new work-permit regulations allowing employed Japanese to remain in the territory for two years. By year's end, the government reported that new industries, including a cultured-pearl project and a logging operation, had sprung up in the territory.

The University of Papua-New Guinea, established in Port Moresby in 1965, was officially opened by the governor-general of Australia, Lord Casey, in mid-August. With an enrollment of 200 students, the university was considered of special importance because it would provide educated young people to help fill essential jobs as Papua-New Guinea approached full self-government.

The New Guinea Corporation, a mainly Australian-financed development company, was building the first large office building at Port Moresby.

NEW ORLEANS advanced a number of major public works projects in 1967 although few were completed, and one, the controversial Vieux Carre Expressway, was stalled. The six-lane freeway, in the planning stage for more than 20 years, was to follow the waterfront skirting the historic French Quarter. The proposal, however, ran into formidable local outcries. Opponents charged it would destroy the unique character of the section. An April confrontation between preservationists and the U.S. Bureau of Public Roads held up immediate construction, but little hope was held that the facility would be built elsewhere.

During the year, three buildings of a new $9,000,000 police complex were dedicated: a central police garage, a house of detention, and traffic courts. The fourth structure, a police administration building, was to open in 1968.

In May, construction began on a $72,000,000 crossing of Lake Ponchartrain, parallel to the existing two-lane causeway.

In December, the city received a $300,000 federal grant to plan rehabilitation of the lower 9th ward, devastated by Hurricane *Betsy* in 1965. A proposed community renewal project of $18,000,000 would help restore the area.

Behind the scenes, city hall, business, and civic groups prepared for a year-long observance of New Orleans' 250th anniversary in 1968. [DONALD W. LIEF]

New York City's Mayor John V. Lindsay took to the streets to help cool disturbances that erupted in Spanish Harlem during the summer.

NEW YORK CITY. Public confidence in the local government services of welfare, health, education, and law enforcement declined in 1967, giving the nation's largest city problems to match its size. With 700,000 clients, Human Resources Administration head, Mitchell I. Ginsberg, repeatedly cited the inadequacy and inefficiency of the traditional welfare system. In December, a mayor's task force scathingly criticized the quality of city hospitals and health services.

Public education, with its racial overtones, mounting costs, personnel problems, and insular bureaucracy, was the most turbulent issue. Adding to parent discontent, the fall term started two weeks late due to a strike by the 50,000-member United Federation of Teachers Union. On November 8, a vast reorganization of New York's 900 public schools was recommended by an expert panel, headed by Ford Foundation President McGeorge Bundy. The sweeping plan called for decentralizing control of the schools by means of largely autonomous community school boards. Mayor John V. Lindsay sought approval for the plan from the state legislature in December.

The scale and significance of New York's problems convinced federal officials to award the city three separate model neighborhood planning grants, making New York the only city to be so treated. Mayor Lindsay was unsuccessful in an attempt to persuade the New York Constitutional Convention to grant municipal governments more fiscal authority. In November, he and other leaders voiced disapproval of the proposed constitution, and it was overwhelmingly defeated. Voters at the same time approved by over a two-thirds majority a $2,500,000,000 transportation bond issue for the state's roads, airports, and transit systems.

Waterfront. The city looked to its riverfront in 1967 for economic and social benefits. The city and the Port of New York Authority jointly planned a $76,500,000 consolidated ship terminal to replace three existing Hudson River piers. On December 22, the Board of Estimates gave final approval to construction of a six-acre project to be built on a platform over the East River. Its four towers and row of townhouses will contain 1,468 apartments for families in different income levels.

Construction. Architectural gem of the year was the opulent $17,000,000 headquarters of the Ford Foundation. Less distinguished was a 41-story federal office building, the nation's tallest, completed in December in the Civic Center area. On June 24, after lengthy negotiation, the way was cleared for construction of twin 110-story towers for the World Trade Center. In 1967, Mayor Lindsay supported planning for creation of a "Linear City" in mid-Brooklyn to combine highways, rapid transit, schools, housing, and stores. [DONALD W. LIEF]

NEW ZEALAND. The government, in an emergency budget, announced on May 4, 1967, that it was instituting tax increases on automobiles, gasoline, liquor, and tobacco. The new taxes formed the third part of a program of economic measures that had been introduced earlier in the year to deflate the economy.

The deflation had been made necessary by years of economic expansion that had caused a sharp decline in foreign exchange reserves, and by the collapse in world prices for coarse wool, a major New Zealand export. In two seasons, wool prices had fallen by 50 per cent–from about 43 pence in 1965 to 24 pence a pound in 1967.

The first part of the deflation program, introduced in February, involved the cancellation of subsidies on many food items. This resulted in increases in prices and in rentals on government housing. The move also brought tightened credit. The second step, taken in April, was a 20 per cent reduction in import licenses on a wide range of goods.

The new taxes were the harshest since the Labour government's 1958 budget but they were expected to yield $70,000,000 yearly and to tighten the credit squeeze further. These measures, while they helped dampen business activity, also brought cuts in the demand for labor. As a result, the minister of labor announced in August that unemployment was the highest since World War II.

On July 10, New Zealand switched to a decimal currency. The change from pounds, shillings, and pence to dollars and cents was accomplished with little confusion. Dual currencies, however, would remain in use until early 1968.

The new New Zealand dollar was pegged at $1.40 to the U.S. $1. In November, however, Prime Minister Keith J. Holyoake announced that the currency would be devalued. The decision to devalue put the New Zealand dollar on a par with the Australian dollar. Both are now valued at $1.12. See INTERNATIONAL TRADE AND FINANCE; MONEY.

Plans went forward for the building of three hydroelectric stations with a total capacity of 370 megawatts in the Lake Taupo area on New Zealand's North Island. The project would require 32 miles of tunnels, 12 miles of canals, 10 1/2 miles of pipelines, 72 miles of access roads, two pumping stations, 15 stream intakes, and seven dams.

Facts in Brief. Population: 2,781,000. Government: Governor-General Sir Bernard Fergusson; Prime Minister Keith J. Holyoake. Monetary Unit: dollar (1=U.S. $1.12). Foreign Trade: exports, $1,076,000,000; imports, $1,095,000,000; Principal Exports: wool, lamb and mutton, butter.

NEWBERY MEDAL. See LITERATURE FOR CHILDREN (Awards).

NEWFOUNDLAND. See CANADA.

NEWSPAPER. See PUBLISHING.

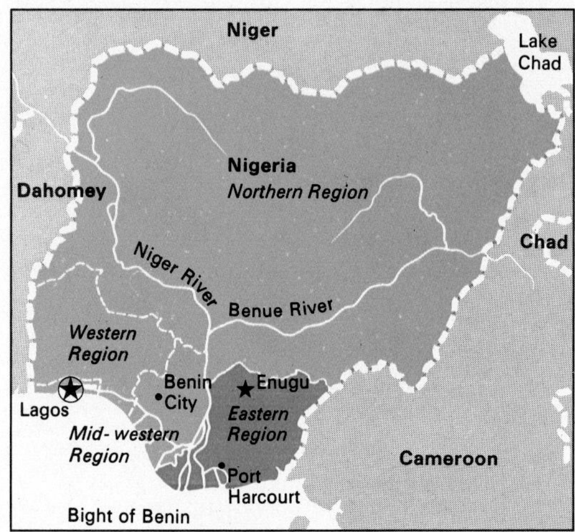

NICARAGUA. General Anastasio Somoza Debayle, presidential candidate of the ruling Nationalist Liberal party, won the elections held on Feb. 5, 1967, thus continuing the 35-year-old "Somoza dynasty" in Nicaragua. Sworn into office on May 1, Somoza promised a government committed to private enterprise and to political stability.

Earlier in the year, on January 23, a 24-hour uprising occurred against the Somoza-controlled regime following a pre-election rally. During their rampage, the rioters held 117 foreigners as hostages in a Managua hotel. Included among them were 89 North Americans. About 34 Nicaraguans were killed and 69 were wounded during the fighting.

Despite its political problems, Nicaragua continued to enjoy one of the highest economic growth rates in Central America. The gross national product for 1967 was expected to rise by at least 5 per cent, a rate that was materially higher than the 3.6 per cent of 1966, but below the average annual growth rate of nearly 8 per cent. Domestic business did rather well, with retail sales at midyear about 15 per cent above the 1966 level. [MARY C. WEBSTER]

Facts in Brief. Population: 1,789,000. Government: President Anastasio Somoza Debayle. Monetary Unit: cordóba (7.05=U.S. $1). Foreign Trade: exports, $137,600,000; imports, $181,900,000. Principal Exports: cotton, coffee, meat.

NIGER. See AFRICA.

NIGERIA was torn by civil war between the federal government of Lieutenant Colonel Yakubu Gowon and the nation's Eastern Region. The central government, at Lagos, was formerly supported by the Northern, Eastern, Mid-western, and Western Regions, divided during British colonial days. But intertribal riots and massacres in mid-1966 had destroyed civilian control. The year began, however, with Gowon's attempt to maintain order and unity. The Supreme Military Council, including the governors of the four regions of Nigeria, met at Aburi, Ghana, on January 4 and 5, and agreed on policies calling for the prevention of further bloodshed.

Soon after the meeting, Lieutenant Colonel Odumegwu Ojukwu, governor of the Eastern Region, charged that his region was being denied the autonomy promised at Aburi. As a result, the rift widened. Other Nigerian leaders as well as those from other African countries attempted to settle their differences. American Negro leaders, among them the Reverend Martin Luther King, A. Philip Randolph, Roy Wilkins, and Whitney Young, also offered their help. But all efforts failed. On May 30, the Eastern Region declared its independence as the Republic of Biafra.

The Nigerian navy blockaded Biafra's ports in June, and army units started a "police action" against the rebellious region on July 6. The weak military forces of both sides fought only light skirmishes but on August 9, Biafra's army, assisted by local Ibos, conquered the Mid-western Region and then invaded the Western Region.

Rebel Successes caused Gowon, now a general, to escalate from "police action" to "total war." He abolished the old regional boundaries in favor of 12 states. He obtained aircraft and other military equipment from the Soviet Union. Some supplies also came from Great Britain; the United States refused aid.

The central government, with its strengthened forces, retook the Mid-western Region in September and then occupied part of Biafra, but, at year's end, Gowon had not restored complete control. Though oil production in Biafra was halted by the naval blockade, farming and other industries continued operation outside the combat areas.

Nigeria accepted Communist economic aid for the first time. Loans came from Czechoslovakia, Poland, the Soviet Union, and Yugoslavia. Soviet experts studied the feasibility of an iron and steel industry. Work on the Kainji Dam on the Niger River in the Northern Region continued with assistance from the United States. [BENJAMIN E. THOMAS]

Facts in Brief. Population: 60,450,000. Government: Federal Military Government Head Yakubu Gowon. Monetary Unit: pound (1 = U.S. $2.79). Foreign Trade: exports, $793,000,000; imports, $718,000,000. Principal Exports: crude petroleum, cocoa beans, peanuts.

NOBEL PRIZES in literature and science were presented at ceremonies in Stockholm, Sweden, on Dec. 10, 1967. The Norwegian storting (parliament) Nobel Committee in Oslo, Norway, withheld the peace prize for the second consecutive year.

Literature Prize was awarded to *Miguel Angel Asturias* (1899-), Guatemalan ambassador to France. The poet and novelist was cited "for his highly colored writings rooted in a national individuality and Indian traditions." His first novel, *The President*, published in 1946, has been translated into many languages. *Men of Corn* and *Poetry: Pulse of the Skylark*, an anthology, were published in 1949. *Strong Wind* (1950) was followed by the sequels *The Green Pope* (1954) and *Eyes of the Interred* (1954). *Mulatto* (1963) was published in English in 1967. Much of Asturias' writings are about dictators and oppressed Indians. He lived in exile from 1953 until early 1967, and spent most of those years in Argentina and France.

Chemistry Prize was awarded to three scientists for "their studies of extremely fast chemical reactions effected by disturbing the equilibrium by means of very short pulses of energy." *Manfred Eigen* (1927-), chairman of the Max Planck Institute of Physical Chemistry, Göttingen, West Germany, received half of the chemistry prize. He started research in 1953 on fast chemical reactions. Eigen found that the equilibrium of molecules could be upset, or changed, by a sudden increase in temperature or pressure. He measured electronically the time required for the molecules to return to a state of equilibrium. *Ronald G. W. Norrish* (1897-), Cambridge University professor emeritus of physical chemistry, and *George Porter* (1920-), director of the Royal Institution in London, shared the other half of the chemistry prize. They worked together from 1949 to 1955, and developed a research technique known as flash photolysis. They used extremely powerful and brief light pulses to create molecular changes, and then timed and studied those molecular changes as they occurred.

Physics Prize was awarded to *Hans Albrecht Bethe* (1906-), Cornell University professor of theoretical physics. He was cited for "his contributions to the theory of nuclear reaction, especially his discoveries concerning the energy production of stars." He concluded from his research that energy radiated by stars is produced by the process in which hydrogen fuses to form helium. Bethe was born in Strasburg when it was a part of Germany. He came to the United States in 1935, and was director of the theoretical division at the Los Alamos, N.Mex., Scientific Laboratory from 1943 to 1946.

Physiology and Medicine Prize was shared by three scientists "for their discoveries concerning the primary chemical and physiological visual processes in the eye." *Ragnar Arthur Granit* (1900-), retired neurophysiology professor at the Royal Caroline Institute, Stockholm, Sweden, was honored as the first to show how different neutral units in the retina react to colors. He was born in Finland when it was a province of Russia. Granit began his research when a Helsinki University faculty member, from 1929 to 1937. *Haldan Keffer Hartline* (1903-), a Rockefeller University biophysics professor, was honored for his work on the electrical impulses that carry images to the brain and for being able "to explain how the eye, by sharpening contrasts, is able to differentiate form and movement." Hartline was born in Bloomsburg, Pa. He was chairman of the biophysics department at Johns Hopkins University before going to Rockefeller University in 1953. *George Wald* (1906-), Harvard University biology professor, was honored as a world renowned authority on the biochemistry of perception. His primary contribution was described as increasing the understanding of how light activates the photoreceptive cells in the retina. Wald was born in New York City. He received his Ph.D. degree at Columbia University in 1932, and joined the Harvard faculty in 1934 as a biology instructor.

The Nobel Laureates in 1966 were: *Literature*, Shmuel Yosef Agnon and Nelly Sachs; *Chemistry*, Robert Sanderson Mulliken; *Physics*, Alfred Kastler; and *Physiology and Medicine*, Charles Brenton Huggins and (Francis) Peyton Rous.

NORRISH, RONALD G. W. See NOBEL PRIZES.

NORTH ATLANTIC TREATY ORGANIZATION (NATO) said farewell to France without pomp or circumstance on Oct. 15, 1967. The NATO flag and those of the 15 member nations were lowered at the Paris headquarters, and, on the following day, Paul Vanden Boeynants, the Belgian prime minister, handed over new temporary headquarters to the North Atlantic Council near Brussels, Belgium. Permanent buildings, in Casteau, 35 miles away, will be completed in five years.

All NATO operational forces were out of France by March 31, the last day of the 12-month notice served on the council by French President Charles de Gaulle. On March 30, Supreme Headquarters Allied Powers in Europe (SHAPE) left Rocquen fort, near Paris, for Casteau, Belgium. The NATO Defense College moved from Paris and was opened in Rome, Italy, in February.

New Strategy. The NATO defense ministers, meeting in Paris in May, agreed on new directives to help the military chiefs match their planning to available forces and not to theoretical strengths, while, at the same time, taking account of Soviet capabilities.

At a ministerial meeting in the city of Luxembourg, in June, NATO topics were overshadowed by discussions of the Middle East crisis. In September, NATO's Nuclear Planning Group (NPG), set up late in 1966, met with Robert S. McNamara, U.S. Secretary of Defense to hear an explanation of the U.S. decision to place a "thin" antiballistic missile defense around the country (see ARMED FORCES OF THE WORLD; NATIONAL DEFENSE).

Rhine Army. President Lyndon B. Johnson announced in August that he and Kurt Kiesinger, West German chancellor, would consult fully with their NATO allies before making any decision to reduce U.S. forces in Europe. In April, after tripartite talks that included Great Britain, new plans were agreed to for offsetting the costs of troops stationed in Germany. Great Britain and the United States will withdraw 35,000 to 40,000 men and four air squadrons in 1968, allowing savings of $15,000,000 for Great Britain and over $100,000,000 for the United States.

Appointment: Paul-Henri Spaak of Belgium, former NATO secretary-general, was appointed chairman of a NATO working group for ensuring closer relations between the 15 member nations.

Total Strength of NATO units included: 56 divisions, plus 30 in reserve in land forces; 4,000 tactical aircraft, based at 150 NATO airfields; 7,000 nuclear warheads, with 2,250 delivery vehicles, both aircraft and missiles; 500 escort vehicles for naval forces; 150 nuclear submarines (potential); and 800 antisubmarine aircraft. [KENNETH BROWN]

Flags of member nations, as well as the NATO flag, flutter over the newly-built headquarters of the North Atlantic Treaty Organization in Brussels, Belgium.

NORWAY turned its September local elections into a nationwide opinion poll to test the popularity of the two-year-old coalition government–the first nonsocialist administration in 30 years. Labor made some gains, as did the Center Party (Agrarian), but there were no significant changes.

The budget, presented in October, called for total expenditure of $2,300,000,000, a 9.9 per cent increase over the previous year. Postal and telephone charges were raised, family allowances were to be increased, and the workweek was to be cut from 45 to 42 1/2 hours in 1968.

Recessions in Great Britain, the Netherlands, and West Germany made difficulties for Norway's exporters and increased a balance of payments deficit. Domestic demand threatened inflation in 1968.

Norway clashed with Britain in the fall over plans to develop an aluminum smelter industry. Norway, whose aluminum industry exports 120,000 tons a year to Britain, complained to the European Free Trade Association of unfair competition from a state-subsidized industry. [KENNETH BROWN]

Facts in Brief. Population: 3,797,000. Government: King Olav V; Prime Minister Per Borten. Monetary Unit: krone (7.16=U.S. $1). Foreign Trade: exports, $1,563,000,000; imports, $2,403,000,000. Principal Exports: ships and boats, aluminum, paper and pulp, fish and fish meal.

NOVA SCOTIA. See CANADA.

OCEAN. The National Council on Marine Resources and Engineering Development, created by the Congress of the United States late in 1966, began to influence all facets of the national oceanographic program in 1967. Edward Wenk, Jr., was appointed secretary for the newly created council, which absorbed the staff and functions of the Interagency Committee on Oceanography.

The membership for the council's companion organization, the Commission on Marine Science, Engineering, and Resources, was selected, with Julius A. Stratton as the chairman. Stratton, who also is chairman of the board of the Ford Foundation and a past president of Massachusetts Institute of Technology, established seven panels to evaluate and plan activities in particular areas of oceanology. The seven panels are: Basic Science and Research, Marine Engineering and Technology, Marine Resources, Environmental Problems, Industrial and Private Investment, International Aspects of Marine Affairs, and Education and Training.

Bills were introduced in both houses of Congress to extend the lifetimes of the commission and the council to Jan. 9, 1969, and June 30, 1969, respectively.

Universities began mobilizing their facilities and talent to participate in the new and widely popular Sea Grant College program created in 1966 by the 89th Congress. Under this program, federal funds will be given to educational institutions with special programs in ocean science, including oceanographic engineering, economy, law, medicine, and fishery science. The first large institutional grant was expected to be awarded in the first quarter of 1968.

Reports. Three important publications released in 1967 documented the first results of this new focus on the oceans. The first was issued in February by the National Council on Marine Resources and Engineering Development. It was entitled *Marine Science Affairs–A Year of Transition.*

One month later, the National Academy of Science's Committee on Oceanography, in its report *Oceanography 1966–Achievements and Opportunities*, outlined major recommendations for support of ocean science. These included a new, comprehensive, well-balanced, national ocean policy, coupled with new budgeting concepts, and a new management structure to cope with the rapid growth of ocean science and use activities.

The U.S. Navy, taking its cue from the President's Scientific Advisory Committee report of 1966, revamped the naval management structure for ocean sciences and listed its accomplishments and prospects in a June report entitled *The Ocean Science Program of the U.S. Navy.*

Man in the Sea. *Sealab III*, the most complex ocean engineering experiment attempted to date, was delayed as a result of problems with deck decompression chambers. Originally set for late 1967, this experiment was rescheduled for early 1968. *Sealab III* will test man's effectiveness and endurance at depths greater than 400 feet and will also provide an opportunity to test some of the equipment and techniques developed since the 1965 *Sealab II* experiment.

Man's increasing capability to operate at greater and greater depths was marked by a record dive of 636 feet, in August, at a site 40 miles south of Grand Isle, La. Arthur Pashette and Glen Taylor spent a total of six hours in the dive, which required six days of decompression time.

Submarine Mapping. Marine scientists from Flinders University, Adelaide, Australia, reported the discovery of the world's deepest submarine canyon, 25 miles off Western Australia near Esperance. The canyon is 20 miles wide and 6,000 feet deep, 1,000 feet deeper than the previous record holder–California's Monterey Canyon. The U.S. research ship *Oceanographer* found vast fishing grounds near the mouth of this and other submarine canyons in the vicinity.

The Antarctic research vessel *Eltanin* returned to the United States in September after traveling 194,000 miles over five years.

A Scripps expedition discovered two Western Pacific submarine volcanoes considered to be among the largest yet found. Both were discovered in the same flat abyssal plain, 1,200 miles southwest of Hawaii. They rise to within one mile of the ocean surface from a depth of 18,000 feet. [ARTHUR G. ALEXIOU]

OLD AGE. A major increase in Social Security retirement benefits was approved by the Congress of the United States in 1967, raising the payments to retired people about 20 per cent. The minimum payment to a couple was raised from $66 a month to $82. Maximum payment to a couple was increased from $252 a month to $323. See SOCIAL SECURITY.

Most of the recipients of Old Age Assistance also receive Social Security payments, and their livelihood depends on the combination of Social Security benefits and Old Age Assistance payments. The states set the level of Old Age Assistance, which varies from state to state. Social Security benefits were increased in 1939, 1950, 1952, 1954, 1958, 1961, 1965, and 1967. But generally the states reduced Old Age Assistance payments, which negated the increased Social Security benefits. Thus, the intent of Congress to increase the real income of Social Security recipients was partially nullified by state practices.

On Aug. 21, 1967, the Senate Subcommittee on Employment and Retirement Incomes recommended that future Social Security increases should contain a provision prohibiting reduction of Old Age Assistance grants due to a Social Security increase, but granting the Secretary of Health, Education, and Welfare the right to allow such reductions for states that prove that their Old Age Assistance program already pays enough for minimum subsistence needs.

Cost of Living. Information on the general social situation of older people in the United States is obtained through periodic surveys made by the Social Security Administration. The latest of these surveys was published by the U.S. Government Printing Office in August, and was entitled, *The Aged Population of the United States: The 1963 Social Security Survey of the Aged*. This report covers the population aged 62 and over in the year 1962. For that year, nearly two-fifths of the income of people over 65 came from retirement programs, 30 per cent of this from Social Security benefits. Medium income for married couples 65 and over was $2,875, and $1,130 for unmarried men and women aged 65 and over.

When a cost-of-living level for minimum needs was calculated, it was found that below that level were 24 per cent of the 5,400,000 married couples with at least one member over 65, and 65 per cent of the 8,700,000 unmarried persons over 65.

Growing Old Gracefully. Among the *gerontologists* (scientists who study human aging) there are two theories about the nature of social disengagement after age 60. According to one theory, most people beyond 60 or 65 disengage from the activities and roles of middle age with relief and pleasure that they no longer have to work so much.

An opposite theory argues that older people would like to maintain their social engagement in the society around them, but they are pushed out by the attitudes of younger people, by the rules of society, and by their own decreasing vigor.

The two opposing points of view lead to radically different attitudes on such matters as office holding in church and social organizations by people over 65.

Some light was shed on the situation in November at the annual meeting of the Gerontological Society of America in St. Petersburg, Fla., where a team of sociologists from the University of Chicago reported on a study comparing retired schoolteachers and retired steelworkers–all men, aged 69 to 76. The Chicago scientists were members of a research team that studied these two occupational groups in Bonn, West Germany; Chicago, Ill.; London, England; Milan, Italy; Nijmegen, the Netherlands; Vienna, Austria; and Warsaw, Poland. They found that the retired teachers were considerably more "engaged" in economic, social, religious, and political activities than the retired steelworkers in all of the cities of the study. There was some evidence that the retired teachers were better satisfied with their life than were the retired steelworkers who were tested. [ROBERT J. HAVIGHURST]

ONTARIO. See CANADA.

OPERA. See MUSIC.

OUTDOOR RECREATION. See CONSERVATION.

OUTER MONGOLIA, PEOPLE'S REPUBLIC OF. See MONGOLIAN PEOPLE'S REPUBLIC.

PACIFIC ISLANDS emerged in varying degrees from their traditional isolation into modern patterns of economic and social life in 1967. A prime force was the Congress of Micronesia, an interisland commission formed to study and propose ways in which members of the Pacific Island communities could improve their economic, political, and social welfare.

Polynesia. French Polynesia enjoyed a new affluence brought on by the location of a French nuclear-testing center there. Independent Western Samoa continued its efforts to improve its agriculture and attract tourists. In American Samoa, the United States continued to spend large sums for public works and education, at the same time expanding the local tuna industry and encouraging tourism.

Melanesia. The Fiji Islands, as a Pacific crossroads, were fast becoming the South Pacific's largest tourist center. They were also the site of the newly organized University of Fiji. The British Solomons and the French-British New Hebrides Islands, moving toward self-determination, made economic progress with the help of Australian investments.

Micronesia. The return of the Bonin Islands to Japanese jurisdiction was the subject of talks between Japanese Prime Minister Eisaku Sato and U.S. President Lyndon B. Johnson in 1967 as was Eniwetok and the Volcano Islands (see JAPAN). Nauru, an Australian-administered United Nations Trust Territory moved toward independence.

PAINTING AND SCULPTURE

During the course of any year, the works that will prove to be really significant trends in the visual arts are all but impossible to spot. There may be—and usually are—major events of the moment, but what real and permanent significance such events have is impossible to gauge. There were some significant events and also, to use a now-fashionable phrase, an unusually large number of nonevents as well.

The most significant event of the year by all apparent standards was the great exhibition of Pablo Picasso's sculpture, first held at the Tate Gallery in London, England, then, in October, at the Museum of Modern Art in New York City. The bulk of the work, spanning 65 years, came from the artist's own collection and was, thus, new to the public. While some of the 290 pieces had been seen in photographs throughout the years, this was the first opportunity to examine the stature of the most famous of living painters and printmakers as a sculptor. The examination suggests that Picasso at age 86 is indeed great and influential as a sculptor. In fact, the influence of his brilliant and seemingly endlessly inventive plastic creations may just possibly be more influen-

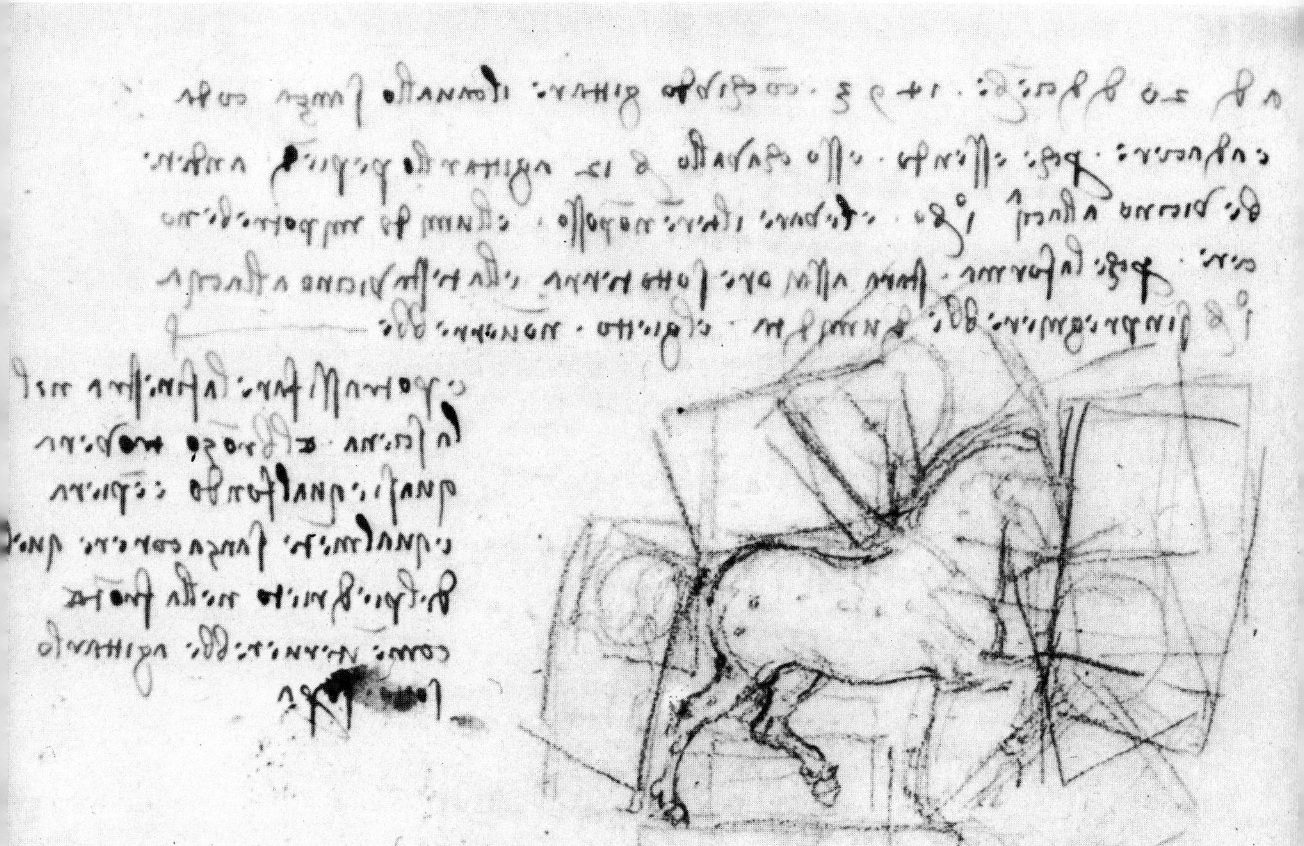

Augusto Meneses, *Life* © Time Inc., courtesy The National Museum of Madrid

Leonardo da Vinci's design for a bronze horse, annotated with the artist's curious right-to-left script, was found among "lost" notebooks in Madrid.

tial in the history of 20th century art than his two-dimensional works. The exhibition, which included Picasso's *maquette* (preliminary model) for the monumental work done for the Civic Center in Chicago, had special interest for Americans. The 50-foot, 163-ton sculpture, dedicated in August, proved that the master's eye and power of projection remain undiminished, even if the popular reception of the piece was somewhat equivocal.

Other Major Exhibitions. If Picasso proved to be as endlessly inventive as one had always supposed, the enormous retrospective exhibition devoted to André Derain held first in September at the Edinburgh (Scotland) Festival and then at the Royal Academy, London, England, proved to be just as disastrously destructive as most such exhibitions usually are. Derain emerged as a promising minor figure in his youth who later retreated into a vulgar and sentimental eclecticism that was bolstered only by his superb technical facility. Nor was the large exhibition devoted to Sir John Everett Millais, also at the Royal Academy, any more helpful to that charming but slight Victorian figure. The exhibition merely proved how talent alone without real sensibility can prove disastrous. The exhibition of the complete works of Gilbert Stuart at the National Gallery of Art in Washington, D.C., and at the Rhode Island School of Design, Providence, was more rewarding. Stuart was only a portraitist, but he was one of uncommon distinction and technical security, and he emerged as indeed America's first, true "old master." New York City's Museum of Modern Art held its long-projected retrospective exhibition of the late Jackson Pollock. The painter appeared as a sensitive, even charming, artist but one, unfortunately, of second rank, something some viewers had long suspected. The Los Angeles County Museum of Art, The Art Institute of Chicago, and the Guggenheim Museum in New York City each held large, retrospective displays of sculpture of the last few years. For selection and presentation, the Los Angeles show seemed the most provocative.

Acquisitions. The most important museum acquisition of the year, timed to coincide with its 25th anniversary, was the purchase by the National Gallery of Art of Leonardo's portrait of *Ginevra di Benci*. The painting was sold by the Prince of Liechtenstein at what was said to be a record price of $5,000,000 to $6,000,000. The Metropolitan Museum of Art bought the second version of the *Perseus* by the most famous of neoclassic sculptors, Antonio Canova, while The Art Institute of Chicago made two acquisitions: one of the finest portraits by Jacques-Louis David and one of the few that had remained in private hands; and a major figure composition by Rubens, an oil painted about 1615.

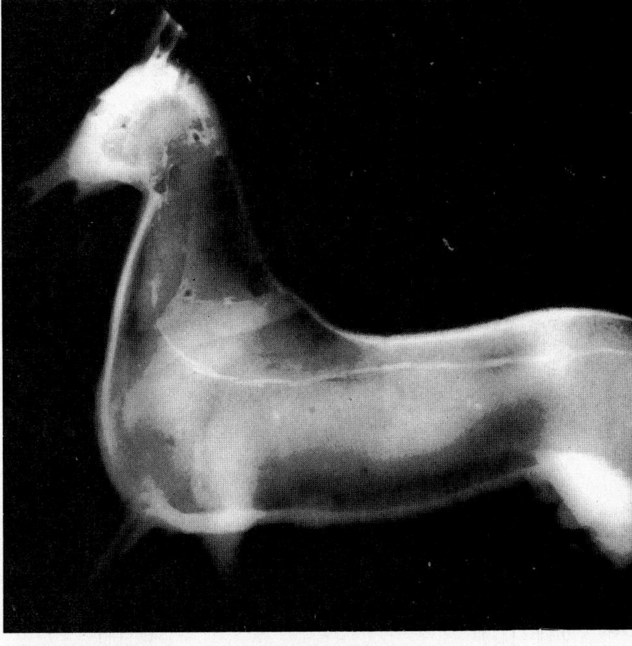

A supposedly 2,400-year-old bronze statue in the Metropolitan Museum, *left*, proved to be 50-year-old fake when a gamma-ray shadow-graph, *above*, revealed it had been cast by modern methods.

Peter Hurd's portrait of President Johnson achieved notoriety in 1967, when the President called it "the ugliest thing I ever saw."

The state of the art market continued on its merry and expensive way. Prices for major works continued to mount. As works by the greatest and most famous of masters disappeared into public collections, the prices of the works of artists of second and even third rank continued to skyrocket.

New Museums. More museums continued to be founded or to be expanded. For example, after a generation of discussion, a group of Chicagoans opened a Museum of Contemporary Art in October. The Abegg-stiftung, a small museum devoted to the study of textiles as well as to the display of decorative arts, opened near Bern, Switzerland, in 1967.

New Museum Directors. Thomas P. F. Hoving, who had made a brilliant record both at the Cloisters and as park commissioner of New York City, became director of the Metropolitan Museum of Art. The Museum of Modern Art chose an academic scholar, Bates Lowry, as its director.

Final Impressions of the year's activities lie with the continuing frenetic pace of the market and the increasingly keen competition for supreme works of art. It now becomes almost too clear that the generation of great exhibitions begun in Europe at the end of World War II is now practically over. The works are too fragile to move, and the costs are too high. The brilliant exhibition, "Man and His World," at Expo 67 may well have been the last of its kind. [John Maxon]

PAKISTAN celebrated the 20th anniversary of its independence in the midst of an economic boom. Under President Mohammed Ayub Khan, its domestic political problems had become less acute and its foreign policy more independent of either East or West influences. The death, in July, of Fatimah Jinnah, sister of Pakistan's founder, removed one of President Ayub Khan's most formidable opponents from the political scene. Four opposition parties – the Awami League, the Council of the Muslim League, Jamaat-e-Islam, and Nizam-i-Islam – united to form the Pakistan Democratic Movement during the year. Their union, however, was more of a collection of regional interests than a national challenge to the president. In East Pakistan, Governor Abdul Monem Kahn, by emphasizing the region's Islamic culture and instituting well-planned development programs, successfully maintained the loyalties of the East Pakistanis to Pakistan as a whole.

A Model Economy. Pakistan made steady progress in its economic growth. The gross national product for 1967 rose 5.4 per cent versus 4.8 per cent for the preceding year. Industrial production was up 8.6 per cent. Agricultural output increased 3.2 per cent versus .8 per cent for 1966. Per capita income rose 2.7 per cent, to $80.22. As the year neared its close, the nation's balance of payments actually showed a surplus of $34,000,000 as compared to a $13,000,000 deficit for the previous year.

Although Pakistan imported more than 2,000,000 tons of wheat in 1967, there were indications that the nation stood on the threshold of an agricultural revolution that might eventually end its grain imports. A dwarf Mexican wheat with dramatic yields per acre was planted extensively and gave promise of producing bumper crops. The Tarbela dam project on the Indus River, which would double the irrigation area in West Pakistan, got off to a promising start with a $550,000,000 loan from an Aid Pakistan consortium of Western nations. In East Pakistan work began on a 2,600-mile system of dikes which would shore up the fertile Ganges River delta against seawater and help bring 2,700,000 acres under cultivation.

Foreign Policy. Pakistan's relations abroad continued to be shaped by a fear of India and a suspicion of the United States. The title of President Ayub's new book, *Friends Not Masters*, suggested the relationship Pakistan wanted with the United States. Its policy on Vietnam became increasingly anti-American during the year, and in the Middle East crisis Pakistan sponsored a resolution in the United Nations bidding Israel to withdraw its annexation of Jerusalem. See United Nations. [Keki R. Bhote]

Facts in Brief. Population: 108,388,000. Government: President Mohammed Ayub Khan. Monetary Unit: rupee (4.8=U.S. $1). Foreign Trade: exports, $601,000,000; imports, $900,000,000. Principal Exports: jute, textiles, cotton.

PAN AMERICAN GAMES. Athletes from the United States dominated the fifth Pan American Games, held in July and August, 1967, at Winnipeg, Man. The U.S. athletes took 120 gold medals of the 173 available. Their supremacy had been expected – the gold medal total tied a record set by the United States in Chicago in 1959 – but there were major surprises in the team's victories in baseball and volleyball and in the gigantic assault on the world record book by swimmers from the United States and from Canada.

Pan American records fell by the dozens in track and field, generally the most popular phase of the games, but no world track marks were set. The U.S. men won 22 of 24 events, with Van Nelson of St. Cloud (Minn.) State College scoring the only double victory. Nelson won both the 5,000- and 10,000-meter runs.

Swimming. Mark Spitz, a 17-year-old high school student from Santa Clara, Calif., broke two world records in swimming, the 100- and 200-meter butterfly. He also captured three more gold medals in relay races that were won by the U.S. swimming team. Others to break more than one world record in the 70-x-25-yard pool, the largest in North America, were 14-year-old Debbie Meyer of Sacramento, Calif. (400-meter and 800-meter free-style); 17-year-old Claudia Kolb of Sacramento, Calif. (200-meter and 400-meter individual medleys); and Canada's Elaine Tanner, 16, of Vancouver, B.C. (100-meter and 200-meter backstroke).

World swimming marks were also shattered by Catie Ball of Jacksonville, Fla. (100-meter breast stroke); Ken Walsh of East Lansing, Mich. (100-meter free-style); Don Schollander of Lake Oswego, Ore. (200-meter free-style); and the U.S. relay squads in the men's 800-meter free-style and women's 400-meter medley.

Other Sports. In baseball, the United States upset defending champion Cuba by beating the Cubans in the third game of a best-of-three play-off series, after losing to them twice in the double round robin that determined qualifiers for the finals. It was the first time the U.S. baseball team won a Pan American gold medal. Both the U.S. men's and women's volleyball teams surprised the defending champions from Brazil to win gold medals.

The United States swept all eight weight classes in wrestling, captured six of seven rowing titles, and five of seven in weight lifting. A Pan American mark and tie of the world mark was set in rifle shooting by Lieutenant Margaret L. Thompson of Topeka, Kans., who scored 1,152 of a possible 1,200 points in small-bore competition.

The highlight of boxing was a gold medal triumph by a New York City high school boy, Forest Ward, a 200-pounder who turned professional three months after his championship-round knockout of Cuba's Luis Cabrera. [JOHN LAKE]

PANAMA. After almost three years of negotiations, representatives of the United States and Panama agreed in June, 1967, to three new accords governing the control, defense, and neutrality of the Panama Canal. The accords also provided for the possibility of a new sea-level canal between the Atlantic and Pacific Oceans. All were subject to ratification by Panama's legislature and the U.S. Senate.

The new accords replaced the 1903 agreement which, because it favored U.S. interests, had given rise from time to time to violent anti-U.S. demonstrations in Panama. Under its clauses, the United States had permanent rights over the use of the canal. Panama was excluded from exercising any administrative power over the waterway.

Eliminating Causes of Discord. It was hoped that the new agreement would eliminate the former causes of ill-feeling. Specifically, the agreements would abolish the Panama Canal Company and the Canal Zone. The former was to be replaced by a bilateral organization to be called the Panama Canal Joint Administration having a rotating presidency and nine directors – five named by the United States and four by Panama. The annual fee received by the republic would be increased from $1,930,000 to an estimated $28,000,000 to $30,000,000 in the first four years. It would rise to $40,000,000 after the fifth year. Panama, subject to the authority of the joint administration, would be given full control over the new canal area as well as over public security.

Further Agreements. In other clauses, the treaty provided that (1) the U.S. government stores in the area would become private property after five years; (2) the joint administration would have the authority to modify toll fees; (3) the treaty would be effective for a 40-year period or until a new sea-level canal was built; and (4) the United States would maintain its bases in the area and participate in its defense.

Certain U.S. Congressmen considered the various new provisions excessively liberal; in Panama, many politicians were offended by what they considered inadequate concessions to the republic.

Other Developments. The country's "gradual and progressive" entry into the Central American Common Market was agreed to by that body's policy-making economic council during the year. Work was completed on the final 28.5-mile unpaved section of the Pan American Highway connecting the city of Panamá and the Costa Rican border. Panama joined five other Latin-American nations, Argentina, Chile, Costa Rica, Ecuador, and Peru, in extending its territorial waters to 200 miles offshore. [MARY C. WEBSTER]

Facts in Brief. Population: 1,338,000. Government: President Marco Aurelio Robles. Monetary Unit: balboa (1 = U.S. $1). Foreign Trade: exports, $89,000,000; imports, $253,000,000. Principal Exports: bananas, petroleum products, fish.

PARAGUAY. See LATIN AMERICA.

PARENTS AND TEACHERS, NATIONAL CONGRESS OF (PTA), intensified its campaign against smoking, initiated a major drive to recruit members from low-income neighborhoods, and completed the first phase of a program to improve and strengthen its organizational structure and services.

Members of local PTAs in 21 states distributed brochures on smoking and health to parents of 7th and 8th grade children. The pamphlet pointed out that (1) each day nearly 4,500 children light their first cigarette, (2) one in three high school students smokes, and (3) half the nation's teen-agers are regular smokers by age 18. The PTA also called on the television industry to ban cigarette commercials before 9 P.M. local time in any community.

The Office of Economic Opportunity awarded a grant of $51,802 to underwrite the cost of the special program to enlist the interest and participation of parents living in low-income communities. A new source of leadership in the program came from state units of the National Congress of Colored Parents and Teachers.

Delegates to the 1967 annual convention, held May 22 to 24 in Minneapolis, Minn., elected the following officers: president, Mrs. Irvin E. Hendryson, Albuquerque, N. Mex.; 1st vice-president, Mrs. Leon S. Price, Dallas, Tex.; secretary, Mrs. William C. Baisinger, Washington, D.C.; treasurer, Glenn E. Holmes, Ames, Iowa. [JOSEPH P. ANDERSON]

PEACE CORPS. The School Partnership Program, designed to help build schools in underdeveloped countries, enjoyed its biggest year in 1967. Under this program, U.S. student groups raise from $1,000 to $1,500 each to pay for construction materials of a school overseas. Peace Corps volunteers provide the link between the U.S. groups and the overseas communities and help in the construction.

Of the 519 schools sponsored since the program was inaugurated by the Peace Corps in June, 1964, 396 were funded from June, 1966, to October, 1967. This represented more than 900 new classrooms in which approximately 45,000 schoolchildren will be educated annually. President Lyndon B. Johnson has set a goal of at least 1,000 partnership schools by June, 1968.

Milestone. The Peace Corps passed a significant milestone in August, 1967, when the number of returned volunteers, 14,573, outnumbered the 14,452 still serving abroad. A majority of the volunteers who had taught abroad were in great demand by U.S. schools upon their return, because of their experiences and the teacher shortage.

By the end of 1967, 12,800 volunteers were serving in 58 countries, compared to 12,006 in 53 countries at the end of 1966. The drop in year-end figures, in comparison with the number of volunteers abroad in August, reflected the usual heavy return of workers at the close of a year. Another 1,350 were in training in the United States. More and more trainees worked in city slums, depressed rural areas, and migrant labor camps before going overseas.

Politics and War. As in the past, the Peace Corps was again caught up in the political and armed crossfires of countries in which it served. It withdrew from Mauritania after that country had broken diplomatic relations with the United States during the Arab-Israeli war, and from the eastern and midwestern regions of Nigeria after civil war broke out there. In previous years, programs had been withdrawn from Ceylon, Cyprus, Guinea, and Indonesia. In 1967, however, Ceylon invited the Peace Corps to return.

Bruce Murray of Newport, R.I., a 25-year-old volunteer who protested in Chile against U.S. policy in Vietnam, was dismissed on June 28. Murray, who served as a music teacher at the Universidad de Concepción, objected to a ruling issued by Peace Corps Director Jack Hood Vaughn on June 7. This prohibited the volunteers from identifying themselves as corpsmen when voicing opinions on U.S. foreign policy. Murray's termination came after he wrote to *The New York Times* and a Chilean newspaper.

In July, Vaughn revised his ruling and informed corpsmen they were free to write to newspapers in the United States. He said Murray was discharged because he expressed his opinion in a publication of a host country. [WILLIAM MCGAFFIN]

PERCY, CHARLES HARTING (1919-), junior U.S. senator from Illinois, was mentioned prominently in 1967 as a possible Republican nominee for President in 1968. He was not an avowed candidate, but was increasingly active in party affairs and made frequent criticisms of the Democratic administration.

Percy was born in Pensacola, Fla., Sept. 27, 1919. He worked his way through the University of Chicago, earning a B.A. degree in economics in 1941. In 1938, he started working as a sales trainee for Bell & Howell Company, a Chicago-based firm manufacturing photographic equipment. He was elected president of the company in 1949 at the age of 30 and was one of the nation's youngest business executives. Percy was made chairman of the board in 1961, a position he held until 1966.

Percy headed the platform committee at the 1960 Republican National Convention. He ran for governor of Illinois in 1964, and was defeated by the incumbent, Otto Kerner. In 1966, Percy unseated Senator Paul H. Douglas (D., Ill.), his former economics teacher at the University of Chicago.

Percy and his wife Loraine visited Vietnam in December, 1967. While Percy was inspecting Dak Son, the site of a Viet Cong massacre, Communist guerrillas fired on his party. Percy was scratched and bruised on both arms. No one else in the group was injured, and they were quickly rescued by helicopters. [WALTER F. MORSE]

PERSONALITIES OF 1967. Americans chose former President Dwight D. Eisenhower as the man they admired most in 1967. He had placed second on the list five times in six years. President Lyndon B. Johnson, who had been first for the last four years, was second in 1967, according to the Gallup Poll. The Reverend Billy Graham, the evangelist, came up from fourth place to third place on the list. Senator Robert F. Kennedy of New York, third on the list for the last two years, placed fourth. Pope Paul VI was fifth for the third straight year. Senator Everett M. Dirksen of Illinois was sixth. Richard M. Nixon and former Governor George C. Wallace of Alabama tied for seventh place, and California Governor Ronald Reagan was ninth on the list.

Other Personalities in the news during 1967 included the following:

Alcock, Robert, defeated 23 women to win the title of champion knitter of King's Lynn, England. He had been practicing the craft for several years as part of his treatment for rheumatism.

Ball, Peggy, of Muncie, Ind., was spared disaster when her purse was stolen while taking a nap in Los Angeles, Calif. Her money and ticket were gone and she could not board the Trans World Airlines plane. It crashed near Constance, Ky., on November 20. See DISASTERS (Aircraft Crashes). Mrs. Ball was returning to Muncie, after visiting her husband in Hawaii. He was wounded in Vietnam.

Belote, David, of Virginia Beach, Va., visited President Johnson on July 20, and got to sit in his chair. When the President asked, "What's my name–the 36th President?" David flashed back, "Lyndon B. Johnson." Then came, "Who was the first President?" Taking longer to reply this time, David said, "George Washington." The four-year-old boy, on a White House tour with his mother and other relatives, greatly impressed the guides by reciting the names of all the Presidents of the United States in the chronological order of their terms in office.

Bradley, Reginald, was honored with a party at the U.S. Army Presidio in San Francisco, Calif., on October 25, his 100th birthday. A letter from President Johnson read: "Your devotion while serving this nation in the Indian Wars and the full and varied life you continue to live are an inspiration to us all." Bradley migrated from England in 1888, worked as a cowboy, joined the army, fought the Apaches in the Arizona Territory, and was mustered out as a sergeant in 1894. Then came 10 years as a forest ranger and a career as a rancher. Bradley now lives with a daughter near Grass Valley, Calif., and spends his time painting.

Chichester, Sir Francis, completed his solo ocean voyage around the world on May 28, having sailed farther and faster alone than any other man in recorded history. He brought *Gipsy Moth IV*, his 53-foot ketch, into Plymouth, England, at dusk. On July 7, Sir Francis was dubbed a Knight of the Order of the British Empire at Greenwich. The outdoor ceremony at the Royal Naval College was televised. As he knelt, Queen Elizabeth II tapped him on each shoulder with a sword that Queen Elizabeth I presented to Sir Francis Drake in 1581. Chichester made his 28,500-mile voyage in 226 days. He embarked from Plymouth on Aug. 27, 1966, sailed down the Atlantic and celebrated his 65th birthday on September 17, went around Africa's Cape of Good Hope, crossed the Indian Ocean to Australia, and arrived in Sydney on December 12. The badly damaged *Gipsy Moth IV* was repaired and supplied for the return voyage. The knighthood for Chichester was announced on Jan. 27, 1967, and two days later, he embarked from Sydney as Sir Francis. He crossed the South Pacific, rounded South America's Cape Horn, into the South Atlantic, and then sailed on to Plymouth. The other Sir Francis, the first Englishman to circumnavigate the world, was nearly three years on his global journey.

Stifled Initiative

Billy Churchill of Satellite Beach, Fla., had official assistance in reopening his television-tray pop stand at the end of the family drive on October 24. Governor Claude R. Kirk, Jr., flew in from Tallahassee and bought a glass of Billy's Florida orange juice. The stand was closed by Brevard County Health officials because the 11-year-old boy did not have a proper license. Governor Kirk said, "It was symbolic of a nationwide problem of individual initiative stifled by governmental red tape and foolishly administered regulation."

Couzens, Bert, a 67-year-old janitor, arrived for work three hours late in May, and was given a champagne party. He had just made a 208-mile nonstop walk from York to Barkin, England, in 36 hours 6 minutes. Couzens also got the rest of the day off.

Daly, Robert Cliff, on April 26, entered the army as the smallest soldier ever to be inducted. He is 4 feet 10 1/2 inches tall and weighs 135 pounds. Lieutenant Colonel Bill Dutton, towering to six and a half feet, administered the oath at the Denver, Colo., induction center. Daly, a former high school wrestler, wanted to go to Vietnam as a "tunnel rat," and flush out Viet Cong there. Unable to keep up with the tall men on long hikes at Fort Ord, in California, he was reassigned to train as a paratrooper.

Mr. and Mrs. John D. Rockefeller IV, smiling and happy after the wedding ceremony, leave Rockefeller Memorial Chapel at the University of Chicago.

Caroline Kennedy christens the aircraft carrier U.S.S. *John F. Kennedy* in memory of her father as her mother and brother John watch the champagne ceremony.

Dostal, James, who lives in a Chicago suburb, has four sons in the U.S. armed forces. Identical twins James R. and John R., age 19, were sworn into the army in August by their brother, Lieutenant Ronald Dostal. He is 24, and a helicopter pilot at the Van Buren Street Induction Center, Chicago. Airman 1/c Donald, age 21, was stationed in Vietnam when the swearing in took place.

Friedman, Harvey M., is the youngest person to receive a doctor's degree at the Massachusetts Institute of Technology (M.I.T.). He was granted a Ph.D. degree in mathematics on September 20, three days before his 19th birthday. He went on to Stanford University as an assistant professor of logic in the philosophy department, the youngest professor in that institution's history. The Highland Park, Ill., youth began studying mathematics at the age of seven, entered M.I.T. without a high school diploma when he was just under 16 years of age, and entered the graduate division at 18.

Gandy, Lillian G., was elected to her 11th four-year term as city collector in Corbin City, N.J., on November 7. She was unopposed and did not campaign. "The folks know I'm here," the 93-year-old widow said. She is a lifelong Republican and also holds the appointive offices of city treasurer and custodian of school funds.

"I Got It, I Got My Boa."

Adam Gilmore, a five-year-old Dayton, Ohio, boy, opened his box from under the family Christmas tree on Christmas morning and squealed, "I got it, I got it, I got my boa." He saw the boa constrictor snake in a pet shop, and had his heart set on it.

Guenther, Minnie, was chosen the 1967 American Mother of the Year by the American Mothers Committee, Inc. She was cited for bringing religious education and medical treatment to Apache Indian children. The 76-year-old widow of a Lutheran minister has lived at the Lutheran mission in Whiteriver, Ariz., since 1911. Her nine children are all college graduates. She has 22 grandchildren and three great-grandchildren.

Kazhe, Peter D., received the gold bars of a lieutenant at Fort Sills, Oklahoma, in July, the first Mescalero Apache Indian to be commissioned in the United States Army. Lieutenant Kazhe's home is in Mescalero, N.Mex. His grandfather, Rogers Tuo-Clanny, was an Indian scout for the armed forces.

Kennedy, Mrs. John F., visited Cambodia in early November. She was the guest of Chief of State Norodom Sihanouk, and received the traditional welcome reserved for high-ranking official visitors. Three days were spent among ancient ruins in northwestern Cambodia, including Angkor, or Angkor Thom, the capital of the Khmer Empire. On November 6, Mrs. Kennedy was in Sihanoukville, where she dedicated Avenue J. F. Kennedy in memory of her husband. She and her party ended their visit on November 8.

Léger, Paul-Emile Cardinal, who had served as Roman Catholic archbishop of Montreal since 1950, sailed for Africa in December as a missionary. He had long desired to work with lepers in Africa, but had been released from his archdiocesan duties by Pope Paul VI only a short while before. An earlier missionary assignment had been as superior at the Seminary of Fukuoka in Japan, from 1933 to 1939. Cardinal Léger also served as rector of the Canadian College in Rome, Italy, from 1947 to 1950.

Leinsdorf, Erich, conductor of the Boston Symphony Orchestra, and his two sons received degrees at Columbia University's commencement in June. It was the first such incident in the university's history. An honor-

Secretary of the Interior Stewart L. Udall, *left*, leads the pack in a jog along the Potomac River to publicize the healthful joys of jogging.

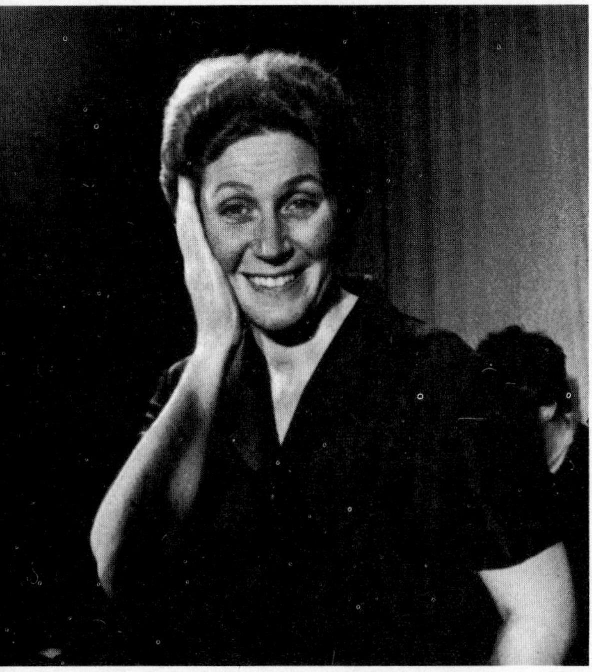

Svetlana Alliluyeva, the only daughter of Joseph Stalin, meets the press in New York City and discusses her defection from the Soviet Union.

ary degree of Doctor of Humane Letters was conferred on the father. Son Joshua received his bachelor's degree, and David was graduated from the law school.

Lindsay, John V., mayor of New York City, was named the National Father of the Year by the National Father's Day Committee. He was cited for giving new hope to urban America as a resourceful and inspired chief executive of "the world's No. 1 metropolis." Lindsay is the father of three daughters and one son.

Nixon-Eisenhower Betrothal

Julie Nixon received a diamond ring from David Eisenhower. Former Vice-President Richard M. Nixon, thinking the news was getting around, let the secret out on a television interview in late November. Young Eisenhower, the only grandson of former President Dwight D. Eisenhower, confirmed the engagement. Both are 19 and sophomores at Massachusetts colleges. Julie attends Smith College in Northampton, and David attends Amherst College in Amherst. They plan to graduate before making wedding plans. Nixon said, "They are both remarkable young people. And I'd say that even if they weren't both Republicans."

O'Brien, Mr. and Mrs. Michael, of Oak Park, Ill., became parents of a baby girl in June. Bridget is the first girl born in the O'Brien family in 60 years. She has one cousin, a boy. Mrs. O'Brien is the only girl in a family of boys, and her husband comes from a family of 10 boys.

Percy-Rockefeller Wedding

Sharon Lee Percy and John D. Rockefeller IV were married on April 1 in Chicago. The double-ring ceremony was held in the University of Chicago's Rockefeller Memorial Chapel on a rainy Saturday afternoon. The bride carried violets, rhododendrons, and roses, the state flowers of Illinois, West Virginia, and New York. Her father, Charles H. Percy, is the junior U.S.Senator from Illinois and a Republican presidential hopeful. The bridegroom, known as Jay Rockefeller, is a Democrat and a member of the West Virginia house of delegates, and a nephew of New York Governor Nelson A. Rockefeller.

Pincombe, Mrs. Winifred, of Wadsworth, Ill., is an accomplished hand with horses. She and her husband own a 22-acre horse farm, where she helps feed, groom, exercise, and also shoes the horses. Mrs. Pincombe learned her shoeing skill as an economy measure at the age of 15. A horse, bought with $150 of her own money, kept losing its shoes all the time. So, she just learned to nail on those shoes herself.

Ramoboa, Ernestine, a housewife, found a 601.25 carat diamond, the world's seventh largest, in a small mining stake in Lesotho on May 26. A New York jeweler, Harry Winston, bought it. He reportedly paid $302,400 for the diamond, with the Ramoboas getting $150,400. Ernestine, her husband Petrus, and daughter Maria came to New York in November. Winston sponsored the trip to get medical treatment for the Ramoboa's crippled and deaf daughter. Petrus liked New York City, but prefers his mountain village of Letseng-la-Draai. He would like to build a skyscraper in Maseru, the capital of Lesotho, like the ones in New York.

Sanford, Terry, and his mother, Mrs. Betsy Martin Sanford, were recipients of the American Association of School Administrators Golden Key award in 1967. Sanford was honored for his efforts to better education when governor of North Carolina during the early 1960s. He named his seventh grade mathematics teacher, his mother, as "the teacher who influenced him decisively in his formative years."

Queen Elizabeth II dubs Sir Francis Chichester a Knight Commander of the Order of the British Empire with a sword Elizabeth I presented to Sir Francis Drake in 1581.

Petrus Ramoboa holds 601.25 carat diamond found by his wife Ernestine when she was sifting gravel in the African kingdom of Lesotho.

"A Prayer in Stone."

Sir Basil Spence, the architect of England's new Coventry Cathedral, told a group of medical students that the design came to him when he had an abscessed tooth. A dentist gave him an anesthetic. "I passed out. Then the whole idea came to me. The Cathedral is built as I saw it at that time." Completed in 1962, the famous cathedral has been described as "a prayer in stone," and "an aesthetic outrage."

Tabor, Hans R., Denmark's permanent representative at the United Nations, received some 8,500 letters from television viewers in the summer. As president of the Security Council in June, he presided over the Arab-Israeli war debates. The sessions were televised, and Tabor was on for more than 51 hours. He was complimented on his fairness in conducting the heated sessions. One viewer said that Tabor had helped restore his faith in the world organization. One young girl thought the ambassador had a "darling accent." Some suggested that he enter show business.

Tenney, Roger, a teacher of vocal music at the Owatonna Junior-Senior High School in Minnesota, received the Teacher of the Year award from President Johnson on April 19. His 81-voice high school choir sang at the White House ceremony. Tenney, a dedicated teacher, came to Owatonna seven years before. He is the father of three girls: Dianne, 7; Christie, 5; and Sharon, 3.

Worthington, Bill, when attending an American Association of Retired Persons luncheon in Baltimore, Md., told how he spent much of his time reading, the Bible mostly. Asked why he had not done that earlier in life, the oldster, now 91, said, "Oh, I've read it before, but now I'm cramming for the finals."

PERU. Economic crises plagued the country in 1967. Included among them were a large trade deficit, a sizable budgetary deficit, financial woes in the fish meal industy, and a drop in cotton production, the smallest crop since 1951. To help the republic, a group of American banks lent $40,000,000 and the International Monetary Fund granted it a $42,500,000, 12-month stand-by arrangement. Monetary reserves continued to fall, however, and by mid-September they were down to $68,000,000 versus about $151,000,000 at the outset of 1967. Tight money conditions prevailed throughout the year. Living costs, meanwhile, rose an estimated 20 to 25 per cent between January and September. To halt an outbreak of strikes and violence protesting the rampant inflation, the government ordered a general wage increase.

Congress remained reluctant to act on such government proposals to relieve the situation as raising taxes and sharply increasing duties on a wide range of imports. At one point, the senate was unable to convene for a 38-day period because of an interparty argument over the validity of the election of a senate president. [MARY C. WEBSTER]

Facts in Brief. Population: 12,656,000. Government: President Fernando Belaúnde Terry. Monetary Unit: sol (38.70=U.S. $1). Foreign Trade: exports, $763,200,000; imports, $817,200,000. Principal Exports: copper, fish meal, cotton.

PET. At the last Westminster Kennel Club dog show to be held in the old Madison Square Garden in New York City, a Scottish terrier, Champion Bardene Bingo, owned by Elbridge H. Stuart of Carnation, Wash., took best-in-show honors. The February event drew 2,548 entries. It was the 24th best-in-show performance by Bardene Bingo, although the terrier had been shut out in his two previous appearances in the Westminster show.

The International Kennel Club show in Chicago, Ill., saw an English springer spaniel, Champion Salilyn's Aristocrat, owned by Mrs. Frederick H. Gasow of Troy, Mich., chosen best-in-show. Entries totaled 2,696, well under the record 1966 total of 3,420. The decline was attributed to the fact that the show had to be shifted from April to July because of scheduling conflicts resulting from the multi-million dollar fire that destroyed McCormick Place early in the year.

Leading Breeds. American Kennel Club registration figures showed the poodle maintaining its place as the most popular breed in the United States. It was the seventh year in a row that this dog held the top spot.

The first 10 in order behind the poodles were German shepherds, beagles, dachshunds, Chihuahuas, Pekingese, collies, miniature schnauzers, cocker spaniels, and basset hounds. All showed a marked increase in popularity except Chihuahuas. The only change among the first 10 was the replacement of basset hounds for Pomeranians in 10th place. Saint Bernards jumped from 23rd place to 19th.

Because of greatly increased activity in the purebred dog field, the American Kennel Club raised some of its basic fees for the first time in 46 years. In July, the fee for registering a litter was raised from $2 to $3, and for transferring an ownership from $1 to $2.

Headliners. A small white mongrel from Texas became the White House dog most favored by President Lyndon B. Johnson. Named Yuki, the Japanese word for snow, the dog was discovered wailing at an Austin, Tex., service station in November, 1966, by the President's daughter and son-in-law, Mr. and Mrs. Patrick Nugent. They adopted him.

When the Nugents went to the Bahamas in August for a vacation, they left their young son and three dogs, including Yuki, at the White House. Upon their return, they found the President had become so attached to Yuki that Mrs. Nugent told her father to keep him. Yuki has frequently been seen in the President's office, and has attended at least one news conference as well as a bill-signing ceremony in the White House rose garden.

Mijo, a powerful 180-pound Saint Bernard, received the 14th annual Ken-L-Ration Dog Hero gold medal in August. The dog is owned by Mr. and Mrs. Jake Bennett of Anchorage, Alaska. It saved the life of the Bennett's 13-year-old daughter, Philiciann, after the girl had become mired in a water-filled gravel pit. Mijo came to the girl, who grasped the dog's collar. It yanked her free. Mijo then pulled the 105-pound Philiciann to safety.

Cats. Special Grand International Champion Mizpah's Ferdnand of Briarwood, a sable Burmese male, owned by John E. Baker of Pittsburgh, Pa., took *Cat of the Year* honors. It is the only cat in the world to be a grand champion seven times. *Opposite Sex Cat of the Year* was Grand Champion Silva-Wyte of J.B., a black Persian female owned by John Bannon of Denville, N.J. *Opposite Sex Shorthair of the Year* was Double Grand Champion Mai Hai Demitasse, a sable Burmese female owned by Mr. and Mrs. R. L. Erhart of Monterey Park, Calif. Quadruple Grand Champion and Grand Champion Chestermere Kinuba of Nevah-Tep, a blue point Himalayan male, owned by Larry Keely of Chicago, Ill., was *Opposite Sex Longhair of the Year. Kitten of the Year* was Grand Champion Halton Ridge's Moontreasure, a copper-eyed white Persian female owned by Mr. and Mrs. Eric Johnston of Ontario, Canada. *Alter of the Year* was Quadruple Grand Champion Gloretta Pearl of Groot's, a shaded silver Persian belonging to Marie Groot of Portland, Ore.

Milan J. Greer, New York City pet shop owner and author, estimated that in 1967 there were 25,500,000 cats, 24,500,000 dogs, 20,000,000 pet birds, and 650,000,000 tropical fish in the United States. [THEODORE M. O'LEARY]

PETROLEUM AND GAS. In August, 1967, a 360-foot petroleum ship that displaces 11,500 tons was drilling into the great oil and gas pool under Alaska's Cook Inlet. The ship, *Wodeco IV*, served as a floating, self-propelled platform for a giant rig capable of sending a drill down through 1,000 feet of ocean water to probe for oil 10,000 feet or more below the bottom of the sea.

This big ship, and others even larger, represented one facet of an intensified, world-wide effort to find new sources of oil. There were two reasons for the stepped-up exploration. One was the increasing world demand in the face of decreasing reserves, which now total only about 30 times the current annual consumption. At the present rate of consumption, if no new sources are discovered, the last drop of the world's oil will be used up within 30 years.

The second reason for the new activity underlines the first. In June, 1967, the Arab-Israeli war temporarily cut off the flow of oil from the Middle East. This dramatized the dependence of other countries, including the United States, on Middle East oil. At least two-thirds of the world's oil reserves are located in that area. Prolonged trouble in the Arab states could mean a fuel crisis for Europe.

The closing of the Suez Canal, jammed with sunken ships at the end of the war added greatly to transportation costs. Oil tankers, along with other ships, were forced to take the long voyage around Africa. To add to the difficulties, oil prices rose in Europe. The closing of the canal reinforced a trend to larger and larger tankers that has been underway for several years. In the fall of 1967, 189 supertankers with a 100,000-deadweight tonnage were on order. All these ships will be too large to navigate the Suez Canal when it is reopened.

Growth Prospects. The need for exploration and discovery was clearly indicated by John K. Jamieson, president of Standard Oil Company of New Jersey, who said:

"The future is going to bring an immense demand for energy throughout the Free World. Our most recent projections indicate that through 1980 the average rate of growth in energy consumption will be about 4 1/2 per cent a year. On that basis, Free World demand in 1980 will be nearly double what it was in 1965.

"The rate of growth for oil and gas will be even more impressive. An average annual gain of about 5 per cent is forecast in Free World oil consumption, while gas demand is expected to rise at a rate of 5 1/2 per cent a year."

For the petroleum industry, 1967 was the sixth record year in a row. John E. Swearingen, chairman of the board of Standard Oil Company (Indiana), summed up 1967 in these words: "Both in the United States and abroad, it has been a year characterized by growth in oil and gas demand and production, a Middle East supply crisis faced and solved, and reasonably firm prices. For U.S.-based companies, profits should be in the range of 8 to 9 per cent above the 1966 level."

Total demand for petroleum products gained 4 per cent in 1967 to a level of 12,500,000 barrels a day. The largest gain in demand was in the kerosene-jet fuel products category, a 17 per cent rise.

New Sources. The Netherlands reported that significant quantities of natural gas were taken from wells under the North Sea, and drilling for new gas and oil fields in the area was continuing. Africa opened as a new source, with Occidental Petroleum drilling four large wells in Libya. Drilling was also underway in a number of other African countries. Australia, which now produces far less than one-third of the 400,000 barrels of oil the country consumes each day, made promising discoveries.

New drilling in the United States has declined steadily since 1956 when major companies went overseas to participate in the huge new oil pools that were opened. The war in the Middle East, however, encouraged a resurgence of wildcatting in Oklahoma, Texas, and Wyoming. But the most important exploratory drilling took place offshore.

The year's most exciting exploratory effort, Operation Gasbuggy, took place on December 11. This was an attempt to release oil and gas in underground New Mexico rock through the use of nuclear explosion. See MINES AND MINING. [EDWIN DARBY]

PHILADELPHIA. In a tight contest, Mayor James H. Tate won a second term by defeating District Attorney Arlen Specter by 10,892 votes. The absence of major racial outbreaks aided Tate who, in addition to giving strong support to his police department, banned any public assembly of more than 12 persons for six weeks during the summer.

In the November elections, voters approved three bond issues totaling $51,200,000 by more than 2 to 1 margins. Some 150 public projects will be affected. In May, voters passed a $13,000,000 bond issue for additional costs connected with the city's planned multipurpose sports stadium. Groundbreaking for the $38,000,000 facility took place on October 2. Near the site, in South Philadelphia, a privately financed $12,000,000 sports and entertainment center opened in October. On September 29, ground was broken for the $18,000,000 Tioga Marine Terminal, the first major construction project of the Philadelphia Port Corporation, formed in 1966.

Urban design gained support in May when a federal interagency task force recommended lowering, covering, and landscaping four blocks of the 10-lane Delaware Expressway that would have sliced through historic Penn's Landing and the Independence Hall area. The $9,000,000 required will come from state and federal funds. In turn, the city will similarly develop Delaware Avenue, parallel to the freeway. [DONALD W. LIEF]

PHILIPPINES, THE, held general elections on November 15, 1967, for eight senatorial posts, 65 provincial governorships, and 14,000 mayoral and other city-level offices. When the votes were tallied, the Nationalist party of President Ferdinand E. Marcos had made a clean sweep of most of the offices. The party already controlled the 150-member House of Representatives.

President Marcos had campaigned vigorously on behalf of his party's candidates, not only because his chances for re-election to a second term in 1969 were dependent on the outcome but also because the vote would reflect national reaction to his two-year-old "rice and roads" program. The outcome convinced Marcos that he had a solid political base from which to push lagging economic and social programs. The mandate, he announced shortly after the election, would also enable him to carry out his pledge to make all of central Luzon – the site of renewed Communist Hukbalahap activity – a land reform area by 1970. The U.S. government, he announced, would equip five more Filipino army engineer battalions for road building in the hinterland. Five units were already at work in 1967.

Economic Prospects. The country's economic growth rate – estimated at about 4.2 per cent for 1967 – was running barely ahead of population growth. Excessive luxury imports had produced a chronic trade deficit; unemployment in the cities had risen to 13 per cent.

Nevertheless, the nation continued to enjoy a potential that might well make it a showcase of Southeast Asia. The rapid acceptance by farmers of the newly developed high yield "IR-8" rice seed promised to end Filipino dependence on rice imports by 1970. The country's proven mineral wealth remained largely unexploited but a number of foreign consortiums were showing interest in exploring its possibilities.

U.S.-Philippine Relations. On April 3, the United States refused to comply with a Philippine request that it turn over Sangley Point naval air station to the Philippine navy. The base, located on the south shore of Manila Bay, had been leased to the United States until 1991. The Philippine navy had wanted to use it as a center for antismuggling operations in the bay.

In September, the United States signed a pact permitting Filipinos to exploit natural resources within American bases in the Philippines. Negotiations on the pact had begun in 1957 after U.S. officials at Clark Air Force Base near Manila had barred Filipino prospectors from land used as a U.S. airfield.

Facts in Brief. Population: 35,158,000. Government: President Ferdinand E. Marcos. Monetary Unit: peso (3.92=U.S. $1). Foreign Trade: exports, $838,000,000; imports, $957,000,000. Principal Exports: copra, wood, sugar.

PHONOGRAPH. See RECORDINGS.

PHOTOGRAPHY. The Pulitzer prize committee announced in December, 1967, that it had established a new prize for feature photography, which would be awarded in future years. In 1967 there also was an upgrading of camera and projection equipment through many new models that incorporated electronic and mechanical features to simplify picture taking and showing.

New Cameras. Several innovations unveiled at Photokina 66, held in Cologne, Germany, in 1966, made their U.S. debut. Among them were the Rolleiflex SL 66 reflex, small Rollei 35, and compact 2 1/4 x 2 3/4-inch Linhof 220.

Polaroid expanded its color-pack line, adding four new models – the 210, 220, 230, and 240 – to replace the older 100 series. It also added the 250, with a Zeiss rangefinder-viewfinder and a flashgun. The prices for these cameras ranged from under $50 to $160, with the top four models able to make automatically controlled time exposures. Eastman Kodak introduced a pair of compact Instamatic cameras, the S-10 and S-20. Both use instant-loading 126-size film cartridges, have automatic flashcube advance, and weigh 11 ounces.

Leitz announced an M4 Leica, which combines features of the M3 and M2. The addition of a three-pronged, nonremovable take-up spool permits fast and simplified film loading. A folding rapid-rewind crank fits into the body. Zeiss Ikon-Voightlander introduced its Contarex Super 35mm single-lens reflex with a behind-the-lens exposure meter. The light-measuring field is in the center of the picture format, and is indicated by a small circle in the viewfinder. The spot reading is particularly effective with telephoto lenses where small objects at great distances may be accurately exposed, regardless of the surrounding light conditions.

A specialty close-up camera outfit, designed for taking pictures in three ranges, was announced by Kodak. The 126-film cartridge-loading Instatech is a modified version of the Instamatic 104. It can be coupled to attachments consisting of lenses and frames for pictures with a 1-to-1 ratio at distances from 5 to 8 inches. The frames establish the correct position of the subject. A lens and chain system is attached for subjects at distances of 15 to 24 inches.

Slide projectors featuring electronic, automatic focusing became increasingly popular in 1967. The systems automatically bring each slide into focus after the first slide has been manually focused by the operator. Among the models with this new feature were the Honeywell Auto/Sharp 642, B & H Monitor, Miranda Auto-Sensor, Nikkormat Autofocus, Kodak Carousel 850, Sawyer's 707 AQ, and the Airequipt 450/EF.

Lenses that became available in 1967 included the first quality aspheric lens, the 50mm *f*/1.2 Leitz Noctilux, which was unveiled at Photokina 66. Spiratone introduced a low-cost 180-degree auxili-

Top Pictures of 1967

Among the award-winning pictures of 1967 were a study of fishermen, *below*, in the Northern Illinois annual ice fishing derby by Gary Settle of the *Chicago Daily News;* a picture of a chimney sweep in Basel, Switzerland, *upper right*, by Bruce Dale of *National Geographic;* "Morning Mist," by Albert Sadler of San Diego, Calif., *lower right;* and a photograph of five horses, *bottom*, trotting across a strip of land between two ponds by Jozee Salinas of the *Los Angeles Herald-Examiner*.

Bruce Dale, © National Geographic Society

ary fisheye lens, said to fit almost any camera. When fitted in front of the regular lens, the fisheye changes its effective angle of view to less than 1/6 of its original focal length.

Film News. Two extremely high-speed 35mm films, available in 36-exposure magazines, were announced. One was General Aniline & Film Corporation's Anscochrome 500, a daylight-type color transparency film for general photography under low-level lighting. The other was Kodak's 2475 Recording Film (ASA 1000 and higher). This is a panchromatic film for applications requiring low-level illumination or exposures of short duration. It was recommended for high-speed and law enforcement photography, as well as scientific work.

Awards in 1967 in various categories of photography included the following:

29th Annual Newspaper National Snapshot Awards. Grand Prize Winners ($1,000 plus 30-day around-the-world photo safari for two): *Color*–Jozee Salinas, Mt. Center, Calif.; *Black-and-white*–Geoffrey Gove, San Mateo, Calif. Second Prize ($500 plus 21-day European photo safari for two): *Color*–Donald C. Skilling, Palos Verdes Peninsula, Calif.; *Black-and-white*–Robert M. Rosenblatt, Washington, D.C. Third Prize ($250 plus 14-day Mexican photo safari for two): *Color*–Claude Chamberland, Lauzon, Quebec, Can.; *Black-and-white*–Thomas D. Riddell, Irvine, Ky. Fourth Prize ($100 plus 7-day Hawaiian photo safari for two): *Color*–Dr. Perry A. Peterson, Salt Lake City, Utah; *Black-and-white*–Edwin S. Roseberry, Charlottesville, Va. Fifth Prize ($100 plus 7-day West Indies photo safari for two): *Color*–Madelaine Tetinek, Cleveland, Ohio; *Black-and-white*–Bill Adams, Perry, Okla.

22nd Annual Collegiate Competition, sponsored by Kappa Alpha Mu (KAM), National Press Photographers Association (NPPA), University of Missouri School of Journalism, and World Book Encyclopedia Science Service, Inc. NPPA's Colonel William Lookadoo $500 Scholarship to Johnny B. Jenkins and first Milt Freier Memorial Scholarship to David A. Harvey, both of the University of Missouri. First place winners –from Washburn University: *News*, George Olson; from East Texas State: *Category X*, Raymond Adler; from the University of Minnesota: *Portrait/Personality*, Kent Robersteen; from the University of Missouri: *College Life*, *Picture Story*, *Portfolio*, Johnny B. Jenkins, named College Photographer of the Year; *Feature*, *Sports*, *Pictorial*, David A. Harvey; *Color*, James Holland.

1967 Scholastic Photography Awards, sponsored by *Scholastic Magazine* and Eastman Kodak Company. $1,000 senior scholarship to Dennis Pierce, Santa Monica (Calif.) High School. In addition to the scholarship and three $200 Special Merit awards, there were 288 cash awards totaling $6,215 to 208 winners.

Photographic Society of America 1967 Progress Medal Award to Captain Edward J. Steichen, Hon. FPSA, in recognition of his many contributions to photography culminating in "The Family of Man" exhibition.

White House News Photographers Association 1967 Grand Award to *Look* Magazine staff photographer Stanley Tretick for his color picture of Senator Robert F. Kennedy greeting crowds.

1967 Pulitzer Prize for News Photography to Jack Thornell, Associated Press, for his photo of James Meredith ambushed in Mississippi.

Joseph A. Sprague Memorial Award by NPPA, to Arthur Rothstein, *Look*, and Robert E. Gilka, *National Geographic* Magazine. [FRANK E. FENNER]

PHYSICS. Among the phenomena that physicists understand best are those related to electromagnetic and gravitational forces. Occasionally, however, they discover unusual effects whose explanations lie outside the scope of existing theory. This happened in 1967, when important experimental results were reported that may require significant modifications of established theories.

Quantum Electrodynamics (QED) is a term that refers to the theory of electromagnetic forces in the world of subnuclear particles. The present theory of QED has had impressive success in describing many phenomena, though it is not expected to be accurate when the forces act within an extremely small distance.

Physicists would like to know just how small this limiting distance is. One way to find out involves the use of high energy gamma rays from a huge particle accelerator. In the presence of matter, some of these gamma rays undergo an electromagnetic interaction that converts them into electron-positron pairs. The opening angle of the pairs can be measured. The smaller the distance over which the interaction takes place, the wider the angle between the electron and positron.

In 1966, Francis M. Pipkin and his collaborators at Harvard University announced the results of an experiment of this type. They found that for interactions characterized by distances of about a hundred-trillionth of an inch, the observed rate at which wide angle pairs were produced differed significantly from the predictions of the theory of QED. In January, 1967, results were published of a similar experiment carried out at the Deutsches Elektronen-Synchrotron (DESY) in Hamburg, Germany, by physicists from DESY and Columbia University. These results appear to be more accurate than the Harvard data and indicate no significant deviation from QED theory at these distances.

These contradictory results have generated great interest among physicists throughout the world. They hope soon to carry out experiments, with much improved accuracy, that will push the test of QED to even smaller distances.

Gravitation. The forces of gravitation are far weaker than electromagnetic forces. Observation of subtle effects frequently requires astronomical masses acting over vast distances. Up to the present time, the best known and most successful theory of gravitation has been Albert Einstein's theory of general relativity. This theory has been most accurately tested through observations of the planet Mercury. The point in Mercury's orbit that lies nearest the sun–known as the "perihelion"–appears to move, or "precess," slowly along the orbit. Until 1967, this precession could best be explained only by Einstein's theory. According to this theory, gravity is not a force acting on bodies but a consequence of the curvature of space.

The most powerful linear accelerator in the world was dedicated on September 9 at Palo Alto, Calif., by Glenn T. Seaborg, chairman of the Atomic Energy Commission.

In 1964, Robert H. Dicke of Princeton University suggested that part of Mercury's perihelion rotation might be due to a rapidly spinning core within the sun. If such a core exists, it should cause the sun to appear slightly flattened at its poles. Accordingly, Dicke and H. Mark Goldenberg, a colleague at Princeton, constructed a precision optical telescope, equipped it with sensitive electronic detection equipment, and in January, 1967, carefully measured the circular symmetry of the sun's disk. They reported their finding, that the sun is indeed slightly oblate. If this flatness is due to a rapidly spinning core beneath the sun's surface, then Dicke's belief that gravitation is more than a purely geometrical phenomenon is confirmed, and general relativity is no longer accurate in accounting for the excess precession of Mercury's perihelion. Dicke's results agree with a "scalar-tensor" theory of gravitation that he and Carl Brans proposed in 1961.

Of course, some important questions remain to be answered: Are present data on Mercury's orbit completely accurate? How can we discover if the sun's flattening is due to something other than a spinning core? Many physicists have faith in general relativity's ultimate correctness because of its workability and past success. The issue, however, can be settled only by experimentation. [THOMAS O. WHITE]

PLASTICS. See CHEMICAL INDUSTRY.

POETRY. See LITERATURE.

POLAND gave its usual firm support to the Soviet Union's foreign policy in 1967. Twice during the year–once in Poland in January, and again in Moscow in September–Soviet leader Leonid I. Brezhnev conferred with Poland's Wladyslaw Gomulka. More than once during the year, Polish leaders supported Soviet calls for an international Communist conference. A visit to Hanoi by a top Polish leader, Zenon Kliszko, indicated continuing support for North Vietnam. Following a Soviet-bloc conference in Warsaw on Germany, Poland not only concluded a 20-year friendship pact with Bulgaria, Czechoslovakia, and the (East) German Democratic Republic, but it also re-emphasized its stand against West Germany's policies. See GERMANY.

Poland did not neglect its relations with the non-Communist world, especially France. A visit by President Charles de Gaulle in September produced no striking results but it was dramatic evidence of a mutual desire for friendship. De Gaulle paid tribute to Poland and urged it to play a larger role in European affairs, subtly suggesting a more independent course. He did not reiterate his earlier acceptance of the Western boundaries but traveled to points in those territories during his extensive tour of the country. The Polish foreign minister, Adam Rapacki, made official visits to Britain, France, and Turkey during the year. A noteworthy event in the economic field was the admission of Poland, as a full member, to the General Agreement on Tariffs and Trade (GATT). See EUROPE; INTERNATIONAL TRADE AND FINANCE.

The domestic scene was relatively quiet on the surface, but serious stresses were present. Ideological unrest had been created among intellectuals at the close of 1966 by the expulsion of a leading philosopher, Professor Leszek Kolakowski, from the party.

Relations between the Roman Catholic Church and the regime in 1967 were somewhat more peaceful than in 1966. Church-state talks took place on the disputed question of the closing of seminaries. A new cardinal, Karol Cardinal Wojtyla, the second in Poland, was appointed in Kraków. The Vatican appointed apostolical administrators in dioceses in the western territories, thus moving closer to recognition of Polish sovereignty. Several visits by a papal envoy seemed to point toward a rapprochement, or at least a lessening of tension. Prominent party leaders, however, continued to denounce the Polish hierarchy. [H. GORDON SKILLING]

Facts in Brief. Population: 32,531,000. Government: Communist Party First Secretary Wladyslaw Gomulka; Premier Josef Cyrankiewicz; State Council Chairman Edward Ochab. Monetary Unit: zloty (24=U.S. $1). Foreign Trade: exports, $2,272,000,000; imports, $2,495,000,000. Principal Exports: coal, meat, ships and boats.

POPULATION, WORLD. The world's population continued its tremendous growth in 1967, reaching 3,400,000,000 by midyear. It took 130 years, from 1800 to about 1930, for world population to grow from 1,000,000,000 to 2,000,000,000. The next billion increase in world population is expected within 15 years, with the present population expected to more than double by the end of the century.

Population growth is most rapid in those parts of the world where existence is the most precarious. In the developing countries of Africa, Asia, and Latin America, hunger, illiteracy, and poverty are endemic. About 85 per cent of the births occur in these poverty-stricken areas.

In the United States, the 1967 birth rate–about 18.3 births per 1,000 population–was the lowest in the history of the nation. The decline began in 1956 and continued through 1967. In November, the U.S. Bureau of the Census announced that the country's population had grown to 200,000,000. It said that, in view of the declining birth rate, the population may not exceed 300,000,000 by the year 2000. See CENSUS; VITAL STATISTICS.

Family Planning. The International Planned Parenthood Federation announced in November that it would spend $6,500,000 on its 1968 program. The federation, which represents voluntary family-planning groups in more than 50 countries, said the figure was double its 1967 budget and six times that of 1966. The largest share of the 1968 funds, an allocation of $2,350,000, would go to Latin America, an increase of $500,000 over the 1967 expenditure.

The federation, which meets every four years, held its eighth conference in Santiago, Chile, in April. About 1,250 delegates representing more than 80 countries and international organizations attended.

The Ford Foundation, in November, announced grants totaling $15,700,000 to scientists exploring simpler, safer, and more effective contraceptive techniques. McGeorge Bundy, president, said the largest such grant, $1,600,000, went to the Bio-Medical Division of the Population Council to establish a monkey colony for contraceptive research. The foundation also gave the Population Council $5,000,000 to extend its overseas assistance and to strengthen its educational program in family planning. In May, $435,000 was allotted for a program to train 32 Latin American doctors and medical researchers in scientific family planning.

The U.S. Agency for International Development (AID) reported that in 1967 about $20,000,000 was made available to support population-control and family-planning programs in countries requesting assistance. This compared with $4,000,000 used during 1966 to assist such programs in 20 countries. AID increased the staff of its reorganized Population Division from 4 to 28. [ROBERT C. COOK]

PORTER, GEORGE. See NOBEL PRIZES.

PORTUGAL. Premier António de Oliveira Salazar marked the 39th anniversary of his rise to power as head of the Portuguese government on April 28, 1967. Shortly thereafter, he announced an ambitious new six-year development plan aimed at bringing the Portuguese economy up to a European standard. The plan's principal targets included a 7 per cent annual growth rate of the gross national product and an 8.2 per cent rate of increase of fixed capital investment. The six-year plan also called for a total investment of $5,862,000,000 with about one-quarter of the projected outlay going to Portugal's overseas provinces.

The problems created by Portugal's determination to retain its overseas provinces of Angola and Mozambique continued to produce economic stresses at home and diplomatic problems abroad. The strain of maintaining a 120,000-man expeditionary army to fight the nationalist guerrillas in Africa was increasingly taxing the Portuguese economy. Civilian priorities continued to be sacrificed to meet the military requirements. In November, Portugal was assailed in the United Nations because of its policies in Africa. [KENNETH BROWN]

Facts in Brief. Population: 9,330,000. Government: President Américo Deus Rodrigues Tomaz; Premier António de Oliveira Salazar. Monetary Unit: escudo (29.02=U.S. $1). Foreign Trade: exports, $627,000,000; imports, $1,012,000,000. Principal Exports: textiles, fish, wine.

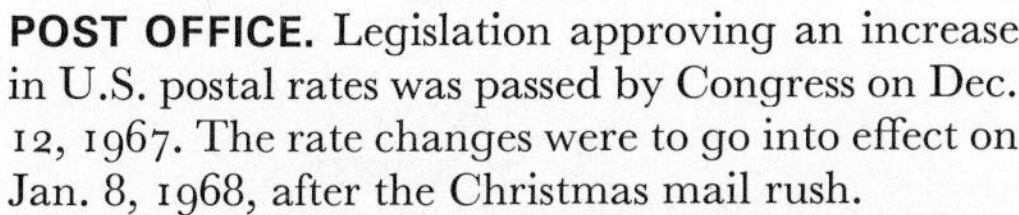

Closed-circuit television in the main Detroit post office, *right*, was used to cope with the growing volume of mail. Postmaster General Lawrence F. O'Brien, *above*, called it "a race with catastrophe."

POST OFFICE. Legislation approving an increase in U.S. postal rates was passed by Congress on Dec. 12, 1967. The rate changes were to go into effect on Jan. 8, 1968, after the Christmas mail rush.

The new rates require 6 cents postage for first-class mail, which had been 5 cents; 10 cents for airmail letters, a rise of 2 cents; 5 cents for postal cards, which had been 4 cents; and 8 cents for airmail postal cards, a 2-cent increase. The rate increases were expected to produce about $900,000,000 a year in new revenue.

It was the most extensive postal rate change in history. Postmaster General Lawrence F. O'Brien predicted, however, that the changes would be the smoothest ever put into effect. Among the steps he planned to take to ensure a smooth changeover was the sending of 200,000 posters and signs on the new rates to post offices throughout the country for display in many public buildings. Public service announcements were also prepared for radio and television stations.

In addition to the increases in first-class mail and airmail, rates also were to be increased on other classes in 1968.

The rates for third-class mail–bulk mail and unsolicited direct-mail advertising–were to increase from 2.8 cents to 3.5 cents, and then to 4 cents in 1969. For mailings of 250,000 or more pieces, however, the rate would be 3.8 cents.

The legislation also abolished the special 4-cent rate for greeting cards and other single-piece mailings entitled to third-class privileges. In effect, this makes the cost of mailing unsealed Christmas cards the same as that of first-class letters–6 cents.

New York Fire. The Morgan annex of the New York General Post Office burned out of control for more than eight hours on December 16, in what was described by O'Brien as "the worst postal facility fire in many decades." The annex handled 85 per cent of the country's international mail routed for ship transportation. It also was a concentration point for large-volume bulk mailings, chiefly advertising circulars, and for newspapers and magazines. According to postal officials, the blaze destroyed more than 6,000,000 pieces of mail and parcels.

Firemen found a partly opened package containing $44,000 in cash among the charred debris, the water-soaked packages, and the sludge of fallen plaster mixed with water. The money was turned over to postal authorities.

Statistics. The 716,603 employees in the Post Office Department handled a total of 79,165,000,000 pieces of mail in fiscal 1967, a 4.7 per cent increase over 1966. The department received $6,133,449,396 in appropriations. As of June 30, there were 32,626 post offices, and 11,524 contract and classified stations and branches.

POULTRY. See AGRICULTURE.

POVERTY. "I recommend that we intensify our efforts to give the poor a chance to join in the nation's progress," President Lyndon B. Johnson told the Congress of the United States in his January, 1967, State of the Union address. But the money was still lacking for a full-scale offensive as it had been every year since Mr. Johnson declared "unconditional war on poverty in America" in his first major speech as President, on Jan. 8, 1964.

When he sent his fiscal 1968 budget to Congress, the President requested only a modest increase in anti-poverty funds, $2,060,000,000 in contrast to the $1,600,000,000 appropriated by Congress for fiscal 1967. But the cost of the other war in Vietnam had become so excessive, an estimated $30,000,000,000 a year, that Congress decided the country could not, in addition, afford even a slight acceleration of the war on poverty.

The more liberal Senate did authorize more than the President requested – $2,225,000,000 – but the House, after a three-day debate, cut the amount in its authorization bill to $1,600,000,000. The Office of Economic Opportunity (OEO) had insisted that a minimum of $1,788,000,000 was necessary to prevent cutbacks in the poverty program. The final compromise figure, approved on the last day of the session, was $1,773,000,000 – $15,000,000 short of the OEO request and $287,000,000 short of the President's budget request. However, the poverty program was still one of the few programs that was authorized more money in fiscal 1968 than in 1967.

Civil rights leaders complained that spending on this scale would not make a serious dent in the nation's poverty. Whitney M. Young, Jr., executive director of the Urban League, compared it to "applying Band-Aids as a cancer cure." The Reverend Martin Luther King, Jr., president of the Southern Christian Leadership Conference, described the anti-poverty war as "scarcely a skirmish." It was generally agreed by the critics that a much larger budget would be necessary to accomplish the President's proclaimed goal of eliminating poverty in the United States. An estimate by the A. Philip Randolph Institute called for combined expenditures by government and private industry of $185,000,000,000 over a 10-year period.

Ghetto Proposal Defeated. Had the administration not been confronted with the staggering expense of a major land war in Asia, it probably would have greatly increased its anti-poverty budget. As matters stood, however, it did not react sympathetically to the attempt of a group of Senators, led by Joseph S. Clark (D., Pa.), to add $2,800,000,000 to the war on poverty. Alarmed by racial riots in the summer of 1967 in Newark, N.J.; Detroit, Mich.; and other cities, the Clark group was convinced that whatever the strains on the economy, Congress should act to relieve the pent-up pressures of the ghettos (see CITY; CIVIL RIGHTS). Clark was additionally motivated by a study of poverty conditions in cities and rural areas conducted by his Senate Subcommittee on Employment, Manpower, and Poverty. In Mississippi, the subcommittee found some Negroes suffering from what it declared was a near-starvation diet – a charge that was challenged by Mississippi members of Congress.

Clark's group proposed a $2,800,000,000 emergency program to create 200,000 jobs over a two-year period. The proposal had little chance in the Senate, which defeated it 54 to 28. A compromise $925,000,000, one-year job program, jointly sponsored by Clark and Senator Winston L. Prouty (R., Vt.), drew the support of both Democrats and Republicans, however, and was only narrowly defeated, 47 to 42.

Poverty Bill Changes. Democratic supporters of the administration were encouraged, nevertheless, due to failure of Republicans to put through a series of amendments that would have dismantled the OEO, placed anti-poverty programs under other agencies, and required more involvement by the states and by private business. The Democrats, who had worked for weeks to line up votes, proclaimed a moral victory in keeping the programs alive, if not entirely intact. An important administrative change in the anti-poverty program was granted as a concession to Southern Democrats and big-city Demo-

cratic mayors. Nearly all anti-poverty Community Action grants will be funneled through local governmental agencies instead of going directly from Washington to nongovernmental agencies. The poor will still have representation on various boards, but their policy-making power will be restricted. This was a sharp departure from the original conception of the 1964 anti-poverty act, which required the "maximum feasible participation" of the poor in planning and operating poverty programs. This participation was considered indispensable, at the time, as a means of breaking down barriers of hostility between the poor and the outside world. The House minority leader, Gerald R. Ford of Michigan, reminded Democrats that they had formerly argued that the poor could help themselves only if city halls and county courthouses, the traditional dispensers of patronage, were by-passed.

Under the new provision, local governments will either run the Community Action programs or will designate a private agency they wish to take on the task. It will no longer be possible for private Community Action agencies to by-pass their local governments and deal directly with the OEO in Washington, D.C. The change in the law won the support of the Southern Democrats and big-city Democratic machines. Their viewpoint was stated by Representative Carl D. Perkins (D., Ky.), who said, "If we are going to have a program that will endure . . . we must get the local governments more involved."

There was speculation during the year that R. Sargent Shriver, Jr., the 52-year-old OEO director, would resign sometime in 1968. In his annual report to Congress, he gave this accounting of major developments during fiscal 1967:

Community Action Programs (CAP) included a series of programs operated by 1,050 Community Action Agencies to help the poor "break out of the iron circle of poverty" through stimulation of a broad-based "hometown effort." Among them were:

Head Start, the program for prekindergarten children that helps prepare them for entry into the public schools, had 465,000 enrolled for an eight-week session in the summer of 1967. In addition, 215,000 children attended classes during the school year. A total of $352,000,000 was allocated for Head Start. See EDUCATION.

Upward Bound. This educational experiment enrolled 23,000 high school students in 249 projects in the summer of 1967, at a cost of $27,000,000. About 6,000 students were enrolled for the first time, with the rest returning for a second "Upward Bound summer" designed to give inspiration and "catch-up" knowledge for a college career. In the fall of 1967, 4,750 Upward Bound students entered college. Entrance requirements in most instances were waived, special tutorial programs were set up, and complete financial support was provided for the student's first year.

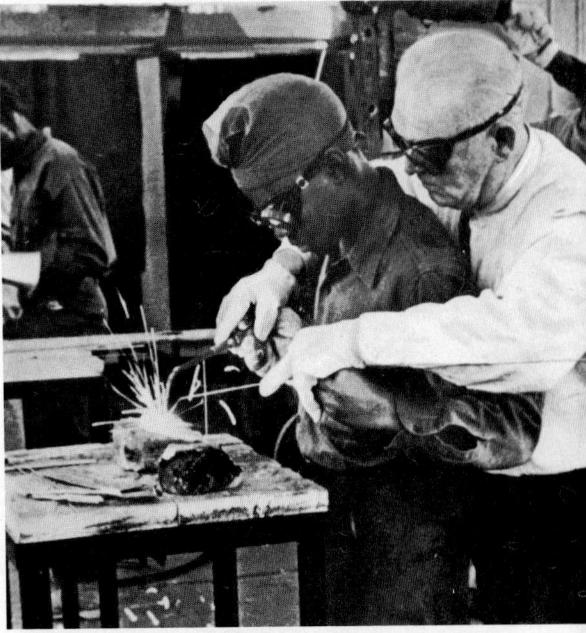

Manpower training project in Detroit was one of many efforts to teach disadvantaged persons job skills and lift them out of the ghettos.

Legal Services were provided free to 313,000 persons by 1,800 lawyers employed in 850 nationwide neighborhood law offices. The cost of this program was $24,700,000.

Neighborhood Health Centers. By the end of June, 1967, 41 centers had been approved and seven were in full or partial operation. Under a $60,200,000 program, mental health services, drugs and appliances, social service follow-up, and medical, dental, and related services were offered within one centrally located facility.

Foster Grandparents supplied 3,927 men and women in their 60s with work caring for 8,000 neglected children in 38 states and Puerto Rico, under a budget of $8,300,000.

Project Find for the "friendless, isolated, needy, disabled" was created to help locate needy older persons. It had a budget of $1,200,000 and employed 372 low-income persons to aid in the search.

Job Corps. Training in new vocational careers was provided 41,000 high school drop-outs, aged 16 to 21, at 123 Job Corps centers under a program costing $209,200,000.

VISTA, the "Volunteers in Service to America" program, informally called the domestic Peace Corps, had 4,250 volunteers working on 412 projects in 48 states, the District of Columbia, the Virgin Islands, and Puerto Rico. Its budget was $26,300,000. [WILLIAM MCGAFFIN]

PRESIDENT OF THE UNITED STATES

President Lyndon Baines Johnson conferred with many of the world's leaders and traveled widely in 1967. But neither conferences nor trips could conceal the growing opposition to his policies – the war on poverty at home, and the war in Vietnam abroad. He asked Congress, unsuccessfully, to raise personal and corporate income taxes to pay for the escalated fighting in Vietnam, and he urged Congressmen to further his anti-poverty program.

The President's surprise conference with Soviet Premier Aleksei N. Kosygin at Glassboro, N.J., was a highlight of 1967. Kosygin was in the United States to participate in the discussion at the United Nations (UN) on the Middle East crisis. At Glassboro State College, halfway between Washington, D.C., and the UN headquarters in New York City, the two leaders of the world's most powerful nuclear-armed nations met face to face for the first time. For five and a half hours on June 23 and again for four hours on June 25, they talked about the Middle East

Historic Glassboro meeting included, left to right, Secretary of Defense McNamara, Premier Kosygin, Secretary of State Rusk, and President Johnson.

crisis, the war in Vietnam, and the possibility of an arms control agreement. Some progress was reported on arms control, but there was no agreement on the Middle East crisis or on a way to end the war in Vietnam. Nevertheless, President Johnson had opened friendly personal relations with the Russian premier, and he had silenced critics who doubted that he would talk with Kosygin. See DISARMAMENT; UNITED NATIONS.

Travels. The President left the continental United States six times in 1967, visiting Guam, Uruguay, West Germany, Canada, Mexico, Australia, Thailand, Vietnam, and Italy. On March 20, he flew to Guam to meet with South Vietnamese Premier Nguyen Cao Ky and Chief of State Nguyen Van Thieu. He also talked with General William C. Westmoreland, United States military commander in South Vietnam, and received a copy of South Vietnam's new constitution.

In April, President Johnson flew to Punta del Este, Uruguay, for a three-day conference with Latin American heads of state. He addressed an informal closed session of the presidents of the Western Hemisphere on April 12, and pledged United States support for a Latin American common market. Following the Punta del Este meeting, he flew to West Germany to attend the funeral of former West German Chancellor Konrad Adenauer on April 24. After the funeral, he talked with German Chancellor Kurt Georg Kiesinger, French President Charles de Gaulle, and British Prime Minister Harold Wilson.

On May 25, the President visited Expo 67, the world's fair at Montreal, and lunched with Canadian Prime Minister Lester B. Pearson. On October 28, he met Mexican President Gustavo Díaz Ordaz in Ciudad Juárez, Mexico, and turned 437 acres of land over to Mexico in settlement of a century-old boundary dispute that had been resolved by agreement in 1963.

The President flew to Australia, on December 19, to honor the memory of a loyal supporter of the U.S. commitment in Vietnam, Prime Minister Harold Holt, who had apparently drowned while swimming. This was the occasion for another gathering of the allied leaders in Vietnam and many other dignitaries, with whom he conferred. Then the President flew to the war zone to talk to U.S. troops and airmen in Thailand and Vietnam. He then went to Rome, where he discussed the prospects for peace with Pope Paul VI at the Vatican before he returned to the White House for Christmas.

War in Vietnam. The frustrating and costly war in Vietnam caused much popular discontent with the Johnson administration. Throughout the year the President repeated his hope that an "honorable peace" would soon be negotiated, but no peace talks were held. On March 21, North Vietnam disclosed that the President had written the North Vietnamese President Ho Chi Minh, in February, proposing direct negotiations to end the war. The North Vietnamese leader maintained that the bombing and all the other American hostilities must stop before peace talks could begin.

In May, the Associated Press reported that the President had banned all bombing of Hanoi, capital of North Vietnam, from December, 1966, to April, 1967, hoping that North Vietnam would agree to open peace talks. The ban was lifted on May 20, and after that Hanoi suffered intensive bombing.

President Johnson, at a March press conference, virtually named Vice-President Humphrey as his running mate should he choose to run in 1968.

By midsummer, the need for more American troops in Vietnam was the subject of wide debate. At a joint news conference with General Westmoreland and Chief of Staff General Earle Wheeler, on July 13, the President told newsmen that modest troop increases would be necessary. On August 3, he announced that he would send 45,000 to 50,000 additional soldiers to Vietnam, and that the total number of troops in the area would reach 525,000 by June 30, 1968. See NATIONAL DEFENSE.

In September, responding to his critics, President Johnson defended the U.S. policy of selective bombing of targets in North Vietnam. He denied that there was a difference of opinion between his military and civilian advisers. In early November, the President made seven major speeches during a continent-wide, 5,000-mile trip to explain and defend his policies and to denounce his critics.

The explanations did not satisfy a growing and articulate group of Congressmen and intellectuals who challenged the President's conduct of the war. With the President in attendance at a Sunday-morning service in the Bruton Parish Church in Williamsburg, Va., on November 12, its minister asked for "some logical, straightforward explanation" of the American presence in Vietnam. At year's end, critics of the war continued to challenge the President.

Middle East War. President Johnson also worried about the Arab-Israeli war, in June, 1967, and its aftermath. When Egyptian President Gamal Abdel Nasser closed the Gulf of Aqaba to Israeli shipping in May, President Johnson advised the United Arab Republic to avoid the illegal blockade and warned that the United States supported the territorial integrity of all Middle Eastern states and the right of "free innocent passage of all ships" through the gulf.

Following the rapid Israeli victory in the subsequent war, the President and his advisers worked out a five-point program to settle the Middle East dispute. Late in June, he announced that the United States would extend $5,000,000 in emergency relief for Arab-Israeli war victims. See MIDDLE EAST.

Other Foreign Policy Actions. In line with UN sanctions, the President signed an executive order halting United States trade with Rhodesia on January 5. On January 14, he asked Undersecretary of State for Political Affairs Eugene Rostow to organize an Aid to India consortium to help meet India's food shortage. On February 2, in a special message to Congress, he said he was sending 2,000,000 tons of grain to India and asked Congress to approve sending 3,000,000 tons more, if this shipment were matched by other nations.

In March, the President asked Congress to increase Latin America's share of United States aid by 30 per cent a year. On June 29, acting on authority granted by Congress, President Johnson gave his approval to the Kennedy Round of tariff-cutting talks and authorized the United States to sign the agreement. Tariff cuts of up to 50 per cent will be made gradually after Jan. 1, 1968. In July, he announced an agreement with Mexico to build and operate an international flood control project for the Tijuana River.

Relations with the 90th Congress disappointed President Johnson. In his State of the Union message, he asked for increased Social Security benefits, for a flexible draft law, for an anticrime program, for a tax rise, and for vigorous prosecution of the war on poverty at home and the war against Communism in Southeast Asia. But the 90th Congress rejected many of the President's requests and sharply reduced others. See CONGRESS OF THE UNITED STATES.

CIA Exposure. Criticism of the Central Intelligence Agency (CIA) troubled the President during 1967. The public learned in February that for years the CIA had given secret funds to private organizations, including student associations and labor unions. Responding to widespread criticism, on March 29, the President ordered such secret funding to stop, except in cases where the Departments of State and Defense have "overriding security reasons" for secret action. Even in such cases, cultural, educational, and philanthropic groups were excluded. The President acted on the recommendations of a five-man committee, chaired by Undersecretary of State Nicholas deB. Katzenbach, that had investigated the actions of the CIA.

The Middle East crisis brought President Johnson's closest advisers together in the tense atmosphere of the situation room located in the White House basement.

Selective Service and its inequities were reevaluated by a special presidential commission that reported in 1967. Acting on their recommendation, President Johnson asked Congress to revise the Selective Service System. The legislation passed by the 90th Congress, however, did not give the President the flexibility he had requested.

In November, the Director of Selective Service, Lieutenant General Lewis B. Hershey, said that he had checked with the White House before he ordered local draft boards in the nation to deprive war protestors of their deferments, declare them delinquents, and draft them as soon as possible. The action led to protests by some members of Congress, civil liberties lawyers, and college officials.

Riots and Slums. On July 27, President Johnson appointed an 11-member Advisory Commission on Civil Disorders to study problems of the urban slums and the causes of the rioting and to recommend remedial measures. The action was taken after the President sent troops to Detroit, Mich., to quell a disastrous riot (see Civil Rights). On September 14, in an address to the International Association of Chiefs of Police, he criticized rioters and their leaders.

Other Domestic Actions. Throughout the year, the President was busy naming commissions and evaluating their reports. He named commissions to study the CIA, crime, civil disorders, Selective Service, pornography, and the postal system.

President Johnson was welcomed by the First Lady when he arrived at airport in Nashville, Tenn., to dedicate a junior college in nearby Columbia.

On February 20, the President addressed a conference on national farm policy called by Secretary of Agriculture Orville L. Freeman. In May, he met with six New England governors and promised that he would order a study of the problems of the New Haven Railroad. In September, he urged a $5,000,000,000 plan to expand the nation's air traffic system. The expansion would be financed by the aviation industries, communities with air service, and the flying public.

Democratic Party Leader. President Johnson, in his role as Democratic party leader, worked to pave the way for the presidential elections in 1968. Within party ranks, there was growing dissatisfaction with his conduct of the war, and public opinion surveys indicated popular disapproval of his handling of the presidency. Yet the President gave every indication that he would be his party's candidate in 1968. In March, he described his presidency as "the greatest era of American progress known since our Constitution was adopted." He attacked critics of the Vietnamese war, charging that they weakened the American position in Vietnam, and he blamed the Republicans for the failures of his program in Congress. See DEMOCRATIC PARTY; ELECTIONS.

Presidential Succession. The 25th Amendment became part of the U.S. Constitution on Feb. 10, 1967, when it was ratified by the 38th state. It was formally proclaimed by the White House on February 23. It had been submitted to the states on July 6, 1965.

Under its provisions, the Vice-President was to become President if the President died or resigned. In case of a vacancy in the office of the Vice-President, the amendment, said that the President was to nominate one, who would take office on confirmation by a majority vote of both houses of Congress.

The amendment further provided that if the President declared in writing that he was disabled, the Vice-President would be Acting President. If the Vice-President and a majority of the cabinet "or of such other body as Congress may by law provide" declared in writing that the President was disabled, the Vice-President would become Acting President.

Under other provisions of the amendment, the President could return to office if he declared in writing that no disability existed, unless the Vice-President and a majority of the cabinet "or . . . other body" declared otherwise. In the latter case, Congress would determine the issue by a two-thirds vote of both houses. [CAROL L. THOMPSON]

See also JOHNSON, LYNDON BAINES; U.S. GOVERNMENT; Section One, JAMES B. RESTON: FOCUS ON THE NATION.

PRINCE EDWARD ISLAND. See CANADA.

PRISON. See CRIME.

PRIZES. See AWARDS AND PRIZES; NOBEL PRIZES; PULITZER PRIZES.

"The question is, Mr. President, which of us is on the mainland?"

PROTESTANT. World Protestantism celebrated its 450th anniversary in 1967 and encountered some of the most troublesome issues in its history. Most Protestants consider Oct. 31, 1517, as the symbolic beginning of the Reformation. On that day, Martin Luther issued his Ninety-Five Theses criticizing the Roman Catholic Church and pointing toward a fresh understanding of God's grace. In October, 1967, Protestants gathered – quite often with Roman Catholics – in countries throughout the world, to recall that event.

The fact that Communists in Eastern Europe tried to appropriate Martin Luther as a hero of the peoples' revolutions of the 16th century and to honor him, was one sign of a continuing problem as well as a new potential for Protestants. While Christians suffered inconvenience and harassment in many nations under Communist control, there also were signs of moderation and change in the countries of the Free World. The French Communist theoretician, Roger Garaudy, toured North America and took part in dialogues with Christians. Martin Niemöller, the German Lutheran clergyman who had once opposed Hitler and who now was a tireless agitator for peace programs, was awarded the Lenin Peace Prize in April. *The Baptist World* reported that the Baptist faithful were gathering as worshiping groups in the Soviet Union despite the official encouragement given atheism by the government.

Many Protestant theologians joined Roman Catholics in expressing interest for more interaction with Communist theorists.

The 450th anniversary of the Reformation represented a significant change in Catholic-Protestant relations. Whereas "Reformation Day" as recently as 10 years ago was often the occasion for anti-Catholic rallies, some Reformation observances in 1967 were addressed by Roman Catholic priests and laymen.

Protestant-Catholic Interaction had two sides as did Christian-Communist interaction. While some Catholics had urged Pope Paul VI to remove the old ban of excommunication against Luther, hostility and mistrust remained in many countries. Spain, a stronghold of conservative Catholicism, passed a new law purportedly granting religious liberty. Most Protestants, among them Lutherans, Pentecostals, and Spanish Presbyterians, complained loudly that the law's guarantees were minor and that they were accompanied by offensive demands, among them the requirement that Protestant churches register as "associations," falling under government surveillance.

In the state of New York, many Protestant groups organized to oppose what they considered to be Roman Catholic attempts to rewrite the state constitution to make possible financial aid for parochial schools. Protestant leaders joined others in placing a major newspaper advertisement complaining that "Catholic Bishops Assail Birth Control as Millions Face Starvation."

Such tensions were the exception and not the rule, however. Protestant proposals relating to Catholicism rarely went so far as those of Episcopal Bishop C. Kilmer Myers of California, who foresaw and advocated an eventually reunited church under the pope as chief pastor and spokesman. But at the other end of the Protestant spectrum, the Southern Baptist Convention magazine, *Home Missions*, reported that the large conservative body was in ever-increasing dialogue with Catholicism.

War in Vietnam. In a time of rapid social change it was inevitable that much news affecting Protestantism concerned social issues. In the United States, Protestants were as divided as most of their fellow citizens over the continuing war in Vietnam. The Central Committee of the World Council of Churches, meeting in late August on the Greek island of Crete, issued a statement strongly critical of U.S. bombing and escalation policies.

Throughout the year, Protestant clergymen and laymen debated Vietnam. Many clerics were serving in the chaplaincy, and most of these supported the war effort. In February, a group called "Clergy and Laymen Concerned About Vietnam" brought together in Washington, D.C., 2,600 church leaders, many of them Protestants, for a conference and a demonstration. They were joined by thousands of other churchmen in the April 16 Spring Mobilization for Peace, in New York City, in which the Reverend Martin Luther King, Jr., took an active role. In October, a massive antiwar demonstration in Washington, D.C., numbered many Protestants in its leadership (see DEMOCRACY). The Reverend William Sloane Coffin, chaplain of Yale University, was a Protestant spokesman at the latter event, which he helped organize.

Dr. Arthur Michael Ramsey, Archbishop of Canterbury, right, spoke at a Christian unity service in Chicago. With him are, from left, Episcopal Bishop Gerald Francis Burrill; John Cardinal Cody, Roman Catholic Archbishop of Chicago; and Eastern Orthodox Archbishop Iakovos.

Few denominations were able to make an unambiguous and clear statement on the morality or immorality of the war. A Methodist Commission asked for withdrawal, while the American Baptist Convention asked for an end to the bombing. Some members of the Society of Friends (Quakers) sent medical supplies to North Vietnam, but Episcopalians, the Missouri Synod Lutherans, and Presbyterians were unable, during their summer conventions, to unite their delegates in outright support of, or opposition to, the war policies.

Other Social Issues had to do with civil rights and with city rioting. The first National Conference on Black Power, held in Newark, N.J., July 20 to July 23, convened on Episcopal church premises. Episcopal cleric Nathan Wright, Jr., of Newark, was a spokesman for the conference. This conference and many other expressions of "black power" were critical of conventional Christianity, but by no means all Protestants abandoned their desire to communicate meaningfully with Negro militants. When urban riots occurred in Newark and Detroit, Mich., Protestant churches joined with other agencies in ministering to the victims and in aiding the rebuilders. They tended to unite in acknowledging that their work had become newly complicated and that white Christians shared a large measure of the guilt for helping create circumstances that produced such riots. See CITY; CIVIL RIGHTS.

Church Reunion. The year was not particularly productive of new formal ecumenical ventures or gains toward church reunion. The Consultation on Church Union, which could eventuate in the merger of 25,000,000 persons into a single Protestant body, pursued a largely undramatic course and set a new, leisurely timetable at its May meeting in Cambridge, Mass. The Methodist Church and The Evangelical United Brethren Church nearly completed their work toward union. But intra-Protestant union activities, which had dominated Protestant news in recent years, were receding, while Protestant-Catholic events attracted new attention.

Current Beliefs of two church bodies were stated during the year. The General Assembly of the 3,300,000-member United Presbyterian Church, meeting in Portland, Ore., in May, overwhelmingly adopted a "Confession of 1967," which was relatively outspoken on social issues and which updated church teaching. A poll of the Unitarian Universalist Association, on the other hand, showed that the extreme theological "left" on the Protestant spectrum included in its membership a 59 per cent majority that no longer thought of itself as Christian, and only a 3 per cent minority that conceived of God as a supernatural being.

The year revealed few demonstrable tendencies toward a single theological trend. The "death of God" furor of 1965 and 1966 was dying down, though a number of books on the theme appeared in 1967. Representative of a major line of thought was the English translation of Jürgen Moltmann's *The Theology of Hope*, which appeared in November. This theology aspires to be revolutionary in character, since it claims to be prophetic about the present and is strongly future-oriented. Whether or not "a theology of hope" will come to dominance in Protestantism is still uncertain. The best-selling book published under general Protestant auspices was an inexpensive new translation of the Bible, *Good News for Modern Man*. The American Bible Society sold more than 5,000,000 copies in 1967.

Deaths. Perhaps the most prominent Protestant church leader to die during the year was Bishop Otto Dibelius, 86, a German Evangelical (Lutheran) Church leader who, from his post as bishop of Berlin, had opposed both Nazism and Communism. Dibelius had been chairman of the World Council of Churches from 1954 to 1961. [MARTIN E. MARTY]

PSYCHIATRY. See MENTAL HEALTH; PSYCHOLOGY.

PSYCHOLOGY. Howard Moltz, David Geller, and Robert Levin, working at Brooklyn College in New York City, conducted experiments, in 1967, that suggest the mammary glands contribute little to either the initiation or maintenance of maternal behavior in rats. Female rats are often used in studies of maternal behavior because they display a predictable pattern of infant care. Psychologists would like to be able to determine exactly what triggers the nursing response in these female rats. In rats, as in many other mammals, the mammary glands are already distended with milk when the mother gives birth to its young. Some investigators have suggested that the engorgement of these glands gives rise to the nursing behavior.

The Brooklyn College researchers surgically removed the mammary glands from one group of prepubertal female rats and performed mock operations on another group. When the rats grew to adulthood, all mated, became pregnant, and gave birth to normal litters. While the females without mammary glands could not lactate and their young had to be fed by foster mothers, they cared for their young in a manner indistinguishable from the mock-operated, normal mothers. The females without mammary glands built nests, retrieved young, and adopted the stereotyped nursing crouch while hovering over their young as often as did the control females.

Psychosomatic Conditioning. Some experiments showing that visceral responses (reactions of the heart, liver, intestines, and other internal organs) can be learned by conventional reward techniques were successfully carried out by Neal Miller and Alfredo Carmona at Yale University. The traditional view has been that only the responses of striated skeletal muscles can be learned by the law of effect (reward and punishment). Visceral responses were thought to be learned only by the law of contiguity (classical Pavlovian conditioning). But if the acquisition of visceral responses can be achieved only through classical conditioning, then the persistence of such responses requires the frequent recurrence of an eliciting stimulus, and such a stimulus has never been identified in any psychosomatic disorder.

Miller and Carmona rewarded thirsty dogs with water each time they salivated spontaneously. Gradually the training procedure led to progressive increases in salivation. Conversely, when other dogs were rewarded with water for not salivating, the amount of salivation decreased. The best efforts of these scientists failed to reveal any skeletal response, such as chewing or panting, that might have been learned by the dogs and that might indirectly have caused the changes in salivation. While subtle muscle movements do not seem to account for the changes, the possibility exists that the salivary changes may have been part of a larger pattern of responses detected by electrical recordings of brain activity. [ROBERT W. GOY]

Early Bird Spans the Atlantic

Satellite Transmission Route — Land cable — Undersea cable

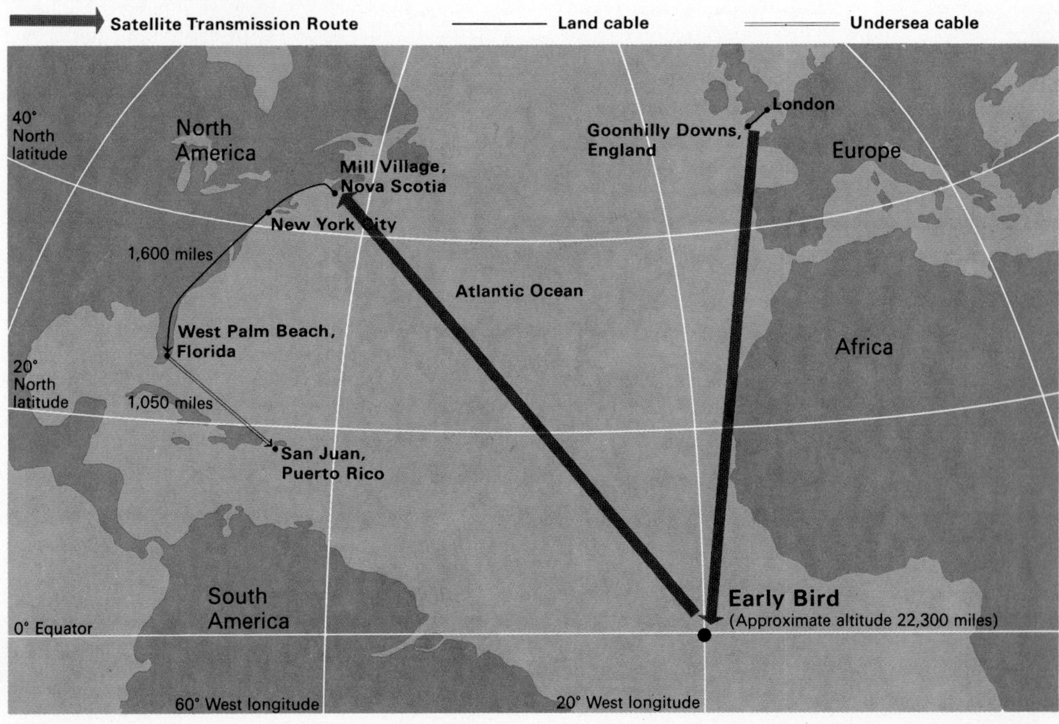

PUBLISHING. The *World Journal Tribune*, New York City's newest newspaper, stopped publication on May 5, 1967, less than eight months after its first issue. Management blamed the unions for high labor costs, interference with operations, and insistence that personnel be retained from the three consolidated papers, *Herald Tribune*, *Journal-American*, and *World Telegram and Sun*. Losses were reported to have been about $700,000 a month.

Its demise left the largest city in the United States with only three newspapers: two morning dailies and one afternoon paper. *The New York Times*, with a morning circulation of a little less than 1,000,000, seriously investigated the possibilities of starting a new afternoon daily. After printing 200 closely guarded copies of two 40-page pilot issues, however, the *Times* decided not to risk it. With a circulation of more than 2,000,000, New York City's other morning paper, the *Daily News*, may take up the challenge. The city's only afternoon paper, the *New York Post*, increased its circulation from 400,000 to 700,000 and has increased production facilities to meet the demand for more copies.

In Washington, D.C., the Senate Antitrust and Monopoly Subcommittee started hearings on July 12 on a bill to exempt joint newspaper operations and combinations from antitrust laws. Called the "Failing Newspaper Bill," the legislation had been introduced by Senator Carl T. Hayden (D., Ariz.) on March 16. Statements by 42 witnesses for and against the bill revealed that opinion was divided on the need for the bill, and it was not expected to be reported out of committee. On September 10, however, the subcommittee decided to expand its inquiry of newspapers in four specific areas: pricing practices of the wire services, the handling of syndicated features and columns, rising newsprint costs, and the death of the *World Journal Tribune*.

Figures published by the American Newspaper Publishers Association in New York City point out that readers in the United States and Canada buy about 61,000,000 newspapers a day and spend more than $2,250,000,000 for newspapers a year. When advertising volume is included, total expenditures come to about $7,000,000,000 per year.

Technological Advances in methods of transmission, reproduction, and dissemination of the printed word continued to have a pronounced effect on all fields of publishing. On October 17, a full front page of the *Daily Express* of London was sent 50,000 miles from London, England, to the office of *El Mundo* in San Juan, Puerto Rico, by facsimile transmission via the Early Bird satellite. It was the first time a commercial satellite had been used for such a purpose. The process is basically similar to that used for many years in transmitting photos by wire and radio but is now so refined that the reproduced page is much like the original page.

PUBLISHING

Acquisitions and Mergers. Roy Herbert Thomson of Canada who, in Great Britain, is Lord Thomson of Fleet, continued to be an abiding force in the newspaper business. The owner of 169 newspapers in Canada, Great Britain, and the United States, the 73-year-old Lord Thomson reportedly paid $72,000,000 for the Brush-Moore chain of 12 daily newspapers operating in five states in the United States. "I am confident in the future of newspapers no matter what Marshall McLuhan and other communications experts say about the printed word being outdated," Lord Thomson said. Earlier in 1967, Samuel I. Newhouse bought the Ohio *Cleveland Plain Dealer* for an estimated $53,400,000. The *Boston Traveler*, an evening daily founded in 1824, and the *Boston Herald*, a morning paper founded 22 years later, merged in July to become the *Boston Herald Traveler*. Bill D. Moyers, former press secretary to President Lyndon B. Johnson, became publisher of *Newsday*, an evening daily of 415,000 circulation, published on Long Island, N.Y., and serving suburban New York City. Washington, D.C., got a new newspaper in *The Washington Examiner*, which published its first issue on September 7. In a full-page editorial, the newspaper declared that it hoped to be "a link between . . . haves and have-nots, black and white, city and suburb." Initial circulation was announced at 150,000.

In Magazines, the year's major event was the death of Henry R. Luce, founder and head for 41 years of Time Inc., publisher of *Time*, *Life*, *Fortune*, and *Sports Illustrated* magazines. See DEATHS OF NOTABLE PERSONS (Close-Up).

Magazine publishing, centered chiefly in New York City, continued at about the same rate as in 1966 with advertising revenues up a little more than 1 per cent to a total for the year of slightly over $1,000,000,000. The largest magazine circulation, about 16,000,000, belongs to *The Reader's Digest*, which marked its 45th year in 1967. *Printer's Ink*, the 79-year-old trade publication serving the advertising and publishing fields, stopped publishing and became *Marketing/Communications*, a new monthly with a circulation of more than 84,000.

On December 11, the Internal Revenue Service announced that the advertising revenues of magazines of certain tax-exempt organizations would be subject to corporate tax. Among the magazines were *The Journal of the American Medical Association* and *Nation's Business*, published by the U.S. Chamber of Commerce.

Book Publishing moved up faster. More than 30,000 books are published in the United States annually. The Department of Commerce expected sales to reach $2,450,000,000 in 1967, an increase of 11.4 per cent over 1966. There were many mergers of publishing houses; some 44 of them have "gone public" and now sell stock on the exchange or over the counter. [MALCOLM MERRITT]

PUERTO RICO held a national referendum on July 23, 1967, in which voters were offered a choice of statehood, independence, or continuing status as a commonwealth of the United States. In the final balloting, nearly 60 per cent of the electorate chose the latter. The election results were considered a major victory for former governor Luis Muñoz Marín, who had been a leading advocate of continuing the island's commonwealth status.

A short time after the national plebiscite, the government's Economic Development Administration – commonly known as Fomento – announced the establishment of the 1,500th plant under its "Operation Bootstrap" industrialization program. Total Operation Bootstrap investment as of August, 1967, was about $1,200,000,000. The industries involved in it had a roster of 94,000 workers and a combined annual payroll of $212,000,000. Under Fomento's leadership, industry, commerce, and tourism continued to make progress in 1967. To maintain the rate of growth, the government in January had approved a $713,000,000 budget for fiscal 1967-1968. Late in the year, a huge $61,000,000 petrochemical project was opened near Guayama.

Facts in Brief. Population: 2,780,000. Government: Governor Roberto Sánchez Vilella. Monetary Unit: U.S. $1. Foreign Trade: exports, $1,136,000,000; imports, $1,735,000,000. Principal Exports: food products, textiles, vegetables.

PULITZER PRIZES in journalism, literature, music, and art were announced on May 1, 1967. Prizes in all categories were awarded for the first time since 1961 as follows:

For the Most Disinterested and Meritorious Public Service Rendered by a U.S. Newspaper: gold medals to *The Louisville Courier-Journal* for its "successful campaign to control the Kentucky strip-mine industry," and to *The Milwaukee Journal* for its "successful campaign to stiffen Wisconsin laws against water pollution."

For a Distinguished Example of Reporting on International Affairs: $1,000 to R. John Hughes, *The Christian Science Monitor* Far East correspondent, for his reporting on the attempted Communist coup d'état in Indonesia and the purge that followed.

For a Distinguished Example of Reporting on National Affairs: $1,000 to Monroe W. Karmin and Stanley W. Penn of *The Wall Street Journal* for their reporting of the link between American crime and gambling in the Bahamas.

For a Distinguished Example of Local Reporting: *General Reporting*, $1,000 to Robert V. Cox of *The Chambersburg* (Pa.) *Public Opinion* for deadline reporting on a mountain country manhunt for a deranged fugitive. *For Special Reporting*, $1,000 to Gene Miller of *The Miami* (Fla.) *Herald* for helping to free two persons wrongfully convicted of murder.

For a Distinguished Example of Editorial Writing: $1,000 to Eugene C. Patterson of *The Atlanta Constitution*, among the first to protest when the Georgia House of Representatives refused to seat Negro Julian Bond.

For an Outstanding Example of News Photography: $1,000 to Jack R. Thornell of The Associated Press New Orleans Bureau for his picture of civil rightist James H. Meredith felled by a sniper's bullet.

For an Outstanding Example of a Cartoonist's Work Published in a U.S. Newspaper: $1,000 to Patrick B. Oliphant of *The Denver* (Colo.) *Post*, whose cartoon pictures Ho Chi Minh of North Vietnam with the body of a Vietnamese in his arms.

For the Best Fiction by a U.S. Author: $500 to Bernard Malamud for *The Fixer*. See MALAMUD, BERNARD.

For the Best Nonfiction by an American Author: $500 to David Brion Davis for *The Problem of Slavery in Western Culture*. See DAVIS, DAVID BRION.

For a Distinguished Book of the Year on U.S. History: $500 to William H. Goetzmann for *Exploration and Empire: The Explorer and the Scientist in the Winning of the American West*. See GOETZMANN, WILLIAM H.

For a Distinguished Biography or Autobiography Preferably on an American Subject: $500 to Justin Kaplan for *Mr. Clemens and Mark Twain*. See KAPLAN, JUSTIN.

For a Distinguished Volume of Verse by an American Author: $500 to Anne Sexton for *Live or Die*. See SEXTON, ANNE.

For the Best Original American Play: $500 to Edward Franklin Albee for *A Delicate Balance*. See ALBEE, EDWARD FRANKLIN.

For a Distinguished Musical Composition: $500 to Leon Kirchner for his *String Quartet No. 3*. See KIRCHNER, LEON.

Fellowship in Creative Writing, $1,500 to Phyllis Leslie Meras, a *New York Times* copy editor.

Traveling Fellowships to graduates of the Columbia University Graduate School of Journalism, $1,500 each to: David Rorvik of Missoula, Mont.; Carey Winfrey of Coral Gables, Fla.; David Ablett of Vancouver, B.C.

QUEBEC. See CANADA.

RACING. See AUTOMOBILE RACING; BOATS AND BOATING; HORSE RACING; TRACK AND FIELD.

RADIO. Diversity was the key to radio programming in 1967 for local AM-FM stations and at least one of the networks, American Broadcasting Company (ABC). *The New York Times Magazine* aptly described the year as radio's "fractionalization" period.

Although almost 50 per cent of the radio stations across the country still featured something-for-everybody, "middle-of-the-road" programming, more and more outlets were switching to all-talk, all-news, all-female, all-hippie, all-jazz, and a variety of ethnic and foreign-language formats.

The trend was accelerated when the Federal Communications Commission (FCC) demanded in 1966 that certain AM-FM outlets in top markets discontinue simultaneous programming and instead feature separate material on their AM and FM bands. As a result, a survey of FM programming by the National Association of Broadcasters (NAB) showed in March, 1967, that 23 per cent of the nation's FM stations had changed their formats.

The ABC radio network officially recognized the new trend when it announced a plan, starting in 1968, to provide its affiliates with a choice of four separate radio feeds, each featuring a different format–American-contemporary; FM; personality-entertainment; and information.

Other Developments. Radio proved more popular than ever in 1967. According to a December poll reported in *Variety*, more than 95 per cent of all people over 11 years of age listen to radio programs during the course of a week.

A consent decree signed early in 1967 settled the government's antitrust suit against Broadcast Music Inc. (BMI). The decree left BMI's ownership by broadcasters undisturbed but imposed some curbs on its operation.

People. John Charles Daly, moderator of the now defunct "What's My Line," succeeded John Chancellor as director of the "Voice of America" in June. Chancellor returned to National Broadcasting Company (NBC) news. A survey by the "Voice of America" in September indicated that its overseas broadcasts were attracting about 43,000,000 listeners each week.

Martin Block, 64, who was the host on radio's first disk jockey show, "Make Believe Ballroom," in New York City for 20 years (1935-1954), died in September after heart surgery.

The 1967 Peabody Awards in radio went to Edwin Newman (NBC) for news; Elmo Ellis (WSB, Atlanta, Ga.) for local public service; and "Community Opinion" (WLIB, New York City), a hotline telephone interview show that permitted Harlem citizens to voice their candid opinions about ghetto life, thereby giving the residents of the Harlem area "an essential safety valve during the hot summer." [JUNE BUNDY CSIDA]

RAILROAD. See TRANSPORTATION.

REAGAN, RONALD WILSON (1911-), a conservative Republican, was sworn in Jan. 2, 1967, as the 33rd governor of California. He was considered by many voters as a leading prospect for the 1968 Republican presidential nomination.

Reagan was born at Tampico, Ill., on Feb. 6, 1911. He majored in economics and sociology at Eureka (Ill.) College, receiving his B.A. degree in 1932. After graduation, he worked as a radio sportscaster at Davenport and Des Moines, Iowa. In 1937, he began a motion picture career that included appearances in at least 50 films. His first featured part was in *Kings Row* in 1941. Poor eyesight kept him from combat duty in World War II, during which he made training films for the U.S. Air Force. He served as president of the Screen Actors Guild from 1947 to 1952 and in 1959.

Long a liberal Democrat, be began his move to the Republican side as a Democrat-for-Eisenhower campaigner in 1952. He became a Republican in 1962, and, in October, 1964, delivered a television speech, "A Time for Choosing," on behalf of Barry Goldwater, the Republican presidential nominee.

Reagan and his wife, former actress Nancy Davis, have two children, Patricia Ann and Ronald Prescott. Reagan's first wife was actress Jane Wyman. They had a daughter, Maureen Elizabeth, and an adopted son, Michael Edward. Reagan's chief hobby is a 395-acre ranch. [WALTER F. MORSE]

Senator Everett McKinley Dirksen (R., Ill.) of the dulcet voice, became one of the country's top-selling recording artists, with three albums out.

RECORDINGS. World-wide sales of records grossed well over $1,500,000,000 in 1967. The United States accounted for half this total. Great Britain was second with 7 per cent, Japan third with 5 1/4 per cent, and West Germany next with 4 3/4 per cent.

Confusion grew as music recorded for albums became available through four different media: long-playing (LP) disks, reel-to-reel tapes, cartridges, and cassettes.

Recording Artists most consistently represented on the best-selling-album charts were Herb Alpert and the Tijuana Brass, with seven hit LPs; and Bill Cosby, with six–five as a comedian, one as a singer.

Among the 42 "Grammy" award winners for the best performances of the previous year were Frank Sinatra and Eydie Gorme (vocal), The Mamas and the Papas (rock group), Jeannie Seely and David Houston (country and western vocal), Ray Charles (rhythm and blues), and Duke Ellington and Wes Montgomery (jazz).

An unusual hit was a patriotic monologue, "Letter to My Teen-Age Son," narrated by Victor Lundberg, a Michigan businessman. Its criticism of long hair and draft-card burning led to rebuttals on six other recordings.

Finances and Sales. The trend toward financing Broadway musicals by record companies receded in 1967, and the output of albums by original casts was reduced. In a money-saving move, expected to save millions of dollars in copyright royalties, the standard number of tunes in a popular album was reduced from 12 to 10 or 11.

In June, the price of monaural albums was raised to equal stereo albums, which previously were generally a dollar higher. It was hoped that this would simplify production by eliminating monaural sales.

The number of disks receiving Gold Record awards, representing $1,000,000 gross sales for albums or 1,000,000 single records sold, increased sharply. The top pop singles of the year included "Groovin' " by the Young Rascals; "Windy" by the Association; "Light My Fire" by the Doors, and others by Lulu, Aretha Franklin, Sam and Dave, The Rolling Stones, The Box Tops, and the Beatles.

Among the top pop albums receiving Gold Record awards were the Beatles' "Sergeant Pepper's Lonely Hearts Club Band"; the Monkees' "Pisces, Aquarius, Capricorn and Jones Ltd."; Andy Williams' "Born Free"; the Jefferson Airplane's "Surrealistic Pillow"; and Sergio Mendes' "Brasil '66."

Among the classical artists, violinist Yehudi Menuhin and Indian sitarist Ravi Shankar scored a unique success with their album "East Meets West." The leading operatic soloist was Leontyne Price with her LP "Prima Donna, Vol. 2." [LEONARD G. FEATHER]

See also MUSIC, POPULAR.

RECREATION. See CONSERVATION; FAIRS AND EXHIBITIONS; HUNTING AND FISHING.

RED CROSS expanded its program and services in 1967 by establishing an independent overseas area headquarters in Southeast Asia. The number of U.S. servicemen in Vietnam receiving assistance each month climbed from an average of 11,000 in 1966 to 20,000 in 1967. The Red Cross refugee camp project in South Vietnam, begun in 1966 in cooperation with the Agency for International Development, included 31 camps caring for over 31,000 displaced persons in 1967.

In response to an appeal from the International Committee of the Red Cross (ICRC), the American Red Cross sent pharmaceutical products valued at $350,000 to the Middle East. In addition to these supplies, which were donated by drug companies, the ICRC received $20,000 for use in behalf of the victims of the Arab-Israeli conflict.

American Red Cross Youth representatives joined 400 high school and college students from 50 countries in "Rendezvous '67," a seminar held at Carleton University in Ottawa, Ont., to discuss ways to strengthen Red Cross youth programs.

National disaster specialists assisted Red Cross volunteers with flood relief programs in Fairbanks, Alaska, and in southern Texas following the devastation caused by hurricane *Beulah*. Flood victims in Malaysia and Iraq and earthquake sufferers in Turkey were helped through the League of Red Cross Societies. [JOSEPH P. ANDERSON]

RELIGION. News of religion from the non-Western world ordinarily reaches the West in political and ideological disguises. In Europe and North and South America, it is possible to document religious change chiefly by reporting on church councils and congresses, theological trends, new books, and the activities of ecclesiastical leaders. These forms are not always the best indicators of change elsewhere in the world.

In 1967, the non-Western event that most dramatized the role of religion in human affairs was the Arab-Israeli war. President Gamal Abdel Nasser of the United Arab Republic joined other Arab leaders in calling for a "holy war" to put an end to Israel. Military forces of Moslem nations were inspired to undertake action for religious reasons; the *Koran*, the Moslem's sacred book, justifies only religious wars. Similarly, the counteractions by Israel were not merely political. For Jews, Israel is a state as well as a state of mind and spirit. The ancient promises concerning their people are in no small measure connected with Israel's fate.

When the six-day war ended on June 10, the picture of Israeli soldiers triumphant at the Wailing Wall and the debate over access to the "holy places" in the Old City of Jerusalem served to remind the world of these religious dimensions. On the other side of the world, in the prolonged Vietnamese conflict, religious issues also surfaced from time to time,

U.S. Church Membership Reported for Bodies with 150,000 or More Members.*

Adventists, Seventh-Day	374,433
Assemblies of God	576,058
Baptist Bodies	
American Baptist Association	731,000
American Baptist Convention	1,538,988
Conservative Baptist Association of America	('65) 325,000
Free Will Baptists	178,450
General Association of Regular Baptist Churches, The	170,299
National Baptist Convention of America	('56) 2,668,799
National Baptist Convention, U.S.A., Inc.	('58) 5,500,000
National Primitive Baptist Convention in the U.S.A.	1,255,000
North American Baptist Association	200,000
Progressive National Baptist Convention, Inc.	521,581
Southern Baptist Convention	10,947,389
Brethren (German Baptists)	
Church of the Brethren	191,402
Christian Churches (Disciples of Christ) International Convention	1,894,927
Churches of God	
Church of God (Cleveland, Tenn.)	220,405
Church of God in Christ	('65) 425,500
Church of the Nazarene	350,882
Churches of Christ	('65) 2,350,000
Eastern Churches	
Greek Orthodox Archdiocese of North and South America	('65) 1,770,000
Russian Orthodox Catholic Church in America Patriarchal Exarchate	('65) 152,973
Evangelical United Brethren Church	732,377
Jehovah's Witnesses	('65) 330,358
Jewish Congregations	('65) 5,725,000
Latter-Day Saints	
Church of Jesus Christ of Latter-day Saints	2,480,899
Reorganized Church of Jesus Christ of Latter Day Saints	182,251
Lutherans	
Lutheran Council in the U.S.A.	
American Lutheran Church, The	2,566,581
Lutheran Church in America	3,147,959
Lutheran Church–Missouri Synod	2,729,897
Other Lutheran Bodies	
Wisconsin Evangelical Lutheran Synod	('64) 358,466
Methodist Bodies	
African Methodist Episcopal Church	('51) 1,166,301
African Methodist Episcopal Zion Church	('65) 1,100,000
Christian Methodist Episcopal Church	('65) 466,718
The Methodist Church	10,310,619
Polish National Catholic Church of America	('60) 282,411
Presbyterian Bodies	
The United Presbyterian Church in the U.S.A.	3,298,583
Protestant Episcopal Church, The	3,429,153
Reformed Bodies	
Christian Reformed Church	275,530
Reformed Church in America	377,671
Roman Catholic Church, The	46,864,910
Salvation Army	294,201
Spiritualists, International General Assembly of	('65) 164,072
Unitarian Universalist Association	('65) 166,622
United Church of Christ	2,063,481

*Statistics mainly for calendar year 1966
Source: 1968 Yearbook of American Churches

as was the case in the controversy between various Buddhist sects and between Buddhists and Roman Catholics during the South Vietnamese elections.

Ideological Conflict. Not all the news of world religion was connected with military activities and holy wars. Much of it had to do with ideological clashes in those parts of the world where new and old faiths were in conflict. The new faiths may seem to be antireligious, but they make demands on peoples' ultimate commitments of the kind men usually associate with religious appeals.

Communist China. Nowhere was this clash of the old and the new more prominent in 1967 than on Chinese soil. In China, where Confucianism had contributed to a more or less religious philosophy for millions of people for thousands of years, a new generation found spiritual sustenance in the little book, *Quotations from Chairman Mao Tse-tung*. This collection of writings served to unite a militant people against its own inherited religious past and against cultural traces left by other religions, especially Christianity. Many monuments of China's spiritual past were threatened by the Cultural Revolution. *Sinologists* (students of China) discussing the Chinese future urged scholars to become informed concerning the interaction of residual religions and Maoism.

In India, the clash was between old religions and new secularity; it was based on urgent practical demands. An estimated 250,000,000 sacred cows and 2,500,000,000 rats are allowed to live in an overpopulated and starving nation because of Hindu religious beliefs associated with living things. Many practical politicians urge a change in beliefs and an end to such customs in order to produce a more prosperous India. Meanwhile, millions found solace in Hinduism and Buddhism as they faced seemingly insuperable human problems in India.

In Japan, the old met the new as historic faiths lived on in a modernizing nation, even as a Buddhist-backed "Value Creation Society" called *Soka Gakkai* took on increasing political importance.

Eastern Influence. Finally, news of non-Western religion came to the West in 1967 through the efforts of individuals and groups that might be described as commuters between value systems. The "hippie" phenomenon, which reached a peak in midsummer, was an example. Hippies turned to Zen Buddhism, the Vedas, the writings of Rabbi Hillel, and the teachings of Jesus, implying that these could provide meaning for a nonviolent generation. The Beatles were the best known of the celebrities who turned to Eastern religion as they sought "transcendental meditation" through contact with Maharishi Mahesh Yogi, their chosen spiritual leader. Timothy Leary advocated a religion based not only on mind-expanding drugs like LSD, but also on literary resources of Eastern religion. [MARTIN E. MARTY]

See also EASTERN ORTHODOX; JEWS AND JUDAISM; PROTESTANT; ROMAN CATHOLIC.

REPUBLICAN PARTY. Republicans were eager and expectant in 1967 as they contemplated the 1968 elections. Encouraged by public opinion polls and a deepening conviction that President Lyndon B. Johnson was in serious trouble with the voters, the GOP was convinced that 1968 would offer them the best opportunity in years. But even if voter alienation were as extensive as they believed, Republican leaders knew they could not put their own man in the White House unless he were able to attract the votes of Democrats and independents as well as Republicans. By the end of the year, the Republicans had five potential presidential candidates. Governor Nelson A. Rockefeller of New York, their strongest candidate, with the best chance of defeating Mr. Johnson, was unlikely to receive the nomination. And Richard M. Nixon, the former Vice-President, who was considered to have the best chance of getting the nomination, was not expected to run nearly as well against the President.

Other Candidates. Nixon and Governor George W. Romney of Michigan were regarded as the two front runners as 1967 drew to a close. But both had drawbacks. Romney had slipped from the lead he enjoyed at the end of 1966, after his landslide re-election to another term as governor, chiefly because his bewildering confusion of comments on Vietnam led some observers to believe he lacked any real understanding of U.S. foreign policy. Nixon was the favorite of the party regulars, for whom he had performed many favors. He was more experienced in foreign affairs than any of his rivals, and, because he was more or less acceptable to all factions, could claim to be a unifying force in the party. But he had the reputation of being a loser after his defeats by John F. Kennedy in 1960 and by Governor Edmund G. "Pat" Brown of California in 1962.

Nixon and Romney, it was generally agreed, would probably be the principal contenders in 1968's presidential preference primaries. If they should cancel each other out before the Republican nominating convention convenes at Miami Beach, Fla., in August, 1968, the three "fallback" candidates would be Rockefeller, Governor Ronald Reagan of California, and Charles H. Percy, the junior senator from Illinois.

Rockefeller, reiterating in 1967 his support for Romney, insisted that he himself was not a candidate, as he had been in 1960 and 1964. Rockefeller's name, however, continued to head the list in the public opinion polls. Nixon supporters were cheered when a Gallup Poll in October showed that he would beat Mr. Johnson 49 to 45 per cent, and a Harris Poll in November showed him winning by 48 to 41 per cent. But the same polls showed Rockefeller crushing the President by 54 to 40 per cent, and 52 to 35 per cent, respectively. The Harris Poll, in fact, pictured Mr. Johnson as so unpopular that he would run behind not only Rockefeller, Romney,

Republican party leaders who might be picked as presidential nominees in 1968 included, left to right, Ronald Reagan, Richard Nixon, George Romney, and Charles Percy.

and Nixon, but also Reagan, Mayor John V. Lindsay of New York City, and Percy.

Elections. The Republicans were encouraged by this, as they were by their two major accomplishments in the off-year elections in November, 1967. They took the Kentucky statehouse away from Democrats for the first time in 20 years when they elected 43-year-old attorney Louie B. Nunn governor. And they recaptured, with a 3-to-1 majority of the vote, both houses of the New Jersey legislature, which they had lost to the Democrats in 1965.

But they also suffered disappointments. In the Philadelphia mayoral race, they made a strenuous effort to elect Arlen Specter, an erstwhile Democrat who had switched to the Republican party and won the district attorneyship in 1965. Specter, who would have been Philadelphia's first Jewish mayor, was a slight favorite. But he lost a close race to Mayor James H. Tate, a Roman Catholic who received 50.9 per cent of the vote. In Cleveland, Ohio, the Republican candidate for mayor was Seth C. Taft, 44-year-old grandson of President William Howard Taft. Although he did not wage a white backlash campaign, many white Democrats defected to him rather than vote for Negro candidate Carl B. Stokes. Yet Taft lost to Stokes, the 40-year-old great-grandson of a slave, by 1,679 votes. In the Gary, Ind., race for mayor, another white Republican, Joseph B. Radigan, failed by 1,871 votes to defeat Negro

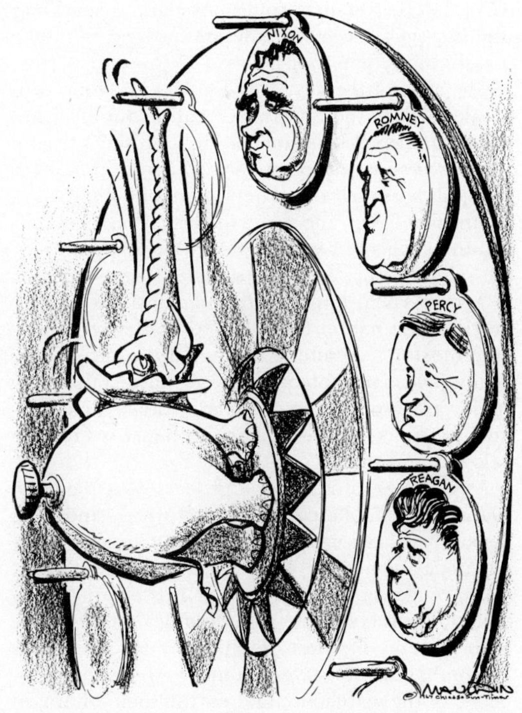

Any Number Can Play

Democrat Richard G. Hatcher. No one, not even the Democrats, could be sure, but there was a possibility that the breakthroughs they achieved in the Cleveland and Gary elections could mean that the Republicans would have difficulty in winning a larger share of the Negro vote from the Democrats in 1968. See CIVIL RIGHTS; ELECTIONS.

But if the Democrats were strong in the big cities of the North, the Republicans had managed to obtain a 26 to 24 majority of the nation's governors after their Kentucky victory. Republicans governed in states with approximately 58 per cent of the nation's population and 302 electoral votes. Only 270 are needed to elect a President. This, of course, did not guarantee them success at the polls in 1968, but they were confident it would help.

In Congress, House leader Gerald R. Ford of Michigan and Senate leader Everett M. Dirksen of Illinois were effective in their opposition roles, even though outnumbered by Democrats (64 to 36) in the Senate, and 245 to 187 in the House, with three Democratic vacancies. Ford, making skillful use of the 47 additional seats which the Republicans picked up in the 1966 election, proved troublesome to the Democrats. A coalition of Republicans and Southern Democrats was responsible for many of the cuts made in the Great Society programs. Some Republicans, however, felt this opposition would harm them in the 1968 campaign. [WILLIAM MCGAFFIN]

RETAILING. Retailers could not claim a sparkling year in 1967, even though the American public bought more than ever before.

The start of the year was dreary. The long economic surge of the 1960s was running out of steam, and consumers became increasingly cautious, fearful that a recession was on the way. Savings mounted, and purchases fell off. The automobile companies felt the slowdown, and so did the television set manufacturers. This last was particularly disappointing; the sale of color television sets had been expected to boom. Then, too, a cold and rainy spring over much of the nation helped keep housewives away from the stores. As summer began, this same weather factor gave many potential buyers the idea that they could get through the summer without air conditioning. Sales of this major appliance were also below expectations.

As the year progressed and fears of a recession evaporated, public confidence returned, and sales generally picked up. With a strong Christmas season, department stores recorded an advance of about 5 per cent over 1966. Although this meant a new record, it was below the plans and projections of the industry and of most retailing companies. This meant that the stores were caught with inventories–goods in the warehouse and on the shelf–that cost money to finance and to buy but did not bring a return. Furthermore, many stores expanded or opened branches on the basis of false expectations. The end result was often lower profits despite the final gain in sales. For 1967, personal disposable income in the United States increased an estimated 7.9 per cent to the $545,000,000,000 level, while consumer expenditures increased 6.5 per cent to about $495,000,000,000.

What a decision on the part of the public to increase their savings can do to retailing is seen in one set of figures. Savings rose by an estimated 1 1/2 per cent in the first half of 1967. That may seem slight. But when figured on the basis of the more than a half trillion dollars in personal disposable income, the 1 1/2 per cent could have meant a loss in retail sales of more than $7,500,000,000.

Of Interest During the Year: The discounters were running into increasing trouble from the competition of the traditional stores, but discounters still accounted for an estimated $15,000,000,000 of the nation's total household goods and food expenditures. Mini and mod styles, forcing major wardrobe changes, caused sales of clothing to boom. More than 500 representatives of 60 consumer groups formed the Consumer Federation of America. Bank credit cards swept the Midwest, and were offered to customers by six supermarket chains in California. In Europe, an American institution–mail-order buying–boomed. In France, for instance, mail-order sales jumped 30 per cent in 1967. [EDWIN DARBY]

RHODESIA continued steady under the white-dominated illegal government of Prime Minister Ian D. Smith despite pressure from international sanctions. Rhodesia had declared itself independent from Great Britain in 1965 in defiance of Britain's refusal to grant the territory independence until its African majority was given an important voice in government.

The boycott on petroleum shipments to Rhodesia, voted by the United Nations (UN) in 1966 and enforced by the British navy throughout 1967, was not effective. Rhodesia rationed gasoline and obtained some supplies from its sympathetic neighbor, the Republic of South Africa. Sanctions against the purchase of Rhodesian products also failed to bring the fall of Smith's government. To sustain its agriculture, Rhodesia guaranteed prices, held secret sales of tobacco in March, and granted subsidies to white farmers. Agricultural production still fell, though, and the government was left with some unsold tobacco on its hands, as well.

British efforts to bring Rhodesia back to legal colonial status continued through diplomacy as well as by economic pressure. Britain's Lord Alport visited Rhodesia in June, met with Smith, and interviewed Rhodesians. But Smith's government, encouraged by its ability to withstand economic sanctions, rejected all suggestions to compromise. See GREAT BRITAIN; UNITED NATIONS.

Armed Resistance by African nationalists caused occasional flare-ups. On August 8, a guerrilla force ambushed a Rhodesian army patrol in the Wankie area. Another clash occurred on August 13. The government said that the guerrillas had entered Rhodesia from Zambia. Government forces put up roadblocks around Bulawayo, Rhodesia's second largest city, and conducted a house-to-house search of African districts for weapons. Rhodesia reported that by August 31, 28 guerrillas had been killed and that six security forces members had been killed and 13 wounded.

In both the UN and at African conferences, independent African nations demanded that the white government of Rhodesia be replaced by a black government. On August 29, Zambia accused Rhodesia of accepting military forces from South Africa and urged Britain to put down Smith's Rhodesian rebellion. Rhodesia, on the same day, demanded that Britain exert pressure on Zambia to stop supporting guerrillas in Rhodesia. [BENJAMIN E. THOMAS]

Facts in Brief. Population: 4,612,000. Government: Prime Minister Ian D. Smith. Monetary Unit: pound (1=U.S. $2.79). Foreign Trade: exports, $274,000,000; imports, $266,000,000. Principal Exports: tobacco, asbestos, iron and steel.

ROADS AND HIGHWAYS. See BUILDING AND CONSTRUCTION; TRANSPORTATION.

ROCKEFELLER, NELSON ALDRICH (1908-), governor of New York, continued to be mentioned as a possible Republican presidential nominee in 1968. Though several organizations were formed to support him, he insisted he was not seeking the nomination and declared his support for Michigan Governor George W. Romney. See ROMNEY, GEORGE W.

Rockefeller began his third term on Jan. 2, 1967. He was first considered a presidential possibility in 1958, the year he was elected governor despite a national Democratic trend. A possible impediment to nationwide support came in 1962 when his wife, Mary Todhunter Clark Rockefeller, divorced him after 31 years of marriage. Rockefeller married Mrs. Margaretta "Happy" Fitler Murphy in 1963.

Rockefeller was born July 8, 1908, at Bar Harbor, Me. He was a Phi Beta Kappa graduate of Dartmouth College in 1930. His first job was that of a clerk in the Chase National (now Chase Manhattan) Bank in New York City. He was coordinator of Inter-American Affairs under President Franklin D. Roosevelt from 1940 to 1944, and helped to formulate the "good neighbor" policy. He served as chairman of the International Development Advisory Board under President Harry S. Truman and as special assistant to President Dwight D. Eisenhower. The governor has five children by his first wife and two by his second. [WALTER F. MORSE]

Rhodesia's major export, tobacco, piled up in warehouses as a result of United Nations sanctions against Ian Smith's illegal but sturdy government.

ROMAN CATHOLIC. Pope Paul VI again became the pilgrim for peace in 1967. Preaching at Fátima, Portugal, on May 13, he warned that world peace was threatened when moral progress lagged behind scientific and technical progress. The occasion commemorated the 50th anniversary of the apparition of the Blessed Mother. Sister Lúcia, 60, now a cloistered nun, and the only survivor of three children who witnessed the apparition in 1917, appeared in public for the first time in 20 years.

Ecumenism. One of the chief concerns of Vatican Council II (1962 to 1965) was Christian unity. To this end, ecumenical meetings of great importance were held in 1967. On July 25, Pope Paul visited the once Christian capital of the East, Istanbul, Turkey. It was the first such visit made by a Roman Catholic Pope in almost 1,000 years. A visit with the 81-year-old Patriarch Athenagoras I, senior prelate of Orthodox Christianity, recalled their meeting three years previously in the Holy Land.

The patriarch in turn paid a three-day visit to the Vatican in October. At that time, the patriarch and the pope again exchanged the kiss of peace. This was the first visit to Rome made by the leader of the Greek Orthodox Church since 1451.

World-Wide Ministry. Appealing to the leaders of Communist China on January 6, Pope Paul requested that the 3,000,000 Catholics of Communist China be given the right to be heard. He expressed the desire to re-establish contact with the Chinese people of the continent and to discuss peace with their leaders.

On February 2, Pope Paul held an unprecedented meeting in Rome with Nikolai V. Podgorny, chairman of the presidium of the Supreme Soviet Union. Vatican sources stated that they discussed "questions relative to the maintenance of peace and to the development of better relations among peoples."

Although the vigorous persecution of the church in Communist Czechoslovakia had come to a halt, religious functions remained virtually under civil control. With the clergy under strict supervision, the church was still deprived of access to radio, television, motion pictures, and publishing houses.

On October 31, Pope Paul, although ailing and facing surgery, issued a 7,000-word "message to Africa." In it, the pope outlined the moral and religious values in African tradition. Indicating that "the transition to independence was made almost universally in an orderly and peaceful manner," he also made a strong appeal for cessation of existing racism, violence, and strife.

Pleas for World Peace. Pope Paul's unflagging dedication to the cause of peace during 1967 was apparent to the entire world. Pleading with the United States on May 24 to stop bombing North Vietnam, he called for a halt at the same time to "infiltration of arms and war materials into the south" by North Vietnam. In calling for the cessation of every form of violence, he also asked that the peace he sought was "with justice, liberty, and respect for the human person"–not peace at any cost.

With the defeat of the Arab nations by Israel in the June war, the pope urged the internationalization of Jerusalem, so that the Middle East, as well as the entire world, would be spared "suffering and destruction" (see MIDDLE EAST).

Peace was discussed by the pope and President Lyndon B. Johnson during the latter's historical visit to Rome on December 23. In his own Christmas message, the President stated: "I felt once more what all the world knows; the human sympathy, the passion for peace that fills the heart of the pope."

Pope Paul designated Jan. 1, 1968, a Day of Peace for all Roman Catholics, urging all men of good will to celebrate the day every year on their own initiative. He stated that within a nation, peace in international relations must be founded on liberty, sincerity, justice, and love.

New Cardinals. In July, the pope crowned 27 new cardinals, including four Americans, and opened a Year of Faith. The occasion commemorated the 19th centenary of the martyrdoms of Saint Peter and Saint Paul; a concelebrated Mass took place on the steps of St. Peter's Basilica, and the pope presented children of South and North Vietnam and of both sides of the Middle East war.

New Encyclicals. Pope Paul's fifth encyclical was made public on May 28. Entitled *Populorum Progressio* (Development of Peoples) and consisting of 18,000 words, it appealed to all for the resolution of social, cultural, and economic problems of the developing countries. He repeated his suggestion made at Bombay, India, that a world fund be established to relieve the destitute. A second encyclical, the sixth, appeared on June 24, 1967. Entitled *Sacerdotalis Caelibatus* (On Priestly Celibacy), it reaffirmed the church's teaching on clerical celibacy.

Curial Reform. The pope's desire to internationalize the Curia was demonstrated by his appointment in April of French Cardinal Jean Cardinal Villot as prefect of the Congregation of the Council. In a *Motu Proprio* dated August 6, the pope included diocesan bishops in the Curia, which previously had been restricted to cardinals. Other curial reforms included increase in power of the papal secretariat, replacement of lifetime tenures by five-year terms, and the use of modern languages in curial communication.

Other Events. May 7 marked the first World Communications Day as proposed by the Vatican Council. The pope warned that a lack of moral responsibility on the part of those whose duty it is to bring the truth to the public was dangerous for all, but especially for the young.

Implementing decisions of Vatican Council II, a *Motu Proprio*, dated June 27, defined rules for the restoration of a permanent diaconate in Latin Amer-

Sister Lúcia kisses ring of Pope Paul VI at Fátima, Portugal, where the Virgin Mary is said to have appeared before her and two other children in 1917.

ica. As a result, deacons are to be ordained in South America in 1968, and approval has been granted for a permanent diaconate in France.

The responsibility assigned to the laity by the Vatican Council brought about increased lay activity within the church in many parts of the world. The Third World Congress of the Lay Apostolate, meeting in Rome, expressed the laity's increasing concern for environmental problems in the light of Christian principles.

The first meeting in Rome of the Synod of Bishops opened on September 29. In addressing the synod, the pope emphasized the forced absence of representatives from Poland due to interference by the Communist regime. He indicated the ecumenical importance of the synod and explained that other Christian churches look to it for continued progress.

Brother Benilde became the first teaching brother to be canonized. Paul-Émile Cardinal Léger resigned as archbishop of Montreal, Canada, to serve as a missioner among African lepers. Francis Cardinal Spellman, Archbishop of New York, died of a stroke in December. Other church leaders who died during the year were: Francisco Cardinal Bracci; Joseph Cardinal Cardijn of Belgium; James Louis Cardinal Copello; Enrico Cardinal Dante; Alfredo Cardinal Pacini; Antonio Cardinal Riberi; Joseph Cardinal Ritter of St. Louis; Ernesto Cardinal Ruffini; Maximos IV Cardinal Saigh, Melkite Rite Patriarch of Antioch; and Thomas Cardinal Tien, first Chinese cardinal.

In the United States. The first session of the newly named National Conference of Catholic Bishops, formerly the National Catholic Welfare Conference, met in Washington, D.C. Proposals made at the synod were reported in matters concerning canon law and decentralization of administration.

Archbishop Luigi Raimondi became the U.S. apostolic delegate and Monsignor Edward T. O'Meara took office as national director of the Society for the Propagation of the Faith.

English was used for the first time in the canon of the Mass. Lay councils were organized in various dioceses. There was also a growing tendency for the church to go out to the people. In Rochester, N.Y., changes in priestly training include a lay teacher on the seminary staff and internships for deacons in the "inner city."

In New York City, another example of ecumenism occurred when Archbishop Iakovas, primate of the Greek Orthodox Church of North and South America, officiated at a pre-requiem for Francis Cardinal Spellman. The ceremony was the first of its kind for a Roman Catholic prelate since A.D. 1054.

Total Catholic Population in the U.S. reached 46,964,910 in 1967, an increase of 618,735 over 1966 and representing 23.6 per cent of the total U.S. population. [FULTON J. SHEEN]

ROMANIA once again demonstrated its independence within the Communist world in 1967. In January, it established diplomatic relations with the Federal Republic of (West) Germany, and later strenuously defended its action despite East German criticism (see GERMANY). In June, during the Middle East crisis, Romania was unwilling to follow the Soviet lead in placing all the blame on Israel and it called for a settlement through peaceful negotiations between the nations involved.

Although Romania was represented at the Moscow conference on the Middle East crisis in June, its representatives declined to sign the final communiqué, nor did they attend the subsequent Budapest meeting to coordinate assistance to the Arab countries. Similarly, Romania was not present at the Karlsbad conference on the German question that was held in April (see COMMUNISM).

In May, Romanian Communist party leader Nicolae Ceausescu published an article asserting the right of each Communist party to determine its policy in the light of its own interests. Ceausescu, in his article, also rejected the interference of other parties in the Romanian party's internal affairs.

The active foreign policy of Romania was further demonstrated by the election of its foreign minister, Corneliu Mănescu, to the presidency of the United Nations (UN) General Assembly. Mănescu thus became the first Communist leader to hold the post.

During the special UN session on Israel, Romania's Prime Minister Ion Gheorghe Maurer was also the first Communist leader other than the Soviet Union's Aleksei Kosygin to visit President Lyndon B. Johnson. In April, Maurer paid an unofficial visit to Communist China. In September, the prime minister visited Hanoi in North Vietnam, a visit that was also cloaked in secrecy.

Domestic Affairs. Some significant changes occurred in Romania's domestic affairs. The Central Committee's meetings were devoted primarily to such economic matters as the reorganization of the state farms and reforms in local government.

Ceausescu was elected state council president at the end of the year, thus combining the offices of chief of state and party secretary-general. Earlier, in July, Ceausescu had expressed an extensive criticism of past security police activities. Subsequent changes made in the security ministry included a law safeguarding the citizens' constitutional rights to claim damages for actions attributable to illegal administrative procedures. [H. GORDON SKILLING]

Facts in Brief. Population: 19,386,000. Government: Communist Party Secretary-General and State Council President Nicolae Ceausescu; Council of Ministers President Ion Gheorghe Maurer. Monetary Unit: leu (18=U.S. $1). Foreign Trade, exports, $1,186,000,000; imports, $1,213,000,000. Principal Exports: food, lumber, fuel.

ROMNEY, GEORGE (1907-   ), the 60-year-old, three-term governor of Michigan, announced on Nov. 18, 1967, that he would seek the Republican party's nomination for President of the United States in 1968. Romney thus became the first major candidate to declare for the presidency. See REPUBLICAN PARTY.

Romney, who was born on July 8, 1907, in Chihuahua, Mexico, returned to the United States in 1912, living with his family in Texas and California before settling in Idaho in 1921. From 1922 to 1926, Romney worked his way through Latter-Day Saints University in Salt Lake City, Utah. After two years in England and Scotland as a Mormon missionary, he returned to the United States.

Between 1930 and 1954, Romney held a variety of jobs; for six years, he was a lobbyist for the aluminum industry in Washington D.C., and general manager of the Automobile Manufacturers Association for another six years. In 1948, he joined the Nash-Kelvinator Corporation. When that company merged with the Hudson Motor Corporation in 1954, he became its chief executive. He took a leave of absence in 1962 to campaign for the governorship of Michigan. He was inaugurated governor in 1963.

ROTARY INTERNATIONAL. See SERVICE CLUBS.

RUBBER. See MANUFACTURING.

RULERS OF THE WORLD. See Facts in Brief under various country articles.

RUSSIA marked its 50th year under the Soviet system of government with ceremonial fanfare in almost every sphere of Soviet life in 1967. The regime, headed by Communist Party General Secretary Leonid I. Brezhnev, pursued the even tenor of its ways; its policy, both in domestic and in foreign affairs, was marked by the absence of radical experiments or of militant moves. This caution was strikingly inconsistent with the radical poses struck in the course of the anniversary celebrations. Although lip service was paid to the revolutionary origins of the regime and its revolutionary international objectives, the Soviet government acted like a satisfied great power, conscious of its strength and its national interests, and determined to defend these interests with moderation and without excessive risks. See COMMUNISM.

Anniversary Events. The anniversary was the occasion for celebrating Soviet achievements and for granting awards to those who had fulfilled their pledges of greater production. A new order, that of the October revolution, was established and was conferred first on the city of Leningrad where the revolution had occurred in 1917. Dimitri Shostakovich composed a symphonic poem, *October*, in honor of the anniversary. The actual celebrations were conventional, however, and did not seem to catch fire. Brezhnev occupied the center of the stage at all the commemorative meetings, unveiling an enormous statue of Lenin and delivering a four-hour speech on November 4.

A very long and dull set of theses was issued setting forth the significance of the October revolution and its aftermath. The theses did not mention Joseph Stalin, who had been supreme ruler for 30 years, nor his successor, Nikita S. Khrushchev, who had begun the transition toward a de-Stalinized Russia. Leon Trotsky, a chief architect of the revolution itself, was mentioned only to be denounced for the heresy of Trotskyism. The absence of Communist China's Mao Tse-tung and Albania's Enver Hoxha from the ceremonies was to be expected, but the failure of Cuba's Fidel Castro and North Vietnam's Ho Chi Minh to attend weakened the international significance of the event. This was somewhat offset by the presence of most other leading foreign Communists, including the two widely known Communist dissidents–Yugoslavia's Tito and Romania's Nicolae Ceausescu.

A much more spectacular event was an astronautical achievement that coincided with the anniversary celebrations. In October, two Soviet rockets were linked together in space, a further evidence of Soviet achievement in the field of science and a crucial first step toward an ultimate landing on the moon. An even greater triumph for the Soviet Union had been the landing of an automatic space station on the planet Venus in October. See SPACE EXPLORATION.

Russia's celebration of the 50th anniversary of the Bolshevik revolution began officially on November 3, with ceremonies in the Kremlin's Palace of Congresses.

Important Changes. The defection of Stalin's daughter, Svetlana Alliluyeva, awakened little apparent interest within the Soviet Union (see ALLILUYEVA, SVETLANA). News of her defection was kept to a minimum, and only an occasional propaganda attack was launched against her. Most Russians were no doubt more interested in the inauguration of the five-day week and the reduction of military service. The shorter working week, with the same number of hours, 41, distributed over five instead of six days, was gradually introduced during the year. The reduction of service in the army from three to two years, and from four to three in the navy, was combined with the introduction of military training in secondary schools.

Significant, too, was the sweeping amnesty announced in October, which freed certain persons serving five years, and cut in half the sentence of those serving more than two years. Excluded were those imprisoned for "particularly dangerous state crimes," or "gross violations of public order." Throughout the year there was a growing attention to consumer needs and greater emphasis on more fashionable clothing and better foods.

High Politics remained relatively dull and beyond the ken of the ordinary Russian. Collective leadership was maintained, with a dominant triumvirate consisting of party general secretary Brezhnev, Premier Aleksei N. Kosygin, and Nikolai V. Podgorny, chairman of the Presidium. The voice of

Svetlana Alliluyeva from the United States, charging some of the present leaders with responsibility for Stalin's crimes and accusing them of failing to fulfill the promises of reform made after Khrushchev's removal, had no repercussions.

There were dismissals and promotions at the topmost level but their significance, although perhaps great, was obscure to most observers. The dismissal of V. Y. Semichastny as chairman of the State Security Committee, and his replacement by Y. V. Andropov, who later became an alternate member of the Politburo, suggested an upgrading of the secret police. The transfer of Alexander N. Shelepin from the party secretariat to become head of the trade unions, seemed to represent a demotion for a leader who had also been responsible earlier for police affairs. The removal of another reputed party hard-liner, N. G. Yegorychev, from the important Moscow city party secretaryship, and the appointment of a Politburo member, V. V. Grishin, to this position, may have reflected a conflict over policy.

These moves were interpreted by some abroad as evidence of a clash of "hawks" and "doves" in the Soviet leadership and of rivalry for power among Brezhnev's associates. Brezhnev's position seemed, however, to be strengthened as a result of these shifts. The death of Marshal Rodion Y. Malinovsky led to speculation that a civilian might be placed in charge of the ministry of defense but he was succeeded by Marshal A. A. Grechko, a deputy minister and former chief commander of the Warsaw Pact forces. The party's control of the army was reasserted in the military newspaper, *Krasnaya Zvezda*.

Meanwhile, the general political structure remained unchanged, and the main organs functioned in their traditional manner. Although a new constitution might well have been expected as part of the anniversary, the five-year-old Constitutional Committee did not offer a single amendment. Major decisions continued to be made in the Politburo, the topmost level of the party hierarchy, with the 13,000,000 party members playing little part.

Routine Meetings. A plenary session was held in June to adopt the theses on the revolution and to discuss the crisis in the Middle East. The removal of Yegorychev immediately thereafter hinted at serious differences of view. Another session was held in September to approve the plan and the budget. Between these sessions, decrees were issued in the name of the Central Committee dealing with such prosaic matters as state farm accounting and soil erosion, and to discuss measures to improve living standards. The Supreme Soviet, which had met in routine session in December, 1966, to approve the plan and the budget, did not meet again until October, 1967, again to ratify the same items for 1968.

The new economic system passed through its second year uneventfully. By the end of 1967, about one-half of industry was scheduled to go over to the new system. Bureaucratic resistance seemed to have been an impediment to the progress of the new order, as was the absence of a reform in pricing.

Chinese diplomats leave May Day ceremonies in Moscow, another sign of tense relations between Russia and Communist China.

Freer Expression Continues. In the cultural sphere, the party continued to follow a middle-of-the-road course and to avoid interfering too drastically with the freer expression gained since Stalin's era. Early in the year, for example, a *Pravda* article sharply took to task both the organ of the more liberal writers, *Novy mir*, and that of the more conservative, *Oktyabr*. No doubt it was thus hoped to avoid a major conflict during the congress of the Writers Union which, after two postponements, was finally held in May. Its proceedings were, in fact, quiet and free of disputation. A number of major writers, including Ilya Ehrenburg and Andrei Voznesensky, were absent from the meetings.

International Relations. In foreign affairs, the Soviet Union was unable to mend or improve relations with either of its main rivals, Communist China and the United States. Diplomatic relations with China hung by a thread, following mob attacks on the embassies in Peking and Moscow, and constant denunciation on both sides. Soviet delegates walked out on China's 18th anniversary meeting in Peking; the Chinese refused to attend the Moscow celebrations. Soviet propaganda more and more centered on Mao Tse-tung and his "group," and included open appeals for his replacement. Proposals for united action in aid of Vietnam fell on deaf ears in Peking. Direct contacts between the Chinese and the Russian parties virtually ceased. Weak as was the position of China in the Communist camp, however, the Soviet party failed entirely in its effort to secure concerted action against it by the Communist parties throughout the world.

The continuing war in Vietnam persisted as the major stumbling block to an improvement in the Soviet Union's relations with the United States. As American intervention escalated, the Soviet Union increased its denunciation of the United States and its aid to North Vietnam.

Agreements Reached. There were some positive features of Soviet-American relations, especially the signing of a treaty on outer space, and an agreement to discuss mutual reduction of the arms race, particularly in antimissile defense systems. A meeting of Kosygin and President Lyndon B. Johnson in Glassboro, N.J., in June provided an opportunity for a frank exchange of views but the meeting failed to produce any significant shift in relations between the two countries.

The greatest Soviet setback came in the Middle East crisis of the summer. The ignominious defeat of the United Arab Republic to whose armed strength the U.S.S.R. had contributed so much was a blow to the Soviet Union's reputation. Its denunciation of Israeli aggression and demands for withdrawal could not alter this fact. Nor could Soviet policy at the United Nations conceal the fact that it was unable to rally a majority or effect any actual change in the situation in the Middle East.

Fireman

Alliances Formed. In Europe, alliances with Hungary and Bulgaria, top-level visits by Brezhnev to Poland, Czechoslovakia, Berlin, and Bulgaria, and to talks in Czechoslovakia and Hungary were important in solidifying the Communist bloc. Similarly, the appointment of Marshal Ivan J. Yakubovsky, Soviet deputy minister of defense, as head of the Warsaw Pact forces, maintained the Soviet primacy in the alliance. The Soviet Union was not able, however, to prevent its close ally, Romania, from entering into diplomatic relations with West Germany (see ROMANIA). The Soviet Union maintained its hard line toward Bonn and threw its weight behind the East German and Polish pressure on other Communist countries not to follow Romania's example. [H. GORDON SKILLING]

Facts in Brief. Population: 239,701,000. Government: Communist Party General Secretary Leonid I. Brezhnev; Premier Aleksei N. Kosygin; Supreme Soviet Presidium Chairman Nikolai V. Podgorny. Monetary Unit: ruble (1 = U.S. $1.11). Foreign Trade: exports, $8,840,000,000; imports, $7,909,000,000. Principal Exports: machinery, fuels, iron and steel.

RWANDA. See AFRICA.

SAFETY. The number of deaths from accidents in the United States declined in 1967 as the result of decreases in two of the four major categories of accidents. Accidents took 112,000 lives, decreasing 1 per cent from 1966. The accidental death rate was reduced to 56.6 per 100,000.

Among the four major types of accidents, the number of deaths from public and motor-vehicle accidents showed no change in 1967 compared with the previous year. On the job fatalities decreased

Accidental Deaths and Death Rates

	1966		1967	
Type of Accident	Number	Rate†	Number	Rate†
Motor-vehicle	53,000	27.1	53,000	26.8
Public nonroad	19,500	10.0	19,500	9.9
Home	29,500	15.1	28,500	14.4
Work	14,500	7.4	14,200	7.2
TOTAL*	113,000	57.7	112,000	56.6

†Deaths per 100,000 population.
*Total does not add up because of some duplications of motor vehicle and home and work deaths.

2 per cent. Accidental deaths at home were reduced by 3 per cent. Approximately 10,600,000 persons received injuries that disabled them beyond the day of the accident.

During 1967, accidents cost the nation an estimated $21,000,000,000. The largest portion of this amount, about $6,000,000,000, was charged to lost wages. Medical expenses totaled $2,200,000,000; insurance administrative costs, $4,500,000,000, and property loss in fires, $1,700,000,000.

The National Safety Council said that the increasing use of dividers on Interstate expressway systems was one factor in the decrease in traffic deaths. The Interstate system carried 91,000,000,000 miles of vehicle travel in 1966, compared to 64,000,000,000 in 1965. The death rate on these expressways was 2.9 per cent per 100,000,000 vehicle miles of travel. This compared with a death rate of 7.5 per cent on rural roads.

The Congress of the United States reduced its financial support in 1967 for the safety legislation passed the previous year. The House of Representatives Appropriations Committee cut President Lyndon B. Johnson's total budget request for highway safety activities from $131,000,000 to $41,000,000. In mid-October, a committee of both houses increased the appropriation to $46,000,000.

Congress initiated legislation during the year in the area of product safety, passing a bill that expanded the Flammable Fabrics Act to include additional articles of clothing, bedding, and household furnishings. It was signed by President Johnson in December. On November 20, the President signed a bill creating a seven-member Commission on Product Safety that would identify household products presenting unreasonable hazards. [HOWARD PYLE]

SAILING. See BOATS AND BOATING.

SAINT LOUIS took further steps in 1967 to rejuvenate its waterfront as its cultural and commercial hub. In March, voters passed a $2,000,000 bond issue that, with $6,000,000 in federal aid, will complete the 90-acre Jefferson National Expansion Memorial at the base of the 630-foot Gateway Arch. The visual highpoint will be a monumental stairway leading from the river to the arch. Visitors to the arch during its first year totaled 2,000,000. City fathers also approved a design for Gateway Mall, which will extend a mile west from the arch.

To the south, a handsome Spanish Pavilion is being erected, and the 2,165-foot-long Poplar Street Bridge opened in October. Its orthotropic design, in which the roadway deck is also part of the support structure, is unusual for major bridges. It includes a center span of 600 feet. When Interstate highways are fully linked to it, the bridge will carry 100,000 autos daily.

Downtown, construction began on a 34-story office tower and a second major bus terminal. Lambert Field, the city's airport, underwent enlargement and renovation of terminal facilities to handle the growing volume of passengers and cargo. In the future, the airport will undergo a massive $188,000,000 expansion program to meet anticipated future traffic needs. The area's economic future is considered so bright, however, that a second airport, costing about $140,000,000, was planned. [DONALD W. LIEF]

SALVATION ARMY units throughout the world gave special attention to a program designed to enlist layman participation in Army programs in 1967. U.S. units also launched a project called Operation Manpower to recruit men for Salvation Army ranks in such activities as club work, Scouting, and fellowship camps.

In Canada, the Salvation Army established its first advisory council of laymen. The council provides a channel through which laymen may contribute effectively to the planning, development, and ministry of the Salvation Army. Consisting of a self-governing association of senior soldiers, the advisory council of laymen was formed with the approval of the organization's international and Canadian territorial headquarters.

The Salvationist Service Corps, which began its work in three South American countries in 1966, was expanded to serve in Central American countries and in the West Indies in 1967. Student volunteers for the program were recruited from many sections of the United States.

The Ethel H. Wise Award of the Columbia University School of Social Work, New York City, was given to Edward C. Boyle of the Salvation Army in Los Angeles, Calif. The award cited "his achievement in establishing and successfully maintaining several 'halfway houses' for discharged prisoners and parolees." [JOSEPH P. ANDERSON]

SAN FRANCISCO. The Bay Area Rapid Transit District released plans on Aug. 8, 1967, to cut the proposed 75-mile system down to 57 miles. The shortened system became necessary due to increased construction costs.

In November, voters chose Democrat Joseph L. Alioto to succeed John F. Shelley as mayor. Alioto received a plurality among the field of 18 candidates. Voters also approved a $98,000,000 bond issue to improve crowded San Francisco International Airport. In a special referendum, San Franciscans opposed by a 2 to 1 margin any immediate withdrawal from Vietnam. The results had national implications because of the city's many antiwar demonstrations and its role as focal point of the "hippie" movement.

"Hippie" headquarters in the Haight-Ashbury District were a summer tourist attraction, but more substantial tourism was fostered by continued expansion of waterfront shops, stores, and restaurants located in old candy and glue factories and woolen mills. Five new hotels and major extensions to three others will add 4,000 rooms. A 172-room hotel will be part of the $15,000,000 Japanese Cultural and Trade Center under construction.

Homeowners were jolted in November by a state law requiring more equal assessment for residences and industrial property. The measure could mean a tripling of present rates. [DONALD W. LIEF]

SASKATCHEWAN. See CANADA.

King Faisal of Saudi Arabia inspected an honor guard shortly after his arrival in London in May. It was the first state visit to Britain by an Arabian monarch.

SAUDI ARABIA continued its support for the royalists in Yemen's civil war, sharpening King Faisal's differences with United Arab Republic President Gamal Abdel Nasser. Nasser, backing Yemen's republicans, seized the Saudi royal family's properties in Egypt, and Radio Cairo urged Arabs to carry out acts of sabotage toward "liberating" the Arabian Peninsula from imperialism. After a series of bombings hit Riyadh, Arabia's capital, the Saudis struck back with counter-terror. They arrested 32 Yemenis and publicly executed 17 of them, then deported 35,000 Yemenis, charging them with subversion.

The oil embargo imposed by the Arab states after Israel's swift victory in the June war was lifted in a few days due to pressure from the American-owned Arabian American Oil Company.

Construction began on a $6,200,000 desalination plant to replace Jidda's well-drawn water supply. Another $1,000,000 U.S. grant financed water surveys. King Faisal inaugurated the King Abd al-Aziz University, and pledged support for a sister Islamic university in Somalia. [WILLIAM SPENCER]

Facts in Brief. Population: 7,040,000. Government: King Faisal. Monetary Unit: riyal (4.5=U.S. $1). Foreign Trade: exports, $1,640,000,000; imports, $394,000,000. Principal Exports: petroleum and petroleum products.

SCHOOL. See CIVIL RIGHTS; EDUCATION; Section One, LAWRENCE CREMIN: FOCUS ON EDUCATION.

SCIENCE AND RESEARCH. There was growing concern in the Congress of the United States, in 1967, over possibly harmful consequences of sciences and technology and its inefficient use. Two committees were established, one in the Senate and the other in the House, to study the issues related to science and society. The Senate group, a temporary Select Committee on Technology and the Human Environment, is headed by Senator Edmund S. Muskie (D., Me.). The House body is the Subcommittee on Science, Research, and Development. Its chairman is Representative Emilio Q. Daddario (D., Conn.).

Both committees were assigned two broad objectives. One objective was to determine how the federal government could most effectively utilize science and technology to solve environmental problems such as crime, poverty, and pollution. The other objective was to develop an early warning system to foresee undesirable technological consequences so that corrective measures might be taken.

In establishing the committees, it was pointed out that the expenditure of public funds has been inefficiently and often ineffectively employed because funds were provided after a crisis developed rather than in anticipation of one. Water pollution, for example, is so severe that experts believe it will cost $100,000,000,000 during the next 20 years to clean up the nation's lakes and streams. See Section Two, THE KILLING OF A GREAT LAKE.

The issue was articulated by Glenn T. Seaborg, chairman of the U.S. Atomic Energy Commission. "The year 2000," he said before the Muskie committee, "is not waiting for the fulfillment of our Utopian dreams. In less than 33 years, it will be here with a vengeance, and whether we welcome it in jubilation or in despair will largely depend on how quickly we can act in the coming years."

Classified Research. Mounting student and faculty protest against classified government research on university campuses resulted in a policy decision by the Department of Defense to discontinue such projects. About 8 per cent of the defense research at universities in 1967 was classified.

Expenditures. The National Science Foundation estimated that $24,000,000,000 would be spent on research and development in 1967 and $25,000,000,000 in 1968. Their report, entitled *National Patterns of Research and Development Resources*, also cited these trends in funding from 1953 to 1968:

- The annual growth rate of research and development has dropped from 12 per cent to 5 per cent.
- During the past 15 years the federal government's share of research funding has increased from 53 per cent to 63 per cent, while industry's share has dropped from 43 to 33 per cent.
- Expenditures for basic research have climbed from 9 to 14 per cent of the total. [JAMES A. PEARRE]

SCIENCE CLUBS OF AMERICA held the 18th national Science Fair-International in San Francisco, Calif., from May 10 to 13, to honor the most promising student-scientists of the year.

Top Winners from among the 425 finalists were:

Douglas Milton Brenner, 18, of Chesapeake, Va., for *Formation of Septal Pores and the Nature of Woronin Bodies in Ascodesmis sphaerospora.*

Rosmarie Lehmann, 20, of Thun, Switzerland, for *Comparison of the Lichen Vegetable from Oberdiessbach and Thun.*

Martha C. Cragoe, 17, of Fairview Village, Pa., for *Synthesis and Investigation of Cholesteric Liquid Crystals.*

Robert M. Swift, 16, of Chicago, Ill., for *Biochemical Study of Prostanoic Hormones.*

Neil F. Martin, 16, of Bethesda, Md., for *Research and Design Procedures Resulting in a Variable Camber and Thickness Airfoil.*

Kathleen Reavette Page, 18, of Tulsa, Okla., for *Factors Influencing the Orientation of Shells on a Beach.*

Ronald Stephen Hencin, 17, of Melbourne, Fla., for *Separation of Mammalian Immunological Capacities: A Functional Equivalent of the Avian Bursa of Fabricius.*

Eileen Moffitt, 17, of Berkeley, Calif., for *Messenger RNA Comparison in Inducible and Constitutive E. coli.*

Paul B. Ré, 17, of Albuquerque, N.Mex., for *Coanda Effect Propulsion by Negative Drag.*

Gary Ray Rylander, 16, of Austin, Tex., for *Field-Effect Transistors and Field-Effect Transistor Amplifiers at −195°C.*

Sheldon Jay Axler, 17, of Miami, Fla., for *Original Investigations of the Calculus of Complex Numbers.*

Dorcas Harley, 15, of Morgantown, W.VA., for *Identification of 55 Naturally-Occurring Equine Blood Factors.*

Distribution of Research and Development Dollars Fiscal 1965

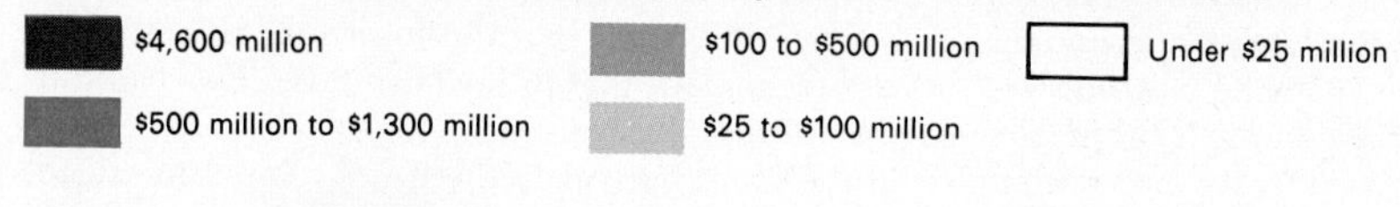

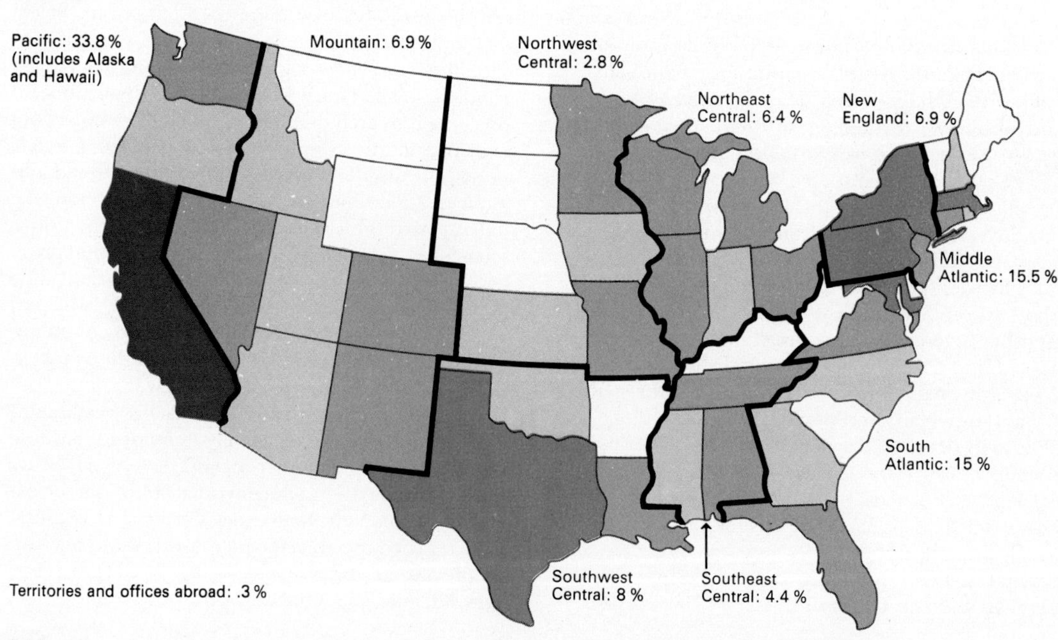

Nevin Morris Summers, Jr., 17, of Jacksonville, Fla., for *Radiochemical Studies on the Biogenesis of the Crab Cuticle Hardening Agent.*

Health Awards were given by the following organizations: *American Dental Association*—Gaines W. Hammond of Spartanburg, S.C., and Jerald D. Malone of El Paso, Tex. *American Medical Association*—Susan T. Bertrand of New Albany, Ind., and Stephen R. Igo of Winterset, Iowa. *American Pharmaceutical Association*—Philip W. Payne of Richmond, Ind. *American Veterinary Medical Association*—Dorcas J. Harley of Morgantown, W. Va.

Special Awards were made by the following organizations; *American Association of Petroleum Geologists*—S. Thomas Mast of Laramie, Wyo. *American Chemical Society*—Martha C. Cragoe of Fairview Village, Pa., and Robert A. Lipson of St. George, N.Y. *American Institute of Chemical Engineers*—F. Stephen Beckman of Burlington, Iowa. *American Institute of Mining, Metallurgical, and Petroleum Engineers*—Lawrence E. Eiselstein of Huntington, W.Va., and Hans Dieter Hoelzer of Huntsville, Ala. *American Patent Law Association*—Curtis Bryant of LeMars, Iowa. *American Psychological Association*—Cozette Stiles of Snohomish, Wash. *American Society for Metals*—Stephen M. Zvolner of Chicago, Ill. *American Society for Microbiology*—Douglas Milton Brenner of Chesapeake, Va. **Other Special Awards** were: *Entomological Society of America*—Bruce Christian Black of Falls Church, Va. *National Committee for Careers in Medical Technology*—Jeffrey Howard Hill of Columbus, Ohio. *National Pest Control Association*—Susan Lee Campbell of Bossier City, La. *Optical Society of America*—Curtis Bryant of LeMars, Iowa. *Society of Exploration Geophysicists*—Ronald Franklin Nichols of Ada, Okla., and Carolyn Ann Ross of Berkeley Heights, N.J. *Society of Women Engineers*—Carolyn Ann Ross of Berkeley Heights, N.J.

The National Aeronautics and Space Administration (NASA) awarded two-day visits to NASA facilities to: Patrick J. Gerstle of Louisville, Ky.; Hans Dieter Hoelzer of Huntsville, Ala.; Scott A. Jenkins of Albuquerque, N.Mex.; Larry Lewis of Gadsden, Ala.; Gary Stuart Settles of Maryville, Tenn.; and Robert A. Warriner III of New Orleans, La.

The Atomic Energy Commission awarded trips to Argonne National Laboratory to: Glenn Merrill Brackett of Atlanta, Ga.; Marilyn Ann Finn of New York, N.Y.; Larry C. Ford of Provo, Utah; Glenn Eric Hager of Lovington, N.Mex.; Evelyn D. Jankowski of Lodi, N.J.; Nicolette Danielle Orlando of Frederick, Md.; Robert H. Roswell of Bartlesville, Okla.; Randall Allen Schaefer of Bettendorf, Iowa; Nevin Morris Summers, Jr., of Jacksonville, Fla.; and Michael P. Taff of Chapel Hill, N.C.

The U.S. Air Force (USAF) honored finalists in 10 special categories with plaques and expense-paid trips to USAF research facilities. The 10 USAF winners were: Thomas S. Messer of Cape Girardeau, Mo.; Martha C. Cragoe of Fairview Village, Pa.; Gary Stuart Settles of Maryville, Tenn.; Carolyn Ann Ross of Berkeley Heights, N.J.; Curtis Bryant of LeMars, Iowa; Sheldon Jay Axler of Miami, Fla.; Robert A. Warriner III of New Orleans, La.; John Gordon Boland of Wichita Falls, Tex.; Ronald James Wilson of Dickinson, Tex.; and John Martin Seward of Oklahoma City, Okla.

Westinghouse 26th Annual Science Talent Search scholarships went to: Nevin Summers, Jr., 17, of Jacksonville, Fla., $7,500; Steven Binder, 17, of Glenview, Ill., $6,000; and Daniel Weisser, 17, of Washington, D.C., $5,000. Scholarship awards of $3,000 went to Frank Wilczek, 15, of Glen Oaks, N.Y.; and Mark Cullen, 16, of Wyncote, Pa. [FOSTER P. STOCKWELL]

SCULPTURE. See PAINTING AND SCULPTURE.

SENEGAL. See AFRICA.

SERVICE CLUBS and organizations in 1967 continued to emphasize programs of international exchange and cooperation.

Kiwanis International began a new program designed to strengthen clubs by combining community service and membership development. The program, called Let's Match, stimulated club growth by enlisting the aid of prospective Kiwanians in a significant project and then inviting these men to join the club. As a result of the Let's Match approach, membership reached a new high in 1967. There were 273,305 members in 5,471 clubs in 22 countries, as of August 1.

The international extension program, started in 1962, also contributed to the increase in membership. New clubs were organized in Australia, Colombia, New Zealand, Nicaragua, and Sweden.

The first Kiwanis Mexico-U.S. friendship marker was erected at the International Bridge, Hidalgo, Tex. Additional markers were placed in Brownsville and El Paso. The plaques follow a Kiwanis tradition of 35 similar peace and friendship markers along the Canada-U.S. border.

The 52nd Annual Kiwanis International Convention was held in Houston, Tex., June 25 to 29. James M. Moler of Charleston, W. Va., was elected president. Harold M. Heimbaugh of West Hollywood, Calif., was named president-elect.

Lions International completed its year-long, world-wide essay contest on the topic "Peace Is Attainable." The contest brought entries from more than a million boys and girls between the ages of 14 and 21 in 132 countries. The grand prize-winning essay was submitted by A. Russell Wodell, 17, from Cranbrook, B.C., Canada. He received $25,000 to be used as an educational or career-assistance grant.

The other seven finalists, each of whom received $1,000, were: Montserrat F. Campos, 18, Mexico City; William A. Curry, 18, Carrolton, Alabama; Khalid Jamai, 21, Rabat, Morocco; Masahiro Sahara, 21, Tokyo, Japan; Roger Schawinski, 21, Zurich, Switzerland; Andrew Wyatt, 18, Wellington, New Zealand; and José B. Russó Zarza, 21, Asunción, Paraguay.

In a new program, the Lions planned to pair towns and cities of South Vietnam with Lions communities in all parts of the world to foster a two-way exchange of ideas. The Lions Clubs in Saigon, with help of the South Vietnamese government, assumed responsibility for selecting 1,000 towns, cities, and hamlets to participate in the program.

As of Aug. 31, 1967, there were 827,776 Lions International in 21,522 clubs in 140 countries and geographical locations. Texas became the first state with 900 clubs.

The 50th annual convention of Lions International was held in Chicago, Ill., July 5 to 8. Jorge Bird from San Juan, Puerto Rico, was elected international president.

Rotary International added a new program called Rotary Volunteers Abroad as a supplement to the Small Business Clinic program. The Small Business Clinic enables Rotarians to share their business experience with local small business men in a wide variety of occupations. Rotary Volunteers Abroad is designed to help an individual company or owner in another country deal with a problem.

The Rotary Foundation observed its 50th anniversary by establishing 50 new undergraduate scholarships and by increasing to 50 the number of awards for group study exchange. The former will provide a year of undergraduate study abroad for highly qualified young men and women between the ages of 18 and 24. Under the group study exchange, a group of six young businessmen, selected by a Rotary District, will study the business methods, institutions, and culture of a country other than their own for three months.

As of Aug. 29, 1967, there were 12,939 Rotary Clubs and an estimated 621,250 members in 135 countries and geographical regions.

Interact, Rotary's organization for high school age boys, observed its 5th anniversary in 1967. There were 45,000 members in 1,860 Interact Clubs located in 59 countries.

The 58th convention of Rotary International, held in Nice, France, May 21 to 25, elected Luther H. Hodges as president. [JOSEPH P. ANDERSON]

SEXTON, ANNE (1928-), was awarded the 1967 Pulitzer prize for poetry on May 1 for her third book of verse, *Live or Die*, a journal of poems written from 1962 to 1966. A fellow poet, Millen Brand, reviewing the work in 1966, said that in it and in her earlier *To Bedlam and Part Way Back* (1960), Mrs. Sexton "unhesitatingly made her (mental) illness her central subject, fully exposing her inner darkness as 'feverish and frowning'." Her poetry is generally associated with Robert Lowell and Sylvia Plath in what has been called the "confessional school."

Mrs. Sexton, who now lives in Newton Lower Falls, Mass., was born at nearby Newton, Mass. She attended Garland Junior College, Wellesley, and the Radcliffe Institute for Independent Study. In 1950 and 1951, she was a fashion model in Boston, Mass. Her second book of verse, *All My Pretty Ones*, was published in 1962. In that year, she won the Levinson Prize for seven poems published in *Poetry* magazine. In 1965, she was elected a fellow of the Royal Society of Literature. She is a frequent contributor to magazines and is co-author of a children's book, and she has given many poetry readings, chiefly at colleges. She and her husband, Alfred M. Sexton II, a salesman, have two daughters, Linda and Joyce. [WALTER F. MORSE]

SHIPS AND SHIPPING. See TRANSPORTATION.

SHIPWRECK. See DISASTERS.

SHOOTING. See SPORTS.

SIERRA LEONE had two bloodless military coups in March, 1967, following political disputes and election tensions. With the elections approaching, interparty disputes had become so violent that a state of emergency was declared in the Eastern Region on March 1, and in the Western Region on March 3. Police prevented further fighting, and the elections were held on March 17. On the next day–before the election results were announced–Governor General Henry Lightfoot-Boston appointed Siaka P. Stevens, leader of the opposition All-People's Congress, as prime minister. The armed forces commander, Brigadier David Lansana, declared the action illegal and arrested both Lightfoot-Boston and Stevens.

Lansana met with the newly elected parliament on March 22. But a day later, a group of junior officers, with police cooperation, seized power. They set up a national reformation council, which dissolved all political parties and suspended the constitution. Lieutenant Colonel Andrew T. Juxon-Smith became chairman on March 27. His government adopted a nonaligned position. [BENJAMIN E. THOMAS]

Facts in Brief. Population: 2,412,000. Government: National Reformation Council Chairman Andrew T. Juxon-Smith. Monetary Unit: leone (1=U.S. $1.20). Foreign Trade: exports, $83,000,000; imports, $100,000,000. Principal Exports: diamonds, iron ore, palm kernels.

SKATING. See ICE HOCKEY; ICE SKATING.

SKIING. Jean-Claude Killy dominated Alpine skiing as no one had since Austria's Toni Sailer won three gold medals in the 1956 Winter Olympics. Killy, a 23-year-old French customs inspector from Val d'Isere, France, won 16 out of 23 races against world class competition, which is comparable to a major league baseball player hitting 120 home runs or a pitcher winning 60 games in a single season.

As a result, Killy won the new World Cup, symbol of skiing supremacy, with a perfect score of 225 points. Heini Messner of Austria was a distant second with 114, followed by Guy Perillat, Leo LaCroix, and Georges Mauduit, all of France. Jim Huega, the American champion, was sixth.

In contrast to Killy's runaway victory, the women's World Cup was won in the final race of the season. Nancy Greene of Canada won the trophy with 176 points after capturing the giant slalom at Jackson Hole, Wyo., by 7/100 of a second. Second in the race, and in the World Cup competition, was Marielle Goitschel of France, with 172 points. Annie Famose of France was a close third with 158. Isabelle Mir Florence Steurer followed.

Miss Greene's victory was spectacular since she had missed many of the meets that counted in the scoring. After taking a substantial lead in Europe, she returned to Canada in late January to compete in local meets. Miss Goitschel then took over the European lead. But Miss Greene re-entered the

World Cup competition in the United States in March, and achieved the victory.

France easily won the team World Cup competition, and also the five-nation World Series at Vail, Colo., by a surprisingly small three-point margin over Austria, 231 to 228. The United States was third with 148 points.

Nordic Skiing. The 1966 world champion Bjorn Wirkola of Norway again captured most of the honors in ski-jumping. He won the Four Hills competition, held in Germany and Austria in January, with three firsts and a third, set a North American record of 335 feet at Leavenworth, Wash., in February, and took the prestigious Holmenkollen at Oslo in March.

Wirkola, however, lost his world record in ski-flying, where distance alone counts and form is not scored. The record of 479 feet was broken three times in two days at Oberstdorf, Germany. First, Lars Grini of Norway leaped 482 feet on February 10, only to be topped 90 minutes later by Kjell Sjoeberg of Sweden with 485 feet. The next day Grini came back with a 492-foot jump to nail down the record.

The University of Denver won the National Collegiate Athletic Association (NCAA) championship for the seventh year in a row. A good score in the jumping competition, the final event, gave Denver 376.7 points, just enough to pass Wyoming's 375.9 and Dartmouth's 374. [JAMES O. DUNAWAY]

SOAP BOX DERBY. See SPORTS.

SOCCER experienced a stormier year than usual throughout the world. At a game in Kayseri, Turkey, Sept. 17, 1967, a spectator riot resulted in the deaths of 42 fans and injuries to an estimated 600. At the World Club title game in Montevideo, Uruguay, in July, police were called out to halt repeated brawls between the rival Racing Club of Buenos Aires, Argentina, and the European Cup winner, Glasgow (Scotland) Celtics. Five players, three from the Scottish team, were ejected from the game, which was won by the Argentines. In May, the Glasgow Celtics had defeated Milan, Italy, to become the first British team to take the European soccer cup.

U.S. Rivalry. In the United States, two new leagues struggled for survival. The United Soccer Association (USA) ended its season in July with an overtime title game at Los Angeles that lasted two hours and six minutes. The Los Angeles, Calif., Wolves finally outlasted the Washington Whips, 6 to 5. One Washington player was tossed out for rough play in the first half of the game. But with only 10 men to the Wolves' 11 for the rest of the match, the Whips–actually an entire squad imported from Aberdeen, Scotland–tied the score with 70 seconds left in regulation time. The team then tied the score again on a penalty kick in the final two seconds of the first overtime period. The winning team, representing Los Angeles, was the English Wolverhampton Wanderers.

In the rival National Professional Soccer League (NPSL), which imported its foreign players singly rather than en masse and played until September, the two-game play-off for the championship was decided by total goals. The Baltimore Bays won the first game in Baltimore, 1 to 0, but the Oakland Clippers came back six days later to beat them for the title, 4 to 1, in Oakland.

A merger of the two leagues seemed likely after the season, but first the NPSL sued its rival, along with the parent bodies, the U.S. Soccer Football Association and the International Federation of Football Associations, claiming a violation of the anti-trust laws. The $18,000,000 suit charged the three groups with blacklisting foreign players who competed in the NPSL and conspiring to exclude its members from world-wide organized soccer. Finally, however, the two leagues did agree to merge into one, the North American Soccer League.

Other Cup Winners. Tottenham Hotspur beat Chelsea to win the English Football Association Cup, and Manchester United captured the championship of the English League. Manchester fans later did $2,400 worth of damage to a train en route to London for a game against Chelsea.

In the United States, the National Open Challenge Cup was won by the New York Greek-American Club, and the National Amateur title by the Italian-American Stars of Hartford, Conn. [JOHN LAKE]

SOCIAL SECURITY legislation passed by the 90th Congress in December, 1967, will provide the largest single benefits increase in the history of the program. The 1967 amendments to the Social Security Act call for an increase of at least 13 per cent for everyone presently receiving benefits, with a 25 per cent hike for those at the bottom of the scale. The minimum monthly benefit for an individual will range from $55 to $218, compared with the present $44 to $168. The minimum monthly benefit for a man and wife will range from $82.50 to $323, instead of the present $66 to $252.

The maximum individual payment will be $218, a 30 per cent increase over the $168 possible under the old law. The maximum payment for a couple will be $323 instead of $252 now being paid.

Special Benefits for persons 72 years of age and over who lack the necessary Social Security qualification to receive full payments will be increased to $40 for an individual and $60 for a couple.

Under the new law, benefits for wives with no earnings record will be limited to $105 per month. Under the old law, they received half of the amount paid to their husbands when their wives had reached the age of 65.

Disabled widows and widowers between the ages of 50 and 62 will receive benefits ranging from 50 to 82 1/2 per cent of the amount to which the deceased worker would have been entitled if living.

Monthly Social Security Benefits Under the Old and New Plans

Average yearly earnings after 1950....	$800 or less		$1,800		$3,000	
Average monthly earnings after 1950...	$67 or less		$150		$250	
	Old law	New bill	Old law	New bill	Old law	New bill
1. Retirement at 65 or disability benefit......	$ 44.00	$ 55.00	$ 78.20	$ 88.40	$101.70	$115.00
2. Retirement at 62......................	35.20	44.00	62.60	70.80	81.40	92.00
3. Wife's benefit at 65 or with child in her care..	22.00	27.50	39.10	44.20	50.90	57.50
4. Wife's benefit at 62....................	16.50	20.70	29.40	33.20	38.20	43.20
5. One child of retired or disabled worker.....	22.00	27.50	39.10	44.20	50.90	57.50
6. Widow 62 or older....................	44.00	55.00	64.60	73.00	84.00	94.90
7. Widow at 60, no child.................	38.20	47.70	56.00	63.30	72.80	82.30
8. Disabled widow at age 50..............	....	33.40	....	44.30	....	57.60
9. Widow under 62 and 1 child............	66.00	82.50	117.40	132.60	152.60	172.60
10. Widow under 62 and 2 children..........	66.00	82.50	120.00	132.60	202.40	202.40
11. One surviving child....................	44.00	55.00	58.70	66.30	76.30	86.30
12. Two surviving children.................	66.00	82.50	117.40	132.60	152.60	172.60
13. Maximum family benefit................	66.00	82.50	120.00	132.60	202.40	202.40
14. Maximum lump-sum death payment.......	132.00	165.00	234.60	255.00	255.00	255.00

The new law substitutes a more restrictive definition of those persons entitled to disability payments. A person will be determined to be disabled only if he is unable to engage in any kind of substantial gainful work that exists in the national economy, even if such work is not available in the area in which he lives.

Other provisions of the law influencing the amount of benefits payments deal with earnings exemption and wage credits for military personnel.

The wages a retired worker or survivor may earn before losing part of his Social Security payments was increased to $1,680 a year from $1,500. A person is allowed to earn $140 a month without losing benefits in that month, whatever his annual earnings. When earnings exceed the new annual limits, $1 of benefits will be lost for each $2 earned up to $2,880. After that there will be a $1 for $1 loss.

For Social Security benefit purposes, pay of persons in the military services will be considered $100 per month more than the basic pay received.

The revisions in the Social Security Act will mean the payment of an additional $3,600,000,000 in benefits to 24,000,000 persons during the first full year of operation. The increased benefits were to become effective in February, 1968, with the first checks to be mailed early in March of that year.

They will be financed by raising the taxable wage base to $7,800 a year from $6,600, effective Jan. 1, 1968. The tax rate now of 4.4 per cent each for workers and employers will remain at that figure in 1968, but will go up to 4.8 per cent in 1969.

The New Legislation also provided:

- An increased authorization for child welfare programs from $55,000,000 to $100,000,000 in fiscal 1969 and from $60,000,000 to $110,000,000 in succeeding years.
- An increased ceiling on federal participation in public welfare programs in Puerto Rico from $9,800,000 to $12,500,000 in 1968 and eventually up to $24,000,000 in 1972.
- A total of $20,000,000 over the next four years in grants to colleges and universities to improve training in professional social work.

Although there was agreement on the need for the increase in benefits and other amendments to the Social Security Act that would improve services for older Americans, a controversy developed about the public welfare and Medicaid proposals. A group of liberal Senators threatened to delay enactment of the bill until the second session of the 90th Congress. In spite of the heated debate, however, the 1967 amendments to the Social Security Act were approved by both houses and sent to the President for his signature.

The legislation was passed in the House of Representatives by a vote of 388 to 3 and in the Senate by 62 to 14. It was signed by President Lyndon B. Johnson Jan. 2, 1968. [JOSEPH P. ANDERSON]

	$3,600		$4,200		$4,800		$6,600	$7,800
	$300		$350		$400		$550	$650
Old law	New bill	Old law	New bill	Old law	New bill	Old law	New bill	New Plan Maximum*
$112.40	$127.10	$124.20	$140.40	$135.90	$153.60	$168.00	$189.90	$218.00
90.00	101.70	99.40	112.40	108.80	122.90	134.40	152.00	174.40
56.20	63.60	62.10	70.20	68.00	76.80	84.00	95.00	105.00
42.20	47.70	46.60	52.70	51.00	57.60	63.00	71.30	78.80
56.20	63.60	62.10	70.20	68.00	76.80	84.00	95.00	109.00
92.80	104.90	102.50	115.90	112.20	126.80	138.60	156.70	179.90
80.50	91.00	88.90	100.50	97.30	109.90	120.20	135.90	156.00
....	63.60	....	70.30	....	76.90	....	95.00	109.10
168.60	190.80	186.40	210.60	204.00	230.40	252.00	285.00	327.00
240.00	240.00	279.60	280.80	306.00	322.40	368.00	395.60	434.40
84.30	95.40	93.20	105.30	102.00	115.20	126.00	142.50	163.50
168.60	190.80	186.40	210.60	204.00	230.40	252.00	285.00	327.00
240.00	240.00	280.80	280.80	309.20	322.40	368.00	395.20	434.40
255.00	255.00	255.00	255.00	255.00	255.00	255.00	255.00	255.00

*Amount of earnings subject to Social Security taxes raised in new law.

SOCIAL WELFARE legislation adopted by Congress in 1967 revealed a deep concern about the increasing number of welfare recipients and the mounting costs of federal and state programs. Sweeping changes were made in the largest and most controversial of all the public assistance programs, Aid to Dependent Children (ADC).

The changes were a part of the Social Security Amendments of 1967. They included these requirements:

- That states develop programs for each relative and dependent child that will assure, to the maximum extent possible, that they can enter the labor force in order to become self-sufficient.
- That states provide day care services for the children of mothers who wish to work or take training, and to offer services for children who can contribute toward making the family self-sustaining.
- That states establish community work training programs in areas where a significant number of ADC families live.

Strong criticisms of the new welfare legislation and of welfare programs in general were expressed by delegates to the First Annual National Welfare Rights Convention held in Washington, D.C., August 25 to 28. The convention participants were representatives of organizations of welfare recipients in 58 cities. These groups staged demonstrations in June to protest inadequacies in welfare programs.

Reorganization. Secretary of the Department of Health, Education, and Welfare John W. Gardner announced the establishment of a new agency, the Social and Rehabilitation Service, in a major reorganization of its welfare, rehabilitation, and social service programs, effective on August 15. The agency now has five major divisions. These are the Administration on Aging, the Assistance Payments Administration, the Children's Bureau, the Medical Services Administration, and the Rehabilitation Services Administration.

The new agency is designed to bring a unified approach to the problems of special groups and to achieve greater efficiency and more productive use of resources. Mary E. Switzer, formerly Commissioner of Vocational Rehabilitation Administration was appointed the director.

Awards in 1967 included:

National Conference on Social Welfare 1967 Distinguished Service Award to Vice-President Hubert H. Humphrey for "his courageous leadership and dedicated service in the area of social reform."

Planned Parenthood-World Population Distinguished Service Awards to Howard F. Gustafson (posthumous), former President of the National Association of Social Workers and Ruth M. Williams (posthumous), former National Conference on Social Welfare Assistant Executive Secretary and International Conference Executive Secretary. [JOSEPH P. ANDERSON]

SOMALIA. Somali warriors in northeastern Kenya continued guerrilla attacks against Kenya forces in their efforts to make their territory part of Somalia. Kenya called the Somalis *shiftas* (bandits), and killed and captured scores of them during 1967. On May 1, Somali's foreign minister proposed negotiations on the future of Kenya's northeastern province and its Somali inhabitants. But Kenya rejected negotiations on the grounds that it would not give its territory to Somalia. It also demanded that Somalia stop aiding the guerrillas or run the risk of war. Later discussions between the two countries avoided war, but did not end the dispute. See KENYA.

The national assembly elected Dr. Abdirascid Ali Scermarche, former prime minister, to a six-year term as president on June 10. He replaced Aden Abdulla Osman, who had held the office since Somalia's independence in 1960. Mohammed Ibrahim Egal became prime minister on July 10.

Somalia objected to the outcome of a March referendum in neighboring French Somaliland. It had hoped the area would choose independence and then join Somalia. But the voters rejected independence in favor of remaining under French control. Somalia accused France of expelling large numbers of Somalis as nonresidents and of not permitting Somali women to vote, thus permitting the pro-French voters to win the referendum. Somalia called on the United Nations and the Organization of African Unity for assistance against the French policies, and attempted to move 8,000 persons across the border, claiming that they had come originally from French Somaliland.

Peace Corps Spying? A small Arabic-language weekly newspaper published documents in December, 1966, and January, 1967, that indicated the United States had instructed Peace Corps volunteers in Somalia to engage in espionage. The United States denounced the documents as forgeries. Somali's minister of education defended the Peace Corps and claimed the volunteers had served well as teachers. On January 25, the national assembly rejected a motion requesting withdrawal of the 94-man Peace Corps by a vote of 46 to 19.

The International Monetary Fund granted $5,000,000 in credit to Somalia to ease its financial difficulties, caused partly by the end of the protected market for Somali bananas in Italy. United Nations technical experts in Somalia increased in number from 85 to more than 120 in 1967. West German aid to Somalia totaled more than $20,000,000; road building, a technical school, and a textile factory were the major projects. [BENJAMIN E. THOMAS]

Facts in Brief. Population: 2,617,000. Government: President Abdirascid Ali Scermarche; Prime Minister Mohammed Ibrahim Egal. Monetary Unit: shilling (7.14=U.S. $1). Foreign Trade: exports, $33,800,000; imports, $50,500,000. Principal Exports: bananas, livestock, hides and skins.

SOUTH AFRICA, REPUBLIC OF. The United Nations (UN) General Assembly voted on May 19, 1967, to set up a council that would take over the territory of South West Africa from South Africa and administer it until independence was granted. Prime Minister Balthazar Johannes Vorster refused to recognize the UN action. See UNITED NATIONS. His country has held the territory since it was taken from Germany after World War I and mandated to South Africa by the League of Nations in 1920. South Africa's plans for dividing the territory into racially segregated areas continued. One area, Ovamboland, with 45 per cent of the population, was offered local self-rule on March 21.

South Africa and the United States clashed over racial segregation during the visit of U.S. aircraft carrier *Franklin Delano Roosevelt* to Cape Town from February 4 to 6. South Africa had invited the crew ashore without racial restrictions. But the ship's captain, under orders to permit crewmen to attend only integrated activites, canceled all shore leaves. Public irritation was somewhat lessened when the ship accepted 100,000 visitors of all races.

Official Policies strengthened security at home and expanded relations with black African nations. The government stockpiled strategic goods of many types for use should economic sanctions be applied against South Africa. It extended the length of compulsory military service for white South Africans. An anti-terrorism law further increased the police's power to detain and interrogate prisoners and invoked the death penalty for terrorism and sabotage. The army obtained a fleet of 16 troop-carrying helicopters from France and arranged for French loans to purchase additional military supplies. Discussions with the African nations of Botswana, Lesotho, and Malawi led to several economic agreements.

The economy continued to expand. Trade with Great Britain increased substantially; trade with Asia, especially Japan, almost doubled in 1967.

Theophilus Ebenhaezer Donges was elected president of South Africa for a seven-year term on February 28, succeeding Charles R. Swart. But before the inauguration date of May 11, the 69-year-old Donges fell seriously ill and President of the Senate Jozua F. T. Naude was appointed acting president.

Albert J. Luthuli, 69, African nationalist, former president-general of the banned African National Congress, and 1960 Nobel Peace prize winner, was killed by a train on July 21 as he walked across a railway bridge. [BENJAMIN E. THOMAS]

Facts in Brief. Population: 18,948,000. Government: Acting State President Jozua F. T. Naude; Prime Minister Balthazar Johannes Vorster. Monetary Unit: rand (1=U.S. $1.39). Foreign Trade: exports, $1,706,000,000; imports, $2,530,000,000. Principal Exports: gold, diamonds, wool.

SOUTH AMERICA. See LATIN AMERICA and articles on various countries.

South Arabians cheered the end of 128 years of British occupation and the first days of independence for their Arab homeland in November.

SOUTH ARABIA, FEDERATION OF, renamed the People's Republic of South Yemen, became the world's newest nation on Nov. 30, 1967, as British troops evacuated Aden after 128 years of colonial rule. The Federation had originally been stitched together in 1959 by Great Britain from 17 feudal sultanates and Aden colony. The new state incorporated the former federation with three larger sultanates, Kathiri, Mahri, and Quaiti, that had been previously independent under British protection as the Hadhramaut. The republic also acquired Kamaran and Perim, small islands in the Red Sea.

Independence for South Arabia followed four years of terrorism. Attacks by Arab nationalists were directed first against British troops – 57 of them were killed and hundreds injured during the four years. In 1967, the combination of the withdrawal of British troops to comply with a deadline of independence for the federation on Jan. 9, 1968, and the pressures of Arab nationalism was too strong. For several months, civil war flared between two rival nationalist groups, the National Liberation Front (NLF) and the Front for the Liberation of Occupied South Yemen (FLOSY).

Unhappy Anniversary. The federation's eighth anniversary in February was celebrated by terrorism and a general strike, one of many called jointly by the two nationalist groups. And when a three-member United Nations peace mission went to Aden in April it was unable to mediate or determine the people's wishes, since both the nationalist groups boycotted the mission and the mission itself refused to deal with the federation government.

The tempo of civil strife increased as British forces withdrew and all their dependents were evacuated. In September, the new British high commissioner, Sir Humphrey Trevelyan, admitted that the federation government troops were no longer in control of their territory.

During the summer, the NLF had gradually extended its authority over the individual members of the federation and emerged as the stronger of the two nationalist groups. Subsequently, the NLF and FLOSY accepted Britain's call for a cease-fire and began talks toward a provisional government in Cairo with representatives of both groups. Late in November, Great Britain reached agreement with NLF representatives in Geneva, Switzerland, for the transfer of sovereignty. Britain agreed to continue subsidizing the state, but set no fixed amount. See GREAT BRITAIN. [WILLIAM SPENCER]

Facts in Brief. Population: 921,000. Government: President Qahtan ash-Sha'bi; Premier Faisal ash-Sha'bi. Monetary Unit: dinar (1 = U.S. $2.79). Foreign Trade: exports, $190,000,000; imports, $285,000,000. Principal Exports: petroleum products, hides and skins, coffee.

SOUTH WEST AFRICA. See SOUTH AFRICA, REPUBLIC OF.

USA
USA
UNITED STATES
USA
USA

SPACE EXPLORATION

Efforts by the United States and the Soviet Union to land men on the moon were set back by the deaths of spacemen in 1967, but by year's end both countries were recovering their momentum.

Fire killed three American astronauts in a ground test of an Apollo spacecraft at Cape Kennedy, Fla., on January 27. A Soviet cosmonaut died in his Soyuz I spacecraft on April 24 when its parachute tangled during re-entry into the atmosphere. Three of the dead were space veterans. They were Air Force Colonel Virgil I. Grissom, 40, who had flown in the Mercury and Gemini programs; Lieutenant Colonel Edward H. White II, 36, who had achieved the first U.S. "space walk"; and Soviet Colonel Vladimir M. Komarov, 40, who had commanded man's first three-man space flight. The fourth was Lieutenant Commander Roger B. Chaffee, 31.

Three other astronauts were killed during non-space missions in 1967: Air Force Major Edward G. Givens, 37, on June 6 in a car accident; Marine Major Clifton C. Williams, Jr., 35, on October 5 in a jet crash; and Air Force Major Robert H. Lawrence, Jr., 31, on December 8 during a flight at Edwards Air Force Base, Calif. See ASTRONAUTS.

Neither country committed man to space again in 1967, but both made other major achievements late in the year in their preparations for the manned lunar mission. The United States conducted a successful maiden flight of the mighty Saturn V, the vehicle to be used for the manned lunar mission, and returned an unmanned spacecraft through a baptism of fire more intense than it will undergo on return from the moon. The Soviet Union accomplished the first rendezvous and docking of two unmanned spacecraft, preparing for the day when cosmonauts will employ such a technique on their lunar mission. There were reports that a giant Soviet rocket, presumably intended for the lunar mission, was being readied for flight in 1968.

Other Major Accomplishments of 1967:

- A series of unmanned soft-landing and orbiting spacecraft greatly increased knowledge of the moon, in preparation for the manned landings, and supplied the first chemical analysis of lunar soil.
- There was increasing talk of the possibility of Soviet-U.S. cooperation in space exploration.
- Soviet and U.S. probes returned data indicating that Venus is too hot and its atmospheric pressure is too high to permit life as we know it.

Apollo Disaster. A special nine-member review board of the National Aeronautics and Space Administration (NASA) reported that the Apollo fire probably originated in an electrical arc in the spacecraft wiring.

The review board, headed by Director Floyd L. Thompson of the Langley Research Center, Hampton, Va., in the final official report on April 9 listed six other conditions as leading to the disaster:

- A sealed cabin, pressurized with an oxygen atmosphere.
- An extensive distribution of combustible materials in the cabin.
- Vulnerable wiring carrying spacecraft power.
- Vulnerable plumbing carrying a combustible and corrosive coolant.
- Inadequate provisions for the crew to escape.
- Inadequate provisions for rescue or medical aid.

NASA and contractor officials paraded before congressional committees to take their share of the blame for what they had done or left undone. One issue that generated considerable controversy related to an investigation of the management of the Apollo spacecraft project, North American Aviation, Inc., conducted in 1965 and 1966 by Major General Samuel C. Phillips, Apollo program director. Senators and Congressmen expressed displeasure that NASA had not informed them at the time that there were such problems.

In response to demands that the Phillips findings be made public, NASA provided a summary to a congressional committee, but maintained that release of the entire document would injure the company unfairly by exposing its inner workings to competitors.

At the conclusion of the hearings, Senator Clinton P. Anderson (D., N.Mex.), chairman of the Senate Space Committee, said: "An admitted mood of overconfidence by NASA and North American, based on past successes, proved fatal." He added: "The accident has taken a toll in morale and in momentum within the program. I am confident that momentum will be regained and NASA will emerge stronger."

New Precautions. As the result of the accident and conditions highlighted by the report of the review board, steps were taken to:

- Use noncombustible and fire-resistant materials to the widest possible extent in the spacecraft.
- Study further the pros and cons of oxygen atmospheres in spacecraft used in the Mercury and Gemini programs.
- Install water hoses for extinguishing fires.
- Conduct full-scale fire and vibration tests of all spacecraft.
- Strengthen procedures for management of testing, quality control audits, and contractor relations.

A mock-up of Saturn V, dwarfing the trucks in the lower left corner, inches to its pad at Cape Kennedy for try-outs of new launch facilities.

Yale Joel, *Life* © Time Inc.

- Increase contractor activity in support of the total space vehicle integration.
- Establish two safety review offices independent of the Apollo program organization.

Apollo-Saturn V Moon Shot. The first Apollo manned flight was delayed a year and a half, to mid-1968. But on November 9, a major milestone was passed in the successful first flight of the 364-foot, 36-story Apollo-Saturn V, powered by a three-stage rocket eight times more powerful than any rocket previously launched by the United States. The Saturn V, weighing about as much as a U.S. Navy destroyer, generated 7,500,000 pounds of thrust in its first stage and orbited a total load of 140 tons. Then its third stage ignited a second time to propel the Apollo spacecraft into an elliptical path that carried it more than 11,000 miles from the earth.

The spacecraft propulsion system, which one day will maneuver it into orbit around the moon, fired twice during the mission, the second time accelerating the craft to seven miles a second, the speed of return to earth from the moon. The heat shield protected it during the fiery re-entry and the intact craft landed by parachute less than nine miles from its aiming point in the Pacific Ocean, where it was recovered by the carrier U.S.S. *Bennington.*

At year's end, preparations were underway for an unmanned test of the lunar module and one or two additional unmanned Apollo-Saturn V flights in preparation for the long-awaited manned phases of the Apollo program.

The Soviet Space Tragedy investigation produced no public report comparable to the Apollo disaster, but the subsequent course of the Soviet program gave clear indications of caution.

On October 30, however, a major first was achieved when two unmanned spacecraft, Cosmos 186 and 188, were docked together for three and a half hours before separating and flying individual paths again. Cosmos 186 returned to earth the next day. Some Western observers interpreted this as meaning that Soviet engineers had solved the problem that had caused the Komarov accident.

In 1967, for the first time in a decade, the number of Soviet satellite launchings exceeded those of the United States. At year's end, the totals were: Soviet Union, 66 and United States, 57.

Surveyor V, which arrived at the moon on September 10, transmitted the first chemical analysis of the surface. An instrument designed by Anthony Turkevich of the University of Chicago irradiated the lunar soil with alpha particles, which are helium atoms stripped of their two electrons. Measurement of the energy of reflected radiation enable the chemical composition of material at the top few thousandths of an inch to be estimated.

The surface seemed to be basalt, a dark-colored and relatively light rock of volcanic origin. Basalt is the most common volcanic rock on earth, found in the Hudson Palisades, the Snake River plain in the western United States, and the Columbia River area of the Northwest. The chemical composition of the soil tested by Surveyor V was about three-fifths oxygen, one-fifth silicon, and smaller amounts of aluminum, sulfur, iron, cobalt, and nickel. Scientists said these findings indicated the moon had been hot enough in the past to melt rock into lava, and that gravity had caused the lava to differentiate, the heavier materials sinking and the lighter basalt rising to the top.

Charred exterior of Apollo capsule attests to the heat of the flash fire that killed Roger Chaffee, Virgil Grissom, and Edward White at Cape Kennedy.

Moon Mapped. With the Lunar Orbiter photos, the entire surface of the moon was mapped with a resolution many times better than the best obtainable by earth telescopes. The maps showed the back of the moon to be quite different from the front, having considerably fewer "seas" or smooth areas and a more even distribution of craters.

The maps permitted the number of potential lunar landing sites for Apollo astronauts to be reduced from 30 to eight. It was planned that further analysis would reduce them to three or four. One will be in the Sea of Tranquillity, one in the Central Bay, and one in the Ocean of Storms.

The Planet Venus was reached by two spacecraft within a period of two days. On October 18, the Soviet Venus IV made the first landing on a planet other than the earth. On October 19, the U.S. Mariner V passed within 2,480 miles of Venus.

Both returned reports indicating high concentrations of carbon dioxide in the atmosphere under pressure at least seven times that of earth. The Soviet spacecraft confirmed the report of the 1962 U.S. Mariner II, that the surface temperature is more than 500° F. Scientists said the atmospheric density would produce weird optical illusions. The curvature of sunlight in the atmosphere would make it appear that the sun never sets on Venus, while the horizon would appear high in the sky.

Space Cooperation. During the year, a long-distance dialogue took place between U.S. and Soviet officials on the possibility of greater cooperation in space.

NASA administrator James E. Webb told an April news conference the loss of spacemen's lives indicated the desirability of cooperation in the interest of flight safety. Soviet academician Leonid I. Sodov said in September that large future projects will require international cooperation.

Space Disarmament Treaty. President Lyndon B. Johnson in October marked the adoption of an 84-nation treaty that committed the signatories to permanent disarmament in outer space. He said: "The next decade should increasingly become a partnership, not only between the Soviet Union and America, but among all nations under the sun and stars." Later that month, Mstislav V. Keldysh, head of the Soviet Academy of Sciences, said U.S.-Soviet cooperation could be discussed.

In December, U.S. and Soviet delegates to the United Nations (UN) reached agreement on a draft treaty on the rescue and return of astronauts and of objects launched in space. The treaty, approved by the UN General Assembly, was submitted to the UN member governments for ratification.

Two Other International Efforts achieved fruition. An Italian satellite, San Marco II, was launched by a U.S. rocket on April 26 from a platform in the Indian Ocean. It was the first launching from the Equator. A British satellite, Ariel III, was orbited from California on May 5.

Other Developments in 1967 were:

- Pepper plants and wheat seedlings grown on a two-day orbital flight of a U.S. biological satellite appeared to demonstrate that plants depend on gravity for their orientation.
- Orbiting Solar Observatory III, launched March 8, continued the study of the sun, while Orbiting Geophysical Observatory IV, orbited July 28, made possible a wide variety of measurements of the space environment near earth.
- Applications of space technology moved ahead with the flights of two Applications Technology Spacecraft, three weather satellites of the Environmental Science Services Administration (ESSA) of the U.S. Department of Commerce, two Comsat Corporation communications satellites, and three Soviet Molniya communications satellites.

Saturn V Moon Rocket

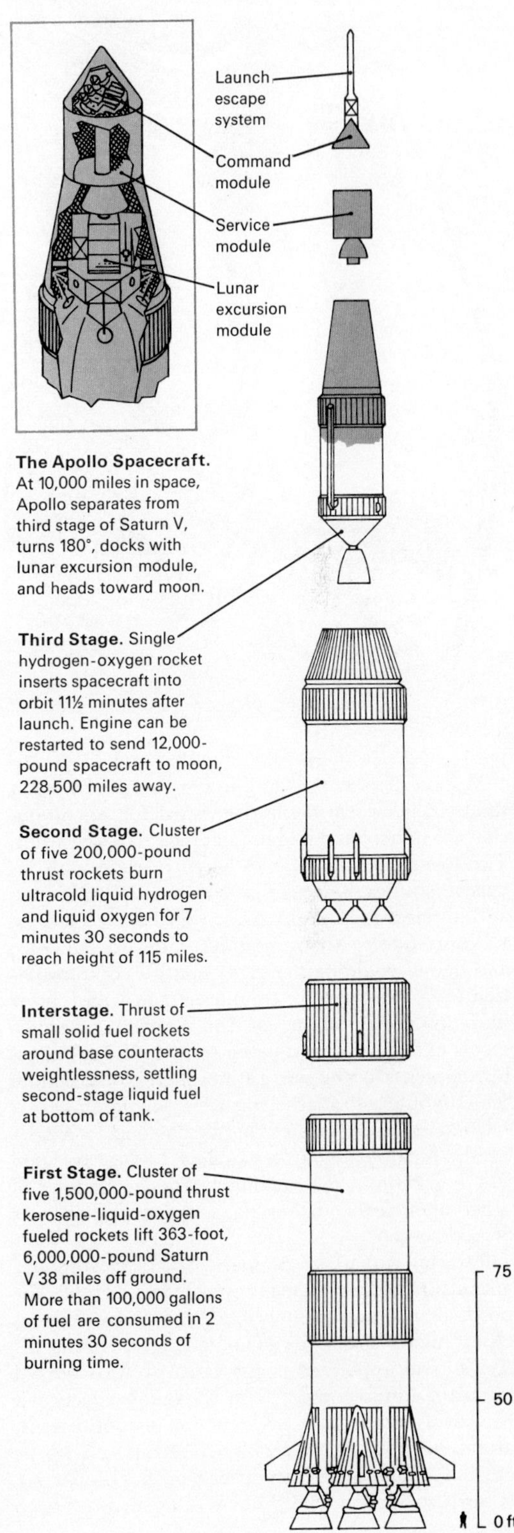

The Apollo Spacecraft. At 10,000 miles in space, Apollo separates from third stage of Saturn V, turns 180°, docks with lunar excursion module, and heads toward moon.

Third Stage. Single hydrogen-oxygen rocket inserts spacecraft into orbit 11½ minutes after launch. Engine can be restarted to send 12,000-pound spacecraft to moon, 228,500 miles away.

Second Stage. Cluster of five 200,000-pound thrust rockets burn ultracold liquid hydrogen and liquid oxygen for 7 minutes 30 seconds to reach height of 115 miles.

Interstage. Thrust of small solid fuel rockets around base counteracts weightlessness, settling second-stage liquid fuel at bottom of tank.

First Stage. Cluster of five 1,500,000-pound thrust kerosene-liquid-oxygen fueled rockets lift 363-foot, 6,000,000-pound Saturn V 38 miles off ground. More than 100,000 gallons of fuel are consumed in 2 minutes 30 seconds of burning time.

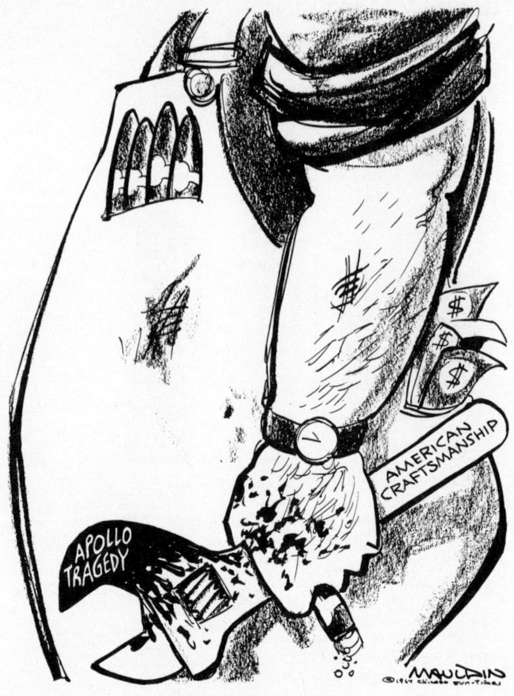

Death Weapon

▪ At Lucerne, Switzerland, in October, the world's weathermen pressed plans forward for an all-out effort to understand and predict the earth's weather. The two-stage plan was to begin in 1972 with intensive studies of areas that spawn tropical storms and hurricanes in the Atlantic and Pacific Oceans.
▪ From 1973 to 1976, satellites, aircraft, balloons, and buoys would gather vast quantities of information for processing by computers 500 times faster than any now in existence. Simultaneous measurements of temperatures, pressures, winds, and moisture contents for the entire atmosphere would enable the computers to make long-term predictions.
▪ Congress appropriated $4,589,000,000 to NASA for the fiscal year that began July 1–$511,000,000 less than requested. Combined with the budgets of other agencies, the total U.S. space budget was $6,600,000,000.

People. Robert C. Seamans, Jr., NASA deputy administrator, retired to private life Jan. 4, 1968. His post was not immediately filled, however. Among other major space personnel changes Homer E. Newell was appointed to the vacant NASA post of associate administrator, John E. Naugle succeeded Newell as head of space science and applications, and George M. Low replaced Joseph F. Shea as chief of Apollo spacecraft development. [JAY HOLMES]

See also Section One, JOHN H. GLENN, JR.: FOCUS ON SPACE.

SPAIN held a national parliamentary election on Oct. 10, 1967, to choose 108 deputies to the 595-seat *Cortes* (legislature). The nation thus experienced its first democratic election since the eruption of the civil war in 1936. The election, however, did not produce any immediately measurable impact on the national political scene; the remaining 487 deputies still came from official appointments.

On September 10, an attempt was made to settle a long-standing dispute between Spain and Great Britain over the status of Gibraltar, a British Crown colony. A British-sponsored referendum held in the colony offered the Gibraltarians the choice of remaining under British sovereignty or uniting with Spain. The Gibraltarians voted overwhelmingly for continued British rule. Spain and the United Nations Special Committee of 24 on Colonialism, however, assailed the referendum and rejected the results. See GREAT BRITAIN.

A religious freedom law was enacted in June. It guaranteed free worship to officially recognized non-Roman Catholic religions. To be recognized, religious groups had to register with the government. [KENNETH BROWN]

Facts in Brief. Population: 32,275,000. Government: President Francisco Franco; Vice-President Luis Carrero Blanco. Monetary Unit: peseta (70=U.S. $1). Foreign Trade: exports, $1,254,000,000; imports, $3,574,000,000. Principal Exports: citrus fruits, vegetables, wine.

SPORTS. The business, politics, and chemistry of sports all made headlines in 1967. Sometimes newspaper sports pages seemed to read like the financial section. New highs were reached on the professional golf tour, with more than $4,500,000 in prize money, and in legal betting on horse racing, with a total of $4,852,890,970 wagered on flat and harness races. In both bowling and rodeo competition, the top professionals won more than $50,000 apiece.

In a surprise action the British Lawn Tennis Council voted to make its Wimbledon tournament, the world's leading amateur event, open to professionals in 1968. They took this move to eliminate "shamateurism," in which top amateur players receive hidden expense payments, sometimes more than $10,000 a year.

The International Lawn Tennis Federation, which has repeatedly rejected open tennis, declared it would suspend British or any other amateur players who participated in the Wimbledon if it were actually held as an open tournament. But most leading amateurs said they would play in an open Wimbledon tournament, and many indicated they might turn professional in 1968. This would strip amateur tennis of its top box-office attractions.

The feud between the Amateur Athletic Union (AAU) and the National Collegiate Athletic Association (NCAA) sputtered past its sixth birthday in a state of uneasy truce. Neither side modified its

"Thin Air" Olympic Concern

Records fall with regularity every time the Olympic Games are held. Records will assuredly continue to fall in the 1968 Olympics at Mexico City, October 12 to 27. It will be surprising, however, if many are broken in running races, swimming races, or other contests that take much longer than one minute. This is because Mexico City, standing at an altitude of 7,400 feet above sea level, has so-called "thin air"–an oxygen shortage that imposes harsh demands on the lungs of any athlete who is not accustomed to competition at that altitude.

More than 60 nations are expected to take part in the Mexico City Games. Many, including England, the Soviet Union, the United States, and West Germany, began their studies of the thin-air problem shortly after the close of the 1964 Olympics in Tokyo. Mexican officials cooperated by playing host to a series of annual "Little Olympics" each autumn. By 1967 it was clear that warnings of possible fatal overexertion in the Olympics were unfounded.

It seems certain that the struggle for gold medals will be dominated, at least in swimming, by the United States. The United States dominates world swimming, and the Mexico City schedule calls for 29 aquatic events.

Track and field, however, is the showcase of the Olympics. With this in mind, the Soviet Union set up a training camp for individual athletes in mountainous Alma-Ata, and scheduled its 1967 national track championships for Leninakan, in the mountains of Armenia.

Individual members of the U.S. team such as Jim Ryun, holder of the world mile record, experimented on their own with practice running at high altitudes. Ryun did his running in the Rocky Mountains.

When Mexico City was selected as the site for the 1968 Olympiad, there were protests over the unfair advantage it might offer athletes who live in mountainous lands. Indeed, his year-round running in the oxygen-thin air of Ethiopia may be partly responsible for the superiority of Abebe Bikila, runaway victor in the Olympic marathon both at Rome in 1960 and at Tokyo in 1964.

There was interest, therefore, in Jim Ryun's July, 1967, race against Kipchoge Keino of Kenya, since Keino lives and trains at more than a mile above sea level.

Ryun's first reaction to his practice runs at Alamosa, Colo., was almost frightening. "It's just as if there were something in your throat and chest, stopping you from breathing," Ryun said. "But each day you run, the easier it gets. When you come down from the mountains, you can't get over how much air there seems to be. Being able to handle the altitude will decide who does what in Mexico City, that's for sure."

Ryun lowered his own mile record to 3 minutes 51.1 seconds after his first strenuous struggles up in the Rockies. He did this at the Amateur Athletic Union (AAU) meet in Bakersfield, Calif., which is near sea level. Then he returned to Alamosa for several more weeks of mountain running, met Keino in a highly publicized 1,500-meter race at Los Angeles, Calif., and not only outran Keino but also set a world mark of 3 minutes 33.1 seconds.

The U.S. Olympic Committee selected four high-altitude sites for a 21-day experimental program in August and September, 1967. The committee also picked 32 middle-distance and long-distance runners who rated fair chances to earn places on the national Olympic team. These athletes were separated into groups of eight who worked out at Alamosa; South Lake Tahoe, Calif.; Flagstaff, Ariz.; and Los Alamos, N.Mex.

Medical tests during the three-week program included blood-count and oxygen-intake checks, but the committee was unable to finance sufficient research to establish specific time-lag figures for running various distances. The U.S. training looked thorough enough, however, to convince Olympic officials in West Germany. They promptly requested reservations for their own athletes in Flagstaff, Ariz., and plan to spend a month there, just prior to the Olympic Games.

The three-day Olympic equestrian competition was shifted from Mexico City to Oaxtepec, 2,900 feet lower, to protect the animals from the hazards of "thin air." [JOHN LAKE] position, but the U.S. Senate-appointed Sports Arbitration Board managed to keep further overt disputes from erupting. As the feud's threat to the U.S. Olympic effort faded, however, a new one arose in a proposed Negro boycott of the U.S. team.

East Germany was involved in two international sports disputes. In one, the world weight lifting championships were canceled after Japan refused to fly the East German flag or play their national anthem. East Germany and Cuba withdrew at the last minute from the North American rowing championships in Canada for similar reasons.

Drugs. The problem of the use of stimulating drugs by athletes received widespread attention after the death of Tom Simpson, a 29-year-old former world champion bicycle rider from England. Simpson, who had previously admitted the regular use of stimulating drugs, collapsed and died while competing in the Tour de France.

Three months later, a world cycling record was refused recognition by the International Cycling Union because the cyclist, Jacques Anquetil of France, would not undergo a drug test after setting the record. In other sports, drug tests were rapidly becoming a standard procedure. Plans were even made to test athletes for drug use at the Mexico City Olympic Games.

Awards. Carl Yastrzemski, the Boston Red Sox left fielder who led the American League in home runs, runs batted in, and batting average, was named sportsman of the year by *Sports Illustrated.* In the poll taken by the Associated Press, Yastrzemski also won the male athlete award, while tennis star Billie Jean King won women's honors.

Among the Winners in other sports competitions in 1967 were:

Curling. The world championship and the Scotch Cup were won by Scotland. The U.S. men's title was won by Seattle, Wash., and the women's championship by the Glengarries of Utica, N.Y.

Handball. Paul Haber of San Francisco, Calif., won his second straight U.S. Handball Association four-wall singles championship, while Jimmy Jacobs and Marty Decatur of New York City took the doubles crown. In AAU play, Steve Sandler of New York City retained his one-wall singles title, and Carl and Ruby Obert of New York City won the doubles. The Obert family swept the AAU four-wall titles, Carl winning the singles and Oscar and Ruby the doubles.

Rowing. Harvard, undefeated for the fourth year in a row, was rated as the best American college crew. In international competition, Harvard won the Pan American Games, but was beaten by New Zealand in the U.S. championships; by New Zealand, Australian, and West German crews in the North American title event; and by West Germany in the European championships. The American single sculls champion was Bill Maher of Detroit, Mich.

Shooting. James Bellows of Lackland Air Force Base won the National Skeet Shooting Association's all-around men's championship, and Mrs. Valerie Johnson of San Antonio, Tex., captured the women's all-around. In trapshooting, Herman Welch of Downers Grove, Ill., won the men's Grand American, while Mary Lou Hvizdos of Uniontown, Pa., took the women's prize. Italy won the world trapshooting title, followed by the United States and Russia. The national service-rifle championship went to James Bowen of the U.S. Marine Corps, and perennial champion W. B. Blankenship of the air force won the U.S. pistol title.

Kenneth D. Cline, 13, of Lincoln, Nebr., bested 242 other entries in the 30th All-American Soap Box Derby held at Akron, Ohio, on August 19.

Weight Lifting. Poland and Russia took five of the seven gold medals in Mexico's pre-Olympic meet, with world records being set by lightweight Waldemar Baszanoski of Poland with 968 pounds and middleweight Viktor Kurentsov of Russia with 1,034 pounds. The United States team placed third. The AAU championships went to: Gary Hanson, bantamweight; Walter Imahara, featherweight; Homer Brannum, lightweight; Russell Knipp, middleweight; Joe Puleo, light heavyweight; Phil Grippaldi, middle heavyweight; and Bob Bednarski, heavyweight.

Wrestling. Russia led the way in the world free-style championships in New Delhi, India, winning three gold and four silver medals out of eight classes. The best U.S. showing was a silver medal in the flyweight class by Richard Sanders of Portland, Ore., while featherweight Mike Young of Provo, Utah, and heavyweight Larry Kristoff of Carbondale, Ill., won bronze medals. In AAU competition, Kristoff repeated his 1966 feat by winning both the free-style and Greco-Roman heavyweight titles. In the wide-open NCAA tournament, Michigan State, the only school to have two champions, captured the team title. Individual Spartan winners were Dale Anderson in the 137-pound class and George Radman in the 167-pound class.

Other champions: *Archery*, world championships: men, Ray Rogers, Muskogee, Okla.; women, Maria Maczynska, Poland. U.S. champions: men, Ray Rogers; women, Mrs. Ardelle Mills, Minnetonka, Minn. *Bicycling*, Tour de France winner: Roger Pingeon, France. *Billiards*, world professional pocket title:

Luther Lassiter, Elizabeth City, N.C. *Bobsledding*, world two-man: Austria. *Canoeing*, U.S. singles: Andy Weigand, Washington, D.C. Kayak singles: John Van Dyke, Washington, D.C. *Fencing*, world championships: foil, Romania, épeé, Russia; saber, Russia; women's foil, Hungary. NCAA champion: New York University. *Gymnastics*, AAU championships: men's all-around, Yoshi Hayasaki, Seattle, Wash.; team, Northwestern Louisiana State; women's all-around, Carolyn Hacker, Southern Connecticut Girl's Club; team, Southern Illinois. NCAA championships: all-around, Steve Cohen, Penn State; team, Southern Illinois. *Judo*, AAU grand champion: Yashuhiko Nagatoshi, Los Angeles. *Lacrosse*, club champion: Mount Washington of Baltimore, Md.; intercollegiate champions: (tie) Johns Hopkins, Maryland, and Navy. *Modern Pentathlon*, world championships: individual, Andras Balczo, Hungary; team, Hungary. U.S. championships: individual, Bjorn Ferm, Sweden. *Polo*, open: Bunntyco, Oak Brook, Ill. Intercollegiate: Yale. *Rodeo*, U.S. national professional all-around champion: Larry Mahan, Brooks, Ore., $51,996.37. *Surfing*, world championships: men, Nat Young, Australia; women, Joyce Hoffman, Capistrano Beach, Calif. U.S. championships: men, Corky Carroll, Dana Point, Calif.; women, Joyce Hoffman, Capistrano Beach, Calif. *Synchronized swimming*, AAU outdoor championships: solo, Margo McGrath, San Francisco; duet, Margo McGrath and Carol Redmond, San Francisco; team, San Francisco Merionettes. *Volleyball*, women's world championships: Japan. U.S. open championships: men, Fresno, Calif.; women, Shamrocks, Long Beach, Calif. Intercollegiate: UCLA. *Water skiing*, world championships: men, Mike Suyderhoud, San Anselmo, Calif.; women, Jeanette Stewart-Wood, Great Britain. [JAMES O. DUNAWAY]

STAMP COLLECTING. See HOBBIES.

STATE GOVERNMENT. Racial problems plagued a number of states in 1967. Governors called out the National Guard 23 times to prevent or control violence resulting from racial antagonisms. Legislatures of 13 states debated bills to forbid racial discrimination in the sale and rental of housing. Bills passed in Hawaii, Iowa, Maryland, Vermont, and Washington, but were defeated elsewhere. Twenty-one states, including all of the 15 largest states outside the South, except Illinois, have adopted open occupancy laws since the first law was passed in New York in 1958. Coverage, administrative procedures, and penalties for violations vary extensively from state to state.

Some states improved their ability to deal with the problems in their cities. Connecticut, Ohio, and Wisconsin established community affairs departments in 1967, as have 12 other states since 1959. Arizona and Nevada created advisory councils of local officials.

State Constitutions. Conventions to revise state constitutions met in four states. Rhode Island's convention adjourned September 11 after almost three years of deliberations, but decided in October, to make further revisions before submitting a revised constitution to the voters for approval. A New York convention worked from April to September, 1967, but its new constitution was rejected in a referendum on November 7. Hawaii will hold a convention in 1968, and voters in Illinois and New Mexico will decide whether to call constitutional conventions in their respective states.

Annual legislative sessions are now held in 20 states and more are adopting the plan. Pennsylvania voters approved an annual sessions referendum in 1967; citizens of Idaho, Iowa, and New Hampshire will vote on the question in 1968. The legislatures of Illinois, Ohio, Tennessee, and Vermont, although required to meet only once every two years, decided not to wait until 1969 to meet again, but to reconvene in the interim to deal with possible gubernatorial vetoes and other matters.

Education again was the costliest state activity. It also took a larger share of state appropriations and grew faster than most others. State expenditures for education, including universities and local schools, accounted for 38.6 per cent of general state appropriations in fiscal 1966, according to figures released in 1967. The total spent on education was $17,700,000,000, compared to $14,500,000,000 in fiscal 1965, when 36 per cent of state spending was for education.

Expenditures in education rose 22.1 per cent in fiscal 1966, due in large part to increased federal aid under the Elementary and Secondary School-Improvement Act of 1965. Public welfare expenditures increased 10.8 per cent, hospitals 10.1 per cent, and highways 5.1 per cent. These four categories accounted for 80 per cent of state appropriations, the same share as in 1965. Total state expenditures in fiscal 1966 were $46,000,000,000, 13.8 per cent higher than the year before. All states but Illinois had larger budgets.

General Revenue to the states in fiscal 1966 was $46,760,000,000, an increase of 14.2 per cent over 1965. Most tax revenue came from levies on general sales (27 per cent), motor fuel (15.7 per cent), personal income (14.5 per cent), and corporation income (6.9 per cent). Miscellaneous charges and fees brought 11 per cent, 26.2 per cent came from intergovernmental payments. Altogether, state taxes accounted for 62.8 per cent of general revenue.

The federal government provided 25.1 per cent of state revenue, almost as much as general sales taxes and individual income taxes combined. While money from state taxes went up 12.5 per cent, money from Washington increased 18.7 per cent.

Even so, the states levied new taxes and raised rates on old taxes in 1967. Minnesota and Nebraska became the 43rd and 44th states to adopt a general sales tax. Michigan and Nebraska passed personal income tax laws, as had 36 other states previously. Maryland shifted from a flat rate to a graduated income tax. A corporation income tax was passed in Michigan, Nebraska, and West Virginia. Nine states raised the sales tax rate; eight states increased taxes on motor fuel; and eight states increased the tax on cigarettes. [JAMES H. ANDREWS]

STEEL INDUSTRY. For the 75th consecutive year, the United States maintained its position as the world's leading producer of steel, although its lead was narrowed. In 1967, U.S. industry produced an estimated 126,000,000 tons of steel, 26 per cent of the world's total production. Russia, in second place, increased its output to an estimated 110,000,000 tons from 106,000,000 in 1966.

The U.S. steel industry's capital outlays reached a record $2,400,000,000 in 1967, which makes a total of $13,000,000,000 for new production facilities since 1957. Most of the outlay went for basic oxygen furnace (BOF) installations, which can make 300 tons of steel in 50 minutes, compared to 10 hours in a conventional open hearth process. Though in 1957 the BOF process accounted for only one-half of one per cent of the nation's steel, today it accounts for more than one-third of the production.

Nevertheless, a feeling of urgency and concern pervaded the industry as 1967 drew to a close. Shipments of finished steel totaled only 85,000,000 tons, down from the 1966 total of 91,000,000 tons.

Earnings were down in the first half of 1967. Two labor union strikes–one against the Ford Motor Company and a teamsters strike against steel haulers in seven Midwestern states–were major factors in the reduction of third-quarter earnings by 28 per cent. The downward trend was finally stopped in the last quarter when users began all-out efforts to catch up on lost production. Buyers also began an inventory build-up because of a possible steel strike in mid-1968 and as a hedge against the threat of inflation. The industry benefited further from a 3 per cent increase in exports that broke a three-year declining export cycle.

Imports also increased 3 per cent, setting a new import record of 11,000,000 tons. The devaluation of the British pound sterling in November, 1967, and the growing concern by manufacturing nations about reducing their balance of payments deficits made it seem inevitable that imports would continue to increase. For this reason, the U.S. steel industry was one of the groups trying to change the mood of the Congress from one of trade liberalization to one of protectionism.

Labor. The steel industry continued to be a prime employer, with more than 200 companies having plants in 36 states. Hourly and salaried employees were paid a record $5,000,000,000 in 1967.

In July, 1968, the industry will be faced with the expiration of labor contracts. Spokesmen expressed hope in 1967 that a new kind of agreement might be developed with binding labor negotiations that could eliminate the threat of strikes. One major steelmaker, Kaiser Steel Corporation, has already pioneered such an agreement. Known as the "Kaiser Long Range Sharing Plan," it aims to eliminate strike threats through the equitable sharing of productivity gains. [MEL F. BRDLIK]

STOCKS AND BONDS. The New York Stock Exchange (NYSE) and the American Stock Exchange (Amex) experienced a soaring volume of transactions in 1967. For the first time in history, annual trading volume topped 2,000,000,000 shares on the NYSE in October (2,500,000,000 for the year) and 1,000,000,000 on the Amex in November. This high trading volume exerted heavy pressure on commercial banks that act as agents and bookkeepers for security transactions. Robert W. Haack, who was appointed NYSE president on April 25, and other security industry representatives met with a committee of New York Clearing House Association banks to consider security transaction reforms (see HAACK, ROBERT W.).

Security Markets reflected an unusual sensitivity to borrowing costs in 1967, after the experience of the 1966 "credit crunch." Although the Dow Jones Index (DJI) average of blue-chip stock prices advanced to a peak of 943 in September, this was well below the historic high of nearly 1000 (995.15) in early 1966. The DJI's 1967 low was 786 in early January. At year's end, it was 905. The 1967 stock market was one of the most speculative in years. During the first nine months, the DJI rose only 18 per cent while the broadly based NYSE index climbed 30 per cent and the Amex index soared 66 per cent to record levels. Short interest levels leaped to successive records on both the NYSE and Amex.

The Federal Reserve Board (FRB) clamped down on stock market credit. Its minimum cash requirement for purchases of stock listed on major security exchanges remained at 70 per cent. But it extended margin requirements to previously unregulated lenders and made convertible bonds and other securities convertible into registered stocks subject to margin requirements. Convertible bonds rose in popularity, largely because investors stood to gain if stock values rose sharply. Before the new FRB regulation, it was estimated that 90 per cent of the convertible bond business was done on 70 to 90 per cent credit. Previously unregulated lenders could lend up to 100 per cent of the purchase price of listed stocks at interest costs of 1 to 2 per cent per month. Under the FRB's ruling, lenders were subjected to the same regulations as banks and stock exchange firms.

Other Credit Controls were used by the stock exchanges themselves to limit some speculative activity. In Amex listed stocks, 1 out of 10 tripled in price from its low to its high over the first nine months of 1967. Many fell equally hard. Through September, trading was so feverish that the ratio of Amex shares traded to the total listed ran about 57 per cent, over 2 1/2 times the 22 per cent NYSE turnover ratio. Ralph S. Saul, Amex president, expressed his concern by writing to all member brokerage firms, urging that they limit their customer's speculative purchases, particularly low-priced shares and day-trading. The ultimate weapon, a ban on credit purchases of a stock, was imposed on 73 Amex issues through September, 1967, in comparison with only 23 in all of 1966. Only 14 NYSE listed stocks had been made subject to a 100 per cent down payment as of Nov. 20, 1967. Despite cautious policies, speculation was a major factor in giving Amex both the highest volume day and week in its 118-year history. It was mostly low-priced shares that pushed trading volume to 33,459,514 shares during the week ended October 28. Trading on Thursday, October 26, was a record 8,290,000 shares, exceeding the previous record 7,090,000 set on "Black Tuesday," Oct. 29, 1929.

Stock Ownership. The number of individuals owning stocks in the United States rose to more than 23,000,000 in 1967, up 3,000,000 from the NYSE's last census of stockholders in 1965. American Telephone and Telegraph still headed the list with 2,841,000 shareholders.

The Securities and Exchange Commission (SEC) urged that its proposals to reduce mutual fund sales and management charges be enacted by Congress. The SEC wanted charges cut to 5 per cent from the prevalent 9.3 per cent fee.

People. R. John Cunningham, who set up a computerized clearing organization for the Midwest Stock Exchange, was named NYSE executive vice-president, effective Feb. 1, 1968. [WILLIAM G. DEWALD]

SUDAN held elections in March, 1967, in three provinces in the rebellious southern region to fill 34 vacant seats in the constituent assembly. The Umma party, the majority party in the country's coalition government, won 14 seats.

Premier Sadiq el Mahdi reported that the 12-year southern revolt had been ended, but operations against the rebels continued, nevertheless. In its border dispute with Ethiopia, Sudan's troops became involved in several clashes (see ETHIOPIA).

Sadiq el Mahdi lost a vote of confidence in June and resigned. He was replaced by former Premier Mohammed Ahmed Mahgoub, ousted in July, 1966, who continued El Mahdi's economic plans and scheduled general elections for 1968.

A conference of Arab leaders was convened in Khartoum, Sudan, on August 31, following the Arabs' disastrous war with Israel. Reflecting the conference's anti-Western stance, Sudan contracted for the first time to obtain arms from the Soviet Union. Earlier, Sudan had received a $3,325,000 loan from the U.S. Agency for International Development for a food plant in Khartoum North.

Facts in Brief. Population: 14,458,000. Government: Supreme Council of State President Ismail al-Azhari; Premier Mohammed Ahmed Mahgoub. Monetary Unit: pound (1 = U.S. $2.87). Foreign Trade: exports, $203,000,000; imports, $217,000,000. Principal Exports: cotton, peanuts, gum arabic.

SUPREME COURT OF THE UNITED STATES. The most significant decision of the Supreme Court in 1967 was handed down in May in the *In re Gault* case. The Gault decision was a virtual bill of rights for children as defendants in juvenile proceedings.

Associate Justice Abe Fortas wrote the 8-to-1 majority opinion which declared that a child brought into court on a juvenile delinquency charge that could result in incarceration must be afforded certain basic rights under the due process clause of Amendment 14. See COURTS AND LAWS.

Free Speech. In two landmark opinions in January, the Court held that Amendment 1 guarantees state legislators and public school teachers the same right of free speech enjoyed by every other citizen. The Court unanimously ruled that the state of Georgia could not deny Julian Bond, a civil rights leader and a Negro, his seat in its house of representatives after he publicly attacked the draft and U.S. military activities in Vietnam. In the second opinion, the Court condemned, 5 to 4, New York state's loyalty oath for public school teachers as unconstitutional, holding that it made teachers unwilling to discuss controversial issues in the classroom for fear of losing their jobs.

Civil Rights Demonstrations. As a result of one of many switches to the conservative side during the year by the usually liberal Justice Hugo L. Black, the Court, in contrast to previous decisions, upheld a state action against civil rights demonstrators. In June, the Court sustained, 5 to 4, Alabama's prosecution of eight Negro ministers, including the Reverend Martin Luther King, Jr., for violation of a local injunction that forbade a civil rights march in Birmingham in 1963.

Searches. On June 5, the Court announced two decisions, 6 to 3, which expanded the protection of Amendment 4 against unreasonable searches. The Court held in separate decisions that municipal health inspectors and municipal fire inspectors could not conduct routine inspections of private dwellings and commercial establishments without the occupant's permission unless armed with search warrants. Both rulings reversed an eight-year-old Court opinion that had exempted this type of inspection from the protection of Amendment 4.

In Other Decisions in 1967, the Supreme Court ruled:

- California's controversial "Proposition 14," regarding freedom of choice in the sale or rental of housing, violated the equal protection clause of Amendment 14 because it authorized racial discrimination in housing, and was thus unconstitutional. The vote was 5 to 4.
- Virginia's statute prohibiting marriages between whites and Negroes was unconstitutional as a violation of the due process and the equal protection clauses of Amendment 14, in a unanimous vote. In 1967, there were similar laws in 15 other states.

▪ An American under Amendment 14 can be deprived of citizenship only by voluntarily renouncing it. This 5-to-4 ruling overturned a decade-old Court decision which held that the Congress of the United States could take away citizenship if a U.S. citizen voted in a foreign election.

▪ In a ground-breaking decision, the Court ordered the Procter and Gamble Company to divest itself of the Clorox Chemical Company, the nation's leading manufacturer of household bleach. The Court held that Procter and Gamble, in acquiring Clorox instead of going into competition with it had acted to lessen competition.

New Court Member. Thurgood Marshall, 59, the U.S. Solicitor General, became the first Negro member of the Court when he was appointed, in June, to replace Associate Justice Tom C. Clark, who retired after 18 years service (see MARSHALL, THURGOOD). The other members of the Court during 1967 were Chief Justice Earl Warren, 76, and, in order of seniority, Associate Justices Hugo L. Black, 81; William O. Douglas, 68; John Marshall Harlan, 68; William J. Brennan, Jr., 61; Potter Stewart, 52; Byron Raymond White, 50; and Abe Fortas, 57. [ALLEN HARRIS]

See also Section Four, SUPREME COURT OF THE UNITED STATES.

SWAZILAND. See AFRICA.

SWEDEN switched from left- to right-hand driving on Sept. 3, 1967. The changeover, which followed four years of planning and an investment of $120,000,000, involved a brief no-traffic period and the instituting of a new, nationwide speed-limit system. A survey taken two months after the switch indicated a marked decrease in traffic deaths.

In January, the government introduced its most deflationary budget since World War II. The budget, which was designed in part to offset a trade deficit as well as cut down on domestic demand, included a sales tax increase, higher taxes on tobacco, and on nonessential building construction. In a further attempt to offset the trade deficit by increasing its exports, Sweden applied for membership in the European Economic Community.

In March, after 13 years of bargaining, representatives of the nation's four major political parties agreed on a reform of the Swedish constitution promulgated in 1809. The main reform would replace the present two-chamber parliament with a unicameral legislature. [KENNETH BROWN]

Facts in Brief. Population: 7,853,000. Government: King Gustav VI Adolf; Prime Minister Tage Erlander. Monetary Unit: krona (5.16=U.S. $1). Foreign Trade: exports, $4,272,000,000; imports, $4,574,000,000. Principal Exports: machinery, paper and pulp, iron and steel.

After four years of preparation, Swedish motorists who formerly had driven on the left side of the road, *top*, moved over to the right, *bottom*, in September.

Claudia Kolb of Santa Clara, Calif., set a world record for the 200-meter individual medley at the AAU swimming meet in Philadelphia in August.

SWIMMING. United States swimmers continued to lead the way as the record book took its annual pounding in 1967. A total of 26 out of the 31 major metric world records were broken, with U.S. swimmers setting new marks in 19 events.

The U.S. swimmers also took most of the medals in major international competition. They won 24 of the 29 gold medals in the Pan American Games at Winnipeg, Canada; 21 out of 22 in the World University Games in Tokyo, Japan, and 15 out of 29 in the Mexico City Pre-Olympics.

Don Schollander, of the Santa Clara (Calif.) Swim Club and Yale University, extended his remarkable mastery of the 200-meter free-style by lowering the world record to 1 minute 55.7 seconds.

In the butterfly, Mark Spitz, also of the Santa Clara Swim Club, set new records of 55.7 seconds for 100 meters and 2 minutes 5.7 seconds for 200 meters. Spitz also briefly held the world 400-meter free-style mark at 4 minutes 8.8 seconds before Greg Charlton of Los Angeles, Calif., brought it down to 4 minutes 8.2 seconds.

Other U.S. record-breakers included Ken Walsh of East Lansing, Mich., with 52.6 seconds for the 100-meter free-style; Mike Burton of Carmichael, Calif., with 16 minutes 34.1 seconds for the 1,500-meter free-style; and Greg Buckingham of Santa Clara, who set a new 200-meter individual medley record of 2 minutes 11.3 seconds.

East Germany's 17-year-old Roland Matthes captured both backstroke world records with 58.4 seconds for 100 meters and 2 minutes 7.9 seconds for 200 meters. Matthes also swam a leg on the East German 400-meter medley relay team that lowered the world record to 3 minutes 56.5 seconds.

Women's Records. In women's swimming, two 15-year-olds from the United States outshadowed all others. Debbie Meyer of Sacramento, Calif., took nine seconds off the 400-meter free-style record by swimming the distance in only 4 minutes 29 seconds. She also set equally impressive free-style marks for 800 meters (9 minutes 22.9 seconds) and 1,500 meters (17 minutes 50.2 seconds). Catie Ball of Jacksonville, Fla., captured both breast stroke records from the Russians with 1 minute 14.6 seconds for 100 meters and 2 minutes 39.5 seconds for 200 meters.

Other U.S. women record setters were Claudia Kolb of the Santa Clara Swim Club, who swam the 200- and 400-meter individual medleys in 2 minutes 25 seconds and 5 minutes 8.2 seconds, respectively, and Pam Kruse of Fort Lauderdale, who swam the 200-meter free-style in 2 minutes 9.7 seconds.

Canada's Elaine Tanner, of Vancouver, B.C., backstroked her way to two world records with times of 1 minute 7.1 seconds for 100 meters and 2 minutes 24.4 seconds for 200 meters. And Ada Kok of Holland set a new 200-meter butterfly mark of 2 minutes 21 seconds. [James O. Dunaway]

SWITZERLAND elected Foreign Minister Willy Spühler as its president on Dec. 14, 1967. Spühler, who succeeded Roger Bonvin, was to take office in January, 1968, and serve for one year. Ludwig von Moos was elected vice-president. Although the four parties constituting the government coalition lost ground in the October elections, they still held 165 of the 200 seats in the national assembly.

An economic slowdown in West Germany directly affected Swiss export levels and widened the gap in the balance of payments. Inflation remained a serious danger. Restrictions on employment of foreign labor at a time when the labor situation was strained, and a voluntary limit on credit expansion cut economic growth.

An even more serious threat to the economy was a massive influx of foreign funds following the Middle East crisis in June. To discourage the inflow, the Swiss national bank trimmed the discount rate from 3.5 per cent to 3 per cent. The reduction not only resulted in a return to the customary situation in which Swiss interest rates were lower than those in other nations but also discouraged the further transfer of foreign funds to Switzerland. [Kenneth Brown]

Facts in Brief. Population: 6,237,000. Government: President Roger Bonvin. Monetary Unit: franc (4.33=U.S. $1). Foreign Trade: exports, $3,275,000,000; imports, $3,944,000,000. Principal Exports: machinery, chemicals, clocks and watches.

SYRIA. President Nur al-Din al-Atasi achieved the near-impossible as he completed a second year in office. His government was unshaken by even an attempted coup or the Arab-Israeli war (see MIDDLE EAST). He was elected International Secretary-General of the ruling Ba'ath Party for another term as the party healed its internal dissensions.

The economy remained sluggish despite a 50 per cent increase in fees for oil transit through Syria granted by the Iraq Petroleum Company, with a lump sum payment of $11,000,000. Aid also flowed freely into Syria from the Communist countries. East Germany granted $25,000,000 for new industries. Communist China contributed $3,600,000 to help build a combed-yarn factory at Hama. Russia sent experts and heavy machinery to expand Syrian oil production. Four-fifths of Syria's cotton crop of 140,000 tons was sold to Communist customers.

The trend toward socialism continued. All private schools were nationalized, and their headmasters were replaced by education ministry employees. Rigid censorship struck U.S. publications; the American Friends of the Middle East office in Damascus was shut down. [WILLIAM SPENCER]

Facts in Brief. Population: 5,712,000. Government: Chief of State Nur al-Din al-Atasi; Premier Yusuf Zuayn. Monetary Unit: pound (4.19=U.S. $1). Foreign Trade: exports, $169,000,000; imports, $293,000,000. Principal Exports: cotton, barley, vegetables.

TANZANIA. President Julius K. Nyerere announced new socialist policies on Feb. 5, 1967, which resulted from a political conference at Arusha from January 26 to 29. The Arusha Declaration provided for the end of "feudalism and capitalism" by the control of banks, factories, plantations, and other means of production, as well as the government, by peasants and workers. The government implemented the plan on February 11. Banks, food factories, insurance companies, and several export-import companies were nationalized. The government acquired majority holdings in breweries and several factories. Foreign banks were told to replace European employees with Africans.

In January, a search started for aliens who did not hold valid entry permits, and it was announced that permits would not be renewed for foreigners whose jobs could be done by local people. Panic-stricken Asians and Arabs without permits attempted to hide, but scores were found and given two months to leave Tanzania. In February and March, the expulsion orders were reviewed to avoid serious hardships or unfair treatment of aliens.

Education. Nyerere called for major changes in the education system on March 9. Primary schools would be required to grow some of their own food and to prepare pupils for agricultural and local work. On March 14, the ministry of education ordered that Tanzanians be given the headships of all secondary schools and teachers' colleges by the end of April. It further announced that Swahili would displace English as the language of instruction in Tanzanian elementary schools, starting with the first grade in the 1967 school year and adding a grade each year until English is eliminated. A conference in March on "The Role of the University College in Socialist Training" recommended compulsory teaching of socialism, "East Africanization" of the university staff, and membership of all university students in a government Youth League.

In June, 392 university students who were expelled in October, 1966, for demonstrating against serving in the National Youth Service were readmitted after obtaining pardons from Nyerere.

Tanzania received aid from many countries. Volunteers from Denmark, East Germany, Japan, and Sweden came officially as teachers and community development workers. Tanzanian marine police went to West Germany to train on four patrol boats they would later operate in Tanzania. Canada provided a $1,800,000 loan for the construction of power lines, and the United States gave a $1,600,000 loan for highway improvement. [BENJAMIN E. THOMAS]

Facts in Brief. Population: 11,078,000. Government: President Julius K. Nyerere. Monetary Unit: shilling (7.14=U.S. $1). Foreign Trade: exports, $235,000,000; imports, $180,000,000. Principal Exports: sisal, cotton, coffee.

TAXATION triggered a major controversy between President Lyndon B. Johnson and the first session of the 90th Congress in 1967. When the session convened on January 10, the President asked for a 6 per cent surcharge on personal and corporation income taxes. The increase was needed, he said, to pay for the war in Vietnam, the war against poverty at home, and to help curb inflation.

The costs of the war were rising sharply. According to a report from the U.S. Treasury and the Bureau of the Budget, the federal deficit for fiscal 1967, which ended June 30, totaled $9,900,000,000 in the administrative budget. This was the second highest deficit since World War II, topped only by the 1959 deficit of $12,400,000,000. With $68,400,000,000 budgeted for defense, including $20,000,000,000 for Vietnam alone, total expenses had soared to $125,700,000,000. Receipts totaled only $115,800,000,000. The deficit according to figures in the national incomes account budget was $7,500,-

Fiscal 1967 Federal Tax Collections
(millions of dollars)

Type of Tax	1967	1966
Corporation income	$ 34,918	$ 30,834
Individual income	69,371	61,298
Employment	26,958	20,256
Estate and gift	3,014	3,094
Excise and other	14,114	13,398
Total	148,375	128,880

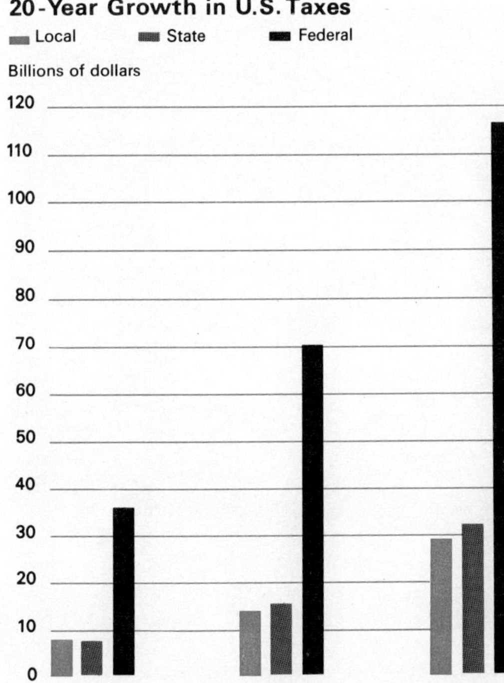

Figures for 1967 estimated by U.S. Department of the Treasury

000,000; according to the cash budget, the deficit was only $1,800,000,000, because it included receipts from Social Security and highway funds.

In July, the President warned that if the 6 per cent surcharge was not passed to yield some $5,000,000,000 in additional revenue, the fiscal 1968 deficit might reach $20,000,000,000. In August, he revised his request and asked for a 10 per cent surcharge. But the first session of the 90th Congress refused to act on the tax increase, demanding instead that the administration economize and reduce its requests for appropriations.

On June 13, the President signed an administration-supported bill restoring the 7 per cent tax credit on business investments, plus an accelerated system of depreciation allowances for new business or industrial construction. These provisions had been suspended in October, 1966, and were restored to stimulate business. The tax saving for businesses for fiscal 1967 through 1970 was estimated at $1,710,000,000. Federal tax receipts for fiscal 1967 totaled $148,374,815,000, a rise of nearly $20,000,000,000 over fiscal 1966.

State Tax Collections totaled $31,900,000,000 in fiscal 1967, an 8.6 per cent rise over the $29,400,000,000 collected by the states in fiscal 1966. New York collected the most, $4,056,000,000; California was next with a total collection of $3,485,000,000. Pennsylvania, Michigan, Illinois, Texas, and Ohio followed, in that order. The average per capita amount of state tax revenue collected varied extensively. In seven states, the per capita state tax revenue in fiscal 1967 was $200 or more, and in four states, the per capita tax revenue was less than $120.

All states showed some increase in tax revenue, but in 19 states the increase between 1966 and 1967 was less than 6 per cent. The five states with the greatest percentage rise from the preceding fiscal year were: New Jersey, 41.6 per cent; Massachusetts, 21.6 per cent; Virginia, 20 per cent; New York, 18.3 per cent, and Hawaii, 16.4 per cent. [CAROL L. THOMPSON]

Major States Tax Sources in Fiscal 1967
(millions of dollars)

Type of Tax*	Amount	Rise in Year
General sales (42)	$8,924	13.4%
Selective sales:		
Motor fuels (50)	4,839	4.6%
Tobacco products (49)	1,602	3.9%
Alcoholic beverages (50)	1,041	5.7%
Insurance (50)	866	6.6%
Individual income (36)	4,909	14.1%
Corporation income (38)	2,227	9.3%
Property (42)	862	3.4%
Death and gift (49)	795	−1.6%
Severance (29)	577	5.8%

*Number of states with tax shown in parentheses.

See also CONGRESS OF THE UNITED STATES.

TELEPHONE AND TELEGRAPH. See COMMUNICATIONS; TELEVISION.

TELEVISION. Two important events, the Public Broadcasting Act of 1967, and the Ford Foundation's $10,000,000 Public Broadcasting Laboratory (PBL) TV series, highlighted the 1967 television year. The broadcasting act, regarded by many as the most important television-radio legislation since the adoption of the Communications Act that created the Federal Communications Commission (FCC) in 1934, was signed on November 7 by President Lyndon B. Johnson.

The act had been recommended in a report on public television by the Carnegie Foundation. It provided the first federal subsidy for television programming, and was to be administered by a 15-man Public Television Corporation.

A PBL program, the first regular network show ever produced for noncommercial television, was shown on the National Educational Television (NET) network in November. That same month, the Ford Foundation contributed another $6,000,000 to NET, bringing its total donations over the years to NET and noncommercial television stations throughout the country up to $142,000,000.

Commercial Television, embroiled in the usual pursuit of ratings and revenue, weathered one of its most harrowing years. In 1967, commercial television was blighted by strikes, disappointing ratings for many of its new shows and special programs, and multiple conflicts with the FCC.

At the same time, the FCC was deluged with complaints from the public about programming and commercials. In September, the FCC said that its television "gripe" mail was pouring in at a record rate of 5,000 pieces a month.

Two of television's major disagreements with the FCC–the "Fairness Doctrine" (particularly in relation to cigarette commercials and antismoking spots) and the copyright responsibilities of television's newest extension, community antenna television (CATV) systems–were still unresolved by the end of 1967. However, the Supreme Court of the United States was scheduled to hear the two separate challenges sometime during the first half of 1968.

On New Year's Eve, time ran out for the long pending merger between International Telephone and Telegraph Corp. (IT&T) and the American Broadcasting Company. Terms of the merger agreement gave either party the right to cancel after Dec. 31, 1967, and–after two years of government opposition to the plan–IT&T elected to do so.

Movies continued to receive the highest ratings, with feature films chalking up high ratings during prime evening hours six nights a week. In addition to making multimillion-dollar deals for television rights to old Hollywood films, both ABC and the Columbia Broadcasting System (CBS) decided to go into movie production on their own. Fearful of losing their lucrative market, major Hollywood producers retaliated by asking the U.S. Department of Justice to investigate possible antitrust infringements on the part of the two networks.

NBC's Edwin Newman stopped long enough to sign an autograph as he joined other television personalities on the picket line in April.

CBS honored Ed Sullivan, second from right, on his 20th year in television by renaming its Studio 50 The Ed Sullivan Theater.

New Shows. None of the year's new shows was an all-out winner, but "The Smothers Brothers Comedy Hour" scored a surprise hit early in the year when it outrated the previously unbeatable "Bonanza." Among other new programs with solid audience appcal were "The Flying Nun," Raymond Burr's "come-back" vehicle "Ironsides," and "Gentle Ben."

Favorite Personalities. Andy Griffith, "Lucy," Dean Martin, Jim Nabors, Jackie Gleason, Red Skelton, and Ed Sullivan, continued to lead in the ratings. However, two venerable oldies, "Candid Camera" and "What's My Line," were dropped.

Specials dominated 1967 programming. The National Broadcasting Company (NBC) alone aired 15 specials in prime time during the first two weeks in December.

Some of the outstanding 1967 specials were a three-part report on the Warren Commission; a four-hour-long study on Africa; Frank Sinatra's "A Man and His Music Plus Ella Plus Jobim"; "Losers Weepers" from Budd Schulberg's Watts Writers Workshop; "Mark Twain Tonight"; the National Geographic Society's "Grizzly!"; Barbra Streisand's "The Belle of 14th Street"; and the Hallmark Hall of Fame's "St. Joan."

The networks were alternately praised and criticized for their coverage of the war in Vietnam, protest demonstrations, and riots in 1967. The critics accused the networks of attempting to make their own news in some cases and questioned the possible inflammatory impact of radio-television coverage of such controversial events.

Emmy Awards. Specials also walked off with the major share of the Emmy awards. Emmys went to *Brigadoon, Death of a Salesman,* the revival of Sid Caesar's "Show of Shows," Geraldine Page for "A Christmas Memory"; Peter Ustinov for "Barefoot in Athens"; Gene Kelly's "Jack and the Beanstalk"; and veteran broadcasting executive Pat Weaver for introducing the special to television during the 1950s.

Emmy winners among the regular programs included Don Adams, Barbara Bain, Lucille Ball, Bill Cosby, The Monkees, and Andy Williams.

Sales of Color Television sets in 1967 failed to live up to the bonanza predictions, although they were still ahead of 1966. According to the Electronic Industries Association, almost 23 per cent of U.S. television households owned color sets as of October 1. The total was placed at 12,670,000.

Color or black and white, more people were watching television than ever before. An A. C. Nielsen survey estimated that, as of September 1, there were 56,000,000 television homes in 1967–95 per cent of all U.S. households. [June Bundy Csida]

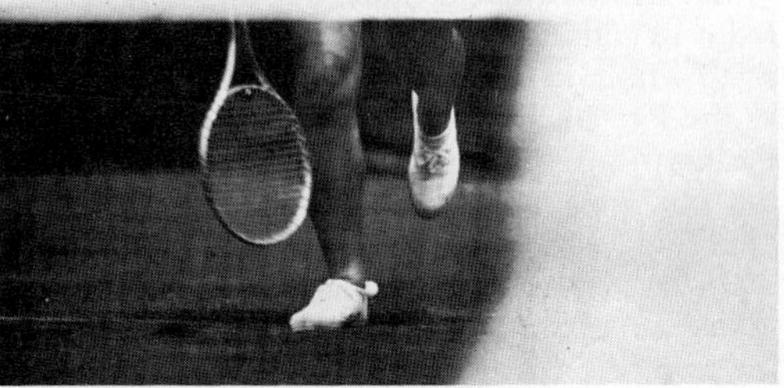

Richard Meek, *Life* © Time Inc.

Billie Jean King became first American woman in 28 years to win singles, doubles, and mixed doubles tennis titles in both Britain and the United States.

TENNIS. John Newcombe of Australia and Mrs. Billie Jean King of Long Beach, Calif., ended the season as the year's outstanding amateur players.

Newcombe's chief rival for men's honors was his fellow countryman Roy Emerson, who was attempting to win a "Grand Slam" of the Australian, French, Wimbledon, and United States tennis championships.

Emerson had started off well by winning the Australian title for the sixth time, and also the French championship. But at Wimbledon, the unofficial world championship tournament, Emerson was caught in a wave of upsets, which eliminated six of the eight top players before the quarterfinals. Newcombe swept through to the finals with the loss of only two sets. In the final, he won in straight sets from Wilhelm Bungert of West Germany.

Newcombe then clinched honors for the year by winning the U.S. crown at Forest Hills. His opponent in the final was Clark Graebner of Beechwood, Ohio, the first U.S. player to make these finals since 1963. Newcombe's straight-set victory made it 12 times in a row that a foreigner has won the U.S. championship.

Women. On the distaff side, Nancy Richey of Dallas, Tex., began the year by winning the Australian championship. In the French championship, Françoise Durr became the first native Frenchwoman to win the title since 1939.

Mrs. King's turn came at Wimbledon, where she beat Mrs. Ann Haydon Jones of England in the final of the singles. Mrs. King then joined with Rosemary Casals of San Francisco, Calif. and Owen Davidson of Australia to win the women's doubles and mixed doubles titles. It was the first sweep at Wimbledon since Doris Hart of the United States did it in 1951.

At Forest Hills, Mrs. King and Mrs. Jones again met in the final, and again Mrs. King was the winner in straight sets.

American women won the Wightman Cup match with Britain, 6 to 1, for the seventh straight time. In the Federation Cup, women's equivalent of the Davis Cup, Mrs. King and Miss Casals teamed to defeat Britain in the final round.

Davis Cup. Australia won its fourth consecutive Davis Cup and its 11th in 13 years by defeating Spain 4 to 1 in the challenge round at Brisbane, Australia. Earlier, the United States had suffered a stunning 3 to 2 upset by Ecuador in the American Zone final at Guayaquil, Ecuador.

Professional tennis was brightened by the entry of former U.S. amateur star, Dennis Ralston, of Bakersfield, Calif., and Australia's Fred Stolle. The top player, however, was still Rodney Laver of Australia. The expanded professional "tour" included 39 weekly tournaments in nine countries. Laver won most of them. [James O. Dunaway]

See also Sports.

THAILAND continued to support the United States war effort in Vietnam in 1967. About 2,000 Thai troops were fighting in South Vietnam and, in November, the Thai government agreed to send 10,000 more. The United States, too, continued to use Thailand as a base for air strikes against the North Vietnamese. Although the extent of U.S. military involvement in Thailand was veiled in diplomatic secrecy, reports indicated that there were about 40,000 U.S. servicemen stationed there and at least six U.S.-built air bases in operation, including the one at Korat that President Lyndon B. Johnson visited in December. See PRESIDENT OF THE UNITED STATES; VIETNAM.

The United States continued to aid the Thai government's efforts to control the guerrilla bands operating within its borders. The guerrillas, organized as the Patriotic Front, were particularly active in the northeastern area of the country. In October, the Thai government imposed martial law on the area and in December extended it to cover five southern and central provinces as part of a determined effort on the part of Thailand to wipe out the terrorists. [JOHN N. STALKER]

Facts in Brief. Population: 32,889,000. Government: King Phumiphon Aduldet; Premier Thanom Kittikachorn. Monetary Unit: baht (20.75=U.S. $1). Foreign Trade: exports, $694,000,000; imports, $1,168,000,000. Principal Exports: rice, rubber, tin.

Impresario David Merrick produced an all-Negro version of the hit musical, *Hello, Dolly!,* starring Pearl Bailey and Cab Calloway.

THEATER. At the beginning of 1967, English playwright Harold Pinter caused a revolution on Broadway with *The Homecoming.* An unknown cast, a distasteful story, and an earlier mild reception in England seemed to forecast box-office failure. But it succeeded beyond expectations. It extended ordinary characters, story, and setting to a dimension where they became extraordinary and disturbing. Its audiences did not sit back; they sat up. Distinguished persons and average playgoers deluged newspaper drama pages with letters of opinion as to the meaning of the play. Pinter said it was not for him but for the play to say what it meant. It played to packed theaters and won both the New York Drama Critics' Circle and Antoinette Perry awards as the year's best play.

In *The Homecoming,* a usually sentimental situation in which a son brings his wife home to meet the family turns into a nightmare when the father, a butcher, and two brothers, a racketeer and a fighter, make love to the wife. She decides to stay with them and sell her love professionally. Her husband leaves. At once superreal and symbolic, comic and tragic, Pinter's family is the family of man, selfishly exploiting others or selfishly withdrawing.

Other Plays. Pinter's play paved the way for the fall arrival of other impressive and unconventional British plays. The best was *Rosencrantz and Guildenstern Are Dead,* a line from Shakespeare's *Hamlet,* which set playwright Tom Stoppard wondering about these two characters whom Hamlet sends to their death for prying. Rosencrantz and Guildenstern, says Stoppard, are "the most expendable people of all time. Their very facelessness makes them dramatic; the fact that they die without ever really understanding why they lived makes them somehow cosmic." With humor, style, and compassion for the "two guys waiting for something to happen," Stoppard weaves his story into the frame of *Hamlet* to show that those who matter little in the grand design matter mightily as human beings. John Wood as the sharp Guildenstern and Brian Murray as the slower Rosencrantz were excellent.

Pinter's *The Birthday Party,* though written before *The Homecoming,* also centered around a sentimental occasion–a birthday party. Stanley, a lodger at a rundown seaside boarding house, is visited by two men, Goldberg and McCann, who he fears have come to "get" him. Even the frenzied beating of his birthday present, a toy drum, cannot ward off sinister destiny. At the birthday party they arrange for him, his fear and hopelessness mount to a climax in a frightening game of blindman's buff. When they take Stanley away the next morning, he is a walking corpse, hardly noticed by the paternal landlord and his cheerfully inane wife.

Eugene O'Neill's *More Stately Mansions,* left unfinished at his death, was impressive if disappointing. Completed and staged by José Quintero, the play, a sequel to *A Touch of the Poet*, starred Ingrid Bergman and Arthur Hill. It further explored O'Neill's theme of the deep-rooted American conflict between the idealism of the founding fathers and the materialism of those who developed the country.

Edward Albee's contribution for the year was *Everything in the Garden*, an adaptation of an English play by Giles Cooper. It concerned the battle of a suburban couple to live within their means. See Albee, Edward.

On the Lighter Side. The two best comedies of the year were Robert Anderson's *You Know I Can't Hear You when the Water's Running* and Peter Shaffer's *Black Comedy*. Anderson's four playlets viewed physical love with humor and pathos. *Black Comedy* was a facile romp which disintegrated when the variations on its clever idea – a lighted stage representing darkness and vice versa – became monotonous.

Musicals. *Cabaret* dominated the musical stage and won eight Antoinette Perry awards, including "best musical." Based on Christopher Isherwood's *Goodbye to Berlin*, and set in that city in 1929 and 1930, the musical impressively re-created that era's desperate search for fun to hide an emptiness soon to be filled by Nazism. The music by John Kander and lyrics by Fred Ebb caught the era perfectly.

Off-Broadway Theater again appealed to the mind. Most successful and most original was *America Hurrah* by Jean-Claude van Itallie. In the three one-act plays, van Itallie abandoned realism for effects that were fragmentary and dreamlike, and dominated by a "metaphor" by which, he explained, the audience would recognize "its own dreams of unrecognized hatreds and aggressions, twisted motives, bodies cut off from minds, aimless spirits. . . ." In the last of the three one-acters, "Motel," a motel room is the metaphor of a rootless society living day-to-day on sex and violence in a stainless-steel cube. There are no flesh-and-blood actors, only the taped voice of the motel owner uttering sentimental clichés while two gigantic papier-mâché figures make love, deface the walls with obscenities, and destroy the room. The near-perfect ensemble acting was directed by Jacques Levy and Joseph Chaikin.

Novelist Bruce Jay Friedman's bitter, grotesque comedy *Scuba Duba* also commented on social patterns. Hero Harold is a tense, complex modern male, a liberal who is outraged when his wife runs away with a Negro. Harold finds solace in a garden scythe and a bikini-clad girl.

The most controversial off-Broadway play was *MacBird!* by Barbara Garson, a political satire based on Shakespeare's *Macbeth*. In obvious reference to current political personalities, a vice-president gets

Actor Stacy Keach played the title role in *MacBird!*, an off-Broadway Shakespearean parody critical of President Lyndon B. Johnson, caricatured in the background.

the top job when a president is assassinated in the vice-president's hometown. The brother of the deceased president plots revenge and finally kills MacBird, who has become a maniacal tyrant.

Repertory Theater. Because of audience support for plays of substance, professional repertory continued to grow steadily in 1967. The season's favorite at the Tyrone Guthrie Theatre in Minneapolis, Minn., was Jean Anouilh's *Thieves' Carnival*, a wry commentary on the dance of life. The Guthrie's first new play to be offered was Barry Stavis' *Harper's Ferry*. Although the endeavor was praised, the historical play about John Brown was judged superficial.

San Francisco, Calif., became the new permanent home of the American Conservatory Theater (ACT), founded by director William Ball in Pittsburgh, Pa., in 1965. A 40-week, 31-production 1967-1968 season was made possible by grants from the National Endowment for the Arts and from the Ford Foundation, as well as from funds raised locally. The season, which opened in October with *Twelfth Night*, included Albee's *A Delicate Balance* and Molière's *The Misanthrope*.

In Houston, Tex., the Alley Theater balanced two major activities: producing six plays (including Duerrenmatt's *The Physicists* and Pinter's *The Caretaker*) for 10,000 subscribers, and planning the opening of a new theater. [ALICE GRIFFIN]

See also MERRICK, DAVID.

THIEU, NGUYEN VAN (1923-), lieutenant general in the South Vietnam army, was elected president of the Republic of Vietnam Sept. 3, 1967. He is regarded as a man of high integrity in financial matters, unlike many in Vietnamese public life.

Thieu was born in Phan Rang, the capital of Ninhthuan, one of the poorest provinces of the central lowlands of Vietnam and about 150 miles northeast of Saigon. He was the youngest of five children of a small landowner. During the Japanese occupation days of World War II, he worked in his father's rice fields. Later, with the help of his brother, a Paris-educated lawyer, he was able to enroll in the Merchant Marine Academy at Saigon. He spent a year there and then transferred to the newly established Vietnamese Military Academy, from which he graduated in 1949.

By 1954, when the French withdrew from Vietnam and the country was partitioned, Thieu had become a colonel and a regimental commander. On Nov. 2, 1963, when President Ngo Dinh Diem was overthrown, it was General Thieu, as commander of the Fifth Infantry Division, who personally led the attack on the barracks of the presidential bodyguard. He continued to remain an important figure in the military leadership during the successive series of governmental changes. On June 19, 1965, when the military junta took power, Thieu became its chairman.

TOGO. On April 24, President Etienne Eyadema escaped assassination when a notebook in his hand deflected a pistol bullet. It caused only a minor wound. The shot was fired by a 20-year-old corporal in the presidential palace guard. Eyadema blamed the plot on Major Emmanuel Bodjollé, a relative of the would-be assassin and former chief of staff, who was being held for the illegal possession of firearms. Bodjollé was sentenced in May to 26 months in jail.

Eyadema, a lieutenant colonel, had led a military coup that seized power on January 13, unseating President Nicolas Grunitzky. In April, Eyadema, now military dictator, dissolved the governing *Comité de Reconciliation Nationale.* He declared himself president and appointed a council of ministers. In a message on April 27, Togo's Independence Day, Eyadema blamed Togo's former leaders and political strife for the nation's troubles. On May 12, the council abolished Togo's four political parties. On July 11, Eyadema pardoned 32 prisoners who had been jailed by previous regimes on charges of treason. [BENJAMIN E. THOMAS]

Facts in Brief. Population: 1,728,000. Government: President Etienne Eyadema. Monetary Unit: CFA franc (246.85=U.S. $1). Foreign Trade: exports, $36,200,000; imports, $47,600,000. Principal Exports: phosphates, cocoa beans, coffee.

TORNADOS. See DISASTERS; WEATHER.

TOYS. See GAMES, HOBBIES, AND TOYS.

TRACK AND FIELD. For the second year in a row, Jim Ryun of Kansas University lowered the world record for a mile. On June 24, in the Amateur Athletic Union (AAU) championships at Bakersfield, Calif., he led every step of the way to register a time of 3 minutes 51.1 seconds, two-tenths of a second under his former record.

Ryun followed this by setting a new world record for 1,500 meters, in the British Commonwealth vs. U.S.A. meet at Los Angeles, on July 8. He came from behind to defeat Kipchoge Keino of Kenya with a sizzling 53.9-second last lap. Ryun's time, 3 minutes 33.1 seconds, knocked 2 1/2 seconds off the record set by Herb Elliott of Australia in the 1960 Olympic Games.

Tommie Smith of San Jose State College also set two world records, both in the same race. He made record times of 44.5 seconds for 400 meters and 44.8 seconds for 440 yards over his home track on May 20. A week earlier, Smith had anchored San Jose State to a new 880-yard relay record of 1 minute 22.1 seconds.

Threatened Boycott. In November, Smith was one of a number of prominent young American Negro athletes who voted to boycott the 1968 Olympics in protest against racial conditions in the United States. Others who are equally prominent opposed the boycott, and the issue remained in doubt as the year came to a close.

Perhaps the most impressive world record, on a percentage basis, was that set by four University of Southern California (USC) sprinters in the 440-yard relay. Fred Kuller, Earl McCullouch, Lennox Miller, and O. J. Simpson took a full second off the world mark with a 38.6-second clocking in the National Collegiate Athletic Association (NCAA) championships. McCullouch also tied the world record of 13.2 seconds for the 110-meter high hurdles in winning the Pan American Games trials.

Ron Clarke of Australia set the only other running record with a time of 8 minutes 19.8 seconds for two miles. West Germany produced a new record holder in the decathlon; he was Kurt Bendlin, whose score of 8,319 points took the record away from Russ Hodge of the United States.

Field Records. Only two field event records were broken. USC teammates Bob Seagren and Paul Wilson took turns raising the pole vault record, with Wilson having the last word by clearing 17 feet 7 3/4 inches at the AAU meet. In the shot-put, Randy Matson of Texas A&M University improved his own record to 71 feet 5 1/2 inches. On the same day, Matson also achieved the year's longest discus throw, 213 feet 9 inches, just two inches short of Ludvik Danek's 1965 record.

The AAU championship was won by the Southern California Striders, and the NCAA title by USC.

Distaff Results. Women's track and field took a giant step forward with the establishment of world records for the 1,500 meter and mile distances.

Australia's Judy Pollock ran 800 meters in 2 minutes 1 second to reduce the world record by one-tenth of a second. Anne Smith of Great Britain became the mile record holder with a time of 4 minutes 37 seconds, while Mia Gommers of Holland claimed the 1,500-meter mark by running it in 4 minutes 15.6 seconds.

In the discus throw, Liesel Westermann of West Germany set a new world record, with a throw of 200 feet 11 3/4 inches.

U.S. women also reached a new level of prominence. Madeline Manning was the top-ranked 800-meter runner, with victories over both Judy Pollock (after Miss Pollock made the record at Helsinki) and European champion Vera Nicolic. Others who excelled were Charlette Cook, whose 52.4 second U.S. record was the fastest 400-meter time of the year; Cherrie Sherrard, who set a new U.S. record of 10.5 seconds for the 80-meter hurdles; Eleanor Montgomery, whose 5-foot 10 1/8-inch high jump ranked her second in the world for the year; and javelinists RaNae Bair and Barbara Friedrich, both with throws over 195 feet.

A sex-test incident marred the year. At the Women's European Cup finals in Kiev, Russia, Ewa

New World Track and Field Records Established in 1967

Subject to recognition by the International Amateur Athletic Federation (IAAF)

Event	Holder	Country	Where made	Date	Record
Men					
400 meters	Tommie Smith	U.S.A.	San Jose, Calif.	May 20	0:44.5
440 yards	Tommie Smith	U.S.A.	San Jose, Calif.	May 20	0:44.8
1,500 meters	Jim Ryun	U.S.A.	Los Angeles, Calif.	July 8	3:33.1
Mile	Jim Ryun	U.S.A.	Bakersfield, Calif.	June 24	3:51.1
2 miles	Ron Clarke	Australia	Vasteras, Sweden	June 27	8:19.8
440-yard relay	U. of Southern California (McCullouch, Kuller, Simpson, Miller)	U.S.A.	Provo, Utah	June 17	0:38.6
880-yard relay	San Jose State (Shackleford, Talmadge, Evans, Smith)	U.S.A.	Fresno, Calif.	May 13	1:22.1
Pole vault	Paul Wilson	U.S.A.	Bakersfield, Calif.	June 24	17 feet, 7¾ inches
Shot-put	Randy Matson	U.S.A.	College Station, Texas	April 22	71 feet, 5½ inches
Decathlon	Kurt Bendlin	W. Germany	Hamburg, W. Germany	May 13-14	8,319 pts.
Women					
800 meters	Judy Pollock	Australia	Helsinki, Finland	June 28	2:01.0
1,500 meters	Mia Gommers	Holland	Sittard, Holland	October 25	4:15.6
Mile	Anne Smith	England	Chiswick, England	June 3	4:37.0
100-meter hurdles (33-inches)	Christine Perera	England	Blackburn, England	June 3	0:13.7
200-meter hurdles	Roza Babich	Russia	Leninakan, Russia	October 2	0:27.1
800-meter relay	Russia (Pechenkina, Tkachenko, Borchikova, Samotyesova)	Russia	Leninakan, Russia	October 2	1:34.4
2,400-meter relay	Britain (Stirling, Lowe, Piercy)	England	London, England	August 28	6:20.0
Discus throw	Liesel Westermann	W. Germany	Sao Paulo, Brazil	November 6	200 feet, 11¾ inches

Klobukowska of Poland, co-holder of the 100-meter dash record, was barred from competition because of an unspecified genetic irregularity.

Although suspicions about other women athletes had been voiced in the past, Miss Klobukowska was the first prominent athlete to suffer the embarrassment of failing a sex test. A five-step sex examination system was announced for athletes at the Mexico City Olympic Games.

International Competition. Athletes from the United States dominated the track and field events at the Fifth Pan American Games, held in Winnipeg, Canada, July 23 to August 6. They won 22 of 24 men's events and 8 of 11 women's events.

Russia won repeat victories in both the men's and the women's European Cup competition. The Russian men barely made it, however, with only 81 points to 80 each for East and West Germany. The Russian women scored 51 points for an 8-point margin over runner-up East Germany. Europe won the Europe versus America meet at Montreal in August.

Cross Country. Ken Moore of the Oregon Track Club won the AAU individual cross-country title, with the team championship going to the Toronto Olympic Club. In the NCAA championship, Gerry Lindgren of Washington State University won his third straight individual crown, while Villanova University won the team title for the second year in a row. [JAMES O. DUNAWAY]

TRANSPORTATION. Most transportation companies were to remember 1967 as the year of the "profit squeeze." The earnings pinch was the result of a general sluggishness in the economy, which tended to hold down the demand for transportation services, and of rising operating costs, particularly labor.

The Transportation Association of America (TAA) estimated the nation's total transportation bill for 1967 at $153,100,000,000, including outlays for all types of private and for-hire transport. Of that total, $72,100,000,000 was spent for freight and $81,000,000,000 for passenger transportation. The TAA's preliminary estimates on total United States traffic volume, not including international movements, follow:

Freight (billions of intercity ton-miles)	1966	1967
Rail	757	732
Truck	396	403
Pipeline	332	353
Barge	158	159
Lakes	115	102
Air	2	2.7
Total freight	1,760	1,751.7

Passenger (billions of intercity passenger-miles)	1966	1967
Auto	880	937
Air	68.7	87
Bus	25	25
Rail	17.3	15
Water	3.3	4
Total passenger	994.3	1,068

For the second time in five years, transportation failed to grow faster than the gross national product (GNP). For 1967, freight volume declined 1 per cent from the 1966 high, while the GNP, as it was measured in constant 1958 dollars, increased. Overall passenger volume rose 5 per cent, as the airlines continued to widen their lead over all other modes of public transportation in intercity passenger-miles.

Department of Transportation. The Department of Transportation (DOT), which was created by law in October, 1966, became operational in 1967. In January, Alan S. Boyd was officially approved by the Senate as the first Secretary of Transportation.

On March 30, President Lyndon B. Johnson issued Executive Order 11340, prescribing April 1, 1967, as "the date on which the Department of Transportation Act shall take effect." He forecast "a new era for transportation in America" and stressed safety in travel, expanded technology, and enhanced foreign trade, as priority "tasks."

As in any new organization with 100,000 employees, DOT's beginning stages were not without start-up problems. During the year, a great deal of the time and attention of top DOT management was devoted to problems of finance, housekeeping, organization, and recruitment of personnel. Since no money had been appropriated for DOT for fiscal 1968, it had to operate from April 1 to June 30 with funds from its constituent agencies. The $1,600,000,000 finally appropriated in mid-October for fiscal 1968 was 11 per cent less than requested. As a result, DOT was forced to make major reductions in two main areas. It allotted $11,700,000 for high-speed ground transportation research and development compared to the $18,600,000 it had requested. The $25,000,000 for state and community safety was a reduction of $75,000,000 from its original budget.

The agency's actions and statements indicated that during the next few years particular attention would be given to urban transportation problems, a more comprehensive airport development plan and program, matters of transportation safety, and the environmental aspects of transportation, such as air pollution, congestion, and noise.

Airlines

The regularly scheduled U.S. domestic airlines, stimulated by promotional fares and the increasing popularity of air travel, flew a record 76,000,000,000 passenger-miles, 25.5 per cent above the 1966 level. However, while the number of passenger-miles was at an all-time high, profits were down. The sluggish economy and declining yields on passenger fares tended to hold down revenues, while costs were adversely affected by delayed jet deliveries, congested air traffic, and higher wages.

The cargo end of the air transport business was also disappointing in 1967. The slower pace of cargo growth, as compared with that of previous years,

Sleek and streamlined, a three-car TurboTrain begins low speed test runs in Chicago. Powered by gas turbines, it will be capable of traveling 160 miles per hour.

reflected the lack of vigor in the economy and decreased demand for military airlifts to Vietnam. For the full 1966 year, domestic air freight traffic rose 18 per cent; for 1964 and 1965, the rate of gain had been 27 per cent. As such, the 12 per cent increase during 1967 was the lowest for a non-strike period in three years.

Railroads

The year was a disappointing one for the nation's railroads, which had their second most prosperous year on record in 1966. Freight volume, at 720,000,000,000 ton-miles, was 2.5 per cent below 1966. Gross revenues of $10,400,000,000 were 2.3 per cent below 1966. Net profits slumped to about $575,000,000 from $904,000,000 in 1966.

The major factors contributing to this decline were (1) a general leveling off in business; (2) decreased grain shipments; (3) inclement weather; (4) prolonged strikes in the automobile, copper, and other industries; (5) labor agreements that resulted in large cost increases; (6) material cost increases; and (7) removal of railway post office cars from passenger trains.

Labor Relations. In mid-July a two-day strike involving six rail shopcraft unions, totaling 137,000 members, effectively shut down 95 per cent of the nation's railroad mileage. On July 17, Congress passed a law requested by President Johnson to end the "chaos." The law provided for the appointment of a five-man mediation board that was given power to impose settlement terms if no accord had been reached at the end of 90 days. In September, the board voted unanimously to grant the unions a two-year wage increase totaling 11 per cent.

The railroads estimated that the total additional cost of the package, as measured against 1966 wage payments, called for $64,100,000 in 1967, $110,000,000 in 1968, and $145,600,000 in 1969.

Freight Rate Increase. The Interstate Commerce Commission (ICC) authorized a general railroad freight rate increase, the first such increase requested since 1960. Effective on August 19, it averaged about 3 per cent and was expected to add $300,000,000 in annual revenue and help cover $441,000,000 in higher costs.

The Merger Movement. For four railroads, consolidation became a reality in 1967. With ICC approval, the Missouri Pacific took control of the Chicago and Eastern Illinois on May 12. The Atlantic Coast Line-Seaboard Air Line merger had been approved by the ICC on Dec. 13, 1963, but four years of court litigation followed. On July 1, 1967, the merger was completed and the two began operations as the Seaboard Coast Line Railroad.

At year's end, the merger outlook for eight other railroads was hopeful. A series of appeals to the courts continued to delay the Pennsylvania-New York Central merger, approved by the ICC in April, 1966. The Chicago & North Western had ICC and court approval for its merger with the Chicago Great Western. The outlook for the Northern Lines merger –Great Northern, Northern Pacific, Chicago, Burlington & Quincy, and Spokane, Portland & Seattle –was more favorable the second time around because the Milwaukee Road and the Chicago & North Western withdrew their opposition.

Rail Passenger Service. The long downward trend in rail intercity passenger travel, which began in 1951, was accelerated in 1967 by the U.S. Post Office Department's decision to remove first class mail from rail passenger trains. The dropping of railway post office cars meant a total revenue loss to the industry of $60,000,000, and this accelerated the demise of some well-known passenger trains. For example, in September, the Atchison, Topeka & Santa Fe Railway, long renowned for operating fine passenger trains, announced plans for eliminating 33 of its trains. Two of the nation's most famous passenger trains gave in to the economic pressure. The Twentieth Century Limited and the Broadway Limited, both 65 years old, ended their New York City to Chicago runs in December.

The inauguration of high speed rail passenger service between Washington, D.C., and New York City, which was scheduled to begin in October, 1967, was delayed until 1968. In a joint announcement made late in September, DOT, the Pennsylvania Railroad, and the Budd Company explained the delay was needed to provide more time for reliability and performance tests of the 160 mph self-

Status of the U.S. Interstate Highway System as of Sept. 30, 1967

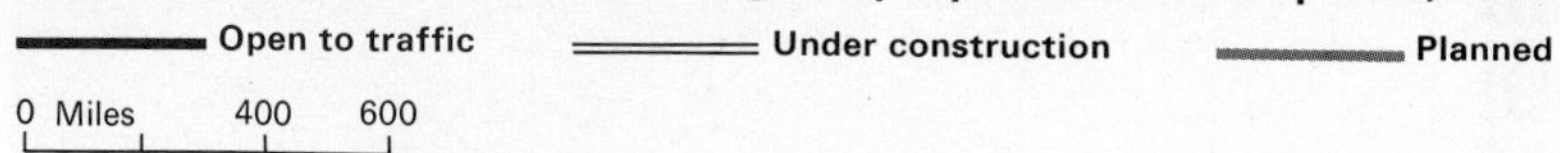

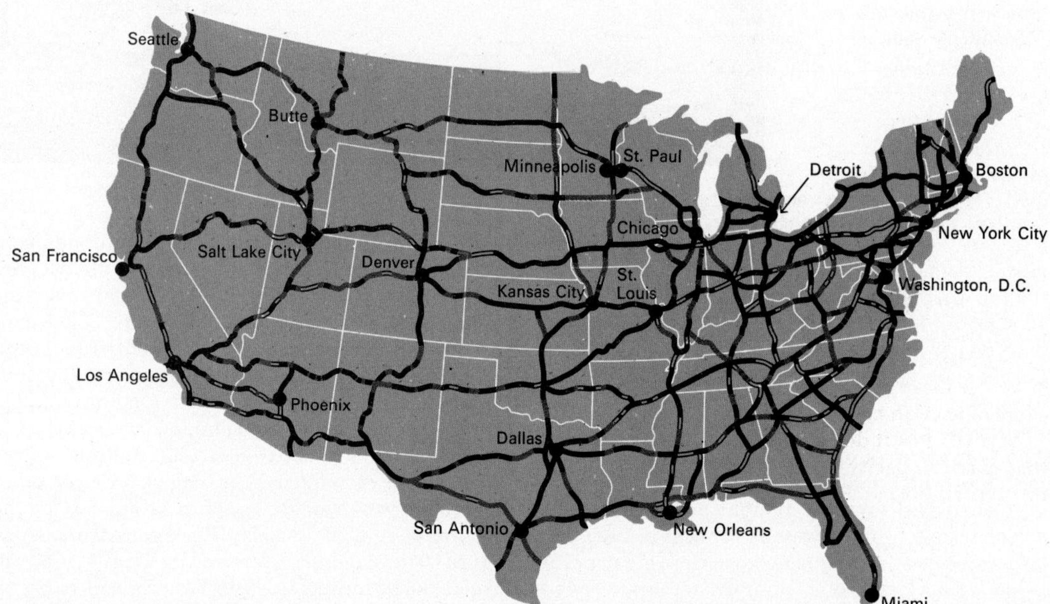

propelled cars. It was also announced that the start of turbine train service between New York City and Boston, Mass., would be delayed several months.

Trucking

Earnings of most trucking companies declined in 1967 as a result of a general traffic decline due to a letup in the economy, labor shutdowns, and rising wage costs.

Probably the year's biggest trucking development was the national settlement agreed to by Trucking Employers, Inc., and the International Brotherhood of Teamsters. In addition to the settlement itself, the negotiations were significant because they firmly established nationwide bargaining in the trucking industry.

The final settlement with the Teamsters called for a 5.4 per cent annual wage increase over three years; 6.7 per cent the first year, 4.7 per cent the second, and 4.7 per cent the third. In dollars, this settlement would cost the motor carriers $135,000,000 the first year, $110,000,000 more the second, and $107,000,000 more the third.

Rate Increase. During the summer, regulated motor carriers around the country filed for a series of rate increases with the ICC in such a fashion as to amount to a general rate rise. Relief granted truckers by the ICC varied by geographic region, with boosts averaging around 5 per cent. Because of their timing, the increases were not sufficient, however, to counter the effects of rising operating and labor costs on 1967's profit statements.

Air Freight Forwarding Authority. In September the Civil Aeronautics Board (CAB), by a 4 to 1 vote, permitted three long-haul general commodity truckers–Consolidated Freightways, Navajo Freight, and Pacific Intermountain Express–to enter the air freight forwarder field on a five-year trial basis, the majority of the board calling the ruling a means for providing a "real breakthrough in stimulating intermodal air-truck service." However, in November, a federal appellate court stayed the order as a result of a petition by air freight forwarders, who claimed that the CAB's decision violated congressional intent to keep surface and air modes mutually independent.

Roads and Highways

At the end of the year, motor vehicle registrations totaled over 97,500,000. This was a 3,400,000 gain over 1966, with trucks and buses up 4 per cent and autos up 3.4 per cent. By Dec. 31, 1967, traffic was running on over 25,000 miles, or 61 per cent of the 41,000-mile Interstate Highway System. Construction was underway on 6,000 miles; only 3 per cent of the system was in a preliminary state.

Ocean Shipping

Profits of most shipping companies declined in 1967 from 1966 levels. This was largely due to large expenditures for containerization, and to the slowing of foreign trade, which was, in turn, a reflection of sluggish economies in a number of the world's leading industrialized nations.

Containerization. While the cargo container began to assert its significance in international transport just a few years before, it began to have an enormous impact on the maritime industry in 1967. A cargo container is essentially a sturdy, demountable truck trailer van that can move by air, highway, rail, sea, or by a combination of these on a single trip. It protects cargo from damage and from widespread pilferage, a large element in the cost of ocean shipping. Containerization also allows discharge and receipt of cargo in port much faster, in some instances in one-fifth the time of conventional methods.

In the face of such large potential savings, shipowners and port directors felt forced to pursue containerization or risk being left out of the maritime future. However, this placed a substantial financial strain on those venturing into containerization because of its high cost.

At year's end, industry authorities were concerned that excess capacity might lead to cutthroat competition for the limited volume of freight suitable for containerized shipments.

New Maritime Policy. Public disclosure of President Johnson's long-awaited maritime program was again postponed. In September, it was reported that DOT and congressional maritime leaders had agreed on a program to revitalize the merchant marine, but without the proposal to build ships abroad. However, the program collided with high costs of the war in Vietnam, economy reductions in other programs, and the President's battle with Congress for a tax increase.

In November, refusing to wait any longer for a program, congressional maritime interests introduced legislation that they said reflected general agreement between the administration and congressional advocates of higher subsidies. The White House did not publicly endorse the legislation.

World Shipping. According to Lloyd's Register of Shipping the number of merchant ships under construction on Dec. 31, 1967, was 1,775. This was a decline from a high of 1,782 ships in December, 1966. However, shipbuilding orders, including those under construction, hit a new peak in tonnage with 3,260 vessels of 40,351,369 gross-tons on the total world order book compared with 3,251 vessels of 33,639,292 gross-tons on Dec. 31, 1966.

Japan stayed in first place with 4,762,036 tons of merchant shipping under construction plus orders for 12,402,477 tons more. Great Britain remained in second place with 1,248,232 gross-tons under construction plus 2,386,151 on order. The United States climbed from 10th place to 8th with 507,092 gross-tons under construction plus 588,010 tons on order. Information was incomplete from Communist China and Russia.

Inland Waterways. Barge traffic on the nation's inland waterways continued to rise during 1967 and showed a 5.9 per cent increase over 1966. The low cost of shallow-draft carriage continued to encourage a growing number of industrial firms to locate plants near navigable rivers. Expansion of economic activity in the South and the Southwest continued to be a favorable factor in 1967. [KENNETH E. SCHAEFLE]

Transit

A long-standing downward trend in the number of transit riders was broken in 1967. For the first time since 1945, there was a slight increase over the previous year's figures in revenue passengers. The news had major significance for the nation's traffic-choked cities. The transit decline had been paralleled by dramatic increases in the number of automobiles and by steady decreases in the number of passengers carried in each automobile.

Greater public awareness of the need for good transit facilities in a healthy urban environment was evident during the year. Six new subway systems were in various stages of planning or construction in Atlanta, Ga.; Baltimore, Md.; Los Angeles, Calif.; San Francisco, Calif.; Seattle, Wash.; and Washington, D.C. Proposals for improving the efficiency of bus facilities were receiving increased national attention. Pittsburgh, Pa., for example, reported favorably on experiments with the "skybus"–a semiautomated buslike electric vehicle that runs singly or in trains on rubber tires along a special concrete track.

Overall, the transit industry at the end of 1967 was experiencing a mood of optimism and progress –a feeling that the year was an important turning point in transit history.

Other Notable Events of the year were:

- The National Academy of Sciences received a $150,000 grant from the U.S. Department of Housing and Urban Development (HUD) for the development of design and performance criteria for a new "nonrail surface transit vehicle," a project that aims at the eventual production of an improved type of bus or a substitute for the bus.
- A March 17 grant of $46,000,000 from HUD enabled the Chicago Transit Authority to begin a $69,000,000, 15-mile extension of its rail transit lines.
- New York voters approved a $2,500,000,000 transportation bond issue in a November 7 referendum. The funds are to be used for improvement of transit and other transportation facilities.

Early in 1967, at the recommendation of Governor Nelson A. Rockefeller, the New York assembly established the Metropolitan Transportation Authority to unify mass transportation administration in New York City. Into the new organization were merged the New York City Transit Authority, the Manhattan and Bronx Surface Transit Operating Authority, the Triborough Bridge and Tunnel Authority, and the Metropolitan Commuter Transportation Authority. [EUGENE B. MCCAUL]

TRAVEL, the single largest item in world trade, reached record heights in 1967. The year was celebrated throughout the world as International Tourist Year (ITY) by unanimous proclamation of the United Nations. Some 86,000,000 citizens of 128 countries spent $13,720,000,000 on foreign travel, compared to the 80,000,000 who had spent a total of $12,990,000,000 in 1966.

In honor of ITY, frontier formalities were eased by immigration, customs, and fiscal authorities in many countries. These included Yugoslavia, which eliminated visas for all visitors; the United States, which reduced paperwork and permitted visitors to remain in the country up to 10 days without visas; and Hong Kong, India, Japan, and South Korea, all of which simplified their entrance requirements.

Balance of Payments. The United States experienced a record-breaking volume of outbound, inbound, and domestic travel. Nearly 18,850,000 U.S. citizens spent $4,600,000,000 on foreign travel in 1967, a sharp advance of 15 per cent over the amount spent in 1966. This accelerated gain was due chiefly to the 13,600,000 Americans who visited Canada's Expo 67 (see FAIRS AND EXHIBITIONS).

The United States also earned $1,895,000,000 from 8,125,000 foreign visitors. None of 1967's other leading host countries, Canada, Italy, and Spain, approached this total tourist income. But in spite of these earnings, the United States had the worst travel deficit in its history, $2,085,000,000. This sum was the largest single factor in the total U.S. balance of payments deficit and the largest travel gap ever experienced by any country.

President Lyndon B. Johnson, confronted by the pressure on the stability of the dollar, appointed a Travel Task Force in November, 1967, to make specific recommendations to the federal government for closing the travel gap. The President made it clear that his purpose was to develop measures for stimulating foreign travel to the United States, not to limit American travel abroad. The Travel Task Force, composed of 22 leaders in industry, finance, and government, was expected to submit its report early in April, 1968. But on Jan. 1, 1968, the President appealed to Americans to restrain their travel outside the Western Hemisphere "for the next two years." He raised the possibility of legislation to help achieve that objective.

One of the many questions that is likely to be resolved by the Task Force is how to increase the budget of the United States Travel Service (USTS), the federal agency charged with the responsibility of promoting travel to the United States. The Congress has refused to provide more than minimal funds–$3,000,000 in 1967–for USTS, even though travel industry leaders have repeatedly recommended budgets ranging from $10,000,000 to $15,000,000, even to $30,000,000, for a strong positive effort to reduce the critical billion-dollar travel gap.

Discover America, the private, industry-financed program to promote more travel within the United States, gathered momentum in 1967 after a somewhat delayed start in 1966. Organized under White House and congressional auspices, the private agency mobilized an impressive and diversified array of cooperative travel tie-in promotions from automotive, oil, tire, hotel, and transportation companies. This helped push the U.S. domestic travel market up an estimated 6 per cent to a record high of $24,306,000,000.

Other highlights of the 1967 travel year were:

- The completion of diplomatic and technical details for the establishment of the first direct scheduled air service between Moscow and New York City.
- Authorization for the construction of a multibillion-dollar U.S. supersonic transport plane that will carry 300 passengers at 1,850 mph.
- The retirement of the Cunard line's celebrated *Queen Mary* to the role of a floating museum, convention hall, and hotel in Long Beach, Calif.
- The entry of more airlines into the hotel field, with Trans World Airlines, a major international U.S. carrier, acquiring the Hilton International Hotel chain of 43 hotels abroad. [WILLIAM D. PATTERSON]

See also CONSERVATION; FAIRS AND EXHIBITIONS; TRANSPORTATION.

TRINIDAD AND TOBAGO. See LATIN AMERICA; WEST INDIES.

TROWBRIDGE, ALEXANDER BUEL (1929-   ), officially joined the Cabinet as its youngest member and the youngest ever to hold the post of Secretary of Commerce when he was sworn in on June 14, 1967. He had been acting secretary since the resignation of John T. Connor on Jan. 18, 1967.

A handsome six-footer, Trowbridge left a promising career in the petroleum industry as division manager for Esso Standard Oil Company in Puerto Rico, to take the post of assistant Secretary of Commerce for domestic and international business in April, 1965. He had also seen oil industry duty in Cuba, El Salvador, Panama, and the Philippines. Earlier, he had served in the Korean War and was awarded the Bronze Star.

Trowbridge was born on Dec. 12, 1929, in Englewood, N.J. He attended Phillips Academy in Andover, Mass., and was graduated from Princeton University with honors, with his major courses taken in the Woodrow Wilson School of Public and International Affairs. It was on the advice of diplomat George F. Kennan, then at Princeton, that Trowbridge chose the international oil business as a career rather than the foreign service.

Trowbridge, whose nickname is Sandy, married the former Nancy Horst of Greenwich, Conn. Their three children, two boys and a girl, attend District of Columbia public schools.

TRUCKING. See TRANSPORTATION.

TRUMAN, HARRY S. (1884-), 33rd President of the United States, joined with former President Dwight D. Eisenhower, several former Cabinet members, and others in October, 1967, to form the nonpartisan Citizens Committee for Peace with Freedom in Vietnam. The group gave strong support to U.S. military presence in Vietnam, although it avoided supporting President Lyndon B. Johnson personally.

For the first time since he left the White House in 1953, Truman was unable to attend the annual birthday celebration held for him by the Eddie Jacobson Memorial Foundation. The former President, who was 83 on May 8, felt that too much strain would be put on his health if he attended.

The Jacobson Memorial Foundation, named for Truman's old haberdashery partner, announced that it would sponsor an annual Harry S. Truman Foreign Policy Award to be given to a member of the U.S. Senate. The $1,000 award and a scroll will be presented at Truman's birthday party in 1968.

In March, Greece honored Truman during its 20th anniversary celebration of the Truman Doctrine, the U.S. policy that sent military and economic aid to Greece after World War II. First, Truman was awarded an honorary law degree by the University of Salonika. Then, he was given an ancient Athenian helmet as a gift from the Greeks to the American people. [CAROL L. THOMPSON]

TUNISIA. President Habib Bourguiba suffered a heart attack in March but recovered and celebrated his 64th birthday in full command of Tunisia's affairs. His partial incapacitation revealed not only his importance to Tunisia but also the risks of one-party totalitarianism. In his absence, the government seized the private newspaper *La Presse* because of its hostile criticism. Its editor, Henry Smadja, though a close friend of the ailing president, was convicted of currency smuggling.

Reaction in Tunis to Israel's attack on the Arabs in June was unexpectedly violent. Rioters sacked the British and U.S. embassies and burned Jewish-owned shops for a full day before the army could restore order. In July, 54 students were sentenced to long prison terms for starting the riots. A new draft law made a year's military service obligatory for males over 20.

Tunisia broke relations with the weakening Yemen republican government in February and with Communist China in September because of its anti-Bourguiba propaganda. A major obstacle to North African unity was removed when the Algerian-Tunisian border dispute was settled. [WILLIAM SPENCER]

Facts in Brief. Population: 4,920,000. Government: President Habib Bourguiba. Monetary Unit: dinar (1=U.S. $1.93). Foreign Trade: exports, $140,000,000; imports, $250,000,000. Principal Exports: phosphates, olive oil, fruits and vegetables.

TURKEY. Premier Suleyman Demirel ordered his nation on a war alert in November, 1967, and hinted Turkey would invade Cyprus to assure the safety of Turkish Cypriots. The killing of 24 persons by Greek Cypriot police had caused mass demonstrations in Turkish cities. The U.S. library at Ankara was stoned. Hurried meetings in December temporarily cooled tempers. See CYPRUS; GREECE.

An improved economy and continuing resentment over lack of Western, principally American, support for its position on Cyprus, pushed the Turks toward nonalignment and closer contacts with Russia. Demirel visited Moscow in September to discuss the $250,000,000 aid program offered to Turkey in 1965. In June, Russia agreed to build a $60,000,000 oil refinery at Izmir.

In contrast, the United States completed the 310-mile Batman-Iskenderun oil pipeline. The U.S. aid program stated that all aid to Turkey would end in 1972 with completion of the $337,000,000 Keban Dam on the Euphrates River. Good harvests and industrial growth pushed the national growth rate to 8.5 per cent. [WILLIAM SPENCER]

Facts in Brief. Population: 33,203,000. Government: President Cevdet Sunay; Premier Suleyman Demirel. Monetary Unit: lira (9=U.S. $1). Foreign Trade: exports, $490,000,000; imports, $725,000,000. Principal Exports: cotton, tobacco, hazel nuts.

TYPHOONS. See DISASTERS; WEATHER.

UGANDA. A plot to assassinate President A. Milton Obote and his cabinet and seize control of the government was discovered in February, 1967. In March, 17 plotters were charged with treason. By June, 22 persons were implicated.

On July 14, the government announced that 123 prisoners detained since the 1966 Buganda riots and fighting would be released; 52 were being held.

A new constitution, providing for a strong central government, was debated from June to September. It abolished the traditional kingdoms of Ankole, Buganda, Bunyoro, and Toro and pensioned the former rulers. Obote was accorded the right to extend the terms of national assembly members, and to hold persons in detention in an emergency. Opposition to this extension of powers was finally overcome, and the constitution was accepted by the assembly on September 8.

Uganda planned to build 24 high schools and expand 15 now operating. The International Development Association loaned $10,000,000 to cover 70 per cent of the cost. [BENJAMIN E. THOMAS]

Facts in Brief. Population: 7,916,000. Government: President A. Milton Obote. Monetary Unit: shilling (7.14=U.S. $1). Foreign Trade: exports, $188,000,000; imports, $120,000,000. Principal Exports: coffee, cotton, copper.

UNION OF SOVIET SOCIALIST REPUBLICS (U.S.S.R.). See RUSSIA.

UNITED ARAB REPUBLIC (U.A.R.), caught unprepared by Israel's swift attack in early June, suffered a military defeat more catastrophic than that of 1956. This time, 90 per cent of the U.A.R. air force was destroyed on the ground before operations even began. U.A.R. tanks and troops were quickly marooned in the Sinai Desert. Israel occupied vast reaches of U.A.R. territory. See MIDDLE EAST.

When news of the disaster reached Cairo, Gamal Abdel Nasser announced his resignation as president. But a vast display of popular support soon changed Nasser's mind. Late in June, he reassumed the presidency and formed a new cabinet.

Evidence of negligence, even incompetence, in the conduct of the war piled up after the defeat. Nasser dismissed the minister of war, Shanshamseddin Badran, as well as his old comrade, Deputy Chief of Staff Marshal Abdel Hakim Amer. He retired more than 40 senior officers. Partly as the result of the dismissals, a plot to overthrow Nasser took shape. But it was leaked to the intelligence services in August, and a wave of arrests followed. Amer subsequently committed suicide.

Economic Woes. The economy was in serious trouble even before the war began in June. In February, the U.A.R. defaulted on two back payments of $4,000,000 owed the International Monetary Fund (IMF). The IMF agreed to a postponement as long as the U.A.R. followed a new economic

Defeat, epitomized by the surrender of Arab soldiers, *above*, was far from the minds of Jordan's King Hussein and U.A.R.'s Gamal Abdel Nasser, *below*, when they signed a defense pact in Cairo in May.

stabilization program. France, Great Britain, and Italy also rescheduled Egypt's debt obligations over a five-year period.

There were a few bright spots. Oil was found in the Gulf of Suez – 100 barrels per hour. The first of 12 hydroelectric turbines in the Aswan High Dam complex began generating electricity. Some 150,000 acres of land, newly irrigated from the dam's channels, were under cultivation.

Except for the United States, which cut off all technical assistance, foreign aid continued to flow into the U.A.R. France contributed 120,000 tons of flour, Poland an $18,000,000 aluminum plant. Russia replaced 80 per cent of the military equipment lost in the war. Britain resumed diplomatic relations, broken off in 1965.

The closing of the Suez Canal because of the war and the loss of $50,000,000 in oil revenues from wells captured by the Israeli in Sinai forced the U.A.R. to adopt a strict austerity program. Expenditures were cut from $900,000,000 to $575,000,000. Tax and price increases were announced. Both Kuwait and Saudi Arabia loaned the U.A.R. $100,000,000. [William Spencer]

Facts in Brief. Population: 31,855,000. Government: President and Premier Gamal Abdel Nasser. Monetary Unit: pound (1 = U.S. $2.30). Foreign Trade: exports, $605,000,000; imports, $1,070,000,000. Principal Exports: cotton, textiles, rice.

UNITED COMMUNITY FUNDS AND COUNCILS OF AMERICA (UCFCA) continued a study of the respective roles played by voluntary and governmental programs in meeting present and emerging health and welfare needs in metropolitan areas. In its first report, the study urged affiliated organizations to (1) stimulate and support innovative programs, (2) press for adoption of creative approaches in new federal programs, and (3) help finance nontraditional programs.

The 1967 Citizens' Conference on Community Planning was held in Oklahoma City, Okla., February 1 to 3. The conference cited the following social service projects for outstanding merit:

- Allegheny County, Pennsylvania, for establishing a new public child welfare agency.
- Cleveland, Ohio, for developing a model for a healthy community.
- Lima and Allen counties, Ohio, for improving and expanding services for the mentally retarded.
- Peoria, Ill., for an agency self-study program.
- Philadelphia, Pa., for a sound program for public and private financing of child care services.

The Very Reverend Robert F. Royster, dean of the Cathedral of St. James, South Bend, Ind., was given the Newton D. Baker II Award for his leadership in providing re-employment services for 4,000 persons left jobless after age 50 when the Studebaker plant closed there. [Joseph P. Anderson]

UNITED NATIONS

A war in the Middle East rocked the world's peace-keeping organization in 1967. Israel's six-day war with the United Arab Republic (U.A.R.), Jordan, and Syria, from June 5 to June 10, ended when the defeated Arabs bowed to a series of cease-fire demands by the UN Security Council. Efforts to bring stability to Arab-Israeli relations dominated UN concerns the rest of the year.

The 10 years of shaky, UN-aided Arab-Israeli co-existence collapsed after the U.A.R., on May 18, formally requested the removal of the UN Emergency Force (UNEF) stationed as a buffer on the U.A.R. side of the Israel border since the 1956 Suez Canal war. Secretary-General U Thant accepted the U.A.R. request, recalling that UNEF was on U.A.R. territory by permission of Cairo. U Thant noted that U.A.R. forces had moved up to the border. He said the new situation endangered UNEF's lightly armed volunteers. U.A.R. forces replaced the blue-helmeted UNEF at the entrance to the Gulf of Aqaba. Cairo announced it was blockading the gulf entrance to Israeli ships and all shipping bound for Israel's southern port, Elath.

The Security Council met in emergency session beginning on May 24. U Thant flew to Cairo and urged all parties to forego belligerence. Israel denounced the blockade as "an act of aggression." Troops massed on both sides of Israel's frontiers. U.A.R. President Gamal Abdel Nasser rejected an appeal from United States President Lyndon B. Johnson to restore UNEF and end the blockade. The Soviet Union accused Israel of provoking the Arabs, with U.S. and British backing. Deadlocked by the big-power split, the Security Council adjourned, without acting, on May 31.

The war began on June 5. Israel and the U.A.R. accused each other of firing the first shots. As Israeli forces swept over the Arabs, the UN Security Council, meeting day and night, issued three unanimous calls for a cease-fire. Russia voted "Yes" along with Western delegates. Jordan accepted first, on June 7; the U.A.R., June 8; and Syria, June 9 and 10. On June 12, the Security Council condemned all cease-fire violations and any further forward military movements. On June 14, the Council called on Israel to ensure the welfare of Arab residents of the occupied areas and to assist the return of residents who had fled. Also on June 14, the Council rejected a Soviet proposal to condemn Israel and to demand Israeli withdrawal from newly occupied territory. The withdrawal demand was backed in the 15-nation Council by Bulgaria, Ethiopia, India, Mali, Nigeria, and the Soviet Union, three votes short of the nine needed for passage.

The Soviet Union, which had seen Israel destroy or capture the jet fighters, tanks, and rockets it had supplied to the U.A.R. and Syria, then called for an emergency session of the 122-nation General Assembly to be attended by the heads of government. The Kremlin and the White House, using the Hot Line, conferred repeatedly during the June

Soviet Foreign Minister Andrei A. Gromyko, center, discusses political strategy with Communist country representatives in a UN lounge.

war, assuring each other they would not take part in the fighting. This refusal to escalate was reaffirmed despite false Arab propaganda charges that U.S. and British planes were providing air cover for Israel, and also during a dangerous period of uncertainty following an attack by Israeli planes on the U.S.S. *Liberty*, an American message-relay ship cruising in the Mediterranean near the Sinai battle area.

Premier Aleksei Kosygin repeated the Soviet demand for UN condemnation of Israel and called for the withdrawal of Israeli forces when the General Assembly met in emergency session June 17 to July 21. Two heads of state, 14 prime ministers, and many other officials attended, but the Assembly was able to muster the necessary two-thirds vote on only two subjects. One involved the status of Jerusalem; the other concerned war victims.

Jerusalem. The Assembly voted 99 to 0, with 20 countries abstaining, to call on Israel to rescind its annexation of the Old City, formerly held by Jordan. (The U.S. abstained.) When Israel ignored the call, the Assembly repeated it on a similar vote, deploring Israel's failure to accept the recommendation. U Thant later reported Israel refused to restore the political division of Jerusalem, while leaving open future arrangements for the Christian, Moslem, and Jewish holy places. Israel declared its policy was to ensure that these places should be scrupulously respected and revered, U Thant reported.

Humanitarian. The Assembly called for relief aid for those who lost relatives, homes, and jobs during the war.

While formal results of the emergency Assembly were meager, it was an exercise that released psychological pressure on the Soviets to "do something" about the Arab defeat. It also made possible the Glassboro, N.J., "summit" meeting of Premier Kosygin and President Johnson.

New violations of the cease-fire were unanimously condemned by the Security Council on October 25, after a major flare-up during which U.A.R. naval rockets sank the Israeli destroyer *Elath* on October 21, and Israeli artillery replied on October 24 by destroying U.A.R. oil refineries in the city of Suez. U Thant increased his UN observers to 90 in nine posts on each side of the Suez Canal. He added four UN helicopters and four patrol boats.

The U.A.R. called the Security Council back into session on the Middle East crisis on November 9, complaining that Israel had refused to evacuate Arab territory taken in June. Israel offered to negotiate a withdrawal from part of the territory, if the Arab nations would accept Israel formally and would deal directly with the Jerusalem government. After strenuous behind-the-scenes diplomacy led by U.S. Ambassador to the UN Arthur J. Goldberg, the Council unanimously adopted a British-sponsored resolution on November 22. It said that peace in the Middle East should be based on the principles of (1) withdrawal of Israeli armed forces from occupied territory; and (2) ending all claims of (Arab) belligerency, and acknowledgment of the sovereignty of every state and its right to live in peace, free from threats or acts of force.

The resolution also affirmed the need to guarantee freedom of navigation through Middle East international waterways–the Gulf of Aqaba and the Suez Canal–the need to achieve a just settlement for the Arab refugees displaced by the 1948 and 1967 wars, and the need to set up demilitarized zones to help guarantee territorial borders. Also under the resolution, U Thant appointed Swedish diplomat Gunnar Jarring as his special representative to promote a peaceful and agreed settlement.

Vietnam. UN attention returned to the war in Vietnam as American delegates began consultations for a Security Council debate requested by the U.S. Senate. The Viet Cong's National Liberation Front (NLF) circulated its latest political program to UN members at the formal request of Romania. The NLF put out feelers on sending lobbyists to the UN. The United States announced it would not object to NLF participation in any Security Council consideration of the war. But the United States opposed purely propaganda exploitation of the UN. U Thant repeatedly appealed for de-escalation, warning that otherwise the war in Vietnam could mark the beginning of World War III.

Cyprus. A war scare over the eastern Mediterranean island was averted through coordinated United States, North Atlantic Treaty Organization (NATO), and UN diplomacy. U Thant sent UN Undersecretary José Rolz-Bennett to help work out an agreement for withdrawal of Greek and Turkish troops stationed illegally on Cyprus. See CYPRUS.

Aden. The 24-nation UN anti-colonialism committee sent a mission to the British protectorate of Aden with orders to arrange a UN-supervised handover to the Cairo-backed Front for the Liberation of South Yemen. The UN mission was snubbed amid rioting. A rival nationalist group, the Front for National Liberation, won out. Britain gave the strategic Southern Arabian territory independence on November 30. As the People's Republic of South Yemen, it became the UN's 123rd member nation. See SOUTH ARABIA, FEDERATION OF.

Congo (Kinshasa). Beset by a rebellion led by white mercenary officers, Congo won new UN Security Council backing. The Council demanded that Portugal cease aiding the mercenaries via neighboring Portuguese Angola. Later, the General Assembly condemned Portugal for resisting national independence movements in Angola, Mozambique, and other overseas territories. The Assembly called on Portugal to let the territories choose their rulers by self-determination. See CONGO (KINSHASA).

South West Africa. A special session of the General Assembly established an 11-nation UN Council "to administer South West Africa until its independence." The new Council was ignored by the Republic of South Africa, which claimed it had absorbed the former League of Nations mandate territory. The Assembly also condemned South Africa's apartheid laws, calling on the United States and Britain, as leading investors, to apply economic pressure. See SOUTH AFRICA, REPUBLIC OF.

Rhodesia. A UN-sponsored economic boycott of Rhodesia failed to overturn the white-minority leadership. The Assembly called on Britain to use force, but London, with American and French backing, declined. See RHODESIA.

Communist China. The Assembly again rejected a proposal to replace Nationalist Chinese delegates with representatives of Communist China. Also on Asia, the Assembly reaffirmed its call for a unified Korea under representative, democratic government, rejecting Soviet demands to end the UN role in Korea. See KOREA.

Disarmament. Hopefully awaiting agreement in the Geneva 18-nation disarmament talks on a new treaty, the Assembly delayed most action. When the Geneva negotiators present a treaty to halt the spread of nuclear weapons to nonnuclear countries, a special Assembly will be called. See DISARMAMENT.

Discriminatory Practices. The Assembly unanimously approved a new Declaration on the Elimination of Discrimination Against Women. It calls on governments, other agencies, and individuals to bring about equal rights for women in all countries. Specified are women's rights to vote and hold public office. The declaration also forbids child marriage.

Population Control. Under auspices of the UN Economic and Social Council, U Thant announced a Population Trust Fund of $5,500,000 for a five-year program to aid population control.

Financial Problems. U Thant reported that 23 countries gave special contributions totaling $23,600,000 during the year. The Soviet Union and France, however, still withheld funds they had promised to help clear up the remaining UN deficit of more than $35,000,000.

World Weather Watch. The UN-affiliated World Meteorological Congress approved a system of weather-watching using satellites and computers.

Elections. For the first time, a Communist, Foreign Minister Corneliu Mănescu of Romania, was elected president of the General Assembly (see MĂNESCU, CORNELIU). He succeeded Abdul Rahman Pazhwak of Afghanistan. New Security Council members elected in 1967 were Algeria, Hungary, Pakistan, Paraguay, and Senegal. They replaced Argentina, Bulgaria, Japan, Mali, and Nigeria. The permanent members are the United States, Britain, the Soviet Union, France, and China, and the remaining members are Brazil, Canada, Denmark, Ethiopia, and India. [MILT FREUDENHEIM]

U.S. GOVERNMENT. Americans, 200,000,000 strong as of November 10, faced rising frustration in 1967 from the threat of inflation, intensified rioting in the urban slums, and the costly, escalating war in Vietnam. News that the Soviets had developed an orbital nuclear bomb and that the Chinese Communist nuclear potential was growing worried many Americans. The Arab-Israeli war in June, and the threat of involvement by the United States and the Soviet Union, added to American anxiety.

On the home front, the report of President Lyndon B. Johnson's crime commission confirmed fears that crime was becoming a major problem in the United States. The "do-little" 90th Congress reflected the national mood and the President's declining popularity. At year's end, Americans were fretting most about rising taxes and prices and the continuing war in Southeast Asia. Looking toward the 1968 election year frenzy, Democrats were wondering whether Mr. Johnson would be able to unite his party behind him, and leading Republicans were jockeying for position on their party's ticket. See ARMED FORCES OF THE WORLD; CONGRESS OF THE UNITED STATES; CRIME; ECONOMY, THE; MIDDLE EAST; PRESIDENT OF THE UNITED STATES; VIETNAM.

The Cabinet. After almost seven years of service, Secretary of Defense Robert S. McNamara announced his resignation late in November to take the presidency of the International Bank for Reconstruction and Development (World Bank). His resignation left four appointees of President John F. Kennedy still serving in the Cabinet: Secretary of State Dean Rusk, Secretary of the Interior Stewart L. Udall, Secretary of Agriculture Orville Freeman, and Secretary of Labor W. Willard Wirtz. Alan S. Boyd took over as Secretary of the Department of Transportation in January. His appointment had been announced in November, 1966.

In February, the President named Acting Attorney General Ramsey Clark as the new Attorney General. Clark replaced Nicholas deB. Katzenbach, who had resigned from the office to become Undersecretary of State.

In May, Alexander B. Trowbridge was appointed Secretary of Commerce, replacing John T. Connor. See CABINET; CLARK, RAMSEY; TRANSPORTATION; TROWBRIDGE, ALEXANDER B.

The Supreme Court. In June, President Johnson appointed U.S. Solicitor General Thurgood Marshall as an Associate Justice on the Supreme Court. Confirmed by the Senate on August 30, Marshall was the first Negro to serve on the high bench. He replaced Justice Tom C. Clark, who retired to avoid any conflict of interest with his son, Attorney General Ramsey Clark. See MARSHALL, THURGOOD; SUPREME COURT OF THE UNITED STATES.

Other Federal Appointments in 1967 included the following:

In January, Deputy Assistant Phil G. Goulding as Assistant Secretary of Defense for Public Affairs, succeeding Arthur S. Sylvester; First Deputy Comptroller of the Currency William B. Camp, as Comptroller, succeeding James J. Saxon. *In March*, Richard B. Smith to the Securities and Exchange Commission (SEC), succeeding Byron D. Woodside; William McChesney Martin, Jr., to continue to serve as chairman of the Federal Reserve Board. *In May*, television actress Betty Furness as the President's Special Assistant for Consumer Affairs (see FURNESS, BETTY); John Charles Daly, Jr., as director of the Voice of America, succeeding John Chancellor. *In June*, Secretary of the Navy Paul H. Nitze as Deputy Secretary of Defense, succeeding Cyrus R. Vance; Clifford L. Alexander, Jr., as chairman of the Equal Employment Opportunity Commission. *In August*, Assistant Secretary of Defense Paul Robert Ignatius as Secretary of the Navy, replacing newly appointed John T. McNaughton, who was killed in a plane crash July 19. *In September*, Dean of Harvard Law School Erwin N. Griswold as Solicitor General, succeeding Thurgood Marshall. *In November*, Stephen J. Pollack as head of the Civil Rights Division of the Department of Justice, succeeding John M. Doar. *In December*, Joe G. Moore, Jr., as commissioner of the Federal Water Pollution Control Administration, replacing James M. Quigley, who resigned.

Major Military Appointments in 1967 included:

In March, Lieutenant General James Polk, as commander in chief of the U.S. Army in Europe, replacing General Andrew O'Meara. *In April*, General Creighton Williams Abrams, Jr., as deputy commander of the U.S. Military Assistance Command in Vietnam, succeeding Lieutenant General John A. Heintges as second in command to General William C. Westmoreland. *In July*, Presidential aide Robert Komer, as civilian deputy to General Westmoreland, with the rank of Ambassador. *In December*, Navy Admiral Horacio Rivero, Jr., as commander in chief for Allied Forces in Southern Europe, replacing Admiral Charles D. Griffin, retiring Feb. 1, 1968.

Major Diplomatic Appointments in 1967 included:

In March, Ellsworth Bunker, as Ambassador to South Vietnam, replacing Henry Cabot Lodge, who became Ambassador at Large; Karl F. Rolvaag, former governor of Minnesota, as Ambassador to Iceland. *In May*, Winthrop G. Brown as state department representative to the 50 states, a new position; William J. Porter, formerly Deputy Ambassador to South Vietnam, as Ambassador to South Korea, succeeding Winthrop Brown. *In November*, former Deputy Secretary of Defense Cyrus R. Vance as the President's special envoy to Cyprus.

Central Intelligence Agency (CIA). In February, Americans were surprised to learn that since 1952 the CIA had been secretly giving money to various organizations for the purpose of offsetting the influence of Communism. On February 13, the National Student Association disclosed the CIA action in answer to a query about an article that was to appear in *Ramparts* magazine. Other organizations made similar disclosures. The money had been channeled through foundations that served as "conduits" for the CIA. Following the recommendations of a three-man committee, the President ordered the CIA to stop giving funds secretly to private voluntary organizations, except for "overriding security reasons." Even in these cases, cultural, educational, and philanthropic groups were to be excluded.

Post Office. On April 3, Postmaster General Lawrence F. O'Brien suggested that the Post Office be removed from the Cabinet and established as a governmental corporation. O'Brien said the postal system should be run by a board of directors with a professional executive. Removed from political pressures, he maintained, hopefully it would be managed more efficiently. Following O'Brien's suggestion, the President set up a 10-man commission on April 8 to make an "exhaustive review" of the postal system. He also asked Congress to raise postal rates to increase revenues by about $800,000,000 annually. The postal increases were approved by Congress on December 12. See POST OFFICE.

Department of Defense. In January, Secretary of Defense McNamara announced plans to consolidate, reduce, or eliminate 39 military bases and other operations run by his department in the United States and overseas. He said this would save $47,400,000 a year. Long a pioneer against segregation in the armed services, McNamara directed in June that all segregated housing near the Andrews Air Force Base in Maryland would be off-limits to servicemen. This was the government's first attempt to enforce off-base desegregation by military order.

Department of Health, Education, and Welfare (HEW). In January, HEW Secretary John W. Gardner announced that federal support for Alabama's welfare programs would stop unless Alabama complied with the nondiscriminatory provisions of the Civil Rights Act of 1964. HEW's zeal for civil rights irritated some Southern Congressmen. In May, Congress directed HEW to consolidate all its civil rights activities. The five bureau chiefs of HEW programs would no longer be involved in asking compliance with the Civil Rights Act. See CIVIL RIGHTS; HEALTH AND DISEASE; MEDICARE; OLD AGE; SOCIAL SECURITY.

Other Government Action in 1967 included:

In January, the Department of State announced that passport applicants would no longer have to sign an oath of allegiance; the National Traffic Safety Agency issued 20 federal standards to further auto, truck, bus, and motorcycle safety. *In February*, the President's Commission on Law Enforcement and Administration of Justice published a 308 page report, with more than 200 specific recommendations for combating crime in America. *In September*, the Federal Communications Commission (FCC) said it would not reconsider its unanimous decision that broadcasters must give free time on radio and television for announcements of the hazards of cigarette smoking to balance the advertisements sponsored by cigarette manufacturers.

Amendment 25 to the United States Constitution concerning succession in case of presidential disability went into effect February 10, with Nevada the 38th state to ratify (see PRESIDENT OF THE UNITED STATES). [CAROL L. THOMPSON]

UPPER VOLTA. See AFRICA.

URUGUAY mourned the loss of its president, Oscar Daniel Gestido, who died on Dec. 6, 1967. Gestido, who had won a five-year term that began on March 1, 1967, had been the first permanent president elected in 15 years. Previously, Uruguay had been governed by a nine-man national government council whose members rotated the presidential office among themselves.

Gestido was succeeded by Vice-President Jorge Pacheco Areco, who indicated he would carry on the late president's austerity program. Gestido had first submitted the program to congress as an emergency bill designed to end frequent strikes and rampant inflation. Congress, however, had opposed the measures, and it was not until October that Gestido invoked his full powers, declared a limited state of siege, and began instituting reforms.

The nation was still struggling against inflation at year's end. The cost of living had risen 107 per cent; the gross national product was down 10 per cent while agricultural production was off an estimated 20 per cent. [MARY C. WEBSTER]

Facts in Brief. Population: 2,806,000. Government: President Jorge Pacheco Areco. Monetary Unit: peso (200=U.S. $1). Foreign Trade: exports, $186,000,000; imports, $164,000,000. Principal Exports: wool, meat, hides and skins.

UTILITIES. See COMMUNICATIONS; ELECTRIC POWER AND EQUIPMENT; PETROLEUM AND GAS.

VENEZUELA. In November, 1967, Venezuela reinstated constitutional rights that had been suspended when a wave of terrorism swept various parts of the country. The suspension, in March, had allowed the authorities to make arrests without warrants, hold suspects for indefinite periods, open private mail, and by-pass other constitutional guarantees.

The terrorism was attributed to Communist infiltrators trained in guerrilla tactics and equipped with weapons in Cuba. At the urgings of Venezuela, the Organization of American States met, and in a subsequent report it confirmed Venezuela's accusation that Cuba had been behind the terrorism.

During the year, the economy recovered from the slump that had overtaken it in 1966. The annual growth rate of the gross national product was up by an estimated 4.5 per cent to 5 per cent for the year. New tax measures had also substantially bolstered government revenues. The crisis in the Middle East in June had helped boost the republic's oil exports and, later in the year, Venezuela amended its laws governing oil to expedite new service contract agreements with private firms for exploration and exploitation of its oil resources. [MARY C. WEBSTER]

Facts in Brief. Population: 9,549,000. Government: President Raúl Leoni. Monetary Unit: bolívar (4.5= U.S. $1). Foreign Trade: exports, $2,713,000,000; imports, $1,331,000,000. Principal Exports: petroleum and petroleum products, iron ore, coffee.

VETERANS and their dependents became eligible for an increase in pension payments and higher financial grants for education and job training through the Veterans Pension and Readjustment Assistance Act of 1967, signed into law August 31. The law was set up to eliminate the inequity of benefits between those currently in the armed forces and those who served during previous wars. Its principal provisions include:

- A cost-of-living increase averaging 5.4 per cent in pensions of veterans, wives, and children, and an average 8.5 per cent increase for widows and children in lowest income brackets.
- An increase of $5 per month in pensions for Spanish-American War widows and widows of earlier wars; pensions for disabled veterans who need regular care were increased the same amount.
- Payment for special educational and medical services, including a $1,600 allowance for the purchase of a specially equipped automobile for seriously disabled veterans serving on or after Jan. 31, 1955.
- An increase in educational assistance allowances for full-time college students. Payments range from $130 per month for a veteran without dependents to $175 for a veteran with two dependents; $10 monthly is added for each additional dependent.
- A provision that veterans who did not finish high school can do so without losing eligibility for subsequent college benefits.
- Payment of allowances for on-the-job, on-the-farm, and commercial flight training to veterans enrolled in federal- or state-approved programs.
- Extension to June 25, 1970, of the period during which World War II veterans can apply for home and small business loans. The Veterans Administration can make direct home loans up to $25,000 in high-cost areas.

The cost of the new benefits was expected to amount to about $286,000,000 for the first year and an estimated $1,500,000,000 over a five-year period.

Veterans returning to civilian life were promised special assistance in getting jobs. President Lyndon B. Johnson directed that the Public Employment Service extend its help beyond the confines of the office and that "every returning veteran be personally contacted by a representative from one of the nation's 2,200 Employment Service offices . . . ."

The Urban League set up 10 Veterans Affairs offices to assist 81 local affiliates in developing a program to ease readjustment to civilian life of Negro servicemen now in Vietnam. The program, financed by a $175,000 grant from the Rockefeller Brothers Fund, will inform Negro veterans about benefits for which they are eligible. It also will encourage them to take advantage of opportunities available for advanced education and on-the-job training.

American Legion reached a record high membership in 1967. There were 2,568,049 members in September, an increase of more than 14,000 over the total for all of 1966. The membership increase was due partly to the large number of veterans of the war in Vietnam who became eligible for membership.

Alan L. Keyes, a 16-year-old Negro from San Antonio, Tex., won the Legion's 1967 National Oratorical title and was awarded a $4,000 scholarship. He also was elected president of the Legion's Boys Nation. Keyes was the youngest boy to win both honors and the first Negro to gain either title.

William Eugene Galbraith of Beemer, Nebr., was elected national commander for 1967-1968.

American Veterans Committee (AVC) began a program to offer information and advice on veterans benefits to new Vietnam veterans. Eugene D. Byrd, of Baltimore, Md., was elected national chairman.

American Veterans of World War II and Korea (AMVETS) urged each state to set aside land dedicated for national cemeteries to assure veterans a burial place of honor. Anthony Caserta, of Alliance, Ohio, was elected national commander.

Veterans of Foreign Wars (VFW) reported its 13th consecutive year of membership growth in 1967. As of June 30, it had 1,356,862 members.

Plans were completed for the erecting in Paris, France, of a memorial statue of General John J. Pershing, who was commander of the American Expeditionary Forces in World War I. Joseph A. Scerra of Gardner, Mass., was elected commander in chief. [JOSEPH P. ANDERSON]

VIETNAM

Vietnam was a name heard throughout the world during 1967. From the depths of Africa and the mountain fastnesses of Latin America, to remote regions of Asia and in every major city of the West, the war in Vietnam was the single most important issue of the year. It was debated everywhere; it was the subject of riots and demonstrations, of earnest and often painful self-inquiry by serious men everywhere. For Americans, Vietnam became the subject of one of the most painful soul-searchings that their nation had ever had to face. And while the controversy boiled all over the world, men fought and died in the rice paddies, jungle thickets, or steep mountains of Vietnam to the constant scream of jet bombers, the clickety-clack of helicopters, and the whomp of bombs, the swoosh of rockets, and the staccato of gunfire.

Regardless of the endless stream of words, the war ground on, broadening and escalating in almost every phase. It was a war that pitted the most modern technological systems against the human sophistication of a grimly determined nation dedicated to Communism. Initially, it was a war of jets, napalm bombs, and electronically controlled rockets turned against Vietnamese peasants who often had

General William C. Westmoreland, U.S. commander in chief in Vietnam, holds a briefing in the White House for the President and his Cabinet.

no more than a handful of rice, a rifle, a grenade, or a mine. Yet as the war progressed both the United States and North Vietnam began to verge toward each other in the techniques of war. The Viet Cong, both in the south and in the north, began to display the most modern weaponry. Most of it was from the Soviet Union and included 140-millimeter rocket-propelled mortar shells, 5-inch fin-stabilized rockets, and the latest in Soviet MIG fighter planes, as well as highly technical anti-aircraft systems. The United States, in turn, began to uncrate older World War II systems as the more modern technology failed to achieve desired results. In fact, both sides were approaching the essence of all war – the pitting of man against man with weaponry becoming a stand-off.

New Areas of Action. The war itself was ushered in with the usual holiday truces that had been declared by both sides as 1966 ended and 1967 began. After the brief pause, the war went back into high gear. Two new areas became the scene of increasing action. The first was the Mekong delta area which, with its rich rice paddies, was a major food source for both the Viet Cong and the South Vietnamese. Repeated sweeps, carried out jointly by U.S. and Vietnamese forces, began to clear the paddies of the Viet Cong. Pacification efforts by the South Vietnamese government also seemed to pay off as hamlet after hamlet began to deny food to the Viet Cong guerrillas and to cooperate with U.S. military forces in their areas.

But the major area of concentrated military action came far to the north and revolved around the so-called demilitarized zone (DMZ). There, a constant build-up of Viet Cong forces – coupled with artillery attacks on Da Nang mounted from the DMZ – prompted the United States to decide it would move its troops into what had been called a "neutral" area. U.S. Marines knifed their way into the DMZ, destroying major enemy artillery emplacements and seizing high ground which controlled the approaches used to the south. The positions were hotly contested by both sides, but the United States had definitely committed itself to the strategy that the DMZ would no longer serve as a sanctuary for the Viet Cong, and its troops remained in the zone.

The newly increased military thrusts, and stiffening Viet Cong resistance meant a steadily increasing need for additional manpower. By the year's end, about 525,000 U.S. servicemen were in the country and there were indications that General William C. Westmoreland, the U.S. commander in Vietnam, might require still more. Nor, of course, were the American troops the sole force engaged in the war. A number of other nations were contributing their support. The Republic of (South) Korea led this effort with two of its best divisions; Thailand sent a special regiment; the Philippines dispatched a special 3,000-man support unit. Both Australia and New Zealand beefed up their support, especially after South Vietnam's Nguyen Cao Ky, then premier, visited both countries early in 1967. These forces, combined with those of the South Vietnamese army, brought the total military strength of the forces fighting the Viet Cong and the North Vietnamese regulars to around 900,000.

Escalation in the Air. Not all the action was being fought on the ground, however, and the air and sea aspects of the war also attracted increasing

Posters, *left*, proclaim merits of candidates in South Vietnamese elections in September. Elected, *above*, were Chief of Staff Nguyen Van Thieu, left, president, and Premier Nguyen Cao Ky, vice-president.

attention in 1967. U.S. naval forces began a more concentrated effort to prevent the Viet Cong from using the seacoasts and waterways as either supply depots or staging areas. Certain areas in the approaches to the port of Haiphong were mined, and a fleet of special armored river boats began patrolling the inland waterways to halt the flow of Viet Cong supplies southward.

Carrier-based planes were extremely active during the year, not only on the tactical but also on the strategic front. The principal air thrusts, however, were mounted by land-based air force units operating almost around the clock. Under its policy of escalating the air war, the United States carried its air raids deep into North Vietnam, often close to the border of Communist China.

U.S. air power based on Guam–and with alternate bases in Thailand, the Philippines, and Okinawa–as well as in Vietnam, carried the air war close to Communist China's border. Targets in the densely populated Hanoi-Haiphong complex, which had formerly been off target, were now subjected to pinpoint raids. So telling were such air strikes that the degree of anti-aircraft resistance was increased both in efficiency and in numbers. The installation of Soviet-made anti-aircraft systems, however, meant increasing losses to U.S. aircraft. Soviet MIGs also stepped-up their scrambles against invading U.S. aircraft.

The effectiveness of the air war could be measured in several ways. First, its success could be gauged by the repeated insistence of North Vietnam that it would not come to the conference table unless the air bombing was halted. A second clue was the announcement by the North Vietnamese government of large-scale evacuations of civilians from the Hanoi area and the dispersal of certain industrial complexes that were prime bombing targets. Despite these reactions, U.S. Secretary of Defense Robert McNamara indicated that the air strikes in the north did not appear to have substantially reduced the flow of men and supplies from the north to the south.

The most heartening aspect of the war from the American point of view was the rising number of desertions from the Viet Cong ranks. Government authorities announced that some 20,398 Viet Cong had surrendered in the first seven months of 1967; by the end of the year the number had increased to an estimated 38,000. A more sobering aspect of the war was to be found in the mounting casualty figures for both sides. According to official U.S. figures released by the Pentagon, 9,353 U.S. servicemen lost their lives in Vietnam in 1967, bringing U.S. losses to a total of 15,997 since 1961. South Vietnamese troop losses over the same seven-year period totaled 53,137, while other allied dead reached 1,700 for the same period. Viet Cong losses in 1967 were 90,401, bringing their death toll to 249,145 since 1961. As a pathetic sidelight of the fighting, an estimated 20,000 Vietnamese civilians had been murdered by the Viet Cong since 1961.

While the mounting casualty figures were one indication of the heightening of the conflict, financial costs were also reflective of the escalation. From 1961 to 1966, the cost of the war in Vietnam to the United States had totaled about $20,000,000,000 for the entire period. In 1967, the cost was running about $2,000,000,000 a month, or $24,000,000,000 a year, and the costs were rising. The U.S. defense budget, as a result of the war, was not far from the peak it had reached in World War II.

Finally, the intensity of the war and the emotions it aroused made it a central issue in virtually every major power in the world. The United Nations (UN) heard endless motions asking that negotiations for peace begin. United Nations Secretary-General U Thant, on a number of occasions, met with representatives of North Vietnam in an effort to get them to the conference table but to no avail. Other nations made similar efforts without success. Nor were the North Vietnamese any more receptive to direct U.S. efforts to negotiate a peaceful settlement. See PRESIDENT OF THE UNITED STATES.

Yet, if peace seemed far away, the newly formed government of the republic of South Vietnam became extremely active on the diplomatic front as it pushed its cause among the peoples of Asia. Premier Ky paid important visits to Australia and New Zealand to enlist additional support for his cause, and was successful. But perhaps the most important support came from Japan. Prime Minister Eisaku Sato, despite violent opposition from Japanese leftists, journeyed to Saigon in the fall and offered to help bring about some form of settlement of the war, and although Japan did not offer any concrete aid to South Vietnam, its expression of interest and open sympathy with the South Vietnamese cause was of great significance to Asians.

The Elections. While the military conflict seemed no closer to resolution during the year, substantial progress was made on the political front. It was in this development that there seemed a hope for the future of South Vietnam. As the year began, Premier Ky had promised to end military rule and provide for a restoration of civilian rule. This was to be done through the formulation and promulgation of a new constitution and the holding of national elections. Few observers, however, were very hopeful that the South Vietnamese military junta would honor its pledge, and there were many reasons, indeed, which could be found for delaying the process.

In a sense, the movement toward civilian government began quietly in January, with the lifting of news censorship on agricultural, educational, and social affairs. For the next two months, the constituent assembly labored hard to draft a new constitution for the country. The final draft, providing for a presidential election within seven months and the end of military rule, was approved by the military without amendment. Although a few Roman Catholics and some Buddhists demonstrated against the secular nature of the constitution, it was accepted in general. On April 2, and continuing for the following four Sundays, local balloting was held to elect people's councils in about 1,000 villages. Next, following the restoration of local village councils, a second series of elections was held between May 14 and June 11 to choose the chiefs of about 4,500 hamlets, thus restoring local government in the rural areas. It was also decided in May that presidential and senatorial elections would be held simultaneously in September. A number of candidates promptly announced they would run for the presidency. Among them were Premier Ky and Chief of State Nguyen Van Thieu (see THIEU, NGUYEN VAN). An open conflict between the two was averted when Premier Ky withdrew his candidacy and, instead, agreed to run for the vice-presidential office. Some 480 announced their candidacy for the 60 seats at stake in the senate.

Early in the campaign, rival civilian candidates charged they and their campaign workers were being intimidated by the military. Although some of the charges had the ring of truth, the government did its best to achieve a relatively free election.

U.S. Troop Strength in Vietnam

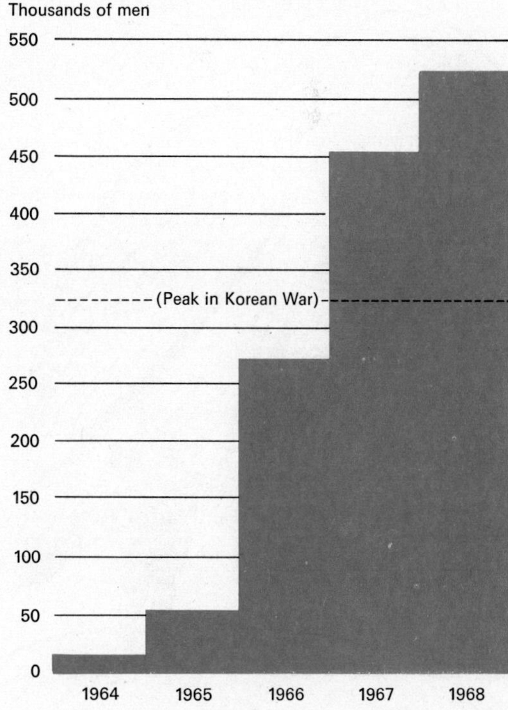

*Announced figure for mid-1968

Helicopters fly in with loads of South Vietnamese Rangers who joined U.S. troops in Operation Shelby, a sweep of the Mekong Delta area southwest of Saigon.

Falconer.

The United States, with its overpowering military presence in South Vietnam, also took steps to make sure there would be no grounds for charges that it had interfered in the election. The U.S. embassy in Saigon announced a 31-hour curfew would be in effect during the election period for all Americans, whether they were employed by the military government or by U.S. firms under government contract in South Vietnam. Similar precautions were extended to cover U.S. troops in the field. Finally, in order to assure the world at large and the U.S. public in particular that the elections were being fairly held, the United States sent a 22-man official observer delegation to South Vietnam. The delegation, headed by former U.S. Ambassador to Vietnam Henry Cabot Lodge, and composed of U.S. Senators and Congressmen, as well as other officials was permitted free access to the election areas. They reported no serious incidents of intimidation or fraud.

On September 3, despite Viet Cong terrorism and threats of reprisals, about 83 per cent of the registered voters streamed to the polls. The joint military-civilian ticket headed by Thieu and Ky won easily, outstripping their nearest rival by more than 830,000 votes. There were, however, post-election difficulties. The runner-up candidate, Truong Dinh Dzu, promptly charged fraud and protested the election. Dzu was detained, subsequently, for illegal financial activities. Tri Quang, the leader of the militant Buddhists in Hue and Da Nang, demanded that the election results be annulled and that the national assembly elections scheduled for September be postponed. Tri Quang, in an attempt to directly embarrass the government, went on a hunger strike before the presidential palace. Although his action revived a certain amount of unrest, the Thieu government remained firm and refused to bend before this pressure. Tri Quang consequently ended his hunger strike after 13 days.

The national assembly elections, held simultaneously with the presidential election, came off without incident. Again, the Thieu-Ky ticket swept the nation and as a result their party held a clear majority in the legislature. President Thieu was inaugurated on October 31. U.S. Vice-President Hubert H. Humphrey represented President Johnson at the inaugural ceremonies.

All in all, under the circumstances, the election was a remarkable demonstration of the ability of Ky's caretaker government to actually move toward civilian rule. Although no one could say that the military influence was thereby lessened, the fact that an election was even held was reassuring. There was further reassurance in the fact that, with an 83 per cent voter turnout, the South Vietnam government was beginning to relate itself to the country as a whole and not just to Saigon. This held out the most important hopes for the future inasmuch as no real decision affecting the war with the Viet Cong was possible without popular support at home.

Domestic Problems. South Vietnam still faced some incredible problems on the domestic front. The continuing inflow of vast U.S. military and economic aid added immeasurably to an inflationary trend. Although rigorous attempts at currency reform did halt the price spiral for a time, the really basic problem of inflation had yet to be solved. A second, and perhaps more important, problem facing the South Vietnamese government was the vast number of refugees it had to care for. In part, the situation was created by both the Viet Cong guerrillas as well as U.S. military strategy. By the end of the year, about 2,000,000 people were classed as refugees. [JOHN N. STALKER]

Facts in Brief. **Vietnam (North)** Population: 20,063,000. Government: President Ho Chi Minh; Premier Pham Van Dong. Monetary Unit: dong (2.94=U.S. $1). Foreign Trade: no statistics available. Principal Exports: agricultural products, minerals.

Vietnam (South) Population: 17,091,000. Government: President Nguyen Van Thieu; Vice-President Nguyen Cao Ky. Monetary Unit: piaster (118=U.S. $1). Foreign Trade: exports, $35,400,000; imports, $370,500,000. Principal Exports: rubber, tea.

Fallen U.S. marines, their bodies piled atop the tank that retrieved them, are carried from a battlefield after bitter hand-to-hand fighting near Con Thien.

VITAL STATISTICS. In 1967, there were fewer births, fewer deaths, more marriages, and more divorces in the United States than in 1966.

There were 2,951,000 live births during the first 10 months of 1967. This is 2.5 per cent fewer than for the same period of 1966. From January through October, there were 1,584,000 marriages, about a 4 per cent increase over the first 10 months of 1966.

U.S. Vital Statistics

	1966	1967
Live births*	3,645,000	3,556,000
Birth rate†*	18.6	18.0
Infant deaths (under age 1)*	86,300	79,200
Deaths*	1,871,000	1,839,000
Death rate†*	9.6	9.3
Marriages*	1,825,000	1,903,000
Divorces (39 reporting areas Jan.-Oct.)	303,428	322,837

*12 months through October. †Per 1,000 population.
Source: U.S. Public Health Service

The January-October cumulative total of divorces was 4.5 per cent above the 1966 period. California led the 39 reporting areas with 59,691 divorces. Through the first 10 months of 1967, there were 1,528,000 deaths, about 30,000 fewer than during the same period in 1966. Heart disease continued as the leading cause of death.

VOCATIONAL EDUCATION. See EDUCATION.

WALD, GEORGE. See NOBEL PRIZES.

WALLACE, GEORGE CORLEY (1919-), former Alabama governor and militant advocate of states' rights and segregation, developed as a possible third-party nominee for President in 1967. His backers claimed that organizations supporting him for President had been set up in 27 states. Virginia's Conservative Party filed petitions for a Wallace-Ronald Reagan national ticket.

Wallace was well received in many of his speaking appearances around the nation, but some of his college campus talks set off a few disturbances. In California, Wallace collected more than the 66,069 signatures to put his American Independent party on the 1968 ballot. Public opinion polls in 1967 indicated that if Wallace ran for the presidency in 1968, he would take more votes from the Republican candidate than from the Democratic nominee.

Wallace served two terms in the Alabama legislature, 1947 to 1953, and was a circuit court judge and in private practice in Clayton, Ala., before serving as governor from 1963 through 1966.

Since Alabama governors cannot succeed themselves, Wallace's wife, the former Lurleen Burns (1926-), ran for the office. She was elected governor in 1966 for a four-year term. Her husband is her $1-a-year administrative assistant. Mrs. Wallace's work has been somewhat hampered by recurring illness. [WALTER F. MORSE]

WAR ON POVERTY. See POVERTY.

WASHINGTON, D.C., will recall 1967 as the end of one era and the beginning of another. President Lyndon B. Johnson successfully reorganized the District of Columbia government through his executive powers, and gave residents a greater measure of self-rule than at any time since 1874, the last year of territorial government. Walter E. Washington was named as the capital's chief executive. Officially the post is commissioner, but Washington was immediately called "mayor." He and a nine-member city council, also appointed by the President, were installed November 3, replacing the much-criticized three-man board of commissioners. Reflecting the city's 62 per cent Negro population, five city councilmen are Negroes, as is Mayor Washington.

In June, Federal Judge J. Skelly Wright, in a far-reaching decision, ruled that segregated Washington schools resulting from all-Negro neighborhoods are as unconstitutional as deliberately segregated schools (see EDUCATION). He ordered the transfer of students from crowded slum area schools to less-crowded schools in white populated neighborhoods. In the face of the ruling, School Superintendent Carl Hansen resigned. He was replaced by William Manning of Lansing, Mich. [DONALD W. LIEF]

WATER AND FLOOD CONTROL. See CONSERVATION.

WATER BALLET. See SWIMMING.

WATERWAYS. See TRANSPORTATION.

WEATHER. Representatives of the 125 member nations of the World Meteorological Organization (WMO) met in Geneva, Switzerland, in April to plan an international weather research effort to begin in 1972. The plan is known as the Global Atmospheric Research Program (GARP). It will consist of three phases: intense study of equatorial zone weather phenomena in the Pacific, starting in 1972; broader observations in the Pacific, starting in 1973; and the study of weather throughout the world in areas now unreported, to begin in 1976. At least four satellites will be used in the study as well as several thousand balloon-borne telemetry systems to gather and relay data to computers for analysis.

Numerical Forecasting. Also discussed at the WMO meeting was a powerful new forecasting tool that is replacing long-standing, hand-plotted weather map forecasting methods. Called "numerical forecasting," the method uses mathematical equations to determine weather changes on a global scale. Such equations can accurately predict the behavior of world weather when sufficient data is provided on temperatures, wind velocities, and humidity from many points throughout the world. Meteorologists foresee the day when such data will be collected from land, sea, and air with no reporting points more than 400 miles apart.

Computers that are at least 100 times faster than any present computer will be required to carry out

Fast-moving traffic in Chicago was immobilized by a January blanket of snow that piled up an all-time city record of 23 inches.

the calculations for global numerical forecasting in a practical amount of time. Such computers will be available by 1972. When a world-wide data system is established, numerical forecasting is expected to produce global forecasts two weeks in advance with 90 per cent accuracy.

Numerical forecasting was in limited use in 1967 to predict the behavior of high and low pressure areas and storms over the United States. Similar forecasting methods were also used in Britain, Japan, Norway, Russia, and West Germany.

GARP Study. A rehearsal for GARP took place in February and March, 1967, when about 80 meteorologists gathered weather data from a mid-Pacific area known as the equatorial trough. The experiment was prompted by the launching of Applications Technology Satellite I (ATS-I), which was placed in orbit 23,000 miles above the mid-Pacific in December, 1966. Planes, balloons, radiosondes, island bases, and the oceanographic vessel *Surveyor* were used to collect weather data that were correlated with the time-lapse cloud photos transmitted from ATS-I.

The study accumulated new knowledge of tropical cumulus-cloud growth in the influential zone. Prior to this, it was known that tropical cumulus clouds play an important role in determining world-wide weather patterns, but little was known of their size and formation.

ATS-I was used later in the year as part of an experimental system for providing early warning of potential floods. Automatic measuring devices were stationed at sites in Arkansas, California, and Oregon to record river level and accumulated precipitation at 15-minute intervals. The measurements were sent to ATS-I periodically on radio command and then relayed to a National Aeronautics and Space Administration (NASA) receiving station at Mojave, Calif.

Soviet Meteorology. According to the National Science Foundation's eighth annual report on weather modification, the Soviet Union devotes more manpower and money to weather modification research than does the United States. Evgenii K. Fedorov, director of the Leningrad Institute for Experimental Meteorology, outlined Russian proposals for large scale climate control at the Fifth World Meteorological Congress, held at Geneva, Switzerland, in April. Included was a proposal for forced melting of the Arctic icecap, resulting in a warmer Arctic Ocean.

ESSA IV, the fourth in a series of Environmental Survey Satellites, was launched in January, 1967. The satellite transmitted its first pictures on January 28 of storm systems over the North Atlantic. The spacecraft has taken over the duties of ESSA II, launched in February, 1966. [JAMES A. PEARRE]

WEIGHT LIFTING. See SPORTS.

WEST INDIES drew a considerable amount of international attention in 1967 because of a wave of independence that swept the area. In March, five more tiny West Indies islands–Antigua, Dominica, Grenada, St. Kitts-Nevis-Anguilla, and St. Lucia–ceased to be British colonies and became "associated states" within the British Commonwealth. Each island had control of its own domestic affairs and the right to become totally independent whenever it chose.

Bahamas, The

The Bahamas was rocked by a scandal with international implications in 1967. The scandal involved financial dealings between former government officials and gamblers and land developers. As a result of an investigation, Prime Minister Lynden O. Pindling announced in July that the Bahamian residence permits of three American gamblers would not be renewed when they expired in 1968.

Pindling, the 36-year-old leader of the Progressive Liberal party, had been sworn in as Bahama's second prime minister in January. His was the first all-Negro cabinet in the centuries-old history of the Bahama Islands.

Facts in Brief. Population: 151,000. Government: Governor Sir Ralph Grey; Prime Minister Lynden O. Pindling. Monetary Unit: dollar ($1.04=U.S. $1). Foreign Trade: exports, $19,000,000; imports, $105,000,000. Principal Exports: fish, vegetables, pulpwood, salt.

Jamaica
In February, Jamaica elected a new government for the first time since the country achieved full independence in 1962. The voters chose Donald Sangster, head of the Jamaican Labor party, to succeed Prime Minister Sir Alexander Bustamente. In April, Sangster died of a brain hemorrhage. He was succeeded by Hugh Shearer, who called for continued economic growth based on foreign investment, tourism, and expanded industry. Overcrowded living conditions, unemployment, and illiteracy, however, continued to impede the nation's growth.

Facts in Brief. Population: 1,850,000. Government: Governor-General Sir Clifford Campbell; Prime Minister Hugh Shearer. Monetary Unit: pound (1 = U.S. $2.40). Foreign Trade: exports, $225,000,000; imports, $321,000,000. Principal Exports: aluminum, bauxite, sugar.

Trinidad and Tobago
In August, Trinidad and Tobago celebrated the fifth anniversary of its independence from Great Britain. Under the leadership of Prime Minister Eric Eustace Williams and his People's National Movement party, the political situation was stable.

Facts in Brief. Population: 1,051,000. Government: Governor-General Sir Solomon Hochoy; Prime Minister Eric Eustace Williams. Monetary Unit: dollar (2 = U.S. $1). Foreign Trade: exports, $426,000,000; imports, $457,000,000. Principal Exports: petroleum, sugar.

WESTMORELAND, WILLIAM CHILDS (1914-), commander of U.S. forces in Vietnam since 1963, became the first battle commander in history to address Congress during wartime when he spoke on April 28, 1967, to a joint session. He reported progress in the conflict with North Vietnam and declared, "Backed at home by resolve, confidence, patience, determination, and continued support, we will prevail over the Communist aggressor." General Westmoreland returned to Washington, D.C., in July, when he reportedly sought more troops.

Westmoreland was born March 26, 1914, in Spartanburg County, S.C. He was graduated from West Point in 1936. During World War II, he served in North Africa, Italy, France, and Germany. During the Korean War, he led a paratroop regiment. From 1958 to 1960, he commanded the 101st Airborne Division. Early in his command, five paratroopers were killed by freak winds in a mass practice jump. After that incident, Westmoreland always jumped ahead of his men in order to test wind conditions.

In 1960, at the age of 47, he became the second-youngest superintendent of West Point. He left West Point in 1963 for Fort Bragg, N.C., where he was the commanding general of the XVIII Airborne Corps. He was then assigned to Vietnam. Westmoreland has three children. [WALTER MORSE]

WILDLIFE. See CONSERVATION.

WRESTLING. See SPORTS.

WYETH, ANDREW (1917-), became America's most popular and highly paid artist following shows in New York City, Philadelphia, Baltimore, and Chicago. In 1967, the William A. Farnsworth Library and Art Museum in Rockland, Me., paid $65,000, an all-time record for a living American artist, for one of his paintings. It was titled *Her Room.*

Wyeth was born and still lives at Chadds Ford, Pa. (pop. 140), on July 12, 1917. He studied under private tutors, and began his career as a landscape painter in 1936. In 1937, he held his first one-man show in New York City. He is married, and one of his two sons, James, is also an artist. His wife, the former Betsy James, is the subject of many of his paintings. His father also was a noted artist.

Wyeth is noted for scenes of loneliness, which he paints with realism. "You don't just admire a Wyeth painting," says one admirer, "you can see it and smell the grass; feel the afternoon, the quiet."

Among the honors and awards he has received for his work are the Obrig Prize of the American Watercolor Society (1945), the Medal of Merit of the American Academy of Arts and Letters (1947), and the Gold Medal of the National Institute of Arts and Letters (1964).

Wyeth, however, seems unaffected by the wide acclaim for his work. "I'm just a country boy," he says. "I think I'll stay right here in Chadds Ford, out of all the hullabaloo."

YEMEN. The civil war between royalists and republicans remained at a standstill. Until October, 1967, the United Arab Republic (U.A.R.) troops had held their positions around Sana'ā', Ta'izz, and Al Ḫudaydah, leaving the rest of the country to the royalists. U.A.R. aircraft gas-bombed several royalist-held villages during the year.

The massive defeat of U.A.R. forces in the Arab-Israeli war in June shifted the stalemate. The U.A.R. agreed at the Arab summit conference in August, at Khartoum, Sudan, to withdraw its 25,000 troops from Yemen if Saudi Arabia stopped financing the royalists. But when representatives from Iraq, Morocco, and Sudan went to Sana'ā' to supervise the withdrawal, President Abdullah al-Sallal refused to receive them. The U.A.R. withdrawal was completed on November 30. In November, too, the army ousted al-Sallal; Abdul Rahman al-Iryani became the new republican council president. With U.A.R. withdrawal, hostilities resumed. In December, army chief Hassan al-Amri became premier.

Russia agreed to build a fish meal processing plant. Soviet geologists discovered large coal and limestone deposits. [WILLIAM SPENCER]

Facts in Brief. Population: 5,235,000. Government: Premier Hassan al-Amri; Republican Council President Abdul Rahman al-Iryani. Monetary Unit: riyal (1.1 = U.S. $1). Foreign Trade: no information available. Principal Exports: coffee, hides and skins, salt.

YOUNG MEN'S CHRISTIAN ASSOCIATION (YMCA) took the final legal step in 1967 to end racial segregation in the YMCA movement when delegates to the 41st annual meeting of the National Council, held in Philadelphia, Pa., May 12 to 14, voted to amend its constitution by a vote of 294 to 11. Under the change, only associations "which annually certify that their policies and practices provide that eligibility for membership or participation in a program shall be without any discrimination on the basis of race, color, or national origin" may apply for council membership.

The council also received reports of significant ecumenical developments, among them a series of meetings between the National Board of the YMCA and the National Conference of Catholic Bishops. These were viewed as having special importance in developing more productive relationships between the YMCA and leaders of Roman Catholicism.

The YMCA World Service announced the completion of its "Buildings for Brotherhood" project, which raised $19,000,000 for the construction of 112 YMCA buildings in 35 countries.

George E. Gullen, Jr., Detroit, Mich., was reelected president of the National Council of the YMCA. Vice-presidents were: Bernard F. Jefferson, Los Angeles; Richard Kautz, Muscatine, Iowa; Oscar T. Martin II, Springfield, Ohio; and William R. Robbins, Sr., Miami. [JOSEPH P. ANDERSON]

YOUNG WOMEN'S CHRISTIAN ASSOCIATION (YWCA) adopted a new statement of purpose to broaden its membership and to outline its image as a movement open to change. The action was taken by delegates to the YWCA's 24th triennial convention held in April in Boston, Mass. The redefined purpose was included in a statement presented by a national commission that had been studying the YWCA as a Christian movement since 1964.

The approved statement of purpose is as follows: "The Young Women's Christian Association of the U.S.A., a movement rooted in the Christian faith . . . seeks to respond to the barrier-breaking love of God in this day. The association draws together into responsible membership women and girls of diverse experiences and faiths, that their lives may be open to new understandings and deeper relationships and that together they may join in the struggle for peace and justice, freedom, and dignity for all people."

Delegates to the convention elected Mrs. Robert W. Claytor of Grand Rapids, Mich., as president. Mrs. Claytor is the first Negro to hold the office. Elected as vice-presidents were Mrs. Ambrose L. Cram, Jr., Bronxville, N.Y.; Mrs. Paul McClellan Jones, White Plains, N.Y.; Mrs. Ralph A. McCanse, Madison, Wis.; Mrs. Fred J. Church, Natick, Mass.; Mrs. Howard Grimes, Dallas, Tex.; and Mrs. Chester Root, Los Gatos, Calif. [JOSEPH P. ANDERSON]

YOUTH ORGANIZATIONS expanded their activities during 1967 and experimented with new programs to reach young people in low-income neighborhoods. Special attention was given to problems of youth employment, with agencies providing work opportunities in camps and clubs, and assisting their members in finding jobs in business and industry.

Through conferences, seminars, and workshops, opportunities were provided for discussion of the major changes taking place throughout the world. Also discussed was the need to eliminate barriers that separate blighted communities from affluent communities.

Boy Scouts of America were hosts to nearly 12,000 Scouts and Scout leaders from 100 countries at the 12th Boy Scout World Jamboree, held at Farragut State Park, Idaho, August 1 to 9. The gathering–first World Jamboree to be held in the United States–celebrated the 60th anniversary of the experimental Boy Scout camp on Brownsea Island off the English coast. It was established by Lord Baden-Powell, the founder of the Scouting movement.

The Jamboree theme, "For Friendship," was reflected in the daily program and in activities carried on before and after the gathering. Every participant from another country was invited to visit in the home of a U.S. Scout. Also six hundred U.S. Eagle Scouts and their leaders served as "hosts" to each Scout troop from a visiting association.

Boys' Clubs of America undertook a special program to find opportunities for summer employment for their teen-age members. The organization also set a record during the first six months of 1967 for building clubs and camps. A total of $16,600,000 was authorized to cover 97 building and development projects. Among the buildings completed in 1967 was the Herbert Hoover Boys' Club, on the site of the old Busch Stadium in St. Louis, Mo.

The 61st Annual Boys' Club Convention was held in Pittsburgh, Pa., May 1 to 4. Gerald Simila, 17, from the Denison, Tex., Boys' Club was named "1967 Boy of the Year."

Camp Fire Girls continued to work on the problem of potential delinquency. Special programs were developed in disadvantaged neighborhoods to prevent explosive unrest among adults and teen-agers.

A demonstration research project carried on by the Los Angeles Area Camp Fire Council ended in 1967. It made possible a group treatment service for girls from deprived families who had problems in school performance and social relationships.

The Quadrennial Camp Fire Girls Conference was held in Kansas City, Mo., November 5 to 9. Delegates heard that planning was in its final stages for "Adventure '68," the national Horizon Club Conference to be held July 8 to 27, 1968.

Four-H Clubs assisted with planning and coordination of the first National Outlook Conference on Rural Youth, called by President Lyndon B.

Vice-President Hubert H. Humphrey told of his days as a scoutmaster at the 12th World Boy Scout Jamboree held in Farragut Park, Idaho, in August.

Girl Scouts of the United States of America held their 1967 National Senior Girl Scout Conference at Marian College, Indianapolis, Ind., August 7 to 17. There were 200 Senior Girl Scouts and adults, representing councils in all major metropolitan areas, in attendance. They made plans to start a recreational and teaching program for Chinese immigrant children in San Francisco, Calif.; to create "friendship troops" linking Negro and white members in Houston, Tex.; and to provide portable service centers in Detroit, Mich.

The 1967 All-States Encampment was again held in Nantahala National Forest near Andrews, N.C. The project is designed to test the camper's initiative and resourcefulness under primitive conditions, as well as to prepare experienced adults to direct similar events in their own regions.

Girls Clubs of America (GCA), Inc., began a physical fitness program, with the aim of preparing 100,000 club members to be examples and teachers of physical fitness throughout the United States and Canada. The program was launched at three training institutes, held in different sections of the country and conducted by Bonnie Pruden, an authority on physical fitness.

The organization also acquired a permanent home in 1967 with the purchase of a building in New York City that was to serve as its national headquarters. [JOSEPH P. ANDERSON]

Johnson. It was held in Washington, October 23 to 26. The delegates agreed to promote state and local action to develop effective programs to meet the needs of rural young people.

A delegation of 35 4-H Club members began their International Farm Youth Exchange (IFYE) experience with an orientation program to prepare them for a six-month stay in another country. They then lived with host families in Argentina, Australia, Botswana, Chile, Costa Rica, Cyprus, India, Jamaica, Kenya, Nepal, New Zealand, Paraguay, Thailand, and Uruguay.

The 46th National 4-H Club Conference was held in Washington, D.C., April 23 to 28.

Future Farmers of America (FFA) embarked on a program of study and preliminary architectural work toward the development of a $2,000,000 leadership training center to be located on former George Washington property about 15 miles southwest of Washington, D.C. The center would have meeting and housing facilities for about 300 persons.

Delegates to the annual convention at Kansas City, Mo., October 11 to 13, defeated constitutional amendments to give larger states more representation in the delegate body and to permit participation by girls in FFA activities at the national level. David J. Mosher, 19, of Greenwich, N.Y., was named Star Farmer of America. Greg Lynn Bamford, 20, of Haxtun, Colo., was elected president.

YUGOSLAVIA. President Tito was re-elected to his fourth term in office in May, 1967. While continuing his policy of economic liberalization, he also sought to extend the political reforms launched after the dismissal of Alexsandar Ranković in 1966.

A major change in the role and character of the Yugoslav Communist party was introduced during the year in order to make it a "guiding force" rather than the dominating element in the political system. In the elections held for the federal assembly, there were more candidates than seats to be filled and official party candidates were defeated in a number of constituencies. In the top echelons of the government some party veterans were removed and younger nonparty members replaced them. The state criminal code was revised to eliminate the role of the security police and extend the citizen's right of defense. Measures also were taken to free more prices from central control.

One-Party System. The measures taken by the government testified to the seriousness of Tito's efforts to make Yugoslav Communism more democratic. It was equally clear, however, that he had no intention of abandoning the one-party system. On more than one occasion, Tito reasserted the party's authority and called for drastic action against dissidents. The release of Milovan Djilas after nine years of imprisonment was counterbalanced by a second trial of the young journalist and professor, Mihajlo

Mihajlov, and his imprisonment for four and one-half years for "hostile propaganda." When several Croatian writers called for wider rights for the Croatian language, disciplinary measures were taken and grave warnings issued against national discord.

Nonaligned Policy. Yugoslavia maintained its nonaligned and independent position but moved closer to the Soviet Union on a number of issues. Tito paid a visit to Moscow in January, and returned in October for the 50th anniversary celebrations. He also attended the conference in Moscow on the Middle East crisis, endorsed the denunciation of Israeli aggression, and broke off relations with Israel. Belgrade was later the site of a Communist conference to discuss aid for the Arab states. Tito visited the United Arab Republic (U.A.R.) and conferred with President Gamel Abdel Nasser twice during the year.

Yugoslavia continued to oppose the convening of an international Communist conference and refrained from attending the Karlsbad meeting. Relations with the United States were marred by attacks on some consulates in the United States, by some of Belgrade's policies, and by a congressional cut in U.S. food aid to Yugoslavia. [H. GORDON SKILLING]

Facts in Brief. Population: 20,308,000. Government: President Josip Broz Tito; Premier Mika Spiljak. Monetary Unit: dinar (12.5=U.S. $1). Foreign Trade: exports, $1,220,000,000; imports, $1,575,000,000. Principal Exports: meat, machinery, ships and boats.

ZAMBIA supported the United Nations (UN) and Great Britain in their blockade of white-dominated Rhodesia. Relations between Zambia and Rhodesia were tense throughout the year. In April, white miners in Zambia's copper belt went on strike to protest the detention of five white men charged with spreading alarm and despondency and with spying for Rhodesia. In June, the Rhodesian Railways, which formerly operated in both countries, was divided into separate lines. Zambia's airways withdrew from Central African Airways, which had been operated jointly by Malawi, Rhodesia, and Zambia.

Zambia still managed to export copper and import petroleum. A UN mission visited Zambia in February to study problems caused by the sanctions against Rhodesia. Britain provided aid of more than $35,000,000, mostly to improve supply routes. On March 3, Zambia awarded an $11,000,000 contract to a Japanese company to construct a fertilizer plant. Negotiations were started with several countries to help establish an iron and steel industry as well as to develop a large new agricultural region on the Kafue Flats located in the southwestern part of the country. [BENJAMIN E. THOMAS]

Facts in Brief. Population: 3,983,000. Government: President Kenneth David Kaunda. Monetary Unit: pound (1=U.S. $2.79). Foreign Trade: exports, $691,000,000; imports, $388,000,000. Principal Exports: copper, zinc, tobacco.

ZOOLOGY. Prehistoric man's failure to practice conservation caused the extinction of hundreds of species of large prehistoric mammals over the past 50,000 years, according to a theory advanced in 1967 by geochronologist Paul Martin of the University of Arizona. He based his theory on the fact that the pattern of mammal extinction throughout the world corresponded consistently with the arrival of prehistoric hunters. Many scientists have attributed the disappearance of these prehistoric species to sudden climatic changes and to the advance and retreat of glacial ice sheets. Martin pointed out in November, however, that the large mammals that perished during the Ice Age of the late Pleistocene Epoch had survived the earlier ice ages.

Whales. Conservationists continued to express alarm over a decline in the world whale population, despite limitations set on catches. At the annual meeting of the International Whaling Commission (IWC), held in London, England, in June, the ban on killing humpback whales in the North Pacific was extended for three more years.

Dolphin Talk. Marine biologists, in 1967, trained dolphins to respond to artificial "words" transmitted through water by electronic devices. They hoped soon to be able to determine whether dolphins could be trained to respond to the sounds with speech sounds of their own as well as through actions. This attempt to establish two-way spoken communication was conducted at the University of Hawaii's Oceanic Institute on Coconut Island near Oahu, Hawaii, under a contract with the United States Navy. Dolphins communicate with whistles of varying frequency. The ultimate goal of the research program is to train dolphins to convey meaningful information to human beings by their form of speech.

Snake Tastes. Gordon M. Burghardt of the University of Chicago found that snakes, like some children, are born with definite likes and dislikes for various foods. His studies showed that these food preferences vary from species to species.

Burghardt found that no amount of force-feeding could coax a snake into changing its tastes. A snake born with a preference for earthworms, for example, but force-fed nothing but liver for the first six months of its life, would still gobble up earthworms at its first chance. The reason for this is that snakes are equipped with a chemical sense organ, called Jacobson's organ, that tells them what is good among the available foods.

To be sure that the snakes were responding only to a chemical cue, Burghardt prepared water-based extracts of various snake foods–crickets, fish, frogs, mice, slugs, and worms. The newborn snakes were presented with cotton swabs that had been dipped in one of the several extracts. A cricket-eating Western smooth green snake would rapidly lick a swab that was ignored by a worm-eating Eastern plains garter snake. [JAMES A. PEARRE]

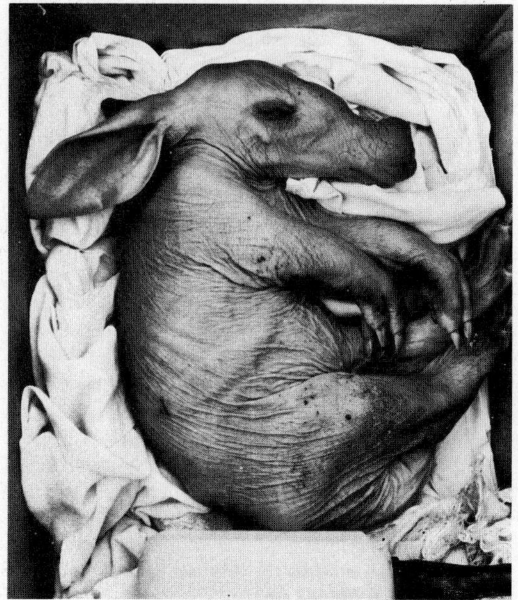

Flip Schulke, *Life* © Time Inc.

A baby albino gorilla, *left*, and an aardvark born in the Miami Zoo, *right*, made headlines in 1967. The gorilla was found in Spanish Equatorial Guinea after its mother had been shot.

ZOOS AND AQUARIUMS. Discovery of the world's first known white gorilla was announced in February, 1967. The gorilla was found in Río Muni, a province of Spanish Equatorial Guinea, on the west coast of Africa. The male albino gorilla was found clinging to the back of its dead mother, shot by a plantation owner for raiding his banana grove. The baby gorilla was only about two years old and had white fur, pink skin, and blue eyes. It weighed 19 1/2 pounds. Ordinarily, gorillas are black.

The baby gorilla was sold to a naturalist who runs an animal acclimation station in Río Muni for the zoo at Barcelona, Spain. It was then shipped to the home of the Barcelona Zoo's chief veterinarian, Roman Luera Carbo, where it is living until it can be moved to the zoo for public viewing. Nicknamed Little Snowflake, the gorilla will not be fully grown until it is 12 to 15 years old. At that time, it may weigh as much as 500 pounds.

Albinoism is extremely rare among primates, but the fact that the baby was clinging to its mother when found shows that other gorillas did not reject it because of its unusual color.

Zoo Births. Twin gorillas were born in captivity at the Frankfurt Zoo in West Germany, on May 3. They were the first such twins to be born in a zoo and are both females. One of the gorillas weighed three pounds, nine ounces; the other weighed three pounds, three ounces.

At the zoo in Melbourne, Australia, iguanas were hatched for the first time in captivity. The female iguana laid 38 eggs, each about the size of a large hen's egg. Zoo officials placed them in jars of damp sand in their artificially heated reptile house, and the baby iguanas hatched progressively in a two-day period.

Rosie, a whooping crane at the San Antonio, Tex., zoo and the only female whooping crane in captivity, laid two eggs that hatched in July. The eggs aroused interest among naturalists because the known whooping crane population before the hatching totaled only 57—45 free and 12 in captivity. But Rosie proved to be an uninterested mother, and after the first one was born, she accidentally sat on it and crushed or suffocated it. When the second hatched, zoo officials took the chick away from her to save its life.

The Bronx Zoo in New York City reported in August that two scarlet ibises were hatched successfully. The scarlet ibis is a rare type of wading bird, native to Trinidad and other islands in the West Indies. These are the first hatched in the United States, though they have been successfully hatched in the zoos at Frankfurt and Stuttgart, Germany.

Remodeling. An indoor jungle where llamas may roam free and there will be a rainstorm every hour is one of the many exhibits planned for the Brookfield Zoo near Chicago. [R. Marlin Perkins]

Section Four

World Book Supplement

In its function of keeping all *World Book* owners up-to-date, *The World Book Year Book* herewith offers significant new articles from the 1968 edition of *The World Book Encyclopedia*. These articles should be indexed in *The World Book Encyclopedia* by means of *The Year Book* cross-reference tabs.

544 **Earth**

A new article by Samuel P. Ellison, Jr., of the University of Texas.

561 **Education**

Four timely articles chosen from new material in the field of education.

561 Learning

563 Motivation

564 Perception

566 Testing

568 **Heart**

A new article by Dr. Michael E. DeBakey and Dr. Edward B. Diethrich.

579 **Sports**

Articles on three of the fastest growing sports in the United States.

579 Skiing

582 Soccer

590 Surfing

586 **Supreme Court of the United States**

An article by William R. Forrester of the Cornell University Law School; critically reviewed by Associate Justice Byron R. White.

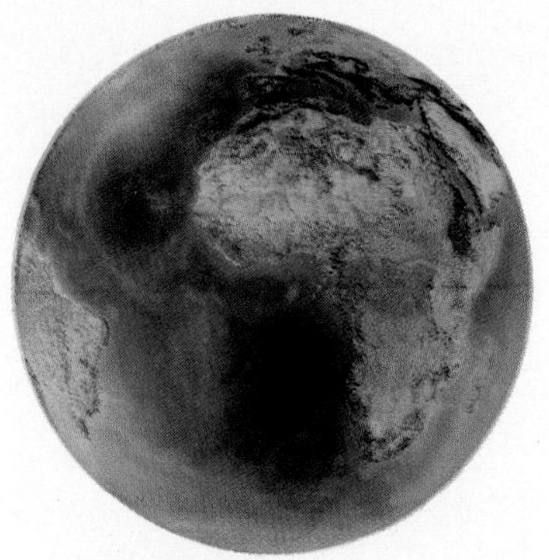

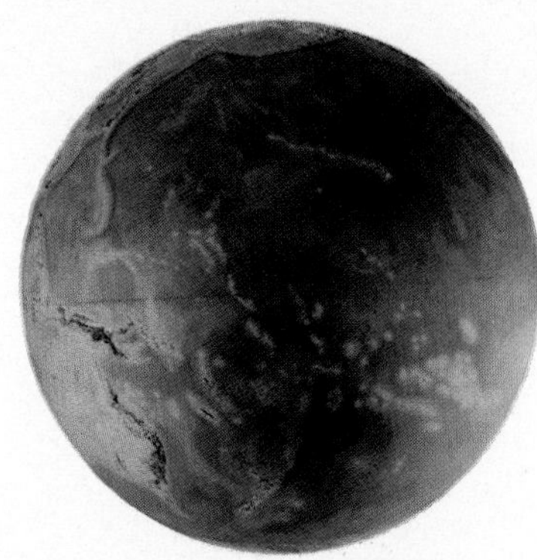

EARTH

EARTH means many things to the people who live on it. To a farmer, earth is rich soil. To a road builder, earth means tons of hard rock. For a sailor, earth is water as far as he can see. A pilot's view of earth may include part of an ocean, a mountain, and patches of farmland. An astronaut speeding through space sees the earth's round shape and the outline of lands and oceans beneath the clouds. All these ideas help describe the earth, but they do not tell what it is.

The earth is a huge ball covered with water, rock, and soil, and surrounded by air. It is one of nine *planets* that travel through space around the sun. The sun is a star—one of billions of stars that make up a *galaxy* called the Milky Way. The Milky Way and billions of other galaxies make up the *universe.*

Samuel P. Ellison, Jr., the contributor of this article, is Professor of Geology at the University of Texas.

The planet earth is only a tiny part of the universe, but it is the home of man and many other living things. Animals and plants live almost everywhere on the earth's surface. They can live on the earth because it is just the right distance from the sun. Living things need the sun's warmth and light for life. If the earth were too close to the sun, it would be too hot for living things. If the earth were too far from the sun, it would be too

NASA

A Photograph of the Earth shows clouds over the Pacific Ocean. The Gulf of California and part of Mexico can be seen through a break in the clouds, *upper right.* A space satellite took this picture from a height of 22,300 miles.

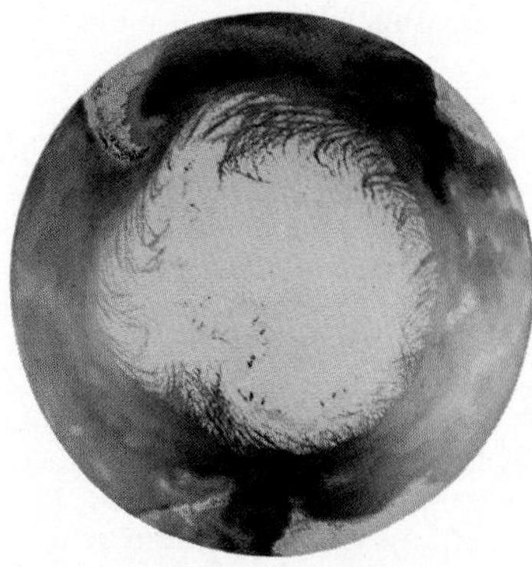

Globes © Rand McNally & Co.

Looking at the Earth. Between each of the four views, *far left*, the earth has turned a fourth of the way around. The two views *above* show regions around the North Pole, *left*, and South Pole, *right*.

cold for anything to live. Most living things also must have water and a gas called oxygen, or they will die. The earth has plenty of both. Water covers most of the earth's surface. Oxygen is mixed with other gases in the air that surrounds the earth.

All life on the earth is found on and above a skinlike *crust* made of rock. The crust lies below all soil, and under the hills, plains, deserts, lakes, rivers, and oceans that we know as the earth's surface. Beneath the crust, the earth is a hot, lifeless ball of rock and metal that no man has ever seen.

The earth is always moving. It spins like a top and also travels around the sun at the same time. We use these two motions of the earth to measure the length of days and years. One day is the time it takes the earth to spin around once. One year is the time it takes the earth to travel once around the sun. The earth, like some of the other planets, has a ball-shaped moon traveling around it. The other planets that have moons all have two or more.

The study of the earth is called *geology*, and scientists who study the earth are geologists. This article deals with the planet earth as it is studied in geology. For information on the earth as the home of man, see the article on World in World Book.

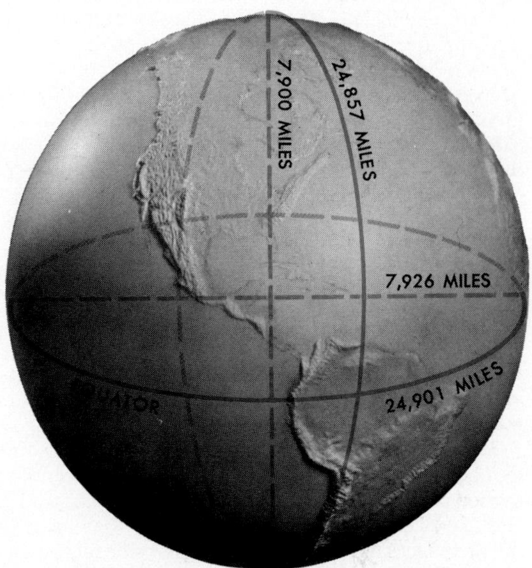

The Earth Is Not Perfectly Round. Distances measured through the poles are shorter than those measured at the equator.

THE EARTH AT A GLANCE

Age: 4,500,000,000 (4½ billion) years.

Weight: 6,600,000,000,000,000,000,000 (6.6 sextillion) tons.

Motion: *Rotation* (spinning motion around an imaginary line connecting the North and South poles)—once every 23 hours, 56 minutes, 4.09 seconds. *Revolution* (motion around the sun)—once every 365 days, 6 hours, 9 minutes, 9.54 seconds.

Size: *Polar Diameter* (distance through the earth from North Pole to South Pole)—7,899.86 miles. *Equatorial Diameter* (distance through the earth measured at the equator)—7,926.39 miles. *Polar Circumference* (distance around the earth measured through the poles)—24,857 miles. *Equatorial Circumference* (distance around the earth measured along the equator)—24,901 miles.

Area: *Total Surface Area*—196,940,400 square miles. *Land Area*—approximately 59,000,000 square miles, about 30 per cent of total surface area. *Water Area*—approximately 138,000,000 square miles, about 70 per cent of total surface area.

Surface Features: *Highest Land*—Mount Everest, 29,028 feet above sea level. *Lowest Land*—shore of Dead Sea, 1,286 feet below sea level. *Average Height of Land Above Sea Level*—2,757 feet.

Ocean Depths: *Deepest Part of Ocean*—Challenger Deep in Pacific Ocean southwest of Guam, 36,198 feet below surface. *Average Ocean Depth*—12,450 feet.

Temperature: *Highest*, 136° F. at Azizia, Libya. *Lowest*, −126.9° F. at Vostok in Antarctica. *Average Surface Temperature*, 57° F.

Atmosphere: *Height of Atmosphere*—99 per cent of the atmosphere is less than 100 miles above the earth's surface, but particles of the atmosphere are 1,000 miles above the surface. *Chemical Makeup of Atmosphere*—78 per cent nitrogen, 21 per cent oxygen, 1 per cent argon with small amounts of other gases.

Chemical Makeup of the Earth (in per cent of the earth's total weight): oxygen 46.6, silicon 27.7, aluminum 8.1, iron 5.0, calcium 3.6, sodium 2.8, potassium 2.6, magnesium 2.1, and other elements totaling 1.5.

The Earth in the Universe

The Earth as a Planet. The earth ranks fifth in size among the planets. It has a diameter of about 8,000 miles. The diameter of Jupiter, the largest planet, is more than 10 times that of the earth. The diameter of Mercury, the smallest planet, is less than half the diameter of the earth.

The earth is about 93 million miles from the sun. Only two planets—Mercury and Venus—are closer to the sun. Scientists believe these planets have surface temperatures of 700° or 800° F. (about 370° to 430° C.). The average temperature of the earth's surface is 57° F. (about 14° C.). All the other planets except Mars are very cold, with temperatures ranging from −225° to −325° F. (about −140° to −200° C.).

The temperature on Mars varies greatly. It drops to perhaps −150° F. (−101° C.) on the side of Mars away from the sun. But it may reach as high as 80° F. (27° C.) at noon on the Martian equator. If the atmosphere of Mars contained oxygen, scientists might expect to find living things on Mars similar to living things on the earth. But only the earth's atmosphere contains enough oxygen to support life as we know it. The atmosphere of Mars contains carbon dioxide and water vapor. The atmosphere of Venus consists mainly of carbon dioxide. Jupiter, Saturn, Uranus, and Neptune all have atmospheres that include methane, a gas that makes up most of the natural gas found on the earth. Mercury and Pluto have no known atmosphere.

How the Earth Moves. The earth has three motions. It (1) spins like a top, (2) travels around the sun, and (3) moves through the Milky Way galaxy with the rest of the solar system.

The earth spins around its *axis*, an imaginary line that connects the North and South poles. The spinning motion makes the sun appear to move from east to west, and causes day and night on earth. The "day" side of the earth faces the sun, and the "night" side faces away from the sun. As the earth spins eastward, some parts of the earth move from the night side to the day side. People who live in these regions see the sun "come up" in the east. Other parts of the earth move from the day side to the night side. Persons living there see the sun "set" in the west. It takes 23 hours, 56 minutes, and 4.09 seconds for the earth to spin around once. This length of time is called a *sidereal day*. See DAY.

The earth travels 595 million miles around the sun in 365 days, 6 hours, 9 minutes, and 9.54 seconds. This length of time is called a *sidereal year*. During this period, the earth travels at an average speed of 66,600 miles an hour. As the earth moves around the sun, the night sky changes slowly. Some groups of stars become visible in the night sky, and other groups disappear into the sunlit day sky. See YEAR; ASTRONOMY (Skies of the Seasons).

The path of the earth around the sun is called the earth's *orbit*. The orbit lies on an imaginary flat surface that cuts through the sun. This surface is the earth's *orbital plane*. The earth's axis does not stick straight up from the orbital plane. It tilts about 23½° from the straight-up position. This tilt and the earth's motion around the sun cause the change of seasons. For example, the northern half of the earth tilts toward the sun in summer. In winter, the northern half of the earth tilts away from the sun. See SEASON.

The whole Milky Way galaxy spins around like a giant wheel once every 200 million years. The solar system is about three-fifths of the way from the center to the edge of the galaxy. The solar system and the earth revolve around the center of the galaxy at a speed of 43,000 miles an hour.

The Earth and Its Moon. The earth has only one moon. Mercury, Venus, and Pluto have none. All the other planets have two or more moons. The earth's moon has a diameter of a little more than 2,100 miles—about a fourth that of the earth. The sun's gravity acts on the earth and the moon as though they were a single body with its center about 1,000 miles below the earth's surface. This spot is the earth-moon *barycenter*. It is the point of balance between the heavy earth and the lighter moon. The earth and the moon circle around the barycenter as they travel around the sun. The path of the barycenter around the sun is a smooth curve. Because the earth circles the barycenter, the earth follows a "wobbly" path around the sun.

THREE MOTIONS OF THE EARTH

WORLD BOOK diagram by Cynthia Fujii

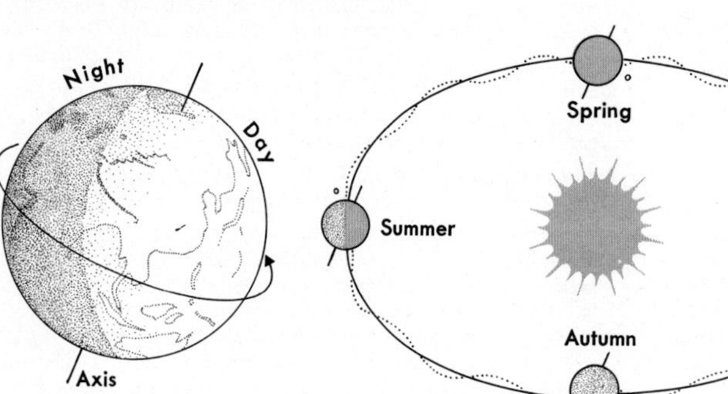

The Earth Spins around its axis once every 24 hours. This motion creates day and night.

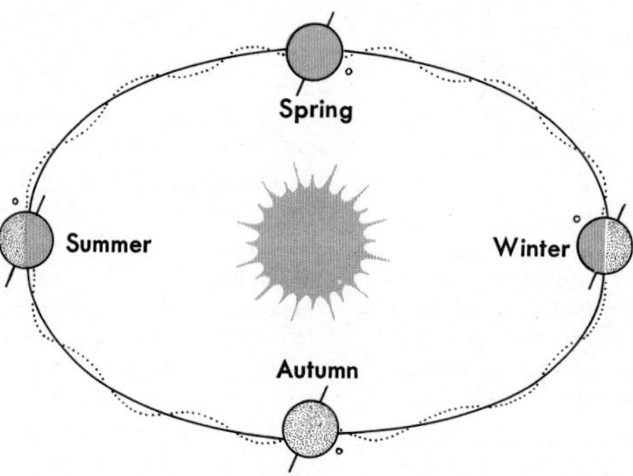

The Earth Travels Around the Sun once every 365 days. This motion creates years. The moon's gravitation makes the earth follow a wobbly path, *dotted line.*

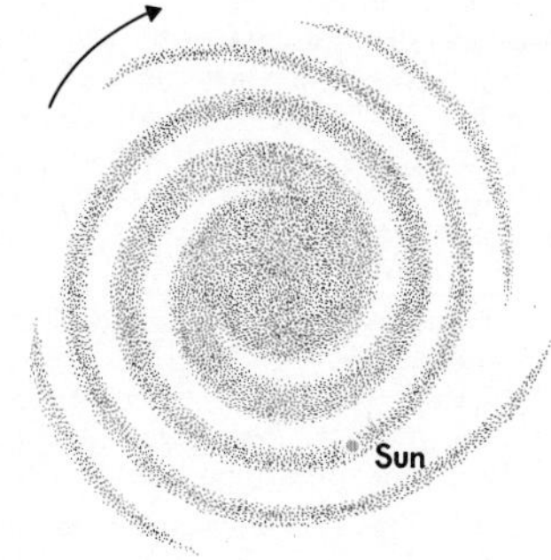

The Earth Moves with the Sun as the sun circles the center of the Milky Way once every 200 million years.

EARTH / *Outside and Inside the Earth*

The Earth's Shape and Size. The earth may be thought of as a ball with the North Pole at the top and the South Pole at the bottom. Halfway between the poles is an imaginary circle around the earth called the *equator*. The earth is not perfectly round, but is slightly flattened at the poles. Thus, the diameter of the earth measured from pole to pole is shorter than the diameter measured at the equator. At the poles, the earth's diameter is 7,899.86 miles. This distance is 26.53 miles shorter than the diameter of the earth at the equator—7,926.39 miles.

Similarly, the distance around the earth is shorter at the poles than at the equator. At the poles, the earth measures 24,857 miles around. At the equator, it measures 24,901 miles around. It takes almost two days for a jet airplane to fly around the earth. An astronaut in space circles the earth in about 90 minutes.

The equator does not mark the earth's "fattest" part. The distance around the earth is greatest along a circle slightly south of the equator. The earth's shape is somewhat like that of a pear, which has its fattest part just below its "middle." But this bulge is so small that the earth still looks like a perfectly round ball.

The Earth's Atmosphere. Air surrounds the earth and extends as far as 1,000 miles above the surface. This air is called the *atmosphere*. Nitrogen makes up 78 per cent of the atmosphere, and oxygen makes up 21 per cent. The remaining 1 per cent consists mainly of argon and small amounts of other gases. Air also contains water vapor and particles of dust. Clouds float in the lowest part of the atmosphere, called the *troposphere*. Wind, storms, and other features of the earth's weather all take place in the troposphere. Other parts of the atmosphere are above the troposphere. The air gets thinner and thinner the farther it is from the earth. About 1,000 miles above the earth, the atmosphere gradually fades into space. See AIR.

The Earth's Surface is about 70 per cent water—almost all of it in the ocean. Land makes up only about 30 per cent of the earth's surface. The oceans have an average depth of 12,450 feet. The deepest part of any ocean is the Challenger Deep, a steep-sided valley in the floor of the Pacific Ocean southwest of Guam. The bottom of this valley lies 36,198 feet below the ocean's surface. The earth's land rises to an average height of 2,757 feet above the level of the oceans. The highest land is the top of Mount Everest in Asia, 29,028 feet above the sea level. The lowest spot on earth, the shore of the Dead Sea in southwest Asia, is 1,286 feet below sea level.

Oceans, lakes, rivers, and all other bodies of water and ice make up a part of the earth called the *hydrosphere*. The waters of the hydrosphere are important in many ways. Man, animals, and plants need water to live. Plants use water to make food, and are eaten by man and animals. Water also wears away the rocks that make up the land. It slowly turns rocks into soil that is necessary for growing crops. Oceans and other large bodies of water also help control the earth's weather and climate. The temperature of water does not change so fast as that of land. Wind blowing over a large body of water can keep land from becoming extremely hot or extremely cold.

The largest bodies of land are called *continents*. Their surfaces vary from low, green valleys to high, rocky mountains where almost nothing grows. Antarctica, the continent at the South Pole, is completely buried under a layer of ice and snow. Near the equator, thick forests cover hot and rainy parts of Africa and South America. Temperatures at the earth's surface range from the highest ever recorded, 136° F. at Azizia, Libya, to the lowest, −126.9° F. at Vostok in Antarctica.

All the earth's animals and plants live on the earth's surface or close to the surface—underground, underwater, or in the atmosphere. The region where life is found is called the earth's *biosphere*.

The Earth's Crust. Continents and *ocean basins* (lands beneath the oceans) are part of a rocky "skin" that surrounds the main body of the earth. This skin is called the earth's *crust*. The thickness of the crust varies from about 5 miles under the oceans to about 20 miles under the continents. Temperatures within the deepest parts of the crust may reach as high as 1,600° F. (870° C.)—hot enough to melt rocks.

WHERE OCEANS OVERFLOW THE LAND

The dark gray areas of this map show where the continents extend under the oceans, forming *continental shelves*. The curving lines in the Pacific Ocean represent deep valleys in the ocean floor.

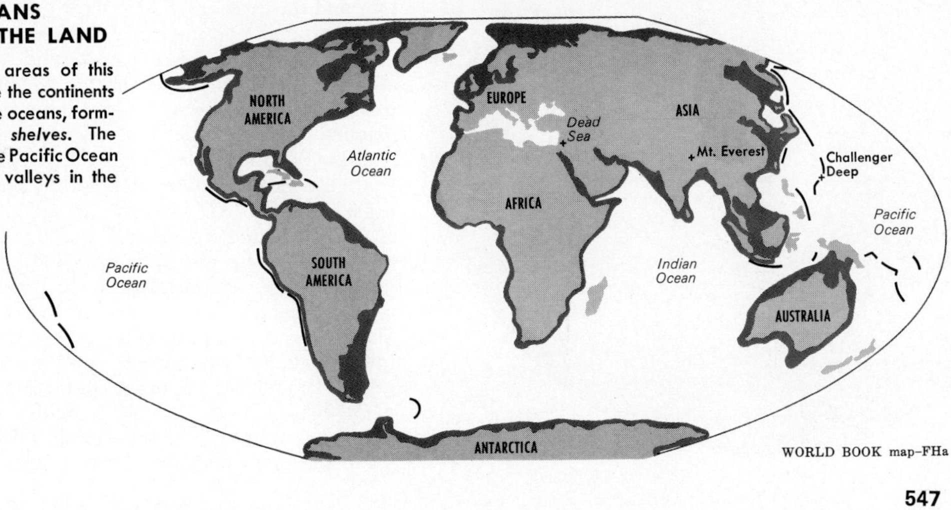

WORLD BOOK map-FHa

THE EARTH'S THREE KINDS OF ROCKS

Pictured *below* are an igneous rock (granite), a sedimentary rock (sandstone), and a metamorphic rock (quartzite). All were made from the same basic materials.

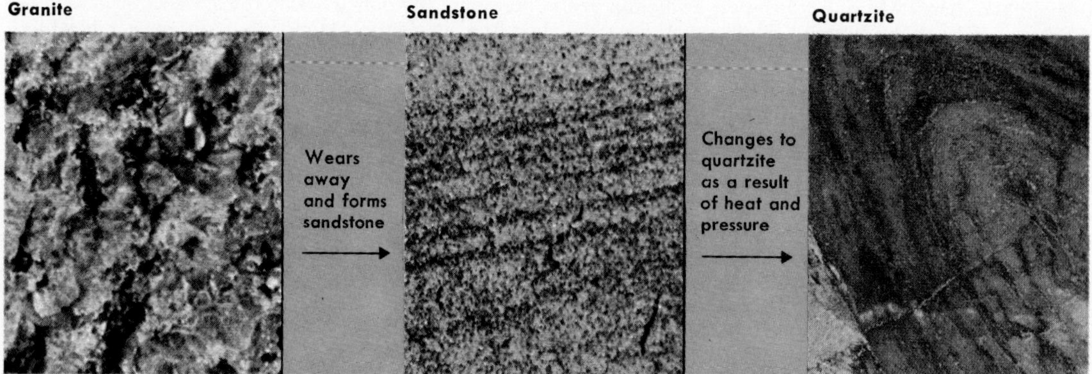

WORLD BOOK photos courtesy the Field Museum of Natural History, Chicago

The crust is made up of three kinds of rock: *igneous*, *sedimentary*, and *metamorphic*. Igneous rocks were formed when melted rock deep inside the crust cooled and hardened. Sedimentary rocks developed from material worn away from the land by water and the weather. This material collected in low places, layer upon layer, and hardened into rock. Many sedimentary rocks contain shells, bones, and other remains of living things. Such remains, or the outlines of remains in sedimentary rocks, are called *fossils*. Metamorphic rocks were formed deep in the crust when igneous and sedimentary rocks were chemically changed by heat and the weight of the crust pressing on them.

INSIDE THE EARTH

Beneath the earth's skinlike crust are the hot, lifeless mantle, the outer core, and the inner core. Scientists learn about the inside of the earth by studying how earthquakes affect the crust.

WORLD BOOK illustration by Raymond Perlman

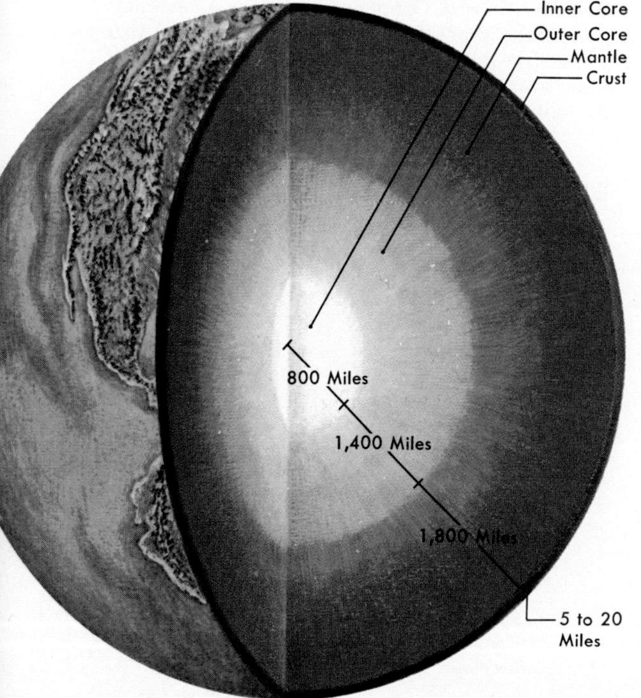

Rocks in the earth's crust are made up mostly of two chemicals—silicon and oxygen. These two chemicals account for more than 74 per cent of the crust's weight. The next most common chemicals in the crust are, in order: aluminum, iron, calcium, sodium, potassium, and magnesium.

Beneath the continents, the crust is divided into two rock layers. The continents make up a layer consisting chiefly of silicon, oxygen, aluminum, calcium, sodium, and potassium. This rock layer is called *sial*. The sial, in turn, rests on a layer consisting mainly of silicon, oxygen, iron, and magnesium. This layer of rock is called *sima*. The sima layer extends under the oceans and forms the ocean basins. There is no sial under the oceans. The bottom of the crust is called the *Mohorovičić discontinuity* or *Moho*. The Moho marks the boundary between the crust and the inner parts of the earth.

Inside the Earth. Beneath the crust, the earth is a ball of hot rock and metal. By studying the records of earthquakes, scientists have learned that the inside of the earth is divided into three parts: the *mantle*, the *outer core*, and the *inner core*. These three parts, together with the crust, make up the earth's *lithosphere*.

The mantle is a thick layer of solid rock below the crust. It goes down about 1,800 miles. The rock in the mantle is made of silicon, oxygen, aluminum, iron, and magnesium. The upper part of the mantle has a temperature of about 1,600° F. (870° C.). This temperature gradually increases down through the mantle to about 4,000° F. (2,200° C.) where the mantle meets the next lower section, the outer core.

The outer core begins about 1,800 miles below the earth's surface. Scientists believe the outer core is about 1,400 miles thick and is made of melted iron and nickel. The temperature of the outer core ranges from about 4,000° F. (2,200° C.) in the uppermost parts to perhaps 9,000° F. (5,000° C.) in the deepest parts.

The ball-shaped inner core lies within the outer core and makes up the center of the earth. The boundary between the outer and inner cores is about 3,200 miles

THE EARTH'S CRUST HAS TWO LAYERS

Continents have an upper layer of granitelike rocks called *sial*. The lower layer, called *sima*, extends under the oceans and consists of materials similar to hardened lava. Continents appear to "float" like icebergs in the heavier rock of the mantle.

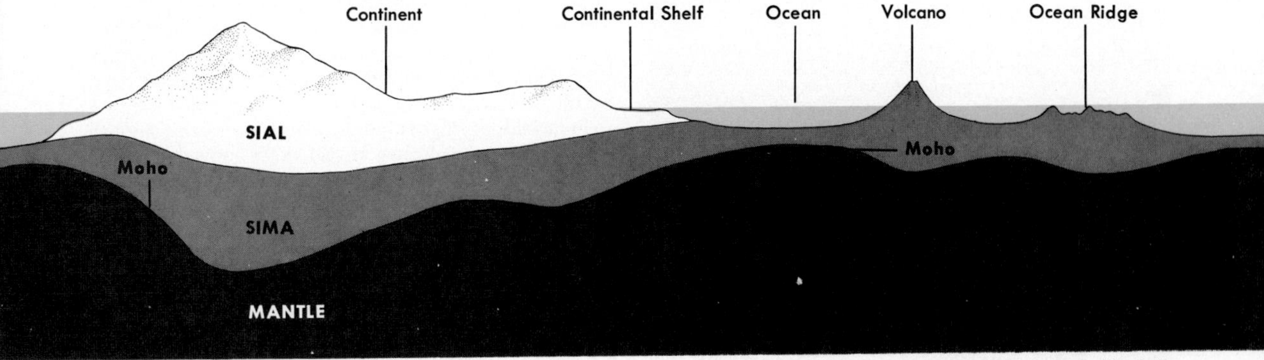

WORLD BOOK diagram by Cynthia Fujii

below the earth's surface. The center of the inner core is about 800 miles below this boundary, or about 4,000 miles below the earth's surface. Scientists believe the inner core consists of solid iron and nickel. The temperature in this core may be as high as 9,000° F. (5,000° C.).

The Earth's Gravity is the force that causes objects to fall when they are dropped. Gravity acts between all bodies in the universe. The earth and the other planets travel around the sun because gravity pulls them toward it. In the same way, gravity keeps the moon traveling around the earth instead of flying off into space. On the earth, gravity works to change the land's surface. For example, it makes rivers and glaciers move downhill. This motion wears away the land and carries soil and rock to low places on the surface.

The force of gravity varies slightly on the earth. It is stronger at the poles than at the equator because the poles are closer to the earth's center. For the same reason, gravity is stronger at sea level than on mountaintops. Gravity also increases above sections of the crust that contain large amounts of heavy rocks. See GRAVITATION.

The combined gravities of the earth and moon cause the ocean level to rise and fall twice a day in *tides*. The earth's rock crust rises and falls in a similar way, but this motion is extremely slight. See TIDE.

The Earth's Magnetism. The earth spins around an imaginary line that connects the North Pole and the South Pole. Near each of these poles, the earth also has a *magnetic pole*. The magnetic poles act like the ends of a magnet and make compass needles point north. The north magnetic pole is under Prince of Wales Island in Canada, about 1,000 miles from the North Pole. The south magnetic pole is in Wilkes Land, a part of Antarctica, about 1,600 miles from the South Pole.

The magnetism of the earth is similar to that which surrounds a coil of wire when electricity flows through it. Scientists believe the magnetism surrounding the earth comes from electricity flowing within the earth's inner core. The earth's magnetic force operates in a region called the *magnetosphere*, which has a shape somewhat like that of a doughnut.

The earth's magnetism acts on bits of matter called *electrons* and *protons* that move through space. The Van Allen radiation belts are parts of the magnetosphere that contain large numbers of particles. Disturbances on the sun cause changes in the magnetosphere. For example, sunspots may cause particles in the magnetosphere to produce the *aurora borealis* (northern lights).

WORLD BOOK diagram by Cynthia Fujii

THE EARTH HAS A MAGNETIC "TAIL"

The earth's magnetism operates in a region called the *magnetosphere*. Radiation from the sun acts like a wind that blows the magnetosphere into a long tail. The magnetosphere includes the Van Allen radiation belts, which consist of large numbers of electrons and protons trapped by the magnetism.

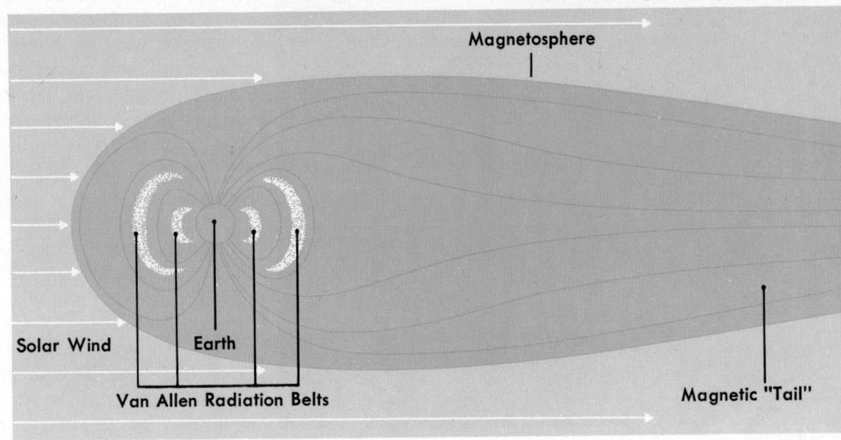

Williams, APF

Rocks Begin to Crumble when rootless plants called *lichens* spread over them. Lichens produce an acid that dissolves parts of rocks. Bits of rock then mix with decayed matter, forming soil.

Solid Rock Once Filled the Grand Canyon, but the Colorado River wore away the rock bit by bit. In some parts of the canyon, the river has cut its way more than 7,000 feet down.

Josef Muench

The earth changes continuously. Some changes, such as the wearing away of the Grand Canyon, take millions of years. Others, including earthquakes, happen in a few minutes. Rocks tell the story of these changes. When geologists discover seashells in rock high on a mountain, they know the mountain was once a lowland, covered by the sea.

Four main kinds of changes affect the earth's surface: (1) weathering, (2) erosion, (3) mass movement, and (4) changes in the earth's crust.

Weathering is the breaking up of rocks by such forces as water, ice, chemicals, growing plants, and changing temperature. Soil is an important product of weathering. Soil consists of bits of weathered rock mixed with living things and their remains. Geologists speak of two types of weathering: (1) physical weathering, which is also called mechanical weathering, and (2) chemical weathering.

Physical Weathering breaks rock into pieces. One of the main causes of physical weathering is the formation of ice in cracks within rocks. First, water soaks into the cracks. Then, if the temperature falls low enough, the water near the rock's surface freezes and seals in the water that is deep in the cracks. After the rest of the water freezes, it expands in the cracks and may push hard enough to split the rock. In a similar way, tree roots may grow through cracks in rocks and cause the rocks to split.

Chemical Weathering affects the substances that make up rocks and soil. One of the main causes of chemical weathering is the dissolving action of water. Rain, streams, and seawater dissolve some substances from rock, and may cause the remaining substances to crumble. For example, water dissolves the mineral feldspar from granite, leaving grains of the mineral quartz, a form of sand.

Erosion is a combination of weathering and the movement of weathered material from one place to another. Eroded material generally moves from high places to low places on the earth's surface. For example, erosion wears away rock from mountainsides and carries it down into valleys. Water, glaciers, and wind are three important causes of erosion.

Erosion by Water combines the weathering action of water with water's ability to move pieces of rock. Rainwater drains from the land into streams that flow downhill. The moving water cuts into the land as it wears away soil and rock. The faster the stream flows, the more it wears away the land around it. Bits of rock picked up by the stream add to the grinding action. Soft rock wears away first, and then hard rock. Sometimes this action leaves towering masses of hard rock standing alone on a plain. The rock remains long after the disappearance of the water that wore away soft surrounding rock. The Grand Canyon of the Colorado River is a spectacular example of water's eroding power. There, after millions of years, the river has cut more than a mile deep into the earth.

When rivers reach the sea, they leave behind the materials they picked up while flowing over the land. At the mouths of some rivers, this material forms a fertile land area called a *delta*. At the mouths of other rivers, the materials are swept away into the ocean. All along the seashore, water gradually changes the shape of the land. Waves and tides wear away the rocky shore and create sand bars, beaches, cliffs, and headlands that stick out into the sea.

Water moving underground also changes the land. Spouts of water called *geysers* shoot out of the earth and carry minerals and bits of rock to the surface. Underground rivers dissolve limestone and other rock, and form caves deep in the ground.

Erosion by Glaciers has shaped and leveled large areas of the earth's surface. The northern midwestern plains of the United States were formed hundreds of thousands of years ago when huge glaciers slid over the land and smoothed it out. Today, glaciers cover all of Antarctica and most of Greenland. In mountainous areas throughout the world, glaciers flow among rocky peaks like frozen rivers.

Mountain glaciers form when fallen snow builds up and becomes so thickly packed that it turns into ice. Many glaciers are more than 1,000 feet thick. Gravity pulls a glacier downhill. The thick, heavy ice scrapes away any soil in its path and digs U-shaped valleys in the mountains. It grinds away rock, sometimes polishing it smooth and at other times leaving deep scratches. Pieces of rock become frozen inside the ice and add to the grinding action. When the glacier melts, it drops the rock and soil that were frozen inside it. Water from the melting ice then spreads out the loose material.

Erosion by Wind involves the movement of dust and particles of sand. Wind also carries ashes from volcanoes great distances before dropping them to earth. During dry seasons, strong winds pick up large quantities of soil and blow it away. In deserts and on some beaches, windblown sand forms hills called *dunes*. Some dunes move little by little because the wind blows sand from one side of the dunes to the other. Some of these dunes cover and destroy forests. Sand particles driven by wind also scrape and wear away rock surfaces.

Mass Movement is the slipping of large amounts of rock and soil, as occurs in a landslide or a mudslide. Most landslides and other forms of rapid mass movement take place along steep-sided hills and mountains. Slow movement, such as the gradual downhill creep of soil, takes place unnoticed on gently sloping land. Weathering and erosion help loosen large chunks of earth and start them sliding downhill. Earthquakes also sometimes cause sections of hills and mountains to break off and slide down.

Mass movement may produce a variety of effects. For example, a landslide may fall across a river, damming the water and causing it to form a lake. The slipping of soil down the sides of a river valley gradually widens the valley and makes the sides slope more gently. One type of landslide called a *rock glacier* moves through mountains in much the same way that an ice glacier does. A rock glacier consists mostly of rocks. Pieces of ice mixed with the rocks make it possible for the rock to flow downhill.

Changes in the Earth's Crust include earthquakes and volcano eruptions. They also include many land motions that occur so slowly that they are unseen or hardly noticed. Many of the earth's major land features result from changes in the crust. The Rocky Mountains and other mountain ranges were formed millions of years ago when the crust buckled, wrinkled, and snapped. Even today, islands rise from the ocean when a new volcano shoots out lava and ashes from deep inside the crust.

The earth's crust may move in any direction. It can move up or down, and sometimes causes sections of land to rise or fall a fraction of an inch in a year. The crust also tilts, changing a level plain to a gentle slope. It may move sideways along great cracks, changing the course of a river or shifting part of a mountain range.

Changes in the earth's crust were largely responsible for the development of the continents. See the section *The Shaping of the Continents* in this article.

HOW TWO KINDS OF MOUNTAINS WERE FORMED

The simplified diagrams *below* show the crust of North America and two kinds of mountains formed by changes in the crust.

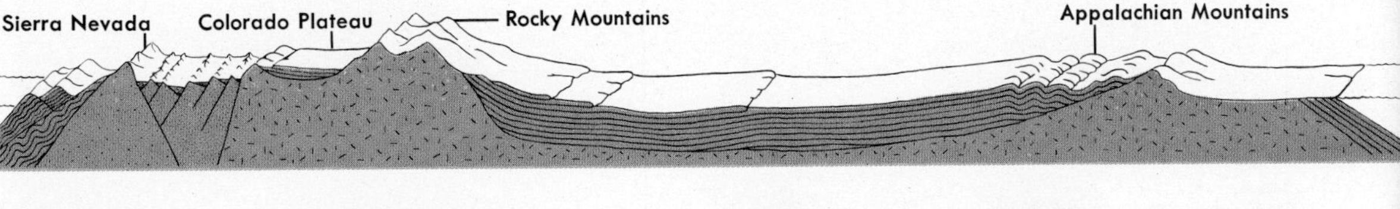

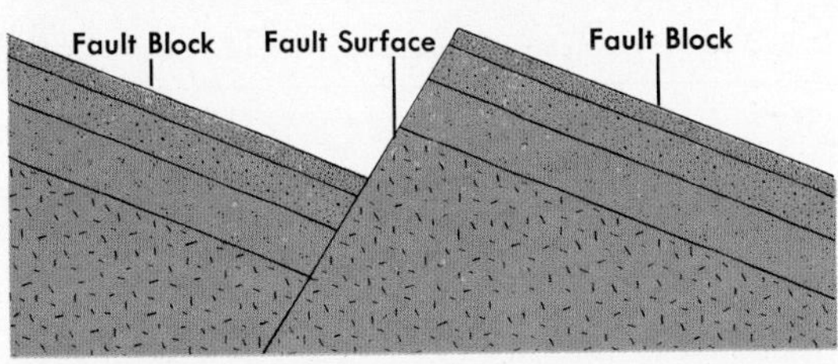

Fault-Block Mountains formed when the crust broke into great blocks that were then tilted or lifted. The Sierra Nevada and many other mountains in the western United States were formed this way.

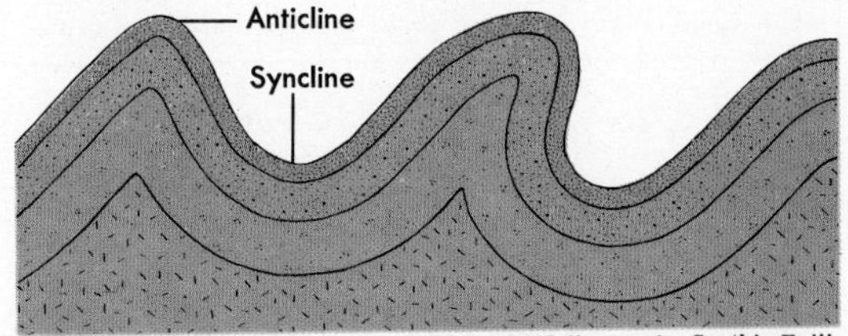

WORLD BOOK diagram by Cynthia Fujii

Folded Mountains formed when layers of the crust wrinkled into wavelike *folds*. Such folding produced the Appalachian Mountains. Folding and block faulting sometimes occurred at the same time.

How the Earth Began

There is no single, generally accepted scientific theory as to when or how the earth was formed. However, scientists agree that it was probably formed at the same time as the other planets in the solar system. They also have several ideas about the formation of the solar system. But they cannot be certain that their explanations are correct. New information about the chemical makeup of the moon and the planets might help prove or disprove these explanations. Scientists hope that astronauts and instruments sent into space will provide such information.

The Earth's Age. The earth is probably at least $4\frac{1}{2}$ billion years old. The oldest rocks ever discovered are almost $3\frac{1}{2}$ billion years old. Scientists believe that the earth itself must be at least 1 billion years older than these rocks.

Scientists learn the age of rocks by measuring the amount of radioactive substances in them. A radioactive substance gives off invisible rays and changes into a different substance. For example, uranium gives off rays and slowly changes into lead. Scientists know the time it takes for uranium to change to lead. They can find a rock's age by comparing the amount of uranium in it to the amount of lead in it. See RADIOGEOLOGY.

The Birth of the Solar System. Most scientists believe that the solar system developed from a huge *nebula* (cloud of gas and dust) that once swirled around the sun. The sun itself may have been formed from the central part of this nebula. As the nebula whirled around the sun, it slowly flattened out. Sections of the cloud began to spin like *eddies* (whirlpools) in a stream. Gas and dust collected near the centers of these eddies. The collections of gas and dust grew by attracting nearby particles of matter. They slowly developed into the spinning planets that now travel around the sun.

Immanuel Kant, a German philosopher, proposed a nebular theory for the origin of the solar system in 1755. A French astronomer, Pierre Simon Laplace, refined Kant's theory in 1796. Laplace suggested that the original nebula was much larger than the present solar system, and left behind eddies of matter as it became smaller. This theory assumes that the earth was first a gas and then a liquid, and finally cooled enough to have a solid crust.

In 1905, Thomas Chamberlin, an American geologist, and Forest Moulton, an American astronomer, proposed the *planetesimal theory*. According to this theory, a rapidly moving star passed close to the sun but did not collide with it. The gravity of the passing star pulled long, threadlike "arms" of gas from the sun. Eddies swirled within the arms of gas. The gas cooled and formed solid particles called *planetesimals*. The planetesimals gradually collected in the centers of the eddies, and formed planets. The planetesimal theory assumes that the earth was made of solid particles from the beginning. Meteorites that fall to the earth each day may be evidence that the earth is still growing by the gradual collection of solid particles.

Two English scientists, Sir James Jeans and Harold Jeffreys, proposed the *tidal* or *gaseous theory* in 1919. Like the planetesimal theory, the tidal theory begins with arms of hot gas pulled from the sun by the gravity of a passing star. The gas gathers in eddies which turn into liquid balls. Each liquid ball slowly cools, and a hard crust forms around it. This theory assumes that the earth was first a gas and then a liquid before it developed a solid crust.

In the 1930's, the English astronomer R. A. Lyttleton proposed the *double star theory*. Our galaxy contains many two-star combinations called double stars. Lyttleton assumed that the sun and a "companion" star once formed a double star. The companion star exploded into a cloud of gas which was "captured" by the sun's gravity. The planets developed from this cloud in much the same way as described in the tidal theory.

Many scientists support *condensation theories* that begin

HOW THE SOLAR SYSTEM BEGAN: A Nebular Theory

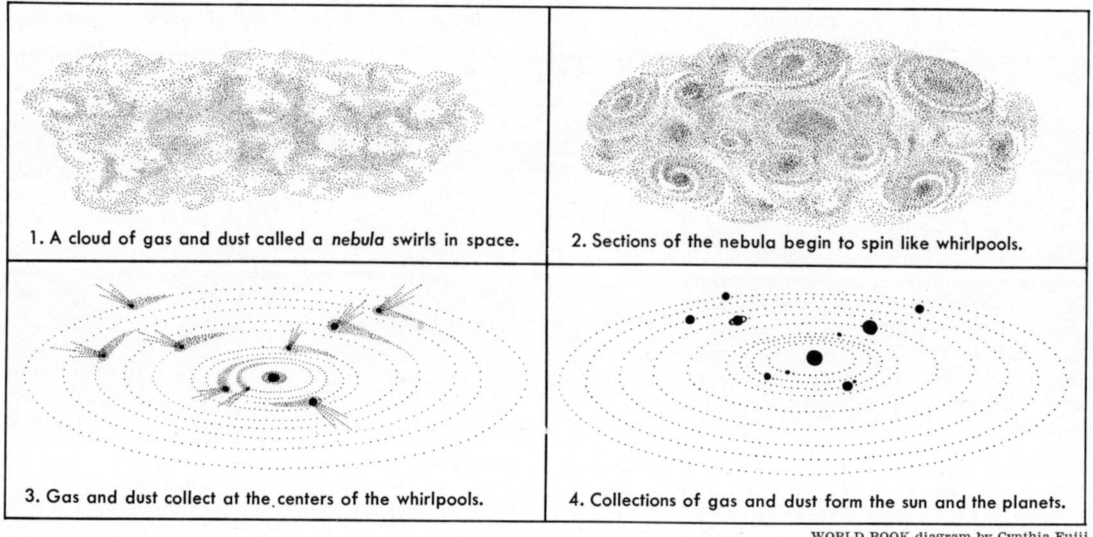

1. A cloud of gas and dust called a *nebula* swirls in space.
2. Sections of the nebula begin to spin like whirlpools.
3. Gas and dust collect at the centers of the whirlpools.
4. Collections of gas and dust form the sun and the planets.

WORLD BOOK diagram by Cynthia Fujii

THE EARTH'S OLDEST EXPOSED ROCKS

This map shows where the oldest rocks lie exposed at the earth's surface. These rocks are parts of *shields* that formed the earliest continents. Large parts of the shields are now underground. A geologist, *right*, chips samples from the Canadian shield.

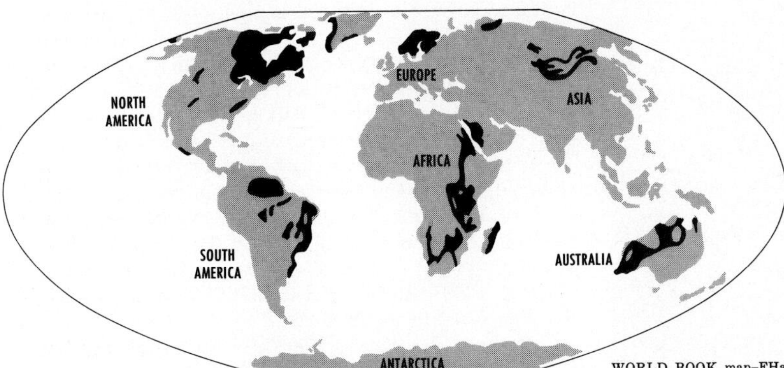

WORLD BOOK map–FHa

Data for map from *Historical Geology* by Carl O. Dunbar. 2nd ed. Wiley, 1960.

Geological Survey of Canada

with a single exploding star. These theories were developed during the 1940's and 1950's. They assume that a star exploded and that most of the exploded material escaped into space. A small part of the material remained behind to form a nebula that was captured by the sun's gravity. Eddies of gas then changed into liquid balls which finally developed solid crusts.

The Earth's Early Development. Scientists do not know any more about the earth's earliest stages than they do about the birth of the solar system. They suppose that the earth began as a waterless mass of rock surrounded by a cloud of gas. Radioactive materials in the rock and increasing pressure in the earth's interior gradually produced enough heat to melt the interior of the earth. The heavy materials, such as iron, then sank. The light *silicates* (rocks made of silicon and oxygen) rose to the earth's surface and formed the crust. These rocks became the ocean floors and the land areas called *shields*, which were the original continents.

The heating of the earth's interior also caused other chemicals inside the earth to rise to the surface. Some of these chemicals formed water and others formed the gases of the atmosphere. Over many years, the water slowly collected in low places of the crust and formed the oceans. As land developed, rain water and rivers dissolved salts and other substances from rocks and carried them to the oceans, making the oceans salty.

The earth's earliest atmosphere may have been a combination of methane and ammonia, similar to the present atmosphere of Jupiter. Or it may have contained a large amount of carbon dioxide, as does the atmosphere of Venus. The earth's earliest atmosphere probably did not contain much oxygen. Oxygen collected gradually in the atmosphere as the earth aged. The oxygen was originally combined with other chemicals in rocks. The melting of these rocks freed the oxygen and allowed it to escape to the surface. As the amount of oxygen increased, conditions on earth became favorable for plants and animals to develop.

The Shaping of the Continents. The earth's early continental shields were much smaller than the continents of today. Many scientists believe the continents gradually grew outward into the sea as mountains developed along their shorelines. The shields themselves are now relatively flat areas on the continents. These areas contain the "roots" of the earliest mountains whose tops have been worn away.

Many coastal mountain ranges developed from long, low areas in the earth's crust called *geosynclines.* A geosyncline might appear as a narrow waterway cutting across an early continent near the shoreline. This seaway collects large amounts of *sediment* (bits of rock and soil) worn from the high land alongside it. The weight of the sediment pushes the bottom of the seaway deeper and deeper into the hot part of the crust. The sediment finally melts and hardens into new rock, and the crust buckles under the great weight. The broken edges of the crust push against one another and rise, forming mountain ranges.

Geologists are not sure why the crust buckles. One explanation is that the earth is slowly cooling off and its crust is shrinking. Parts of the crust squeeze against each other and finally break and push up where the crust is weakest. Another explanation is that there may be a slow, continuous movement of the mantle under the crust. This movement drags the crust along and causes it to buckle, mainly at the edges of continents. Such movement could be caused by the heat of the earth's core. The heat makes the rock in the mantle flow slowly in great loops beneath the crust.

Still another explanation is that entire continents might be drifting away from one another. Such drifting could cause the edge of a continent to "roll up" into a mountain as it pushes over rock beneath it. This idea is based on the close match between the shorelines of South America, Africa, and other continents. It is supported by a similarity between rocks and fossils found along these shorelines. See CONTINENTAL DRIFT.

Lyn, APF

Rocks Tell the Earth's History. Tilted layers of rock, *above*, show that this hillside was once a level plain. A piece of limestone, *below*, formed more than 100 million years ago, contains fossils of snail-like sea animals that have since died out.

WORLD BOOK photo courtesy the Field Museum of Natural History, Chicago

The history of the earth is recorded in the rocks that make up the earth's crust. Rocks have been forming, wearing away, and re-forming ever since the earth took shape. This continual changing of rocks has resulted in the formation of layers of rock called *strata*. Strata contain many clues that tell geologists what the earth was like in the past. These clues include the thickness and position of the layers, the chemicals that make them up, and the fossils they contain.

Geologists base their explanations of rock clues on their observations of the earth today. They assume that the laws of chemistry and physics have remained unchanged, and that such forces as gravitation have operated continuously. Geologists also assume that the earth has developed in the past in the same way it is developing now. This idea was first proposed by James Hutton, a Scottish scientist, in 1785. It is now called the *principle of uniformitarianism*.

Geologists know that some rock strata were once hot and liquid because hot, liquid lava from volcanoes hardens and forms layers of rock. Geologists also know that erosion supplied the materials from which other strata were made because erosion produces layers of sediment. If a slab of rock has a rippled surface, geologists assume that the rock was once mud or sand at the bottom of a body of water. They make this assumption because they still find such ripples on the bottoms of streams, rivers, lakes, and oceans. Geologists can even tell which way the current once flowed by the shape of the ripples in the rock.

Many rocks contain fossils that reveal the history of life on earth. A fossil may be an animal's body, a tooth, or a piece of bone. It may simply be an outline of a plant or an animal made in a rock when the rock was soft mud or liquid lava. The study of fossils is called *paleontology*, and scientists who collect and study fossils are *paleontologists*.

Fossils help geologists figure out the ages of rock strata and the times at which animals and plants lived. Fossils of the simplest animals and plants are found in the oldest strata. The youngest strata contain fossils of animals and plants much like those living today. See EVOLUTION.

Fossils also are clues to changes that have taken place on the earth. For example, paleontologists find fossil seashells in strata high in a mountain, many miles from an ocean. These discoveries indicate that the strata formed a muddy ocean bottom long before the rocks were lifted to form a mountain.

Rocks contain only an incomplete history of the earth. Many rocks—together with their geological records—are destroyed or changed by heat and pressure deep in the earth's crust, or by weathering at the surface. In addition, geological clues in rocks help describe conditions on the earth only at the time the rocks hardened. Geologists have learned the story of the earth's development by piecing together clues from rocks of many ages. But the complete history of the earth will probably never be known.

The known history of the earth is divided into six lengths of time called *eras*. The eras are, from oldest to youngest: Azoic, Archeozoic, Proterozoic, Paleozoic,

Mesozoic, and Cenozoic. Some historical geologists group the first three eras into one unit called the Precambrian. Eras are divided into *periods*, and periods are divided into *epochs*. These divisions and subdivisions represent various stages in the development of life as indicated by fossils. As a result, the lengths of eras, periods, and epochs are not equal.

A chart showing an outline of the earth's history by using the various time divisions is called a *geological time scale*. On such a chart, the earth's earliest history is at the bottom, and its recent history at the top. This arrangement resembles the way rock strata are formed, with the newest on top of the oldest. A geological time scale appears later in this article.

The Earth's Earliest History. The Azoic, Archeozoic, and Proterozoic eras make up almost the first 4 billion years of the earth's earliest history. This length of time covers about 80 per cent of the earth's total history. It is often called Precambrian Time.

During the Azoic Era, the earth had its very beginning. It may first have been part of a cloud of gas and dust, and then a ball of liquid. After millions of years, a rock crust finally formed. Geological evidence shows that the crust repeatedly melted and hardened. The continental shields took shape and the continents began to grow. The oceans and atmosphere also were formed during the Azoic Era. No evidence of life has been found in rocks of this era.

Rocks of the Archeozoic Era contain fossils of the first and most primitive life—bacteria and tiny plants called *algae*. Archeozoic rocks include types of marble, slate, and other metamorphic rocks. These rocks were made from sandstones, shales, limestones, iron ores, lava, and volcanic ash by the action of heat, pressure, and chemicals in the earth's crust. Among the Archeozoic rocks are great blocks of granite. These blocks were formed when melted rock flowed through cracks in the crust during periods of mountain building. The mountains themselves have been worn away, leaving only their bases in the shield areas.

Fossils of the first animals appear in rocks of the Proterozoic Era. These animals include worms, sponges, jellyfish, corals, and other primitive *invertebrates* (animals without backbones). Algae and bacteria also were still plentiful. Flakes of graphite in limestones of the Proterozoic Era may represent the remains of other kinds of living things. Graphite is a form of carbon, a basic chemical in the makeup of living things.

In southern Canada, Proterozoic rocks including sandstones, shales, limestones, lava, and volcanic ash form strata more than 80,000 feet thick. These rocks contain large amounts of iron ore. During the Archeozoic and Proterozoic mountain-building periods, melted rock rose through the earth's crust and hardened among the rocks there. This melted rock contained copper, nickel, gold, silver, and uranium. The hardening of the rock created the rich mineral resources for which the shield areas are well known.

The Paleozoic Era began 600 million years ago and ended 225 million years ago. It included seven periods. These periods were, from oldest to youngest: Cambrian, Ordovician, Silurian, Devonian, Mississippian, Pennsylvanian, and Permian. The Mississippian and Pennsylvanian periods are sometimes considered a single unit called the Carboniferous Period.

Rocks of the Paleozoic Era contain a large number and variety of fossils. The appearance of such a great number of fossils of invertebrates suggests that much of the earlier fossil record was destroyed by erosion at the end of the Proterozoic Era.

Plants of the Cambrian Period include water-dwelling algae from the Proterozoic Era. By Devonian times, the first land plants had developed. These plants were fern trees that grew on swampy land and reproduced by means of tiny bodies called *spores*, not seeds. Mosses appeared during the Mississippian Period. During the Pennsylvanian Period, there was a great variety of ferns. Some grew 100 feet high in the coal-making swamps of the Pennsylvanian Period. The first true seed plants, the *conifers* (cone-bearers), are found as fossils in strata formed during the Permian Period.

Cambrian animals include insectlike *trilobites*, shelled animals called *brachiopods*, many kinds of snails and clams, and primitive fish. Animals of later Paleozoic periods include corals, sea buds, sea lilies, sea urchins, crayfishlike animals called *eurypterids*, sharks, armored fish, lungfish, amphibians, and reptiles. The variety and number of fish in the Devonian Period were so great that the period is usually called the Age of Fish. Lungfish were probably the first air-breathing animals with backbones. Amphibians were the first air-breathing animals with backbones to walk on land. Fossils of warm-blooded animals have not been found in Paleozoic rocks.

Two long, narrow seaways called *geosynclines* made up an important part of the Paleozoic geography of North America. The Appalachian geosyncline in the east and the Cordilleran geosyncline in the west were sinking areas that received large amounts of sediments from the surrounding lands. The Appalachian geosyncline disappeared when the Appalachian Mountains were built near the end of the Paleozoic Era.

Many times during the Paleozoic Era, the seas which flooded the Appalachian and Cordilleran seaways would overflow to cover the low, flat shield areas of the continent. The greatest of these floods occurred during the Ordovician Period, when about 70 per cent of the continent was under water. The shallow seas were good places for large numbers of living things to develop. The strata laid down in these seas originally contained many tiny spaces between bits of sediment. These rocks were not disturbed much because mountain making took place mainly in the areas of the geosynclines. As a result, the tiny spaces remained in the strata. Substances produced by decaying plants collected in these spaces and slowly formed deposits of oil and natural gas.

In Europe, disturbances in the crust created two important mountain chains during the Paleozoic Era. The Caledonian Mountains were formed in Norway, Sweden, and Scotland, and the Variscan Mountains were formed in France, Belgium, and Germany. Later, erosion partly wore down both these mountain chains.

The Mesozoic Era began 225 million years ago and ended 65 million years ago. It had three periods. These

Precambrian Time included almost all of the earth's first 4 billion years. The crust melted and hardened, the atmosphere and oceans were formed, and the simplest kinds of life appeared.

The Paleozoic Era lasted 375 million years. Many kinds of animals and plants developed in the seas and on land. This painting shows some early land plants from about the middle of the era.

periods were, from oldest to youngest: Triassic, Jurassic, and Cretaceous.

Fossil plants of the Mesozoic Era include algae, ferns, mosses, and conifers, all of which continued from the Paleozoic Era. Conifers became the main land cover during the Mesozoic Era. Fossils of flowering seed plants, including grasses, appear in Cretaceous rocks.

Single-celled animals called *protozoa* lived in the warm seas of the Mesozoic Era. Each of these animals grew a tiny shell made of lime. Deposits of the shells form the main ingredient of such chalk rocks as the white cliffs of Dover, England. The Cretaceous Period was named for *creta*, the Latin word for *chalk*.

Other plentiful animals, including corals, snails, and clams, also developed during the Mesozoic Era. There were many kinds of mollusks, and fish, amphibians, and reptiles also flourished. Dinosaurs, a group of giant reptiles, lived only during the Mesozoic Era. Dinosaurs died out completely at the end of the era. The first warm-blooded mammals appeared during the Triassic Period, and birds appeared during the Jurassic Period.

The Mesozoic Era began with most of North America exposed as land. The sea flooded only the Cordilleran geosyncline in the west. During the Mesozoic Era, the seas overflowed the Cordilleran seaway and covered the shield areas. This shallow flooding again provided good conditions for the development of living things. It again resulted in deposits of sediment where oil and natural gas could form. Mesozoic flooding ended during the Cretaceous Period, when more of North America was flooded than at any other time.

During the Triassic Period, the action of volcanoes created lava beds in what is now the eastern United States. Mountain-making disturbances of the crust, and the rising of melted rock, created the Sierra Nevada Mountains in California during the Jurassic Period. The end of the Mesozoic Era was marked by mountain-making disturbances that affected the whole North

A Mountain of Precambrian Rock rises in the harbor of Rio de Janeiro, Brazil. The rounded shape of Sugar Loaf Mountain resulted from hundreds of millions of years of erosion.

Annan Photo

Paleozoic Sandstones make up part of the rock formations in Monument Valley, Utah. The rocks that once surrounded these formations have been worn away by water and the weather.

Josef Muench

The Mesozoic Era was the Age of Reptiles. Dinosaurs roamed the earth, and then died out. Ferns and fern trees thrived before flowering plants and modern trees appeared during the era.

WORLD BOOK illustrations by Tom Dolan

The Cenozoic Era included an Ice Age when great glaciers swept slowly across northern lands and then melted. Sheets and rivers of ice forced men and animals to move to warmer regions.

American continent and produced the Rocky Mountains. This brought an end to the Cordilleran seaway.

The Cenozoic Era began 65 million years ago and is still going on. It covers the Tertiary Period, which lasted until $3\frac{1}{2}$ million years ago, and the Quaternary Period, which includes the present time. The Tertiary Period is divided into five epochs: Paleocene, Eocene, Oligocene, Miocene, and Pliocene. The Quaternary Period consists of two epochs, the Pleistocene Epoch or "Ice Age," and the Recent Epoch. Many scientists believe the Ice Age is still going on.

The Alps, Andes, and Himalaya mountains were formed during the Cenozoic Era. In western North America, many volcanoes erupted and lava covered much of what is now Oregon and Washington. Four times during the Pleistocene Epoch, glaciers covered much of the earth and then melted. As the ice pushed across the land, men and animals moved ahead of it to find food and places to live.

The wide variety of plants and animals that we know today came into existence during the Cenozoic Era. Small mammals that first appeared during the Mesozoic Era lived during the Paleocene Epoch. During the Eocene Epoch, ancestors of the horse, rhinoceros, and camel roamed Europe and North America. These animals were much smaller than they are today. By the Oligocene Epoch, dogs and cats had appeared, along with three-toed horses about as large as sheep. The mammals grew larger as prairies spread over the land during the Miocene Epoch. By the Pliocene Epoch, many kinds of mammals had grown to giant size. Elephantlike mammoths and mastodons, huge saber-toothed cats, and giant ground sloths roamed the prairies and forests. All these animals gradually died out.

The earliest fossils of man are in rocks of the Pleistocene Epoch. Man's years on the earth are only a brief moment among the billions of years during which the earth has developed.

SAMUEL P. ELLISON, JR.

A Block of Mesozoic Limestone, the Rock of Gibraltar, formed on a lowland during the Jurassic Period. Changes in the crust later lifted the block more than 1,400 feet above the sea.

Slim Aarons, Photo Researchers

Cenozoic Glaciers Cut Deep Valleys through mountains such as those along the coast of Norway, *below*. The ice scraped away mountainsides, and then melted and dropped the ground-up rock.

Fritz Henle, Photo Researchers

Outline of Earth History

This geological time chart outlines the development of the earth and of life on the earth. The earth's earliest history appears at the bottom of the chart, and its most recent history is at the top.

Era	Period	Period or Epoch and Its Length	Beginning (Years Ago)	Development of Life on Earth	
CENOZOIC ERA	Quaternary Period	RECENT EPOCH 10-25 Thousand Years	10-25 Thousand	Man hunted and tamed animals; developed agriculture; learned to use metals, coal, oil, gas, and other resources; and learned to put the power of wind and rivers to work.	 Cultivated Plants
CENOZOIC ERA	Quaternary Period	PLEISTOCENE EPOCH 3½ Million Years	3½ Million	Man appeared before the first glaciers swept down from the north. Mammoths, woolly rhinos, and other animals roamed parts of the world, but died out near the end of the epoch.	 Primitive Man
CENOZOIC ERA	Tertiary Period	PLIOCENE EPOCH 10½ Million Years	14 Million	Sea life became much like that of today. Birds, camels, cats, elephants, horses, monkeys, and other mammals became like modern kinds and spread from continent to continent.	 Horses
CENOZOIC ERA	Tertiary Period	MIOCENE EPOCH 12 Million Years	26 Million	Apes appeared in Asia and Africa. Other animals included bats, monkeys, and whales, and primitive bears, dogs, and elephants. Flowering plants and trees resembled modern kinds.	 Apes
CENOZOIC ERA	Tertiary Period	OLIGOCENE EPOCH 14 Million Years	40 Million	Primitive apes appeared. Camels, cats, dogs, elephants, horses, rhinos, and rodents developed. Huge rhinoceroslike animals disappeared near the end of the epoch.	 Early Horses
CENOZOIC ERA	Tertiary Period	EOCENE EPOCH 15 Million Years	55 Million	Fruits, grains, and grasses developed. Birds, amphibians, small reptiles, and fish were plentiful. Primitive bats, camels, cats, horses, monkeys, rhinoceroses, and whales appeared.	 Grasses
CENOZOIC ERA	Tertiary Period	PALEOCENE EPOCH 10 Million Years	65 Million	Flowering plants became plentiful. Invertebrates, fish, amphibians, reptiles, and small mammals were common.	 Small Mammals
MESOZOIC ERA		CRETACEOUS PERIOD 65 Million Years	130 Million	Flowering plants appeared. Invertebrates, fish, and amphibians were plentiful. Dinosaurs with horns and armor became common. Dinosaurs died out at the end of the period.	 Flowering Plants
MESOZOIC ERA		JURASSIC PERIOD 50 Million Years	180 Million	Cone-bearing trees were plentiful. Sea life included primitive squids. Dinosaurs reached their largest size. The first birds appeared. A few small, primitive mammals lived on land.	 Birds
MESOZOIC ERA		TRIASSIC PERIOD 45 Million Years	225 Million	Cone-bearing trees were plentiful. Many fish resembled modern kinds. Insects were plentiful. The first turtles, crocodiles, and dinosaurs appeared, as did the first mammals.	 Dinosaurs
PALEOZOIC ERA		PERMIAN PERIOD 50 Million Years	275 Million	Algae were plentiful. The first seed plants—cone-bearing trees—appeared. Fish, amphibians, and reptiles were plentiful. Trilobites and eurypterids died out near the end of the period.	 Seed Plants
PALEOZOIC ERA	Carboniferous Period	PENNSYLVANIAN PERIOD 35 Million Years	310 Million	Algae were plentiful. Fern trees grew from seedlike bodies. Fish and amphibians were plentiful. The first reptiles appeared. Giant insects lived in forests where coal later formed.	 Reptiles
PALEOZOIC ERA	Carboniferous Period	MISSISSIPPIAN PERIOD 35 Million Years	345 Million	Algae were plentiful and the first mosses appeared. Trilobites were dying out. Shelled animals, fish, and amphibians were plentiful. Many coral reefs were formed.	 Amphibians
PALEOZOIC ERA		DEVONIAN PERIOD 60 Million Years	405 Million	The first forests grew in swamps. Many kinds of fish, including sharks, armored fish, and lungfish, swam in the sea and in fresh waters. The first amphibians and insects appeared.	 Fish
PALEOZOIC ERA		SILURIAN PERIOD 30 Million Years	435 Million	Algae were plentiful and spore-bearing land plants appeared. Trilobites, fish, and mollusks were common. Coral reefs formed, and air-breathing animals called eurypterids appeared.	 Eurypterids
PALEOZOIC ERA		ORDOVICIAN PERIOD 45 Million Years	480 Million	Algae became plentiful. Trilobites, corals, and shelled animals were common. Tiny animals called 'graptolites grouped together and formed branching colonies. Jawless fish appeared.	 Mollusks
PALEOZOIC ERA		CAMBRIAN PERIOD 120 Million Years (?)	600 Million (?)	Plentiful fossils appeared for the first time. Insectlike animals called trilobites, and some shelled animals were common in the sea. Fossil teeth give evidence of the first fish.	 Trilobites
PRECAMBRIAN TIME Almost 4 Billion Years (?)			4½ Billion (?)	Corals, jellyfish, sponges, and worms lived in the sea about 1,100 million years ago. Algae and bacteria lived as long ago as 2,200 million years. Before that, no living things are known.	 Bacteria

Development of the Earth	Mountain Building: North America	Mountain Building: Europe and Asia
Streams, glaciers, and oceans eroded the land. Present river deltas and coastlines were formed. Ice Age glaciers melted and water collected, forming the Great Lakes in North America.		
Four times during this Ice Age, glaciers covered large areas of North America and Europe. The climate was cool. Mountains rose in western North America, and volcanoes erupted.		
The Oligocene, Miocene, and Pliocene epochs were much alike. Rocks that formed during these epochs included clays, limestones, and sands. The climate was uniform and mild through the Oligocene and Miocene, but began to get cooler during the Pliocene, leading up to the following Ice Age. Mountain making was common, and many volcanoes erupted. Oil and natural gas formed in rocks made during these epochs.	Cascade Mountains	Alps and Himalaya
Seas flooded the shores of the continents. Large areas were covered by swamps where lignite, a kind of coal, later formed. Oil and gas also formed in clays, limestones, and sands.		
Thick soil formed in hot, rainy lands. Mountains, not yet worn by erosion, were high. The climate was varied. Coal, gas, and oil formed in clays, limestones, and sands.	Rocky Mountains	
Oceans flooded large areas. Coal swamps developed. Rocks included chalk, limestones, sandstones, and shales. Coal, gas, oil, and ores of gold, silver, and other metals were formed.		
Shallow seaways cut across the continents. Some volcanic action occurred. Rocks included limestones, sandstones, and shales. Gas, oil, salt, and ores of gold and uranium formed.	Sierra Nevada; California Coast Ranges	
Layers called *red beds* developed along with shales, sandstones, and limestones. Gas, oil, and ores of copper and uranium formed. *Faults* (cracks) occurred in eastern North America.	Palisades	Caucasus Mountains
Glaciers in the southern hemisphere melted and left sedimentary layers. Rocks in the northern hemisphere included limestones, sandstones, and shales. Gas, oil, gypsum, and salt formed.		Ural Mountains
Swamps covered the lowlands. Oil, gas, and large amounts of coal formed among limestones, sandstones, and shales. River deltas partially filled the Appalachian seaway.	Appalachian Mountains	
Large amounts of limestone formed among layers of shale and sandstone in deltas in the Appalachian and Cordilleran seaways. Coal, gas, oil, and deposits of lead and zinc formed.		Variscan Mountains
Red sandstones, shales, and limestones formed in Europe, and black shales, reef limestones, and sandstones formed in North America. Gas, oil, and quartz sand formed.	Acadian Mountains	Caledonian Mountains
Limestones, coral reefs, sandstones, and shales formed, with the deepest deposits in the Appalachian and Cordilleran seaways. Gas, oil, gypsum, iron ore, and salt formed.		
Greatest floods of the era covered two-thirds of North America. A delta formed in the Appalachian seaway. Gas, oil, lead, and zinc formed in limestones, sandstones, and shales.	Taconian Mountains	
Seas spread across North America from the Appalachian seaway in the east and the Cordilleran seaway in the west. Lead and zinc formed in sandstones, shales, and limestones.	Vermont Mountains	
Copper, gold, iron, nickel, and silver formed in shales, siltstones, lava, volcanic ash, and metamorphic rocks. The earth's crust melted and cooled repeatedly during this time.	Killarneyan Mountains; Algoman Mountains; Laurentian Mountains	

Development of North America

These maps compare North America's present shape with its shape (white) during four periods. Blue represents oceans.

Miocene Epoch

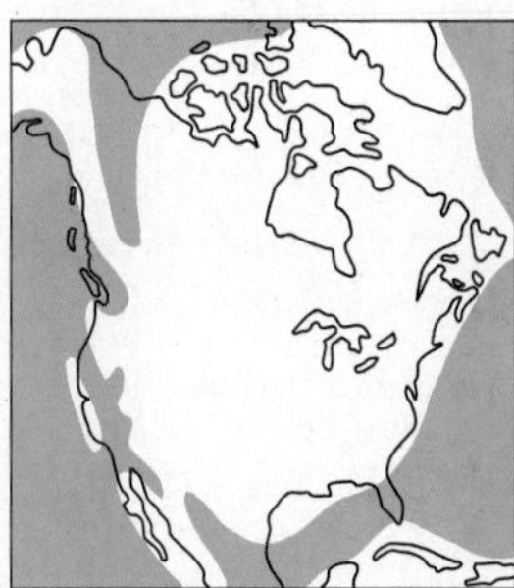

Late Triassic Period

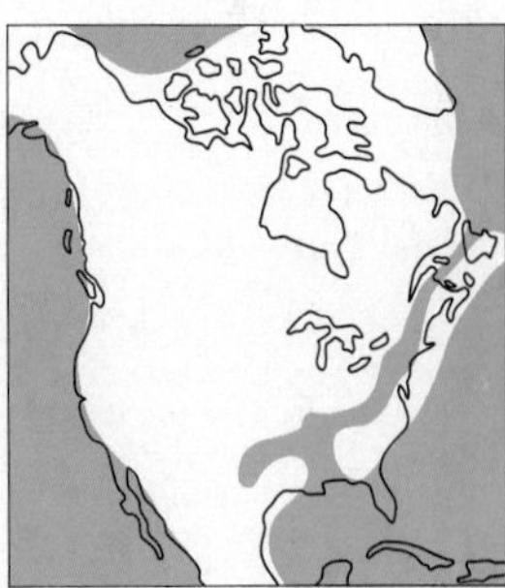

Early Devonian Period

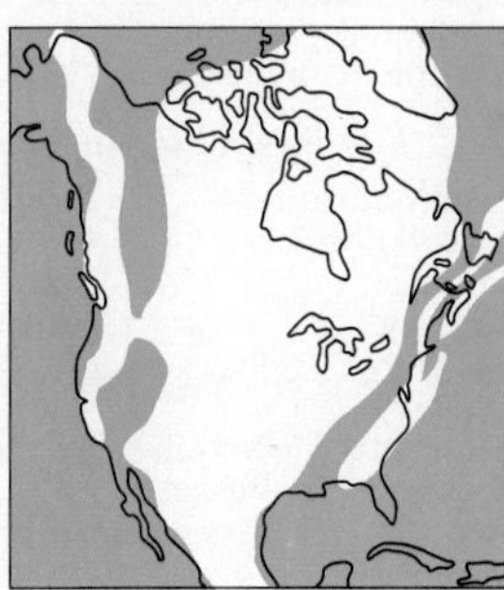

Early Cambrian Period

Data for maps from *Historical Geology*, by Carl O. Dunbar. 2nd ed. Wiley, 1960.

EARTH / Study Aids

Related Articles. See GEOLOGY with its list of Related Articles. See also the following articles:

MOTIONS AND FORCES OF THE EARTH

Climate	Gravitation	Season
Equinox	Magnet and Magnetism	Zone

THE ATMOSPHERE (AIR)

Air	Meteor	Troposphere
Aurora Borealis	Rain	Van Allen Radiation
Cloud	Sky	Weather
Frost	Snow	Wind
Horizon	Stratosphere	
Ionosphere	Tropopause	

THE LITHOSPHERE (ROCKS)

Continent	Mineral	Soil
Island	Rock	

THE HYDROSPHERE (WATER)

Deep	Hydrosphere	River
Geyser	Lake	Water
Ground Water	Ocean	Waterfall

THE EARTH AS MAN'S STOREHOUSE

Atomic Energy	Food	Petroleum
Clothing	Gas (fuel)	Radiation
Coal	Iron and Steel	Shelter
Conservation	Natural Resources	Water Power
Element, Chemical		

THE EARTH AS A HISTORY BOOK

Cambrian Period	Ice Age	Prehistoric Man
Cenozoic Era	Paleontology	Reptiles, Age of
Cretaceous Period	Pennsylvanian Epoch	
Devonian Period	Petrified Forest	
Dinosaur	Prehistoric Animal	
Fossil		

EXPLORING AND MAPPING THE EARTH

Equator	International Geophysical Year	Meridian
Exploration and Discovery		Mohole
		North Pole
Geodesy	Latitude	Pole
Geophysics	Longitude	South Pole
Hemisphere	Map	Space Travel

SURFACE FEATURES

Alluvial Fan	Delta	Lava	Plateau
Atoll	Desert	Mesa	Polder
Basin	Divide	Moor	Pothole
Beach	Dune	Mountain	Prairie
Canyon	Fall Line	Muskeg	Silt
Cave	Glacier	Oasis	Swamp
Coral	Hill	Ooze	Valley
Crevasse	Hogback	Peneplain	Vein
Dalles	Kettle Hole	Plain	Volcano

THE CHANGING EARTH

Continental Drift	Floods and Flood Control
Earthquake	Wind
Erosion	

THE EARTH AS THE HOME OF LIVING THINGS

Acclimatization	Environment	Plant
Adaptation	Geography	Population
Animal	Man	World
Ecology	Nature Study	

THE EARTH'S "FAMILY"

Asteroid	Nebular Hypothesis	Solar System
Eclipse	Planet	Sun
Moon	Planetesimal Hypothesis	Universe

Outline

I. The Earth in the Universe
- A. The Earth as a Planet
- B. How the Earth Moves
- C. The Earth and Its Moon

II. Outside and Inside the Earth
- A. The Earth's Shape and Size
- B. The Earth's Atmosphere
- C. The Earth's Surface
- D. The Earth's Crust
- E. Inside the Earth
- F. The Earth's Gravity
- G. The Earth's Magnetism

III. How the Earth Changes
- A. Weathering
- B. Erosion
- C. Mass Movement
- D. Changes in the Earth's Crust

IV. How the Earth Began
- A. The Earth's Age
- B. The Birth of the Solar System
- C. The Earth's Early Development
- D. The Shaping of the Continents

V. History of the Earth
- A. The Earth's Earliest History
- B. The Paleozoic Era
- C. The Mesozoic Era
- D. The Cenozoic Era

Questions

What two chemicals make up most of the earth's crust?
When did the first bird live on the earth?
Which motion of the earth causes day and night?
Who first suggested a nebular theory about the birth of the solar system?
What gas makes up most of the earth's atmosphere?
What are three important causes of erosion?
How does the earth rank in size among the planets?
What part of the earth is believed to be made of melted iron and nickel?
During what geological period did the first land plants appear?
What parts of the earth make up the lithosphere? What is the biosphere?

Books to Read

FENTON, CARROLL L. *Earth's Adventures*. Day, 1942. With MILDRED A. FENTON: *Rocks and Their Stories*. Doubleday, 1951. *The Fossil Book: A Record of Prehistoric Life*. 1958.

GALLANT, ROY A. *Exploring Under the Earth: The Story of Geology and Geophysics*. Doubleday, 1960.

LIFE MAGAZINE. *The World We Live In*. Simon & Schuster, 1955. Another edition, published in 1956, was prepared for young readers.

MOORE, PATRICK A. *The Earth, Our Home*. Abelard Schuman, 1957. A history of the earth for the layman.

PLACE, MARIAN T. *Our Earth: Geology and Geologists*. Putnam, 1961.

REED, WILLIAM M. *The Earth for Sam*. Rev. ed. Harcourt, 1960.

RICHARDS, HORACE G. *The Story of Earth Science*. Lippincott, 1959. A broad survey of geology for the amateur collector.

SCHNEIDER, HERMAN and NINA. *Rocks, Rivers and the Changing Earth: A First Book About Geology*. W. R. Scott, 1952.

SEVREY, O. IRENE. *The First Book of the Earth*. Watts, 1958.

SOOTIN, HARRY and LAURA. *The Young Experimenter's Workbook*. Norton, 1965.

WYCKOFF, JEROME. *The Story of Geology: Our Changing Earth Through the Ages*. Golden Press, 1960.

LEARNING is an important field of study in psychology. Psychologists define learning as the process by which changes in behavior result from experience or practice. By *behavior*, psychologists mean any response that an organism makes to its environment. Thus, behavior includes actions, emotions, thoughts, and the responses of muscles and glands. Learning can produce changes in any of these forms of behavior.

All changes in behavior are not the result of learning. Some changes result from *maturation* (physical growth). Other behavior changes, including those caused by illness or fatigue, are only temporary and cannot be called learning.

How We Learn

We can see learning taking place around us all the time, but there is no simple explanation of the process. Psychologists have examined four kinds of learning in detail: (1) classical conditioning or respondent learning, (2) instrumental conditioning or operant learning, (3) multiple-response learning, and (4) insight learning.

Classical Conditioning is perhaps the simplest kind of learning. This learning process is based on stimulus-response relationships. A *stimulus* is an object or a situation that excites one of our sense organs. A light is a stimulus because it excites the retina of the eye, allowing us to see. Often a stimulus makes a person *respond* in a certain way, as when a sudden flash of light makes us blink. Psychologists say that in this instance the stimulus *elicits* (draws forth) the response.

In classical conditioning, learning occurs when a new stimulus elicits behavior similar to that originally produced by an old stimulus. Suppose a person tastes some lemon juice, which makes him salivate. While he is tasting it, a tone is sounded. Suppose these two stimuli—the lemon juice and the tone—occur together many times. Eventually, the tone by itself will make the person salivate. Classical conditioning has occurred because the new stimulus (the tone) elicits the response of salivation in much the same way as the lemon juice did.

Any condition that makes learning occur is said to *reinforce* the learning. When a person learns to salivate to a tone, the reinforcement is the lemon juice that the tone is paired with. Without the lemon juice, the person would not learn to salivate to the tone.

The classical conditioning process is particularly important in understanding how we learn emotional behavior. When a person develops a new fear, for example, he learns to fear a stimulus that has been combined with some other frightening stimulus.

Studies of classical conditioning are based on experiments performed in the early 1900's by the Russian physiologist Ivan P. Pavlov. He trained dogs to salivate to such signals as lights, tones, or buzzers by using the signals when he gave food to the dog (see Reflex Action). Pavlov called the learned response a *conditioned response* because it depended on the conditions of the stimulus. To emphasize the fact that a stimulus produces a response in this kind of learning, classical conditioning is often called *respondent learning*.

Instrumental Conditioning. Often a person learns to perform a response as a result of what happens after the response is made. A child may learn to beg for candy. There is no one stimulus that elicits the response of begging. The child begs because such behavior occasionally results in receiving candy. Every time he receives candy, his tendency to beg becomes greater. Candy, therefore, is the reinforcer. Instrumental conditioning is also called *operant learning* because the learned response *operates* on the environment to produce some effect.

The American psychologist B. F. Skinner performed important experiments with instrumental conditioning in the 1930's. He trained rats to press levers to get food. In one experiment, a hungry rat was placed in a special box containing a lever attached to some concealed food. At first, the rat ran around restlessly. Eventually, it happened to press the lever, and the food dropped into the box. The food reinforced the response of pressing the lever. After repeating the process many times, the rat learned to press the lever for food.

Skinner's experiments were based on those performed earlier in the 1900's by the American psychologist E. L. Thorndike. In Thorndike's experiments, an animal inside a puzzle box had to pull a string, press a pedal, or make some other response that would open the box and expose some food. Thorndike noted that the animal learned gradually. It improved on a puzzle in time, but the entire learning process was slow and gradual. Thorndike called this type of learning *trial-and-error behavior*.

Multiple-Response Learning. When we learn skills, we first learn a sequence of simple movement-patterns. We combine these movement-patterns to form a more complicated behavior pattern. In most cases, various stimuli guide the process. For example, operating a typewriter requires putting together many skilled finger movements. These movements are guided by the letters or words that we want to type. At first, a person has to type letter-by-letter. With practice, he learns to type word-by-word or phrase-by-phrase. In verbal learning, such as memorizing a poem or learning a new language, we learn sequences of words. We then combine these sequences of responses into a complex organization. Learning which involves many responses requires much practice to smooth out the rough spots.

To examine this kind of learning, psychologists have observed animals learning to run through a maze. Starting at the beginning, the animal wanders through the maze until it finds food at the end. The animal periodically comes to a choice-point, where it must turn right or left. Only one choice is correct. Eventually the animal learns the correct sequence of turns. Psychologists have found that the two ends of the maze are learned more easily than the parts near the middle. In the same way, when we learn a list of things, we usually find the middle part hardest.

Insight Learning. The term *insight* refers to solving a problem through understanding the relationships of various parts of the problem. Insight often occurs suddenly, as when we look at a problem for some time and then suddenly grasp the solution.

The psychologist Wolfgang Köhler performed important insight experiments in the early 1900's. He showed that chimpanzees sometimes use insight instead of trial-and-error responses to solve problems. When a banana was placed high out of reach, the chimpanzees stacked boxes on top of each other to reach it. They also put two sticks together to reach an object that was too far away to reach with just one stick. The chimpanzees appeared to see and use the relationships involved in reaching their goals.

Theories of Learning are based on facts obtained from experiments such as those on classical and instrumental conditioning. Psychologists differ in their interpretation of these facts. As a result, there are a number of learning theories. These theories can be divided into two groups.

One group of psychologists emphasizes stimulus-response relationships and the experiments with classical and instrumental conditioning. They say all learning is the forming of habits. When we learn, we connect a stimulus and a response that did not exist before, thus forming a habit (see HABIT). Habits can range from the simplest ones to complex ones that are involved in learning skills. These psychologists believe that when a learner meets a new problem, he uses appropriate responses learned from past experience to solve it. If this procedure does not lead to the solution, the learner uses a trial-and-error approach. He uses one response after another until he solves the problem.

The second group of psychologists stresses *cognition* (the act of knowing) above the importance of habit. These experts feel that experiments with classical and instrumental conditioning are too limited to explain such complex learning as understanding concepts and ideas. They emphasize insight, understanding, and other thought processes.

Learning involves changes in the nervous system. Through research, scientists are trying to discover the processes that take place in the brain to produce learning. Such experiments may lead to a physiological theory of learning. See BRAIN (Research on the Brain).

Efficient Learning

Readiness to Learn. Learning occurs more efficiently if a person is ready to learn. This readiness results from a combination of growth and experience. A child cannot learn to read until his eyes and nervous system are mature enough. He also must have a sufficient background of spoken words and prereading experience with letters and pictures.

Motivation. Psychologists and educators also recognize that learning is best when the learner is motivated to learn (see MOTIVATION). Rewards are often used to increase motivation to learn. Punishment, particularly the threat of punishment, is also used to control learning. Experiments have shown that reward serves as a more effective aid to learning than punishment. This is due largely to two factors: (1) a learner can recognize the direct effects of reward more easily than he can the effects of punishment; and (2) the by-products of reward are more favorable. For example, reward leads to liking the rewarded task, but punishment leads to dislike of the punished deed.

Psychologists also look at the motivation of learning from the point of view of the learner. They tend to talk about success and failure, rather than reward and punishment. Success consists of reaching a goal that the learner sets for himself. Failure consists of not reaching the goal. An ideal learning situation is one in which the learner sets progressively more difficult goals for himself, and keeps at the task until he succeeds.

Skill Learning and Verbal Learning. Through research, psychologists have discovered some general rules designed to help a person learn.

The following rules apply particularly to learning skills. (1) Within a given amount of practice time, you can usually learn a task more easily if you work in short practice sessions spaced widely apart, instead of longer sessions held closer together. (2) You can learn many tasks best by imitating experts. (3) You should perform a new activity yourself, rather than merely watch or listen to someone. (4) You learn better if you know immediately how good your performance was. (5) You should practice difficult parts of a task separately and then try to incorporate them into the task as a whole.

Two additional rules apply mainly to verbal learning. (1) The more meaningful the task, the more easily it is learned. You will find a task easier to learn if you can relate it to other things you have learned. (2) A part of a task is learned faster when it is distinctive. When studying a book, for example, underlining a difficult passage in red makes it distinctive and easier to learn.

Transfer of Training. Psychologists and educators recognize that new learning can profit from old learning because learning one thing helps in learning something else. This process is called *transfer of training.*

Transfer of training can be either positive or negative. Suppose a person learns two tasks. After he learns Task 1, he might find Task 2 easier or harder. If Task 2 is easier, then the old learning has been a help and positive transfer of training has occurred. If Task 2 is harder, the old learning is a hindrance and negative transfer has occurred.

Whether transfer is positive or negative depends on the relationship between the two tasks. Positive transfer occurs when the two tasks have similar stimuli and both stimuli elicit the same response. For example, if we know the German word *gross*, it is easier to learn the French word *gros* because both words mean *large*. In this case, similar stimuli (*gross* and *gros*) elicit the same response (*large*).

Negative transfer occurs when the two tasks have similar stimuli, but these stimuli elicit different responses. After you learn the German word *Gras* (grass), it is harder to learn the French word *gras* (fat). The words are similar, but they have different meanings. In this case, similar stimuli (*Gras* and *gras*) elicit different responses.

Psychologists believe new learning can profit from old learning because of three factors: (1) positive transfer of training, (2) general principles that we learn in one task and apply to another task, and (3) good study habits that we learn in one task which help us learn another task. ERNEST R. HILGARD and LEONARD M. HOROWITZ

Related Articles in WORLD BOOK include:

Animal (Behavior; Intelligence of Animals)
Association
Behavior
Comparative Psychology
Developmental Psychology
Educational Psychology
Instinct
Memory
Mind
Pavlov, Ivan P
Psychology (History)
Teaching Machine
Thought

MOTIVATION is a word that is popularly used to explain why people behave as they do. In psychology and the other behavioral sciences, the word has a more limited use. Some scientists view motivation as the factor that determines behavior, as expressed in the phrase "All behavior is motivated." This usage expresses a general attitude or conviction, and is similar to the popular usage. However, when studying motivation, other scientists focus on two specific aspects of motivated behavior—the energization or arousal of behavior, and the direction of behavior.

Some scientists view motivation as the factor that energizes behavior. That is, motivation arouses an organism and causes it to act. According to this viewpoint, motivation provides the energy in behavior, but habits, abilities, skills, and structural features of organisms give direction or guidance to what they do. Other scientists, however, say that motivation serves some direction-giving function. Thus, in the behavioral sciences, motivation can mean energization or direction of behavior or both.

Energization is like arousal or activation, and means being "stirred up" or "ready for action." Energization can take place in several ways. An organism can be aroused by stimuli from outside or inside its body. If you touch a hot burner, pain from the external stimulus arouses behavior. A new or unexpected stimulus can arouse fear in some cases, and curiosity in other cases. Stomach contractions that produce hunger pangs are an internal stimulus. Thirst, which is often said to consist of dryness in the mouth and throat, is another internal stimulus.

Physiological conditions can make organisms sensitive to stimuli from the environment. For example, when hormones, the chemical secretions of the endocrine glands, reach a certain level in many species of birds, the birds begin nest-building activities.

After an organism has been aroused, its actions depend on the external or internal stimuli that call forth habits or other dispositions to respond in particular ways. An aroused organism with no habits or dispositions, or with no stimuli available to evoke habits or dispositions, acts aimlessly or restlessly. With such stimuli and habits present, the aroused organism acts purposefully and effectively.

Motivational conditions themselves may provide stimuli that direct behavior. For example, hunger or some other internal motive may direct an organism toward food. Or a motive state such as sex may make the organism sensitive to external stimuli, including a mate. But the directing function of the stimulation arising from motives differs from the arousal function of motives.

Kinds of Motives suggested by behavioral scientists usually include four groups: (1) homeostatic motives, (2) non-homeostatic motives, (3) learned motives, and (4) incentive-like motives.

Homeostatic Motives include hunger, thirst, respiration, and excretion. Just as a thermostat works to maintain a balanced temperature in a room, homeostatic motives work to keep the body in a balanced internal state. (The term *homeostasis* refers to the body's tendency to maintain such a balanced internal state.) Homeostatic motives are set in motion either by bodily deficits or by bodily excesses. When a person's body needs water, for example, bodily changes occur that make the individual thirsty and motivate him to seek something to drink.

Non-homeostatic Motives, like homeostatic ones, are biological in character, but they do not function homeostatically. Non-homeostatic motives include sex, such maternal activity as nest-building, and motives dealing with curiosity about the environment.

Learned Motives are acquired through reward and punishment in social situations, especially those of early childhood. These motives include anxiety, dependency, aggression, and a desire for social approval.

Incentive-like Motives include such incentives as money, prizes, status, and other goals. Through learning, we come to value these incentives so that the possibility of attaining them is motivating. Many homeostatic, non-homeostatic, and learned motives may also function through incentive-like processes. Food, for example, can arouse an animal because a hungry animal has learned that obtaining and eating food will reduce its hunger. In animals, also, a learned motive such as fear is usually associated with and aroused by a specific place where the animal experienced fear previously.

Theories of Motivation. Most general theories of motivation identify important sources of motives and describe their operation. Some theories stress sex and aggression, and others emphasize a variety of homeostatic, biological motives. Both groups of theories state that the organism seeks to remove a state of tension or arousal.

Still other theories emphasize such motives as curiosity, information-seeking, and interest in problem-solving. These theories indicate that organisms seek an intermediate level of arousal rather than the complete reduction of tension.

Some psychologists believe organisms tend to seek pleasure and avoid pain or unpleasantness. Other students of motivation say that realization of one's potentialities is the basic motivational factor.

In addition to general theories of motivation, there are theoretical descriptions of specific motivated behavior including sex, aggression, hunger, thirst, achievement, and dependency. A complete theory of motivation has not yet been formulated. CHARLES N. COFER

See also DEVELOPMENTAL PSYCHOLOGY (Psychoanalytic Theory; Cognitive Theory); LEARNING (How We Learn; Efficient Learning); PERCEPTION (Factors Affecting Perception); PSYCHOLOGY.

MOTIVATION RESEARCH tries to learn how people choose things they buy. It also seeks to find out what people learn from advertising. Motivation researchers explore the feelings and points of view of consumers. They use knowledge from psychology, sociology, and other social sciences to interpret these emotions and attitudes. Motivation researchers interview people in a conversational way, and sometimes give them tests that must be analyzed by psychologists and sociologists. This type of research has shown that people do not shop with only price and quality in mind. They may buy something to impress others, or to keep up with their group. A person may also buy something to imitate someone he admires. BURLEIGH B. GARDNER

See also ADVERTISING (Research).

PERCEPTION. The world around us consists of various kinds and levels of physical energy. Our knowledge of the world comes through our sense organs, which react to these energies. Certain wavelengths of electromagnetic energy stimulate our eyes. Our ears sense certain kinds of mechanical vibrations in the air. Our noses and tongues are sensitive to certain chemical stimuli. Sense organs in our skin respond to pressure, temperature changes, and various stimuli related to pain. Sense organs in our joints, tendons, and muscles are sensitive to body movement and position.

The sense organs change the various environmental energies into nervous impulses, and these impulses then go to the brain. Through the psychological process of perception, the patterns of energies become known as objects, events, people, and other aspects of the world.

The process of perception does not reveal objects and events of the world. We see light and color, but there is no light or color in the electromagnetic waves that stimulate the eyes. In the same way, there is no music or noise in the vibrations that stimulate the ear. The brain organizes and interprets nervous impulses from the eyes as light and color, and impulses from the ears as sound. Together, the sense organs and the brain transform physical energy from environmental stimuli into information about the events around us.

When looking at the illustration on this page, you may first see only a complicated pattern of dark and light areas. As you study the pattern, your first perception may change, particularly if you are told that a bearded man is in the picture. After you have seen the man, it will be almost impossible not to see him when you look at the picture again. This picture emphasizes two important points about perception. First, stimulation of the sense organs alone does not determine the nature of what is perceived. Second, perception is a dynamic process of "working on" sensory data to produce perceptual objects and events. The "work" involves many physical, physiological, and psychological factors.

William M. Smith

Hidden Figure Designs show how we must "work on" sensory stimulation to perceive something recognizable. The face of a man with a beard and long hair appears in the top half of this design, in the center. It is a front view, cut off above the eyes. Do not look for such details as the eyes, but concentrate on getting an overall impression.

Factors Affecting Perception

Various factors influence what and how we perceive. Our perceptions are influenced by the ways our bodies are structured to receive and process stimuli from the environment. Our perceptions also reflect our emotions, needs, expectations, and learning.

Receptors. Each sensory system, such as vision, hearing, or touch, has its own specialized body parts. These parts are called *receptors*, and they change energies from the environment into nervous impulses. The human eye, for example, has two major kinds of receptors in the *retina* (the light-sensitive part of the eye). These receptors are called *rods* and *cones*. The rods respond to light, but not to color (different frequencies of light). The cones do respond to different frequencies of light, and are called color receptors. The rods allow us to see in dim light, and the cones enable us to see colors and sharp detail in bright light. Thus, the particular ways that receptors are structured and function help determine the perceptual effects related to them.

The Brain. Certain physical and functional features of the brain also determine some aspects of perception. The part of the brain that serves vision has different kinds of cells that respond only under certain conditions of stimulation. Some of these cells respond only when a light goes off. Others respond when a light goes on, but they stop responding if the light stays on. Such cells also are arranged in special ways in the brain, and this fact is related to how we perceive. For example, some cells are arranged in columns or in clusters. Such arrangements are related to how we perceive edges and forms.

Learning, Emotion, and Motivation. Much evidence points to the conclusion that early experience, learning, emotion, and motivation are important in defining what and how we perceive. Part of this accumulating evidence comes from experiments that compare how persons in different cultures perceive things. The perception of such things as form, color, pain, and touch may differ from culture to culture, depending on habits and customs, and training of children.

A simple example of how learning can affect perception is provided by reading the phrases inside the two triangles in the illustration on the next page. Did you fail to see the duplicate word in each phrase? Most persons do, and some continue to do so even with many repeated readings. In learning to perceive words and sentences, we learn not to perceive each letter and word separately. Instead, we become able to scan the overall pattern and "fill in" the remainder. A poor reader is more likely than a good reader to see the duplicate word in each phrase.

Some illusions are related to learning and past experience. An illusion is not a false perception, as many people believe, but one that is inconsistent with another perception. Since perception does not literally reveal the environment, no sensory system is closer to some absolute truth than any other. We tend to check visual illusions against touch, but touch can involve illusory effects, too. Look at the two triangular patches of gray containing black and white detail in the illustration on this page. If you see the patches as being different shades of gray, you are experiencing an illusion. The patches were made with the same paint.

Emotions and motivation can have an important effect on perception. Sometimes a severe emotional disturbance can prevent perception completely, as when emotional shock causes an individual to lose his hearing temporarily. We are more likely to perceive those aspects of our environment that are related to our motives. For example, motivation can affect the perceived characteristics of objects. To a hungry man, food may appear larger or more colorful than usual.

PERCEPTUAL EFFECTS

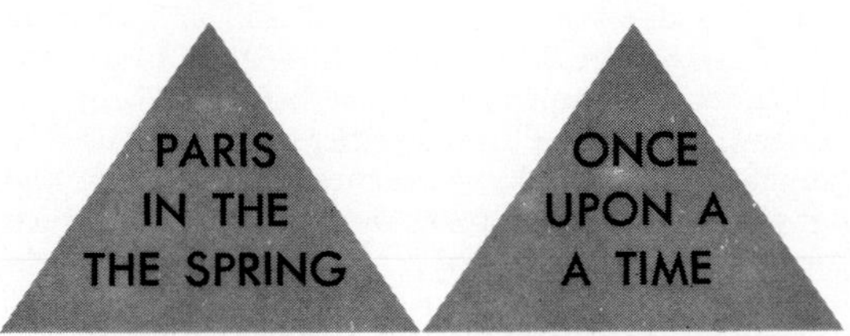

What are the two phrases printed in the two triangles above? Read them carefully. Did you read them correctly the first time?

How many complete cubes do you see in the drawing at the left? Three or five?

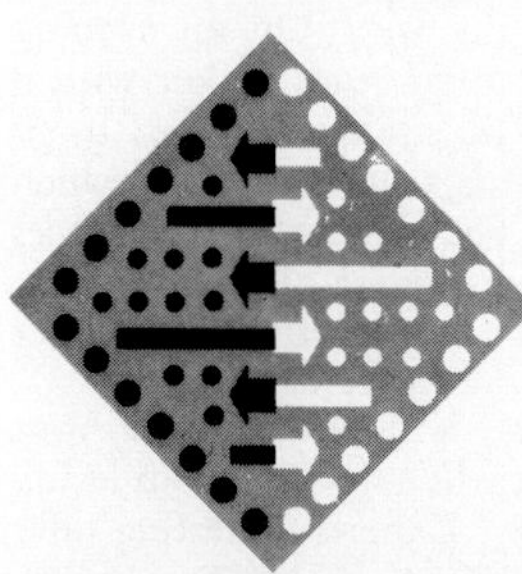

How do the two gray triangles at the left compare in brightness? In the drawings below, does the rectangle surrounded by black appear brighter than the rectangle surrounded by white? The text of this article discusses each of the perceptual effects shown here.

William M. Smith

Understanding Perception

Types of Perception. Perception has three levels of complexity: (1) *detection,* (2) *recognition,* and (3) *discrimination.* Detection refers to whether a person can sense that he is being stimulated by some form of energy. For example, a light may be so dim that he can barely detect its presence. Recognition means being able to identify as well as detect a particular pattern of stimulation. Discrimination means being able to perceive patterns of stimulation as different. For example, a person may hear slight differences between two similar musical tones.

The field of study that deals with the levels of perception is called *psychophysics.* Experimental psychologists investigate the relationships between the physical properties of stimulus patterns and the perceived effects. They may try to find the relationship between sound frequency and the perceived pitch of the sound.

Principles of Perception. There are a number of general principles that help us understand the process of perception. One of the most important is the principle of *closure.* It tells us that we have the general tendency to perceive things as complete and unified. We tend to "fill in" parts that are missing, or parts that conform to an overall impression.

The principle of *constancy* states that despite changes that occur in stimulation, we have a strong tendency to perceive objects as constant in size, shape, color, and other qualities. For example, an orange will be perceived with its characteristic color under different kinds of light.

The opposite of the principle of constancy is also important. Sometimes an object or pattern of stimulation will remain constant, but the perceived effect will vary. Look at the gray and black cubes in the illustration on this page. At one moment you will see three complete cubes, and at another you may see five.

Another important principle relates to *perceptual context.* The perception of an object or event depends in part on the *context* (surrounding conditions). Look at the two gray rectangles in the illustration on this page. One rectangle is surrounded by a black area, and the other by a white area. Do the two gray rectangles seem identical? To most persons, gray surrounded by black appears brighter and somewhat larger. This effect is called *visual induction.* Notice, too, that the effect is opposite to that observed with the two gray triangles with black and white detail. In this case, the gray with black detail appears darker rather than brighter. But all four figures—rectangles and triangles—were made with the same paint.

William M. Smith

Related Articles in World Book include:

Color (How the Eye Sees Color; How Color Fools the Eye)
Ear (Parts of the Ear; How We Hear)
Eye (Parts of the Eye; How We See)
Human Engineering
Nervous System
Optical Illusion
Psychology
Senses
Smell
Taste
Touch

TESTING—in psychology, education, and industry—involves making estimates of individual characteristics. Tests are used to help estimate differences between people in learning ability, school achievement, mechanical skills, clerical aptitude, and many other special abilities. To a lesser extent, tests are also used to estimate a person's attitudes and personality traits.

Information gained from tests has many important uses. Teachers test their students' ability and achievement to discover what the students have learned, what they should try to learn next, and how rapidly they can be expected to learn. Employers test employees and job applicants to determine the kinds of skills these individuals possess and the kinds of work they can be expected to do well. Psychologists use special kinds of tests to study personality characteristics, especially when they suspect emotional problems.

Most tests used by schools and employers are given for at least one of three purposes: (1) to help estimate what and how much an individual has already learned, (2) to help predict what he probably can learn next in school or on the job, and (3) to help estimate how well he is likely to get along with other people.

Most printed tests taken by students and employees are *standardized*. A test has been standardized when it has been used, revised, and used again until its results are uniform under certain conditions. The person who gives a standardized test knows the average test scores earned by others tested at various ages or at different stages of training. Many teachers also use *nonstandardized* tests that they devise themselves, but this article is about standardized tests.

Any standardized test is nothing more than a standard job which you do according to directions. The results of your performance are compared with those of other persons who have taken the same test. The test may measure learning ability, recall of American history, accuracy in arithmetic, or skill in using your hands. Every test is simply a job designed to let you show what you can do.

In order to work properly, a standardized test must be both valid and reliable. A test is *valid* if it measures what it is intended to measure. For example, a test of reading comprehension could lose much of its validity if the time allowed for taking it were so brief that the test measured reading speed rather than comprehension.

A test is *reliable* if it yields about the same score every time the same individual takes it. To establish the reliability of a test, it is given to the same group of people on different occasions. The more consistent the scores for each individual, the more reliable the test. Generally, long tests are more reliable than short tests because they provide a larger sample of a person's performance.

Tests of Learning Ability are the best known standardized tests. These tests are often called intelligence tests, "IQ" tests, or academic aptitude tests. But all of them are standard jobs on which an individual can demonstrate intellectual skills that he has been learning for most of his life.

Tests of learning ability measure in a comparative way some of the many intellectual skills you have learned in and out of school. Contrary to what most people believe, no test can open a window to let someone see how bright you are, and no test can measure the amount of brightness you inherited from your ancestors. "Intelligence" is simply a general term used to describe, in a comparative way, a person's capability in solving intellectual problems. Intelligence is not something that can be measured directly. Tests of intelligence call for a demonstration of certain intellectual skills, and that performance is then used to make estimates of "intelligence." See INTELLIGENCE.

Achievement Tests are similar to tests of learning ability. But the content of achievement tests is much more closely related to a specific field of learning. Achievement tests measure learning accomplished over a short period of time—a semester, a year, or two years. Ability tests measure learning acquired during an individual's lifetime.

Thousands of achievement tests are made just for school use. There are tests of achievement in division of fractions, in American history before 1776, in the biology of fishes, and in many other subjects. In its most familiar form, an achievement test is designed to find out whether a student has learned what his teacher has tried to teach him. The test is no more than a set of jobs on which the student can demonstrate his learning.

Aptitude Tests and Interest Tests are special kinds of measurements used mainly for guidance in school. A person does not "have" an aptitude in the same sense that he has blue eyes or large feet. But he does have a combination of interest and experience in certain kinds of activity. A boy who likes to tinker with machinery will do better on a test of mechanical aptitude than a boy who has never tinkered with machinery. A school counselor would say that the first boy has an *aptitude* for mechanics. That is, he has a better chance of succeeding in mechanics than in some other field where he has had little interest or experience.

Interest tests are not really tests at all. They are usually called *interest inventories*, and resemble check lists of activities, ideas, and circumstances. A question on an interest inventory might ask: "On an evening alone at home, would you rather read, tinker with a radio, or paint a picture?" The student is asked to go through a list of such questions and indicate which items interest him the most. The sum of his preferences offers a good clue to his main interests. Used together, aptitude tests and inventories help a student discover his own areas of strength and experience.

Learning how to take tests will not improve your ability or achievement, but it will help you avoid losing test score points unnecessarily. Experts in testing offer the following pointers:

(1) Get all the experience you can in taking tests. As in everything else you do, your testmanship will improve with practice.

(2) Cramming before a test is better than no study at all. But careful review, spread over several days, is better than cramming.

(3) Get a good night's sleep, because rest before a test is important.

(4) Find out ahead of time what any test is to cover. Ask enough questions to protect yourself from surprises.

(5) Be sure you understand the directions at the beginning of every test. If you begin a test before you are

Learning Ability Tests measure intellectual skills that an individual has learned from many sources, including his home, school, and community. These tests are used to estimate a student's capacity for learning. They can help teachers instruct a student better, and direct him toward kinds of learning that best suit his abilities.

Test 1. *Information*

Mark the word that makes the sentence TRUE.

Our first President was—

1. Adams 2. Washington 3. Lincoln 4. Jefferson 5. Monroe

Test 2. *Synonyms*

Mark the word which has the SAME or most nearly the same meaning as the first word.

Correct 1. Neat 2. Fair 3. Right 4. Poor 5. Good

Test 3. *Logical Selection*

Mark the word which tells what the thing ALWAYS has or ALWAYS involves.

A cat always has—

1. Kittens 2. Spots 3. Milk 4. Mouse 5. Hair

Test 4. *Classification*

In each line below, four of the words belong together. Pick out the ONE WORD which does not belong with the others.

1. Dog 2. Cat 3. Horse 4. Chicken 5. Cow

Test 5. *Analogies*

Hat is to head as shoe is to—

1. Arm 2. Leg 3. Foot 4. Fit 5. Glove

Test 6. *Opposites*

Choose the word which is OPPOSITE, or most nearly opposite, in meaning to the beginning word of each line.

North 1. Hot 2. East 3. West 4. Down 5. South

Test 7. *Best Answer*

Read the statement and mark the answer which you think is best.

We should not put a burning match in the wastebasket because:

1. Matches cost money. 2. We might need a match later.
3. It might go out. 4. It might start a fire.

Reproduced by permission of Harcourt, Brace, & World, Inc.

Achievement Tests measure information, skills, and ideas that are learned in a short time and are taught in schools. These tests are used to determine whether a student has learned what a teacher has tried to teach him. One kind of social science test, *right*, requires a student to use his knowledge of interpreting maps, as well as his understanding of geography and economics.

The shading on the map at right is used to indicate
(A) population density
(B) percentage of total labor force in agriculture
(C) per capita income
(D) death rate per thousand of population

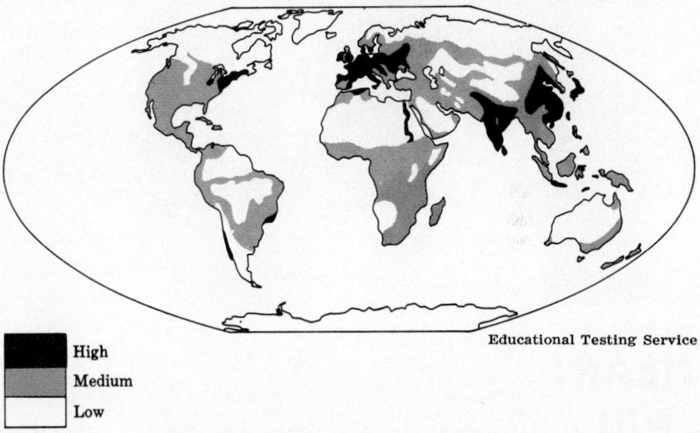

High
Medium
Low

Educational Testing Service

absolutely clear about what you are supposed to do, your score will probably be low.

(6) Answer first the questions or problems that are easy for you. Answer them quickly, and then go back to the harder ones. This is the single most important rule in taking a test.

(7) Unless there is a clearly stated penalty for guessing, put down an answer for every question. This is the second most important rule in test-taking.

There are several things to keep in mind about the score you make on a test. First, any test takes only a sample of your skill or knowledge in any subject. Your score cannot tell you all about yourself, but only how well you performed on one particular test.

Second, every test score is simply a comparison of your test performance with the performances of other persons. If the others are like you in some important way, such as being the same age or in the same grade, the comparison of your score with theirs will provide some useful information.

Third, every test score is an estimate rather than a precise measurement. To remind you that your score is an estimate, some test scores are reported as *bands* rather than as single points. The bands show the range over which your scores would probably spread if you took the same test many times.

Personality tests are interpreted differently than tests of learning ability, achievement, or performance. Scores on measurements of personal characteristics are often used simply as clues for further inquiry by a trained specialist. They are not regarded as conclusive indicators of human traits. JOHN E. DOBBIN

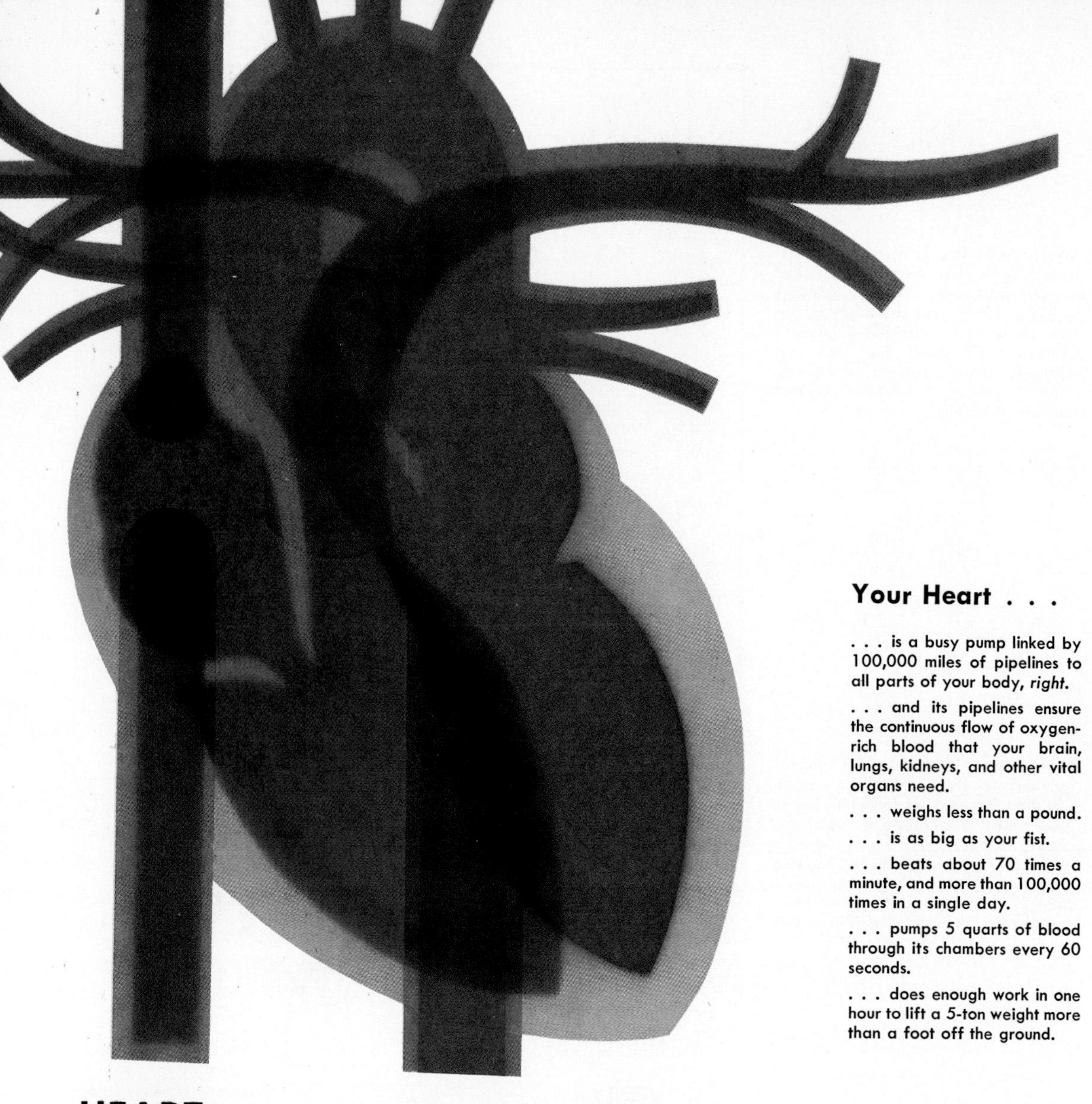

Your Heart . . .

. . . is a busy pump linked by 100,000 miles of pipelines to all parts of your body, *right.*

. . . and its pipelines ensure the continuous flow of oxygen-rich blood that your brain, lungs, kidneys, and other vital organs need.

. . . weighs less than a pound.

. . . is as big as your fist.

. . . beats about 70 times a minute, and more than 100,000 times in a single day.

. . . pumps 5 quarts of blood through its chambers every 60 seconds.

. . . does enough work in one hour to lift a 5-ton weight more than a foot off the ground.

HEART

HEART is a busy machine that pumps blood to all parts of the body. Blood carries oxygen to the brain and all other parts of your body. As long as your heart pumps blood, your body gets the oxygen it needs. If your heart stops, the oxygen is cut off and you will die unless a special device is used to circulate your blood.

The heart is a large hollow muscle. Tubes called *veins* bring blood to the heart. Other tubes called *arteries* carry blood away from the heart. Regulators called *valves* control the flow of blood through the heart itself.

A person's heart is about the size of his fist, and his heart and his fist grow at about the same rate. The heart of an adult is about 5 inches long, $3\frac{1}{2}$ inches wide, and $2\frac{1}{2}$ inches thick. A man's heart weighs about 11 ounces, and a woman's heart weighs about 9 ounces.

Michael E. De Bakey and Edward B. Diethrich are the contributors of this article. Dr. De Bakey is Professor and Chairman of the Department of Surgery at Baylor University College of Medicine, in Houston, Tex. Dr. Diethrich is an Assistant Professor of Surgery in the same department. The illustration consultant was Arnold Ryan Chalfant.

The heart lies in a slanting position near the middle of the chest toward the front. It is wider at the top than at the bottom. The wider end points toward the person's right shoulder. The narrower end points downward, toward the front of his chest and to his left. The lower end is the part you can feel beating.

This article is about the human heart, but many kinds of animals have hearts. For example, earthworms, houseflies, snails, and some other *invertebrate animals* (animals without backbones) have hearts. Their hearts are not as well developed as human hearts. Often, they are just a simple tube with thick walls. All *vertebrate animals* (animals with backbones) have hearts. These animals include frogs, toads, lizards, snakes, and all birds and mammals.

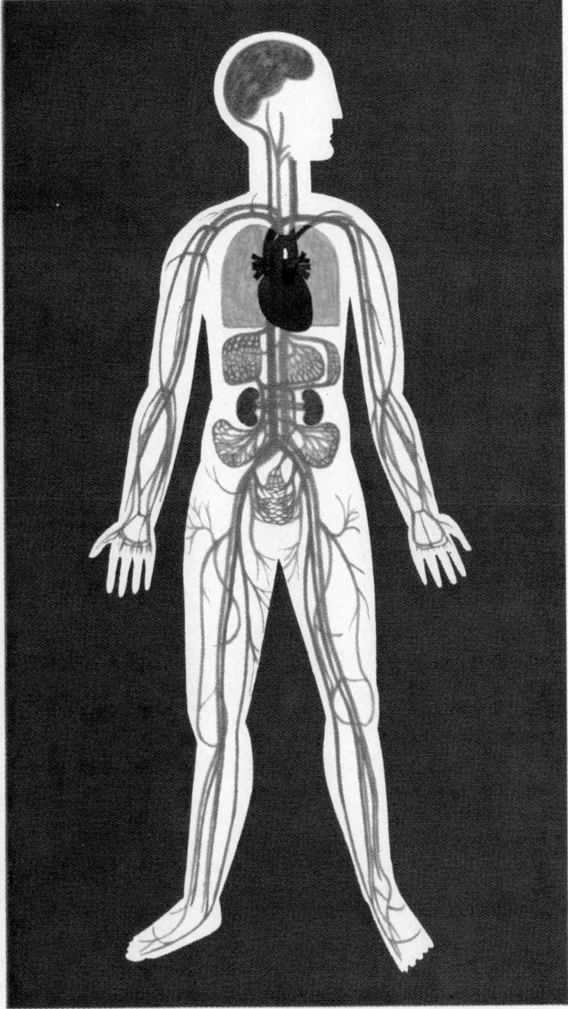

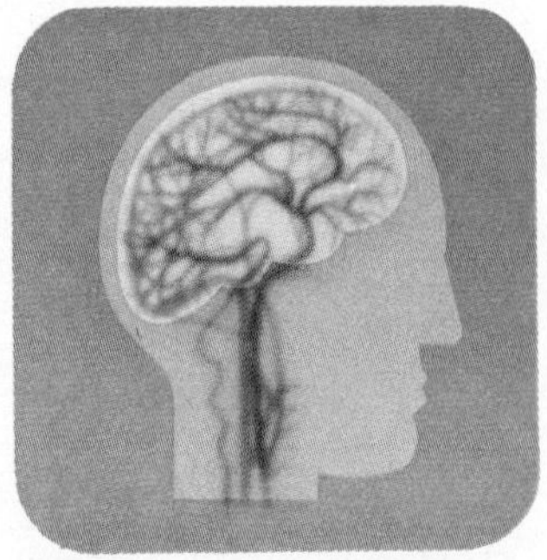

The Brain suffers permanent damage if its supply of blood fails for more than a few minutes. The carotid arteries, which supply the brain with blood, come from a point just off the aorta, very close to the heart.

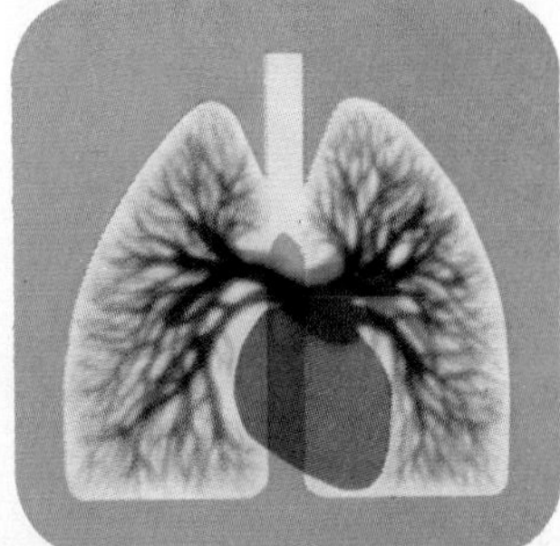

The Lungs refresh the blood pumped to them from the right side of the heart. They remove carbon dioxide from the blood, and add fresh oxygen to it. The blood re-enters the heart, and is then pumped to the body.

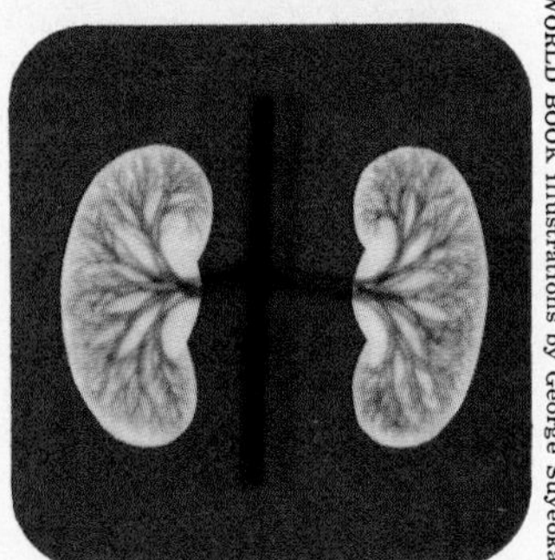

The Kidneys lie very close to the aorta, and only a short distance from the heart itself. The high pressure in this area forces blood through a filtering process in the kidneys that takes wastes out of the blood.

WORLD BOOK illustrations by George Suyeoka

HEART/*Its Parts and Development*

Parts of the Heart. The heart is completely enclosed by a thin sac called the *pericardium.* The pericardium is made of tough tissue. It protects the heart from rubbing against the lungs and the wall of the chest. The inside of the pericardium has a smooth lining that *secretes* (discharges) a slippery liquid. The heart beats smoothly and with little friction against the moistened lining of the pericardium.

A muscular wall called the *septum* divides the heart lengthwise. Two chambers, one above the other, are on each side of the septum. The upper chamber on each side is called an *atrium.* The thin-walled *atria* (plural of *atrium*) collect the blood flowing into the heart from the veins. Below each atrium is another chamber called a *ventricle.* The two ventricles pump the blood into the arteries.

The walls of the ventricles are made of thick, strong muscles. The right ventricle pumps blood only to the lungs, but the left ventricle pumps blood to the entire body. The left ventricle has walls three times as thick as those of the right ventricle because it has to pump the blood so much farther.

Valves control the flow of blood through the heart. The *tricuspid valve* is between the right atrium and the right ventricle. The *mitral valve* is between the left atrium and the left ventricle. The *semilunar valves* control the flow of blood from the ventricles to the arteries. The semilunar valve that controls blood-flow from the left ventricle to the *aorta* (the main artery of the body) is also called the *aortic valve.*

Arteries carry blood from the heart to other parts of the body, but the heart itself also must receive nourishment. Blood flows to the heart muscle through *coronary arteries.* The coronary arteries lie over the walls of the heart in a complicated network, and carry oxygen to all parts of the hardworking heart muscle.

PARTS OF THE HEART

The heart lies between the lungs at the center of the chest. The lower part of the heart points toward the left side of the body. Because the beating, or pumping, takes place in the lower part, many persons incorrectly think the heart is entirely on the left side of the body. This illustration shows the heart about two thirds normal size.

Superior Vena Cava
Aorta
Pulmonary Artery
Left Atrium
Right Atrium
Coronary
Arteries
and Veins

The Outer Covering of the Heart is a strong, thin membrane called the *pericardium*. The superior vena cava, aorta, and other large blood vessels lead in and out of the heart. Smaller blood vessels nourish the heart itself.

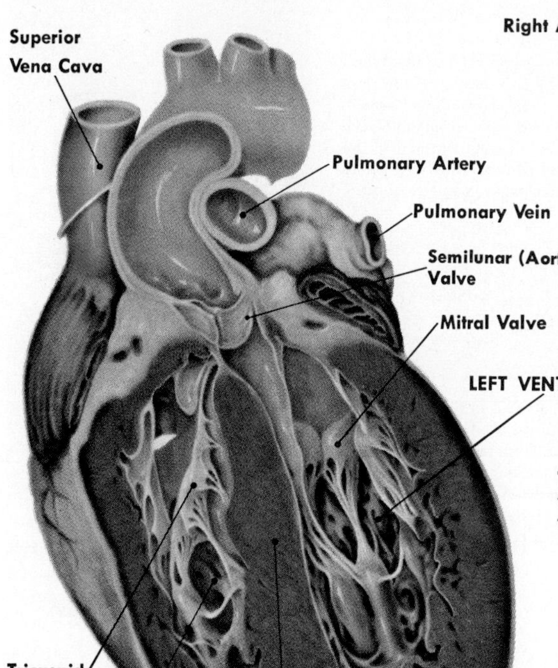

The Ventricles, *left,* make up the largest part of the heart. They form the whole lower portion. Their thick, strong muscles pump blood throughout the body.

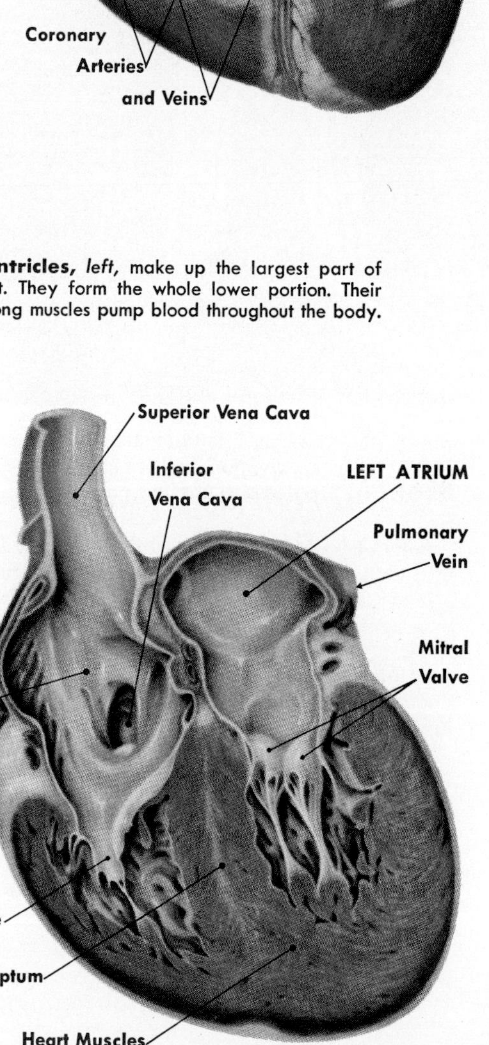

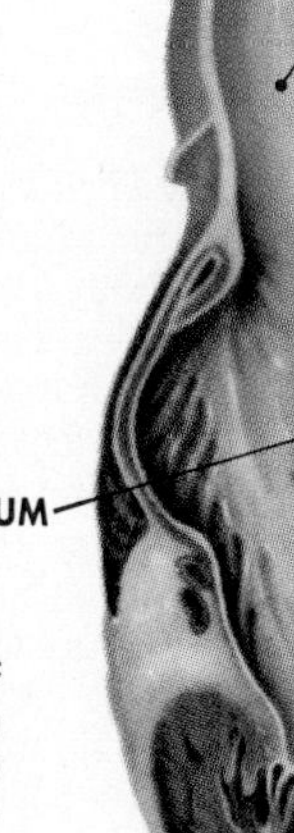

The Atria, *right,* form the upper, smaller part of the heart. They have thin walls, and are smaller than the ventricles. Each atrium serves as a collecting station for the blood that flows into the heart.

Courtesy of Abbott Laboratories International Company. Color reconstructions by Virginia Samter and Arnold Ryan Chalfant.

Development of the Heart. The heart starts to form as soon as the embryo begins to develop inside the mother's body. The walls that divide the heart into chambers are forming when the embryo is only six weeks old.

At first, the human heart is a simple tube that soon begins to beat regularly. It grows so fast that there is no room for it to become longer inside the embryo. It doubles back on itself, twists around, and begins to look like the heart as we know it. A layer of tissue grows down the middle of the tube, dividing it into the right and left sides. A little later, the partitions between the atria and ventricles start to form.

The human heart goes through stages in which it resembles the hearts of various animals, before it is finally divided into four chambers. First, when it is a simple tube, it is like the heart of most fishes. Later, when the partitions begin to form, there is a time when the atria are partly separated but the ventricles have no wall between them. At this stage, the human heart looks like the heart of a frog. After the atria have divided, but the division between the ventricles is incomplete, the human heart resembles that of a snake or a turtle.

During the first weeks of growth, the human heart is nine times as large in proportion to the size of the whole body as it is in an adult. It lies high up in the chest. Later it moves into its permanent position in the middle of the chest.

The next striking change in the human heart occurs after birth. Before birth, there is no need for the blood to go through the lungs, because there is no air in them. The blood flows from the right atrium directly to the left atrium through an opening in the septum called the *foramen ovale*. Another short circuit occurs through a blood vessel called the *ductus arteriosus*. The ductus arteriosus extends from the *pulmonary artery*, which connects the heart and lungs, to the aorta.

After the baby's supply of oxygen from its mother has been cut off following birth, the baby must use its own lungs. The openings through the ductus arteriosus and foramen ovale are no longer needed, and they gradually close. In most infants, the ductus arteriosus closes within three months. The foramen ovale usually closes before the end of the first year.

Three changes gradually take place in the heart as the baby grows into a child and then into an adult. First, the heart slowly increases in weight along with the rest of the body. At birth, the heart weighs only about ⅔ of an ounce. At two years, it weighs about 1½ ounces. At nine years, it weighs 3⅓ ounces, and at 15 or 16 years, about 7 ounces. Second, the heart lies almost horizontal in small children. As the chest lengthens, the lower end of the heart shifts downward so that it lies in a more nearly vertical position. Third, the child's heart beats more slowly as he grows older. An infant's heart beats about 120 times a minute. The heart of a 7-year-old child beats about 90 times a minute. An adult's heart beats about 70 times a minute.

HEART/*How the Heart Works*

Each side of the heart performs a different pumping job. The right side takes blood from the body and pumps it to the lungs. The left side collects blood from the lungs and pumps it to the body.

Blood entering the right side of the heart contains *carbon dioxide*, a waste product of the body. All blood entering the right side of the heart goes to the lungs before it reaches the left side of the heart. In the lungs, the carbon dioxide is removed, and oxygen is added to the blood. Blood that flows to the body from the left side of the heart contains fresh oxygen. The oxygen is used in the body cells to produce energy. See CIRCULATION; BLOOD.

Right Side. Blood from the body flows into the right atrium through two large veins. One of these veins, the *superior vena cava*, carries blood from the head and arms. The other vein, the *inferior vena cava*, carries blood from the trunk and legs.

Blood from the body fills the right atrium. The atrium then contracts, squeezing blood through the tricuspid valve into the ventricle. The tricuspid valve is made of three little triangular flaps of thin, strong fibrous tissue. These flaps permit the blood to flow into the ventricle, but they prevent it from flowing back into the atrium. They are like doors that open only in one direction.

At first, the ventricle is relaxed, but it contracts when it is filled with blood. The resulting pressure closes the tricuspid valve and opens the semilunar valve between the ventricle and the *pulmonary artery*. Blood gushes through the valve into the artery, which leads to the lungs. The valve is called *semilunar* because it has three flaps that are shaped like half-moons. Blood squeezed from the ventricle pushes the flaps against the walls of the pulmonary artery.

Left Side. From the lungs, the blood flows back to the heart through the four *pulmonary veins*. It flows out of the pulmonary veins into the left atrium. The left atrium, like its neighbor on the right, then contracts, squeezing blood through the mitral valve into the left ventricle. The mitral valve is similar to the tricuspid valve, except that it has only two flaps. The left ventricle contracts, forcing blood through another semilunar valve into the aorta. The aorta, with its numerous branches, carries blood throughout the body.

Phases. The two sides of the heart relax and fill, and then contract and empty themselves at the same time. The atria contract only a split second before the ventricles do. The relaxing and filling phase is called the *diastole*. The contracting and pumping phase is called the *systole*. The action felt as a heart beat is the systole.

Blood Pressure. The blood in the circulatory system is always under pressure, as is the water in the pipes of a water system. Blood pressure depends upon the amount of blood in the system, the strength and rate of the heart's contraction, and the elasticity of the arteries. Doctors measure two phases of blood pressure—the *systolic pressure* and the *diastolic pressure*. The systolic pressure is the blood pressure when the heart is contracted. The diastolic pressure is the pressure when the heart relaxes between beats. Doctors use a device called a *sphygmomanometer* to measure a patient's blood pressure. See BLOOD PRESSURE; MANOMETER.

HOW YOUR HEART WORKS

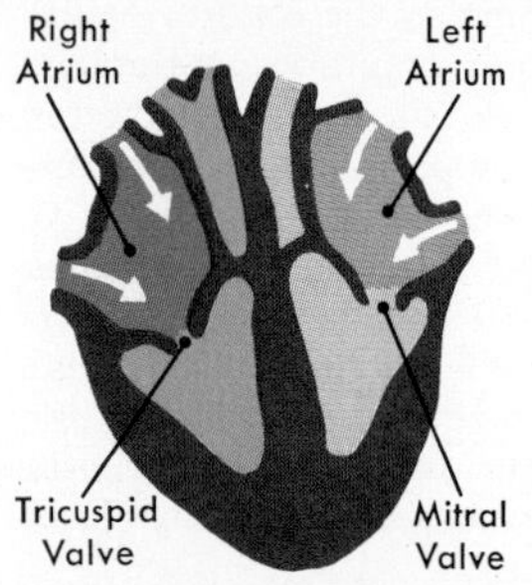

The Heart Relaxes between beats in the *diastole* phase. Blood flows into the heart, filling both atria. The mitral and tricuspid valves open.

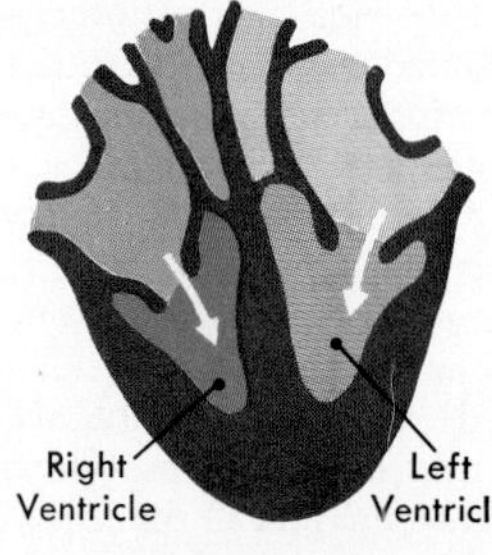

The Pumping Phase, or *systole*, begins when the atria contract. They push blood through the mitral and tricuspid valves into the ventricles.

Pulmonary Artery
Aorta
Semilunar Valves

The Ventricles Contract and force the blood through the semilunar valves into the aorta, the body's largest artery, and the pulmonary artery.

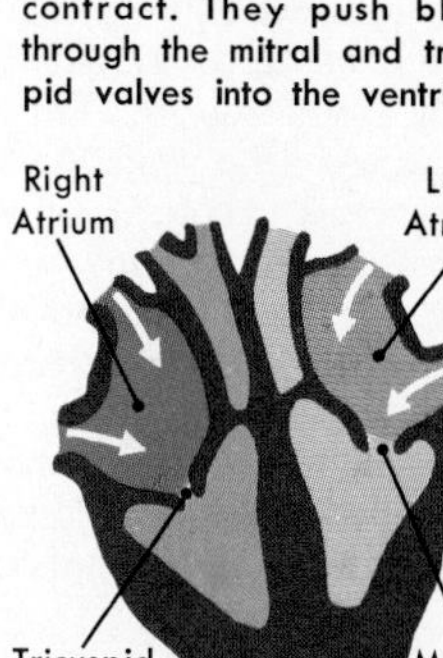

The Heart Relaxes again, and the semilunar valves close. Blood flows into the atria, the mitral and tricuspid valves open, and the cycle begins again.

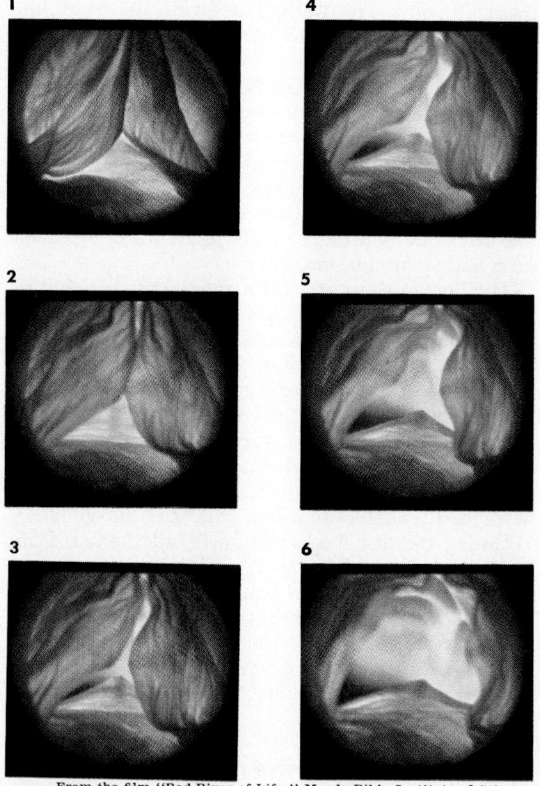

From the film "Red River of Life," Moody Bible Institute of Science

The Aortic Valve, *above*, controls the flow of blood from the left ventricle to the aorta, the largest artery in the body. This sequence of photographs was taken inside a heart taken from a dead person. It shows how the flaps of the valve open to let out blood as the powerful left ventricle contracts.

Beat of the Heart. The walls of the heart are made of a special kind of muscle. The heart muscle contracts and relaxes regularly and automatically. A beat is one complete contraction and relaxation of the heart muscle.

A special system of muscles in the heart causes it to beat with a regular rhythm. One part of this system, the *sinoatrial* (*sinoauricular*) or *S-A node*, has the job of starting each heartbeat, setting the pace, and causing contraction of the heart muscle. It has been called the "pacemaker" of the heart. The impulse from this node spreads through the atria and reaches a second node, the *atrioventricular*, or *A-V node*. A part of this specialized system, called the *atrioventricular bundle* or the *bundle of His*, conducts the beating impulse from the atria and the A-V node to the rest of the heart. This system causes the heart to contract as a single unit.

Sometimes the heart may stop beating because of an accident, a heart attack, or surgical shock. If the heart stops during an operation, a doctor may open the patient's chest and massage the heart until it starts to beat again. In other emergency situations, doctors or other specially trained persons may give the victim *external heart massage*. They apply pressure to the chest in a certain way to restart the heartbeat.

Rate of Beating. Without oxygen, the body cells stop working. Sometimes the body needs much oxygen. At other times, it requires little. The heart responds automatically to these needs. A man's heart normally beats about 70 times a minute, but the rate changes to provide as much oxygen as his body needs. See PULSE.

The body needs a lot of fuel for such strenuous exercises as swimming or ice skating. For this reason, the heart beats rapidly when a person swims or skates. It is rushing more oxygen to the body by speeding the flow of blood. If the person stops exercising, his heart gradually slows down. It is regulating the flow of blood to the body's slower tempo.

There are many other examples of how the heart changes its rate of beating to meet a particular need. The heart beats faster when a person is angry, afraid, or excited. It is rushing more oxygen to his muscles to prepare him for fighting or for running away. If a person is wounded and loses some blood, his heart speeds up in an effort to make the remaining blood do extra duty. During pregnancy, a woman's heart takes care not only of her own needs, but also the needs of the unborn baby. Her heart increases its output by half to three-fourths more than normal.

HEART/*Heart Diseases*

Diseases of the heart and blood vessels are called *cardiovascular diseases.* The word *cardiovascular* comes from the word *cardiac,* meaning heart, and *vascular,* meaning blood vessel. Each year, deaths from cardiovascular diseases account for more than half of all deaths in the United States. This number is twice as many as result from the next five leading diseases together.

The three most important kinds of heart disease are (1) *arteriosclerosis,* or hardening of the arteries; (2) *hypertension,* or high blood pressure; and (3) *rheumatic fever,* which often leads to *rheumatic heart disease* later in life. Certain infections, such as diphtheria, and syphilis in its late stages, can produce heart disease. But these forms are fairly rare. Some children are born with imperfectly formed hearts. They suffer from *congenital heart disease.*

Diagnosis. When a doctor examines the heart, he looks for signs of trouble. First, he notes carefully anything the patient reports that indicates the heart is not working as it should. He asks questions to help discover whether the patient may have a heart ailment. Next, the doctor examines the heart by trying to feel its tip pushing against the wall of the chest. The position of the heart tells him its size. He thumps on the chest over the heart to get an idea of its shape.

The doctor places a stethoscope on the chest over the heart to hear its beat. The heart makes two sounds each time it beats: first, a low-pitched, long sound, "lubb," and then a high-pitched, more snapping sound, "dup." The first sound is made by the closing of the tricuspid valve and the mitral valve. The second sound is caused by the snapping shut of the semilunar valves just as the heart begins to relax. If one of the valves is faulty, it does not close tightly and lets some blood leak through. The returning blood causes a rushing or blowing sound called a *heart murmur.* Heart murmurs can also be caused by other conditions. Sometimes they are present in normal hearts, but these murmurs sound different. See HEART MURMUR.

In some cases, a doctor uses an *electrocardiograph.* This instrument makes a record of the electrical changes that occur as the heart beats. The doctor also may use an X-ray machine. This machine gives off rays that pass through the body and make a shadow picture of the heart. With a *fluoroscope,* a kind of X-ray machine, a doctor can look directly at the heart shadow. He can study its size and shape, and the way it beats.

If certain types of heart operations are being considered for a patient, the doctor may insert a *catheter* (long tube) into a vein in the arm. He pushes the catheter into the heart itself by way of the vein, and watches its course with the fluoroscope. Blood pressures in the heart can be measured by means of the catheter. The doctor also withdraws blood samples to measure the oxygen content and to make other tests.

Arteriosclerosis is a condition in which the arteries harden. Deposits of fatty material and calcium narrow the arteries and roughen their normally smooth lining. These deposits, called *plaques,* cause cells in the artery walls to break down. Substances from the ruptured cells irritate nearby tissues, causing scars to form. As a result, the artery wall becomes hard, rough, and narrow.

The coronary arteries, which nourish the heart muscle itself, are more frequently affected by arteriosclerosis than are any others. Hardening of these arteries reduces

A. B. Shaffer, M.D.

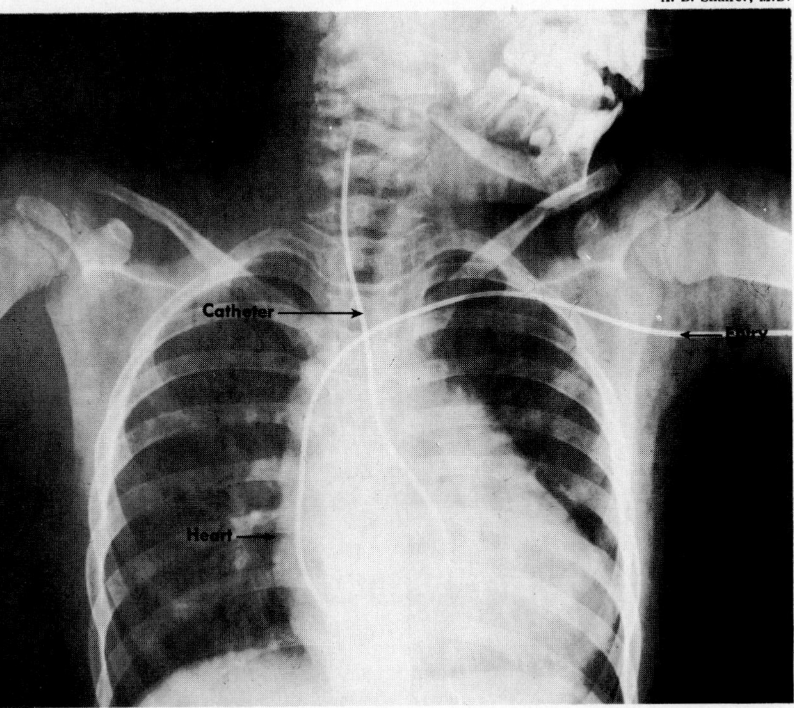

Using a Catheter (thin tube) and tracing its route on an X-ray screen, doctors find a hole between the two ventricles of a patient's heart. The *catheter* was pushed into the interior of the heart through a vein in the patient's arm, found its way through the hole, and is on its way up the carotid artery.

the heart's blood supply, and may cause a pain in the chest known as *angina pectoris* (see ANGINA PECTORIS).

The rough surface of the wall, together with the sluggish flow of blood through the narrowed channels, may cause a blood clot to form. A clot of this type is called a *thrombus*. A thrombus may break away from the place where it formed and be carried in the bloodstream. A moving clot is called an *embolus* (see EMBOLISM). A thrombus or an embolus may block an artery altogether. A blocked artery in the brain causes a *stroke*. Blockage in a coronary artery causes a *heart attack*, which is described in another section of this article. See ARTERIOSCLEROSIS; CORONARY THROMBOSIS.

Hypertension is caused by an increased resistance to the flow of the blood. The increased resistance occurs as a result of prolonged *constriction* (narrowing) of the smallest arteries, the *arterioles*. As a result, the heart has to beat harder to pump the blood through the body. Constriction of the *renal arteries* (main arteries to the kidneys) can also cause hypertension. If hypertension exists without other signs of illness, and no cause can be found, it is called *essential hypertension*. In a small proportion of cases, the disease becomes progressively and rapidly more severe, and is called *malignant hypertension*. See BLOOD PRESSURE.

Rheumatic Fever is caused by bacteria that belong to the *Streptococcus* group, the same group that causes blood poisoning and scarlet fever. It is usually, but not always, a disease of young persons. It ranks among the leading causes of heart disease among children. It is also responsible for much serious heart disease later in life. Rheumatic fever may damage the heart valves so that blood cannot flow through them normally. As a result, the heart must work harder to keep up with the needs of the body. These aftereffects of rheumatic fever are called *rheumatic heart disease*.. See RHEUMATIC FEVER.

Congenital Heart Disease describes a heart disorder which is present at birth. A *blue baby* has a congenital heart disorder. Some of his blood passes directly from the right side of the heart to the left side, without being pumped to the lungs. Having bypassed the lungs, the blood still contains carbon dioxide when it re-enters the body, and it has not picked up oxygen. Such blood gives a baby's skin a bluish tinge. See BLUE BABY.

Bacterial Endocarditis is a serious infection of the *endocardium* (the lining of the chambers of the heart). It sometimes occurs when persons with congenital or rheumatic heart disease undergo an operation. Bacteria that enter the bloodstream during operations infect the heart and damage it even further. Most cases of endocarditis can be prevented by giving patients prone to infection adequate doses of antibiotics before and after operations, even minor ones such as tooth extractions.

Fibrillation is a condition in which the muscle fibers of the heart work without coordination, with an irregular rhythm, and usually at a far faster rate than normal. The result is a quivering or fluttering of the heart, instead of the strong, regular contractions that result when the muscle fibers work together properly. When fibrillation affects the ventricles, as in *ventricular fibrillation*, it usually is fatal, because the irregularly quivering ventricles cannot pump blood out of the heart. Doctors can correct ventricular fibrillation by giving the victim's heart a powerful electric shock. Fibrillation of the atria is not as serious as ventricular fibrillation.

Heart Failure is a condition in which the heart does not pump efficiently. It does not mean the heart stops beating. It is usually an advanced stage of heart disease.

HEART/*Heart Attacks*

Heart attacks are the greatest single cause of death in the United States. Every day they kill about 1,400 persons and leave thousands of others crippled to some extent for the rest of their lives.

What Happens to the Heart? Almost all heart attacks are caused by a clot of blood blocking a coronary artery that has become hard and narrow because of arteriosclerosis. The clot cuts off the blood supply to part of the heart, and a portion of the heart muscle dies. If the clot blocks a major coronary artery, cutting off the blood supply to a large area of the heart, the attack is usually fatal. About 40 per cent of the persons who suffer a heart attack die shortly afterwards.

However, in the majority of cases, the patient recovers. The blood clot may not block a major artery, and only a small portion of his heart may be involved. The patient's body eventually replaces the dead heart muscle with scar tissue, and smaller arteries take over the job of supplying the scar tissue with blood.

What Causes a Heart Attack? A heart attack occurs suddenly, but the build-up of fatty deposits and calcium in the coronary arteries is a slow process. It may take years before an artery is narrow enough to be sealed off by a blood clot. There is probably no single cause of arteriosclerosis or heart attacks. Several factors are involved, including diet, smoking, and hereditary traits.

Diet. The fatty deposits that coat the inside of arteries contain large amounts of a substance called *cholesterol*. High levels of cholesterol form in the bodies of persons whose diets are rich in animal fats. Foods rich in animal fats include meat, butter, cheese, cream, and whole milk. Persons who eat a lot of such foods are more likely to suffer a heart attack through arteriosclerosis than those whose diets are low in animal fats. As a result, many doctors urge their patients to replace most of the animal fats in their diets with vegetable oils. These oils do not lead to overproduction of cholesterol in the body.

Persons who eat too much and are overweight also run a greater risk of a heart attack than those who eat sensibly and maintain the proper weight.

Smoking. Persons who smoke cigarettes are two to three times more likely to have a heart attack than nonsmokers, former smokers, or persons who smoke pipes or cigars. Smoking does not cause heart attacks, but it increases the likelihood of an attack.

Hereditary Traits may play a part in heart attacks by making a person more susceptible to arteriosclerosis. On the other hand, a person aware of a family history of arteriosclerosis is likely to take care of his heart. Many experts believe a person's habits and his environment are far more important factors in heart attacks than any traits he may have inherited from his parents.

CASE HISTORY OF A HEART ATTACK

A heart attack occurs suddenly, but the factors that cause it take many years to build up.

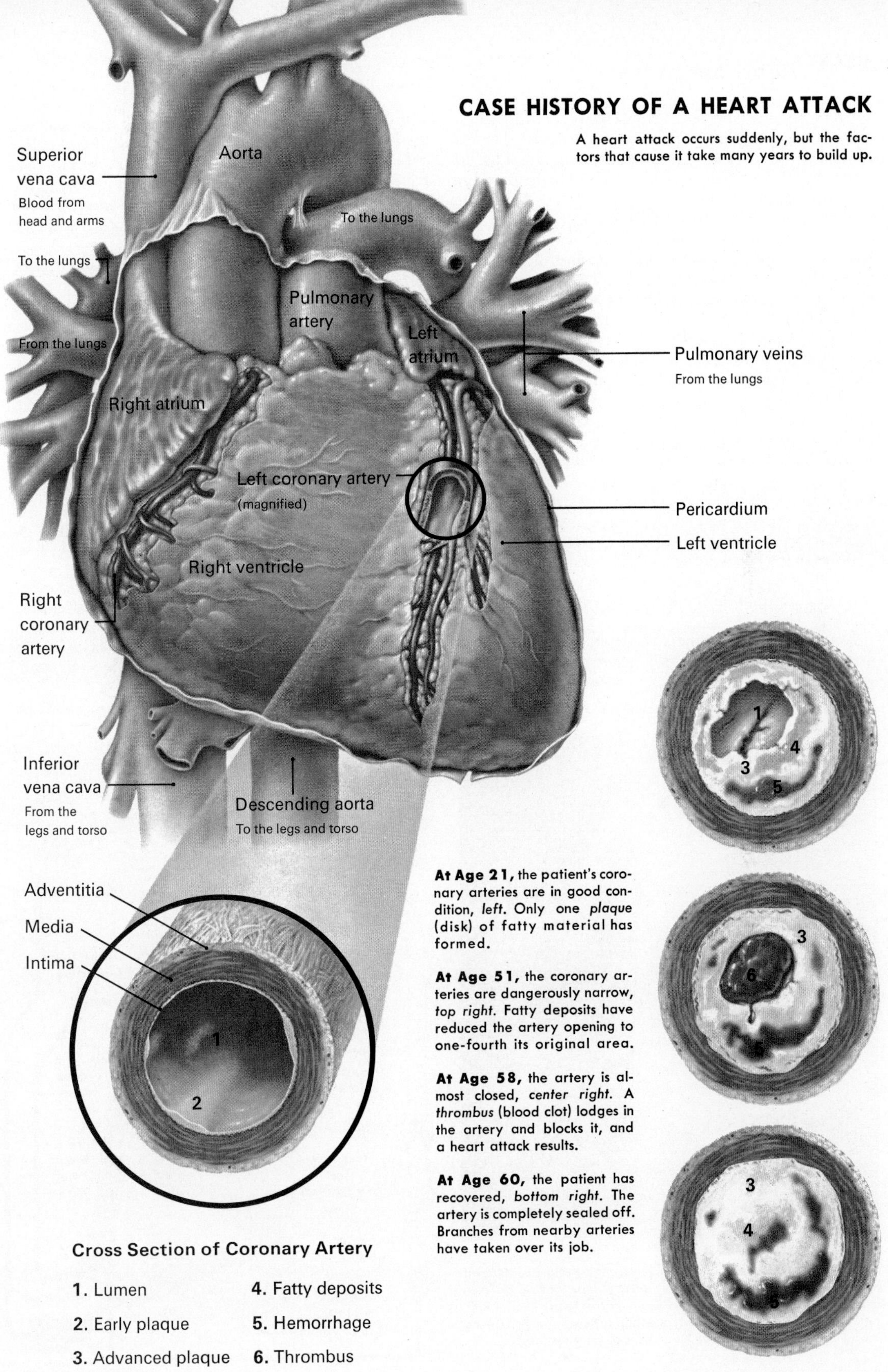

At Age 21, the patient's coronary arteries are in good condition, *left*. Only one *plaque* (disk) of fatty material has formed.

At Age 51, the coronary arteries are dangerously narrow, *top right*. Fatty deposits have reduced the artery opening to one-fourth its original area.

At Age 58, the artery is almost closed, *center right*. A *thrombus* (blood clot) lodges in the artery and blocks it, and a heart attack results.

At Age 60, the patient has recovered, *bottom right*. The artery is completely sealed off. Branches from nearby arteries have taken over its job.

Cross Section of Coronary Artery

1. Lumen
2. Early plaque
3. Advanced plaque
4. Fatty deposits
5. Hemorrhage
6. Thrombus

Some persons suffer such serious heart conditions that they undergo surgery to have them corrected. For example, babies with congenital heart diseases and adults with faulty heart valves need a surgeon's help before they can lead normal lives.

Before the 1940's, there was often little hope for persons with serious heart conditions. But heart surgery has since made spectacular advances. Many of these advances have come about through the development of a device called a *heart-lung machine* or *pump-oxygenator*. In this machine, an electrically driven pump takes over the job of the heart. In addition, an oxygenator takes over the job of the lungs. It removes carbon dioxide from the blood and replenishes it with oxygen.

At the start of an operation, the surgeon opens the patient's chest and exposes the heart. He then connects the heart-lung machine to the patient's circulatory system and switches on the pump. He can now stop the heart, open it, examine it for defects, and repair it. This type of surgery is called *open-heart surgery*. Several heart conditions once considered incurable can now be corrected using this technique.

Holes in the Heart are congenital defects in the chamber walls of the heart. If they are not repaired, the holes will cause a strain on the heart and eventually lead to heart failure.

Normally, the two atria of the heart are separated by a membrane called the *atrial septum*. Babies are born with a small hole through this membrane. In most cases, the hole closes within the first year, preventing the flow of blood from one atrium to the other. However, in some babies the hole does not close. This kind of hole in the heart, called *patent foramen oval*, is one kind of *atrial septal defect*. Similarly, a *ventricular septal defect* is a hole between the heart's two ventricles.

Surgeons can repair holes in the heart. In some cases, surgeons close the hole by *suturing* (sewing) the edges together. If the hole is very big, they mend it by sewing a patch of synthetic fabric over the hole.

Defective Heart Valves may be present at birth, or may develop later in life. Most persons who develop defective heart valves had rheumatic fever when they were young. A damaged valve may be *stenotic* (too tight) or *insufficient* (too loose). The two most frequently affected valves are the mitral valve and the aortic valve. Both valves may be faulty at the same time.

In *mitral stenosis*, the flaps of the mitral valve stick together, narrowing the valve opening. This narrowing interferes with the flow of blood from the left atrium to the left ventricle. A surgeon can correct the defect by separating the leaflets of the valve.

An insufficient valve leaks blood. *Mitral insufficiency* is a leaking mitral valve. *Aortic insufficiency* is a leaking aortic valve. To repair insufficient valves, a surgeon usually removes the faulty valve and replaces it with an artificial one. Several types of artificial valves are avail-

REPAIRING A DAMAGED HEART

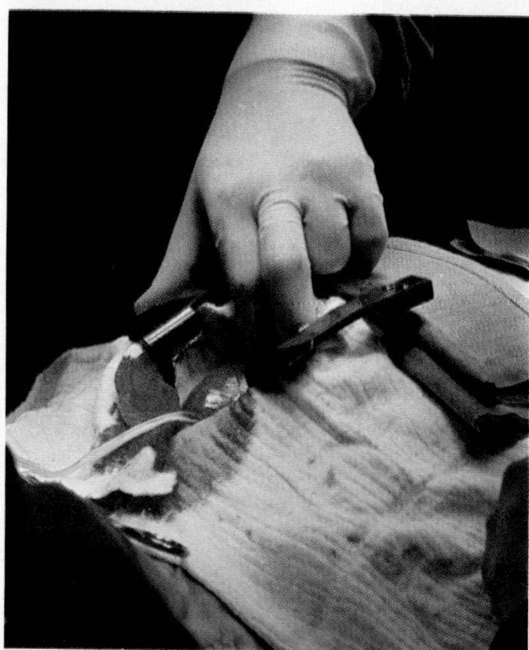

WORLD BOOK photo by E. F. Hoppe

Open-Heart Surgery is a technique for repairing a damaged heart. The surgeon first opens the patient's chest, *above*. He then cuts through the pericardium and exposes the heart itself. Next, he connects the patient's heart and leg artery to a heart-lung machine, *right*, and stops the heart by clamping the aorta.

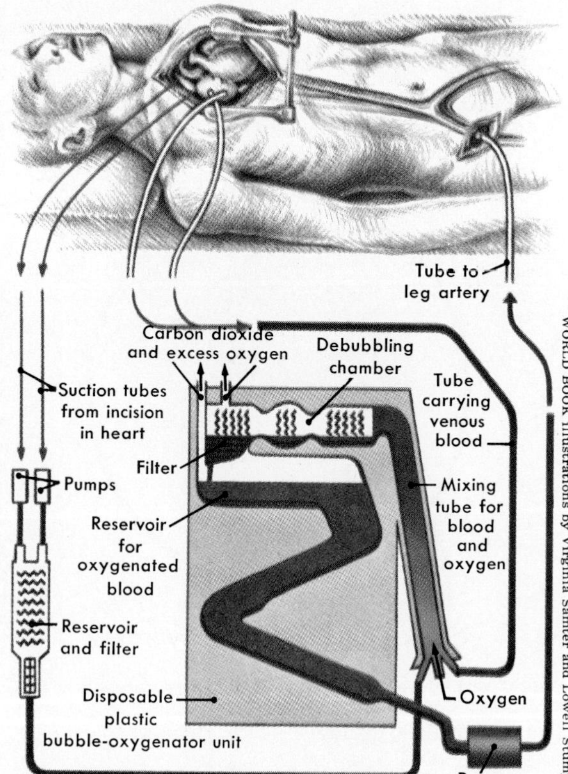

WORLD BOOK illustrations by Virginia Samter and Lowell Stumpf able. One type, called a *caged-ball valve*, is a tiny, stainless-steel cage enclosing a silicone-coated, plastic ball. The cage has a soft ring of synthetic fabric attached to it so that the surgeon can sew the valve into the heart. Like all ball valves, the artificial heart valve allows blood to pass only in one direction. Back flow is prevented because any reverse pressure forces the ball backward and closes the valve.

Clearing Coronary Arteries. In coronary artery disease, a person's coronary arteries become dangerously narrow. Narrower arteries supply less blood to the heart, and the heart cannot do its job properly.

If only a short section of a coronary artery is affected, the surgeon opens it, and removes the deposits inside that interfered with the flow of blood. Then he sews it up again. Usually, however, many of the arteries are affected. In this case, the surgeon has to provide a new route for blood to reach the patient's heart. He uses the *internal mammary artery*, which normally runs beneath the breast bone, for this. The surgeon frees the mammary artery from the breast bone and tunnels it into the heart muscle. Over a period of several months, the mammary artery gradually takes over the job of supplying blood to the heart muscle.

Correcting Heart Blocks. The heart has its own system for regulating the heart beat. Occasionally, a condition known as *heart block* develops when this system is disturbed and the normal impulse from the atrium to the ventricle is interrupted. Electronic pacemakers are used to correct heart block. A pacemaker consists of a small battery implanted in the body that transmits an impulse to the heart through an attachment.

Helping the Heart Pump. A heart that has become seriously weakened by disease will not pump blood properly unless it is helped in some way. Surgeons help the heart by installing a mechanical pump in the patient's body. These pumps are called *artificial hearts* or *assisting hearts.*

Assisting hearts are generally designed to help a failing left ventricle. For example, one type removes some of the blood entering the left atrium and pumps it back into the blood stream through the *axillary artery* in the patient's arm. This bypass lowers the pressure in the left atrium and relieves much of the strain on the patient's left ventricle.

Another type of assisting heart removes blood from the aorta at the point where the aorta leaves the heart, and pumps it back into the aorta a little farther on. The pump removes blood from the aorta as the left ventricle contracts, and drives it back into the aorta as the ventricle relaxes. The overall effect of this device is to ease the left ventricle's pumping job.

Several models of complete artificial hearts have been developed and tried out in animals. An artificial heart is intended to replace a human heart completely, not just to assist it. Michael E. De Bakey and Edward B. Diethrich

The Methodist Hospital, Houston, Tex.

Caged-Ball Valve

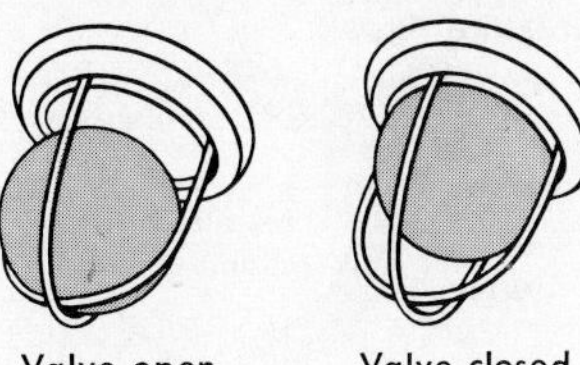

An Artificial Valve is used to replace a damaged mitral valve. A ball and cage control the direction and rate of blood-flow. The fabric on the ring is used to sew the valve to the heart.

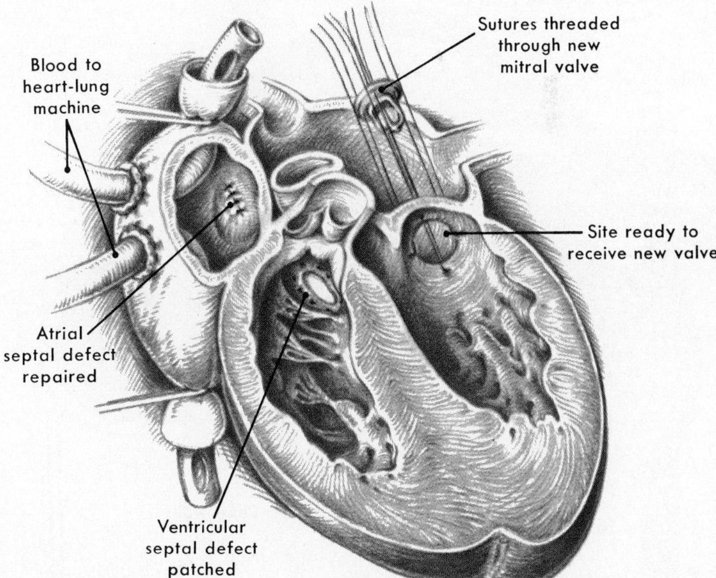

WORLD BOOK illustration by Virginia Samter

The Heart Is Opened to expose its defects, *above*. The surgeon mends small holes by sewing their edges together, *left*. Larger holes are repaired with a patch of synthetic fabric, *center*. The surgeon removes a faulty valve, and sews a ring of *sutures* (threads) around the opening. The sutures are threaded through the fabric around the ring of the ball-valve, *right*, which is then slipped into place, cage downward, and sewed to the heart.

1628 Circulation of the Blood through the body was described by William Harvey, an English physician.

1706 The Structure of the Left Ventricle and Distribution of Coronary Vessels were described by Raymond de Vieussens, a French anatomy professor.

1733 Blood Pressure was measured by Stephen Hales, an English clergyman and scientist.

1785 Digitalis, in the form of dried foxglove leaves, was introduced by William Withering, English physician. The drug is still used to treat heart failure.

1816 The Stethoscope was invented by René T. H. Laënnec, a French physician.

1893 The Atrioventricular Bundle, a muscle bundle connecting the right atrium with the ventricles of the heart, was discovered by Wilhelm His, Jr., a Swiss anatomist. It is also called the *bundle of His.*

1903 The Electrocardiograph, for showing the heart's electrical activity, was developed by Willem Einthoven, a Dutch physiologist.

1904 The Effect of Rheumatic Fever on the heart was described by Ludwig Aschoff, a German pathologist.

1908 Congenital Heart Disease was described and classified by Maude Abbott, a Canadian physician.

1912 First Diagnosis of Coronary Thrombosis and description of heart disease resulting from hardening of the arteries were made by James B. Herrick, an American cardiologist.

1930 Modern Method of Electrocardiography was developed by Frank N. Wilson, an American physician.

1939 First Surgery for Congenital Heart Disease was performed by Robert E. Gross, an American surgeon.

1945 First Surgery for Blue Babies was performed by Alfred Blalock, an American surgeon, and Helen B. Taussig, an American cardiologist.

1948 First Successful Operations for rheumatic heart disease were performed independently by Charles P. Bailey and Dwight E. Harken, American surgeons.

1951 Plastic Ball Valve for a leaky aortic (semilunar) valve was developed by Charles Hufnagel, an American surgeon.

1952 Open Heart Surgery was first successfully performed by F. John Lewis, an American surgeon. He used ice to lower the body temperature and slow down circulation so that the heart remained dry during surgery.

1953 Mechanical Heart and Blood Purifier was used successfully for the first time by John H. Gibbon, an American surgeon.

1954 Human Cross-Circulation, permitting a second person's heart and lungs to pump blood of a person under surgery, was developed by C. Walton Lillehei, an American surgeon.

1959 Coronary Arteriography, an X-ray technique for examining the coronary arteries and diagnosing coronary artery disease, was perfected by F. Mason Sones, Jr., an American cardiologist.

1961 External Cardiac Massage, a treatment for restarting a stopped heart without opening the chest, was introduced by J. R. Jude, American cardiologist, and his associates.

1962 Cardioversion, a method of correcting fibrillation and irregular heart beat by electric shock, was introduced by B. Lown, an American cardiologist.

1965 Assisting Hearts, mechanical devices to help a diseased or overworked left ventricle, were first successfully implanted by Michael E. De Bakey, and by Adrian Kantrowitz, American surgeons.

Ventricular Bypass Pump

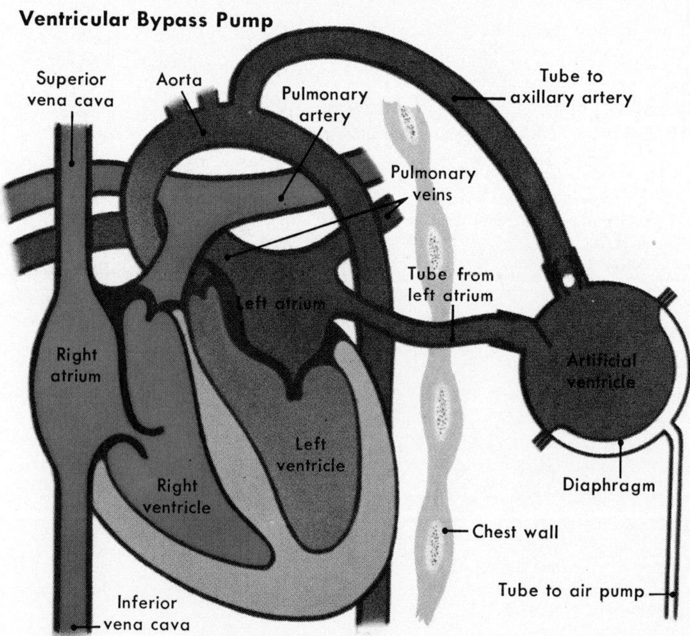

WORLD BOOK diagram by Lowell Stumpf

The Ventricular Bypass Pump, *above,* helps a failing left ventricle. It takes blood from the left atrium and then forces it into the arm artery. As a result, the left ventricle has to pump less hard and the strain on the heart is relieved. Tubes connect the device to the arm artery and left atrium. Another tube goes to a pump, which controls the rate of "beating."

The Methodist Hospital, Houston, Tex.

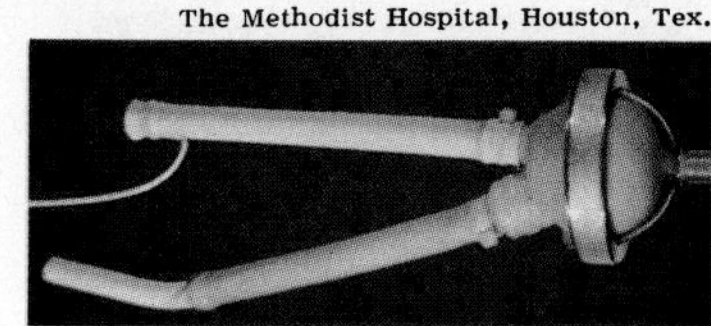

Artificial Ventricle

Relaxing Phase

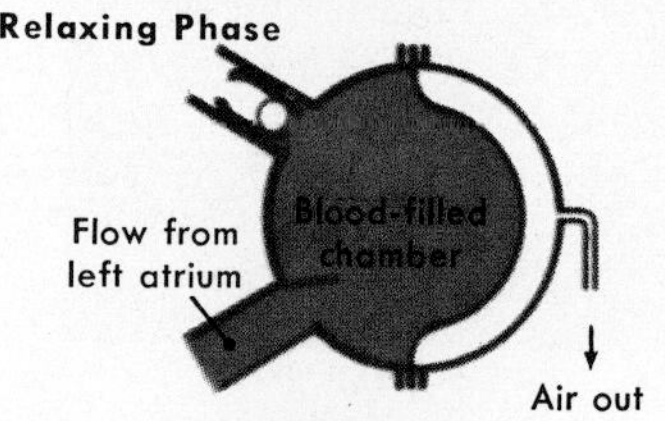

Contracting Phase

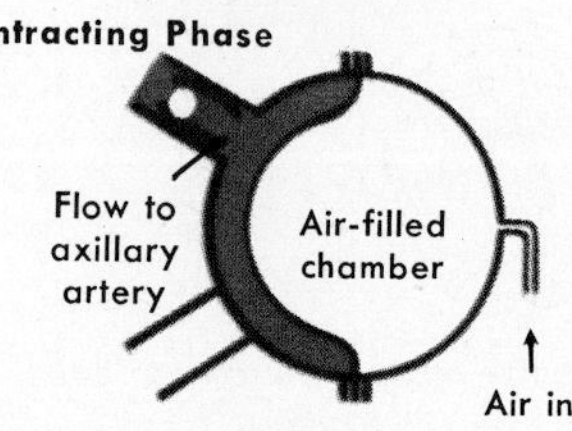

The Artificial Ventricle, *top,* is about the size of an orange. It continuously fills and empties as the pump moves the diaphragm back and forth, *above.* Valves control the direction of blood-flow.

Margaret Durrance, Photo Researchers

SKIING, *SKEE ing*, is the exciting sport of speeding down a snow-covered slope or soaring through the air on two slats, or runners, called skis. People of almost every country enjoy the thrill of skimming over the snow on skis. In recent years, skiing has gained increasing popularity in the United States. Machines that produce artificial snow have made it possible for people to ski when no natural snow is available. Hundreds of ski resorts provide facilities to make the sport more comfortable and convenient.

Equipment. A *ski* is a long, narrow, flat runner that is turned up at the front end. Skis are made of wood, metal, or sometimes fiber glass that is reinforced with *epoxy* (a strong plastic). Most skis have a plastic running surface and metal edges. Skis are about 3 to 4 inches wide. Most experts use skis that are stiff and more than a foot longer than the skier is tall. Other skiers use more flexible, shorter skis. Skis 8 feet long or longer are used for cross-country racing.

The skier carries two *poles*. These are made of metal, cane, fiber glass, or bamboo, and are shaped to a point at one end. Several inches above the point is a circular *basket*, about 3 inches in diameter and attached to the pole by spokes. The basket prevents the pole from plunging too deeply into the snow. When a person skis downhill, he uses the poles to help keep his balance. They are also used as walking sticks on flat land and for uphill climbing.

Among the most important safety items for the skier are the *boots*. They are made of stout, pliable leather, and have thick soles that are usually reinforced with steel. The boots fit snugly around the ankles and support the ankles so that they do not tire. The boots can be attached to the skis by several methods. One of the safest methods requires metal attachments, called *safety-release bindings*, on the skis and boots. These clamp the boot firmly to the ski, but allow the ski to come off when pressure is exerted in an emergency. This release of the ski helps prevent skiers from twisting, spraining, or breaking their ankles.

Where to Ski. Almost any hill that is free from rocks, trees, and other obstructions can be a good place to learn to ski. Special *ski areas* provide many kinds of skiing for persons with all degrees of ability. Such ski areas as Aspen and Vail, Colo., Sun Valley, Ida., Stowe, Vt., Banff, Alta., and Mont Tremblant, Que., attract thousands of skiers every winter. A ski area has one or more *slopes*, the steep sides of hills or mountains. In some areas, the slopes are more than 3,000 feet high.

Most ski areas offer the advantage of *lifts*. These mechanically operated devices transport the skier to the top of the slope. The *rope tow* is a rope attached to two pulleys, one at the top of the slope and one at the bottom, and driven by a motor. The skier hangs on to the rope and it pulls him up the slope. The *T-bar* con-

Bob Beattie, the contributor of this article, is Head Alpine Coach of the United States Ski Team.

Skiers Skim Through the Snow at speeds as high as 80 miles per hour. They turn and twist to control their speed and to avoid trees and rocks. This slope is one of several at Aspen, Colo.

sists of a motor-driven cable from which metal bars shaped like upside-down letter T's are suspended. The skier leans against the crossbar and holds on to the upright as he goes up the slope. The *chair* lift is a series of chairs hung from a high motor-driven cable. *Gondola* and *cable car* lifts operate in a similar manner, but skiers ride in enclosed cars.

Types of Skiing

Skiing may be divided roughly into two general categories, noncompetitive and competitive. Noncompetitive skiing is recreational. Competitive skiing includes specialized and regulated events.

Noncompetitive Skiing. The most common kind of noncompetitive skiing is the downhill run. When a skier points straight down a slope without trying to turn or slow down, he is said to be *schussing*. A skier *traverses* a slope when he skis at an angle to the *fall line* (a straight line from the skier to the bottom of the slope). He must learn to traverse properly and turn by edging. A skier edges by shifting his weight to the edges of his skis, causing the skis to dig into the snow.

The *snowplow* is usually the first turn a skier learns. It is also used to stop or slow down. To stop or turn, a skier forces out his heels and brings the tips of his skis almost together to form a *V*. At the same time, he shifts his weight to the inside edges of his skis. This helps slow down for his forward motion. A turn occurs when the skier shifts his weight to the ski that is opposite to the direction of the turn.

The *stem christie*, sometimes called a *stem turn*, is more difficult than the snowplow. To turn right, a skier *stems* when, by pushing out his left heel, he places his left ski at an angle to the direction of motion. This puts his weight on the left ski and causes it to turn toward the fall line. At the end of the turn, the skis are parallel. The skier reverses the procedure to turn left.

A *parallel christie* is a difficult turn usually done at high speeds. It is sometimes called a *full christiana* or *parallel turn*. To turn right, the skier keeps his skis parallel and shifts his weight to the right edges of his skis by turning his body. To turn left, the skier reverses the procedure. A *wedeln* is a series of short, connected parallel turns.

A skier must also know how to climb the slope. Two common methods are the *herringbone* and *sidestepping*. Both of these methods require edging at an angle to the slope.

Competitive Skiing. One of the most exciting competitive races is the *downhill*. The object of this event is to start from the top of a 1,500- or 2,500-foot slope and ski down by the straightest, fastest route possible. *Moguls* (snow mounds), ruts, and other obstacles are added to make many downhill courses more difficult.

The *slalom* is an obstacle course with a vertical drop of 400 to 700 feet. Pairs of closely spaced flag poles mark the edges of the path, which winds about in a snakelike fashion. The skier must weave his way between each pair of poles. The *giant slalom* has a drop of 1,000 to 1,300 feet. The sets of flags are farther apart, and the course is studded with steep pitches, moguls, and ruts. Competitors in the downhill and slalom are judged on the basis of speed.

A Snowplow is a beginner's way to stop, slow down, or turn. He places his weight on the inside edges of the skis.

A Stem Christie is a more advanced method of turning. At the end of the turn, the skis are parallel.

WORLD BOOK illustrations by William Gorman

A Parallel Christie requires great coordination. The skier's feet remain close together and parallel throughout the turn. Skiers try to keep their feet together throughout a run.

SKI EQUIPMENT

Ski Poles help skiers to push themselves forward and to keep their balance. The *baskets* prevent the poles from sinking deep into soft snow. Ski poles should be long enough so that the grip fits under the skier's arm.

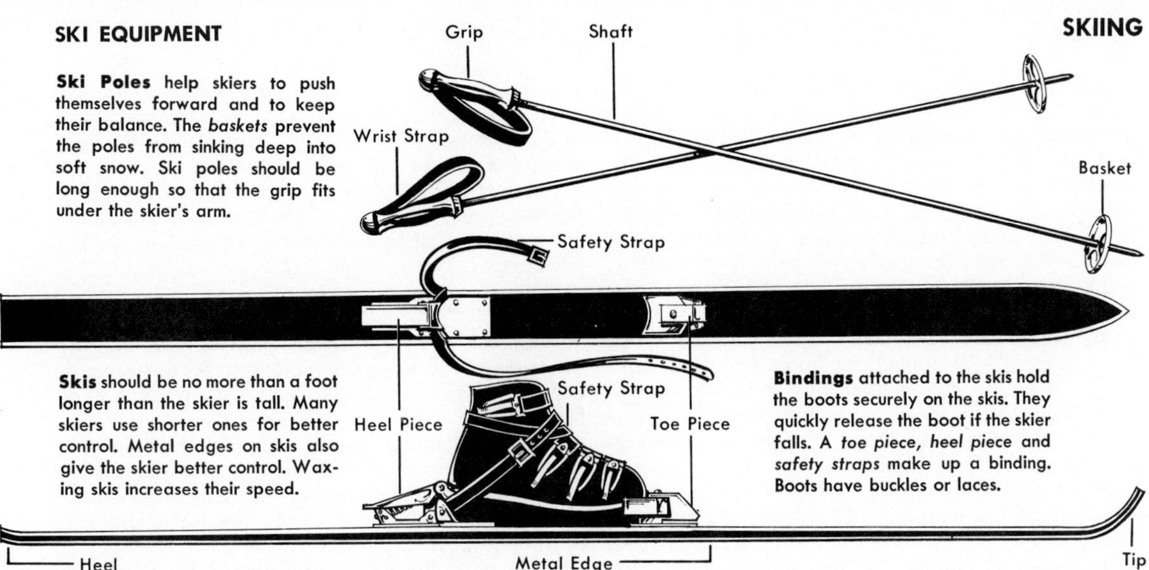

Skis should be no more than a foot longer than the skier is tall. Many skiers use shorter ones for better control. Metal edges on skis also give the skier better control. Waxing skis increases their speed.

Bindings attached to the skis hold the boots securely on the skis. They quickly release the boot if the skier falls. A *toe piece, heel piece* and *safety straps* make up a binding. Boots have buckles or laces.

Wide World

Throngs of Spectators gather to watch competition at Olympic Ski Jumping Hill at Garmisch, Germany.

In *ski-jumping*, the skier speeds down a long, steep take-off that levels off for a few feet before ending suddenly, high above the ground. He is judged on the basis of the distance of his jump, and on his control and style in the air and in his landing.

The fourth competitive event is the *cross-country race*. This event tests the stamina, endurance, and all-around technique of the skier. The course consists of natural terrain, and includes uphill, downhill, and flat-land skiing. There are no artificial obstacles, but many trees and rugged trails provide challenges. The Olympic Games include all four of these competitive events.

History

Skiing was developed as a method of transportation by peoples who lived in regions with heavy snowfall. Originally, skis were probably made from the bones of large animals. A pair of skis on exhibit in Stockholm, Sweden, is about 5,000 years old.

Skis later came into use for military purposes. During the battle of Oslo between Norway and Sweden in 1200, the Norwegians used skiers as scouts. Sweden used ski troops in 1521 against Denmark. United States ski troops fought in the Alps during World War II.

Skiing as a sport probably began about the early 1800's. Norwegian immigrants brought it to the United States in the mid-1800's. Fédération Internationale de Ski (FIS) was founded by 26 countries in 1924. This organization convinced the Olympic Games committee to add competition in the winter sports to the program. The first winter games took place in France in 1924.

Outstanding U.S. skiers of the 1940's and 1950's included Arthur Devlin, Alf Engen, and Toger Tokle. All three achieved fame as ski jumpers, but Devlin and Engen also excelled in other events. In the 1960's, outstanding skiiers in the slalom and downhill events included Gordon Eaton, Charles Ferries, Jim Heuga, Billy Kidd, Jean Saubert, and the late Bud Werner. Gene Kotlarek excelled in jumping. Bob Beattie

See also Michigan (Places to Visit [American Ski Hall of Fame]); Water Skiing.

SOCCER is one of the most popular sports in the world. It is the "national sport" of several European and South American countries, and of many countries in Asia. Soccer games often attract huge crowds of up to 200,000 persons. Soccer's most famous international competition, the World Cup matches, pits national teams from many countries against each other every four years. World Cup matches arouse as much interest and excitement in many countries as the World Series does in the United States each October.

In a soccer game, two teams of 11 men each try to knock a round ball through the opponent's goal. The speedy, muscular players wear only shirts and shorts, heavy knee-length socks, and cleated soccer shoes. Some players wear shin guards. The team that scores the most goals wins the game.

Only the goalkeepers, playing within a certain area, can touch the ball with their hands. Other players must kick it with their feet or hit it with their heads or bodies. Acrobatic soccer players leap high to bounce the ball away with their heads or turn in midair to kick the ball back over their heads.

Soccer is a tough, fast, exciting game that requires great physical endurance. Play rarely stops once the game begins, and the players move up and down the field almost continuously. Play is stopped only when a goal is scored, a foul occurs, or if a player is seriously injured. A player taken out of a game cannot play again in that game. So soccer players often stay on the field in spite of painful injuries.

George E. Fishwick, the contributor of this article, is Director of Promotion and Publicity of the United States Soccer Football Association.

In Great Britain, soccer is called *football* or *association football.* The word soccer comes from *assoc.*, an abbreviation for *association.* American and Canadian football and rugby developed from soccer.

Soccer Field and Equipment

The Field. Most adult teams play on fields that are from 100 to 130 yards long and from 50 to 100 yards wide. Children may play on fields that are about 80 by 60 yards.

The boundary lines on the long sides of the field are called *touch lines.* Those on the short sides are called *goal lines.* When a player knocks the ball out of bounds, play stops until a player from the opposing team kicks or throws the ball into the playing area. The *halfway line* runs across the center of the field, halfway between the two goal lines.

The Goals stand in the center of the goal lines. Each goal consists of two wooden posts 24 feet apart and joined at the top by a crossbar that is 8 feet above the ground. A net is usually attached to the back of the crossbar and posts and pegged to the ground behind them. The net is helpful, because it stops the ball when it goes in the goal. In this way everyone can be sure that the ball has passed between the posts and under the crossbar to score a goal.

Soccer Is One of the World's Most Popular and Exciting Sports. In many countries, huge crowds pack big stadiums to watch soccer teams play. Soccer players move the ball quickly and cleverly with the feet, head, or body, and try to knock it into the opposing team's goal.

Pictorial Parade

Two rectangles are marked in front of each goal. The smaller rectangle is called the *goal area.* It is 60 feet wide and extends 18 feet in front of the goal. The larger rectangle is called the *penalty area.* The penalty area is 132 feet wide and extends 54 feet in front of the goal.

The goalkeeper cannot be charged by an opponent in the goal area, unless he is holding the ball and has both feet on the ground. The penalty area is important, because defenders are seriously penalized if they break certain rules in that area. In such cases, a member of the offensive team gets a kick from the *penalty spot* 12 yards in front of the goal. Only the goalkeeper can attempt to block the shot.

The Ball is a leather casing inflated by a rubber bladder. A ball about 27-28 inches in circumference is used for adult games and one about 25 inches is generally used for children's games.

Soccer Rules

The Officials are the *referee* and two *linesmen.* The referee acts as the timekeeper and enforces the rules. He blows a whistle to stop and start play whenever (1) a goal is scored, (2) the ball goes out of bounds, (3) a player commits a foul, and (4) play is stopped for an injury. He may put a player out of the game for repeated fouling.

A linesman stands on each touch line and decides which team throws the ball in when it goes out of bounds. The linesmen also call fouls.

Time. Most games last 90 minutes. Games are divided into two halves, and there is usually a short rest period between the two halves. Sometimes, the teams play an overtime period to determine a winner if the score is tied at the end of the second half.

Starting Play. Before a game starts, the team captains flip a coin to decide which team will kick off and to choose the goals their teams will defend. The teams change goals at the beginning of the second half, and the team that did not kick off to start the game kicks off for the second half.

Teams kick off from the *center spot,* a point in the middle of the halfway line. Players line up on their own half of the field with three players on the kicking team generally standing close to the ball. Opponents must be at least 10 yards away from the ball. One of the attackers kicks the ball forward to a teammate to start play again. Play resumes with a kickoff after each goal.

Fouls. The referee may penalize a team for a foul by sending the offending player off the field for the rest of the game, and perhaps awarding a free kick to the opponents. The kick may be a *direct free kick,* a *penalty kick,* or an *indirect free kick.*

A direct free kick is taken toward the opponent's goal from the spot where the foul occurred. Opponents must stay at least 10 yards from the ball. A direct free kick may be awarded for (1) deliberately kicking or attempting to kick an opponent; (2) tripping, striking, holding, or pushing an opponent; (3) deliberately running into an opponent, and (4) jumping so as to endanger another player while trying to get the ball. If a player other than the goalkeeper touches the ball with his hands, the other team gets a direct free kick.

A penalty kick is awarded if a defender commits one of these fouls within his own penalty area. The offended team takes the penalty kick from the *penalty spot,* 12 yards directly in front of the goal. All players, except the opposing goalkeeper and the kicker, must stand outside of the penalty area.

The referee awards indirect free kicks for less serious fouls. The kicker must kick the ball so that it touches another player before it enters the opponent's goal. All opponents must stay at least 10 feet from the ball. Indirect free kicks are awarded for (1) dangerous play such as kicking the ball when the goalkeeper is holding it, (2) blocking an opponent, (3) pushing an opponent when the ball is not nearby, and (4) running into the goalkeeper when he is not holding the ball, when he is in his goal area, or when he is not blocking an opponent. The referee awards an indirect free kick against the goalkeeper if the goalkeeper takes more than four steps with the ball without bouncing it.

The referee also awards an indirect free kick if a

A Soccer Field is a rectangular area divided by the halfway line, which runs across the center of the field. The diagram, *below,* shows how the soccer players line up for the kickoff.

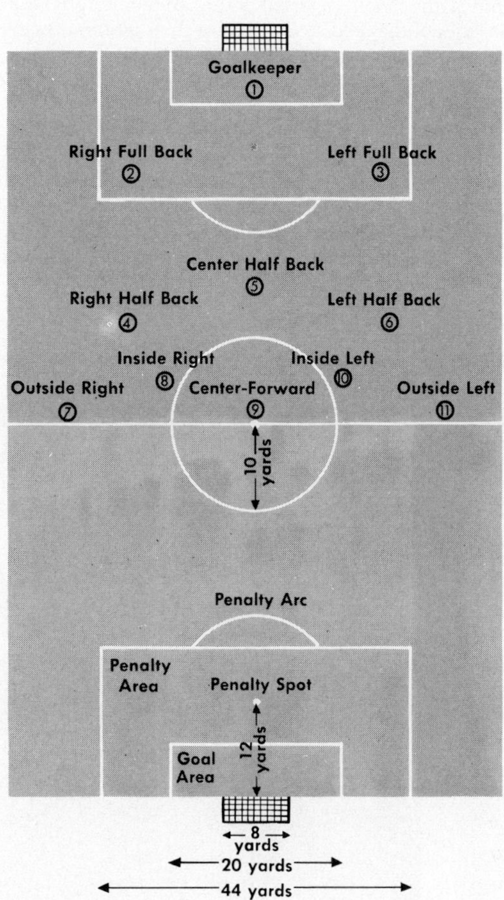

player is offside. Generally, an attacking player who is in his opponent's half of the field is offside if he is between the ball and the goal line. But he is not offside if (1) two opponents are closer to their goal line than he is, (2) he moved between the ball and goal line after a teammate kicked the ball, (3) the ball touched an opponent, or (4) he received the ball from a *goal kick*, a *throw-in*, a *corner kick*, or a *dropped ball*. These terms are explained in the table: *Soccer Terms* elsewhere on this page.

Soccer Players

A soccer team is divided almost equally into attackers and defenders. As the teams line up on either side of the halfway line to start a game, the first line for each team has five forwards. They are the left and right outside (*wing*) players; a center forward; and left and right inside players. The second line consists of the left, center, and right halfbacks. The left and right fullbacks play in front of the goalkeeper.

The forwards are offensive players, and they try to score goals. They must be fast, agile, and able to move the ball accurately and quickly with their feet or their heads. The *center forward* plays close to his opponent's goal and usually has the most opportunity to score. The *wing forwards* must be able to *center* the ball accurately. That is, they kick it in front of the opponent's goal from the sides of the field so that one of their teammates can knock the ball into the goal.

The *inside forwards* must be able to *dribble* (run while moving the ball along with one foot to the other), pass accurately, and receive passes from their own defenders.

The defense consists of the goalkeeper and the five *backs*. The backs on a soccer team are generally bigger than the forwards. The *left* and *right fullbacks* and the *center halfback* form the main defensive barrier in front of the goalkeeper. The center halfback plays near his own goal. He is the most important back, because he often stops attacks by *clearing* the ball (pushing it away from his own goal area) with his head. He stays very close to the opposing center forward to prevent him from scoring.

The *wing halfbacks* play both defense and offense. They try to stop opponents' attacks on their own goal, and then they pass the ball out to teammates to start moving the ball toward the opponent's goal. Wing halfbacks occasionally score goals from 20 to 30 yards out in front of the goal.

The goalkeeper stands between the goal posts and moves quickly to all parts of the penalty area to stop shots. He is the only player that can use his hands and arms to stop the ball.

Soccer Skills

Kicking includes those kicks that (1) attempt to score a goal, (2) put the ball in play, or (3) put the ball into a particular area of the field. Good players should be able

SOCCER TERMS

Goal Kick is made by a defender when a ball last touched by a member of the attacking team passes over the goal line without going into the goal. He must kick the ball from inside his team's goal area, and it must go beyond his team's penalty area.

Corner Kick is made by an offensive player when a ball last touched by a defensive player over the goal line without going into the goal. The player kicks the ball from the nearest corner of the field.

Throw-In takes place after a player knocks the ball over one of the touch lines. A member of the other team throws the ball back into play. The thrower must have both feet on the ground either on the touch line or outside the playing area and he must throw the ball with both hands from above his head.

Dropped Ball. The referee drops the ball onto the ground between opposing players. This starts play again after the referee has stopped it for some reason other than foul, such as injury to a player.

A Soccer Player Tries to Score a Goal with a Header. He dove through the air, *right,* and hit the ball with his forehead, trying to knock it past the goalkeeper, *left.* Skilled soccer players can hit the ball in almost any direction quickly and accurately with a header.

Pictorial Parade

to kick the ball well with either foot. A player who can kick best with his right foot generally plays on the right side of the field, and a left-footed kicker will play on the left side. For example, a left wing forward must be able to kick the ball well with his left foot.

A player may kick the ball with (1) his *instep* (top of the foot), (2) the outer or inner sides of his foot, or (3) his heel. The instep is perhaps the most effective kick. A player can control the length, accuracy, and power of his kick much better with the instep.

Players kick with greater accuracy if they kick the ball so that it travels close to the ground. A player about to kick the ball along the ground should place his nonkicking foot near the ball. He should keep his head down and his eyes on the ball. He swings the kicking leg so that his foot hits the ball squarely. After his foot hits the ball, it should *follow through* (continue to move forward) to make the ball travel in the right direction and to keep the ball low.

To *chip* the ball, a player kicks it with his instep or the inside of his foot, lifting the ball over the head of an opponent. A player who chips cannot always be sure that the ball will travel the right distance and in the right direction. Also, an opponent may anticipate the chip, back up quickly, and intercept the ball with his head or his body.

Other common kicks are the *volley* and the *half volley*. A player volleys when he kicks hard, just as the ball bounces off the ground. Volleys make powerful shots, but the ball is likely to sail high and go over the goal's crossbar.

Passing the ball to teammates is one of the most important skills in soccer. For accuracy, especially for quick, short passes, a player usually passes with the inside of his foot. Quick passes often fool opponents who are unable to recover in time to get the ball or get into the proper defensive position. Most passing is done to the right or left, but soccer players also pass the ball forward to a teammate.

A player sometimes passes the ball 20 yards or more with the inside of his foot. But if he wants to make a long pass, he is much more likely to reach a teammate by kicking the ball with his instep. The ball travels much faster this way and it is much more difficult for opponents to intercept it.

Players occasionally *back-heel* (pass the ball backwards by kicking it with the heel). Players sometimes use the back heel to send the ball to a teammate in one direction after getting the opposing player's moving in the opposite direction.

Dribbling means to move the ball down the field by kicking it gently or nudging it with one foot to the other. Dribbling allows the player to keep the ball in his possession as he runs. By faking with his head or body to go one way, then actually going in another direction, a player may dribble quickly past several opponents. The ball will never be more than a few inches from the player's feet as he moves down the field.

Trapping occurs when a player uses his chest, thigh, foot, or his head to stop a ball and gain control of it. He may wedge it between his foot and the ground, or he may allow it to hit his chest, thigh, or head and drop to the ground at his feet. If the ball bounces even a foot away from him, he is likely to lose possession of it.

Heading means hitting the ball with the head. Forwards score many goals by running into the goal area as the ball is kicked there, and heading it into the goal. Good players can head the ball long distances. Goalkeepers seldom head the ball, because the rules allow them to use their hands.

Players head the ball with their foreheads. A player may head the ball directly from the front, or flick it with his head. If a player heads the ball with the top or back of his head, he cannot control the ball as well, and the impact of the ball as it hits may stun him.

Tackling is hooking or kicking the ball away from an opponent with the feet. In the most common type of tackle, a player faces his opponent and lunges at the ball, reaching with one foot to take it away from his opponent. In the *sliding tackle*, the player slides along the ground with one leg extended to kick the ball away from his opponent. In the shoulder charge, the player meets shoulder to shoulder with his opponent and tries to move him away from the ball. Players must never push with their elbows or arms, or deliberately kick or trip an opponent.

Soccer History

A game similar to soccer was probably played as early as 400 B.C. by the Chinese. In the A.D. 200's, the Romans played a game in which two teams tried to move a ball across a line on the field. During the 1100's, London children played a form of soccer in the streets.

During the early 1800's, many English schools played a game similar to soccer. The players made a number of rules that changed and developed the game. But each school interpreted the rules differently. In 1848, an association of school representatives met at Trinity College, Cambridge, to draw up the first set of rules.

In 1863, representatives of English football clubs founded the Football Association. In 1871, the association introduced the Football Association Challenge Cup Competition. This competition is still one of the most famous in soccer. Professional soccer began in 1885 in England, and three years later 12 clubs formed the Football League of England.

Soccer began to spread throughout the world in the late 1800's. By 1900, associations were founded in Belgium, Chile, Denmark, Italy, The Netherlands, and Switzerland. In 1904, the national associations founded the *Federation Internationale de Football Association* (FIFA). Soccer rules are made by a 20-man board made up of equal numbers of representatives from the FIFA, England, Northern Ireland, Scotland, and Wales. Board members have a total of eight votes, with the FIFA representatives having four of them.

In 1930, Jules Rimet, a Frenchman who was president of the FIFA, presented a cup for the winner of an international competition. This competition is now called the World Cup, and its winner is determined in a famous series between national teams from many countries. The World Cup games are held every four years.

The United States Soccer Football Association (U.S.S.F.A.), founded in 1913, is a member of the FIFA. Until the mid-1960's, it was mainly concerned with amateur soccer. In 1967, two professional leagues began play in the United States. GEORGE E. FISHWICK

SUPREME COURT OF THE UNITED STATES is the highest court in the nation. One of its basic duties is to determine whether federal, state, and local governments are acting according to the United States Constitution. The Supreme Court does its job by deciding specific legal cases on the basis of established legal rules. Much of the court's work involves rules that are laid down in the Constitution. Although many of these rules are stated in words that are not entirely clear, the Supreme Court must determine their meaning and apply them to the cases presented for decision. For a discussion of the relationship between the Supreme Court and the Constitution, see the article GOVERNMENT (Constitutional Government).

A Supreme Court decision has great importance. Once a decision has been reached by the court, all other courts throughout the United States are required to follow the decision in similar cases. In this way, the Supreme Court helps guarantee equal legal justice to all Americans. The court is not required to consider every case presented to it. It accepts only a few, most of which involve problems of national importance.

The Supreme Court heads the judicial branch of the federal government. It is the only court specifically created by the Constitution. The judicial system of each state is also headed by a supreme court. In some states, the court is known by another name, such as *court of appeals*. For the most part, state courts hear cases concerning state laws. However, the U.S. Supreme Court may review the decisions of the highest state courts that involve the U.S. Constitution or acts of Congress. This article deals only with the U.S. Supreme Court. For information on the entire federal court system and on the state courts, see the article COURT.

William Ray Forrester, the contributor of this article, is Dean of the Cornell University Law School, and the author of Cases and Materials on Constitutional Law. *The article was critically reviewed by Byron R. White, Associate Justice of the Supreme Court of the United States.*

The role of the Supreme Court and its interpretation of the law change occasionally. These changes depend partly on the political, social, and economic beliefs of its members, and partly on the national conditions of the time. In our early days as a nation, for example, the court concerned itself chiefly with the proper division of authority between the federal government and state governments. A major concern today is the protection of the rights and liberties of individuals.

How the Supreme Court Is Organized

Article III of the Constitution provides for the creation of the Supreme Court and states the limits of its jurisdiction. But details of the court's exact organization and the work it can do are left largely to Congress. Congress established the federal court system in the Judiciary Act of 1789. This act included provisions governing the Supreme Court.

Membership. The Supreme Court has nine members —a chief justice and eight associate justices. The exact number is set by Congress and has changed through the years. The first Supreme Court had six members. Since 1869, the court has consisted of nine members.

The Constitution sets no qualifications for justices, but states that they shall be appointed by the President, with the advice and consent of the Senate. However, all members have had some legal training and experience, and most justices have been prominent

From "Equal Justice Under Law"

Courtroom of the Supreme Court Building in Washington, D.C., is shown here as the justices see it from the bench. Spectators sit in the rear of the courtroom. The space between the spectators and the bench is reserved for lawyers pleading cases, for other members of the bar, and for the press. The building, completed in 1935, was designed by Cass Gilbert.

Hugo L. Black W. J. Brennan, Jr.

John M. Harlan Thurgood Marshall

THE SUPREME COURT

Chief Justice Earl Warren

William O. Douglas Abe Fortas

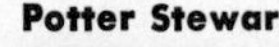

Potter Stewart Byron R. White

Harris & Ewing; United Press Int.; Wide World

judges, lawyers, law teachers, or government officials.

Once appointed, justices may remain in office for life, or "during good behavior," and Congress cannot reduce their salary. These provisions protect the justices from political control, and help ensure the independence of the court.

Salary and Terms. The Court meets regularly in the Supreme Court Building in Washington, D.C. The annual term of the court begins the first Monday in October and usually ends in June.

The chief justice receives $40,000 a year, and each associate justice receives $39,500. A justice 70 years of age, who has served 10 or more years, may retire and continue to receive his salary. A justice may also retire at 65 if he has served at least 15 years.

Authority of the Supreme Court

The Supreme Court declares what the law is only when an actual case comes before it under established rules of legal procedure. A matter before the court must involve a real dispute between opposing parties. The court does not give legal advice or advisory opinions, even if requested by the President or Congress.

The Constitution permits the court to decide cases "arising under" the Constitution, federal laws, and treaties. The court also decides disputes involving the United States or two or more states. The most important of these cases are those that require the court to interpret the Constitution or the laws enacted by Congress.

The Supreme Court has the power to decide whether a federal or state law or executive action is constitutional. This power, known as *judicial review*, is not expressly granted in the Constitution. However, the Constitution by its own terms is the "supreme law of the land." The court has ruled that it must review conflicts between the Constitution and an act of Congress or of a state legislature.

Most of the work of the Supreme Court comes under its *appellate jurisdiction*. This is the authority to confirm or reverse the decisions of lower courts. Appellate courts can call a lower court decision up for review when requested to do so by the losing party. The appeal is usually made on grounds that the judge has made an error in declaring the law that applies to the facts of the case. Most cases reviewed by the Supreme Court come from the federal courts of appeals and the highest state courts. The decisions of federal district courts are normally reviewed first by the courts of appeals. But in a few cases, the Supreme Court reviews the decisions of federal district courts directly. It also reviews the decisions of the federal Court of Claims and the Court of Customs and Patent Appeals.

The Supreme Court may try a few types of cases from their beginning. This authority is called *original jurisdiction*. The court has original jurisdiction in cases ". . . affecting ambassadors, other public ministers and consuls, and those in which a state shall be party. . . ." These cases, however, make up only a small fraction of the court's workload.

The Court in Action

Accepting Cases. The Supreme Court cannot possibly review all the cases decided by lower courts. It can select only a few that it considers to be of sufficient importance. Questions of individual justice are most often left to the judgment of lower courts.

However, Congress has provided that the Supreme Court must grant review in a few types of cases. Such cases are brought to the court by *appeal*.

Most cases are brought before the court by a *writ of*

U.S. SUPREME COURT JUSTICES

Name	Term	Appointed By
CHIEF JUSTICES		
*John Jay	1790-1795	Washington
*John Rutledge	1795	Washington
*Oliver Ellsworth	1796-1800	Washington
*John Marshall	1801-1835	J. Adams
*Roger B. Taney	1836-1864	Jackson
*Salmon P. Chase	1864-1873	Lincoln
*Morrison R. Waite	1874-1888	Grant
*Melville W. Fuller	1888-1910	Cleveland
*Edward D. White	1910-1921	Taft
*William H. Taft	1921-1930	Harding
*Charles E. Hughes	1930-1941	Hoover
*Harlan F. Stone	1941-1946	F. D. Roosevelt
*Frederick M. Vinson	1946-1953	Truman
*Earl Warren	1953-	Eisenhower
ASSOCIATE JUSTICES		
*James Wilson	1789-1798	Washington
*John Rutledge	1790-1791	Washington
William Cushing	1790-1810	Washington
*John Blair	1790-1796	Washington
*James Iredell	1790-1799	Washington
*Thomas Johnson	1792-1793	Washington
*William Paterson	1793-1806	Washington
*Samuel Chase	1796-1811	Washington
Bushrod Washington	1799-1829	J. Adams
Alfred Moore	1800-1804	J. Adams
William Johnson	1804-1834	Jefferson
H. Brockholst Livingston	1807-1823	Jefferson
Thomas Todd	1807-1826	Jefferson
Gabriel Duval	1811-1835	Madison
*Joseph Story	1812-1845	Madison
Smith Thompson	1823-1843	Monroe
Robert Trimble	1826-1828	J. Q. Adams
John McLean	1830-1861	Jackson
Henry Baldwin	1830-1844	Jackson
James M. Wayne	1835-1867	Jackson
Philip P. Barbour	1836-1841	Jackson
John Catron	1837-1865	Van Buren
John McKinley	1838-1852	Van Buren
Peter V. Daniel	1842-1860	Van Buren
Samuel Nelson	1845-1872	Tyler
Levi Woodbury	1845-1851	Polk
Robert C. Grier	1846-1870	Polk
Benjamin R. Curtis	1851-1857	Fillmore
John A. Campbell	1853-1861	Pierce
Nathan Clifford	1858-1881	Buchanan
Noah H. Swayne	1862-1881	Lincoln
Samuel F. Miller	1862-1890	Lincoln
*David Davis	1862-1877	Lincoln
*Stephen J. Field	1863-1897	Lincoln
William Strong	1870-1880	Grant
Joseph P. Bradley	1870-1892	Grant
Ward Hunt	1873-1882	Grant
*John M. Harlan	1877-1911	Hayes
William B. Woods	1881-1887	Hayes
Stanley Matthews	1881-1889	Garfield
Horace Gray	1882-1902	Arthur
Samuel Blatchford	1882-1893	Arthur
*Lucius Q. C. Lamar	1888-1893	Cleveland
David J. Brewer	1890-1910	Harrison
Henry B. Brown	1891-1906	Harrison
George Shiras, Jr.	1892-1903	Harrison
Howell E. Jackson	1893-1895	Harrison
*Edward D. White	1894-1910	Cleveland
Rufus W. Peckham	1896-1909	Cleveland
Joseph McKenna	1898-1925	McKinley
*Oliver W. Holmes, Jr.	1902-1932	T. Roosevelt
William R. Day	1903-1922	T. Roosevelt
William H. Moody	1906-1910	T. Roosevelt
Horace H. Lurton	1910-1914	Taft
*Charles E. Hughes	1910-1916	Taft
*Willis Van Devanter	1911-1937	Taft
Joseph R. Lamar	1911-1916	Taft
Mahlon Pitney	1912-1922	Taft
James C. McReynolds	1914-1941	Wilson
*Louis D. Brandeis	1916-1939	Wilson
John H. Clarke	1916-1922	Wilson
*George Sutherland	1922-1938	Harding
Pierce Butler	1923-1939	Harding
Edward T. Sanford	1923-1930	Harding
*Harlan F. Stone	1925-1941	Coolidge
*Owen J. Roberts	1930-1945	Hoover
*Benjamin N. Cardozo	1932-1938	Hoover
*Hugo L. Black	1937-	F. D. Roosevelt
Stanley F. Reed	1938-1957	F. D. Roosevelt
*Felix Frankfurter	1939-1962	F. D. Roosevelt
*William O. Douglas	1939-	F. D. Roosevelt
*Frank Murphy	1940-1949	F. D. Roosevelt
*James F. Byrnes	1941-1942	F. D. Roosevelt
*Robert H. Jackson	1941-1954	F. D. Roosevelt
Wiley B. Rutledge	1943-1949	F. D. Roosevelt
*Harold H. Burton	1945-1958	Truman
*Tom C. Clark	1949-1967	Truman
Sherman Minton	1949-1956	Truman
*John M. Harlan	1955-	Eisenhower
*William J. Brennan, Jr.	1956-	Eisenhower
*Charles E. Whittaker	1957-1962	Eisenhower
*Potter Stewart	1958-	Eisenhower
*Byron R. White	1962-	Kennedy
*Arthur J. Goldberg	1962-1965	Kennedy
*Abe Fortas	1965-	Johnson
*Thurgood Marshall	1967-	Johnson

*Has a separate biography in WORLD BOOK.

certiorari (pronounced *ser shee uh RARE ee*). This is a written order to call a case up from a lower court for review. The opposing attorney is given copies of the petition for certiorari and the supporting *brief* (written reasons for appeal). He has a short time to file a brief in opposition. If four justices vote to grant the petition, the court agrees to hear the case. The court controls its work load by granting only a small percentage of the requests for a writ of certiorari.

Pleading Cases before the Supreme Court is normally done by attorneys who have been admitted to the bar of the court. However, a *litigant* (person engaged in a lawsuit) may argue his own case. Each litigant usually hires and pays his own attorney. If a litigant has no money, free legal service may be provided, particularly in criminal cases.

When the United States government has an interest in a case before the Supreme Court, it is represented by the solicitor general of the United States. Actually, the solicitor general himself appears before the court in only a few cases. Most of the cases are argued by members of his staff or by other government lawyers.

Deciding Cases. The justices decide a case after they have considered written and oral arguments from each side. During oral arguments, the justices are free to interrupt and to ask questions.

After the attorneys' oral arguments, the justices discuss the case *in conference* (in private). The chief justice begins the discussion. Then, in order of seniority, each associate justice gives his opinion. After discussion ends, the justices vote in reverse order of seniority. The latest member to be appointed to the court votes first.

The chief justice votes last, immediately after the associate justice who has served longest on the court. Cases are decided by majority vote.

If the chief justice has voted with the majority, he selects a justice to write the *opinion of the court*. This opinion is also called the *majority opinion*. If the chief justice has not voted with the majority, the senior justice of the majority assigns the opinion. A justice who disagrees with this opinion may write a *dissenting opinion*. A justice may write a *concurring opinion* if he agrees with the conclusion but not with the reasons for reaching it, or if he wishes to express similar reasons in his own words. Authors of the opinions announce them in a public session. All opinions are published in the *United States Reports*.

The practice of putting opinions in writing requires the justices to explain and justify their decisions. Any citizen is free to read and criticize the opinions. This is an important tradition in a free society, and a strong safeguard against unreasonable use of power. The publishing of opinions also enables the public to know and understand the decisions of the court.

Effects of Decisions. Supreme Court decisions have importance far beyond the particular facts and parties involved. Once the court decides a case, lower courts are required to follow the decision in similar cases. The Supreme Court itself usually follows its earlier decisions. The policy of following rules laid down in previous decisions is known as *stare decisis*. This practice lends stability and predictability to the law. It allows persons to plan their future knowing that the rules will not be changed without a good reason.

The Supreme Court, however, is not bound by an earlier decision if it is convinced that an error has been made or that changed circumstances require a different approach. This provides for the court's recognition of social, political, and economic change.

Landmark Decisions

The Marshall Court. Many of the most important and historic Supreme Court opinions were written by John Marshall, one of the most famous of all American judges. Marshall served as chief justice from 1801 to 1835. The Supreme Court during those years is sometimes referred to as the "Marshall court."

Marshall's most historic opinion was written in 1803, in the case of *Marbury v. Madison*. His majority opinion stated that the court may rule an act of Congress unenforceable if the act violates the U.S. Constitution. This power of *judicial review* is *implied* (expressed indirectly) but not clearly granted in the Constitution.

Some persons have protested vigorously against the court's exercise of judicial review. However, this power has become firmly established as a basic part of the American constitutional system. For a discussion of the case of *Marbury v. Madison*, see JEFFERSON, THOMAS (The Courts).

Several other Marshall court decisions also have had far-reaching application. In 1819, in *Dartmouth College v. Woodward*, the court ruled that private charters are contracts. It held that the Constitution protects such charters against violation by the states. This decision strengthened the rights of private property. See DARTMOUTH COLLEGE CASE.

Also in 1819, in *McCulloch v. Maryland*, the court supported the doctrine of implied powers. It ruled that the federal government possesses powers in addition to those specifically granted in the Constitution. It said that the U.S. government has any powers that are necessary and proper in carrying out its specified powers. This decision broadened the scope and authority of the federal government. See MARSHALL, JOHN.

Regulating Commerce. An important concern of the court has been the proper relationship between government and business. The Constitution gives Congress the power to regulate interstate commerce. In 1824, in *Gibbons v. Ogden*, the Marshall court gave a broad interpretation to the word *commerce*. Since the mid-1930's, the court has interpreted the commerce clause in a way that gives Congress wide regulatory powers in matters affecting business. For information on important commerce decisions, see INTERSTATE COMMERCE.

Civil Rights and Liberties. Through the years, the role and interpretations of the Supreme Court have shifted with changes in national conditions and public opinion. This has been true of the court's position on civil rights, especially in the area of race relations.

In 1857, in *Dred Scott v. Sandford*, the court held that Negroes were not and could not become U.S. citizens (see DRED SCOTT DECISION). But the 14th Amendment to the Constitution (1868) made all former slaves citizens and gave them full civil rights. In 1896, in the case of *Plessy v. Ferguson*, the court upheld a law providing for "separate but equal" public facilities for the white and Negro races. But in 1954, in *Brown v. Board of Education of Topeka*, the court ruled that racial segregation in public schools is unconstitutional. In 1964, in *Atlanta Motel v. United States*, the court upheld the Civil Rights Act of 1964. This act prohibits racial discrimination in many public accommodations. See NEGRO (The Civil Rights Movement).

Several cases in the 1960's dealt with voting rights. In 1962, the court ruled in *Baker v. Carr* that unfair districting of state legislatures could be challenged in federal courts. It ruled in other cases that congressional districts must be about equal in population, and that both houses of state legislatures must be apportioned on the basis of equal population.

Several recent decisions have dealt with the rights of persons accused of crimes. In 1963, in *Gideon v. Wainwright*, the court held that states must provide free legal counsel to any person accused of a felony who is without funds. In 1964, in *Escobedo v. Illinois*, the court ruled that a confession cannot be used as evidence if it is obtained after the defendant has been denied permission to see his lawyer. The court went even further in the 1966 case of *Miranda v. Arizona*. It held that prior to any questioning, the defendant must be informed of his constitutional rights, including the right to remain silent.

Other important civil rights decisions have dealt with Bible reading and prayers in public schools, freedom of speech and of the press, and pretrial publicity that is *prejudicial* (unfair) to the accused.

Controversy on the Court

The Supreme Court has been sharply divided on some cases brought before it. This has been especially true of cases involving questions that have divided the American public, such as minority rights. The court's lack of complete agreement in such cases is not unexpected nor undesirable. It reflects the seriousness of the cases and the presence of different points of view.

Since the Supreme Court was established, a strong debate has continued concerning the extent of its power. One side has insisted that the court should interpret and apply the Constitution to agree with the meaning and intent of those who wrote it. Another group has insisted on a more creative role for the court. They would interpret the Constitution so that it would apply to the new and changing problems of the nation. The second group also draws support from the original intent of the founding fathers, but disagrees as to the scope and meaning of that intent. Outstanding judges and legal scholars have been found on both sides of this debate.

The Supreme Court possesses great power over the Constitution and the nation. But this power is based on the respect of the American people. Throughout most of its history, the court has held the streams of government within their proper channels. It has largely succeeded in the delicate task of protecting the rights of unpopular minorities while relying for its support on the approval of the majority. WILLIAM RAY FORRESTER

Critically reviewed by BYRON R. WHITE

SURFING is a thrilling water sport for persons of all ages. In *surfboard riding*, the surfer stands on a board that skims along the *crest* (top) of a wave. However, body surfers are swept along by the wave without using a board. Both kinds of surfing demand split-second timing. The surfer must have sharp reflexes to maintain the delicate balance he needs for a thrilling ride.

SURFING TERMS

Backwash, Rip, or **Riptide** is a current that reverses itself and moves out from the shore.

Big Gun is a heavy surfboard used on big waves.

Break is the point in shallow water where a wave slows and builds up, then scatters.

Cornering occurs when a surfer shoots across a wave at an angle to the shoreline.

Crack a Wave means to ride a big wave successfully.

Dumper, or **Fall** is a wave that builds up sharply and drops straight down into shallow water.

Going Down the Mine occurs when a surfer misses the proper take-off point in a wave and is thrown in front of the wave.

Green Wave is a long, uninterrupted wave.

Hanging Five, or **Ten** occurs when the surfer hooks his toes over the end of the board.

Hot Dogger is an expert surfer who can do gymnastic and balancing tricks on the board.

Howler, or **Zipper** is a big wave that only an expert can ride.

Pig Board, or **Tear Drop** is a board that is shaped like a pie wedge.

Roller is a long, smooth wave that rolls to the shore line.

Wipe Out occurs when a rider is bumped from a board by a wave.

Surfers usually train for surfboard riding by body surfing. To body surf, a surfer swims out from the shore a few hundred yards and waits for a high wave. When a high wave starts in toward the shore, he does a *scissors kick* (spreads his legs apart and kicks them together) in the direction of the shore and swims a few strokes at the crest. He then puts his head down, arches his back, and puts his hands at his sides. The wave sweeps him toward shore in this position. As it dies out, the surfer pushes his hands out and spreads his legs to slow down. The feel of the surf and the sense of balance gained in body surfing is good training for surfboard riding.

For a surfboard ride, the surfer lies on his stomach on the board and paddles out to the area where the waves build up. When a big wave starts in toward shore, the surfer paddles his board ahead of it. As the wave begins to carry the board toward shore, the surfer stands up. He tries to guide the board across the face of the wave by shifting the weight of his body. Expert surfers may move to the front of the board, but most surfers stand at the middle or rear of the board to keep it from turning over. A long rolling wave will bring a surfer onto the sands of the shore. The bigger the wave, the better the ride will be.

Surfing began in Hawaii hundreds of years ago. The sport is now popular in most parts of the world. Surfing in the United States centers on the beaches of Hawaii and southern California. Many styles of surfboards are used, but most U.S. surfers use a fiberglass board that is tapered at both ends. It is about 10 feet long, 30 inches wide, 3 inches thick, and weighs from 8 to 15 pounds. SAM J. GRELLER

Don James

Surfing requires good balance and quick reflexes. Many expert surfers can perform gymnastic tricks on the board. For their own safety, all surfers should be good swimmers.

Section Five

Dictionary Supplement

The following supplement has been prepared under the direction of the editors of *The World Book Encyclopedia* in cooperation with Clarence L. Barnhart, editor in chief of *The World Book Dictionary*. This dictionary, first published by Field Enterprises Educational Corporation in 1963, keeps abreast of our living language with a program of continuous editorial revision. This section, presented as a service to owners of the dictionary and as an informative feature to subscribers of *The World Book Year Book*, contains six new articles and features to be included in the 1968 edition of *The World Book Dictionary*.

592 **New Views of Grammar**

593 **So You Think You Speak English?**

593 **What's in a Name?**

594 **Words That Have Changed with Time**

595 **Be-Careful Words**

596 **Fun with Words**

New Views of Grammar

Recently, American linguists have presented new ways of looking at English that depart from traditional grammar. One approach, "structural linguistics," analyzes English by concentrating on word endings, signal words, and location of words in sentences.

Nouns, verbs, adjectives, and adverbs have endings that help identify them. Common noun endings are *-ance*, *-ence*, *-er*, *-ion*, *-ity*, *-ment*, *-ness*, and *-or*. Common verb endings are *-ate*, *-d*, *-ed*, *-en*, *-fy*, *-ing*, *-ize*, and *-t*. Common adjective endings are *-able*, *-al*, *-ant*, *-ary*, *-ed*, *-en*, *-ent*, *-ful*, *-ic*, *-ish*, *-less*, *-ous*, *-some*, and *-y*. A common adverb ending is *-ly*.

Certain words are called signal words when they announce that certain parts of speech are coming. *A*, *an*, *the*, *both*, *some*, and similar words signal nouns. Auxiliaries such as *may*, *have*, *will*, *can*, and *should* signal verbs. Prepositions such as *on*, *in*, and *of* signal nouns or pronouns. Of course, *both* and *some* are sometimes used as nouns, and *have* and other auxiliaries are sometimes verbs.

The position of a word in a sentence is also a good clue to part of speech because the English language contains certain sentence patterns.

Consider the sentence "The ________ fumbled the ball." Without knowing the missing word, you can tell it will be a noun. How? Because of its place in the sentence and its link with the signal word *the*.

Or consider the sentence "The trugy deer gimfeled the grass." Even though you don't know the meaning of *gimfeled*, you can tell that it is a verb because of its position in the sentence and its *-ed* ending. You also know that *trugy* is an adjective because of its *-y* ending and its place in the sentence.

Another new approach to grammar, "generative transformational grammar," formulates logical procedures for "generating" new sentences. The basic unit of this grammar is the kernel sentence—an active, positive statement such as "Ruth is happy." By applying certain procedures, you can "transform" this kernel sentence into the following sentences:

Ruth is not happy. (negative transform)
Is Ruth happy? (question transform)

You also can transform two or more kernel sentences into a more complicated sentence. The sentence "John smiled and walked away" is a transform of the kernel sentences "John smiled" and "John walked away." The sentence "The hungry man eats the pie" is a transform of "The man is hungry" and "The man eats the pie." The sentence "I found somebody's ring" is a transform of "Somebody had a ring" and "I found the ring."

These two new approaches to grammar use terms not found in traditional grammar. For example, they discuss *morphemes*, which are single units of meaning expressed by a word or a part of a word.

boy is one morpheme
boy's is two morphemes (boy+possessive)
boys is two morphemes (boy+plural)

The past tense morpheme is whatever is done to a verb to make it past tense. Usually, *-ed* is added to the end of the word. However, the past tense morpheme is not always shown this way.

help is one morpheme
helped is two morphemes (past+help)
teach is one morpheme
taught is two morphemes (past+teach)

The new grammars also classify words in a way slightly different from that of traditional grammar. All the parts of speech are classified under two main headings—content words and function words.

Content words contain many of the words that traditional grammar calls nouns, verbs, adjectives, and adverbs. This category of words is constantly expanding because when new words are added to the language, they are almost always content words.

Even though they rarely change, function words are very important. Function words are the little words, like prepositions and conjunctions, that connect content words and hold sentences together. Some other important function words are:

Auxiliaries. The auxiliaries are the familiar verb-helpers like *may*, *might*, *have*, *has*, *had*, *can*, *could*, *should*, and similar words.

Determiners. A determiner is used with a noun and determines something about the meaning of the noun. A determiner can be an article like *a*, *an*, or *the;* a demonstrative like *this*, *that*, *these*, or *those;* a number like *one*, *six*, or *thirteen;* a quantifier like *several of* or *many of;* or a possessive like *his* or *hers*. A determiner differs from an adjective in that a determiner usually does not make sense when it is used alone in the predicate. For example, *green* when it is used with a noun is an adjective. You can say "The green sweater shrank," or "The sweater is green." However, *the* when it is used with a noun is a determiner. You can say "The sweater shrank," but you cannot say "Sweater is the."

Intensifiers. Intensifiers are words like *very*, *rather*, *quite*, and *somewhat*. They intensify or give more specific meaning to adjectives and adverbs.

Structural linguistics and transformational grammar are two new views on the study of the English language. No one knows how soon, if ever, either one will replace traditional grammar. However, many teachers of English are incorporating some of the ideas from these new grammars with the traditional approach. For example, consider the sentence "The lion devoured his trainer." In traditional grammar, the third word is called a verb because it expresses action. In structural linguistics, it is called a verb because of its position in the sentence and its *-ed* ending. When both the traditional and structural descriptions of a verb are combined into one definition, the advantages of both views are utilized, and the idea of what a verb is becomes clearer.

So You Think You Speak English?

The British and Americans both speak a language called English. For the most part we have little difficulty understanding one another. There are times, however, when certain words and expressions may cause confusion.

Exercise I

Can you match the list of British words on the left with their American counterparts? Answers are on page **596.**

Example:

British	American
1. petrol	(a) automobile
2. windscreen	(b) windshield
3. motorcar	(c) gasoline

Answers: 1. petrol, (c) gasoline
2. windscreen, (b) windshield
3. motorcar, (a) automobile

1. bonnet	(a) truck	9. maize	(i) elevator
2. wings	(b) newsstand	10. fortnight	(j) cookies
3. cooker	(c) tavern	11. public house	(k) radio
4. wireless	(d) turn signal	12. waistcoat	(l) hood
5. lift	(e) vest	13. lorry	(m) rare
6. holiday	(f) thumbtack	14. underdone	(n) vacation
7. kiosk	(g) two weeks	15. drawing pin	(o) corn
8. indicator	(h) oven	16. biscuits	(p) fenders

Exercise II

One word in each of the following sentences is British. Find the word and match it to its American counterpart in the column opposite the sentences. Answers are on page **596.**

1. He collected the old newspapers and put them in the dustbin.	raincoat
2. John hung his waterproof on a hook in the kitchen.	hardware store
3. Mrs. Pryce-Jones bought a frying pan at the ironmonger's.	hot water heater
4. It was a new car, but something was wrong with the silencer.	garbage can
5. Signs alerted Peter to the road works ahead.	undershirt
6. Nora put a coin in the geyser and waited for the water to turn hot.	highway repairs
7. She disapproved when he came to the dinner table in his vest.	muffler

What's In a Name?

Many words in the English language come from the names of persons and places. In the exercise below, column I describes a person or a place and gives the meaning of the word derived from the name. Match these descriptions with the names and the words listed in column II. Answers are on page **596.**

Example:

Dame Nellie_______, an opera singer, liked her toast sliced thin and evenly browned. This toast now bears her name.

Answer: (c) Melba—melba toast

(a) Chauvin–chauvinist
(b) Kameryk–cambric
(c) Melba–melba toast

1. Samuel_______, a Texas cattleman, refused to brand his cattle. Now his name is used to describe anyone who is unconventional.	(a) Derrick–derrick
2. This device lifts and moves heavy objects. It gets its name from a 17th century hangman.	(b) Xeres–sherry
3. A county in England gave its name to this four-wheeled vehicle with two seats facing inward.	(c) Shrapnel–shrapnel
	(d) Surrey–surrey
4. Henry_______, an English army officer, invented an artillery shell that explodes in the air and scatters pellets over a wide area.	(e) Maverick–maverick
5. Jerez, Spain, once called Xeres, was mispronounced and thus gave its name to a wine which varies in color from pale yellow to dark brown.	(f) Meander River–meander
6. Gabriel D._______ invented a scale for measuring temperature.	(g) Boycott–boycott
7. Blue jeans are made from this cloth named for a town in France.	
8. Meaning to follow a winding course, this word comes from the name of a winding river in Caria, Asia Minor.	(h) Fahrenheit–Fahrenheit
	(i) Nîmes–denim

Words That Have Changed with Time

Words are the symbols with which we communicate. A common knowledge of these symbols makes it possible for us to tell others what we think and to make ourselves understood. But the words themselves are only symbols. The meanings of these symbols may change.

One important factor in changing the meaning of words is time. In some instances a word takes on a broader meaning than it had originally. *Town*, from the Old English *tun*, once meant any enclosure. It related to the time when a group of people came together and built a wall or fence around their collective buildings to protect themselves from strangers and wild beasts. *Town* now means a large group of houses and other buildings, smaller than a city but larger than a village. The word *demon* is from the Greek *daímōn* and originally meant divinity, or a divine thing. Christian writers changed the meaning to that of a thing of evil, and this is the sense in which it is used today.

Words and their original meanings are listed in column I. Column II lists their present meanings. See whether you can match the present meanings to their counterparts in column I. Answers are on page **596.**

Example:

rumor—a great uproar

(a) thunderstorm
(b) news without proof
(c) an assembly hall

Answer: (b) news without proof

I

1. rummage—to stow cargo in the hold of a ship
2. senate—a gathering of old men
3. infant—not speaking
4. comrade—roommate
5. pretty—tricky, crafty
6. nice—stupid, ignorant
7. school—leisure
8. companion—one who shares his bread with another
9. carpenter—a carriage maker
10. garble—to sift spices
11. hospital—a place where travelers are entertained and sheltered
12. plunder—household goods
13. measles—wretch
14. umbrage—a shadowy outline
15. rival—one who uses the same stream
16. risk—to skirt the cliffs while sailing
17. silly—rustic, happy, innocent
18. chimney—furnace, oven
19. handsome—easy to handle
20. foyer—fireplace
21. villain—a farm hand
22. cunning—skillful, knowing
23. sarcasm—act of stripping the flesh
24. stomach—throat or gullet
25. nerve—sinew, tendon
26. explode—to drive out by clapping the hands

II

(a) a very young child
(b) agreeable, pleasing
(c) to search thoroughly by moving things about
(d) resentment
(e) making fun of a person to hurt his feelings
(f) to rob by force
(g) an entrance hall
(h) the legislative assembly of a state or nation
(i) danger, chance of harm
(j) a friend
(k) competitor
(l) pleasing in appearance
(m) pleasing, dainty
(n) a place for teaching and learning
(o) a very wicked person, a scoundrel
(p) clever in a deceitful way
(q) one who goes along with another
(r) a virus disease
(s) structure connected with fireplace to carry away smoke
(t) one who builds or repairs with wood
(u) distort meaning by scrambling words
(v) a place where the sick are cared for
(w) without sense or reason
(x) in man, the saclike dilation of the alimentary canal occupying the upper part of the left side of the abdomen
(y) a fiber or bundle of fibers connecting the brain or the spinal cord with the eyes, muscles, glands, etc.
(z) to blow up, burst with a loud noise

Be-Careful Words

Can you find five misspelled words in the next paragraph?

Last summer my family and I went too Canada for our vacation. We visited Toronto and Ottawa, the capitol of Canada; but if I had to chose my favorite city, I would pick Montreal. We climbed Mount Royal their and also toured the imminent McGill University.

Some of the misspelled words are homonyms. Homonyms are words that sound alike but do not have the same spelling or meaning. They are a common source of spelling errors. The sentences below illustrate homonyms which may cause spelling errors if you aren't careful.

1. **aisle** (noun meaning "passage between rows of seats")
   The aisle was blocked by boxes.
   I'll (contraction meaning "I will")
   I'll wait by the State Street entrance.
   isle (noun meaning "small island")
   The isle was swept by the tidal wave.
2. **all ready** (completely ready)
   Everyone is all ready.
   already (adverb meaning "by this time")
   Everyone had eaten already.
3. **allowed** (verb meaning "permitted")
   Reading aloud is not allowed.
   aloud (adverb meaning "loud enough to be heard")
   Please do not read aloud.
4. **altar** (noun meaning "a place of worship")
   The church was known for its stone altar.
   alter (verb meaning "to change")
   Sharon tried to have the coat altered.
5. **canvas** (noun meaning "a type of cloth")
   The ship's sails were made of canvas.
   canvass (verb meaning "to inspect," verb meaning "to discuss", verb meaning "to solicit votes, opinions, etc.")
   She canvassed the paper for want ads.
   Congress canvassed the President's plan.
6. **capital** (noun meaning "the city which is the official seat of government," noun meaning "the center of some industry, group, or interest," noun meaning "the amount a person uses in carrying on a business")
   Rome is the capital of Italy.
   New York is the financial capital of the world.
   The Walter Company has a capital of $100,000.
   capitol (noun meaning "the building in which a legislature meets")
   Illinois' capitol in Springfield was completed in 1888.
7. **cite** (verb meaning "to quote")
   Can you cite another example?
   sight (verb meaning "to see")
   Did he sight land?
   site (noun meaning "location")
   This is a good site for our home.
8. **currant** (noun meaning "a small, seedless raisin")
   Mother baked currant cookies.
   current (adjective meaning "of the present time," noun meaning "flow")
   She always wears the current fashions.
   The current carried the boat out to sea.
9. **dyeing** (coloring of fabrics with dye)
   Chris is dyeing her dress yellow.
   dying (at the point of death)
   The gooseberry bush is dying.
10. **principal** (noun meaning "chief person," adjective meaning "most important," noun meaning "sum of money")
    Mr. Jones is the principal.
    Their principal crop was corn.
    The principal was $6,500.
    principle (noun meaning "a basic truth")
    We believe in the principle of freedom.
11. **stationary** (adjective meaning "not movable," adjective meaning "not changing")
    The kitchen table is stationary.
    The school's enrollment has been stationary for three years.
    stationery (noun meaning "writing materials")
    He gave her a gift of stationery.
12. **their** (possessive pronoun)
    We saw their new car.
    they're (contraction of "they are")
    They're all coming tomorrow.
    there (adverb)
    We will see you there.
13. **to** (preposition)
    Can you carry them to the office?
    too (adverb of degree)
    The third one is too heavy to lift.
    two (adjective)
    The first two boxes are heavy.

You've probably already found the five misspelled words in the opening paragraph, but here's the way the paragraph should be written.

Last summer my family and I went *to* Canada for our vacation. We visited Toronto and Ottawa, the *capital* of Canada; but if I had to *choose* my favorite city, I would pick Montreal. We climbed Mount Royal *there* and also toured the *eminent* McGill University.

Fun with Words

A pleasant way to add to your vocabulary is to play word games. They exercise your ability to spell, your knowledge of the parts of speech, and your use of antonyms, synonyms, affixes, and combining forms. Word games challenge your ability to think quickly, and they help you to reinforce your memory of the words you already know. Here are a few of the most popular word games.

Group Games

Turn Arounds. Players are divided into two groups. Each group makes up a list of five sentences containing the definitions of two words. When each of the defined words is inverted, it spells the other. For example; "Turn around this drop of moisture and you'll be married." (dew - wed) A reasonable time limit is set to compose the sentences. Then the groups exchange lists, and a time limit for solution is set. Here are two suggestions to start you off.

1. Turn around this nasty look and you have a fish line. (leer - reel)
2. Turn around this cooking utensil and you have a toy that spins. (pot - top)

Hidden Words. Each player receives a sheet of paper on which the same long word is printed. Five minutes is the time limit. At a signal from the leader each player writes down as many words as he can find hidden in the long word. Proper names do not count.

Telegrams. Each player writes 15 different letters on a sheet of paper allowing enough space between each so that words can be formed. He then passes the sheet to the player on his right. At a signal from the leader, each player composes a message. He uses as initials each letter in the order in which it appears on the sheet of paper he has received. Time limit is five minutes.

Hidden Animals. A list of sentences is given to each player. Each sentence contains the name of an animal which is well-hidden in one or a series of consecutive words. It is as much fun to make up the sentences as it is to find the hidden animal. Before the game begins, players may divide into two groups, make up a list of sentences and then exchange lists. The following examples will give you some idea of the kinds of words that may be used.

1. His pres*tige r*ose with each promotion. (tige r)
2. He*r at*titude was good. (r at)

Ghost. The group sits in a semicircle. The first player calls out the first letter of a word. The second player adds a letter. The trick is to keep the word going as long as possible because the player who is first to end a word loses the round and receives the letter G. No word of fewer than four letters may be used. If a player loses a second round he is GH and so on. During the round a player has the right to challenge if he thinks a letter as given in sequence cannot be part of a word. If the challenged player is unable to prove that he has a legitimate word, he receives a letter from GHOST. The player who is first to receive all the letters in GHOST is out of the game.

Coffee Pot. This game is especially appropriate for very young children. Choose one player to be "it." When he leaves the room, the remaining players choose a verb that is to be guessed by "it." When "it" is called back into the room, he must ask questions that can be answered by *yes* or *no*. He substitutes the words "coffee pot" for the verb he is looking for. For example, he may ask "Does the Queen of England coffee pot?" "Do I coffee pot?" and so on. "It" continues to ask questions until he finds the word or gives up.

Games That Can be Played Alone

Cryptograms. In a cryptogram one letter is used without change in place of another throughout the message to be deciphered. No clues to the hidden message are given. It is up to the player to find the clue by looking for: one letter words (usually *I* and *a*), common prefixes and suffixes, common two and three letter words, and frequently used double letters. Cryptograms are easier to solve if you remember that the letters most used in the English alphabet are, in order of frequency, E, T, A, O, N, R, I, and S. For example, the cryptogram for *A stitch in time saves nine* might read X FNZNOQ ZE NZRP FXIPF EZEP.

Anagrams. In anagrams a series of letters is rearranged to make a word. For example, the following anagrams can be rearranged to spell the names of flowers. EROS (ROSE), LOVEIT (VIOLET), EARST (ASTER).

Acrostics. Words are arranged so that the initial of each word when taken in sequence spells another word which answers a definition. For example, the adjectives *happy*, *ordinary*, *rough*, *sad*, *empty* contain the name of what quadruped? (Answer: horse)

Answers

So You Think You Speak English?

Exercise I

1. (l)	5. (i)	9. (o)	13. (a)
2. (p)	6. (n)	10. (g)	14. (m)
3. (h)	7. (b)	11. (c)	15. (f)
4. (k)	8. (d)	12. (e)	16. (j)

Exercise II

1. dustbin—garbage can
2. waterproof—raincoat
3. ironmonger's—hardware store
4. silencer—muffler
5. road works—highway repairs
6. geyser—hot water heater
7. vest—undershirt

What's in a Name?

1. (e)	3. (d)	5. (b)	7. (i)
2. (a)	4. (c)	6. (h)	8. (f)

Words That Have Changed with Time

1. (c)	8. (q)	15. (k)	22. (p)
2. (h)	9. (t)	16. (i)	23. (e)
3. (a)	10. (u)	17. (w)	24. (x)
4. (j)	11. (v)	18. (s)	25. (y)
5. (m)	12. (f)	19. (l)	26. (z)
6. (b)	13. (r)	20. (g)	
7. (n)	14. (d)	21. (o)	

Section Six

Index

How to Use the Index

This index covers the contents of all editions of *The World Book Year Book* from 1964 to 1968. It indexes subjects discussed in the first four sections of each edition, and lists the titles of all new or revised articles from *The World Book Encyclopedia* appearing in the supplement section.

Each index entry is followed by the edition years (in italics) and the page numbers, as:
ADVERTISING, *68*–192, *67*–200, *66*–210, *65*–206, *64*–204

This means that information about advertising begins on the pages indicated for each of the editions.

An index entry that is the title of an article appearing in *The Year Book* is printed in capital letters, as: **AUTOMOBILE.** An entry that is not an article title, but a subject discussed in an article of some other title is printed: **Tires.**

The various "See" and "See also" cross references in the index list are to other entries within the index. Clue words or phrases are used when two or more references to the same subject appear in the same edition of *The Year Book.* These make it easy to locate the material on the page, since they refer to an article title or article subsection in which the reference appears, as:
Air pollution: automobile *66*–236; botany, *67*–247; conservation, *68*–283; electric power, *68*–323; health, *64*–357; Houston, *67*–366; *Special Report, 66*–165.

The indication "*il.*" means that the reference is to an illustration only.
An index entry in capital letters followed by "*WBE*" refers to a new or revised *World Book Encyclopedia* article, which is printed in the supplement section as:
EARTH, *WBE, 68*–544

INDEX

A

Aaltonen, Wäinö, 67–296
Ababda, 67–106
Abu Simbel, 66–220, 64–212
Abyssinia. See **ETHIOPIA**
Accelerator, particle, il., 68–459
Accidents. See **DISASTERS; SAFETY**
Acheson, Dean, 65–231
ACKLEY, (HUGH) GARDNER, 67–200
ACTH: chemistry, 64–268; science, 64–33
Adams, Michael J., 66–229
Addiction, 66–435
ADEN. See **SOUTH ARABIA, FEDERATION OF**
Adenauer, Konrad: Erhard, Ludwig, 64–321; deaths, 68–293; Germany, il., 67–353, 65–346; 64–343, 64–346
Administration on Aging, 66–463
Adoption, 68–262, 67–266
Adult education, 67–465
ADVERTISING, 68–192, 67–200, 66–210, 65–206, 64–204
drugs, 65–314; food, 67–340; motion pictures, il., 64–416; newspapers, 64–464; packaging, 65–449, 64–437; publishing, 68–471; radio, 67–478, 66–500, 65–479, 64–466; television, 67–519
AFGHANISTAN, 68–193, 67–201, 66–210, 65–206, 64–204; Pazhwak, Abdul Rahman, 67–450
AFL-CIO. See **American Federation of Labor-Congress of Industrial Organizations**
AFRICA, 68–194, 67–98, 67–202, 66–211, 65–207, 64–204; anthropology, 68–204; Asia, 68–212; democracy, 68–301, 67–304; engineering, 68–328; international relations, 67–18; petroleum, 68–455; Portugal, 67–462; Roman Catholic, 68–480, 67–483; United Nations, 67–535. See also by name of country
Afro-Asian Conference: China, 66–277; India, 66–385
AGNON, SHMUEL YOSEF, 67–206
Agranoff, Bernard W., 66–251
AGRICULTURE, 68–198, 67–206, 66–214, 65–210, 64–208
Albania, 68–202; aviation, 66–240; botany, 64–247; Brazil, 68–242; Bulgaria, 64–253; Canada, 67–258, 64–260; census, 67–263; child welfare, 65–261; China, 66–117, 66–279, 65–264, 64–271; Congress, 66–295, 65–280; dairying, 65–289, 64–293; economy, 67–318; employment, 68–102; Europe, 67–332, 65–326, 64–324; farm equipment, 68–410, 67–412, 65–333, 64–330; food, 68–339; forestry, 64–335; Four-H Clubs, 66–353, 65–337, 64–335; France, 68–346; Future Farmers of America, 66–357, 65–340, 64–339; garden and lawn, 67–350, 66–358; Germany, 64–344; Girl Scouts, 66–363; India, 66–132, 66–383, 65–367; insect, 68–372, 67–374; international trade, 64–369; Iran, 65–373; labor, 67–390; livestock, 65–407, 64–400; livestock show, 68–406, 67–406, 66–424, 65–408, 64–401; manufacturing, 66–429; Mekong River, 68–79; Mexico, 67–420; Pakistan, 68–447; Peace Corps, 67–450; Philippines, 65–463; poverty, 67–464, 66–485; poultry, 65–468, 64–456; prices, 65–250, 64–256; Russia, 67–486, 66–515, 64–14, 64–478; science, 68–33; soil conservation, 65–503, 64–486; Special Report, 65–123; youth organizations, 68–539
Agriculture, U.S. Department of: agriculture, 64–208; library, 68–397
Aguiyi-Ironsi, Johnson, 67–441
Aid to Dependent Children: child welfare, 64–269; social welfare, 64–486
AILES, STEPHEN, 65–211
Air force: armed forces, 68–210, 67–216, 66–223, 65–216, 64–214; Australia, 64–229; Germany, 67–353; Middle East, il., 68–425
Air Force, U.S.: atomic energy, 67–224; aviation, il., 65–229; Brown, Harold, 66–261; McConnell, John Paul, 66–431; national defense, 68–435, 67–435, 66–451, 65–431, 64–423; Science Clubs, 67–495, 66–519, 65–497, 64–482; Vietnam, 68–531, 66–555
Air pollution: automobile, 66–236; botany, 67–247; conservation, 68–283; electric power, 68–323; health, 64–357; Houston, 67–366; Special Report, 66–165
Aircraft carrier, 67–436, 66–455, 65–434
Airplane, model, 68–347, 65–342, 64–412
Airport: aviation, 68–222, 67–233, 66–240, 65–229, 64–235; Dallas, 66–300; fairs and exhibitions, 64–330; Los Angeles, 64–401; New York City, 65–439; St. Louis, 68–486; San Francisco, 66–517, 64–480
Aitken, Virginia, 66–470
Akhmatova, Anna, 67–296
Alabama: civil rights, 66–286, 64–276; Negro, 66–456, 64–429; President of the United States, 64–459; U.S. government, 68–528; Wallace, George C., 68–536, 64–525
Alaska: celebrations, 68–256; civil defense, 65–266; conservation, 68–283, 67–291; courts and laws, 65–285; disasters, il., 68–309; earthquakes, 65–312, 65–343; exploration, 64–328; fishery, 64–332; iron and steel, 65–374; mines and mining, 65–417; petroleum, 67–456
ALBANIA, 68–202, 67–210, 66–217, 65–212, 64–209
Albareda, Anselmo Cardinal, 67–296
ALBEE, EDWARD FRANKLIN, 68–202; theater, 68–513, 67–522, 66–540, 64–506
Alberta: Canada, 68–252, 67–259, 66–268, 65–256 il., 64–106, 64–262
Albinoism, 68–542
Alcindor, Lew, 68–233
Alcock, Albert, 68–450
Alcoholism: courts, 68–287; crime, 67–294; mental health, 67–418
Aldrin, Edwin E., Jr., 67–505
Alewife, 68–365, 66–380
Alexander, Franz, 65–293
ALGERIA, 68–203, 67–210, 66–217, 65–212, 64–209; Boumedienne, Houari, 66–256; civil rights, 66–283; democracy, 64–303; France, 65–340; Morocco, 65–419, 64–414
Ali, Muhammad. See **CLAY, CASSIUS**
Allen, Florence E., 67–296
Allergy, 67–138, 66–317
Alliance for Progress: Latin America, 67–392, 66–410, 65–392, 64–386
ALLILUYEVA, SVETLANA, 68–203; literature, 68–399; personalities, il., 68–452; Russia, 68–482
Allingham, Margery, 67–296
Alpert, Herb, il., 68–433
Alps: bridge and tunnel, 66–259; celebrations, 66–271
Aluminum, 68–443
Amateur Athletic Union: sports, 65–513, 64–494; track and field, 67–526, 66–542, 65–528, 64–509
Ambassador. See **DIPLOMAT**
American Bar Association, 68–287, 67–292, 65–284
American Dental Association, 67–306
American Federation of Labor-Congress of Industrial Organizations, 68–390, 67–390, 66–407
American Federation of Teachers, 68–39
American Hospital Association, 66–377
American Indian. See **INDIAN, AMERICAN**
American Legion, 68–529, 67–540, 66–553, 65–536, 64–520
AMERICAN LIBRARY ASSOCIATION, 68–203, 67–211, 66–218, 65–212, 64–210
American Medical Association: drugs, 67–134, 65–314; hospital, 66–377; Medicare, 66–432; medicine, 65–411, 64–403
American Veterans Committee, 68–529, 67–540, 66–553
American Veterans of World War II and Korea, 68–529, 67–540, 66–553, 65–536
Ammann, Othmar H.: bridge and tunnel, 66–259; deaths, 66–303
Ammonia, 66–428
Amphetamines, 67–145
Anatomy, 67–81; heart, WBE, 68–568
Andrews, Julie, 65–423, il., 64–501
Andrews, La Verne, 68–293
Angell, Sir Norman, 68–293
Anglican. See **England, Church of**
ANGOLA, 68–196, 66–218, 65–213, 64–211
Africa, 67–206, 65–208; international relations, 65–17; Portugal, 68–460, 67–462, 65–467, 64–455; United Nations, 64–517
Anguilla, 68–358
Animal. See **AGRICULTURE; LIVESTOCK; LIVESTOCK SHOW; PET; WILDLIFE; ZOOLOGY; ZOOS AND AQUARIUMS**
Animal migration, 67–553
Ankrah, Joseph A., 67–354
Anniversaries. See **CELEBRATIONS**
Antarctica: exploration, 66–347, 65–329; insect, 66–388
ANTHROPOLOGY, 68–204, 67–212, 66–219, 65–213
American Indian, 64–364; Beja, 67–98; education, 64–38; literature for children, 64–394; Mayans, 68–160; population, 64–187; Special Report, 65–107. See also **ARCHAEOLOGY**
Antibiotics: dentistry, 66–317; medicine, 66–432; Special Report, 67–134
Antibodies, 67–243
Antigen, 68–236
Antihistamines, 67–143
Antimatter, 67–460, 66–461
Anti-trust laws: banks, 68–21; chemical industry, 68–259
ANZUS Treaty, 65–220
Apartheid: international relations, 64–17; South Africa, 66–523, 65–503, 64–487; United Nations, 65–534; Vorster, Balthazar, 67–547
Ape, 68–205, 65–110, 65–213
Apollo, Project, 68–497, 66–527
Focus, 67–45; space exploration, 67–507
Appalachia: Congress, 66–294; PTA, 66–468; roads and highways, 66–507
Appleton, Sir Edward, 66–303
Appliances. See **ELECTRICAL EQUIPMENT**
Aquariums. See **ZOOS AND AQUARIUMS**
Arabia. See **MIDDLE EAST; SAUDI ARABIA; SOUTH ARABIA, FEDERATION OF**
Arabs: Ethiopia, 68–329; Kuwait, 66–405; Middle East, 68–418, 67–420, 66–437; Morocco, 68–427; world affairs, 68–17, 66–19
ARBUTHNOT, MAY HILL, 65–213
ARCHAEOLOGY, 68–206, 67–213, 66–219, 65–214; Jews, 68–381; Mayans, 68–160, 68–503; Rowley, Graham W., 64–476. See also **ANTHROPOLOGY**
Archery, 67–511, 66–528, 65–513, 64–494
Archipenko, Alexander, 65–293
ARCHITECTURE, 68–208, 67–214, 66–221, 65–214, 64–213
Australia, il., 67–226; awards and prizes, 68–227, 67–235, 66–242, 65–231, 64–237; Detroit, 67–306; Focus, 67–51; Kennedy memorials, 65–386; libraries, 64–388; memorials, 65–411; WBE, 64–537. See also **BUILDING AND CONSTRUCTION**
Arctic: exploration, 66–347, 64–327; Rowley, Graham W., 64–476
Arden, Elizabeth, 67–296
ARGENTINA, 68–209, 67–215, 66–222, 65–215, 64–214
celebrations, 67–261, 66–271; Illia, Arturo, 64–362; Paraguay, 66–468
Arithmetic: numeration systems, WBE, 65–598; set theory, WBE, 65–592
Arizona: dam, 65–290, 64–293; Supreme Court, 67–514, 64–498
Arlington National Cemetery: Kennedy assassination, 64–69; Washington, D.C., 64–525
ARMED FORCES OF THE WORLD, 68–210, 67–215, 66–223, 65–215, 64–214. See also **NATIONAL DEFENSE** and the names of the various countries
Armstrong, Neil, 67–505, 66–229, 64–224
Army, 68–210, 67–215, 66–223, 65–216, 64–215
Army, U.S.: civil defense, 66–281; Johnson, Harold, 65–379; national defense, 68–436, 67–436, 66–451, 65–431, 64–423; Resor, Stanley R., 66–505; Vietnam, 66–555; Westmoreland, William C., 68–538
Arntz, Heinz, 67–451
Arp, Jean (Hans), 67–296
ARRUPE, PEDRO, 66–223
Arts: archaeology, 65–214; awards and prizes, 68–226, 67–235, 65–231, 64–237; Burningham, John, 65–247; Canada, 68–251; Chicago, 68–261; educational foundations, 66–338; Focus, 68–50, 67–50, 66–53, 65–50, 64–48; Kennedy, John F., 64–380; museums, 67–427, 65–424, 64–417; state government, 64–497. See also **ARCHITECTURE; DANCING; LITERATURE; MUSIC; PAINTING AND SCULPTURE; THEATER**
Ashe, Arthur, 66–537
ASIA, 68–211, 67–216, 66–225, 65–217, 64–217. See also by name of country
Asian Games, 67–510
Assassination of John F. Kennedy: business, 64–26; courts and laws, 65–284; Garrison, Jim, 68–348; Johnson, Lyndon B., 64–587; literature, 67–400; national affairs, 64–20; Oswald, Lee Harvey, 64–436; President of the United States, 64–457, 64–518; publishing, 67–477; Roman Catholic, 64–474; Ruby, Jack, 65–490, 64–476; Special Report, 64–60; stocks and bonds, 64–497; television, 64–501; Warren Commission, 65–540; Warren Report, 65–550. See also **KENNEDY, JOHN F.**
Astor, William Waldorf, 67–296
ASTRONAUTS, 68–213, 67–219, 66–228, 65–220, 64–222
awards, 64–236; Bykovsky, Valery F., 64–257; Cooper, L. Gordon, Jr., 64–287; exploration, 68–497, 67–503; space travel, 66–525, 64–44, 64–490
ASTRONOMY, 68–214, 67–220, 66–229, 65–221, 64–224

awards, 68–227, 66–244; balloons, 65–234, 64–239; biology, 66–252; moon, 64–168; physics, 68–458, 67–460; science, 65–32, 64–32; space exploration, 68–497, 66–149, 66–526, 65–46, 65–508, 64–490; *Special Report*, 65–63
Astrophysics: astronomy, 64–226; science, 64–32; *Special Report*, 65–63
Asturia, Miguel A., 68–441
Aswân High Dam: archaeology, 66–220, 64–212; Middle East, 65–416; United Arab Republic, 65–530, 64–512; water, 66–190
Athenagoras I: Eastern Orthodox, 68–312, 65–315; Roman Catholic, 68–480
Atkinson, J. Robert, 65–293
ATLANTA, 67–222, 66–231
Atlantic Community Development Group for Latin America, 65–392
Atmosphere: air pollution, 66–170; astronomy, 65–222; atomic energy, 64–228; balloons, 65–234; health, 64–357; Mars, 66–230, 64–226; science, 64–32; space exploration, 67–505; weather, 65–543
ATOMIC ENERGY, 67–223, 66–232, 65–223
armed forces, 68–210, 67–216, 66–223, 65–215; Asia, 65–217; awards, 68–228, 66–243; China, 68–265, 65–262; Chicago, 67–265; Congress, 67–282; desalination, 67–289; disarmament, 68–307, 67–308, 66–318, 65–307, 64–309; electric power, 68–324, 67–328, 66–341; energy, 68–325; Europe, 66–347, 64–325; France, 67–346, 66–356; Great Britain, 64–354; India, *il.*, 66–146; memorials, 66–434; metallurgy, 65–412; national defense, 67–436, 65–431; North Atlantic Treaty Organization, 64–430; Norway, 66–411; nuclear physics, 66–461, 65–442, 64–434; Pacific Islands, 64–437; science, 67–493; science clubs, 66–519, 65–497; space travel, 66–159; Spain, 67–509; water and flood control, 64–526
Atomic Energy Commission, U.S.: atomic energy, 67–224, 64–228; inventions, 68–377; Oppenheimer, J. Robert, 64–436; Science Clubs, 68–489, 67–495
Attlee, Clement R., 68–293
Auchincloss, Louis, 65–397
Auctions and sales: coin collecting, 64–279; painting and sculpture, 67–447, 66–464, 64–439; stamp collecting, 68–361, 67–363, 65–358, 64–496
Auer, Misha, 68–293
Aurelio Robles, Marco, 66–468
Auriol, Vincent, 67–296
Auslander, Joseph, 66–303
AUSTRALIA, 68–216, 67–224, 66–233, 65–224, 64–229
Asia, 65–220; boats, 67–247; bridge and tunnel, 65–245; Casey, Lord Richard, 66–271; celebrations, 64–265; dam, 66–300; Holt, Harold E., 67–363; mines and mining, 64–412; money, 67–423; national defense, 64–426; New Guinea, 68–438, 67–439, 66–457, 65–439, 64–430; petroleum, 68–455, 67–456; Spender, Sir Percy, 65–512; Vietnam, 67–542
AUSTRIA, 68–219, 67–227, 66–233, 65–224, 64–229
celebrations, 66–271; Europe, 68–331; Italy, 68–379, 67–381, 64–373; Jonas, Franz, 66–402; Klaus, Josef, 65–387; Olympic Games, 65–447; opera, *il.*, 68–430
AUTOMATION, 66–233, 65–224, 64–229
business, 64–29; computers, 67–279, 66–290, 65–274, 64–283; courts and laws, 64–28; industry, 65–369; labor, 68–391, 67–390; library, 68–397, 65–394; national affairs, 64–21; post office, 66–481, 65–467; publishing, 66–498; stocks and bonds, 66–530; taxation, 64–500
AUTOMOBILE, 68–219, 67–228, 66–235, 65–225
automation, 66–233; Belgium, 66–250; bus, 65–247, 64–253; business, 65–249; Canada, 66–269, 64–260; Congress, 67–286; disasters, 67–310, 66–320, 65–312; energy, 68–327; engine, 67–330; Europe, *il.*, 68–330, *il.*, 66–345; Iacocca, Lee A., 65–363; insurance, 68–372, 66–388, 65–371; international trade, *il.*, 66–389; labor, 68–388, 66–407, 65–389; literature, 67–400; Los Angeles, 68–406; manufacturing, 68–410; Mexico, 65–413; Nova Scotia, 67–259, 64–262; old age, 65–444; petroleum, 67–456; recordings, 66–501; roads and highways, 65–486; Roche, James, 66–508; rubber, 65–490, 64–476; safety, 68–485, 67–489, 66–516, 65–494, 64–479; state government, 66–529, 64–497; trucking, 67–527, 66–543, 65–529, 64–511
AUTOMOBILE RACING, 68–221, 67–231, 66–237, 65–227, 64–233
Avalanche: disasters, 67–312, 66–322, 64–314; floods, 64–294
AVIATION, 68–222, 67–231, 66–239, 65–229, 64–235; armed forces, 68–210, 66–223, 65–216; arts, 66–56; balloons, 65–233; celebrations, *il.*, 68–257; Corrigan, Douglas, 64–447; crime, 65–285; disasters, 68–307, 67–308, 66–319, 65–311, 64–312; engine, 64–320; espionage, 65–324; Europe, 64–324; fairs and exhibitions, 64–330; France, 68–346, 67–348, 66–356; Great Britain, 65–353; Guinea, 66–372; invention, 64–370; Klaben, Helen, 64–447; labor, 64–382; manufacturing, 68–408, 66–429; McKee, William F., 66–431; metallurgy, 66–435; Miller, Betty, 64–448; Murphy, Charles S., 66–445; national defense, 68–435, 67–435, 65–431, 64–423; New York City, 65–439; Pacific Islands, 64–437; space exploration, 67–503; transportation, 68–516, 67–527, 66–543; travel, 68–520, 67–531, 65–528, 64–510
AWARDS AND PRIZES, 68–226, 67–234, 66–242, 65–231, 64–237. See also by name of organization and activity
Aymé, Marcel, 68–293
Ayub Khan, Mohammed, 68–447, 67–449, 66–467, 65–453, 64–440

B

Badoux, D. M., 66–219
BAHAMAS, 66–244, 65–233, 64–239; Latin America, 68–395; money, 67–423; West Indies, 68–537, 67–549
Bail bond, 67–292
BAKER, ROBERT G., 65–233; Congress, 68–282, 65–283; crime, 68–288; Johnson, Lyndon B., 65–383; politics, 68–64
BALAGUER Y RICARDO, JÓAQUIN, 67–237
Dominican Republic, 68–395, 67–312
Balance of payments: business, 65–29, 64–26; economy, 68–28, 68–316, 66–31; international trade, 68–375, 67–376, 66–389; money, 66–440, 65–419, 64–412; travel, 68–520, 67–530, 66–546, 65–528
Balanchine, George, 66–300
Balewa, Sir Abubakar Tafawa, 67–441
Ball, Peggy, 68–450
Ballet: arts, 64–52; dancing; 68–290, 67–295, 66–300, 65–290, 64–296
BALLOONS, 65–233, 64–239; weather; 67–547, 66–563
Balokovic, Zlatko, 66–303
BANDA, HASTINGS KAMUZU, 65–234
Malawi, 67–408, 65–409
Bandaranaike, Sirimavo, 66–273
BANKS AND BANKING, 68–229, 67–237, 66–245, 65–234, 64–239
business, 65–251; Canada, 68–248, 67–256; crime, 67–294; economy, 68–315, 67–317, 66–328; Germany, 68–350, 66–362; Great Britain, 65–352; housing, 68–364; insurance, 67–375; international monetary fund, 66–390; international trade, 68–374, 67–376; Latin America, 68–396, 65–392, 64–387; Lebanon, 67–394; money, 67–423, 66–440, 65–419, 64–412; Schweitzer, Pierre-Paul, 64–481; Switzerland, 67–516, 66–532; United Nations, 67–535
Baptist, 68–468, 66–541, 65–474
Barbados, 68–394, 67–549
Barbiturates, 67–144, 66–435
Barghoorn, Elso S., 66–359
Barker, Shirley F., 66–303
Barnard, Christian N., 68–412
Barnes, Margaret Ayer, 68–293
Baron, Melissa, 66–470
Barraquer y Barraquer, Ignacio, 66–304
Barreras, Antonio Imbert, 66–324
Barrientos Ortuño, René, 67–394, 65–242
Barrow, Edward, 67–57
Barton, Bruce, 68–293
Baruch, Bernard, 66–304
BASEBALL, 68–231, 67–239, 66–247, 65–235, 64–240
Eckert, William D., 66–325; Monaco, *il.*, 67–454; Musial, Stanley, 65–425; Pan American Games, 68–448; *Special Report*, 68–57, 67–148; sports, 67–57, 66–59, 65–59, 64–54; television, 65–520
Bashir, Antony: deaths, 67–296; Eastern Orthodox, 67–313
BASKETBALL, 68–233, 67–241, 66–249, 65–236, 64–243
Olympic games, 65–447
BASOV, NIKOLAI GENNADIEVICH, 65–237
Bassett, Charles A., II, 67–219, 66–229, 64–223
BASSETT, LESLIE, 67–242
BASUTOLAND, 66–250, 65–237, 64–244
Africa, 65–207. See also **LESOTHO**
BATE, WALTER JACKSON, 65–237
Bathyscaph, ocean, 65–443
Batman: battery, 67–330; games, 67–348; television, 67–520
Bea, Augustin Cardinal, 66–90
Beame, Abraham D.: Democratic Party, 66–316; New York City, 66–458
Beatles, the: arts, 65–54; Great Britain, 66–371; motion pictures, 65–424; personalities, *il.*, 66–471; popular music, 68–149, *il.*, 67–433, 66–449, 65–429; recordings, 65–480
Beatrix, Princess, *il.*, 67–334, 66–457
Beatty, Clyde Raymond, 66–304
Beautification: arts, 66–57; conservation, 67–288; garden and lawn, 66–359; parks, 66–468; roads and highways, 66–507; youth organizations, 67–551
Bechuanaland. See **BOTSWANA**
Beebe, Lucius Morris, 67–296
Beemer, Brace Bell, 66–304
Beetle: garden, 66–358; insect, 66–388, 64–366
Behan, Brendan, 65–294
Beja, 67–98
Belaúnde, Victor Andrés, 67–297
BELAÚNDE TERRY, FERNANDO, 64–244
Peru, 66–474, 64–449
Belgian Congo. See **CONGO (KINSHASA)**
BELGIUM, 68–235, 67–242, 66–250, 65–238, 64–244
Congo, 65–208; Congo (Léopoldville), 66–291, 65–277; Harmel, Pierre, 66–373; North Atlantic Treaty Organization, 68–442; memorials, 64–405; Vanden Boeynants, Paul, 67–538
Belgrade Conference. See **Neutral Nations Conference**
Bell, Clive, 65–294
BELLOW, SAUL, 66–251
literature, 65–397
Belote, David, 68–450
Ben Barka, Mehdi: France, 67–346; Morocco, 67–423
BEN BELLA, AHMED, 65–212
Algeria, 66–217; Boumedienne, Houari, 66–256
Ben-Gurion, David, 66–393, 64–373
Bendix, William, 65–294
Beni Amer, 67–106
Bennett, Charles E., 67–451
Bennett, Constance, 66–304
Bennett, John B., 65–294
Berg, Gertrude, 67–297
Berlin: Germany, 68–350, 67–352, 66–360, 65–345, 64–343; international relations, 64–15; music, 64–420; Russia, *il.*, 67–171
BERMUDA, 65–238, 64–244
Bernstein, Leonard, 67–432
Berra, Yogi: baseball, 65–235; sports, 65–59
BERRYMAN, JOHN, 66–251
Berton, Pierre, 66–496
Bethe, Hans Albrecht, 68–441
Bevilacqua, Giulio Cardinal, 66–304
Bhabha, Homi Jehangir 67–297
BHUTAN, 65–239
Biafra, 68–440
Bible: celebrations, 67–261; civil liberties, 64–278; education, 64–317; Protestant, 64–460; Roman Catholic, 67–483; Salvation Army, 64–480; Supreme Court, 64–498
Bickford, Charles A., 68–293
Bicycling, 68–502, 67–511, 66–528
Bill of Rights, 67–262
Billiards, 68–502, 67–511, 66–528, 65–513, 64–494
Billner, Karl P., 66–304
BIOCHEMISTRY, 68–235, 67–243, 66–251, 65–239
awards, 68–228; biology, 68–236, 67–244, 64–245; Bloch, Konrad Emil, 65–241; botany, 66–255, 65–242, 64–247; chemistry, 67–264, 65–260, 64–268; engine, 66–342; insect, 67–374; Lake Erie, 68–128; Lynen, Feodor, 65–409; medicine, 66–432, 65–410, 64–403; mental health, 66–435; psychology, 67–474, 66–497; science, 65–36, 64–32; science clubs, 65–496, 64–482; Woodward, Robert B., 66–565
Biography: awards, 66–242; Bate, Walter Jackson, 65–237; Canadian literature, 68–255, 67–260, 66–270, 64–264; Edel, Leon, 64–316; Eisenhower, Dwight D., 66–339; Kaplan, Justin, 68–385; Kennedy, John F., 66–404; literature, 68–399, 67–398, 66–415, 65–398, 64–392; literature for children, 66–423, 65–403, 64–395; Pulitzer prizes, 68–473, 67–477, 66–500, 65–478, 64–466; Samuels, Ernest, 66–517. See also **DEATHS OF NOTABLE PERSONS; PERSONALITIES;** also names of individuals
BIOLOGY, 68–236, 67–244, 66–252, 65–240, 64–245
astronomy, 66–229; awards and prizes, 68–

227, 66–244, 65–232, biochemistry, 68–235, 67–243, 66–251, 65–239, 64–245; botany, 68–239, 67–247, 66–255, 65–242, 64–247; careers, 64–264; geology, 66–359; insect, 68–372; North America (*Trans-Vision*), 65–84; psychology, 68–470; science, 64–30; *Special Report*, 67–70; *WBE*, 64–562; zoology, 68–541, 67–553, 66–568, 65–548
Biophysics: awards and prizes, 65–232; Hodgkin, Alan, 64–358
Birch Society. See **John Birch Society**
Birds: wildlife, 66–564, 64–529; zoology, 66–568, 65–548; zoos, 68–542
Birmingham, Ala.: civil liberties, 64–276; Negro, 64–429; United States, 64–518
Birnbaum, Abe, 67–297
Birth control: Formosa, 66–353; India, 67–372, 66–139; population, 68–460, 67–462, 66–480, 64–190; Roman Catholic, 66–510; state government, 66–529; Supreme Court, 66–531
Births: elephants, 64–532; Kennedy, Patrick, 64–378; Fischer quintuplets, *il.*, 64–404; Great Britain, 65–354; Japan, 66–397; population, 66–480, 65–467; Prieto quintuplets, 64–449; quintuplets, 64–447; vital statistics, 68–536, 67–547, 65–540, 64–524
Bissier, Julius, 66–304
Black Muslims, 65–410
Black power, 67–275
Blackmur, Richard, 66–304
Blackstone, Harry, 66–304
BLAKE, EUGENE CARSON, 67–245
church unity, *il.*, 66–85; Protestant, 67–473
Blake, George, 68–329
Blanton, Smiley, 67–297
Blatz, William E., 65–294
BLINDNESS, 68–237, 67–245, 66–253, 65–240, 64–246
Atkinson, J. Robert, 65–293; Boswell, Charles, 66–470; Camp Fire Girls, 66–263; handicapped, 65–356
Bliss, Ray C., 66–503
Blizzards, 68–308, 65–543, 64–312
BLOCH, KONRAD EMIL, 65–241
Block, Martin, 68–473
Blood, 68–235, *il.*, 67–86, 65–213
BOATS AND BOATING, 68–238, 67–245, 66–253, 65–241, 64–246
Chichester, Sir Francis, 68–450; Manry, Robert, 66–473; Olympic Games, 65–447; rowing, 68–502, 67–510, 66–528, 65–513, 64–494; sailing, 65–494, 64–480
Bobsledding, 68–502, 67–511, 65–448
Boland, Mary, 66–304
BOLIVIA, 68–239, 66–255, 65–242, 64–247
civil rights, 66–284; Chile, 64–269; Latin America, 67–394, 64–386
Bond, James, 66–443
Bond, Janet M., 66–470
Bone, 68–305, *il.*, 67–85
Bonifay, Eugène, 66–219
Bonin Islands: Japan, 68–380; Pacific Islands, 68–444
Bonner, Charles, 66–304
Bonner, Herbert C., 66–304
Book collecting, 65–358
Book publishing: advertising, 64–204; Civil War Centennial, 64–278, education, 67–39; Post, Elizabeth, 67–454; publishing, 68–472, 67–476, 66–499, 65–477, 64–465. See also **LITERATURE**
Boone, Daniel VI, 67–451
Boone, Pat, 66–470
Borman, Frank: astronauts, 66–228; 65–220, 64–224; space exploration, 67–503, 66–525
Borneo, 66–386, 64–402
Bosch, Juan D., 66–323, 64–315
Bossom, Lord Alfred, 66–304
BOSTOCK, HUGH SAMUEL, 66–255
BOSTON, 68–239, 67–247, 66–255, 65–242, 64–247
architecture, 64–213; baseball, 68–231; building and construction, 66–261; crime, 64–289; elections, 68–322, 66–339; New England, 66–195; opera, 67–430; poverty, 66–486; transit, 66–545
Boswell, Charles, 66–470
Bosworth, William W., 67–297
BOTANY, 68–239, 67–247, 66–255, 65–242, 64–247
awards, 68–227; chemistry, 67–264; garden and lawn, 68–348, 67–350, 66–358, 65–342; Mars, 65–510; science, 64–32; science clubs, 65–496, 64–482; space exploration, 68–499. See also **AGRICULTURE; GARDEN AND LAWN**
BOTSWANA, 68–196, 67–248
Botvinnik, Mikhail, 66–274
BOUMEDIENNE, HOUARI, 66–256
Algeria, 67–210, 66–217
Bourguiba, Habib: Middle East, 66–438; Tunisia, 68–521, 67–531, 66–546
Bow, Clara, 66–304
BOWLING, 68–240, 67–248, 66–256, 65–242, 64–248
BOXING, 68–240, 67–248, 66–256, 65–243, 64–248
Clay, Cassius, 65–269; Olympic games, 65–447; sports, 68–58, 67–150, 66–60, 65–58
BOY SCOUTS OF AMERICA, 66–258, 65–244, 64–250; youth organizations, 68–539, 67–551
Boyd, Alan S., 68–516, 67–253
BOYS' CLUBS OF AMERICA, 66–258, 65–244; juvenile delinquency, 64–376; youth organizations, 68–539, 67–551
Brabham, Jack, 67–231
Bracci, Francesco Cardinal, 68–293
Bradley, Bill, 66–249
Bradley, Reginald, 68–450, 67–451
Braille, 67–245, 66–253, 65–241
Brain, 64–463; medicine, 68–413; science, 65–37
Braley, Burton, 67–297
Brandt, Willy, *il.*, 68–351
Brauner, Victor, 67–297
BRAZIL, 68–241, 67–249, 66–258, 65–244, 64–251
bridge and tunnel, 66–259; Castelo Branco, Humberto, 65–258; celebrations, 66–271; civil rights, 66–284; Costa e Silva, Arthur da, 68–287; mines and mining, *il.*, 66–439; money, 66–441
Breedlove, Craig, 66–237
Breen, Joseph I., 66–304
Breton, André, 67–297
Bretton Woods agreement, 66–390
BREZHNEV, LEONID ILYICH, 65–245; communism, 66–289, 65–273; Russia, 68–482, 67–486, 66–513, 65–491, 64–478
BRIDGE AND TUNNEL, 66–259, 65–245, 64–251; building and construction, 68–244, 67–251; Chicago, 64–268; disasters, 68–311; Great Britain, 65–354; New York City, 65–439, *il.*, 64–431; St. Louis, 68–486; Switzerland, 65–519
BRIDGE, CONTRACT, 68–242, 67–249, 66–260, 65–246, 64–252
Bristow, James J. R., 66–305
British Columbia: Canada, 68–253, 67–259, 66–268, 65–254, 64–262; dam, 66–300
British Commonwealth. See **GREAT BRITAIN;** also articles on the various countries of the Commonwealth
British Commonwealth Games, 67–526
BRITISH GUIANA, 66–260, 65–246, 64–252. See also **GUYANA**
British Honduras, 68–395
British West Indies. See **JAMAICA; TRINIDAD AND TOBAGO; WEST INDIES FEDERATION**
Broadcasting. See **RADIO; TELEVISION**
Brodie, John Riley, 67–146
Brokenshire, Norman E., 66–304
Brooke, Edward W., 67–327; *il.*, 66–207
BROSIO, MANLIO, 65–246; North Atlantic Treaty Organization, 65–442
Brouwer, Dirk, 67–297
Brown, Arthur W., 67–297
Brown, Clarence J., 66–304
Brown, George, 68–356, 67–359, 66–368, 65–351
BROWN, HAROLD, 66–261
Brown, Nacio Herb, 65–294
Brown, Walter, 65–237
Browne, Irene, 66–304
Brumel, Valeri, 64–509
Brunner, Emil H., 67–297
Buber, Martin: deaths, 66–304; Jews, 66–398; Protestant, 66–495
Bucher, Walter H., 66–305
Buckley, William F.: New York City, 66–458; Republican party, 66–505
Buddhism: religion, 68–476; Vietnam, 68–533
Budget, national. See **CONGRESS; ECONOMY; NATIONAL DEFENSE; United States government;** see also entries on various countries
BUILDING AND CONSTRUCTION, 68–242, 67–250, 66–261, 65–246, 64–252
Atlanta, 67–222, 66–231; Australia, *il.*, 68–217; banks and banking, 67–238; Boston, 66–255; 65–242, 64–247; bridge, 66–259, 65–245, 64–251; Canada, 66–268; Canadian Library Association, 68–255; Chicago, 67–265, 66–274, 64–268; city, 67–272, 65–265; city planning, 67–273; dam, 66–300, 65–290, 64–293, Detroit, 66–317, 65–306, 64–306; economy, 67–319; electronics, 66–342; fairs and exhibitions, 64–330; forest products, 67–342; hotel, 67–530, 66–378, 65–360; housing, 68–363, 67–365, 66–378, 65–360, 64–360; Houston, 68–365, 67–366, 64–361; labor, 68–388; Los Angeles, 68–406, 67–407, 65–408, 64–401; museums, 67–427, 64–417; music, 65–427; New Orleans, 68–438, 67–439; 66–457, 64–430; New York City, 68–439, 66–458, 65–439, 64–431; Philadelphia, 66–475, 65–463; prison, 65–473; roads and highways, 66–507, 65–486, 64–471; Saint Louis, 67–491, 66–516, 64–480; San Francisco, 66–517; shipbuilding, 64–484; space travel, 66–527; tunnel, 65–245, 64–251; Washington, D.C., 66–562. See Also **ARCHITECTURE**
BULGARIA, 68–244, 67–252, 66–261, 65–246, 64–253
Bullitt, William C., 68–293
BUNDY, McGEORGE, 67–252; *il.*, 66–491
Burch, Dean, 66–503, 65–485
Burchfield, Charles E., 68–293
Burco, Ferruccio, 66–305
Burdick, Eugene, 66–305
Burg, Stanley and Ellen, 66–255
Burgess, Thornton W., 66–305
Burka, Petra, 66–380
Burlingame, Roger, 68–293
Burliuk, David, 68–293
BURMA, 68–245, 67–252, 66–262, 65–247, 64–253
Burnette, "Smiley," 68–293
Burnham, Forbes, 66–260
BURNINGHAM, JOHN, 65–247
Burris, Robert H., 66–255
Burton, Richard: motion pictures, 65–424; theater, 65–526
BURUNDI, 67–252, 66–262, 65–247, 64–253
Africa, 67–204, 66–211
BUS, 65–247, 64–253
disasters, 68–308, 67–310, 66–320, 65–312, 64–312; roads and highways, 65–487; transit, 64–510; transportation, 68–516, 67–527
Bushman, Francis X., 67–297
BUSINESS, 65–248, 64–254
awards and prizes, 64–235; careers, 64–264; census, 68–258; Junior Achievement, 68–384, 66–403, 65–383, 64–375; poverty, 66–485. See also **ECONOMY, THE**
Butts, Wally: football, 64–333; publishing, 64–465; sports, 64–57
Byrd, Harry F.: deaths, 67–297; Democratic party, 66–470, *il.*, 65–472

C

CABINET, 68–245, 67–253, 66–262, 65–251 64–257
Ailes, Stephen, 65–211; Brown, Harold, 66–261; Canada, 68–246, 65–254; city, 66–280; Clark, Ramsey, 68–272; Connor, John T., 65–284; Fowler, Henry H., 66–353; Gardner, John W., 66–359; Great Britain, 65–351; Gronouski, John S., Jr., 64–355; housing, 66–378; Ignatius, Paul, 68–367; Katzenbach, Nicholas, 66–404; Kennedy assassination, 64–64; O'Brien, Lawrence F., 66–462; President of the United States, 66–491, 65–472; transportation, 68–516, 67–527; Trowbridge, Alexander, 68–521; U.S. government, 68–527, 67–537
Caldecott medal, 68–405, 66–441, 65–407, 64–400
Calendar: 1968, 68–621; 1967, 67–629; 1966, 66–625; 1965, 65–629; 1964, 64–533. See also **CELEBRATIONS**
California: agriculture, 67–209; atomic energy, 64–228; automobile, 66–236; banks and banking, 64–239; bridge, 67–251; building and construction, 68–244; census, 65–259, 64–266; child guidance; 66–275; city planning, 66–281; computers, 66–290; courts and laws, 65–285; desalination, 67–289; education, 68–321, 66–338, 65–40, 65–317; elections, 65–321; fairs and exhibitions, 64–330; forestry, 66–352, 65–337; geology, 66–360; Los Angeles, 68–406, 67–407, 66–425, 65–408, 64–401; Negro, 65–437; prison, 64–460; Reagan, Ronald, 68–473; television, 65–522; San Francisco, 68–486, 67–491, 66–517, 64–480; Supreme Court, 68–505, 66–531, 64–498; transit, 67–530
Callaghan, James, 66–367, 65–351
Calmat, Alain, 66–380
Calver, George W., 67–451
CAMBODIA, 68–245, 67–253, 66–263, 65–251, 64–257
Asia, 68–212; Mekong River, 68–80; Thailand, 65–523, 64–504
Camel, 67–103, 65–548
Camera, 68–457, 67–458, 66–477, 65–463, 64–452; photography, *WBE*, 65–571

CAMEROON, 66–263, 65–251, 64–257; Africa, 68–196, 67–204
Camm, Sir Sidney, 67–297
CAMP FIRE GIRLS, 66–263, 65–251, 64–257 youth organizations, 68–539, 67–551
Campbell, Alexander B., 67–260
Campbell, Donald, 68–238
CANADA, 68–246, 67–254, 66–265, 65–252, 64–258
advertising, 68–193, 66–210; aviation, 67–234; Bostock, Hugh, 66–255; bridge, 66–259; Bulgaria, 64–253; curling, 64–494; dam, 67–251, 65–290; Diefenbaker, John G., *il.*, 64–445; electric power, 66–340; energy, 68–325; espionage, 67–331; fairs and exhibitions, 68–334, 67–335, 66–348, 65–331, 64–330; football, 65–336, 64–334; forestry, 64–335; France, 68–345; history: *Trans-Vision*, 64–109; ice hockey, 64–361; immigration and emigration, 66–381; insurance, 67–374; international trade, 66–392; libraries, 66–270, 65–257; 64–264; livestock show, 66–424, 64–401; Michener, Donald, 68–417; mines and mining, 64–412; museums, 68–429; painting and sculpture, 65–451; parks, 65–455; petroleum, 67–456, 66–475; Protestant, 67–472, 66–496; Rowley, Graham W., 64–476; Salvation Army, 68–486; *Special Report*, 64–96; theater, 64–506; transit, 66–545; water, 66–188; waterways, 65–543, 64–526; whooping crane, 66–564; wildlife, 64–529; world affairs, 66–19
CANADIAN LIBRARY ASSOCIATION, 68–254, 67–260, 66–270, 65–257, 64–264
CANADIAN LITERATURE, 68–255, 67–260, 66–270, 65–257, 64–264
Cancer: biochemistry, 64–245; dentistry, 67–306, 66–317, 65–305, 64–306; drug, 64–315; electronics, 66–342; health, 65–356, 64–357; lasers, 65–322; medicine, 68–412, 67–414, 66–433, 65–410, 64–404; science, 67–33; smoking, 64–484; vital statistics, 65–540
Canoeing, 68–502, 67–511
Capital punishment, 66–494, 65–514
Capitol: Kennedy assassination, 66–494, 64–70; memorials, 64–405
Cardijin, Joseph Cardinal, 68–293
Cardin, Lucien, 67–254
Cardinals, Sacred College of; Paul VI, 64–442; Roman Catholic, 68–480, 66–511
Carl Gustav V, 67–515
CARLSON, PAUL EARLE, 65–258, 65–276
CARMICHAEL, STOKELY, 68–256, 67–275
Carnegie Corporation of New York, 68–343, 67–343, 66–338, 65–318, 64–318
Carnegie medal, 66–481, 65–247, 64–279
Carnera, Primo, 68–293
Carpenter, Malcolm Scott: astronauts, 68–213, 65–221, 64–224; ocean, 67–63, 66–462
Carra, Carlo, 67–297
Carson, Rachel, 65–294, 64–366
Carter, John Stewart, 66–414
Cartoon: Block, Herbert L., 64–446; computers, 65–274; Goldberg, "Rube," 64–447; Pulitzer prizes, 68–473, 67–477, 65–478
CASEY, LORD RICHARD GARDINER, 66–271
Casper, Billy, *il.*, 67–160, 67–355
Castaldo, Alfonso Cardinal, 67–297
CASTELO BRANCO, HUMBERTO DE ALENCAR, 65–258; Brazil, 67–249, 66–258
Castro, Fidel: Communism, *il.*, 64–282; Cuba, 68–289, 66–297, 65–286, 64–291
Cat, pet, 68–454, 67–454, 66–474, 65–462
Cavanagh, Jerome P., 68–305, 66–317
Ceausescu, Nicolae, 66–512
CELEBRATIONS, 68–256, 67–261, 66–271, 65–258; astronomy, 65–221; Austria, 66–233; Belgium, 66–250; calendar 1968, 68–621; calendar 1967, 67–629; calendar 1966, 66–625; calendar 1965, 65–629; calendar 1964, 64–533; Canada, 68–246, 67–254, 65–253; Canadian Library Association, 68–254; Churchill, Sir Winston, 65–459; Civil War centennial, 66–286, 65–269, 64–278; Communism, 68–273; energy, 68–326; hobbies, *il.*, 67–362; India, 68–368; Iran, 68–377; iron and steel, 65–373; Kiwanis, 65–498; library, 64–388; Lincoln day, 64–305; Lions International, 67–496; literature for children, 67–401; Luxembourg, 64–401; magazines, 66–499; memorials, 68–414; Monaco, 67–422; museums, 67–427, 65–425; music, 68–431, 65–428, 64–420; painting and sculpture, 67–447; Poland, 67–460, 66–479; Protestant, 68–468; Red Cross, 65–481, 64–468; Rockefeller foundation, 64–318; Roman Catholic, 66–511; Russia, 68–482; St. Louis, 65–494; Salvation Army, 66–517, 65–495
Cell: biochemistry, 65–239; biology, 66–252, 65–240, 64–245; botany, 64–247
Cellini, Renato, 68–293
Censorship: arts, 65–51; motion pictures, 68–427, 67–426, 66–443, 65–422; Poland, 65–466; Supreme Court, 67–514
CENSUS, 68–258, 67–262, 66–272, 65–259, 64–266
blindness, 67–245; Canada, housing, 64–360; Nigeria, 64–432; population, 68–460, 67–461, 64–455; vital statistics, 65–540
CENTRAL AFRICAN REPUBLIC, Africa, 68–196, 67–263
Central America. See **LATIN AMERICA**
Central American Common Market, 68–393, 67–392
Central Intelligence Agency: Helms, Richard M., 67–362; President of the U.S., 68–466; Raborn, William, 66–500; U.S. government, 68–528
Cernan, Eugene, 67–504
Cervantes, Alphonso J., 67–491, 66–516
CEYLON, 68–258, 67–263, 66–273, 65–260, 64–267
CHAD, 68–196, 66–273, 65–260; Africa, 67–204
Chaffee, Roger B., 68–497, 67–219
Chaikoff, Israel Lyon, 67–297
Chalmers, Thomas, 67–298
Charoux, Siegfried, 68–293
CHEMICAL INDUSTRY, 68–258, 67–263, 65–260
drugs, 68–311, 67–313; engine and energy, 64–320; forestry and forest products, 65–337; gas, 64–341; glass, 64–348; insect, 65–370; interior design, 67–375; manufacturing, 67–412, 66–429; metallurgy, 64–406; plastics, 65–466, 64–455; pollution, 65–466; rubber, 65–490
CHEMISTRY, 68–259, 67–264, 66–273, 65–260, 64–267
awards and prizes, 68–227, 67–235, 66–243, 65–232, 64–238; biochemistry, 68–235, 67–243, 66–251, 65–239, 64–245; careers, 64–264; chemical industry, 68–258, 67–263, 66–429, 64–267; drugs, 67–130; engineering, 66–343; food, 66–350; garden and lawn, 64–340; insect, 66–387; Nobel prizes, 68–441, 66–460, 64–433
Cherkasov, Nikolai K., 67–298
CHESS, 68–260, 67–265, 66–274, 65–261, 64–268
Chiang Ching, 67–270
Chiang Kai-shek, 68–117
CHICAGO, 68–260, 67–265, 66–274, 65–261, 64–268
airports, 67–233; architecture, 68–208, 67–215, 66–221; banks and banking, 65–234; building and construction, 68–243, 66–261; civil liberties, 64–276; civil rights, *il.*, 67–274; computers, 66–290; conservation, *il.*, 68–285; dancing, 66–301; education, 66–44, 66–336; elections, 68–323; fashion, 65–333; hospital, 67–365; library, 65–394; museum, 65–424; music, 66–447, 64–419; opera, 68–431, 67–430; painting and sculpture, 68–446, 67–447; post office, 67–462
Chichester, Sir Francis, 68–450
CHILD GUIDANCE, 68–261, 67–265, 66–275, 64–269
education, 65–42; juvenile delinquency, 66–403, 64–376; Kennedy, Rose, 66–66; Parents and Teachers, National Congress of, 64–441; social welfare, 66–522
CHILD WELFARE, 68–261, 67–266, 66–275, 65–261
Camp Fire Girls, 65–251; dentistry, 68–304, 67–306; mental health, 68–415; Salvation Army, 64–480; social welfare, 68–493; state government, 65–514; Supreme Court, 68–505; toys, 65–341; United Nations Children's Fund, 66–551; veterans, 66–553; youth organizations, 68–539
Children's recordings. See **RECORDINGS FOR CHILDREN**
Children's theater. See **THEATER, AMATEUR**
CHILE, 68–262, 66–275, 65–262, 64–269
Frei Montalva, Eduardo, 65–340; Latin America, 67–394
CHINA, 68–263, 67–266, 66–277, 65–262, 64–270
Albania, 68–202, 67–210, 65–212, 64–209; archaeology, *il.*, 68–206; armed forces, 68–210, 66–223, 65–216, 64–215; Asia, 68–211, 67–216, 66–225, 65–217, 64–217; atomic energy, 65–223; Burma, 68–245; Cambodia, 68–245, 66–263; Central African Republic, 67–263; Communism, 68–273, 67–277, 66–289, 65–273, 64–281; Cuba, 67–294; disarmament, 67–308, 66–318, 65–307; energy, 68–325; Formosa, 68–343, 67–343, 65–337, 64–335; France, 65–339; Great Britain, 68–357; India, 66–383; 64–363; Indonesia, 68–371, 66–386; international relations, 68–16, 67–15, 65–14, 64–367; international trade, 66–392; Ivory Coast, 66–396; Japan, 68–380, 67–382; Korea, 66–405; Lin Piao, 67–269; Mao Tse-tung, 68–111; Nepal, 66–457; North Atlantic Treaty Organization, 66–460; Outer Mongolia, 68–427, 67–445, 66–464, 65–449, 64–437; Nepal, 68–438; Pakistan, 66–467, 64–440; religion, 68–476; Roman Catholic, 68–480; rural life, 66–115; Russia, 68–484, 67–163, 67–486, 66–515; Tanzania, 66–533; track and field, 66–542; United Nations, 68–526, 67–535, 66–551, 64–515; Vietnam, 68–531, 66–556; world affairs, 66–18
Cholesterol, 68–412
Chou En-lai, 68–264, 65–262, 64–271
Christian Church. See **EASTERN ORTHODOX; PROTESTANT; RELIGION; ROMAN CATHOLIC; SALVATION ARMY**
Christian Science, 67–261
Christophoros II, 68–294
Churchill, Billy, 68–450
Churchill, Winston: Congress, 64–287; deaths, 66–305; Great Britain, 66–368; hobbies, 66–376; literature, 67–398; memorials, 68–414, 67–417, 66–435, 65–411
CITY, 68–266, 67–272, 66–280, 65–265, 64–273
air pollution, *il.*, 68–283; arts, 67–50; Canada, 64–104; city planning, 68–268, 66–281, 65–265, 64–273; civil rights, 68–269; conservation, 68–283; Congress, 67–285; cultural centers, 66–42; Democratic party, 68–303; 66–316; education, 66–42; elections, 66–339; housing, 68–363, 67–365, 66–378, 65–360, 64–360; insurance, 68–372; poverty, 68–463; Republican party, 68–477; retailing, 67–482, 66–506; safety, 64–479; state government, 68–503; taxation, 67–517, 66–534; transit, 68–519, 67–530, 66–543, 65–528, 64–510; United Community Funds, 68–523
CITY AND REGIONAL PLANNING, 68–268, 67–273, 66–281, 65–265, 64–273
CIVIL DEFENSE, 66–281, 65–266, 64–274
Civil engineering. See **BUILDING AND CONSTRUCTION**
CIVIL RIGHTS, 68–269, 67–273, 66–283. See also **CIVIL LIBERTIES,** 64–274
American Library Association, 64–210; Atlanta, 67–222; awards and prizes, 68–226, 67–235; Brooke, Edward T., 67–327; Carmichael, Stokely, 68–256; Chicago, 67–265, 64–268; city, 68–266, 67–272, 65–265; Collins, LeRoy, 65–270; Congress, 67–287, 66–294, 65–279, 64–286; courts and laws, 68–287, 67–292, 66–296; crime, 67–294; democracy, 68–301, 66–314, 64–303; Democratic party, 64–304; Detroit, 68–305; education, 68–320, 67–322, 66–336, 65–317, 64–36; elections, 68–322; Evers, Medgar W., 64–326; France, 66–357; Great Britain, 66–371; hospitals, 65–360; housing, 64–360; Humphrey, Hubert H., 65–362; international relations, 64–17; Jews, 66–397, 65–379; Kerner, Otto, 68–385; King, Martin Luther, Jr., 65–386, 64–381; labor, 65–389, 64–383; literature, 68–400; Los Angeles, 67–407, 66–425; Medicare, 67–412; national affairs, 68–23, 67–22, 65–21, 64–21; Negro, 66–455, 65–437, 64–427; new words and phrases, 64–430; poverty, 68–462; President of the United States, 68–467, 67–471, 66–489, 65–470, 64–458; Protestant, 68–469, 66–496, 65–474, 64–461; radio, 66–500; religion, 67–480; Roman Catholic, 66–510; Roosevelt, Franklin D., Jr., 66–512; Russia, 66–514; San Francisco, 67–491; South Africa, 67–501, 66–523, 65–503, 64–487, *Special Report*, 65–165; state government, 68–503, 66–529; Supreme Court, 68–505, 67–514, 66–531, 65–515, 64–498; travel, 66–546; United Nations, 66–552, 64–516; United States government, 68–528, 64–518; Wallace, George C., 64–525; Washington, D.C., 68–536, 64–525; YMCA, 68–539, 67–550, 64–530; YWCA, 65–547, 64–530
CIVIL WAR CENTENNIAL, 66–286, 65–269, 64–278
celebrations, 64–265; history, 64–393; literature for children, 65–401
Clark, Jim, 67–231, 66–237, 64–233
Clark, June, 67–451
CLARK, RAMSEY, 68–272; Cabinet, 67–253; U.S. government, 68–528
CLAY, CASSIUS MARCELLUS, JR., 65–269
boxing, 68–240, 67–248, 66–256, 65–243, 64–248; draft, 67–437; sports, 68–58; *il.*, 67–150; 66–60
Clift, Montgomery, 67–298
Clubs. See **Organizations**
Cluytens, André, 68–294

Clyde, Andy, 68–293

COAL, 65–270, 64–279
conservation, 67–292; employment, 68–102; industry, 65–369; Lewis, John L., 64–448; mines and mining, 67–422, 66–440

Coast and Geodetic Survey, U.S., 66–563

Coast Guard, U.S.: boats and boating, 65–241, 64–246; national defense, 68–438, 67–438, 66–455, 65–434, 64–425

Cockcroft, Sir John, 68–293

Coffee: agriculture, 65–211; Costa Rica, 65–284; El Salvador, 66–342; Ethiopia, 66–343

Coho, 68–365

Coin: Congress, 66–295; money, 68–426, 67–423, 66–441, 65–419

COIN COLLECTING, 68–361, 66–375, 65–357, 64–279; hobbies, 67–362

Cold War. See **COMMUNISM; INTERNATIONAL RELATIONS; NATIONAL DEFENSE**

Cole, George, 67–451

Cole, Nat King, 66–305

Cole, Thomas, 66–471

Coles, Cyril Henry, 66–305

Collins, John F., 66–200

Collins, Michael, 67–504

COLLINS, (THOMAS) LeROY, 65–270

Collip, James B., 66–305

COLOMBIA, 68–272, 67–276, 66–286, 65–270, 64–279
civil rights, 66–284; disasters, *il.*, 68–309; Lleras Restrepo, Carlos, 67–407; Peace Corps, 65–149

Colonialism: Africa, 64–206; Portugal, 64–455; United Nations, 65–535

COLOR: *WBE*, 64–568
photography, 64–452; psychology, 65–476

Colorado: architecture, *il.*, 68–208; conservation, 68–283; courts and laws, 67–292; geology, 67–351; tunnel, 67–251

Columbia River: Canada, 65–254, 64–260; conservation, 67–289; dam, 66–300

COMECON: Communism, 66–290, 64–283; Europe, 64–326; Romania, 64–476

Commerce. See **BUSINESS; ECONOMY; INTERNATIONAL TRADE**

Commerce, U.S. Department of: economy, 66–327; Lindley, Jonathan, 67–396; transportation, 66–543; Trowbridge, Alexander B., 68–521; weather, 66–563

Committee for Economic Development, 67–272

Common Market: Austria, 68–219, 67–227, 64–229; business, 65–29; Denmark, 64–306; economy, 68–313; Europe, 68–331, 67–332, 66–345, 65–324, 64–322; France, 66–355, 65–339; Great Britain, 68–356, 64–352; international relations, 65–16, 64–16; international trade, 67–377, 66–389, 65–371, 64–369; Ireland, 68–378, 64–371; Latin America, 68–393, 67–392, 66–410, 65–393, 64–387; Luxembourg, 68–406; Paraguay, 64–441; Schuman, Robert, 64–481; Spain, 65–512

Commonwealth Fund, 68–343, 67–343, 66–338, 65–318, 64–318

Commonwealth of Nations. See **GREAT BRITAIN;** also articles on various countries of the Commonwealth

COMMUNICATIONS, 68–272, 67–277, 66–286, 65–270
biology, 67–244; boats, 66–254; civil rights, 68–270; computers, 65–274; democracy, 67–304; education, 67–39; electronics, 66–342, 64–319; "hot line," 64–311; Hyde, Rosel H., 67–368; insect, 66–387; manufacturing, 67–411; science, 66–36; Sealab, 67–70; stocks and bonds, 65–514; travel, *il.*, 67–530. See also **LITERATURE; MOTION PICTURES; POST OFFICE; PUBLISHING; RADIO; RECORDINGS; SPACE TRAVEL; TELEPHONE AND TELEGRAPH; TELEVISION; TELSTAR**

COMMUNISM, 68–273, 67–277, 66–289, 65–272, 64–280
agriculture, 67–206, 66–214; civil rights, 66–283; armed forces, 68–210, 67–216; democracy, 66–314; international trade, 67–378, 66–392; Mao Tse-tung, 68–111; post office, 66–481; Protestant, 68–468, 67–472; *Special Report*, 67–163; world affairs, 68–15, 67–15, 66–20. See also articles on individual countries

Community Action Programs, 68–463, 66–483

Community Funds. See **UNITED COMMUNITY FUNDS AND COUNCILS**

Community theater, 67–525

COMPUTERS, 68–274, 67–279, 66–290, 65–274, 64–283
archaeology, 67–213; automation, 66–233, 65–224, 64–230; aviation, 66–240; blindness, 64–246; census, 64–266; communications, 67–277; courts and laws, 64–289; education, 67–42; electronics, 64–319; electronics industry, 65–369; insects, 65–370; invention, 67–378, 64–370; library, 64–388; manufacturing, 67–412; post office, 67–462; publishing, 66–498

Conant, James Bryant: education, 68–321, 66–336, 65–316

CONGO (BRAZZAVILLE), 66–291, 65–274, 64–283; Africa, 67–204, 64–206

CONGO (KINSHASA), 68–275, 67–280, 66–291, 65–275, 64–284
Africa, 68–196, 66–213, 65–208, 64–207; Belgium, 68–235, 66–250, 65–238; Carlson, Paul Earle, 65–258; international relations, 67–18, 65–17, 64–17; United Nations, 68–526, 65–534

CONGRESS OF THE UNITED STATES, 68–276, 67–280, 66–293, 65–278, 64–284
agriculture, 67–209, 66–214, 65–210, 64–208; American Library Association, 66–218; automation, 65–224, 64–230; automobile, 67–228, 66–236; Baker, Robert G., 65–233; banks and banking, 66–245, 64–239; blindness, 68–237, 67–245; boxing, 65–243; Byrd, Harry F., 66–470; chemical industry, 65–260; child welfare, 68–261, 65–261; city, 68–266, 67–52, 67–262, 66–280, 64–273; city planning, 68–268, 66–281; civil defense, 66–281, 64–274; civil rights, 67–273, 65–165, 65–266, 64–277; conservation, 68–283, 67–288; courts and laws, 67–292, 65–284; crime, 67–294; dairying, 64–293; Democratic party, 68–302, 67–304, 66–315, 65–303, 64–305; dentistry, 64–306; disarmament, 64–310; drug, 68–311, 67–130; education, 67–322, 66–41, 66–334, 65–38, 65–315, 64–39, 64–316; elections, 67–324, 65–321; electric power, 65–322; ethics, 68–75; fishery, 67–339, 65–335; football, 67–342; Ford, Gerald R., 66–352; gas, 64–341; handicapped, 67–361; health, 67–361, 66–374; housing, 68–363, 67–365, 66–378, 65–360, 64–360; hunting and fishing, 66–380; immigration and emigration, 68–367, 66–381; Indian, American, 68–371, 66–385, 65–368, 64–365; insurance, 67–375; Johnson, Lyndon B., 64–583; juvenile delinquency, 65–384; Kennedy, Jacqueline, 64–381; labor, 68–387, 67–390, 66–407, 64–382; library, 67–395, 66–411, 65–394, 64–388; Medicare, 68–411, 66–431; Medicine, 66–434; mental health, 66–435, 65–412, 64–405; Middle East, 66–438; mining, 67–422; money, 68–426, 66–441, 64–414; motion pictures, 66–443; national affairs 67–21, 66–24, 66–452, 64–22; national defense, 68–434, 67–436, 65–433, 64–426; Negro, 66–455, 64–429; ocean, 68–443, 67–444, 64–435; old age, 67–444, 66–463, 65–444, 64–435; outdoor recreation, 65–449, 64–437; parks, 66–468, 65–455; Peace Corps, 66–469, 64–444; Percy, Charles H., 68–449; personalities, 67–451; pet, 67–454; pollution, *Special Report*, 66–179; population, 67–462; post office, 68–461; poverty, 68–462, 67–464, 66–483; prayer, 65–474; presidential succession, 66–392; publishing, 68–471; railroad, 67–528; religion, 67–480; Republican party, 68–478, 67–480, 66–504, 64–469; roads and highways, 66–507; safety, 68–485, 67–489; science and research, 68–487, 67–34, 67–493, 66–518, 64–481; social security, 68–491, 67–499, social welfare, 68–493, 65–502; stocks and bonds, 67–513; taxation, 68–508, 67–517, 66–533; transit, 66–543, 65–528, 64–510; veterans, 67–539, 66–553, 65–536; Vietnam, 64–522

Connecticut: architecture, 65–215; fluoridation, 66–317; population, 66–480; roads and highways, 66–508; Supreme Court, 66–531; theater, 64–506

CONNOR, JOHN T., 65–284; Cabinet, 68–245

Conrad, Charles, Jr.: astronauts, *il.*, 66–228, 64–224; space exploration, 67–504, 66–525

CONSERVATION, 68 283, 67–288
Congress, 67–285, 65–280; forestry, 68–342, 64–335; hunting and fishing, 68–365, 66–380, 65–362; land utilization, 65–126; literature for children, 67–405; national parks and monuments, 66–468; outdoor recreation, 66–463, 65–449, 64–437; parks, 66–468; petroleum, 67–456; pollution, 66–164; soil conservation, 65–503, 64–486; water, *Special Report*, 66–183; 64–526; water and flood control, 66–562, 65–542; wilderness, 65–189; wildlife, 66–564, 65–545, 64–149, 64–529; youth organizations, 67–551; zoology, 68–541, 66–568

Conservative party (Britain), 68–357, 66–368, 65–351, 64–350

Conservative party (Canada), 68–248, 66–265

Conservatives: John Birch Society, 66–398; national affairs, 65–20; Republican Party, 66–503

CONSTANTINE XIII, 65–284; Greece, 68–358, 66–371

Constitution of the United States, 68–528, 66–492, 65–514, 64–288

Construction. See **BUILDING AND CONSTRUCTION**

Consumers, 68–347, 67–285

Continental drift, 68–349, 67–444, 64–341

COOPER, LEROY GORDON, 64–287
astronauts, *il.*, 66–228, 64–224; space travel, 66–525, 64–46, 64–490

Copello, James Cardinal, 68–294

Copenhagen, 68–256

Coppens, Yves, 66–219

Copper: Chile, 68–262, 67–394, 66–275; energy, 68–327; manufacturing, 67–411; metal industry, 67–394, 64–405; mines and mining, 67–422, 66–439, 65–417

Cory, David, 67–298

Cosby, Bill, 67–478

Cosmology: astronomy, 65–223; physics, 67–460; science, 65–32; *Special Report*, 65–63

COSTA E SILVA, ARTHUR DA, 68–287; Brazil, 68–241, 67–249

COSTA RICA, 66–296, 65–284, 64–288; Latin America, 68–394, 67–392; Trejos Fernandez, José, 67–531

Costain, Thomas B., 66–305

Cotton: agriculture, 68–199, 67–207, 66–216, 65–210; manufacturing, 66–428; textile, 65–523, 64–504

COULSON, SIR JOHN ENTRINGHAM, 66–296

Courrèges, André, 66–348

COURTS AND LAWS, 68–287, 67–292, 66–296, 65–284, 64–288
arts, 65–51; banks and banking, 68–231, 64–239; boats and boating, 64–246; Butts, Wally, 64–57, 64–333; civil rights, 68–271, 67–273, 66–286, 64–278; Communism, 64–283; congress, 67–285, 64–287; crime, 68–288, 67–294, 66–297, 65–285; Great Britain, 64–353; Indian, American, 68–371; prison, 65–473; Ruby, Jack, 65–490; South Africa, 64–487; Spender, Sir Percy, 65–512; sports, 67–154; state government, 64–496; Supreme Court, 68–505, 67–514, 66–531, 65–515, 64–498; Supreme Court of the United States, *WBE*, 68–586; Tunisia, 64–511. See also **CONGRESS OF THE UNITED STATES; STATE GOVERNMENT**

Cousins, Frank, 67–359

Couve de Murville, Maurice, 66–345

Couzens, Bert, 68–450

Cowell, Henry, 66–307

Craig, Edward G., 67–298

Credit: banks and banking, 67–238; consumer credit, 64–414; economy, 66–328; money, 66–440; stocks and bonds, 64–497

Creech-Jones, Arthur, 65–294

Crerar, Henry D. G., 66–307

Crews, Albert H., 66–229

CRIME, 68–288, 67–294, 66–297, 65–285, 64–289
Canada, 66–266; computers, 66–290; Congo (Brazzaville), 66–291; courts and laws, 67–292; espionage, 67–331, 65–323; Evers, Medgar W., 64–326; Germany, 66–362; Great Britain, 67–360; hobbies, 67–362; juvenile delinquency, 66–403, 65–383, 64–376; Negro, 65–437; Oswald, Lee Harvey, 64–436; payola, 65–522; Philippines, 66–476; prison, 66–494, 65–473, 64–460; Quebec, 66–269, 64–125; Ruby, Jack, 64–476; Russia, 64–478; Supreme Court, 66–531; television, 65–520; U.S. Government, 68–527. See also **Assassination of John F. Kennedy**

Crossman, Richard, 67–359

Crouse, Russel, 67–298

CUBA, 68–289, 67–294, 66–297, 65–286, 64–290
civil rights, 66–284; hurricanes, 64–313; Latin America, 64–386; President of the United States, 64–459; United Nations, 64–515; Venezuela, 68–529

Cunningham, R. Walter, 67–219, 65–220

Curling, 68–502, 67–510, 66–528, 65–513, 64–494

Custer, James Holly II, 67–451

Cybernetics. See **COMPUTERS**

CYPRUS, 68–289, 67–360, 66–298, 65–286, 64–292; Finland, 65–334; Greece, 65–354; Turkey, 68–521, 65–530; United Nations, 68–526, 65–534

CZECHOSLOVAKIA, 68–289, 67–295, 66–299, 65–289, 64–292
anthropology, 68–204; Roman Catholic, 68–480

D

Daddah, Moktar Ould, 66–430
DAHOMEY, 68–194, 66–299, 65–289, 64–293
Africa, 67–202, 66–212, 65–209
DAIRYING, 65–289, 64–293
agriculture, 68–201, 67–207; food, 65–335; livestock show, 67–406; plastics, 65–466
Daley, Richard J.: Chicago, 68–260, 67–265; Democratic Party, 68–303, 67–265; elections, 68–323
DALLAS, 68–290, 66–300, 64–293
civil liberties, 64–278; Kennedy assassination, 65–552, 64–61; Stevenson, Adlai, *il.*, 64–516
Daly, John Charles, 68–473
Daly, Robert Cliff, 68–450
DAM, 66–300, 65–290, 64–293
building and construction, 68–244, 67–251; Canada, 68–253, 65–254; conservation, 68–283, 67–289; India, *il.*, 66–145; Los Angeles, 64–401; Mekong River, 68–85; Mexico, 64–407; Middle East, 65–416; United Arab Republic, 65–530; Venezuela, 65–535; water and flood control, 65–542
DANCING, 68–290, 67–295, 66–300, 65–290, 64–296
arts, 64–52; awards and prizes, 66–242; popular music, 68–148
Dandridge, Dorothy, 66–307
Dane, Clemence, 66–307
Daniels, Josephus, Jr., 65–295
Dante Alighieri, 66–271
Dante, Enrico Cardinal, 68–294
Darnell, Linda, 66–307
Darwell, Jane, 68–294
Data processing. See **COMPUTERS**
Dating, 68–206
Davidson, George, 66–307
DAVIS, DAVID BRION, 68–292
Davis, Stuart, 65–295
Davis, Watson, 68–294
DAYAN, MOSHE, 68–292; *il.*, 68–378
Daylight saving time, 67–285
Dayton, Mona, 67–451
Dean, Sir Patrick Henry, 66–301
Deaths: boxing, 64–248; child welfare, 64–269; literature, 66–413; medicine, 64–404; population, 65–467, 64–198; publishing, 66–499; safety, 67–489; smoking, 64–484; space travel, 66–527; television, 66–537; vital statistics, 68–536, 67–547
DEATHS OF NOTABLE PERSONS, 68–293, 67–296, 66–303, 65–292, 64–296
DeBakey, Michael E., 67–414
DEBATE, 64–302
Debye, Peter J. W., 67–298
Decathlon, 68–516, 67–525
Defense. See **ARMED FORCES OF THE WORLD; CIVIL DEFENSE; NATIONAL DEFENSE**
Defense, U.S. Department of, 68–528, 65–434
De Gaulle, Charles: Asia, 65–220; Canada, 68–248; Europe, 68–332, 67–332, 66–345, 65–326, 64–322; France, 68–344, 67–344, 66–355, 65–339, 64–337; international relations, 67–16, 65–16, 64–15, 64–367; international trade, 66–389, 65–371; Latin America, 65–391; Monaco, 66–440; North Atlantic Treaty Organization, 66–460, 65–442; Poland, 68–459; world affairs, 68–18, 66–20
De Havilland, Sir Geoffrey, 66–307
Delaware Water Gap, 66–468
Demerec, Milislav, 67–298
Demirel, Suleyman, 68–521
DEMOCRACY, 68–301, 67–303, 66–314, 64–303
Afghanistan, 67–201; Asia, 64–219; Brazil, 68–241; civil rights, 68–269, 66–283, 64–276; Dominican Republic, 67–312, 64–315; *Focus*, 65–20; Ghana, 66–363, 65–347, 64–348; Greece, 68–358; Haiti, 65–355, 64–356; Korea, 64–381; Latin America, 64–385; Middle East, 66–439; New Guinea, 67–439; Senegal, 66–520; South Africa, 66–523; Spain, 68–500; Supreme Court, 68–505; Venezuela, 68–529; Yugoslavia, 68–540
DEMOCRATIC PARTY, 68–302, 67–304, 66–315, 65–303, 64–304
congress, 67–281, 66–293, elections, 68–322, 67–324, 66–339, 65–319; Humphrey, Hubert H., 66–379, 65–361; Johnson, Lyndon B., 65–381, 64–583; Kennedy, John F., 65–384, 64–62, 64–380; McCarthy, Eugene, 68–411; national affairs, 66–24, 65–20; President of the U.S., 68–468
DENMARK, 68–304, 67–306, 66–317, 65–305, 64–360
Dennis, Wesley, 67–298
Denny, Reginald, 68–294
DENTISTRY, 68–304, 67–306, 66–317, 65–305, 64–307
Desalination of water, 64–526
atomic energy, 67–224, 66–232, 65–223; chemistry, 65–260; conservation, 68–284, 67–289; Saudi Arabia, 68–487; United Arab Republic, 65–530; water and flood control, 66–186, 66–562
DeSalvo, Albert, 68–288
Desegregation: civil rights, 68–271, 66–283, 65–266, 64–274; education, 66–44, 66–336, 65–317; Great Britain, 66–371; hospital, 66–377, 65–360; libraries, 64–210; Negro, 65–437; Parents and Teachers, National Congress of, 65–455; Protestant, 64–461; Red Cross, 66–501; South Africa, 68–494, 66–523; Supreme Court, 64–498. See also **NEGRO; CIVIL RIGHTS**
DETROIT, 68–305, 67–306, 66–317, 65–306, 64–306; city, 68–266; civil rights, 68–269
De Valéra, Éamon, 67–379
Devine, George, 67–298
Dewey, Thomas E., 66–503
Diabetes, 67–142
DÍAZ ORDAZ, GUSTAVO, 67–419, 65–306; Mexico, 68–416, 66–436, 65–413
Dibelius, Otto: deaths, 68–294; Protestant, 68–470, 66–497
Dictionary: *World Book Encyclopedia Dictionary* supplement 68–591, 67–599, 66–597, 65–603, 64–607
Diefenbaker, John G., 68–248, 67–254, 66–265, 64–259, *il.*, 64–445
Dieting: food, 66–350; health, 66–374, 65–357
Dillon, C. Douglas, 66–262, 65–541
Dinges, Madeline, 67–452
Diori, Hamani, 66–459, 64–432
DIPLOMAT, 68–306, 67–307, 66–318, 65–306, 64–307
Dirksen, Everett M.: civil rights, 65–166; Congress, 66–293; garden and lawn, 68–348; personalities, *il.*, 67–453; politics, 68–65; poverty, 66–485; religion, 67–480; recordings, *il.*, 68–474; Republican Party, 66–503
DISARMAMENT, 68–307, 67–308, 66–318, 65–307
atomic energy, 64–228; congress, 64–287; Europe, 68–333; Great Britain, 64–354; international relations, 64–12, 64–367; Schweitzer, Albert, 64–148; space exploration, 68–499, 67–49; United Nations, 68–527, 67–533, 66–551, 65–535, 64–515
DISASTERS, 68–307, 67–308, 66–319, 65–311, 64–312
astronauts, 68–213; automobile racing, *il.*, 65–227; British Columbia, 68–253, 66–268; Chicago, 68–260; Chile, 66–275; civil defense, 65–266; 64–274; communications, 66–287; Costa Rica, 65–284, 64–288; crime, 65–285; Cuba, 64–291; dam, 64–294; electric power, 66–339; flood control, 68–284, 65–543, 64–526; forestry, 68–342, 66–562; insurance, 68–372, 67–375, 66–388, 65–371; Italy, 67–380; Los Angeles, 64–401; Mexico, 66–436; New Orleans, 66–457; painting and sculpture, 67–446; nuclear physics, 66–461; radio, 66–500; Red Cross, 68–475; safety, 64–479; submarines, 64–425; weather, 67–549, 65–543, 64–527
Discothèque: fashion, 65–334; words and phrases, 65–546
Discount rate, 66–330, 65–419
Discus throwing, 68–515
Disease: dentistry, 66–317; drugs, 67–128; Egypt, 66–190; livestock, 64–400; mental health, 66–435; psychology, 66–497; population, 64–191; vital statistics, 67–547, 65–540. See also **HEALTH AND DISEASE; MEDICINE**
Disney, "Walt," Walter E., 67–302
District of Columbia. See **WASHINGTON, D.C.**
Divine, Father, 66–307
Diving: exploration, 65–329; ocean, *il.*, 67–443; Olympic Games, 65–448; Sealab, 67–68
Divorces, 66–296, 65–540, 64–525
Dixon, Sir Pierson, 66–307
DNA, 64–245
biochemistry, 68–236, 65–239; biology, 65–240
Dobie, James Frank: awards and prizes, 65–231; deaths, 65–295
Dodd, Thomas J.: Congress, 68–283; politics, 68–64
Dogs, 68–454, 67–454, 66–474, 65–462, 64–450
Doll, 66–358
Dolphin, 68–541, 67–64
DOMINICAN REPUBLIC, 67–312, 66–323, 65–314, 64–315
Balaguer y Ricardo, Jóaquin, 67–237; civil rights, 67–276, 66–284; democracy, 64–303; Haiti, 64–356; Latin America, 68–395
Donath, Ludwig, 68–294
Donges, Theophilus E., 68–494
Dorion, Frederic, 66–266
Dostal, James, 68–450
DOUGLAS-HOME, SIR ALEXANDER FREDERICK, 64–315
Great Britain, 66–368, 65–351, 64–350
Doxiadis, Constantinos A., 67–214
Draft. See **Selective Service**
Dresser, Louise, 66–307
Drop-outs: business, 64–29; child guidance, 64–269; education, 64–317; job corps, 65–379; juvenile delinquency, 67–465, 66–403, 64–376; poverty, 66–483; social welfare, 64–486; vocational education, 64–525
DRUG, 68–311, 67–313, 65–314, 64–315
botany, 66–256; dentistry, 66–317; garden and lawn, 67–350; Goddard, James L., 67–355; health, 66–374; manufacturing, 66–428; medicine, 68–412; mental health, 67–418, 66–435, 65–412; psychology, 64–463; *Special Report*, 67–128; sports, 68–502
Dryden, Hugh L., 66–527
Drysdale, Don 67–148
Ducks, 67–291, 66–564, 65–545, 64–529
Duhamel, Georges, 67–298
Dumont, Wayne, Jr., 66–504
Dunn, James, 68–294
Durham, Elliot, 67–452
Durkee, William P., 66–281
Durocher, Leo, 66–249
Duryea, J. Frank, 68–294
Duvalier, François, 68–395, 66–372, 65–355, 64–356
Duvivier, Julien, 68–294

E

Early Bird: communications, 66–286; space travel, 66–526; television, 66–537
EARTH, *WBE*, 68–544; *il.*, 67–221
Earthquakes: disasters, 68–308, 67–311, 66–320, 65–312, 64–312; El Salvador, 66–342, 66–360; geology, 68–349, 67–351, 65–343, 64–341; Japan, 65–378; Turkey, 67–532
East Africa, Federation of, 64–381
East Germany. See **GERMANY**
EASTERN ORTHODOX, 68–312, 67–313, 66–325, 65–315, 64–316
ecumenical movement, 66–87; Roman Catholic, 68–480, 66–511, 65–488
EBERHART, RICHARD, 67–314
ECKERT, WILLIAM D., 66–325; baseball, 66–249
Eclipse, 67–222, 66–230, 64–224
ECONOMY, THE, 68–312, 67–314, 66–327. See also **BUSINESS,** 65–248, 64–254
agriculture, 68–198, 67–206, 66–214, 65–210, 64–208; automation, 66–233, 64–229; census, 68–278, 67–263; Congress, 67–282; *Focus*, 68–27, 67–26, 66–29, 65–26, 64–24; food, 67–339; invention, 64–370; New England, 66–198; national affairs, 67–21, 64–18; national defense, 64–426; President of the U.S., 67–470; sports, 68–57; Supreme Court, 65–518, 64–498; taxation, 65–519. See also **BANKS AND BANKING; MANUFACTURING; INTERNATIONAL TRADE; LABOR;** also entries on specific businesses, industries, countries, and regions
ECUADOR, 68–396, 67–394, 66–332, 65–315, 64–316
Latin America, 64–385
Ecumenical movement: Eastern Orthodox, 67–313, 66–325, 65–315; Jews and Judaism, 68–380, 67–383, 64–375; Protestant, 68–469, 67–472, 66–496, 64–461, religion, 67–480; Roman Catholic, 68–480, 67–485, 65–487, 64–472; *Special Report*, 66–82
Eddy, Nelson, 68–294
Edson, Gus, 67–298
EDUCATION, 68–318, 67–322, 66–333, 65–315, 64–316
American Indian, 64–364; astronauts, 64–222; automation, 64–229; awards, 67–235, 66–243; blindness, 68–237, 67–245, 66–253, 65–240, 64–246; Boys' Clubs of America, 64–250; business, 64–28; Canada, 67–256, 66–269; careers, 64–264; Chicago, 64–268; child guidance, 68–261, 66–275, 64–269; child welfare, 67–266, 65–261; China, 66–279, *il.*, 66–120; city, 64–273; civil rights, 67–274, 64–277; computers, 66–290, 64–283; congress, 68–278, 67–282, 66–294, 64–287; dentistry, 67–306, 64–306, employment, 68–99; engineering, 68–328, 67–330, 66–343, 64–321; Filbey, Emery T., 64–447; *Focus*, 68–38, 67–38, 66–41, 65–38, 64–36; Formosa, 68–343; foundations, 68–343, 67–

343, *66*–338, *65*–318, *64*–318; Gardner, John W., *66*–359; Great Britain, *65*–354, *64*–354; handicapped, *67*–361; hospital, *68*–363; Howe, Harold, *66*–379; Indian, American, *66*–385; interior design, *66*–389; job corps, *65*–379; juvenile delinquency, *66*–403; labor, *68*–387; learning, *WBE*, *68*–561; Liberia, *65*–394; library, *68*–396, *67*–395, *66*–411, *65*–394, *64*–211, *64*–388; Medicare, *67*–414; mental health, *68*–415; museums, *68*–429, *67*–427, *66*–445, *65*–424, *64*–417; national affairs, *64*–22; Negro, *65*–437, *64*–429; New England, *66*–202; New York City, *68*–439; old age, *67*–444; Ousley, Elmon, *64*–448; Parents and Teachers, National Congress of, *68*–449, *67*–449, *66*–468, *65*–455, *64*–441; Peace Corps, *68*–449, *67*–450, *65*–457, *64*–442; poverty, *68*–463, *67*–464, *66*–483; President of the U.S., *66*–491; Protestant, *66*–496, *64*–460; publishing, *67*–477; Quebec, *65*–257; recordings for children, *64*–468; religion, *67*–480; Rotary International, *67*–496; safety, *66*–516; science, *66*–518; science clubs, *64*–482; social welfare, *65*–501, *64*–486; space travel, *64*–44; sports, *66*–61; state government, *68*–503, *66*–529, *65*–514, *64*–496; Supreme Court, *64*–498; television, *67*–519, *66*–536, *65*–522, *64*–503; Tanzania, *68*–508; testing, *WBE*, *68*–566; United Nations, *64*–517; UNICEF, *66*–551; veterans, *68*–529, *67*–539, *65*–535; vocational education, *64*–525; Washington, D.C., *68*–536

EDUCATIONAL FOUNDATIONS, *66*–338, *65*–318, *64*–318. See also **Foundations**

Edwards, Hartley Benson, *67*–452

Egypt. See **UNITED ARAB REPUBLIC**

Ehrenburg, Ilya, *68*–294, *68*–399

Eigen, Manfred, *68*–441

Einstein, Albert, *65*–74

Eire. See **IRELAND**

EISENHOWER, DWIGHT D., *68*–322, *67*–324, *66*–339
Kennedy assassination, *64*–69; memoirs, *66*–415, *66*–469, *il.*, *64*–362; personalities, *68*–450, *66*–470, *il.*, *66*–472, *il.*, *64*–448; Republican party, *66*–503, *64*–470; vice-presidency, *64*–82

ELECTIONS, *68*–322, *67*–324, *66*–339, *65*–319; Baker, Robert G., *65*–233; city, *68*–266; civil rights, *68*–270, *67*–275, *66*–285, *65*–269, *64*–277; Congress, *67*–280, *66*–294; Democratic party, *68*–302, *67*–304, *66*–316, *65*–303, *64*–304; democracy, *68*–301; *Focus*, *65*–20; Goldwater, Barry M., *65*–348; governors, *67*–356, *65*–349, *64*–350; Humphrey, Hubert H., *65*–361; Johnson, Lyndon B., *65*–382; Kennedy, Robert F., *65*–386; Miller, William E., *65*–417; national affairs, *67*–24; Negro, *66*–455, *65*–437; President of the U.S., *65*–471, *64*–83; publishing, *65*–476; Republican party, *68*–476, *67*–480, *66*–504, *65*–483, *64*–469; *Special Report*, *68*–62; state government, *65*–514, *64*–496; television, *65*–520; wheat, *64*–208. See also entries on various countries, states, and cities

ELECTRIC POWER AND EQUIPMENT, *68*–323, *67*–328, *66*–339, *65*–322, *64*–318

ELECTRICAL EQUIPMENT, *65*–322, *64*–319

Electricity: physics, *66*–478, *65*–465, *64*–454; psychology, *64*–463

Electromagnetism, *68*–458

ELECTRONICS, *68*–324, *67*–329, *66*–341, *65*–322
automation, *65*–224; communications, *66*–287, *65*–270; computers, *68*–274, *67*–279, *66*–290, *65*–274, *64*–283; education, *67*–39; manufacturing, *67*–411; publishing, *67*–477

ELECTRONICS INDUSTRY, *64*–320

Elements, table of, *65*–260

Elephant: Africa, *64*–160; zoos, *64*–532

Eliot, T. S.: awards, *65*–231; deaths, *66*–307; literature, *66*–417

Elisabeth of Belgium, *66*–307

Elizabeth II: Belgium, *67*–243; Canada, *68*–246, *65*–254; Great Britain, *66*–369, *65*–354, *64*–354; personalities, *il.*, *68*–453; Salvation Army, *66*–517

Elliott, Alonzo, *65*–295

Ellis Island, *66*–469

Elman, Mischa, *68*–294

Elmore, Daniel, *65*–460

EL SALVADOR, *68*–394, *66*–342, *65*–323, *64*–320; Latin America, *67*–392

Emerson, Roy, *67*–521

Emigration. See **IMMIGRATION AND EMIGRATION**

Encephalitis: health, *67*–361, *65*–357; Houston, *65*–361

ENGINE AND ENERGY, *67*–330, *66*–342, *65*–323, *64*–320

ENGINEERING, *68*–328, *67*–330, *66*–343, *64*–321
Abu Simbel, *66*–220, *64*–212; atomic energy, *66*–232; bridge, *64*–251, building and construction, *68*–242, *67*–250, *64*–252; dam, *66*–300, *64*–293; water, *66*–187

England, Church of: Johnson, Hewlett, *64*–447; Protestant, *67*–472; Roman Catholic, *67*–483

Engle, Clair, *65*–295

English Channel tunnel, *il.*, *67*–250, *65*–245

English language: education, *64*–38; India, *68*–368; Malaysia, *68*–407; new words and phrases, *65*–546, *64*–430. See also **Dictionary**

Environmental Science Services Administration, *66*–563

Epidemiology, *67*–361

Episcopalian. See **Protestant Episcopal Church**

ERHARD, LUDWIG, *64*–321
Europe, *67*–335; Germany, *67*–352, *66*–362, *65*–345, *64*–343

Ericson, Leif, *66*–347

Erie, Lake, *68*–127

Eritrea, *68*–329

Erlanger, Joseph, *66*–307

Erosion, *67*–351

Erwin, Stuart, *68*–294

ESHKOL, LEVI, *66*–393, *64*–321
Israel, *65*–374, *64*–373

ESPIONAGE, *68*–328, *67*–331, *66*–343, *65*–323, *64*–321; anthropology, *68*–206; Canada, *67*–256; France, *67*–346; Great Britain, *64*–353; Helms, Richard M., *67*–362; Sweden, *64*–499; television, *66*–534; toys, *67*–348; United Arab Republic, *66*–547; U.S. government, *68*–528

Estes, Billie Sol: Congress, *65*–283

Ethics, *68*–282

ETHIOPIA, *68*–329, *67*–331, *66*–343, *65*–324, *64*–322
anthropology, *68*–204; Elizabeth II, *66*–369; Liberia, *65*–394; Somalia, *65*–503

EUROPE, *68*–330, *67*–332, *66*–345, *65*–324, *64*–322. See also by name of country

European Economic Community. See **Common Market**

European Free Trade Association: Coulson, Sir John, *66*–296; Europe, *68*–332, *67*–332, *66*–347, *65*–324, *64*–324; Iceland, *66*–381; international trade, *65*–372, *64*–369

Evangelical United Brethren, *64*–462

Evans, Patsy, *66*–471

Evatt, Herbert Vere, *66*–307

Evelyn, Judith, *68*–294

Everest, Mount, *64*–328

EVERS, MEDGAR W., *64*–326
civil liberties, *64*–276

Evolution: anthropology, *65*–110, *Trans-Vision*, *65*–81, *64*–211

Excise taxes: congress, *66*–295; taxation, *66*–533, *65*–519

Exhibitions. See **FAIRS AND EXHIBITIONS**

EXPLORATION, *66*–347, *65*–329, *64*–326
Beja, *67*–98; East Africa, *64*–150; Fortier, Yves, *65*–337; garden and lawn, *64*–340; oceanography, *65*–443; Rowley, Graham, *64*–476; Sealab, *67*–63. See also **SPACE EXPLORATION**

Explosions: disasters, *68*–309, *67*–311, *66*–320, *65*–312, *64*–313; nuclear physics, *66*–461; Quebec, *64*–125, *il.*, *64*–260; stars, *64*–224

Expo 67: architecture, *68*–209, *67*–214; Canada, *68*–246, *il.*, *67*–258; fairs and exhibitions, *68*–334

Exports. See **INTERNATIONAL TRADE**

Eyadema, Etienne, *68*–514

F

Fabreau, Guy, *68*–247

FAIRS AND EXHIBITIONS, *68*–334, *67*–335, *66*–348, *65*–331, *64*–328
American Library Association, *65*–212; architecture, *68*–209, *67*–214, *65*–214, *64*–213; aviation, *il.*, *66*–241; building and construction, *64*–253; Canada, *68*–246; garden and lawn, *68*–348; interior decoration, *65*–371; Japan, *66*–397; livestock show, *68*–406, *67*–406, *65*–408, *64*–401; Montreal, *il.*, *66*–269, *65*–257, *64*–262; motion pictures, *65*–424; painting and sculpture, *67*–447; pets, *68*–454, *67*–454, *66*–474, *65*–462, *64*–450; plastics, *65*–466; Roman Catholic, *65*–489; science clubs, *68*–488, *67*–494, *66*–519, *65*–496

FAISAL, ABDEL AZIZ AL SAUD AL FAISAL, *65*–332; Middle East, *65*–415; Saudi Arabia, *68*–487, *67*–491, *66*–517, *65*–495, *64*–481; Yemen, *65*–546

Famine, *68*–370

FANFANI, AMINTORE, *66*–348
Italy, *66*–395, *64*–373; science, *67*–494; United Nations, *66*–551

Farm Equipment: manufacturing, *68*–410, *67*–412, *65*–333, *64*–330

Farrar, Geraldine, *68*–294

FASHION, *68*–336, *67*–337, *66*–348, *65*–333, *64*–330. See also **INTERIOR DESIGN; TEXTILE**

Fatima, Our Lady of, *68*–257

Faulkner, Barry, *67*–298

Favreau, Guy, *66*–266

Federal Aviation Agency: aviation, *66*–239, *64*–235; McKee, William, *66*–431

Federal Bureau of Investigation: civil liberties, *65*–267; democracy, *67*–304; espionage, *67*–331; Kennedy assassination, *65*–541

Federal Communications Commission: communications, *67*–277, *66*–287, *65*–270; Henry, E. William, *64*–358; Hyde, Rosel H., *67*–368; radio, *68*–473, *64*–466; television, *68*–509, *65*–522, *64*–503; U.S. government, *68*–528

Federal Power Commission: electric power, *66*–340, *64*–341; petroleum, *66*–475

Federal Reserve Board: banks, *68*–230, *67*–237, *66*–245, *64*–240; economy, *67*–29, *67*–317, *66*–330; money, *66*–440; stocks and bonds, *68*–504

Fencing, *68*–503, *67*–511, *66*–528, *65*–447

Festivals: dancing, *68*–290, *66*–300, *65*–291, *64*–296; music, *68*–432, *64*–421; poetry, *66*–417; popular music, *68*–433; theater, *64*–505

FEYNMAN, RICHARD PHILLIPS, *66*–349

Field, Marshall IV: deaths, *66*–307; publishing, *66*–499

Field Foundation, Inc., *67*–343, *65*–318, *64*–318

Fields, Joseph, *67*–298

Fiene, Ernest, *66*–307

Fiji Islands, *68*–444, *67*–446, *64*–437

Film, *68*–458, *67*–458, *66*–477, *65*–464, *64*–452

FINLAND, *68*–338, *67*–338, *66*–350, *65*–334, *64*–332

Finley, John L., *66*–229

Fires: botany, *66*–256; Chicago, *68*–260; disasters, *68*–309, *67*–311, *66*–320, *65*–312, *64*–313; forestry, *68*–342, *67*–291, *66*–352, *65*–337, *64*–335; insurance, *64*–366; Jews, *67*–383; post office, *68*–461; Quebec, *67*–260; safety, *67*–490, *65*–494, *64*–479; space exploration, *68*–497

Fischer, Bobby, *68*–260, *67*–265, *66*–274, *65*–261

Fish: biology, *66*–253; ocean, *67*–64, *64*–435

Fish, tropical, *65*–462, *64*–450

Fisher, Vardis, *66*–414

FISHERY, *68*–338, *67*–339, *66*–350, *65*–334, *64*–332
conservation, *67*–291; France, *66*–357; hunting and fishing, *68*–365, *66*–380; Iceland, *66*–381; Lake Erie, *68*–128; ocean, *64*–435; pollution, *65*–467; zoology, *66*–568

Fishing. See **HUNTING AND FISHING**

Fitzgerald, John, *66*–66

Fitzsimmons, James E., *67*–298

Flag, *66*–265, *65*–254, *64*–440

Flanner, Janet, *il.*, *67*–399

Fleming, Eric, *67*–298

Fleming, Ian, *65*–295

Fleming, Peggy, *68*–366, *67*–369

Fletcher, Lorena C., *66*–471

Flood Control, *64*–526. See also **WATER AND FLOOD CONTROL**

Floods: conservation, *68*–284, *67*–289; disasters, *68*–309, *67*–311, *66*–320, *65*–313, *64*–313; Italy, *68*–379, *67*–380; Outer Mongolia, *67*–445; painting and sculpture, *67*–446; weather, *65*–543

Florida: governors, *65*–349; Indian, American, *68*–371; waterways, *65*–543; zoos, *66*–568

Flowers, *68*–348, *67*–350, *66*–359, *65*–342, *64*–340

Fluoridation: dentistry, *il.*, *68*–305, *66*–317, *65*–306; state government, *66*–529

Fock, Jenö, *68*–365

Fogarty, John E., *68*–294

Folk music: music, popular, *66*–449, *64*–421; recordings, *65*–480, *64*–467

Fonteyn, Margot, *il.*, *68*–291

FOOD, *68*–339, *67*–339, *66*–350, *65*–335, *64*–333
agriculture, *68*–201, *67*–206, *66*–214, *65*–210; Asia, *65*–218; chemistry, *65*–260; China, *66*–117, *66*–279; dairying, *65*–289, *64*–293; economy, *67*–30, *67*–316; fishery, *68*–338, *67*–339, *66*–350, *65*–334, *64*–332; food stamps, *65*–211, *65*–280; health, *64*–357; India, *68*–370, *67*–372, *66*–132, *66*–383, *65*–367; invention, *64*–371; ocean, *67*–70,

population, *67*–461, *64*–191; poultry, *65*–468; prices, *65*–250, *64*–256; science, *68*–33. See also **AGRICULTURE**
Food and Agricultural Organization, *68*–85, *65*–129
Food and Drug Administration: drug, *68*–311, *67*–130, *67*–313, *65*–314, *64*–315; food, *68*–339, *67*–340; foot and mouth disease, *68*–357; Goddard, James L., *67*–355; mental health, *65*–412
FOOTBALL, *68*–340, *67*–340, *66*–351, *65*–335, *64*–333
Forbes, Esther, *68*–294
FORD, GERALD RUDOLPH, *66*–352
Republican Party, *68*–478, *66*–504
Ford, Wallace, *67*–298
Ford Foundation: arts, *64*–52; Bundy, McGeorge, *67*–252; Chicago, *66*–274; dancing, *67*–295, *65*–290, *64*–296; education, *68*–321, *67*–323; foundations, *67*–343, *66*–338, *65*–318, *64*–318; library, *65*–389; literature, *66*–417; music, *64*–419; population, *68*–460; television, *68*–509, *67*–519, *66*–447, *64*–503; vocational education, *64*–525
Foreign exchange: international monetary fund, *66*–390; money, *67*–423, *66*–440, *65*–418, *64*–412
FOREST PRODUCTS, *68*–342, *67*–342, *66*–352, *65*–337, *64*–335
atomic energy, *66*–232; conservation, *68*–285, *67*–291; Honduras, *65*–359; memorials, *68*–414
Forester, Cecil Scott, *67*–299
FORMOSA, *68*–343, *67*–343, *66*–353, *65*–337, *64*–335
agriculture, *il.*, *65*–125; *Special Report*, *65*–135
FORTAS, ABE, *66*–353
President of the U.S., *il.*, *66*–489; Supreme Court, *66*–531
Fossati, Maurilio Cardinal, *66*–307
Fossils, *68*–204, *67*–212, *66*–359, *65*–107, *65*–213
FOUNDATIONS, *68*–343, *67*–343
arts, *64*–52; awards, *66*–242; Boys' Clubs of America, *64*–250; Canada, *65*–256; city planning, *64*–274; dancing, *67*–295, *65*–290; educational foundations, *68*–321, *66*–338, *65*–318, *64*–318; engineering, *64*–321; Kennedy foundation, *65*–384. See also **Ford Foundation**
FOUR-H CLUBS, *68*–539, *66*–353, *65*–337, *64*–335
FOWLER, HENRY HAMILL, *66*–353
Foxx, James E., *68*–294
FRANCE, *68*–344, *67*–344, *66*–355, *65*–339, *64*–336
Algeria, *66*–217, *64*–210; armed forces, *68*–210; Canada, *68*–248, *64*–105; Chad, *66*–273, *65*–260; civil rights, *66*–283; dam, *67*–251; democracy, *66*–314; electric power, *64*–318; Europe, *67*–332, *66*–345, *65*–324, *64*–322; Gabon, *65*–341; Germany, *66*–360, *64*–345; Guinea, *65*–355, *64*–355; international relations, *68*–18, *67*–16, *65*–16, *64*–15; international trade, *66*–389; Latin America, *65*–391; Monaco, *64*–412; Morocco, *68*–427, *67*–423; motion pictures, *64*–417; North Atlantic Treaty Organization, *68*–442, *67*–441, *66*–460; Pacific Islands, *68*–444, *67*–446, *65*–449, *64*–437; Poland, *68*–459; Schuman, Robert, *64*–481; Schweitzer, Pierre-Paul, *64*–481; Senegal, *67*–203, *66*–520; space exploration, *67*–47; Tunisia, *65*–530, *64*–511; tunnel, *66*–259, *64*–252; United Nations, *67*–536, *66*–550; Vietnam, *66*–560; weather, *67*–548
Frank, Albert Rudolf, *66*–307
Frank, Philipp, *67*–299
Frankau, Pamela, *68*–294
Frankfurter, Felix, *66*–307
Frawley, William, *67*–299
Free Society Association, *66*–503
Freedom March: arts, *64*–52; civil liberties, *65*–173, *il.*, *64*–275; King, Martin Luther, Jr., *64*–381; national affairs, *64*–21; Negro, *64*–429; Protestant, *64*–461
Freedoms Foundation, *66*–435
Freeman, Orville L., *68*–200
Freeman, Theodore C.: astronauts, *65*–221, *64*–223; deaths, *il.*, *65*–294
FREI MONTALVA, EDUARDO RODRÍGUEZ, *65*–340
Chile, *66*–275, *65*–262; Latin America, *66*–410
French Canadians: Canada, *68*–246, *66*–268, *65*–253, *64*–103, *64*–123, *64*–262; Canadian Library Association, *65*–257, *64*–264
French Somaliland, *68*–346
Friedlander, Leo, *67*–299
Friedman, Harvey M., *68*–451
Fruit: botany, *66*–255; garden, *67*–350, *66*–359; insect, *68*–372; inventions, *68*–377
Fulbright, J. William, *67*–304
Fuller, John F. C., *67*–299
Fuller, R. Buckminster, *68*–209
Funk, Casimir, *68*–294
Funk, Wilfred John, *66*–307
Fuqua, Janice, *67*–452
Furman, N. Howell, *66*–309
FURNESS, BETTY, *68*–347
Furniture, *68*–373, *67*–375, *66*–388, *65*–371, *64*–367
FUTURE FARMERS OF AMERICA, *68*–540, *66*–357, *65*–340, *64*–339
FUTURE HOMEMAKERS OF AMERICA, *66*–357, *65*–341, *64*–339

G

GABON, *68*–196, *66*–357, *65*–341, *64*–340; Africa, *67*–204
Gaitskell, Hugh: deaths, *64*–298; Great Britain, *64*–350
Galaxies: astronomy, *66*–231, *65*–223; science, *65*–32
Galloway, Robert E., *66*–471
GAMBIA, *66*–358, *65*–341, *64*–340
Africa, *68*–194, *67*–204, *65*–207; United Nations, *66*–552
Gambling: football, *64*–56, *64*–334; harness racing, *64*–357
GAMES, MODELS, AND TOYS, *68*–347, *67*–348, *66*–358, *65*–341
bridge, *68*–242, *67*–249, *66*–260, *65*–246, *64*–252; chess, *68*–260, *67*–265, *66*–274, *65*–261, *64*–268; models, *64*–412. See also **SPORTS**
GANDHI, INDIRA NEHRU, *67*–349; India, *68*–368, *67*–370
Gandy, Lillian G., *68*–451
Garbutt, Elizabeth, *66*–432
Garcia-Godoy, Hector, *66*–324
Gardella, Danny, *67*–154
Garden, Mary, *68*–294
GARDEN AND LAWN, *68*–348, *67*–350, *66*–358, *65*–342, *64*–340
GARDNER, JOHN WILLIAM, *66*–359
education, *66*–338; health and disease, *68*–360; social welfare, *66*–522
Garner, John Nance, *68*–294
GARRISON, JIM C., *68*–348
Garriott, Owen K., *66*–228
Gary (Ind.), *68*–322
GAS. See **PETROLEUM AND GAS**
Gas turbine, *64*–232
Gases: chemistry, *66*–273, *64*–267; engine and energy, *64*–320
Gasoline, *66*–475, *64*–451
Gassner, John W., *68*–296
Gates, Ruth, *67*–299
GAUD, WILLIAM S., *67*–350
Gbenye, Christophe, *65*–276
Gell-Mann, Murray, *65*–442
Gemini project: *Focus*, *67*–45; space exploration, *67*–503
General Electric Company, *67*–273
Genetics: agriculture, *67*–208; biochemistry, *68*–235, *66*–251, *65*–239, *64*–245; Jacob, François, *66*–396; Lwoff, André, *66*–425; Monod, Jacques, *66*–441
Geography: awards, *68*–228, *67*–236, *66*–255; Russia, *67*–179
GEOLOGY, *68*–349, *67*–351, *66*–359, *65*–343, *64*–341
awards and prizes, *68*–228, *65*–232; biology, *66*–252; Bostock, Hugh, *66*–255; Earth, *WBE*, *68*–544; earthquakes, *68*–308; moon, *68*–498, *67*–506; ocean, *68*–443, *67*–443, *66*–463, *65*–443, *64*–435; science clubs, *65*–496, *64*–482; *Trans-Vision*, *65*–81
Geomagnetism, *68*–350, *65*–222
Geometry: *WBE*, *65*–593
Geophysics: geology, *66*–360; ocean, *67*–443; science, *66*–494; space exploration, *67*–505
Georgia: Atlanta, *67*–222, *66*–231; civil liberties, *65*–268; state government, *64*–496; Supreme Court, *64*–498
Gerbil, *67*–454
Gerlier, Pierre Cardinal, *66*–309
GERMANY, *68*–350, *67*–352, *66*–360, *65*–345, *64*–342
armed forces, *68*–210; bridge and tunnel, *il.*, *64*–251; communism, *68*–274; Czechoslovakia, *68*–289, *67*–295; democracy, *68*–301, *67*–303, *66*–314; disarmament, *66*–319; Elizabeth II, *66*–369; espionage, *68*–328; Erhard, Ludwig, *64*–321; Europe, *68*–332, *67*–335, *65*–326, *64*–325; fairs and exhibitions, *64*–330; France, *65*–339; *64*–338; Hungary, *64*–361; international relations, *65*–16; Israel, *66*–393, *65*–374; Kiesinger, Kurt, *67*–387; memorials, *64*–405; Middle East, *66*–438; national defense, *64*–423; Netherlands, *64*–430; North Atlantic Treaty Organization, *68*–442; sports, *68*–502, *66*–528; Stoph, Willi, *65*–515; United Arab Republic, *66*–548
Gestido, Oscar Daniel, *68*–528
GHANA, *68*–352, *67*–354, *66*–363, *65*–347, *64*–348
Giacometti, Alberto, *67*–299, *il.*, *66*–464
Giannini, Vittorio, *67*–299
GI Bill of Rights, *65*–535
Gibraltar: Great Britain, *67*–359; Spain, *68*–500, *67*–509, *66*–528, *65*–512
Gibson, Edward G., *66*–228
Gildersleeve, Virginia C., *66*–309
Gilliard, Ernest T., *66*–309
Gilmore, Adam, *68*–451
GILROY, FRANK DANIEL, *66*–363
Gimbel, Bernard F., *67*–299
GIRL SCOUTS, *66*–363, *65*–347, *64*–348
youth organizations, *68*–540, *67*–552
GIRLS CLUBS OF AMERICA, *66*–363, *65*–347, *64*–348
youth organizations, *68*–540, *67*–552
Givens, Edward G., *68*–213
Gland, *68*–470
GLASS, *64*–348
Glenn, John Herschel, Jr.: astronauts, *65*–220, *64*–224; awards and prizes, *65*–231; personalities, *il.*, *66*–471
Glenny, Alexander T., *66*–309
GODDARD, JAMES LEE, *67*–355
drugs, *67*–130, *67*–313; food, *68*–339
Godwin, Mills E., Jr., *66*–339
GOETZMANN, WILLIAM H., *68*–352
Gold: international monetary fund, *66*–390; international trade, *67*–376, *66*–391; medicine, *66*–433; money, *65*–419, *64*–412
Goldberg, Arthur Joseph: disarmament, *67*–308; United Nations, *il.*, *67*–123, *66*–550
Goldberg, "Rube," *64*–447
GOLDMAN, ERIC F., *65*–347
GOLDWATER, BARRY MORRIS, *65*–348
elections, *65*–320; national affairs, *65*–20; Protestant, *65*–474; publishing, *65*–476; Republican party, *66*–503, *65*–483, *il.*, *64*–469; vice-presidency, *64*–88
GOLF, *68*–352, *67*–355, *66*–364, *65*–348, *64*–349
Gomulka, Wladyslaw, *il.*, *67*–487, *65*–466
Goodenough, Erwin R., *66*–309
Goodyear, Ansen Conger, *65*–295
Gorbach, Alfons, *65*–224
Gordon, Richard, *67*–504
Gordon, Walter L., *68*–247, *65*–256, *64*–261
GORDON-WALKER, PATRICK CHRESTIEN, *66*–368, *65*–348; Great Britain, *65*–351
Gorilla, *68*–542
Gorton, John, *68*–216
Goulart, João Belchior, Brazil, *66*–314, *65*–244, *64*–251
Government: Afghanistan, *66*–210; democracy, *67*–303, *66*–314, *64*–303. See also **CITY; STATE GOVERNMENT; U.S. GOVERNMENT**
GOVERNORS OF THE STATES, *68*–354, *67*–356, *66*–365, *65*–349, *64*–350
Democratic party, *66*–316; elections, *65*–321; Kerner, Otto, *68*–385; Reagan, Ronald, *68*–473; Republican party, *67*–480, *65*–483; Rockefeller, Nelson, *68*–479; Romney, George W., *68*–482, *65*–489; Scranton, William, *65*–497; Wallace, George C., *68*–536, *64*–525
Gowers, Sir Ernest, *67*–299
Gowon, Yakubu, *68*–441, *67*–441
Grace, Princess, *il.*, *67*–454
Graham, Billy, *67*–472, *65*–474
Graham, Martha, *67*–295, *66*–301, *65*–291
Grand Canyon, *67*–289
Granit, Ragnar Arthur, *68*–441
GRAU, SHIRLEY ANN, *66*–365
literature, *65*–398
Gravity, *68*–458, *65*–75, *64*–531
GREAT BRITAIN, *68*–354, *67*–356, *66*–367, *65*–351, *64*–350
Africa, *66*–212; armed forces, *68*–210; automobile, *67*–230, *65*–226; Bahamas, *65*–233, *64*–239; banks, *68*–230, *66*–245; Basutoland, *65*–237, *64*–244; Botswana, *67*–248; Boy Scouts, *67*–551; bridge and tunnel, *67*–251, *65*–245; British Guiana, *66*–260, *64*–252; Canada, *64*–105; celebrations, *67*–261; civil rights, *66*–283; coins, *66*–376; communications, *67*–277; crime, *67*–294; Cyprus, *66*–299, *65*–287, *64*–292; dancing, *64*–296; Dean, Sir Patrick, *66*–301; democracy, *67*–303, *66*–314; Denmark, *64*–306; disarmament, *65*–308, *64*–309; Douglas-Home, Sir Alexander Frederick, *64*–315; economy, *68*–30; espionage, *68*–329, *67*–331, *64*–322; Europe, *68*–332, *67*–333, *66*–346, *65*–328, *64*–322; fairs

and exhibitions, 64–330; fashion, 66–348; France, 67–348, 66–356; Gambia, 66–358, 65–341, 64–340; gas, 67–456, 65–327; Germany, 68–351, 66–360; Gordon-Walker, Patrick, 65–351; Greece, 64–354; Guyana, 67–360; Heath, Edward, 66–374; India, 64–364; Indonesia, 64–366; interior design, 66–388; international relations, 65–17, 64–16; international trade, 67–377, 66–389, 65–372; Ireland, 66–393; Kenya, 65–386, 64–381; Laos, 64–384; library, 64–390; Libya, 65–395; literature, 67–396; Malaysia, 68–407, 66–426, 65–409, 64–402; Malta, 68–407, 67–410, 65–410; memorials, 66–434; Middle East, 65–415; money, 68–426, 65–419; music, 65–428; New Zealand, 67–440, 66–459, 65–440, 64–432; Nigeria, 64–432; North Atlantic Treaty Organization, 66–460, 65–442; Pacific Islands, 65–449; painting, 65–451; prison, 66–494; Rhodesia, 68–478, 67–482, 66–506, 64–471, 63–433; Saudi Arabia, 64–481; Somalia, 64–487; South Arabia, Federation of, 68–495, 67–501, 66–523, 65–503, 64–487; Spain, 68–500, 66–528, 65–512; Swaziland, 67–206, 66–532, 65–518, 64–498; theater, 66–540, 64–507; Trinidad-Tobago, 65–529, 64–510; tunnel, 64–252; United Nations, 67–535, 66–550, 64–516; West Indies, 68–537; Wilson, Harold, 65–545, 64–529; Zambia, 66–567, 65–547; Zanzibar, 64–531

Great Lakes: Canada, 65–255; fishery, 68–338, 66–350; hunting and fishing, 66–380; labor, 64–260; water, 66–173, 65–542; waterways, 65–543, 64–526; *Special Report*, 68–127

Great Society: city and regional planning, 67–273; Congress, 67–281, 66–293; democracy, 67–304; national affairs, 66–25; President of the U.S., 66–487. See also **POVERTY**

GREECE, 68–358, 67–360, 66–371, 65–354, 64–354
agriculture, *il.*, 65–123; architecture, 64–213; Boy Scouts, 64–250; Bulgaria, 65–247; city, 64–273; civil rights, 68–271; Constantine XIII, 65–284; Cyprus, 68–289, 66–298, 65–287, 64–292; democracy, 68–301; labor, 68–391

Greek Orthodox Church, 68–312, 64–316
Green, Theodore F., 67–299
Greenbelt, 67–55
Greene, Nancy, 68–490
Greene, Wallace M., 66–453, 64–426
Gregory, Dick, *il.*, 68–270
Grew, Joseph C., 66–309
Gribanovsky, Anastassy, 66–309
Griffin, Gwyn, 68–296
Griffin, Robert P., *il.*, 67–325
Grissom, Virgil Ivan: astronauts, 67–219, 65–220, 64–224; space travel, 68–497, 66–525
Grivas, George, 67–360, 66–298, 65–288
GRONOUSKI, JOHN A., JR., 66–262, 64–257, 64–355
Groppi, James, *il.*, 68–270
Gross national product, 68–313, 67–314, 66–327, 65–249, 64–255
Grosvenor, Gilbert Hovey, 67–299
Growth process, 66–252
Gruenberg, Louis, 65–296
GRUNITZKY, NICOLAS, 64–355
Togo, 66–541, 64–507
Guam, 66–464
GUATEMALA, 65–355, 64–355
democracy, 64–303; Latin America, 68–394, 67–392; Mayans, 68–160; Méndez Montenegro, Julio César, 67–418
Guenther, Minnie, 68–451
Guess, Fred, 66–471
Gueverra, Che, 68–239, 66–298
Guggenheim Memorial Foundation, John Simon, 68–343, 66–338, 65–318, 64–318
Guggenheimer, Minnie, 67–299
Guided missiles: armed forces, 68–210, 67–215, 66–223, 65–216, 64–214; engine, 64–320; Great Britain, 65–353; Middle East, 64–411; national defense, 68–434, *il.*, 67–435, 66–452, 65–434, 64–425
GUINEA, 67–360, 66–372, 65–355, 64–355
Africa, 68–194; diamonds, 64–341; Ghana, 67–354
Guinness, Rupert E. C. L., 68–296
Gunn, Ross, 67–299
Guns, 67–294, 66–380
Guthrie, Tyrone, 64–505
Guthrie, "Woody," 68–296
GUYANA, 68–359, 67–360. See also **BRITISH GUIANA**
Gymnastics: Olympic Games, 65–447; sports, 68–503, 67–511, 66–528, 65–513, 64–494

H

HAACK, ROBERT W., 68–359
Hadas, Moses, 67–299
Hageman, Richard, 67–299
HAIDER, MICHAEL LAWRENCE, 66–372
Haile Selassie I: Elizabeth II, 66–369; Ethiopia, 68–329, 66–343, 64–322
Hairdressing, 68–337, 65–333, 64–330
HAITI, 66–372, 65–355, 64–356; hurricanes, 64–313; Latin America, 68–395, 67–393
Hale, Creighton, 66–309
Hallstein, Walter, 68–330
Hamey, Ted, 67–453
Hamilton, George, 67–437
Hammarskjöld, Dag: memorials, 66–434, 65–411; United Nations, 67–121
Hammond, John Hays, Jr., 66–309
Handball, 68–502, 67–510, 66–528, 65–513, 64–494
HANDICAPPED, THE, 68–359, 67–361, 66–373, 65–356, 64–356
blindness, 68–237, 67–245, 66–253, 65–240, 64–246; child guidance, 67–265; invention, 64–371; library, 67–395; Russell, Harold, 65–490; sports, 65–513
Hansberry, Lorraine V., 66–309
Hanson, Lars, 66–309
Harbor, 68–439
Harding, Warren G., 66–271
Hargrove, Christopher P., 66–471
HARMEL, PIERRE CHARLES JOSÉ MARIE, 66–373
HARNESS RACING, 68–363, 66–373, 65–356, 64–357
horse racing, 67–364
HARPER, JOHN DICKSON, 66–373
Harrigan, William, 67–299
Harrington, "Pat," 66–309
Harris, Elmer Blaney, 67–299
HARRIS, PATRICIA ROBERTS, 66–374
Hartford Foundation, Inc., John A., 68–343, 67–344, 66–338, 65–318, 64–318
Hartline, Haldan Keffer, 68–441
Harvard University, 67–262
HASSAN II, 66–441, 64–414
Morocco, 68–427
Hatcher, Richard G., 68–322
Hayatsu, Ryoichi, 66–252
Hayford, Mrs. Delbert, 65–460
Hayward, John Davy, 66–309
Head Start, Project: education, 67–323, 66–336; Indian, American, 66–385; library, 66–411; poverty, 68–463, 67–464, 66–483
HEALTH AND DISEASE, 68–360, 67–361. See **HEALTH,** 66–374, 65–356, 64–357
awards and prizes, 65–232; Canada, 66–269; city, 65–265; Congress, 66–294; dentistry, 66–317, 64–306; educational foundations, 66–338; food, 68–339; Great Britain, 68–357; hospitals, 68–363, 65–360; Houston, 65–361; insect, 65–370; insurance, 66–269; Medicare, 68–411, 66–431; medicine, 66–432; mental health, 68–415, 67–418, 66–435, 65–412, 64–405; Musial, Stanley, 65–425; old age, 67–444; pollution, 65–466; population, 67–495; poverty, 68–463, 67–465; science clubs, 68–489, 66–519, 65–496, 64–482; Sauter, Arnold, 67–493; smoking, 64–484; social security, 65–500; state government, 66–529; United Nations, 66–551; vital statistics, 65–540. See also **MEDICINE**
Health, Education, and Welfare, U.S. Department of: child welfare, 64–269; education, 67–322, 66–338; Gardner, John W., 66–359; hospital, 66–377; old age, 66–463; social security, 64–485; social welfare, 68–493, 66–522, 64–486; U.S. government, 68–528, 67–538
HEART, *WBE*, 68–568
health, 66–374, 65–357, 64–357; medicine, 68–412, 67–414; *Special Report*, *il.*, 67–91
HEATH, EDWARD RICHARD GEORGE, 66–374; Great Britain, 68–357, 67–356, 66–368
Heating, 66–341
Hecht, Ben, 65–296
Helicopter: aviation, 66–239; Vietnam, 66–555
Helium, 67–222, 66–479, 65–465
Heller, Walter, 67–28
Hellyer, Paul, 68–247
HELMS, RICHARD M., 67–362
HELOU, CHARLES, 65–357
Hemingway, Ernest: literature, 67–398
Hench, Philip Showalter, 66–309
Hennessey, Luella, 66–471
HENRY, E. WILLIAM, 64–358
television, 66–536, 64–503
Hepburn, Samuel, 67–491
Hershey, Lewis B., 68–467, 67–437
Herter, Christian A., 67–299
Hess, Dame Myra, 66–309
Hévésy, Georg von, 67–299
Heyrovsky, Jaroslav, 68–296
Hicks, Louise Day, 66–339
Higgins, Marguerite, 67–299
Highway. See **ROADS AND HIGHWAYS**
Hiking: health, 64–357; sports, 64–494
Hinduism, 68–476
HINES, JOHN ELBRIDGE, 66–375
Hinshelwood, Sir Cyril, 68–296
"Hippie": religion, 68–476; San Francisco, 68–486
History: awards and prizes, 67–235, 66–242, 65–231, 64–238; Canadian literature, 68–255, 67–261, 65–257; Civil War Centennial, 65–269; literature, 68–400, 67–399, 66–415, 65–400, 64–393; literature for children, 68–404, 67–405, 66–418, 65–401, 64–394; Pulitzer prizes, 68–473, 67–477, 66–500, 65–478, 64–466; Russia, *Trans-Vision*, 67–181; *WBE*, 66–570
Hives, Lord Ernest Walter, 66–309
Hobart, Alice Tisdale, 68–296
Ho Chi Minh, 66–559
HOBBIES, 68–361, 67–362, 66–375, 65–357
amateur radio, 64–466; coin collecting, 64–279; model building, 65–341, 64–412; photography, 64–452; stamp collecting, 64–496. See also **GAMES, MODELS, AND TOYS; PET; SPORTS**
Hochens, Mary, 67–453
Hockenjos, William, 67–453
Hockey. See **ICE HOCKEY**
Hocking, William E., 67–299
HODGES, C. WALTER, 66–376
Hodges, Luther H., 66–376
HODGKIN, DOROTHY CROWFOOT, 65–358
personalities, 66–472
Hoffa, Jimmy: labor, 68–390, 67–390; sports, 67–510
Hoffman, Malvina, 67–299
Hoffmann, Arnold, 67–299
Hofmann, Hans, 67–299
HOFSTADTER, RICHARD, 65–359
Holcomb, Thomas, 66–309
Holidays: 1967, 67–629; 1966, 66–625; 1965, 65–630; 1964, 64–553; literature for children, 64–394
Holland, Sir Henry, 66–309
Holland. See **NETHERLANDS, THE**
Holley, Robert W., 66–251
Holliday, Judy, 66–309
Holt, Bertha M., 67–453
HOLT, HAROLD EDWARD, 67–363; Australia, 68–216, 67–224; deaths, 68–296
Holton, A. Linwood, Jr., 66–505
Holyoake, Keith J., 67–440, 64–432
Home, Earl of. See **DOUGLAS-HOME, SIR ALEXANDER FREDERICK**
***"Homo habilis"*:** anthropology, 66–219, 65–213; *Special Report*, 65–110
HONDURAS, 66–376, 65–359, 64–358; Latin America, 68–395, 67–393
Hong Kong: Asia, 68–212; Great Britain, 68–357
Hoogstraaten, Willem van, 66–309
Hoover, Herbert C.: Boys' Clubs of America, 66–258, 65–244, 64–250; deaths, 65–300
Hoover, J. Edgar, 67–551
Hopper, Edward, 68–296
Hopper, Hedda, 67–299
Hormones: biochemistry, 67–243, 66–252, 64–268; botany, 68–239; drugs, 67–142; insect, 67–374; psychology, 67–474; science, 67–33
Hornby, Lesley, 68–337
HORNIG, DONALD FREDERICK, 64–358
science, 66–518
Horowitz, Vladimir, 66–448
HORSE RACING, 68–362, 67–363, 66–377, 65–359, 64–358; harness racing, 66–373, 65–356, 64–357
HOSPITAL, 68–363, 67–365, 66–377, 65–360, 64–359; Canada, 64–263; civil rights, 67–274; Medicare, 68–411, 67–412, 66–432; mental health, 65–412, 64–405; veterans, 66–553
HOTEL, 66–378, 65–360, 64–360; Ghana, 68–352; travel, 68–520, 67–530
Houdon, Jean Antoine, 65–451
Houphouet-Boigny, Felix, 66–396, 65–376
HOUSING, 68–363, 67–365, 66–378, 65–360, 64–360
banks, 68–230; building and construction, 68–242; Chicago, 66–274; city, 68–268, 66–280; city planning, 66–281; civil liberties, 65–265; civil rights, 68–270; Congress, 66–294; Detroit, 66–317; economy, 67–319; Indian, American, 65–368; insurance, 68–372; interior design, 67–375, 65–371; Latin America, *il.*, 66–409; Los Angeles, 65–408; New York City, 65–439, 64–431; old age,

65–444, 64–436; Philadelphia, 65–463; Puerto Rico, 64–465; Singapore, *il.*, 68–212; state government, 68–503; veterans, 65–535; Washington, D.C., 67–547, 66–562
Housing and Urban Development, U.S. Department of: cabinet, 67–253; city, 66–280; housing, 67–365, 66–378; U.S. government, 67–538; Supreme Court, 68–505; Weaver, Robert C., 67–549
HOUSTON, 68–365, 67–366, 66–379, 65–361
baseball, *il.*, 66–248; health, 65–357; space travel, 65–512; theater, 68–513; zoos and aquariums, 65–548
How a Bill Becomes a Law, 65–165
Howard, Eugene, 66–309
Howard, John Tasker, 65–296
Howe, Gordie, 67–368
HOWE, HAROLD (II), 66–379
education, 66–338
Howe, Mark D. Wolfe, 68–296
Howell, F. Clark, 66–219
Huddleston, I. Forest, 66–310
Hudson River, 66–176
HUGGINS, CHARLES BRENTON, 67–366; science, 67–33
Hughes, Langston, 68–296
Hughes, Richard J., 66–339
Hull, Bobby, 67–368
Human rights: civil liberties, 65–266, 64–274; *Special Report*, 65–164; United Nations, 67–536, 66–551, 64–517. See also **Civil Rights**
HUMPHREY, HUBERT HORATIO, 68–365, 67–367, 66–379, 65–361
civil rights, 65–166; Democratic Party, *il.*, 67–305, 66–316, 65–304; 64–305; elections, 65–319; travel, 67–530. See also **Vice-President of the United States**
HUNGARY, 68–365, 67–367, 66–379, 65–362, 64–361; anthropology, 68–204; archaeology, 65–214; Kallai, Gyula, 66–403; United Nations, 64–516
HUNTING AND FISHING, 68–365, 67–367, 66–380, 65–362; anthropology, 67–213; conservation, 68–286, 67–291; wildlife, 66–564, 65–545
Hurricanes: communications, 66–287; Cuba, 64–291, 64–313; disasters, 68–309, 67–310, 66–321, 65–313; Haiti, 65–355; insurance, 66–388; Latin America, 64–386; New Orleans, 66–457; Tobago, 64–510; weather, 67–549, 66–563, 65–543, 64–527
Hussein I, 67–420, 66–402, 65–383, 64–375
Hutchins, Robert M., 66–472
Huxley, Aldous Leonard, 64–299
HUXLEY, ANDREW FIELDING, 64–361
HYDE, ROSEL HERSCHEL, 67–368
Hyderabad, Nizam of, 68–296
Hydrogen: astronomy, 67–221; biology, 67–244; chemistry, 67–264
Hydroponics, *il.*, 66–163
Hylton, Jack, 66–310
Hylton-Foster, Sir Harry, 66–310

I

IACOCCA, LEE A., 65–363
Ibis, 68–542
ICE HOCKEY, 68–366, 67–368, 66–380, 65–363, 64–361; *Special Report*, 67–160
ICE SKATING, 68–366, 67–369, 66–380, 65–363, 64–362
Olympic Games, 65–447
ICELAND, 67–370, 66–381, 65–364, 64–362
Idaho: celebrations, 66–272; courts, 64–265; Girl Scouts, 66–363
Idris I, 66–412, 65–395
IGNATIUS, PAUL ROBERT, 68–367; cabinet, 68–245; national defense, 68–437
Iguana, 68–542
Ikeda, Hayato, deaths, 66–310; Japan, 65–378, 64–374
Ikeya, K., 66–231
ILLIA, ARTURO UMBERTO, 64–362
Argentina, 67–215, 66–222, 65–215, 64–214
Illinois: boats, 65–241; Chicago, 68–260, 67–265, 66–274, 65–261, 64–268; child guidance, 66–275; disasters, *il.*, 68–308; elections, 65–321; Kerner, Otto, 68–385; Percy, Charles H., 68–449; science, 67–493; state government, 64–497
Illiteracy: social welfare, 65–502
IMMIGRATION AND EMIGRATION, 68–367, 67–370, 66–381, 65–364, 64–363
Australia, 68–218, 67–226; Canada, 64–104; Congress, 66–294; Great Britain, 66–371; Jamaica, 66–396; Switzerland, 67–516; Trinidad-Tobago, 65–529, 64–510
Immunization, 66–374
Imports. See **INTERNATIONAL TRADE**
Inauguration, 65–470
Incaparina, 66–350
Income tax: automation, 64–230; business, 64–28; politics, 68–72; state government, 66–529; taxation, 65–519, 64–500
INDIA, 68–368, 67–370, 66–383, 65–365, 64–363,
Asia, 66–225, 64–217; Ceylon, 68–258; China, 66–277, 64–271; communism, 66–290; dam, 66–300; earthquakes, 64–313; food, 68–339; Gandhi, Indira, 67–349; land reform, *il.*, 65–127; Nepal, 65–438; Pakistan, 67–449, 66–467, 65–453, 64–440; Peace Corps, 67–450; religion, 68–476; Roman Catholic, 65–488; science, 68–33; *Special Report*, 66–132; Shastri, Lal Bahadur, 65–498; United Nations, 66–550
INDIAN, AMERICAN, 68–371, 67–373, 66–385, 65–368, 64–364
archaeology, 67–213, 66–219; Canadian literature, 66–270; celebrations, 67–261; Clark, Ann Nolan, 64–278; conservation, 67–290; Mayans, 68–160
Indian Ocean, 66–347
Indianapolis, 68–429, 67–490, 66–498
INDONESIA, 68–371, 67–373, 66–386, 65–368, 64–365
Asia, 67–218, 66–226, 65–218, *il.*, 64–216; China, 66–277, 64–272; Communism, 67–278, 66–290; Malaysia, Federation of, 67–408, 65–409, 64–402; New Guinea, 68–438, 67–439, 66–457, 64–430; Peace Corps, 66–469, 64–444; Philippines, 65–463; United Nations, 67–535, 66–549, 65–534
INDUSTRY, 65–369. See **MANUFACTURING.** See also **BUSINESS; INTERNATIONAL TRADE; LABOR;** also entries on specific industries, countries, and states
Influenza, 67–361
INSECT, 68–372, 67–374, 66–387, 65–370, 64–366
Insulin, biochemistry, 67–243, 66–252; drugs, 67–142
INSURANCE, 68–372, 67–374; Belgium, 67–242, 66–388, 65–371, 64–366
health, 66–269; housing, 68–364; medicare, 67–412, 66–431, 64–263; old age, 64–435; veterans, 65–536, 64–519. See also **SOCIAL SECURITY**
Intelligence, 67–279, 66–275, 65–42
Intelligence services, 66–500. See also **Espionage**
Interest rates, 67–29, 66–330, 65–251
Interior, U.S. Department of the: American Indian, 67–373, 65–368, 64–364; national parks and monuments, 64–427; outdoor recreation, 64–437; wildlife, 64–529
INTERIOR DESIGN, 68–373, 67–375, 66–388. See **INTERIOR DECORATION,** 65–371
Internal Revenue Service, 64–500
International Bank for Reconstruction and Development, 65–512, 64–530
International Biological Program, 68–237
International Court of Justice, 67–535, 65–512
International Geophysical Year, 65–222
International Hydrological Decade, 66–184
International Labor Organization, 64–487
International law, 67–536
International Monetary Fund: banks and banking, 68–230; Costa Rica, 68–394; economy, 68–30, 66–31; international trade, 68–374, 67–377, 66–389; money, 68–426; Somalia, 68–494
INTERNATIONAL RELATIONS, 64–367
INTERNATIONAL TRADE AND FINANCE, 68–374, 67–376, 66–389, 65–371, 64–369. See also entries on specific industries and countries
INVENTION, 68–376, 67–378, 66–392, 65–372, 64–370
agriculture, 68–201, 67–208; aviation, 67–231; automobile, 68–220; boats, 66–253; building, 68–243; chemistry, 68–259; communications, 68–272; computers, 68–274; electronics, 66–341, 65–322; engine, 66–342, 64–320; food, 68–339, 65–335; forestry, 65–337; glass, 64–348; handicapped, 68–359, 65–356, 64–356; industry, 65–369; iron and steel, 65–374; manufacturing, 68–408, 67–411, 66–429; metallurgy, 68–415, 65–412; photography, 68–457, 67–458, 66–477, 64–452; physics, 65–463, 64–454; publishing, 68–472
INVESTMENTS AND SAVINGS, 65–234
housing, 65–360; insurance, 65–371, 64–367, Latin America, 65–392; Mexico, 65–413. See also **BANKS AND BANKING; ECONOMY; STOCKS AND BONDS**
Ion energy: engine, 66–342; physics, 66–479; space travel, 66–159
IRAN, 68–377, 67–378, 66–393, 65–373, 64–371
Afghanistan, 64–204; dam, 64–293; land reform, *il.*, 65–127, 65–130
IRAQ, 68–378, 67–379, 66–393, 65–373, 64–371; Iran, 67–378; Kuwait, 64–382; Middle East, 67–421, 66–439, 65–416, 64–409
IRELAND, 68–378, 67–379, 66–393, 65–373, 64–371
IRON AND STEEL, 65–373, 64–372, Australia, 68–217, 67–226; Newfoundland, 67–259. See **STEEL INDUSTRY**
Irradiation, 68–340
Irrigation: archaeology, 68–207; dam; 66–300; Israel, 66–393; Mekong River, 68–79; water, 65–543, 64–526
Isaacs, Alick, 68–296
ISRAEL, 68–378, 67–379, 66–393, 65–374, 64–373
archaeology, 68–207; Dayan, Moshe, 68–292; desalinization, *il.*, 66–189; Gambia, 64–340; international relations, 68–17, 64–17; Jordan 67–386, 66–402; kibbutz, *il.*, 65–129; Middle East, 68–418, 67–420, 66–438, 65–415; Palestine, *Trans-Vision*, 66–97; Paul VI, 65–488; 64–474; Shazar, Schneor Zalman, 64–484; Syria, 67–516, 65–519; Tunisia, 66–546; United Arab Republic, 68–522; United Nations, 68–524, 67–533, 66–550, 65–534, 64–517. See also **JEWS AND JUDAISM**
ITALY, 68–379, 67–380, 66–395, 65–374, 64–373
Austria, 67–227; Brosio, Manlio, 65–246; dam, 64–294; espionage, 68–328, 65–323; Ethiopia, 64–322; Fanfani, Amintore, 66–348; fashion, 64–332; motion pictures, 64–417; opera, 65–428; painting, 65–453; Saragat, Giuseppe, 65–495; tunnel, 66–259
Ives, Charles, 66–448
IVORY COAST, 68–195, 66–396, 65–376, 64–374; Africa, 67–203

J

JACOB, FRANÇOIS, 66–396
Jagan, Cheddi Berret: British Guiana, 66–260, 65–246
JAMAICA, 66–396, 65–376, 64–374; democracy, 68–301; Latin America, 68–395; West Indies, 68–538, 67–549
Janssen, Herbert, 66–310
JAPAN, 68–379, 67–382, 66–396, 65–377, 64–374
architecture, 65–214; Asia, 68–213; bridge and tunnel, 64–251; building and construction, *il.*, 68–243; Burma, 64–253; democracy, 68–301; disasters, *il.*, 67–311; earthquakes, 65–312; fairs, 68–335, 66–348, 66–405; fishery, 68–338, 66–350, 64–332; Formosa, 65–138; jazz, 65–430; Korea, 66–405; MacArthur, Douglas, 65–297; Malagasy Republic, 64–401; Malaysia, 68–407; motion pictures, 64–417; Olympic Games, 67–509, 65–445, 64–436; population, 64–187; Sato, Eisaku, 65–495; steel industry, 67–512; tunnels, 68–244
Jarrell, Randall, 66–310
Jarvis, DeForest Clinton, 67–299
Jeanneret, Charles. See **Le Corbusier**,
Jerusalem: archaeology, 66–219; architecture, *il.*, 66–221; Israel, 68–378; Jews, *il.* 68–381; Middle East, 68–420; Roman Catholic, 68–480; United Nations, 68–525
Jesus, Society of, 66–223
JEWS AND JUDAISM, 68–380, 67–383, 66–397, 65–379, 64–375
civil rights, 66–285, 64–274; education, 66–43; memorials, 68–414; Middle East, 68–421; religion, 68–475, 67–479; Roman Catholic, 66–510, 65–487; Saudi Arabia, 67–491. See also **ISRAEL**
JOB CORPS, 65–379
child welfare, 65–261; education, 65–39, 65–316; Indian, American, 66–385; poverty, 68–463, 67–465, 66–483; Singletary, Otis A., 65–499; VISTA, 65–540
Joffrey, Robert, 67–295, 65–291
John XXIII: awards and prizes, 64–237; civil liberties, 64–274; deaths, 64–299; ecumenical movement, *il.*, 66–84; memorials, *il.*, 68–414; Paul VI, 64–442; Protestants, 64–461; Roman Catholic, 64–472
JOHN BIRCH SOCIETY, 66–398
Johnson, Daniel, 67–260
JOHNSON, HAROLD KEITH, 65–379
national defense, *il.*, 66–453
Johnson, Hewlett, 67–299
Johnson, Lady Bird: arts, 66–57; communications, 65–271; fashion, 66–349; garden, 66–359; Johnson, Lyndon B., 68–383, 67–385, 66–402, 65–381, 64–583; personalities, 66–470, 65–458, 64–445; President of the U.S., *il.*, 68–467; roads and highways, 66–507; youth organizations, *il.*, 67–551

Johnson, Luci Baines, 67–384, fashion, 67–338; Johnson, Lyndon B., 68–382, 67–384, 66–402

Johnson, Lynda Bird, 68–382, 67–385, 65–382

JOHNSON, LYNDON B., 68–382, 66–399, 65–381; *WBE*, 64–582
Baker, Robert G., 65–233; Boys' Clubs of America, 66–258; Boy Scouts of America, 65–244; business, 64–27; cabinet, 64–257; civil liberties, 65–166, 65–268; congress, 64–286; Democratic party, 68–302, 67–304, 66–315, 65–303, 64–304; economy, *il.*, 67–314; education, 66–335; Eisenhower, Dwight D., 66–339; elections, 65–319; Fortas, Abe, 66–353; Kennedy assassination, 65–552, 64–67; Korea, 67–387; livestock show, 67–406; Mexico, *il.*, 68–416; national affairs, 65–20; Negro, 64–427; painting and sculpture, *il.*, 68–447; personalities, 66–470, 65–458, 64–445; pet, 68–454, *il.*, 67–455, 66–474, 65–462; Truman, Harry S., 67–531; United Nations, 64–515; Valenti, Jack, 67–538; vice-presidency, 64–80; Vietnam, *il.*, 67–544; youth organizations, *il.*, 67–551. See also **PRESIDENT OF THE UNITED STATES**

Johnson, Susan, 67–453

Johnson, Wilfrid E., 67–224

Johnston, Olin DeWitt, 66–310

JONAS, FRANZ, 66–402
Austria, 66–233

Jonathan, Leabua, 68–196, 67–395, 66–250

JONES, HOWARD MUMFORD, 66–402

Jones, Howard P., *il.*, 66–387

Jones, "Spike," 66–310

JORDAN, 68–384, 67–386, 66–402, 65–383, 64–375
Israel, 67–379; Middle East, 67–420, 64–410; Palestine, *Trans-Vision*, 66–97, 66–393, Paul VI, 65–488, 64–474; Saudi Arabia, 66–517; United Nations, 67–533, 66–550; Yemen, 64–530

Jordan River Project, 66–393, 65–415

Journalism. See **NEWSPAPERS AND MAGAZINES; PUBLISHING**

Judo, 68–503, 67–511

Juin, Alphonse Pierre, 68–296

Jung, Paul, 66–310

JUNIOR ACHIEVEMENT, 68–384, 67–386, 66–403, 65–383, 64–375

Jupiter, 66–230, 65–35

Jury, 67–292, 66–296

Justice, Department of: Clark, Ramsey, 68–272; courts and laws, 65–284; Katzenbach, Nicholas, 66–404; Negro, 66–455; U.S. government, 68–528

JUVENILE DELINQUENCY, 66–403, 65–383, 64–376
Boys' Clubs of America, 66–258; Camp Fire Girls, 64–257; courts, 68–287; Great Britain, 65–354; Kiwanis, 64–483; Supreme Court, 68–505

K

Kádár, János, 67–367, 66–379

Kaiser, Henry J., 68–296

KALLAI, GYULA, 66–403

Kaltenborn, H. V., 66–310

Kamuzu, Hastings, 66–426

Kane, Helen, 67–299

KAPLAN, JUSTIN, 68–385

Karami, Rachid, 66–411

Kasavubu, Joseph, 66–291, 65–275

Kashmir: Asia, 66–225; India, 65–368, 64–364; Pakistan, 67–449, 66–467, 64–440

KASTLER, ALFRED, 67–386

Kate Greenaway Medal, 66–376, 65–274, 64–400, 64–529

Katzen, Sally, 67–453

KATZENBACH, NICHOLAS deBELLEVILLE, 66–404
cabinet, 67–253, 65–251; civil liberties, 65–170; courts and laws, 67–293; crime, 66–297; U.S. government, 67–537

Keane, John J.: baseball, 65–235; sports, 67–151, 65–59

Keating, Kenneth B., 65–386

Keaton, "Buster," 67–299

Kefauver, Estes, 67–417, 64–299

Keino, Kipchoge, 68–501

Kejimkujik National Park, 66–269

Keller, Helen, 65–231

Kemeny, Zoltan, 66–310

Kennedy, Edward M., 66–297, 65–304

Kennedy, Jacqueline: assassination of JFK, 65–552, 64–60; Great Britain, 66–367; Kennedy, John F., 65–384, 64–63, 64–377; personalities, 68–451, 66–470, 65–458, 64–445; President of the United States, *il.*, 64–457; publishing, 67–477

KENNEDY, JOHN F., 66–404, 65–384, 64–376
awards, 66–242; biography, 64–392; cabinet, 64–257; civil liberties, 65–166; coins, 66–375; congress, 64–286; deaths, 64–299; Democratic party, 64–305; disarmament, 64–309; education, 64–40; Germany, 64–343; Great Britain, *il.*, 66–367; hobbies, 65–357; housing, 66–378, 64–360; immigration and emigration, 64–363; Ireland, 64–371; Johnson, Lyndon B., 64–587; Kennedy, Rose, 66–66; labor, 64–382; Latin America, 64–387; library, 65–394, 64–389; literature, 66–415; memorial, 68–414, 67–417, *il.*, 66–434; music, 64–420; national affairs, 64–20; Negro, 64–429; O'Brien, Lawrence F., 66–462; politics, 68–65. See also **Assassination of John F. Kennedy**

Kennedy, Joseph P., 66–66, 64–378

Kennedy, Margaret, 68–296

KENNEDY, ROBERT FRANCIS, 65–386
cabinet, 65–251; civil liberties, 65–172; Democratic party, 68–302, 67–305, 66–316, 65–304; Kennedy, John F., 66–404, 65–384, 64–60, 64–65, 64–378; Kennedy, Rose, 66–70; personalities, 66–470, 64–445; South Africa, 67–500

Kennedy, Rose, 66–66

Kennedy, Tom, 66–310

"Kennedy Round," 66–392, 65–328, 65–372

Kentucky: celebrations, 68–256; civil rights, 67–273; conservation, 67–292; dam, 67–251; elections, 68–322

KENYA, 68–385, 67–386, 66–404, 65–386, 64–381; Africa, 65–208, 64–206; anthropology, 68–204; Ethiopia, 65–324; Kenyatta, Jomo, 64–381; Somalia, 68–494, 67–204, 65–503, 64–487; United Nations, 64–517; wildlife, 64–150

KENYATTA, JOMO, 66–404, 64–381
Great Britain, *il.*, 65–354; Kenya, 67–386

Kenyon, Kathleen, 66–219

Keppel, Francis: American Library Association, 65–212; education, 66–44, 66–338, 64–38; Howe, Harold, 66–379

KERNER, OTTO, 68–385; civil rights, 68–269; Democratic Party, *il.*, 67–305

Kerr, Clark, 68–321, 65–41

Kerwin, Joseph P., 66–228

Kesselring, Joseph, 68–296

Key West, 68–284

Khama, Sir Seretse, 67–248

Khrushchev, Nikita S.: China, 65–262; Communism, 66–289, 65–273, 64–282; disarmament, 64–309; Germany, 64–343; Hungary, 65–362; international relations, 65–14, 64–14, *il.*, 64–368; Middle East, 65–416; Nixon, Richard M., *il.*, 64–90; Norway, 65–442; personalities, *il.*, 66–470; Poland, 65–466; Russia, 67–164, 67–486, 66–513, 65–491, 64–478; United Arab Republic, 65–530; Yugoslavia, 64–531

Kiepura, Jan, 67–300

KIESINGER, KURT GEORG, 67–387; Germany, 68–350, 67–352

Kilgore, Bernard, 68–297

Killy, Jean-Claude, 68–490

Kilpatrick, William H., 66–310

KING, MARTIN LUTHER, JR., 65–386, 64–381; civil rights, 67–275, *il.*, 66–284; Negro, 66–456, *il.*, 65–437, 64–428; Nobel prizes, *il.*, 65–441; personalities, 65–458, 64–445; Protestant, 64–461

King-Hall, Sir Stephen, 67–300

Kiplinger, Willard M., 68–297

KIRCHNER, LEON, 68–386

Kiwanis International: service clubs, 68–489, 67–496, 66–520, 65–498, 64–483

KLAUS, JOSEF, 65–387; Austria, 67–227

Klinck, Richard E., 66–472

Knappertsbusch, Hans, 66–310

Kodály, Zoltán, 68–297

Köhler, Wolfgang, 68–297

Kolehmainen, Hannes, 67–300

Kollias, Constantine, 68–358

Komarov, Vladimir M., *il.*, 68–214, 68–497

KOREA, 68–386, 67–387, 66–405, 65–387, 64–381; China, 65–264; Communism, 67–278; Japan, 66–397; United Nations, 67–535, 64–516; Vietnam, 67–542

Korolev, Sergey P., 67–300

KOSYGIN, ALEKSEI NIKOLAEVICH, 65–388; Communism, 66–289; President of the U.S., 68–464; Russia, 68–482, 67–486, 66–513, 65–491

Kotoga, Emmanuel R., 67–354

Koufax, Sandy, 66–247; baseball, 67–239, 64–242; personalities, 67–453; sports, 67–148, 66–60, 66–528, 64–56, 64–494

Kozlov, Frol R., 66–310, 64–478

Kraeling, Carl Herman, 67–300

Krag, Jens Otto, 68–304, 67–306

Kresge, Sebastian S., 67–300

Krock, Arthur, 67–474

Krupp von Bohlen und Halbach, Alfried, 68–297

Kuhn, Richard, 68–297

Kurds: Iran, 67–378; Iraq, 68–378, 67–379, 66–393, 65–373, 64–371; Middle East, 66–439, 65–417, 64–410

KUWAIT, 68–387, 67–388, 66–405, 65–388, 64–382

KY, NGUYEN CAO, 67–388
President of the U.S., 67–467; Vietnam, 68–533, 67–542, 66–556

L

LABOR, 68–387, 67–389, 66–406, 65–388, 64–382; agriculture, 68–199, 67–209; Africa, 65–208; Argentina, 68–209; automation, 66–234, 64–229; automobile, 68–219, 65–226, 64–233; aviation, 67–231; Bolivia, 66–255; Brazil, 64–251; building and construction, 68–242; business, 65–249, 64–27, 64–255; Canada, 67–259, 66–268, 65–255, 64–260; careers, 64–264; celebrations, 64–265; child welfare, 64–269; city, 67–272; civil liberties, 64–277; congress, 68–282, 67–287, 64–287; Denmark, 68–304; Detroit, 68–305; economy, 68–315, 67–320; education, 68–39, 68–320, 66–338; El Salvador, 64–320; engineering, 68–328, 66–343; France, *il.*, 67–348, 64–338; Germany, 64–345; Great Britain, 66–371; handicapped, 66–373; hospital, 67–365; India, 68–370; iron and steel, 64–372; Israel, 68–378; Italy, 68–379; Kenya, 66–404; Lewis, John L., 64–448; Liberia, 67–202; manufacturing, 68–408, 67–410; mining, 67–422; music, 68–431, 67–430, 66–447, 64–420; Negro, 65–437, 64–428; newspapers, 64–21, 64–463; Nigeria, 65–441; Norway, 67–443, 65–442; old age, 65–444; Peace Corps, 65–457; poverty, 67–464; President of the United States, 67–470, 66–490; publishing, 66–498; Quebec, 68–254; railroad, 68–517, 67–528, 65–479, 64–467; science, 65–496; ship, 65–499; *Special Report*, 68–97; sports, 67–160; steel industry, 68–504, 66–529; Supreme Court, 66–531, 64–498; Sweden, 67–515, 66–532; Switzerland, 66–532; Tanganyika, 64–499; television, 68–510; transportation, 66–545; Trinidad, 66–546; trucking, 65–529; Upper Volta, 67–538

Labouisse, Henry, 66–551

Labour Party (Britain), 68–357, 66–367, 65–351

Lacrosse, 68–503, 66–528, 65–513, 64–494

La Follette, Philip, 66–310

Lahr, Bert, 68–297

Laise, Carol C., 67–453

Lamizana, Sangoule, 67–538

Lamprey, 68–338, 65–380

Land, Edwin H., *il.*, 66–207

Langbein, Walter B., 66–191

Language: archaeology, 65–214; Beja, 67–102; Belgium, 64–244; Canada, 64–127; Chinese, *il.*, 68–206; education, 64–38; India, 66–384; Malaysia, 68–407; new words and phrases, 66–565, 65–546, 64–430; Roman Catholic, 65–489; travel, 67–530. See also **English language**

Lanning, Edward, 66–219

LAOS, 68–391, 67–391, 66–407, 65–389, 64–383; Asia, 66–226, 65–218, 64–217; Mekong River, 68–80; Thailand, 65–523, 64–504

Laser: chemistry, 67–264, 66–273; electronics, 67–329, 66–341, 65–322, 64–319; Kastler, Alfred, 67–386; medicine, 65–410; physics, 64–454

LATIN AMERICA, 68–393, 67–392, 66–409, 65–391, 64–384; disarmament, 68–307. See also by name of country

Latin American Free Trade Association, 68–393, 67–392, 66–410

Laurel, Stanley, 66–310

Lausanne, 65–331

Lausche, Frank J., 66–472

Lawson, Samuel, 66–472

Lawyer, Richard E., 66–229

Le Corbusier: architecture, 66–221, 64–213, deaths, 66–310

Lead, 67–422, 65–417

Leakey, Louis S. B.: anthropology, 68–204, 67–212, 66–219, 65–213, 64–212; *Special Report*, 65–107

Leakey, Mary, 67–213

LEARNING, *WBE*, 68–561; biochemistry, 66–251; psychology, 66–497

LEBANON, 68–396, 67–394, 66–411, 65–394, 64–388
Middle East, 67–420

Lecaunet, Jean, *66*–355
Lee Kuan Yew, *66*–426
Legal aid: civil liberties, *64*–278; courts and laws, *66*–297, *64*–288
Legislation. See **CONGRESS OF THE UNITED STATES; STATE GOVERNMENT**
Leigh, Vivien, *68*–297
Leinsdorf, Erich, *68*–451
Lemass, Séan F., *66*–393
Lenin, Nikolai, *67*–165, *il.*, *67*–263
Leonardo da Vinci, *il.*, *68*–445
Leonov, Aleksei A., *66*–525
Leonty, Metropolitan, *66*–311
Leprosy, *66*–432
Lesage, Jean, *67*–260, *66*–267, *65*–253
LESOTHO, Africa *68*–197, *67*–395. See also **BASUTOLAND**
Leukemia, *68*–412, *65*–410
Lewis, Fulton, Jr., *67*–478
Lewis, Meade Lux, *65*–298
Lewis Carroll Shelf Award, *66*–418
Liberal Party (Canada), *66*–265
LIBERIA, *66*–411, *65*–394, *64*–388; Africa, *68*–195, *67*–203
Liberte, Jean, *66*–311
LIBRARY, *68*–396, *67*–395, *66*–411, *65*–394, *64*–388
American Library Association, *68*–203, *67*–211, *66*–218, *65*–212, *64*–210; Canadian Library Association, *68*–254, *67*–260, *66*–270, *65*–257, *64*–264; education, *66*–334; Greenwood, Mrs. May M., *65*–460; Jews and Judaism, *67*–383; Kennedy Memorial Library, *65*–386, *64*–380; Library of Congress, *68*–396; memorials, *65*–412
LIBYA, *68*–397, *67*–395, *66*–412, *65*–395, *64*–390; earthquakes, *64*–312
Lie, Trygve, *67*–120
Life: astronomy, *64*–226; biochemistry, *66*–252; biology, *68*–236, *67*–244, *66*–252; geology, *66*–359; science, *64*–30
Life insurance, *68*–372, *67*–374, *66*–388, *65*–371, *64*–366
Light: astronomy, *65*–222; chemistry, *66*–274; Doppler effect, *65*–73; electronics, *65*–322; invention, *65*–372; physics, *66*–479, *64*–454
Lighting, *68*–373
Limón, José, *65*–291
Lin Piao, *68*–122, *67*–269
Lincoln, Abraham, *66*–286
Lind, Samuel C., *66*–311
LINDLEY, JONATHAN, *67*–396
LINDSAY, JOHN VLIET, *66*–412
civil rights, *65*–176; New York City, *68*–439, *67*–440, *66*–458; personalities, *68*–451; Republican party, *66*–505
Lions International, *68*–489, *67*–496, *66*–520, *65*–498
L'Isle, Viscount de, *66*–233
Liston, Sonny: *66*–256, *65*–243; boxing, *64*–248; sports, *66*–60, *65*–58, *64*–58
Literacy, *66*–552
LITERATURE, *68*–398, *67*–396, *66*–413, *65*–397, *64*–390
awards and prizes, *68*–226, *67*–235, *66*–242, *65*–231, *64*–237; book reviews, *64*–465; Canadian, *68*–255, *67*–260, *66*–270, *65*–257, *64*–264; Czechoslovakia, *68*–289; literature for children, *68*–402, *67*–401, *65*–401, *64*–394; Nobel prizes, *68*–441, *67*–441, *66*–460, *65*–441, *64*–433; publishing, *67*–476; Pulitzer prizes, *68*–473, *67*–477, *66*–500, *65*–478, *64*–466; Russia, *68*–484, *67*–486, *64*–478. See also **THEATER**
LITERATURE FOR CHILDREN, *68*–402, *67*–401, *66*–418, *65*–401, *64*–394
amateur theater, *66*–541; Canadian Library Association, *67*–260, *66*–270, *64*–264; recordings for children, *64*–468
Liu Shao-chi, *68*–123, *66*–278
Liver, *il.*, *67*–94
LIVESTOCK, *66*–214, *65*–407, *64*–400
agriculture, *68*–199, *67*–207; Australia, *67*–226; dairying, *65*–289; Great Britain, *68*–357; inventions, *68*–377; poultry, *65*–468, *64*–456
LIVESTOCK SHOW, *68*–406, *67*–406, *66*–424, *65*–408, *64*–401
LLERAS RESTREPO, CARLOS, *67*–407; Colombia, *67*–276
Lloyd George, Lady Megan, *67*–300
Lodge, Henry Cabot, Jr., Johnson, Lyndon B., *64*–73; Republican party, *64*–470; vice-presidency, *64*–89; Vietnam, *66*–559, *il.*, *65*–538, *64*–523
London: celebrations, *67*–262; music, *65*–428
Long, Edward V., *68*–283
Long, Marguerite, *67*–300
Long, Russell, B., *il.*, *66*–315
Loomis, Roger Sherman, *67*–300
López Arellano, Osvaldo, *66*–376, *64*–358
LOS ANGELES, *68*–406, *67*–407, *66*–425
Lothrop, Samuel K., *66*–311
Louisiana, *65*–290; disasters, *il.*, *66*–319; elections, *68*–323; New Orleans, *68*–438, *66*–457
Louisville, *66*–339, *65*–259
Lovell, James A., *67*–503, *65*–220, *64*–224; astronauts, *66*–228; electronics, *66*–341; space travel, *66*–525
LSD, *67*–143
Luce, Henry R., *68*–298, *il.*, *65*–476
Luckner, Count Felix von, *67*–300
Lumber industry. See **FORESTRY AND FOREST PRODUCTS**
Lurçat, Jean-Marie, *67*–300
Lutheran: celebrations, *65*–259; Protestant, *66*–497, *65*–474
Luthuli, Albert John, *68*–297
LUXEMBOURG, *68*–406, *67*–407, *66*–425, *65*–408
LWOFF, ANDRÉ, *66*–425
LYNEN, FEODOR, *65*–409

M

Maas, Melvin J.: deaths, *65*–298; handicapped, *65*–356
Macao, *68*–212
Macapagal, Diosdado, Asia, *il.*, *65*–218; Philippines, *66*–476, *65*–463, *64*–451
MacArthur, Douglas A.: deaths, *65*–297; literature, *65*–398; memorials, *66*–435, *65*–412
MacDonald, Jeannette, *66*–311
MacEachen, Allan, *67*–254
Machine. See **ENGINE AND ENERGY; MANUFACTURING**
Machine tools: automation, *66*–233; manufacturing, *68*–408, *67*–411, *66*–428
Macken, Walter, *68*–297
Macleay, Lachlan, *66*–229
MacMillan, Donald B., *65*–460
Macmillan, Lady Dorothy, *67*–300
Madagascar. See **MALAGASY REPUBLIC**
Maddy, Joseph Edgar, *67*–300
Magazines: advertising, *67*–200, *65*–206; literature for children, *65*–401; Luce, Henry, *68*–297, *68*–298; photography, *66*–478, *65*–465, *64*–393, *64*–454; poetry, *67*–400; publishing, *68*–472, *67*–476, *66*–499, *65*–477
Magnetism: engine and energy, *66*–342, *65*–323; metallurgy, *65*–412; physics, *66*–479, *65*–465
Magritte, René, *68*–297
Maher, Mrs. Gay, *66*–473
Makarios, *67*–360, *65*–287, *64*–292
MALAGASY REPUBLIC, *66*–426, *65*–409, *64*–401; Africa, *68*–197, *67*–206
MALAMUD, BERNARD, *68*–407, *64*–390
MALAWI, *67*–408, *66*–426, *65*–409; Africa, *68*–197, *65*–207; Banda, Hastings, *65*–234; civil liberties, *65*–266; United Nations, *65*–535
MALAYSIA, FEDERATION OF, *68*–407, *67*–408, *66*–426, *65*–409, *64*–402. See **MALAYA,** Asia, *66*–226, *65*–218, *64*–219; Great Britain, *66*–370, *65*–353; Indonesia, *67*–374, *66*–386, *65*–368, *64*–365; Japan, *64*–374; Philippines, *65*–463, *64*–451; United Nations, *65*–535
MALCOLM X, *66*–297, *65*–410
Maldive Islands, *66*–552
MALI: Africa, *68*–195, *67*–204, *66*–427, *65*–410, *64*–402
Malotte, Albert Hay, *65*–298
MALTA, *68*–407, *67*–410, *65*–410; United Nations, *65*–535
Man: anthropology, *68*–204, *66*–219, *65*–213, *64*–211; archaeology, *66*–219, *65*–214; population, *65*–467, *64*–187; space travel, *65*–505, *64*–45, *64*–490; *Special Report*, *65*–107; sports, *64*–495
Manchester, William, *67*–477
MANESCU, CORNELIU, *68*–408
Manitoba: Canada, *68*–253, *67*–259, *66*–268, *65*–256
Mann, Anthony, *68*–297
Mann, Edwin, *65*–460
Mann, Thomas C., *64*–460
Manry, Robert Neal: boats, *il.*, *66*–254; personalities, *66*–473
Mansfield, Jayne, *68*–297
Mansfield, Mike, *68*–303, *il.*, *66*–315, *65*–178, *il.*, *64*–304
Manship, Paul, *67*–300
Mansur, Hassan Ali: Iran, *66*–393; Middle East, *il.*, *66*–438
Mantz, Albert, *66*–311
MANUFACTURING, *68*–408, *67*–410, *66*–428
automation, *66*–233, *65*–224; metallurgy, *68*–415, *67*–418, *65*–412. See also **ECONOMY, THE; INVENTION; TECHNOLOGY;** also entries on specific industries and specific nations
Mao Tse-tung, *66*–279, *65*–273, *il.*, *64*–271, *64*–272; China, *68*–263, *67*–266; Communism, *il.*, *67*–271; international relations, *68*–16; Russia, *il.*, *67*–175; *Special Report*, *68*–111
Maoris, *67*–440
Mapmaking: moon, *68*–498; ocean, *68*–443
Marchand, Jean, *67*–254
March on Washington. See **Freedom March**
MARCOS, FERDINAND EDRALIN, *68*–457, *66*–430
Philippines, *67*–457, *66*–476
Margaret, Princess, *65*–354, *64*–354; Great Britain, *66*–371; personalities, *66*–470
Margrethe, Princess, *67*–306
Marichal, Juan, *il.*, *66*–247
Marine biology, *68*–541, *66*–347, *64*–435
Marine Corps, U.S., *66*–451, *64*–425
Bishop, Barbara J., *64*–446; national defense, *68*–437, *67*–438, *65*–432, *64*–424; Vietnam, *il.*, *66*–556
Markle Foundation, John and Mary R., *68*–343, *67*–344, *66*–338, *65*–318, *64*–318
MARKS, LEONARD HAROLD, *66*–430, *il.*, *66*–490
Marriage, *68*–536, *65*–540
Mars (planet): astronomy, *66*–229, *64*–226; science, *64*–34; space travel, *66*–152, *65*–46, *65*–510
Marshall, Edison, *68*–297
Marshall, George C., *65*–412, *64*–405
Marshall, Herbert, *67*–300
MARSHALL, THURGOOD, *68*–410
Negro, *66*–456; Supreme Court, *68*–506; U.S. government, *68*–528
Martinez Ruiz, José, *68*–297
Marx, Groucho, *66*–473
Maryland, *65*–321, *64*–496; city planning, *66*–281; courts, *66*–296; elections, *65*–321; parks, *66*–468; state government, *64*–496
Masaryk, Alice G., *67*–300
Masefield, John, *68*–297, *65*–460
Massachusetts: atomic energy, *64*–228; Boston, *67*–247, *66*–255, *65*–242, *64*–247; Brooke, Edward W., *67*–327; mental retardation, *68*–415; Negro, *65*–437; New England, *66*–195; state government, *65*–514; transit, *65*–528
Massey medal, *66*–255, *65*–337, *64*–476
Mathematics: awards and prizes, *68*–228, *67*–236, *66*–244, *65*–232; braille, *67*–245; careers, *64*–264; Japan, *68*–380; numeration systems, *WBE*, *65*–595; relativity, *65*–75; Science Clubs, *65*–496, *64*–482; set theory, *WBE*, *65*–589; weather, *68*–536
Matisse, Henri, *67*–447
Matter: biochemistry, *64*–245; nuclear physics, *64*–434; physics, *67*–460, *66*–478, *64*–454
Matthiessen, Peter, *66*–414
Maugham, William Somerset: deaths, *66*–311; literature, *66*–413
Maurer, Ion Gheorghe, *68*–482
MAURITANIA, *66*–430, *65*–410, *64*–402 Africa, *68*–195, *67*–202; Mali, *64*–402
Maurois, André, *68*–297
Maya Indians, *68*–160
Mays, Willy, *67*–240
M'ba, Leon: Africa, *68*–196, *65*–209; Gabon, *66*–357, *65*–341
McAdoo, Eleanor Wilson, *68*–259
McAuliffe, Anthony C., *65*–460
McBride, Lester, *66*–472
McCallum, David, *il.*, *66*–534
McCARTHY, EUGENE JOSEPH, *68*–411; Democratic party, *68*–303
McCollum, Elmer, *68*–299
McCone, John A., *66*–425
McCONNELL, JOHN PAUL, *66*–431, *65*–435
national defense, *il.*, *66*–453, *65*–435
McCormack, John William, Democratic party, *68*–303, *il.*, *64*–304; Johnson, Lyndon B., *il.*, *64*–586; President of the United States, *64*–458
McCullers, Carson, *68*–299, *64*–506
McCulloch, William M., *65*–166
McDivitt, James A., *65*–220, *64*–224; space travel, *66*–525
McDonald, Admiral David L., *il.*, *66*–453
McEwen, John, *68*–216
McKechnie, William, *66*–311
McKEE, WILLIAM FULTON, *66*–431
McLean, Kathryn Forbes, *67*–300
McLean, Sir Robert, *65*–298
McNamara, Patrick V., *67*–300
McNamara, Robert: armed forces, *68*–210; cabinet, *68*–245; disarmament, *68*–307; Kennedy assassination, *64*–67; mines and mining, *66*–439; national defense, *68*–434, *67*–434, *66*–451, *65*–434, *64*–424; personalities, *il.*, *65*–458; U.S. government, *68*–527; Vietnam, *il.*, *65*–538

McNaughton, Andrew G. L., *67*–300
McNeil, C. F., *66*–522
McNeill, Sir James, *65*–298
McPhee, Colin, *65*–298
McVeigh, Linda, *67*–454
Measles, *68*–360, *il.*, *67*–416, *64*–403
Measurement: chemistry, *66*–273; electronics, *66*–342
Meat: agriculture, *68*–199, *67*–207, *66*–214; food, *68*–339; labor, *68*–387. See also **LIVESTOCK**
Medicaid, *67*–414
MEDICARE, *68*–411, *67*–412, *66*–431
Canada, *64*–263; Congress, *66*–294; Evans, Patsy, *66*–471; health, *66*–374; hospital, *67*–365, *66*–377; old age, *67*–444, *66*–463, *64*–435; social security, *65*–500, *64*–485
MEDICINE, *68*–412, *67*–414, *66*–432, *65*–410, *64*–403
awards and prizes, *68*–228, *67*–235, *66*–244, *65*–232, *64*–238; Beja, *67*–110; Belgium, *67*–242, *65*–238; blindness, *65*–240; Canada, *67*–256, *64*–263; celebrations, *67*–261; computers, *il.*, *68*–274, *64*–283; Congress, *66*–294; dentistry, *68*–304, *67*–306, *66*–317, *65*–305, *64*–306; drug, *68*–311, *67*–128, *67*–313, *66*–428, *65*–314; education, *64*–316; electronics, *67*–329, *66*–342; Fischer quintuplets, *64*–447; foundations, *68*–343, *66*–338, *65*–318, *64*–318; garden and lawn, *67*–350; handicapped, *65*–356, *64*–356; heart, *WBE*, *68*–574; hospital, *68*–363, *67*–365, *66*–377, *64*–359; Jacob, François, *66*–396; Johnson, Lyndon B., *66*–400; library, *66*–411; Lwoff, André, *66*–425; Medicare, *68*–411, *67*–412, *66*–431; Nobel prizes, *68*–441, *66*–460, *64*–433; pet, *67*–454; Prieto quintuplets, *64*–449; smoking, *64*–484; science, *68*–33, *67*–33; space travel, *65*–505; *Special Report*, *67*–81. See also **DRUG; HEALTH; MENTAL HEALTH**
Mekong River, *68*–79, *66*–227, *65*–218
Melachrino, George, *66*–311
Mele, Sam, *66*–60
MEMORIALS, *68*–414, *67*–417, *66*–434, *65*–411, *64*–405
Great Britain, *il.*, *68*–356, *il.*, *66*–367; Kennedy, John F., *66*–404, *65*–384; music, *65*–427; national monuments, *66*–469, *64*–427; Saint Louis, *68*–486, *66*–516, *64*–480; veterans, *68*–529
Memory: biochemistry, *66*–251; computers, *67*–279; psychology, *66*–497, *64*–463
MÉNDEZ MONTENEGRO, JULIO CÉSAR, *67*–418; Guatemala, *67*–393
Meng, S. Y., *67*–221
Menken, Helen, *67*–301
Menninger, William C., *67*–301
MENTAL HEALTH, *68*–415, *67*–418, *66*–435, *65*–412
child guidance, *68*–261, *67*–265, *66*–275, *64*–269; child welfare, *65*–261; drugs, *67*–139; psychology, *68*–470, *66*–497; PTA, *67*–449
Mental retardation: Camp Fire Girls, *64*–257; child guidance, *68*–261, *66*–275, *64*–269; Kennedy, John F., *65*–384; mental health, *68*–415, *67*–418, *64*–405; state government, *65*–514
Menzies, Sir Robert, *67*–363
Mercury: astronomy, *66*–230; physics, *68*–458; space travel, *66*–154, *65*–465
Meredith, James Howard: civil rights, *67*–275; Negro *64*–429
Meriwether, Lee, *67*–301
MERRICK, DAVID, *68*–415
METALLURGY, *68*–415, *67*–418, *66*–435, *65*–412, *64*–406
iron and steel, *65*–373, *64*–372; manufacturing, *68*–408; physics, *66*–478
Meteorite, *67*–222, *66*–252, *65*–240, *64*–226
Meteorology. See **WEATHER**
Methodist, *65*–534, *65*–474; celebrations, *67*–261; Protestant, *67*–473, *65*–474; Taylor, Prince Albert, Jr., *66*–534
Methadone, *66*–435
Metropolitan government, *66*–379, *64*–273
Metropolitan Opera, *67*–428, *66*–448, *64*–419
MEXICO, *68*–416, *67*–419, *66*–436, *65*–413, *64*–406
archaeology, *64*–213; city planning, *64*–274; dam, *66*–300; Díaz Ordaz, Gustavo, *65*–306; Kiwanis International, *68*–489; Latin America, *67*–392; Olympic Games, *66*–528; *64*–436; President of the U.S., *67*–470; sports, *68*–501, *67*–509
Meyer, Albert Cardinal, *66*–311
Miami, *68*–222
Micara, Clemente Cardinal, *66*–311
Michel, F. Curtis, *66*–228
MICHENER, DANIEL ROLAND, *68*–417
Michener, James A., *66*–414
Michenfelder, Sister Marita, *67*–454
Michigan: city, *68*–266; conservation, *67*–290; Detroit, *68*–305, *66*–317, *65*–306, *64*–306; education, *66*–338; Ford, Gerald R., *66*–352; Romney, George W., *68*–482, *65*–489
Michigan, Lake, *68*–365
Micombero, Michel, *67*–252
Micronesia, *68*–444, *67*–446, *66*–464
MIDDLE EAST, *68*–418, *67*–420, *66*–437, *65*–415, *64*–408; communism, *68*–274; international relations, *68*–17; Jews, *68*–380; petroleum, *68*–455; President of the U.S., *68*–466; religion, *68*–475; United Nations, *68*–524. See also under names of countries
Mies van der Rohe, Ludwig, *67*–214
Mikoyan, Anastas I., *66*–514, *65*–492
MILLER, PERRY, *67*–421
Miller, Stanley L., *66*–229, *64*–32
Miller, Warren, *67*–301
MILLER, WILLIAM EDWARD, *65*–417
elections, *65*–320; Republican party, *65*–484
Mills, Billy: Olympic Games, *65*–446; sports, *65*–67
Minerals, *67*–292, *65*–343
MINES AND MINING, *67*–422, *66*–439, *65*–417
Australia, *68*–217, *67*–225; Bolivia, *68*–239, *66*–255, *64*–247; Canada, *68*–253; chemical industry, *65*–260; coal, *65*–270, *64*–279; conservation, *68*–286, *67*–292; diamonds, *64*–341; disasters, *68*–310, *66*–321, *65*–313, *64*–313; France, *64*–338; Gabon, *66*–357, *64*–340; iron and steel, *65*–374; Lewis, John L., *64*–448; metals, *64*–405; Morocco, *67*–423; Newfoundland, *67*–259; Ontario, *65*–257; South Africa, *66*–523; Supreme Court, *66*–531; uranium, *67*–223. See also **PETROLEUM AND GAS**
Miniaturization, *67*–329, *66*–341
Minnesota: governors, *64*–350; iron and steel, *65*–374; McCarthy, Eugene, *68*–411; mines and mining, *64*–412
Minow, Newton N.: Henry, E. William, *64*–358; radio, *64*–466; television, *64*–503
Minting. See **Coins**
Minton, Sherman, *66*–311
Missile. See **Guided Missile**
Mississippi: celebrations, *68*–256; civil liberties, *65*–267; courts and laws, *68*–287; elections, *68*–323, *64*–305, *64*–469; Evers, Medgar W., *64*–326; Negro, *65*–437
Missouri, *67*–491, *65*–494, *64*–480
roads and highways, *66*–508; Saint Louis, *66*–516
Mitchell, David F., *66*–317
Mitchell, James P., *65*–298
Mitterand, François, *66*–355
Mobutu, Joseph, *68*–275, *67*–280, *66*–291
MODEL BUILDING, *64*–412. See also **GAMES, MODELS, AND TOYS**
Mohammed Riza Pahlevi, *68*–377
Mohole project, *67*–352, *66*–359, *65*–343
MONACO, *68*–426, *67*–422, *66*–440, *64*–412
Monckton, Walter, *66*–311
MONEY, *68*–426, *67*–423, *66*–440, *65*–419, *64*–412
Argentina, *68*–209; Australia, *67*–225, *66*–233; Bahamas, *67*–549; banks and banking, *68*–229, *67*–237, *66*–330, *65*–234, *64*–239; business, *65*–27; Brazil, *68*–242, *64*–251; coin collecting, *68*–361, *65*–357, *64*–279; Colombia, *68*–272; Congress, *66*–295, *64*–287; Costa Rica, *66*–296; economy, *68*–27, *68*–315, *67*–29, *67*–314, *66*–31, *66*–330; Europe, *68*–332, *65*–326; Finland, *68*–338, *64*–332; Germany, *68*–350; Great Britain, *68*–354, *67*–356, *66*–367, *65*–352; Haiti, *66*–372; hobbies, *67*–362, *66*–375; India, *67*–371, *64*–363; insurance, *67*–375; international trade, *68*–374, *67*–376, *66*–389; Ireland, *67*–379; Latin America, *68*–394; Mexico, *66*–436, *64*–406; New Zealand, *65*–440; Nicaragua, *68*–440, *65*–440; Peru, *68*–454; Switzerland, *67*–516; Uruguay, *68*–528; *66*–552, *64*–519; Vietnam, *66*–558
MONGOLIAN PEOPLE'S REPUBLIC, *68*–427. See also **OUTER MONGOLIA**
MONOD, JACQUES, *66*–441
Montana, *67*–212, *66*–300, *65*–258
Montreal: architecture, *67*–214; Canada, *68*–246; city planning, *67*–273; fairs and exhibitions, *68*–334, *67*–335, *66*–348, *65*–331, *64*–330; Quebec, *67*–260; transit, *67*–530
Mont Saint Michel, *66*–271
MONTRESOR, BENI, *66*–441
Moon: astronauts, *65*–220; astronomy, *68*–216, *67*–220, *66*–230, *65*–221; geology, *68*–350; photography, *65*–463; science, *65*–35; space exploration, *68*–497, *67*–45, *67*–505, *66*–151, *66*–526, *65*–44, *65*–508, *64*–44, *64*–488; *Special Report*, *64*–168
Moore, Henry, *il.*, *68*–432
Moore, John, *66*–349
Morgenthau, Henry, Jr., *68*–299
Moro, Aldo, *67*–380, *66*–395, *65*–374, *64*–373
MOROCCO, *68*–427, *67*–423, *66*–441, *65*–419, *64*–414
Algeria, *64*–209; France, *67*–346; Mauritania, *65*–410, *64*–402
Morrison, Charles C., *67*–301
Morrissey, Francis X., *66*–297
Morrisson, Herbert Stanley, *66*–311
Moslem: Palestine, *Trans-Vision*, *66*–97; religion, *68*–475; Somalia, *66*–523; United Arab Republic, *66*–548
Mosquito: biology, *67*–244; health, *67*–361; Houston, *66*–361; insect, *65*–370
MOTION PICTURES, *68*–427, *67*–425, *66*–443, *65*–421
American Library Association, *66*–218; arts, *68*–51, *66*–56; Canada, *68*–251; recordings, *67*–478, *64*–467; recordings for children, *65*–481; television, *68*–510, *67*–519; Temple, Shirley, *64*–449; Valenti, Jack, *67*–538
MOTLEY, CONSTANCE BAKER, *67*–426
Motley, Willard, *66*–311
Motorboat racing: boats and boating, *68*–238, *67*–245, *66*–254, *65*–241, *64*–247
Mott, Frank Luther, *65*–298
Mountain climbing: exploration, *65*–329, *64*–327; Kennedy, Robert F., *66*–404
Moyers, Bill D., *il.*, *66*–488; *64*–444
MOZAMBIQUE, *66*–445, *65*–424, *64*–417
Africa, *68*–197, *67*–206, *65*–208; Portugal, *68*–460, *67*–462, *65*–467, *64*–455
Mueller, Paul, *66*–311
Muller, Hermann Joseph, *68*–299
MULLIKEN, ROBERT SANDERSON, *67*–427
Mumps, *67*–416
Muni, Paul, *68*–299
Munich, *67*–509
Munsinger, Gerda: Canada, *67*–254; espionage, *67*–331
MURPHY, CHARLES SPRINGS, *66*–445
Murray, Bruce, *68*–449
Murray, Mae, *66*–311
Murrow, Edward R.: awards and prizes, *65*–231; deaths, *66*–311; memorials, *66*–434; personalities, *il.*, *64*–446; television, *66*–537
MUSEUMS, *68*–429, *67*–427, *66*–445, *65*–424, *64*–417
Detroit, *67*–306; exploration, *65*–329; Jews, *68*–381; memorials, *65*–412; painting and sculpture, *68*–445, *67*–447, *66*–464, *65*–451, *64*–439
MUSIAL, STANLEY FRANK, *65*–425; baseball, *64*–242; sports, *68*–58
MUSIC, *68*–431, *67*–428, *66*–447, *65*–427, *64*–418; awards and prizes, *67*–235, *66*–242, *65*–231, *64*–237; Barber, Samuel, *64*–240; botany, *64*–247; celebrations, *64*–265; *Focus*, *65*–54; Kirchner, Leon, *68*–386; literature for children, *67*–402, *64*–398; Price, Leontyne, *66*–494; Pulitzer prizes, *68*–473, *67*–477, *64*–466; recordings, *68*–474, *67*–478, *66*–501, *65*–480, *64*–467; recordings for children, *66*–501, *64*–468
MUSIC, JAZZ, *66*–449, *65*–430, *64*–421
MUSIC, POPULAR, *68*–433, *67*–432, *66*–449, *65*–429, *64*–421; *Special Report*, *68*–144
Musicals: arts, *64*–51; theater, *67*–522; motion pictures, *65*–423; recordings, *68*–474, *67*–478; theater, *68*–513, *65*–526; theater, amateur, *64*–507
Mutual funds: banks, *66*–245
Muzzey, David Saville, *66*–311

N

Nabokov, Vladimir, *68*–399, *65*–401
Nabrit, Samuel N., *67*–224
Nace, Raymond L., *66*–191
Nader, Ralph, *il.*, *67*–229
Narcotics: courts and laws, *68*–287; crime, *65*–285; drug addiction, *67*–418; Jamaica, *64*–374; mental health, *66*–435
Nasser, Gamal Abdel: Iraq, *64*–371; Middle East, *68*–418, *66*–438, *64*–409; United Arab Republic, *68*–522, *67*–532, *66*–547, *65*–530, *64*–512; Yemen, *65*–546
Natcher, William H., *65*–460
NATO. See **NORTH ATLANTIC TREATY ORGANIZATION**
National Aeronautics and Space Administration: astronauts, *67*–219, *66*–228, *65*–220, *64*–222; building and construction, *67*–251; electronics, *64*–319; Houston, *66*–519, *65*–361; science clubs, *68*–489, *67*–495, *65*–496, *64*–482. See also **SPACE EXPLORATION**
National Association for the Advancement of Colored People: Evers, Medgar W., *64*–326; Negro, *64*–427; Supreme Court, *65*–516; Wilkins, Roy, *65*–545

National Collegiate Athletic Association: sports, 65–513, 64–494; track and field, 67–526, 66–542, 65–528, 64–509
National Council of Churches, 66–494
National Dance Foundation, 67–296
NATIONAL DEFENSE, 68–434, 67–434, 66–451, 65–431, 64–422
Ailes, Stephen, 65–211; armed forces, 68–210, 67–215, 65–215, 64–214; atomic energy, 66–232; Bahamas, 64–239; Brown, Harold, 66–261; cabinet, 68–245; Canada, 67–257, 64–259; civil defense, 66–281, 65–266, 64–274; Congress, 68–278, 66–294, 64–287; disarmament, 68–307, 65–307, 64–308; economy, 66–323; espionage, 67–331; Europe, 64–325; "hot line," 64–311; insurance, 66–388; Johnson, Harold Keith, 65–379; Libya, 65–395; MacArthur, Douglas, 65–297; manufacturing, 67–410, 66–429; national affairs, 68–22; North Atlantic Treaty Organization, 68–442, 65–442; Resor, Stanley, 66–505; science and research, 64–481; space exploration, 67–508, 66–50, 66–527, 65–46; transportation, 67–529; U.S. government, 68–528; veterans, 64–519; Vietnam, 68–530, 67–540, 66–555, 64–538, 65–522
National Education Association: education, 68–39, 68–320, 66–338, 64–41; labor, 68–387
National Foundation for the Arts and Humanities: arts, 66–56; motion pictures, 66–443; music, 66–447
NATIONAL PARKS AND MONUMENTS, 64–427. See also **PARKS**
Canada, 66–269; Congress, 67–286; conservation, 68–283, 67–290; forest products, 68–342; museums, 66–445; Serengeti, 64–150
National Science Foundation: exploration, 66–347; geology, 66–359; Haworth, Leland J., 64–357; science and research, 68–488, 67–493, 64–481
National Teacher Corps: Congress, 67–281; education, 67–322, 66–336
Natural resources, 67–292, 66–164
Navy, U.S.: disasters, *il.*, 68–310; espionage, 64–322; exploration, 66–347; Ignatius, Paul, 68–367; national defense, 68–437, 67–436, 66–451, 65–431, 64–424; Nitze, Paul H., 64–433; Philippines, 68–457; South Africa, 68–494; Vietnam, 66–555, 65–539
Ne Win, 67–252, 65–247, 64–253
NEGRO, 66–455, 65–437, 64–427; advertising, 67–201; arts, 64–52; awards, 67–235; Brooke, Edward, 67–327; Carmichael, Stokely, 68–256; census, 68–258; city, 68–266, 67–272; civil rights, 68–269, 67–273, 66–283, 65–165, 65–266, 64–276, 64–303; Congress, 66–294; democracy, 68–301, 66–314; Democratic party, 64–304; education, 68–41; elections, 68–322, 67–326, 66–339; Evers, Medgar W., 64–326; food, 66–350; foundations, 66–338; Future Farmers of America, 66–357; Great Britain, 66–371; Harris, Patricia, 66–374; housing, 64–360; King, Martin Luther, Jr., 65–386, 64–381; labor, 64–383; literature, 64–392; Los Angeles, 66–425; Malcolm X, 65–410; Marshall, Thurgood, 68–410; Motley, Constance, 67–426; music, popular, 68–158, 68–433, 64–421; national affairs, 68–23, 67–22, 64–21; New York City, 65–440; poetry, 65–401; post office, 67–463; poverty, 68–462; Price, Hollis F., 66–493; Price, Leontyne, 66–494; Protestant, 65–474, 64–461; Rowan, Carl T., 65–490; Supreme Court, 65–516, 64–498; Taylor, Prince, 66–534; Tolbert, William, 66–541; track and field, 68–514; veterans, 68–529; Weaver, Robert C., 67–549; Wilkins, Roy, 65–545
Nehru, Jawaharlal: India, 65–366
Neighborhood Youth Corps, 66–483, 65–502
Nelson, Nels, 65–298
NEPAL, 68–438, 67–439, 66–457, 65–438, 64–429
Nervi, Pier Luigi: architecture, 65–215; awards, 65–232
Nervous system, *il.*, 67–88, 67–243
NETHERLANDS, THE, 68–438, 67–439, 66–457, 65–439, 64–430
Belgium, 64–244; celebrations, 64–265; Europe, *il.*, 67–334, 66–347; gas, 68–455, 67–456, 65–327
Neubeck, F. Gregory, 66–229
Nevada: celebrations, 65–258; census, 65–259, 64–266; state government, 64–497
NEVILLE, EMILY CHENEY, 65–439
New Brunswick: bridge, 66–259; Canada, 68–253, 67–259, 66–268, 65–256, 64–262
New England: *Special Report*, 66–195
New Farmers of America, 66–357
NEW GUINEA, PAPUA AND, 68–438, 67–439, 66–457, 65–439, 64–430
Indonesia, 64–365; United Nations, 64–517
New Hampshire, 66–196
New Haven, 68–269, 67–263
New Jersey: celebrations, 65–258; Democratic party, 66–316, 64–305; elections, 68–322, 66–339, 64–469; parks, 66–468; Republican party, 66–504; transportation, 66–544
New Mexico, 67–213, 65–321, 64–497
NEW ORLEANS, 68–438, 67–439, 66–457, 64–430
New York (state): bridge, 64–251; census, 64–266; courts and laws, 68–287; dancing, 65–291; Democratic party, 66–316; education, 68–321; elections, 68–323, 66–339, 65–321; Kennedy, Robert F., 65–386; labor, 68–391; prison, 66–494; Protestant, 68–469; Republican party, 67–481; Rockefeller, Nelson A., 68–479
NEW YORK CITY, 68–439, 67–440, 66–458, 65–439
advertising, *il.*, 67–201; airports, 65–229; amateur theater, 66–541; architecture, 66–222, 65–214, 64–213; arts, 64–50; bridge, 65–245, 64–251; building and construction, 68–243, 67–250, 66–261, 65–246, 64–253; celebrations, 65–258; child welfare, 68–262; civil liberties, 65–269; crime, 65–285, 64–289; dancing, 68–290, 66–300, 65–290, 64–296; Democratic party, 66–316, 65–303; education, 68–41, 68–320, 67–322, 66–336, 65–317; elections, 66–339; electric power, 67–328, 66–339; fairs and exhibitions, 66–348, 65–331, 64–329; fluoridation, 65–306; hospital, 67–365; hotel, 66–378, 65–360, 64–360; housing, *il.*, 68–364; Jews, 66–397; Lindsay, John V., 66–412; memorials, 66–434, 64–405; motion pictures, 64–416; museums, 67–427, 65–424; music, 68–431, 67–428, 66–447, 65–427, 64–419; national monuments, 66–469; newspapers, 64–21, 64–463; painting and sculpture, 65–452; poverty, 66–486; publishing, 68–471, 67–474, 66–498; Republican party, 66–505; Roman Catholic, 66–511; sports, 67–57; taxation, 67–517; theater, 68–512, 67–523, 66–539, 65–525, 64–506; transit, 68–519, 67–530, 66–543; zoos, 67–553, 66–568, 65–548, 64–532
NEW ZEALAND, 68–439, 67–440, 66–459, 65–440
Newark: celebrations, 67–262; city, 68–266; civil rights, 68–269
Newbery medal, 68–405, 66–565, 65–407, 64–400
Newfoundland: Canada, 68–253, 67–259, 66–269
Newspapers and magazines: advertising, 67–200, 65–206; awards and prizes, 66–243, 64–238; Beaverbrook, Lord, 65–294; civil rights, 66–283; courts and laws, 67–292; Detroit, 65–306; Johnson, Lyndon B., 65–381; photography, 68–458, 67–458, 66–478, 65–464, 64–452; publishing, 68–471, 67–474, 66–498, 65–476, 64–463; Pulitzer prizes, 68–472, 67–477, 66–499, 65–478, 64–465; Reedy, George E., 65–481; strikes, 64–21, 64–382; Supreme Court, 67–514
Ngendandumwe, Pierre: Africa, 66–211; Burundi, 66–262
NICARAGUA, 68–440, 66–459, 65–440, 64–432
Latin America, 67–393
Nichols, Anne, 67–301
Nichols, "Red," 66–311
Nicklaus, Jack, 68–352, 67–355, 66–364, 65–348
NIGER, 66–459, 65–440, 64–432
Africa, 68–196, 67–204; Dahomey, 65–289
NIGERIA, 68–440, 67–441, 66–459, 65–441, 64–432
Nimitz, Chester W., 67–301
Nirenberg, Marshall W., 65–239
Nitrogen: biology, 66–252; botany, 66–255; chemistry, 68–259; gas, 64–341
NITZE, PAUL H., 64–433; national defense, 68–437
Nixon, Pat, 65–460
Nixon, Richard Milhous: personalities, 68–451; Republican party, 68–476, 67–480, 66–503, 64–470; vice-presidency, 64–80
Nkrumah, Kwame: Ghana, 67–354, 66–363, 65–347; Guinea, 67–360; international relations, 67–18
NOBEL PRIZES, 68–441, 67–441, 66–460, 65–441
Norblad, Walter, 65–299
Norden, Carl, 66–311
Norodom Sihanouk, 65–251
Norris, Kathleen, 67–301
Norrish, Ronald G. W., 68–441
North America: *Trans-Vision*, 65–81
NORTH ATLANTIC TREATY ORGANIZATION, 68–442, 67–441, 66–460, 65–442, 64–433
armed forces, 67–216, 66–223, 65–216, 64–215; Belgium, 67–243; Brosio, Manlio, 65–246; Cyprus, 65–288; disarmament, 66–318, 65–309, 64–310; espionage, 68–328; Europe, 68–333, 67–335, 66–345, 65–324, 64–322; France, 68–344, 67–344, 66–355, 65–339, 64–337; international relations, 67–15, 65–16; Luxembourg, 67–407; Portugal, 64–455; Republican party, 66–504
North Sea: Europe, 65–327; Netherlands, 65–439
Northern Rhodesia. See **ZAMBIA**
Northwest Territories, 66–268, 65–256, 64–262
NORWAY, 68–443, 67–443, 66–461, 65–442, 64–434
Nova Scotia: Canada, 68–253, 67–259, 66–269, 65–256, 64–262
Novotny, Antonin, 66–299, 65–289
NUCLEAR PHYSICS, 66–461, 65–442, 64–434
chemistry, 66–273; computers, 65–274; Jensen, J. Hans D., 64–375; metallurgy, 65–412; science, 65–34; space travel, 65–508; Wigner, Eugene Paul, 64–528. See also **ATOMIC ENERGY; PHYSICS**
Nugent, Patrick J., 68–383, 67–384
Nureyev, Rudolf, *il.*, 68–291
Nursing home: hospital, 67–365, 66–377; Medicare, 66–432
Nutrition: food, 67–339; mental health, 67–418
Nyasaland. See **MALAWI; RHODESIA AND NYASALAND, FEDERATION OF**
Nyerere, Julius, 68–508, 65–519

O

OAS. See **Organization of American States**
Oats: agriculture, 68–202, 67–207; food, 68–339
Obando Candia, Alfred, 66–255, 65–242
Obesity: health, 67–361; psychology, 67–474
Obituaries. See **DEATHS OF NOTABLE PERSONS**
O'BRIEN, LAWRENCE FRANCIS, 66–462
civil rights, 65–174; Democratic party, 65–304; post office, 68–461, 66–481; U.S. government, 68–528
Observatory: astronomy, 67–222, 65–223; Icarus, *il.*, 66–157; *Special Report*, 65–63
Obsidian, 68–206
O'Casey, Sean, 65–299
OCEAN, 68–443, 67–443, 66–462, 65–443, 64–435
awards and prizes, 66–244, 64–239; exploration, 66–347, 65–329, 64–327; fishery, 67–339; geology, 68–349, 67–351, 64–341; petroleum, 67–456; pollution, 65–467; *Special Report*, 67–63; United Nations, 67–536
O'Connor, Frank D., 67–301, 66–316
Odinga, Oginga, 67–386
O'Donnell, P. Kenneth, 65–304
OECD. See **Organization for Economic Cooperation and Development**
Office of Economic Opportunity, 67–464
O'Hara, John, 66–414, 64–390
Oil. See **PETROLEUM**
O'Kelly, Seán Thomas, 67–301
Okinawa, 68–380
Oklahoma, 67–213, 66–300
OLD AGE, 68–444, 67–444, 66–463, 65–444, 64–435
Canada, 67–256, 66–266; Congress, 66–294; food, 66–350; Medicare, 68–411, 67–412, 66–431; personalities, 65–458; poverty, 67–464, 66–485; social security, 68–491, 67–499, 66–522, 64–485; social welfare, 66–522
Olduvai Gorge, 67–212, 65–110
Olsen, John S. "Ole," 64–300
OLYMPIC GAMES, 65–445, 64–436
architecture, 65–214; Detroit, 64–306; Japan, 65–377; Mexico, 68–417, 66–528; sports, 68–501; track and field, 68–514. See also **SPORTS**
Olympio, Sylvanus, 64–507
Omega-minus, 65–442
Onassis, Aristotle, 68–426, 67–422, 66–440
O'Neil, Nance, 66–311
O'Neill, Eugene, 68–513
O'Neill, Terence M., 66–393
Ongania, Juan Carlos, 67–215
Onions, Charles Talbut, 66–312
Ontario: Canada, 68–254, 67–260, 66–269, 65–256, 64–262; mines and mining, 65–417
Op art: arts, 66–54; fashion, 66–348; interior design, 66–389

Opera: Australia, *il.*, *67*–226; building and construction, *67*–250; dancing, *66*–301; music, *68*–431, *67*–428, *66*–448, *65*–428, *64*–419
OPPENHEIMER, J. ROBERT, *64*–436
atomic energy, *64*–228; deaths, *68*–299
Oregon, *67*–251, *65*–514, *64*–293
Organization of African Unity: Africa, *65*–208, *64*–206; Algeria, *64*–210; Angola, *64*–211; Ethiopia, *64*–322; South Africa, *64*–487
Organization of American States: Cuba, *68*–289, *65*–286; Dominican Republic, *67*–312, *66*–324; Latin America, *68*–393, *67*–392, *66*–409, *65*–391, *64*–386
Organizations: agriculture, *68*–200; American Bar Association, *68*–287; awards and prizes, *68*–226, *65*–231, *64*–237; celebrations, *67*–261; education, *66*–43; engineering, *67*–330; garden and lawn, *67*–350; library, *68*–203, *68*–254, *67*–211, *67*–260, *66*–218, *66*–411, *65*–212, *65*–257; Negro, *64*–428; science, *66*–35; service clubs, *68*–489, *67*–496, *66*–520, *65*–498, *64*–483; social welfare, *65*–498; veterans, *68*–529, *67*–540, *66*–553, *65*–535. See also **YOUTH ORGANIZATIONS;** also names of specific organizations
Oroville Dam, *68*–244
Orr, Carey Cassius, *68*–299
Orr, Douglas William, *67*–301
Orr, Louis, *67*–301
Osborn, Albert W. T., *68*–299
OSWALD, LEE HARVEY, *64*–436
civil liberties, *64*–278; Garrison, Jim C., *68*–348; Kennedy assassination, *64*–63; Ruby, Jack, *64*–476; Warren Report, *65*–555
Otto of Hapsburg, Archduke, *67*–227
OUTDOOR RECREATION, *67*–290, *66*–463, *65*–449, *64*–437
Congress, *65*–280; conservation, *68*–285; national parks and monuments, *64*–427; hunting and fishing, *65*–362; parks, *66*–468, *65*–455; *Special Report*, *65*–189. See also **SPORTS**
OUTER MONGOLIA, *67*–445, *66*–464, *65*–449
Mongolian People's Republic, *68*–427
Outram, Harry, *66*–473
Owen, Catherine Dale, *66*–312

P

PAASIO, RAFAEL, *67*–446
PACIFIC ISLANDS, *68*–444, *67*–446, *66*–464, *65*–449
New Guinea, *67*–439, *66*–457, *65*–439; Western Samoa, *65*–544
PACKAGING, *65*–449, *64*–437
Congress, *67*–285; food, *68*–339, *67*–340, *64*–333
PAINTING AND SCULPTURE, *68*–445, *67*–446, *66*–464, *65*–451, *64*–438
agriculture, *il.*, *67*–209; anatomy, *67*–81; Archipenko, Alexander, *65*–293; awards and prizes, *66*–242, *64*–237; Canadian literature, *67*–260; celebrations, *64*–265; Chicago, *67*–265; crime, *68*–288; fashion, *66*–348; *Focus*, *66*–53, *65*–53; interior decoration, *64*–367; library, *64*–389; literature for children, *64*–398; memorials, *68*–414, *67*–417, *66*–434, *65*–411; museums, *68*–429, *66*–445, *65*–451, *64*–417; Pietà, *il.*, *65*–331; Wyeth, Andrew, *68*–538
PAKISTAN, *68*–447, *67*–449, *66*–467, *65*–453, *64*–440
Afghanistan, *64*–204; Asia, *66*–225; Bashir Ahmed, *64*–446; Communism, *66*–290; earthquakes, *64*–313; India, *66*–383, *64*–364; Kashmir, *65*–368; United Nations, *66*–550
Palestine: archaeology, *66*–219; ecumenical movement, *66*–96; Middle East, *68*–421; *Trans-Vision*, *66*–97. See also **ISRAEL; JORDAN**
Palmer, Arnold, *68*–352, *67*–355, *66*–364, *65*–348
Palmeri, Robert J., *66*–473
Palombo, David, *67*–301
PANAMA, *68*–448, *67*–449, *66*–468, *65*–453, *64*–440
Pan American Games, *68*–448, *64*–509
Papadopoulos, George, *68*–358
Papandreou, George, *66*–371, *65*–354, *64*–354
Paper: British Columbia, *66*–268; forestry, *67*–342, *66*–352; interior design, *68*–373; manufacturing, *66*–429; United Arab Republic, *66*–548
Papua. See **NEW GUINEA**
PARAGUAY, *66*–468, *65*–455, *64*–441; Latin America, *68*–396, *67*–394; bridge and tunnel, *66*–259
PARENTS AND TEACHERS, NATIONAL CONGRESS OF, *68*–449, *67*–449, *66*–468, *65*–455
Park, Chung Hee, *68*–386, *66*–405, *65*–387, *64*–381
Parker, Dorothy, *68*–299
PARKS, *66*–468, *65*–455
Congress, *65*–280; conservation, *68*–285, *67*–290; St. Louis, *64*–480; zoos and aquariums, *68*–542, *67*–553, *66*–568, *65*–548. See also **NATIONAL PARKS AND MONUMENTS**
Parochial education, *67*–480, *66*–335
Parrish, Maxfield, *67*–301
Particle: biology, *64*–245; nuclear physics, *65*–442, *64*–434; physics, *68*–458, *67*–460
Passport, *68*–528
Pate, Maurice, *66*–312
Pathet Lao, *67*–391, *66*–407, *64*–383
Patri, Angelo, *66*–312
Patterson, Arthur L., *67*–301
Patterson, Elizabeth, *67*–301
Patterson, Floyd: boxing, *66*–61, *66*–256, *64*–248
PAUL VI, *64*–442
celebrations, *68*–257, *66*–271; Eastern Orthodox, *68*–312; ecumenical movement, *il.*, *66*–83; New York City, *66*–458; personalities, *66*–470; Poland, *66*–479; Roman Catholic, *68*–480, *67*–483, *66*–508, *65*–487, *64*–472; United Nations, *66*–549; Vietnam, *66*–556
PAZHWAK, ABDUL RAHMAN, *67*–450; *il.*, *67*–534; Afghanistan, *68*–193
Peabody, Ernest H., *66*–312
PEACE CORPS, *68*–449, *67*–450, *66*–457, *65*–469
blindness, *64*–246; Vaughn, Jack Hood, *67*–539; Somalia, *68*–494; *Special Report*, *65*–149; VISTA, *65*–540
Peale, John S., *66*–473
Pearce, Alice, *67*–301
Pearlfish, *67*–244
Pearson, Lester B.: Canada, *68*–246, *67*–254, *66*–265, *65*–253, *64*–126, *64*–259; fairs and exhibitions, *68*–335; international trade, *il.*, *66*–389
Peck, Paul, *67*–81
Pelikan, Jaroslav, *66*–82
Pendleton, "Nat," *68*–299
Peng Chen, *67*–271
Penicillin, *67*–134
Penkovskiy, Oleg V., *66*–343, *64*–321
Pennel, John: sports, *64*–494; track and field, *64*–508
Pennsylvania: harness racing, *64*–357; parks, *66*–468; pet, *66*–474; Philadelphia, *68*–455, *65*–463, *64*–451; Scranton, William W., *65*–497
Pensions: Canada, *66*–266; labor, *65*–389; veterans, *67*–540, *65*–536, *64*–519. See also **SOCIAL SECURITY**
Pentathlon, *68*–503, *67*–511
Peralta Azurdia, Enrique, *66*–372, *64*–445
PERCY, CHARLES HARTING, *68*–449
elections, *il.*, *67*–325, *65*–321; personalities, *68*–452; Republican party, *68*–476, *67*–480
Periodontal diseases, *66*–317
Perkins, Frances, *66*–312
Perón, Juan D., *66*–222, *65*–215, *64*–214
PERSONALITIES, *68*–450, *67*–451, *66*–470, *65*–458. See also **Biography**
PERU, *68*–454, *66*–474, *65*–462, *64*–449; archaeology, *66*–219, Belaúnde Terry, Fernando, *64*–244; disasters, *65*–311; Latin America, *67*–394; Peace Corps, *64*–444
Pesticides: chemical industry, *65*–260, *64*–267; dairying, *65*–289; forestry, *64*–335; garden and lawn, *66*–358, *65*–342, *64*–340; health, *65*–357; insect, *65*–370, *64*–366; pollution, *65*–457; snake poison, *65*–373; wildlife, *65*–545
PET, *68*–454, *67*–454, *66*–474, *65*–462, *64*–450
Peterson, Esther Eggertsen: food, *65*–335; retailing, *65*–486
PETROLEUM AND GAS, *68*–455, *67*–456, *66*–475, *65*–462, *64*–451
Africa, *il.*, *67*–202, *65*–210; Alberta, *67*–259, *65*–256; Algeria, *67*–211, *66*–217; Australia, *68*–216, *67*–225; chemical industry, *68*–259; China, *66*–280; conservation, *68*–286; Europe, *65*–327; food, *68*–339; gas, *65*–343, *64*–341; Haider, Michael, *66*–372; Iran, *66*–393; Iraq, *68*–378, *66*–393; Kenya, *65*–386; Kuwait, *65*–388, *64*–382; Libya, *68*–397, *67*–395, *66*–412, *64*–390; Middle East, *67*–420, *il.*, *66*–437, *64*–411; Puerto Rico, *66*–499; Rhodesia, *68*–478; Saudi Arabia, *68*–487, *67*–492; Senegal, *65*–497; United Arab Republic, *67*–533; Venezuela, *68*–529, *67*–539
Petrosian, Tigran, *67*–265
Peugeot, Jean-Pierre, *67*–301
Phenylketonuria (PKU), *66*–497
Pheremones, *66*–388
PHILADELPHIA, *68*–455, *67*–457, *66*–475, *65*–463
elections, *68*–323, *66*–339, *64*–304, *64*–469; music, *64*–420; Republican party, *66*–505; transit, *66*–544; zoos and aquariums, *66*–568
Philby, Harold A. R. (Kim), *68*–329
PHILIPPINES, *68*–457, *67*–457, *66*–476, *65*–463, *64*–451
Aguinaldo, Emilio, *65*–293; celebrations, *68*–256; disasters, *il.*, *66*–321; Malaysia, Federation of, *65*–409, *64*–402; Marcos, Ferdinand, *66*–430; Vietnam, *67*–542
Phillips, Duncan, *67*–301
Phonograph. See **RECORDINGS; RECORDINGS FOR CHILDREN**
PHOTOGRAPHY, *68*–457, *67*–458, *66*–477, *65*–463
Asia, *il.*, *67*–126; astronomy, *67*–220, *66*–229; biology, *65*–240; invention, *65*–372; Pulitzer prizes, *68*–472, *67*–477, *65*–478, *64*–466; space exploration, *67*–46, *67*–505, *66*–526, *65*–508
Photosynthesis: biochemistry, *67*–244; biology, *66*–252; botany, *65*–242, *64*–247; chemistry, *67*–264
PHYSICS, *68*–458, *67*–460, *66*–478, *65*–465, *64*–454
astronomy, *68*–214, *65*–222, *64*–226; atomic energy, *67*–223, *65*–223, *64*–228; awards and prizes, *68*–227, *67*–235, *66*–243, *65*–232, *64*–238; careers, *64*–264; chemistry, *66*–273; electronics, *68*–324, *67*–329, *65*–322, *64*–319; engine, *66*–342; Feynman, Richard, *66*–349; *Focus*, *66*–38; metallurgy, *67*–418; Nobel prizes, *68*–441, *66*–460, *64*–433; nuclear physics, *66*–461, *65*–442, *64*–434; science, *65*–34; Oppenheimer, J. Robert, *64*–436; Schwinger, Julian, *66*–518; Science Clubs, *64*–482; Tomonaga, Sin-Itiro, *66*–541
Physiology: Nobel prizes, *68*–441; psychology, *68*–470; Sealab, *67*–69; *Special Report*, *67*–81
Phytochrome, *68*–239, *67*–247
Picasso, Pablo: Chicago, *67*–265; painting and sculpture, *68*–445, *67*–448
Pickett, Clarence, *66*–312
Pickford, Mary, *66*–473
Pig, *67*–553
Pike, James A., *67*–473
Pimentel, George, *66*–273
Pincombe, Mrs. Winifred, *68*–452
Pindling, Lynden O., *68*–537
Pininfarina, Battista, *67*–301
Pinter, Harold, *68*–512
PLASTICS, *65*–466, *64*–455; chemical industry, *68*–258, *65*–260; packaging, *65*–449
Player, Gary, *66*–364
Podgorny, N. V., *66*–514, *64*–478
Poetry: awards and prizes, *68*–227, *67*–235, *66*–242, *65*–231, *64*–237; Canadian, *68*–255, *65*–257; literature, *68*–400, *67*–400, *66*–417, *65*–400, *64*–393; literature for children, *68*–405, *67*–402, *66*–419, *65*–405, *64*–398; Pulitzer prizes, *68*–473, *67*–477, *66*–500, *65*–478, *64*–466; Sandburg, Carl, *68*–298; Sexton, Anne, *68*–490
Poff, Richard H., *67*–454
POLAND, *68*–459, *67*–460, *66*–479, *65*–466, *64*–455
celebrations, *67*–261; France, *68*–345; Protestant, *67*–472; Roman Catholic, *67*–483
Polar bear: conservation, *67*–291; wildlife, *66*–564; zoology, *66*–568
Polasek, Albin, *66*–312
Pole vault, *68*–515
Police: city, *67*–272; civil liberties, *65*–269; computers, *66*–290; Congress, *67*–287; courts and laws, *67*–293; crime, *67*–294; Detroit, *67*–306; New York City, *67*–440; Supreme Court, *67*–514
Political parties: *Special Report*, *68*–62. See also **COMMUNISM;** the various parties and countries
Poll tax, *65*–514
POLLUTION, *65*–466
boats and boating, *65*–241; Congress, *66*–295; electric power, *68*–323; fishing, *65*–362; Great Lakes, *68*–127; health, *65*–356; insect, *66*–387, *65*–370; science, *67*–493; *Special Report*, *66*–164; water, *66*–562; wildlife, *65*–545
Polo, *68*–503, *67*–511, *65*–513, *64*–494
Polynesia. See **PACIFIC ISLANDS**
Pompidou, Georges, *68*–344
Ponnamperuma, Cyril, *66*–252, *64*–33
Pop art: arts, *66*–54; fashion, *66*–348
Pope. See **JOHN XXIII; PAUL VI**
Popular music. See **MUSIC, POPULAR**

POPULATION, WORLD, *68*–460, *67*–461, *66*–480, *65*–467, *64*–455
Porter, Cole, *65*–299
Porter, George, *68*–441
PORTER, KATHERINE ANNE, *67*–462; *il.*, *67*–399
PORTER, SHEENA, *66*–481
Porter, Quincy, *67*–302
PORTUGAL, *68*–460, *67*–462, *66*–481, *65*–467, *64*–455
Africa, *68*–196, *67*–206, *65*–208, *64*–206; Angola, *66*–218, *65*–213, *64*–211; bridge and tunnel, *67*–251, *66*–259; international relations, *64*–16; Mozambique, *66*–445, *65*–424, *64*–417; United Nations, *67*–535, *64*–516
Portuguese Guinea, *68*–196
Post, Elizabeth L., *67*–454
POST OFFICE, *68*–461, *67*–462, *66*–481, *65*–467, *64*–456
Europe, *64*–324; Gronouski, John A., Jr., *64*–355; O'Brien, Lawrence, *66*–462; stamp collecting, *68*–361, *66*–376, *64*–496; U.S. government, *68*–528
Postal savings, *67*–463
Potatoes, *68*–202, *67*–207
Potomac River, *66*–177
Potter, Beatrix, *67*–401
Poultry: agriculture, *68*–199, *67*–207; food, *67*–339, *65*–468, *64*–456
POVERTY, *68*–462, *67*–464, *66*–483
agriculture, *68*–198, *65*–211; child welfare, *66*–275, *65*–261; city, *66*–280; civil rights, *66*–285; Congress, *68*–278, *67*–282, *66*–294, *65*–279; courts and laws, *68*–287, *66*–297; education, *67*–322, *66*–334; Indian, American, *66*–385; juvenile delinquency, *66*–403; library, *67*–395; old age, *67*–444, *66*–463; PTA, *66*–468; population, *66*–480; President of the U.S., *66*–489; roads and highways, *66*–507; social welfare, *67*–499, *66*–522, *65*–501; United Nations, *66*–552; politics, *68*–64; VISTA, *65*–540; YWCA, *67*–550
Powell, Adam Clayton: Congress, *68*–282, *67*–287; poverty, *66*–485
Powell, Dawn, *66*–312
POWELL, SUMNER CHILTON, *65*–468
Prayer: Protestant, *68*–470, *67*–480, *65*–474
Presbyterians, *67*–245, *66*–496, *65*–474, *64*–461
PRESIDENT OF THE UNITED STATES, *68*–464, *67*–467, *66*–487, *65*–469, *64*–457
agriculture, *68*–200; cabinet, *68*–245, *67*–253, *66*–262, *65*–251; Canada, *68*–249; city, *68*–266, *68*–269; civil rights, *67*–273, *66*–285; Congress, *68*–276, *67*–280, *66*–293, *65*–279; conservation, *68*–283, *67*–288; crime, *66*–297; desalination, *65*–543; disarmament, *67*–308, *65*–307; Dominican Republic, *66*–324; economy, *68*–313, *67*–28, *67*–315, *66*–30; education, *67*–322; Europe, *67*–335; Ford, Gerald R., *66*–352; Goldman, Eric, *65*–347; health, *66*–374; hobbies, *66*–375; Hoover, Herbert, *65*–300; housing, *67*–365, *66*–378; Humphrey, Hubert, *66*–379; immigration, *66*–381; international trade, *67*–378, *66*–389; invention, *66*–392; Latin America, *68*–393, *66*–409; library, *67*–395; literature, *66*–417; Medal of Freedom, *65*–231, *64*–237; Medicare, *66*–431; medicine, *66*–434; mental health, *67*–418, *66*–435; mines, *66*–439; national affairs, *67*–22, *66*–41; national defense, *68*–434, *66*–451; Negro, *66*–456; parks, *66*–468; pet, *67*–454; political campaigns, *68*–74; population, *67*–461; post office, *66*–481; poverty, *68*–462, *67*–464, *66*–483, *65*–502; presidential succession, *66*–492; Reedy, George, *65*–481; Roman Catholic, *68*–480; Rostow, Walt, *67*–485; safety, *67*–489; science, *67*–34, *67*–494, *66*–518; social security, *67*–499; space exploration, *68*–499; steel industry, *66*–529; taxation, *68*–508, *66*–533; transportation, *67*–527, *66*–543; travel, *68*–520; U.S. government, *67*–537; Vietnam, *67*–546, *66*–555; Washington, D.C., *68*–536, *66*–562; water and flood control, *66*–562; weather, *66*–563.
PRICE, HOLLIS FREEMAN, *66*–493
PRICE, LEONTYNE, *66*–494
Prices. See **ECONOMY, THE**
Primaries. See **ELECTIONS**
Primates, *67*–212
Prince Edward Island: bridge and tunnel, *66*–259; Canada, *68*–254, *67*–260, *66*–269, *65*–257, *64*–262
Printing: braille, *66*–253; invention, *64*–370; library, *65*–394; photography, *65*–463
PRISON, *66*–494, *65*–473, *64*–460; courts and laws, *68*–287; crime, *68*–288, *67*–294; Great Britain, *67*–360; pets, *66*–474; Salvation Army, *64*–480
Proconsul, *68*–205
Programmed learning, *67*–41
PROKHOROV, ALEKSANDR MIKHAILOVICH, *67*–473
Protein: biochemistry, *67*–243; food, *68*–339, *67*–339, *66*–350; psychology, *66*–497; science, *65*–36
PROTESTANT, *68*–468, *67*–472, *66*–494, *65*–474, *64*–460
celebrations, *68*–256; ecumenical movement, *66*–85; religion, *67*–479; Roman Catholic, *67*–483
Protestant Episcopal Church, *66*–375, *64*–462
PSYCHOLOGY, *68*–470, *67*–474, *66*–497, *65*–476
child guidance, *66*–275; child welfare, *65*–262; learning, *WBE*, *68*–561, *66*–251; mental health, *68*–415, *66*–435; science, *64*–39
PTA. See **PARENTS AND TEACHERS, NATIONAL CONGRESS OF**
Public Health Service, U.S., *68*–360, *67*–361
PUBLISHING, *68*–471, *67*–474, *66*–498, *65*–476, *64*–463
advertising, *68*–192; astronauts, *64*–224; awards and prizes, *65*–231; blindness, *65*–241, *64*–246; dancing, *68*–292; education, *66*–335; science, *66*–36; Warren Commission, *65*–540.
PUERTO RICO, *68*–472, *66*–499, *65*–477, *64*–465
Latin America, *67*–393
PULITZER PRIZES, *68*–457, *67*–477, *66*–499, *65*–478

Q

QUAISON-SACKEY, ALEX, *65*–478; United Nations, *65*–535
Quasi-star (quasar): astronomy, *68*–214, *67*–220, *66*–231, *65*–64, *65*–221; science, *65*–34
Quebec: Canada, *68*–246, *68*–254, *67*–257, *66*–267, *65*–253, *64*–104, *64*–125, *64*–262; Canadian literature, *66*–270
Quintuplets: Fischer, *64*–447, *il.*, *64*–404; Lawson, *66*–472; Prieto, *64*–449

R

Rabbage, *68*–240
RABORN, WILLIAM FRANCIS, JR., *il.*, *66*–489, *66*–500
Rachewiltz, Prince Boris de, *67*–97
Radiation: balloons, *64*–239; biochemistry, *67*–243; biology, *64*–245; chemistry, *64*–267; dairying, *64*–293; exploration, *64*–328; fishery, *65*–335; physics, *67*–460; space travel, *66*–152. See also **ATOMIC ENERGY; CIVIL DEFENSE**
RADIO, *68*–473, *67*–478, *66*–500, *65*–478, *64*–466
Australia, *68*–219; advertising, *67*–200, *65*–206; communications, *68*–272, *67*–277; electronics, *67*–329, *66*–342; Great Britain, *68*–358; science, *65*–32, *64*–34; space travel, *65*–508
Radio telescope, *65*–32, *il.*, *65*–76, *64*–35
RAILROAD, *65*–479, *64*–467
Canada, *67*–259, *64*–100; celebrations, *64*–266; congress, *64*–287; disasters, *68*–311, *67*–312, *66*–322, *65*–313, *64*–314; Gabon, *66*–357; labor, *68*–387, *65*–388, *64*–382; Mauritania, *64*–402; transportation, *68*–517, *67*–527, *66*–543
Rainier III, *68*–426, *67*–422, *66*–440
Rains, Claude, *68*–299
Ramoboa, Ernestine, *68*–452
Ramos, Sugar, *67*–248
Ramsey, Arthur Michael: ecumenical movement, *il.*, *66*–86; Protestant, *il.*, *68*–469; Roman Catholic, *67*–483
Randall, Clarence B., *68*–299
Randolph, Philip, *67*–275, *64*–428
Ranković, Aleksandar, *67*–552
Rann of Kutch, *66*–384
Ransome, Arthur, *68*–299
Rathbone, Basil, *68*–299
Rayburn, Sam, *66*–435
Raynolds, Robert, *66*–312
REAGAN, RONALD WILSON, *68*–473
elections, *il.*, *67*–325; Republican party, *68*–476, *67*–480
Reapportionment: city, *64*–273; state government, *66*–529, *65*–513, *64*–496; Supreme Court, *65*–515
Reclamation, *67*–486
RECORDINGS, *68*–474, *67*–478, *66*–501, *65*–480
jazz, *66*–449, *64*–421; music, *68*–432, *67*–432, *66*–448, *65*–428, *64*–420; popular music, *68*–433, *64*–421
RECORDINGS FOR CHILDREN, *66*–501, *65*–481, *64*–468
RED CROSS, *68*–475, *67*–479, *66*–501, *65*–481, *64*–468
Redfield, Edward, *66*–312
Redwoods, *68*–342, *67*–291
REEDY, GEORGE EDWARD, *66*–297, *65*–481
Refrigeration, *68*–340
Refugees: Cuba, *64*–292; Middle East, *68*–423, *65*–415; Outer Mongolia, *64*–437; Rwanda, *66*–516
Regina medal, *68*–405, *66*–518, *65*–213, *64*–400
Rehabilitation. See **HANDICAPPED**
Reicher, Frank, *66*–312
Reines, Frederick, *66*–461
Relativity: astronomy, *68*–214; physics, *68*–458
Relief. See **SOCIAL WELFARE**
RELIGION, *68*–475, *67*–479
Barth, Karl, *67*–479; Bermuda, *65*–238; Carlson, Paul E., *65*–258; civil rights, *68*–270, *66*–285, *64*–278; courts and laws, *66*–296; Eastern Orthodox, *68*–312, *67*–313, *65*–315, *64*–316; ecumenical movement, *66*–82; education, *68*–320, *64*–36, *64*–317; Israel, *64*–373; jazz, *67*–433; Jews and Judaism, *68*–380, *67*–383, *66*–397, *65*–379, *64*–375; memorials, *65*–411; Palestine, *Trans-Vision*, *66*–97; prison, *66*–494; Protestant, *68*–468, *67*–472, *66*–494, *65*–474, *64*–460; Roman Catholic, *68*–480, *67*–483, *66*–508, *65*–487, *64*–472; Salvation Army, *68*–486, *67*–491, *66*–517, *65*–495, *64*–480; Schweitzer, Albert, *64*–133; Spain, *68*–500; Supreme Court, *64*–498; theater, amateur, *67*–525; Vietnam, *64*–522; YWCA, *68*–539
Religious education: education, *64*–36, *64*–317; Protestant, *64*–460
Rennie, James, *66*–313
Reptiles, *67*–553
REPUBLICAN PARTY, *68*–476, *67*–480, *66*–503, *65*–482
congress, *67*–281, *66*–293; Eisenhower, Dwight D., *66*–339; elections, *68*–322, *67*–324, *66*–339, *65*–320; Ford, Gerald R., *66*–352; Goldwater, Barry M., *65*–348; John Birch Society, *66*–398; Lindsay, John V., *66*–412; Miller, William E., *65*–417; national affairs, *67*–24; Percy, Charles H., *68*–449, *68*–482; Philadelphia, *66*–475; Reagan, Ronald, *68*–473; Rockefeller, Nelson, *68*–479; Romney, George W., *65*–489; Scranton, William W., *65*–497
Research. See **INVENTION; SCIENCE AND RESEARCH**
Reserves, military, *66*–455, *65*–435, *64*–426
RESOR, STANLEY R., *66*–505
Respiratory diseases, *67*–361
Reston, Va., *68*–268, *66*–281
RETAILING, *68*–478, *67*–482, *66*–506, *65*–486, *64*–470
agriculture, *67*–208; automobile, *65*–226; boats, *66*–253; business, *65*–250; city, *66*–281; Congress, *67*–285; economy, *67*–318, *66*–328; food, *68*–339, *67*–339, *64*–333; industry, *65*–370; interior decoration, *64*–367; packaging, *65*–449, *64*–437; recordings, *67*–478, *66*–501; state government, *66*–529; taxation, *67*–517
Retirement: labor, *65*–389; old age, *65*–444
Reuther, Walter, *68*–390
Reynaud, Paul, *67*–302
Reynolds, Quentin, *66*–312
Rhee, Syngman, *66*–312
Rhode Island, *68*–503, *67*–251, *66*–196
RHODESIA, *68*–478, *67*–482, *66*–506, *65*–486
Africa, *68*–196, *66*–212; Botswana, *67*–248; civil rights, *66*–283; democracy, *66*–314; Great Britain, *68*–357, *67*–359, *66*–370, *65*–352; international relations, *67*–18; South Africa, *67*–500; United Nations, *68*–526, *67*–535, *66*–550, *65*–535; world affairs, *66*–19; Zambia, *68*–541, *66*–567
RHODESIA AND NYASALAND, FEDERATION OF, *64*–471. See also **MALAWI; RHODESIA;** United Nations, *64*–517
Rhyne, Charles S., *66*–296
Rice, Elmer, *68*–299
Rice: agriculture, *68*–202, *67*–207; food, *67*–339, *66*–396; Malaysia, *68*–407; Mekong River, *68*–79; science, *68*–33
Rickey, Branch, *66*–312
Rifle shooting, *68*–502
Riggs, Tommy, *68*–300
"Right-to-work," *66*–407
Riiser-Larsen, Hjalmar, *66*–312
Rineri, Antonio Cardinal, *68*–299
Rio de Janeiro, *66*–271
Rio Grande, *66*–300, *64*–407
Ritter, Joseph Cardinal, *68*–300
Rivard, Lucien, *66*–266

RNA: biochemistry, *66*–251, *65*–239, *64*–245; biology, *68*–236; Jacob, François, *66*–396; Monod, Jacques, *66*–441; psychology, *66*–497

ROADS AND HIGHWAYS, *66*–507, *65*–486
arts, *66*–57; automobile, *67*–228; bridge and tunnel, *66*–259, *65*–245, *64*–251; Congress, *67*–285, *66*–295; garden and lawn, *66*–359; Honduras, *66*–376; Johnson, Lyndon B., *66*–402; Nepal, *66*–457, *65*–438; New England, *66*–200; Nicaragua, *66*–459; Pan American Highway, *64*–387; Philadelphia, *68*–455; safety, *68*–485, *il.*, *67*–490, *64*–479; state government, *64*–497; Sweden, *68*–506; Thailand, *66*–537; transportation, *68*–518, *67*–529; trucking, *64*–511; tunnel, *67*–251

Robb, Charles S., *68*–382

Robbins, Jerome, *67*–295

Roberto, Holden, *66*–218, *65*–213, *64*–211

Robinson, Frank, *67*–239

Robinson, Fred Norris, *67*–302

Roblin, Dufferin, *68*–248

ROCHE, JAMES MICHAEL, *66*–508

Rockefeller, John D. IV, *68*–452

ROCKEFELLER, NELSON ALDRICH, *68*–479
Republican party, *68*–476, *67*–481, *65*–483, *64*–470; vice-presidency, *64*–88

Rockefeller Foundation, *68*–343, *67*–344, *66*–338, *65*–318, *64*–318

Roethke, Theodore: deaths, *64*–301; literature, *67*–400; poetry, *67*–398, *64*–393

Rogoff, Julius M., *67*–302

Rolamite, *68*–377

Rolling Stones, *il.*, *68*–150

ROMAN CATHOLIC, *68*–480, *67*–483, *66*–508, *65*–487, *64*–472; celebrations, *68*–257; education, *68*–319; Poland, *68*–460; Protestant, *68*–469

ROMANIA, *68*–481, *67*–485, *66*–512, *65*–489, *64*–476

ROMNEY, GEORGE WILCKEN, *68*–482, *65*–489
elections, *il.*, *67*–325, *65*–321; Republican party, *68*–476, *67*–480, *65*–483, *64*–470

Roosevelt, Anna Eleanor: memorials, *67*–417, *64*–405; stamp collecting, *64*–496

Roosevelt, Franklin D.: Johnson, Lyndon B., *64*–584; memorials, *66*–434; vice-presidency, *64*–93

ROOSEVELT, FRANKLIN DELANO, JR., *66*–512

Roosevelt, Theodore, *68*–414, *64*–405

Roques, Clement Emile Cardinal, *65*–299

Rorimer, James J., *67*–302

Rose, Billy, *67*–302

Roses, *67*–350, *66*–359, *65*–342, *64*–340

Ross, Barney, *68*–300

Rossen, Robert, *67*–302

ROSTOW, WALT WHITMAN, *67*–485

Rotary International: service clubs, *68*–490, *67*–496, *66*–520, *65*–498, *64*–483

Rothberger, Jeannette Grauberg, *65*–460

Rouleau, Guy, *66*–266

ROUS, (FRANCIS) PEYTON, *67*–486

Roush, J. Edward, *68*–73

ROWAN, CARL THOMAS, *65*–490

Rowing: Olympic Games, *65*–447; sports, *68*–502, *67*–510, *66*–528, *65*–57, *65*–513, *64*–494

ROWLEY, GRAHAM WESTBROOK, *64*–476

RUANDA-URUNDI. See **BURUNDI; RWANDA**

Ruark, Robert, *66*–312

RUBBER, *65*–490, *64*–476
Malaysia, *68*–407; manufacturing, *68*–410, *67*–412, *66*–430

Ruben, Samuel, *67*–378

Rubinstein, Helena, *66*–312

RUBY, JACK, *65*–490, *64*–476
courts and laws, *67*–292, *65*–284; Kennedy assassination, *64*–70; Warren Report, *65*–562

Ruffini, Ernesto Cardinal, *68*–300

Running: Olympic Games, *65*–446; sports, *68*–501; track and field, *68*–514, *67*–525, *66*–542, *65*–527, *64*–508

Rusk, Dean: Asia, *il.*, *65*–218; international relations, *il.*, *64*–368; Vietnam, *il.*, *65*–538

Russell, Bertrand, *68*–399

RUSSELL, HAROLD, *65*–490; handicapped, *65*–356

Russell, Richard B., *65*–166

RUSSIA, *68*–482, *67*–486, *66*–513, *65*–491, *64*–477
agriculture, *66*–216; Albania, *66*–217, *64*–209; Alliluyeva, Svetlana, *68*–203; armed forces, *68*–210, *67*–216, *66*–223, *65*–216, *64*–214; Asia, *66*–225, *65*–220, *64*–219; atomic energy, *65*–223, *64*–228; aviation, *67*–234; Brezhnev, Leonid, *65*–245; Bulgaria, *68*–244, *67*–252; chemistry, *65*–260; China, *66*–277, *65*–262, *64*–271; civil rights, *66*–283, *65*–266; communications, *68*–272; Communism, *68*–273, *67*–277, *66*–289, *65*–273, *64*–281; Cuba, *64*–291; Czechoslovakia, *68*–289; Denmark, *65*–305; disarmament, *68*–307, *67*–308, *66*–319, *65*–307, *64*–309; Eastern Orthodox Church, *67*–314, *66*–325, *64*–316; economy, *66*–327; espionage, *68*–328, *67*–331, *66*–343, *65*–324, *64*–321; Europe, *65*–324, *64*–322; exploration, *66*–347; fairs and exhibitions, *68*–335; fishery, *68*–338, *66*–350; *Focus*, *65*–14; France, *67*–346; geology, *66*–359; "hot line," *64*–311; Hungary, *67*–367; international relations, *68*–16, *67*–15, *64*–12, *64*–367; international trade, *64*–369; invention, *66*–392; Iran, *68*–377; Italy, *68*–379, *67*–381; Japan, *67*–382; Jews, *66*–397, *65*–379, *64*–375; Korea, *66*–405; Kosygin, Aleksei, *65*–388; Middle East, *68*–423, *64*–411; Mongolia, *68*–427, *67*–445, *66*–464, *65*–449, *64*–437; Pakistan, *66*–467; petroleum, *64*–451; Poland, *68*–459, *67*–461, *65*–466; President of the United States, *66*–488, *64*–459; Roman Catholic, *68*–480; Romania, *66*–512, *65*–489, *64*–476; science, *65*–496; Somalia, *64*–487; space exploration, *68*–44, *68*–497, *67*–45, *67*–508, *66*–50, *66*–525, *65*–47, *65*–505, *64*–46, *64*–488; *Special Report*, *67*–161; Tereshkova, Valentina V., *64*–503; track and field, *67*–525, *66*–542, *65*–527, *64*–509; *Trans-Vision*, *67*–177; Turkey, *68*–521; Uganda, *66*–547; United Nations, *67*–536, *66*–550, *65*–533, *64*–515; Vietnam, *68*–531, *66*–556; weather, *68*–537; world affairs, *66*–18; *WBE*, *67*–556; wrestling, *64*–530; Yemen, *68*–538; Yugoslavia, *68*–541, *65*–547

Russian Orthodox Church, *68*–312, *66*–325, *65*–315

Rutgers College, *67*–261

RWANDA, *66*–516, *65*–494, *64*–479
Africa, *68*–196, *67*–204, *65*–209; Burundi, *67*–252

Ryan, Sister Michael Thérèse, *67*–454

RYUN, JIM, *67*–489; sports, *68*–501; track and field, *68*–514, *67*–525

S

SACHS, NELLY, *67*–489

Sadiq el Mahdi, *68*–505

Safdie, Moshe, *67*–214

SAFETY, *68*–485, *67*–489, *66*–516, *65*–494, *64*–479
astronauts, *68*–214; automobile, *68*–220, *67*–228, *66*–236; aviation, *68*–225, *65*–230; boats and boating, *67*–245, *65*–241, *64*–246; Congress, *67*–285; dentistry, *65*–306; games, models, and toys, *66*–358; mining, *67*–422; PTA, *66*–468; space exploration, *68*–497; state government, *66*–529, *64*–497; vital statistics, *67*–547. See also **DISASTERS**

Saigh, Maximos IV Cardinal, *68*–300

SAILING, *65*–494, *64*–480
boats and boating, *68*–238, *67*–246, *66*–254

Saint Augustine, Fla., *66*–271

Saint Lawrence Seaway: Canada, *65*–256; transportation, *67*–530, *66*–545; waterways, *65*–543, *64*–526

SAINT LOUIS, *68*–486, *67*–491, *66*–516, *65*–494
architecture, *66*–222; baseball, *68*–231; bridge and tunnel, *66*–259; building and construction, *67*–251; zoos, *65*–548

Saliba, Philip, *67*–313

SALVATION ARMY, *68*–486, *67*–491, *66*–517, *65*–495

Samoa, *68*–444, *67*–446, *66*–464. See also **WESTERN SAMOA**

SAMUELS, ERNST, *66*–517

San Antonio, *68*–335, *67*–336, *65*–332

SAN FRANCISCO, *68*–486, *67*–491, *66*–517, *64*–480
bridge and tunnel, *66*–259; city, *68*–267; civil rights, *il.*, *67*–274; elections, *68*–323; opera, *67*–430; publishing, *66*–498; theater, *68*–513; transit, *66*–545, *65*–528

Sandage, Allan, *66*–231

Sandburg, Carl: deaths, *68*–298; literature for children, *68*–402

Sandoz, Mari, *67*–302

Sanford, Terry, *68*–452

Sanger, Margaret, *67*–302

Sangster, Donald, *68*–538

Santee, Ross, *66*–313

SARAGAT, GIUSEPPE, *65*–495; Italy, *65*–374

Sargent, Sir Malcolm, *68*–300

Saskatchewan: Canada, *68*–254, *67*–260, *66*–270, *65*–257; medicare, *64*–263

Sassoon, Siegfried, *68*–300

Satellite, artificial. See **SPACE TRAVEL**

SATO, EISAKU, *65*–495; Japan, *68*–379, *67*–382, *66*–397, *65*–378

Saturn (planet), *68*–215

Saturn (rocket), *68*–498, *66*–527, *64*–488

SAUDI ARABIA, *68*–487, *67*–491, *66*–517, *65*–495, *64*–481

SAUL, RALPH SOUTHEY, *67*–492

SAUTER, ARNOLD, *67*–493

Savings. See **INVESTMENTS AND SAVINGS**

Savings and loan associations, *68*–230, *67*–237, *66*–245, *64*–240

Sawyer, Charles B., *65*–299

SAWYER, RUTH, *66*–518

Scandinavia. See **DENMARK; FINLAND; NORWAY; SWEDEN**

Scharf, Kurt, *67*–472

Scherchen, Hermann, *67*–302, *65*–428

Schick, Béla, *68*–300

Schipa, Tito, *66*–313

SCHIRRA, WALTER MARTY, JR.
astronauts, *68*–214, *67*–220, *66*–228, *65*–220, *64*–224; space exploration, *67*–504, *66*–526

Schizophrenia, *68*–415

Schlesinger, Arthur M., *il.*, *67*–399, *66*–313

Schmitt, Harrison H., *66*–228

Schmidt, Maarten, *66*–231, *65*–63

Schoendienst, Albert, *68*–58

School. See **EDUCATION**

Scholarships: education, *66*–42, *66*–334; foundations, *66*–338; Four-H Clubs, *66*–353, *65*–337; Junior Achievement, *66*–403; Parents and Teachers, National Congress of, *64*–441; Rotary International, *65*–498; Science Clubs, *66*–519, *64*–482; United Community Funds, *67*–533

Schollander, Don, *67*–515, *65*–518

Schuyler, Phillipa Duke, *68*–300

Schweickart, Russell L., *64*–223

Schweitzer, Albert, *66*–306, *64*–133

SCHWEITZER, PIERRE-PAUL, *64*–481

SCHWINGER, JULIAN SEYMOUR, *66*–518

SCIENCE AND RESEARCH, *68*–487, *67*–493, *66*–518, *65*–496, *64*–481. See also the various sciences

SCIENCE CLUBS OF AMERICA, *68*–488, *67*–494, *66*–519, *65*–496, *64*–482

Science of science, *67*–494

Scott, David R., *67*–505, *66*–229, *64*–223

Scott, Zachary, *66*–313

SCRANTON, WILLIAM WARREN, *65*–497
Republican party, *65*–483, *64*–470

Screwworm, *67*–374, *64*–400

Sculpture. See **PAINTING AND SCULPTURE**

Seagrave, Gordon S., *66*–313

Sealab II, *68*–443, *67*–64, *66*–462

SEATO. See **Southeast Asia Treaty Organization**

Securities and Exchange Commission, *67*–513, *66*–530, *65*–515, *64*–497

See, Elliot M., Jr., *67*–219, *66*–229, *64*–224

Seed, *67*–247, *65*–129

Selassie, Haile, *67*–331

Selective Service, *68*–437, *66*–455, *65*–435; President of the U.S., *68*–466; boxing, *68*–240; national defense, *68*–435

Selma, Ala.: civil rights, *66*–286; Negro, *66*–456

Selznick, David O., *66*–313

Seminole Indians, *68*–371

Senanayake, Dudley, *66*–273

Senayake, Senake, *66*–473

SENEGAL, *66*–520, *65*–497, *64*–483
Africa, *68*–196, *67*–203; Gambia, *66*–358, *65*–341; Mali, *66*–427, *64*–402

Serbian American Church, *66*–325

Sert, Jose Luis, *il.*, *66*–207

SERVICE CLUBS AND ORGANIZATIONS, *68*–489, *67*–496, *66*–520, *65*–498, *64*–483

Set Theory: *WBE*, *65*–589

Severini, Gino, *67*–302

Sévigny, Pierre, *67*–256

Sevitzky, Fabien, *68*–300

Sewage disposal, *68*–133, *66*–173

SEXTON, ANNE, *68*–490

Shafer, Burr, *66*–313

Shakespeare Quadricentennial: literature, *65*–399; literature for children, *65*–401; memorial, *65*–412; museums, *65*–425; poetry, *65*–400; stamp collecting, *65*–358; theater, *65*–526, *64*–505

Shapley, Harlow, *65*–70

Shaporin, Yuri, *67*–302

Sharett, Mose, *66*–313

Sharp, Mitchell, *67*–254

SHASTRI, LAL BAHADUR, *66*–383, *65*–498; deaths, *67*–302; India, *65*–367

Sheeler, Charles, *66*–313

Shepard, Alan B., Jr.: astronauts, *65*–221, *64*–224

Shepard, Odell, *68*–300

Sheppard, Samuel, *67*–514

Sheridan, Ann, *68*–300

Sherry, Al, *65*–461

SHIP, *65*–499, *64*–484
disasters, *68*–310, *67*–311, *66*–321, *65*–313, *64*–313; electronics, *64*–319; engine and energy, *64*–320; Great Britain, *il.*, *67*–357; Great Lakes, *65*–255; Italy, *66*–395; labor, *65*–388, *64*–382; national defense, *64*–425; ocean, *64*–435; petroleum, *68*–455; transportation, *68*–516, *67*–529, *66*–543; travel, *64*–510. See also **WATERWAYS**
Shooting: Olympic Games, *65*–448; sports, *68*–502, *67*–510, *66*–528, *65*–513, *64*–494
Shostakovich, Dimitri, *66*–448
Shotwell, James, *66*–313
Shriver, R. Sargent, Jr.: Kennedy, John F., *64*–378; Peace Corps, *67*–450, *65*–457, *64*–442; personalities, *65*–461; poverty, *67*–465, *66*–483; social welfare, *65*–502
Sibelius, Jan, *68*–414, *66*–271
SIERRA LEONE, *68*–490, *66*–521, *65*–499, *64*–484
Sihanouk, Norodom, *68*–245, *66*–263, *65*–251, *64*–257
Sikkim, *65*–458, *64*–447
India, *66*–384; personalities, *66*–471
Sillanpää, Frans Eemil, *65*–301
Silver: coins, *66*–375; Congress, *66*–295; metals, *64*–406; money, *68*–426, *67*–423, *66*–441, *65*–419, *64*–414; retailing, *66*–506
Simon and Garfunkel, *68*–153
SIMPSON, LOUIS, *65*–499
Simpson, O. J., *il.*, *68*–341
Sinatra, Frank, *il.*, *66*–536
Singapore, *65*–409, *64*–402
Asia, *il.*, *68*–212; Great Britain, *66*–370; Malaysia, *66*–426; United Nations, *66*–552
SINGLETARY, OTIS A., *65*–499
Sirén, Osvald, *67*–302
Sites, Sharon, *66*–473
Sitwell, Dame Edith, *65*–301
Skate boards, *66*–358
Skating. See **ICE HOCKEY; ICE SKATING**
Skeet shooting, *68*–502, *67*–510, *66*–528, *65*–513
SKIING, *68*–490, *67*–496, *66*–521, *65*–500, *64*–484; Olympic Games, *65*–448; *WBE*, *68*–579
Skin, *68*–235, *il.*, *67*–87
Skinner, B. F., *67*–41
Skyscrapers, *66*–221
Slayton, Donald K., *64*–224
Sleep, *68*–239
Sloan, Alfred P., Jr., *67*–302
Sloan Foundation, Inc., Alfred P.: education, *68*–321; engineering, *64*–321; foundations, *68*–343, *67*–343, *66*–338, *65*–318, *64*–318; science, *67*–494
Small business, *68*–489
Smathers, George A., *il.*, *66*–315
Smith, David, *66*–313
Smith, Holland M., *68*–500
Smith, Ian: Africa, *66*–212; Great Britain, *67*–359, *66*–370; Rhodesia, *68*–478, *67*–482, *66*–506
Smith, Joan Merriam, *65*–230
Smith, Lillian, *67*–303
Smith, Margaret, *67*–521
Smith, Margaret Chase, *66*–473
Smith, Pamela Sue, *67*–454
Smith, Tommy, *67*–525
Smithson, James, *66*–272
Smithsonian Institution, *65*–424, *64*–417; fashion, *66*–349; museums, *65*–424, *64*–417; zoos, *66*–568
Smog, *66*–167, *65*–466, *64*–357
SMOKING, *64*–484
advertising, *65*–206; cancer, *66*–433; dentistry, *65*–306; health, *65*–356; PTA, *68*–449, *67*–449
Smuggling, *67*–457
Smylie, Robert E., *66*–398, *65*–485
Snake: invention, *65*–373; zoology, *68*–541, *65*–548
Snow, Charles P., *65*–398
Snowy Mountain project, *il.*, *68*–218
SOAP BOX DERBY, *65*–500; sports, *67*–510
SOCCER, *68*–491, *67*–497, *66*–521, *65*–500
disasters, *65*–314; Great Britain, *67*–360; Olympic Games, *65*–448; *WBE*, *68*–582
Social Credit Party, *65*–254, *64*–262
Social sciences, *64*–38. See also **ANTHROPOLOGY; ARCHAEOLOGY**
SOCIAL SECURITY, *68*–491, *67*–499, *66*–522, *65*–500
Congress, *66*–294; Medicare, *68*–411, *67*–412, *66*–431; old age, *68*–444, *67*–444; retailing, *66*–506
SOCIAL WELFARE, *68*–493, *67*–499, *66*–522, *65*–501
agriculture, *65*–211; awards and prizes, *65*–231; Congress, *67*–282, *66*–293, *65*–279; drugs, *68*–311; education, *65*–39, *65*–316; employment, *68*–108; Girl Scouts, *65*–347; housing, *66*–378; Indian, American, *68*–371, *65*–368; Job Corps, *65*–379; Medicare, *68*–411, *67*–412, *66*–431; mental health, *67*–418; national affairs, *66*–24; New York City, *68*–439; Norway, *67*–438; old age, *68*–444, *67*–444, *65*–444; Peace Corps, *64*–445; poverty, *68*–462, *67*–464, *66*–483; Red Cross, *68*–475; Roman Catholic, *68*–480; Salvation Army, *68*–486, *67*–491, *64*–480; service clubs, *68*–489; state government, *66*–529, *65*–514; United Community Funds, *68*–523; veterans, *68*–529; VISTA, *65*–540; YMCA, *65*–546. See also **CHILD WELFARE**
Socialism: Burma, *66*–262, *65*–247, *64*–253; India, *65*–367; Italy, *65*–374, *64*–373; Norway, *66*–461; Saskatchewan, *65*–257; Syria, *66*–533, *65*–519; United Arab Republic, *64*–512
Soglo, Christophe, *66*–299, *64*–293
SOMALIA, *68*–494, *66*–523, *65*–503, *64*–487
Africa, *68*–196, *67*–204; Ethiopia, *67*–331, *65*–324; Kenya, *68*–385, *67*–386, *65*–386
Somaliland, French, *68*–346
Somoza Debayle, Anastasio, *68*–440
Sonny and Cher, *66*–449
South, The: civil liberties, *64*–276; Democratic party, *67*–305, *65*–303, *64*–305; elections, *65*–320; libraries, *64*–210; Negro, *66*–455, *65*–437, *64*–428; Protestant, *64*–461; Republican party, *67*–481
SOUTH AFRICA, REPUBLIC OF, *68*–494, *67*–500, *66*–523, *65*–503, *64*–487
Africa, *68*–196, *65*–210; Botswana, *67*–248; civil liberties, *65*–267, *64*–274; international relations, *67*–18, *64*–17; Lesotho, *67*–395; mines and mining, *65*–417; nuclear physics, *66*–461; sports, *67*–509; United Nations, *68*–526, *67*–535, *66*–551, *65*–534, *64*–516; Vorster, Balthazar, *67*–547
SOUTH ARABIA, FEDERATION OF, *68*–495, *67*–501, *66*–523, *65*–503, *64*–487
Great Britain, *68*–357; Middle East, *65*–415; United Nations, *68*–526
Southeast Asia Treaty Organization: Asia, *65*–219, *64*–221; France, *65*–340; international relations, *65*–15; Laos, *64*–384
South West Africa: Africa, *68*–197, *65*–210; international relations, *67*–18; South Africa, *68*–494, *67*–500; United Nations, *68*–526, *67*–535
South Yemen, People's Republic of, *68*–495
Souvanna Phouma: *67*–391, Laos, *66*–407
Soviet Union. See **RUSSIA**
Soybeans, *68*–199, *67*–207
Spaak, Paul-Henri, *68*–442, *il.*, *67*–242, *66*–346, *65*–238, *il.*, *64*–13, *64*–324
SPACE EXPLORATION, *68*–497, *67*–503; **SPACE TRAVEL,** *66*–525, *65*–505, *64*–488
agriculture, *68*–201; astronauts, *68*–213, *67*–219, *66*–228, *65*–220, *64*–222; astronomy, *68*–216, *67*–220, *66*–229, *65*–221; awards and prizes, *64*–236; balloons, *64*–239; biochemistry, *il.*, *68*–235; biology, *65*–240; botany, *68*–240; building and construction, *65*–246; Bykovsky, Valery F., *64*–257; chemistry, *65*–260; cockroaches, *64*–366; communications, *68*–272, *67*–277, *66*–286, *65*–270; Cooper, L. Gordon, Jr., *64*–287; disarmament, *68*–307, *67*–308; dogs, *64*–450; electronics, *66*–341, *64*–319; engine, *66*–342; espionage, *65*–324; Europe, *il.*, *65*–325; *Focus*, *68*–44, *67*–44, *66*–47, *65*–44, *64*–42; Houston, *66*–379, *64*–361; Italy, *67*–382, invention, *64*–370; Johnson, Lyndon B., *64*–586; Kennedy, John F., *64*–62; manufacturing, *66*–429; moon, *64*–171; museums, *64*–417; new words and phrases, *64*–430; photography, *65*–463; President of the U.S., *67*–470; Russia, *68*–482, *64*–478; science, *65*–36, *64*–34, *64*–481; Science Clubs, *64*–482; *Special Report*, *66*–149; television, *64*–502; Tereshkova, Valentina V., *64*–503; United Nations, *68*–526, *67*–533; weather, *68*–537, *67*–547, *66*–563, *65*–544, *64*–527; zoology, *67*–553
Spaeth, Sigmund, *66*–313
SPAIN, *68*–500, *67*–509, *66*–528, *65*–512, *64*–494
Africa, *68*–196; atomic energy, *67*–224; civil rights, *67*–276; Great Britain, *67*–359; national defense, *65*–432; painting, *65*–451; Portugal, *64*–455
Spassky, Boris, *67*–265
Speck, Richard F., *68*–288
"Special drawing rights," *68*–374
Specter, Arlen, *66*–505
Speech, *68*–505, *67*–70
Spellman, Francis Cardinal, *68*–300
Spence, Sir Basil, *68*–452
Spiegelman, Sol, *66*–251
Spingarn Medal, *66*–494, *65*–545, *64*–326
SPORTS, *68*–500, *67*–509, *Special Report*, *67*–146, *66*–528, *65*–513, *64*–494
Stafford, Thomas P., *65*–220, *64*–224; astronauts, *66*–228; space exploration, *67*–504, *66*–526
Stagg, Amos Alonzo, *66*–313
Stalin, Joseph, *68*–203, *67*–173
STAMP COLLECTING, *64*–496; Civil War Centennial, *65*–269; hobbies, *68*–361, *67*–363, *66*–376, *65*–358
Stanfield, Robert L., *68*–248
Starr, Ringo, *66*–471
State Department, U.S.: diplomat, *68*–306, *67*–307, *66*–318, *65*–306, *64*–307; Gaud, William S., *67*–350; immigration and emigration, *64*–363; Peace Corps, *64*–442; U.S. government, *68*–528, *67*–537
STATE GOVERNMENT, *68*–503, *66*–529, *65*–513
city, *66*–280, *65*–265, *64*–273; civil defense, *66*–281; civil liberties, *65*–269; Congress, *67*–287; courts and laws, *66*–296, *65*–285; crime, *66*–297; Democratic party, *68*–302, *67*–304, *66*–316, *65*–303, *64*–304; economy, *66*–331; education, *66*–42, *66*–336; elections, *68*–322, *67*–324, *66*–339, *65*–320; governors, *68*–354, *67*–356, *66*–365, *65*–349, *64*–350; labor, *68*–391; Medicare, *68*–411; old age, *68*–444, *66*–463, *64*–435; outdoor recreation, *66*–463, *64*–437; Philadelphia, *64*–451; population, *67*–462; Republican party, *68*–477, *67*–481; roads and highways, *66*–507, *64*–511; social welfare, *68*–493, *64*–486; Supreme Court, *66*–531, *65*–515, *64*–498; taxation, *68*–509, *67*–517, *66*–533, *65*–520; teacher education, *64*–41
STEEL INDUSTRY, *68*–504, *67*–512, *66*–529. See also **IRON AND STEEL,** *65*–373, *64*–372; Luxembourg, *68*–406; metallurgy, *68*–415
Steinbeck, John: personalities, *67*–454
Stengel, Casey, *67*–240
Sterry, Charlotte, *67*–303
Stevenson, Adlai Ewing: Chicago, *66*–274; civil liberties, *64*–274; deaths, *66*–308; Democratic party, *64*–305; disarmament, *il.*, *64*–308; memorials, *68*–414; United Nations, *65*–534
STOCKS AND BONDS, *68*–504, *67*–512, *66*–530, *65*–514, *64*–497; economy, *68*–317; Haack, Robert W., *68*–359
Stokes, Carl B., *68*–322, *66*–339
Stonehenge, *67*–213
STOPH, WILLI, *65*–515; Germany, *68*–350
Stott, Earl C., *65*–301
Stratton, William G., *68*–71
Strauss, Franz Josef, *il.*, *68*–351
Strauss, Richard: celebrations, *65*–258; music, *65*–428
Strayhorn, William T., *68*–300
Streisand, Barbra: popular music, *66*–449, *64*–421; television, *il.*, *66*–537
Stribling, Thomas S., *66*–313
Stroessner, Alfredo, *68*–396, *65*–455, *64*–441
Styron, William, *68*–398
Submarine: armed forces, *67*–216; boats, *66*–253, *64*–246; engine, *65*–323; national defense, *il.*, *65*–436, *64*–425; ocean, *65*–443, *64*–435; Sealab, *67*–64
Subway, *68*–519, *67*–530, *66*–545, *64*–510
SUDAN, *68*–505, *66*–531, *65*–515, *64*–498; Africa, *68*–196, *67*–205; anthropology, *65*–213; Beja, *67*–100; Chad, *66*–273; Elizabeth II, *66*–369
Suez Canal: petroleum, *68*–455; UAR, *68*–522
Sugar: agriculture, *68*–202, *67*–207; Cuba, *67*–294, *66*–298; Dominican Republic, *67*–312; Trinidad, *66*–546
Suharto, *68*–371, *67*–373
Sukarno, *68*–371, *67*–373, *66*–386, *65*–368, *64*–365
Sulfur, *68*–417, *67*–263, *66*–436, *65*–260
Sun: astronomy, *68*–215, *67*–222, *66*–230, *65*–222; balloons, *65*–234; eclipse, *64*–224; energy, *67*–330; science, *64*–32; space exploration, *67*–505, *66*–157, *66*–526
SUNAY, CEVDET, *67*–514
Superconductivity, *66*–478
Superfluidity, *66*–479
Supersonic aircraft, *il.*, *68*–225, *il.*, *67*–232, *65*–230
Suppes, Patrick, *67*–42
SUPREME COURT OF THE UNITED STATES, *68*–505, *67*–514, *66*–531, *65*–515, *64*–498
banks and banking, *65*–234, *64*–239; Bible, *64*–278; Burton, Harold H., *65*–294; city, *67*–272, *65*–265; civil rights, *68*–271, *67*–273, *65*–269; courts and laws, *68*–287, *67*–293, *64*–288; crime, *67*–294, *66*–297; Fortas, Abe, *66*–353; gas, *64*–341; hospital, *65*–360;

Indian, American, *64*–364; invention, *67*–378; labor, *66*–407; Marshall, Thurgood, *68*–410; motion pictures, *66*–443; Negro, *64*–429; population, *66*–480; post office, *66*–481; Protestant, *64*–460; publishing, *65*–477; reapportionment, *65*–515, *64*–273; sports, *67*–154; state government, *66*–529, *65*–513; transportation, *66*–544; trucking, *65*–529; U.S. government, *68*–528; water and flood control, *64*–526; *WBE*, *68*–586
SURFING: *WBE*, *68*–590; sports, *68*–503, *67*–511; recordings, *64*–467
Surgery: dentistry, *65*–305; electronics, *67*–329; medicine, *67*–414, *65*–411, *64*–403
Surtees, John, *67*–231, *65*–227
SWAZILAND, *66*–532, *65*–518, *64*–498; Africa, *68*–197, *67*–206
SWEDEN, *68*–506, *67*–515, *66*–532, *65*–518, *64*–499
Christina, Princess, *64*–446
SWIMMING, *68*–507, *67*–515, *66*–532, *65*–518, *64*–499
Olympic Games, *65*–446; Pan American Games, *68*–448; sports, *68*–503, *65*–58
Swine: livestock, *65*–407, *64*–400; livestock show, *64*–401
SWITZERLAND, *68*–507, *67*–516, *66*–532, *65*–519
architecture, *65*–215; celebrations, *66*–271; fairs and exhibitions, *65*–331; tunnel, *66*–259
Symbols: numeration systems, *WBE*, *65*–595; set theory, *WBE*, *65*–589
Symphony, *68*–431, *67*–430, *66*–447, *65*–427, *64*–420
SYRIA, *68*–508, *67*–516, *66*–533, *65*–519, *64*–499
Israel, *65*–374; Lebanon, *64*–388; Middle East, *67*–420, *66*–439, *64*–409; United Arab Republic, *64*–512; United Nations, *67*–533, *65*–534, *64*–517
Szilard, Leo, *65*–301

T

Tabor, Hans R., *68*–452
Tahiti, *68*–257, *65*–449, *64*–437
Taiwan. See **FORMOSA**
Takin, *67*–553
Takruni, *67*–116
Tallchief, Maria, *66*–300
TANGANYIKA, *64*–499
Africa, *64*–206; anthropology, *65*–110; Kenya, *64*–381; wildlife, *64*–150. See also **TANZANIA**
Tange, Kenzo, *67*–214
Tank, *68*–442
Tantalum, *66*–435, *64*–406
TANZANIA, *68*–508, *66*–533, *65*–519; Africa, *67*–204; Malawi, *67*–408
Tape recordings, *67*–478, *66*–501
Tariffs: chemical industry, *68*–259; Europe, *68*–332, *67*–334, *65*–326, *64*–324; international trade, *68*–374, *67*–377, *66*–392, *65*–372, *64*–370; Latin America, *65*–393
Tate, H. J., *68*–455
Tatum, "Goose," *68*–300
TAXATION, *68*–508, *67*–517, *66*–533, *65*–519, *64*–500
automobile, *66*–236; Bahamas, *66*–244; Boston, *67*–247; business, *65*–28, *64*–26; Canada, *67*–256, *66*–267, *65*–254, *64*–261; communications, *67*–277; congress, *68*–278, *67*–282, *66*–295, *65*–279, *64*–286; Detroit, *64*–306; Dominican Republic, *68*–313, *65*–314; economy, *67*–28, *67*–315; excise taxes, *65*–251; Great Britain, *67*–358, *65*–352; Houston, *68*–365; India, *64*–363; Latin America, *64*–386; Luxembourg, *68*–406; Medicare, *66*–432; Monaco, *64*–412; motorboats, *64*–247; national affairs, *64*–22; New Zealand, *68*–439; outdoor recreation, *66*–463; Philippines, *64*–451; President of the United States, *67*–470, *64*–458; railroad, *64*–467; retailing, *66*–506; San Francisco, *68*–486; social security, *67*–499, *66*–522; state government, *68*–503, *66*–529, *65*–514, *64*–496; stocks and bonds, *67*–513; travel, *66*–546; Venezuela, *67*–539
Taylor, Deems, *67*–303
Taylor, James M., *66*–229
TAYLOR, PRINCE ALBERT, JR., *66*–534
Teacher: education, *68*–39, *68*–320, *67*–322, *66*–45, *66*–334, *65*–316, *64*–40; labor, *68*–387; old age, *68*–444; Sweden, *67*–515
Teaching machines, *67*–41
TEALE, EDWIN WAY, *67*–517
Technology. See **ENGINEERING; INVENTION; MANUFACTURING; SCIENCE AND RESEARCH**
Tedder, Arthur William, *68*–300
Teen-agers: child guidance, *64*–269; dropouts, *64*–29; fashion, *67*–337, *66*–348, *64*–331; popular music, *65*–429; vocational education, *64*–525. See also **JUVENILE DELINQUENCY**
TELEPHONE AND TELEGRAPH, *65*–270, *64*–500; automation, *64*–230; civil rights, *68*–270; communications, *68*–272, *67*–277, *66*–286; computers, *65*–274; courts and laws, *68*–287; Europe, *64*–324; handicapped, *66*–373, *65*–356, *64*–356; "hot line," *64*–311; Niger, *66*–459. See also **COMMUNICATIONS**
TELEVISION, *68*–509, *67*–519, *66*–534, *65*–520, *64*–501
advertising, *68*–192, *67*–200, *65*–206; arts, *64*–52; awards and prizes, *65*–232; baseball, *66*–249; communications, *68*–272, *67*–277, *66*–287, *65*–270; electrical equipment, *65*–322; electronics, *67*–329, *66*–341; electronics industry, *64*–320; foundations, *67*–343; Henry, E. William, *64*–358; ice hockey, *67*–368; Iceland, *66*–381; Johnson, Lyndon B., *65*–383; Kennedy assassination, *64*–64; manufacturing, *67*–411, *66*–429; motion pictures, *67*–425, *65*–424; post office, *il.*, *68*–461; soccer, *67*–498; space travel, *66*–526, *65*–511, *64*–492; sports, *68*–57, *67*–150, *67*–510; Supreme Court, *66*–531; weather, *65*–544
Telstar: electronics, *64*–319; space travel, *64*–492; television, *64*–502
Tennessee Valley Authority, *68*–324, *66*–300, *65*–270
Tenney, Roger, *68*–452
TENNIS, *68*–511, *67*–521, *66*–537, *65*–523, *64*–503; sports, *68*–500
Testing and measurements: child guidance, *64*–269; education, *66*–44, *64*–41; *WBE*, *68*–566
Texas: conservation, *67*–290; Dallas, *68*–290, *66*–300, *64*–293; dam, *65*–290; fairs and exhibitions, *68*–335; Houston, *68*–365, *66*–379, *65*–361, *64*–361; Kennedy assassination, *64*–61; Mexico, *68*–417, *64*–407
TEXTILE, *65*–523, *64*–504; fashion, *64*–330; manufacturing, *il.*, *68*–409, *67*–412, *66*–428; metallurgy, *66*–435; museums, *68*–447; prices, *65*–250; safety, *68*–485
THAILAND, *68*–512, *67*–521, *66*–537, *65*–523, *64*–504; dam, *65*–290; marketing, *il.*, *65*–132; Mekong River, *68*–79
Thalidomide, *67*–130
Thant, U: civil liberties, *65*–267; Laos, *64*–384; Middle East, *68*–418; United Nations, *68*–524, *66*–549, *65*–533; *Special Report*, *67*–119; *67*–533
Thapa, Surya Bahadur, *66*–457
Thatcher, Ross, *65*–257
THEATER, *68*–512, *67*–522, *66*–539, *65*–525, *64*–505
Albee, Edward F., *68*–202; amateur, *67*–525, *66*–541, *64*–507; arts, *66*–55, *65*–54, *64*–50; awards and prizes, *66*–242, *65*–231; celebrations, *64*–265; Chevalier, Maurice, *64*–446; Clogg, Hallye, *64*–446; Communism, *il.*, *66*–289; democracy, *68*–301; dancing, *66*–300, *65*–290; Gilroy, Frank, *66*–363; Jews, *65*–379; Martin, Mary, *64*–448; Marx, Harpo, *64*–448; Merrick, David, *68*–415; Metropolitan Opera, *67*–431; poetry, *67*–400; Pulitzer prizes, *68*–473, *66*–500; recordings, *67*–478; Shakespeare Quadricentennial, *65*–399. See also **MOTION PICTURES**
THEATER, AMATEUR, *67*–525, *66*–541, *64*–507
Theodosius, *68*–312
Theology: Jews, *68*–381; Protestant *68*–470, *67*–473; religion, *67*–479, *66*–497, *65*–475, *64*–462
Thermonuclear energy, *67*–223
THIEU, NGUYEN VAN, *68*–514; Vietnam, *68*–533
Thomas, Albert, *67*–303
Thomas, Dylan, *il.*, *66*–413
Thomson, Roy H., *68*–471
***Thresher*, U.S.S.,** *il.*, *65*–436, *64*–425
Tibet, *67*–439, *66*–551
Tidal power, *67*–251
Tien, Thomas Cardinal, *68*–300
Tiger, Dick, *67*–248
Tikal, *68*–160
Tillich, Paul: deaths, *66*–313; Protestant, *66*–495
Timber. See **FORESTRY AND FOREST PRODUCTS**
Time, *67*–285, *66*–461, *65*–443
Tin, *66*–530
Tires, *68*–410, *65*–490, *64*–476
Titanium, *68*–408, *67*–422, *66*–435
Tito, *68*–540, *67*–552, *66*–567, *65*–547, *64*–531
Tobacco, *68*–202, *67*–207, *65*–211, *64*–484
Tobago. See **TRINIDAD-TOBAGO**
Tobias, Philip V., *66*–219
Toch, Ernst, *65*–301
TOGO, *68*–514, *66*–541, *65*–527, *64*–507
Africa, *67*–204, *64*–206; Grunitzky, Nicolas, *64*–355
Toklas, Alice B., *68*–300
Tokyo, *66*–397
TOLBERT, WILLIAM RICHARD, JR., *66*–541
Tombalbaye, François, *66*–273
TOMONAGA, SIN-ITIRO, *66*–541
Tonga, *64*–496
Tornadoes: disasters, *68*–310, *67*–312, *66*–322, *65*–313, *64*–314; insurance, *66*–388; weather, *67*–548, *65*–543
Toronto: architecture *66*–222; Canada, *66*–269; museums, *67*–427; Ontario, *67*–260
Touré, Sékou, *67*–360, *66*–372, *64*–355
TRACK AND FIELD, *68*–514, *67*–525, *66*–542, *65*–527
Olympic Games, *65*–446; Pan American Games, *68*–448; records, *64*–495; Ryun, Jim, *68*–501, *67*–489; sports, *65*–56, *64*–494
Tracy, Spencer, *68*–300
Trade. See **ECONOMY, THE; INTERNATIONAL TRADE**
Trade fairs. See **FAIRS AND EXHIBITIONS**
Tranquilizers, *67*–140, *65*–412
Trans-Vision, *68*–177, *67*–177, *66*–97, *65*–81, *64*–109
Transistor, *67*–329, *66*–341, *64*–319
TRANSIT, *65*–528, *64*–510
aviation, *68*–222; Boston, *67*–247; bus, *65*–247, *64*–253; city, *65*–265, *64*–273; Congress, *67*–285, *65*–280; Los Angeles, *68*–406, *65*–408, *64*–401; New York City, *67*–440, *66*–458; Philadelphia, *67*–457, *64*–451; roads and highways, *65*–487; Saint Louis, *64*–480; San Francisco, *68*–486, *67*–491, *66*–517, *64*–480; Toronto, *64*–262; transportation, *68*–519, *67*–530, *66*–544
TRANSPORTATION, *68*–516, *67*–527, *66*–543
Congress, *67*–285, *66*–295. See also **AUTOMOBILE; AVIATION; BUS; DISASTERS; RAILROAD; SHIP; TRANSIT; TRAVEL; TRUCKING; WATERWAYS**
Transportation, U.S. Department of: cabinet, *67*–253; transportation, *68*–516, *67*–527; U.S. government, *67*–538
Trapshooting, *68*–502, *66*–528, *64*–494
TRAVEL, *68*–520, *67*–530, *66*–546, *65*–528, *64*–510
Bahamas, *67*–549, *66*–244, *65*–233; bus, *64*–253; Camp Fire Girls, *66*–263; fairs and exhibitions, *67*–337; France, *66*–356; Greece, *65*–354; hotel, *66*–378, *65*–360, *64*–360; Hungary, *66*–379, *64*–361; immigration and emigration, *65*–364; Italy, *66*–395; Monaco, *66*–440; national parks, *64*–427; Paul VI, *65*–488; Portugal, *66*–481; ship, *64*–484; Spain, *66*–528
Treasury Department, *68*–426, *67*–423, *66*–353
Treece, Henry, *67*–303
Trees, *67*–247. See also **FORESTRY AND FOREST PRODUCTS**
TREJOS FERNÁNDEZ, JOSÉ JOAQUIN, *67*–531; Costa Rica, *67*–392
Tremblay, Paul, *il.*, *67*–123
TRINIDAD-TOBAGO, *66*–546, *65*–529, *64*–510; Latin America, *68*–395; West Indies, *68*–538, *67*–549
Trotsky, Leon, *il.*, *67*–165
TROWBRIDGE, ALEXANDER BUEL, *68*–521
U.S. government, *68*–528
TRUCKING, *65*–529, *64*–511
disasters, *67*–310, *66*–320, *65*–312; labor, *68*–388; transportation, *68*–518, *67*–527, *66*–543
Trudeau, Pierre Elliot, *68*–246
Truly, Richard H., *66*–229
TRUMAN, HARRY S., *68*–521, *67*–531
awards, *66*–242; Medicare, *67*–413, *66*–431; memorials, *67*–417, *64*–405
Trumpeter swan, *64*–529
Trust Territory of the Pacific, *67*–446; Peace Corps, *67*–450, *66*–464, *65*–449
Tshombe, Moise: Africa, *65*–208; Algeria, *68*–203; Congo (Kinshasa), *68*–275, *67*–280, *66*–291, *65*–275, *64*–284; international relations, *65*–18; Middle East, *65*–417
Tsiranana, Philibert, *66*–426
Tubman, William V. S., *66*–411, *65*–394
TUCHMAN, BARBARA WERTHEIM, *64*–511
Tucker, Sophie, *67*–303
TUNISIA, *68*–521, *67*–531, *66*–546, *65*–530, *64*–511
Lebanon, *65*–394; Middle East, *66*–438
TUNNEL. See **BRIDGE AND TUNNEL,** *64*–251; building and construction, *68*–244, *67*–251
Tuomioja, Sakari S., *65*–288

TURKEY, *68*–521, *67*–532, *66*–547, *65*–530, *64*–511
archaeology, *65*–214; Cyprus, *68*–289, *66*–298, *65*–287, *64*–292; earthquakes, *il.*, *67*–310; Eastern Orthodox Church, *66*–325; Greece, *65*–354; Middle East, *67*–421, *64*–411; Sunay, Cevdet, *67*–514
Turkey: hunting, *65*–363; poultry, *65*–468, *64*–456
Turner, John, *68*–247
"Twiggy." See **Hornby, Lesley**
Typhoons: *68*–309, *67*–310, *66*–321, *65*–313, *64*–313

U

Udall, Stewart L.: housing, *66*–378; personalities, *il.*, *68*–452; President of the United States, *64*–458; water and flood control, *64*–526
UGANDA, *68*–521, *66*–547, *65*–530, *64*–511
Africa, *65*–208, *64*–206; Kenya, *64*–381
Ulbricht, Walter, *64*–343
Germany, *66*–362, *64*–343; Middle East, *66*–438
UNESCO, *64*–212
archaeology, *66*–220, *64*–212; education, *66*–337; library, *66*–411; science, *66*–38; United Nations, *66*–552; water, *66*–184
UNGER, IRWIN, *66*–547
UNICEF. See **United Nations Children's Fund**
Unidentified flying objects, *68*–216
Union of Soviet Socialist Republics. See **RUSSIA**
Unitarian, *68*–470
UNITED ARAB REPUBLIC, *68*–522, *67*–532, *66*–547, *65*–530, *64*–512
anthropology, *68*–206; archaeology, *66*–220, *64*–212; Beja, *67*–100; bridge and tunnel, *64*–251; civil liberties, *65*–266; dam, *65*–290; espionage, *65*–323; Germany, *66*–362; Iran, *67*–378; Iraq, *65*–373, *64*–371; irrigation, *il.*, *65*–128; Jordan, *65*–383; Kenya, *68*–385; Kuwait, *65*–388; Malawi, *67*–408; Middle East, *68*–418, *67*–420, *66*–437, *65*–415, *64*–409; museums, *68*–429; population, *64*–200; Saudi Arabia, *68*–487, *67*–491; Syria, *67*–516, *64*–499; Tunisia, *66*–546; United Nations, *68*–524; water, *66*–190; Yemen, *68*–538, *67*–550, *66*–566, *65*–546, *64*–530
United Church of Canada, *66*–496
United Church of Christ, *66*–493
UNITED COMMUNITY FUNDS AND COUNCILS, *68*–523, *67*–533, *66*–548, *65*–531, *64*–513
UNITED NATIONS, *68*–524, *67*–533, *66*–549, *65*–533, *64*–515
Africa, *68*–197, *66*–212, *64*–206; architecture, *68*–208; Asia, *66*–226; atomic energy, *64*–228; Canada, *66*–267, *65*–255; civil liberties, *65*–267, *64*–274; Congo (Léopoldville), *65*–275, *64*–284; Cyprus, *68*–289, *66*–298, *65*–287; disarmament, *67*–308, *66*–318; Fanfani, Amintore, *66*–348; fishery, *66*–350; food, *65*–129; Gambia, *64*–340; Indonesia, *67*–374, *66*–386, *65*–369; international relations, *65*–18, *64*–16, *64*–367; Kuwait, *64*–382; Manescu, Corneliu, *68*–408; Mekong River, *68*–80, *65*–219; memorials, *65*–411; Middle East, *68*–418, *67*–420, *66*–439, *65*–415, *64*–410; New Guinea, *66*–457, Pakistan, *66*–467; Panama, *65*–455; Pazhwak, Abdul Rahman, *67*–450; population, *66*–480; Portugal, *64*–455; Protestant, *il.*, *64*–461; Quaison-Sackey, Alex, *65*–478; Rhodesia, *68*–479, *67*–482, *66*–506; Roman Catholic, *66*–511; Russia, *66*–515; San Francisco, *66*–517; Sosa Rodriguez, Carlos, *64*–487; South Africa, *68*–494, *66*–523, *65*–503, *64*–487; space exploration, *67*–49, *66*–50; *Special Report*, *67*–119; stamps, *68*–361; *66*–376; Sweden, *65*–518, *64*–499; travel, *67*–530, *64*–510; Vietnam, *68*–533; world affairs, *66*–21; Yemen, *64*–530; Zambia, *68*–541
United Nations Children's Fund: child welfare, *66*–275; Nobel prize, *66*–460; United Nations, *66*–551
UNITED STATES GOVERNMENT, *68*–527, *67*–537
agriculture, *65*–210; Atomic Energy Commission, *66*–232, *64*–228; aviation, *68*–224, *67*–233, *66*–239; Baker, Robert G., *65*–233; banks, *66*–245; Cabinet, *68*–245, *67*–253, *66*–262, *65*–251, *64*–257; city, *66*–280; city planning, *66*–281; civil defense, *65*–266, *64*–274; Congress, *68*–276, *67*–280, *66*–293, *65*–279, *64*–284; conservation, *68*–283; courts and laws, *66*–296, *65*–284; crime, *66*–297; Democratic party, *66*–315, *65*–303; diplomat, *68*–306, *67*–307, *66*–318, *65*–306; disarmament, *66*–318; economy, *66*–330; education, *67*–42, *66*–41, *66*–333, *65*–38; elections, *67*–324, *65*–320; *Focus*, *68*–20, *67*–20; housing, *66*–378; immigration and emigration, *66*–381, *65*–364, *64*–363; invention, *66*–392; Job Corps, *65*–379; money, *68*–426, *67*–423; national defense, *68*–434, *67*–434, *66*–451, *65*–431, *64*–214, *64*–422; national parks and monuments, *65*–455, *64*–427; old age, *66*–463; outdoor recreation, *65*–189, *65*–449, *64*–437; Peace Corps, *67*–450, *66*–469, *65*–457, *64*–442; Post Office, *68*–461, *67*–462, *66*–481, *65*–467, *64*–456; poverty, *67*–464, *66*–483, *65*–502; President of the United States, *68*–464, *67*–467, *66*–487, *65*–469, *64*–457; prison, *65*–473; Protestant, *66*–496; Social Security, *68*–491, *67*–499, *66*–522, *65*–500, *64*–485; social welfare, *66*–522, *65*–501, *64*–486; Supreme Court, *68*–505, *67*–514, *66*–531, *65*–515, *64*–498; taxation, *68*–508, *67*–517, *66*–533, *65*–519; transportation, *67*–527, *66*–543; travel, *68*–520; veterans, *68*–529, *67*–540, *66*–553, *65*–535, *64*–519; vice-president, *64*–80; VISTA, *65*–540; Warren Commission, *65*–540; Washington, D.C., *66*–562; weather, *66*–563. See also biographies of individual government officials and entries on various government agencies
United States Information Service, *66*–430
UNITED STATES OF AMERICA, *64*–518
census, *67*–262, *66*–272, *65*–259, *64*–266. See also various states and cities and various specific subjects
Universe, *67*–460, *65*–63
Universities and colleges: Africa, *64*–206; architecture, *64*–213; Canadian Library Association, *66*–270; celebrations, *65*–258, *64*–265; Chicago, *66*–274, *64*–268; congress, *66*–294, *64*–287; courts and laws, *65*–284; Dallas, *66*–300; democracy, *68*–301; Detroit, *67*–306; draft, *67*–437; education, *68*–318, *67*–323, *66*–42, *66*–334, *65*–38, *65*–316, *64*–317; engineering, *66*–343, *64*–321; foundations, *65*–318, *64*–318; Great Britain, *64*–354; jazz, *67*–433, *64*–421; Jews, *67*–383; library, *67*–395, *il.*, *65*–395, *64*–389; memorials, *64*–405; Mexico, *67*–419; Negro, *64*–429; New Guinea, *68*–438; ocean, *68*–443, *67*–444; poverty, *66*–485; science and research, *68*–488, *67*–36, *66*–518; social welfare, *65*–502; teacher education, *64*–40; theater, amateur, *67*–525; United Arab Republic, *65*–531; Vietnam, *66*–556. See also **SPORTS**
Untermeyer, Louis, *66*–473
Untouchables, *66*–140
Updike, John, *66*–414
UPPER VOLTA, *67*–538; Africa, *68*–196
Upward Bound program, *68*–463
Uranium: atomic energy, *67*–223; energy, *68*–325; mines and mining, *67*–422
Urban renewal. See **CITY; CITY PLANNING**
Urban transportation. See **ROADS AND HIGHWAYS; TRANSIT**
URUGUAY, *68*–528, *66*–552, *65*–535, *64*–519, Latin America, *67*–394
Utah, *65*–455

V

Vaccine: dentistry, *68*–304; health and disease, *68*–360; medicine, *67*–416, *64*–403
VALENTI, JACK JOSEPH, *67*–538
motion pictures, *67*–426; President of the U.S., *il.*, *67*–471, *il.*, *66*–488
Valleta, Vittorio, *68*–300
Vance, Cyrus Roberts: Ailes, Stephen, *65*–211
Van de Graaff, Robert J., *68*–300
Vance, Marguerite, *66*–313
VANDEN BOEYNANTS, PAUL, *67*–538
Vanier, Georges P., *68*–300
Varèse, Edgard, *66*–313
Vatican, *66*–297. See also **ROMAN CATHOLIC**
Vatican Council II: civil rights *66*–284; Eastern Orthodox, *65*–315; ecumenical movement, *66*–92; Protestant, *64*–461; Jews, *66*–397, *65*–379; Roman Catholic, *67*–483, *66*–508, *65*–487, *64*–472
VAUGHN, JACK HOOD, *68*–449, *67*–539; Peace Corps, *67*–450
Vegetable, *68*–240, *67*–350, *66*–359
Veksler, Vladimir I., *67*–303
Venereal disease, *66*–374
VENEZUELA, *68*–529, *67*–539, *66*–553, *65*–535, *64*–519
bridges, *68*–244; celebrations, *68*–256; democracy, *64*–303; Latin America, *64*–386; Leoni, Raul, *65*–394; Prieto quintuplets, *64*–449; Sosa Rodriguez, Carlos, *64*–487
Venice, *il.*, *67*–380
Vening Meinesz, Felix, *67*–303
Venturi, Ken, *65*–348
Venus: astronomy, *68*–216, *66*–231, *65*–223; science, *65*–35; space exploration, *68*–497, *67*–508, *66*–154, *64*–492
Vermont: Civil War Centennial, *65*–269; elections, *66*–339; New England, *66*–196
Verwoerd, Hendrik F., *67*–500
VETERANS, *68*–529, *67*–539, *66*–553, *65*–535, *64*–519
Congress, *67*–282
Veterans of Foreign Wars, *68*–529
Veterinary Medicine: livestock, *65*–407, *64*–400; zoology, *65*–548
Vice-President of the United States: Democratic party, *64*–304; Garner, John Nance, *64*–447; Humphrey, Hubert H., *68*–365, *67*–367, *66*–379, *65*–361; Johnson, Lyndon B., *64*–73, *64*–583; President of the U.S., *65*–471; presidential succession, *66*–492; *Special Report*, *64*–80; television, *66*–536; travel, *66*–546; Warren Commission, *65*–541
Victoria Alexandra Alice Mary, *66*–313
Vienna, *66*–233
VIETNAM, *68*–530, *66*–555, *65*–537, *64*–520
Asia, *68*–211, *67*–217, *66*–225, *65*–218, *64*–217; Cambodia, *67*–253, *65*–251, *64*–257; Canada, *67*–257; China, *67*–267, *66*–277; Communism, *68*–273, *67*–277, *66*–289; Congress, *68*–278, *67*–287; democracy, *68*–301; economy, *68*–29; education, *66*–338; Great Britain, *66*–370; India, *66*–385; international relations, *68*–15; Ky, Nguyen Cao, *67*–388; Laos, *68*–391; literature, *66*–417; Mekong River, *68*–80; national affairs, *68*–21, *67*–21; national defense, *68*–434, *67*–434, *66*–451, *65*–432, *64*–424; Philippines, *67*–457, *66*–476; President of the U.S., *68*–465, *67*–467, *66*–488, *65*–472; Protestant, *68*–469, *66*–496; Red Cross, *67*–479; religion, *68*–475; Russia, *68*–512, *66*–515; Thailand, *67*–521; Thieu, Nguyen Van, *68*–514; Truman, Harry S., *68*–521; United Nations, *68*–526, *66*–550, *65*–534; U.S. government, *67*–537; veterans, *67*–540; Westmoreland, William C., *68*–538; world affairs, *67*–15, *66*–18
Vinson, Carl: awards and prizes, *65*–231; personalities, *65*–461, *64*–449
Virgin Islands, *68*–256
Virginia: bridge and tunnel, *64*–252; city planning, *66*–281; Civil War Centennial, *66*–286; Democratic party, *66*–316; elections, *66*–339; parks, *66*–468; Republican party, *66*–505; Supreme Court, *68*–505, *66*–531
Virolainen, Johannes, *65*–334
Virus, *68*–236
Vishinsky, Andrei, *il.*, *67*–166
Vision, *65*–476
Visser't Hooft, Willem A., *il.*, *66*–84
VISTA, *65*–540
old age, *66*–463; Peace Corps, *65*–457; poverty, *68*–463, *67*–465, *66*–485; social welfare, *65*–502
VITAL STATISTICS, *68*–536, *67*–547, *66*–562, *65*–540, *64*–524
population, *68*–460, *67*–461, *66*–480, *65*–467; safety, *68*–485, *67*–489. See also **CENSUS**
Vitamins: drugs, *67*–143; food, *67*–340
Vittorini, Elio, *67*–303
VOCATIONAL EDUCATION, *64*–525
automation, *64*–230; blindness, *68*–237; business, *64*–28; congress, *64*–287; education, *65*–38, *65*–317; employment, *68*–103; Future Farmers of America, *65*–340, *64*–39, *64*–317; handicapped, *64*–356; Indian, American, *64*–364; social welfare, *64*–486; state government, *64*–496; veterans, *68*–529, *66*–553
Volcano: Costa Rica, *65*–284, *64*–288; disasters, *67*–312, *il.*, *66*–321, *64*–314; geology, *68*–350, *67*–351; Indonesia, *64*–365; moon, *67*–506; ocean, *68*–443
Volleyball, *68*–503, *67*–511, *66*–528, *65*–513, *64*–494
Volunteers in Service to America. See **VISTA**
VORSTER, BALTHAZAR JOHANNES, *67*–547
South Africa, *67*–500
Voting: civil rights, *66*–285; Negro, *66*–455; Supreme Court, *67*–514. See also **ELECTIONS**

W

Wages. See **LABOR**
Wagner, Robert S., *66*–473, *64*–431
Wagner, Wieland: deaths, *67*–303; music, *67*–430
Walbrook, Anton, *68*–300

Wald, George, *68*–441
Wales: disasters, *il.*, *67*–309; Great Britain, *67*–356
Waley, Arthur, *67*–303
Walker, Kenneth M., *67*–303
WALLACE, GEORGE CORLEY, *68*–536, *64*–525
Democratic party, *67*-305; elections, *67*–326; Negro, *66*–456
Wallace, Henry Agard, *66*–313
Walter, Francis, *64*–302
Waner, Paul G., *66*–313
War: Algeria, *64*–209; Asia, *67*–217, *66*–225, *64*–217; India, *66*–383; Indonesia, *66*–386, *64*–365; international relations, *68*–15, *64*–368; Iraq, *66*–393; Israel, *68*–378; Jordan, *68*–384; Korea, *64*–382; Laos, *66*–407, *64*–383; Malaysia, *65*–409; Middle East, *68*–418; Morocco, *64*–414; Pakistan, *66*–467; Somalia, *68*–494; United Nations, *68*–524, *66*–550; Vietnam, *68*–530, *67*–540, *66*–555, *65*–537, *64*–520; Yemen, *68*–538, *66*–566, *64*–512, *64*–530. See also **ARMED FORCES OF THE WORLD; NATIONAL DEFENSE**
War of 1812, *66*–271
"WAR ON POVERTY." See **POVERTY**
Warner, Albert, *68*–300
WARREN COMMISSION, *65*–540
courts and laws, *65*–284; President of the U.S., *65*–471; Ruby, Jack, *65*–490
WARREN REPORT, *65*–550; Kennedy, John F., *65*–384; publishing, *65*–477
Washington, Walter E., *68*–536
Washington (state): bridge and tunnel, *67*–251, *64*–251; dam, *66*–300, *64*–293; forestry, *66*–352; parks, *66*–469; *Special Report*, *65*–189; transit, *66*–545
WASHINGTON, D.C., *68*–536, *67*–547, *66*–562, *65*–542, *64*–525
Congress, *67*–287; Freedom March, *64*–429, *il.*, *64*–275; garden and lawn, *65*–343; Kennedy, John F., *65*–384, *65*–424; Kennedy assassination, *64*–65; memorials, *68*–414, *66*–434; museums, *65*–424, *64*–417; music, *65*–427, *64*–420; transit, *64*–510; United States, *64*–419; zoos and aquariums, *66*–568, *65*–548
WATER AND FLOOD CONTROL, *66*–562, *65*–542, *64*–526
atomic energy, *66*–232, *65*–223; Canada, *65*–254; chemistry, *65*–260; Chicago, *65*–261; Congress, *67*–285, *66*–295; conservation, *68*–283, *67*–288, *65*–126; dam, *66*–300, *65*–290; dentistry, *66*–317; desalination, *67*–224; Detroit, *66*–317; disasters, *66*–321, *65*–313; electric power, *68*–323; Houston, *64*–361; hunting and fishing, *66*–380; Israel *65*–374; Mars, *65*–510, *64*–226; Mexico, *64*–407; Middle East, *65*–415; New York City, *66*–458; outdoor recreation, *65*–449; pollution, *68*–127; science, *65*–496; soil conservation, *64*–486; *Special Report*, *66*–183; Supreme Court, *64*–498; United Arab Republic, *65*–530
Water Skiing, *68*–503, *66*–528, *65*–513
Waterloo, Battle of, *66*–271
WATERWAYS, *65*–543, *64*–526
Belgium, *64*–244; Congress, *66*–295; conservation, *67*–289; dam, *65*–290; Finland, *66*–350; floods, *68*–309; health, *65*–356; Mekong River, *68*–79, *65*–219; outdoor recreation, *64*–437; Panama, *68*–448, *66*–468, *65*–455, *64*–441; pollution, *66*–172, *65*–466; transportation, *67*–529, *66*–545
Watkins, Charles L., *65*–461
Watson, Minor, *66*–313
Watts, Custer, *67*–454
Waugh, Evelyn, *67*–303
Waxman, Franz, *68*–300
Weapons. See **ARMED FORCES; Guided Missiles; NATIONAL DEFENSE**
WEATHER, *68*–536, *67*–547, *66*–563, *65*–543, *64*–527
agriculture, *66*–214; astronomy, *65*–222; balloons, *65*–234; disasters, *68*–308, *67*–310, *66*–320, *65*–313, *64*-312; Europe, *il.*, *65*–325; floods, *65*–542; health, *64*–357; Italy, *67*–380; ocean, *67*–74; President of the U.S., *66*–490; soil conservation, *65*–503; space exploration, *68*–499, *67*–505, *66*–49, *66*–527, *65*–45, *65*–508; water and flood control, *66*–562, *66*–183
Weather Bureau, U.S., *66*–563
WEAVER, ROBERT CLIFTON, *67*–549
cabinet, *67*–253; city planning, *67*–273; housing, *67*–365
Webb, Clifton, *67*–303
Weight lifting: Olympic Games, *65*–448; sports, *68*–502, *67*–510, *66*–528, *65*–513, *64*–494
Weightlessness, *66*–151
Weiss, George, *67*–57
Welch, Robert, *66*–398
Welfare. See **CHILD WELFARE; SOCIAL WELFARE**
Wellman, Paul I., *67*–303
Wessin y Wessin, Elias, *66*–323
West Germany. See **GERMANY**
WEST INDIES, *68*–537, *67*–549; Great Britain, *68*–358; Latin America, *68*–395, *67*–393
West Irian. See **NEW GUINEA**
West Virginia, *68*–286, *66*–469, *65*–269, *64*–265
WESTERN SAMOA, *65*–544
Westminster Abbey, *67*–261, *66*–271
WESTMORELAND, WILLIAM CHILDS, *68*–538; Congress, *68*–278; personalities, *66*–470; Vietnam, *68*–531
Westover, Russ, *67*–303
Weygand, Maxime, *66*–313
Whale, *68*–541, *67*–553, *66*–568, *65*–548, *64*–332
Wheat: agriculture, *68*–201, *67*–206, *66*–214, *65*–210, *64*–208; Canada *64*–261; China, *66*–280
WHEELER, EARLE GILMORE, *66*–453, *65*–545
White, Edward H.: astronauts, *67*–219, *65*–220, *64*–224; space travel, *68*–497, *66*–525
WHITE, ROBERT M., *66*–563, *64*–527
White, Terence Hanbury, *65*–301
White, Theodore Harold: literature, *66*–415
White House: Kennedy assassination, *il.*, *64*–66; library, *64*–380
Whitney, Eli, *66*–272
Whitney, John Hay, *67*–475
Whooping crane, *68*–542, *67*–291, *66*–564, *64*–529
Wiesner, Jerome Bert, *64*–358
WIGNER, EUGENE PAUL, *64*–528
Wilderness: outdoor recreation, *65*–449; *Special Report*, *65*–189
WILDLIFE, *66*–564, *65*–545, *64*–529
conservation, *68*–283, *67*–290; health, *66*–374; hunting and fishing, *68*–365, *67*–367, *66*–380, *65*–362; Schweitzer, Albert, *64*–133; *Special Report*, *66*–166, *64*–149; wilderness, *65*–189; zoology, *68*–541, *66*–568; zoos and aquariums, *67*–553, *65*–548, *64*–532
Wilhelm (Sweden), *66*–313
WILKINS, ROY, *65*–545; civil rights, *67*–275
Wilkinson, Louis U., *67*–303
Willcox, Walter F., *65*–301
Williams, Clifton C., Jr., *68*–213, *65*–221, *64*–223
Williams, Eric Eustace, *68*–538
Williams, Tennessee, *67*–522
WILLIAMS, WILLIAM CARLOS, *64*–529
deaths, *64*–302; poetry, *64*–393
Williamson, John Finley, *65*–301
Wilson, Edward O., *66*–387
WILSON, (JAMES) HAROLD, *65*–545, *64*–529
Africa, *66*–212; Europe, *66*–346; Great Britain, *68*–354, *67*–356, *66*–367, *65*–351, *64*–350; Rhodesia, *67*–482
Wilson, Mary, *67*–454
Wind, *65*–544
Windsor, Duke of, *il.*, *68*–356
Winston-Salem, *67*–261
Winters, Robert H., *67*–254
Wiretapping: civil rights, *68*–270; espionage, *68*–329
WOJCIECHOWSKA, MAIA, *66*–565
Wolfson, Louis E., *67*–513
Women: civil rights, *66*–283; employment, *68*–107; France, *66*–357; Middle East, *66*–439; United Nations, *68*–527
WOODS, GEORGE DAVID, *64*–530
WOODWARD, ROBERT BURNS, *66*–565
WORDS AND PHRASES, NEW, *66*–565, *65*–546, *64*–430; ***World Book Encyclopedia Dictionary*** supplement, *68*–591, *67*–599, *66*–597, *65*–603, *64*–607
World affairs. See **INTERNATIONAL RELATIONS**
World Book Encyclopedia: ALA award, *67*–211, *66*–218, *65*–212, *64*–211; astronauts, *64*–224; Braille edition, *64*–246; dictionary supplement, *68*–591, *67*–599, *66*–597, *65*–603, *64*–607; Peace Corps, *63*–406; photography, *64*–452; science service, *64*–464
World Council of Churches: Blake, Eugene Carson, *67*–245; ecumenical movement, *66*–86; Protestant, *67*–472, *64*–462
WORLD HISTORY: *WBE*, *66*–570
World Law Center, *66*–296
World Series, *68*–231, *67*–239, *66*–247, *65*–235, *64*–241
World Veterans Federation, *66*–553
World War I, *67*–262
World War II: celebrations, *68*–256, *66*–271, *65*–258; Germany, *67*–353, *66*–362; literature for children, *65*–402; memorials, *64*–405; veterans, *65*–535
World's Fair. See **FAIRS AND EXHIBITIONS**
Worthing, Bill, *68*–452
WRESTLING, *68*–502, *66*–566, *65*–546, *64*–530
Olympic Games, *65*–448; sports, *67*–510
Wright, Lawrence, *65*–301
WYETH, ANDREW, *68*–538
Wynn, Ed, *67*–303
Wyoming, *67*–290, *66*–272
Wyszynski, Mrs. Bernice, *66*–473
Wyszynski, Stefan Cardinal, *67*–460

X

Xceron, Jean, *68*–301
Xenon, *64*–267
X ray, *68*–260, *67*–222, *65*–34

Y

Yachting. See **SAILING**
Yadin, Yigael, *68*–381
Yastrzemski, Carl: baseball, *68*–231; sports, *68*–502
Ydígoras Fuentes, Miguel, *64*–355
Yeats, William Butler, *66*–272
YEMEN, *68*–538, *67*–550, *66*–566, *65*–546, *64*–530
Great Britain, *65*–353; Middle East, *68*–425, *67*–420, *65*–415, *64*–410; Saudi Arabia, *68*–487, *67*–491, *66*–517; South Arabia, *67*–501; United Arab Republic, *67*–533, *64*–512; United Nations, *65*–534, *64*–517
York, Alvin C., *65*–301
York, William, *67*–454
Yorty, Samuel W., *67*–407
Yoshi, Prince, *il.*, *65*–377
Yoshida, Shigeru: deaths, *68*–301; Japan, *68*–380
Youlou, Fulbert, *64*–283
Young, Desmond, *67*–303
Young, John W., *67*–504, *66*–525, *65*–220
Young, Marguerite, *66*–414
YOUNG MEN'S CHRISTIAN ASSOCIATION, *68*–539, *67*–550, *66*–566, *65*–546, *64*–530; juvenile delinquency, *64*–376
YOUNG WOMEN'S CHRISTIAN ASSOCIATION, *68*–539, *67*–550, *66*–567, *65*–547, *64*–530
Younger, J. Arthur, *68*–301
Youssoupoff, Prince Felix, *68*–301
YOUTH ORGANIZATIONS, *68*–539, *67*–551
Boy Scouts of America, *66*–258, *65*–244, *64*–250; Boys' Clubs of America, *66*–258, *65*–244, *64*–250; Camp Fire Girls, *66*–263, *65*–251, *64*–257; Four-H Clubs, *66*–353, *65*–337, *64*–335; Future Farmers of America, *66*–357, *65*–340, *64*–339; Future Homemakers of America, *66*–357, *65*–341, *64*–339; Girl Scouts, *66*–363, *65*–347, *64*–348; Girls Clubs of America, *66*–363, *65*–347, *64*–348; Junior Achievement, *68*–384, *67*–386, *66*–403, *65*–383, *64*–375; juvenile delinquency, *65*–383; Science Clubs of America, *68*–488, *67*–494, *66*–519, *65*–496, *64*–482; Young Men's Christian Association, *68*–539, *67*–550, *66*–566, *65*–546, *64*–530; Young Women's Christian Association, *68*–539, *67*–550, *66*–567, *65*–547, *64*–530
YUGOSLAVIA, *68*–540, *67*–552, *66*–567, *65*–547
architecture, *68*–208; Communism, *64*–283; earthquakes, *64*–313; Eastern Orthodox, *68*–312; Greece, *65*–355; Nepal, *66*–457; Roman Catholic, *67*–483
Yukon, *66*–255

Z

ZAMBIA, *68*–541, *66*–567, *65*–547
Africa, *67*–205, *65*–207; civil liberties, *65*–266; Kaunda, Kenneth, *65*–384; Rhodesia, *68*–479, *66*–506; United Nations, *65*–535
ZANZIBAR, *64*–531. See also **TANZANIA**
United Nations, *64*–517
Zayyin, Youssef, *67*–516
Zernike, Frits, *67*–303
Zhivkov, Todor, *66*–261, *64*–253
ZIEGLER, KARL, *65*–417, *64*–531
Zinc, *67*–422, *65*–417
Zionism, *68*–421
ZOOLOGY, *68*–541, *67*–553, *66*–568, *65*–548, *64*–531
insect, *68*–372, *67*–374, *66*–387, *65*–370, *64*–366; literature for children, *66*–422; pet, *67*–454, *65*–462; psychology, *64*–463; science clubs, *65*–496, *64*–482; tropical fish, *64*–450; wildlife, *66*–564, *65*–545
ZOOS AND AQUARIUMS, *68*–542, *67*–553, *66*–568, *65*–548, *64*–532; Los Angeles, *67*–407
Zorach, William, *67*–303

Acknowledgments

The publishers of the 1968 *World Book Year Book* gratefully acknowledge the courtesy of the following artists, photographers, publishers, institutions, agencies, and corporations for the illustrations in this volume. Credits should be read from left to right, top to bottom, on their respective pages. All entries marked with an asterisk (*) denote illustrations created exclusively for *The World Book Year Book*. All entries marked with a dagger (†) denote photographs entered in the National Press Photographers Association Pictures of the Year contest. All maps were created by the World Book Cartographic Staff. All charts and diagrams were prepared by artists of *The World Book Year Book* staff unless otherwise noted.

Preface

3 NASA

Focus Reports

14 James Hill*; Wide World; Eastfoto; Pictorial Parade; United Press Int.; Wide World; United Press Int.
16-17 Wide World
18 Pictorial Parade
20 James Hill*; United Press Int.; *Chicago Sun-Times;* Wide World; Wide World; Wide World; Eddie Adams†, Associated Press
23 Wide World
24 *The New York Times*
26 James Hill*; *U.S. News & World Report;* United Press Int.; Wide World; Wide World; Wide World; David F. Penney†, *Des Moines Register and Tribune*
28 Wide World
32 James Hill*; E. F. Hoppe*; E. F. Hoppe*; Pictorial Parade; High Altitude Observatory; E. F. Hoppe*; E. F. Hoppe*; Dr. Russell P. Sherwin, University of Southern California
34 Wide World
38 James Hill*; *U.S. News & World Report;* Washington University; Wide World; *U.S. News & World Report;* Steve Lasker†, *Chicago's American*
40-42 *The New York Times*
44 James Hill*; Wide World; NASA; NASA; Ralph Morse; Hughes Aircraft Company; NASA
46-47 NASA
50 James Hill*; Bert Andrews; Bill Yoscary from Nancy Palmer; Wide World; United Press Int.; *The New York Times;* Reg Wilson, Pix from Publix; Wide World
52 Warner Bros.
54 Terry Schutte
56 James Hill*; Dick Darcey†, *Washington Post;* Wide World; Wide World; Wide World; Pictorial Parade; Wide World; Wide World
58-59 Wide World

Special Reports

63-70 Phil Renaud*
72 Bruce Harlan*
75 Phil Renaud*
78-79 Stockpile
83 Jerry Cooke, Photo Researchers; Jules Bucher, Photo Researchers; Gilbert F. White, University of Chicago
84 Frederick Ayer, Photo Researchers; James A. Harder,* University of California
89 United Nations
90-91 James A. Harder*, University of California
92-93 Bill Strode, Black Star
94 United Nations
96-97 Los Alamos Scientific Laboratory
99 E. F. Hoppe*
100 E. F. Hoppe*; Donald Stebbing*
101 Inland Steel Company; E. F. Hoppe*
103 E. F. Hoppe*
104 Donald Stebbing*
105 Bethlehem Steel Corporation
106-107 Shel Hershorn, Black Star
108 Vories Fisher*
109 Los Alamos Scientific Laboratory
110 P.I.P.
111 Black Star
112 From *Mao Tse-tung* by Stuart Schram, courtesy Simon and Schuster
113 Huston Collection, Hoover Institution
114 United Press Int.
115 René Burri, Magnum; Bosshard, Black Star
116 Eastfoto; United Press Int.
117 Jack Wilkes, *Life* ©Time Inc.; Pix from Publix
118 Brian Brake, Magnum
119 Birnback Publishing Service
120 Harry Redl, Black Star
121-122 Richard Harrington
124 Pictorial Parade
126 U.S. Department of the Interior; U.S. Dept. of the Interior; U.S. Department of the Interior; Frank Aleksandrowicz*; U.S. Department of the Interior; U.S. Dept. of the Interior; U.S. Dept. of the Interior
127-130 Frank Aleksandrowicz*
131 N. Wilson Britt; Harold Hungerford, Photo Researchers; N. Wilson Britt
132 U.S. Department of the Interior
132-133 Frank Aleksandrowicz*
134 Fred Eckhardt*; U.S. Department of the Interior
135 U.S. Dept. of the Interior
138 Frank Aleksandrowicz*; Frank Aleksandrowicz*; U.S. Department of the Interior; Frank Aleksandrowicz*
140 U.S. Department of the Interior
142 U.S. Department of the Interior; Fred Eckhardt*
144 United Press Int.; Culver; United Press Int.
145 E. F. Hoppe*; Globe Photos; Pictorial Parade
147 John Hamilton, Globe Photos; Pictorial Parade
148 Ken Regan; Miller-Barbier, Globe Photos
149 Henry Grossman; Henry Grossman; Ted Streshinsky; Galaxy International, Inc.
150 Galaxy International, Inc.
151 E. F. Hoppe*
152 ©Daniel Kramer; Merka
153 Bob Bonis
154 Ken Regan; Roy Cummings, Inc.; Ken Regan
155 Roy Cummings, Inc.; Curt Gunther
156 Jim Marshall
157 Burris Sarlin and Assoc.*
158 Jack Stager, Globe Photos
160-161 William R. Coe, University of Pennsylvania Museum
162 John J. McGinn, University of Pennsylvania Museum
164 William R. Coe, University of Pennsylvania Museum
166-167 George Holton, University of Pennsylvania Museum
168-175 William R. Coe, University of Pennsylvania Museum

Year on File

192 The Advertising Council
193 Wells, Rich, Greene, Inc.

194-195 *The New York Times*
200 Wide World
206 The Sackler Collections
207 James Mavor, Jr.
208 © Ezra Stoller
211 Robert Ellison, Empire News; Felix Greene, Magnum
212 United Press Int.
213 Ralph Morse, *Life* © Time Inc.
214 Wide World
215 Jet Propulsion Laboratory
216-217 Wide World
218 *Engineering News-Record* © McGraw-Hill, Inc.
220 Pictorial Parade; Ford Motor Company
221 Wide World
222-223 Port Authority of New York
224-225 Wide World
229 John Reader, *Life* © Time Inc.
231 Wide World
234 Rich Clarkson†, *Topeka Capital-Journal*
235 California Institute of Technology
236 NASA
238 Stanley Rosenfeld
241 Wide World
243 United Press Int.
246-247 Canada Centennial Commission
248 Pictorial Parade
251 Canada Centennial Commission
252 Wide World
257 Pictorial Parade
261 Donald Stebbing*
263 Wide World
264 Pictorial Parade
265 Wide World
267 Jack Dykinga†, *Chicago Sun-Times*
268-269 Jerry Hostetler†, *The Detroit News*
270 Frank Lodge, *The Milwaukee Journal*
271 United Press Int.
273 Kyodo News
274 Aerojet-General Corporation
275 Black Star
276 Charles Tasnadi†, Associated Press; Wide World
277 Wide World; United Press Int.
284 © National Geographic Society
285 United Press Int.
289 Wide World
291 Reg Wilson, Pix from Publix
293 Pictorial Parade; United Press Int.; Culver
295 Bernard Hoffman, *Life* © Time Inc.
296 Wide World; © Philippe Halsman; United Press Int.
297 Culver; Wide World; Pictorial Parade
298 Drawing by Robert Vickrey, *Time* © Time Inc. 1967
299 Thomas MacAvoy, *Life* © Time Inc.; Culver; M-G-M Corporation
302 Wide World
303 *The New York Times;* Wide World
307 United Press Int.
308 Curt Kitchen†, *Rockford Morning Star*
309 United Press Int.; Wide World
310 Richard Swanson, *Life* © Time Inc.
311 Wide World
312-313 The White House, Washington, D.C.
318-319 Fred Devan, *Life* © Time Inc.
322 Wide World
324 Texas Instruments; IBM
326 Donald Stebbing*
327 United Press Int.
330-333 Pictorial Parade
334-335 Fred Maroon; Miller Services Ltd.
336 United Press Int.; United Press Int.; Pictorial Parade
341 Wide World
344-346 Pictorial Parade
347 E. F. Hoppe*
351 Robert Lackenbach, Black Star
353 Wide World
355 Pictorial Parade
356 Wide World
357 Associated Newspapers, Ltd.
361 United Nations
362 Jerry Cooke, *Sports Illustrated* © Time Inc.
364 *New York Daily News; Engineering News-Record* © McGraw-Hill, Inc.; *New York Daily News*
367 United Press Int.
368-369 Wide World
370 Baldev, Pix
372 Harvard University
373 Callaway Mills, Inc.
377-378 Pictorial Parade
380 T. Tanuma
381 Capa-Bar-Am, Magnum; David Rubinger, *Life* © Time Inc.
382 The White House, Washington, D.C.
383 Wide World
384 Pictorial Parade
386 Wide World
388-389 Tony Spina
391 Wide World
392 Francis Miller, *Life* © Time Inc.
397 Rosario Cassata
398 Sovfoto
401 B & G International
409 Woven Structures Inc.
413 Murrie-White and Associates, Inc.*; Wide World
414 United Press Int.
416 Wide World
417 Keystone
418-419 Gamma from Pix
420 Pictorial Parade; Wide World
424 Hubert Le Campion, *Life* © Time Inc.; Gilles Caron, Pix from Publix
428 Columbia Pictures; Bernard Gotfryd, *Newsweek*
429 Warner Bros.
430 Siegfried Lauterwasser
432 Fernando Turchi, *Time* © Time Inc.
433 Wide World
434 Eugene Anthony
437 Pictorial Parade
439 *New York Daily News*
442 Pictorial Parade
445 Augusto Meneses, *Life* © Time Inc., courtesy The National Museum of Madrid
446 The Metropolitan Museum of Art, New York, Fletcher Fund, 1923; The Metropolitan Museum of Art, New York
450 Wide World
451 Frank Hurley†, *New York Daily News*
452 United Press Int.; Anthony Camerano†, Associated Press
453 Wide World; Harry Winston, Inc.
457 Gary Settle†, *Chicago Daily News;* Bruce Dale† © National Geographic Society; Anscochrome of the Year: Albert Sadler; National Newspaper Snapshot Award: Jozee Salinas
459-461 Wide World
463 Ron Unternahrer
464-466 *The New York Times*
467 The White House, Washington D.C.; Wide World
469 *Chicago Sun-Times*
474-477 Wide World
479 Authenticated News Int.
481 United Press Int.
483-484 Sovfoto
487 Wide World
495 Keystone
496 Yale Joel, *Life* © Time Inc.
498 NASA
499 Dick Larson
501 1968 Olympic Organization of Mexico
502-507 Wide World
510 CBS Television; Greg Harris
511 Richard Meek, *Life* © Time Inc.
512 Friedman-Abeles
513 Bert Andrews
517 United Aircraft Corporation
522-523 Gilles Caron, Pix from Publix; United Press Int.
524-525 Wide World
530-531 The White House, Washington D.C.
532 United Press Int.; Wide World
534 Rick Merron†, Associated Press
535 Dana Stone†, United Press Int.
537 Ed Wagner, Sr.†, *Chicago's American*
540 Wide World
542 Flip Schulke, *Life* © Time Inc.; Keystone

A Preview Of 1968

January

1 **New Year's Day.**
March of Dimes through January 31.
United Cerebral Palsy Month through January 31.
International Human Rights Year through December 31, commemorates the 20th anniversary of the Universal Declaration of Human Rights.
6 **Epiphany,** Twelfth Day after Christmas.
7 **Universal Week of Prayer** through January 14.
15 **90th Congress of U.S. Opens** its second session in Washington, D.C.
18 **Week of Prayer for Christian Unity** through January 25.
21 **World Religion Day.**
National YMCA Week through January 28.
28 **Youth Week** through February 4.
30 **Franklin D. Roosevelt Day** (Ky., W.Va.).

February

1 **National Freedom Day.**
American Heart Month.
American History Month.
American Music Month.
2 **Candlemas Day.**
Ground-Hog Day.
4 **National Children's Dental Health Week** through February 10.
6 **X Winter Olympic Games,** Grenoble, France, through February 18.
7 **Boy Scout Week** through February 13.
11 **National Crime Prevention Week** through February 17.
Negro History Week through February 17.
12 **Abraham Lincoln's Birthday.**
14 **Saint Valentine's Day.**
16 **National Date Festival,** Indio, Calif., through February 25.
17 **Future Farmers of America Week** through February 24.
18 **Catholic Book Week** through February 24.
Brotherhood Week through February 25.
22 **George Washington's Birthday.**
27 **Shrove Tuesday:** *Mardi Gras of the French; Pancake Day of the English;* and *Carnival of the Italians.*
28 **Ash Wednesday.**
29 **Leap Year Day.**

March

1 **Saint David's Day,** patron saint of Wales.
American Red Cross Month.
Children's Art Month.
Easter Seal Campaign through April 14.
5 **National Teachers Day.**
10 **Girl Scout Week** through March 16.
14 **Purim,** Jewish Festival of Lots.
17 **Saint Patrick's Day.**
Camp Fire Girls Birthday Week through March 23.
National Wildlife Week through March 23.
20 **First Day of Spring** (8:22 A.M., E.S.T.).
25 **Annunciation Day.**
28 **Partial Eclipse of Sun,** visible in South Pacific Ocean.
31 **National Boys' Club Week** through April 6.

April

1 **April Fools' Day.**
Cancer Control Month.
Freedom Shrine Month.
National Hobby Month.
Teaching Career Month.
6 **HemisFair '68** through October 6, commemorates 250th anniversary of San Antonio, Tex.
7 **Palm Sunday.**
World Health Day.
9 **Bataan Day** (Philippines).
Sir Winston Churchill Day (U.S.).
12 **Good Friday.**
Total Eclipse of Moon through April 13, visible in North America, Europe, most of Africa, Atlantic Ocean, South America, southeastern Pacific Ocean, and Antarctica.
13 **Thomas Jefferson's Birthday.**
Passover through April 20.
14 **Easter Sunday.**
Pan American Day.
15 **Catholic Library Association Conference,** St. Paul, Minn., through April 18.
16 **World Congress of Catholic Youth Organizations,** West Berlin, through April 20.
21 **National Garden Week** through April 27.
National Library Week through April 27.
Youth Temperance Education Week through April 27.
National YWCA Week through April 28.
26 **Confederate Memorial Day** (Ala., Fla., Ga., and Miss.).
28 **Daylight Saving Begins** in many U.S. communities.
Canada-U.S. Goodwill Week through May 4.

May

1 **May Day.**
Law Day.
Loyalty Day.
Mental Health Week through May 7.
4 **Kentucky Derby,** Louisville, Ky.
5 **Be Kind to Animals Week** through May 11.
National Family Week through May 12.
8 **V-E Day.**
10 **Confederate Memorial Day** (N.C., S.C.).
12 **Mother's Day.**
National Girls Club Week through May 18.
National Hospital Week through May 18.
Multiple Sclerosis Hope Chest Campaign through June 16.
15 **Royal Danish Ballet and Music Festival,** Copenhagen, Denmark, through May 31.
18 **Armed Forces Day.**
19 **Rogation Sunday.**
National Salvation Army Week through May 25.
Opera Festival, Glyndebourne, England, through July 31.
20 **Victoria Day and Queen's Birthday,** official celebration, in Canada.
Girl Guide Anniversary Week through May 26.
23 **Ascension Day.**
International Festival of Music, Drama, and Folklore, Bergen, Norway, through June 9.
29 **Festival Casals,** San Juan, Puerto Rico, through June 12.
30 **Memorial (Decoration) Day.**
Confederate Memorial Day (Va.).
500-Mile Speedway Race, Indianapolis.

June

2 **Pentecost,** or Whitsunday.
Shabuot, Jewish Feast of Weeks, through June 3.
3 **Confederate Memorial Day** (Ky., La., Tenn.).
Jefferson Davis' Birthday.
8 **Queen's Birthday,** official celebration, London, England.
Mozart Music Festival, Augsburg, West Germany, through June 14.
9 **Trinity Sunday.**

January

Sun	Mon	Tue	Wed	Thu	Fri	Sat
	1	2	3	4	5	6
7	8	9	10	11	12	13
14	15	16	17	18	19	20
21	22	23	24	25	26	27
28	29	30	31			

February

Sun	Mon	Tue	Wed	Thu	Fri	Sat
				1	2	3
4	5	6	7	8	9	10
11	12	13	14	15	16	17
18	19	20	21	22	23	24
25	26	27	28	29		

March

Sun	Mon	Tue	Wed	Thu	Fri	Sat
					1	2
3	4	5	6	7	8	9
10	11	12	13	14	15	16
17	18	19	20	21	22	23
24/31	25	26	27	28	29	30

April

Sun	Mon	Tue	Wed	Thu	Fri	Sat
	1	2	3	4	5	6
7	8	9	10	11	12	13
14	15	16	17	18	19	20
21	22	23	24	25	26	27
28	29	30				

May

Sun	Mon	Tue	Wed	Thu	Fri	Sat
			1	2	3	4
5	6	7	8	9	10	11
12	13	14	15	16	17	18
19	20	21	22	23	24	25
26	27	28	29	30	31	

June

Sun	Mon	Tue	Wed	Thu	Fri	Sat
						1
2	3	4	5	6	7	8
9	10	11	12	13	14	15
16	17	18	19	20	21	22
23/30	24	25	26	27	28	29

A Preview Of 1968

July

Sun	Mon	Tue	Wed	Thu	Fri	Sat
	1	2	3	4	5	6
7	8	9	10	11	12	13
14	15	16	17	18	19	20
21	22	23	24	25	26	27
28	29	30	31			

August

Sun	Mon	Tue	Wed	Thu	Fri	Sat
				1	2	3
4	5	6	7	8	9	10
11	12	13	14	15	16	17
18	19	20	21	22	23	24
25	26	27	28	29	30	31

September

Sun	Mon	Tue	Wed	Thu	Fri	Sat
1	2	3	4	5	6	7
8	9	10	11	12	13	14
15	16	17	18	19	20	21
22	23	24	25	26	27	28
29	30					

October

Sun	Mon	Tue	Wed	Thu	Fri	Sat
		1	2	3	4	5
6	7	8	9	10	11	12
13	14	15	16	17	18	19
20	21	22	23	24	25	26
27	28	29	30	31		

November

Sun	Mon	Tue	Wed	Thu	Fri	Sat
					1	2
3	4	5	6	7	8	9
10	11	12	13	14	15	16
17	18	19	20	21	22	23
24	25	26	27	28	29	30

December

Sun	Mon	Tue	Wed	Thu	Fri	Sat
1	2	3	4	5	6	7
8	9	10	11	12	13	14
15	16	17	18	19	20	21
22	23	24	25	26	27	28
29	30	31				

10 **Festival Canada,** Stratford, Ontario, through October 12.

14 **Flag Day.**

16 **Father's Day.**

21 **First Day of Summer** (3:13 A.M., E.S.T.).

23 **American Library Association Conference,** Kansas City, Mo., through June 29.
National Music Camp, Interlochen, Mich., through August 18.

24 **All-England Lawn Tennis Championships,** Wimbledon, England, through July 6.

29 **Feast of Saints Peter and Paul.**

30 **National Safe Boating Week** through July 6.

July

1 **Dominion Day** (Canada).
National Arts and Crafts Month.

4 **Independence Day** (U.S.).
American Philippine Friendship Day (Philippines).

5 **Berkshire Festival,** Lenox, Mass., through August 25.

7 **Hans Christian Andersen Festival,** Funen Village, Denmark, through August 11.

9 **International Musical Eisteddfod,** LLangollen, Wales, through July 14.

13 **Sea Festival,** Vancouver, British Columbia, through July 22.

14 **Bastille Day** (France).

20 **Oregon Shakespearean Festival,** Ashland, through September 8.

21 **Captive Nations Week** through July 27
National Farm Safety Week through July 27.

25 **Richard Wagner Festival,** Bayreuth, West Germany, through August 28.

26 **International Music and Drama Festival,** Salzburg, Austria, through August 30.

August

5 **Republican Party National Convention Opens** in Miami Beach, Fla.

6 **Feast of the Transfiguration.**

8 **International Festival of Music and Drama,** Edinburgh, Scotland, through September 7.

14 **Atlantic Charter Day.**
V-J Day (original).
World Space Conference, Vienna, Austria, through August 27.

15 **Feast of the Assumption.**

24 **Pacific National Exhibition,** Vancouver, B. C., through September 2.

26 **Democratic Party National Convention Opens** in Chicago.

September

1 **Youth Month.**

2 **Labor Day.**
V-J Day (official).

4 **National Child Safety Week** through September 11.

11 **Boy Scouts of America Fall Roundup** through December 15.

17 **Citizenship Day.**
Constitution Day.

22 **First Day of Autumn** (6:26 P.M., E.S.T.).
Total Eclipse of Sun, visible in northern Asia.

23 **Rosh Hashanah,** Jewish New Year, through September 24.

28 **Kiwanis Kids' Day.**
National 4-H Club Week through October 5.

29 **National Gold Star Mothers Day.**
National Sunday School Week through October 6.

October

1 **National Science Youth Month.**

2 **Yom Kippur,** Jewish Day of Atonement.

6 **Total Eclipse of Moon,** visible in North America.
Fire Prevention Week through October 12.
National Employ the Physically Handicapped Week through October 12.

7 **Child Health Day.**

12 **Columbus Day.**
XIX Olympiad, Mexico City, Mexico, through October 27.

13 **National Y-Teen Roll Call Week** through October 19.

14 **Thanksgiving Day** (Canada).

15 **World Poetry Day.**

21 **English Thanksgiving Day.**

24 **United Nations Day.**

27 **Daylight Saving Ends** in many U.S. communities.

31 **Halloween,** or **All Hallow's Eve.**
Reformation Day.

November

1 **All Saints' Day.**
March for Muscular Dystrophy through November 30.

2 **All-Souls' Day.**

3 **National Children's Book Week** through November 9.

5 **General Election Day** (U.S.).

10 **American Education Week** through November 16.
YMCA-YWCA World Fellowship Week through November 16.

11 **Remembrance Day** (Canada).
Veterans Day (U.S.).

13 **Christmas Seal Campaign** through December 31.

15 **Jewish Book Month** through December 15.

22 **National Farm City Week** through November 28.

24 **Latin America Week** through November 30.

28 **Thanksgiving Day** (U.S.).

29 **International Live Stock Exposition,** Chicago, through December 7.

December

1 **First Sunday in Advent.**
National 4-H Club Congress, Chicago, through December 6.

2 **Pan American Health Day.**

3 **Illinois Sesquicentennial,** admitted to Union as 21st state in 1818.

6 **Feast of Saint Nicholas.**

7 **Pearl Harbor Day.**

8 **Feast of the Immaculate Conception**
Universal Bible Week through December 15.

10 **Nobel Prizes Presentation** in Stockholm, Sweden, and Oslo, Norway.
United Nations Human Rights Day.

15 **Bill of Rights Day** (U.S.).

16 **Hanukkah,** Jewish Feast of Lights, through December 23.

21 **First Day of Winter** (2:00 P.M., E.S.T.).

22 **Fourth Sunday in Advent.**

24 **"Silent Night, Holy Night!" Sesquicentennial** commemorates writing of carol in 1818.

25 **Christmas Day.**

31 **New Year's Eve.**